Contemporary Authors®
NEW REVISION SERIES

ISSN 0275-7176

Contemporary Authors®

A Bio-Bibliographical Guide to
Current Writers in Fiction, General Nonfiction,
Poetry, Journalism, Drama, Motion Pictures,
Television, and Other Fields

NEW REVISION SERIES volume 134

THOMSON
GALE

Detroit • New York • San Francisco • San Diego • New Haven, Conn. • Waterville, Maine • London • Munich

Contemporary Authors, New Revision Series, Vol. 134

Project Editor
Tracey L. Matthews

Editorial
Katy Balcer, Sara Constantakis, Michelle Kazensky, Julie Keppen, Lisa Kumar, Mary Ruby, Lemma Shomali, Maikue Vang

Permissions
Denise Buckley, Kim Smilay, Sheila Spencer

Imaging and Multimedia
Leslie Light, Michael Logusz

Composition and Electronic Capture
Carolyn Roney

Manufacturing
Drew Kalasky

LIBRARY OF CONGRESS CATALOG CARD NUMBER 81-640179

ISBN 0-7876-6726-9
ISSN 0275-7176

Printed in the United States of America
10 9 8 7 6 5 4 3 2 1

Contents

Indexing note: All *Contemporary Authors* entries are indexed in the *Contemporary Authors* cumulative index, which is published separately and distributed twice a year.

As always, the most recent Contemporary Authors cumulative index continues to be the user's guide to the location of an individual author's listing.

Preface

Contemporary Authors (*CA*) provides information on approximately 115,000 writers in a wide range of media, including:

- Current writers of fiction, nonfiction, poetry, and drama whose works have been issued by commercial publishers, risk publishers, or university presses (authors whose books have been published only by known vanity or author-subsidized firms are ordinarily not included)

- Prominent print and broadcast journalists, editors, photojournalists, syndicated cartoonists, graphic novelists, screenwriters, television scriptwriters, and other media people

- Notable international authors

- Literary greats of the early twentieth century whose works are popular in today's high school and college curriculums and continue to elicit critical attention

A *CA* listing entails no charge or obligation. Authors are included on the basis of the above criteria and their interest to *CA* users. Sources of potential listees include trade periodicals, publishers' catalogs, librarians, and other users.

How to Get the Most out of *CA*: Use the Index

The key to locating an author's most recent entry is the *CA* cumulative index, which is published separately and distributed twice a year. It provides access to *all* entries in *CA* and *Contemporary Authors New Revision Series* (*CANR*). Always consult the latest index to find an author's most recent entry.

For the convenience of users, the *CA* cumulative index also includes references to all entries in these Thomson Gale literary series: *Authors and Artists for Young Adults, Authors in the News, Bestsellers, Black Literature Criticism, Black Literature Criticism Supplement, Black Writers, Children's Literature Review, Concise Dictionary of American Literary Biography, Concise Dictionary of British Literary Biography, Contemporary Authors Autobiography Series, Contemporary Authors Bibliographical Series, Contemporary Dramatists, Contemporary Literary Criticism, Contemporary Novelists, Contemporary Poets, Contemporary Popular Writers, Contemporary Southern Writers, Contemporary Women Poets, Dictionary of Literary Biography, Dictionary of Literary Biography Documentary Series, Dictionary of Literary Biography Yearbook, DISCovering Authors, DISCovering Authors: British, DISCovering Authors: Canadian, DISCovering Authors: Modules* (including modules for Dramatists, Most-Studied Authors, Multicultural Authors, Novelists, Poets, and Popular/Genre Authors), *DISCovering Authors 3.0, Drama Criticism, Drama for Students, Feminist Writers, Hispanic Literature Criticism, Hispanic Writers, Junior DISCovering Authors, Major Authors and Illustrators for Children and Young Adults, Major 20th-Century Writers, Native North American Literature, Novels for Students, Poetry Criticism, Poetry for Students, Short Stories for Students, Short Story Criticism, Something about the Author, Something about the Author Autobiography Series, St. James Guide to Children's Writers, St. James Guide to Crime & Mystery Writers, St. James Guide to Fantasy Writers, St. James Guide to Horror, Ghost & Gothic Writers, St. James Guide to Science Fiction Writers, St. James Guide to Young Adult Writers, Twentieth-Century Literary Criticism, 20th Century Romance and Historical Writers, World Literature Criticism,* and *Yesterday's Authors of Books for Children.*

A Sample Index Entry:

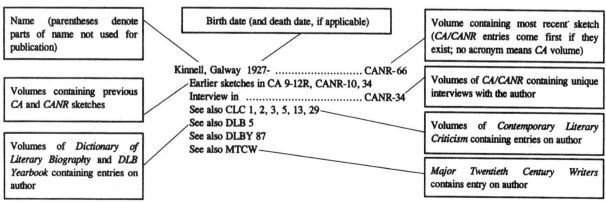

Name (parentheses denote parts of name not used for publication)

Birth date (and death date, if applicable)

Volume containing most recent sketch (*CA/CANR* entries come first if they exist; no acronym means *CA* volume)

Volumes containing previous *CA* and *CANR* sketches

Kinnell, Galway 1927- CANR-66
Earlier sketches in CA 9-12R, CANR-10, 34
Interview in CANR-34
See also CLC 1, 2, 3, 5, 13, 29
See also DLB 5
See also DLBY 87
See also MTCW

Volumes of *CA/CANR* containing unique interviews with the author

Volumes of *Contemporary Literary Criticism* containing entries on author

Volumes of *Dictionary of Literary Biography* and *DLB Yearbook* containing entries on author

Major Twentieth Century Writers contains entry on author

How Are Entries Compiled?

The editors make every effort to secure new information directly from the authors; listees' responses to our questionnaires and query letters provide most of the information featured in *CA*. For deceased writers, or those who fail to reply to requests for data, we consult other reliable biographical sources, such as those indexed in Thomson Gale's *Biography and Genealogy Master Index,* and bibliographical sources, including *National Union Catalog, LC MARC,* and *British National Bibliography.* Further details come from published interviews, feature stories, and book reviews, as well as information supplied by the authors' publishers and agents.

An asterisk (*) at the end of a sketch indicates that the listing has been compiled from secondary sources believed to be reliable but has not been personally verified for this edition by the author sketched.

What Kinds of Information Does An Entry Provide?

Sketches in *CA* contain the following biographical and bibliographical information:

- **Entry heading:** the most complete form of author's name, plus any pseudonyms or name variations used for writing

- **Personal information:** author's date and place of birth, family data, ethnicity, educational background, political and religious affiliations, and hobbies and leisure interests

- **Addresses:** author's home, office, or agent's addresses, plus e-mail and fax numbers, as available

- **Career summary:** name of employer, position, and dates held for each career post; resume of other vocational achievements; military service

- **Membership information:** professional, civic, and other association memberships and any official posts held

- **Awards and honors:** military and civic citations, major prizes and nominations, fellowships, grants, and honorary degrees

- **Writings:** a comprehensive, chronological list of titles, publishers, dates of original publication and revised editions, and production information for plays, television scripts, and screenplays

- **Adaptations:** a list of films, plays, and other media which have been adapted from the author's work

- **Work in progress:** current or planned projects, with dates of completion and/or publication, and expected publisher, when known

- **Sidelights:** a biographical portrait of the author's development; information about the critical reception of the author's works; revealing comments, often by the author, on personal interests, aspirations, motivations, and thoughts on writing

- **Interview:** a one-on-one discussion with authors conducted especially for *CA*, offering insight into authors' thoughts about their craft

- **Autobiographical essay:** an original essay written by noted authors for *CA*, a forum in which writers may present themselves, on their own terms, to their audience

- **Photographs:** portraits and personal photographs of notable authors

- **Biographical and critical sources:** a list of books and periodicals in which additional information on an author's life and/or writings appears

- **Obituary Notices** in *CA* provide date and place of birth as well as death information about authors whose full-length sketches appeared in the series before their deaths. The entries also summarize the authors' careers and writings and list other sources of biographical and death information.

Related Titles in the *CA* Series

Contemporary Authors Autobiography Series complements *CA* original and revised volumes with specially commissioned autobiographical essays by important current authors, illustrated with personal photographs they provide. Common topics include their motivations for writing, the people and experiences that shaped their careers, the rewards they derive from their work, and their impressions of the current literary scene.

Contemporary Authors Bibliographical Series surveys writings by and about important American authors since World War II. Each volume concentrates on a specific genre and features approximately ten writers; entries list works written by and about the author and contain a bibliographical essay discussing the merits and deficiencies of major critical and scholarly studies in detail.

Available in Electronic Formats

GaleNet. *CA* is available on a subscription basis through GaleNet, an online information resource that features an easy-to-use end-user interface, powerful search capabilities, and ease of access through the World-Wide Web. For more information, call 1-800-877-GALE.

Licensing. *CA* is available for licensing. The complete database is provided in a fielded format and is deliverable on such media as disk, CD-ROM, or tape. For more information, contact Thomson Gale's Business Development Group at 1-800-877-GALE, or visit us on our website at www.galegroup.com/bizdev.

Suggestions Are Welcome

The editors welcome comments and suggestions from users on any aspect of the *CA* series. If readers would like to recommend authors for inclusion in future volumes of the series, they are cordially invited to write the Editors at *Contemporary Authors*, Thomson Gale, 27500 Drake Rd., Farmington Hills, MI 48331-3535; or call at 1-248-699-4253; or fax at 1-248-699-8054.

Contemporary Authors Product Advisory Board

The editors of *Contemporary Authors* are dedicated to maintaining a high standard of excellence by publishing comprehensive, accurate, and highly readable entries on a wide array of writers. In addition to the quality of the content, the editors take pride in the graphic design of the series, which is intended to be orderly yet inviting, allowing readers to utilize the pages of *CA* easily and with efficiency. Despite the longevity of the *CA* print series, and the success of its format, we are mindful that the vitality of a literary reference product is dependent on its ability to serve its users over time. As literature, and attitudes about literature, constantly evolve, so do the reference needs of students, teachers, scholars, journalists, researchers, and book club members. To be certain that we continue to keep pace with the expectations of our customers, the editors of *CA* listen carefully to their comments regarding the value, utility, and quality of the series. Librarians, who have firsthand knowledge of the needs of library users, are a valuable resource for us. The *Contemporary Authors* Product Advisory Board, made up of school, public, and academic librarians, is a forum to promote focused feedback about *CA* on a regular basis. The seven-member advisory board includes the following individuals, whom the editors wish to thank for sharing their expertise:

- **Anne M. Christensen,** Librarian II, Phoenix Public Library, Phoenix, Arizona.

- **Barbara C. Chumard,** Reference/Adult Services Librarian, Middletown Thrall Library, Middletown, New York.

- **Eva M. Davis,** Youth Department Manager, Ann Arbor District Library, Ann Arbor, Michigan.

- **Adam Janowski, Jr.,** Library Media Specialist, Naples High School Library Media Center, Naples, Florida.

- **Robert Reginald,** Head of Technical Services and Collection Development, California State University, San Bernadino, California.

- **Stephen Weiner,** Director, Maynard Public Library, Maynard, Massachusetts.

International Advisory Board

Well-represented among the 115,000 author entries published in *Contemporary Authors* are sketches on notable writers from many non-English-speaking countries. The primary criteria for inclusion of such authors has traditionally been the publication of at least one title in English, either as an original work or as a translation. However, the editors of *Contemporary Authors* came to observe that many important international writers were being overlooked due to a strict adherence to our inclusion criteria. In addition, writers who were publishing in languages other than English were not being covered in the traditional sources we used for identifying new listees. Intent on increasing our coverage of international authors, including those who write only in their native language and have not been translated into English, the editors enlisted the aid of a board of advisors, each of whom is an expert on the literature of a particular country or region. Among the countries we focused attention on are Mexico, Puerto Rico, Spain, Italy, France, Germany, Luxembourg, Belgium, the Netherlands, Norway, Sweden, Denmark, Finland, Taiwan, Singapore, Malaysia, Thailand, South Africa, Israel, and Japan, as well as England, Scotland, Wales, Ireland, Australia, and New Zealand. The sixteen-member advisory board includes the following individuals, whom the editors wish to thank for sharing their expertise:

- **Lowell A. Bangerter,** Professor of German, University of Wyoming, Laramie, Wyoming.

- **Nancy E. Berg,** Associate Professor of Hebrew and Comparative Literature, Washington University, St. Louis, Missouri.

- **Frances Devlin-Glass,** Associate Professor, School of Literary and Communication Studies, Deakin University, Burwood, Victoria, Australia.

- **David William Foster,** Regent's Professor of Spanish, Interdisciplinary Humanities, and Women's Studies, Arizona State University, Tempe, Arizona.

- **Hosea Hirata,** Director of the Japanese Program, Associate Professor of Japanese, Tufts University, Medford, Massachusetts.

- **Jack Kolbert,** Professor Emeritus of French Literature, Susquehanna University, Selinsgrove, Pennsylvania.

- **Mark Libin,** Professor, University of Manitoba, Winnipeg, Manitoba, Canada.

- **C. S. Lim,** Professor, University of Malaya, Kuala Lumpur, Malaysia.

- **Eloy E. Merino,** Assistant Professor of Spanish, Northern Illinois University, DeKalb, Illinois.

- **Linda M. Rodríguez Guglielmoni,** Associate Professor, University of Puerto Rico—Mayagüez, Puerto Rico.

- **Sven Hakon Rossel,** Professor and Chair of Scandinavian Studies, University of Vienna, Vienna, Austria.

- **Steven R. Serafin,** Director, Writing Center, Hunter College of the City University of New York, New York City.

- **David Smyth,** Lecturer in Thai, School of Oriental and African Studies, University of London, England.

- **Ismail S. Talib,** Senior Lecturer, Department of English Language and Literature, National University of Singapore, Singapore.

- **Dionisio Viscarri,** Assistant Professor, Ohio State University, Columbus, Ohio.

- **Mark Williams,** Associate Professor, English Department, University of Canterbury, Christchurch, New Zealand.

CA Numbering System and Volume Update Chart

Occasionally questions arise about the *CA* numbering system and which volumes, if any, can be discarded. Despite numbers like "29-32R," "97-100" and "226," the entire *CA* print series consists of only 289 physical volumes with the publication of *CA* Volume 227. The following charts note changes in the numbering system and cover design, and indicate which volumes are essential for the most complete, up-to-date coverage.

CA First Revision
- 1-4R through 41-44R (11 books)
  Cover: Brown with black and gold trim.
  There will be no further First Revision volumes because revised entries are now being handled exclusively through the more efficient *New Revision Series* mentioned below.

CA Original Volumes
- 45-48 through 97-100 (14 books)
  Cover: Brown with black and gold trim.
  101 through 228 (128 books)
  Cover: Blue and black with orange bands.
  The same as previous *CA* original volumes but with a new, simplified numbering system and new cover design.

CA Permanent Series
- *CAP*-1 and *CAP*-2 (2 books)
  Cover: Brown with red and gold trim.
  There will be no further Permanent Series volumes because revised entries are now being handled exclusively through the more efficient *New Revision Series* mentioned below.

CA New Revision Series
- CANR-1 through CANR-134 (134 books)
  Cover: Blue and black with green bands.
  Includes only sketches requiring significant changes; **sketches are taken from any previously published CA, CAP, or CANR volume.**

If You Have:	You May Discard:
CA First Revision Volumes 1-4R through 41-44R and *CA Permanent Series* Volumes 1 and 2	*CA* Original Volumes 1, 2, 3, 4 and Volumes 5-6 through 41-44
CA Original Volumes 45-48 through 97-100 and 101 through 228	**NONE:** These volumes will not be superseded by corresponding revised volumes. Individual entries from these and all other volumes appearing in the left column of this chart may be revised and included in the various volumes of the *New Revision Series*.
CA New Revision Series Volumes *CANR*-1 through *CANR*-134	**NONE:** The *New Revision Series* does not replace any single volume of *CA*. Instead, volumes of *CANR* include entries from many previous *CA* series volumes. All *New Revision Series* volumes must be retained for full coverage.

A Sampling of Authors and Media People
Featured in This Volume

Maeve Binchy

Binchy, who once reported on daily life in London for the *Irish Times,* is the Irish-born author of best-selling novels like *Circle of Friends* and *Tara Road.* Praised for her astute and affectionate portrayal of her characters, Binchy often writes about women learning to take charge of their lives while coping with problems like alcoholism, adultery, and divorce. *Quentins,* her most recent novel, was published in 2002. She is working on a book of linked short stories titled *Avoid Disappointment.*

Bebe Moore Campbell

Campbell, author of the best-seller *Brothers and Sisters,* is an NAACP Image Award-winner who depicts the effects of racism and family problems in both fiction and nonfiction. Critics applaud the sensitivity and understanding she brings to her characters, like the father-daughter relationship in *Sweet Summer* and the intertwined family relationships in *Your Blues Ain't Like Mine.* In 2003, Campbell published *Sometimes My Mommy Gets Angry,* a children's picture book on bipolar disease. She is now at work on a novel, *Where I Useta Live.*

Sue Grafton

Grafton is the creator of the female private eye Kinsey Millhone. Her mega-hit series began with *A is for Alibi* and worked through the alphabet to *R is for Ricochet,* published in 2004. Lauded by a host of awards and a legion of fans, Grafton's books feature a feminine variation on the hard-boiled private-eye molded by Dashiell Hammett, Raymond Chandler and Ross MacDonald. With more than twenty years on the job, Millhone has developed and mellowed, but will no doubt return in *S is for....*

David Halberstam

Halberstam, a former war correspondent and political reporter, is the Pulitzer Prize-winning author of *The Best and the Brightest, The Powers That Be,* and *The Reckoning,* all best-sellers that examine power in America. Known for his voluminous research and novelistic style, Halberstam tackles a wide range of subjects, from the Japanese auto industry to basketball's Michael Jordan. His most recent books include *Teammates* and *Defining a Nation: Our America and the Sources of Its Strength,* both published in 2003.

Tony Hillerman

Hillerman is best known for his popular mystery novels set in the Southwest's Four Corners region of Arizona, Utah, Colorado, and New Mexico and featuring Jim Chee and Joe Leaphorn, detectives with the Navajo Tribal Police. The international award-winning author often draws his themes from the conflict between modern society and traditional Native American values and customs, weaving intricate plots with detailed descriptions of people, places, and exotic rituals. His most recent novel is *Skeleton Man,* published in 2004.

Stephen King

King is a world-renowned master storyteller whose prolific fiction, like his best-sellers *The Shining* and *Salem's Lot,* combines elements of horror, fantasy, science fiction, and humor. Placing him within the American Gothic tradition of Edgar Allan Poe, critics note that King has the distinctive ability to transform the ordinary into the horrific. In 2004, King published his most recent novel, under the pseudonym Eleanor Druse, *The Journals of Eleanor Druse: My Investigation of the Kingdom Hospital Incident.*

J. R. R. Tolkien

Tolkien's tales of Middle-Earth are considered by many the most important fantasy stories of modern times, and he remains a lively presence on the literary scene three decades after his death. In 2003, British readers voted *The Lord of the Rings* their best-loved novel and put *The Hobbit* in the top 100. A popular motion picture cycle based on *The Lord of the Rings* was produced between 2001 and 2003, winning a 2004 Academy Award for best picture. New editions of *The Hobbit* and *Beowulf and the Critics* were published in 2002.

Stuart Woods

Woods, a former advertising executive, is the author of best-selling adventures like *L.A. Dead* and *Capital Crimes,* that are often set against the backgrounds of high society, power politics, and the entertainment world. Critics and readers alike commend his sophisticated blend of fast action, beautiful women, and tongue-in-cheek humor. Stone Barrington, ex-cop turned lawyer and detective—and one of the author's most popular protagonists—is featured in *The Two-Dollar Bill,* published in 2005.

Acknowledgments

Grateful acknowledgment is made to those publishers, photographers, and artists whose work appear with these authors' essays. Following is a list of the copyright holders who have granted us permission to reproduce material in this volume of *CA*. Every effort has been made to trace copyright, but if omissions have been made, please let us know.

Photographs/Art

Claribel Alegría: Alegría, photograph by Joe Kohen. AP/Wide World Photos. Reproduced by permission.

A. Alvarez: Alvarez, 1972, photograph. AP/Wide World Photos. Reproduced by permission.

Jennifer Armstrong: Armstrong (right) with sister Sarah, photograph. Reproduced by permission of Jennifer Armstrong.

Madison Smartt Bell: Bell, photograph by Sophie Bassouls. © Bassouls Sophie/Corbis Sygma.

Maeve Binchy: Binchy, photograph by Tim Boyle. Getty Images. Reproduced by permission.

Jewel Spears Brooker: Brooker, photograph. Reproduced by permission.

Ed Bullins: Bullins, photograph. AP/Wide World Photos. Reproduced by permission.

Chris Crutcher: Crutcher, photograph by Tony Omer. Reproduced by permission.

Carl Deuker: Deuker, in Seattle, Washington, 2003, photograph. Photo by Anne Mitchell. Courtesy of Carl Deuker. Reproduced by permission.

Peter Dickinson: Dickinson, photograph by Jerry Bauer. © Jerry Bauer. Reproduced by permission.

Carlos M. N. Eire: Eire, photograph by Stuart Ramson. AP/Wide World Photos. Reproduced by permission.

Oriana Fallaci: Fallaci, photograph by Gianangelo Pistoria. AP/Wide World Photos. Reproduced by permission.

Rosario Ferré: Ferré, photograph by Ricardo Figueroa. AP/Wide World Photos. Reproduced by permission.

Dario Fo: Fo, photograph. Getty Images. Reproduced by permission.

Marilyn French: French, photograph by Jerry Bauer. © Jerry Bauer. Reproduced by permission.

Bruce Goldberg: Goldberg, photograph. Reproduced by permission.

Sue Grafton: Grafton, photograph by Gino Domenico. AP/Wide World Photos. Reproduced by permission.

David Halberstam: Halbertstam, photograph by Mark Lennihan. AP/Wide World Photos. Reproduced by permission.

Ursula Hegi: Hegi, photograph by Gordon Gagliano. Reproduced by permission.

Tony Hillerman: Hillerman, photograph. AP/Wide World Photos. Reproduced by permission.

A

ALEGRÍA, Claribel (Joy) 1924-

PERSONAL: Born May 12, 1924, in Esteli, Nicaragua; daughter of Daniel Alegría (a medical doctor) and Ana Maria Vides; married Darwin J. Flakoll (a journalist), 1947 (died, 1995); children: Maya, Patricia, Karen, Erik. *Education:* George Washington University, B.A., 1948.

ADDRESSES: Home—Apt. Postal A 36, Managua, Nicaragua. *Office*—c/o Curbstone Press, 321 Jackson St., Willimantic, CT 06226.

CAREER: Poet, novelist, and essayist.

AWARDS, HONORS: Cenizas de Izalco was a finalist in the Seix Barral competition, Barcelona, Spain, 1964; Casa de las Americas poetry award, 1978, for *Sobrevivo;* honorary doctorate from Eastern Connecticut State University.

WRITINGS:

Anillo de silencio (poetry; title means "Ring of Silence"; also see below), Botas (Mexico), 1948.
Suite de amor, angustia y soledad (poetry), Brigadas Liricas (Mendoza, Argentina), 1950.
Vigilias (poetry; also see below), Ediciones Poesia de America (Mexico City, Mexico), 1953.
Acuario (poetry; also see below), Editorial Universitaria (Santiago, Chile), 1955.

Claribel Alegría

Tres cuentos (children's stories; title means "Three Stories"), illustrations by Agustin Blancovaras, El Salvador Ministerio de Cultura (San Salvador, El Salvador), 1958.
Huesped de mi tiempo (poetry; also see below), Americalee (Buenos Aires, Argentina), 1961.
(Editor and translator, with husband, Darwin J. Flakoll) *New Voices of Hispanic America,* Beacon Press (Boston, MA), 1962.

Via unica (poetry; title means "One Way"; includes *Auto de fe* and *Comunicacion a larga distancia*), Alfa (Montevideo, Uruguay), 1965.

(With Darwin J. Flakoll) *Cenizas de Izalco* (novel), Seix Barral (Barcelona, Spain), 1966, translated by Darwin J. Flakoll as *Ashes of Izalco,* Curbstone Press/Talman (Willimantic, CT), 1989.

(Translator, with Darwin J. Flakoll) Miguel Angel Asturias, *The Cyclone,* Peter Owen (London, England), 1967.

(Translator, with Darwin J. Flakoll) Morris West, *El Hereje,* Pomaire (Barcelona, Spain), 1969.

(Translator, with Darwin J. Flakoll) *Unstill Life: An Introduction to the Spanish Poetry of Latin America,* edited by Mario Benedetti, Harcourt, Brace & World (New York, NY), 1969.

Aprendizaje (title means "Apprenticeship"; includes poetry from *Anillo de silencio, Vigilias, Acuario, Huesped de mi tiempo,* and *Via unica*), Universitaria de El Salvador (San Salvador, El Salvador), 1970.

Pagare a cobrar y otros poemas, Ocnos (Barcelona, Spain), 1973.

El Deten (novel; also see below), Lumen (Barcelona, Spain), 1977.

Sobrevivo (poetry; title means "I Survive"), Casa de las Americas (Havana, Cuba), 1978.

(With Darwin J. Flakoll) *La Encrucijada salvadorena* (historical essays), CIDOB (Barcelona, Spain), 1980.

(Author of introduction) *Homenaje a El Salvador,* edited by Alberto Corazon, Visor (Madrid, Spain), 1981.

(Editor and translator, with Darwin J. Flakoll) *Nuevas voces de norteamerica* (bilingual edition), Plaza y Janes (Barcelona, Spain), 1981.

Suma y sigue (anthology), Visor (Madrid, Spain), 1981.

(Translator, with Darwin J. Flakoll) Robert Graves, *Cien poemas* (anthology), Lumen (Barcelona, Spain), 1982.

Flores del volcan/Flowers from the Volcano (anthology; parallel text in English and Spanish), translated by Carolyn Forche, University of Pittsburgh Press (Pittsburgh, PA), 1982.

(With Darwin J. Flakoll) *Nicaragua: La Revolucion sandinista; Una Cronica politica, 1855-1979* (history), Ediciones Era (Mexico), 1982.

(With Darwin J. Flakoll) *No me agarran viva: La Mujer salvadorena en lucha,* Ediciones Era (Mexico), 1983, translated by Amanda Hopkinson as *They Won't Take Me Alive: Salvadoran Women in Struggle for National Liberation,* Women's Press (London, England), 1987.

Poesia viva (anthology), Blackrose Press (London, England), 1983.

Album familiar (novel; title means "Family Album"; also see below), Editorial Universitaria Centroamericana (San Jose, Costa Rica), 1984.

Para romper el silencio: Resistencia y lucha en las carceles salvadorenas (title means "Breaking the Silence: Resistance and Struggle in Salvadoran Prisons"), Ediciones Era (Mexico), 1984.

Pueblo de Dios y de mandinga: Con el asesoriamiento cientifico de Slim (also see below), Ediciones Era (Mexico), 1985.

(Translator, with Darwin J. Flakoll) Carlos Fonseca, *Viva Sandino,* Vanguardia (Managua, Nicaragua), 1985.

Pueblo de dios y de mandinga (contains *El Deten, Album familiar,* and *Pueblo de dios y de mandinga*), Editorial Lumen (Barcelona, Spain), 1986, translated by Amanda Hopkinson as *Family Album,* Curbstone Press (Willimantic, CT), 1991.

Despierta, mi bien, despierta (title means "Wake up, My Love, Wake up"), UCA Editores (San Salvador, El Salvador), 1986.

Luisa en el pais de la realidad/Luisa in Realityland (parallel text in English and Spanish), translated by Darwin J. Flakoll, Curbstone Press/Talman (Willimantic, CT), 1987.

(Editor and translator, with Darwin J. Flakoll) *On the Front Line: Guerrilla Poems of El Salvador,* Editorial Nueva Nicaragua (Managua, Nicaragua), 1988.

Y este poema rio, Editorial Nueva Nicaragua (Managua, Nicaragua), 1988.

Mujer del rio/Woman of the River (poetry; parallel text in English and Spanish), translated by Darwin J. Flakoll, University of Pittsburgh Press (Pittsburgh, PA), 1989.

Fuga de Canto Grande, UCA Editores, 1992, translated by Darwin J. Flakoll as *Tunnel to Canto Grande,* Curbstone Press (Willimantic, CT), 1996.

Fugues (parallel text in English and Spanish), translated by Darwin J. Flakoll, Curbstone Press (Willimantic, CT), 1993.

Somoza: Expediente cerrado: La Historia de un ajusticiamiento, Editorial el Gato Negro (Managua, Nicaragua), 1993, translation published as *Death of Somoza,* Curbstone Press (Willimantic, CT), 1996.

Variaciones en clave de mi, Libertarias/Prodhufi (Madrid, Spain), 1993.

Clave de mi, EDUCA (San Jose, Costa Rica), 1996.

(Editor, with Darwin J. Flakoll) *Blood Pact and Other Stories,* translated by Daniel Balderston and others, Curbstone Press (Willimantic, CT), 1997.

El Niño que buscaba a ayer (title means "The Boy Who Searched for Yesterday"), 1997.

Umbrales = Thresholds: Poems, translated by Darwin J. Flakoll, Curbstone Press (Willimantic, CT), 1997.

Saudade = Sorrow (poems), translated by Carolyn Forche, Curbstone Press (Willimantic, CT), 1999.

In Soltando Amarras = Casting Off (poems), translated by Margaret Sayers Peden, Curbstone Press (Willimantic, CT), 2003.

Una vida en poemas (poems), Editorial Hispamer (Managua, Nicaragua), 2003.

Contributor to books including *Lives on the Line: The Testimony of Contemporary Latin American Authors,* edited by Doris Meyer, University of California Press (Berkeley, CA) 1988; and *You Can't Drown the Fire: Latin American Women Writing in Exile,* edited by Alicia Portnoy, Cleis Press (Pittsburgh, PA), 1988; contributor to periodicals such as *Casa de las Americas* and *Massachusetts Review.*

SIDELIGHTS: Considered one of the most prolific and significant voices in late twentieth-century Latin-American literature, Claribel Alegría, a poet, novelist, and testimony writer, was born in Nicaragua and spent her childhood in exile in El Salvador. Alegría lived in the United States, Mexico, Chile, Uruguay, and Majorca, Spain, before returning to her native Nicaragua upon the victory of the Sandinista Front for National Liberation (FSLN) in 1979. According to Jan Clausen in the *Women's Review of Books,* Alegría represents a writer of "an educated class which is relatively privileged by Central American standards, yet has suffered enough at the hands of repressive oligarchs who represent North American imperial interests to be acutely sensitized to the plight of workers and campesinos."

Alegría's mother loved to read poetry, her father loved to recite it, and both loved to recite it to their young daughter. She, in turn, loved to create it, and her mother insisted she dictate it to her while she wrote it down. Although she learned to read French from her grandfather who had an extensive library containing many books written in French, Alegría had no real interest in literature other than poetry. As a child, she dreamt of becoming an actress or a performer of tragic theater and as an adolescent, of becoming a scientist or a doctor. When she was fourteen, she read Rainer Maria Rilke's 1903 *Letters to a Young Poet,* which made such an impression on her that she decided there and then that poetry would become her life's pursuit; her first poems were published in *Repertorio Americano* when she was seventeen. At the age of eighteen, she was admitted to a girls' finishing school in Hammond, Louisiana, and in 1944, she was awarded a scholarship to summer school at Loyola University in New Orleans. There she met poet Juan Ramon Jiménez who lived in Washington, D.C., but who had read some of her poems in *Repertorio Americano.* He invited her to move to Washington, D.C., where he could mentor her while she attended college. She forfeited a four-year scholarship elsewhere, enrolled at Georgetown University, acquired a job as a translator at the Pan-American Union, pursued her degree in philosophy and letters, and studied writing verse under Jiménez's mentorship. Within three years, Jiménez had chosen twenty-two of her poems, which were published as *Anillo de silencio.*

Political discord, however, galvanized Alegría's desire to become a writer. She told Marjorie Agosin in *Americas* that it was not until the Cuban Revolution in the early 1950s that she began to write about more serious topics. "I was living in Paris," she explained, and "Carlos Fuentes and other friends . . . encouraged me to write down those memories" precipitated by the revolution. For Alegría, this meant writing "about what was happening around me, to go outside of my bourgeois family." Her first prose novel, *Cenizas de Izalco (Ashes of Izalco),* was the result; it went on to become one of the Salvadoran education system's official texts.

Often employing feminist and political themes, Alegría's novels are sometimes classified as "resistance narratives." *Ashes of Izalco* is a love story cowritten with her husband, Darwin J. Flakoll, that recounts the repressive aspects of small-town life in El Salvador. The narrative focuses on events that occurred in 1932, the year the Salvadoran government massacred hundreds of political dissidents in Alegría's adopted hometown of Santa Ana. Focusing on a daughter's discovery of her mother's love affair, the novel provides little direct discourse on the massacre itself. Some critics have interpreted the detachment of

Alegría's characters from their political surroundings as a commentary on the United States' involvement in the war-torn countries of El Salvador and Nicaragua.

With *Despierta, mi bien, despierta* ("Wake up, My Love, Wake Up"), Alegría focuses on Lorena, an upper-middle-class Salvadoran woman who is married to a member of the oligarchy in 1980. Although her social class affords her many privileges, she is lonely and bored, and her marriage is dull. When she has an affair with a young guerrilla poet, however, she becomes more attuned to the political and social situation in her country. Seymour Menton observed in *World Literature Today* that "the novel ends melodramatically with Lorena's discovering her lover's severed head on her car seat."

Linda Gregory in the *American Book Review* praised the way Alegría's language in her novel *Luisa in Realityland,* "delights and astounds in its presence as words, sounds, and images." A novel that blends poetry and prose in telling about the coming of age of a young girl in El Salvador, *Luisa in Realityland* employs the techniques of magic realism to blend traditional Central American fables with actual historic events in order to emphasize Latin America's cultural heritage. The novel "moves the reader through a narrative mixing present with past, dreams with reality, the personal with the political," commented Gregory, who concluded that the work is a "complexly textured piece of literature which is as concerned with modes of perception as with that which is perceived and just as dependent on the resonance between images as on the images themselves."

Despite her prolific and acclaimed prose output, Alegría considers poetry, which she has been writing since 1948, to be her primary passion. But her verse was not widely known among English-speaking North Americans until the publication in 1982 of *Flowers from the Volcano,* a bilingual collection of poetry drawn from more than two decades of work. Helene J. F. De Aguilar, in a *Parnassus* essay, quoted translator Carolyn Forche from her preface to this collection: "In her poems, we listen to the stark cry of the human spirit, stripped by necessity of its natural lyricism, deprived of the luxuries of cleverness and virtuosity enjoyed by poets of the north." Calling the poems neither easy nor comfortable, a *Publishers Weekly* contributor wrote that although the poems "ask us to share the loss of friends and country, to stand witness

to torture and violent death," there is a spirit of hope in them as well, "of belief in the power of the word and in the value of one human memory."

Like *Flowers from the Volcano,* Alegría's poetry collection *Woman of the River* is concerned with political turmoil, repression of citizens, and torture in Central America. Alegría's later poetry collection, *Fugues,* translated by her husband Darwin J. Flakoll, was faulted by one critic for its failure to match the level of insight and accomplished imagery revealed in her previous volumes. Others critics, however, emphasized the distinctly personal voice of *Fugues,* arguing that the collection presents a deliberate contrast with her previous work in its use of classical imagery and concern with the theme of death from an individual, rather than political, perspective.

With *On the Front Line: Guerrilla Poems of El Salvador,* a bilingual anthology of poetry, Alegría turned to translation and editorship, again in collaboration with her husband. Reviewers have observed that while the terror of war provides the dark background to the poems, the central focus of the verse is human and life-affirming.

In *No me agarran viva: La Mujer salvadorena en lucha,* translated in a 1987 English version as *They Won't Take Me Alive: Salvadoran Women in Struggle for National Liberation,* Alegría recounts the life of Eugenia, a Salvadoran guerrilla leader who was killed by army troops in 1981. Through interviews with Eugenia's family and friends, Alegría offers a portrait of a committed, brave woman who lost numerous friends in battles with the government. Some critics faulted the book for being overly doctrinaire and one-dimensional. Writing in the *New Statesman,* Jane Dibblin observed that the work is "stiff with political jargon" but remarked that Alegría's verse nonetheless "challenges and lingers in the mind."

When Flakoll, to whom Alegría had been married for forty-seven years, died in 1995, the poet told Agosin she felt "mutilated." Yet this loss became the source of yet another poetry collection, *Saudade = Sorrow,* published in a bilingual edition with an English translation by Forche. The book was welcomed as a sensitive, tender, and powerful collection that, according to Forche, records "the passage of the human soul through searing grief and separation." *Bloomsbury*

Review critic Cristian Salazar hailed *Sorrow* as a "gorgeous and brave" work that "pulses with the rhythm of grief and grieving." A writer for *Kirkus Reviews* observed that "these simple lyrics of solitude and sorrow, with their haiku-like brevity, at their best achieve the purity and clarity of classical verse." The book was chosen for the Academy of American Poets Book Club catalog, and the American Booksellers Association selected it for its Book Sense program.

When reviewing *In Soltando Amarras = Casting Off*—a natural sequel to *Saudade = Sorrow,* in which Alegría immortalizes her dead husband as she struggles with her loss—Juana Ponce de Leon commented in *School Library Journal* that Alegría "comes from a culture where the living stay in constant conversation with the dead. With an ease and laughter that register clearly over our long-distance telephone connection, she says, 'Since I was very young the two main themes in my writing have been love and death. When I was young, however, death was distant. Now death is near, especially since Bud passed away. Now death is my friend. I speak to her.'" Ponce de Leon added that, in *In Soltando Amarras,* "the past looms large as the future diminishes. The poems illuminate the open road that lies before the prize-winning poet and evoke the feelings that go with charting new terrain."

BIOGRAPHICAL AND CRITICAL SOURCES:

BOOKS

Alegría, Claribel, *Saudade = Sorrow,* translated by Carolyn Forche, Curbstone Press (Willimantic, CT), 1999.

Boschetto-Sandoval, Sandra M., *Claribel Alegría and Central American Literature: Critical Essays,* Ohio University Center for International Studies (Athens, OH), 1994.

Contemporary Literary Criticism, Volume 75, Gale (Detroit, MI), 1993.

Dictionary of Literary Biography, Volume 145: *Modern Latin-American Fiction Writers, Second Series,* Gale (Detroit, MI), 1994.

Encyclopedia of World Literature in the Twentieth Century, St. James Press (Detroit, MI), 1999.

PERIODICALS

American Book Review, July, 1988, Linda Gregory, review of *Luisa in Realityland.*

Americas, February, 1999, interview with Marjorie Agosin, p. 48.

Bloomsbury Review, March-April, 2000, Cristian Salazar, review of *Saudade = Sorrow.*

Library Journal, February 15, 2000, Judy Clarence, review of *Sorrow,* p. 166.

New Statesman, April 24, 1987, Jane Dibblin, review of *No me agarran viva: La Mujer salvadorena en lucha,* p. 28.

Parnassus, spring, 1985, Helene J. F. De Aguilar, review of *Flowers from the Volcano.*

Publishers Weekly, October 22, 1982, review of *Flowers from the Volcano;* October 18, 1993, review of *Fugues,* p. 69; October 25, 1999, review of *Sorrow,* p. 78.

School Library Journal, June, 2003, Juana Ponce de Leon, "Acetylene Rose" (interview), p. 30.

Times Educational Supplement, May 29, 1987, p. 23.

Women's Review of Books, October, 1984.

World Literature Today, spring, 1988, Seymour Menton, review of *Despierta, mi bien, despierta.**

*   *   *

ALLABY, (John) Michael 1933-

PERSONAL: Born September 18, 1933, in Belper, Derbyshire, England; son of Albert (a chiropodist) and Jessie May (King) Allaby; married Ailsa Marthe McGregor, January 3, 1957; children: Vivien Gail, Robin Graham. *Ethnicity:* British. *Politics:* "My political views are definitely left of center." *Hobbies and other interests:* "Reading (for pleasure as well as work), watching movies, listening to music, gardening, walking (gently!)."

ADDRESSES: Home—Braehead Cottage, Tighnabruaich, Argyll PA21 2ED, Scotland. *E-mail*—mike@michaelallaby.com.

CAREER: Variously employed as police cadet, 1949-51, and actor, 1954-64; Soil Association, Suffolk, England, member of editorial department, 1964-72, editor of *Span,* 1967-72; Ecosystems Ltd., Wadebridge, Cornwall, England, member of board of directors, associate editor of *Ecologist,* 1970-72, managing editor, 1972-73; freelance writer, 1973—. *Military service:* Royal Air Force, 1951-54, served as pilot; became pilot officer.

MEMBER: Society for the History of Natural History, Planetary Society, Society of Authors, New York Academy of Sciences, Association of British Science Writers.

AWARDS, HONORS: Runner-up, Times Educational Supplement Information Book Award, 1984, for *The Food Chain*; *Dangerous Weather: Hurricanes* selected as one of New York Public Library's 1998 books for the teenage; Aventis Junior Prize for Science Books, 2001, for *How the Weather Works*; *Encyclopedia of Weather and Climate* listed among top ten Science Reference Sources in *Booklist*, 2002; Society of School Librarians, honor book selection, science 7-12 category, 2002.

WRITINGS:

DICTIONARIES

(Editor) *A Dictionary of the Environment*, Macmillan (New York, NY), 1977, 2nd edition, New York University Press (New York, NY), 1983, 3rd edition, Macmillan (New York, NY), 1988, 4th edition published as *Macmillan Dictionary of the Environment*, Macmillan (London, England), 1994.

(Editor) *The Oxford Dictionary of Natural History*, Oxford University Press (New York, NY), 1985.

(Editor, with wife, Ailsa Allaby) *The Concise Oxford Dictionary of Earth Sciences*, Oxford University Press (New York, NY), 1990, 2nd edition, 1999, 3rd edition, 2003.

(Editor) *The Concise Oxford Dictionary of Zoology*, Oxford University Press (New York, NY), 1991, 2nd edition, 1999, 3rd edition, 2003.

(Editor) *The Concise Oxford Dictionary of Botany*, Oxford University Press (New York, NY), 1992; 2nd edition published as *Oxford Dictionary of Plant Sciences*, Oxford University Press (New York, NY), 1998.

The Concise Oxford Dictionary of Ecology, Oxford University Press (New York, NY), 1994, 2nd edition, 1998, 3rd edition, 2004.

(Advisory editor) *Illustrated Dictionary of Science* (previously issued with a different advisory editor as *Encyclopedic Dictionary of Science*, 1988), Facts on File (New York, NY), 1995.

"ELEMENTS" SERIES

Air: The Nature of Atmosphere and the Climate, Facts on File (New York, NY), 1992.

Water: Its Global Nature, Facts on File (New York, NY), 1992.

Earth: Our Planet and Its Resources, Facts on File (New York, NY), 1993.

Fire: The Vital Source of Energy, Facts on File (New York, NY), 1993.

"DANGEROUS WEATHER" SERIES

Hurricanes, Facts on File (New York, NY), 1997, 2nd edition, 2003.

Blizzards, Facts on File (New York, NY), 1997, 2nd edition, illustrated by Richard Garratt, 2004.

Droughts, Facts on File (New York, NY), 1998, 2nd edition, 2003.

Tornadoes, Facts on File (New York, NY), 1997, 2nd edition, illustrated by Richard Garratt, 2004.

Floods, Facts on File (New York, NY), 1998, 2nd edition, illustrated by Richard Garratt, 2003.

A Chronology of Weather, Facts on File (New York, NY), 1998, 2nd edition, illustrated by Richard Garratt, 2004.

Fog, Smoke, and Poisoned Rain, illustrated by Richard Garratt, Facts on File (New York, NY), 2003.

A Change in the Weather, illustrated by Richard Garratt, Facts on File (New York, NY), 2004.

MULTIVOLUME SETS

Biomes of the World (nine-volume set including *Polar Regions, Deserts, Oceans, Wetlands, Mountains, Temperate Forests, Tropical Forests, Temperate Grasslands,* and *Tropical Grasslands*), Grolier Educational (Danbury, CT), 1999.

Plants and Plant Life (wrote five volumes of a ten-volume series; titles include *Plant Ecology, Plants Used by People, Conifers, Flowering Plants: The Monocotyledons,* and *Flowering Plants: The Dicotyledons*), Grolier Educational (Danbury, CT), 2001.

(With Derek Gjertsen) *Makers of Science* (five-volume set), Oxford University Press (New York, NY), 2002.

"ECOSYSTEM" SERIES

Temperate Forests, Facts on File (New York, NY), 1999.

Deserts, Facts on File (New York, NY), 2001.

WITH JANE BURTON

Your Cat's First Year, photographs by Jane Burton and Kim Taylor, Simon & Schuster (New York, NY), 1985.

Nine Lives: A Year in the Life of a Cat Family, photographs by Jane Burton and Kim Taylor, Ebury Press (London, England), 1985.

A Dog's Life, Howell Book (New York, NY), 1986.

A Pony's Tale: A Year in the Life of a Foal, photographs by Jane Burton and Kim Taylor, Half Halt Press (Gaithersburg, MD), 1987.

OTHER

The Eco-Activists, Knight (London, England), 1971.

Who Will Eat? The World Food Problem, Stacey (London, England), 1972.

(With others) *A Blueprint for Survival,* Houghton Mifflin, 1972.

(With Colin Blythe and Colin Hines) *Losing Ground: The First of Three Discussion Papers on United Kingdom Food Prospects,* Friends of the Earth (London, England), 1974.

(With Floyd Allen) *Robots behind the Plow: Modern Farming and the Need for an Organic Alternative,* Rodale Press (Emmaus, PA), 1974.

Ecology, Hamlyn (New York, NY), 1975.

(With Marika Hanbury-Tenison, Hugh Sharman, and John Seymour) *The Survival Handbook: Self-Sufficiency for Everyone,* Macmillan (London, England), 1975.

Inventing Tomorrow: How to Live in a Changing World, Hodder & Stoughton (London, England), 1976.

World Food Resources: Actual and Potential, Applied Science Publishers (London, England), 1977.

(With Colin Tudge) *Home Farm: Complete Food Self-Sufficiency,* Macmillan (London, England), 1977.

Animals That Hunt, Hamlyn (New York, NY), 1979.

Wildlife of North America, Hamlyn (New York, NY), 1979.

Making and Managing a Smallholding, David & Charles (North Pomfret, VT), 1980.

(With Peter Bunyard) *The Politics of Self-Sufficiency,* Oxford University Press (New York, NY), 1980.

A Year in the Life of a Field, David & Charles (North Pomfret, VT), 1981.

Le Foreste Tropicale, Instituto Geografico de Agostini (Italy), 1981.

Animal Artisans, Knopf (New York, NY), 1982.

(With Peter Crawford) *The Curious Cat,* M. Joseph (London, England), 1982.

(With James Lovelock) *The Great Extinction: The Solution to One of the Great Mysteries of Science, the Disappearance of the Dinosaurs,* Doubleday (Garden City, NY), 1983.

(With James Lovelock) *The Greening of Mars,* St. Martin's Press (New York, NY), 1984.

2040: Our World in the Future, Gollancz (London, England), 1985.

Your Child and the Computer, Methuen (London, England), 1985.

The Woodland Trust Book of British Woodlands, David & Charles (North Pomfret, VT), 1986.

Ecology Facts, Hamlyn, 1986, 2nd revised edition published as *Green Facts,* 1989.

A Guide to Gaia, Macdonald-Optima (London, England), 1989, published as *A Guide to Gaia: A Survey of the News Science of Our Living Earth,* Dutton (New York, NY), 1990.

Into Harmony with the Planet: The Delicate Balance between Industry and the Environment, Bloomsbury Publishing (London, England), 1990.

(With Neil Curtis) *Planet Earth,* Kingfisher (New York, NY), 1993.

How the Weather Works, Reader's Digest (Pleasantville, NY), 1995.

Facing the Future, Bloomsbury Publishing (London, England), 1995.

Basics of Environmental Science, Routledge (New York, NY), 1996, 2nd edition, 2000.

DK Guide to the Weather, Dorling Kindersley (New York, NY), 2000.

The Environment, illustrated by Mike Saunders and others, Gareth Stevens (Milwaukee, WI), 2000.

Tornadoes and Other Dramatic Weather Systems, Dorling Kindersley (New York, NY), 2001.

(With Robert Anderson and Ian Crofton) *Deserts and Semideserts,* Raintree Steck-Vaughn (Austin, TX), 2002.

The Facts on File Weather and Climate Handbook, Facts on File (New York, NY), 2002.

Encyclopedia of Weather and Climate (two volumes), Facts on File (New York, NY), 2002.

The World's Weather, Gareth Stevens (Milwaukee, WI), 2002.

Also author of *The Changing Uplands,* Countryside Commission, 1983; *The Food Chain,* Andre Deutsch, 1984; *The Ordnance Survey Outdoor Handbook,*

Macmillan/Ordnance Survey, 1987; *Conservation at Home: A Practical Handbook,* Unwin-Hyman, 1988; and *Living in the Greenhouse,* Thorsons, 1990; and edited *Thinking Green: An Anthology of Essential Ecological Writing,* Barrie & Jenkins, 1989.

Contributor to books, including *The Environmental Handbook,* edited by John Barr, Ballantine, 1971; *Can Britain Survive?,* edited by Edward Goldsmith, Stacey, 1971; *Teach-In for Survival: A Record of the Teach-In on a Blueprint for Survival, Held at Imperial College, London, in May 1972,* edited by Michael Schwab, Robinson & Watkins, 1972; *Ecology,* edited by Jonathan Benthall, Longmans, Green, 1973; *Nightwatch,* edited by Linda Gamlin, M. Joseph, 1983; and *Ecology 2000: The Changing Face of the Earth,* edited by Edmund Hillary, Beaufort Books, 1984. Also contributor to *Encyclopaedia Britannica,* and to magazines, journals, and newspapers.

Most of Allaby's works have been published in both the United Kingdom and the United States and several titles have been translated into foreign languages including French, German, Italian, Norwegian, Swedish, and Finnish.

WORK IN PROGRESS: Research into the positive influence technology has made on the quality of human life.

SIDELIGHTS: Born in Belper, Derbyshire, England, in 1933, writer Michael Allaby's early careers included training as a police cadet, working in a morgue, acting in a children's repertory theater, piloting planes for the Royal Air Force, and writing for an environmentalist magazine. Since 1973, however, the author has worked as a freelance writer, penning many books that focus primarily on scientific topics such as ecology and weather. He has written, edited, and revised numerous encyclopedias and dictionaries for prominent publishers such as Facts on File, Macmillan, and Oxford University Press. Allaby wrote on his Web site, "In my books you'll find simply written explanations of what really goes on in the world around us. Over the years I've written about ecology, animal behaviour, farming, and the countryside. More recently a lot of my work has been about weather and climate. . . . Many of my books are for young readers, but I like to think I'm talking to anyone who'll listen."

Allaby's science writings include dictionaries that define terms related to subjects ranging from botany to zoology. *The Concise Oxford Dictionary of Botany,*

later published as *Oxford Dictionary of Plant Sciences,* includes about 5,500 clear, concise entries about plant life. In *The Concise Oxford Dictionary of Ecology,* Allaby defines and discusses ecological topics such as acid rain and the greenhouse effect. Serving as advisory editor, Allaby revised and updated the *Encyclopedic Dictionary of Science* to produce Facts on File's *Illustrated Dictionary of Science.* According to a *Booklist* reviewer, the updated dictionary is "written in clear, nonspecialist language" and includes definitions of terms related to biology, medicine, geology, physical geography, astronomy, and technology.

In his *Basics of Environmental Science,* according to Jonathan Horner of the *Geographical Journal,* "Allaby considers a very wide range of topical environmental concerns including global warming, eutrophication, soil erosion, overfishing, and pollution." Horner praised the author, writing, "Allaby is to be commended for producing a very readable up-to-date introduction to the major disciplines comprising environmental science." In *The Environment,* Allaby writes about nutrient cycles, biomes, the ozone layer, and other topics. Kathleen Isaacs of *School Library Journal* commented, "[*The Environment*] presents a broad, browsable introduction . . . [to] the make-up and natural systems of our planet." Among Allaby's other science writings are the nine-volume *Biomes of the World,* which describes polar regions, oceans, wetlands, and other ecosystems throughout the world; five-volumes of a ten-volume set titled *Plants and Plant Life;* the "Elements" series, which explains earth, fire, water, and air; and the "Ecosystem" series, which discusses topics such as temperate forests and deserts. Claudia Moore of *School Library Journal* called *Deserts* from the "Ecosystem" series "a wonderful, reader-friendly work" full of "outstanding color photographs and clear diagrams." The book discusses the geography, geology, biology, history, economics, health, and management of deserts.

Another major focus of Allaby's works has been weather and climate. He has written encyclopedias, dictionaries, and handbooks on weather and climate, and has penned an entire series on dangerous weather conditions. The "Dangerous Weather" series includes volumes on severe weather conditions such as droughts, blizzards, floods, hurricanes, tornadoes, and even fog. *Booklist*'s Mary Romano Marks observed that the examples in *Droughts* "vividly bring to life the reality of extreme forms of weather." Shauna

Yusko of *School Library Journal* commented that while the chapters in *Fog, Smog, and Poisoned Rain* were "somewhat dense," the "well-written" book will "provide enough material for students researching meteorology, climatology, and the environment." In his *DK Guide to Weather,* Allaby presents information on each type of weather phenomenon on a two-page spread, complete with color photographs. *Booklist*'s Carolyn Phelan called the photographs "clear, colorful, and dramatic," and noted that "students researching specific topics will find themselves browsing widely through this impressive volume."

In Allaby's *Encyclopedia of Weather and Climate,* the author provides a comprehensive overview of weather-related terms, and offers biographical information on those who contributed to the study of weather. Included in the book is a bibliography, references to helpful books, Web sites, and other resources, and five appendices with titles such as "Chronology of Disasters," "Chronology of Discoveries," and "Tornadoes of the Past." *School Library Journal*'s Dana McDougald labeled the *Encyclopedia of Weather and Climate* "a much-needed resource that does not disappoint." Similarly, Mary Ellen Quinn wrote in *Booklist,* "This book stands out because it is an easy-to-understand, well-put-together text." Allaby's *Facts on File Weather and Climate Handbook* also received good reviews from critics. Robin N. Sinn of *Reference and User Services Quarterly* called the volume "a nice reference work covering the basic terms in climate and weather."

Turning his attention away from environmental science, Allaby wrote *Makers of Science* with Derek Gjertsen. According to a *Booklist* critic, *Makers of Science* takes "a slightly different approach to ordinary biographical information on scientists. . . . This set," the reviewer continued, "incorporates the political and social setting as well as the scientific achievements of each scientist. . . . Scientific principles are clearly explained [and] . . . intriguing personal stories are woven in." The book documents the lives of forty-one important scientists beginning with Aristotle and ending with Stephen Hawking. Brief biographies of other important figures are also included. *School Library Journal* contributor John Peters believed, "For scope, ease of use, and clarity of presentation, this set . . . is likely to become the first choice of middle graders on research missions." The *Booklist* critic concluded, "Science teachers will love the connections made between different inventors' works and how science is relevant to our life today."

Allaby once told *CA:* "In recent years I have become increasingly disturbed by the shift away from scientific, indeed rational, thought in popular culture. Fed by the exaggerated propaganda of the populist environmental movement and by wide, but uninformed concern over ethical issues raised by potential scientific or technological developments, the distrust of scientists and technologists has developed into a fear and rejection of the future itself. The evidence can be seen in the quest for spurious certainties by adherents of fundamentalist religions, the invention of new pseudo-religions that rely on magic to achieve control of the natural forces, and the sentimental yearning for a world in which plants and animals can live in cozy harmony with humans enjoying the supposedly simple life that our ancestors are alleged to have enjoyed in the distant past.

"I believe these views must be challenged in the strongest possible terms, lest their gloomy forebodings become self-fulfilling prophecies, and I am working to develop an argument that will achieve this. The resulting book will re-assert the positive contribution to the quality of our lives that has been made in the past by scientific discoveries and technological development and will list some of the contributions that may be made in years to come."

BIOGRAPHICAL AND CRITICAL SOURCES:

PERIODICALS

American Reference Books Annual, 1996, review of *The Concise Oxford Dictionary of Ecology,* p. 777, review of *Illustrated Dictionary of Science,* p. 639; 1999, review of *Blizzards,* p. 634, review of *A Chronology of Weather,* p. 634, review of *Droughts,* p. 634, review of *Floods,* p. 634, review of *Hurricanes,* p. 634, review of *Tornadoes,* p. 635.

American Scientist, November, 1995, review of *Illustrated Dictionary of Science,* p. 563.

Appraisal: Science Books for Young People, Volume 29, 1996, review of *Illustrated Dictionary of Science,* p. 6.

Booklist, January 15, 1995, review of *The Concise Oxford Dictionary of Ecology,* p. 950, review of *A Dictionary of the Environment,* p. 950; October 1, 1995, review of *Illustrated Dictionary of Science,* p. 350; March 1, 1997, review of *Enciclopedia*

Visual: El Planeta Tierra, p. 1196; December 1, 1997, Mary Romano Marks, review of *Droughts,* p. 621; December 1, 2000, Carolyn Phelan, review of *DK Guide to Weather,* p. 729; May 1, 2002, Mary Ellen Quinn, review of *Encyclopedia of Weather and Climate,* p. 1542; June 1, 2002, review of *Makers of Science,* p. 1776.

Book Report, January-February, 1998, James Gross, review of *Blizzards,* p. 53, review of *Hurricanes,* p. 53, review of *Tornadoes,* p. 53; September, 1998, review of *Floods,* p. 72; September-October, 1999, Sandra J. Morton, review of *Temperate Forests,* p. 70; November, 1999, review of *Biomes of the World,* p. 85; March, 2002, review of *Makers of Science,* p. 57.

Books for Keeps, May, 2001, review of *DK Guide to Weather,* p. 25.

Children's Bookwatch, March, 1998, review of *Droughts,* p. 2.

Choice: Current Reviews for Academic Libraries, January, 1995, N. Chipman-Shlaes, review of *The Concise Oxford Dictionary of Ecology,* p. 744; June, 2002, J. C. Stachacz, review of *Encyclopedia of Weather and Climate,* p. 1740.

Christian Science Monitor, August 31, 1983.

Geographical Journal, November, 1997, Jonathan Horner, review of *Basics of Environmental Science,* pp. 310-311.

Horn Book Guide, spring, 1998, review of *Blizzards,* p. 122, review of *Droughts,* p. 122, review of *Hurricanes,* p. 122, review of *Tornadoes,* p. 122; fall, 1998, review of *A Chronology of Weather,* p. 374, review of *Floods,* p. 374; spring, 2001, review of *DK Guide to Weather,* p. 108; fall, 2001, review of *The Environment,* p. 359; spring, 2002, review of *Tornadoes and Other Dramatic Weather Systems,* p. 133.

Kirkus Reviews, September 1, 1997, review of *Tornadoes,* p. 1384; November 1, 1997, review of *Droughts,* p. 1640.

Library Journal, October 15, 1995, Laura Lipton, review of *Illustrated Dictionary of Science,* p. 54; November 1, 2002, Nancy R. Curtis, review of *Encyclopedia of Weather and Climate,* p. 76.

Nature, June 2, 1994, John Lawton, review of *The Concise Oxford Dictionary of Ecology,* p. 368; February 1, 1996, review of *Facing the Future,* p. 412; February 29, 1996, review of *The Concise Oxford Dictionary of Ecology,* p. 784.

New Scientist, April 8, 1995, review of *How the Weather Works,* p. 41; June 10, 1995, review of *Facing the Future,* p. 43; October 11, 1997, review of *Basics of Environmental Science,* p. 48.

New Technical Books, May, 1994, review of *The Concise Oxford Dictionary of Ecology,* p. 575.

New York Times Book Review, January 6, 1985.

Personal Computer World, May, 1996, Jessica Hodgson, review of *Facing the Future,* p. 228.

Population Studies, November, 1995, Richard Sandbrook, review of *Macmillan Dictionary of the Environment* (4th edition), p. 537.

Publishers Weekly, August 28, 2000, "A Wonderful World," review of *DK Guide to Weather,* p. 85.

Reference and Research Book News, March, 1994, review of *Fire: The Vital Source of Energy,* p. 52; December, 1994, review of *The Concise Oxford Dictionary of Ecology,* p. 41; September, 1995, review of *Illustrated Dictionary of Science,* p. 57.

Reference and User Services Quarterly, spring, 2003, Robin N. Sinn, review of *The Facts on File Weather and Climate Handbook,* p. 265.

Reference Reviews, May, 2001, review of *Deserts,* p. ONL; March, 2002, review of *Encyclopedia of Weather and Climate,* p. ONL.

School Librarian, winter, 1999, review of *Temperate Forests,* p. 219.

School Library Journal, February, 1994, John Peters, review of *Planet Earth,* p. 108; September, 1995, review of *Illustrated Dictionary of Science,* p. 237; April, 1998, Jeffrey A. French, review of *Hurricanes,* p. 140, review of *Tornadoes,* p. 140; November, 1999, review of *Biomes of the World,* p. 75; March, 2001, Kathleen Isaacs, review of *The Environment,* p. 259; August, 2001, Claudia Moore, review of *Deserts,* p. 211; May, 2002, Dana McDougald, review of *Encyclopedia of Weather and Climate,* p. 91; February, 2002, John Peters, review of *Makers of Science,* p. 84; May, 2003, John Peters, review of *Makers of Science,* p. 101; October, 2003, review of *Makers of Science,* p. 46, Shauna Yusko, review of *Fog, Smog, and Poisoned Rain,* p. 103.

Science Books and Films, October, 1995, review of *Illustrated Dictionary of Science,* p. 206; November, 1999, review of *Biomes of the World,* p. 274.

SciTech Book News, December, 1994, review of *The Concise Oxford Dictionary of Ecology,* p. 17; July, 1995, review of *The Illustrated Dictionary of Science,* p. 4; June, 1999, review of *Temperate Forests,* p. 70; March, 2001, review of *Deserts,* p. 61; September, 2001, review of *Basics of Environmental Science* (2nd edition), p. 10.

Times (London), January 23, 1986.

Times Educational Supplement, July 7, 1995, Dennis Ashton, review of *How the Weather Works,* p. R4.

Times Literary Supplement, July 29, 1986.

Voice of Youth Advocates, December, 1995, review of *How the Weather Works,* p. 319; June, 2001, review of *Deserts,* p. 149.

ONLINE

Michael Allaby Web site, http://www.michaelallaby. com/ (June 30, 2004), author's homepage.*

*　　*　　*

ALVAREZ, A(lfred) 1929-

PERSONAL: Born August 5, 1929, in London, England; son of Bertie and Katie (Levy) Alvarez; married Ursula Graham Barr, 1956 (divorced, 1961); married Audrey Anne Adams, 1966; children: (first marriage) Adam Richard; (second marriage) Luke Lyon, Kate. *Education:* Attended Corpus Christi College, Oxford, B.A., 1952, M.A., 1956. *Hobbies and other interests:* Rock climbing, poker, classical music.

ADDRESSES: Agent—c/o Aitken and Stone Ltd., 29 Fernshaw Rd., London SW10 0TG, England. *E-mail*—aalvarez@compuserve.com.

CAREER: Oxford University, Corpus Christi College, Oxford, England, senior research scholar, 1952-55, and tutor in English, 1954-55; Princeton University, Princeton, NJ, Procter visiting fellow, 1953-54; Rockefeller Foundation, New York, NY, visiting fellow, 1955-56, 1958; *Observer,* London, England, poetry editor and critic, 1956-66; freelance writer, 1956; *Journal of Education,* poetry critic and editor, London, 1957; Gauss Seminarian and visiting lecturer, Princeton University, 1957-58; D. H. Lawrence fellow, University of New Mexico, 1958; drama critic, *New Statesman,* London, England, 1958-60; visiting professor at Brandeis University, Waltham, MA, 1960-61, and State University of New York—Buffalo, NY, 1966; Penguin Modern European Poets in Translation, advisory editor, 1965-75; *Voices* program, presenter, Channel 4 Television, 1982.

MEMBER: Climbers' Club, Alpine Club.

A. Alvarez

AWARDS, HONORS: Rockefeller fellowship, 1955-56; Vachel Lindsay Prize for Poetry (Chicago, IL), 1961.

WRITINGS:

(Poems), Fantasy Press (Oxford, England), 1952.

Stewards of Excellence: Studies in Modern English and American Poets, Scribner (New York, NY), 1958, published as *The Shaping Spirit: Studies in Modern English and American Poets,* Chatto & Windus (London, England), 1958.

The End of It, privately printed, 1958.

The School of Donne, Chatto & Windus (London, England), 1961, Pantheon (New York, NY), 1962.

(Editor and author of introduction) *The New Poetry,* Penguin (Harmondsworth, England), 1962, revised edition, 1966.

Under Pressure: The Writer in Society, Eastern Europe and the U.S.A., Penguin (Baltimore, MD), 1965, published as *Under Pressure: The Artist and Society, Eastern Europe and the U.S.A.,* Penguin (Harmondsworth, England), 1965.

Lost (poems), Turret Books (London, England), 1968.

Beyond All This Fiddle: Essays, 1955-1967, Allen Lane (London, England), 1968, Random House (New York, NY), 1969.

(With Roy Fuller and Anthony Thwaite) *Penguin Modern Poets 18* (poems), Penguin (Harmondsworth, England), 1970.

Apparition (poems), University of Queensland Press (St. Lucia, Australia), 1971.

The Savage God: A Study of Suicide, Weidenfeld & Nicolson (London, England), 1971, Random House (New York, NY), 1972.

The Legacy, Poem-of-the-Month Club (London, England), 1972.

Samuel Beckett, Viking (New York, NY), 1973, published as *Beckett,* Fontana (London, England), 1973.

Hers (novel), Weidenfeld & Nicolson (London, England), 1974, Random House (New York, NY), 1975.

Autumn to Autumn, and Selected Poems, 1953-1976, Macmillan (London, England), 1978.

(Editor, with David Skilton) Thomas Hardy, *Tess of the D'Urbervilles,* Penguin (Harmondsworth, England), 1978.

Hunt (novel), Simon & Schuster (New York, NY), 1978.

Life after Marriage: Love in an Age of Divorce, Simon & Schuster (New York, NY), 1982, published as *Life after Marriage: Scenes from Divorce,* Macmillan (London, England), 1982.

The Biggest Game in Town, Houghton Mifflin (Boston, MA), 1983.

Offshore: A North Sea Journey, Houghton Mifflin (Boston, MA), 1986.

(With Charles Blackman) *Rainforest,* Macmillan (Melbourne, Australia), 1988.

Feeding the Rat: Profile of a Climber, Bloomsbury (London, England), 1988, Atlantic Monthly Press (New York, NY), 1989.

Day of Atonement (novel), J. Cape (London, England), 1991.

(Editor) *The Faber Book of Modern European Poetry,* Faber (London, England), 1992.

Night: An Exploration of Night Life, Night Language, Sleep and Dreams, Norton (New York, NY), 1995.

Where Did It All Go Right? (autobiography), Morrow (New York, NY), 1999.

Poker: Bets, Bluffs, and Bad Beats, edited by Kelly Duane, Chronicle Books (San Francisco, CA), 2001.

Feeding the Rat: A Climber's Life on the Edge, Thunder Mouth Press (New York, NY), 2001.

The Biggest Game in Town, Chronicle Books (San Francisco, CA), 2002.

New and Selected Poems, Waywiser (London, England), 2002.

The Writer's Voice, Norton (New York, NY), 2005.

Also author of screenplay *The Anarchist,* 1969. Contributor to *Observer, New Yorker, Cosmopolitan, Daily Telegraph Magazine, Times, New York Review of Books,* and other periodicals. Advisory editor, "Penguin Modern European Poets" series, 1966-75.

SIDELIGHTS: A. Alvarez first made a name for himself in literary circles with his work as critic, particularly with his meditation on suicide, *The Savage God: A Study of Suicide,* but his career moved in a more creative direction in the late 1960s when, as he once explained, he "had grown weary of writing books about other people's books, so effectively [I] gave up criticism in order to concentrate on [my] own creative work." Since then, he has published several poetry collections and a handful of novels, in which, according to Carol Simpson Stern in *Contemporary Novelists,* "his passion for language and curiosity about the human condition find expression." Though she found some fault in these creative writings, she concluded that Alvarez "writes well and is always eminently readable."

Alvarez published his first poems in 1952, while still at Corpus Christi College at Oxford, and six years later, he privately published a collection called *The End of It.* Three years later, he won a poetry prize for a group of poems about the breakup of his first marriage, which, remarked John Ferns in the *Dictionary of Literary Biography,* "are written in a style that combines natural and violent images to express states of alienation and separation . . . and attempts to capture almost suicidal states of isolation."

However, Alvarez did not fully embrace creative writing until the late 1960s. By the beginning of the next decade, he was established "as a recognized, if minor, contemporary British poet," Ferns related. Despite these early successes, Alvarez has never produced a large body of poetry. Stern wrote in *Contemporary Poets* that the "published poetry of A. Alvarez is slight indeed in volume, but it is rich in its economy." His body of work is consistent in its preoccupation with themes of love, separation, and death.

Alvarez's later poems often concern mates divided by fears. Noted Stern in *Contemporary Poets,* "They are poems of ephemera, in which an emotion is briefly isolated, felt, and wafted away, leaving the persona with a sense of perplexity and regret." The collection *Autumn to Autumn, and Selected Poems, 1953-1976,* contains one new, seven-sequence poem along with poems that had appeared over the previous two decades. Alvarez stated that *Autumn to Autumn* "contains all the poems I want to preserve." The new work, depicting a cycle of loss and renewal, is full of "delicate, lyric particularity and subtle rhythms," observed Ferns, "reminiscent in places of Lawrence and the Thomas Hardy of the 1912-1913 poems." Stern, in *Contemporary Poets,* also commented that some of the earlier poems in the collection "recall Plath's stridency and savage treatment of love's anger." Derek Sanford of *Books and Bookmen* further praised this work as "good, very good, strictly minor poetry, much of which poets with bigger names might justifiably be proud."

Alvarez first turned to fiction writing in the early 1970s with *Hers,* a novel about a middle-aged woman married to an older university professor, who has an affair with one of her husband's students. Stern, in *Contemporary Novelists,* found that Alvarez's "portrait of the professor Charles is both entertaining and honest." *Hers,* drawing upon some of Alvarez's personal experiences, also shares themes of his poetry in his characters' inability to forge meaningful communication; when Charles discovers his wife's affair, he cannot even speak his own words and instead quotes Shakespeare's Othello.

Alvarez's other novels, *Hunt* and *Day of Atonement,* are written in the thriller tradition. In *Hunt* he tells the story of Conrad Jessup, whose quest for excitement leads him to the discovery of a murdered body and a charge by the police that he is the killer. Jessup, once released, seeks the real killer and so becomes involved in a game of international intrigue. Stern, in her *Contemporary Novelists* essay, deemed the plot "slow and obvious." A *Contemporary Review* critic, though, declared of the book, "Taut, disturbing and expertly constructed, this is a novel not to be missed."

Day of Atonement finds a married couple, Joe and Judy Constantine, implicated after their friend Tommy Apple mysteriously dies. The Constantines are hounded by drug traffickers and the police alike, and Joe finds that a questionable favor he once did for Tommy now endangers his relationship to Judy. Stern, in *Contemporary Novelists,* looked on *Day of Atonement* in a far more favorable light than *Hunt.* "At one level," she remarked, "the book is a who-dunnit. . . . At another, it is a rich exploration of friendship, love, guilt, and reparation." She also found that the characters are "compelling" and that the dialogue "rings true." Stern also praised Alvarez's portrayal of the underworld: "His sense of detail, the excitement, and the people is unerring."

Where Did It All Go Right? is Alvarez's exploration of his life. He describes himself as "not quite an Englishman . . . a Jew with a Spanish surname disguised as a true Brit." His forebears had enjoyed success in business, and although this was followed by reverses of fortune, Alvarez grew up in a world of privilege; he was attended by servants and educated at elite schools. He still felt like an outsider, though, because of being Jewish. He writes of this feeling, of his sometimes difficult relationship with his family, of his happy second marriage, and of his literary career and friendships, especially his role in promoting the poetry of Sylvia Plath, John Berryman, and Robert Lowell. He also details his experiences in World War II and his penchant for dangerous hobbies—boxing, rock climbing, stunt flying—leading an *Economist* reviewer to call him "the Hemingway of poetry." The reviewer described Alvarez's autobiography as "a good read, with lots of page-turning anecdote."

Independent on Sunday contributor William Scammell deemed *Where Did It All Go Right?* an "engaging but exasperating memoir." Scammell remarked of Alvarez, "As a critic he deserves honor for championing the unhappy few, for his fighting spirit—and sometimes deserves flaying for his glibness and exhibitionism." Stephen Pile, writing in the *New Statesman,* found both faults and virtues in the book. "The greatest fault in this autobiography," Pile observed, "is that he gives us, for example, little sense of his life as a poet, novelist or a writer of rather good non-fiction books about divorce, poker and life on North Sea oil rigs. . . . He is also frustratingly silent on his bizarre first marriage," to D. H. Lawrence's granddaughter Ursula, whom Alvarez had known for only seven weeks before they wed. Pile continued, "The greatest virtue of this book lies in the vivid pen portraits he gives of the leading poets of the second half of the twentieth century." Similarly, Ian Sansom, critiquing for the

London Review of Books, pointed out, "There are in fact more than enough highly polished little gems about family and friends and twentieth-century writers, artists and critics to merit the price of the book." Pile added, "What stops this being the club-room ramblings of a senior contributor is that they are expertly written with irony and humor." Michael Schmidt, writing in the daily *Independent,* praised Alvarez's "unostentatious rightness of style. . . . He believes in this world—its people and passions—and he brings it wonderfully alive."

After nearly twenty-five years since his last book of poems, *Autumn to Autumn and Selected Poems 1953-1976,* Alvarez followed up with *New and Selected Poems.* Maintaining the theme of love, which was mixed with death and separation in his last poetry collection, this time around Alvarez delves into the purity of love, not only between individuals, but between man and the world as a whole. "The new poems . . . lack the bustle and energy of the earlier . . . but the best make up for it with a Keatsian appreciation of the sensual possibilities of the world and of human love," commented Martin Crucefix of *Poetry London.* Christopher Levenson of *World Literature Today* commented that for Alvarez, the collection is "surprisingly traditional, even neoclassical." However, he continued, "The evidence of these later poems, which infuse his characteristic wit and imagery with greater colloquial ease, suggests there may be even better things to come."

Alvarez is still primarily known as a critic, but his literary contributions in other capacities are undeniable. As his criticism delves into topics of concern to both literary circles and to contemporary society, his creative work also explores relevant issues, such as suicide, religious prejudice, infidelity, divorce, and crime. In both his poetry and his fiction, Alvarez finds "his own colloquial, modern voice," observed Stern in *Contemporary Poets.* His novels, like his poetry, "offer lyrical descriptions of the urban wasteland or the mood of the day," she wrote. She also maintained in *Contemporary Novelists* that "Alvarez is a writer one wants to read."

BIOGRAPHICAL AND CRITICAL SOURCES:

BOOKS

Alvarez, A., *Where Did It All Go Right?,* Morrow (New York, NY), 1999.

Contemporary Literary Criticism, Gale (Detroit, MI), Volume 5, 1976, Volume 13, 1980.
Contemporary Novelists, 6th edition, St. James Press (Detroit, MI), 1996.
Contemporary Poets, 6th edition, St. James Press (Detroit, MI), 1996.
Dictionary of Literary Biography, Gale (Detroit, MI), Volume 14: *British Novelists since 1960,* 1983, Volume 40: *Poets of Great Britain and Ireland since 1960,* 1985.
Fraser, G. S., *The Modern Writer and His World,* Deutsch (London, England), 1964.
Hamilton, Ian, *The Modern Poet,* Macdonald (London, England), 1968, Horizon Press (New York, NY), 1969.

PERIODICALS

Books and Bookmen, April, 1968; June, 1978.
Book World, August 10, 1969; April 25, 1972.
Christian Science Monitor, January 4, 1962; August 2, 1969.
Contemporary Review, July, 1978, review of *Hunt.*
Detroit News, February 14, 1982.
Economist (U.S.), November 13, 1999, "English Writers: Wish Him Well," p. 11.
Guardian, February 24, 1961.
Independent (London, England), September 18, 1999, Michael Schmidt, "Hearts Are Trumps in a Long-Winning Streak," p. 11.
Independent on Sunday (London, England), October 24, 1999, William Scammell, "Been There, Donne That," p. 13.
Insight on the News, April 24, 1995, p. 25.
Listener, February 29, 1968.
London Review of Books, August 24, 2000, Ian Sansom, "What's This?," pp. 19-20.
Los Angeles Times, February 3, 1982.
Los Angeles Times Book Review, April 20, 1986; April 30, 1989.
New Review (London, England), March, 1978.
New Statesman, March 22, 1968; November 19, 1971; April 14, 1978; June 2, 1978; September 27, 1999, Stephen Pile, review of *Where Did It All Go Right?,* p. 85.
New Statesman & Society, February 3, 1995, p. 38.
Newsweek, February 1, 1982.
New Yorker, March 31, 1974.
New York Times, July 5, 1969; April 7, 1972; March 19, 1975; January 30, 1979; January 25, 1982; March 1, 1982; May 6, 1983.

New York Times Book Review, July 20, 1969; August 17, 1969; April 16, 1972; March 30, 1975; June 1, 1975; February 11, 1979; February 1, 1981; January 31, 1982; May 8, 1983; May 18, 1986.

Observer, March 3, 1968; December 20, 1970; May 7, 1978.

Poetry, November, 1959.

Poetry London, spring, 2003, Martin Crucefix, review of *New and Selected Poems.*

Saturday Review, August 2, 1969; April 5, 1975.

Spectator, December 18, 1971.

Sunday Times, July 7, 2002.

Time, February 8, 1982; May 30, 1983.

Times Literary Supplement, May 9, 1958; March 3, 1961; February 29, 1968, November 26, 1971; November 8, 1974; April 21, 1978; June 2, 1978; July 2, 1982; October 10, 1986; July 22, 1988.

Washington Post, July 5, 1986.

Washington Post Book World, February 14, 1982; May 29, 1983; June 25, 1989.

World Literature Today, July-September, 2003, p. 100.*

*   *   *

Jennifer Armstrong

ARMSTRONG, Jennifer 1961-
(Kate William, Julia Winfield)

PERSONAL: Born May 12, 1961, in Waltham, MA; daughter of John (a physicist) and Elizabeth (a master gardener; maiden name, Saunders) Armstrong; married James Howard Kunstler (a writer and painter), 1996. *Education:* Smith College, B.A., 1983. *Hobbies and other interests:* Gardening, teaching, music, reading.

ADDRESSES: Office—P.O. Box 335, Saratoga Springs, NY 12866. *Agent*—Susan Cohen, Writers House, 21 West 26th St., New York, NY 10010. *E-mail*—mail@jennifer-armstrong.com.

CAREER: Author of children's fiction. Cloverdale Press, New York, NY, assistant editor, 1983-85; freelance writer, 1985—. Girl Scout leader, 1987-89; Smith College, recruiter, 1990—; Literacy Volunteers of Saratoga, board president, 1991-93; Guiding Eyes for the Blind, puppy raiser; leader of writing workshops. Also worked as a teacher.

MEMBER: Society of Children's Book Writers and Illustrators, Saratoga County Arts Council.

AWARDS, HONORS: Best Book Award, American Library Association (ALA), and Golden Kite Honor Book Award, Society of Children's Book Writers and Illustrators, both 1992, both for *Steal Away;* Notable Book citations, ALA, 1992, for *Steal Away* and *Hugh Can Do;* Children's Book Choices, International Reading Association/Children's Book Council, 1995, for *That Terrible Baby;* Children's Books of Distinction (young adult fiction), *Hungry Mind Review,* 1997, for *The Dreams of Mairhe Mehan;* Children's Books of Distinction (young adult fiction), *Riverbank Review,* 1998, for *Mary Mehan Awake;* Orbis Pictus Award for Outstanding Nonfiction, National Council of Teachers of English, *Boston Globe/Horn Book* Honor Book in nonfiction, and Children's Books of Distinction (nonfiction), *Riverbank Review,* all 1999, all for *Shipwreck at the Bottom of the World: The Extraordinary True Story of Shackleton and the Endurance;* Cuffies Award for Best Autobiography, *Publishers Weekly,* 1999, Children's Books of Distinction (nonfiction), *Riverbank Review,* 2000, Anisfield-Wolf Book Award, 2000, and Children's Booksellers Choices Award in nonfiction, Association of Booksellers for Children (ABC), 2000, all for *In My Hands: Memories of a Holocaust Rescuer;* Children's Booksellers Choices

Award in nonfiction, ABC, 2000, for *The Century for Young People;* Best Children's Books of the Year, Bank Street College, 2001, for *Spirit of Endurance: The True Story of the Shackleton Expedition to the Antarctic;* Best Books for Young Adults selection, and Notable Book in Social Studies, National Council for the Social Studies/CBC, both 2002, both for *Shattered: Stories of Children in War;* Book Links Lasting Connections, 2002, for *The Kindling.* Various titles have been selected by *Horn Book,* the New York Public Library, and the American Library Association as "Best Books" on a yearly basis.

WRITINGS:

PICTURE BOOKS

Hugh Can Do (picture book), illustrated by Kimberly Bulcken Root, Crown (New York, NY), 1992.

Chin Yu Min and the Ginger Cat (picture book), illustrated by Mary GrandPré, Crown (New York, NY), 1993.

That Terrible Baby (picture book), illustrated by Susan Meddaugh, Tambourine Books (New York, NY), 1994.

Little Salt Lick and the Sun King (picture book), illustrated by Jon Goodell, Crown (New York, NY), 1994.

The Whittler's Tale (picture book), illustrated by Valery Vasiliev, Tambourine Books (New York, NY), 1994.

Wan Hu Is in the Stars, illustrated by Barry Root, Tambourine Books (New York, NY), 1995.

King Crow, illustrated by Eric Rohmann, Crown (New York, NY), 1995.

Pockets, illustrated by Mary GrandPré, Crown (New York, NY), 1998.

Pierre's Dream, illustrated by Susan Gaber, Dial (New York, NY), 1999.

Sign of the Times, illustrated by David Jarvis, Simon & Schuster (New York, NY), 2004.

Magnus at the Fire, illustrated by Owen Smith, Simon & Schuster (New York, NY), 2005.

FICTION FOR MIDDLE-GRADE AND YOUNG ADULT READERS

Steal Away (novel), Orchard Books (New York, NY), 1992.

Black-Eyed Susan, illustrated by Emily Martindale, Crown (New York, NY), 1995.

The Dreams of Mairhe Mehan (young adult novel; also see below), Knopf (New York, NY), 1996.

Patrick Doyle Is Full of Blarney (chapter book), illustrated by Krista Brauckmann-Towns, Random House (New York, NY), 1996.

Lili the Brave (chapter book), illustrated by Uldis Klavins, Random House (New York, NY), 1997.

Foolish Gretel (chapter book), illustrated by Donna Diamond, Random House (New York, NY), 1997.

Mary Mehan Awake (young adult novel; also see below), Knopf (New York, NY), 1997.

Theodore Roosevelt: Letters from a Young Coal Miner (middle-grade novel), Winslow Press (Delray Beach, FL), 2000.

Thomas Jefferson: Letters from a Philadelphia Bookworm (middle-grade novel), Winslow Press (Delray Beach, FL), 2000.

Becoming Mary Mehan: Two Novels (includes the novels *The Dreams of Mairhe Mehan* and *Mary Mehan Awake*) Random House (New York, NY), 2002.

(Editor) *Shattered: Stories of Children and War* (short story anthology), Knopf (New York, NY), 2002.

(With Nancy Butcher) *The Kindling* (young adult novel; first book in the "Fire-us" series), HarperCollins (New York, NY), 2002.

(With Nancy Butcher) *The Keepers of the Flame* (young adult novel; second book in the "Fire-us" series), HarperCollins (New York, NY), 2002.

(With Nancy Butcher) *The Kiln* (young adult novel; third book in the "Fire-us" series), HarperCollins (New York, NY), 2003.

(Editor) *What a Song Can Do: Twelve Riffs on the Power of Music* (short story anthology), Knopf (New York, NY), 2004.

"PETS, INC." SERIES; MIDDLE-GRADE FICTION

The Puppy Project, Bantam (New York, NY), 1990.

Too Many Pets, Bantam (New York, NY), 1990.

Hillary to the Rescue, Bantam (New York, NY), 1990.

That Champion Chimp, Bantam (New York, NY), 1990.

"WILD ROSE INN" SERIES; YOUNG ADULT HISTORICAL FICTION

Bridie of the Wild Rose Inn, Bantam (New York, NY), 1994.

Ann of the Wild Rose Inn, Bantam (New York, NY), 1994.

Emily of the Wild Rose Inn, Bantam (New York, NY), 1994.

Laura of the Wild Rose Inn, Bantam (New York, NY), 1994.

Claire of the Wild Rose Inn, Bantam (New York, NY), 1994.

Grace of the Wild Rose Inn, Bantam (New York, NY), 1994.

NONFICTION

Shipwreck at the Bottom of the World: The Extraordinary True Story of Shackleton and the Endurance, Crown (New York, NY), 1998.

The Century for Young People (adapted from *The Century* by Peter Jennings and Todd Brewster), Random House (New York, NY), 1999.

(With Irene Gut Opdyke) *In My Hands: Memories of a Holocaust Rescuer,* Knopf (New York, NY), 1999.

Spirit of Endurance: The True Story of the Shackleton Expedition to the Antarctic (picture book), illustrated by William Maughan, Crown (New York, NY), 2000.

Audubon: Painter of Birds in the Wild Frontier (picture book), illustrated by Jos. A. Smith, Abrams (New York, NY), 2003.

A Three-Minute Speech: Lincoln's Remarks at Gettysburg, illustrated by Albert Lorenz, Simon & Schuster (New York, NY), 2003.

Photo by Brady: A Picture of the Civil War, Simon & Schuster (New York, NY), 2005.

UNDER PSEUDONYM JULIA WINFIELD; YOUNG ADULT FICTION

Only Make-Believe (part of "Sweet Dreams" series), Bantam (New York, NY), 1987.

Private Eyes (part of "Sweet Dreams" series), Bantam (New York, NY), 1989.

Partners in Crime (part of "Private Eyes" series), Bantam (New York, NY), 1989.

Tug of Hearts (part of "Private Eyes" series), Bantam (New York, NY), 1989.

On Dangerous (part of "Private Eyes" series), Bantam (New York, NY), 1989.

OTHER

The Snowball (beginning reader), illustrated by Jean Pidgeon, Random House (New York, NY), 1996.

Sunshine, Moonshine (beginning reader), illustrated by Lucia Washburn, Random House (New York, NY), 1997.

Also worked as a ghostwriter, under the pseudonym Kate William, for the "Sweet Valley High" and "Sweet Valley Kids" series. Contributor to periodicals, including *Riverbank Review, Horn Book,* and *Five Owls.*

WORK IN PROGRESS: Researching nineteenth-century American history.

SIDELIGHTS: Jennifer Armstrong once commented, "I came to write children's books by accident. When I left college I took the first publishing job I could get, and it turned out to be with the packager of many of the best-known juvenile and young adult series on the market. After a year and a half of working on these books, I was convinced that I could do a creditable job of writing them, too. And so I began to write for 'Sweet Valley High.'" She continued, "After a number of years working as a full-time writer for the packager, I teamed up with my agent, Susan Cohen of Writers House. With my mass market experience firmly behind me, I was ready to set to work on my own projects.

"The idea for my novel, *Steal Away,* came to me a number of years before I wrote it. At first, it was conceived of as a straightforward adventure story. Having written so many of those books, however, I felt I was ready to tackle something more complex and ambitious. And so, after much thought and nail biting, I settled on the form of the novel as I wrote it—with two narratives interwoven, emphasizing the effect that telling and hearing stories has on us. I intertwined so many threads in *Steal Away* that I was often in danger of getting hopelessly confused. But those issues—race relations, feminism, friendship, and loyalty, and the importance of telling stories—were and still are important to me."

Armstrong's desire to write about what is important to her is evident in *Steal Away.* The book begins in the year 1896 when Mary, a thirteen-year-old, travels with her grandmother to visit Gran's sick friend, Bethlehem. Gran (Susannah) and Bethlehem soon relate the story of how they became fast friends when they, too, were thirteen years old. *Steal Away* is a tale of courage, friendship, and interracial understanding. The title is derived from a spiritual which was used in those days as a signal to slaves that the time had come for them to run for freedom.

In the story, both of Susannah's parents die in an accident in 1855, and she is sent to live with an uncle who keeps slaves on a plantation in Virginia. Susannah believes that slavery is wrong, and so, when she is given Bethlehem as her own personal slave, Susannah befriends her. The basic difference between her uncle's beliefs and what Susannah believes drives the story, becoming the catalyst for relationships among the characters. Emotions in the story run high as Bethlehem deals with her hatred of slavery, resentment of her white "friend," and her need to leave Susannah and go her own way. Young Susannah must resolve her own feelings about black people just as her granddaughter, Mary, must do when Susannah, or Gran, tells her the story years later. Ann Welton, writing in *School Library Journal,* commented that "the issues explored in this book run deep. . . . This will go a long way toward explicating the damage done by slavery."

After the success of *Steal Away,* Armstrong wrote a series of historical fiction novels, the "Wild Rose Inn" series, revolving around six girls in a single family over three centuries. A family-run tavern in the town of Marblehead, Massachusetts, provided the setting for the novels. By maintaining a single setting and family, she was able to plunge into the historical periods spanned by three centuries and create a cumulative narrative that transcended the individual volumes. She once commented, "This is one of the great attractions of writing series books—although the books stand on their own, the whole can be greater than the sum of the parts."

The versatile Armstrong has also written several picture books, including *Hugh Can Do* and *Chin Yu Min and the Ginger Cat.* The first of these books, with its cumulative theme and rhythmic text, is similar to poetry and is fun to read aloud, as many reviewers have noted. Moreover, as is typical of many folktales, the story offers "a valuable lesson presented in a book to be valued," wrote a contributor to *Publishers Weekly.* Kate McClelland, in a *School Library Journal* review, decided that *Hugh Can Do* is "an especially nice balance of dramatic tension, droll humor, and positive philosophy."

Chin Yu Min and the Ginger Cat is based on a tale that Armstrong learned from a Chinese visitor to upstate New York. She developed her version of the story and set it appropriately, she thought, in China. The response of the critics was mixed. Armstrong commented, "The illustrator of this book, Mary GrandPré, later took some hits for what some critics thought was chinoiserie—old-fashioned stereotypes of Chinese people. I am convinced that if either of us had been Chinese, the critics would have agreed wholeheartedly that this was a wonderful book with fabulous pictures."

She mused, "I have learned that some critics will not allow writers to be writers. . . . There is a widely held belief that only an African American can write the African-American experience . . . and so on. There were people who thought that *Chin Yu Min and the Ginger Cat* was some kind of scam—as though we had tricked people into believing it was an authentic Chinese folktale. . . . It didn't occur to me that I should be limited to setting my stories in the Westchester County, New York, of the 1960s and 1970s."

Black-Eyed Susan is set far from contemporary Westchester County, during frontier days on the western prairie, where young Susan lives with her parents in a sod house. The prairie was a bleak place in those days: primitive, isolated, and for the most part colorless. The theme of the book is, according to the author, "the geography of the prairie, and its power to uplift or crush a human soul." Susan's mother has fallen into a malaise of depression and loneliness, and the girl's challenge is to revive her mother's sagging spirits. She does so with the gift of a bright, yellow canary, acquired from a family of passers-by. "Told in a highly readable text that is almost poetic at times," Elizabeth S. Watson wrote in *Horn Book,* "the story has a satisfying roundness that will elicit contented sighs from young readers."

This novel was followed by *The Dreams of Mairhe Mehan,* a work that Armstrong called "the most challenging one I have yet written." In it, she relates the tale of an Irish family transported to America at the time of the Civil War. Mairhe's peace of mind is torn apart by her father, a sad, defeated man who wants nothing more than to return to his native Ireland, and her brother, who joins the Union forces to fight for his new homeland. As the war progresses, Mairhe retreats into a series of dreams, fractured by flashes of ancient myth and contemporary events. "Everything she sees is falling into fragments," Armstrong once explained, "and her frantic attempts to keep all things together is breaking her heart." A *Publishers Weekly* reviewer called *The Dreams of Mairhe Mehan* a "finely wrought historical novel [that] also captures a powerful measure of the magnitude and depth of the pain" of war.

A sequel, *Mary Mehan Awake,* follows the Americanized Mairhe of the first novel to upstate New York, where she has moved with the help of the poet Walt Whitman, who had befriended her during the war. Mary, devastated by the war and the death of her brother, has so completely withdrawn from life that she has lost much of the intensity of her senses. In a new setting on Lake Ontario, rich with plant and animal life and other sensory delights, and under the care of a kindly naturalist and his wife, Mary slowly begins to recover. Jennifer M. Brabander commented in *Horn Book,* "The story unfolds effortlessly and richly; the metaphors and similes allow the reader to experience what Mary cannot." Brabander called the novel "*The Secret Garden* for an older audience," a story of "healing and wholeness." In 2002, Armstrong combined *The Dreams of Mairhe Mehan* and *Mary Mehan Awake* into one volume titled *Becoming Mary Mehan.*

Many of Armstrong's books challenge young readers' minds and inspire them to imagine the world from a different perspective. In *Pockets,* Armstrong tells the story of a woman who arrives in a sheltered town and becomes the town's seamstress. The people of the town like plain clothes, in plain colors, but when the woman lines the pockets of their clothing with images of ships, oceans, and faraway lands, the townspeople change their way of thinking. *Booklist*'s John Peters called the book a "grand, lyrical tale of imagination's transformative power."

In *Pierre's Dream,* Armstrong weaves a tale that mixes fantasy and reality. Armstrong describes Pierre as a lazy man who enjoys naps under the olive trees. When Pierre falls asleep and wakes up in the middle of a circus, he assumes he is dreaming. With no fear, Pierre joins the circus and catches an escaped lion, rides horses, and swings from the trapeze. After a long day, he takes a nap and awakens to find the ringmaster's top hat and a parasol lying beside him, only to realize that his dream was reality. *Pierre's Dream* is "a wonderfully imaginative tale that reveals the potential that each of us carefully hides within," noted Karyn Miller-Medzon in the *Boston Herald.*

Armstrong teamed with Nancy Butcher to pen the "Fire-us" series of young adult science-fiction novels. The first book in the trilogy, *The Kindling,* begins five years after a strange virus (Fire-us) has wiped out most of the adult population. A group of teens and children have banded together to go on a quest to find the president and learn more about the virus. In the

second book, *The Keepers of the Flame,* the children are taken in by a group of adults who call themselves the "Keepers of the Flame." The children soon learn that the adults are members of a religious cult who have plans to put the youngest children to "the test." After escaping from the cult, the determined youngsters continue their journey to find the president. In the final book, *The Kiln,* the children discover a retirement community filled with elderly women who somehow survived the virus. Using the retirement community's solar-powered golf carts, the kids finally reach the president, who turns out to be the Supreme Leader of the Keepers of the Flame, and the person responsible for releasing the virus. Together, the children must figure out a way to stop the president from releasing a second wave of Fire-us. *School Library Journal*'s Mara Alpert called the "Fire-us" series "an exhilarating thrill-ride of a tale." In her review of the final book in the series, Alpert noted, "Armstrong and Butcher have crafted a chillingly realistic picture of events that unfortunately isn't that hard to imagine. . . . A strong finish to an engrossing . . . series."

In addition to her fiction, Armstrong has written several nonfiction works, including *The Century for Young People,* an adaptation of Peter Jennings and Todd Brewster's best-selling *The Century.* The book outlines some of the most amazing and radical changes brought about during the twentieth century. In *Audubon: Painter of Birds in the Wild Frontier,* Armstrong presents the life of John James Audubon, and the adventures he had while painting birds in uncharted territories. Calling the work "stunning," *School Library Journal*'s Robyn Walker commented, "The flowing narrative engages readers' interest and simply does not let go."

Two of Armstrong's nonfiction books, *Shipwreck at the Bottom of the World: The Extraordinary True Story of Shackleton and the Endurance* and *Spirit of Endurance: The True Story of the Shackleton Expedition to the Antarctic,* describe the adventures of Ernest Shackleton and his crew, who were trapped in the ice packs of the Antarctic for almost a year. As Stephanie Zvirin noted in *Booklist, Spirit of Endurance,* a picture book meant for younger readers, "provides an excellent outline of the extraordinary expedition." *School Library Journal*'s Patricia Manning mentioned that the book "presents a good picture of human survival under almost unimaginable conditions."

Armstrong coauthored Irene Gut Opdyke's autobiography titled *In My Hands: Memories of a Holocaust Rescuer.* The book details Opdyke's life as the servant to a Nazi officer during World War II. The book describes the sacrifices Opdyke made to hide twelve Jews in the basement of the officer's home. Some of the scenes are shocking and disturbing, noted reviewers, but they capture the truth and reality of war. A *Publishers Weekly* contributor commented, "Armstrong and Opdyke demonstrate an almost uncanny power to place readers in the young Irene's shoes."

Another war-themed book, *Shattered: Stories of Children and War,* is a collection of short stories edited by Armstrong. Each story describes not only the physical toll of war on children, but the mental and emotional toll as well. Each story features a footnote that describes the facts of the war behind the story. While the stories are fictional in nature, the reality of the wars about which they are written is captured in detail. "It puts a human face on conflicts in various parts of the world . . . , driving home the point that no one is left untouched in wartime," wrote *School Library Journal*'s Saleena L. Davidson.

On the topic of books in general, Armstrong once commented, "In my experience there are two broad categories of writers for children . . . those who write for children because they have a teaching agenda, and . . . those who write for children because they are writers and children's books are what they happen to write." Armstrong wants herself to be considered one of the latter. "Art enriches our lives, feeds our spirits, strengthens the ties between one human being and all others. Children should be allowed to participate in the experience of art equally with adults. . . . Art does not have a didactic soul. Art has an artistic soul."

She wrote, "More and more these days I see people— grown-up people—trying to control what kids can see and do and read. I know teachers and librarians who scorn the mass market books which I wrote . . . , and insist on giving kids exclusively 'good' books. But adults have access to a variety of fiction, and I think all kinds of fiction should be available to kids so that they can make their own decisions about what they enjoy."

BIOGRAPHICAL AND CRITICAL SOURCES:

BOOKS

Children's Literature Review, Volume 66, Gale (Detroit, MI), 2000.

St. James Guide to Young Adult Writers, 2nd edition, St. James Press (Detroit, MI), 1999.

Something about the Author Autobiography Series, Volume 24, Gale (Detroit, MI), 1997.

PERIODICALS

Audubon, December, 2003, David Seideman, review of *Audubon: Painter of Birds in the Wild Frontier,* p. 98.

Booklist, October 1, 1990, p. 344; August, 1998, John Peters, review of *Pockets,* p. 2012; December 1, 1998, Stephanie Zvirin, review of *Shipwreck at the Bottom of the World: The Extraordinary True Story of Shackleton and the Endurance,* p. 657; March 15, 1999, review of *Shipwreck at the Bottom of the World,* p. 1308; June 1, 1999, Ilene Cooper, review of *In My Hands: Memories of a Holocaust Rescuer,* p. 1826; August, 1999, Kay Weisman, review of *Pierre's Dream,* p. 2062; January 1, 2000, review of *In My Hands,* p. 820; March 15, 2000, review of *Shipwreck at the Bottom of the World,* p. 1339; April 1, 2000, Stephanie Zvirin, review of *In My Hands,* p. 1430; June 1, 2000, Ted Hipple, review of *In My Hands,* p. 1921; July, 2000, Karen Harris, review of *In My Hands,* p. 2052; September 15, 2000, Stephanie Zvirin, review of *Spirit of Endurance: The True Story of the Shackleton Expedition to the Antarctic,* p. 233; March 1, 2001, Kay Weisman, review of *Theodore Roosevelt: Letters from a Young Coal Miner,* p. 1275; May 15, 2001, Randy Meyer, review of *Thomas Jefferson: Letters from a Philadelphia Bookworm,* p. 1749; December 15, 2001, Hazel Rochman, review of *Shattered: Stories of Children and War,* p. 722; April 15, 2002, Sally Estes, review of *The Kindling,* p. 1412; August, 2002, Sally Estes, review of *The Keepers of the Flame,* p. 1962; January 1, 2003, review of *The Kindling,* p. 795; April 1, 2003, Carolyn Phelan, review of *Audubon,* p. 1391; April 15, 2003, Sally Estes, review of *The Kiln,* p. 1464; September 1, 2003, Carolyn Phelan, review of *A Three-Minute Speech: Lincoln's Remarks at Gettysburg,* p. 117.

Book Report, March, 1998, review of *Mary Mehan Awake,* p. 28.

Boston Herald, May 30, 1999, Karyn Miller-Medzon, review of *Pierre's Dream,* p. 59.

Bulletin of the Center for Children's Books, March, 1992, p. 173; February, 1999, review of *Shipwreck at the Bottom of the World,* p. 195; July, 1999, review of *Pierre's Dream,* p. 379; May, 2001, review of *Thomas Jefferson,* p. 330; May, 2002, review of *Shattered,* p. 309.

Children's Digest, June, 1999, review of *Shipwreck at the Bottom of the World,* p. 28.

Globe and Mail (Toronto, Ontario, Canada), February 16, 2002, review of *Shattered,* p. D14.

Guardian (London, England), January 30, 2001, Lindsey Fraser, review of *In My Hands,* p. 55.

Horn Book, March-April, 1996, Elizabeth S. Watson, review of *Black-Eyed Susan,* p. 193; November-December, 1997, Jennifer M. Brabander, review of *Mary Mehan Awake,* p. 675; July, 1999, review of *Shipwreck at the Bottom of the World,* p. 478, review of *In My Hands,* p. 486; January, 2000, review of *Shipwreck at the Bottom of the World,* p. 50; May, 2000, Kristi Beavin, review of *In My Hands,* p. 341, review of *Shipwreck at the Bottom of the World,* p. 340; May-June, 2002, Peter D. Sieruta, review of *Shattered,* pp. 323-324; November-December, 2003, Kristi Elle Jemtegaard, review of *Thomas Jefferson,* pp. 773-774.

Instructor, May, 2001, review of *Spirit of Endurance,* p. 37.

Journal of Adolescent and Adult Literacy, November, 1998, review of *The Dreams of Mairhe Mehan,* p. 231.

Kirkus Reviews, July 15, 1992, p. 917; December 1, 1998, review of *Shipwreck at the Bottom of the World,* p. 1730; May 1, 1999, review of *Pierre's Dream,* p. 718; December 1, 2001, review of *Shattered,* p. 1681; March 1, 2002, review of *The Kindling,* p. 329; October 15, 2002, review of *The Keepers of the Flame,* p. 1526; March 1, 2003, review of *The Kiln,* p. 379; March 15, 2003, review of *Audubon,* p. 458.

Kliatt, March, 1998, review of *The Dreams of Mairhe Mehan,* p. 6; November, 1998, review of *Mary Mehan Awake,* p. 10; July, 1999, review of *Shipwreck at the Bottom of the World,* p. 3; March, 2002, review of *The Kindling,* p. 6; November, 2002, Paula Rohrlick, review of *The Keepers of the Flame,* pp. 5-6; March, 2003, review of *The Kiln,* pp. 5-6; May, 2003, Paula Rohrlick, review of *The Kindling,* p. 23; November, 2003, Paula Rohrlick, review of *The Keepers of the Flame,* pp. 20-21; June 1, 2004, review of *What a Song Can Do: Twelve Riffs on the Power of Music,* p. 533.

New York Times Book Review, April 15, 2001, review of *Thomas Jefferson,* p. 24.

Publishers Weekly, March 24, 1989, p. 73; July 13, 1990, p. 55; June 29, 1992, review of *Hugh Can Do,* p. 62; April 17, 1995, p. 59; May 8, 1995, p. 295; July 10, 1995, p. 58; July 8, 1996, review of *The Dreams of Mairhe Mehan,* p. 84; July 13, 1998, review of *Mary Mehan Awake,* p. 79; October 19, 1998, review of *Pockets,* p. 78; January 25, 1999, review of *Shipwreck at the Bottom of the World,* p. 97; May 31, 1999, review of *Pierre's Dream,* p. 92; July 19, 1999, review of *In My Hands,* p. 197; November 1, 1999, review of *Shipwreck at the Bottom of the World,* p. 58, review of *In My Hands,* p. 58; July 17, 2000, review of *Spirit of Endurance,* p. 196; February 25, 2001, review of *Becoming Mary Mehan,* p. 69; January 21, 2002, review of *Shattered,* p. 90.

Reading Teacher, December, 1999, review of *Shipwreck at the Bottom of the World,* p. 349; May, 2001, review of *Theodore Roosevelt,* p. 827.

Reading Today, February-March, 2002, Lynne T. Burke, review of *Shattered,* p. 32.

School Library Journal, June, 1989, p. 125; July, 1990, p. 74; February, 1992, p. 85; October, 1992, Kate McClelland, review of *Hugh Can Do,* p. 78; January, 1998, Marie Wright, review of *Mary Mehan Awake,* p. 108; August, 1998, Ann Welton, review of *Steal Away,* p. 25; October, 1998, Miriam Lang Budin, review of *Pockets,* p. 86; April, 1999, Edward Sullivan, review of *Shipwreck at the Bottom of the World,* p. 144; June, 1999, Barbara Elleman, review of *Pierre's Dream,* p. 85, Cyrisse Jaffe, review of *In My Hands,* p. 151; October, 2000, Patricia Manning, review of *Spirit of Endurance,* p. 177; April, 2001, Janie Schomberg, review of *Theodore Roosevelt,* p. 138; June, 2001, Janet Gillen, review of *Thomas Jefferson,* p. 142; January, 2002, Saleena L. Davidson, review of *Shattered,* p. 131; April, 2002, review of *Shipwreck at the Bottom of the World,* p. 66; October, 2002, Trish Anderson, review of *The Kindling,* p. 154; December, 2002, Mara Alpert, review of *The Keepers of the Flame,* p. 132; April, 2003, Cindy Lombardo, review of *Thomas Jefferson,* p. 87; May, 2003, Robyn Walker, review of *Audubon,* p. 134, Mara Alpert, review of *The Kiln,* p. 144; September, 2003, Laura Scott, review of *A Three-Minute Speech,* p. 224; July, 2004, Renee Steinberg, review of *What a Song Can Do,* p. 98.

Science Books & Films, May, 1999, review of *Shipwreck at the Bottom of the World,* p. 130; March, 2002, review of *Shipwreck at the Bottom of the World,* p. 348.

Times Educational Supplement, January 12, 2001, Victoria Neumark, review of *In My Hands,* p. B21.

Voice of Youth Advocates, August, 1992, p. 165; April, 1998, review of *Steal Away,* p. 43; August, 2001, review of *Theodore Roosevelt,* p. 196, review of *Thomas Jefferson,* p. 196.

ONLINE

Jennifer Armstrong Web site, http://www.jennifer-armstrong.com/ (April 2, 2004).

What You Need to Know about Women Writers Web site, http://womenwriters.about.com/ (February 1, 2003), review of *Shattered.**

* * *

ASHTON, Lorayne
   See GOTTFRIED, Theodore Mark

* * *

AVISON, Margaret (Kirkland) 1918-

PERSONAL: Born April 23, 1918, in Galt, Ontario, Canada; daughter of Harold Wilson (in the clergy) and Mabel (Kirkland) Avison. *Education:* University of Toronto, B.A., 1940, M.A., 1964.

ADDRESSES: Home—17 Lascelles Blvd., Apt. 108, Toronto M4V 2B6, Ontario, Canada.

CAREER: Poet. Worked at North American Life Insurance Co. and Gage Press, Toronto, Ontario, Canada; Canadian Institute of International Affairs, editor, until 1945; University of Toronto, Toronto, worked at registrar's office and library, 1945-55, also lecturer; worked as a nursemaid, 1955, and at Presbyterian Home Missions, Toronto; University of Western Ontario, Waterloo, Ontario, Canada, writer in residence, 1972-73; Canadian Broadcasting Corp., worked in Archives Division, 1973-78; Mustard Seed Mission, Toronto, staff member, beginning 1978.

AWARDS, HONORS: Guggenheim fellowship, 1956; Governor-General's Literary Awards for poetry, 1960, for *Winter Sun,* for poetry and drama, 1970, for *The Cosmic Chef: An Evening of Concrete,* for the *Winter*

Sun: The Dumbfounding; Poems, 1940-66, and 1990, for *No Time;* Griffin Poetry Prize, 2003, for *Concrete and Wild Carrot.*

WRITINGS:

History of Ontario, Gage Press (Toronto, Ontario, Canada), 1951.

(With A. I. Wolinsky) *A Doctor's Memoirs,* Macmillan (New York, NY), 1960.

Winter Sun (poetry), University of Toronto Press (Toronto, Ontario, Canada), 1960, new edition published as *Winter Sun: The Dumbfounding; Poems, 1940-66,* McClelland & Stewart (Toronto, Ontario, Canada), 1982.

(Translator, with Ilona Duczynska and Karl Polanyi) *The Plough and the Pen: Writings from Hungary, 1930-1956,* McClelland & Stewart (Toronto, Ontario, Canada), 1963.

(With Albert Rose) *The Research Compendium,* University of Toronto Press (Toronto, Ontario, Canada), 1964.

The Dumbfounding (poetry), Norton (New York, NY), 1966.

Silverick, Ganglia Press (Toronto, Ontario, Canada), 1969.

The Cosmic Chef, Oberon Press (Ottawa, Ontario, Canada), 1970.

(Translator, with Ilona Duczynska) Jozsef Lengyel, *Acta Sanctorum and Other Tales,* Peter Owen (London, England), 1970.

Sunblue (poetry), Lancelot Press (Hantsport, Nova Scotia, Canada), 1978.

No Time, Lancelot Press (Hantsport, Nova Scotia, Canada), 1989, Brick Books (London, Ontario, Canada), 1998.

Selected Poems, Oxford University Press (New York, NY), 1992.

A Kind of Perseverance, Lancelot Press (Hantsport, Nova Scotia, Canada), 1994.

Not Yet but Still, Lancelot Press (Hantsport, Nova Scotia, Canada), 1997.

Concrete and Wild Carrot (poetry), Brick Books (London, Ontario, Canada), 2003.

Contributor to anthologies, including *The Book of Canadian Poetry,* University of Chicago Press (Chicago, IL), 1943, *Recent Canadian Verse,* Jackson Press, 1959, and *The Country of the Risen King: An*

Anthology of Christian Poetry, Baker Book House (Grand Rapids, MI), 1978. Contributor to periodicals, including *Canadian Forum, Manitoba Arts Review,* and *Origin.*

SIDELIGHTS: Although Margaret Avison is recognized by many critics as one of Canada's finest and most sensitive poets, she is relatively unknown internationally. Several reasons have been suggested for her lack of fame and attention. A very private person, Avison has not actively promoted her books. Another factor contributing to her lack of public recognition can be attributed to the fact that several of her books are hard to find—either published by a small press or not widely distributed by the publisher.

In the *Dictionary of Literary Biography,* Ernest H. Redekop explained: "Margaret Avison has always been a relatively unknown poet, except among readers and critics of Canadian verse. Since 1966, critical essays on her work have increased, but the verbal and imaginative complexities of her poems have not won over many casual readers. . . . Her stature as a Canadian poet, to judge from the distribution of her poems today, is low; but those readers who have taken the trouble to study her work acknowledge the scope of her intelligence, the uniqueness of her imagination, and a virtuosity in the use of language perhaps unparalleled among contemporary Canadian poets."

Daniel W. Doerksen commented on Avison's poems in *Canadian Literature:* "Their rich sensitivity to all aspects of life, amounting to a wholesome 'secularity,'

their deep and incisive engagement in the world of thought and meaning, their full exploitation of all the modern resources of language and technique—all these mark them with the vitality which is the essence of true poetry."

BIOGRAPHICAL AND CRITICAL SOURCES:

BOOKS

Contemporary Literary Criticism, Gale (Detroit, MI), Volume 2, 1974, Volume 4, 1975.
David, Jack, and Robert Lecker, editors, *Annotated Bibliography of Canada's Major Author,* Volume 6, ECW Press (Toronto, Ontario, Canada), 1985.
Dictionary of Literary Biography, Volume 53: *Canadian Writers since 1960,* Gale (Detroit, MI), 1986.
Kent, David, *Margaret Avison and Her Works,* ECW Press (Toronto, Ontario, Canada), 1989.
Redekop, E. H., *Margaret Avison,* Copp Clark (London, Ontario, Canada), 1970.

PERIODICALS

Books in Canada, summer, 2003, Harold Heft, review of *Concrete and Wild Carrot.*
Canadian Literature, autumn, 1959; spring, 1974.
Twentieth Century Literature, July, 1970.*

B

BACHMAN, Richard
   See KING, Stephen (Edwin)

*   *   *

BANNISTER, Patricia Valeria 1923-
   (Gwyneth Moore, Patricia Veryan)

PERSONAL: Born November 21, 1923, in London, England; immigrated to the United States, 1946; married Allan Louis Berg, 1946 (deceased, 1980); children: Carol (deceased, 2002), David. *Education:* Attended Miss Lodge Secretarial School, London, 1937-38. *Religion:* Presbyterian. *Hobbies and other interests:* History, classical music, animal welfare.

ADDRESSES: Home—9805 Northeast 116th St., PMB 7239, Kirkland, WA 98034.

CAREER: Novelist. Worked as a secretary for British Navy, Army, and Air Force Institutes in London, England, 1938-40, Columbia Pictures, London, 1940-42, U.S. Army in London, Paris, France, and Frankfurt, Germany, 1942-46, Pacific Telephone, Sacramento, CA, 1949, National Cash Register Company, Los Angeles, CA, 1950, Southern Counties Gas Company, Los Angeles, 1951-52, and Humble Oil and Refining Company, Los Angeles, 1952-55; University of California, Riverside, secretary for graduate affairs, 1971-85. Freelance novelist, 1978—.

AWARDS, HONORS: Barbara Cartland Loving Cup award, Booklovers Convention, and *Romantic Times* Award for Best Regency Novel, both 1983, both for *Married Past Redemption; Romantic Times* Award for Best Regency Novel, 1984, for *The Noblest Frailty,* 1986, for *Sanguinet's Crown,* and 1987, for *Give All to Love; Romantic Times* Lifetime Achievement Award.

WRITINGS:

HISTORICAL ROMANCE NOVELS; UNDER PSEUDONYM PATRICIA VERYAN

The Lord and the Gypsy, Walker (New York, NY), 1978, published as *Debt of Honour,* Souvenir (London, England), 1980.

Love's Duet, Walker (New York, NY), 1979, published as *A Perfect Match,* Souvenir (London, England), 1981.

Mistress of Willowvale, Walker (New York, NY), 1980, Souvenir (London, England), 1982.

Some Brief Folly, St. Martin's Press (New York, NY), 1981.

The Wagered Widow, St. Martin's Press (New York, NY), 1984.

Logic of the Heart, St Martin's Press (New York, NY), 1990.

Poor Splendid Wings, Severn House (London, England), 1992.

Lanterns, St. Martin's Press (New York, NY), 1996.

The Riddle of Alabaster Royal, St. Martin's Press (New York, NY), 1997.

The Riddle of the Lost Lover, St. Martin's Press (New York, NY), 1998.

The Riddle of the Reluctant Rake, St. Martin's Press (New York, NY), 1999.

The Riddle of the Shipwrecked Spinster, St. Martin's Press (New York, NY), 2001.

The Riddle of the Deplorable Dandy, St. Martin's Press (New York, NY), 2002.

Contributor to books, including *Autumn Loves,* Fawcett (New York, NY), 1993.

"SANGUINET SAGA"; UNDER PSEUDONYM PATRICIA VERYAN

Nanette, Walker (New York, NY), 1981.

Feather Castles, St. Martin's Press (New York, NY), 1982.

Married Past Redemption, St. Martin's Press (New York, NY), 1983.

The Noblest Frailty, St. Martin's Press (New York, NY), 1983.

Sanguinet's Crown, St. Martin's Press (New York, NY), 1985.

Give All to Love, St. Martin's Press (New York, NY), 1987.

"GOLDEN CHRONICLES"; UNDER PSEUDONYM PATRICIA VERYAN

Practice to Deceive, St. Martin's Press (New York, NY), 1985.

Journey to Enchantment, St. Martin's Press (New York, NY), 1986.

Cherished Enemy, St. Martin's Press (New York, NY), 1987.

The Tyrant, St. Martin's Press (New York, NY), 1987.

Love Alters Not, St. Martin's Press (New York, NY), 1988.

The Dedicated Villain, St. Martin's Press (New York, NY), 1989.

"JEWELED MEN" SERIES; UNDER PSEUDONYM PATRICIA VERYAN

Time's Fool, St. Martin's Press (New York, NY), 1991.

Had We Never Loved, St. Martin's Press (New York, NY), 1992.

Ask Me No Questions, St. Martin's Press (New York, NY), 1993.

A Shadow's Bliss, St. Martin's Press (New York, NY), 1994.

Never Doubt I Love, St. Martin's Press (New York, NY), 1995.

The Mandarin of Mayfair, St. Martin's Press (New York, NY), 1995.

ROMANCE NOVELS; UNDER PSEUDONYM GWYNETH MOORE

Men Were Deceivers Ever, Harlequin (New York, NY), 1989.

The Dirty Frog, Harlequin (New York, NY), 1990.

Love's Lady Lost, Harlequin (New York, NY), 1991.

Also contributor to *Regency Quartet* (novella), Pride House, 1992.

WORK IN PROGRESS: Whimsy, an adventure romance set in the 1800s.

SIDELIGHTS: Patricia Valeria Bannister is the author of historical romance novels published under the pseudonyms Patricia Veryan and Gwyneth Moore. Her works include the "Sanguinet Saga," the "Golden Chronicles," and the "Jeweled Men" series. Her books under the Veryan pseudonym have been her most acclaimed. According to Barbara E. Kemp in *Twentieth-Century Romance and Historical Writers,* "Veryan is one of the most outstanding authors of historical romance writing today. She is adept at creating fascinating characters, and has written some of the most original and intriguing stories to be found in the genre."

Bannister was born in 1923, in London, England. She completed secretarial school and worked for Columbia Pictures and the U.S. Army. After moving to the United States, Bannister married an California G.I. she had met while working in Frankfurt, Germany, and set about raising a family, until her husband's failing health prompted her to get a job at the University of California. In 1977 she took up writing at the urging of a friend.

Bannister published her first work, 1978's *The Lord and the Gypsy,* under the Veryan pseudonym, This tale features the protagonist Lucian St. Clair, who, as Kemp noted, "endures great emotional and physical suffering as the ultimate atonement for past wrongs committed." Kemp also observed that Bannister's works create a multifaceted view of Regency society.

Bannister's "Sanguinet Saga" is held together by the theme of nine heroes fighting against the antagonistic Sanguinet brothers. Her "Golden Chronicles," set in the Georgian period of English history, follow the adventures of several Jacobites—people who plot to replace the Hanoverian royal line with the Catholic descendants of the deposed James II. The "Jeweled Men" series, also set in the Georgian era, involves a plot to replace the monarchy with a republic.

In her Veryan romance-adventure novels with the word "riddle" in the title, Bannister has created a series revolving around a group of central characters, among them Captain Jack Vespa, newly retired from the Napoleonic Wars. In *The Riddle of Alabaster Royal* Vespa and several friends try to determine whether his estate is haunted or not, uncovering strange secrets along the way. Elizabeth Mary Mellett in *Library Journal* called the novel an "exciting, humorous, romantic adventure." A critic for *Publishers Weekly* praised the novel as "charming and droll," adding that "the story is further enlivened by well-drawn secondary characters" and that "skilled pacing and dramatization carry events along."

Vespa returns in *The Riddle of the Lost Lover,* in which the captain searches for his true father's identity in hopes that his family background will make him worthy of the noble woman he loves. The search eventually involves him in a dangerous mission on behalf of England's war effort. Ann Bouricius in *Booklist* described Vespa as "a pure Veryan hero to die for—courageous, loyal, and honorable." Mellett found that "this work blends wonderful characters, a breathlessly exciting plot, and just the right touch of humor."

The Riddle of the Reluctant Rake focuses on Vespa's friend Hastings Chatteris Adair, who is wrongly accused of stealing a maiden's virtue. Enlisting the help of his friends, Hastings works on clearing his name, a quest that takes him into his family's disreputable past. A critic for *Publishers Weekly* believed that "Veryan sets a sprightly pace for her engaging plot, serving up a sparkling romance and a mystery with a subtle denouement." Alexandra Shrake in *Booklist* noted that "readers of this polished period mystery romance will relish Veryan's charming British characters and their innocent, 'proper' beliefs and values that are so refreshing to the modern reader."

The Riddle of the Shipwrecked Spinster tells two stories. The first concerns Cordelia, whose mother maneuvers a local dandy into proposing marriage to her against his wishes. Cordelia flees to Egypt and, presumed lost in a shipwreck, stays away from England for a year. The second story concerns Piers Cranford, who is struggling to keep the family estate financially afloat. Inevitably, the two characters get together. A *Publishers Weekly* critic praised the "deliciously entangled plot," while Diana Texier Herald in *Booklist* believed that *The Riddle of the Shipwrecked Spinster* "will delight both Veryan fanatics and readers new to her books."

Bannister once told *CA:* "I like to find humour, characterization, tenderness and lots of action in a book, so I try to incorporate these in my books. I am most grateful to my devoted readers, and to the loyalty and efforts of my fan club."

More recently, she added: "It's been quite a while, but I suspect that my initial interest in writing was fostered by a great deal of reading. In my youth I was a devotee of tales of adventure and derring-do. I devoured science fiction and historical books and became much interested in the stories of British authors Jeffery Farnol and Georgette Heyer besides the works of Jane Austen and others.

"My writing schedule in earlier years was quite heavy—about eight hours a day sandwiched between a full time job, a home, and family tasks. Much accomplished with the help of my loyal husband. At this stage of my life it has become whenever I can find available hours.

"I don't know that I have a 'favorite book'. I'm rather fond of most of my tales. I tend to refer new readers to *Lanterns,* which had some plot twists I thought worked out quite well. And I was pleased with *Love Alterns Not,* many readers have praised the hero of this story as being particularly appealing.

"My ambition for my works is that they may enable some reader to escape today's frightening (to me) world for a little while and perhaps inspire a chuckle or even a laugh now and then. And also that the plots remind us that there are countless men and women who live quiet and honorable lives spreading kindness and caring to others despite the efforts of much of the 'entertainment' industry to undermine such old fashioned morality.

BIOGRAPHICAL AND CRITICAL SOURCES:

BOOKS

Twentieth-Century Romance and Historical Writers, 3rd edition, St. James Press (Detroit, MI), 1994.

PERIODICALS

Booklist, March 15, 1994, Denise Perry Donavin, review of *A Shadow's Bliss,* p. 1329; February 1, 1995, Denise Perry Donavin, review of *Never Doubt I Love,* p. 992; October 15, 1996, Jennifer Henderson, review of *Lanterns,* p. 406; September 15, 1998, Ann Bouricius, review of *The Riddle of the Lost Lover,* p. 214; October 15, 1999, Alexandra Shrake, review of *The Riddle of the Reluctant Rake,* p. 423; March 1, 2001, Diana Tixier Herald, review of *The Riddle of the Shipwrecked Spinster,* p. 1232; December 1, 2002, Kaite Mediatore, review of *The Riddle of the Deplorable Dandy,* p. 651.
Kirkus Reviews, February 1, 1995, p. 102; September 1, 1995, p. 1218; September 15, 1996, p. 1351.
Library Journal, October 1, 1995, Paula M. Zieselman, review of *The Mandarin of Mayfair,* p. 121; February 15, 1997, p. 184; November 1, 1997, Elizabeth Mary Mellett, review of *The Riddle of Alabaster Royal,* p. 118; September 15, 1998, Elizabeth Mellett, review of *The Riddle of the Lost Lover,* p. 115.
Publishers Weekly, March 21, 1994, review of *A Shadow's Bliss,* p. 56; September 16, 1996, review of *Lanterns,* p. 71; September 15, 1997, review of *The Riddle of Alabaster Royal,* p. 51; Oct 5, 1998, review of *The Riddle of the Lost Lover,* p. 81; October 4, 1999, review of *The Riddle of the Reluctant Rake,* p. 65; April 2, 2001, review of *The Riddle of the Shipwrecked Spinster,* p. 40.
School Library Journal, March, 1997, Linda A. Vretos, review of *Lanterns,* p. 217; April, 1998, Claudia Moore, review of *The Riddle of Alabaster Royal,* p. 159.

ONLINE

Patricia Veryan Fanclub Web site, http://www.patricia veryanfanclub.com/ (October, 2003).

BARRY, Lynda (Jean) 1956-

PERSONAL: Born January 2, 1956, in Richland Center, WI. *Education:* Graduated from Evergreen State College, c. 1978.

ADDRESSES: Agent—c/o Author Mail, Sasquatch Books, Suite 260, 615 Second Ave., Seattle, WA 98104.

CAREER: Artist, author, and playwright. Commentator for National Public Radio; guest on television programs, including *Late Night with David Letterman.* Exhibitions include "Naked Ladies! Naked Ladies! Naked Ladies!," Linda Farris Gallery, Seattle, WA, 1984, and "The Good Times Are Killing Me," Linda Farris Gallery, 1986.

AWARDS, HONORS: Alex Award, Young Adult Library Services Association, 2003, for *One Hundred Demons.*

WRITINGS:

COMICS

Girls + Boys, Real Comet Press (Seattle, WA), 1981.
Big Ideas, Real Comet Press (Seattle, WA), 1983.
Naked Ladies! Naked Ladies! Naked Ladies!, Real Comet Press (Seattle, WA), 1984.
Everything in the World, Perennial Library (New York, NY), 1986.
The Fun House, Perennial Library (New York, NY), 1987.
Down the Street, Perennial Library (New York, NY), 1988.
Come over, Come Over, Harper Perennial (New York, NY), 1990.
My Perfect Life, Harper Perennial (New York, NY), 1992.
It's So Magic, HarperCollins (New York, NY), 1994.
The Freddie Stories, Sasquatch Books (Seattle, WA), 1999.
The Greatest of Marlys, Sasquatch Books (Seattle, WA), 2000.
One Hundred Demons, Sasquatch Books (Seattle, WA), 2002.

Contributor of cartoon strips "Girls and Boys," "Ernie Pook's Comeek," and "Modern Romance;" to periodicals, including *Esquire* (1984-89), *Village Voice, New York Times,* and *Raw.*

OTHER

The Last House (play), produced by Pioneer Square Theater, Seattle, WA, 1988.

The Good Times Are Killing Me (novel), Real Comet Press (Seattle, WA), 1988, with new illustrations, Sasquatch Books (Seattle, WA), 1998.

(With Arnold Aprill) *The Good Times Are Killing Me* (play; adapted from her novel), first produced in Chicago, IL, 1989, produced Off-Broadway, 1991.

Cruddy: An Illustrated Novel, Simon & Schuster (New York, NY), 1999.

Contributor of articles and book reviews to periodicals, including *American Film, Life, Los Angeles Times, Newsweek,* and *New York Times.* Contributor of short stories to periodicals, including a monthly fiction column for *Mother Jones,* 1989—.

WORK IN PROGRESS: A sequel to the novel *The Good Times Are Killing Me,* showing Edna from ages twelve to thirteen; plans for a screenplay adaptation of *The Good Times Are Killing Me* and for a musical.

SIDELIGHTS: "Imagine having a job like mine where you sit around all day and think about dirt bombs!," commented Lynda Barry in the *San Jose Mercury News.* In such writings as her "Ernie Pook" comic strip and the novel-turned-play, *The Good Times Are Killing Me,* Barry ranges over the whole comic/tragic experience of growing up, from dirt bombs to divorced parents to the strains that pull friendships apart. The lives of young people, Barry suggests, offer major insights about life in general. "I think about my own childhood all the time," she told an interviewer for the *Los Angeles Times.* "It's the only place to go if you're looking for answers. It's where all our motivations, feelings and opinions come from."

While many adults prefer to remember their youth as a "simpler" time, Barry grew up knowing that life is complicated. She was born in a small Wisconsin town into a multicultural family, daughter of a Filipino mother and a Norwegian-Irish father. Her mother soon

felt out of place in the Midwest, so the family moved to Seattle, Washington, where her father felt out of place—surrounded by Filipino in-laws who could not speak English. Though Barry inherited her father's European looks—"Norwegian blood," she told the Chicago *Sun-Times,* "can suck the color out of anything"—she was received as a fellow Filipino by her mother's relatives, who talked to her routinely about "white" people. "I never felt completely Filipino and I never felt completely white," she told the *San Jose Mercury News.* "I felt completely different. I didn't even feel like a girl; I didn't feel like a boy, either. I could not find a peer."

Barry settled as best she could into her new neighborhood—the multiracial, working-class south end of Seattle, where dozens of her Filipino relatives lived. Music became one of the joys of her life. "Filipinos are really cool people. They have a tradition of a lot of dancing, a lot of group activity," Barry recalled in the Chicago *Sun-Times.* "The radio's always going, there's always music playing. We had our record player in the kitchen, which was the center of where people sat around and hung out. They were always listening to the hippest things. Still, to this day, my aunts and uncles listen to Top 40. They listen to the same music kids do." Also in the kitchen was her "exuberant" Filipino grandmother, who served up delicious potfuls of chicken *adobo,* boiled in vinegar and soy sauce. "I worship and adore her," Barry wrote in the *Los Angeles Times,* "because she has made my life incredibly rich."

Despite the vitality exhibited by her family, life was never easy. Money was tight, and her parents eventually broke up. She started to realize that society was not very equitable, and that her family had to struggle more than most. Nevertheless, Barry became the first in her family to attend college and enrolled at Evergreen State, where her goal, as she told the *New York Times,* was "to be the best, the most depressed, bohemian in the world and make the most serious paintings." Being cast off by a boyfriend changed her life. "I couldn't sleep, going through my first heartbreak, and I drew a lot of comics about women and men," she told *Mother Jones.* "The men were cactuses who would talk to women and say, you know, 'Come to bed with me' and stuff. And a lot of them were friendly, too. It was just that they would be really bad to lay [sic] on top of." She called her drawings "Spinal Comics" and, for all the pointy spines, men seemed to like them as well as women. Eventually her work would become known as "Ernie Pook's Comeek," in honor of her little brother, who liked to call everything he owned by that name.

One of Barry's earliest fans was the editor of the Evergreen school paper, Matt Groening, who went on to fame as the creator of "Life in Hell" comics and *The Simpsons* television series. "Lynda's stuff," he told the *Washington Post,* "was funny, wild, had a very strong point of view, and it was obviously what *Lynda* thought was funny." Soon Barry's work was appearing in the papers at Evergreen State and the University of Washington.

Barry had qualms about switching her focus from painting to cartoons, but a nasty boss made up Barry's mind for her. "I had a job selling popcorn in a movie theater when I was twenty-one," she told the New York *Daily News,* "and then they found out I could draw and so I started doing paste-up for their little ads. I worked really hard. One day my boss came in—he was an alcoholic, I hated him—and his highball breath was blowing on me and he told me I was skating on thin ice. And I thought, 'This is what having a job is all about. That you can be alone in a room working hard on something you don't care about and a complete ass can come in and blow his nasty breath on you and tell you you're skating on thin ice.'" She promptly quit and, on the bus home, wrote a pledge to herself that she would never work for anyone ever again.

Fresh out of college in the late 1970s, Barry did not have much of a cartooning career except continued appearances in the University of Washington *Daily* and ten dollars a week from the Seattle *Sun*—a struggling alternative paper that finally went out of business. Just as she was ready to give up, her friendship with Groening helped to save her. Groening, himself a struggling cartoonist/writer in Los Angeles, wrote an article describing his friends in the "Evergreen mafia" that came to the attention of Bob Roth, publisher of the thriving alternative weekly the *Chicago Reader.* Roth liked Barry's work. "She was drawing a hipper kind of strip that you couldn't find anywhere else," he told the *San Jose Mercury News.* "She was addressing adult concerns in a way that comic strips almost never do." Barry liked Roth's offer of eighty dollars a week—at last she could live. "I had a telephone answering machine," she observed,

"and for the next year, whenever Roth called I wouldn't pick up the phone because I was too scared he would fire me."

By the early 1980s, Barry's comic strip was ensconced in alternative weeklies nationwide. She had stopped drawing men as spiny plants, but she remained interested in male-female relationships—"the whole luuuv thang," as she was quoted in the *Seattle Times.* In strips that were later collected in the volumes *Girls + Boys, Big Ideas,* and *Everything in the World,* she satirized dating, parties, fashions, two-faced boyfriends, and the illusions of romance. She became known for quips such as "Cupid is a monster from hell" and "Love is an exploding cigar which we willingly smoke"; interviewers likened her live delivery to that of a stand-up comedian. "Cupid *is* a monster," Barry explained in *Interview,* "because he shoots you and then you suddenly have to do all these things that you ordinarily wouldn't do. To operate a car you must have a driver's license. Love is a hundred times more dangerous than driving a car and you do it completely unprepared. You can fall in love with anybody, even people who hit you or steal your money or make you feel like you have a giant butt."

To satirize popular culture, Barry studied it avidly, poring through magazines, catalogs, and even junk mail. "Basically there is no idea *too* small," she told *Interview.* She became an accomplished eavesdropper: overheard conversations were not only a source of subject matter, but a way to understand how people actually talk. She visited singles bars a lot—for business reasons. "I go there with my boyfriend," she explained, "who is very good at making me look occupied, but not saying much, so I can eavesdrop." By 1984 Barry was supplementing her weekly newspaper strip with a monthly "Modern Romance" strip she wrote especially for *Esquire* magazine. "Her screwy depictions of the mating game," wrote Margot Sims in *Mother Jones,* "are so dead-on they make you cringe."

A favorite target of Barry's barbs became what sociologists call "women's body image": specifically, the difference between the glamour that society expects women to exude and their actual appearance. Her pop culture studies gave her plenty of ammunition. "Magazines like *Cosmopolitan* . . . really capitalize on women feeling horrible about themselves," Barry told *Interview.* "They resemble porno magazines. . . . You're supposed to look at the pictures of models standing around with no clothes on trying to look as sexy as possible and think to yourself, 'Oh, that's me looking like that for so-and-so.' Women yell about *Playboy* for its sexist treatment of women, while *Glamour* and *Mademoiselle* slip under the rug, no sweat. Women's magazines are as guilty, if not more so, of creating an image of how women think they should be." False expectations were deeply entrenched, going back all the way to childhood. "Girls have an idea of how their bodies should be," said Barry in *Ms.* "They don't play with their Barbie dolls because they are looking for intellectual idols."

Barry created her own gallery of more authentic women. In *Naked Ladies! Naked Ladies! Naked Ladies!*, she uses a coloring-book format to present cartoon portraits of dozens of different (undressed) women, including fashionable women, fat women, anorexic women, and a groggy woman with curlers in her hair wearing "Foxy Lady" underwear. Along with the pictures is a first-person narrative in which an adolescent girl describes the uneasy blossoming of her own sexuality. "We got Bras and they got Jock Straps," the narrator recalls of her school days. "Like everything was suddenly going out of control and your mom had to buy you something to stop it."

The book was another daring move for Barry. Friends warned her against it; some feminists criticized it; some pornographers liked it. "I couldn't figure out who was going to kill me—the Moral Majority or the lesbian separatists," Barry told *Ms.* "But the thing that surprised me most was that it seemed to work on enough levels that everyone saw it totally differently, and most found a reason to like it." Wrote B. Ruby Rich in the *Voice Literary Supplement:* "Barry stakes her position not on the good or bad essence of sexuality, but rather on the tragicomic inevitability of it all, traumas and yearnings included. It is a testimony to her skill that she confronts so complicated a subject in so simple a format."

Meanwhile, Barry had mixed feelings about her work for *Esquire,* even if it did help her become more widely known. Unlike her usual comic strips, in which she followed her own creative instincts, "Modern Romance" was made to order for a particular audience—*Esquire*'s affluent, young, male readers. The stories were not supposed to be whimsical or darkly satirical; they had to be quick, lively, and unambiguously funny. At first Barry tried to take the

assignment in stride, viewing it as chance to develop her versatility. "I really like being in *Esquire* because it *is* a man's magazine," she told *Mother Jones.* "It makes me feel just like the girls in high school who would take electronics or machine shop. You know, you would take those classes not only because you wanted to learn about machines, but mostly because you wanted to be in there with the guys, and just kind of messing up their act, too." Eventually, though, the need to conform to someone else's ideas took its toll, and Barry discontinued the *Esquire* strip. "I had to work with an editor, whose job it was to make sure my cartoons conformed to the 'Esquire Man' way of looking at things," she told the *Los Angeles Times.* "Thing is, I don't see the world through the eyes of a successful, thirty-year-old white guy."

Instead of quips about modern romance, Barry increasingly wanted to express the concerns of growing up. The adolescent narrator of *Naked Ladies!* was her inspiration. "That was my first character, my first encounter with the fact that you can take a character and then they'll do all the work and you just sit behind them and jot down everything they're saying," she told the *San Jose Mercury News.* "To me it is simply a marvel that you could have various characters that speak in different voices!" By the time Barry produced the comic strips that appear in *Down the Street,* she had settled on four elementary schoolers for her focus: Arna, the sensitive, observant narrator; Arnold, her rowdy brother; Marlys, a cousin who is smart, self-assured, even bratty; and Freddie, brother of Marlys, who lives with the humiliating knowledge that his parents had him "by accident." "With those four characters," she told the Chicago *Sun-Times,* "you can pretty much tell any story."

Barry's work was not as predictably funny anymore. Along with Freddie's bug collection, Marlys's beauty makeovers, and Arnold's chewing-gum map of South America came narratives about child abuse, poverty, and the man at the candy store who had not said much to anyone since his wife left him. Some readers thought Barry was saying that childhood unhappiness was funny; some thought she was too depressing; others assumed the traumas were all autobiographical. The last assumption especially troubled Barry ("My God, what kind of life would I have had?" she remarked in the *Seattle Times*), and she ran disclaimers at the front of several of her books. A few papers canceled the strip. For a while Barry was worried.

"You always have fears of pushing your audience away," she told the *San Jose Mercury News.* "If you made your reputation doing these sorts of snappy jokes about relationships and then you move into some other field, you're going to definitely lose a lot of people who feel there's something wrong with you. And then I'm going to wonder whether there's something wrong with me. But there's really no choice," she said. "When I found a story that I thought was so good and so authentic, I wasn't going to write one about somebody eating hot dogs just because I was scared to send the stronger one out."

Why should a comic strip about children be painful at times? "Pain for kids is much sharper," Barry explained to the *Chicago Tribune.* "As a kid, you're stuck, no matter what's going on. As an adult, if you're at your friend's house and she and her boyfriend have a wild fight, you can leave. As a kid you can't." Wouldn't it be better to just forget about it? "It's important to go back and decide what happened back then," she said in the *St. Paul Pioneer Press-Dispatch.* "Making an adult decision about it really works wonders. . . . [As a child] when you're not invited to a party, you figure it's because you're a jerk, when really maybe the other kids just needed someone to boast to or you just lived in the wrong neighborhood. People do go through their lives hurt by these things. There's a beauty about reconciling it. It's like music; it has the same kind of power." Barry likened her strips to short stories, and increasingly observers agreed, describing her less as a cartoonist than as an author. "This isn't just a smart cartoon," wrote Katherine Dieckmann in the *Voice Literary Supplement.* "It's strong writing." In the long run, Barry's bold move to change her comic strip was amply rewarded. Fewer than twenty papers carried her work in 1983; five years later the number had grown to nearly fifty; she topped sixty in the early 1990s.

Meanwhile Barry had begun another ambitious project, inspired by a vision she had while driving through a pineapple field during a Hawaiian vacation. "I saw a series of portraits," she told the *Los Angeles Times,* "in funky metal frames, of my favorite musicians—most of them black, most of them dead. Suddenly, I knew what my next project would be." Using the bright, flat, multicolored style of American folk art, Barry created eighteen portraits of American musicians, ranging from pioneering blues singer Gertrude ("Ma") Rainey to soul singer Otis Redding. The paintings were exhibited at a Seattle gallery, which asked Barry to write a short introduction for the exhibition catalog.

She read up on the musicians, many of whom endured poverty and racial discrimination, and began to ponder how thoroughly racism had saturated American society. Determined to explain how closely the history of American music was intertwined with the history of American racism, Barry struggled with her essay for months without success. "[I] was telling instead of showing," she explained in the New York *Daily News.* Instead of finishing the essay, she decided to dramatize her concerns in a work of fiction, using the setting she knew best: the poor, interracial neighborhood where she had grown up. In particular, she told the *New York Times,* "I wanted to paint a picture of adolescence, because one of the things that's incredible about adolescence is that you start to see the problems of the world, and when they first hit, you think you know how to fix things."

The resulting novel, *The Good Times Are Killing Me,* is set in the 1960s and narrated by Edna Arkins, a white junior high school student looking back on her last year in elementary school. Edna's downscale neighborhood exemplifies the interracial tensions of the sixties: while the ideals of the civil rights era preached a new interracial harmony, whites were fleeing from the racially mixed inner cities as quickly as they could. "In the beginning of this street it was a mainly white street," Edna recalls. "The houses went White, White, White, Japanese, White, White. . . . Then it seemed like just about everybody kept moving out until now our street is Chinese, Negro, Negro, White, Japanese, Filipino." As the novel progresses, Edna describes her abortive friendship with Bonna Willis, a hip, assertive black girl from the nearby housing projects. The bridge between the two girls is music: Bonna has records she wants to play, and Edna is lucky enough to have a battered old record player. Their friendship blossoms as Bonna teaches Edna about black singers like James Brown and dances like the Tighten Up while the girls cavort in Edna's Record Player Nightclub—actually Edna's basement, redone in a sixth-grader's notion of glamour and style.

The girls' friendship is never free of tension. Edna's aunt, reeking with condescension, takes Bonna along on a family camping trip to acquaint her with the finer things in life (Bonna has been camping many times). Edna is utterly afraid when Bonna starts taking her on a tour of the housing projects. Things deteriorate further when Edna attends a slumber party from which black girls have been excluded, and the two girls start avoiding each other. Then comes the more grown-up, hostile world of junior high, where "from the second we walked through the doors we all automatically split apart into groups of who was alike. . . . This was our new main rule of life even though it wasn't us who created it. It just grew there, like big permanent teeth after baby teeth." Fights erupt. Edna gets pushed around in the girl's bathroom by one of Bonna's friends, then Edna blames Bonna, and Bonna smacks Edna. The friendship is over. "In the vice principal's office we acted like we had never met," Edna concludes. "Like all it was was any black girl slapping any white girl who had mouthed off to her, something that happened every single day and would just keep on happening world without end." "I really wanted to show how the problem of racism affects people for their entire lives," Barry told the *New York Times.* "Edna and Bonna are a couple of kids who became friends at a time when they each really needed a friend. And that need isn't about to stop. I wanted to make them the first casualties. Because it is a war. To me [*Good Times* is] a tragedy—or perhaps a feel-bad comedy."

Barry's novel brought her a new level of fame, including her first major critical notice. Writing in the *New York Times Book Review,* Deborah Stead praised Barry's "impeccable ear" for Edna's way of speaking and declared: "This funny, intricate and finally heartbreaking story exquisitely captures an American childhood." *The Good Times Are Killing Me* also piqued the interest of the theater world, particularly Arnold Aprill, head of Chicago's City Lit Theater Company. After meeting with Barry, he roughed out a dramatic adaptation of the novel, and then Barry joined him to work with the cast and write a final script. The play debuted in Chicago in 1989, and then, after further rewriting by Barry, was produced Off-Broadway in 1991 and became a hit with audiences and theater critics alike. A writer for the *New York Post* praised its "masterly sense of progression, construction, and dramatic form." *The Good Times Are Killing Me,* the reviewer concluded, "hits us in places we had forgotten, and tells us things we never knew we knew." Some reviewers suggested that the play had too many short scenes—the result, they surmised, of Barry's comic-strip background—but they nonetheless lauded her as an acute observer of human nature. Edith Oliver of the *New Yorker* called Edna Arkins "the most enchanting heroine of the Off-Broadway season."

The Good Times Are Killing Me ends as Edna and Bonna enter junior high school, and Barry prepared to follow them, writing about their further adventures in short stories for *Mother Jones,* beginning in 1989. She also moved her weekly comic strip into the world of adolescence, changing its focus from four elementary schoolers to Marlys and her fourteen-year-old sister Maybonne. "I've pretty much exhausted what I know about [childhood]," she told the Chicago *Sun-Times.* Writing about adolescence was a new gamble. "It's hard because people hate that time of their lives. And in general, I think society does not like adolescence. It's really hard to find the right voice of the narrator."

As part of her search, Barry explored yet another aspect of popular culture: the diaries of teenage girls. Spotlighted in cartoon collections beginning with *Come over, Come Over,* Maybonne's adventures include coping with her overburdened, inadequate parents, getting snubbed by girlfriends, and acting out the role of the small intestine for science class ("I swear to God I hate my life"). She confides in her diary frequently, and Marlys, of course, reads it. Somehow Maybonne survives all the emotional ups and downs. "Life," she declares, "can magically turn cruddy then turn beautiful . . . and then back to cruddy again." *The Freddie Stories* and *The Greatest of Marlys* collect more adventures of Maybonne, Marlys, and Freddie. In the former, Freddie suffers indignities that include sexual abuse, name-calling, and incarceration for a crime he did not commit, but he manages to weather it all. *The Freddie Stories* is "a foray into the perceptions of children growing up in a callous and destructive culture" and "Barry's newest testimony of genius," commented Inga Muscio in *Lambda Book Report.* A *Mother Jones* reviewer added that "Freddie's charm is the sense he makes of the bleak, adult-infested world." *The Greatest of Marlys* shows how "simple pleasures" allow the siblings to cope in a world of "callous teachers, ruthless classmates, and vicious dogs," related Gordon Flagg in *Booklist.* A *Publishers Weekly* critic noted that the book displays Barry's talent for "the very nearly poetic invocation of moments of pubescent joy and humiliation."

Horror rather than joy is at the center of *Cruddy: An Illustrated Novel.* The year is 1971, and the protagonist, Roberta Rohbeson, is a sixteen-year-old living a "cruddy" life with her mother, sister, and misfit friends. Five years earlier, Roberta was the only survivor of a mass murderer's attack on a group of people in a motel in the Nevada desert. Roberta had arrived at that motel with her father, who had gone on a cross-country crime spree after the breakup with her mother. Roberta narrates this harrowing story in flashback. A *Publishers Weekly* reviewer thought "Barry goes over the top with alarming details," and felt readers may have trouble following this "labyrinthine" story. *Booklist* contributor Donna Seaman, however, praised Barry's "galvanic prose" and "daredevil literary wizardry"; mixed in with the story's darker aspects, Seaman wrote, is a "stubborn affection for our seriously flawed species." *Library Journal* reviewer Reba Leiding commented that "Roberta's wacky, irrepressible outlook makes her story fresh, compelling, and sometimes hilarious." And Alanna Nash, writing in the *New York Times Book Review,* called *Cruddy* "a work of terrible beauty," marked by Barry's "ability to capture the paralyzing bleakness of despair, and her uncanny ear for dialogue."

In *One Hundred Demons,* Barry presents a collection of twenty autobiographical comic strip stories from an ongoing *Salon.com* feature "Mothers Who Think," which appeared online semi-monthly between April 7, 2000 and January 15, 2001. Barry, who calls the ink brush and watercolor drawings "autobifictionalgraphy," produced the strips by practicing an Asian painting exercise called "One Hundred Demons." In the drawings, Barry once again delves into the vagaries of adolescence ("Head Lice and My Worst Boyfriend"), family, and love, as well as abused dogs, doing acid, and even the 2000 presidential election. Writing in the *Library Journal,* Steve Raiteri commented, "Barry's text-heavy panels fit a lot of story into a few pages, and her child-like drawings seem almost designed to encourage budding artist readers." Noting that this book "may be her breakthrough," Lev Grossman of *Time* added that "*One Hundred Demons* deserves a place on the shelf with serious graphic novels like Art Spiegelman's Maus." Writing in *MELUS,* Melinda L. de Jesus noted that the book "is an exploration of events and memories that deeply affected the artist, namely, her childhood and its manifold tragedies, large and small. It deftly exhibits the hallmarks of Barry's powerful storytelling aesthetic: her deliberately 'naíve' graphic style complements the brutally honest musings of its young narrator and the often harsh subjects of the strips themselves."

BIOGRAPHICAL AND CRITICAL SOURCES:

BOOKS

The Good Times Are Killing Me (novel), Real Comet Press (Seattle, WA), 1988.

PERIODICALS

Booklist, January 1, 1987, p. 674; June 1, 1988, p. 1635; October 1, 1988, p. 185; April 15, 1994, p. 1496; August, 1999, Donna Seaman, review of *Cruddy: An Illustrated Novel,* p. 2020; August, 2000, Gordon Flagg, review of *The Greatest of Marlys,* p. 2093; August, 2002, Gordon Flagg, review of *One Hundred Demons,* p. 1907.
Chicago Tribune, August 9, 1987; April 19, 1989, section 5, p. 1.
Daily News (New York, NY), April 14, 1991.
Denver Post, February 12, 1989.
Interview, November, 1985, p. 119.
Lambda Book Report, July-August, 1999, Inga Muscio, review of *The Freddie Stories,* p. 20.
Library Journal, March 1, 1999, Stephen Weiner, review of *The Freddie Stories,* p. 78; September 15, 1999, Reba Leiding, review of *Cruddy,* p. 110; November 1, 2002, Steve Raiteri, review of *One Hundred Demons,* p. 64.
Los Angeles Times, October 18, 1990, p. H13; April 28, 1991.
Los Angeles Times Book Review, October 21, 1990, p. 10.
MELUS, spring, 2004, Melinda L. de Jesus, "Liminality and Mestiza Consciousness in Lynda Barry's *One Hundred Demons,*" p. 219.
Mother Jones, December, 1984, p. 17; March, 1999, review of *The Freddie Stories,* p. 75.
Ms., October, 1983, p. 106; April, 1985, p. 23.
New Straits Times, July 9, 2001, review of *Cruddy.*
Newsweek, August 19, 1991, p. 54.
New York, April 29, 1991, p. 84.
New Yorker, May 6, 1991, Edith Oliver, "The Theatre: Back Then," p. 81.
New York Post, April 19, 1991.
New York Times, November 27, 1988; August 14, 1991, p. C11.
New York Times Book Review, November 20, 1988, Deborah Stead, review of *The Good Times Are Killing Me,* p. 53; September 5, 1999, Alanna Nash, "Bad Trip."
Oregonian (Portland, OR), April 21, 1991.
People, March 30, 1987, p. 109; September 27, 1999, Anne-Marie O'Neill, review of *Cruddy,* p. 53.
Philadelphia Inquirer, September 27, 1991.
Publishers Weekly, March 15, 1999, review of *The Freddie Stories,* p. 48; July 12, 1999, review of *Cruddy,* p. 72; August 28, 2000, review of *The Greatest of Marlys,* p. 57; September 9, 2002, review of *One Hundred Demons,* p. 45.

St. Paul Pioneer Press-Dispatch, April 2, 1988.

San Jose Mercury News, May 22, 1988.

Sassy, November, 1991, p. 43.

School Library Journal, March, 2003, Jody Sharp, review of *One Hundred Demons,* p. 262.

Seattle Times, November 6, 1988; April 25, 1991.

Sun-Times (Chicago, IL), April 30, 1989.

Time, August 26, 1991, p. 63; September 2, 2002, Lev Grossman, review of *One Hundred Demons,* p. 72.

Voice Literary Supplement, July, 1985, p. 13; January, 1989, p. 5.

Washington Post, December 12, 1988.

Washington Post Book World, December 20, 1987, p. 12; October 30, 1988, p. 16.

OTHER

Salon.com, http://www.salon.com/ (May 21, 1999), Pamela Grossman, "Barefoot on the Shag: An Interview with Cartoonist, Novelist Lynda Barry."*

*   *   *

BASS, Kingsley B., Jr.
    See BULLINS, Ed

*   *   *

BELL, Madison Smartt 1957-

PERSONAL: Born August 1, 1957, in Nashville, TN; son of Henry Denmark (an attorney) and Allen (a farmer; maiden name, Wigginton) Bell; married Elizabeth Spires (a poet), June 15, 1985; children: Celia. *Education:* Princeton University, B.A. (summa cum laude), 1979; Hollins College, M.A., 1981.

ADDRESSES: Home—Baltimore, MD. *Office*—Department of English, Goucher College, Towson, MD 21204. *Agent*—Jane Gellman, 250 West 57th St., New York, NY 10107. *E-mail*—mbell@goucher.edu.

CAREER: Security guard at Unique Clothing Warehouse (boutique), 1979; production assistant for Gomes-Lowe Associates (commercial production house), 1979; sound man for Radiotelevisione Italiana (Italian national network), 1979; Franklin Library

Madison Smartt Bell

(publishing firm), New York, NY, picture research assistant, 1980, writer of reader's guides, 1980-83; Berkley Publishing Corp., New York, NY, manuscript reader and copy writer, 1981-83; Goucher College, Towson, MD, assistant professor of English, 1984-86, writer-in-residence, 1988—. Visiting writer, Poetry Center, 92nd Street Y, New York, NY, 1984-86, Iowa Writers Workshop, 1987-88, and Johns Hopkins Writing Seminars, 1989-93. Director of 185 Corporation (media arts organization), 1979-84.

MEMBER: PEN American Center, Authors Guild, Authors League of America, Poets and Writers, Phi Beta Kappa.

AWARDS, HONORS: Ward Mathis Prize, 1977, for short story "Triptych," Class of 1870 Junior Prize, 1978, Francis LeMoyne Page Award, 1978, for fiction writing, and Class of 1859 Prize, 1979, all from Princeton University; Lillian Smith Award, 1989; Guggenheim fellowship, 1991; Maryland State Arts Council Individual Artist Award, 1991-92; George A. and Eliza Gardner Howard Foundation Award, 1991-92; National Endowment for the Arts fellowship, 1992;

National Book Award finalist, 1995, PEN/Faulkner Award finalist, Maryland Library Association Award, and Anisfield-Wolf Award, all 1996, all for *All Souls' Rising;* selected as one of the "Best American Novelists under Forty," *Granta,* 1996; Andrew James Purdy Fiction Award, Hollins College.

WRITINGS:

NOVELS

The Washington Square Ensemble, Viking (New York, NY), 1983.
Waiting for the End of the World, Ticknor & Fields (New York, NY), 1985.
Straight Cut, Ticknor & Fields (New York, NY), 1986.
The Year of Silence, Ticknor & Fields (New York, NY), 1987.
Soldier's Joy, Ticknor & Fields (New York, NY), 1989.
Doctor Sleep, Harcourt (San Diego, CA), 1991.
Save Me, Joe Louis, Harcourt (New York, NY), 1993.
All Souls' Rising, Pantheon (New York, NY), 1995.
Ten Indians, Pantheon (New York, NY), 1996.
Master of the Crossroads, Pantheon (New York, NY), 2000.
Anything Goes, Pantheon (New York, NY), 2002.

OTHER

History of the Owen Graduate School of Management (nonfiction), Vanderbilt University (Nashville, TN), 1985.
Zero db (short fiction), Ticknor & Fields (New York, NY), 1987.
(With others) *George Garrett: An Interview,* Northouse & Northouse (Dallas, TX), 1988.
Waiting for the End of the World (screenplay), Cine Paris, 1988.
The Safety Net (screenplay), New Horizons, 1990.
Barking Man and Other Stories (contains "Holding Together," "Black and Tan," "Customs of the Country," "Finding Natasha," "Dragon's Seed," "Barking Man," "Petit Cachou," "Witness," "Move on Up," and "Mr. Potatohead in Love,") Ticknor & Fields (New York, NY), 1990.
Choc en Retour (screen adaptation of *Straight Cut*), Thomas Kuchenreuther (Munich, Germany), 1993.
New Millennium Writings, Spring & Summer 1996, New Messenger Books (Nashville, TN), 1996.

Narrative Design: A Writer's Guide to Structure, Norton (New York, NY), 1997.
(Author of introduction) George Garrett, *The King of Babylon Shall Not Come against You* (novel), Harcourt (New York, NY), 1998.

Contributor of short fiction to periodicals and anthologies, including *Best American Short Stories, New Writers of the South, New Stories from the South, Atlantic, Harper's, Best of Intro, Editors' Choice, Louder Than Words, A Pocketful of Prose, Sound of Writing, Elvis in Oz, That's What I Like about the South, Antaeus, Boulevard, Cosmopolitan, Literary Review* (London, England), *Ploughshares, Columbia, Crescent Review, Northwest Review, Lowlands Review, Poughkeepsie Review, Stories, Tennessee Illustrated, Switch, Southern Review, Witness, Hudson Review,* and *North American Review.* Contributor of reviews and essays to *Harper's, Antaeus, Chronicles, Switch, World and I, A Wake for the Living, Critical Essays on Peter Taylor, New York Times Magazine, USA Today, Philadelphia Inquirer, London Standard, North American Review, Boston Globe, Southern Magazine, New York Times Book Review, Village Voice,* and *Los Angeles Times Book Review.* Work included in anthologies, including *It's Only Rock and Roll,* edited by Janice Eidus and John Kastan, D. Godine; and *Sudden Fiction (Continued),* edited by Robert Shapard and James Thomas. Contributor of essay to *Joyful Noise: The New Testament Revisited,* edited by Rick Moody and Darcey Steinke, Little, Brown, and to *Outside the Law: Narratives on Justice in America,* edited by Susan Richards Shreve and Porter Shreve, Beacon Press. Author of readers' guides, Franklin Library, 1979-83.

Several of Bell's works have been translated into other languages, including German, Danish, Spanish, Portuguese, Japanese, French, and Dutch.

SIDELIGHTS: "Madison Smartt Bell has been called a postmodernist, a minimalist, a prose poet of aloneness, and the best writer of his generation," stated Donna Seaman in *Booklist.* "His distinctively riling fiction sizzles with tension and menace." Bell, who had published six novels and two short-story collections by the time he was thirty-five years old, usually writes about society's misfits. Most of his main characters are petty criminals, drifters, and lost souls whose lives Seaman describes as "fateful and apocalyptic."

Save Me, Joe Louis exemplifies the themes and situations found in much of Bell's fiction. In this novel, Macrae, an AWOL Southerner, and Charlie, an unstable ex-con, forge a dangerous partnership soon after meeting in New York City. Together they embark on a small-time crime spree that eventually leads them to flee for Macrae's backcountry homeland. There, the relationship sours and violence erupts. Macrae and Charlie are typical of Bell's protagonists in that there is little to like about them; many commentators find that one of the great strengths of Bell's writing is his ability to generate characters for such people. Andy Solomon wrote in the *Chicago Tribune* that Bell "moves among modern thieves and lepers with charity. His is a Robert Browning empathy that creates no character so defiled that Bell cannot ask, 'What is at the heart of this man that is in me as well?' In Macrae, Bell once again takes a character you'd be disturbed to find living anywhere near your neighborhood, then moves relentlessly against the grain of popular thought to find the embers of Macrae's humanity beneath the ashes of his pain." Reviewing the novel for *Booklist,* Seaman called *Save Me, Joe Louis* "a work of ferocious intensity and poetic nihilism" in which Bell examines the "soul's disturbing capacity for both good and evil and the pointlessness of unexamined lives lived wholly by instinct and rage."

Rage is at the center of *All Souls' Rising,* an epic history of Haiti's war for independence, which broke out shortly after the French revolution in the late 1700s. The strange alliances, hatred, and tensions among Haiti's rich white ruling class, the poor whites, the free mulattoes, and the island's mistreated slave population culminated in a fifteen-year bloodbath. In just the first few months of the revolution, 12,000 people perished and nearly 200 plantations were burned. Writing in the *New York Times Book Review,* John Vernon described Bell's historical novel as a "carefully drawn roadmap through hell." "*All Souls' Rising,*" he continued, "is historical fiction in the monumental manner, heavily prefaced, prologued, glossaried and chronologized. It admirably diagrams the complex muddle of eighteenth-century Haiti, a slave society constructed along clearly racist lines but with surprising alliances. Haitian whites, split into royalists and revolutionaries, alternately compete for and spurn the loyalties of free mulattoes, for whom gradations of color are of central importance. . . . This bizarre and rich stew is the perfect stuff of fiction, whose subject is never reality but competing realities."

Countless atrocities were committed on all sides in the Haitian revolution, and Bell's book details many

examples. For some reviewers, the gore was too much. Brian Morton expressed little enthusiasm for the novel, stating in the *New Statesman* that *All Souls' Rising* "is an ugly book about ugly times. The author can claim historical veracity. . . . But there are undercurrents that recall the violent pornography of another triple-barrelled American novelist, Bret Easton Ellis." Vernon also found the scenes of mutilation, rape, and violence relentless and warned that such repeated gore may numb the novel "into a handbook of splatter-punk. To his credit," Vernon continued, "Bell knows that violence may be the writer's hedge against mawkishness, but it also threatens to become mere slush, the sentimentality of gore." Still, Vernon found much to praise, especially Bell's ability to humanize all types of characters and concluded that while there are flaws in the novel, they are overshadowed by its power and intelligence: "*All Souls' Rising,* refreshingly ambitious and maximalist in its approach, takes enormous chances, and consequently will haunt readers long after plenty of flawless books have found their little slots on their narrow shelves."

A *Publishers Weekly* reviewer expressed unreserved enthusiasm for *All Souls' Rising,* deeming it an "astonishing novel of epic scope." The reviewer argued that "Bell avoids the sense of victory that mars so many novels about revolution." After the many scenes of massacre, rape, and violence, the critic continued, "there can be no question of a winner of the battle for Haitian liberation. Surviving it was feat enough. In Bell's hands, the chaos . . . that surrounds these characters somehow elucidates the nobility of even the most craven among them."

Discussing *All Souls' Rising,* with Ken Ringle of the *Washington Post,* Bell compared Haiti's race conflict with conditions in the contemporary United States. "Haiti's was a full-blown race war," he explained, "over issues we've never really come to terms with in this country. Now we're having our own race war. But it's a slow-motion race war, disguised as crime in the streets. And nobody, black or white, wants to admit what's happening."

Bell's next novel, *Ten Indians,* centers on a white, middle-aged therapist for children named Mike Devlin who creates in the black ghetto of Baltimore a school for Tae Kwon Do, which ends up drawing people from two rivaling drug gangs—one member becomes involved with Devlin's seventeen-year-old daughter,

Michelle. A reviewer for *Publishers Weekly* said that in the novel, which switches between first- and third-person narratives, "Devlin's motivations . . . remain personally unclear, if admirable in the abstract," but the reviewer called Bell "a natural storyteller." John Skow, in a review for *Time,* noted that "the working out, told partly from Devlin's viewpoint and partly, in convincing street language, from that of the drug dealers and their women, is spare and cinematic," and concluded, "Good ending, good novel." In a review of *Ten Indians, Booklist*'s Michael Cart mentioned that the novel "would be a wonderful book for mature young adult readers" because it "captures the mix of literary quality and right-on relevance that, if put into the right readers' hands, can change lives—one individual at a time. It can, in fact, translate good intentions into redeeming reality."

Anything Goes, which centers on a bass player in a bar band, reflects a world Bell has some personal experience with. He has collaborated with poet Wyn Cooper, who came to fame as the author of the lyrics of the Sheryl Crow song *All I Wanna Do.* The two have collaborated on a CD, *Anything Goes,* which contains the songs mentioned in Bell's book. The CD garnered the duo a recording contract and a second album, titled *Forty Words for Fear.*

BIOGRAPHICAL AND CRITICAL SOURCES:

PERIODICALS

Atlanta Journal-Constitution, April 22, 1990, p. N8; January 13, 1991, p. N10; June 13, 1993, p. N8; November 26, 1995, p. C1.
Booklist, April 15, 1993, pp. 1468-1469; September 1, 1995, p. 4; January 1, 1997, p. 834.
Boston Globe, May 23, 1993, p. B40; October 22, 1995, p. B38.
Chicago Tribune, January 13, 1991, section 14, p. 1; May 30, 1993, section 14, p. 6; October 22, 1995, section 14, p. 1.
Entertainment Weekly, November 10, 1995, p. 55.
Harper's, August, 1986.
Library Journal, October 1, 1995, p. 118.
Los Angeles Times, September 16, 1985; September 15, 1986; February 20, 1987; November 3, 1987.
Los Angeles Times Book Review, February 27, 1983; September 30, 1990, p. 12; January 20, 1991, p. 8; July 11, 1993, p. 7.

New Statesman, February 9, 1996, pp. 37-38.
New York Times Book Review, February 20, 1983; August 18, 1985; October 12, 1986; February 15, 1987; November 15, 1987; December 27, 1987; April 8, 1990, p. 11; January 6, 1991, p. 11; June 20, 1993, p. 9; November 24, 1994; October 29, 1995, p. 12.
Publishers Weekly, August 28, 1995, p. 102; November 6, 1995, p. 58; August 26, 1996, p. 75.
Time, October 28, 1996, p. 110.
Times (London, England), November 14, 1985; November 19, 1987.
Times Literary Supplement, August 26, 1983; November 22, 1985; November 6, 1987.
Tribune Books (Chicago, IL), November 22, 1987.
Washington Post, October 25, 1986; January 24, 1991, p. B3; November 28, 1995, pp. C1-C2; March 19, 1996.
Washington Post Book World, February 16, 1983; September 1, 1985; October 26, 1986; February 1, 1987; November 22, 1987; April 15, 1990, p. 7; June 24, 1993, p. C2; November 5, 1995, p. 4.

ONLINE

Goucher College Web site, http://www.faculty.goucher.edu/ (January 15, 2000).*

*   *   *

BENFORD, Gregory (Albert) 1941-
(Sterling Blake, a pseudonym)

PERSONAL: Born January 30, 1941, in Mobile, AL; son of James Alton (a colonel in the U.S. Army) and Mary Eloise (a teacher; maiden name, Nelson) Benford; married Joan Abbe (an artist), August 26, 1967; children: Alyson Rhandra, Mark Gregory. *Education:* University of Oklahoma, B.S., 1963; University of California—San Diego, M.S., 1965, Ph.D., 1967.

ADDRESSES: Home—84 Harvey Court, Irvine, CA 92612. *Office*—Department of Physics and Astronomy, 4176 Frederick Reines Hall, University of California, Irvine, CA 92697. *E-mail*—gbenford@uci.edu.

CAREER: Lawrence Radiation Laboratory, Livermore, CA, fellow, 1967-69, research physicist, 1969-71, and consultant; University of California, Irvine, assistant professor, 1971-73, associate professor, 1973-79, professor of physics, 1979—. Former foreign correspondent, *Frankfurt Zeitung* (newspaper). Visiting fellow at Cambridge University, 1976 and 1979, Torino University, 1979, and MIT, 1992. Consultant to Department of Energy, Physics International Co., and National Aeronautics and Space Administration (NASA).

MEMBER: Royal Astronomical Society, American Physical Society, Science Fiction Writers of America, Phi Beta Kappa.

AWARDS, HONORS: Woodrow Wilson fellowship, 1963-64; Nebula Award, Science Fiction Writers of America, 1974, for *If the Stars Are Gods* (with Gordon Eklund), and 1980, for *Timescape;* British Science Fiction Association Award, John W. Campbell Award for Best Science Fiction Novel, World Science Fiction Convention, and (Australian) Ditmar Award for International Long Fiction, all 1980, all for *Timescape;* SF Chronicle Award, 1997, for "Immersion"; United Nations Medal in Literature; grants from National Science Foundation, 1972-76, Office of Naval Research, 1975 and 1982, Army Research Organization, 1977-82, Air Force Office of Scientific Research, 1982, and California Space Office, 1984-85; Lord Foundation Award, 1995.

WRITINGS:

NOVELS

Deeper Than the Darkness, Ace Books (New York, NY), 1970, revised edition published as *The Stars in Shroud,* Putnam (New York, NY), 1979.
Jupiter Project (for children), Thomas Nelson (Nashville, TN), 1975, 2nd edition, 1980.
(With Gordon Eklund) *If the Stars Are Gods* (based on the authors' novella of the same title), Putnam (New York, NY), 1977.
(With Gordon Eklund) *Find the Changeling,* Dell (New York, NY), 1980.
(With William Rotsler) *Shiva Descending,* Avon (New York, NY), 1980.
Timescape, Simon & Schuster (New York, NY), 1980.
Against Infinity, Simon & Schuster (New York, NY), 1983.
Time's Rub, Cheap Street (New Castle, VA), 1984.

Artifact, Tor (New York, NY), 1985.
Of Space-Time and the River, Cheap Street (New Castle, VA), 1985.
In Alien Flesh, Tor (New York, NY), 1986.
(With David Brin) *Heart of the Comet* (for young adults), Bantam (New York, NY), 1986.
Great Sky River, Bantam (New York, NY), 1987.
(With others) *Under the Wheel,* Baen (New York, NY), 1987.
(With Arthur C. Clarke) *Beyond the Fall of Night,* Putnam (New York, NY), 1990.
Centigrade 233, Cheap Street (New Castle, VA), 1990.
(Under pseudonym Sterling Blake) *Chiller,* Bantam (New York, NY), 1993.
Foundation's Fear (continuation of Isaac Asimov's "Foundation" series), HarperPrism (New York, NY), 1997.
Cosm, Avon Eos (New York, NY), 1998.
The Martian Race, Warner Books (New York, NY), 1999.
Eater, Avon Eos (New York, NY), 2000.
Beyond Infinity, Aspect/Warner Books (New York, NY), 2004.

"GALACTIC CENTER SAGA" SERIES

In the Ocean of Night, Dial (New York, NY), 1977.
Across the Sea of Suns, Bantam (New York, NY), 1984, Warner (New York, NY), 2004.
Great Sky River, Bantam (New York, NY), 1987.
Tides of Light, Bantam (New York, NY), 1989.
Furious Gulf, Bantam (New York, NY), 1994.
Sailing Bright Eternity, Bantam (New York, NY), 1995.

EDITOR OF SPECULATIVE FICTION; ANTHOLOGIES

(With Martin H. Greenberg) *Hitler Victorious: Eleven Stories of the German Victory in World War II,* Berkley (New York, NY), 1987.
(With Martin H. Greenberg; and contributor of story, "We Could Do Worse") *What Might Have Been? Volume I: Alternate Empires,* Bantam Spectra (New York, NY), 1989.
(With Martin H. Greenberg) *What Might Have Been? Volume II: Alternate Heroes,* Bantam Spectra (New York, NY), 1990.
(With Martin H. Greenberg; also author of introduction) *What Might Have Been? Volume IV: Alternate Americas,* Bantam (New York, NY), 1992.

Far Futures, Tor (New York, NY), 1995.

(And author of introduction and notes, with George Zebrowski) *Skylife: Space Habitats in Story and Science,* Harcourt (New York, NY), 2000.

OTHER

Matter's End (stories), Cheap Street (New Castle, VA), 1991, illustrated by Judy J. King, Bantam, 1994.

Deep Time: How Humanity Communicates across Millennia (nonfiction), HarperCollins (New York, NY), 2000.

Worlds Vast and Various (stories), Avon Eos (New York, NY), 2000.

Immersion and Other Short Novels, Five Star (Waterville, ME), 2002.

Also author, with others, of *Thread of Time,* Amereon. Contributor to anthologies, including *Again, Dangerous Visions,* edited by Harlan Ellison, Doubleday (New York, NY), 1972; *Universe 4,* Random House (New York, NY), 1974, *Universe 8,* Doubleday, 1978, and *Universe 9,* Doubleday, 1979, all edited by Terry Carr; and *New Dimensions, 5,* edited by Robert Silverberg, Harper (New York, NY), 1975. Contributor of articles and stories to magazines, including *Amazing, Analog, Magazine of Fantasy and Science Fiction, Natural History, Omni, Science Fiction Age,* and *Smithsonian.*

SIDELIGHTS: American astrophysicist and science fiction writer Gregory Benford "is one of the major talents to bring the science back into SF," averred *Publishers Weekly* contributor Rosemary Herbert. In fact, Benford's achievements in the field of physics, wrote Mark J. Lidman in the *Dictionary of Literary Biography Yearbook,* may overshadow his literary accomplishments. Benford holds a doctorate in theoretical physics and has done research on solid state physics, plasma physics, and high energy astrophysics, as well as astronomical research on the dynamics of pulsars, violent extragalactic events, and quasars. At the same time, his science fiction novels have earned him the respect of critics, fans, and his fellow writers, and "he has made no small achievement in writing since he took it up as a 'hobby' to distract himself from the pressures of studying for his doctorate in physics," Herbert related.

As a scientist, Lidman believed, Benford is "acutely aware of modern society's fascination with technology, but his novels also stress the negative aspects of living in a technological age. His works about alien contact have an appeal that is widespread . . . and his works which deal with science show us that we must learn to live intelligently in a technological world." The essayist stated that Benford's novels "are characterized by thoughtful composition and scientific expertise, and his work experience lends authenticity to his perspective on science."

Against Infinity is set on the immensely cold, frozen surface of Ganymede, one of Jupiter's moons, whose limited atmosphere is lethally poisonous to humans. A man and a boy must survive this savage environment in their hunt for an alien artifact called an "Aleph" that has ruled Ganymede for uncounted millennia. This immensely dangerous foe has blocked all efforts to terraform the planetoid and has the ability to enter and haunt human's dreams. For the boy, their hunt is a search to claim his manhood; for the man, it is a quest for enlightenment.

In the *Voice Literary Supplement,* Debra Rae Cohen listed Benford among those writers who "represent the idea of science as technology, of plot as problem solving. . . . SF has always been a forum for scientists to work out ideas that are unproven yet still right. . . . Benford and others . . . test interdisciplinary limits between fiction and science, not the limits of technology." For example, *Fantasy Review* contributor Gary K. Wolfe noted that Benford's *Artifact,* a thriller involving an archaeological find that has the potential to destroy the Earth, combines "enough nonstop action and international intrigue . . . to satisfy the most jaded Robert Ludlum fan" together with "the familiar Benford elements—a very believable and at times satirical portrayal of academic politics, a fully-realized near-future world which is kept discretely in the background . . . and a lot of real physics, carefully worked out and meticulously confined to a few plausible speculations." Like other reviewers, Wolfe observed that this attempt to crossbreed the science fiction novel and the international thriller yields "mixed results." Even so, maintained Gregory Feeley in a *Los Angeles Times* review, "It is the scientific side of *Artifact* that redeems the novel. . . . It is the subject matter and authority of the writer that intrigue, not the style of presentation." Writing in the *Washington Post Book World,* Feeley remarked, "As before, Benford effectively dramatizes the excitement and procedures of discovery, and his evocation of academic research, its protocols and rivalries, is impeccable."

Benford won the coveted Nebula Award in 1980 and the praise of reviewers with the novel *Timescape*. "Its protagonists are physicists deeply and obsessively involved in the entangled arduous pursuit of (relatively) pure knowledge," John Clute reported in the *Times Literary Supplement*. Benford closed the gap between science and fiction in the novel by narrating the scientific activities of two groups of physicists; one group, living in 1998, is desperately trying to communicate to scientists in the 1960s the message that will prevent the destruction of the Earth's ecosystem at the end of the twentieth century. The message consists of imaginary but plausible faster-than-light particles called tachyons sent in Morse code to a California physicist who is working with a substance that is "sensitive to tachyon bombardment," explained Clute. *Washington Post Book World* reviewer George R. R. Martin commented that Benford "makes research fully as intense and gripping as the events of any thriller, without compromising a whit, and manages the extremely difficult feat of conveying not only the meaning of his speculations in physics and cosmology, but the excitement as well. . . . *Timescape* is not only splendid science fiction, it is a thoroughly splendid novel."

Benford's 1986 novel *Heart of the Comet,* coauthored with David Brin, involves an attempt by humans to set up a colony on Halley's Comet when it makes a return trip back through our solar system. Plot complications include predatory aliens already in residence on the comet and conflicts on Earth between the Percells (genetically altered superhumans) and the Orthos (normal, non-modified humans) and their impact upon the struggling colonists.

Set 37,000 years in the future, *Sailing Bright Eternity,* the final novel of the popular, six-volume "Galactic Center Saga" series, sees the return of the twenty-first-century Earth's first starship voyager, Nigel Walmsley, protagonist of the first series installment, *Ocean of Night*. Walmsley returns to recount the most recent adventures inside the Esty to Toby Bishop, teen protagonist in *Furious Gulf*. The Esty is a haven of space-time existing near the galaxy's true center, just outside of a black hole. Bishop's family and fellow humans have been destroyed by the mechs, a machine-based life-form who now threaten to penetrate the Esty and decimate all remnants of human life. Aided by Toby and the surviving members of Toby's family, Walmsley is the only hope of stopping this impending threat to human existence.

In a *Booklist* review of *Sailing Bright Eternity,* Carl Hays asserted, "Benford makes up for his somewhat pedantic prose with a wealth of fascinating scientific speculations in a dazzling finish to one of the best hard-sf sagas ever written." And a *Publishers Weekly* reviewer praised, "This novel stands as a worthy conclusion to what now should be acknowledged as the most important and involving hard SF series yet written."

Published in 1997, *Foundation's Fear* is the first volume of "The Second Foundation Trilogy," a continuation of Isaac Asimov's famous "Foundation Trilogy" (1951-1953)—with the subsequent books written by David Brin and Greg Bear. The series is a prequel to the original books, and its primary goal is to reveal the career events of Hari Seldon, discoverer of psychohistory, prior to those previously detailed. In *Foundation's Fear,* Seldon is engaged in a project to slow and soften the impact when the dreaded inevitable occurs and the universe-spanning empire collapses, ushering in the Dark Ages that must surely follow in its wake. As the leading candidate for First Minister of the Empire, he attracts the animosity of rivals, but when the current emperor appoints him to the position, Seldon is thrown into a dangerous sphere of political intrigue and assassination plots. Seldon and his wife Dors—a humanlike robot—are forced to flee the whirlwind of court machinations of the imperial capital city on Trantor, experiencing a perilous adventure when their minds are transferred to the bodies of primates on a far-off, primitive planet. In the meantime, computer simulations of the dynamically opposite intelligences of Joan of Arc and Voltaire—the ultimately trusting versus the ultimately skeptical—assert their own freedom of action and uncover the destructive handiwork of aliens who themselves survive only as electronic memories—a potentially devastating computer virus. With the help of an elder statesman of the humaniform robot community, R. Daneel Olivaw, Seldon and Dors eventually return to Trantor.

Susan Hamburger, in a *Library Journal* review of *Foundation's Fear,* maintained that the author "makes the characters come alive." In *Booklist,* Roland Green stated, "The book continues, more successfully, Asimov's late efforts to reconcile the Foundation stories with his robot novels and also profits from the fact that Benford is a more visual writer than Asimov." And a *Publishers Weekly* critic lauded, "Benford . . .

writes up to his usual high standard and excels in bringing Asimovian concepts . . . to vivid, visually compelling life."

The protagonist of Benford's next novel, *Cosm,* is Alicia Butterworth, a black female small-particle researching physicist from the University of California—Irvine, who is using the Brookhaven National Laboratory's Relativistic Ion Collider on Long Island in an attempt to recreate the conditions existing just prior to the theoretical Big Bang. During one of the collider runs, something goes haywire, and part of the machine explodes, leaving behind a strange artifact, a small, reflective metallic sphere floating amidst the wreckage. Butterworth steals the sphere, surreptitiously taking it back to Irvine, where she and her team of physicists and graduate students investigate the phenomenon and decide it is actually a space-time wormhole, a window into a miniature universe called a "cosm." This cosm is evolving at an infinitely faster rate than our own universe, giving Butterworth a unique vantage to a fast-forward play of the history of creation. Her theft of the sphere initiates an adventurous intrigue among academic, scientific, political, and religious circles, as they all struggle for control of the sphere.

In his *Booklist* review of *Cosm,* Eric Robbins noted that Benford has proven a "great favorite" of readers who are interested in the "techie," hard-science side of science fiction, and said that "his newest won't disappoint them." Likewise, a *Publishers Weekly* reviewer observed, "His novel depicts cutting-edge science the way it's actually done in the cluttered, fund-starved laboratories of a modern university. His highly believable characters have little in common with the unrealistic scientists of so much SF. They're complex human beings, each with a full array of strengths and weaknesses."

In the nonfiction work *Deep Time: How Humanity Communicates across Millennia,* Benford explores humankind's need to communicate with the inhabitants of the far future, in words—whether in books or as graffiti, such as the Greek mercenaries who carved their names onto Egyptian monuments, Lord Byron's carving his name into the Temple of Poseidon, or modern-day "taggers"—or artifacts and deeds—from the Seven Wonders of the Ancient World to modern monuments, tombs, and cathedrals. Benford discusses how we may accurately convey information over

prolonged spans of time, even millions of years, to warn those denizens of the future about our other, current, long-time "messages," such as the disposal of nuclear waste, the threat posed by climatic changes, and extinction of the species.

Dayne Sherman, reviewing *Deep Time* for *Library Journal,* called the book "hearty and compelling," adding that Benford's work "elucidates some of the inherent problems humanity faces in communicating over the expanse of time." Moreover, a *Publishers Weekly* critic asserted that, "In his first foray into book-length nonfiction . . . Benford . . . combines a scientist's perspective and a novelist's imagination to produce a provocative and disturbing look into 'deep time.'"

Benford's *The Martian Race* is a near-future story set in the 2020s about astronaut Julia Barth and her Russian husband, Viktor. Financed by the Mars Consortium and its CEO, biotech-billionaire John Axelrod, they and their crew head for Mars in a race against a European-Chinese-backed expedition, struggling to reach the Red Planet first and return to Earth, in order to win the thirty billion dollar Mars Prize. The prize has been offered by the U.S. government following a launching pad disaster that destroyed NASA's dream of a manned flight to Mars, and in lieu of investing in the 450 billion dollar venture proposed by NASA as its replacement. Technical problems with their spaceship, interpersonal conflicts, and the hostile Martian environment all pose challenges to the crew's survival. During the span of their stay, Julia discovers evidence of the much-speculated and much-debated life on Mars.

In a *Booklist* review of *The Martian Race,* Roland Green averred, "Benford is as expert as ever at seamlessly melding characterization, technology, and narrative drive in an effective novel that takes its place near the front of the pack of Martian-yarn contenders." A *Publishers Weekly* reviewer similarly noted, "A practicing physicist, [Benford] writes plausible hard SF as well as anyone on the planet, and his portrait of Mars is among the most believable in recent genre literature. His strange and beautiful ecology is so well described, in fact, that most readers will hope to explore it further, in a sequel." And Jackie Cassada, writing in *Library Journal,* praised Benford as "one of the premier crafters of the genre."

The protagonist of *Eater* is Benjamin Knowlton, a Hawaii-based physicist who discovers a strange interstellar object many light years away in space. He first thinks his find is a gamma-ray burster—a black hole swallowing a star. Only thirteen hours later, a second burst is spotted, an extremely disconcerting fact, since, because of the vast distance between stars, the phenomenon should be physically impossible. Knowlton's old rival and competing theorist, British astronomer Kingsley Dart—who also once had an affair with Knowlton's ex-astronaut wife, Channing, now dying of cancer—inveigles his way into the investigation of this phenomenon. They learn that the object is a black hole only a few yards wide but with a mass approximately that of the Moon, and that it is currently entering the boundaries of the Earth's solar system. Further revelations show that this "Eater," which consumes everything it encounters, is an intelligent entity billions of years old, one that has destroyed entire civilizations in its travels. And Eater is now headed for Earth. When Eater begins communicating with Knowlton's team, his operation is taken over by the mysterious U Agency. When Eater starts detailing techniques for brain destruction so the contents of selected minds—including those of both Dart and Knowlton—can be downloaded for its assimilation, the U.S. government, thinking it can lay the blame on China if it fails in its mission, risks an abortive attempt to destroy Eater with nuclear missiles. Unfooled and undamaged, Eater devastates vast tracts of America in merciless retaliation. The brave Channing, near death from cancer, offers to pilot a reconnaissance probe to Eater in the hope she can help direct another, more successful strike against this threat to all humanity.

A *Publishers Weekly* reviewer commented on *Eater,* saying, "One of Benford's specialties is presenting science the way it's really done, and this is clearly the case here. . . . Full of astronomical pyrotechnics and the kind of intelligent verbal fencing that seems to go along with creative scientific thinking, this Benford novel should delight any serious reader of SF."

In *Beyond Infinity,* Benford expands his 1990 novella *Beyond the Fall of Night.* The story revolves around Cley, an "Original" human being on Earth who works for the "Supras," genetically and physically enhanced humans. A vengeful "trans-dimensional" creature called the "Malign" attacks Earth, killing all the Originals except Cley and most of the Supras. Aided by an alien helper called Seeker-After-Patterns, Cley flees Earth and the controlling Supras and sets out to

find the reasons behind the Malign's attack in order to keep it from killing her.

In *Library Journal,* Jackie Cassada described *Beyond Infinity* as a "wildly imaginative coming-of-age story" with a "grounding in hard science." Benford, she noted, "writes clearly about space and time without forgetting the human perceptions that give those concepts meaning." A contributor to *Kirkus Reviews* took a less enthusiastic view of the novel, however, calling it "inexplicable except in terms of a deep-seated obsession," a book that "goes nowhere in particular." On a much more positive note, a *Publishers Weekly* critic dubbed *Beyond Infinity* a "dense, lively, far-future SF novel . . . that sweeps readers away in a taut adventure that examines humanity's role in steering the fate of the universe." "With its thoughtful extrapolation and mind-bending physics," the review continued, "this book reinforces Benford's position as one of today's foremost writers of hard SF."

BIOGRAPHICAL AND CRITICAL SOURCES:

BOOKS

Bridges to Science Fiction, Southern Illinois University Press (Carbondale, IL), 1981.
Carr, Terry, editor, *Universe 6,* Popular Library (New York, NY), 1976.
Contemporary Literary Criticism, Volume 52, Gale (Detroit, MI), 1989.
Dictionary of Literary Biography Yearbook, 1982, Gale (Detroit, MI), 1983.
Platt, Charles, *Dream Makers: The Uncommon People Who Write Science Fiction,* Berkley Books (New York, NY), 1980.

PERIODICALS

Analog Science Fiction & Fact, November, 1985, p. 179; June, 1986; March, 1988, p. 178; March, 1995, Tom Easton, review of *Furious Gulf,* pp. 162-179; December, 1995, Tom Easton, review of *Sailing Bright Eternity,* pp. 181-189; June, 1998, review of *Cosm,* p. 132.
Booklist, March 15, 1985, p. 1010; October 15, 1987, p. 345; May 15, 1994, p. 1644; December 1, 1994, p. 657; August, 1995, Carl Hays, review of *Sail-*

ing Bright Eternity, p. 1908; November 15, 1995, Carl Hays, review of *Far Futures,* p. 538; March 1, 1997, Roland Green, review of *Foundation's Fear,* p. 1114; January 1, 1998, Eric Robbins, review of *Cosm,* p. 785; November 1, 1999, Roland Green, review of *The Martian Race,* p. 512; March 1, 2000, Roland Green, review of *Skylife,* p. 1200.

Christian Science Monitor, May 16, 1986; February 9, 1988, p. 20; February 18, 1999, Frederick Pratter, review of *Deep Time,* p. 19.

Fantasy Review, September, 1985, p. 17; February, 1986; July, 1986.

Foundation, winter, 1977-1978.

Kirkus Reviews, February, 2004, review of *Beyond Infinity,* p. 113.

Library Journal, December, 1995, Jackie Cassada, review of *Far Futures,* p. 164; March 1, 1997, Susan Hamburger, review of *Foundation's Fear,* p. 93; March 15, 1997, p. 93; February 1, 1999, Dayne Sherman, review of *Deep Time,* p. 116; December, 1999, Jackie Cassada, review of *The Martian Race,* p. 192; February, 2004, Jackie Cassada, review of *Beyond Infinity,* p. 166.

Locus, April, 1991, p. 40; September, 1992, p. 13; October, 1992, p. 27; November, 1992, p. 53; August, 1994, p. 27.

Los Angeles Times, December 16, 1985; April 18, 1986.

Los Angeles Times Book Review, December 27, 1987, p. 11.

New York Times Book Review, January 27, 1977; March 27, 1977; November 25, 1984, p. 20; December 27, 1987, p. 11; August 14, 1994, p. 30; April 6, 1997, Gerald Jonas, review of *Foundation's Fear,* p. 24.

Publishers Weekly, May 23, 1986; July 4, 1994, p. 56; July 24, 1995, review of *Sailing Bright Eternity,* p. 52; November 6, 1995, review of *Far Futures,* p. 86; February 24, 1997, review of *Foundation's Fear,* pp. 67-68; December 8, 1997, review of *Cosm,* p. 59; January 4, 1999, review of *Deep Time,* p. 84; November 1, 1999, review of *The Martian Race,* p. 78; February 1, 2000, review of *Eater,* p. 69; February, 2004, review of *Beyond Infinity,* p. 63.

Science Fiction and Fantasy Book Review, September, 1983.

Science Fiction Chronicle, October, 1985, p. 42; June, 1986; July, 1986.

Science Fiction Review, August, 1984; August, 1985, p. 17; November, 1985, p. 23; February, 1986; May, 1986; June, 1986.

Times Literary Supplement, December 5, 1980.

Tribune Books (Chicago, IL), March 23, 1986.

Voice Literary Supplement, December, 1983.

Washington Post Book World, June 22, 1980; May 29, 1983; February 26, 1984; October 27, 1985, p. 6; March 23, 1986; October 25, 1988, p. 6.*

* * *

BERESFORD-HOWE, Constance 1922-

PERSONAL: Born November 10, 1922, in Montreal, Canada; daughter of Russell (an insurance salesman) and Marjory (a homemaker; maiden name, Moore) Beresford-Howe; married Christopher W. Pressnell (a teacher), December 31, 1960; children: Jeremy. *Education:* McGill University, B.A., 1945, M.A., 1946; Brown University, Ph.D., 1950.

ADDRESSES: Home—c/o Taylor, 55 Argowan Crescent, Toronto M1V 1B4, Ontario, Canada.

CAREER: McGill University, Montreal, Quebec, lecturer, 1948-49, assistant professor, 1949-61, associate professor of English, 1961-69; Ryerson Polytechnical Institute, Toronto, Ontario, professor of English, 1970-88.

MEMBER: International PEN.

AWARDS, HONORS: Dodd, Mead intercollegiate literary fellowship, 1945, for *The Unreasoning Heart;* Canadian booksellers annual award, 1974, for *The Book of Eve;* Canadian Council Senior Arts Award, 1975; Ontario Arts Council Grants, 1976, 1983, 1985.

WRITINGS:

The Unreasoning Heart, Dodd, Mead (New York, NY), 1946.

Of This Day's Journey, Dodd, Mead (New York, NY), 1948.

The Invisible Gate, Dodd, Mead (New York, NY), 1949.

My Lady Greensleeves, Ballantine (New York, NY), 1955.

The Book of Eve, Little, Brown (Boston, MA), 1974.

A Population of One, Macmillan of Canada (Toronto, Ontario, Canada), 1977, St. Martin's Press (New York, NY), 1978.

The Marriage Bed, St. Martin's Press (New York, NY), 1981.

Night Studies, Macmillan Canada (Toronto, Ontario Canada), 1985.

Prospero's Daughter, Macmillan Canada (Toronto, Ontario, Canada), 1988.

A Serious Widow, Macmillan Canada (Toronto, Ontario, Canada), 1991.

Author of television script *The Cuckoo Bird,* Canadian Broadcasting Corp., 1981. Contributor to periodicals, including *Maclean's, Writer,* and *Chatelaine.*

ADAPTATIONS: The Book of Eve was adapted for the stage by Larry Fineberg and performed at the Stratford Festival in Stratford, Ontario, in 1976, and made into a film in 2002; *A Population of One* was adapted to television for the Canadian Broadcasting Corp. in 1980; *The Marriage Bed* was produced for television by CBC-TV in 1986.

SIDELIGHTS: Constance Beresford-Howe gained acclaim in her native Canada as a voice of twentieth-century women, particularly "in their struggle for freedom against popular expectations—both sexist and feminist," according to Barbara Pell in a *Dictionary of Literary Biography* essay. The only daughter of an insurance salesman and a homemaker, Beresford-Howe was the product of Depression-era Notre Dame de Grace, Montreal, Quebec. With her parents and brother, she lived in a series of low-rent flats; an attack of rheumatic fever at age eleven further challenged the young girl. Confined to bed for months during her recovery, Beresford-Howe "strengthened her inclination to introspection, reading, and writing," as Pell noted. By the time she reached college age, Beresford-Howe had set her sights on becoming a high-school teacher. But Beresford-Howe excelled at writing, winning McGill University's Shakespeare Gold Medal in 1945, as well as the Peterson Prize for creative writing.

A year later, Beresford-Howe published her first novel, *The Unreasoning Heart.* This story of an orphaned teenage girl finds acceptance and eventually love within a prosperous Montreal family features "a rather melodramatic plot," said Pell. Still, *The Unreasoning*

Heart was named the Dodd, Mead Intercollegiate Literary Fellowship winner. Other early Beresford-Howe novels include *Of This Day's Journey* and *The Invisible Gate.* Both books trace the love lives of young Canadian women. In the former, the freshly minted lecturer arrives in America to begin teaching at a small college; her "doomed romance," as Pell put it, with the school's married president propels the narrative. *The Invisible Gate,* set in postwar Montreal, "portrays the cynical exploitation of two sisters by a returned serviceman." While Beresford-Howe's early novels tended to attract critical epithets like "cardboard figures" and "hammock fiction," *The Invisible Gate* began to show the author in a better light. A reviewer of the day, Claude Bissell of the *University of Toronto Quarterly,* cited this novel for the author's "lively talent" and her "easy fluency" of prose style, according to Pell's essay. In 1955 Beresford-Howe published *My Lady Greensleeves,* a historical novel based on an authentic Elizabethan love triangle and the lawsuit that followed it. But it would be nearly twelve years between that book and the publication of the author's fifth novel.

In the ensuing years Beresford-Howe had a long teaching career at McGill, her alma mater; she reluctantly left Quebec for Toronto, Ontario, in 1969, accepting a teaching position at the Ryerson Polytechnical Institute. In 1974 she published *The Book of Eve,* which tells of a sixty-five-year-old woman who abruptly leaves her husband of forty years. She also abandons "the bourgeois wilderness of Notre Dame de Grace to descend into a tenement flat and an eccentric existence as a scavenger," as Pell described it. "But, in her freedom from convention and materialism, she finds an independent identity, strength for survival, new values, fellowship, and even love."

The Book of Eve was the first of a "Voice of Eve" trilogy that focuses on women finding their own fulfillment outside of society's conventions. Beresford-Howe's second work of the series, *A Population of One,* concerns Wilhelmina (Willy) Doyle, a thirtyish Ph.D. who arrives in Montreal in 1969 with a dual purpose: to teach college English and to marry, "or at the very least to have an affair," as she put it. That Willy succeeds in her career and not her personal goal speaks to her character's rejection of the casual-sex ethos of the era; she "accept[s] her very Canadian isolation with dignity," said Pell. *Canadian Forum's* Raymond Shady found the scenes of Willy's professional life lacking; the counterculture college atmosphere Beresford-Howe created reveals her "prejudices . . . as she portrays the leader of the radical reform group as a self-serving American who cares nothing for his students; the student radicals themselves are uniformly characterized as shabby, vulgar and confused, while much of the 'power-to-the-people' dialogue sounds contrived." But Shady concluded that the "ultimate success" of *A Population of One* is in the story of Willy's romantic adventures. "The dignity she achieves in the face of her 'incurable' loneliness offers us a glimpse into the human condition," he said. Willy "is marvelous," stated a *Publishers Weekly* contributor, "funny, rueful, tentative, filled with yearnings." To know Willy, the critic continued, "is to know ourselves better."

Beresford-Howe wrapped up her "Voices of Eve" trilogy with *The Marriage Bed,* about a young wife and mother in contemporary Toronto. Anne Graham, pregnant and abandoned by her lawyer husband, attempts to draw meaning from her life of drudgery. "The thematic inversion," noted Pell, "is that she refuses all offers to be liberated and wins back her husband by delivering their baby on the floor of his mistress's communal rooming house." Paul Stuewe of *Quill & Quire* dubbed this novel "Diary of a Moderately Mad Housewife," and faulted the author for having her protagonist, who remained passive through much of the book, take an out-of-character turn into an activist during the story's childbirth climax. But if *The Marriage Bed* "never grows into anything resembling sustained and coherent fiction," Stuewe added, "it does offer other enjoyments that partially redeem this failure." He praised Beresford-Howe's "polished and highly readable prose," and said that the Toronto setting is put to good use. A Publishers Weekly critic found more to recommend in *The Marriage Bed,* saying that "Anne's witty and ironic optimism transforms the petty into something wonderful."

In an interview with Michael Ryval for *Quill & Quire,* Beresford-Howe discussed the divergent personalities of Willy and Anne in the two novels. In the case of *A Population of One,* "I'm upside-downing ideas," she said. "Willy discovers it isn't possible to go to bed with anyone. Today's kids say, 'What's wrong with one-night stands?' Everything. I had a lot of women who were delighted with a book that dealt with celibacy." Anne's homebound status is the author's response to an era that depicts domesticity as undesir-

able. "It is not," she declared to Ryval. "I know a lot of women who say, 'I *like* staying home with my children.' Yet they're made to feel as if they're stupid or wrong." Ultimately, "I don't see the books as old-fashioned," the author said. "Instead, they take a number of popular attitudes and rattle them loose."

Night Studies, published in 1985, uses the setting of a Toronto community college evening course to study the "many characters who toil there nightly," as Louise Longo described it for *Books in Canada.* Two "world-weary" teachers, Imogen and Tyler, escape unhappy marriages in the school hallways; they interact with the many students, faculty and staff of the multicultural college and eventually discover one another. "Beresford-Howe has a fine ear for the everyday chit-chat that passes for conversation," noted Sherrill Cheda of *Quill & Quire,* "but her characters suffer from a lack of a spiritual centre." With *A Serious Widow,* the author explores how middle-aged Toronto homemaker Rowena, suddenly widowed when her husband "dropped dead in his Adidas" while jogging, learns to fend for herself. Complications ensue when a young man shows up at the funeral claiming to be her husband's son by a secret wife in Ottawa; Rowena's successful daughter, Marion, views her unworldly mother with some scorn.

"Initially angry at being the dupe of her bigamist husband," wrote *Canadian Literature* critic Michele O'Flynn, "Rowena quickly begins to feel afraid as she understands her situation." Though the character eventually finds success as a single woman, Rowena "is woefully inadequate if she is to serve as an inspirational symbol for the emancipation of women," said O'Flynn. "Through much of the book, she is a passive observer of her own life. . . . The reader is often frustrated by her inability to think or act on her own behalf." Pat Barclay of *Books in Canada,* however, welcomed Rowena as a character, saying that while "in her darker moments [she] shares her daughter's view of her competence, she can also muster up an ironic detachment." In Barclay's view, Beresford-Howe "understands how genuine charm helps compensate for one's deficiencies."

BIOGRAPHICAL AND CRITICAL SOURCES:

BOOKS

Dictionary of Literary Biography, Volume 88: *Canadian Writers, 1920-1959,* Gale (Detroit, MI), 1989.

PERIODICALS

Best Sellers, October, 1978, R. A. Higgins, review of *A Population of One,* p. 203.

Booklist, February 15, 1982, review of *The Marriage Bed,* p. 743.

Books in Canada, October, 1985, Louise Longo, review of *Night Studies,* pp. 23-24; April, 1988, review of *Prospero's Daughter,* p. 25; October, 1991, Pat Barclay, "Making the Best of It," pp. 35-36.

Canadian Forum, February, 1978, Raymond Shady, "The Second Voice of Eve," pp. 38-39; October, 1985, Fergus Cronin, "Showing the Hands: A Profile of Constance Beresford-Howe," p. 34.

Canadian Literature, winter, 1990, review of *Prospero's Daughter,* p. 180; spring, 1993, Michele O'Flynn, "Serious Widows," pp. 155-156.

Cinema Canada, February, 1987, Edgar Matthews, "Yours, Mine and Ours: Anna Sandor and Constance Beresford-Howe," p. 12.

CM, November, 1988, review of *Prospero's Daughter,* p. 211; July, 1989, review of *The Book of Eve,* p. 172; January, 1992, review of *A Serious Widow,* p. 29.

Kirkus Reviews, March 15, 1978, review of *A Population of One,* p. 318.

Maclean's, September 14, 1981, review of *The Marriage Bed,* p. 76; May 9, 1988, Mark Nichols, review of *Prospero's Daughter,* p. 60.

Publishers Weekly, April 3, 1978, review of *A Population of One;* December 1, 1981, review of *The Marriage Bed,* p. 42.

Quill & Quire, July, 1981, Michael Ryval, "Constance Beresford-Howe's Subversion and Sensibility," p. 64; September, 1981, Paul Stuewe, review of *The Marriage Bed,* p. 64; September, 1985, Sherrill Cheda, review of *Night Studies,* p. 78; March, 1988, review of *Prospero's Daughter,* p. 77; August, 1991, review of *A Serious Widow,* p. 15.

Saturday Night, September, 1977, review of *A Population of One,* p. 69.

Women's Studies, September, 1990, Emily Nett, "The Naked Soul Comes Closer to the Surface," p. 177.

ONLINE

University of Calgary Library, http://www.ucalgary.ca/ (June 10, 2002), Lorraine McMullen, "Constance Beresford-Howe."

BERKIN, Carol (Ruth) 1942-

PERSONAL: Born October 1, 1942, in Mobile, AL; daughter of Saul (a businessman) and Marian (a bookkeeper; maiden name, Goldreich) Berkin; married John Paull Harper (a dean of curriculum), June 21, 1970 (divorced); children: two. *Education:* Barnard College, A.B., 1964; Columbia University, M.A., 1966, Ph.D., 1972. *Religion:* Jewish.

ADDRESSES: Home—118 West 79th St., Apt. 14B, New York, NY 10024. *Office*—Department of History, Graduate School and University Center, City University of New York, 365 5th Ave., New York, NY 10016. *E-mail*—cberkin@gc.cuny.edu.

CAREER: Editorial assistant for "Papers of Alexander Hamilton," New York, NY, 1964; Hunter College of the City University of New York, New York, NY, lecturer in history, 1968; member of editorial staff for "Papers of John Jay," New York, NY, 1972; City University of New York, assistant professor, 1972-75, associate professor, 1975-81, professor of history at Bernard M. Baruch College, 1981—, member of university graduate faculty, 1982—.

MEMBER: American Antiquarian Society (fellow), American Historical Association, Organization of American Historians (member of bicentennial celebration committee, 1975—), Coordinating Committee for Women in the Historical Profession, Smithsonian Institution, Essex Institute, New York Historical Society, Columbia University Seminar in Early American History and Culture.

AWARDS, HONORS: Bancroft Award from Bancroft Foundation and Columbia University, 1972, for doctoral dissertation on Jonathan Sewall; National Endowment for the Humanities grant, 1974; American Council of Learned Societies grant, 1975, study fellowship, 1978; City University of New York Research Foundation grant, 1975; American Association of University Women fellowship, 1978.

WRITINGS:

Jonathan Sewall: Odyssey of an American Loyalist, Columbia University Press (New York, NY), 1974.

Within the Conjurer's Circle: Women in Colonial America (pamphlet), General Learning Press (New York, NY), 1974.

(Compiler) *Women in the American Revolution,* Grossman (New York, NY), 1975.

(Contributor) *The American Revolution: Changing Perspectives,* edited by William M. Fowler, Jr. and Wallace Coyle, Northeastern University Press (Boston, MA), 1979.

Land of Promise: A History of the United States, Scott, Foresman (Glenview, IL), 1982.

(With Leonard Wood) *National Treasures: Source Readings for Land of Promise,* Scott, Foresman (Glenview, IL), 1984.

(With John Patrick) *History of the American Nation,* two volumes, Scribner Educational Publishers (New York, NY), 1986.

(With Joe B. Frantz and Joan Schreiber) *America Yesterday and Today,* Scott, Foresman (Glenview, IL), 1988.

First Generations: Women in Colonial America, Hill & Wang (New York, NY), 1996.

American Colonial History, Houghton Mifflin (Boston, MA), 1997.

(With others) *Making America: A History of the United States,* instructor's annotated edition, Houghton Mifflin (Boston, MA), 1995, 2nd edition, 1999, 3rd edition, 2003.

A Brilliant Solution: Inventing the American Constitution, Harcourt (New York, NY), 2002.

(With Betty S. Anderson) *The History Handbook* Houghton Mifflin (Boston, MA), 2003.

EDITOR

(With Mary Beth Norton) *Women of America: A History,* Houghton Mifflin (Boston, MA), 1979.

(With Clara M. Lovett) *Women, War, and Revolution,* Holmes & Meier, 1980.

(With Leslie Horowitz) *Women's Voices, Women's Lives: Documents in Early American History,* Northeastern University Press (Boston, MA), 1998.

(With others) *Encyclopedia of American Literature,* Facts on File (New York, NY), 2002.

SIDELIGHTS: The role of women in America's past is the forte of historian Carol Berkin. Her 1996 volume, *First Generations: Women in Colonial America,* was widely reviewed. "Inspired" was the term used by Billie Barnes Jensen of *History.* Covering the variety of races, religions, and social classes that comprised the women of early America, Berkin used the technique of profiling in each chapter an individual woman whose "life exemplifies in some way the theme of the narrative," as Jensen noted. Some of the author's subjects are such well-known historical figures as Hannah Duston and Eliza Lucas Pinckney; others, including a slave known only as Mary, are relatively anonymous—"yet the lessons of their lives are no less significant," Jensen stated.

In an article for the *Journal of Social History,* Jacquelyn Miller pointed to Berkin's chapters on the elite classes of the early eighteenth century. The women in these fortunate positions had access to goods and luxuries unheard-of by most of their colonial and indentured sisters who faced a much more demanding struggle to survive. Yet the growth of consumerism in the upper classes "did not necessarily mean expanded independence for women," wrote Miller. "In fact, Berkin argues that the social conventions of gentility placed additional burdens on women's time and energy, while at the same time giving them little control over the wealth of their society." Wealthy or not, the author concluded, "women of all sorts were united in their dependence on men for their economic status." While C. Dallett Hemphill of the *Historian* felt that the author "is not wholly consistent" in her presentation of controversial issues, the critic also acknowledged that *First Generations* "remains a clear and engaging overview."

Berkin explored another aspect of history with her 2002 release, *A Brilliant Solution: Inventing the American Constitution.* In the years following the Revolutionary War of 1776, the new country faced economic, military, and political challenges. When James Madison, George Washington, Benjamin Franklin, and their peers convened the first Constitutional Convention in Philadelphia during the sweltering summer of 1787, anxieties ran high. Small states complained of manipulation by the bigger states; "a few nationalists fretted about America's international impotence," as *Booklist* contributor Gilbert Taylor put it. A *Publishers Weekly* reviewer emphasized that "the framers saw the Constitution as a working document, one that would require revision as the country grew." In the same piece, the author was praised for her novelistic approach, "capturing the human dimensions" of the historic convention. Thomas Karel of *Library Journal* wrote, "With this concise and masterly book, Berkin joins the upper ranks of popular historians."

Carol Berkin once told *CA:* "My primary focus in my work has been to examine the personalities of men or women life style, ideology, or career patterns have placed them on the 'losing side' or out of the mainstream. Thus, the American Loyalists, for whom, in many ways, the world was turned upside down; thus, also, the study of American women who have always been outsiders as the 'second sex' in our history. Recently it has been noted that, 'while the patriots won the revolution, the Loyalists seem to be winning the bicentennial' because of the many sympathetic studies of these men and women in the 1960's and 70's. Perhaps with the new and exciting examination of women in our past, being done by so many able scholars today, it will also be said that women lost many struggles for equality, but they are winning a sense of their past."

BIOGRAPHICAL AND CRITICAL SOURCES:

PERIODICALS

American Historical Review, February, 1998, review of *First Generations: Women in Colonial America,* p. 274.

Biography: An Interdisciplinary Quarterly, spring, 1998, review of *First Generations,* p. 227.

Booklist, September 15, 1996, Kathleen Hughes, review of *First Generations,* p. 185; August, 2002, Gilbert Taylor, review of *A Brilliant Solution: Inventing the American Constitution,* p. 1914.

Bookwatch, January, 1997, review of *First Generations,* p. 3; August, 1998, review of *Women's Voices, Women's Lives: Documents in Early American History,* p. 2; September, 1998, review of *Women's Voices, Women's Lives,* p. 4.

Chicago Daily Law Bulletin, September 17, 2002, Gary Rosen, review of *A Brilliant Solution,* p. 2.

Choice, September, 1987, review of *Women of America: A History,* p. 68.

Come-All-Ye, fall, 1998, review of *Women's Voices, Women's Lives,* p. 1.

Historian, fall, 1998, C. Dallett Hemphill, review of *First Generations,* p. 150.

History: Review of Books, fall, 1997, Billie Barnes Jensen, review of *First Generations,* p. 15.

Journal of American History, September, 1997, Lee Chambers-Schiller, review of *First Generations,* p. 621.

Journal of Social History, spring, 1998, Jacquelyn Miller, review of *First Generations,* p. 733.

Kirkus Reviews, July 1, 1996, review of *First Generations,* p. 937.

Kliatt Young Adult Paperback Book Guide, September, 1998, review of *Women's Voices, Women's Lives,* p. 34.

Library Journal, September 15, 1996, Dorothy Lilly, review of *First Generations,* p. 78; August, 2002, Cynthia Johnson, review of *A Brilliant Solution,* p. 76; Thomas A. Karel, review of *A Brilliant Solution,* p. 114.

New York Review of Books, October 31, 1996, Edmund Morgan, review of *First Generations,* p. 66.

New York Times Book Review, September 15, 2002, Gary Rosen, "A Design for Living," review of *A Brilliant Solution,* p. 29.

Publishers Weekly, July 15, 1996, review of *First Generations,* p. 61; June 24, 2002, review of *A Brilliant Solution,* p. 49.

Seventeenth-Century News, fall, 1998, review of *First Generations,* p. 141.

William and Mary Quarterly, July, 1998, Catherine Clinton, review of *First Generations,* p. 444.

Women's Review of Books, December, 1996, Joni Adamson Clarke, review of *First Generations,* p. 26.

*   *   *

BIANCHI, Eugene C(arl) 1930-

PERSONAL: Born May 5, 1930, in Oakland, CA; son of Natale and Catherine (Mangini) Bianchi; divorced. *Education:* Gonzaga University, B.A., 1954, M.A. (cum laude), 1955; Catholic University of Louvain, S.T.L. (cum laude), 1962; Columbia University and Union Theological Seminary, Ph.D., 1966.

ADDRESSES: Office—Department of Religion, Emory University, 1364 Clifton Rd. NE, Atlanta, GA 30322-0001. *E-mail*—releb@emory.edu.

CAREER: Jesuit priest of California Province, 1961-68; resigned from order, 1968. St. Ignatius High School, San Francisco, CA, teacher, 1955-58; *America,* New York, NY, assistant editor, 1963-66; University of Santa Clara, Santa Clara, CA, assistant professor of theology and director of Center for the Study of Contemporary Values, 1966-68; Emory University, Atlanta, GA, associate professor of religion, 1968—. Visiting summer professor at University of San

Francisco, 1966, and Stanford University, 1969; Distinguished Visiting Professor, California State University, Sacramento, 1975.

MEMBER: American Society of Church History, American Academy of Religion, Religious Education Association, Society for the Scientific Study of Religion.

WRITINGS:

John XXIII and American Protestants, Corpus Books, 1968.
(Contributor) *American Catholic Exodus,* Corpus Books, 1968.
Reconciliation: The Function of the Church, Sheed (Franklin, WI), 1969.
(Contributor) *Why Priests Leave,* Hawthorne, 1969.
The Religious Experience of Revolutionaries, Doubleday (New York, NY), 1972.
(With Rosemary R. Ruether) *From Machismo to Mutuality,* Paulist Press, 1976.
Aging As a Spiritual Journey, Crossroad (New York, NY), 1982.
On Growing Older: A Personal Guide to Life after Thirty-Five, illustrations by Lee Lawson, Crossroad (New York, NY), 1985.
(Editor, with Rosemary Radford Ruether) *A Democratic Catholic Church: The Reconstruction of Roman Catholicism,* Crossroad (New York, NY), 1992.
Elder Wisdom: Crafting Your Own Elderhood, Crossroad (New York, NY), 1994.
(With Peter McDonough) *Passionate Uncertainty: Inside the American Jesuits,* University of California Press (Berkeley, CA), 2002.

Contributor of about forty articles and many reviews to periodicals, including *America, Catholic World, Church History, Commonweal, Ecumenist, National Catholic Reporter,* and *Incunable* (Madrid).

WORK IN PROGRESS: Writing a novel, *The Bishop of San Francisco.*

SIDELIGHTS: Eugene Bianchi's books reflect his career as a former Jesuit priest and as a professor of religion. In 1983 he published *Aging As a Spiritual*

Journey, described by Eugene Dooley of *Best Sellers* as "difficult," because the theme "tends to be more than slightly depressing." This work discusses the aging of America—as people live longer, the elderly population rises, leaving in its wake a spate of sociological and economic issues. Bianchi, the review continued, urges a more religious and contemplative attitude regarding the final years of one's life. "But he may be over-optimistic in thinking that most people approach their last hour with religious thoughts and sentiments," Dooley said. The work contains the thoughts of more than twenty religious scholars, leading *Commonweal*'s John Deedy to state that while the sampling may be limited in scope, the interviews "are the most interesting part of the book." "Persuasive" is the word another *Commonweal* writer, John Shea, used to characterize *Aging As a Spiritual Journey.* On a related topic, Bianchi published *On Growing Older: A Personal Guide to Life after Thirty-Five.* As the title implies, the work guides readers through exercises and meditations (such as "picture yourself as an elderly individual") designed to engender understanding of and empathy for aged people and their concerns.

In *Passionate Uncertainty: Inside the American Jesuits,* Bianchi examines his former order to assess the "current state of the religious community of men known for missionary and teaching work," as a *Publishers Weekly* critic described it. In surveying more than 400 current and former Jesuits for the book, Bianchi and coauthor Peter McDonough chose "snowball sampling," in which respondents nominated their peers to be interviewed. *America* reviewer Katarina Schuth took exception to this nonrandom surveying, saying that the method "may prove information-rich, but . . . is unreliable in that it gives the reader no confidence that the sample is representative." Schuth did, however, find "comprehensive" the authors' eleven subject headings, including spirituality, sexuality, community life, and the meaning of priesthood. In addition, "those who are entertained by clever images and rich vocabulary will find plenty to enjoy in the writing style," though Schuth added that the overall content struck her as "dense, confusing and overstated."

Avery Cardinal Dulles, reviewing *Passionate Uncertainty* for *First Things,* however, saw in the book "a wake-up call" for American Jesuits. Though "flawed," as he put it, by the "heavily slanted" research, the book still "contains an abundance of useful information." And while the authors' use of jargon may be "off-putting," noted a *Kirkus Reviews* contributor, Bianchi and McDonough "[allow] us to listen to an amazing variety of Jesuit voices discussing the calculus of stress and satisfaction that keeps members in the order or prompts them to leave."

"Why shouldn't the Church be democratic," ask Bianchi and coeditor Rosemary Radford Ruether in *A Democratic Catholic Church: The Reconstruction of Roman Catholicism.* Arguing that the contemporary church is modeled after the nondemocratic structures of the Roman Empire, Bianchi and Ruether "lament that church decisions are made by the limited number of men in hierarchy," commented *Christian Century* reviewer David Stagaman. "They seek a church where all members, by virtue of their baptism and faith, participate in decision-making. . . . In such a church, leaders would be accountable to God's people and committed to dialogue. Dogmatic closure of discussion and suppression of dissent would cease."

BIOGRAPHICAL AND CRITICAL SOURCES:

PERIODICALS

America, March 26, 1983, Donald Moore, review of *Aging As a Spiritual Journey,* p. 242; March 25, 2002, Katarina Schuth, "This Least Society," p. 21.

Best Sellers, April, 1983, Eugene Dooley, review of *Aging As a Spiritual Journey.*

Booklist, October 15, 1992, Mary Deeley, review of *A Democratic Catholic Church: The Reconstruction of Roman Catholicism,* p. 381; February 15, 2002, Steven Schroeder, review of *Passionate Uncertainty: Inside the American Jesuits,* p. 974.

Bookwatch, November, 1992, review of *A Democratic Catholic Church,* p. 1.

Christian Century, October 20, 1993, David Stagaman, review of *A Democratic Catholic Church,* p. 1020.

Commonweal, February 25, 1983, John Shea, review of *Aging As a Spiritual Journey,* p. 117; October 21, 1983, John Deedy, review of *Aging As a Spiritual Journey,* p. 573; March 25, 1993, Lawrence Cunningham, review of *A Democratic Catholic Church,* p. 28.

Conscience, autumn, 1994, review of *A Democratic Catholic Church,* p. 46.

First Things, April, 2002, Avery Cardinal Dulles, review of *Passionate Uncertainty,* p. 37.

Jurist, winter, 1993, John Ford, review of *A Democratic Catholic Church,* pp. 223-224.

Kirkus Reviews, January 15, 2002, Steven Schroeder, review of *Passionate Uncertainty,* p. 89.

Library Journal, December, 1985, Elise Chase, review of *On Growing Older: A Personal Guide to Life after Thirty-Five,* p. 118; February 15, 2002, C. Robert Nixon, review of *Passionate Uncertainty,* p. 150.

National Catholic Reporter, November 11, 1983, Mitch Finley, review of *Aging As a Spiritual Journey,* p. 17; August 14, 1987, Jack Dick, review of *On Growing Older,* p. 15; November 20, 1992, William Peatman, review of *A Democratic Catholic Church,* p. 34.

New Catholic World, September-October, 1983, Anthony Padovano, review of *Aging As a Spiritual Journey,* p. 236.

New York Review of Books, March 28, 2002, Garry Wills, "Jesuits in Disarray," p. 12.

Religious Studies Review, April, 1993, review of *A Democratic Catholic Church,* p. 149.*

*   *   *

BILLINGTON, Michael 1939-

PERSONAL: Born November 16, 1939, in Leamington Spa, England; son of Alfred Robert (an accountant) and Patricia (Bradshaw) Billington; married Jeanine Bradlaugh, December 12, 1978; children: Natasha Alexandra. *Education:* St. Catherine's College, Oxford, B.A., 1961. *Hobbies and other interests:* Opera, cricket.

ADDRESSES: Home—15 Hearne Rd., London W4 3NJ, England. *Office*—Guardian, 119 Farringdon Rd., London EC1 3ER, England. *Agent*—Curtis Brown, Haymarket House, 28-29 Haymarket, London SW1Y 4SP. *E-mail*—michael.billington@guardian.cs.uk.

CAREER: Lincoln Theatre Company, public liaison officer and director, 1962-64; *London Times,* London, England, deputy drama and film critic, 1965-71, television critic, 1968-70; *Guardian,* London, drama critic, 1971—. Film critic for *Illustrated London News* and *Birmingham Post,* 1968—; drama critic for *Country Life.* Presenter of *Kaleidoscope* and *Critics' Forum* on British Broadcasting Corp. (BBC) Radio. Visiting professor of Drama, King's College, London.

MEMBER: Critics' Circle.

AWARDS, HONORS: Named critic of the year by International Press Corp., 1974.

WRITINGS:

The Modern Actor, Hamish Hamilton (London, England), 1973.
How Tickled I Am: A Celebration of Ken Dodd, David & Charles (London, England), 1977.
(Editor) *Performing Arts: A Guide to Practice and Appreciation,* foreword by Sir John Gielgud, Facts on File (New York, NY), 1980.
The Guinness Book of Facts and Feats: Theatre, Guinness Superlatives (London, England), 1982.
Alan Ayckbourn, Macmillan (London, England), 1983, Grove Press (New York, NY), 1984, 2nd edition, St. Martin's Press (New York, NY), 1990.
Stoppard, the Playwright, Methuen (New York, NY), 1987.
Peggy Ashcroft, J. Murray (London, England), 1988.
(Editor) *Approaches to "Twelfth Night,"* Nick Hern Books (London, England), 1990.
One Night Stands: A Critic's View of British Theatre from 1971-1991, Nick Hern Books (London, England), 1993, revised as *One Night Stands: A Critic's View of Modern British Theatre,* 2001.
The Life and Work of Harold Pinter, Faber (London, England), 1996.
(Editor) *Stage and Screen Lives,* Oxford University Press (New York, NY), 2001.

Contributor to *TV Guide* and *New York Times.*

SIDELIGHTS: Michael Billington has served as the theatre critic for the *Guardian* newspaper in England since 1971. Commenting on his long tenure at the paper, Billington stated in a brief article posted at the *Guardian* Web site: "People ask me how I keep going and retain my apparent enthusiasm. The short, Johnsonian answer is that the man or woman who is bored with theatre is bored with life."

In *One Night Stands: A Critic's View of British Theatre from 1971-1991,* Billington offers a selection of the many theatrical reviews and articles he has written over the years. Michael Mangan in *Theatre Research*

International believed that Billington's collection "is bound to be one of the books to which future generations of theatre historians will turn in order to build up their picture of theatrical culture in late twentieth-century Britain."

Billington is also the author of *The Life and Work of Harold Pinter,* a look at the career of one of England's most honored playwrights and the first full-length biography to be published on Pinter. While providing a chronicle of Pinter's life, Billington also examines each of his major works and uncovers possible literary and particularly biographical sources for the plays. "In his singular use of biography as context for Pinter's plays," wrote Susan Rusinko in *World Literature Today,* "Billington has succeeded in cracking the myth that Pinter's plays spring solely from his fertile imagination." Jack Helbig in *Booklist* praised Billington's "exhaustive critical biography" for its "fine literary scholarship." John F. Deeney, writing in *Modern Drama,* found that "Billington brings to his study a knowledge and understanding of the work in performance which, hitherto, has been somewhat absent from treatments of Pinter."

Billington once told *CA:* "I am principally a drama critic; I feel the job chose me as much as I chose it. I feel an ungovernable urge to set down my impression of plays and performances that I have seen. But it can be a very monastic profession. Therefore I enjoy the exposure to other arts that comes from doing a monthly film column and from doing radio arts programs which give me a chance to discuss books, television, opera, and ballet."

BIOGRAPHICAL AND CRITICAL SOURCES:

PERIODICALS

American Theatre, September, 1997, Michael Barnwell, review of *The Life and Work of Harold Pinter,* p. 57.
Booklist, March 15, 1997, Jack Helbig, review of *The Life and Work of Harold Pinter,* p. 1220.
Choice: Current Reviews for Academic Libraries, October, 1997, W. Baker, review of *The Life and Work of Harold Pinter,* p. 294.
Modern Drama, fall, 1997, John F. Deeney, review of *The Life and Work of Harold Pinter,* p. 423.

New Theatre Quarterly, February, 1998, John Stokes, review of *The Life and Work of Harold Pinter,* p. 94.

Publishers Weekly, January 20, 1997, review of *The Life and Work of Harold Pinter,* p. 38.

Spectator, October 12, 1996, David Sexton, review of *The Life and Work of Harold Pinter,* p. 42.

Theatre Journal, March, 1997, William C. Boles, review of *One Night Stands,* p. 96.

Theatre Research International, summer, 1994, Michael Mangan, review of *One Night Stands,* p. 177.

World Literature Today, winter, 1998, Susan Rusinko, review of *The Life and Work of Harold Pinter,* p. 142.

ONLINE

Guardian Online, http://www.guardian.co.uk/ (November 4, 2003).

*   *   *

BINCHY, Maeve 1940-

PERSONAL: Born May 28, 1940, in Dalkey, Ireland; daughter of William T. (a lawyer) and Maureen (a nurse; maiden name, Blackmore) Binchy; married Gordon Thomas Snell (a writer and broadcaster), January 29, 1977. *Education:* University College, Dublin, B.A., 1960.

ADDRESSES: Home—Dalkey, Ireland. *Office—Irish Times,* 85 Fleet St., London EC4, England. *Agent*—Christine Green, 2 Barbon Close, Great Ormond St., London WC1 N3JX, England.

CAREER: Zion Schools, Dublin, Ireland, French teacher; Pembroke School for Girls, Dublin, history and Latin teacher, 1961-68; *Irish Times,* Dublin, columnist, 1968—; writer.

AWARDS, HONORS: International Television Festival Golden Prague Award, Czechoslovak Television, Prague, and Jacobs Award, both 1979, both for *Deeply Regretted By;* W. H. Smith Fiction Award, 2001, for *Scarlet Feather.*

Maeve Binchy

WRITINGS:

NOVELS

Light a Penny Candle, Century (London, England), 1982, Viking (New York, NY), 1983.

Echoes, Century (London, England), 1985, Viking (New York, NY), 1986.

Firefly Summer, Century (London, England), 1987, Delacorte Press (New York, NY), 1988.

Silver Wedding, Century (London, England), 1988, Delacorte Press (New York, NY), 1989.

Circle of Friends, Franklin Library (Franklin Center, PA), 1990.

The Copper Beech, Delacorte Press (New York, NY), 1992.

The Glass Lake, Delacorte Press (New York, NY), 1995.

Evening Class, Delacorte Press (New York, NY), 1996.

Tara Road, illustrated by Wendy Shea, Delacorte Press (New York, NY), 1999.

Scarlet Feather, Orion (London, England), 2000, Dutton (New York, NY), 2001.

Quentins, Dutton (New York, NY), 2002.

Two Complete Novels (includes *Circle of Friends* and *The Copper Beech*), Wings Books (New York, NY), 2003.

STORY COLLECTIONS

The Central Line: Stories of Big City Life (also see below), Quartet (London, England), 1978.

Victoria Line (also see below), Quartet (London, England), 1980.

Maeve Binchy's Dublin Four, Ward River Press (Swords, Ireland), 1982, published as *Dublin Four,* Century (London, England), 1983.

London Transports (contains *The Central Line: Stories of Big City Life* and *Victoria Line*), Century (London, England), 1983.

The Lilac Bus: Stories, Ward River Press, 1984, Delacorte Press (New York, NY), 1991.

This Year It Will Be Different and Other Stories: A Christmas Treasury, Delacorte Press (New York, NY), 1996.

The Return Journey, Delacorte Press (New York, NY), 1998.

Ladies' Night at Finbar's Hotel, edited by Dermot Bolger, Harcourt (New York, NY), 2000.

OTHER

My First Book (journalism), Irish Times (Dublin, Ireland), 1976.

End of Term (one-act play), produced in Dublin, Ireland, at the Abbey Theatre, 1976.

The Half Promised Land (play), produced in Dublin, Ireland, 1979, produced in Philadelphia, PA, at Society Hill Playhouse, 1980.

Deeply Regretted By (television screenplay), Radio Telefis Eireann, 1979.

Maeve's Diary (nonfiction), Irish Times (Dublin, Ireland), 1979.

Ireland of the Welcomes (television screenplay), Radio Telefis Eireann, 1980.

Aches & Pains, illustrations by Wendy Shea, Delacorte Press (New York, NY), 2000.

Contributor to books, including *Portrait of the Artist As a Young Girl,* edited by John Quinn, Methuen (London, England), 1986; *Territories of the Voice: Contemporary Stories by Irish Women Writers,* edited by Louise DeSalvo, Kathleen Walsh D'Arcy, and Katherine Hogan, Beacon Press (Boston, MA), 1989; and *In Sunshine or in Shadow,* edited by Kate Cruise O'Brien and Mary Maher, Delacorte Press, 1998. Some of her plays have been produced by the Peacock Theater in Dublin, Ireland.

ADAPTATIONS: Echoes was made into a miniseries, televised in Great Britain in 1988 and in the United States on Public Broadcasting Service in 1990. *Circle of Friends* was made into a film, produced by Savory Pictures, which starred Chris O'Donnell and Minnie Driver.

WORK IN PROGRESS: Avoid Disappointment, a book of linked short stories.

SIDELIGHTS: Maeve Binchy is a versatile Irish writer who once reported on daily life in London for the *Irish Times.* She lived in London for almost fifteen years before taking up residence outside Dublin with husband and fellow writer Gordon Snell. "We have a lovely room with a long, long desk and two word processors," the novelist once said when asked about living with another writer. "We get on perfectly well sitting beside each other. Just the sound of the keyboard and the printer is all we hear. If one of us doesn't like what the other has said, the rule is ten minutes of sulking time. . . . After that the sulks can be construed as being moody or difficult. . . . We're not perfect in our judgment of each other's work, but at least we're honest. And normally we're praising— but if we don't like something, we say it straight out."

Binchy's novels, many of them best sellers, have won her critical acclaim and an international following. Set most frequently in rural Ireland, her stories of family life and intimate friendships appeal to a predominantly female audience. She has been praised as thorough in her storytelling and both astute and affectionate in her characterizations. Many of her female protagonists are women who take control of their lives in the midst of coping with such societal ills as alcoholism, adultery, and divorce. Binchy told a *People* magazine reporter that the message within her novels and short stories is that once people take charge of their lives, they can make things work out for the best. "And maybe that's a reassuring idea," she added. "I wouldn't like to be thought of as patting people on the head, but I wouldn't be at all offended by people who think my books are comforting." Critics note that although her writing sometimes lacks profundity, it transcends the superficiality frequently featured in popular romance novels through such subtle feminist undertones. "In 1963 we all played by the rules," commented Binchy to Cathy Edwards of the *San Francisco Review of Books.* "I want to write about people who make their own decisions. Women of my generation were fooled a bit—maybe all women are."

"Binchy's work, though marketed as romances, by no means fits that category precisely," noted a contributor to *Contemporary Novelists.* "Binchy, a longstanding columnist for the *Irish Times,* presents a realistic picture of the lives of women ordered within the rigidities of Catholic orthodoxy that forbid divorce and abortion. In her work, women's survival is predicated on the creation of powerful, though informal, networks of alliance and friendships that survive the vicissitudes of pregnancy, forced marriage, and alcoholism." As a writer for *Contemporary Popular Writers* elaborated, "Her sprawling narratives express a moral but tolerant sensibility." Critics either dismiss or applaud her particular genre as "women's fiction," or even, as Helen Birch of the *Independent* wrote, "600-page doorstoppers, beach books, fireside books." Most reviewers believe Binchy's work transcends these labels. Her accomplished prose contains shrewd, albeit sentimental, social analysis of Irish women's lives in the mid-to-late twentieth century.

Though best known for her novels, Binchy began her fiction-writing career with short stories and plays. As she once commented: "Because the kind of stories I used to write for the *Irish Times* had a fictional or almost dramatic element to them, sometimes I was approached by people in theater or television asking why didn't I try my hand at writing plays. And because I started everything in life a little bit later than everybody else (to be a cub journalist at twenty-eight was very old), I felt, OK, maybe at thirty-five, thirty-six, thirty-seven I could start to write plays as well." Dublin's Abbey Theatre encouraged new talent and produced Binchy's *End of Term* in 1976.

Although one of her plays, *The Half Promised Land,* was eventually staged as far away as Philadelphia, Pennsylvania, Binchy fared far better with her efforts at writing short fiction. Her collections *London Transports*—originally published in two volumes as *Central Line* and *Victoria Line*—and *Maeve Binchy's Dublin Four* focus on the tedium of city life and the individual

plights of female protagonists. In *London Transports,* for example, the women are often dissatisfied with their relationships with men and drawn into the corruption of Binchy's seedy London. *Times Literary Supplement* contributor Helen Harris pointed out that though the themes of *London Transports* are often bleak, Binchy writes with "ease and buoyancy." Harris also declared that the author's "portrayal of the small skirmishes of day-to-day urban survival is enjoyable; her wry observation of the different layers of London life is uncomfortably acute."

Binchy's 1996 collection, *This Year It Will Be Different and Other Stories: A Christmas Treasury,* received mixed assessments. A *Publishers Weekly* critic appraised the volume's stories as "formulaic and superficial." A *Kirkus Reviews* contributor was more positive, however, recommending the "collection of Christmas-centered feel-good tales" as a "bit of sentimentality and a touch of romance, along with humor and hopeful turns to treat . . . the holiday blues." *The Return Journey,* Binchy's 1998 volume, also received uneven, if not unflattering, reviews. A *Publishers Weekly* reviewer declared the work "unimpressive," faulting Binchy for, among other things, "predictable plot mechanisms" and "conclusions [that] are socked home, often in a chirpy manner." "Too many of these finely wrought tales reach their blissful destinations without hitting a single bump in the road," commented Erica Saunders in *People.*

A small rural town is the primary setting of Binchy's first novel, *Light a Penny Candle.* In this work, she depicts the twenty-year friendship of Elizabeth White and Aisling O'Connor. The girls meet when Elizabeth, a ten-year-old Londoner, is sent by her parents to live with the O'Connor family in Ireland at the start of World War II. Together the two friends experience the joys and hardships of growing up, and their close relationship endures despite such ordeals as Elizabeth's difficulties with her uncaring parents once back in London, Aisling's love affair with a onetime boyfriend of Elizabeth's, and both women's failed marriages. As in many of Binchy's stories, the book's male characters are often presented as insensitive, noncommittal, and the source of the women's problems. "It's been a while since I've enjoyed such a loutish, incompetent, drunken, selfish collection of men in one novel," remarked Carol Sternhell in the *Village Voice.* On the other hand, Sternhell found most of the female characters "practical, competent, and loving." Although some critics complained about what one reviewer, writing in *Harper's*, termed a "too heavy-handed and contrived" ending in which "one disaster after another comes crashing down too quickly," the novel received praise. "With its barreling plot and clamorous characters, *Light a Penny Candle* is a lilting book," asserted Dennis Drabelle in the *Washington Post Book World*. Sternhell called the author's effort an "impressive first novel" and proclaimed that "Binchy's strength is in her honesty: she refuses to trim all edges to get us drunk on easy answers."

In *Firefly Summer* Binchy, observed *New York Times Book Review* contributor Michele Slung, "once again gives us rural Ireland, a frequently maddening yet ultimately seductive place that can render problems only in contrasting shades of old and new, past and present, strange and familiar." Patrick O'Neill, the story's main character, is an American millionaire who comes to the Irish town of Mountfern in the 1960s with the goal of converting a dilapidated manor house into a luxury hotel. His experience in a town made up of people who are either eager or reluctant to accept his business venture is the subject of the novel. Slung thought that *Firefly Summer* "is the best Binchy yet. . . . Here she does what she does best, which is to manufacture experience in which we fully share."

"With *Silver Wedding*," noted Robert Plunket in the *New York Times Book Review*, "Binchy tries something a little bit different, and as she does so you can sense a remarkably gifted writer beginning to flex her muscles." Instead of focusing on the dynamics of small-town life, in her fourth novel, Binchy examines the personal conflicts of the members of one family and their friends. In the last chapter of the book, all of the characters unite for Deidre and Desmond Doyle's twenty-fifth wedding anniversary party. The author devotes each of the previous chapters to one individual in the story, ultimately revealing the emotions, resentments, and ambitions of a cast of characters whose lives are all connected in some way. Plunket pointed out that the author's choice of "guilty secrets" as one theme of *Silver Wedding* left him "wish[ing] she'd come up with something a bit more clever," but he acknowledged that "Binchy is a wonderful student of human nature" and described the book as "an effortless pleasure to read."

The importance that Binchy places on a writer's careful observation of people and places was expressed in a "how-to" article the author wrote for the *Writer*. "To get dialogue right, listen to everyone, everywhere—eavesdrop, follow people so you can hear what they are saying. To get a scene right for *Tara Road*, I spent two days watching mothers and teenage daughters buying clothes in a store. Never hang up on a crossed telephone line, watch people in planes and trains, and be vigilant the whole time." Binchy instructs writers to outline and adhere to a general time schedule for each of their books; to think through the story and the characters, making note cards for each; to plan goals for each chapter; and then to begin writing, and when writing to do so at a quick pace. "Don't pause for breath, punctuation, too much analysis," stated Binchy. She advises writers to fully imagine their characters, their appearance, their actions, and reactions: "If you pretend they are real people, they will become so," she said. Among other pointers, Binchy told writers to refrain from analyzing the worth of their writing. "Just keep going," she urged, advocating a style in the manner of a writer's own speech: "I write exactly as I speak; I don't roll each sentence around and examine it carefully before letting it loose. If you speak in your own voice, you can never be accused of being pretentious or showing off; you can just be yourself, and that's a huge advantage in anybody."

Asked by *Writer* interviewer Lewis Burke Frumkes to explain her theory on her wide appeal—Binchy's writing has been translated into numerous languages and her books have outsold literary giants such as James Joyce and William Butler Yeats—Binchy stated that her writing is geared for a mass audience, unlike Joyce and Yeats: "The thing is, if you were going on a journey and you were thinking, I must read something on the plane, and if you had read any of my books before you would think, well, she tells a good story. . . . For some reason I have hit upon a form of story telling that appeals to people in different languages. I suppose they have also felt love and hope and pain, and they have had dreams and had the delight of close families and the more irritating aspects of close families. They have, perhaps, also loved people who haven't loved them in return and also might have wanted to go up to the bright lights of a big city . . . but the principle is the same. You have people who are young and enthusiastic and want to try to achieve their dream, and I think that is why people everywhere like [the characters]."

Circle of Friends also became a best seller. Set in the 1950s, the book revolves around three young women with contrasting personalities who come of age and develop a close friendship while attending University College in Dublin. Although Susan Isaacs suggested in the *New York Times Book Review* that "a cynical reader might reflect [that] this sort of fiction is so commonplace that the characters will be completely fungible," she lauded Binchy for portraying her protagonists as "modern women, each, in her own way, ambitious, intelligent, perceptive." Isaacs summed up the reason for Binchy's immense popularity when she declared that "the author doesn't daze the reader with narrative bombshells (or, for that matter, with brilliant language), but recounts ordinary events . . . with extraordinary straightforwardness and insight."

The Copper Beech, a set of interlinking stories set in the small Irish village during the 1940s and 1950s, "has its share of murder, adultery, alcoholism, unwanted pregnancies and lots more," Anne Tolstoi Wallach commented in the *New York Times Book Review.* "Bad things happen to good people, good things happen to bad people, but because this is the new Maeve Binchy it all comes right in the end." Of *Evening Class,* a *Publishers Weekly* reviewer wrote, "Fans of Binchy's nimble story telling skills, and of her characters, who are always decent without being dull, won't want to change a thing." Jan Blodgett, writing for *Library Journal,* called the book "a complex tale of loves lost, betrayal, loyalty, and renewed courage." For the type of story it is, *Evening Class* is "satisfying," wrote a *Kirkus Reviews* critic, who described the characters as "a flock of middle- and lower-middle [class] worriers, loners, and groaners, all brooding on their peculiar miseries, until an updraft of love or happy coincidences set them free."

Tara Road revolves around two women who swap houses, and to some extent lives, for a summer. Both are mothers: Marilyn is an American living in New England and mourning the death of her teenaged son; Ria is a resident of Dublin who is completely shocked when her husband leaves her for another woman whom he impregnated. A *Kirkus Reviews* contributor declared *Tara Road* "one of Binchy's best." "Once again, Binchy . . . memorably limns the lives of ordinary people caught in the traps sprung by life and loving hearts," stated the critic. Through the course of the story, the women learn about each other as well as themselves. In a *Booklist* review, Brad Hooper called Binchy "a careful writer and a conscientious plotter."

Scarlet Feather was greeted with critical praise and, according to a *Publishers Weekly* reviewer, "Binchy's

gift for creating a wide range of characters whose foibles and challenges make them lovable and real, coupled with her theme that genuine love can transform lives, add up to another crowd-pleaser." Hooper commented: "Binchy writes domestic drama at its most realistic and moving, and her adoring fans will appreciate her latest work." Her fans might have appreciated it more had Binchy not announced that *Scarlet Feather* would be her last novel. According to Christina Cheakalos writing for *People,* after reading the announcement in Binchy's *Irish Times* column, "More than 800 readers wrote in to say don't go." Writing in *Chatelaine,* reviewer Bonnie Schiedel commented, "She's going out on a proverbial high note," calling *Scarlet Feather* "a delicious read."

Regardless of her announcement, Binchy made a surprise return and produced yet another novel, *The Quentins,* that continued with the modern Dublin theme she used in *Tara Road* and *Scarlet Feather.* A *Publishers Weekly* reviewer commented: "Fans of the bestselling Binchy will be grateful that the basic formula is still intact—decent people pulling through hard times—and that some favorite characters from previous novels reappear." This is a story in which the inhabitants are proud of their cosmopolitan attitudes and, as Christine C. Menefee pointed out in *School Library Journal,* "underlying [the characters'] lives and choices are strengths of family and friendship, and a loving kindness, that still confirm the outsider's hopeful expectations about traditional Irish culture."

BIOGRAPHICAL AND CRITICAL SOURCES:

BOOKS

Bestsellers 90, Issue 1, Gale (Detroit, MI), 1990, pp. 3-4.
Contemporary Novelists, 6th edition, St. James Press (Detroit, MI), 1996.
Contemporary Popular Writers, St. James Press (Detroit, MI), 1997.
Twentieth-Century Romance and Historical Writers, 3rd edition, St. James Press (Detroit, MI), 1994.

PERIODICALS

Booklist, December 15, 1998, Brad Hooper, review of *Tara Road,* p. 706; December 15, 2000, Brad Hooper, review of *Scarlet Feather,* p. 763.

British Book News, May, 1986, p. 308.

Chatelaine, October, 2000, Bonnie Schiedel, "Tea and Empathy," p. 18.

Chicago Tribune, March 17, 1991, section 6, p. 3; October 27, 1991, section 14, pp. 3, 11.

Cosmopolitan, February, 1995, Chris Chase, review of *The Glass Lake,* p. 18.

Detroit Free Press, December 23, 1990.

Harper's, April, 1983, review of *Light a Penny Candle,* pp. 75-76.

Independent, May 12, 1995, Helen Birch, interview with Binchy, p. 25.

Kirkus Reviews, August 1, 1996, review of *This Year It Will Be Different and Other Stories: A Christmas Treasury;* January 1, 1997, review of *Evening Class;* December 1, 1998, review of *Tara Road.*

Library Journal, February 1, 1997, Jan Blodgett, review of *Evening Class,* p. 104; February 1, 1999, Carol J. Bissett, review of *Tara Road,* p. 118; September 1, 1999, Barbara Valle, review of *Tara Road,* p. 252; September 13, 1999, Daisy Maryles, "Irish Eyes Are Smiling," p. 20; March 1, 2000, review of *Aches and Pains,* p. S10.

Los Angeles Times, February 6, 1986; January 14, 1991, p. E3.

New York Times Book Review, January 12, 1986, Kiki Olson, review of *Echoes,* p. 20; September 18, 1988, Michele Slung, review of *Firefly Summer,* p. 13; September 10, 1989, Robert Plunket, review of *Silver Wedding,* p. 18; December 30, 1990, Susan Isaacs, review of *Circle of Friends,* p. 8; December 8, 1991, John Kenny Crane, review of *The Lilac Bus,* p. 22; December 29, 1992, p. 16.

People, December 14, 1992, pp. 34-35; March 30, 1998, Erica Saunders, review of *The Return Journey,* p. 31; August 28, 2000, Christina Cheakalos, "A Novel Retirement," p. 147.

Publishers Weekly, August 26, 1996, review of *This Year It Will Be Different and Other Stories,* p. 74; January 6, 1997, review of *Evening Class,* p. 62; February 16, 1998, review of *The Return Journey,* p. 201; December 21, 1998, review of *Tara Road,* p. 51; April 17, 2000, "June Publications," p. 70; January 8, 2001, review of *Scarlet Feather,* p. 45; September 23, 2002, review of *Quentins,* p. 50.

San Francisco Review of Books, winter, 1992, pp. 6-7.

School Library Journal, February, 2003, Christine C. Menefee, review of *Quentins,* p. 172.

Times Educational Supplement, May 24, 1991, p. 38.

Times Literary Supplement, November 28, 1980, p. 1366; April 1, 1983, p. 324; March 30, 1984, p. 354.

Village Voice, May 17, 1983, Carol Sternhell, review of *Light a Penny Candle,* p. 50.

Washington Post, January 17, 1986; September 11, 1989, p. D3; December 24, 1990, p. C3; November 7, 1991, p. C3.

Washington Post Book World, May 1, 1983, Dennis Drabelle, review of *Light a Penny Candle,* p. 10.

Writer, February, 2000, Maeve Binchy, "Welcome to My Study," p. 12, and Lewis Burke Frumkes, interview with Binchy, p. 14.

*   *   *

BLAKE, Sterling
See BENFORD, Gregory (Albert)

*   *   *

BOARDMAN, Brigid M. 1931-

PERSONAL: Born June 29, 1931, in Winchester, England; daughter of Henry (a soldier) and Lois Neville (Urwick) Boardman. *Ethnicity:* "British." *Education:* University of Bristol, B.A. (with honors), 1970, M.A., 1971; Open University, Ph.D., 1980. *Politics:* Conservative. *Religion:* Roman Catholic.

ADDRESSES: Home—50 Pegasus Ct., Heavitree, Exeter EX1 2RP, England. *E-mail*—mail@bmboardman.fslife.co.uk.

CAREER: Open University, Southwest Region, Bristol, England, course tutor in literary and religious studies, 1972-92.

WRITINGS:

Between Heaven and Charing Cross: The Life of Francis Thompson, Yale University Press (New Haven, CT), 1988.

The Hound of Heaven: Paintings by R. H. Ives Gammell with Commentary by Brigid M. Boardman, Sigo Press (Boston, MA), 1995.

(With Philip Jebb) *In a Quiet Garden,* Downside Abbey Press (Bath, England), 1998.

(Editor) *The Poems of Francis Thompson: A New Edition,* Continuum Publishing (New York, NY), 2002.

Contributor to periodicals, including *Clergy Review* and *Journal of Garden History.*

WORK IN PROGRESS: The Garden in the City, on the symbolic relationship between the garden and the city; a monograph on Christopher Urswick (1459-1521).

SIDELIGHTS: Brigid M. Boardman once told *CA:* "In earlier years I was an artist, rather than a writer. The relationship between the two arts is of great importance to me. This is illustrated by my work on the Boston artist Robert Ives Gammell and his paintings illustrating Francis Thompson's poem 'The Hound of Heaven.' I feel the author and the writer have very vital roles to play in uniting past traditions with present needs, thus creating openings for the future. Present and future must be nourished by the past.

"My research into Thompson's life and work was the outcome of very early reading and love for his poetry, so I chose him as the subject for my M.A. dissertation. I found that neither his life nor his work had been fully examined in the light of the manuscripts held at Boston College, and when I was able to visit the collection five years later I found my suspicions fully confirmed. Thompson became a very different and much more exciting personality than the insipid figure presented by his earlier biographers. His life included very varied experiences apart from the comparatively well-known years as an opium addict on the London streets. He was closely associated with a number of writers and other personalities of the 1890s, although he was notably not one of them, and the reasons for this form an important part of my research. In addition, at the time of his death in 1907 the modernist crisis was at its height in the Catholic Church and was largely responsible for the suppression of much in his writings that can now be viewed very differently.

"I had to interrupt my earlier work on Thompson in order to take advantage of a grant to write my Ph.D. thesis, completed in 1980. It was not possible to use Thompson as my subject, there being no one in this country to supervise the project. But I was able to take up another longstanding interest in exploring the relationship between the ideas associated with the 'Paradisal Garden' and the 'City of God.' I found the symbolic significance became inseparable from the reality of both in shaping much of our outlook in Western society. The book to be based on this topic will also embrace some of the ecological issues that are so much a part of today's concerns.

"Other subjects on which I am working include a continuing interest in Christopher Urswick (c. 1459-1521), an ancestor on my mother's side and chief almoner to Henry VII. He was also a friend of Saint Thomas More and his circle and a collector of manuscripts and the classical works favored by the humanists of the time. I have written on Urswick and lectured in England and America, using slide illustrations connected with his career and the books and manuscripts still extant in British libraries.

"Another important interest is the connection between art and writing. I began my career as an artist and have always kept this as a hobby. While working on the Thompson collection at Boston College I realized how valuable a study could be made of 'The Hound of Heaven' together with the magnificent sequence of paintings based on the poem that was completed by Gammell in 1956.

"All of the above may suggest rather too wide a range of interest. But there is a unifying factor, for in each case I have been drawn to it by a certain sense that this is a personality or a subject that has something to offer to us today, an offering from the past such as we too often neglect to notice in our pursuit of the novel and the new."

BIOGRAPHICAL AND CRITICAL SOURCES:

PERIODICALS

Observer (London, England), July 10, 1988.
Sunday Times (London, England), July 10, 1988.
Times Higher Educational Supplement, December 16, 1988.
Times Literary Supplement, July 1, 1988.

*   *   *

BRISSENDEN, Constance 1947-

PERSONAL: Born 1947, in Canada; companion to Larry Loyie (a writer and speaker). *Education:* University of Guelph, B.A.; University of Alberta, M.A.

ADDRESSES: Home—309-319 East 7th Avenue, Vancouver, British Columbia V5T 1M9, Canada. *E-mail*—livingtraditions@telus.net.

CAREER: Travel and history writer; director of plays by partner, Larry Loyie. Cofounder, Living Traditions Writers Group.

AWARDS, HONORS: Corecipient, with Loyie, Norma Fleck Award for Canadian Children's Nonfiction, 2003, for *As Long As the Rivers Flow: A Last Summer before Residential School.*

WRITINGS:

Factory Lab Anthology, Talonbooks, 1974.
Vancouver Pictorial, Altitude Publishing, 1995.
Portrait of Vancouver, Altitude Publishing, 1995.
Whistler and the Sea to Sky Country, Altitude Publishing, 1995.
Vancouver and Victoria, Formac, 2000.
(With Stephen Brewer, Anita Carmen, and Dorling-Kindersley) *Frommer's Portable Whistler,* Frommer, 2002.
(With Larry Loyie) *As Long As the Rivers Flow: A Last Summer before Residential School,* illustrated by Heather D. Holmlund, Groundwood Books (Berkeley, CA), 2002.

WORK IN PROGRESS: Two nonfiction books with Loyie, *We Were Only Children,* a history of residential schools in the United States and Canada, and *When the Spirits Dance,* a memoir of the Second World War.

SIDELIGHTS: Constance Brissenden is a Canadian writer who is best known for her work with author Larry Loyie on books about Loyie's experiences growing up as a Cree in Northwestern Alberta. For more information, please see the sketch in this volume on Larry Loyie.

BIOGRAPHICAL AND CRITICAL SOURCES:

PERIODICALS

Booklist, April 15, 2003, Hazel Rochman, review of *As Long As the Rivers Flow: A Last Summer before Residential School,* p. 1468.

Books in Canada, November, 2002, review of *As Long As the Rivers Flow.*
Globe and Mail (Toronto, Ontario, Canada), October 14, 2002, Susan Perren, review of *As Long As the Rivers Flow.*
Library Journal, October, 2003, Sean George, review of *As Long As the Rivers Flow,* p. 154.
Wind Speaker, December, 2002, Pamela Sexsmith, review of *As Long As the Rivers Flow,* p. 17.

ONLINE

Living Traditions Writers Group, http://www.first nationswriter.com/ (December 6, 2003), author's home page.*

*   *   *

BROOKER, Jewel Spears 1940-

PERSONAL: Born June 13, 1940, in Jenkins, KY; daughter of William Burnside (in business) and Mae (Johnson) Spears; married Hampton Ralph Brooker (a physicist), December 21, 1962; children: Emily Hope Brooker Langston, Mark Spears. *Education:* Stetson University, B.S., 1962; University of Florida, M.A., 1964; University of South Florida, Ph.D., 1976.

ADDRESSES: Home—501 68th Ave. S, St. Petersburg, FL 33705. *Office*—Eckerd College, 4200 54th Ave. S, St. Petersburg, FL 33733. *E-mail*—jsbrooker@aol.com.

CAREER: University of South Florida, Tampa, adjunct lecturer, 1978-80; Yale University, New Haven, CT, postdoctoral research fellow in English, 1980-81; Eckerd College, St. Petersburg, FL, began as associate professor, became professor of English, 1981—. University of Tampa, adjunct lecturer, 1966-71, 1975; University of South Florida, adjunct lecturer, 1972, 1974-75; St. Edmund's College, Cambridge, visiting scholar, 1987; Columbia University, visiting professor, 1988; Doshisha University, Kyoto, Japan, visiting professor, 1992-94; Harvard University, Stanley J. Kahrl Fellow in Literary Manuscripts, 1999; University of London, John Adams fellow at Institute of United States Studies, 2000; Colorado School of Mines, Hennebach Professor in the Humanities, 2003-04; presenter at conferences and guest speaker at institutions in the

Jewel Spears Brooker

United States and abroad, including Pepperdine University, University of British Columbia, University of Lund, University of Sussex, University of Glasgow, Drury College, and Amherst College. National Endowment for the Humanities, member of National Humanities Council, 2003-08; consultant to Florida Endowment for the Humanities and Social Science and Humanities Research Council of Canada.

MEMBER: International Association of University Professors of English, Modern Language Association of America (member of Delegate Assembly, 1993-96), National Council of Teachers of English, Conference on Christianity and Literature (president, 1992-93, 1994-95), American Association of University Professors, Association of Literary Critics and Scholars, T. S. Eliot Society (member of board of directors, 1984-91; president, 1985-88), Richard Wilbur Society (president, 1996-2000), Katherine Anne Porter Society, Society for the Study of Southern Literature, Asian Society for Literature and Religion, South Atlantic Modern Language Association (chair, Modern British Literature Section, 1982-83, and Christianity and Literature Section, 1988-89; member of executive committee, 1993-96; president, 1998-99).

AWARDS, HONORS: Fellow, National Endowment for the Humanities, 1980-81 and 1987; grants from Florida Endowment for the Humanities, 1983, Regional Arts Commission, Missouri Arts Council, and Southern Regional Educational Board, all 1987, Wilbur Foundation, 1988, and Knight Foundation, 1989; Teaching Excellence and Campus Leadership Award, Sears-Roebuck Foundation, 1989-90; essay prize, South Atlantic Modern Language Association, 1993-94, for "Transcendence and Return: T. S. Eliot and the Dialectic of Modernism"; outstanding service commendation, Conference on Christianity and Literature, 1995; honorary fellow, British Library, 1999—; Pew scholars fellow, 1999-2000; award from Distinguished Christian Scholars Lecture Series, Pew Charitable Trusts, 2001-03; distinguished service award, T. S. Eliot Society, 2002; Chapin Award for excellence in scholarship, 2002-03.

WRITINGS:

(Editor and contributor) *Approaches to Teaching T. S. Eliot's Poetry and Plays,* Modern Language Association of America (New York, NY), 1988.

(With Joseph Bentley) *Reading "The Waste Land": Modernism and the Limits of Interpretation,* University of Massachusetts Press (Amherst, MA), 1990.

(Editor and contributor) *The Placing of T. S. Eliot,* University of Missouri Press (Columbia, MO), 1991.

Mastery and Escape: T. S. Eliot and the Dialectic of Modernism, University of Massachusetts Press (Amherst, MA), 1994.

(Editor and interviewer) *Conversations with Denise Levertov,* University Press of Mississippi (Jackson, MS), 1998.

(Editor and contributor) *T. S. Eliot and Our Turning World,* Macmillan (London, England), 2000, St. Martin's Press (New York, NY), 2001.

(Editor and contributor) *T. S. Eliot: The Contemporary Reviews,* Cambridge University Press (New York, NY), 2003.

Also editor of *T. S. Eliot,* Cambridge University Press. Work represented in anthologies, including *Concise Dictionary of American Literary Biography,* Volume 5: *The Age of Maturity, 1929-1941,* edited by Laura Ingram, Gale (Detroit, MI), 1989; *T. S. Eliot: Man and*

Poet, edited by Laura Cowan, National Poetry Foundation (Orono, ME), 1990; *Making Feminist History: The Literary Scholarship of Sandra M. Gilbert and Susan Gubar,* edited by William E. Cain, Garland Publishing (New York, NY), 1993; *Author-ity and Textuality: Current Views of Collaborative Writing,* edited by James S. Leonard, Christine E. Wharton, and others, Locust Hill Press (West Cornwall, CT), 1994; and *Madison Jones: The Garden of Innocence,* edited by Jan Norby Gretlund, 2003. Contributor of articles and reviews to professional journals, including *Chattahoochee Review, Modern Schoolman, Southern Review, South Atlantic Review, College Literature, Massachusetts Review, Thalia, Centennial Review, Modern Philology,* and *Modernism/Modernity. Christianity and Literature,* guest editor, summer, 1993, winter, 1999, and member of editorial board, 1995—; member of editorial board, *Yeats-Eliot Review,* 1986—, and *South Atlantic Review,* 2002—.

WORK IN PROGRESS: Editing *Letters of Katherine Anne Porter and Mrs. Cleanth Brooks,* for University of Missouri Press (Columbia, MO); editing *The Waste Land: Case Studies in Contemporary Theory,* Bedford Books (Boston, MA); *Violence, Values, Imagination in Modern Literature* (tentative title); *Violence and Desire in Eliot's Poetry and Plays.*

SIDELIGHTS: A respected scholar of T. S. Eliot, Jewel Spears Brooker has written and edited several books on the poet and critic that view Eliot's works from a variety of perspectives. In *Approaches to Teaching Eliot's Poetry and Plays,* Brooker presents an overview of Eliot's place in the contemporary school curriculum and offers possible methods of teaching individual Eliot poems and plays. The collection is, according to Kinley E. Roby in *Theatre Journal,* "very thorough, very broadly based, and generous in its material." Although the critic believed more could have been said of Eliot's political and social beliefs, Roby nonetheless found the book to be "well argued, persuasive, intelligent, and sensitive. It is a valuable guide to anyone who teaches Eliot."

In *Reading "The Waste Land": Modernism and the Limits of Interpretation,* Brooker and coauthor Joseph Bentley provide "a genuinely fresh and insightful analysis of the most explicated modern poem," according to a critic for the *Virginia Quarterly Review.*

Drawing on earlier criticisms of the poem, combining elements from Eliot's biography, and influenced by recent critical theories, the book argues that "The Waste Land" has become a creation of its reading audience as well as of Eliot himself.

The edited work *T. S. Eliot and Our Turning World* contains lectures of a 1996 conference on Eliot's intellectual interests in popular culture and the arts, philosophy, and contemporary literary theory. Noting that the volume "should find a special place on every Eliot scholar's bookshelf," *Christianity and Literature* reviewer Dominic Manganiello added that Brooker's contributions include a discussion of Eliot's interest in the work of German philosopher Immanuel Kant and the links between the writer's Harvard education and his later writings, as well as an "incisive critique" of Anthony Julius's controversial 1995 book *T. S. Eliot, Anti-Semitism, and Literary Form.* Noting that Brooker "is at her best when she is passionately engaged in explicating the historical and philosophical contexts that bear" on Eliot's poetry, Jayme Stayer added in the *Journal of Modern Literature* that *T. S. Eliot and Our Turning World* presents "thoughtful" articles that "reward study."

Brooker's *Mastery and Escape: T. S. Eliot and the Dialectic of Modernism* gathers together her critical essays on Eliot over a fifteen-year span. In his review of the book for *America,* James S. Torrens found that "Brooker weds intellectual history to literary study" in her essays focusing on the philosopher F. H. Bradley, the subject of Eliot's university dissertation. Bradley's view that all of the universe comprised a "living whole" influenced the structures of such Eliot poems as "Gerontion" and "The Waste Land." Brooker's three essays on Bradley's beliefs and how they affected Eliot's writings contain, according to Torrens, "a clarity and conciseness that one certainly will not find in Eliot's dissertation. It is the major contribution of this book." Reviewing *Mastery and Escape* for the *Southern Review,* Lee Oser noted that "Brooker brings a subtle light to Eliot's overanalyzed poems by respecting their elusive mystery." Oser concluded that "most happily, the book succeeds in bringing Eliot's intellectual contexts to bear on his poems. This is not to say that we can now firmly grasp *The Waste Land;* but in their sane and resourceful fashion, Brooker's readings delight and instruct."

BIOGRAPHICAL AND CRITICAL SOURCES:

PERIODICALS

America, April 22, 1995, p. 29.
American Literature, March, 1991, Tim Redman, review of *Reading "The Wasteland": Modernism and the Limits of Interpretation,* pp. 158-159; September, 1995, Robert F. Fleissner, review of *Mastery and Escape: T. S. Eliot and the Dialectic of Modernism,* pp. 598-599.
Choice, December, 1990, p. 625; May, 1995, p. 1445; May, 2001, A. R. Nourie, review of *T. S. Eliot and Our Turning World,* p. 1631.
Christian Century, June 27, 1990, review of *Reading "The Wasteland,"* p. 644.
Christianity and Literature, winter, 1996, Sanford Schwartz, review of *Mastery and Escape,* pp. 256-258; winter, 2003, Dominic Manganiello, review of *T. S. Eliot and Our Turning World,* p. 283.
College English, April, 1996, George S. Lensing, review of *Mastery and Escape,* pp. 460-469.
College Literature, February, 1991, p. 108.
English Literature in Transition, 1880-1920, January, 1997, Richard Badenhausen, review of *Mastery and Escape,* pp. 89-92.
Journal of Modern Literature, summer, 2001, Jayme Stayer, review of *T. S. Eliot and Our Turning World,* p. 525.
Library Journal, December, 1989, p. 122.
Modern Schoolman, January, 1996, William Charron, review of *Mastery and Escape,* pp. 194-196.
Queen's Quarterly, summer, 1991, Edward Lobb, review of *Reading "The Wasteland,"* pp. 463-464.
Review of English Studies, November, 2002, Ronald Bush, review of *T. S. Eliot and Our Turning World,* p. 578.
Sewanee Review, fall, 1991, Sidney Burris, review of *Reading "The Wasteland,"* pp. 617-623; April, 1994, p. 291.
South Atlantic Review, January, 1992, Cleo McNelly Kearns, review of *Reading "The Wasteland,"* pp. 129-132; September, 1995, Nancy Hargrove, review of *Mastery and Escape,* pp. 32-36.
Southern Review, October, 1991, Peter Quartermain, review of *Reading "The Wasteland,"* pp. 949-952; winter, 1996, Lee Oser, review of *Mastery and Escape,* pp. 183-185.
Theatre Journal, December, 1990, Kinley E. Roby, review of *Approaches to Teaching Eliot's Poetry and Plays,* p. 531.

Times Literary Supplement, February 24, 1995, Roger Kojecký, review of *Mastery and Escape,* p. 24.
University Bookman, winter, 1996, p. 21.
Virginia Quarterly Review, winter, 1991, review of *Reading "The Waste Land,"* p. 13.
Yeats-Eliot Review, summer, 1991, Lois A. Cuddy, review of *Reading "The Wasteland,"* pp. 25-26; winter, 1997, Scott R. Christianson, review of *Mastery and Escape,* pp. 34-40.

*   *   *

BULLINS, Ed 1935-
(Kingsley B. Bass, Jr.)

PERSONAL: Born July 2, 1935, in Philadelphia, PA; son of Edward and Bertha Marie (Queen) Bullins; married; wife's name Trixie. *Education:* Attended Los Angeles City College, San Francisco State College (now University), New York School of Visual Arts, New School Extension, Vista College, and University of California Berkeley Extension; William Penn Business Institute, general business certificate; Antioch University, B.A., 1989; Sonoma State University, B.A. candidate; San Francisco State University, M.F.A., 1994.

ADDRESSES: Home—3629 San Pablo Ave., Emeryville, CA 94608. *Agent*—Helen Merrill, 435 West 23rd St., No. 1A, New York, NY 10011.

CAREER: Black Arts/West, San Francisco, CA, cofounder and producer, 1965-67; Black Arts Alliance, cofounder, Black House (Black Panther Party headquarters in San Francisco), cultural director until 1967, also serving briefly as Minister of Culture of the Party. New Lafayette Theatre, New York, NY, joined, 1967, playwright-in-residence, 1968, associate director, 1971-73; American Place Theatre, playwright in residence, beginning 1973; The Surviving Theatre, producing director, beginning 1974; New York Shakespeare Festival, writers unit coordinator, 1975-82; Berkeley Black Repertory, public relations director, 1982; Magic Theatre, public relations director, 1982-83; Julian Theatre, group sales coordinator, 1983. Instructor in playwriting and black theater at various colleges, universities, and workshops, 1971-79; School for Continuing Education, New York University, instructor, 1979; Dramatic Writing Department, New

Ed Bullins

York University, instructor, 1981; Summer Playwrights Conference, Hofstra University, New York, instructor, 1982; People's School of Dramatic Arts, San Francisco, playwriting teacher, 1983; Bay Area Playwrights Festival, Mill Valley, CA, summer drama workshop leader, 1983; City College of San Francisco, instructor in dramatic performance, play directing, and playwriting, 1984-88; Antioch University, instructor in playwriting and administrative assistant in public information and recruitment, 1986-87; Bullins Memorial Theatre, Emeryville, CA, producer and playwright, 1988; Antioch University, San Francisco, student instructor in playwriting, 1986-87; American Multicultural Studies Department, Sonoma State University, Rohnert Park, CA, lecturer, 1988—; Afro-American Studies Department, University of California—Berkeley, lecturer, 1988—; African American Humanities/Afro-American Theatre, Contra Costa College, instructor, 1989-94; Northeastern University, Boston, MA, professor of theater, 1995—. *Military service:* Served in the U.S. Navy, 1952-55.

MEMBER: Dramatists Guild.

AWARDS, HONORS: American Place Theatre grant, 1967; Vernon Rice Drama Desk Award, 1968, for plays performed at American Place Theatre; four Rockefeller Foundation grants, including 1968, 1970, and 1973; Off-Broadway Award for distinguished playwriting, *Village Voice,* and Black Arts Alliance award, both 1971, both for *The Fabulous Miss Marie* and *In New England Winter;* Guggenheim fellowship for playwriting, 1971 and 1976; National Endowment for the Arts playwriting grant, 1972, 1989; grant from Creative Artists Public Service Program, 1973, in support of playwriting; Off-Broadway Award for distinguished playwriting, and New York Drama Critics Circle Award, both 1975, both for *The Taking of Miss Janie;* third Off-Broadway Award; AUDELCO award, Harlem Theater; Litt.D., Columbia College (Chicago, IL), 1976.

WRITINGS:

PUBLISHED PLAYS

How Do You Do?: A Nonsense Drama (one-act; first produced as *How Do You Do* in San Francisco, CA, at Firehouse Repertory Theatre, August 5, 1965; produced off-Broadway at La Mama Experimental Theatre Club, February, 1972), Illuminations Press, 1967.

(Editor and contributor) *New Plays from the Black Theatre* (includes *In New England Winter* [one-act; first produced off-Broadway at New Federal Theatre of Henry Street Playhouse, January 26, 1971]), Bantam (New York, NY), 1969.

Five Plays (includes: *Goin 'a Buffalo* [three-act; first produced in New York, NY, at American Place Theatre, June 6, 1968], *In the Wine Time* [three-act; first produced at New Lafayette Theatre, December 10, 1968], *A Son, Come Home* [one-act; first produced off-Broadway at American Place Theatre, February 21, 1968; originally published in *Negro Digest,* April, 1968], *The Electronic Nigger* [one-act; first produced at American Place Theatre, February 21, 1968], and *Clara's Ole Man* [one-act; first produced in San Francisco, CA, August 5, 1965; produced at American Place Theatre, February 21, 1968]), Bobbs-Merrill (Chicago IL), 1969, published as *The Electronic Nigger, and Other Plays,* Faber (London, England), 1970.

Ya Gonna Let Me Take You out Tonight, Baby? (first produced off-Broadway at Public Theatre, May 17, 1972), published in *Black Arts,* Black Arts Publishing (Detroit, MI), 1969.

The Gentleman Caller (one-act; first produced in Brooklyn, NY, in *A Black Quartet,* Chelsea Theatre Center at Brooklyn Academy of Music, April 25, 1969), published in *A Black Quartet,* New American Library (New York, NY), 1970.

The Duplex: A Black Love Fable in Four Movements (one-act; first produced at New Lafayette Theatre, May 22, 1970; produced at Forum Theatre of Lincoln Center, New York, NY, March 9, 1972), Morrow (New York, NY), 1971.

The Theme Is Blackness: The Corner, and Other Plays (includes: *The Theme Is Blackness* [first produced in San Francisco, CA, by San Francisco State College, 1966], *The Corner* [one-act; first produced in Boston, MA, by Theatre Company of Boston, 1968, produced off-Broadway at Public Theatre, June 22, 1972], *Dialect Determinism* [one-act; first produced in San Francisco, CA, August 5, 1965; produced at La Mama Experimental Theatre Club, February 25, 1972], *It Has No Choice* [one-act; first produced in San Francisco, CA, by Black Arts/West, spring, 1966, produced at La Mama Experimental Theatre Club, February 25, 1972], *The Helper* [first produced in New York, NY, by New Dramatists Workshop, June 1, 1970], *A Minor Scene* [first produced in San Francisco, CA, by Black Arts/West, spring, 1966; produced at La Mama Experimental Theatre Club, February 25, 1972], *The Man Who Dug Fish* [first produced by Theatre Company of Boston, June 1, 1970], *Black Commercial No. 2, The American Flag Ritual, State Office Bldg. Curse, One Minute Commercial, A Street Play, Street Sounds* [first produced at La Mama Experimental Theatre Club, October 14, 1970], *A Short Play for a Small Theatre,* and *The Play of the Play*), Morrow (New York, NY), 1972.

Four Dynamite Plays (includes: *It Bees Dat Way* [one-act; first produced in London, England, September 21, 1970; produced in New York, NY, at ICA, October, 1970], *Death List* [one-act; first produced in New York, NY, by Theatre Black at University of the Streets, October 3, 1970], *The Pig Pen* [one-act; first produced at American Place Theatre, May 20, 1970], and *Night of the Beast* [screenplay]), Morrow (New York, NY), 1972.

(Editor and contributor) *The New Lafayette Theatre Presents; Plays with Aesthetic Comments by Six Black Playwrights: Ed Bullins, J. E. Gaines, Clay Gross, Oyamo, Sonia Sanchez, Richard Wesley,* Anchor Press (Garden City, NY), 1974.

The Taking of Miss Janie (first produced in New York at New Federal Theatre, May 4, 1975), published in *Famous American Plays of the 1970s,* edited by Ted Hoffman, Dell (New York, NY), 1981.

New/Lost Plays: An Anthology, That New Publishing Co. (Honolulu, HI), 1993.

Also author of "Malcolm: '71 or Publishing Blackness," published in *Black Scholar,* June, 1975. Plays represented in anthologies, including *New American Plays,* Volume III, edited by William M. Hoffman, Hill & Wang (New York, NY), 1970.

UNPUBLISHED PLAYS

(With Shirley Tarbell) *The Game of Adam and Eve,* first produced in Los Angeles, CA, at Playwrights' Theatre, spring, 1966.

(Under pseudonym Kingsley B. Bass, Jr.) *We Righteous Bombers* (adapted from Albert Camus's *The Just Assassins*), first produced in New York, NY, at New Lafayette Theatre, April, 1969.

A Ritual to Raise the Dead and Foretell the Future, first produced in New York, NY, at New Lafayette Theatre, 1970.

The Devil Catchers, first produced at New Lafayette Theatre, November 27, 1970.

The Fabulous Miss Marie, first produced at New Lafayette Theatre, March 5, 1971; produced at Mitzi E. Newhouse Theatre of Lincoln Center, May, 1979.

Next Time . . . , first produced in Bronx, NY, at Bronx Community College, May 8, 1972.

The Psychic Pretenders (A Black Magic Show), first produced at New Lafayette Theatre, December, 1972.

House Party, a Soul Happening, first produced at American Place Theatre, fall, 1973.

The Mystery of Phyllis Wheatley, first produced at New Federal Theatre, February 4, 1976.

I Am Lucy Terry, first produced at American Place Theatre, February 11, 1976.

Home Boy, first produced in New York, NY, at Perry Street Theatre, September 26, 1976.

JoAnne!, first produced in New York, NY, at Theatre of the Riverside Church, October 7, 1976.

Storyville, first produced in La Jolla, CA, at the Mandeville Theatre, University of California, May, 1977.

DADDY!, first produced at the New Federal Theatre, June 9, 1977.

Sepia Star, first produced in New York, NY, at Stage 73, August 20, 1977.

Michael, first produced in New York, NY, at New Heritage Repertory Theatre, May, 1978.

C'mon Back to Heavenly House, first produced in Amherst, MA, at Amherst College Theatre, 1978.

Leavings, first produced in New York, NY, at Syncopation, August, 1980.

Steve and Velma, first produced in Boston, MA, by New African Company, August, 1980.

Boy x Man, first produced at the Samuel Beckett Theater, June, 1997.

Also author of the plays *Blacklist* and *City Preacher.*

OTHER

The Hungered One: Early Writings (collected short fiction), Morrow (New York, NY), 1971.

The Reluctant Rapist (novel), Harper (New York, NY), 1973.

Also author of article "The Polished Protest: Aesthetics and the Black Writer," published in *Contact,* 1963. Editor of *Black Theatre,* 1968-73; editor of special black issue of *Drama Review,* summer, 1968. Contributor to *Negro Digest, New York Times,* and other periodicals.

SIDELIGHTS: Ed Bullins is one of the most powerful black voices in contemporary American theater. He began writing plays as a political activist in the mid-1960s and soon emerged as a principal figure in the black arts movement that surfaced in that decade. First as Minister of Culture for California's Black Panther Party and then as associate director of Harlem's New Lafayette Theatre, Bullins helped shape a revolutionary "theater of black experience" that took drama to the streets. In more than fifty dramatic works, written expressly for and about blacks, Bullins probed the disillusionment and frustration of ghetto life. At the height of his militancy, he advocated cultural separatism between races and outspokenly dismissed white aesthetic standards. Asked by *Race Relations Reporter* contributor Bernard Garnett how he felt about white critics' evaluations of his work, Bullins replied: "It doesn't matter whether they appreciate it. It's not for them." Despite his disinterest, by the late 1960s establishment critics were tracking his work, more

often than not praising its lyricism and depth and commending the playwright's ability to transcend narrow politics. As C. W. E. Bigsby pointed out in *The Second Black Renaissance: Essays in Black Literature,* Bullins "was one of the few black writers of the 1960s who kept a cautious distance from a black drama which defined itself solely in political terms." In the 1970s Bullins won three Off-Broadway Awards for distinguished playwriting, a Drama Critics Circle Award, and several prestigious Guggenheim and Rockefeller playwriting grants.

Bullins's acceptance into the theatrical mainstream, which accelerated as the black arts movement lost momentum, presents some difficulty for critics trying to assess the current state of his art. The prolific output of his early years has been replaced by a curious silence. One possible explanation, according to *Black American Literature Forum* contributor Richard G. Scharine, is that Bullins has faced the same artistic dilemma that confronts Steve Benson, his most autobiographical protagonist: "As an artist he requires recognition. As a revolutionary he dare not be accepted. But Bullins has been accepted. . . . The real question is whether, severed from his roots and his hate, Bullins can continue to create effectively." In a written response published with the article, Bullins answered the charge: "I was a conscious artist before I was a conscious artist-revolutionary, which has been my salvation and disguise. . . . I do not feel that I am severed from my roots."

Bullins's desire to express the reality of ordinary black experience reflects the philosophy he developed during his six-year association with the New Lafayette Theatre, a community-based playhouse that was a showpiece of the black arts movement until it closed for lack of funds in 1973. During its halcyon days, the New Lafayette provided a sanctuary wherein the black identity could be assuaged and nurtured, a crucial goal of Bullins and all the members of that theatrical family. "Our job," former New Lafayette director Robert Macbeth told Jervis Anderson in a *New Yorker* interview, "has always been to show black people who they are, where they are, and what condition they are in. . . . Our function, the healing function of theatre and art, is absolutely vital."

Bullins was born and raised in a North Philadelphia ghetto, but was given a middle-class orientation by his mother, a civil servant. He attended a largely white elementary school, where he was an excellent student, and spent his summers vacationing in Maryland farming country. As a junior high student, he was transferred to an inner-city school and joined a gang, the Jet Cobras. During a street fight, he was stabbed in the heart and momentarily lost his life (as does his fictional alter-ego Steve Benson in *The Reluctant Rapist*). The experience, as Bullins explained to *New York Times* contributor Charles M. Young, changed his attitude: "See, when I was young, I was stabbed in a fight. I died. My heart stopped. But I was brought back for a reason. I was gifted with these abilities and I was sent into the world to do what I do because that is the only thing I can do. I write."

Bullins did not immediately recognize his vocation, but spent several years at various jobs. After dropping out of high school, he served in the U.S. Navy from 1952-55, where he won a shipboard lightweight boxing championship and started a program of self-education through reading. Not much is known about the years he spent in North Philadelphia after his discharge, but in a *Dictionary of Literary Biography* essay, Leslie C. Sanders noted "his 1958 departure for Los Angeles quite literally saved his life. When he left Philadelphia, he left behind an unsuccessful marriage and several children." In California, Bullins earned a GED high school equivalency degree and started writing. He turned to plays when he realized that the black audience he was trying to reach did not read much fiction and also that he was naturally suited to the dramatic form. But even after moving to San Francisco in 1964, Bullins found little encouragement for his talent. "Nobody would produce my work," he recalled of his early days in the *New Yorker*. "Some people said my language was too obscene, and others said the stuff I was writing was not theatre in the traditional sense." Bullins might have been discouraged had he not chanced upon a production of two plays by LeRoi Jones, *Dutchman* and *The Slave*, that reminded him of his own. "I could see that an experienced playwright like Jones was dealing with the same qualities and conditions of black life that moved me," Bullins explained.

Inspired by Jones's example, Bullins and a group of black revolutionaries joined forces to create a militant cultural-political organization called Black House. Among those participating were Huey Newton and Bobby Seale, two young radicals whose politics of revolution would soon coalesce into the Black Panther Party.

Between 1967 and 1973, Bullins created and/or produced almost a dozen plays, some of which are still considered his finest work. He also edited the theater magazine, *Black Theatre,* and compiled and edited an anthology of six New Lafayette plays. During this time, Bullins was active as a playwriting teacher and director as well. Despite Bullins's close ties to the New Lafayette, his plays were also produced off-Broadway and at other community theaters, notably the American Place Theatre, where he became playwright in residence after the New Lafayette's demise.

Bullins's plays of this period share common themes. *Clara's Ole Man,* an early drama that established the playwright's reputation in New York during its 1968 production, introduces his concerns. Set in the mid-fifties, it tells the story of twenty-year-old Jack, an upwardly mobile black who goes to the ghetto to visit Clara one afternoon when her "ole man" is at work. Not realizing that Clara's lover is actually Big Girl, a lesbian bully who is home when Jack calls, he gets brutally beaten as a result of his ignorance. Sanders believes that "in *Clara's Ole Man,* Bullins's greatest work is foreshadowed. Its characters, like those in many of his later plays, emerge from brutal life experiences with tenacity and grace. While their language is often crude, it eloquently expresses their pain and anger, as well as the humor that sustains them."

By and large, Bullins's plays fared well artistically during the early 1970s while being criticized, by both black and white critics, for their ideology. Some blacks objected to what Bigsby called the "reductive view of human nature" presented in these dramas, along with "their sense of the black ghetto as lacking in any redeeming sense of community or moral values." Other blacks, particularly those who achieved a measure of material success, resented their exclusion from this art form. "I am a young black from a middle-class family and well-educated," wrote one person in the *New York Times Magazine* in response to a black arts article. "What sense of self will I ever have if I continue to go to the theatre and movies and never see blacks such as myself in performance?" For the white theater-going community, Bullins's exclusively black drama also raised questions of a cultural elitism that seems "to reserve for black art an exclusive and, in some senses, a sacrosanct critical territory," Anderson believed.

In the 1990s Ed Bullins's presence was once again felt in the theater world. His anthology *New/Lost Plays* made available a number of works from the past decades. In 1997 a new play *Boy x Man*—pronounced "boy times man"—was presented by the Negro Ensemble Company at New York's Samuel Beckett Theater. The play concerns family, class, and memory. Though sometimes difficult to perform, its dialogue, in the words of *New York Times* theater reviewer Anita Gates, contains Bullins's brand of "down-home poetry."

Early in his career Bullins distanced himself from the critical fray, saying that if he had listened to what critics have told him, he would have stopped writing long ago. "I don't bother too much what anyone thinks," he told Anderson. "When I sit down in that room by myself, bringing in all that I ever saw, smelled, learned, or checked out, I am the chief determiner of the quality of my work. The only critic that I really trust is me."

In a career that has spanned four decades, Bullins has written more than ninety plays in all. He has also started theatre companies and been a founding member of several writing workshops. When *Black Masks* contributor Pamela Faith Jackson asked him in 1997 what the driving force behind his career has been, Bullins replied, "I did it all to keep from being bored I guess. I mean a lot of things needed to be done."

BIOGRAPHICAL AND CRITICAL SOURCES:

BOOKS

Bigsby, C. W. E., *The Second Black Renaissance: Essays in Black Literature,* Greenwood Press (Westport, CT), 1980.
Black Literature Criticism, Gale (Detroit, MI), 1992.
Contemporary Authors Autobiography Series, Volume 16, Gale (Detroit, MI), 1992.
Contemporary Literary Criticism, Gale (Detroit, MI), Volume 1, 1973, Volume 5, 1976, Volume 7, 1977.
Dictionary of Literary Biography, Gale (Detroit, MI), Volume 7: *Twentieth-Century American Dramatists,* 1981, Volume 38: *Afro-American Writers after 1955—Dramatists and Prose Writers,* 1985.
Gayle, Addison, editor, *The Black Aesthetic,* Doubleday (New York, NY), 1971.
Hay, Samuel A., *Ed Bullins: A Literary Biography,* Wayne State University Press (Detroit, MI), 1997.

Sanders, Leslie C., *The Development of Black Theater in America: From Shadows to Selves,* Louisiana State University Press (Baton Rouge, LA), 1988.

PERIODICALS

Black American Literature Forum, fall, 1979.
Black Creation, winter, 1973.
Black Mask, September 30, 1997, Pamela Faith Jackson, "Ed Bullins: From Minister of Culture to Living Legend," p. 5.
Black World, April, 1974.
CLA Journal, June, 1976.
Dance, April, 1992, p. 86.
Nation, November 12, 1973; April 5, 1975.
Negro Digest, April, 1969.
Newsweek, May 20, 1968.
New Yorker, June 16, 1973, Jervis Anderson, author interview.
New York Times, September 22, 1971; May 18, 1975; June 17, 1977; May 31, 1979; June 3, 1997, Anita Gates, review of *Boy x Man,* p. C16.
New York Times Book Review, June 20, 1971; September 30, 1973.
New York Times Magazine, September 10, 1972.
Plays and Players, May, 1972; March, 1973.
Race Relations Reporter, February 7, 1972.

ONLINE

Ed Bullins Home Page, http://www.edbullins.com/ (August 10, 2004).*

* * *

BUTTERWORTH, Nick 1946-

PERSONAL: Born 1946, in Kingsbury, North London, England; married, 1975; wife's name Annette; children: Ben, Amanda. *Hobbies and other interests:* Skiing, watching television, visiting bookshops.

ADDRESSES: Home—Suffolk, England. *Agent*—c/o Author Mail, HarperCollins Publishers, 77-85 Fulham Palace Rd., Hammersmith, London W6 8JB, England.

CAREER: Author and illustrator of children's books. Graphics and typographic designer; TV AM (England), presenter for "Rub-a-Dub-Tub" children's program.

AWARDS, HONORS: Runner-up, British Book Awards for Illustration, 1992, for *After the Storm.*

WRITINGS:

SELF-ILLUSTRATED

B. B. Blacksheep and Company: A Collection of Favourite Nursery Rhymes, Macdonald (London, England), 1981, published as *B. B. Blacksheep and Company: A Collection of Favorite Nursery Rhymes,* Grosset & Dunlap (New York, NY), 1982.

Julie the Paper Girl and Her Friends (also see below), Walker Books (London, England), 1986.

Tom the Greengrocer and His Friends (also see below), Walker Books (London, England), 1986.

Jack the Carpenter and His Friends (also see below), Walker Books (London, England), 1986.

Jill the Farmer and Her Friends (also see below), Walker Books (London, England), 1986.

My Mum Is Fantastic, Walker Books (London, England), 1989, published as *My Mom Is Excellent,* Candlewick Press (Cambridge, MA), 1994.

My Dad Is Brilliant, Walker Books (London, England), 1989, published as *My Dad Is Awesome,* Candlewick Press (Cambridge, MA), 1992.

(Editor) *Nick Butterworth's Book of Nursery Rhymes,* Aurum (London, England), 1990, Viking (New York, NY), 1991, published as *The Puffin Book of Nursery Rhymes,* Puffin (New York, NY), 1995.

Amanda's Butterfly, Delacorte (New York, NY), 1991.

My Grandma Is Wonderful, Candlewick Press (Cambridge, MA), 1991.

My Grandpa Is Amazing, Candlewick Press (Cambridge, MA), 1992.

Busy People (contains *Julie the Paper Girl and Her Friends, Tom the Greengrocer and His Friends, Jack the Carpenter and His Friends,* and *Jill the Farmer and Her Friends*), Candlewick Press (Cambridge, MA), 1992.

Making Faces, Candlewick Press (Cambridge, MA), 1993.

When It's Time for Bed, Little, Brown (Boston, MA), 1994.

When There's Work to Do, Little, Brown (Boston, MA), 1994.

When We Go Shopping, Little, Brown (Boston, MA), 1994.

When We Play Together, Little, Brown (Boston, MA), 1994.

All Together Now!, Little, Brown (Boston, MA), 1995.

Thud!, Collins (London, England), 1997.

1-2-3—London, Collins (London, England), 1998.

A-B-C—London, Collins (London, England), 1998.

Jingle Bells, Orchard Books (New York, NY), 1998.

Q Pootle 5, Collins (London, England), 2000, Atheneum (New York, NY), 2001.

Albert Le Blanc, Collins (London, England), 2002, published as *Albert the Bear,* HarperCollins (New York, NY), 2002.

"UPNEY JUNCTION" SERIES; SELF-ILLUSTRATED

Treasure Trove at Upney Junction, Macdonald (London, England), 1983.

A Windy Day at Upney Junction, Macdonald (London, England), 1983.

Invasion at Upney Junction, Macdonald (London, England), 1983.

A Monster at Upney Junction, Macdonald (London, England), 1983.

"PERCY THE PARK KEEPER" SERIES; SELF-ILLUSTRATED

One Snowy Night, Collins (London, England), 1989, Little, Brown (Boston, MA), 1990.

After the Storm, Collins (London, England), 1992, published in the United States as *One Blowy Night,* Little, Brown (Boston, MA), 1992.

The Rescue Party, Little, Brown (Boston, MA), 1993.

The Secret Path, Little, Brown (Boston, MA), 1994.

A Year in Percy's Park (contains *One Snowy Night, The Secret Path, The Rescue Party,* and *After the Storm*), Collins (London, England), 1995.

The Cross Rabbit, Collins (London, England), 1995.

Percy the Park Keeper Press-Out Book (contains *The Fox's Hiccups* and *The Hedgehog's Balloon*), Collins (London, England), 1995.

The Fox's Hiccups, Collins (London, England), 1995.

The Treasure Hunt, Collins (London, England), 1996.

The Hedgehog's Balloon, Collins (London, England), 1996.

The Badger's Bath, Collins (London, England), 1996.

Tales from Percy's Park (contains *The Cross Rabbit, The Fox's Hiccups, The Hedgehog's Balloon,* and *The Badger's Bath*), Collins (London, England), 1996.

Percy the Park Keeper Activity Book, Collins (London, England), 1996.

Percy Helps Out: Sticker Book, Collins (London, England), 1996.

The Owl's Flying Lesson, Collins (London, England), 1997.

A Year with Percy Coloring Book, Collins (London, England), 1997.

Percy the Park Keeper Sticker and Story Book, Collins (London, England), 1997.

One Warm Fox, Collins (London, England), 1997.

Four Feathers in Percy's Park, Collins (London, England), 1998.

Percy the Park Keeper A-B-C, Collins (London, England), 1998.

Percy the Park Keeper 1-2-3, Collins (London, England), 1998.

Percy's Bumpy Ride, Collins (London, England), 2000.

Owl Takes Charge, Collins (London, England), 2000.

Other works by Butterworth in the "Percy" series include *Percy in the Park Game Book* and *Percy in the Park Coloring Book,* both published by Collins (London, England).

"PERCY THE PARK KEEPER AND HIS FRIENDS" SERIES; SELF-ILLUSTRATED

Everyone's Friend Percy, Collins (London, England), 2001.

Percy's Friend the Owl, Collins (London, England), 2001.

Percy's Friend the Hedgehog, Collins (London, England), 2001.

Percy's Friend the Fox, Collins (London, England), 2001.

Percy's Friends the Mice, Collins (London, England), 2001.

Percy's Friends the Rabbits, Collins (London, England), 2002.

Percy's Friends the Ducks, Collins (London, England), 2002.

Percy's Friend the Mole, Collins (London, England), 2002.

Percy's Friends the Squirrels, Collins (London, England), 2002.

Percy's Friend the Badger, Collins (London, England), 2002.

AUTHOR AND ILLUSTRATOR; WITH MICK INKPEN

The Nativity Play, Little, Brown (Boston, MA), 1985.

The House on the Rock (also see below), Multnomah Press (Portland, Oregon), 1986.

The Precious Pearl (also see below), Multnomah Press (Portland, Oregon), 1986.

The Lost Sheep (also see below), Multnomah Press (Portland, Oregon), 1986.

The Two Sons (also see below), Multnomah Press (Portland, Oregon), 1986.

Nice and Nasty: A Book of Opposites, Hodder & Stoughton (London, England), published as *Nice or Nasty: A Book of Opposites,* Little, Brown (Boston, MA), 1987.

I Wonder at the Zoo, Zondervan (Grand Rapids, MI), 1987.

I Wonder in the Garden, Zondervan (Grand Rapids, MI), 1987.

I Wonder in the Country, Zondervan (Grand Rapids, MI), 1987.

I Wonder at the Farm, Marshall Pickering (Basingstoke, England), published as *I Wonder on the Farm,* Zondervan (Grand Rapids, MI), 1987.

Who Made . . . In the Country, HarperCollins (London, England), 1987.

Who Made . . . On the Farm, HarperCollins (London, England), 1987.

Who Made . . . At the Zoo, Marshall Pickering (Basingstoke, England), 1987.

Who Made . . . In the Garden, Marshall Pickering (Basingstoke, England), 1987.

Sports Day, Hodder & Stoughton (London, England), 1988.

The Magpie's Story: Jesus and Zacchaeus (also see below), Marshall Pickering (Basingstoke, England), 1988.

The Mouse's Story: Jesus and the Storm (also see below), Marshall Pickering (Basingstoke, England), 1988.

The Cat's Tale: Jesus at the Wedding (also see below), Marshall Pickering (Basingstoke, England), 1988.

The Fox's Tale: Jesus Is Born (also see below), Marshall Pickering (Basingstoke, England), 1988.

Just Like Jasper!, Little, Brown (Boston, MA), 1989.

The Little Gate (also see below), Marshall Pickering (Basingstoke, England), 1989.

The Rich Farmer (also see below), Marshall Pickering (Basingstoke, England), 1989.

The Ten Silver Coins (also see below), Marshall Pickering (Basingstoke, England), 1989.

The Good Stranger (also see below), Marshall Pickering (Basingstoke, England), 1989.

The School Trip, Delacorte (New York, NY), 1990.

Wonderful Earth!, Hunt & Thorpe (Alton, England), 1990.

Field Day, Delacorte (New York, NY), 1991.

Jasper's Beanstalk, Hodder & Stoughton (London, England), 1992, Bradbury Press (New York, NY), 1993.

Stories Jesus Told (contains *The House on the Rock, The Lost Sheep, The Precious Pearl, The Two Sons, The Ten Silver Coins, The Rich Farmer, The Little Gate,* and *The Good Stranger*), Gold 'n' Honey (Sister, OR), 1996.

Opposites, Hodder Children's Books (London, England), 1997.

Animal Tales (includes *The Fox's Tale, The Cat's Tale, The Mouse's Story,* and *The Magpie's Tale*), Marshall Pickering (Basingstoke, England), 1999.

ILLUSTRATOR; WITH MICK INKPEN; ALL WRITTEN BY ELIZABETH LAWRENCE IN CONSULTATION WITH NOREEN WETTON

Can You Do This?, Nelson (Walton-on-Thames, England), 1986.

Come Up and Play, Nelson (Walton-on-Thames, England), 1986.

Do You Like My Hat?, Nelson (Walton-on-Thames, England), 1986.

Do You Like My House?, Nelson (Walton-on-Thames, England), 1986.

I Am Going to Hide, Nelson (Walton-on-Thames, England), 1986.

It Is Too Big, Nelson (Walton-on-Thames, England), 1986.

Look What I Can Do, Nelson (Walton-on-Thames, England), 1986.

May I Come In?, Nelson (Walton-on-Thames, England), 1986.

May I Play with You?, Nelson (Walton-on-Thames, England), 1986.

Where Is the Monster?, Nelson (Walton-on-Thames, England), 1986.

Where Is the Mouse?, Nelson (Walton-on-Thames, England), 1986.

I Like Sausages, Nelson (Walton-on-Thames, England), 1986.

Mrs. Rabbit Gets Locked Out, Nelson (Walton-on-Thames, England), 1987.

Lolli and Pop in Trouble, Nelson (Walton-on-Thames, England), 1987.

ILLUSTRATOR; WRITTEN BY WIFE, ANNETTE BUTTERWORTH

Jake, Hodder & Stoughton (London, England), 1995.

Jake Again, Hodder Children's Books (London, England), 1996.

Jake in Trouble, Hodder Children's Books (London, England), 1997.

The Jake Collection (including *Jake Again* and *Jake in Trouble*), Hodder Children's Books (London, England), 1998.

Jake in Danger, Hodder Children's Books (London, England), 1999.

OTHER

(Illustrator, with Mick Inkpen) Malcolm and Meryl Doney, *Who Made Me?,* Marshall Pickering (Basingstoke, England), 1987, Zondervan (Grand Rapids, MI), 1992.

Also contributed illustrations to a series of Christian instructional booklets for children.

ADAPTATIONS: The "Percy the Park Keeper" series has been adapted as a cartoon for British television and several of the "Percy" books have been recorded on audio cassette.

SIDELIGHTS: Nick Butterworth is a British author-illustrator of children's books best known for his "Percy the Park Keeper" picture books, a series which started in 1989 with *One Snowy Night.* Published in fifteen languages, the series has sold more than two millions copies worldwide. Butterworth also worked in collaboration with the author-illustrator Mick Inkpen for many years, and together they created the popular "Mice of Upney Junction" cartoon strip, as well as the picture books *Just Like Jasper!* and *Jasper's Beanstalk.*

Born in a London suburb in 1946, Butterworth and his family moved to Romford, in the English county of Essex, when the author was three. There his parents took up the running of a sweet shop. From his father—who appeared in amateur reviews as a comedian before World War II—Butterworth inherited a sly sense of humor and an eye for comic situations. In Romford schools, he was something of a passive student, but by the time he reached the Royal Liberty School, Butterworth fared much better academically. Sketching was one of his early passions. He and his brother would fill notebooks with comic-book style drawings; but whereas his brother later went into theology, Butterworth stuck with art. He intended to go to art school, but when his mother heard of a paid apprenticeship in the design department of a printing school, he was talked into that course instead of the study of studio art.

"I don't regret the way my life's gone," Butterworth told Stephanie Nettell in a *Books for Keeps* interview. "But I wish I'd worked harder. I would have liked to have been to art school, though they did send me one day a week to the printing department at Watford College." From an instructor at Watford Butterworth learned of a London design firm looking for new talent. Joining the firm, Butterworth got his first taste of professional design. After some success freelancing, Butterworth decided to start his own design studio. In 1969, along with two colleagues, he set up a design consultancy studio in Romford, working on "a lot of catalogue and packaging work," according to Butterworth. In 1970, his young friend Mick Inkpen joined the firm in his pre-Cambridge year off, and stayed on.

Butterworth's first book was the result of desultory doodling: he developed illustrations for four nursery rhymes which at the time he thought might make good greeting cards. When others saw these illustrations, they convinced Butterworth to make a book of the nursery rhymes and thus was born *B. B. Blacksheep and Company: A Collection of Favourite Nursery Rhymes,* a book which a reviewer for *Growing Point* called a "refreshingly bizarre look at familiar jingles." Butterworth turned many of these nursery rhymes on their heads, looking at them from fresh and often humorous perspectives. Jack and Jill in this rendering are toothy rabbits, the mouse comes down the clock on a parachute, and Humpty Dumpty is a chocolate Easter egg. Brian Alderson, reviewing the book in the *Times Educational Supplement,* noted that Butterworth's collection of favorite nursery rhymes "are stylish and often unexpected."

Publication of this picture book brought an offer from the *Sunday Express* newspaper for a comic strip, and Butterworth and Inkpen subsequently developed the cheeky mice living in the deserted railway station at Upney Junction. The Butterworth-Inkpen collaboration

extended to television, as well, with the two hosting a children's show for eighteen months. "I learned a lot from [Inkpen's] colouring," Butterworth told Nettell in his interview. "My work has always been line-oriented and it used to be more laboured . . . until I realised that reproducing reality isn't necessarily the best way of getting what you want across." Butterworth's draftsmanship rubbed off on Inkpen as much as Inkpen's spontaneity and appreciation for abstract line influenced Butterworth.

The Nativity Play, one of their earliest collaborations, was well received both in England and in the United States. A *Publishers Weekly* contributor commented that the duo "will delight readers of all ages," and went on to note that the "sweet, funny story is illustrated perfectly by brightly colored scenes of feverish activity." In the story, children and their parents at a local school prepare for the Christmas pageant, with all the attendant confusion, missed cues, and last-minute stage fright. A reviewer for *Growing Point* noted of the British publication that "colour, exuberance and mood come over with heart-rending force in a descriptive picture book which encapsulates this infinitely varied once-a-year amateur enterprise." Denise M. Wilms, reviewing *The Nativity Play* for *Booklist,* concluded that "this is a droll diversion that will please children, who will recognize themselves, and amuse their parents, who will find chuckles between the lines."

Butterworth and Inkpen also worked together on *Nice and Nasty: A Book of Opposites,* a volume that offers "immediate appeal," according to a critic for *Publishers Weekly* in a review of the American edition *Nice or Nasty: A Book of Opposites.* "Readers will find a memorable roller-coaster ride between up and down, first and last," continued this same reviewer. *Booklist* critic Ilene Cooper concluded that the "oversize illustrations are expertly executed, and the whole format has a clean, fresh look."

However, the most popular collaborative effort of the two has remained the "Jasper" books, *Just Like Jasper!* and *Jasper's Beanstalk.* "In another effort from this talented British team," noted a *Publishers Weekly* contributor in a review of the first title, "plump, likable Jasper the cat heads for the toy store with his birthday money." The problem once he gets there: what to buy? There are too many choices, but finally he decides on the purchase of a toy kitten, who is a ringer for himself. "Children will sympathize with Jasper's dilemma and appreciate his sound choice," concluded the reviewer. Janie Schomberg remarked in a *School Library Journal* review that the book was a "pleasant offering for toddler story hours," while a *Growing Point* critic concluded that "brilliant primary colours mark each scene and the book as a whole has a sense of excited movement to extend the simple joke of humanising a cat's thoughts but not its appearance."

The two illustrator-writers returned to Jasper in 1992 with *Jasper's Beanstalk,* in which the amiable cat tries unsuccessfully to grow a bean plant. He plants it and lovingly tends to it, but when it fails to sprout, he digs it up and throws it aside. Untended, however, the bean develops into a magnificent beanstalk. "Jasper is a delightful character," noted a reviewer for *Junior Bookshelf,* "and many young children are likely to enjoy this story of his attempt at gardening." Stephanie Zvirin, writing in *Booklist,* called this second Jasper title a "delightful, bubbly book, ideal for group sharing," while Moira Small described it in a *Books for Keeps* review as a "delightful picture book with a simple story to help very young children understand how things grow."

Though Butterworth teamed up with Inkpen for a few more titles, mostly the two have concentrated on their individual work. For Butterworth, that has been primarily the "Percy the Park Keeper" books, a series still growing in number. Starting with *One Snowy Night,* the books highlight the trials and tribulations of a park keeper who looks remarkably like Butterworth himself. In this opening title, Percy finds his hospitality strained to the limit when one animal after the other comes to him seeking refuge from the snow. "The result—too many animals," commented Phyllis G. Sidorski in *School Library Journal.* The bedclothes become tangled, animals get lost in the shuffle. "The illustrations are lighthearted and the penultimate scene of the cluttered room is a wealth of eye-catching details," Sidorski added.

In *The Rescue Party,* Percy takes a day off and relaxes with his animal friends in the park. Things start out fine until a jumping game ends up with a rabbit tumbling down an abandoned well. Percy throws a rope down to rescue the frightened rabbit, who ties it to a log instead of herself. Not to worry; everything turns out happily in the end in this "cozy little story, distinguished by amiable illustrations," according to a

critic for *Kirkus Reviews.* Jan Shephard, writing in *School Library Journal,* concluded that the "bright watercolor illustrations depict the likable and humorous characters" and that the book is a "great read-aloud."

Further adventures of Percy include the aftermath of a storm, the park animals' housing problems, a fox with a serious case of the hiccups, and an angry bunny, among many others. In *The Secret Path,* Percy sets out to get the park maze in order, but his furry friends decide to play a joke on him at the same time, finding their way to the center of the maze to surprise him when finally he gets there. Everyone receives a surprise when he arrives, however, for Percy has trimmed the maze into decorative shapes. Beverley Mathias, writing in *School Librarian,* called the book "great fun for everyone, including those under nine," while Carolyn Phelan dubbed it "simple and beguiling" in a *Booklist* review. "Butterworth's deft line-and-watercolor-wash artwork reflects the general tone of the text," Phelan commented, noting also that the "loving characters and the mild adventure will please young children."

Badger gets filthy digging all day in *The Badger's Bath,* and Percy decides it is time for him to take a bath. But Badger has other ideas about hygiene, so by the time Percy sets the soapy bath out under a tree, Badger has taken off. Instead of wasting the bath water, Percy dons swimming trunks and takes a soak himself. A reviewer for *Junior Bookshelf* called the book a "charming story," remarking also that "Percy is such a realistically rotund and plain featured hero that the reader readily suspends disbelief." In *The Treasure Hunt,* Percy sets up a search for a treasure which he—without thinking—eats. Judith Sharman, writing in *Books for Keeps,* called this "another whimsical tale about Percy the Park Keeper and his friends." Trevor Dickenson commented in *School Librarian* that the illustrations in this book "are up to Nick Butterworth's usual very high standards—clear and quietly amusing."

Though best known for the "Percy" books, as Butterworth told Nettell, he has many ideas for new books and does not want to be simply pegged as Percy the Park Keeper's creator. "There's no next time—this is my go, and I must make the most of it." Indeed, Butterworth has dozens of other books to his credit, among them the popular *Nick Butterworth's Book of*

Nursery Rhymes, Amanda's Butterfly, and *When It's Time for Bed.* His 1995 *All Together Now!* is a popular lift-the-flap book. "The flaps in this chuckly game of hide-and-seek themselves form part of the pictures," explained Nettell in her interview with Butterworth. The premise of this activity book is that a little boy's six animal friends are hiding from him at the outset of a picnic, and he must find them. A *Kirkus Reviews* contributor remarked that "not only do children have the satisfaction of finding the animals, but they have words to shout as they search." Mary Ann Bursk, writing in *School Library Journal,* noted that "toddlers will enjoy this interactive book one-to-one, while beginning readers will delight in sharing it with younger siblings." A Butterworth title dealing with Christmas is his 1998 *Jingle Bells,* a story of Yuletide mice in a stable. "The simply told tale makes a good nonsectarian read-aloud," commented Anne Connor in *School Library Journal.* "Children will enjoy these plucky mice who work together to ensure a happier new year once their enemy is foiled," concluded Connor.

Q Pootle 5 features the alien after whom the book is named. This chubby green creature crash-lands on earth after the failure of one of his rocket boosters ("which look suspiciously like soup cans," commented a *Publishers Weekly* reviewer). Q Pootle 5 begs the earth creatures he meets for assistance, but the frog and birds that he sees cannot help. Then he encounters Henry the cat, who just happens to have a spare cat-food can/rocket booster. Now Q Pootle 5 can go to his party on the moon, and he invites all of his new earth-friends along. They accompany him in their own freshly constructed ships, made out of faucets and other household items. Despite its high-flying setting, the story "is simple, short, and down-to-earth enough for beginning readers," Piper L. Nyman wrote in *School Library Journal.*

First published in England as *Albert Le Blanc, Albert the Bear* is a "brief, clever cautionary take on the dangers of judging by appearances," explained a *Kirkus Reviews* contributor. The other toys in the toy store are alarmed when a sad-looking stuffed polar bear arrives. Together, a jack-in-the-box, a mouse, and Sally the dancing hippo decide to cheer him up, but their efforts at entertainment fail: the mouse forgets the punch line to his joke and the jack-in-the-box falls down when he tries to show off his jumping skills. But when Sally falls on him in the middle of her ballet, Albert the

Bear proves that he is not really sad at all. "This gentle reminder not to judge by appearances slips in unobtrusively, thanks to the buoyant text and illustrations" which include cameos of such famous children's book characters as Paddington Bear, Bob the Builder, and Raymond Brigg's Snowman, noted a *Publishers Weekly* contributor.

In discussing what he enjoys most about being a children's author and illustrator, Butterworth remarked to an interviewer from the *HarperCollins Children's Books Web site,* "I just like the kids. I like the honesty of children, their directness. . . . It's very endearing, and to go out and meet the children is one of the pleasures of what I do. I certainly wouldn't want to be locked up in my studio forever. I get out to schools, I get out to book festivals and do signing sessions in shops when I can. When I can but not as much as I'd like to. It's just very rewarding to see children actually enjoying what you produce in hope." Noting that it is not possible to "road-test a picture book," Butterworth admitted that "You just kind of hope that people are really going to like it and that your judgement . . . has proved to be right. It's nice to have it confirmed when you meet your public."

BIOGRAPHICAL AND CRITICAL SOURCES:

BOOKS

St. James Guide to Children's Writers, 5th edition, St. James Press (Detroit, MI), 1999.

PERIODICALS

Booklist, March 1, 1986, Denise M. Wilms, review of *The Nativity Play,* p. 1014; June 15, 1987, Ilene Cooper, review of *Nice or Nasty: A Book of Opposites,* p. 1598; June 15, 1993, Stephanie Zvirin, review of *Jasper's Beanstalk,* p. 920; April 15, 1995, Carolyn Phelan, review of *The Secret Path,* p. 1505.

Books for Keeps, July, 1991, p. 10; July, 1993, Moira Small, review of *Jasper's Beanstalk,* p. 10; May, 1995, Stephanie Nettell, "Authorgraph No. 32: Nick Butterworth," pp. 16-17; July, 1995, p. 7; March, 1997, Judith Sharman, review of *The Treasure Hunt,* p. 18; July, 1998, Roy Blatchford, review of *Thud!,* p. 21; July, 1999, Gwynneth Bailey, review of *The Hedgehog's Balloon* and *The Badger's Bath,* p. 20; November, 1999, Julia Eccleshare, review of *The School Trip,* p. 21; November, 1999, review of *The School Trip* and *Sports Day* (book and tape pack), p. 21.

Growing Point, November, 1981, review of *B. B. Blacksheep and Company: A Collection of Favourite Nursery Rhymes,* pp. 3980-3981; November, 1985, review of *The Nativity Play,* p. 4528; November, 1989, review of *Just Like Jasper,* p. 5249.

Horn Book, spring, 1999, Patricia Riley, review of *Jingle Bells,* p. 24.

Junior Bookshelf, February, 1990, p. 13; August, 1990, p. 166; December, 1990, p. 276; June, 1992, review of *Jasper's Beanstalk,* p. 100; February, 1994, p. 13; August, 1996, review of *The Badger's Bath,* pp. 140-141; December, 1996, p. 227.

Kirkus Reviews, October 1, 1993, review of *The Rescue Party,* p. 1270; September 1, 1995, review of *All Together Now!,* p. 1277; August 1, 2003, review of *Albert the Bear,* p. 1013.

Liverpool Echo (Liverpool, England), December 28, 2002, Janet Tanslet, review of *Albert Le Blanc,* p. 27.

Publishers Weekly, December 6, 1985, review of *The Nativity Play,* p. 75; June 12, 1987, review of *Nice or Nasty,* p. 83; September 8, 1989, review of *Just Like Jasper,* p. 66; April 17, 1995, p. 56; September 25, 1995, p. 55; April 27, 1998, p. 61; September 28, 1998, review of *Jingle Bells,* p. 56; June 18, 2001, review of *Q Pootle 5,* p. 80; March 3, 2003, review of *My Mom Is Excellent, My Grandma Is Wonderful, My Dad Is Awesome,* and *My Grandpa Is Amazing,* p. 78; September 22, 2003, review of *Albert the Bear,* pp. 102-103.

School Librarian, August, 1991, p. 99; February, 1995, Beverley Mathias, review of *The Secret Path,* p. 16; February, 1995, Beverly Mathias, review of *The Secret Path,* p. 16; February, 1997, Trevor Dickenson, review of *The Treasure Hunt,* p. 17; spring, 1998, Trevor Dickenson, review of *The Owl's Lesson* and *One Warm Fox,* p. 16.

School Library Journal, May, 1990, Janie Schomberg, review of *Just Like Jasper,* p. 81; December, 1990, Phyllis G. Sidorski, review of *One Snowy Night,* p. 70; March, 1991, p. 168; May, 1991, p. 76; December, 1991, p. 80; February, 1994, Jan Shephard, review of *The Rescue Party,* p. 78; July, 1995, p. 55; March, 1996, Mary Ann Bursk, review of *All Together Now!,* p. 167; October, 1998, Anne Connor, review of *Jingle Bells,* p. 40; July, 2001, Piper L. Nyman, review of *Q Pootle 5,* p. 73; January, 2004, Amy Lilien Harper, review of *Albert the Bear,* p. 88.

Teacher Librarian, November, 1998, Shirley Lewis, review of *Jingle Bells,* p. 48.

Times Educational Supplement, January 15, 1992, Brian Alderson, review of *B. B. Blacksheep and Company,* p. 33; November 7, 1997, p. 13; September 17, 1999, Ted Dewan, "New Perspective on Percy's Kingdom," p. 10.

ONLINE

HarperCollins Children's Books Web site, http://www.harpercollinschildrensbooks.co.uk/ (February 14, 2004), interview with Butterworth.

Midlothian Libraries, http://www.midlothian.gov.uk/ (November 11, 2003), "Author Biography: Nick Butterworth."

Tameside MBC Web site, http://www.tameside.gov.uk/ (November 11, 2003), "Nick Butterworth."*

C

CAMP, John (Roswell) 1944-
(John Sandford)

PERSONAL: Born February 23, 1944, in Cedar Rapids, IA; son of Roswell Sandford and Anne (Barron) Camp; married Susan Lee Jones, December 28, 1965; children: Roswell Anthony, Emily Sarah. *Education:* State University of Iowa, B.A., 1966, M.A., 1971. *Religion:* Roman Catholic. *Hobbies and other interests:* Painting, archaeology.

ADDRESSES: Home—Near St. Paul, MN. *Agent*—Esther Newberg, International Creative Management, 40 West 57th St., New York, NY 10019. *E-mail*—js@johnsandford.org.

CAREER: Miami Herald, Miami, FL, reporter, 1971-78; *St. Paul Pioneer Press,* St. Paul, MN, reporter and columnist, 1978-89; writer 1966—. *Military service:* U.S. Army, 1966-68; served in Korea.

AWARDS, HONORS: Pulitzer Prize nomination, 1980, for series of articles on Native Americans in *St. Paul Pioneer Press Dispatch;* Pulitzer Prize for Feature Writing, 1986, for series of articles on a farming family in *Pioneer Press Dispatch;* Distinguished Writing Award, American Society of Newspaper Editors, 1986.

WRITINGS:

The Eye and the Heart: The Watercolors of John Stuart Ingle (nonfiction), Rizzoli (New York, NY), 1988.

Plastic Surgery: The Kindest Cuts (nonfiction), Holt (New York, NY), 1989.
(As John Sandford) *The Night Crew* (novel), Putnam (New York, NY), 1997.

"JASON KIDD" NOVELS

The Fool's Run, Holt (New York, NY), 1989.
The Empress File, Holt (New York, NY), 1991.
(Under name John Sandford) *The Devil's Code,* Putnam (New York, NY), 2000.
(Under name John Sandford) *The Hanged Man's Song,* Putnam (New York, NY), 2003.

"LUCAS DAVENPORT" NOVELS; AS JOHN SANDFORD

Rules of Prey, Putnam (New York, NY), 1989.
Shadow Prey, Putnam (New York, NY), 1990.
Eyes of Prey, Putnam (New York, NY), 1991.
Silent Prey, Putnam (New York, NY), 1992.
Winter Prey, Putnam (New York, NY), 1993.
Night Prey, Putnam (New York, NY), 1994.
Mind Prey (also see below), Putnam (New York, NY), 1995.
Sudden Prey (also see below), Putnam (New York, NY), 1996.
Secret Prey (also see below), Putnam (New York, NY), 1998.
Certain Prey, Putnam (New York, NY), 1999.
Easy Prey, Putnam (New York, NY), 2000.
Three Complete Novels: Mind Prey, Sudden Prey, Secret Prey, Putnam (New York, NY), 2000.
Chosen Prey, Putnam (New York, NY), 2001.

Mortal Prey, Putnam (New York, NY), 2002.
Naked Prey, Putnam (New York, NY), 2004.
Hidden Prey, Putnam (New York, NY), 2004.

ADAPTATIONS: Rules of Prey was adapted for film by Adam Greenman and released as *Mind Prey,* Jaffe/Braunstein, Ltd., 1999.

WORK IN PROGRESS: More "Lucas Davenport" novels.

SIDELIGHTS: Pulitzer Prize-winning journalist John Camp is a versatile writer who has distinguished himself as an author of both nonfiction and mysteries. He is best known under the pseudonym John Sandford for his "Lucas Davenport" novels, a series of thrillers that all feature the word "Prey" in their titles, as well as for the "Jason Kidd" novels which feature a clever computer expert who operates on the fringe of cyberlaw. Throughout the 1990s and into the first decade of the twenty-first century, Camp—as Sandford—has published the "Lucas Davenport" novels at a rate of almost one per year. A *Publishers Weekly* contributor noted the "vast popularity" of the titles and credited it to the author's "clever plotting, sure pacing and fully rounded villains."

As far back as high school, Camp knew he had a talent for writing. After earning a bachelor's degree from the University of Iowa in 1966, he entered the United States Army, and it was there that he began to train as a journalist. Upon completion of his military service, he returned to the University of Iowa, where he earned a master's degree in journalism. He began his career as a newspaper reporter, eventually earning a Pulitzer Prize for a lengthy investigative series first published in the *St. Paul Pioneer Press* about the difficulties facing one farm family in Minnesota.

Camp's experiences as a reporter inform his earliest books, both fictional and nonfictional. He once told *Publishers Weekly* that "most of the hard information in my books comes from a series I did in a newspaper." That series, in fact, was based on a group of incarcerated murderers who had formed a computer corporation in prison. Camp has since said that the opportunity to interview nearly fifty intelligent men serving life sentences was central to his ability to develop villains for his thrillers.

Camp's first book, *The Eye and the Heart: Watercolors of John Stuart Ingle,* is a catalog of Ingle's works seen in a touring exhibition in the late 1980s. Included in the book, which features an essay by Camp, are more than forty color reproductions of the contemporary painter's meticulously realistic works. Camp's next nonfiction publication, *Plastic Surgery: The Kindest Cuts,* relates his insights about cosmetic and restorative surgery. Camp's observations derive from his time spent with surgeon Bruce Cunningham, who allowed Camp operating-room access. Critics found the book to be an engrossing and frank look at plastic surgery.

Camp began publishing fiction in 1989 with *The Fool's Run,* a suspense novel about an eccentric computer criminal hired to undermine a defense contractor. Kidd, the narrator and hero, is a painter, martial arts student, and occult dabbler who possesses considerable computer wizardry. He is hired to disable an aerospace company's information system. Accordingly, he wreaks havoc on the company's computer programs, but in so doing he also discovers the existence of a formidable foe. Critics praised Camp's first fictional effort, and several described *The Fool's Run* as fast-paced, suspenseful, and engaging. A second novel, *The Empress File,* finds Kidd embroiled in racial conflict. His employer, a black activist, engages him to sabotage a band of racist, corrupt officials in Mississippi. Kidd and his lover/accomplice LuEllen, a skilled burglar, soon manage to infiltrate the group and draw them into a scheme designed to result in their downfall. The officials, however, eventually discover that their operation risks exposure, and they retaliate with violence.

Both *The Fool's Run* and *The Empress File* were originally published by Henry Holt under the author's real name, John Camp. When Camp's agent sold the first "Lucas Davenport" novel, *Rules of Prey,* to Putnam, that publisher wanted to print it under a pseudonym. Putnam felt that the "Lucas Davenport" books would become best-sellers, and the company reportedly did not want Holt to cash in on the success by riding the *Prey* books' coattails. Camp cooperated, choosing his great-grandfather's name, Sandford, as a pseudonym. That name is so widely recognized now that Camp is even using it on sequels to *The Fool's Run* and *The Empress File.*

Rules of Prey, the first novel in the series, presents Lucas Davenport, a resourceful Minneapolis detective determined to apprehend a particularly vicious killer,

Maddog, who preys on young women. At the scene of each crime, Maddog leaves a note relating his rules for murder. "Never kill anyone you know," reads one message. "Never carry a weapon after it has been used," reads another. Determined to jar Maddog's sense of gamesmanship, Davenport engages the psychopath in a dangerous cat-and-mouse contest, one with potentially fatal repercussions. *Washington Post Book World* contributor Daniel Woodrell, in his assessment of *Rules of Prey,* deemed it "a big, suspenseful thriller."

In *Shadow Prey,* the next "Lucas Davenport" novel, the detective opposes a terrorist network operated by local Native Americans avenging themselves against their white oppressors. Davenport discovers that one of the group's intended victims is a loathsome FBI director who molests Native-American children. The ensuing action builds to a violent climax. Another book in the series, *Eyes of Prey,* involves a murderous, drug-addicted hospital pathologist, Michael Bekker, and a disfigured actor, Carlo Druze. The two men commit murders for each other, with Bekker killing Druze's theater manager and Druze killing Bekker's wife. By working together, Bekker and Druze are also able to conveniently provide alibis for each other. It is left to Davenport, who is fighting depression and is involved in a rocky love relationship, to apprehend these criminals.

Subsequent "Lucas Davenport" titles have built upon their predecessors without becoming dependent upon one another. Davenport is always present in each story, but in some of them he plays a smaller role. Critics have commended the author for creating, in Davenport, a character whose career choice simultaneously stimulates and depresses him—like an addict, the detective cannot extricate himself from his work no matter how grisly the killings become, not even when they tear apart his relationships with women. It is the author's villains, however, who draw the most praise in the reviews. In *Booklist,* Wes Lukowsky suggested that the series has been sustained "most of all" by its plethora of "great villains." A *Publishers Weekly* correspondent likewise noted that the people Davenport vies against in his labors "are shrewdly conceived originals, cut from fabric way at the back of the bin."

In recent years Camp—again using the Sandford pseudonym—has taken temporary leave of his "Lucas Davenport" series to write independent thrillers featur-ing other heroes. He brought back Kidd in the novel *The Devil's Code,* a work described by a *Kirkus Reviews* critic as "computer skullduggery on an epic scale." He has also introduced Anna Batory, a video freelancer who speeds around Los Angeles, looking for footage of murder and mayhem that she can sell to the television stations. Batory finds herself a target for violence in *The Night Crew,* a thriller that Pam Lambert commended in *People* as "tough, fiercely intelligent and irresistible." Appealing as the heroine is, Sandford explained in an interview published on his Web site, there will not likely be more more Anna Batory novels, because "Anna is basically a female Lucas, minus the badge. And having two characters that similar, by the same author, is just redundant."

Reviewing *The Hanged Man's Song* in *Library Journal,* Denise Garofolo said, "The fourth installment in Sandford's Kidd series finds Kidd's genius hacker friend Bobby brutally murdered and Bobby's laptop missing." Together with LuEllen, Kidd travels from Minnesota to Mississippi, and then Washington, D.C., in pursuit of the killer, along the way encountering "chases, crooked politicians, identity theft, and plenty of peeks into the worlds of burglary and computer hacking." In an interview posted on John Sandford's Web site, the author differentiated between his two major protagonists. Davenport, he said, "is an amalgam of cops I've known, a couple of movie stars, and the characters in any number of thrillers I've read in the past." He added: "There really aren't any cops like Davenport, because he's just too much like Sherlock Holmes, he's a little over the top." Kidd is hardly less extravagant. His creator described Kidd as "a criminal who does industrial espionage to support his watercolor painting habit."

Camp returned to the "Lucas Davenport" series in 2001 with the publication of *Chosen Prey.* In this, the twelfth installment, Deputy Police Chief Lucas Davenport decides to take matters in his own hands when a serial killer begins murdering young women in Wisconsin and Minnesota. Though distracted with sudden changes in his personal life, Davenport soon links the dead women with a prominent art professor at a local university, James Qatar. However, wrapping up the case before Qatar strikes again proves to be a daunting challenge for Davenport, one that nearly claims his life. The author "is in top form here," claimed a *Publishers Weekly* contributor, "his wry humor . . . lighting up the dark of another grisly investigation."

In *Mortal Prey* Lucas is pitted aginst an old nemesis, Clara Rinker, in a novel a *Booklist* contributor called "among the most ambitious" of Sandford's efforts because he effectively "integrates the mundane domesticity of Davenport's life . . . with the terror of a circling killer." *Naked Prey* finds Davenport now a happily married father. However, commented David Koepple in an *Entertainment Weekly* review, "he's lost none of his powers of deduction" as he delves into two murders and "uncovers a corrupt community in which everyone from a mechanic to an ex-nun is keeping secrets." *Hidden Prey* pairs Davenport with a Russian intelligence agent in order to investigate a murder that might be the work of a supposedly defunct Soviet network "forgotten by the motherland," according to Wes Lukowsky in *Booklist*.

Camp once told a *Publishers Weekly* interviewer that he planned to continue writing books featuring his two popular protagonists, Kidd and Davenport, and was contemplating a new pseudonym under which to write mainstream novels of a more literary nature. "Those are the kind of strategies that you have to think about," he remarked, adding: "I like to write books that have real stories in them, but I don't know whether a person who writes thrillers, as I do, *can* write literary books; whether critics will accept them." This is not to suggest that Camp does not see his thrillers as legitimate literature. In his online interview, he said: "What I do is really pretty hard, and I appreciate it when people take my effort with some degree of seriousness, as well as enjoying the stories." He concluded: "Readers are the other half of the essential storytelling partnership. What writers do is create the skeleton of a dream, which is dreamt in full by the readers."

BIOGRAPHICAL AND CRITICAL SOURCES:

PERIODICALS

Booklist, March 15, 1996, Wes Lukowsky, review of *Sudden Prey,* p. 1220; March 1, 1997, Emily Melton, review of *The Night Crew,* p. 1069; March 15, 1998, Wes Lukowsky, review of *Secret Prey,* p. 1180; April 15, 1999, Jenny McLarin, review of *Certain Prey,* p. 1484; March 1, 2000, Wes Lukowsky, review of *Easy Prey,* p. 1148; April 1, 2004, review of *Mortal Prey;* May 1, 2004, Wes Lukowsky, review of *Hidden Prey,* p. 1518.

Entertainment Weekly, May 23, 2003, David Koepple, review of *Mortal Prey.*
Globe and Mail (Toronto, Ontario, Canada), April 27, 1991, p. C7.
Kirkus Reviews, August 1, 2000, review of *The Devil's Code,* p. 1067.
Library Journal, April 1, 2000, Jo Ann Vicarel, review of *Easy Prey,* p. 132; April 15, 2000, Michael Adams, review of *Certain Prey,* p. 141; June 1, 2004, Denise Garofolo, review of *The Hanged Man's Song,* p. 196.
New York Times Book Review, June 7, 1998, Marilyn Stasio, review of *Secret Prey,* p. 47.
People, March 31, 1997, Pam Lambert, review of *The Night Crew,* p. 39.
Publishers Weekly, June 29, 1990, pp. 83-84; April 1, 1996, review of *Sudden Prey,* p. 54; March 10, 1997, review of *The Night Crew,* p. 49; April 20, 1998, review of *Secret Prey,* p. 47; April 19, 1999, review of *Certain Prey,* p. 60; March 20, 2000, review of *Easy Prey,* p. 68; September 4, 2000, review of *The Devil's Code,* p. 79; April 23, 2001, review of *Chosen Prey,* p. 49.
Tribune Books (Chicago, IL), July 2, 1989, p. 4.
Washington Post Book World, July 16, 1989, p. 6.
Writer, September, 2000, Lewis Burke Frumkes, p. 26.

ONLINE

Official John Sandford Web site, http://www.john sandford.org/ (August 23, 2004).*

*   *   *

CAMPBELL, Bebe Moore 1950-

PERSONAL: Born 1950; daughter of George Linwood Peter and Doris (a social worker; maiden name, Carter) Moore; married Tiko F. Campbell (divorced); married Ellis Gordon, Jr. (a banker); children: Maia. *Education:* University of Pittsburgh, B.A. (summa cum laude).

ADDRESSES: Home—Los Angeles, CA. *Agent*—Beth Swofford, William Morris Agency, 151 El Camino Dr., Beverly Hills, CA 90212.

CAREER: Freelance writer. Schoolteacher for five years; commentator on *Morning Edition,* National Public Radio. Guest on television talk shows, including *Donahue, Oprah, Sonya Live,* and *Today,* and numerous radio talk shows.

MEMBER: Alpha Kappa Alpha, Delta Sigma Theta.

AWARDS, HONORS: Body of Work Award, National Association of Negro Business and Professional Women, 1978; National Endowment for the Arts grant, 1980; Golden Reel Award, Midwestern Radio Theatre Workshop Competition, for *Sugar on the Floor;* Certificate of Appreciation, from the mayor of Los Angeles, CA; National Association for the Advancement of Colored People (NAACP) Image Award for outstanding literary work (fiction); National Association for the Mentally Ill (NAMI) Outstanding Literature Award, 2003, for *Sometimes My Mommy Gets Angry.*

WRITINGS:

Successful Women, Angry Men: Backlash in the Two-Career Marriage, Random House (New York, NY), 1986, revised, Berkeley (New York, NY), 2000.
Sweet Summer: Growing Up with and without My Dad, Putnam (New York, NY), 1989.
Your Blues Ain't Like Mine, Putnam (New York, NY), 1992.
Brothers and Sisters, Putnam (New York, NY), 1994.
Singing in the Comeback Choir, Putnam (New York, NY), 1998.
What You Owe Me, Putnam (New York, NY), 2001.
Sometimes My Mommy Gets Angry, illustrated by E. B. Lewis, Putnam (New York, NY), 2003.

Also author of nonfiction work "Old Lady Shoes" and a radio-play adaptation; author of radio play *Sugar on the Floor.* Contributor to periodicals, including *Ebony, Lear's, Ms., New York Times Book Review, New York Times Magazine, Publishers Weekly, Savvy, Seventeen, Washington Post,* and *Working Mother.* Contributing editor of *Essence.*

ADAPTATIONS: Film rights to *Sweet Summer* were bought by Motown Productions, 1989; film rights to *Brothers and Sisters* were bought by Touchstone Pictures, 1995.

WORK IN PROGRESS: A novel, *Where I Useta Live.*

SIDELIGHTS: Bebe Moore Campbell's fiction and nonfiction have earned her widespread acclaim for the insights on racism and divorce that they contain.

Campbell worked as a teacher for several years before turning to a career in freelance journalism following the birth of her daughter. It was an article for *Savvy* magazine that led to the development of her first book, *Successful Women, Angry Men: Backlash in the Two-Career Marriage.* Another article, about Father's Day, prompted the 1989 book, *Sweet Summer: Growing Up with and without My Dad,* her memoir as a child of divorce.

Because her parents separated when she was quite young, Campbell lived a divided existence, spending school years in Pennsylvania with her mother and summers in North Carolina with her father. Campbell draws a sharp contrast between the two worlds. According to *Sweet Summer,* her Philadelphia home was dominated by women—notably her mother, aunt, and grandmother—who urged her to speak well, behave properly, study hard, and generally improve herself. Life with her father, his mother, and his male friends, on the other hand, she describes as a freer one full of cigar and pipe smoke, beer, loud laughter, "roughness, gruffness, awkward gentleness," and a father's abiding love. Wheelchair-bound by a car accident, Campbell's father was nonetheless her hero, a perfect dad who loved her just for herself. When she learned that he was responsible, through speeding, not only for his own crippling accident but also for one that killed a boy, her image of him became tarnished, and Campbell had to come to terms with him as a flawed human being no longer the dream-father she had once idolized.

Critics hailed *Sweet Summer* for its poignant, positive look at a father-daughter relationship and especially for showing such a loving relationship in the black community. *Times Literary Supplement* contributor Adeola Solanke observed that in Campbell's memoir "a black father is portrayed by his daughter as a hero, instead of as the monster stalking the pages of many black American women writers." Similarly, poet Nikki Giovanni, writing in the *Washington Post Book World,* praised the book for providing "a corrective to some of the destructive images of black men that are prevalent in our society." Campbell also earned approval for her treatment of ordinary black life and for the vitality and clarity of her writing. Some reviewers expressed reservations about her work, however, suggesting that she is too hard on women; Martha Southgate, in the *Village Voice,* found "the absolute dichotomy Campbell perceives between men and women . . . disturbing." A few critics pointed out

Campbell's lack of emphasis on social context and analysis, which some deemed a drawback, others an advantage. Stated Solanke, "One of the book's main strengths is that the political and social tumult it presents never eclipses the vitality and immediacy of personal experience."

By sharing her story, Campbell gives readers "the opportunity to reflect on our own fathers," mused Melissa Pritchard in Chicago's *Tribune Books,* "to appreciate their imperfect, profound impact on our lives." The importance of fathers and other men in girls' lives is in fact "perhaps the crucial message in her book," related Itabari Njeri in the *Los Angeles Times,* "one still not fully understood by society." As Campbell explained to Njeri, "Studies show that girls without that nurturing from a father or surrogate father are likely to grow up with damaged self-esteem and are more likely to have problems with their own adult relationships with men." She hoped that reading her book might inspire more divorced fathers to increase their participation in their children's lives. Reflecting on the flurry of Campbell's talk show appearances, the competition for paperback rights, and the interest shown in the book by film producers, Njeri suggested that she was indeed reaching her audience. Noted the critic, "Campbell's gentle, poignant story about her relationship with her father has struck a nerve."

Campbell turned to fiction in 1992 with her novel *Your Blues Ain't Like Mine,* which tells of a young black man murdered in 1955 whose white killer was acquitted by an all-white jury. The novel goes on to trace what happens to the families of the killer and the victim in subsequent years. As Campbell told a *New York Times* reporter: "I wanted to give racism a face. . . . African-Americans know about racism, but I don't think we really know the causes. I decided it's first of all a family problem." The care with which the book's characters are drawn has been cited as one of its greatest strengths. Clyde Edgerton, writing for the *New York Times,* felt that much of the power of the novel "results from Ms. Campbell's subtle and seamless shifting of point of view. She wears the skin and holds in her chest the heart of each of her characters, one after another, regardless of the character's race or sex, response to fear and hate, or need for pity, grace, punishment or peace."

The rioting that broke out in Los Angeles after the 1992 Rodney King trial was the impetus behind Campbell's novel *Brothers and Sisters.* Explained Veronica Chambers in the *New York Times Magazine:* "While many saw the Los Angeles riots as the curtain falling on the myth of racial unity, Campbell . . . saw them as an opportunity to write about race and gender." The setting is a Los Angeles bank during the days after the riots, and the author explores the conflicting loyalties held by two women friends, one black, the other white. In this work the author uses her characters differently than she has previously; *New York Times* reviewer Elizabeth Gleick dubbed the protagonists "a fairly conventional batch," and a *Publisher Weekly* contributor noted that they are "intriguing (if not always three-dimensional)." Instead, *Brothers and Sisters* focuses on the complexities of the characters' relations. *Time* contributor Christopher John Farley praised the work accordingly: "Writing with wit and grace, Campbell shows how all our stories—white, black, male, female—ultimately intertwine." *Ms.* reviewer Retha Powers commended Campbell for her "astute observations about the subtleties of race and race relations in the U.S." The popular success of the novel was proven by its appearance on the *New York Times* best-seller list two weeks after its release. Writing in the *New York Times,* Pamela Newkirk placed Campbell "among a growing number of black women whose writing has mass crossover appeal. One reason for that appeal—to readers as well as to talk show hosts—is that in her characters, and in person, she manages to articulate deftly both black and white points of view."

Campbell's *Sometimes My Mommy Gets Angry* won the National Association for the Mentally Ill's Outstanding Literature Award the same year it was published. As Campbell explained in a preface to the book—a fictional account of a young African-American girl living with a mentally ill mother—she wrote the story "to address the fears and concerns of children who have a parent who suffers from mental illness." Her introductory note to adults discusses bipolar disorder and suggests ways in which the community can play a supportive role for those who suffer from it. In a review for *Publishers Weekly,* a contributor described the picture book narrated from a child's point of view as an "insightful, moving tale." "Most importantly," commented Suzanne Rust in *Black Issues Book Review,* Campbell shows young readers that her young protagonist "is not responsible for her mother's behavior." Anna DeWind Walls added in *School Library Journal* that the book's "multicultural cast is depicted with realistic sensitivity," making *Sometimes My Mommy Gets Angry* a "skillful treatment of a troubling subject."

BIOGRAPHICAL AND CRITICAL SOURCES:

BOOKS

Campbell, Bebe Moore, *Sweet Summer: Growing Up with and without My Dad,* Putnam (New York, NY), 1989.
Newsmakers 96, Gale (Detroit, MI), 1996, pp. 76-77.

PERIODICALS

African American Review, summer, 1997, Kari J. Winter, review of *Brothers and Sisters,* p. 369.
American Visions, October-November, 1994, T. Andreas Spellman, review of *Brothers and Sisters,* p. 38.
Black Enterprise, February, 1995, Sheryl Hillard Tucker, review of *Brothers and Sisters,* p. 224.
Black Issues Book Review, September-October, 2003, Suzanne Rust, review of *Sometimes Mommy Gets Angry,* p. 68.
Booklist, June 1, 1994, Donna Seaman, review of *Brothers and Sisters,* p. 1725; December 15, 1997, Donna Seaman, review of *Singing in a Comeback Choir,* p. 666.
Entertainment Weekly, September 9, 1994, Vanessa V. Friedman, review of *Brothers and Sisters,* p. 78.
Library Journal, August, 1994, Marie F. Jones, review of *Brothers and Sisters,* p. 124; December, 1994, Danna C. Bell-Russel, review of *Your Blues Ain't Like Mine,* p. 154; February 15, 1998, Michele Leber, review of *Singing in the Comeback Choir,* p. 169.
Los Angeles Times, July 25, 1989; December 1, 1989.
Ms., September-October, 1994, Retha Powers, review of *Brothers and Sisters,* p. 78.
Newsweek, April 29, 1996, Malcolm Jones, Jr., "Successful Sisters: Faux Terry Is Better Than No Terry," p. 79.
New York Times, November 15, 1995, Pamela Newkirk, "An Expert, Unexpectedly, on Race," p. C6.
New York Times Book Review, June 11, 1989, Bharati Mukherjee, review of *Sweet Summer,* p. 47; September 20, 1992, Clyde Edgerton, "Medicine for Broken Souls," review of *Your Blues Ain't Like Mine,* p. 13; October 16, 1994, Elizabeth Gleick, review of *Brothers and Sisters,* p. 18; April 12, 1998, Betsy Groban, review of *Singing in the Comeback Choir,* p. 17.
New York Times Magazine, December 25, 1994, Veronica Chambers, "Which Counts More, Gender or Race?," p. 16.
People, November 21, 1994, V. R. Peterson, review of *Brothers and Sisters,* p. 32.
Publishers Weekly, June 30, 1989, Lisa See, "Bebe Moore Campbell; Her Memoir of 'A Special Childhood' Celebrates the Different Styles of Her Upbringing in a Divided Black Family" (interview), pp. 82-83; July 4, 1994, review of *Brothers and Sisters,* p. 51; December 15, 1997, review of *Singing in the Comeback Choir,* p. 49; December, 8, 2003, review of *Sometimes Mommy Gets Angry,* p. 61.
School Library Journal, February, 1995, Ginny Ryder, review of *Brothers and Sisters,* p. 134; September, 2003, Anna DeWind Walls, review of *Sometimes Mommy Gets Angry,* p. 175.
Time, October 17, 1994, Christopher John Farley, review of *Brothers and Sisters,* p. 81.
Times Literary Supplement, October 26, 1990, p. 1148.
Tribune Books (Chicago, IL), June 18, 1989, p. 7.
U.S. Catholic, September, 1987, Gerald M. Costello, review of *Successful Women, Angry Men: Backlash in the Two-Career Marriage,* p. 48.
Village Voice, July 4, 1989, p. 63.
Washington Post Book World, June 18, 1989, pp. 1, 8.

ONLINE

Bebe Moore Campbell Home Page, http://www.bebemoorecampbell.com/ (July 24, 2004).*

*   *   *

CARLSON, Rick J. 1940-

PERSONAL: Born November 17, 1940, in Minneapolis, MN; son of John and Ethel (Anderson) Carlson; married Meg Dredge, September 4, 1965; children: Rebekah, Joshua. *Education:* St. Olaf College, B.A., 1962; University of Minnesota, J.D., 1965.

ADDRESSES: Home—75 Upper Alcatraz, Mill Valley, CA 94941. *Office*—c/o Institute for the Future, 2744 Sand Hill Rd., Menlo Park, CA 94025.

CAREER: Howard, Lefevere, Lefler, Hamilton & Pearson, Minneapolis, MN, attorney, 1965-68; Institute of Interdisciplinary Studies (currently InterStudy), Minneapolis, MN, research attorney, 1968-72; writer, 1972—; NewHealth Centers/Primary Prevention Programs, Inc., president and chief executive officer, 1987-90, special advisor and board member, 1990—; Epstein Becker & Green, P.C., United States, counsel; Age Wave Health Services, San Francisco, CA, vice chair; HealthMagic, Denver, CO, president and CEO; Direct Medical Knowledge (on-line consumer health information company), founder; The Health Strategies Group, LP, Aspen, CO, president. Senior research associate of National Academy of Sciences' Institute of Medicine; vice president and senior associate of Policy Center, Inc. (Denver) and Spectrum Research, Inc. (Washington, DC); research associate of University of California, San Francisco; chair, California Governor's Council on Wellness and Physical Fitness; first director of California Trend Report Project, sponsored by Naisbitt Group; consultant to Blue Cross/Blue Shield Associations of America, American Hospital Association, Health and Human Services Administration, Mac Arthur Foundation, and others; research affiliate for the Institute for the Future, Menlo Park, CA. Adjunct assistant professor at Boston University; instructor at University of Minnesota, 1970; Visiting Fellow at Center for the Study of Democratic Institutions, Santa Barbara, CA, 1972-73.

WRITINGS:

Planning and Law: Planners and Lawyers, American Rehabilitation Foundation Series, R. Carlson (Minneapolis, MN), 1969.

The Need to Study Laws Relating to Health Manpower, InterStudy (Minneapolis, MN), 1970.

(With Paul M. Ellwood, Jr. and others) *Assuring the Quality of Health Care,* InterStudy (Minneapolis, MN), 1973.

The End of Medicine, Wiley (New York, NY), 1975.

(Editor) *The Frontiers of Science and Medicine,* Wildwood House (London, England), 1975, H. Regnery (Chicago, IL), 1976.

(With David DeWolf and Priscilla DeWolf) *The Dilemmas of Corrections,* Lexington Books (Lexington, MA), 1976.

(Editor, with Robert Cunningham) *Future Directions in Health Care: A New Public Policy: Reports from a Conference,* Ballinger (Cambridge, MA), 1978.

(With Clement Bezold and Jonathan C. Peck) *The Future of Work and Health,* Auburn House (Dover, MA), 1986.

(With Brooke Newman) *Issues and Trends in Health,* Mosby (St. Louis, MO), 1987.

(With Gary Stimeling) *The Terrible Gift: The Brave New World of Genetic Medicine,* Public Affairs Publishing (New York, NY), 2002.

Contributor to medical and legal journals, and to *Center, Center Report,* and *Futures Conditional.*

SIDELIGHTS: Attorney, author, and health care consultant Rick J. Carlson was one of the primary framers of the Health Maintenance Organization (HMO) Act (1972). He served as a research attorney at the Institute of Interdisciplinary Studies in Minneapolis, Minnesota, during the late 1960s. Throughout his career, he has served as a consultant in the fields of health care, prevention, health futures, health care information and technology, and U.S. public policy relating to health care. He has served as president or chief executive officer of several organizations providing legal, strategic, and consulting services to the health care industry as well as providing self-help and preventative information to consumers.

Two of Carlson's books, *The End of Medicine* and *The Dilemmas of Corrections,* were written as a result of his work as a Visiting Fellow at the Center for the Study of Democratic Institutions in Santa Barbara, California. In *The End of Medicine,* Carlson challenges the health care system to integrate holistic thinking and wellness programs into the medical care it provides. *The Dilemmas of Corrections* rose out of two major conferences Carlson chaired on Law and Justice for the Center. The book deals with the U.S. correctional system and was written for the Law Enforcement Assistance Administration. Carlson and Robert Cunningham edited the 1978 book *Future Directions in Health Care,* which is a compilation of papers presented at a 1977 conference sponsored by the Blue Cross Association.

With Clement Bezold and Jonathan C. Peck, Carlson published *The Future of Work and Health* in 1986. The book resulted from a report prepared by the Institute for Alternative Futures in partnership with the Washington Business Group on Health. The report was written for the U.S. Office of Disease Prevention and the National Institute of Occupational Safety and Health. Carlson, Bezold, and Peck identify eight trends that would have an impact on work and health over the coming twenty-five years. Those trends deal with the effect of computers and automation on the number of jobs; an increase in the number of elderly people in the work force as a result of longer, healthier life spans; an increase in the number of "alternative" health care practitioners as well as routine self-care; greater attention to the protection of workers from toxic substances in the workplace; and the success of an informal economy in which churches, families, and communities are providing resources and care for the poor and the elderly. After citing demographics, the authors discuss trends that will shape the future of work and health, as well as health care and its financing. E. C. Goldin, in a review for the *Journal of Risk and Insurance,* recommended the book for risk management and insurance teachers and practitioners and for seminar courses in management, insurance, and health administration. "It identifies trends, but steers clear of painting a single picture of the way things will be," Goldin wrote. "It emphasizes that the future will be the result of choices made in the present." Goldin also praised the book's many understandable and text-enhancing figures and tables, as well as its extensive bibliography, which he said "should prove to be very valuable for students."

The Terrible Gift: The Brave New World of Genetic Medicine, written with Gary Stimeling in 2002, was the result of Carlson's work as a principal investigator for a Robert Wood Johnson Foundation-funded project, "Understanding the Human Genome: Implications for Public and Private Decision Makers," and his work as a research affiliate with the Institute for the Future. The book deals with the commercialization of modern medicine and health care, which makes health costs rise and patient-doctor relationships decline. It also deals with the authors' belief that health care is a right, not a privilege, and that research into the human genome could in the future result in abuses by the wealthy, who may pay for human clones to be used as organ donors. Carlson and Stimeling propose that biotechnology has great risks, not the least of which is the likelihood that it will fall into the wrong hands and that it will take away many of the medical freedoms now afforded the average person. In a *Booklist* review, William Beatty concluded that *The Terrible Gift* would be "a book to set genetics wonks a-chattering." A *Publishers Weekly* contributor was skeptical of the authors' reasoning, saying that readers may not accept their "science-fiction-style doomsday scenarios." Nevertheless, Carlson has been widely requested as a guest speaker on the subject since the

book's publication. One of his talks is titled "The Genomics Wave: How It Will Wash across Health Care."

BIOGRAPHICAL AND CRITICAL SOURCES:

PERIODICALS

Booklist, May 15, 2002, William Beatty, review of *The Terrible Gift: The Brave New World of Genetic Medicine,* p. 1563.
Futurist, July-August, 1987, review of *The Future of Work and Health,* p. 46.
Journal of Risk and Insurance, June, 1989, E. C. Goldin, review of *The Future of Work and Health,* p. 364.
Library Journal, June 1, 2002, Mary Chitty review of *The Terrible Gift,* p. 183.
Publishers Weekly, May 6, 2002, review of *The Terrible Gift,* p. 46.

ONLINE

Denver Metro Chamber of Commerce, Business Matters Newsletter Web site, http://www.enewsbuilder. net/denverchamber/ (January 28, 2003), "Exempla Health Care Presents the First-ever Health Care Policy Breakfast."
Office of Disease Prevention and Health Promotion Web site, http://odphp.osophs.dhhs.gov/ (February 13, 2003), "1997 Partnerships for Networked Consumer Health Information Conference, Biographies of Conference Speakers: Rick J. Carlson."
University of California, Irvine, Graduate School of Management Web site, http://www.gsm.uci.edu/ EventSites/ (February 13, 2003), "2002 Conference: Impact of Bio-Technology on Health Care Delivery."
University of Vermont Web site, http://www.uvm.edu/ news/ (October 4, 2002), Jennifer Nachbur, "Genetic Medicine and Health Care Lecture on Oct. 10."*

*   *   *

CARR, Caleb 1955-

PERSONAL: Born August 2, 1955, in New York, NY; son of Lucien Carr (an editor) and Francesca von Hartz (a social worker). *Education:* Attended Kenyon College, 1973-75; New York University, B.A., 1977. *Politics:* Independent.

ADDRESSES: Agent—International Creative Management, 40 West 57th St., New York, NY 10019.

CAREER: Writer and historian, 1980—. *Foreign Affairs,* researcher, c. 1976.

MEMBER: United We Stand America.

AWARDS, HONORS: Anthony Award, First Novel, 1995, for *The Alienist.*

WRITINGS:

Casing the Promised Land (novel), Harper (New York, NY), 1980.
(With James Chace) *America Invulnerable: The Quest for Absolute Security, from 1812 to Star Wars* (nonfiction), Summit Books (New York, NY), 1988.
Bad Attitudes (television movie), Fox, 1991.
The Devil Soldier: The Story of Frederick Townsend Ward (biography), Random House (New York, NY), 1991, published as *The Devil Soldier: The American Soldier of Fortune Who Became God in China,* 1992.
The Alienist (crime novel), Random House (New York, NY), 1994.
The Angel of Darkness (crime novel), Random House (New York, NY), 1997.
Killing Time: A Novel of the Future, Random House (New York, NY), 2000.
The Lessons of Terror: A History of Warfare against Civilians: Why It Has Always Failed (nonfiction), Random House (New York, NY), 2002.

Also author of a screenplay adaptation of *The Devil Soldier.* Author of articles on military history, short stories, screenplays, and plays; wrote and coproduced *The Osiris Chronicles,* a television pilot for Paramount and CBS. Contributor to periodicals, including *World Policy Journal* and *New York Times.* Contributing editor, *Military History Quarterly.*

SIDELIGHTS: Caleb Carr is a military historian and novelist who has written thrillers set in the past and future. The author's father, Lucien Carr, established himself as a national news service editor and, in younger years, was a companion of Beat Generation writers Jack Kerouac, Allen Ginsberg, and William Burroughs. Though Caleb Carr made the acquaintance of some of these well-known authors, he found them "really weird" and was not inspired by them, as he told Mike Capuzzo of the *Knight Ridder/Tribune News Service.* In fact, he added, "I became a writer despite them, basically." His thought and writing was more influenced by the dark circumstances of his upbringing, which involved alcoholism and violence. An intelligent student, he began writing freelance articles on military history after graduating from New York University in 1977. His first novel, *Casing the Promised Land,* was published in 1980 but went largely unnoticed. He followed that with a history of security measures in the United States, *America Invulnerable: The Quest for Absolute Security, from 1812 to Star Wars.*

His first book to attract considerable critical attention was *The Devil Soldier: The Story of Frederick Townsend Ward.* Published in 1991, *The Devil Soldier* recounts the adventures of Ward, an enigmatic American mercenary who was born in 1831 in Salem, Massachusetts. Ward, whose father sent him to Hong Kong at age fifteen as a punishment for truancy, prospected for gold in California in 1849, and served as a soldier of fortune in Mexico, Italy, and the Crimea. Carr's biography focuses on Ward's experiences in China during the late 1850s, when the adventurer was recruited by the Manchu dynasty to form an army which could defend the regime against peasant Taiping rebels. Ward's courage on the battlefield led the Taiping rebels to dub him the "devil soldier." Despite his success as a military leader, the war cost Ward his life at the age of thirty.

The Devil Soldier received complimentary reviews from critics. *New York Times Book Review* contributor Annette Kobak noted that "by marshaling his scholarship well and setting it out as an adventure story, Mr. Carr gives a good picture of the buccaneering milieu of the time, and makes a plausible case for the devil soldier being on the side of the angels." Jonathan Kirsch also praised *The Devil Soldier* in the *Los Angeles Times Book Review,* commenting that the story, "recounted . . . with authority and high spirits, is so marvelously improbable, so rich in exotic detail, that it often reads more like a historical thriller than the serious work of history that it is."

Historical detail also distinguishes *The Alienist,* a novel set in New York City in 1896. Combining historical personalities like police commissioner (and future president) Theodore Roosevelt and crusading journalist Jacob Riis with fictional characters, Carr crafts a story about the manhunt for a serial killer who mutilates young male prostitutes. The investigation is headed by the psychologist Dr. Laszlo Kreizler—an "alienist"—who proposes the idea of creating a psychological profile of the killer, a radical procedure at the time. By studying seemingly minor clues, the investigative team recruited by Kreizler determines that the murderer endured sexual abuse as a child and was raised in a strictly religious household. As the team hunts for the killer, they in turn are stalked by various underworld figures as well as by the very murderer they are attempting to capture.

Reviewers praised *The Alienist* as an engrossing book infused with the authentic atmosphere of turn-of-the-century New York. Some critics, however, found that the story was sometimes overwhelmed by historical detail. According to *New York Times Book Review* contributor Stephen Dobyns, Carr's thorough research "is both a curse and a blessing, for although the novel's ostensible subject is who-is-killing-these-children, the real subject is New York City in the 1890s." Dobyns acknowledged, however, that Carr "knows his history and the details are interesting." *Time* contributor John Skow stated that Carr set up "a good puzzle . . . but it is his ability to re-create the past that is truly impressive. . . . The brooding, detailed cityscapes and rich historical set pieces are the best parts of *The Alienist.*" In the *New Yorker,* a reviewer summed up the novel as "a *really* good book, swift and dense—popular entertainment that brushes important questions with its fingertips."

A sequel to *The Alienist, The Angel of Darkness* is "at least as winning a historical thriller as his bestseller *The Alienist,*" proclaimed the *New York Times Book Review*'s Christopher Lehmann-Haupt. "The quarry [in *The Angel of Darkness*] is more alluring and, if possible, nastier: a woman of beauty and intelligence who murders children and lots of them—both her own and others whom she's kidnaped in a strange perversion of the maternal instinct: Serial Mom in a bonnet and crinoline," explained Ben Macintyre in the *New York Times Book Review*. In "a turn-of-the-century New York City that feels as authentic as a fading tintype," characters first introduced in *The Alienist* "are joined by a vivid gallery of actual historical figures" in "adventures . . . described by a fictional former street urchin, Steve Taggert."

Critics remarked on Carr's choice of narrator as well as the story's frame of reference—Taggert tells the story twenty-two years after the events occurred. Lehmann-Haupt judged Taggert's "uneducated yet colorful vernacular" to be "an improvement on the somewhat musty Victorian prose of *The Alienist,*" yet complained that "Taggert . . . is far too garrulous," speaks with "occasional anachronisms," and deflates the "terror, excitement or whatever" of his stories by "promising too much" prior to recounting the events. However, a more serious flaw in the novel, according to Lehmann-Haupt, is that "the character of the suspect in the kidnaping and murder" remains unclear and flat. "Still," qualified the critic, "she is an extremely intriguing set of hypotheses" aided by "clever plotting."

Driven by "broodings—psychological, moral, [and] legal," recognized a *Publishers Weekly* reviewer, *The Angel of Darkness* "is a talky thriller. . . . whose myriad pleasures exude the essence of intelligent leisure reading." A *Kirkus Reviews* critic, who slightly faulted the "absorbing if overlong sequel" for some "digressive comments" and "needless detailed summaries" of previous murder cases, applauded the story's "rapid pace. . . . ambiance . . . [gruesome] murderous details. . . [and] convincingly presented" ethical issue about a mother killing her children. Also criticizing the novel's length, more than 600 pages, Macintyre maintained that this "intriguing, edifying and pleasingly strange" story can be read on many levels, specifying: "On one level is an earnest if not particularly profound moral inquiry into the nature of criminal behavior and, less comfortably, into the pressures of motherhood. On another, it is a tour of some fine New York monuments, human and architectural. Finally, and most impressively, it is a ripping yarn told with verve, intensity and a feel for historical detail."

The author moved his fiction into a new time setting with his next book, *Killing Time: A Novel of the Future.* In this lengthy novel, the near future is portrayed as bleak. A plague has decimated the world population, the stock market has brought global financial ruin, and the Internet is a pervasive force of misinformation; the air is so polluted that people only venture outdoors when it is urgent to do so. The main character is Gideon Wolfe, a New York psychiatrist and criminal profiler whose work involves him in a decades-old case, a presidential assassination. His activities lead to his kidnaping by an anarchist group, led by a pair of

genetically-engineered siblings. June Naylor, a reviewer for the *Fort Worth Star-Telegram*, took some exception to Carr's prose style, but advised that the author does a "fascinating" and "fairly credible job of illustrating ramifications of the unconscionable, reckless habits universally enjoyed in the year 2000."

Carr turned to nonfiction again with *The Lessons of Terror: A History of Warfare against Civilians: Why It Has Always Failed.* In the wake of the September 11, 2001, terrorist attacks on the United States, Carr turned his knowledge of military history once again to a review of terrorist tactics. Often decried as a new era in human warfare, terrorism is in fact an ancient tactic, according to the author, who provides many examples to prove his point. Often used, it is nevertheless ineffective, as Carr demonstrates in successive chapters. To deter the future use of terrorist tactics, Carr recommends swift, strong, preemptive strikes against nations that support terrorists. A reviewer for the *Christian Science Monitor* noted that while Carr had sometimes been viewed as "too single-minded and too trigger-happy" on the subject, "many Americans now may view Carr's earlier arguments as prescient and his approach as the only one that has a chance of working. *The Lessons of Terror* is fascinating to read and provocative in the best sense of the word."

BIOGRAPHICAL AND CRITICAL SOURCES:

BOOKS

Contemporary Literary Criticism, Volume 86, Gale (Detroit, MI), 1995.

PERIODICALS

Book, March-April, 2002, Chris Barsanti, review of *The Lessons of Terror: A History of Warfare against Civilians: Why It Has Always Failed,* p. 73.

Booklist, May 15, 1998, Whitney Scott, review of *The Angel of Darkness,* p. 1645; April 1, 2000, Brad Hooper, review of *The Alienist* and *The Angel of Darkness,* p. 1442; October 1, 2000, Bill Ott, review of *Killing Time: A Novel of the Future,* p. 291; November 1, 2001, Whitney Scott, review of *Killing Time,* p. 493; February 1, 2002, Brad Hooper, review of *The Lessons of Terror,* p. 906.

Boston Herald, December 10, 2000, Stephanie Schorow, review of *Killing Time,* p. 69.

Christian Science Monitor, August 5, 1994, Kristiana Helmick, review of *The Alienist,* p. 14; February 14, 2002, Peter I. Rose, review of *The Lessons of Terror: A History of Warfare against Civilians,* p. 16.

Commonweal, December 19, 1997, Thomas Deignan, review of *The Angel of Darkness,* p. 21.

Denver Post, January 7, 2001, review of *Killing Time,* p. G3.

Detroit News, November 4, 2000, review of *Killing Time,* p. 26.

Entertainment Weekly, April 1, 1994, p. 48; April 22, 1994; December 30, 1994, p. 117; October 17, 1997.

Esquire, December, 2000, Sven Birkerts, review of *Killing Time,* p. 68.

Fort Worth Star-Telegram, January 24, 2001, June Naylor, review of *Killing Time.*

Houston Chronicle, September 14, 1997, Fritz Lanham, review of *The Angel of Darkness,* p. 24; December 24, 2000, Michael J. Bandler, review of *Killing Time,* p. 12.

Kirkus Reviews, February 15, 1994, p. 158; September 1, 1997, p. 1324.

Knight-Ridder/Tribune News Service, September 7, 1994, Mike Capuzzo, "New York City Epitomizes 'Society's Ultimate Failure' and Caleb Carr's Wounded Heart"; January 24, 2001, June Naylor, review of *The Killing Time;* February 28, 2002, Ernst-Ulrich Franzen, review of *The Lessons of Terror.*

Library Journal, October 15, 1997, David W. Henderson, review of *The Angel of Darkness,* p. 90; December, 1997, Joanna Burkhardt, review of *The Angel of Darkness,* p. 173; November 15, 2000, Laurel Bliss, review of *Killing Time,* p. 95; June 1, 2001, Barbara Hoffert, review of *The Devil's Soldier,* p. S56.

Los Angeles Times, February 1, 2002, Anthony Day, review of *The Lessons of Terror,* p. E3.

Los Angeles Times Book Review, February 2, 1992, p. 4; December 10, 2000, Renee Graham, review of *Killing Time,* p. 10.

Maclean's, December 11, 2000, review of *Killing Time,* p. 52.

Newsweek, April 11, 1994, p. 76; February 11, 2002, Malcolm Jones, review of *The Lessons of Terror,* p. 60; October 6, 1997, review of *The Angel of Darkness,* p. 76.

New York, April 4, 1994, pp. 58-62; December 11, 2000, Daniel Mendelsohn, review of *Killing Time,* p. 77.

New Yorker, June 27, 1994, p. 84.

New York Times, March 29, 1994, Christopher Lehmann-Haupt, review of *The Alienist,* p. C17; May 19, 1994, Matthew Purdy, "A Historian Becomes a Novelist to Flee the Past," p. B5; September 29, 1997, Christopher Lehmann-Haupt, review of *The Angel of Darkness,* p. B6; January 31, 2002, Michiko Kakutani, review of *The Lessons of Terror,* p. B9.

New York Times Book Review, April 10, 1988, p. 12; January 19, 1992, p. 13; April 3, 1994, p. 19; June 18, 1995, p. 32; September 29, 1997; October 12, 1997; December 10, 2000, Daniel Zalewski, review of *Killing Time,* p. 19; February 17, 2002, Michael Ignatieff, review of *The Lessons of Terror,* p. 8.

People, June 20, 1994, pp. 75-76; October 20, 1997, Alec Foegle, review of *The Angel of Darkness,* p. 37.

Publishers Weekly, August 25, 1997, p. 43; September 15, 1997, Jeff Zaleski, interview with Caleb Carr, p. 46; September 25, 2000, review of *Killing Time,* p. 84; January 14, 2002, review of *The Lessons of Terror,* p. 53.

Record (Bergen County, NJ), November 16, 1997, David Shribman, review of *The Angel of Darkness,* p. Y8; December 10, 2000, Renee Graham, review of *Killing Time,* p. Y3.

Rocky Mountain News, November 2, 1997, review of *The Angel of Darkness,* p. 4E; November 26, 2000, review of *Killing Time,* p. 1E.

St. Louis Post-Dispatch, September 28, 1997, Harry Levins, review of *The Angel of Darkness,* p. 5C.

SAIS Review, summer-fall, 2002, Timothy Reuter, review of *Lessons of Terror,* pp. 371-373.

San Francisco Chronicle, September 24, 1997, Colleen Lindsay, review of *The Angel of Darkness,* p. E5; November 7, 2000, David Lazarus, review of *Killing Time,* p. C2.

School Library Journal, February, 2001, Carol DeAngelo, review of *Killing Time,* p. 143.

Seattle Post-Intelligencer, October 3, 1997, review of *The Angel of Darkness,* p. 22.

Time, April 18, 1994, p. 77; September 20, 1997, John Skow, review of *The Angel of Darkness,* p. 92.

Times Literary Supplement, July 1, 1994, p. 20.

Tribune Books (Chicago, IL), April 17, 1994, p. 4.

TV Guide, January 20-26, 1996.

Vanity Fair, April, 1994, p. 108.

Virginian Pilot, February 11, 2001, review of *Killing Time,* p. E4.

Wall Street Journal, January 15, 1992, David Shribman, review of *The Devil Soldier,* p. A10; May 2, 1994, p. A14; October 3, 1997, Tom Nolan, review of *The Angel of Darkness,* p. A8.

Washington Post, January 21, 2001, Gregory Feeley, review of *Killing Time,* p. 1; February 17, 2002, Lorraine Adams, review of *The Lessons of Terror,* p. T4.

Washington Post Book World, March 27, 1994, p. 4; June 11, 1995, p. 12; Feburary 17, 2002, Lorraine Adams, review of *The Lessons of Terror,* p. T4.*

World and I, February, 1998, Linda Simon, review of *The Angel of Darkness,* p. 269; June, 2002, p. 234.

ONLINE

Salon.com, http://www.salon.com/ (May 22, 2003), Dwight Garner, interview with Caleb Carr.

Time, http://www.time.com/ (November 3, 1999), transcript of chat session with Caleb Carr.*

*   *   *

CHALL, Marsha Wilson

PERSONAL: Born in MN; children: Lindsay, Robbie. *Education:* Drake University, B.S., 1975; University of Minnesota, M.A., 1984.

ADDRESSES: Office—Department of Communication and Writing, Metropolitan State University, Suite 205, Energy Park Place, 1380 Energy Lane, St. Paul, MN 55108. *E-mail*—Marsha.Chall@metrostate.edu.

CAREER: Adult Options in Education, Hopkins and St. Louis Park, MN, adult literacy instructor, 1983-2002; Metropolitan State University, St. Paul, MN, community faculty instructor in creative writing, 1998—. Has conducted writing workshops at The Loft Literary Center, Minneapolis, MN, and St. John's Preparatory School, Collegeville, MN. Has given readings and lectures on children's literature at colleges and associations in Minnesota, North Dakota, and elsewhere.

AWARDS, HONORS: Smithsonian Notable Children's Book citation, 2000, for *Bonaparte;* Minnesota State Arts Board Artist Assistance fellowship, and Loft

Literary Center's Minnesota Writers Career Initiative grant, both 2001; Ohio Farm Bureau Outstanding Children's Literature Award, 2002, for *Sugarbush Spring.*

WRITINGS:

Mattie, illustrated by Barbara Lehman, Lothrop, Lee & Shepard (New York, NY), 1992.

Up North at the Cabin, Lothrop, Lee & Shepard (New York, NY), 1992.

Rupa Raises the Sun, illustrated by Rosanne Litzinger, DK Ink (New York, NY), 1998.

Bonaparte, illustrated by Wendy Anderson Halperin, Dorling Kindersley (New York, NY), 2000.

Happy Birthday, America!, illustrated by Guy Porfirio, Lothrop, Lee & Shepard (New York, NY), 2000.

Sugarbush Spring, illustrated by Jim Daly, Lothrop, Lee & Shepard (New York, NY), 2000.

Prairie Train, illustrated by John Thompson, Harper-Collins (New York, NY), 2003.

SIDELIGHTS: Marsha Wilson Chall's picture books have earned praise for their warmth and charm, as well as for their incorporation of the kind of details often left out of books for young readers. In an interview for the *Children's Literature Network* Web site, she said: "Writing for children allowed me [the] joy of experiencing the world over and over again for the first time. Adults lose this childlike appreciation and discovery through over-complication. I like to make the complex simple. Not simple-minded, but pared down to the essential." Chall admits she may work for months or even years on a children's story, searching for just the right phrase or storyline to capture a child's imagination. She is therefore amused when people suggest that writing picture books is easier than creating fiction for adults.

Some of Chall's books are based on childhood memories from her own youth in Minnesota. In *Up North at the Cabin,* she takes readers on a summertime journey to a rustic cabin in the deep woods. The family in *Sugarbush Spring* works together to tap maple trees and turn the sap into syrup, and in *Happy Birthday, America!,* an extended family gathers to celebrate the Fourth of July in a small town. All three titles celebrate not only nature's abundance and seasonal festivals, they also depict the interactions between three generations as grandparents transmit

traditions to grandchildren. *New York Times Book Review* correspondent Beth Dunlop felt that *Up North at the Cabin* "tugs at memory and childhood without being overly sentimental." Chall's words, according to Dunlop, have "a pleasant read-aloud rhythm and imagery that will tickle children." A *Publishers Weekly* reviewer commended *Sugarbush Spring* as an "evocative tale" in which text and pictures combine to produce a "tactile quality." Another *Publishers Weekly* reviewer concluded of *Happy Birthday, America!:* "Ample good cheer, mixed with splashes of patriotism and nostalgia, make this a family outing to which nearly everyone will feel invited."

Two of Chall's more whimsical tales are *Bonaparte* and *Rupa Raises the Sun.* Bonaparte is a French dog who tries in vain to join his beloved owner in school. Throughout the week, Bonaparte adopts many ruses—all of them unsuccessful—until finally he must come to the rescue of his boy. In her *Booklist* review of *Bonaparte,* Lauren Peterson declared: "This humorous and heartwarming tale will engage youngsters." A *Horn Book* contributor likewise found *Bonaparte* a "lighthearted story," concluding: "*Bonaparte est charmant.*" In *Rupa Raises the Sun,* the title character begs for a vacation after rousing the sun 21,954 times. When a substitute sun-raiser cannot be found, the village elders try to solve the problem in innovative ways. "Chall charms the listener with her fondly told tale of foolishness," observed Annie Ayers in *Booklist.* A *Publishers Weekly* critic deemed the book "a quirky, warmhearted work for sophisticated readers."

Chall's *Prairie Train* stems from her recollection of childhood train rides between Iowa and Minnesota. In the book, a young girl describes her first solo trip on the Great Northern to see her grandmother in St. Paul. At first the journey is thrilling, full of exciting sights and sounds and leading to a newfound freedom. Then, when the train halts due to a snowdrift, a note of anxiety creeps in until the other passengers reassure her, in various ways, that all is well. Julie Cummins in *Booklist* described *Prairie Train* as a "poignant glimpse of a time gone by." Tony Hiss in the *New York Times Book Review* praised Chall for being "unusually sensitive to the heightened awareness, the wonder mixed with fear, that travel brings with it."

In her online interview with *Children's Literature Network,* Chall said: "A friend of mine recently reminded me of the axiom that work should be play with a purpose. Writing to me is that kind of work, like being in water; I lose track of time, in the same miraculous way I did as a child in the backyard creating miniature worlds that slipped imperceptibly into nightfall."

BIOGRAPHICAL AND CRITICAL SOURCES:

PERIODICALS

Booklist, April 15, 1992, p. 1527; September 1, 1998, Annie Ayers, review of *Rupa Raises the Sun,* p. 124; September 1, 2003, Julie Cummins, review of *Prairie Train,* p. 128.
Horn Book, September-October, 1992, p. 574.
Kirkus Reviews, June 1, 1992, p. 716.
New York Times Book Review, May 31, 1992, p. 38; November 16, 2003, Tony Hiss, "One-Track Minds," p. 24.
Publishers Weekly, August 17, 1998, review of *Rupa Raises the Sun,* p. 70; January 3, 2000, review of *Sugarbush Spring,* p. 75; June 5, 2000, review of *Happy Birthday, America!,* p. 94; August 7, 2000, review of *Bonaparte,* p. 94.
School Library Journal, June, 1992, p. 89; August, 1992, p. 134; November, 1998, p. 77; March, 2000, Virginia Golodetz, review of *Sugarbush Spring,* p. 189; June, 2000, JoAnn Adams, review of *Happy Birthday, America!,* p. 102.
Star Tribune (Minneapolis, MN), August 24, 2003, Colleen Kelly, "Picture This: There's a Bounty of New Picture Books by Twin Cities Writers and Artists," p. F1.

ONLINE

Children's Literature Network, http://www.childrens literaturenetwork.org/ (December 6, 2003), interview with Chall.*

*   *   *

CHAPMAN, Lynne F(erguson) 1963-

PERSONAL: Born March 14, 1963, in Los Angeles, CA; daughter of James (a professor of English) and Lorice (a library assistant and teacher) Ferguson; married Paul Chapman (a neuroscientist), June 21, 1986; children: Thomas, Samuel. *Education:* DePauw

University, B.A., 1985. *Hobbies and other interests:* Reading, watching films, cooking, playing games, drawing and graphic design, travel.

ADDRESSES: Home and office—7 Westbourne Rd., Cardiff CF4 2BP, Wales.

CAREER: Mayfield Publishing, Mountain View, CA, editorial assistant, 1985-87; Windsor Publications, Northridge, CA, photography editor, 1987-88; Dushkin Publishing, Guilford, CT, annual editions editor, 1988-89; freelance editor and writer, 1989—.

MEMBER: National Childbirth Trust.

WRITINGS:

Sylvia Plath, photographs by Benno Friedman, Creative Education (Mankato, MN), 1994.
Leo Tolstoy, Creative Editons (Mankato, MN), 1997.
Egyptian Pyramids, Creative Education (Mankato, MN), 1999.
Medieval Castles, Creative Education (Mankato, MN), 2000.
Cathedrals, Creative Education (Mankato, MN), 2000.

SIDELIGHTS: Lynne F. Chapman once commented: "Because both of my parents taught English, it was probably inevitable that I, after a proper period of teenage rebelliousness, would want to have a lot to do with books. Publishing seemed an obvious career choice, so I spent several years after college moving from one small publishing company to another as my husband pursued his academic career at various universities. Then I decided to take up freelance editing, not coincidentally before the birth of my first child, and I have worked at home ever since. While living in Minnesota, I was asked to try writing for a small, upmarket publisher of beautiful educational books. I wrote my first book with equal parts nervousness and delight, and three more followed. Now we have settled overseas, in Cardiff, Wales, and as my children get older, I hope to have more time for writing—although those nerves just won't go away!"*

*   *   *

COGHLAN, Margaret M. 1920-
(Jessica Stirling)

PERSONAL: Born January 26, 1920, in Glasgow, Scotland; daughter of Arthur and Jane (McBrien) Walls; married Eugene O. Coghlan; children: Janice A., Rosemary M. Coghlan Gilchrist. *Religion:* Roman Catholic.

ADDRESSES: Home—109 Mugdock Rd., Milngavie, Dunbartonshire, Scotland.

CAREER: Writer.

MEMBER: International P.E.N., Association of Scottish Writers (founding member), Glasgow Writers Club (past president).

WRITINGS:

UNDER PSEUDONYM JESSICA STIRLING

Spoiled Earth, Hodder & Stoughton (London, England), 1974.

Strathmore, Delacorte (New York, NY), 1975.

The Dresden Finch, Delacorte (New York, NY), 1976.

Beloved Sinner, Pan Books, 1976.

Hiring Fair, Pan Books, 1976.

Call Home the Heart, St. Martin's Press (New York, NY), 1977.

The Dark Pasture, St. Martin's Press (New York, NY), 1978.

The Drums of Time, St. Martin's Press (New York, NY), 1979.

Deep Well at Noon, Hodder & Stoughton (London, England), 1979.

Blue Evening Gone, St. Martin's Press (New York, NY), 1982.

The Gates of Midnight, St. Martin's Press (New York, NY), 1983.

Treasures on Earth, St. Martin's Press (New York, NY), 1985.

Creature Comforts, St. Martin's Press (New York, NY), 1986.

Hearts of Gold, St. Martin's Press (New York, NY), 1987.

The Good Provider, St. Martin's Press (New York, NY), 1988.

The Asking Price, St. Martin's Press (New York, NY), 1989.

The Wise Child, St. Martin's Press (New York, NY), 1990.

The Welcome Light, St. Martin's Press (New York, NY), 1991.

A Lantern for the Dark, St. Martin's Press (New York, NY), 1992.

Shadows on the Shore, St. Martin's Press (New York, NY), 1994.

The Penny Wedding, St. Martin's Press (New York, NY), 1995.

The Marrying Kind, St. Martin's Press (New York, NY), 1996.

The Workhouse Girl, St. Martin's Press (New York, NY), 1997.

The Island Wife, St. Martin's Press (New York, NY), 1998.

The Wind from the Hills, St. Martin's Press (New York, NY), 1999.

The Strawberry Season, St. Martin's Press (New York, NY), 2000.

Prized Possessions, St. Martin's Press (New York, NY), 2001.

The Piper's Tune, St. Martin's Press (New York, NY), 2002.

SIDELIGHTS: Under her pseudonym Jessica Stirling, Scottish writer Margaret Coghlan crafts romantic novels that have historical settings, set primarily in Scotland. In *A Lantern for the Dark,* for instance, unmarried Clare Kelso faces trial in 1787 Glasgow for the poisoning of her infant son. Taking her case is attorney Cameron Adams, who suspects that Clare is not the perpetrator of this crime after he learns that the baby's father, Frederick Striker, has vanished. A *Publishers Weekly* critic cited Stirling for creating "fully realized characters against the background of a greedy and corrupt society operating under a thin veneer of respectability."

Clare Kelso appears again in *Shadows on the Shore,* set some years later against the backdrop of the archetypical "dark and stormy night" on the Scottish coast. The storm, wrote a Publishers Weekly contributor, heralds the return of Frederick Striker, the womanizing rogue who disappeared during the murder trial of the previous tale. By now Clare has risen up in the world to become mistress of Headrick House, and she is ready to "[exact] her revenge," said the reviewer. Again, the author was praised for "dry wit and humorous characterizations" that suggest Stirling "is a deft practitioner of the [historical romance] genre." "A stunning sequel" is how *Booklist*'s Denise Perry Donavin characterized *Shadows on the Shore.*

Stirling traveled forward in time for *The Penny Wedding,* set during Depression-era working-class Scotland. Seventeen-year-old Alison Burnside faces calamity when her mother dies and her father loses his job; the young woman believes she must now forego her dream of attending medical school. But an intervention by Alison's favorite teacher, Jim Abbott, saves her career—and opens her life to romance. The Burnside family saga continues in *The Marrying Kind*, which finds Alison too caught up in her medical studies to notice that her fiancée, Jim Abbott, is suffering from tuberculosis. "While Jim languishes in a sanitarium," noted Margaret Flanagan of *Booklist*, "he and Alison must both reevaluate the true depth of their commitment to each other." The pre-World War II setting of *The Marrying Kind* juxtaposes Alison's personal crisis with the rise of the Nazi regime and its eventual effect on Great Britain. Employing themes of class conflict, war and feminism, said a critic for *Publishers Weekly*, Stirling "expertly guides [her characters] through the growing pains of the heart into genuine maturity."

The author is in "top form," according to a *Publishers Weekly* contributor, in *The Workhouse Girl*. This 1997 novel is set in Victorian Scotland, where wealthy young Cassie Armitage is attracted to the new minister in her parish, though she finds a romantic rivalry in the form of her younger sister, Pippa. Though it is Cassie whom the Reverend Montague ultimately marries, their life together does not bode well, as Montague abuses his wife and carries on an affair with Pippa. In a related subplot, the "workhouse girl" of the title, Nancy Winfield, "shares the story's center stage and is as engaging and likeable as her wealthy counterpart," commented *Booklist*'s Alice Joyce.

In *The Island Wife*, the rough and rugged Scottish island of Mull provides the setting for another pair of nineteenth-century sisters, Innis and Biddy Campbell, both of whom are kept under the strict hand of their mother, Vassie. The girls' Protestant upbringing does not prepare them for the arrival of neighbors who hire handsome young shepherd Michael—a Catholic—to work for them. What's more, "the wall Vassie is building will no more keep him away from her daughters than it will keep the encroaching sheep off her cattle's grazing land," as a *Publishers Weekly* reviewer put it. *Library Journal* critic Andrea Lee Shuey labeled Stirling "an excellent storyteller" in this book, noting that *The Island Wife* was the first of a proposed trilogy "that will leave readers eagerly awaiting the second installment."

Readers did not have to wait too long, as *The Wind from the Hills* was published in 1999. No longer poor,

Innis and Biddy face drastically different personal lives. Innis, who has converted to Catholicism to marry Michael, "doggedly obeys her sour and silent" husband, according to a *Publishers Weekly* reviewer. Meanwhile, Biddy is a wealthy but childless widow who finds herself at the edge of a possible new romance. "This enjoyable installment is focused more on plot and less on dark themes," noted Catherine Sias of *Booklist*, and "is sure to entrance Stirling's many fans." *The Strawberry Season* wraps up the trilogy. Now it is 1908, and the sisters meet a newcomer to Mull island, the pregnant runaway wife Fay Ludlow. Biddy rejects Fay, but Innis takes her in because "the husband Fay escaped is none other than her son, Gavin," as Patty Engelmann put it in *Booklist*. A *Publishers Weekly* contributor lauded this work as a "loving chronicle of the hopes and fears of a close knit island community" and concluded that Stirling "provides a pleasing vacation into the past."

The coming of the twenty-first century saw Stirling producing more historical novels. In 2002's *The Piper's Tune*, Edwardian-age Lindsay Franklin finds herself an unexpected shipping magnate after her grandfather wills her a share in the family business. Complications ensue when a distant cousin, Forbes McCulloch, arrives in Scotland with an eye toward taking over the family business and marrying Lindsey. A writer for *Publishers Weekly* commented that *The Piper's Tune* transcends a "formulaic love story" by virtue of Stirling's "bang-up job . . . illustrating how character shapes a person's life."

BIOGRAPHICAL AND CRITICAL SOURCES:

PERIODICALS

Booklist, March 15, 1994, Denise Perry Donavin, review of *Shadows on the Shore*, p. 1329; May 1, 1995, Margaret Flanagan, review of *The Penny Wedding*, p. 1554; June 1, 1996, Flanagan, review of *The Marrying Kind*, p. 1677; June 1, 1997, Alice Joyce, review of *The Workhouse Girl*, p. 1664; September 15, 1998, Sally Estes, review of *The Marrying Kind*, p. 220; November 15, 1998, Catherine Sias, review of *The Island Wife*, p. 568; December 15, 1999, Sias, review of *The Wind from the Hills*, p. 758; November 1, 2000, Patty Engelmann, review of *The Strawberry Season*, p. 522; June 1, 2001, Patty Engelmann, review of *Prized Possessions*, p. 1850.

Library Journal, November 15, 1998, Andrea Lee Shuey, review of *The Island Wife,* p. 92.

Publishers Weekly, July 6, 1990, Sybil Steinberg, review of *The Wise Child,* p. 60; April 20, 1992, review of *A Lantern for the Dark,* p. 37; February 14, 1994, review of *Shadows on the Shore,* p. 80; June 3, 1996, review of *The Marrying Kind,* p. 63; May 26, 1997, review of *The Workhouse Girl,* p. 65; November 2, 1998, review of *The Island Wife,* p. 72; November 22, 1999, review of *The Wind from the Hills,* p. 43; October 30, 2000, review of *The Strawberry Season,* p. 45; March 11, 2002, review of *The Piper's Tune,* p. 51.*

*   *   *

COLLINS, Nancy A(verill) 1959-
(Nanzi Regalia)

PERSONAL: Born 1959, in AR; married Joe Christ (a filmmaker).

ADDRESSES: Agent—Donald Mass Literary Agency, 160 W. 95th St., Suite 1B, New York, NY 10025.

CAREER: Author of horror novels, short stories, comic books, and screenplays. Founder of the International Horror Critics Guild (now the International Horror Guild).

AWARDS, HONORS: Nominated for the Campbell Award, 1989 and 1990, the Eisner Award, 1992, and the Bram Stoker Award for best novelette, Horror Writers of America, 1996, for *The Thing from Lover's Lane;* Bram Stoker Award for best first novel, Horror Writers of America, and the Icarus Award, British Fantasy Society, both 1990, both for *Sunglasses after Dark;* Deathrealm Award for Best Anthology, 1996.

WRITINGS:

NOVELS

Sunglasses after Dark (novel), New American Library (New York, NY) 1989.

Tempter, Onyx Press (New York, NY), 1990, revised edition, Gauntlet Press (Colorado Springs, CO), 2001.

(Under pseudonym Nanzi Regalia) *Love Throbbing Bob* (chapbook), Dark Carnival Press (Berkeley, CA), 1990.

In the Blood, Kinnell (London, England), 1991, Roc (New York, NY), 1992.

The Tortuga Hill Gang's Last Ride: The True Story (chapbook), illustrated by Timothy Standish, Roadkill Press (Arvada, CO), 1991.

Wild Blood, New English Library (London, England), 1993.

Paint It Black, New English Library (London, England), 1995.

Walking Wolf: A Weird Western, Zeising (Shingletown, CA), 1995.

The Fantastic Four: To Free Atlantis, Boulevard (New York, NY), 1995.

A Dozen Black Roses, White Wolf (Stone Mountain, GA), 1996.

Dark Destiny: Proprietors of Fate, White Wolf (Stone Mountain, GA), 1996.

(With artist, Paul Lee) *Dhampire: Stillborn* (based on a work by Ted Naifeh), edited by L. Stathis, DC Comics (New York, NY), 1996.

Angels on Fire, White Wolf (Stone Mountain, GA), 1998.

Lynch: A Gothik Western, Cemetery Dance Publications (Forest Hill, MD), 1998.

Voodoo Chile (chapbook), Gauntlet Press (Colorado Springs, CO), 2001.

Person(s) Unknown (chapbook), Crossroads Press (Honolulu, HI), 2002.

Darkest Heart, White Wolf (Stone Mountain, GA), 2002.

COLLECTIONS

Cold Turkey (chapbook), Crossroads Press (Honolulu, HI), 1992.

Nameless Sins, Gauntlet Press (Colorado Springs, CO), 1994.

Midnight Blue: The Sonja Blue Collection (contains *Sunglasses after Dark, In the Blood,* and *Paint It Black*), White Wolf (Stone Mountain, GA), 1995.

Avenue X and Other Dark Streets, Xlibris (Philadelphia, PA), 2000.

Dead Roses for a Blue Lady, Crossroad Press (New York, NY), 2002.

Knuckles and Tales, illustrated by Bonnie Jacobs, Biting Dog Press (Duluth, GA), 2003.

EDITOR

(With Martin H. Greenberg and Edward E. Kramer; and contributor) *Dark Love,* Roc (New York, NY), 1995.

(With Martin H. Greenberg and Edward E. Kramer; and contributor) *Forbidden Acts,* Avon (New York, NY), 1995.

(With Gahan Wilson; and contributor) *Gahan Wilson's the Ultimate Haunted House,* HarperPrism (New York, NY), 1996.

Writer for the DC Comics series *Swamp Thing,* 1991-93, *Vertigo Jam,* 1993, *Dhampire: Stillborn,* 1996, and *The Big Book of Losers,* 1997. Writer for the Dark Horse comics *Harlan Ellison's Dream Corridor,* 1995-96, *Aliens Special,* 1997, and *Predator,* 1998. Also writer for the comics *Jason vs. Leatherface,* Topps Comics, 1995-96, *2099 Unlimited,* Marvel, 1995, *Sunglasses after Dark,* Verotik Publications, 1995-96, *Verotika,* Verotik Publications, 1995-96, *Those Annoying Post Brothers Annual,* MU/Aeon, 1995, *Weird Business,* Mojo Press, 1995, and *Legend of the Fallen Angel on the World of Magic,* Acclaim/Accadia, 1996.

Contributor to periodicals, including *SF Eye, Cemetery Dance, The Horror Show, Reflex, Midnight Graffiti,* and *Pulphouse.*

Contributor to anthologies, including *Splatterpunks: Extreme Horror,* edited by Paul M. Sammon, St. Martin's Press, 1990; *Splatterpunks 2: Over the Edge,* edited by Paul M. Sammon, St. Martin's Press, 1990; *The Best of Pulphouse: The Hardback Magazine,* edited by Kristine Kathryn Rusch, St. Martin's Press, 1991; *The Ultimate Werewolf,* edited by Byron Preiss, Dell, 1991; *The Fantastic Adventures of Robin Hood,* edited by Martin H. Greenberg, New American Library, 1991; *Year's Best Fantasy and Horror #4,* edited by Ellen Datlow and Terri Windling, St. Martin's Press, 1991; *Nightmares on Elm Street: Freddy Kruger's Seven Sweetest Dreams,* edited by Martin H. Greenberg, St. Martin's Press, 1991; *There Won't Be War,* edited by Harry Harrison and Bruce McAllister, Tor, 1991; *Cold Blood,* edited by Richard T. Chizmar, Zeising, 1991; *Solved!* edited by Ed Gorman and Martin H. Greenberg, Carroll & Graff, 1991; *Hotter Blood: More Tales of Erotic Horror,* edited by Jeff Gelb and Michael Garrett, Pocket Books, 1991; *Under the Fang: Horror Writers of America I,* edited

by Robert R. McCammon, Pocket Books, 1991; *Shock Rock,* edited by Jeff Gelb, Pocket Books, 1992; *Quick Chills II,* edited by Robert Morrish and Peter Enfantino, Deadline Press, 1992; *Narrow Houses,* edited by Peter Crowther and Douglas E. Winter, Little, Brown, 1992; *Still Dead: The Book of the Dead 2,* edited by John M. Skipp and Craig Spector, Bantam, 1992; *The Definitive Best of the Horror Show,* edited by David B. Silva, Cemetery Dance Publications, 1992; *The Further Adventures of Batman: Volume 2,* edited by Martin H. Greenberg, Bantam, 1992; *Best of New Horror #3,* edited by Ramsey Campbell and Stephen Jones, Carroll & Graff, 1992; *After the Darkness,* edited by Stanley Waiter, Maclay Press, 1993; *Confederacy of the Dead,* edited by Richard Gilliam, New American Library, 1993; *Thrillers,* edited by Richard T. Chizmar, Cemetery Dance Publications, 1993; *Shudder Again: Twenty-two Tales of Sex and Horror,* edited by Michele Slung, New American Library, 1993; *Dark Destiny: Proprietors of Fate, The World of Darkness,* edited by Edward E. Kramer, White Wolf, 1994; *Elric: Tales of the White Wolf,* edited by Edward E. Kramer and Michael Moorcock, White Wolf, 1994; *The King Is Dead!: Tales of Elvis Post-Mortem,* edited by Paul M. Sammon, Delta, 1994; *Phobias: Stories of Your Deepest Fears,* edited by Richard Gilliam, Edward E. Kramer, Wendy Webb, and Martin H. Greenberg, New American Library, 1994; *The Earth Strikes Back: New Tales of Ecological Horror,* edited by Richard T. Chizmar, Zeising, 1994; *Year's Best Fantasy and Horror #7,* edited by Ellen Datlow and Terri Windling, St. Martin's Press, 1994; *Adventures of the Batman,* edited by Martin H. Greenberg, MJP Books, 1995; *Fear Itself,* edited by Jeff Gelb, Warner/Aspect, 1995; *Dark Destiny II: Proprietors of Fate,* edited by Edward E. Kramer, White Wolf, 1995; *Tombs,* edited by Edward E. Kramer and Peter Crowther, White Wolf, 1995; *Killing Me Softly: Erotic Tales of Unearthly Love,* edited by Gardner Dozois, Harper Prism, 1995; *Love Bites,* edited by Amarantha Knight, Masquerade, 1995; *Ruby Slippers, Golden Tears,* edited by Ellen Datlow and Terri Windling, St. Martin's Press, 1995; *More Phobias,* edited by Wendy Webb, Pocket Books, 1995; *One Hundred Tiny Tales of Terror,* edited by Stefan R. Dziemianowicz, Martin H. Greenberg, and Robert E. Weinberg, Barnes & Noble, 1996; *Noirotica: An Anthology of Erotic Crime Stories,* edited by Thomas S. Roche, Masquerade, 1996; *It Came from the Drive-In,* edited by Norman Partridge and Martin H. Greenberg, DAW, 1996; *Sandman: Book of Dreams,* edited by Edward E. Kramer and Neil Gaiman, HarperCollins, 1996; *Shades of Noir,* edited by Lisa Manns, Archon Gaming, 1996; *Pawns of Chaos,* edited by

Edward E. Kramer, White Wolf, 1997; *Wild Women,* edited by Melissa Mia Hall, Carroll & Graff, 1997; *One Hundred Twisted Little Tales of Torment,* edited by Stefan R. Dziemianowicz, Martin H. Greenberg, and Robert E. Weinberg, Barnes & Noble, 1998; *Best of Cemetery Dance,* edited by Richard T. Chizmar, Cemetery Dance Publications, 1998; *The Crow: Broken Lives and Shattered Dreams,* edited by Edward E. Kramer and James O'Barr, Berkley/Doubleday, 1998; *Eternal Lovecraft: The Persistence of HPL in Popular Culture,* edited by H. P. Lovecraft and Jim Turner, Golden Gryphon, 1998; *999,* edited by Al Sarrantino, Avon, 1999; *Hellboy: Odd Jobs* (graphic novel edition), edited by Mike Mignola and Christopher Golden, illustrated by Mike Mignola, Dark Horse Comics, 2000; *Skull Full of Spurs,* edited by Jason Bovberg and Kirk Whitham, Dark Highways Press, 2000; *Strange Attractions,* edited by Edward E. Kramer, Shadowlands Press, 2000; *Vampire Sextette,* edited by Marvin Kaye, Doubleday, 2000; *Mammoth Book of Vampire Stories by Women,* edited by Stephen Jones, Carroll & Graff, 2001; *Trick or Treat,* edited by Richard T. Chizmar, Cemetery Dance Publications, 2001; and *Stranger: Dark Tales of Eerie Encounters,* edited by Michele Slung, Perennial, 2002.

Also author of the stage play "Freakababies" based on *Gauntlet #3,* 1992; the radio play *The Thing from Lover's Lane*; and the specs *All the Young Dudes* (with Joe Christ) and *Blood Town.*

ADAPTATIONS: Both *Sunglasses after Dark* and the short story "Rant" were adapted for film. "Walking Wolf" was optioned by New Line Television (1998-2001) and the character Sonja Blue was optioned by Palomar Pictures (beginning in 2001).

WORK IN PROGRESS: A novel, *Absalom's Wake,* for Biting Dog Press.

SIDELIGHTS: Nancy A. Collins has earned kudos for her combination of fantasy and gothic-tinged horror. Her character Sonja Blue, a female part-vampire/vampire huntress who appears in several of Collins's novels, is, according to David Mathew in the *St. James Guide to Horror, Ghost and Gothic Writers,* one of the few recurring characters in horror fiction. "Where other genres (detective fiction, for example) often have long-running characters that are forces for good," Mathew points out, "one of the important points about

horror fiction is that it celebrates the dark side—the forbidden, the taboo—and the book-to-book characters tend to be forces for darkness, or at the very least, unconventionality." Sonja's character is certainly unconventional, and apparently addictive, as devoted Collins fans continue to devour Sonja's stories. John C. Snider, on the *Sci Fi Dimensions* Web site, wrote that "Sonja is sexy, smart, and not to be messed with."

Collins's first novel, *Sunglasses after Dark,* won a Bram Stoker Award and an Icarus Award, and was described as "an energetic, highly inventive, entertaining set of new changes rung on the anything-but-silver bell of vampirism" by Edward Bryant of *Locus.* In the novel, Collins relates the tale of Denise, a wealthy young woman who was attacked by the vampire Lord Morgan, but was found, rushed to the hospital, and given a blood transfusion before her transformation into a creature of the night could fully take place. Instead, Denise, who is now called Sonja Blue, becomes a denizen of a netherworld populated by vampires, shapeshifters, ogres, succubi, werewolves, and other such characters. Known as the Pretenders, this population takes human shape and is represented by characters that are indigent, disabled, or work as exotic dancers or prostitutes. Sonja's quest is to rid the world of the evil Pretenders, who prey on the naivety of humans. Mathew notes that "Collins excels at ripe descriptions of downtown, rundown areas—the sorts of places that a vampire such as Sonja likes to frequent. As Sonja herself puts it, 'The porn shops, titty bars, and adult cinemas are all very busy, like maggots in a corpse. . . . It's my element.'"

By preying on the Pretenders, Sonja tries to avenge what had been done to her by Morgan. Another nemesis of hers in *Sunglasses after Dark* is televangelist Catherine Wheele, who has captured Sonja and immobilized her in a psychiatric ward at the novel's opening. "The whole point of Sonja Blue is, she would really rather be human. She really hates being a vampire. It's self-loathing, but also self-realization, because it's not gonna change," Collins told *Locus.* The novel also incorporates many elements of contemporary culture, including Sonja's visit to the Paris gravesite of rock star Jim Morrison. Bryant called Sonja "deftly characterized" and commended Collins's "seemingly endless fountain of imaginative delights, sometimes grim, mostly perversely funny."

Collins's next book, *Tempter,* started as a voodoo novel, but after the success of *Sunglasses After Dark,*

Collins's editor convinced her to turn it into a vampire novel. The result was not entirely successful, and the author next attempted a true sequel to *Sunglasses after Dark. In the Blood* tracks Sonja and a new companion named Palmer, who has been hired by a doctor to find her. Their adventures are set in New Orleans, a city with a reportedly large population of Pretenders. Sonja and Palmer search for Lord Morgan in order to extract revenge. Bryant remarked, "Collins is developing a hip, romantic style that keeps a honed edge of sardonic humor. It's a killer combination." The critic termed *In the Blood* "crowd-satisfying storytelling with color, movement, excitement, some erotic content, and just enough adroitly twisted violence."

Paint It Black finds Collins writing the most experimental novel in the "Sonja Blue" series and, as Mathew points out, "as is the nature of experiments, some of it works, and some of it does not. Arguably, in fact, *Paint It Black* does not qualify for the term 'novel' in the traditional sense at all; it is a scrapbook of interconnecting diary snippets and vignettes. Multiple voices, cross-indexed and occasionally overlapping, tell the story ostensibly of Sonja's . . . continuing struggles . . . while also providing a curt and ugly parable of Love at the end of the twentieth century. Maybe 'warning' is a better word, for this is Collins's bleakest yet: this is the Dark Age of Love."

Collins has also penned other tales outside of the "Sonja Blue" stories. Among the most praised is the novel *Wild Blood*. The plot involves a young teenager named Skinner who is troubled by dreams that seem to suggest he might be a werewolf. Eventually Skinner encounters a nefarious underworld, similar to the one inhabited by the Pretenders in Collins's "Sonja Blue" tales, and becomes involved with a speed-metal band named Vargr. The musicians are werewolves as well as actual vargr—beings who are able to alter their physical form. In *Locus*, Bryant termed Collins's *Wild Blood* "neither as tight nor as sharp as we readers have become accustomed to in her work. But that doesn't diminish the novel's entertainment value."

In *Walking Wolf: A Weird Western,* Collins crosses the werewolf story with the Western in a tale of a young werewolf boy living in nineteenth-century Texas. Werewolf Billy Skillet works as a bartender, as a musician in a medicine show, and as the assistant to a gunslinger as he makes his way through the American West. A reviewer for *Publishers Weekly* praised "Billy's irreverent portrait of the Wild West and his wry reflections on human nature."

Collins has also edited several collections of stories, including *Dark Love,* an anthology of erotic horror literature, which revolves around "the psychological horror that can arise when relationships, natural or otherwise, go sour," as Roland Green noted in *Booklist.* According to a reviewer for *Publishers Weekly, Dark Love* is "one of the finest horror collections of the year."

After reworking 1990's *Tempter,* Collins re-released the novel in 2001, receiving a much better reception from the critical community and fans of Collins alike. This version of the book focuses on Alex Rossiter, a failed rock star looking for a comeback, which he finds during a descent into the dark world of New Orleans voudou magic. In *Tempter,* Alex starts a new band and is initiated into the voudou community, where he meets Ti, a beautiful dancer, Mad Aggie, a voudou paraphernalia dealer, and other mysterious characters. From Ti, Alex procures an ancient grimoire—a book of voudou spells, some requiring bloody sacrifice—called the *Aegrosomnia.* While Alex tries out different spells for success, he is unknowingly sucked into something much darker as the original owner of the book—the evil spirit of former plantation owner Donatien Legendre, now called Il-Qui-Tente or the Tempter—tries to free himself from self-inflicted, spell-induced centuries of torturous limbo and regain mortality through Alex. As the story progresses, the musician slowly begins to realize that no one is who he or she appears to be. "Although it was not rated very highly at the time, *Tempter* was in its initial form a pretty fair novel," stated reviewer John Grant on the *Infinity Plus* Web site. "It is now much better than that. . . . This is a novel that merits attention." Similarly, *SF Site* reviewer Lisa DuMond called the reworked version of *Tempter* "a whole new ballgame. Gone are the distracting and superfluous vampire plots . . . and the attention is back on the dark voudou dealings that made it a collector's item." DuMond praised the author's ability to "captur[e] the flaws and subtle defects in her characters," and considered the book "another testament to her mastery of dark fantasy." *Books 'n' Bytes* critic Harriet Klausner also commented on Collins's mastery of her characters, calling them "fully developed, making them seem authentic, though pawns in a cosmic chess game played by essences much older than mankind."

Sonja Blue returns in Collins's 2002 novel *Darkest Heart.* After thirty years of hunting vampires, Sonja has her first encounter with a fellow vampire hunter. The human Jack Estes hunts Sonja with the intent of killing her until she reveals her duplicitous nature and her inner battles with "The Other," her internal vampire with whom she struggles, sometimes even injuring herself to keep "The Other" from performing evil acts. Once Jack trusts Sonja, he asks her to help him in a plot of personal vengeance, which he intends to enact on his parents' killer. Jack seeks Noir, a vampire who has been around for countless centuries and is shunned by the vampire community because he is a "strega," a vampire who was created not by "birth" (the traditional bite on the neck), but by a magic spell, and is said to have the darkest heart of all vampires. As Sonja and Jack search for Noir, Sonja must try to help Jack see the hidden, dangerous, and omnipresent "Real World" of the Pretenders, who are visible only to human poets, drunks, and the insane.

"The world Collins gives us is one of uncompromising cruelty," wrote Cindy Lynn Speer on *SF Site.* "She says, in the context, that humans cannot take the reality of the situation, the reality of Sonja's predator-infested world. . . . It is almost as if humans chose not to see." The author, in an interview with Snider, commented on this aspect of her "Sonja Blue" novels: "The 'Real World' is a metaphor for our ability to deceive ourselves. It addresses our unwillingness to deal with the evils we see every day and choose to ignore—whether it's the wife-beater who lives next door, the sexual predator up the street, or the white-collar criminal at work." Speer concluded her review by saying, "Filled with seductive darkness and the brightest lights of hope, *Darkest Heart* may well be, according to the author, the last serving of Sonja Blue we ever get to read." Collins admitted to Snider, "I really don't feel like I have any further novel-length Sonja stories in me. I would rather quit now than grow increasingly tired of the character. I don't want to end up like Arthur Conan Doyle, who came to positively loathe Sherlock Holmes." However, the author teased, "That's not to say I won't write the occasional Sonja Blue short story or novelette." In his own review of the book, Snider commented on the popularity of the "Sonja" series, reporting that "her readers never cease to be excited by the mix of gothic eroticism, the snappy dialogue of an old detective flick, and ass-kicking post-punk attitude."

Collins next published two collections of previously released and new stories: *Dead Roses for a Blue Lady* and *Knuckles and Tales. Dead Roses for a Blue Lady* features a variety of "Sonja Blue" stories, three of which are new. "Knifepoint" is actually the story of Sonja's mentor, Erich Ghilardi, and takes place long before Sonja was created. In "Cold Turkey," which was originally part of the third "Sonja Blue" novel, *Paint It Black,* readers see Sonja's first battles with love as she tries to understand how Judd, the first human to ever romantically pursue Sonja, can have feelings for her. Meanwhile, Sonja must constantly battle "The Other" in an attempt to save Judd. In "Tender Tigers," Sonja tries to save a little girl and her brother from their evil ogress stepmother. "Vampire King of the Goth Chicks" sees Sonja uncover the identity of a pseudo-vampire, whom she loathes for his desire to be part of the world she works to destroy. "*Dead Roses for a Blue Lady* is filled with many different types of stories, and many different moods," wrote Speer in a review of the book. "Sonja Blue is extremely well done, likeable, earthy, and hard out of necessity. . . . It makes me feel better, knowing that if vampires do happen to haunt the night, there might be someone like Sonja standing between us and them," surmised Speer. *Booklist* reviewer Kristine Huntley called the stories in the book "absorbing . . . dark and introspective," observing that they "show just why Sonja Blue is popular."

Knuckles and Tales features a slew of southern gothic stories set in the backwoods fictional town of Seven Devils, Arkansas. "Sunday Go to Meeting Jaw" takes place after the Civil War and relates the sad tale of a little girl who must try to come to terms with her father's war-related disfiguration and artificial jaw. "The Pumpkin Child" takes place post-World War II, when a soldier comes home to find that his girlfriend and business have fallen prey to his arch rival, after which the soldier resorts to witchcraft for revenge. In "Raymond," a little boy undergoes a lobotomy to suppress his werewolf impulses.

In a review of *Knuckles and Tales* for *Publishers Weekly,* a contributor stated that Collins's "strategic deployment of folklore and cornpone colloquialisms gives her homegrown horrors authenticity and helps make these dark slices of southern life as chilling as a mint julep in summer." "Always borderline, always edgy, Nancy Collins is a stylist who handles psychological suspense as intelligently as she does supernatural," wrote Wes Unruh in a review of *Knuckles and Tales* for the *Green Man Review* Web site. "Nancy

Collins's intrigues and private histories are as tangled as the bayous that run through her fictional Choctaw County and the town of Seven Devils," Unruh continued. "Each story . . . hits just the right blend of bizarre erotica, racial tension, and backwoods folklore without ever sacrificing narrative or character." DuMond wrote, "No one outdoes Collins on Southern Gothic; she's practically made the subgenre her very own." DuMond went on to praise the author's "fruitful and frightful imagination," remarking that the book is "well worth the trip down south . . . If you don't value your life."

BIOGRAPHICAL AND CRITICAL SOURCES:

BOOKS

Collins, Nancy A., *Sunglasses after Dark,* New American Library (New York, NY), 1989.
St. James Guide to Horror, Ghost, and Gothic Writers, St. James Press (Detroit, MI), 1998.

PERIODICALS

Booklist, November 1, 1995, p. 454; May 15, 2002, Kristine Huntley, review of *Dead Roses for a Blue Lady,* pp. 1582-1583.
Library Journal, January, 1997, p. 144.
Locus, August, 1989, pp. 21-23, 56; October, 1990, pp. 23-25, 55; February, 1992, p. 31; March, 1992, pp. 21-23, 62; October, 1992, pp. 23-25, 57; September, 1994, pp. 29-31, 70; December, 1994, pp. 4, 80-81; October, 2002, description of *A Darkest Heart,* p. 40.
Publishers Weekly, June 16, 1989, p. 65; April 17, 1995, p. 42; September 25, 1995, p. 44; September 17, 2001, review of *Tempter,* p. 60; December 3, 2001, review of *Knuckles and Tales,* p. 45; March 4, 2002, review of *Dead Roses for a Blue Lady,* p. 61.
Voice of Youth Advocates, February, 1990, p. 370.

ONLINE

Books 'n' Bytes Web site, http://www.booksnbytes.com/ (March 25, 2004), Harriet Klausner, review of *Tempter.*
Fantastic Fiction Web site, http://www.fantasticfiction.co.uk/ (March 25, 2004), "Nancy A. Collins."

Green Man Review Web site, http://www.greenmanreview.com/ (March 25, 2004), Wes Unruh, review of *Knuckles and Tales.*
Infinity Plus Web site, http://www.infinityplus.uk.co/ (April 2, 2004), John Grant, review of *Tempter.*
Sci Fi Dimensions Web site, http://www.scifi dimensions.com/ (March 25, 2004), John C. Snider, reviews of *Knuckles and Tales* and *Darkest Heart,* and "Interview: Nancy A. Collins."
SF Site, http://www.sfsite.com/ (March 25, 2004), Lisa DuMond, reviews of *Knuckles and Tales* and *Tempter;* Cindy Lynn Speer, reviews of *Darkest Heart* and *Dead Roses for a Blue Lady.**

*   *   *

COOPER, Elisha 1971-

PERSONAL: Born February 22, 1971, in New Haven CT; son of Peter (a lawyer and farmer) and Diana (a writer and farmer) Cooper. *Education:* Yale College, B.A., 1993.

ADDRESSES: Home—77A Tamalpais Rd., Berkeley, CA 94708. *Agent*—Darhansoff & Verrill Literary Agency, 179 Franklin St., 4th fl., New York, NY. *E-mail*—elicooper@aol.com.

CAREER: New Yorker magazine, messenger, 1993-95; writer and artist, 1995—.

WRITINGS:

FOR CHILDREN

Country Fair, Greenwillow Press (New York, NY), 1997.
Ballpark, Greenwillow Press (New York, NY), 1998.
Building, Greenwillow Books (New York, NY), 1999.
Henry, Chronicle Books (New York, NY), 1999.
Dance!, Greenwillow Books (New York, NY), 2001.
Ice Cream, Greenwillow Books (New York, NY), 2002.

OTHER

A Year in New York, City & Company (New York, NY), 1995.
Off the Road: An American Sketchbook, Villard (New York, NY), 1997.

A Day at Yale, Yale Bookstore (New Haven, CT), 1998.

California: A Sketchbook, Chronicle Books (New York, NY), 2000.

Paris Night and Day: From the Marais to the Cafe, Artisan (New York, NY), 2002.

WORK IN PROGRESS: A children's book about a large cat.

SIDELIGHTS: Elisha Cooper's books all spring from his love of drawing and observation. Many of his books are intended for children, while others, including *A Year in New York* and *Off the Road: An American Sketchbook* are enjoyable for older readers. Reflecting on his career and how it started, Cooper once told *CA:* "I grew up drawing cows. In the fields below our house there was a herd of Jerseys, and when I was three or four I sat on our porch with pencils and paper and tried to sketch them. The results were pretty lousy, or so I thought at the time, and I remember having tantrums and ripping up the drawings when they didn't look exactly right.

"When I got older, my best friend and I started a lawn-mowing business; we took the money we made and went on trips. I disliked cameras—more accurately, I disliked the loud splashy tourists who used them—so I kept notebooks and wrote down things we saw, what we ate, smells. My mother gave me a tin of watercolors (the same one I use now) and I took that on my trips, too. At home I read a lot, especially *Tintin* and *Asterix.* I took books and newspapers on walks with my goats.

"When I was at Yale and playing football, I brought sketchbooks with me on road trips. I also wrote for the *New Journal,* a magazine, usually about things I had done—like bottling beer at a factory or playing in a game. I spent the summer before my senior year in Idaho working for the Forest Service (inspired by Norman Maclean's short stories) and wrote in a notebook and missed my friends. When I graduated and came to New York, I took a sketchbook along on the subway when I made deliveries as a messenger for the *New Yorker* magazine. That became my first book, *A Year in New York.* I think at this time I fell in love with books, and with New York. They both have a richness to them. Then I quit my job and drove around the country, sleeping in the front seat, showering in rivers, and seeing what I could find. That book was called *Off the Road: An American Sketchbook.*"

The author reflected: "I think most kids' books are stories. I like reading stories, but can't write them. I write what I see. For my first two kids' books, I spent a fall hanging out at country fairs and ballparks. I like nosing around and looking for the weird, something that hits me, a goofy gesture." Nosing around paid off for Cooper's book *Country Fair,* an illustrated look at one day in the life of the popular rural event, from corn-shucking to award-winning cows. *Booklist* reviewer Susan Dove Lempke called the work "as removed from big, splashy preschool books as it can be. It is brimming with tiny, precisely described moments." Lolly Robinson wrote in *Horn Book:* "The small size of this book and the quiet honesty of text and art indicate a book that will be shared one-on-one and frequently revisited by children who enjoy an amiable ramble." A *Kirkus Reviews* critic called Cooper's work "a quirky, engaging look at the sights, sounds, and scents of a country fair."

Next, Cooper turned his gaze to baseball for his book *Ballpark.* A *Kirkus Reviews* critic noted Cooper's attention to detail and his ability to evoke the baseball experience and share it with everyone: "Sports fan or not, spectators or athletes, children will be engaged for the full nine innings." Elizabeth Bush, in *Bulletin of the Center for Children's Books,* noted Cooper's "tidy phrasing . . . and restrained humor" in recommending *Ballpark* as "an elegant visual presentation." *Building,* published in 1999, is a small book that shows in sequential pictures how an empty lot is transformed into a space with an attractive building. Details abound, and the methodical pace found in *Country Fair* and *Ballpark* is also in evidence here. The creation of the building is recorded as if seen through the eyes of a child and "explained in a spare, poetic style," informed Lolly Robinson in *Horn Book.* A *Publishers Weekly* writer stated that "Cooper's latest sketchbook strikes his signature pleasing balance between the facutal and the whimsical." Pencil and watercolors are used to show the action, and "abundant anecdotes bring a refreshing, true-to-life quality to this chronicle."

Cooper's *Dance!,* published in 2001, was warmly reviewed by many critics. The illustrations focus mainly on the human body, and their suggested movements "create an energy and rhythm that more than make up for the lack of props," said Lolly Robinson in *Horn Book.* "With an economy of line and color, Cooper conjures up pain and grace, hard work and camaraderie, stillness and velocity." The reviewer for *Publishers Weekly* took note of the book's "inventive design," which "features cleverly configured type that intermittently mimics the dancers' movements as it gracefully winds and bends across the pages."

Creative typography, subtle humor, and facts about ice cream make up Cooper's book *Ice Cream.* Beginning with cows and proceeding through the manufacturing process, Cooper "balances the relevant facts with his folksy, child-centered descriptions of minutiae," reported Robinson in another *Horn Book* review. "Cooper's relaxed pencil and watercolor drawings imply as much as they show, while the text keeps the atmosphere playful with a design that maximizes Cooper's sense of visual rhythm."

Cooper acknowledges his penchant for reporting on a particular event—be it a fair or a ballgame—but only up to a point. "I think of myself as a lazy journalist," he commented. "If I were more serious, I'd write long pieces with lots of facts. I read too much, the *New York Times* and *Calvin and Hobbes.* In some way, I've never evolved. I'm most happy when I'm about to set off on a trip with a sketchbook in my back pocket. There's a lot of cool stuff out there. For me, books are a way of looking. I still have tantrums when I can't draw cows."

BIOGRAPHICAL AND CRITICAL SOURCES:

PERIODICALS

Booklist, September 15, 1997, p. 240; June 1, 1999, Lauren Peterson, review of *Building,* p. 1832; December 15, 2000, Gillian Engberg, review of *Building,* p. 810; September 15, 2001, Kelly Milner Halls, review of *Dance!,* p. 217; May 15, 2002, Diane Foote, review of *Ice Cream,* p. 1598.
Buffalo News, June 30, 2002, review of *Ice Cream,* p. F5.
Bulletin of the Center for Children's Books, March, 1998, p. 239.
Five Owls, March-April, 1998, pp. 79-80.
Horn Book, September-October, 1997, p. 554; May, 1999, Lolly Robinson, review of *Building,* p. 312; November-December, 2001, Lolly Robinson, review of *Dance!,* p. 733; May-June, 2002, Lolly Robinson, review of *Ice Cream,* p. 343.

Kirkus Reviews, June 15, 1997, pp. 947-948; February 15, 1998, p. 265.
New York Times Book Review, February 25, 1996, p. 20; November 18, 2991, Arnold McCully, review of *Dance!,* p. 50.
Publishers Weekly, January 8, 1996, p. 22; May 26, 1997, p. 85; March 15, 1999, review of *Building,* p. 57; July 30, 2001, review of *Dance!,* p. 84; February 18, 2002, review of *Ice Cream,* p. 96.
School Library Journal, September, 1997, p. 179; March, 1998, p. 194; May, 1999, Carol Ann Wilson, review of *Building,* p. 105; September, 2001, Catherine Threadgill, review of *Dance!,* p. 212; May, 2002, Blair Christolon, review of *Ice Cream,* p. 136.

OTHER

Bulletin of the Center for Children's Books, http://alexia.lis.uiuc.edu/puboff/bccb/ (May 29, 2003), Jeannette Hulick, "Elisha Cooper."

*   *   *

CRUTCHER, Chris(topher C.) 1946-

PERSONAL: Born July 17, 1946, in Cascade, ID; son of John William (a county clerk) and Jewell (Morris) Crutcher. *Education:* Eastern Washington State College (now University), B.A., 1968. *Politics:* Independent.

ADDRESSES: Home—East 3405 Marion St., Spokane, WA 99223. *Office*—Community Mental Health, South 107 Division, Spokane, WA 99202. *Agent*—Liz Darhansoff, 1220 Park Ave., New York, NY 10028.

CAREER: Kennewick Dropout School, Kennewick, WA, teacher of high school dropouts, 1970-73; Lakeside School, Oakland, CA, teacher, 1973-76, director of school, 1976-80; Community Mental Health, Spokane, WA, child protection team specialist, 1980-82, child and family therapist, 1982—.

AWARDS, HONORS: American Library Association's list of best books for young adults, 1983, for *Running Loose,* 1986, for *Stotan!,* 1989, for *Chinese Handcuffs,*

Chris Crutcher

The Crazy Horse Electric Game, Greenwillow (New York, NY), 1987.

Chinese Handcuffs, Greenwillow (New York, NY), 1989.

Athletic Shorts: Six Short Stories, Greenwillow (New York, NY), 1991, HarperTempest (New York, NY), 2002.

Staying Fat for Sarah Byrnes, Greenwillow (New York, NY), 1993, HarperCollins (New York, NY), 2003.

Ironman, Greenwillow (New York, NY), 1995.

(Contributor) Lisa Rowe Fraustino, editor, *Dirty Laundry, Stories about Family Secrets*, Viking (New York, NY), 1998.

Whale Talk, Greenwillow (New York, NY), 2001.

OTHER

The Deep End, Morrow (New York, NY), 1991.

King of the Mild Frontier: An Ill-Advised Autobiography, Greenwillow Books/HarperCollins (New York, NY), 2003.

Contributor to *Spokane* magazine.

ADAPTATIONS: Audio versions have been made of *Athletic Shorts, Ironman, Whale Talk,* and *Staying Fat for Sarah Byrnes*; screenplay for *Staying Fat for Sarah Byrnes* in production.

SIDELIGHTS: Chris Crutcher grew up in a town so small that a local athletic competition would bring business to a standstill. Crutcher played many sports in high school, did well in college swimming, and began participating in triathlons after college. It comes as no surprise then that competitive sports figure heavily in his writing. Throughout his schooling, as he describes in his autobiography, Crutcher was a self-professed academic underachiever, his family life was challenging, and he grew up with a violent temper. Yet he eventually earned a B.A. with a major in psychology and a minor in sociology, and became a high school social studies teacher, a school administrator, and a therapist at a mental health facility. After completing his education, Crutcher taught in tough, inner-city schools and ran an alternative school for inner-city kids in Oakland, California, before becoming a child and family therapist, all of which helped

1991, for *Athletic Shorts,* 1993, for *Staying Fat for Sarah Byrnes,* and 1995, for *Ironman; School Library Journal*'s best books for young adults list, and American Library Association's list of best books for young adults for *The Crazy Horse Electric Game,* both 1988; Michigan Library Association Best Young Adult Book of 1992, for *Athletic Shorts;* ALAN award for Significant Contribution to Adolescent Literature; National Intellectual Freedom Award, National Council of Teachers of English, 1998; ALA Margaret A. Edwards Award for lifetime achievement in writing for teenagers, 2000; Pacific Northwest Booksellers Association and Washington State Book awards for *Whale Talk,* 2002; "Writers Who Make a Difference" Award, *Writer,* 2004.

WRITINGS:

BOOKS FOR YOUNG ADULTS

Running Loose, Greenwillow (New York, NY), 1983, HarperTempest (New York, NY), 2003.

Stotan!, Greenwillow (New York, NY), 1986.

prepare him to write about a wide variety of serious problems with which adolescents are confronted daily in modern day American culture.

"Writing with a vitality and authority that stems from personal experiences in *Running Loose, Stotan!,* and *The Crazy Horse Electric Game,* Chris Crutcher gives readers the inside story on young men, sports, and growing up," wrote Christine McDonnell in *Horn Book.* "His heroes—sensitive, reflective young men, far from stereotypic jocks—use sports as an arena to test personal limits; to prove stamina, integrity, and identity; and to experience loyalty and cooperation as well as competition." In *Staying Fat for Sarah Byrnes,* Crutcher teams a girl whose face is disfigured by a burn and her long-time overweight friend, "Moby" Calhoun, both of whom have the "terminal uglies," in the eyes of their schoolmates. The friends ultimately discover the shameful truth of how Sarah got her burn. In a New York Public Library "Author Chat," Crutcher told a caller: "The 'event' came from a real event in which a man burned his child in a drunken rage, and then handed her back to her mother and said, 'There's your pretty little girl for you.' The real people were very different from those in the story, and I did the 'what if' game to create characters who would help me tell the story the way I wanted to tell it." Crutcher does much to expose the real ugliness of what many children suffer, along with a message of courage and possibilities for healing.

In *Ironman* a high school senior, Bo Brewster, is locked "in a perpetual struggle with an authoritarian father and a battle with a tyrannical teacher," according to *New York Times* reviewer James Gorman. It is the story, Gorman wrote, of "Bo's search for self-understanding, self-possession and self-respect." Gorman noted that even if the book sounds like the plot of a television movie, "[Crutcher's] tale is a lot stronger than the flash that overlays it. He's a terrific storyteller with a wonderful handle on what it's like to be an adolescent." After a gap of six years, Crutcher produced *Whale Talk,* another story set in a small northwest town, where Tao (T. J.) Jones, a mixed-race high school athlete—"witty, self-assured, fearless, intelligent, and wise beyond his years" according to Todd Morning in the *School Library Journal,*—"has refused to play on the school teams and thus condone the Cutter High School cult of athletic privilege. He agrees to lead a startup swim team only to buck the system by signing up every needy misfit he can find—

from a special ed. student to a 'one-legged psychopath'—and ensuring that each will win a Cutter High letterman's jacket. In quintessential Crutcher form, the unlikely athletes build up not only physical strength but emotional support as the team bus becomes a mobile group-therapy session," as a *Horn Book* reviewer described. *Booklist's* Kelly Miller Halls quoted Crutcher on two swim team members: "I actually don't look at either of them as being disabled. I see them as warriors—guys who have really been through it and are struggling to stand up for what they have." T. J. fights elitism among school jocks, extreme racism in the stepfather of a friend, and an arrogant coach to bring his team through.

In 2003, Crutcher broke form by writing *King of the Mild Frontier: An Ill-Advised Autobiography.* A *Horn Book* reviewer praised the new venture: "Crutcher, best known for his novels and short stories, has discovered his most effective voice in this collection of episodic, autobiographical essays." In a *Journal of Adolescent and Adult Literature* interview, James Blasingame asked Crutcher about the ways he deals with death in his essays. The author responded, "The common issue is loss, and death is the trump card of loss. In the preface to one of the short stories in *Athletic Shorts* . . . I said there is a case to be made that from the time of birth, when we lose a warm, enclosed, safe place to be, our lives are made up of a series of losses and our grace can be measured by how we face those losses, and how we replace what is lost. What I'm talking about there is the process of grief, which is one of the most important things we do as humans—taking the risk of losing one thing so we can go on to the next. I believe our culture doesn't understand that very well, and it often tries to force us to hold on to old perceptions and beliefs that have little or no further use and that keep us stuck and afraid. If we do learn to face death, accommodate and accept it, there are few lesser changes that can tip us over, though there are certainly 'fates worse than death.' So, yeah, I think it's common for kids, at their developmental level, and it is common for us at ours." Crutcher, whose work has at times been censored by over-zealous librarians, parents, and teachers for his real-to-life dealing with the complexities—humorous and tragic—of teenage life, addresses these issues and shares stories from his growing up, which Joel Shoemaker in the *School Library Journal* described as "tough and tender reminiscences [which] focus primarily on family, social, and school conflicts, but lessons derived from his career as a teacher, therapist, and writer are also described. Hyperbole lightens the mood as the author portrays himself as a young crybaby, academic misfit, and athletic klutz, utterly without self-aggrandizement." It is his humility, wrote a *Publishers Weekly* reviewer, "that allows readers to laugh with young Chris, rather than at him" when he constantly gets into trouble under his older brother's tutelage, gets hit in the mouth with a softball bat showing off for the girls' team, and trembles as "a terrified 123-pound freshman ('with all the muscle definition of a chalk outline')."

Crutcher shared the following thoughts on writing: "It is a joy to write a tale that is believable, that is real. Writing is also a way to express humor and to present different human perspectives. I like to explore the different ways in which people make sense of what goes on around them—ways in which they respond to the wide range of random things that happen, and to the situations they create.

"Working in the mental health field provides me with some unique perspectives on the human drama—how people get stuck and how they grow. Every client—man, woman, or child, no matter how damaged—has shown me at least a small glimpse of how we're all connected."

BIOGRAPHICAL AND CRITICAL SOURCES:

BOOKS

Authors and Artists for Young Adults, Volume 9, Gale (Detroit, MI), 1992.
Children's Literature Review, Volume 28, Gale (Detroit, MI), 1992.
Davis, Terry, *Presenting Chris Crutcher,* Twayne (Boston, MA), 1997.
Twentieth-Century Young Adult Writers, 1st edition, St. James Press (Detroit, MI), 1994.

PERIODICALS

ALAN Review, fall, 1994, "Chris Crutcher—Hero or Villain?"
Booklist, March 1, 1995, p. 1240; April 1, 2001, pp. 1462, 1463; April 15, 2003, p. 1469.

Buffalo News, July 12, 1998, p. F7.
Denver Post, April 15, 2001, p. F-01.
Detroit News, October 3, 2003, p. 05.
Emergency Librarian, January-February, 1991, pp. 67-71; May-June 1996, interview with Crutcher, p. 61.
English Journal, November, 1989, pp. 44-46; March 1996, 36.
Horn Book, May-June, 1988, p. 332; September-October, 1995, p. 606; May, 2001, p. 320; May-June, 2003, p. 368.
Journal of Adolescent and Adult Literacy, May, 2003, James Blasingame, interview with Crutcher, p. 696.
Kirkus Reviews, April 1, 2003, p. 532.
Knight Ridder/Tribune News Service, June 11, 2003, p. K1815.
Lion and the Unicorn: A Critical Journal of Children's Literature, June, 1992, p. 66.
Los Angeles Times Book Review, June 20, 1993, p. 3.
New York Times, May 18, 2003, p. 24.
New York Times Book Review, September 5, 1993, p. 17; July 2, 1995, p. 13.
Publishers Weekly, March 12, 2001, interview with Crutcher, p. 91; February 20, 1995, interview with Crutcher, p. 183; March 3, 2003, p. 77.
School Library Journal, February, 1996, p. 70; October, 1996, p. 78; January, 1997, p. 36; June 2000, interview with Crutcher, p. 42; May, 2001, p. 148; April, 2003, p. 176; October, 2003, reviews of *Ironman,* p. 99, and *Staying Fat for Sarah Byrnes* (audiobook review), p. S68; November, 2003, Carole Fazioli, review of *King of the Mild Frontier: An Ill-Advised Autobiography,* p. 82.
Teacher Librarian, October, 2003, p. 36.
Tribune Books (Chicago, IL), August 11, 1991, p. 6.
VOYA: Voice of Youth Advocates, April, 1983, p. 36; June 2002, p. 94.

ONLINE

Chris Crutcher Home Page, http://www.aboutcrutcher.com/ (March 8, 2004).
New York Public Library,, http://summerreading.nypl.org/ (July, 2002), interview with Crutcher.
Teenreads.com, http://www.teenreads.com/ (April 2, 2001), interview with Crutcher.*

D

d'ALPUGET, Blanche 1944-

PERSONAL: Surname is pronounced "Dal-pu-*jay*"; born January 3, 1944, in Sydney, Australia; daughter of Louis Albert (a journalist) and Josephine (Curgenven) d'Alpuget; married Anthony Ian Camden Pratt (a civil servant), November 22, 1965 (marriage ended); married R. J. Hawke (former Australian prime minister), July 23, 1995; children: (first marriage) Louis. *Ethnicity:* "Anglo-Celt." *Education:* Attended a Church of England girls' grammar school in Sydney, Australia. *Politics:* Labor.

ADDRESSES: Agent—Robert Gottlieb, William Morris Agency, 1350 Avenue of the Americas, New York, NY 10019.

CAREER: Journalist in Sydney, Australia, London, England, Paris, France, Djakarta, Indonesia, Kuala Lumpur, Malaysia, and Canberra, Australia, between 1962 and 1974; writer. Women's Electoral Lobby, past member.

MEMBER: Women's International League for Peace and Freedom, International PEN (Sydney Centre), Australian Labor Party, Oral History Association of Australia (president of Australian Capital Territory branch, 1980-81), Australian Society of Authors.

AWARDS, HONORS: Novel of the Year Award, *Age* newspaper, 1981, Golden Jubilee Award, Sydney Centre, International PEN, 1981, and Biennial Award for Literature, South Australian Government, 1982, all for *Turtle Beach;* Braille Book of the Year award, 1982, for *Turtle Beach,* and 1983, for *Robert J. Hawke: A Biography;* New South Wales Premier's Award, 1983, for *Robert J. Hawke: A Biography;* Commonwealth Award for Literature, Australasian Division, 1987, for *Winter in Jerusalem.*

WRITINGS:

NOVELS

Monkeys in the Dark, J. Cape (London, England), 1980.
Turtle Beach, Penguin (London, England), 1981, Simon & Schuster (New York, NY), 1983.
Winter in Jerusalem, Simon & Schuster (New York, NY), 1986.
White Eye, Simon & Schuster (New York, NY), 1994.

OTHER

Mediator: A Biography of Sir Richard Kirby, Melbourne University Press (Melbourne, Australia), 1977.
Robert J. Hawke: A Biography, Landsdowne Press (East Melbourne, Australia), 1982.

Work represented in anthologies, including *Eleven Sins,* Random House (Melbourne, Australia), 1993.

SIDELIGHTS: In the novel *Turtle Beach* Blanche d'Alpuget introduces Judith Wilkes, an Australian journalist assigned to cover the arrival of boatloads of

Vietnamese refugees into Malaysia in 1979. The world the press woman encounters in post-colonial Kuala Lumpur is a strange mingling of East and West, full of disturbing juxtapositions and ironies: the people she meets in this chaotic environment are a curious mix as well. As Wilkes reports on the tragic plight of the boat people in a country that does not want them and incarcerates them in cruel camps, she also observes the intricate lives of those she has met and engages in her own journey of self-discovery. Gene Lyons, writing in *Newsweek,* described *Turtle Beach* as "the sort of novel one encounters at very rare intervals: broad in scope, ambitious almost to a fault, yet written with a crisp, breezy intelligence that enlivens the story without concealing for a moment its grave implications. . . . *Turtle Beach* makes us witness to history in the raw—the human tidal wave of Southeast Asia," he added, "without peddling phony guilt or easy answers."

Other critics also noted the gripping plot of *Turtle Beach,* its well-drawn characters, and the skillfulness of d'Alpuget's writing. Toronto *Globe and Mail* reviewer Anne Montagnes remarked that "Blanche d'Alpuget writes in a simple, gripping style. Pages flip over as the reader plunges into the concerns of her characters." Suzanne Freeman voiced a similar observation in a *Washington Post* critique, noting that d'Alpuget "is a strong writer with a particularly sharp sense of character. In a few deft behind-the-scene scenes, we get a good look right into the souls of the people in this book." The critic added that "the sheer force of her story is enough to sweep us along to the end. And it's well worth the trip. The final scenes on Turtle Beach are powerful and haunting." And Joe Klein, writing in the *New York Times Book Review,* reflected: "Mrs. d'Alpuget seems able to enter effortlessly the heads of her characters, both Western and Eastern. . . . Her observations are made all the more powerful by a graceful style of writing that is, at once, lucid and coy. . . . This is an auspicious American debut for Blanche d'Alpuget, and it raises two immediate questions: What else has she written, and when do we get to see it?"

D'Alpuget's fourth novel, *White Eye,* received less enthusiastic reviews. Although written as a thriller, according to *New York Times Book Review* critic Nina Sonenberg, the story is "disappointing" and "packs little suspense." Laurie Clancy described the novel in *Contemporary Novelists:* "Although written in a

deliberately plain and simple style the novel has an extraordinarily intricate plot, involving illegal trafficking in chimpanzees between Thailand and Australia, genetic engineering, and an attempt to destroy the world. . . . The protagonist, Diana Pembridge, is a quintessential d'Alpuget heroine, thirty-two years old, beautiful and patrician in appearance, but vulnerable and unfulfilled in reality. She is a passionate lover of nature without being a fanatic. . . . Against her is pitted John Parker, a deeply misogynistic man whose disgust with a proliferating human race drives him to invent a vaccine that will prevent it breeding." Both Sonenberg and Clancy reported that, in the words of Clancy, "some of the finest writing in the novel is devoted to accounts of [Diana] falconing and her struggle to heal and release a wounded wedgetail eagle."

A *Publishers Weekly* review of *White Eye* faulted d'Alpuget for "striv[ing] so hard to press her fine style and character insights into the thriller genre" and further noted: "More problematic is the way characters drop in and out of the plot without developing cogent relationships." Clancy's summary of the novel also recognized weaknesses in character relations: "Like all of d'Alpuget's work, *White Eye* is a carefully and thoroughly researched novel that at times indeed wears its learning a little ostentatiously. It alternates scenes of lyrical evocation of landscape and the beauty of the colony of birds that Diana looks after with descriptions of violence and cruelty. Like *Winter in Jerusalem* it suffers from a rushed ending in which Diana and a charismatic photographer cum environmentalist meet and fall in love in what seems seconds. D'Alpuget has admitted that she has difficulty in writing scenes of sexual love and this is evident here. . . . However, d'Alpuget does save a couple of ingenious twists in the plot till right near the end."

D'Alpuget once told *CA:* "The Muses were the daughters of Jupiter and Memory. Memory, I think, exists within imagination as the grain in timber. Uncovering it—and memory for me remains utterly mysterious—is a delight."

BIOGRAPHICAL AND CRITICAL SOURCES:

BOOKS

Contemporary Novelists, 6th edition, St. James Press (Detroit, MI), 1996.

PERIODICALS

Globe and Mail, (Toronto, Ontario, Canada), December 3, 1983, Anne Montagnes, review of *Turtle Beach.*

Los Angeles Times, February 3, 1984.

Newsweek, November 14, 1983, Gene Lyons, review of *Turtle Beach.*

New York Times Book Review, October 23, 1983, Joe Klein, review of *Turtle Beach;* August 14, 1994, Nina Sonenberg, review of *White Eye.*

Publishers Weekly, June 6, 1994, review of *White Eye.*

Washington Post, September 20, 1983, Suzanne Freeman, review of *Turtle Beach.*

*   *   *

DAWKINS, Cecil 1927-

PERSONAL: Born October 2, 1927 in Birmingham, AL; daughter of James Toliver and Lucile-Hannah (Thiemonge) Dawkins. *Education:* University of Alabama, B.A., 1950; Stanford University, M.A., 1953.

ADDRESSES: Home—Santa Fe, NM. *Agent*—Charlotte Sheedy Literary Agency, 65 Bleecker St., New York, NY 10012.

CAREER: Writer. Stephens College, instructor in English, 1953-58, writer in residence, 1961-62, 1973-76; Sarah Lawrence College, guest faculty member, 1979-81; University of Hawaii—Manoa, distinguished visiting writer, 1991.

AWARDS, HONORS: Stanford University fellow, 1952-53; McGinnis Award, 1963, for "A Simple Case"; Guggenheim fellow, 1966-67; Harper-Saxton fellow, Harper & Row, 1968, 1971, for *The Live Goat;* grant, National Endowment for the Arts, 1976.

WRITINGS:

The Quiet Enemy (short stories), Atheneum (New York, NY), 1963, reprinted, University of Georgia Press (Athens, GA), 1995.

The Displaced Person (play; adapted from stories by Flannery O'Connor), produced in New York, NY, at American Place Theater, 1966.

The Live Goat (novel), Harper (New York, NY), 1971.

Charleyhorse (contemporary western novel), Viking (New York, NY), 1985.

The Santa Fe Rembrandt (mystery novel), Ivy Books (New York, NY), 1993.

Clay Dancers (mystery novel), Random House (New York, NY), 1994.

Rare Earth (mystery novel), Random House (New York, NY), 1995.

Turtle Truths (mystery novel), Ivy Books (New York, NY), 1997.

(Editor) *A Woman of the Century, Frances Minerva Nunnery (1898-1997): Her Story in Her Own Memorable Voice As Told to Cecil Dawkins,* University of New Mexico Press (Albuquerque, NM), 2002.

Contributor to *Best American Short Stories,* edited by Martha Foley, 1963. Contributor of short stories to magazines, including *Paris Review, Sewanee Review, Georgia Review, Southwest Review, McCall's, Redbook, Pacific Spectator,* and *Saturday Evening Post.*

ADAPTATIONS: The Quiet Enemy was adapted as a sound recording, read by the author, released by American Audio Prose Library (Columbia, MO) in 1983.

SIDELIGHTS: Cecil Dawkins's *The Live Goat* combines history and horror in its presentation of Isaac, the scapegoat referred to in the title. He is mentally disabled and kills a sixteen-year-old girl, Eily, on the morning of her wedding day. Isaac then flees, and a group of men, including Eily's father, pursue him and bring him back to be hanged. Christopher Ricks, a reviewer for the *New York Review of Books,* stated: "The book is markedly unsentimental; the code which pursues Isaac for 500 miles, which halters him and brings him back, and which hangs him, is presented with a very precise sense of what in it is high and proud, and what is gross and vengeful." In a *Best Sellers* article, William A. C. Francis observed that "the point of the novel, however, is that no man whose creed is an eye for an eye will ever be whole again once he is contaminated with the blood of the scapegoat." Hite, the preacher in the novel, echoes this same message right before Isaac is hanged, saying,

"God said let the live goat go! Put on his head all your sins and send him into the wilderness! His is your innocence. Don't destroy it!"

In another novel, *Charleyhorse,* Dawkins moves her wilderness setting to a cattle ranch in Kansas. It is on this ranch that the protagonist, Charlene, challenges her mother's control. This all-female household is completed with the arrival of Juna, a schoolteacher from New York; and with Juna's help, Charlene completes her rebellion and discovers herself. A reviewer for *Publishers Weekly* commented that this story of one girl's initiation into adulthood "confirms Dawkins's skill as a storyteller in the tradition of Flannery O'Connor." In contrast, reviewing the novel for the *New York Times Book Review,* Penelope Ready stated: "Despite the author's accurate accounts of a cow-calf operation, the book has a fakey quality. . . . She misses the heart completely, forcing the reader out back to observe the characters through a fly-covered screen door. This novel never touches upon questions of morality, discipline and dignity, which are as close to the landed Western as are the range grasses and sunsets."

A *Publishers Weekly* reviewer found *The Santa Fe Rembrandt,* Dawkins's first mystery novel, to be "a busy but hollow effort in which crimes abound and characters are delivered with carefully designed doses of charm." The plot revolves around a Rembrandt that has been stolen from Santa Fe's Waldheimer Museum. Ginevra Prettifield, assistant director of the museum, conceals the theft from a visiting tour group of long-time yuppie friends known as "the pod" (short for posse). Ginevra enlists the help of her friend Tina Martinez, who in turn persuades two of her admirers, a local police lieutenant and art expert Pablo Esperanza-Ramos, to undertake a discreet investigation of the Rembrandt theft and the forgery that has been put in its place. Ginevra's next discovery is the unconscious body of Raoul Query, one of "the pod" members, with art expert Pablo kneeling over him. It is Ginevra who eventually exposes the mastermind behind the Rembrandt theft, uncovers Raoul's attacker, and as a bonus, also solves the mystery of a murder that took place prior to the book's action.

Turtle Truths, another mystery novel, is set both in Santa Fe and the West Indies and combines elements of murder mystery and melodrama. A struggling artist named Reuben comes to the aid of celebrity actor Anthony Quayle after Quayle has been injured in a horseback-riding accident. As a reward, Quayle offers Reuben the use of his car and a place to stay in his home. In return, he merely asks that Reuben act as an occasional chauffeur. The "occasional" soon becomes "often" as many of those involved in Quayle's next film come to visit. When one of the visitors turns up dead and Quayle subsequently vanishes, Reuben finds himself without an alibi and the chief suspect in the murder. A reviewer for *Publishers Weekly* commented: "There's a lot of Santa Fe color here but the characters are unpleasant and seem merely to appear on the same page rather than actually interact."

BIOGRAPHICAL AND CRITICAL SOURCES:

BOOKS

Dawkins, Cecil, *The Live Goat,* Harper (New York, NY), 1971.

PERIODICALS

Best Sellers, May 15, 1971, William A. C. Francis, review of *The Live Goat.*
New York Review of Books, July 22, 1971, Christopher Ricks, review of *The Live Goat.*
New York Times, June 12, 1971.
New York Times Book Review, September 22, 1985, Penelope Ready, review of *Charleyhorse,* p. 22.
Publishers Weekly, July 12, 1985, review of *Charleyhorse;* September 6, 1993, review of *The Santa Fe Rembrandt,* p. 88; September 15, 1997, review of *Turtle Truths,* p. 73.
Saturday Review, July 3, 1971.

OTHER

Interview (audio cassette recording), American Audio Prose Library (Columbia, MO), 1983.*

*   *   *

DAWSON, Janet 1949-

PERSONAL: Born October 31, 1949, in Purcell, OK; daughter of Donald E. and Thelma Louise (Metcalf) Dawson. *Education:* University of Colorado—Boulder, B.S.; California State University—Hayward, M.A. *Hobbies and other interests:* Cats, gardening, theater.

ADDRESSES: Agent—Charlotte Sheedy Literary Agency, 65 Bleecker St., 12th Fl., New York, NY 10012.

CAREER: Writer of mystery novels. Also worked as a newspaper reporter. *Military service:* U.S. Navy, served as a journalist; became officer.

MEMBER: Mystery Readers International, Mystery Writers of America, Sisters in Crime, Private Eye Writers of America, American Crime Writers League, Authors Guild, Authors League of America.

AWARDS, HONORS: St. Martin's Press/Private Eye Writer's Association Award for best first private eye novel, 1990, for *Kindred Crimes*.

WRITINGS:

NOVELS; EXCEPT AS NOTED

Kindred Crimes, St. Martin's Press (New York, NY), 1990.
Till the Old Men Die, Fawcett (New York, NY), 1993.
Take a Number, Fawcett (New York, NY), 1993.
Don't Turn Your Back on the Ocean, Fawcett (New York, NY), 1994.
Nobody's Child, Fawcett (New York, NY), 1995.
A Credible Threat, Fawcett (New York, NY), 1996.
Witness to Evil, Fawcett (New York, NY), 1997.
Where the Bodies Are Buried, Fawcett Columbine (New York, NY), 1998.
A Killing at the Track: A Jeri Howard Mystery, Fawcett (New York, NY), 2000.
Scam and Eggs (short stories), Five Star (Waterville, ME), 2002.

SIDELIGHTS: Crime novelist Janet Dawson began her career in the genre with the 1990 novel *Kindred Crimes,* which won a contest sponsored by St. Martin's Press for best first private eye novel. *Kindred Crimes* introduces Dawson's signature heroine, private eye Jerusha "Jeri" Howard, an operative working out of the Oakland-Berkeley region of northern California. Beginning with her debut novel, Dawson demonstrates her fascination with plots and characters that center around family relationships, often involving long-held secrets.

Kindred Crimes begins as Jeri Howard takes on a seemingly straightforward case—tracing a missing wife and her money—but finds it growing to involve a fifteen-year-old domestic homicide. Although some reviewers commented that the identity of the culprit became obvious before the end of the novel, none seemed to regard this as a crippling flaw in Dawson's work. A *Publishers Weekly* reviewer commented that "Dawson keeps suspense and interest at high pitch" even for readers who had guessed the villain. *New York Times* contributor Marilyn Stasio wrote that "there is still something very compelling about the detective's sympathetic examination of the psychic injuries sustained by so-called survivors of family violence. . . . [Jeri Howard] has a streak of decency that makes her a welcome addition to this tough genre." *Armchair Detective* critic Marvin Lachman found *Kindred Crimes* "compelling reading."

After the publication of her first novel, Dawson began to produce an average of a novel per year. In *Take a Number,* missing persons and money are again the motif in a complicated mystery yarn that a *Kirkus Reviews* critic dubbed "too much of a good thing." In *Don't Turn Your Back on the Ocean,* Dawson takes as her setting Monterey, California—Steinbeck country—dotting the landscape with a sequence of crimes that include the mutilation of pelicans as well as a series of sabotage actions at a local restaurant. *Armchair Detective* contributor Liz Currie, comparing Dawson's descriptions of the Monterey peninsula to those of novelist John Steinbeck, liked the way the younger writer used the mystery format to educate readers about the endangered environment. Stated Currie, "The complex story features multidimensional characters who grapple with life-sized issues facing real people and Dawson's level of writing and environmental conscience raise this series above most others." Similarly, *Wilson Library Bulletin* writer Gail Pool praised *Don't Turn Your Back on the Ocean* as "a long, complex, and satisfying mystery that brings to life this stretch of California coast." Emphasizing the novel's solid workmanship rather than its setting, a *Kirkus Reviews* contributor remarked that "despite some rough carpentry in the villains' motivations, Dawson . . . pulls her mysteries together with a logically convincing flourish. . . . The breathless multiple plots . . . for once don't reduce the scurrying characters to ciphers."

In *Nobody's Child,* the action takes place during the Christmas season, although the mood is bleak as protagonist Howard bemoans her loneliness and her impending middle age. Hired to unravel the mystery behind a charred female corpse found at a construction site, she discovers that the victim had recently given birth to a child and was HIV-positive. Howard's search for answers takes her through a variety of socioeconomic groups in the San Francisco Bay Area. What emerges, reported Emily Melton of *Booklist*, is "an entertaining and well-written mystery with a spunky, caring heroine," as well as a story that is "thought provoking and sobering." A *Kirkus Reviews* contributor added that *Nobody's Child* is "a bracingly heartfelt tour of the Bay Area's lowest depths." Maureen Corrigan compared Dawson's view of Christmas with Dickens's *A Christmas Carol* in her *Washington Post Book World* review: "Like Dickens, Dawson manages to blend her social criticism into a rich plum pudding of a story sprinkled throughout with memorable characters."

In *A Credible Threat*, Jeri Howard investigates a series of pranks—which escalate from harmless to sinister—at a Berkeley rooming house for female students. A *Kirkus Reviews* commentator especially liked the early part of Jeri's investigation, feeling that issues were raised that extended the intellectual boundaries of the mystery genre; although later, the reviewer suggested, "a pair of culpable coincidences" kicked in, "feminists should cheer Jeri's fighting instincts." Similarly, a *Publishers Weekly* critic pointed out the introduction of a long-hidden second mystery that added "a sprinkle of coincidence"; what that reviewer liked best in the novel was Jeri's "doubting stance" and her "deliciously suspicion-saturated interest in everyone around." A positive review came from *Booklist* contributor Emily Melton, who called *A Credible Threat* "thoroughly satisfying," declaring that, "as usual, Dawson offers a well-constructed plot and smoothly polished writing."

BIOGRAPHICAL AND CRITICAL SOURCES:

PERIODICALS

Armchair Detective, spring, 1993, p. 57; winter, 1995, Liz Currie, review of *Don't Turn Your Back on the Ocean*, p. 105.
Booklist, October 1, 1995, Emily Melton, review of *Nobody's Child*, p. 253; November 1, 1996, Emily Melton, review of *A Credible Threat*, p. 483;

September 1, 1997, David Pitt, review of *Witness to Evil*, p. 63; November 15, 1998, Emily Melton, review of *Where the Bodies Are Buried*, p. 659.
Kirkus Reviews, August 15, 1993, review of *Take a Number*, p. 1029; September 1, 1994, review of *Don't Turn Your Back on the Ocean*, p. 1168; September 1, 1995, review of *Nobody's Child*, p. 1222; September 1, 1996, review of *A Credible Threat*, p. 1274; September 15, 1998, review of *Where the Bodies Are Buried*, p. 1334.
Kliatt Young Adult Paperback Book Guide, January, 1999, review of *Witness to Evil*, p. 12.
Library Journal, October 1, 1994, Rex E. Klett, review of *Don't Turn Your Back on the Ocean*, p. 118; August, 1995, Rex E. Klett, review of *Nobody's Child*, p. 123.
New York Times Book Review, September 9, 1990, Marilyn Stasio, review of *Kindred Crimes*, p. 39.
Publishers Weekly, June 15, 1990, review of *Kindred Crimes*, p. 58; August 30, 1993, review of *Take a Number*, p. 79; September 12, 1994, review of *Don't Turn Your Back on the Ocean*, p. 84; July 24, 1995, review of *Nobody's Child*, p. 49; September 9, 1996, review of *A Credible Threat*, pp. 67-68; July 21, 1997, review of *Witness to Evil*, p. 187; September 14, 1998, review of *Where the Bodies Are Buried*, p. 53.
School Library Journal, April, 1996, Penny Stevens, review of *Nobody's Child*, p. 166.
Washington Post Book World, December 24, 1995, Maureen Corrigan, review of *Nobody's Child*, p. 4; December 20, 1998, review of *Where the Bodies Are Buried*, p. 4.
Wilson Library Bulletin, January, 1995, Gail Pool, review of *Don't Turn Your Back on the Ocean*, p. 95.*

*   *   *

de DUVÉ, Christian (René Marie Joseph) 1917-

PERSONAL: Born October 2, 1917, in Thames-Ditton, England; immigrated to Belgium, 1920; naturalized Belgian citizen; son of Alphonse and Madeleine (Pungs) de Duvé; married Janine Herman, September 30, 1943; children: Thierry, Anne, Françoise, Alain. *Education:* Catholic University of Louvain, M.D., 1941, Ph.D., 1945, M.Sc., 1946; additional study at the Medical Nobel Institute, Stockholm, Sweden, and Washington University, St. Louis, MO.

ADDRESSES: Office—c/o Christian de Duvé Institute of Cellular Pathology, 75 ave. Hippocrate, B-1200 Brussels, Belgium.

CAREER: Biochemist and cell biologist. Catholic University of Louvain, Louvain, Belgium, instructor in physiological chemistry, 1947-51, professor of biochemistry, 1951-85, professor emeritus, 1985—. Rockefeller University, affiliate, 1962-64, professor, 1964-74, Andrew W. Mellon Professor, 1974-88, professor emeritus, 1988—. Mayne Guest Professor, University of Queensland, 1972; visiting professor at Albert Einstein College of Medicine, 1961-62, State University of Ghent, 1962-63, Free University of Brussels, 1963-64, State University of Liege, 1972-73, Universitaires Notre-Dame de la Paix, Namur, 1990-91. International Institute of Cellular and Molecular Pathology, founder, 1971, president, 1974-91; Christian de Duvé Institute of Cellular Pathology, affiliate; advisor to numerous agencies and organizations, including Ciba Foundation, National Institute for Child Health of National Institute of Health, World Health Organization, Max Planck-Institute for Immunobiology, Ludwig Institute for Cancer Research, Mary Imogene Bassett Research Institute, Clinical Research Institute of Montreal, and Basel Institute for Immunology.

MEMBER: International Society for Cell Biology, European Association for the Study of Diabetes, European Molecular Biology Organization, European Cell Biology Organization, Academia Europaea (foreign associate), American Society for Cell Biology (founding member; member of council, 1966-69), American Society of Biological Chemists, American Chemical Society, American Association for the Advancement of Science (fellow), National Academy of Sciences (United States; foreign associate, 1975), American Philosophical Society, American Academy of Arts and Sciences (foreign associate), Biochemical Society, Royal Academy of Belgium, Societe Belge Biochim. (president, 1962-64), Societe Belge de Physiologie, Koninklyke Akademie voor Geneeskunde, Royal Academy of Medicine, Royal Academy (London, England; foreign associate), Royal Society of Canada (foreign associate), Société Chimie Biologique, Académie des Sciences de Paris (foreign associate), Deutsche Akademie der Naturforscher Leopoldina, Deutsche Gesellschaft für Zellbiologie (foreign associate), Athenian Academy of Sciences (foreign associate), Pontifical Academy of Science, New York Academy of Sciences, Sigma Xi.

AWARDS, HONORS: Therese and Johan Anderson Stiftelse fellow in Stockholm, Sweden, 1946-47; Rockefeller Foundation fellow, 1947-48; Prix Pfizer, Royal Academy of Medicine (Belgium), 1957; Prix Francqui, 1960; Prix Quinquennal Belge des Sciences Medicales, Government of Belgium, 1967; award of merit, Gairdner Foundation International, 1967; Dr. H. P. Heineken Prize, Royal Netherlands Academy of Science, 1973; Nobel Prize in medicine (with Albert Claude and George Palade), 1974; Harden Award, Biochemical Society (England), 1978; Theobald Smith Award, Albany Medical College, 1981; Jimenez Diaz Award, 1985; E. B. Wilson Award, American Society for Cell Biology, 1989; numerous honorary degrees, including ones from University of Turin, University of Leiden, University of Lille, Gustavus Adolphus College, University of Keele, University of Montreal, and Rockefeller University; various awards from Belgian, French, and British biochemical societies.

WRITINGS:

Glucose, insuline, et diabéte, [Paris, France], 1945.
A Guided Tour of the Living Cell, two volumes, Scientific American Library (New York, NY), 1985.
Blueprint for a Cell: The Nature and Origin of Life, N. Patterson (Burlington, NC), 1991.
Vital Dust: Life As a Cosmic Imperative, Basic Books (New York, NY), 1995.
Life Evolving: Molecules, Mind, and Meaning, Oxford University Press (New York, NY), 2002.
À l'écoute du vivant, Odile Jacob (Paris, France), 2002.

Contributor of articles and reviews to periodicals, including *American Scientist, International Review of Cytology, Proceedings of the Royal Society, Journal of Cell Biology,* and *Scientific American.* Member of editorial board, *Subcellular Biochemistry,* 1971-87, *Preparative Biochemistry,* 1971-80, and *Molecular and Cellular Biochemistry,* 1973-80.

SIDELIGHTS: Christian de Duvé's ground-breaking studies of cellular structure and function earned him a Nobel Prize in 1974. However, he did much more than discover the two key cellular organelles—lysosomes and peroxisomes—for which the Swedish Academy honored him. His work, along with that of his fellow recipients, established an entirely new field, that of cell biology. De Duvé introduced techniques that have enabled other scientists to better study cellular anatomy and physiology. De Duvé's research has also been of great value in helping clarify the causes of and treatments for a number of diseases.

De Duvé's parents had fled Belgium after its invasion by the German Army in World War I, escaping to safety in England. There, in Thames-Ditton, Christian de Duvé was born. He returned with his parents to Belgium in 1920, and they settled in Antwerp. As a child, de Duvé journeyed throughout Europe, picking up three foreign languages in the process, and in 1934 enrolled in the Catholic University of Louvain, where he received an education in the "ancient humanities." Deciding to become a physician, he entered the medical school of the university.

Finding the pace of medical training relaxed, and realizing that the better students gravitated to research labs, de Duvé joined a group headed by J. P. Bouckaert. Here he studied physiology, concentrating on the hormone insulin and its effects on uptake of the sugar glucose. De Duvé's experiences in Bouckaert's laboratory convinced him to pursue a research career when he graduated with an M.D. in 1941. World War II disrupted his plans, and de Duvé ended up in a prison camp. He managed to escape and subsequently returned to Louvain to resume his investigations of insulin. Although his access to experimental supplies and equipment was limited, he was able to read extensively from the early literature on the subject. Even before obtaining his Ph.D. from the Catholic University of Louvain in 1945, de Duvé had published several works, including a 400-page book on glucose, insulin, and diabetes. De Duvé then obtained an M.Sc. degree in chemistry in 1946.

After graduation, de Duvé decided that he needed a thorough grounding in biochemical approaches to pursue his research interests. He studied with Hugo Theorell at the Medical Nobel Institute in Stockholm for eighteen months, then spent six months with Carl Ferdinand Cori, Gerty Cori, and Earl Sutherland at Washington University School of Medicine in St. Louis. Thus, in his early postdoctoral years he worked closely with no less than four future Nobel Prize winners. It is not surprising that, after this hectic period, de Duvé was happy to return to Louvain in 1947 to take up a faculty post at his alma mater teaching physiological chemistry at the medical school. In

1951, de Duvé was appointed full professor of biochemistry. As he began his faculty career, de Duvé's research was still targeted at unraveling the mechanism of action of the anti-diabetic hormone, insulin. While he was not successful at his primary effort (indeed the answer to de Duvé's first research question was to elude investigators for more than thirty years), his early experiments opened new avenues of research.

As a consequence of investigating how insulin works in the human body, de Duvé and his students also studied the enzymes involved in carbohydrate metabolism in the liver. It was these studies that proved pivotal for de Duvé's eventual rise to scientific fame. In his first efforts, he had tried to purify a particular liver enzyme, glucose-6-phosphatase, that he believed blocked the effect of insulin on liver cells. Many enzymes would solidify and precipitate out of solution when exposed to an electric field. Most could then be redissolved in a relatively pure form given the right set of conditions, but glucose-6-phosphate stubbornly remained a solid precipitate. The failure of this electrical separation method led de Duvé to try a different technique, separating components of the cell by spinning them in a centrifuge, a machine that rotates at high speed. De Duvé assumed that particular enzymes are associated with particular parts of the cell. These parts, called cellular organelles (little organs) can be seen in the microscope as variously shaped and sized grains and particles within the body of cells. It had long been recognized that there existed several discrete types of these organelles, though little was known about their structures or functions at the time.

The basic principles of centrifugation for separating cell parts had been known for many years. First cells are ground up (homogenized) and the resultant slurry placed in a narrow tube. The tube is placed in a centrifuge, and the artificial gravity that is set up by rotation will separate material by weight. Heavier fragments and particles will be driven to the bottom of the tube while lighter materials will layer out on top. At the time de Duvé began his work, centrifugation could be used to gather roughly four different fractions of cellular debris. This division proved to be too crude for his research, because he needed to separate out various cellular organelles more selectively.

For this reason, de Duvé turned to a technique developed some years earlier by fellow-Belgian Albert Claude while working at the Rockefeller Institute for

Medical Research. In the more common centrifugation technique, the cells of interest were first vigorously homogenized in a blender before being centrifuged. In Claude's technique of differential centrifugation, however, cells were treated much more gently, being merely ground up slightly by hand prior to being spun to separate various components.

When de Duvé used this differential centrifugal fractionation technique on liver cells, he did indeed get better separation of cell organelles, and was able to isolate certain enzymes to certain cell fractions. One of his first findings was that his target enzyme, glucose-6-phosphatase, was associated with microsomes, cellular organelles which had been, until that time, considered by cell biologists to be quite uninteresting. De Duvé's work showed that they were the site of key cellular metabolic events. Further, this was the first time a particular enzyme had been clearly associated with a particular organelle.

De Duvé was also studying an enzyme called acid phosphatase that acts in cells to remove phosphate groups (chemical clusters made up of one phosphorus and three oxygen atoms) from sugar molecules under acidic conditions. The differential centrifugation technique isolated acid phosphatase to a particular cellular fraction, but measurements of enzyme activity showed much lower levels than expected. De Duvé was puzzled. What had happened to the enzyme? He and his students observed that if the cell fraction that initially showed this low level of enzyme were allowed to sit in the refrigerator for several days, the enzyme activity increased to expected levels. This phenomenon became known as enzyme latency.

De Duvé believed he had a solution to the latency mystery. He reasoned that perhaps the early, gentle hand-grinding of differential centrifugation did not damage the cellular organelles as much as did the more traditional mechanical grinding. What if, he wondered, some enzymes were not freely exposed in the cells' interiors, but instead were enclosed *within* protective membranes of organelles. If these organelles were not then broken apart by the gentle grinding, the enzyme might still lie trapped within the organelles in the particular cell fraction after centrifugation. If so, it would be isolated from the chemicals used to measure enzyme activity. This would explain the low initial enzyme activity, and why over time, as the organelles' membranes gradually deteriorated, enzyme activity would increase.

De Duvé realized that his ideas had powerful implications for cellular research. By carefully observing what enzymes were expressed in what fractions and under what conditions, de Duvé's students were able to separate various enzymes and associate them with particular cellular organelles. By performing successive grinding and fractionations, and by using compounds such as detergents to break up membranes, de Duvé's group began making sense out of the complex world that exists within cells.

De Duvé's research built on the work of other scientists. Previous research had clarified some of the roles of various enzymes. But de Duvé came to realize that there existed a group of several enzymes, in addition to acid phosphatase, whose primary functions all related to breaking down certain classes of molecules. These enzymes were always expressed in the same cellular fraction and showed the same latency. Putting this information together, de Duvé realized that he had found an organelle devoted to cellular digestion. It made sense, he reasoned, that these enzymes should be sequestered away from other cell components. They functioned best in a different environment, expressing their activity fully only under acidic conditions (the main cell interior is neutral). Moreover, these enzymes could damage many other cellular components if set loose in the interiors of the cells. With this research, de Duvé identified lysosomes and elucidated their pivotal role in cellular digestive and metabolic processes. Later research in de Duvé's laboratory showed that lysosomes play critical roles in a number of disease processes as well.

De Duvé eventually uncovered more associations between enzymes and organelles. The enzyme monoamine oxidase, for example, behaved very similarly to the enzymes of the lysosome, but de Duvé's careful and meticulous investigations revealed minor differences in when and where it appeared. He eventually showed that monoamine oxidase was associated with a separate cellular organelle, the peroxisome. Further investigation led to more discoveries about this previously unknown organelle. It was discovered that peroxisomes contain enzymes that use oxygen to break up certain types of molecules. They are vital to neutralizing many toxic substances, such as alcohol, and play key roles in sugar metabolism.

Recognizing the power of the technique that he had used in these early experiments, de Duvé pioneered its use to answer questions of both basic biological interest and immense medical application. His group discovered that certain diseases result from the inability of cells to properly digest their own waste products. For example, a group of illnesses known collectively as disorders of glycogen storage result from malfunctioning lysosomal enzymes. Tay Sachs disease, a congenital neurological disorder that kills its victims by age five, results from the accumulation of a component of the cell membrane that is not adequately metabolized due to a defective lysosomal enzyme.

In 1962 de Duvé joined the Rockefeller Institute (now Rockefeller University) while keeping his appointment at Louvain. In subsequent years, working with numerous research groups at both institutions, he studied inflammatory diseases such as arthritis and arteriosclerosis, genetic diseases, immune dysfunctions, tropical maladies, and cancers. This work has led, in some cases, to the creation of new drugs used in combatting some of these conditions. In 1971 de Duvé formed the International Institute of Cellular and Molecular Pathology, affiliated with the university at Louvain. Research at the institute focuses on incorporating the findings from basic cellular research into practical applications.

De Duvé's work has won him the respect of his colleagues. Workers throughout the broad field of cellular biology recognize their debt to his pioneering studies. He helped found the American Society for Cell Biology. He has received awards and honors from many countries, including more than a dozen honorary degrees. In 1974, de Duvé, along with Albert Claude and George Palade, both also of the Rockefeller Institute, received the Nobel Prize in medicine, and were credited with creating the discipline of scientific investigation that became known as cell biology. De Duvé was elected a foreign associate of the U.S. National Academy of Sciences in 1975, and has been acclaimed by Belgian, French, and British biochemical societies. He has also served as a member of numerous prestigious biomedical and health-related organizations around the globe.

BIOGRAPHICAL AND CRITICAL SOURCES:

BOOKS

Magill, F. N., editor, *The Nobel Prize Winners: Physiology or Medicine,* Volume 3: *1970-1990,* Salem Press (Pasadena, CA), 1991, pp. 1177-1187.

PERIODICALS

Booklist, October 1, 2002, Gilbert Taylor, review of *Life Evolving: Molecules, Mind, and Meaning,* p. 293.*

* * *

de HAMEL, Christopher (Frances Rivers) 1950-

PERSONAL: Born November 20, 1950, in London, England; son of Francis Alexander and Joan Littledale (Pollock) de Hamel; married first wife, 1978 (marriage dissolved); married Mette Tang Simpson (art conservator), 1993; children: (first marriage) two sons. *Education:* Otago University (New Zealand), B.A. (honors), 1971; Oxford University, D.Phil., 1979.

ADDRESSES: Office—Corpus Christi College, Trumpington Street, Cambridge CB2 1RH, England.

CAREER: Sotheby's, London, England, cataloguer of medieval manuscripts, 1975-77, assistant director, 1977-82, director of Western illuminated manuscripts, 1982-2000; All Souls College, Oxford, England, visiting fellow, 1999-2000; Corpus Christi College, Cambridge, England, Donnelly Fellow Librarian, 2000—. Lecturer and speaker on illuminated manuscripts.

MEMBER: Roxburghe Club, Grolier Club, Association Internationale de Bibliophile.

AWARDS, HONORS: Honorary Litt.D. from St. John's University (Minnesota), 1994; honorary doctorate in literature degree from Otago University, 2002.

WRITINGS:

Glossed Books of the Bible and the Origins of the Paris Book Trade, Boydell & Brewer (London, England), 1984, Woodbridge (Wolfeboro, NH), 1987.
A History of Illuminated Manuscripts, Phaidon (London, England), 1986.

Syon Abbey, the Library of the Bridgettine Nuns and Their Peregrinations after the Reformation, Roxburghe Club (London, England), 1991.

Scribes and Illuminators, British Museum Press (London, England), 1992.

The Book: A History of the Bible, Phaidon Press (London, England), 2001.

The British Library Guide to Manuscript Illumination: History and Techniques, British Library (London, England), 2001.

SIDELIGHTS: Christopher de Hamel, author and historian, was born in the United Kingdom but moved with his family to New Zealand when he was a young child. It was in New Zealand that he completed his bachelor's degree at the University of Otago, the same institution that would honor him as a distinguished alumnus thirty-one years later. His honorary doctorate degree in literature was bestowed upon him, according to a press release from the university, in recognition of his status as a "widely published international authority on medieval manuscripts and early printing." Over the past twenty years, de Hamel has authored six unique books, emphasizing his special interest of the history of the construction of books and the art of illumination of manuscripts created in Medieval times.

Two such works are his *A History of Illuminated Manuscripts*, first published in 1986, and *Scribes and Illuminators*, published in 1992. In *A History of Illuminated Manuscripts*, de Hamel not only delves into the book-making process in the seventh through the sixteenth centuries, he also discusses the culture that surrounded books-as-objects in these early centuries. For example, in his first chapter, de Hamel looks at the role of the printed manuscript as used by missionaries in the seventh century. This is followed by a reflection of the use of books by emperors, with a special emphasis on the life of Charlemagne (A.D. 742-814), a powerful ruler of the Roman Empire. De Hamel also covers what he refers to as the Golden Age of illuminated manuscripts, the twelfth century, when monks spent much of their days creating extensively decorated publications. He then follows the development of books as it takes on more significance as the demand for the printed word increases with the proliferation of universities in the thirteenth century. During the fifteenth century, a type of religious book, referred to generically as the Book of Hours, became very popular with the general public, thus spreading the use of books beyond the aristocracy,

the universities, and the monasteries. De Hamel discusses why each of these different classes of books was created, where they were made, and all the various challenges that the creators of these manuscripts were forced to overcome. Both the art of text as well as the art of illustration are captured in a series of photographs contained in de Hamel's book.

It is in *Scribes and Illuminators* that de Hamel emphasizes the entire construction process of a medieval book. Here he examines all the trades involved in the creation of a manuscript, from the paper and parchment makers, the ink makers, the scribes who did the actual calligraphy, the artists who created the illustrations, to the binders and the booksellers. This book, like *A History of Illuminated Manuscripts,* is filled with color and black-and-white photographs of not only examples of illuminated books but also pictures of the scribes themselves at work.

Shortly after de Hamel published his study *The Book: A History of the Bible* in 2001, he was asked, as an authority on ancient manuscripts, to give a lecture at the Library of Congress on the famous, rare book that is referred to as the Giant Bible of Mainz. The occasion was meant to celebrate the 550th anniversary that a master scribe in Germany began his work on the huge, two-volume illuminated Bible, which was produced between 1452 and 1453. Who could offer a better history of this publication and the surrounding circumstances of its creation than de Hamel? His own book on the history of the Bible has been praised in a vast number of ways. *Library Journal* reviewer David Bourquin called it a "sumptuous feast for the eyes and mind"; while a reviewer for *Publishers Weekly* tried to capture the essence of de Hamel's work with words such as "most imaginative" and "startling."

De Hamel's *The Book: A History of the Bible* is not a religious study in any way. Rather, as Christopher Howse wrote for London's *Daily Telegraph,* de Hamel's book demonstrates that "the history of the Bible is the history of the book." In other words, in recounting the evolution of the printing of the Bible, one grasps the history of book publishing itself.

De Hamel's book is one of the first to follow the full history of the Christian Bible. He traces its publication through numerous countries and languages, including a translation into Natick, a dialect of the Algonquin people, a language for which speakers no longer exist. De Hamel, according to a review written by Gerald Hammond for the *London Review of Books*, has referred to this Natick translation of the Bible as "the most important unreadable book in the world." Also included are the development of both the Old and the New Testaments as written in Hebrew and Greek, as well as the Latin Vulgate translation of Saint Jerome down through the versions of the Bible as written by Martin Luther and other Protestant reformers and the modern translations of contemporary Bible-publishing industries.

BIOGRAPHICAL AND CRITICAL SOURCES:

PERIODICALS

Commonweal, September 27, 2002, Lawrence S. Cunningham, "Religion Booknotes," review of *The Book: A History of the Bible,* pp. 26-29.

Daily Telegraph (London, England), December 22, 2001, Christopher Howse, "The Older the Better," review of *The Book.*

History Today, April, 2002, Janet Backhouse, review of *The Book,* p. 61.

Library Journal, December, 2001, David Bourquin, review of *The Book,* p. 132.

London Review of Books, July 25, 2002, Gerald Hammond, "Saucy to Princes," review of *The Book,* pp. 19-20.

Publishers Weekly, November 12, 2001, "The Bible for Bibliophiles," review of *The Book,* p. 57.

Theology, May-June, 2002, Richard Coggins, review of *The Book,* p. 211.

ONLINE

University of Otago Web site, http://www.otago.ac.nz/ (April 22, 2002), "University of Otago to Award Two Honorary Degrees."

*   *   *

DEUKER, Carl 1950-

PERSONAL: Born August 26, 1950, in San Francisco, CA; son of John and Marie (Milligan) Deuker; married Anne Mitchell (a teacher), 1978; children: Marian. *Education:* University of California at Berkeley, B.A., 1972; University of Washington, M.A., 1974; University of California at Los Angeles, teaching certificate, 1976. *Politics:* Democrat.

Carl Deuker

ADDRESSES: Home—2827 Northwest 62nd St., Seattle, WA 98107. *E-mail*—carl989@hotmail.com.

CAREER: Saint Luke School, Seattle, WA, teacher, 1977-90; Northshore School District, Bothell, WA, teacher, 1991—. *Seattle Sun* (daily newspaper), film and book critic, 1980-85.

MEMBER: Authors Guild, Authors League of America, Phi Beta Kappa.

AWARDS, HONORS: South Carolina Young Adult Book Award, 1992, for *On the Devil's Court; Heart of a Champion, On the Devil's Court,* and *Panting the Black* were all named to ALA Best Books for Young Adults list; Nebraska Golden Sower Award and Tennessee Volunteer State Book Award, 1996, Pennsylvania Young Readers' Choice Award, 1997, and ALA Best Book for Reluctant Readers citation, all for *Heart of a Champion;* New York Library Books for the Teen Age citation and Young Adult Book of the Year Award from Texas, both 1997, both for *Painting the Black;* Nebraska Golden Sower Award, 2003, for *Night Hoops.*

WRITINGS:

On the Devil's Court, Little, Brown (Boston, MA), 1988.

Heart of a Champion, Little, Brown (Boston, MA), 1993.

Painting the Black, Houghton Mifflin (Boston, MA), 1997.

Night Hoops, Houghton Mifflin (Boston, MA), 2000.

High Heat, Houghton Mifflin (Boston, MA), 2003.

Contributor of short story, "If You Can't Be Lucky," to *Ultimate Sports,* edited by Donald Gallo.

SIDELIGHTS: Carl Deuker once commented that he is often asked by his readers if he writes sports novels for young adults because he was an outstanding athlete. "The answer is—not really," he confessed. "As a high school student, I made a few teams, but I did more sitting on the bench than playing. In college I played on intramural teams. But it wasn't those experiences that laid the groundwork for my becoming a writer.

"Instead I think I was on my way to becoming a writer with the imaginary games I played alone between the ages of eight and twelve. For hour after hour, the dart board in my garage was the strike zone, and I was Juan Marichal baffling the Dodgers. Or the pillow on the sofa was the basketball hoop, the walnut was the basketball, and I was Rick Barry, draining twenty-footers to beat the Lakers. I played football games with marbles, baseball games with clothespins, golf with hula hoops. But really I played those games—literally thousands of them—in my mind."

Deuker still plays games in his mind, but now he does so in the context of sports novels. His characters are high school athletes with differing abilities, ambitions, and psychological baggage, but their stories all unfold within the sports that they choose to play. Far from being just a hinge upon which to hang a plot, sports in Deuker's novels serve as a central metaphor for the complicated process of growing up. As a contributor to the *St. James Guide to Young Adult Writers* put it, "Deuker's ability to move beyond mechanical discussions of various sports and provide insight into the universal struggles of young adults have deservedly earned him the reputation as one of the most promising contemporary writers of sports fiction."

Deuker was born and raised in the San Francisco Bay area. His father died when he was three years old, and to this day he is deeply conscious of the loss and deeply interested in father-son relationships. Deuker's mother encouraged her son to have an active imagination, and he began writing poetry and short stories while still in high school. In college at the University of California at Berkeley, he continued to write, placing some of his work in campus and underground magazines. "I was an English major," he commented, "took lots of writing classes, was never the best writer in class, but persisted with writing anyway." After earning a master's degree, Deuker gravitated into journalism but finally decided to earn a teaching certificate. He has been a middle-school teacher since 1977, writing his books before he goes to work in the morning and revising them at night.

Although Deuker's books are set in high school, he actually writes for the middle-school audience. "My books are ways for them to peek ahead in their lives and perhaps be a little prepared for what might be coming," he said. Unlike most award-winning novelists, he thoroughly enjoys his work as a teacher and draws inspiration from it. "I have no plans to go full time [as a writer]," he admitted. "I don't think I could handle the pressure of writing for a livelihood."

In Deuker's first book, *On the Devil's Court,* Joe Faust, a high-school student with a nearly obsessive interest in basketball, moves with his family from the East Coast to the West. Believing that the move will further his basketball career, Joe convinces his parents to let him attend a large public school with a strong sports program. However, Joe's attendance at a drunken party leads to a run-in with police, after which his parents insist that he enroll at a small private school. One evening in the gym, an angry Joe, who has just been demoted to the junior varsity, hits every shot he takes. Inspired by his recent reading of Christopher Marlowe's *Dr. Faustus,* Joe offers himself to the Devil in exchange for continued prowess and a perfect season. No sooner is the promise made than Joe begins to star on the varsity team, leading his school to the state finals. With each victory, Joe becomes increasingly anxious about his fate. Has he really sold himself to the Devil? In light of his success, Joe wonders if his father's untimely heart attack isn't an early payment. Not until Joe's team wins without him does he realize that the season belongs to his team, and that he has made a bargain with no one but himself.

In a *School Library Journal* review, Gerry Larson called *On the Devil's Court* a "fine addition to sports fiction," and praised Deuker's engaging mixture of suspense, family drama, and athletic competition. *Publishers Weekly* reviewers Kimberly Olsen Fakih and Diane Roback considered Deuker's characters well-rounded and deemed the book a "vivid contemporary morality play." *Horn Book* reviewer Nancy Vasilakis asserted that young readers will enjoy both the story and Joe's ability to deal squarely with his parents by the book's end, "whether or not they fully comprehend what developmental steps were taken to achieve this measure of independence."

In *Heart of a Champion*, Deuker uses baseball to examine the lives of two adolescent boys. Seth has yet to come to terms with his father's death when he meets Jimmy, a budding young baseball star. Inspired by Jimmy's intense pursuit of the game, Seth begins playing baseball, and the competitive nature of the game increases his confidence in other aspects of his life. Seth's grades improve, and, with his mother's help, he begins to address his father's death. Behind their shared success in baseball, however, is Jimmy's father, an alcoholic who drives his son toward perfection on the diamond. His influence proves tragic when Jimmy, a high-school baseball star, dies in an alcohol-related traffic accident. Seth must then deal with the loss of his closest friend, as well as the complexity of the father-son relationship that foreshadowed Jimmy's death.

In a review for *School Library Journal*, Jack Forman speculated that the "well-paced novel will involve many readers." A *Horn Book* reviewer called *Heart of a Champion* a "sensitive, moving portrait of adolescence combined with dramatic sports action." *Bulletin of the Center for Children's Books* reviewer Betsy Hearne praised the detailed relationship between the boys, but was more struck by the book's realistic portrayal of the "balance between talent and discipline."

Painting the Black once again explores the destructive behavior of a star high-school athlete. Josh Daniels is a success in two sports: football and baseball. His exploits on the field are so spectacular that both fellow students and the school administration are tempted to overlook his temperamental outbursts and cruelty to female students. Recruited to serve as a catcher for Josh's pitching, Ryan Ward forms a strong friendship with the athlete and through it finds the courage to regain his own footing as a baseball player. Together the two boys craft a potential championship season for their baseball team, but their aspirations are put to the test when Ryan foils Josh's attempts to assault Monica Robey, an academic star. Ryan faces a difficult choice: Will he, too, overlook Josh's antisocial behavior, or will he report the incident and put an end to his team's championship hopes?

Deuker maintained that *Painting the Black* was based on a real incident in which a star athlete acted inappropriately toward a classmate. Critics of the book praised its realistic detailing of the "double standard" that sometimes surrounds sports heroes. Some reviewers also liked the way the story is filtered through Ryan's perspective, noting that the crux of the conflict lies in Ryan's epic battle with his own conscience. A contributor to *Kirkus Reviews* noted that Deuker, "adept at capturing the thrills during the game, also proves talented at dramatizing Ryan's torment. . . . The depiction of a boy coming into his own is resonant and inspiring." Candace Smith in *Booklist* suggested that Ryan's "moral courage . . . will linger when the reading is done."

Deuker often writes about the one-on-one bonding that young men can experience when they play sports together. In *Night Hoops,* Nick Abbott takes solace in basketball when his parents divorce, but he finds that his emotions spill onto the court and affect his game. It is only when Nick begins to play one-on-one with the grim and antisocial Trent Dawson that he begins to learn how to fit into a team—and how to break down the barriers between himself and others. "This is an excellent novel . . . authentic throughout," observed Todd Morning in *School Library Journal.* Morning added that Deuker "perfectly captures the swirl of ideas in the adolescent mind." A *Publishers Weekly* reviewer called *Night Hoops* "an honest depiction of the contemporary high-school sports scene."

In *High Heat,* Shane Hunter's life is shaken at its roots when his father, facing money laundering charges, suddenly commits suicide. Shane, who has been raised in a life of luxury that includes private schools and a lovely home, must move with his family into subsidized housing, and he begins to fall apart in the new environment. Help comes in the form of his new public school's baseball coach, who convinces Shane to try out for the team. As a relief pitcher, Shane finally finds himself again, but faces a new crisis when he beans an opponent from his former school. Fearful that he has lost his pitching ability and his grip on life in general, Shane forms a friendship with the player he struck. Together they try to make sense of what has happened and how it will affect their futures.

According to John Peters in a review for *Booklist,* *High Heat* contains "enough taut sports action . . . to satisfy the most avid fan." Writing for *School Library Journal,* Todd Morning noted that the story "delivers baseball action along with a rich psychological portrait," and a *Publishers Weekly* critic felt that, although the story builds on a dark premise, "the arc of redemption reminds readers that love conquers all—as does the pursuit of personal excellence."

Deuker commented that he was inspired to write sports novels by the fact that the ones he read as a boy were rarely about sports at all. "Often I'd put the book down and turn to something else, usually historical fiction with a lot of war in it. Those books delivered what they promised. As a writer of sports fiction, I decided early on to make sure I delivered on the promise—that sports be front and center. But I also wanted to make sure that each book gave a little bit more." Deuker commented: "There's a big difference between being alone and being lonely. I was alone often as a child, rarely lonely. Those imaginary games and all that time I 'wasted' playing them—in those hours I was becoming a writer."

BIOGRAPHICAL AND CRITICAL SOURCES:

BOOKS

St. James Guide to Young Adult Writers, 2nd edition, St. James Press (Detroit, MI), 1999.

PERIODICALS

Booklist, June 1, 1997, Candace Smith, review of *Painting the Black;* May 1, 2000, Frances Bradburn, review of *Night Hoops,* p. 1658; August, 2003, John Peters, review of *High Heat,* p. 1982.

Booktalker, September, 1989, p. 11.
Bulletin of the Center for Children's Books, September, 1993, Betsy Hearne, review of *Heart of a Champion,* p. 7.
Horn Book, March-April, 1989, Nancy Vasilakis, review of *On the Devil's Court,* p. 216; May-June, 1993, review of *Heart of a Champion,* p. 337; May-June, 1997, Maeve Visser Knoth, review of *Painting the Black,* p. 317; May, 2000, review of *Night Hoops,* p. 312.
Kirkus Reviews, January 1, 1989, pp. 47-48; May 15, 1993, review of *Heart of a Champion.*
Publishers Weekly, November 11, 1988, Kimberly Olsen Fakih and Diane Roback, review of *On the Devil's Court,* p. 60; May 31, 1993, pp. 56-57; April 10, 2000, review of *Night Hoops,* p. 99; May 19, 2003, review of *High Heat,* p. 75.
School Library Journal, January, 1989, Gerry Larson, review of *On the Devil's Court,* p. 92; June, 1993, Jack Forman, review of *Heart of a Champion,* p. 126; May, 1997, Todd Morning, review of *Painting the Black;* May, 2000, Todd Morning, review of *Night Hoops,* p. 171; July, 2003, Todd Morning, review of *High Heat,* p. 128.
Voice of Youth Advocates, April, 1989, Doris Losey, review of *On the Devil's Court,* p. 27; August, 1997, Susan Dunn, review of *Painting the Black,* p. 182.

*   *   *

DIAMANO, Silmang
See SENGHOR, Léopold Sédar

*   *   *

DICKINSON, Peter (Malcolm de Brissac) 1927-

PERSONAL: Born December 16, 1927, in Livingstone, Northern Rhodesia (Now Zambia); son of Richard Sebastian Willoughby (a colonial civil servant) and May Southey (a tomb restorer; maiden name, Lovemore) Dickinson; married Mary Rose Barnard (an artist), April 20, 1953 (died, 1988); married Robin McKinley (an author), January, 1992; children: (first marriage) Philippa Lucy Anne, Dorothy Louise, John Geoffrey Hyett, James Christopher Meade. *Education:* Attended Eton College, five years; King's College,

Peter Dickinson

Cambridge, B.A., 1951. *Politics:* "Leftish." *Religion:* "Lapsed Anglican."

ADDRESSES: Home—Bramdean Lodge, Nr. Alresford, Hampshire SO24 0JP, England. *Agent*—A. P. Watt, Ltd., 20 John St., London WC1N 2DL, England.

CAREER: Writer of mystery novels and juvenile books. *Punch,* London, England, assistant editor, 1952-69. *Military service:* British Army, 1946-48 ("chaotic period as a conscript").

MEMBER: Crime Writers Association.

AWARDS, HONORS: Crime Writers Association Gold Dagger award for best mystery of the year, 1968, for *The Glass-Sided Ants' Nest,* and 1969, for *The Old English Peep Show;* American Library Association Notable Book Award, 1971, for *Emma Tupper's Diary; Horn Book* nonfiction award, c. 1976, for *Chance, Luck, and Destiny; Guardian* Award, 1977, for *The Blue Hawk; Boston Globe-Horn Book* Award for nonfiction, 1977; Whitbread Award and Carnegie

Medal, both 1979, both for *Tulku; The Flight of Dragons* and *Tulku* were named to the American Library Association's Best Books for Young Adults list, 1979; Carnegie Medal, 1982, for *City of Gold;* Whitbread Award, 1990, for *AK;* Blue Ribbon citation, *Bulletin of the Center for Children's Books,* 1996, for *Chuck and Danielle.*

WRITINGS:

FOR CHILDREN

The Weathermonger (first novel in a trilogy; also see below), Gollancz (London, England), 1968, Little, Brown (Boston, MA), 1969.

Heartsease (second novel in a trilogy; also see below), illustrated by Robert Hales, Little, Brown (Boston, MA), 1969.

The Devil's Children (third novel in a trilogy; also see below), illustrated by Robert Hales, Little, Brown (Boston, MA), 1970.

Emma Tupper's Diary, Little, Brown (Boston, MA), 1971.

The Dancing Bear, illustrated by David Smee, Gollancz (London, England), 1972, Little, Brown (Boston, MA), 1973.

The Iron Lion, illustrated by Marc Brown, Little, Brown (Boston, MA), 1972.

The Gift, illustrated by Gareth Floyd, Gollancz (London, England), 1973, Little, Brown (Boston, MA), 1974.

The Changes: A Trilogy (contains *The Weathermonger, Heartsease,* and *The Devil's Children*), Gollancz (London, England), 1975.

(Editor) *Presto! Humorous Bits and Pieces,* Hutchinson (London, England), 1975.

Chance, Luck, and Destiny (miscellany), illustrated by David Smee and Victor Ambrus, Gollancz (London, England), 1975, Little, Brown (Boston, MA), 1976.

The Blue Hawk, illustrated by David Smee, Little, Brown (Boston, MA), 1976.

Annerton Pit, Little, Brown (Boston, MA), 1977.

Tulku, Dutton (New York, NY), 1979.

Hepzibah, illustrated by Sue Porter, Eel Pie (Twickenham, England), 1978, David R. Godine (New York, NY), 1980.

City of Gold and Other Stories from the Old Testament, illustrated by Michael Foreman, Pantheon (New York, NY), 1980, released as *City of Gold,* illustrated by Foreman, Houghton Mifflin (Boston, MA), 1992.

The Seventh Raven, Dutton (New York, NY), 1981.

Giant Cold, illustrated by Alan E. Cober, Dutton (New York, NY), 1981.

Healer, Gollancz (London, England), 1983, Delacorte (New York, NY), 1985.

(Editor) *Hundreds and Hundreds,* Penguin (London, England), 1984.

Mole Hole, Peter Bedrick (London, England), 1987.

Merlin Dreams, illustrated by Alan Lee, Chivers Press (London, England), 1987, Delacorte (New York, NY), 1988.

A Box of Nothing, illustrated by Ian Newsham, Delacorte (New York, NY), 1988.

Eva, Delacorte (New York, NY), 1989.

AK, Gollancz (London, England), 1990, Doubleday (New York, NY), 1992.

A Bone from a Dry Sea, Delacorte (New York, NY), 1993.

Time and the Clock Mice, Etcetera, illustrated by Emma Chichester-Clark, Delacorte (New York, NY), 1994.

Shadow of a Hero, Delacorte (New York, NY), 1994.

Chuck and Danielle, illustrated by Kees de Kiefte, Bantam (New York, NY), 1996.

The Lion Tamer's Daughter and Other Stories, Delacorte (New York, NY), 1997.

The Ropemaker, Delacorte (New York, NY), 2001.

The Tears of the Salamander, Random House (New York, NY), 2003.

(With Robin McKinley) *Water: Tales of Elemental Spirits* (stories) Putnam (New York, NY), 2002.

Inside Grandad, Random House (New York, NY), 2003, published as *The Gift Boat,* Macmillan (London, England), 2004.

"KIN" SERIES; YOUNG ADULT NOVELS

The Kin (also see below; contains "Noli's Story," "Po's Story," "Suth's Story," and "Mana's Story,") Macmillan (London, England), 1998, Penguin (New York, NY), 2003.

Noli's Story, Grosset & Dunlap (New York, NY), 1998.

Po's Story, Grosset & Dunlap (New York, NY), 1998.

Suth's Story, Grosset & Dunlap (New York, NY), 1998.

Mana's Story, Grosset & Dunlap (New York, NY), 1999.

MYSTERY NOVELS FOR ADULTS

The Glass-Sided Ants' Nest, Harper & Row (New York, NY), 1968, published as *Skin Deep,* Hodder & Stoughton (London, England), 1968.

The Old English Peep Show, Harper & Row (New York, NY), 1969, published as *A Pride of Heroes,* Hodder & Stoughton (London, England), 1969.

The Sinful Stones, Harper & Row (New York, NY), 1970, published as *The Seals,* Hodder & Stoughton (London, England), 1970.

Sleep and His Brother, Harper & Row (New York, NY), 1971.

The Lizard in the Cup, Harper & Row (New York, NY), 1972.

The Green Gene, Pantheon (New York, NY), 1973.

The Poison Oracle, Pantheon (New York, NY), 1974.

The Lively Dead, Pantheon (New York, NY), 1975.

King and Joker, Pantheon (New York, NY), 1976.

Walking Dead, Hodder & Stoughton (London, England), 1977, Pantheon (New York, NY), 1978.

One Foot in the Grave, Hodder & Stoughton (London, England), 1979, Pantheon (New York, NY), 1980.

The Last House-Party, Pantheon (New York, NY), 1982.

Hindsight, Pantheon (New York, NY), 1983.

Death of a Unicorn, Pantheon (New York, NY), 1984.

Skeleton-in-Waiting, Pantheon (New York, NY), 1989.

Play Dead, Bodley Head (London, England), 1991, Mysterious Press (New York, NY), 1992.

The Yellow Room Conspiracy, Mysterious Press (New York, NY), 1994.

Some Deaths before Dying, Mysterious Press (New York, NY), 1999.

OTHER

Mandog (television series), British Broadcasting Co. (BBC-TV), 1972.

(Contributor) Otto Penzler, editor, *The Great Detectives* (nonfiction), Little, Brown (Boston, MA), 1978.

The Flight of Dragons, illustrated by Wayne Anderson, Harper & Row (New York, NY), 1979.

(Contributor) Julian Symons, editor, *Verdict of Thirteen* (contains short story, "Who Killed the Cat?"), Harper & Row (New York, NY), 1979.

A Summer in the Twenties (novel), Pantheon (New York, NY), 1981.

Tefuga: A Novel of Suspense, Bodley Head (London, England), 1985, Pantheon (New York, NY), 1986.

Perfect Gallows: A Novel of Suspense, Pantheon (New York, NY), 1987.

ADAPTATIONS: The British Broadcasting Corp. (BBC) produced a television serial based on Dickinson's *Changes* trilogy, 1975; *The Flight of Dragons* was adapted as an animated television film by the American Broadcasting Co. (ABC) and broadcast January 1, 1982. A cassette recording was made of *A Box of Nothing* by G. K. Hall, 1988.

SIDELIGHTS: "I believe the crucial thing for a writer is the ability to make up coherent worlds," Peter Dickinson explained to *New York Times Book Review* contributor Eden Ross Lipson. "I'm like a beach-comber walking along the shores of invention, picking up things and wondering what kinds of structures they could make. . . . The imagination is like the sea, full of things you can't see but can possibly harvest and use." It is Dickinson's fertile imagination that distinguishes his mystery novels and children's books from those of many of his contemporaries. His mysteries are spiced with such seemingly incompatible elements as aborigine societies living in London, chimpanzees who are murder witnesses, and diseases that have telepathic side-effects. His stories for children contain such oddities as kids with remarkable healing powers and an ancient magician doped up on morphine. "For all their variety," John Rowe Townsend asserted in his *A Sounding of Storytellers: New and Revised Essays on Contemporary Writers for Children,* "the books have much in common: strong professional storytelling, rapid action and adventure, continual invention, a proliferating interest in ideas, and an understanding of how things are done. Behind all this one glimpses an energetic, speculative mind with a leaning towards the exotic."

Like his writing, Dickinson's personal background is also exotic. His father was a British civil servant working in Zambia—what was then the colony of Northern Rhodesia—and it was there that Dickinson was born and lived the first seven years of his life. In 1935 his family returned to England, but not long after their arrival Dickinson's father died. Fortune took a turn for the better, however, when the author won a scholarship in 1941 to attend Eton College. After leaving Eton and serving in the army in the aftermath of World War II as a district signals officer—Dickinson was too young to fight during the war—he studied at King's College, Cambridge. Although he had begun studying Latin, Dickinson later switched to English literature, and it was one of his English tutors who convinced him to apply for a position as assistant editor at *Punch,* the well-known London humor magazine.

Getting an appointment for an interview did not turn out to be as difficult as actually arriving at the *Punch*

offices, for on his way there Dickinson was hit by a tram. Despite the accident, the aspiring editor made it to the interview, his clothing stained with blood, and was accepted for the job. For the next seventeen years Dickinson worked for *Punch,* including five years during which he reviewed crime novels. After reading and analyzing literally thousands of these books, he began to think about writing one of his own. But he did not want his novel to be just another story about a murder. With knowledge of a wide variety of topics, including anthropology, trains, languages, antiques, and history, Dickinson decided to use his learning to add a twist to his writing. Thus his first book, *Skin Deep*—published in the United States as *The Glass-Sided Ants' Nest*—employs certain facts about anthropology to weave a bizarre mystery concerning a tribe of aborigines from New Guinea who have settled in London only to have their chief murdered.

Of his adult mysteries, Dickinson's books featuring detective James Pibble are probably best known, but the author has also written a number of other quirky mysteries featuring out-of-the-ordinary detectives faced with unusual challenges. Dickinson's stories are often set in familiar places made slightly off-balance by science-fiction-like elements. This sort of invention is the key to Dickinson's children's novels, too. A vivid dreamer, the author sometimes sees elements of his plots in his sleep and then builds a story around them. In an online interview with *Mystery World,* he said: "Writing a book in one sense is like having a knock on your door and you open the door and see what comes in. You say, 'I've got to introduce a new character here. . . .' Gradually this person becomes the only person she could be and you know what's right for her. It's like that." Fiction, he told the London *Daily Telegraph,* is "not about preaching messages, but understanding—including the understanding of how people can be so beastly to each other."

Dickinson published his first book for children, *The Weathermonger,* the same year as his first mystery novel. *The Weathermonger* became the first book in a trilogy, including *Heartsease* and *The Devil's Children,* all later published in one book, *The Changes: A Trilogy. The Changes* describes a modern-day England whose populace has developed a mysterious aversion to all types of technology—as well as a general xenophobia—with the result that the entire country is thrown into another Dark Age. Another side effect of the Changes is that it gives some people the power to manipulate the weather. In *The Weathermonger,* Geoffrey, along with his sister, Sally, is sent on a mission to find out what has been causing the Changes. The source turns out to be of a magical nature: a chemist named Furbelow has discovered King Arthur's wizard, Merlin, and revived him from a centuries-old sleep only to manipulate him by getting the magician addicted to morphine. Geoffrey and Sally put an end to England's second Dark Age by curing Merlin of his addiction and returning him to his place of rest.

The next book in the trilogy, *Heartsease,* tells a story that occurs before the events in *The Weathermonger.* England is still in the midst of the Changes when Margaret and Jonathan find an American investigator who has been stoned by the British, who thought he was a witch. The two children, along with their house servant, Lucy, help the American escape back to Gloucester, where he gets a boat to return to the United States. Dickinson backs up yet again in *The Devil's Children,* this time setting his narrative at the very beginning of the time of the Changes, when a group of Sikhs—who have not developed the fear of technology like the British—escapes persecution with the help of a twelve-year-old English girl named Nicola. S. F. Said in the London *Daily Telegraph* noted that the three titles in the "Changes" trilogy "were landmarks of the Sixties, read in schools and broadcast on TV." The trilogy is still in print and is sometimes recommended to students who enjoy challenging and morally ambiguous stories.

Dickinson's next children's book, *Emma Tupper's Diary,* was an American Library Association Notable Book. Set in the present day, this story about a young girl's summer vacation with her cousins, who live near a Scottish loch, at first seems like mainstream fiction. The story begins to delve into fantasy, however, when Emma's cousins decide to contrive a grand ruse by repairing their grandfather's submarine and disguising it as a sea monster much like the famed Loch Ness Monster. The surprise comes when Emma and one of her cousins take the submarine for a spin and discover living Plesiosaurs swimming in the loch.

A number of Dickinson's other children's books, including *The Gift, Annerton Pit,* and *Healer,* have contemporary, realistic settings upon which the author imposes extraordinary elements. In each of these novels, a child possesses—or seems to possess— amazing powers. Davy Price in *The Gift* has inherited the ability to see the images that other people form in their minds. This leads to danger for Davy when he chances upon the thoughts of a murderous psychopath. In *Annerton Pit* the ability of Jake to communicate with a mysterious being is more ambiguous. Kidnapped by a group of environmental terrorists and imprisoned in an abandoned mine, Jake—who is blind—is not put to as much of a disadvantage as his sighted brother, Martin, whom he helps to escape. During their escape, however, Jake comes into telepathic and empathic contact with an unseen creature living inside the hill who tries to chase away the intruders by filling the mine with a sense of terror. At least, this is what Jake believes; but Dickinson keeps open the possibility that the monster exists only in Jake's mind.

The collection *The Lion Tamer's Daughter and Other Stories* consists of four tales that all show characters moving from one world to another. Nancy Vasilakis observed in *Horn Book:* "Complex and unsettling, the stories are above all a testament to the author's potent imagination." With *Healer,* Dickinson explores the emotions and thoughts of not one but two complex characters. Barry is a sixteen-year-old boy with a second, inner personality he names "Bear" because of its more animalistic impulses. The struggle between his two personalities gives him migraine headaches, which are cured one day by a girl named Pinkie who has remarkable healing powers. Pinkie's stepfather takes advantage of his daughter's talent by establishing a cult around her called the "Foundation of Harmony" and charging people huge sums of money for Pinkie's services. Pinkie, however, is restricted to her house by her stepfather, so Barry resolves to rescue her from her imprisonment. Ostensibly a tale of adventure, *Healer* is also one "from which one peels different levels of meaning layer by layer," according to a *Junior Bookshelf* reviewer, as Barry learns to live with his inner self and Pinkie relinquishes some of her overly serious attitudes about life by learning how to laugh.

The Gift, Annerton Pit, and *Healer* are all good illustrations of Dickinson's interest in the psychology of his characters. But *Healer* also explores another one of the author's preoccupations: religion and religious cults. Although Dickinson's parents were religious and he had read through the Bible before he was ten years old, the author revealed in Eden Ross Lipson's *New York Times Book Review* article that he is "completely without faith." Nevertheless, as *Healer* reveals, he is interested in religious faith. This fascination is also manifest in some of the author's other novels, such as the distant-future science fiction work *The Blue Hawk* and the historical work *Tulku.*

The 1987 work *Merlin Dreams* displays Dickinson's talent for language and storytelling. A series of nine stories, all dealing with powers of one sort or another, are presented as the dreams of a sleeping Merlin who is near the end of his life. All of the stories contain medieval elements such as knights and damsels, and Merlin himself appears in some of them. *Horn Book* contributor Ann A. Flowers, while asserting that the interludes of the dreaming Merlin may be "puzzling to the young reader," noted that "all the stories are splendid and a pleasure to read." Christina L. Olson stated in *School Library Journal* that while the collection "works on the level of pure story," the author's "language works *on* readers as well." "It's the language of a spellbinder," Barbara Sherrard-Smith explained in *School Librarian,* concluding that "this is one of those rare joys, a book to be read quickly to find out what happens next, then to be savoured again and again."

One of Dickinson's most controversial works for children is *Eva,* a book that addresses the author's concerns about human society and the impact it has had on the ecology of the earth. Severely injured and paralyzed in a car accident, Eva is "saved" by having her memory transplanted into the body of a chimpanzee. After regaining consciousness, Eva must adjust not only to her new body, with its chimp impulses, but to the corporate sponsorship that makes her the focus of media attention. She eventually decides to leave human society, taking a group of captive chimps with her to a remote island. Calling *Eva* "an astonishing work of biological science fiction," *Horn Book* writer Ethel L. Heins remarked that this adventure story "is also a work of passion and eloquence, and its sobering significance increases in proportion to the reader's maturity." *Times Literary Supplement* reviewer Neil Philip concluded that *Eva* "is one of the better books of a first-rate writer. It is highly provocative, it has tenderness, humour and passion. It involves the reader from the very first page and will not quickly leave the mind."

In an extended *Horn Book* essay, Betty Carter cited *Eva* as a good illustration of Dickinson's place as a thought-provoking author for young adults. "The top-

ics raised in *Eva* transcend the fleeting concerns of adolescence," Carter wrote. "Dickinson shows tremendous respect for his readers and their ability to grapple with hard issues that range from euthanasia to the influence of the media. . . . He gives readers no logical wiggle room in which to build a softer interpretation of this deteriorating society. They can question, challenge, regret, confront, dismiss, or accept it, but they cannot change it. . . . Here readers are on their own, as they should be, full of questions with no certain answers. And that is the power of literature—to provide an arena where young people can encounter unimaginable situations."

A similarly provocative work is *AK,* in which Dickinson writes about a fictional African nation that has been torn by civil war. Paul Kagomi has known nothing but conflict during his twelve years, having known no family except the other members of the Nagala Liberation Army. He defines himself by his weapon— the AK-47 of the title—and is left confused when the war ends and he is sent to school by his foster father, who is now a member of the government. When a coup leads to yet more struggle, Paul escapes his father's enemies, retrieves his gun, and mounts a rescue attempt. Dickinson shows, however, that victories achieved through violence are fragile, and "carefully structures his conclusion so the lesson of ambiguity is the one we carry away," as Michele Slung summarized in the *New York Times Book Review.* Although Dickinson's locale is imaginary, the events are truthful, Margaret A. Bush observed in *Horn Book:* "The absorbing story is disturbing in its plausibility and creates a thoughtful exploration of the dynamics of war." Michael Dirda similarly praised the novel in the *Washington Post Book World:* "When young-adult novels are as riveting as *AK,* by the prolific and imaginative Peter Dickinson, it's a shame that only teenagers are likely to pick them up."

The book *Shadow of a Hero* parallels the Balkan conflicts of the early 1990s. Thirteen-year-old Letta, the granddaughter of the former prime minister of the fictional Eastern European country Varina, lives in London with her family. Letta's grandfather is also a descendant of the Legendary Varinian hero, Restaur Vax. Chapters of the book alternate between Letta's current life in London where her grandfather is teaching her the Varinian language and about the country's contemporary political upheaval, and legendary Varinian history. Readers come to learn about all the bloodshed and betrayal marking Varina's history, and of the pending tragedy in modern Varina. Roger Sutton wrote in the *Bulletin of the Center for Children's Books:* "Dickinson mixes fiction and fact with confidence." *Horn Book* reviewer Ann A. Flowers concluded that the book is "a tour de force of a novel . . . intelligent, complex, and as up-to-date as today's headlines."

In contrast to his historical, political, and other "heavier" novels, Dickinson has written lighthearted books, sometimes featuring animals as the main characters. *Chuck and Danielle* is a story about Danielle and her high-strung dog—a whippet nicknamed Chuck. Danielle has made a bet with her mother that someday Chuck would save the universe. The book details the antics of Chuck, whom a *Kirkus Reviews* critic described as an "antihero," and Danielle—and Danielle wins her bet! Put together in an unusual format, *Time and the Clockmice, Etcetera* uses "a standard animal fantasy to introduce a selection of factual topics," Alasdair Campbell remarked in *School Librarian.* The story begins when the main attraction of Branton, a 99-year-old town hall clock, stops. The clockmaker's grandson, who is now old, comes to repair the clock and discovers a group of super-intelligent mice who can communicate via ESP, and whose safety and existence are threatened by cats and human research scientists. The old man befriends the mice and tells readers, in detail, how to fix the clock and how it works, etc. The book is a series of "essays" on such topics as bells, people, clocks, science, cats, etc.—thus the word in the title. *Time and the Clockmice* is enhanced by the illustrations of Emma Chichester-Clark, and the result, noted Campbell, "becomes a visual treat as well as a literary hotchpotch."

Dickinson's saga *The Kin* was first published in Great Britain in one volume and first published in America as four separate volumes. Set in Africa approximately 200,000 years ago, the stories in *The Kin* follow four children as they venture into adulthood together, struggling to survive after they are separated from their extended family group and threatened by a series of natural disasters and animal predators. What separates *The Kin* from pure adventure yarn is Dickinson's preoccupation with deeper questions of humanity, as represented by these proto-*Homo sapiens* youngsters. They communicate by language, but they befriend a wounded man who does not speak. They must use

their wits to find food, shelter, and to thwart danger, but they also have time to think about what they mean to each other and how the world has come to be. In the London *Daily Telegraph,* Mary Hoffman called the book "a remarkable work. . . . Dickinson has created a completely believable and compelling culture and history from a period which has left virtually no trace." A reviewer for *Books for Keeps* called *The Kin* "writing of the finest quality," and a *Publishers Weekly* reviewer praised one segment of the work, *Noli's Story,* for "the exhilarating mix of ideas the novel so nimbly sets forth."

With *The Ropemaker* and *The Tears of the Salamander* Dickinson returns to fantasy and science fiction themes. In *The Ropemaker,* Tilja and Tahl must undertake a pilgrimage to find a powerful magician who has traditionally protected their homeland from its war-mongering neighbors. Part adventure tale, part character study, *The Ropemaker* explores how young people come to terms with their special skills. "While on one level this tale is a fantasy, it is also a wonderful coming-of-age story," noted Bruce Anne Shook in a starred *School Library Journal* review. A *Publishers Weekly* critic declared Dickinson's mythic world in *The Ropemaker* "as breathtakingly fresh as it is archetypal."

Thirteen-year-old Alfredo is thrust into a fantastic world in *The Tears of the Salamander.* When his beloved father's bakery burns down, Alfredo is orphaned with no prospects, save the unsavory fate of submitting to castration so that he can always sing soprano for the Church. Arriving in the nick of time, Alfredo's Uncle Giorgio offers another option: Alfredo can come and live on the slopes of Mount Etna in the family ancestral home. Alfredo soon discovers that much is amiss in the shadow of the mighty volcano, and as his beautiful singing wrings tears from a magic salamander, he realizes that his uncle has sinister ambitions for immortality and world domination. Offering the work a starred review, a *Publishers Weekly* critic noted that "burning questions" animate the "engrossing, almost operatic novel," recommended for the most thoughtful readers. In *Horn Book,* Joanna Rudge Long concluded that the novel "makes a unique and satisfying addition to Dickinson's remarkable oeuvre."

Inside Grandad is a gentler tale of fantasy and reconciling oneself to the changes wrought by the passage of time. Gavin and his grandfather enjoy a deep bond in their Scottish seacoast town. As Gavin's grandfather completes a model boat, he tells Gavin legends of the selkies—a mystical race of seal-people who can work good or ill in humans' lives. Shortly after completing the boat, Gavin's grandfather suffers a crippling stroke, leaving Gavin to bargain with the selkies for restoration of his beloved family member's health. A *Kirkus Reviews* critic deemed the novel "a touching story of love and determination," and a contributor to the *Bulletin* concluded: "Consistently written from a child's viewpoint, this is a story insightfully developed and satisfyingly unexpected."

Whether in his crime novels or his children's books, creating finely realized fictional worlds has always been a primary concern for Dickinson. "The crucial thing about any act of the imagination," Dickinson maintained in an article for *Children's Literature in Education,* "is its self-coherence, the way in which each part of it fits with all the other parts and by doing so authenticates them. This is the way in which we know and authenticate our real world." But why is this relationship between the imaginary and the real important? "It matters," said Dickinson, "because it is imagination which makes us what we are. It is the core of our humanity." Not only is imagination "humankind's prime evolutionary specialization," which has allowed humans to evolve a high level of intelligence, the author argued, but it is also what "continues to make us what we are." This is why—even with the advent of television—literature remains an important part of living. Dickinson concluded that reading "invites the exercise of the imagination, the enlargement of the imaginative sympathies, the increase of our potential as human beings."

BIOGRAPHICAL AND CRITICAL SOURCES:

BOOKS

Authors and Artists for Young Adults, Volume 49, Gale (Detroit, MI), 2003.
Children's Literature Review, Volume 29, Gale (Detroit, MI), 1993.
Contemporary Literary Criticism, Volume 35, Gale (Detroit, MI), 1985.
Dictionary of Literary Biography, Volume 161: *British Children's Writers since 1960, First Series,* Gale (Detroit, MI), 1996, pp. 109-124.
St. James Guide to Young Adult Writers, 2nd edition, St. James Press (Detroit, MI), 1999.

Townsend, John Rowe, *A Sounding of Storytellers: New and Revised Essays on Contemporary Writers for Children,* Lippincott (Philadelphia, PA), 1979, pp. 41-54.
Townsend, John Rowe, *Writing for Children: An Outline of English-Language Children's Literature,* revised edition, Lippincott (Philadelphia, PA), 1974.
Twentieth-Century Young Adult Writers, St. James Press (Detroit, MI), 1994.

PERIODICALS

Books for Keeps, July, 1999, review of *The Kin,* p. 25.
Bulletin, March, 2004, review of *Inside Grandad.*
Bulletin of the Center for Children's Books, January, 1995, Roger Sutton, review of *Shadow of a Hero,* pp. 163-164.
Children's Literature in Education, spring, 1986, Peter Dickinson, "Fantasy: The Need for Realism," pp. 39-51.
Daily Telegraph (London, England), October 15, 1998, Mary Hoffman, "What It Is to Be Human"; September 15, 2001, S. F. Said, "Power of a Word Wizard: Peter Dickinson Is the Children's Author That All the Rest Admire."
Guardian (London, England), November 9, 2002, "In Their Element," p. 33; July 12, 2003, Jan Mark, "Burning Desire," p. 33.
Horn Book, March-April, 1989, Ann A. Flowers, review of *Merlin Dreams,* p. 210; July-August, 1989, Ethel L. Heins, review of *Eva,* pp. 487-488; September-October, 1992, Margaret A. Bush, review of *AK,* p. 588; March-April, 1995, Ann A. Flowers, review of *Shadow of a Hero,* pp. 199-200; March-April, 1997, Nancy Vasilakis, review of *The Lion Tamer's Daughter and Other Stories,* pp. 195-196; September, 2001, Betty Carter, review of *Eva,* p. 541; November-December, 2001, Anita L. Burkam, review of *The Ropemaker,* p. 745; July-August, 2003, Joanna Rudge Long, review of *The Tears of the Salamander,* p. 453.
Independent, October 24, 1998, Nicholas Tucker, "Visionary Angels on a Bloody Earth."
Kirkus Reviews, December 1, 1995, review of *Chuck and Danielle,* p. 1701; December 15, 2003, review of *Inside Grandad.*
New York Times Book Review, April 20, 1986, Eden Ross Lipson, "Write, Then Research, Then Rewrite"; September 27, 1992, Michele Slung, review of *AK,* p. 33.

Publishers Weekly, June 29, 1998, review of *Noli's Story;* November 5, 2001, review of *The Ropemaker,* p. 70; August 11, 2003, review of *The Tears of the Salamander,* p. 281.

School Librarian, February, 1989, Barbara Sherrard-Smith, review of *Merlin Dreams,* p. 21; May, 1994, Alasdair Campbell, review of *Time and the Clockmice, Etcetera,* p. 60.

School Library Journal, December, 1988, Christina L. Olson, review of *Merlin Dreams,* p. 120; April, 1989, Kathryn Harris, review of *Eva,* p. 118; June, 2002, John Peters, review of *Water: Tales of Elemental Spirits,* p. 142; August, 2003, Renee Steinberg, review of *The Tears of the Salamander,* p. 158.

Times Educational Supplement, October 23, 1998, Michael Thorn, "Back to Africa," p. 10.

Times Literary Supplement, March 3-9, 1988, Neil Philip, "Working with Nature," p. 232.

Washington Post Book World, August 9, 1992, Michael Dirda, review of *AK,* p. 11.

ONLINE

Mystery World, http://www.mystworld.com/young writer/authors/ (December 10, 2003), interview with Dickinson.

Rochester Library, http://www.lib.rochester.edu/camelot/ (May 10, 1989), Raymond H. Thompson, "Interview with Peter Dickinson."

*   *   *

Di FILIPPO, Paul 1954-
   (Philip Lawson)

PERSONAL: Born October 29, 1954, in Woonsocket, RI; son of Frank (a manager of a textile firm) and Claire Louise (a bookkeeper; maiden name, St. Amant) Di Filippo; companion of Deborah Newton (a designer). *Ethnicity:* "Italian and French." *Education:* Attended Rhode Island College, 1973-76.

ADDRESSES: Home and office—2 Poplar St., Providence, RI 02906. *E-mail*—author@pauldifilippo.com.

CAREER: Writer. Rhode Island Blue Cross, programmer, 1980-82; worked at Brown University Bookstore, 1987-94; full-time writer, 1994—.

MEMBER: Science Fiction Writers of America.

AWARDS, HONORS: Nebula nominee, 1987, for "Kid Charlemagne," and 1992, for "Lennon Spex"; British Science Fiction Award, best short story of 1994, for "The Double Felix"; World Fantasy Award nominee, 2001, for "Karuna, Inc"; Hugo Award nominee, 2002, for *A Year in the Linear City.*

WRITINGS:

SHORT STORIES

The Steampunk Trilogy, Four Walls Eight Windows (New York, NY), 1995.

Ribofunk, Four Walls Eight Windows (New York, NY), 1996.

Fractal Paisleys, Four Walls Eight Windows (New York, NY), 1997.

Lost Pages, Four Walls Eight Windows (New York, NY), 1998.

Strange Trades, Golden Gryphon Press (Urbana, IL), 2001.

A Year in the Linear City, PS Publishing (Harrowgate, England), 2002.

Little Doors, Four Walls Eight Windows (New York, NY), 2002.

Babylon Sisters and Other Posthumans, Prime Books (Canton, OH), 2002.

Neutrino Drag, Four Walls Eight Windows (New York, NY), 2004.

NOVELS

Ciphers, Permeable Press (San Francisco, CA), 1997.

(As Philip Lawson, with Michael Bishop) *Would It Kill You to Smile?,* Longstreet (Atlanta, GA), 1998.

(As Philip Lawson, with Michael Bishop) *Muskrat Courage,* St. Martin's Press (New York, NY), 2000.

Joe's Liver, Cambrian Publications (San Jose, CA), 2000.

A Mouthful on Tongues: Her Totipotent Tropicanalia, Wildside Press (Holicong, PA), 2002.

Spondulix, Cambrian Publications (San Jose, CA), 2003.

Fuzzy Dice, PS Publishing (Harrowgate, England), 2003, I Books, 2004.

Work represented in anthologies, including *Best Science Fiction of the Eighties,* edited by Hayakawa; and *What Might Have Been,* Volume 2, edited by Benford. Contributor of about a hundred stories and articles to magazines, including *Amazing, Science Fiction Age, Pirate Writings, Interzone, Shock Waves,* and *Fantasy and Science Fiction.* Contributor to *Cities,* Four Walls Eight Windows (New York, NY), 2004. Writes reviews for *Asimov's,* the *Washington Post,* and *Science Fiction.*

WORK IN PROGRESS: A mimetic novel, *Roadside Bodhisattva; Harp, Pipe and Symphony,* for Prime; *Plumage from Pegasus,* expected publication date, spring, 2005, for Prime; and *The Emperor of Gondwanaland* expected publication date, spring, 2005, for Thunder's Mouth.

SIDELIGHTS: Paul Di Filippo is the author of hundreds of science-fiction and fantasy stories, many of which have been published in collections. Published in 2002, *Little Doors* is a collection of seventeen short fantasies, which a *Publishers Weekly* contributor considered "immaculately told." While the same contributor found the stories to be hilarious, the critic also felt that Di Filippo's writing in the book "verges on the self-consciously clever and is slightly condescending." A *Kirkus Reviews* contributor found *Little Doors* a "grotesquely funny collection." The same contributor noted, "None of the seventeen pieces really outstays its welcome, and a few could possibly have stuck around for a couple dozen more pages." The contributor went on to explain that some of Di Filippo's ideas warranted expansion, such as the title story, in which a professor writing a book about Victorian children's literature discovers a mysterious, unfamiliar volume and then notices little drawn doors appearing around campus. "Still, this is a collection worth reading, even if lacking profundity," concluded the *Publishers Weekly* contributor.

Di Filippo also pens novels, including the 2002 *A Mouthful on Tongues: Her Totipotent Tropicanalia,* which he modeled after Samuel Delany's *Tides of Lust. A Mouthful on Tongues* takes place in 2015 in the jungles of North America, which are dominated by a high-security governmental complex. Humble secretary Kerry Hacket stumbles upon a bio-engineering project—a "She Beast" with incredible powers, including the ability to generate autonomous tongues and change her own appearance and gender as well as that of others. A *Publishers Weekly* reviewer wrote, Di Filippo's "truly wondrous wordcraft—a lush and sometimes playful use of language—is reason enough to admire this short, possibly satiric novel."

In an interview with Claude Lalumière published on the *Strange Horizons* Web site, Di Filippo explains a concurrent theme in his work: a passionate desire to pervert consensus reality and imagine better worlds. He admitted, "I 'fess up to such a starry-eyed nature and program. Perhaps because I had what I like to recall was an idyllic childhood, I continue to believe that life on Earth is infinitely improvable. The tragedy comes in how bad we mess up, and why we can't get out of our way to make the world a better place. (This is true on both the global and personal levels.) In my Buddhistic moments, I also recall the saying, 'Samsara [this mortal life] is nirvana.' If only we could see it. And what's so funny about peace, love, and understanding anyhow?"

BIOGRAPHICAL AND CRITICAL SOURCES:

BOOKS

St. James Guide to Science Fiction Writers, 4th edition, St. James Press (Detroit, MI), 1996.

PERIODICALS

Bookwatch, January, 1999, review of *Lost Pages,* p. 8.
Book World, October 28, 2001, review of *Strange Trades,* p. 13; December 2, 2001, review of *Strange Trades,* p. 7.
Kirkus Reviews, October 15, 2002, review of *Little Doors,* p. 1510.
Magazine of Fantasy and Science Fiction, April, 1999, review of *Lost Pages,* p. 41.
Publishers Weekly, August 20, 2001, review of *Strange Trades,* p. 62; September 30, 2002, review of *A Mouthful on Tongues: Her Totipotent Tropicanalia,* p. 54; November 18, 2002, review of *Little Doors,* p. 46.
Science Fiction Chronicle, February, 1999, review of *Lost Pages,* p. 45.

ONLINE

Strange Horizons Web site, http://www.strange horizons.com/ (November 4, 2002), Claude Lalumière, "Interview: Paul Di Filippo."

*   *   *

DRUSE, Eleanor
See KING, Stephen (Edwin)

E

EBERHART, George M(artin) 1950-

PERSONAL: Born June 6, 1950, in Hanover, PA; son of Richard C. (a craftsman) and Elizabeth (Lautz) Eberhart; married Jennifer Henderson, 1982. *Education:* Ohio State University, B.A., 1973; University of Chicago, M.L.S., 1976. *Politics:* Progressive. *Hobbies and other interests:* History, history of science, cryptozoology, UFOs, parapsychology, collecting postcards.

ADDRESSES: Home—Chicago, IL. *Office*—American Library Association, 50 East Huron St., Chicago, IL 60611.

CAREER: Journal of Law and Economics, Chicago, IL, bibliographic assistant, 1976-77; University of Kansas, Lawrence, serials and reference librarian at library of School of Law, 1977-80; American Library Association, Chicago, editor of *College and Research Libraries News,* 1980-90; American Bar Association, Chicago, managing editor of *Criminal Justice,* 1990-92; American Library Association, Chicago, associate editor of *American Libraries,* 1995-99, senior editor, 1999—.

MEMBER: American Library Association.

AWARDS, HONORS: A Geo-Bibliography of Anomalies was named outstanding academic book by *Choice,* 1980.

WRITINGS:

A Geo-Bibliography of Anomalies: Primary Access to Observations of UFOs, Ghosts, and Other Mysterious Phenomena, Greenwood Press (Westport, CT), 1980.

Monsters: A Guide to Information on Unaccounted for Creatures, including Bigfoot, Many Water Monsters, and Other Irregular Animals, Garland (New York, NY), 1983.

UFOs and the Extraterrestrial Contact Movement: A Bibliography, Garland (New York, NY), 1985.

(Editor) *The Roswell Report: A Historical Perspective,* J. Allen Hynek Center for UFO Studies (Chicago, IL), 1991.

(Compiler) *The Whole Library Handbook: Current Data, Professional Advice, and Curiosa about Libraries and Library Services,* American Library Association (Chicago, IL), 1991, 3rd edition published as *The Whole Library Handbook 3: Current Data, Professional Advice, and Curiosa about Libraries and Library Services,* 2000.

Mysterious Creatures: A Guide to Cryptozoology, two volumes, ABC-Clio (Santa Barbara, CA), 2002.

Also contributor of articles and reviews to magazines, including *American Libraries, Postcard Collector,* and the *International UFO Reporter.*

WORK IN PROGRESS: The Whole Library Handbook, 4th edition.

SIDELIGHTS: George M. Eberhart is a librarian with a special interest in all things unusual, from UFOs and Bigfoot to ESP and ghosts. He is employed at the American Library Association, where he is currently editor of *American Libraries* and is the compiler of *The Whole Library Handbook: Current Data, Professional Advice, and Curiosa about Libraries and Library Services* and its subsequent editions. *The*

Whole Library Handbook is a guide for library professionals that contains "everything you ever wanted to know" about the profession and library facilities, according to Cathleen Bourdon in *American Libraries.*

Eberhart has used similar organizational skills in his books about animals not yet described scientifically (the science of cryptozoology), such as his *Monsters: A Guide to Information on Unaccounted for Creatures, including Bigfoot, Many Water Monsters, and Other Irregular Animals* and the more recent *Mysterious Creatures: A Guide to Cryptozoology.* The latter is an encyclopedic guide to unusual animals, both real and imaginary, with Eberhart including over one thousand descriptive entries on everything from leprechauns and the Loch Ness monster to extremely rare but real species—or those once thought to be extinct that have since been rediscovered. A *Booklist* reviewer concluded that this "useful" guide would "be an asset to public, school, and academic libraries."

Eberhart once told *CA:* "I have long had an interest in events, behavior, conditions, or discoveries that do not conform to prevailing world views—this diverse set of scientific and historical mysteries I collectively call anomalies, and their study can be termed 'anomalistic science.' Anomalies include everything *from* lake monsters, bigfoot, ball lightning, earthquake luminescence, intra-Mercurial planets, falls of ice from the sky, the Bermuda Triangle, spontaneous human combustion, and cattle mutilations, *through* ESP, out-of-body experiences, dowsing, astrology, poltergeists, alchemy, biofeedback, neo-paganism, apparitions, spirit mediums, and haunted houses, *to* phantom panthers, UFO abductions, possession cases, medieval witchcraft, Atlantis, ancient cataclysms, megalithic paleoastronomy, mysterious artifacts, pre-Columbian discoveries of America, lost treasure, assassination conspiracies, the Bavarian Illuminati, and the identities of Kasper Hauser and Anastasia Romanov. And that's merely the beginning!

"One would think that such a vast field of scholarship would require minute specialization. The temptation to specialize certainly exists, although I have managed to avoid it by concentrating on the bibliography of anomalistic literature in general. The literature itself encourages a broad outlook: pick up any ten UFO books and you will find that many of the subjects I have listed above will be mentioned, at least in passing.

"In retrospect, I must say that reading and researching the literature of anomalies for the past forty years has been a very liberal education, since anomalies can occur in any branch of human knowledge. It certainly has given me a grasp on the interconnectedness of all things, an outlook that has proven beneficial in my career as librarian, researcher, and journalist."

BIOGRAPHICAL AND CRITICAL SOURCES:

PERIODICALS

American Libraries, December, 1999, "AL Staff Changes," p. 8; May, 2000, Cathleen Bourdon, "Trivia Treasure Trove," p. 92.

Booklist, July, 2003, review of *Mysterious Creatures: A Guide to Cryptozoology,* p. 1917.

Fate, April, 1981, George W. Earley, review of *A Geo-Bibliography of Anomalies: Primary Access to Observations of UFOs, Ghosts, and Other Mysterious Phenomena,* p. 107; November, 1983, George W. Earley, review of *Monsters: A Guide to Information on Unaccounted for Creatures, including Bigfoot, Many Water Monsters, and Other Irregular Animals,* p. 107; September, 2003, Daniel Perez, review of *Mysterious Creatures,* p. 81.

Library Journal, September 15, 1980, Michael Schuyler, review of *A Geo-Bibliography of Anomalies,* p. 1847; May 1, 1995, Wilda W. Williams, review of *The Whole Library Handbook 2: Current Data, Professional Advice, and Curiosa about Libraries and Library Services,* p. 140.

MUFON UFO Journal, October, 1980, Walt Andrus, review of *A Geo-Bibliography of Anomalies,* p. 18.

New Scientist, July 26, 2003, John Bonner, "Beware the Death Worm," p. 49.

RQ, winter, 1980, review of *A Geo-Bibliography of Anomalies,* p. 145.

School Library Journal, May, 1992, Sharon K. Snow, review of *The Whole Library Handbook: Current Data, Professional Advice, and Curiosa about Libraries and Library Services,* p. 50.

Skeptical Inquirer, July-August, 2003, Kendrick Frazier and Benjamin Radford, review of *Mysterious Creatures,* p. 53.

Whole Earth Review, fall, 1986, Ted Schultz, review of *A Geo-Bibliography of Anomalies,* p. 50.

Wilson Library Bulletin, December, 1980, Charles Bunge, review of *A Geo-Bibliography of Anomalies,* p. 299.

EIRE, Carlos M(ario) N(ieto) 1950-

PERSONAL: Born November 23, 1950, in Havana, Cuba; immigrated to the United States, 1962; naturalized U.S. citizen, 1972; son of Antonio J. Nieto-Cortadellas (an attorney and judge) and Maria Azucena Eire; married Jane Vanderlyn Ulrich, January 6, 1984; children: John Carlo, Grace, Bruno. *Education:* Loyola University of Chicago, B.A., 1973; Yale University, M.A., 1974, M.Phil., 1976, Ph.D., 1979. *Religion:* Roman Catholic.

ADDRESSES: Home—Guilford, CT. *Office*—Department of History, Yale University, New Haven, CT 06520-8324. *E-mail*—carlos.eire@yale.edu.

CAREER: St. John's University, Collegeville, MN, bibliographer and assistant professor of religious studies, 1979-81; University of Virginia, Charlottesville, associate professor of religious studies, 1981-96; Yale University, New Haven, CT, professor of history and religious studies, 1996—, Department of Religious Studies chair, 1999-2002, named T. Lawrason Riggs Professor of History and Religious Studies, 2000. School of Historical Studies at Institute for Advanced Study, Princeton, NJ, member, 1986-87, visitor, 1992-93; Center for Advanced Studies, University of Virginia, member, 1993-93; Whitney Humanities Center, Yale University, member, 2002—. Speaker at international conferences; member of academic conference panels; reader of manuscripts for academic publishers. Series consultant for Public Broadcasting System's *Death: The Trip of a Lifetime,* KCTS-TV (Seattle, WA), 1993; commentator for *The Renaissance* (video), "Just the Facts" learning series, 2001.

MEMBER: American Historical Association, American Catholic Historical Association (John Tracy Ellis Prize committee, 1998-2000), American Society of Church History, American Society for Reformation Research (nominating committee, 1992-94), Sixteenth-Century Studies Conference (council member, 1984-87; nominating committee, 1988-90; Carl Meyer Prize committee, 1986, 1994), Society for Spanish and Portuguese Historical Studies.

AWARDS, HONORS: Carl Meyer Prize, Sixteenth-Century Studies Conference, 1980, for "Iconoclasm As a Revolutionary Tactic: The Case of Switzerland,

Carlos M. N. Eire

1524-1536"; fellow at Newberry Library (Chicago, IL), 1980, 1982; Fulbright fellow in Spain, 1984; Sesquicentennial Associates fellowship, University of Virginia, 1986-87; Board of Trustees Teaching Award, University of Virginia Alumni, 1990; Henry St. George Tucker Faculty Award, University of Virginia, 1992; Distinguished Faculty Award, University of Virginia, 1996; National Book Award for nonfiction, National Book Foundation, 2003, for *Waiting for Snow in Havana: Confessions of a Cuban Boy.*

WRITINGS:

War against the Idols: The Reformation of Worship from Erasmus to Calvin, Cambridge University Press (New York, NY), 1986.

From Madrid to Purgatory: The Art and Craft of Dying in Sixteenth-Century Spain, Cambridge University Press (New York, NY), 1995.

(With John Corrigan, Frederick M. Denny, and others) *Jews, Christians, Muslims: A Comparative Introduction to Monotheistic Religions,* Prentice Hall (Upper Saddle River, NJ), 1997.

Waiting for Snow in Havana: Confessions of a Cuban Boy, Free Press (New York, NY), 2003.

Reviewer and editor, *Archiv fü Reformationsgeschichte Literaturbericht,* 1990-98. Contributor of articles and reviews to history and religion journals and encyclopedias.

WORK IN PROGRESS: Writing a survey history of the Reformation and researching attitudes toward miracles in the sixteenth and seventeenth centuries.

SIDELIGHTS: Carlos M. N. Eire was awarded the 2003 National Book Award for his critically acclaimed memoir, *Waiting for Snow in Havana: Confessions of a Cuban Boy.* The Yale University T. Lawrason Riggs Professor of History and Religious Studies left Cuba when he was only eleven—without his parents. Eire and his older brother were among 14,000 children airlifted out of their homeland during the Cuban revolution. Eire's mother joined the boys three years later when she was finally granted a visa, but Eire never saw his father again.

Prior to immigrating to the United States, Eire enjoyed what he considers a somewhat-privileged, middle-class childhood. While his family was not as rich as some—Eire knew a boy who had his own miniature racecar and another with a zoo in his backyard complete with a tiger—Eire's home was filled with artwork and antiques, collections of his father, a municipal judge. Eire's eccentric family makes for interesting prose; his father was convinced that he was Louis XVI in a former life and his brother electrocuted lizards for entertainment. Eire stresses the importance of religion in his childhood. In his house were many portraits of Jesus that young Eire believed spoke to him in his dreams.

In January, 1959, Fidel Castro took the place of President Batista, and Eire's world was shattered. Christmas was canceled. Religion was outlawed. Eire's classmates began to mysteriously disappear as they were shuttled away to freedom in the United States. While many children escaped, their parents were forced to remain in Cuba. Some, like Eire's father, were never granted visas.

Eire explained to *Yale Alumni Magazine* contributor Cathy Shufro that in 2002, three events inspired him to revisit his memories of a Cuban childhood. First, his oldest son celebrated his eleventh birthday, the same one Eire was on as he was shipped to America.

The debate over whether or not to return child refugee Elián González to Cuba and his only surviving parent was a second. Also in the year 2002, Eire turned fifty years old, "a prospect," claimed Shufro, "that occasioned introspection."

Critics praised both Eire's story and style. "As imaginatively wrought as the finest piece of fiction, the book abounds with magical interpretations of ordinary boyhood events," observed a *Publishers Weekly* contributor, who went on to conclude, "Eire looks beyond the literal to see the mythological themes inherent in the epic struggle for identity that each of our lives represents." A *Kirkus Reviews* contributor reflected, "Between mercurial and leisurely, lush and thorny, jumbled and crystalline, Yale historian Eire's recollection of his Cuban boyhood is to be savored."

In addition to penning *Waiting for Snow in Cuba,* Eire has published several scholarly works, including *From Madrid to Purgatory: The Art and Craft of Dying in Sixteenth-Century Spain,* the first full-length study of Spanish attitudes toward death in the sixteenth century. As Eire explains, death was of monumental importance to the people of this time, since they believed they would not go to heaven without a "good death." Eire divides the volume into three books: the first focuses on ordinary deaths, based on a selection of testaments from Madrid's notarial archives, the second discusses the death of Philip II, and the third centers on the death of Teresa de Avila in 1582. Eire notes that while the Spaniards were fearful of death, they were much more afraid of being sent to purgatory and hell.

Writing in the *Journal of Interdisciplinary History,* Richard L. Kagan was troubled with the sources on which Eire based in his conclusions in book one and book three. "Upon close inspection, the sample upon which Eire bases these conclusions is not much of a sample at all, or at least not one that anyone with a background in social statistics could recognize as viable," he observed. Kagan was much more impressed with book two: "Here the study takes an imaginative leap, as Eire transforms the Escorial into an enormous 'palace of death,' a giant 'liturgical machine' whose vast collection of relics was purposely formed to help launch the souls of both Philip and his family into heaven." Overall, Kagan remarked, *"From Madrid to Purgatory* is an important, provocative, readable, and thoroughly enjoyable book." Remarked William J. Callahan in a review of *From Madrid to Purgatory* for the *Canadian Journal of History,* "Although at times discursive, this is a perceptive and evocative study of death as an immediate and pressing concern of Spaniards who saw it as that terrible yet hopeful moment of transition from earthly to heavenly life." *Journal of Religion*'s Carole Slade dubbed it a "very fine book" and concluded that "Eire makes clear that in sixteenth-century Spain, death was no laughing matter; in fact, laughter about it was considered a sign of prospective damnation."

Eire once told *CA* why he chose Spain as the subject for *From Madrid to Purgatory:* "Since Christianity teaches that the moment of death is that during which an individual crosses over from the material world into the spiritual realm, the phenomenon of death offers a rare opportunity to peer into the metaphysical assumptions of any given society. Since Spain was the staunchest defender of Catholic Christianity in the sixteenth century, it has much to offer to anyone who wishes to study the ethos of the Catholic Reformation.

"On one level, the objective of this book is to analyze the way in which belief shapes society and culture, and how, in turn, society and culture define and express belief. More specifically, by studying Spanish attitudes toward death and the afterlife in the sixteenth century I hope to arrive at a clearer understanding of the way in which the Catholic Reformation worked at various social levels—how Catholic belief was affirmed in specific ways through the projection of a spiritual, unseen world into the material sphere. On another level, the objective is to study the phenomenon of death itself in a particular setting that has heretofore been neglected."

BIOGRAPHICAL AND CRITICAL SOURCES:

BOOKS

Eire, Carlos M. N., *From Madrid to Purgatory: The Art and Craft of Dying in Sixteenth-Century Spain,* Cambridge University Press (New York, NY), 1995.

PERIODICALS

American Historical Review, February, 1997, Jodi Bilinkoff, review of *From Madrid to Purgatory,* p. 132.

Booklist, February 15, 2003, Kristine Huntley, review of *Waiting for Snow in Havana: Confessions of a Cuban Boy,* p. 1034.

Canadian Journal of History, August, 1996, William J. Callahan, review of *From Madrid to Purgatory,* pp. 294-296.

Catholic Historical Review, July, 1996, review of *From Madrid to Purgatory,* p. 563.

Church History, June, 1997, review of *From Madrid to Purgatory,* p. 355.

English Historical Review, July, 1989, review of *War against the Idols: The Reformation of Worship from Erasmus to Calvin,* p. 731; November, 1997, review of *From Madrid to Purgatory,* pp. 1267-1269.

Hispanic American Historical Review, May, 1997, review of *From Madrid to Purgatory,* p. 299.

Historical Journal, March, 1991, Thomas A. Brady, review of *War against the Idols,* pp. 181-183.

Journal of Ecclesiastical History, April, 1997, John Edwards, review of *From Madrid to Purgatory,* pp. 372-374.

Journal of Interdisciplinary History, winter, 1997, Richard L. Kagan, review of *From Madrid to Purgatory,* p. 526.

Journal of the History of Ideas, October, 1995, review of *From Madrid to Purgatory,* p. 687.

Journal of Religion, July, 1997, Carole Slade, review of *From Madrid to Purgatory,* p. 466.

Kirkus Reviews, November 1, 2002, review of *Waiting for Snow in Havana,* p. 1586.

Publishers Weekly, November 13, 2000, John F. Baker, "A Cuban Exile at Yale," p. 16; December 23, 2002, review of *Waiting for Snow in Havana,* p. 54.

Religious Studies Review, July, 1997, review of *From Madrid to Purgatory,* p. 309.

Sixteenth Century Journal, spring, 1996, J. B. Owens, review of *From Madrid to Purgatory,* p. 187.

Spectator, November 23, 1996, review of *From Madrid to Purgatory,* p. 43.

Times Literary Supplement, June 28, 1996, review of *From Madrid to Purgatory,* p. 29.

Yale Alumni Magazine, January-February, 2004, Cathy Shufro, "Cuban Dreams: For National Book Award Winner Carlos Eire, the Road from Sixteenth Century to Personal Memoir Began in Clouds."

ONLINE

Online-NewsHour Web site, http://www.pbs.org/newshour/ (November 25, 2003), interview with Carlos Eire.

Yale University Web site, http://www.yale.edu/ (April 12, 2004), "Carlos M. N. Eire."*

EVANS, Max 1925(?)-

PERSONAL: Born August 29, 1925 (some sources cite 1924 or 1926), in Ropes, TX; son of W. B. and Hazel (Swafford) Evans; married Pat James, August 4, 1949; children: Charlotte and Sheryl (twins). *Education:* Studied art privately.

ADDRESSES: Home—1111 Ridgecrest Dr. SE, Albuquerque, NM 87108. *Agent*—Russell & Volkening, Inc., 551 Fifth Ave., New York, NY 10017.

CAREER: Writer and artist. Began work on a cattle ranch at age twelve; worked as a cowboy, ranch owner, trapper, prospector, and mining promoter; Taos Minerals, Inc., Taos, NM, vice president, 1955-58; Solar Metals, Inc., Taos, president, 1957-59. *Military service:* U.S. Army; served during World War II.

AWARDS, HONORS: Commendation from City of Los Angeles; named honorary member of board of chancellors, University of Texas; Saddleman Award, Western Writers of America, 1990.

WRITINGS:

Southwest Wind (short stories), Naylor (San Antonio, TX), 1958.
Long John Dunn of Taos (biography), Westernlore (Los Angeles, CA), 1959.
The Rounders, Macmillan (New York, NY), 1960.
The Hi Lo Country, Macmillan (New York, NY), 1961, reprinted, Boulevard Books (New York, NY), 1998.
Three Short Novels: The Great Wedding, The One-Eyed Sky, My Pardner, Houghton Mifflin (Boston, MA), 1963 (*My Pardner* reprinted separately, 1972).
Mountain of Gold, Berg (Dunwoody, GA), 1965.
Shadow of Thunder, Swallow Press (Chicago, IL), 1967.
Sam Peckinpah: Master of Violence, Dakota Press (Vermillion, SD), 1972.
Bobby Jack Smith: You Dirty Coward, Nash Publishing (Los Angeles, CA), 1974.
The White Shadow, Joyce Press (San Diego, CA), 1977.

Xavier's Folly and Other Stories, Zia (Castlerock, CO), 1984.
Super Bull and Other True Escapades, University of New Mexico Press (Albuquerque, NM), 1989.
Rounders 3, Doubleday (New York, NY), 1990.
Film Director Sam Peckinpah: Madman and Genius (film script), 1991.
Bluefeather Fellini, University Press of Colorado (Boulder, CO), 1993.
Bluefeather Fellini in the Sacred Realm, University Press of Colorado (Boulder, CO), 1994.
Spinning Sun, Grinning Moon: Novellas, Red Crane Books (Santa Fe, NM), 1995.
This Chosen Place: Finding Shangri-La on the 4UR, University Press of Colorado (Boulder, CO), 1997.
Hi Lo to Hollywood! A Max Evans Reader, Texas Tech University Press (Lubbock, TX), 1998.
Faraway Blue, Forge (New York, NY), 1999.
Madam Millie: Bordellos from Silver City to Ketchikan, University of New Mexico Press (Albuquerque, NM), 2002.
(Editor, with Candy Moulton) *Hot Biscuits: Eighteen Stories by Women and Men of the Ranching West,* University of New Mexico Press (Albuquerque, NM), 2002.

Contributor to anthologies, including *Three West: Conversations with Vardis Fisher, Max Evans and Michael Straight,* by John R. Milton, Dakota Press (Vermillion, SD), 1970; *The Pick of the Roundup,* edited by Stephen Payne, Avon (New York, NY), 1963; *Rivers to Cross,* edited by William R. Cox, Dodd, Mead (New York, NY), 1966; *The Far Side of the Storm,* San Marcos Press (Cerrillos, NM), 1975; and *The New Frontier,* edited by Joe R. Lansdale, Doubleday (New York, NY), 1989. Contributor to screenplays. Contributor of over sixty articles to periodicals, including *Field and Stream, Empire,* and *Contact.*

A collection of Evans's manuscripts is housed at the University of Texas—El Paso.

ADAPTATIONS: The Rounders was filmed by Metro-Goldwyn-Mayer, starring Henry Fonda and Glenn Ford; the book was also adapted for a television series by American Broadcasting Companies in 1966. *The Hi Lo Country* was adapted for a screenplay featuring Woody Harrelson, Billy Crudup, and Patricia Arquette, released by Gramercy Pictures. *Rounders 3* was also adapted as a screenplay, directed by Stephen Friers and produced by Martin Scorsese. Film rights to *Mountain of Gold* have also been sold. An abridged edition of *Hi Lo to Hollywood! A Max Evans Reader* has been recorded as an audio book.

SIDELIGHTS: Max Evans's western novels and short stories are informed by his own years of experience as a ranch hand, rodeo cowboy, and miner. He also made his living for nine years as an artist, selling over 300 oil paintings in his career. Evans's first publication was a short story in the *Denver Post* magazine, and his first book, *Southwest Wind,* was a collection of short stories. According to C. L. Sonnischsen, a contributor to *Twentieth-Century Western Writers,* the vignettes in *Southwest Wind* "probe the dark corners of this little universe" and are "full of life and human feeling and insight."

While working on his second book—*Long John Dunn of Taos,* a biography of a western adventurer—Evans lost a large sum of money on a mining venture. He decided to write a novel to try to raise the cash he needed. The result was *The Rounders,* a contemporary western about two cowboys, both chronic losers, defeated by society. The book is a humorous read, but several critics noted that it would be an error to classify it as simple comedy. Traditionally, the individual is the winner in western fiction; in making his protagonists failures, Evans was making a statement. "They are so funny," Sonnischsen wrote of Evans's protagonists, "but our laughter is at cracked ribs, broken teeth, the frustrations of bachelor life in a lonely line camp, wicked horses hoping to kill their riders, wild debauches when the lonely men come to town. Evans's home country is full of danger, pain, and violence, and that country, as he sees it, is a metaphor for the world." *The Rounders* was made into a very successful film, starring Henry Fonda and Glenn Ford, and it led Evans to do more scriptwriting in Hollywood.

Some of his books, such as *Bobby Jack Smith, You Dirty Coward* and *My Pardner,* are simple examples of "bawdy country humor," in the opinion of Sonnischsen; but Evans's writing after 1963 became "increasingly symbolic, violent, and tragic." The critic summarized: "Evans is a philosopher and teacher as well as a keen observer and this is the lesson he wants to teach: the dependence of every living thing on the earth from which it came, and the interdependence of all the lives involved. . . . Man is not alone, and neither is he independent."

BIOGRAPHICAL AND CRITICAL SOURCES:

BOOKS

Milton, John R., *Three West: Conversations with Vardis Fisher, Max Evans, Michael Straight,* Dakota Press (Vermillion, SD), 1970.
Twentieth-Century Western Writers, St. James Press (Detroit, MI), 1991.

PERIODICALS

Bloomsbury Review, September, 1998, review of *Rounders 3,* p. 17.
Booklist, January 1, 1999, Budd Arthur, review of *Faraway Blue,* p. 831.
Choice, March, 1970, p. 74.
Kirkus Reviews, May 1, 1972, p. 537; December 1, 1998, review of *Faraway Blue,* p. 1695.
Library Journal, November 1, 1974, p. 2871.
New York Times Book Review, September 8, 1974, p. 43; December 29, 1974, p. 20.
Publishers Weekly, August 15, 1966, p. 66; February 24, 1969, p. 65; November 2, 1998, review of *Hi Lo to Hollywood! A Max Evans Reader,* p. 67; November 30, 1998, review of *Faraway Blue,* p. 52.
Reference and Research Book News, May, 1998, review of *Rounders 3,* p. 173.
Roundup, August, 1998, review of *Rounders 3,* p. 30; April, 1999, review of *Faraway Blue* and *Hi Lo to Hollywood!,* p. 33.
Southwestern Historical Quarterly, July, 2001, Russell Goodyear, review of *Hi Lo to Hollywood!,* p. 183.*

*   *   *

EVERETT, Percival L. 1956-

PERSONAL: Born December 22, 1956, in Ft. Gordon, GA; son of Percival Leonard (a dentist) and Dorothy (Stinson) Everett. *Education:* University of Miami, A.B., 1977; attended University of Oregon, 1978-80; Brown University, A.M., 1982.

ADDRESSES: Office—c/o University Park Campus, English Department, University of Southern California, Los Angeles, CA 90089. *E-mail*—peverett@usc.edu.

CAREER: Worked as jazz musician, ranch worker, and high school teacher; University of Kentucky, Lexington, associate professor of English, 1985-89, director of graduate creative writing program, 1985-89; University of Notre Dame, Notre Dame, IN, professor of English, 1989-92; University of California at Riverside, professor of creative writing and chairman of program, 1992-99; University of Southern California, Los Angeles, professor of creative writing, American studies, and critical theory, 1999—; writer.

MEMBER: Writers Guild of America (West), Modern Language Association.

AWARDS, HONORS: D. H. Lawrence fellowship, University of New Mexico, 1984; Lila Wallace-*Reader's Digest* fellowship; New American Writing Award, for *Zulus;* PEN/Oakland Josephine Miles Award, for *Big Picture;* Academy Award for Literature, American Academy of Arts and Letters, 2003; Hurston/Wright Legacy Award; Hillsdale Award.

WRITINGS:

Suder (novel), Viking (New York, NY), 1983.
Walk Me to the Distance (novel), Ticknor & Fields (Boston, MA), 1985.
Cutting Lisa (novel), Ticknor & Fields (Boston, MA), 1986.
The Weather and Women Treat Me Fair (short stories), August House (Little Rock, AK), 1989.
Zulus (novel), Permanent Press (Sag Harbor, NY), 1989.
For Her Dark Skin (novel), Owl Creek Press (Seattle, WA), 1989.
The One That Got Away (children's book), illustrations by Dirk Zimmer, Clarion Books (New York, NY), 1992.
God's Country (novel), Faber (Boston, MA), 1994.
The Body of Martin Aguilera, Owl Creek Press (Seattle, WA), 1994.
Big Picture (short stories), Graywolf Press (St. Paul, MN), 1996.
Watershed (novel), Graywolf Press (St. Paul, MN), 1996.
Frenzy (novel), Graywolf Press (St. Paul, MN), 1996.
Glyph (novel), Graywolf Press (St. Paul, MN), 1999.
Grand Canyon, Inc. (novel), Versus Press, 2001.

Erasure (novel), Hyperion (New York, NY), 2002.
(Author of foreword) *Making Callaloo: Twenty-five Years of Black Literature, 1976-2000,* edited by Charles Henry Rowell, afterword by Carl Phillips, St. Martin's Press (New York, NY), 2002.
American Desert (novel), 2004.
Damned If I Do (short fiction), 2004.
(With James Kincaid) *A History of the African-American People (Proposed) by Strom Thurmond, As Told to Percival Everett and James Kincaid* (novel), Akashic Books, 2004.

Work represented in anthologies, including *From Timberline to Tidepool: Contemporary Fiction from the Northwest,* edited by Rich Ives, Owl Creek Press, 1989. Contributor of stories to periodicals, including *Montana Review, Callaloo, Aspen Journal of the Arts, Modern Short Stories,* and *Black American Literature Forum.*

SIDELIGHTS: Percival L. Everett is an educator and writer who has won acclaim with his comic fiction. Everett gained acclaim in 1983 with his first novel, *Suder,* which tells the story of a baseball player who reacts to a slump and family problems by suddenly embarking on a trip across the American northwest. Carolyn See, writing in the *Los Angeles Times,* described *Suder* as a "mad work of comic genius," and Alice Hoffman affirmed in the *New York Times Book Review* that the novel "gives us a story of a life filled with chance events, some laughable, others tragic." *Walk Me to the Distance,* Everett's second novel, concerns a Vietnam veteran who finds seclusion at a Wyoming ranch house he shares with an aging widow and her mentally impaired son. The hero finds a measure of contentment with the widow, with whom he eventually adopts a Vietnamese girl. But when the widow's son, scorned by his mother, violates the girl, the hero is drawn to vigilante justice. Reviewing *Walk Me to the Distance* in the *Los Angeles Times,* Don Strachan said that the novel "forces us to examine our moral positions," and he added that Everett demonstrates an ability "to plumb a deep emotional well with a detail."

In 1986 Everett produced his third novel, *Cutting Lisa,* and he followed that volume in 1989 with his first short-story collection, *The Weather and Women Treat Me Fair.* In 1989 he also published *Zulus,* a fantasy about the last fertile woman on a post-thermonuclear Earth. The heroine is an obese woman who avoids forced sterilization and subsequently becomes pregnant after being raped. With her potential for childbearing, the heroine proves valuable to rebels interested in rejuvenating the human race. Reviewing *Zulus* in the *Washington Post*, Clarence Major drew comparisons to Aldous Huxley's classic, *Brave New World*, and stated that Everett's novel "is a curious, troublesome and, at times, delightful addition to the literature of the antiheroic and the futuristic." In addition, Major hailed Everett as "one of America's most promising young novelists" and noted that his "gifts as a lyrical writer are vividly on display."

Everett followed *Zulus* with another novel, *For Her Dark Skin*. He then published *The One That Got Away*, a children's book about the high jinks that ensue when a band of cowboys capture the numeral "one." A *Kirkus Reviews* critic conceded that *The One That Got Away* is "sort of a one-joke story" but nonetheless summarized it as a "novel idea, developed with high style and wit."

In 1994 Everett published *God's Country*, a novel about a cowardly racist who requires a black tracker's services after his wife is kidnapped by white men posing as Indians. *Booklist* reviewer Brian McCombie deemed *God's Country* "laugh-out-loud funny, thoughtful, and shocking," and a *Publishers Weekly* critic found it "corrosively funny and disquieting." A *Kirkus Reviews* critic, meanwhile, contended that "as a spoof, this tale hits the mark," and David Bowman, writing in the *New York Times Book Review*, declared that *God's Country* "starts sour, then abruptly turns into Cowpoke Absurdism, ending with an acute hallucination of blood, hate and magic." He added, "The novel sears."

Everett's *Big Picture*, which appeared two years later, contains short stories exemplifying what a *Kirkus Reviews* critic acknowledged as Everett's "usual subtlety and eccentric comic flourishes." Among the tales in *Big Picture* are "Cerulean," where an artist indulges his long-held desire to consume paint; "Dicotyles Tajacu," in which a forlorn painter bonds with a stuffed, one-eyed pig; and "Squeeze," wherein a cowhand falls victim to a prankster sporting a friend's dentures. A *Publishers Weekly* critic, while contending that *Cerulean* "caves in on itself," concluded that other

tales in the collection "steer clear of abstract self-preoccupation and make for good reading." A *Kirkus Reviews* critic similarly summarized the stories in *Big Picture* as "eminently readable," while Maggie Garb, writing in the *New York Times Book Review*, affirmed that Everett sometimes manages to enrich his characters with "a strangely appealing complexity."

In 1996, the same year he issued *Big Picture*, Everett also produced two novels: *Watershed* and *Frenzy*. *Watershed* depicts a black hydrologist contending with both a faltering romance and a federal investigation for murder. The novel begins with the hero surrounded by police in the mountains of Colorado. It then retraces events—including the hero's involvement in a dispute between Indians and the U.S. government—culminating in the standoff. A *Kirkus Reviews* critic claimed that *Watershed* provides "few breathtaking vistas" but conceded that it includes "nice touches of humor and essential humanity." A *Publishers Weekly* critic was likewise ambivalent, noting the novel's "rueful irony and political bite" but adding that the various relationships "lack the nuance of the cultural background [Everett] gives them." James Polk, though, declared in the *New York Times Book Review* that *Watershed* "tells an important story."

Frenzy, meanwhile, is set in the world of Greek mythology. The novel tells of Vlepo, assistant to the half-man, half-God Dionysus. Vlepo, who possesses the ability to read minds, travels back in time in an attempt to help Dionysus grasp his own fate. A *Publishers Weekly* critic deemed *Frenzy* "playful," and *Library Journal* reviewer Robert E. Brown proclaimed it "interesting." A *Kirkus Reviews* critic, however, concluded that some readers might find *Frenzy* "a strained, rather precious exercise."

The novel *Glyph* concerns an infant genius—his studies include philosophy and physics—who blackmails his father before being kidnapped by, successively, a deranged psychologist and conspiratorial government agents. A *Kirkus Reviews* critic described the novel's conclusion as "a final free-for-all that involves [the hero's] previous captors, the Catholic Church, and [former Filipino dictator] Ferdinand Marcos." *Kirkus Reviews* deemed *Glyph* "a smart, rollicking sendup," and a *Publishers Weekly* reviewer described the novel as an "off-kilter academic spoof." Barbara Hoffert, writing in *Library Journal*, was less impressed, claiming that Everett's protagonist is "insufferable enough to leave a sour taste." But *Booklist* critic George Needham called *Glyph* a novel "that can be enjoyed by almost anyone."

Everett continued his prolific production of fiction with the 2001 novella *Grand Canyon, Inc.,* which was followed the next year by the novel *Erasure.* Described by a *Publishers Weekly* critic as an "an over-the-top masterpiece," *Erasure* features as its protagonist one Thelonius "Monk" Ellison, an African-American writer who has built a limited readership for his intellectual essays and experimental novels. Having observed the success of other black writers who have opted to "write black," Monk decides to try his hand at "ghetto prose." His proposal for a novel titled *My Pafology,* written under the pseudonym of Stagg R. Leigh, quickly produces a huge advance from a major publisher and an even larger offer for movie rights to the story. The resulting novel becomes a best-seller and is nominated for an important book award. In the *Review of Contemporary Fiction,* Trey Strecker wrote, "*Erasure*'s acerbic satire on race and publishing is balanced by Monk's heartfelt attempt to reconcile himself to tumultuous—and typically late-twentieth-century—changes in his family life: his sister's murder, his mother's Alzheimer's disease, his brother's coming out, and his father's suicide." In *Publishers Weekly* a reviewer concluded, "Percival's talent is multifaceted, sparked by a satiric brilliance that could place him alongside Wright and Ellison as he skewers the conventions of racial and political correctness."

Everett's *American Desert* projects an even stranger tale. Ted Street, a disgruntled college professor, is en route to commit suicide when he is killed in a car crash. At his funeral he comes back to life, and then embarks on a bizarre journey of soul searching. Reviewing the novel for *Booklist,* Vanessa Bush called *American Desert* a "biting and satirical" story "about the meaning of life and death and one man's search for redemption."

BIOGRAPHICAL AND CRITICAL SOURCES:

PERIODICALS

Booklist, May 15, 1994, Brian McCombie, review of *God's Country;* April 1, 1996, Brad Hooper, review of *Watershed,* p. 1342; January 1, 1997, Brian McCombie, review of *Frenzy,* p. 818; October 15, 1999, George Needham, review of *Glyph;* April 1, 2004, Vanessa Bush, review of *American Desert,* p. 1346.

Kirkus Reviews, March 1, 1992, review of *The One That Got Away;* March 15, 1994, review of *God's Country;* February 15, 1996, reviews of *Watershed* and *Big Picture;* November 1, 1996, review of *Glyph.*

Library Journal, January, 1997, Robert E. Brown, review of *Frenzy;* November 1, 1999, Barbara Hoffert, review of *Glyph.*

Los Angles Times, July 31, 1983, pp. 1, 8.

New York Times Book Review, October 2, 1983, pp. 9, 26; March 24, 1985, p. 24; June 5, 1994, David Bowman, "Cowpoke Absurdism"; September 15, 1996, Maggie Garb, review of *Big Picture;* December 1, 1996, James Polk, review of *Watershed.*

Publishers Weekly, April 18, 1994, review of *God's Country,* p. 46; March 4, 1996, reviews of *Watershed,* p. 53, and *Big Picture,* p. 61; November 18, 1996, review of *Frenzy,* p. 67; November 8, 1999, review of *Glyph;* August 13, 2001, review of *Erasure,* p. 283.

Review of Contemporary Fiction, summer, 2002, Trey Strecker, review of *Erasure,* p. 228.

Washington Post, May 20, 1990, p. 4.

ONLINE

University of Southern California Web site, http://www.usc.edu/ (September 27, 2003).

F

FAITHFULL, Marianne 1946-

PERSONAL: Born 1946, in Hampstead, England; daughter of Glynn Faithfull (an officer in British Intelligence) and Eva Sacher-Masoch (Baroness Erisso); married John Dunbar, an art dealer (divorced); married Ben Brierly, 1979 (divorced); children: Nicholas (first marriage). *Hobbies and other interests:* Reading, cooking, children.

ADDRESSES: Home—Ireland. *Agent*—Ellen Smith, 868 Union St., San Francisco, CA 94133.

CAREER: Folksinger, actress for stage and film, author. Recorded albums, including *Marianne Faithfull,* 1965, *Go Away from My World,* 1965, *Faithfull Forever,* 1966, *Broken English,* 1979, and *A Secret Life,* 1995. Appeared in films, including *Made in U.S. A.,* 1966, *Assault on Agathon,* 1976, and *When Pigs Fly,* 1995. Appeared in theater productions, including *Three Sisters,* 1967, *Hamlet,* 1969, *Alice in Wonderland,* 1973, *The Collector,* 1974, and *The Threepenny Opera.*

WRITINGS:

(With David Dalton) *Faithfull: An Autobiography,* Little, Brown (Boston, MA), 1994.

WORK IN PROGRESS: Chance and Necessity.

SIDELIGHTS: Marianne Faithfull became well-known as a folk singer during the early 1960s, then soon afterward gained notoriety for her relationships with several leading figures of the rock music scene. Her autobiography, *Faithfull,* is a candid account of both her musical career and private life. Claiming Rolling Stones guitarist Keith Richards as the love of her life, Faithfull was most often associated in public with Mick Jagger during the 1960s. In her memoir, Faithfull recounts numerous successful and unsuccessful attempts by other famous men to seduce her. Jeff Giles commented in *Newsweek* that "one of the great pleasures of reading *Faithfull* . . . is watching a generation of rock legends humiliate themselves as they try to hit on one woman." Faithfull is also frank about her years of drug abuse, which sidetracked her career for almost a decade; after the 1979 release of *Broken English,* which restored Faithfull's reputation as a performer, she reemerged "furious and knowing she'd become a cabaret singer for the end of the world," according to Giles in *Newsweek.*

The daughter of aristocrats, Faithfull was educated in a convent before being discovered by Andrew Loog Oldham, the manager of the Rolling Stones. Her first single, "As Tears Go By," which was written by Jagger, Richards, and Oldham, became a hit in 1964. Not long afterward, as Faithfull recounts in her autobiography, she was meeting or touring with many of the names closely associated with the music of the 1960s, including Bob Dylan, the Beatles, and Ike and Tina Turner. It was during this period that Faithfull was—in the words of London *Sunday Times* contributor Christa D'Souza—"inducted, like a kid in a candy store, into the pleasures of getting high." In a *New York Times Book Review* critique of *Faithfull,* David Kelly commented that the singer "has great memory when it comes to acid trips," citing the author's account of

Rolling Stone Brian Jones's urge to play a musical composition for the Barbary apes on the Rock of Gibraltar.

Faithfull's relationship with Jagger came to symbolize a certain rock-and-roll attitude during the late 1960s. "If they weren't the first example of rock royalty, they were certainly the most mythologized—with their King's Road clothes, their aristocratic friends, and their flouting of middle-class conventions," commented Cathy Horyn in *Vanity Fair*. After a four year relationship, Faithfull and Jagger separated in 1970. Her singing career, despite a moderately successful greatest hits album, had ground to a halt, and she was addicted to cocaine and heroin. "Unsupported by Mick's constant disapproval of her drug-taking, she became a street addict and spent the next decade in a smack-induced haze," D'Souza wrote in the London *Sunday Times*.

Faithfull's account of events from the 1970s include two more marriages, several suicide attempts, a recovery from drug addiction, and the revival of her singing career with the release in 1979 of *Broken English*—an album considered a classic by numerous music critics. She resumed her acting career in the late 1970s, having once starred in prestigious productions of Shakespeare and Chekhov a decade earlier. Although Faithfull slid back into drug dependency in the years following the debut of *Broken English,* she definitively kicked her drug addiction in 1986 after a rigorous detox program. Besides penning *Faithfull,* the singer has collaborated on a record with composer Angelo Badalamenti, whose works include the soundtrack for the cult television series *Twin Peaks.* Released in 1995, *A Secret Life* is described by Horyn in *Vanity Fair* as a "searing collaboration . . . which will almost certainly restore this fallen angel to her rightful place: as one of the great interpretive singers of our time."

Critics appreciated *Faithfull* for its insider's view of rock society during a pivotal period in the history of contemporary music. In the London *Sunday Times,* Sarah Miles pointed out that "the section in the book on the elite—Bob Dylan, the Beatles, Jimi Hendrix, the very nub of the Sixties rock'n'roll folklore—is often interesting for those who knew none of it, and, I would have thought, an invaluable document for those rock 'n' roll buffs who mistakenly thought they knew it all." Horyn, in *Vanity Fair,* observed that *Faithfull*

"offers plenty of firsthand Jagger insights, but it's her riffs on Dylan, Hendrix, and, of course, her own well-stimulated life that make for some of the best reading."

BIOGRAPHICAL AND CRITICAL SOURCES:

BOOKS

Contemporary Musicians, Volume 14, Gale (Detroit, MI), 1995.
Encyclopedia of Pop, Rock and Soul, St. Martin's Press (New York, NY), 1989.

PERIODICALS

Interview, February, 1991, pp. 78, 80.
Newsweek, August 22, 1994, pp. 60, 62.
New York Times Book Review, October 16, 1994, p. 37.
Sunday Times, August 14, 1994, section 4, pp. 1-2; August 21, 1994, section 7, p. 3.
Vanity Fair, September, 1994, pp. 102-112.*

*   *   *

FALLACI, Oriana 1930-

PERSONAL: Born June 29, 1930, in Florence, Italy; daughter of Edoardo (a cabinet maker and politician) and Tosca (Cantini) Fallaci; companion of Alexandros Panagoulis (a political activist; died, May 1, 1976). *Education:* Attended University of Florence and medical school. *Politics:* Liberal.

ADDRESSES: Home—New York, NY; Florence, Italy. *Agent*—c/o Rizzoli Editore Corp., 31 West 57th St., 4th Floor, New York, NY 10019; RCS Rizzoli Libri, Via Mecenate 91, 20138 Milan, Italy.

CAREER: Writer. Reporter, *Il Mattino dell'Italia centrale* (newspaper), beginning 1946; reporter, *Epoca* (magazine), 1951; special correspondent, *Europeo* (magazine), 1958-77. Also war correspondent beginning in 1967. Has interviewed internationally known figures, including Nguyen Cao Ky, Yasir Arafat, the Shah of Iran, Henry Kissinger, Walter Cronkite, Indira

Oriana Fallaci

Gandhi, Golda Meir, Nguyen Van Thieu, Zulfikar Ali Bhutto, Willy Brandt, the Aytollah Khomeini, and Mu'ammar Muhammad al-Gaddafi. Collaborator with major publishers throughout the world, including *Washington Post*, 1977-96; *Life* magazine, 1977-96; and *Look* magazine, 1977-96. Lecturer at universities, including University of Chicago, Columbia University, Harvard University, and Yale University. Director, Rizzoli Publishing Corporation.

AWARDS, HONORS: St. Vincent Prize for journalism, 1971, 1973; Bancarella Prize, 1971 for *Nothing, and So Be It;* Viareggio Prize, 1979, for *Un Uomo: Romanzo;* Hemingway prize, Super Bancarella prize, both 1991, both for *Inshallah;* Prix Antibes, 1993, for *Insciallah;* honorary D.Litt., Columbia College (Chicago, IL).

WRITINGS:

I Sette peccati di Hollywood (title means "The Seven Sins of Hollywood"), preface by Orson Welles, Longanesi (Milan, Italy), 1958.
Il Sesso inutile: Viaggio intorno all donna, Rizzoli (Milan, Italy), 1961, translation by Pamela Swing-

lehurst published as *The Useless Sex: Voyage around the Woman*, Horizon Press (New York, NY), 1964.
Penelope alla guerra (novel), Rizzoli (Milan, Italy), 1962, translation by Pamela Swinglehurst published as *Penelope at War*, M. Joseph (London, England), 1966.
Gli antipatici, Rizzoli (Milan, Italy), 1963, translation by Pamela Swinglehurst published as *Limelighters*, M. Joseph (London, England), 1967, published as *The Egotists: Sixteen Surprising Interviews*, Regnery (Chicago, IL), 1968.
Se il sole muore, Rizzoli (Milan, Italy), 1965, translation by Pamela Swinglehurst published as *If the Sun Dies*, Atheneum (New York, NY), 1966.
Niente a cosi sia, Rizzoli (Milan, Italy), 1969, translation by Isabel Quigly published as *Nothing, and So Be It*, Doubleday (New York, NY), 1972, also published as *Nothing and Amen*, M. Joseph (London, England, 1972.
Quel giorno sulla Luna, Rizzoli (Milan, Italy), 1970.
Intervista con la Storia, Rizzoli (Milan, Italy), 1974, translation by John Shepley published as *Interview with History*, Liveright (New York, NY), 1976.
Lettera a un bambino mai nato, Rizzoli (Milan, Italy), 1975, translation by John Shepley published as *Letter to a Child Never Born*, Simon & Schuster (New York, NY), 1976.
Un Uomo: Romanzo (novel), Rizzoli (Milan, Italy), 1979, translation by William Weaver published as *A Man*, Simon & Schuster (New York, NY), 1980.
Insciallah, translation by Oriana Fallaci (from a translation by James Marcus) published as *Inshallah*, Doubleday (New York, NY), 1992.
La Rabbia e l'orgoglio, Rizzoli (Milan, Italy), 2001, translation by Oriana Fallaci published as *The Rage and the Pride*, Rizzoli International (New York, NY), 2002.
La Forza della ragione (title means "Strength of Reason"), Rizzoli International (New York, NY), 2004.

Contributor of articles to periodicals, including *New Republic, New York Times Magazine, Life, La Nouvelle Observateur, Washington Post, Look, Der Stern,* and *Corriere della Sera.*

SIDELIGHTS: Though she has written novels and memoirs, Italian author Oriana Fallaci remains best known as an uncompromising political interviewer, or, as Elizabeth Mehren put it in the *Los Angeles Times,* "the journalist to whom virtually no world figure would say no." Her subjects include Henry Kissinger, Willy Brandt, the Ayatollah Khomeini, and the late Pakistani leader Zulfikar Ali Bhutto, from whom she extracted such criticism of India's Indira Gandhi that a 1972 peace treaty between the two countries almost went unsigned. Already as famous as many of the figures she interviews, Fallaci is a freethinker passionately committed to her craft. "I do not feel myself to be, nor will I ever succeed in feeling like, a cold recorder of what I see and hear," she wrote in the preface to *Interview with History.* "On every professional experience I leave shreds of my heart and soul; and I participate in what I see or hear as though the matter concerned me personally and were one on which I ought to take a stand (in fact I always take one, based on a specific moral choice)."

While Fallaci's morality has seldom been questioned, her interviewing techniques are highly controversial. According to *New York Times Book Review* contributor Francine du Plessix Gray, Fallaci combines "the psychological insight of a great novelist and the irreverence of a bratty quiz kid." Known for her abrasive interviewing tactics, Fallaci often goads her subjects into revelations. "Let's talk about war," she challenged Henry Kissinger in their 1972 interview. "You're not a pacifist, are you?" When a subject refuses to cooperate, he becomes "a bastard, a fascist, an idiot," noted *Esquire* contributor David Sanford.

Fallaci denies her reputation as a brutal interrogator, insisting instead that she merely frames the questions other reporters lack the courage to ask. Where others seek objectivity, Fallaci prefers an approach that she calls "correct" and "honest." Each interview, "is a portrait of myself," she told *Time* contributor Jordan Bonfante. "They are a strange mixture of my ideas, my temperament, my patience, all of these driving the questions."

Although Ted Morgan complained in the *Washington Post* that Fallaci "wants to be more than a brilliant interviewer, she wants to be an avenging angel," Fallaci defends her unique approach on the grounds that she is not simply a journalist but a historian as well. She told Bonfante, "A journalist lives history in the best of ways, that is in the moment that history takes place. He lives history, he touches history with his hands, looks at it with his eyes, he listens to it with his ears." To Jonathan Cott in a *Rolling Stone*

interview, she explained, "I am the judge. I am the one who decides. Listen: if I am a painter and I do your portrait, have I or haven't I the right to paint you as I want?"

Fallaci's commitment to self-expression began at an early age. She once told *CA* that she remembers writing "short naive stories" at age nine. "Yet," she continued, "I really started writing at sixteen when I became a reporter in Florence. I got into journalism to become a writer." When asked what circumstances had been important to her career, Fallaci said, "first of all, the fact of belonging to a liberal and politically engaged family. Also, the fact of having lived—though as a child—the heroic days of the Resistance in Italy through a father who was a leader of it. Then, the fact of being a Florentine. That is, the result of a certain civilization and culture. However, I sometimes wonder if the most motivating factor has not been the fact of being born a woman and poor. When you are a woman, you have to fight more. Consequently, to see more and to think more and to be more creative. The same, when you were born poor. Survival is a great pusher."

Fallaci once told *CA* that the purpose behind her writing is "to tell a story with meaning. Certainly not money. I never wrote for money. I could never write for money—which means by order or for an engagement with a publisher." Instead, the motivating factor of each of her books is "a great emotion, both a psychological or political and [an] intellectual emotion. Think of *Nothing, and So Be It,* the book on Vietnam. For me, it is not even a book on Vietnam, it is a book on the war. (I am obsessed by the uselessness and the stupidity and the cruelty and the folly of the war.) *Letter to a Child Never Born* (which was not written for the issue of abortion as it has been said so often and so gratuitously) was born out of the loss of a child. *A Man* was written out of the death of my companion Alekos Panagoulis and the grief for such loss. However, one should notice that the leitmotif of all my books is the theme of death. These three books always speak of death or refer to death, my hate for death, my fight against death. . . . Freedom is only one of the many other elements. What really pushes me to write is my obsession with death."

In *Letter to a Child Never Born* Fallaci chronicles the fictional dialogue between the narrator and the baby the woman carries inside herself. "The plot proceeds," according to Isa Kapp in the *Washington Post Book*

World, "as a monologue-debate on procreation and the right of a woman who has conceived a child to decide whether she should allow it to live." Based on Fallaci's own three-month pregnancy, the novel "has moments of intense emotional power," allowed Francine du Plessix Gray in the *New York Times Book Review.* But du Plessix Gray went on to say that "it too often lapses into a bathos that is as disconcerting as it is unexpected." Yet du Plessix Gray concluded that *Letter to a Child Never Born* "is a poignant testament" and found that "in her best moments, Fallaci, as always, strips truth down to its naked bone." In her essay on Fallaci for *Feminist Writers,* Maria Elena Raymond explained that *Letter to a Child Never Born* is "considered to be one of the finest feminist writings about pregnancy, abortion, and emotional torture."

In *A Man,* Fallaci attempts to immortalize the martyred poet and Greek resistance leader Alekos Panagoulis, the great love of her life. Though she called the book a novel, *A Man* recounts the real story of Panagoulis's fight for Greece's freedom—a fight he continued until his death. In 1967, Panagoulis attempted to assassinate the fascist Greek dictator Georgios Papadopoulos by planting a series of bombs along the roads he traveled each day. The plan failed, and Panagoulis was captured and imprisoned almost immediately. During the next five years, the revolutionary was subjected to physical abuse as well as psychological torture in an effort to break his spirit and will. Despite the inhuman treatment, Panagoulis refused to succumb, and his repeated escape attempts and uncompromising rebelliousness finally led him to be isolated in a specially constructed cell, not much larger than a double bed, with no windows and only three paces' worth of standing room. He remained there until he was freed under a general amnesty in 1973. Two days after his release, Panagoulis was interviewed by Fallaci, and, firmly convinced that their meeting was an act of fate, the two became lovers within a few weeks.

For the next three years, Fallaci and Panagoulis shared a tempestuous relationship. According to Marcia Seligson in the *Los Angeles Times,* "He told her, 'I don't want a woman to be happy with. The world is full of women you can be happy with. . . . And I want a companion. A companion who will be my comrade, friend, accomplice, brother. I'm a man in battle. I always will be.' She became all those things, surrendering her own full and independent life to follow this difficult, maddening, towering man. She lived an

emotional pendulum of anguish/bliss; there was no serenity, no future, only thrills and chills." Panagoulis was killed by political enemies in an ambush made to look like an auto accident in 1976. Within months of his death, Fallaci began work on the book she would dedicate to him, and, in 1979, published what she considers her most important work, *A Man.*

Critical reaction to the book varied from praise to disdain. Supporters, such as Seligson, hailed *A Man* as "a work of passion, courage, candor and exquisite skill." *Saturday Review* contributor Julie Stone Peters described it as "a majestic and soul-stirring narration," maintaining that Fallaci "has learned from her interviews how to control the novel." Peter Brunette believed that her ideas transcend "the 'merely' political: Fallaci places her subject in the most deeply Greek context of all, that of ancient tragedy, as she marvelously adduces one resonant mythic parallel after another on the way to her lover's final submission to his tragic fate," he wrote in the *New Republic.*

Others eschewed her approach. "Throughout this catalogue of misery, Fallaci never makes the right choice," noted a *Time* reviewer. "When the account needs historical analysis, she offers tantrums; when suffering cries out for a tragic spirit, she substitutes bathos." Vivian Gomick compared it to "an old fashioned dish of hearty melodrama being offered as though it were the cuisine of tragedy."

In the novel *Inshallah,* Fallaci writes a fictional account of Italian troops stationed in Lebanon in 1983. After both the American and French peacekeeping forces are the targets of suicidal truck bombers, the Italian forces ready themselves for what they fear is the inevitable third truck bomb. "Rarely," wrote Christopher Dickey in the *Los Angeles Times Book Review,* "has there been a setting so ready-made for classic tragedy." Unfortunately, Dickey believed that Fallaci "has always had trouble hearing any voice but her own" and that *Inshallah* "might have been a monument to her talents and her passion. Instead it remains as a tribute mainly to her ego." But Thomas Keneally found much of value in *Inshallah.* "Fallaci," Keneally noted in the *New York Times Book Review,* "writes with a muscular eloquence when giving us the squalor, yearning and shadowboxing of the soldiers' existence." Although he saw Fallaci's asides to be the weakest part of her narrative, Keneally concluded that Fallaci "is profligate with plot and detail, and her openhandedness and the inherent tensions of her large story should insure that most readers will overlook her equally spacious faults."

After publishing *Inshallah,* Fallaci lived anonymously in New York City and Florence for two decades as she battled cancer. She broke her silence after the September 11, 2001, terrorist attacks in the United States. Knowing that Fallaci was deeply impressed with New York's skyscrapers and the freedom and security enjoyed by its citizens, Ferraccio de Bortoli, director of Milan's *Corriere della Sera* newspaper, asked Fallaci to describe how she felt about the attacks—and she responded vehemently. "Over the course of two weeks, she covered hundreds of typescript pages with a philippic against Islamist terrorism and the cowardly Western elites who had permitted it to blossom in their midst," explained Christopher Caldwell in *Commentary.* An abridgement of the article was published in *Corriere* on September 29. Remarked Caldwell, "It turned into one of the great sensations in the history of European journalism. Newsstands sold out of a million copies in four hours."

In December, 2002, the Italian publisher Rizzoli printed the article in its entirety in book form under the same name, and the English version of the book was published a year later. Fallaci's fury is even more apparent without the newspaper's edits. Noted Caldwell, "She compared Islamic terrorists to Nazis and fascists, calling them 'the new SS, the new blackshirts,' engaged in a 'reverse crusade' against the West." She laments that Islamic terrorism was not a misinterpretation of a great faith, as most people believe, and that even Muslims living among Americans and Europeans secretly hope to conquer the West. Fallaci held back little in her insults of Islam. As Caldwell recorded, "Fallaci warned that Islamist terrorism was not, as we are so often told, the perversion of a great faith, and not the work of a disillusioned and obscurantist fringe. It was part and parcel of Islam itself, which she referred to as 'this mountain that for fourteen-hundred years has not moved, has not emerged from the abyss of its blindness, has not opened its doors to the conquest of civilization, and has wanted nothing to do with liberty and justice and democracy and progress.'"

The Italian version of *The Rage and the Pride* sold a million copies, ignited a worldwide controversy, and elicited vastly divergent responses from critics, who seemed to either praise the book or regard it as op-

portunistic nonsense. "Understandably, reactions to the piece were strong. Italian daily newspapers published responses from cultural and political thinkers, for and against Fallaci's thinking. In the Roman daily *La Repubblica,* leading Italian intellectual Umberto Eco wrote at length on the need for dialogue and tolerance among cultures," noted Marco Belpoliti in *Foreign Policy.* Belpoliti considered the book's narrative themes a major strength. "As Fallaci mixes together personal and general experience, the reader is drawn to her life story, from youthful journalist to war reporter, novelist, and voluntary exile in New York," he observed. Writing in London's *Guardian,* Rana Kabbani was offended by the book: "One can dismiss Fallaci's rantings as those of an enraged has-been who, even in her heyday, communicated her ego in writing. . . . Fallaci's hatred and fear of Muslims is both visceral and hysterical—no doubt exacerbated by the fact that she lives in New York and seems to have swallowed wholesale the U.S. government's denomination of Arabs and Muslims as synonymous with 'terrorists.'"

Critical opinions matter little to Fallaci, who does not keep reviews of her books. As she once told *CA,* "I do not respect reviewers. They are almost always failed writers, consequently envious and jealous of those who write. I find their profession kind of despicable, because it is so unfair and stupid to snap judgments in a little article after the work of years. I think that the real reviewers are the readers. I care very much for the letters of my readers. I receive them from all over the world, and they always say much more intelligent things than those written by the 'reviewers.'"

BIOGRAPHICAL AND CRITICAL SOURCES:

BOOKS

Almanac of Famous People, Gale (Detroit, MI), 1998.
Contemporary Literary Criticism, Volume 11, Gale (Detroit, MI), 1979.
Fallaci, Oriana, *Interview with History,* Liveright (New York, NY), 1976.
Fallaci, Oriana, *A Man,* Simon & Schuster (New York, NY), 1980.
Fallaci, Oriana, *The Rage and the Pride,* Rizzoli International (New York, NY), 2002.
Feminist Writers, St. James Press (Detroit, MI), 1996.

Gatt-Rutter, John, *Oriana Fallaci: The Rhetoric of Freedom,* Berg (Washington, DC), 1996.

Pattavina, Giovanni, *Alekos Panagulis, il rivoluzionario don Chisciotte di Oriana Fallaci: Saggio politico-letterario,* Edizioni italiane di letteratura e scienze (Rome, Italy), 1984.

PERIODICALS

Best Sellers, May, 1977.

Chicago Tribune Book World, November 30, 1980.

Commentary, October, 2002, Christopher Caldwell, "The Fallaci Affair," pp. 34-44.

Economist (U.S.), November 16, 2002, "Fallacious Fallaci: Italy's Globalisation Debate."

Esquire, November, 1968; June, 1975.

Europe, May, 2002, Niccolo d'Aquino, "The Return of Oriana Fallaci," p. 40.

Foreign Policy, May, 2002, Marco Belpoliti, "The Fallacies of St. Fallaci," pp. 84-87.

Guardian (London, England), June 11, 2002, Rana Kabbani, "Comment & Analysis: Bible of the Muslim Haters: The Popularity of a Virulent New Book Shows How Deeply Islamophobia Has Taken Root in Western Europe," p. 14.

Harper's, November, 1980.

Life, February 21, 1969.

London Review of Books, February 11, 1993, p. 19.

Los Angeles Times, November, 1980; December 2, 1980.

Los Angeles Times Book Review, January 10, 1993, p. 1.

Maclean's, February 8, 1993, p. 55.

M2 Best Books, July 3, 2002, "French Judge Rejects *Rage and Pride* Ban."

New Leader, March 14, 1977.

New Republic, November 22, 1980.

New York, May 22, 1978.

New Yorker, February 21, 1977.

New York Times, January 25, 1973; November 3, 1980; October 31, 2001, Melinda Henneberger, "Provacateur Is Back to 'Spit' on Detractors of U.S.," p. A4.

New York Times Book Review, February 5, 1967; February 13, 1977; November 23, 1980; December 27, 1992, p. 8.

O, The Oprah Magazine, December, 2001, Maria Shriver, "Interview with History," p. 132.

People, March 14, 1977.

Publishers Weekly, November 7, 1980; October 5, 1992, p. 54; November 11, 2002, review of *The Rage and the Pride,* pp. 54-56.

Rolling Stone, June 17, 1976.

Saturday Review, March 18, 1972; November, 1980; January 8, 1981.

Sunday Times (London, England), December 15, 2002, Sarah Baxter, "Italian Firebrand Takes Her Fight to the 'Islamo-Fascists,'" p. 29.

Time, October 20; January 19, 1981.

Times Literary Supplement, August 11, 1972; May 22, 1981; September 28, 1990, p. 1039; December 18, 1992, p. 18.

Washington Post, February 23, 1972; March 13, 1972; May 18, 1976.

Washington Post Book World, February 13, 1977, pp. G7, G10; November 30, 1980; December 13, 1992, p. 5.

World Literature Today, summer, 1991, p. 468.

WWD, September 13, 1999, Susan Smith, "Oriana Fallaci: Views on Power from a 1976 Chat with the Feisty Italian Journalist," p. 113.

ONLINE

Italian Language Web site, http://italian.about.com/ (February 15, 2003), "Rage and Pride Ignites a Firestorm."*

*   *   *

FERRÉ, Rosario 1938-

PERSONAL: Born September 28, 1938, in Ponce, Puerto Rico; daughter of Luis A. (an engineer and former governor of Puerto Rico) and Lorenza Ramirez de Arellano de Ferré; married Benigno Trigo (a businessman), 1960 (divorced); married Jorge Aguilar Mora (a writer; marriage ended); married Agustin Costa (an architect); children: Rosario Trigo Costanzo, Benigno Trigo Ferré, Luis Trigo Ferré. *Education:* University of Puerto Rico, M.A.; University of Maryland, Ph.D., 1986. *Religion:* Roman Catholic.

ADDRESSES: Agent—Susan Bergholz, 17 West 10th St., New York, NY 10011.

CAREER: Writer. Advisory board member, Americas Literary Initiative series, University of Wisconsin Press, 2003.

Rosario Ferré

AWARDS, HONORS: Critics Choice Award, 1995, and National Book Award nomination, 1996, both for *The House on the Lagoon.*

WRITINGS:

Papeles de Pandora (title means "Pandora's Roles"; stories), Joaquin Mortiz (Mexico City, Mexico), 1976, Vintage (New York, NY), 2000, translation by the author published as *The Youngest Doll,* University of Nebraska Press (Lincoln, NE), 1991.

El Medio pollito: Siete cuentos infantiles (title means "The Half Chicken"; children's stories), Ediciones Huracan (Rio Piedras, Puerto Rico), 1976.

La Muñeca menor/The Youngest Doll (bilingual edition), illustrations by Antonio Martorell, Ediciones Huracan (Rio Piedras, Puerto Rico) 1980.

Sitio a Eros: Trece ensayos literarios, Joaquin Mortiz (Mexico City, Mexico), 1980, 2nd edition published as *Sitio a Eros: Quince ensayos literarios,* 1986.

Los Cuentos de Juan Bobo (title means "The Tales of Juan Bobo"; children's stories), Ediciones Huracan (Rio Piedras, Puerto Rico) 1981.

La Mona que le pisaron la cola (title means "The Monkey Whose Tail Got Stepped On"; children's stories), Ediciones Huracan (Rio Piedras, Puerto Rico) 1981.

Fábulas de la garza desangrada, Joaquin Mortiz (Mexico City, Mexico), 1982.

Puerto Rican Writer Rosario Ferré Reading from Her Prose and Poetry (sound recording), recorded for the Archive of Hispanic Literature on Tape in the Library of Congress Recording Laboratory, 1982.

La C Lisa Rowe Fraustino, ed., aja de cristal, La Maquina de Escribir (Mexico), 1982.

Maldito amor (title means "Cursed Love"), Joaquin Mortiz (Mexico City, Mexico), 1986, revised and translated by Ferré and published as *Sweet Diamond Dust* (see also below), Ballantine (New York, NY), 1988.

El Acomodor: Una lectura fantástica de Felisberto Hernández, Fondo de Cultura Economica (Mexico), 1986.

Sonatinas, Ediciones Huracan (Rio Piedras, Puerto Rico) 1989.

El Árbol y sus sombras, Fondo de Cultura Economica (Mexico), 1989.

El Coloquio de las perras, Cultural (San Juan, Puerto Rico), 1990, selections translated by the author and published as "On Destiny, Language, and Translation; or, Ophelia Adrift in the C & O Canal," in *The Youngest Doll,* 1991.

El Cucarachita Martina, Ediciones Huracan (Rio Piedras, Puerto Rico), 1990.

Cortázar, Literal (Washington, DC), 1991.

Las Dos Venecias (title means "The Two Venices"), Joaquin Mortiz (Mexico City, Mexico), 1992.

Memorias de Ponce: Autobiografia de Luis A. Ferré, Editorial Norma (Barcelona, Spain), 1992.

La Batalla de las vírgenes, Editorial de la Universidad de Puerto Rico, (San Juan, Puerto Rico), 1993.

Antología personal: 1992-1976, Editorial Cultural, 1994.

The House on the Lagoon, Farrar, Straus (New York, NY), 1995, translated by the author as *La Casa de la laguna,* Vintage (New York, NY), 1997.

Sweet Diamond Dust and Other Stories, Plume (New York, NY), 1996.

El Sombrero magico (title means "The Magical Hat"), Santillana Publishing, 1997.

La Sapita sabia y otros cuentos (title means "The Smart Frog and Other Stories"), Santillana Publishing, 1997.

Pico Rico Mandorico y otros cuentos (title means "Pico Rico Manorico and Other Stories"), Santillana Publishing, 1997.

Eccentric Neighborhoods, Farrar, Straus (New York, NY), 1998, translated by the author as *Vecindarios eccentricos,* Vintage (New York, NY), 1999.

La Extrana muerte del Capitancito Candelario, Plaza & Janes Editores, 1999.

A la sombra de tu nombre (essays), Alfaguara (Mexico), 2001.

Flight of the Swan, Farrar, Straus (New York, NY), 2001, translated by the author as *Vuelo del cisne,* Vintage (New York, NY), 2002.

Contributor to books, including *Contextos: Literarios hispanoamericanos,* edited by Teresa Mindez-Faith, Holt (New York, NY), 1985; *Anthology of Contemporary Latin American Literature, 1960-1984,* Fairleigh Dickinson University Press, 1986; *Reclaiming Medusa: Short Stories by Contemporary Puerto Rican Women,* Spinsters Aunt Lute (San Francisco, CA), 1988; and *Interviews with Latin American Writers,* edited by Marie-Lisa Gazarian Gautier, Dalkey Archive Press, 1989. Some of Ferré's writings have also been anthologized in *Ritos de iniciacion: Tres novelas cortas de Hispanoamerica,* a textbook for intermediate and advanced students of college Spanish, by Grinor Rojo, and *Anthology of Women Poets.*

SIDELIGHTS: "Rosario Ferré," wrote *Dictionary of Literary Biography* contributor Carmen S. Rivera, "has become the 'translator' of the reality of Puerto Rican women, opening the doors for the feminist movement on the island. By combining classical mythology with indigenous folktales that usurp the traditional actions of female characters, Ferré has interpreted, translated, and rewritten a more active and satisfying myth of Puerto Rican women." Ferré—the daughter of a former governor of Puerto Rico—writes about politics (she favors Puerto Rican independence), about literature, and about the status of women in modern Puerto Rican society. A former student of Angel Rama and Mario Vargas Llosa, she often utilizes magic realist techniques to communicate her points. "Many critics believe that with the publication of her first book," Rivera continued, "Ferré began the feminist movement in Puerto Rico and became, if not its only voice, one of its most resonant and forceful spokespersons."

Chronologically, Ferré's first work was the short-story collection *Papeles de Pandora.* Its original Spanish-language version was published in Mexico in 1976, but it was not until 1991 that an English-language translation by the author became available. "Defiant magic feminism challenges all our conventional notions of time, place, matter and identity in Rosario Ferré's spectacular new book, *The Youngest Doll,*" declared Patricia Hart in the *Nation. New York Times Book Review* contributor Cathy A. Colman stated that "Ferré . . . writes with an irony that cloaks anger about the oppression and danger inherent in being either a protected upper-class woman or a marginalized working-class woman caught in Puerto Rico's patriarchal society." In the story "Sleeping Beauty," for example, a young woman's desire to become a dancer is railroaded by her family, who wants her to marry an aristocratic young man. The protagonist of "The Poisoned Story" starts out as a Cinderella figure (she marries a sugarcane planter) but ends up playing the role of a wicked stepmother to his daughter. "From beginning to end . . . whether she is conceiving stories, translating them or providing commentary," Hart concluded, "Rosario Ferré shines, and it is high time for English-speaking readers to bask in her light."

Ferré's first work to be translated into English was *Sweet Diamond Dust,* a short novel telling the stories of influential Puerto Rican women in different time periods. "Ferré parodies novels about the land, a popular genre during the first half of the [twentieth] century, as she sets out to rewrite Puerto Rican history from a woman's perspective," Rivera declared. "She describes how the island (*isla* is a female noun in Spanish) is oppressed by the government and American businesses—both of which are rendered as masculine in Spanish—while drawing parallels to the situation of women." Reviewer Alan Cheuse, writing in the *Chicago Tribune,* called Ferré "one of the most engaging young Latin American fiction writers at work today," and added, "Ferré shows off her linguistic talent as well as her inventiveness by giving us her own English version of the book."

The House on the Lagoon, Ferré's first work composed in English, was nominated for the National Book Award in 1996. "Most of this novel," declared a *Publishers Weekly* reviewer, "is comprised of . . . semi-fictionalized family history." The book tells of a Puerto Rican couple, Quintin Mendizabal and Isabel Monfort, who come into conflict over politics—she favors independence for the island, he favors close ties with the United States—their attitudes—he believes in traditional women's roles, she favors feminism—and the history she is writing, which includes stories about her husband's family. The family's black servant Petra Aviles also plays a role in the family dynamic. "The novel's conclusion affirms in the strongest terms the necessity of interracial alliances, both sexual and familial, to the future of a Puerto Rican community," wrote Judith Grossman in the *Women's Review of Books*. "Ferré dramatizes the issue of who gets to write history," stated a *Publishers Weekly* contributor, "gracefully incorporating it into a compelling panorama of Puerto Rican experience that is rich in history, drama and memorable characters." "*The House on the Lagoon*," Grossman concluded, "gives us a performance of great accomplishment and wit, and the sense of a world held in measured but deeply affectionate memory."

In *Flight of the Swan*, a novel that melds history and fiction, Ferré tells the story of her version of ballet legend Anna Pavlova, who due to historical upheavals in Russia, finds herself stranded with her dance troupe in Puerto Rico in 1917. She explores the themes of love and betrayal, politics, sex and art, through the voyeuristic narrator Masha, a member of Madame Pavlova's corps de ballet and her slavishly devoted servant. In the end Masha comes to see that, in spite of her mistress's foibles, Pavlova is ready to sacrifice everything for her art, which in turn forces Masha to question her own choices. Praising the novel as "fascinating," *Americas* contributor Barbara Mujica added that *Flight of the Swan* is "an entertaining and thought-provoking book that raises serious questions about class, race, sex, art, and politics. Both Madame and Masha are freely drawn characters whose conflicting perspectives shed light on both Puerto Rican politics during the early decades of the twentieth century and on the hierarchical world of Russian ballet."

Diana Postlethwaite wrote in the *New York Times* that while "the premise of Masha as earthy observer describing the misadventures of an ethereal drama queen is a promising one," "her voice is never consistently sustained." In addition, Postlethwaite noted, Ferré, whose command of English often forces her to rely on prefabricated prose, further complicates her story by telling it in a Russian voice. *Publishers Weekly* contributor Jeff Zaleski concurred that Ferré's writing in her second language "may account for the pedestrian quality of this novel," and that "the imaginatively conceived but strangely lackluster story" is overwhelmed by "an excess of historical details and long monologues." On the other hand, *Washington Post* contributor Laura Jacobs maintained that "Ferré writes beautifully when she is direct . . . but strains language in heated moments." She argued that "there is a shorter, stronger book inside *Flight of the Swan*, if only Ferré had put the manuscript through a final, fat-burning fast."

BIOGRAPHICAL AND CRITICAL SOURCES:

BOOKS

Dictionary of Literary Biography, Volume 145: *Modern Latin-American Fiction Writers,* Gale (Detroit, MI), 1994.
Latina Self-Portraits: Interviews with Contemporary Women Writers, University of New Mexico Press (Albuquerque, NM), 2000.
Sobre castas y puentes: Conversaciones con Elena Poniatowska, Rosario Ferré y Diamela Eltit, Editorial Cuarto Propio (Santiago, Chile), 2000.

PERIODICALS

Americas, January-February, 2002, Barbara Mujica, review of *Flight of the Swan,* p. 60.
Book, July, 2001, Susan Tekulve, review of *Flight of the Swan,* p. 76.
Chicago Tribune, January 13, 1989.
Critique, summer, 2000, Ronald D. Morrison, "Remembering and Recovering Goblin Market in Rosario Ferré's 'Pico Rico, Mandorico,'" p. 365.
Library Journal, August, 1995, p. 115; June 1, 2001, Ed Morales, review of *A la sombra de tu nombre,* p. 37.
Nation, May 6, 1991, pp. 597-598.
New York Times Book Review, March 24, 1991, p. 24; July 29, 2001, Diana Postlethwaite, review of *Flight of the Swan,* p. 21.
Progressive, August, 1998, Lisa Chipongian, review of *Eccentric Neighborhoods,* p. 43.
Publishers Weekly, July 3, 1995, review of *The House on the Lagoon,* p. 47; November 24, 1997, review of *Eccentric Neighborhoods,* p. 51; May 7, 2001, Jeff Zaleski, review of *Flight of the Swan,* p. 219.
Review of Contemporary Fiction, spring, 1996, p. 168.
Studies in Short Fiction, spring, 1995, Augustus Puelo, "The Intersection of Race, Sex, Gender, and Class in a Short Story of Rosario Ferré," p. 227.
Washington Post, July 1, 2001, Laura Jacobs, review of *Flight of the Swan,* p. T09.

Woman's Review of Books, February, 1996, Judith Grossman, review of *The House on the Lagoon,* p. 5.

World Literature Today, summer, 1996, Ilan Stavans, review of *The House on the Lagoon,* p. 690; spring, 2002, Catherine E. Wall, review of *Flight of the Swan,* p. 151.*

*   *   *

FO, Dario 1926-

PERSONAL: Born March 24, 1926, in San Giano, Lombardy, Italy; son of Felice (a railroad stationmaster) and Pina (Rota) Fo; married Franca Rame (a playwright and actress), June, 1954; children: three. *Education:* Attended Accademia di Belle Arti, Milan, Italy.

ADDRESSES: Home—Milan, Italy. *Office*—Michael Imison Playwrights Ltd, 28 Almeida St., London, NI 1 1TD, England; also, CTFR, Corso di Porta Romania 132, 201228 Milan, Italy. *Agent*—Maria Nadotti, 349 East 51st St., New York, NY 10022.

CAREER: Playwright, director, actor, and theatrical company leader. Has written more than forty plays, many of which have been translated and performed in more than thirty countries, 1953—; performs plays in Italy, Europe, and the United States, and runs classes and workshops for actors, 1970s—. Worked as a member of small theatrical group, headed by Franco Parenti, performing semi-improvised sketches for radio before local audiences, 1950; wrote and performed comic monologues for his own radio program, *Poer nana* ("Poor Dwarf"), broadcast by the Italian national radio network RAI, 1951; formed revue company, *I Dritti* ("The Stand-Ups"), with Giustino Durano and Parenti, 1953; screenwriter in Rome, 1956-58; formed improvisational troupe *Compagnia Fo-Rame,* with wife, Franca Rame, 1958; named artistic director of Italian state television network's weekly musical revue, *Chi l'ha visto?* ("Who's Seen It?"), and writer and performer of sketches for variety show *Canzonissima* ("Really Big Song"), 1959; formed theater cooperative *Nuova Scena,* with Rame, 1968, and *La Comune,* 1970.

AWARDS, HONORS: Sonning Award, Denmark, 1981; Off Broadway Award, *Village Voice,* 1987; Nobel Prize in Literature, 1997; Lusanto Jullare Francesco, 1999.

Dario Fo

WRITINGS:

PLAYS

Teatro comico, Garzanti (Italy), 1962.

Le Commedie, Einaudi (Turin, Italy), 1966, enlarged edition published as *Le Commedie di Dario Fo,* six volumes, Einaudi (Turin, Italy), 1974, reprinted, 1984.

Vorrei morire anche stasera se dovessi pensare che no e servito a niente, E.D.B., 1970.

Morte e resurrezione di un pupazzo, Sapere Edizioni, 1971.

Teatro comico, Garzanti (Italy), 1971.

Ordine!, Bertani (Verona, Italy), 1972.

Ordine! Per Dio, Bertani (Verona, Italy), 1972.

Pum, pum! Chi e? La polizia! (title means "Knock, Knock! Who's There? Police!"), Bertani (Verona, Italy), 1972.

Tutti uniti! Tutti insieme! Ma scusa quello non e il padrone?(title means "United We Stand! All Together Now! Oops, Isn't That the Boss?"), Bertani (Verona, Italy), 1972.

Guerra di popolo in Cile (title means "The People's War in Chile"), Bertani (Verona, Italy), 1973.

Mistero buffo: Giullarata popolare, Bertani (Verona, Italy), 1974, reprinted, Einaudi (Torino, Italy), 2003.

Mistero buffo (title means "The Comic Mystery"; first produced in Milan, Italy, 1969; produced on Broadway at the Joyce Theater, May 27, 1986), Bertani (Verona, Italy), 1973, revised, 1974.

Ballate e canzoni (title means "Ballads and Songs"), introduction by Lanfranco Binni, Bertani (Verona, Italy), 1974, reprinted, Newton Compton (Rome, Italy), 1976.

Non si paga, non si paga (first produced in Milan, 1974), La Comune (Milan, Italy), 1974; adapted by Bill Colvill and Robert Walker, Pluto Press (London, England), 1978; translation by Lino Pertite reprinted as *Can't Pay? Won't Pay!,* Pluto Press (London, England), 1982, North American version by R. G. Davis published as *We Won't Pay! We Won't Pay!,* Samuel French (New York, NY), 1984.

Morte accidentale di un anarchico (first produced in Milan, December, 1970; produced on Broadway at Belasco Theater, November 15, 1984), Einaudi (Turin, Italy), 1974, translation by Gavin Richards published as *Accidental Death of an Anarchist,* Pluto Press (London, England), 1980, published as *Morte accidentale di un anarchio [Accidental Death of an Anarchist],* Manchester University Press (New York, NY), 1998.

La Guillarata, Bertani (Verona, Italy), 1975.

Il Fanfani rapito, Bertani (Verona, Italy), 1975.

La Marjuana della mamma e la piu bella, Bertani (Verona, Italy), 1976.

La Signora e da buttare (title means "The Old Girl's for the Scrapheap"), Einaudi (Turin, Italy), 1976.

Il Teatro politico, G. Mazzotta (Milan, Italy), 1977.

Dario Fo parla di Dario Fo, Lerici (Cosenza, Italy), 1977.

(With wife, Franca Rame) *Tutta casa, letto e chiesa* (title means "All House, Bed, and Church"), Bertani (Verona, Italy), 1978, translation published as *Orgasmo Adulto Escapes from the Zoo,* Bertani (Verona, Italy), 1978, translation by Estelle Parsons, Broadway Play Publishing (New York, NY), 1985.

La Storia di un soldato, photographs by Silvia Lelli Masotti, commentary by Ugo Volli, Electa (Milan, Italy), 1979.

Storia della tigre ed altre storie, La Comune (Milan, Italy), 1980.

Storia vera di Piero d'Angera: Che alla crociata non c'era, La Comune (Milan, Italy), 1981.

Fabulazzo osceno, F.R. La Comune (Milan, Italy), 1982.

L'Opera dello sghignazzo: dalla "Beggar's opera di John Gay" e da alcune idee di mio figlio Jacopo, F.R. La Comune (Milan, Italy), 2nd edition, 1982.

Dario Fo and Franca Rame: Theatre Workshops at Riverside Studios, London, April 28th, May 5th, 12th, 13th & 19th, 1983, Red Notes (London, England), 1983.

Coppia aperta, Tip.-Lit. "La Musica moderna," 1984.

Il Ratto della Francesca: Commedia in due tempi, La Comune (Milan, Italy), 1986.

About Face: A Political Farce, translated by Ron Jenkins, S. French (New York, NY), 1989.

Archangels Don't Play Pinball [Arcangeli non giocano a flipper], translated by Ron Jenkins, S. French (New York, NY), 1989.

Dario Fo, dialogo provocatorio sul comico, il tragico, la follia e la ragione con Luigi Allegri, Laterza (Rome, Italy), 1990.

Johan Padan a la descoverta de le Americhe, Giunti (Firenze, Italy), 1992.

(Coauthor) *Parliamo di donne: Il Teatro,* Kaos (Milan, Italy), 1992.

Abducting Diana: Il Ratto della Francesca, adapted by Stephen Stenning, Oberon Books (London, England), 1994.

Toto: Manuale dell'attor comico, Vallecchi (Firenze, Italy), 1995.

(Illustrator) *Una Strega, una pizza e un orco con la stizza,* by Bianca Fo Garambois, FATATRAC (Rome, Italy), 1995.

Il Diavolo con le Zinne, G. Einaudi (Turin, Italy), 1998.

Federico Fellini & Dario Fo: Disegni geniali, Mazzotta (Milan, Italy), 1999.

La Vera storia di Ravenna, F. C. Panini (Modena, Italy), 1999.

OTHER PLAYS; IN ENGLISH TRANSLATION

(With Franca Rame) *Female Parts: One Woman Plays,* translated by Margaret Kunzle and Stuart Hood, adapted by Olwen Wymark, Pluto Press (London, England), 1981.

Car Horns, Trumpets and Raspberries (first produced in Milan, January, 1981; produced in the United States at the Yale Repertory Theater as *About Face,*

1981), translated by R. C. McAvoy and A. H. Giugni, Pluto Press (London, England), 1981, reprinted, 1984.

(With Franca Rame) *The Open Couple—Wide Open Even,* Theatretexts (London, England), 1984.

The Tale of a Tiger: A Comic Monologue [Storia della tigre], Theatretexts (London, England), 1984.

One Was Nude and One Wore Tails: A One-Act Farce [Uomo nudo e l'uomo in frak], Theatretexts (London, England), 1985.

Elizabeth, Almost by Chance a Woman [Quasi per caso una donna, Elisabetta], translated by Ron Jenkins, S. French (New York, NY), 1989.

The Open Couple and an Ordinary Day, Heinemann (London, England), 1990.

The Pope and the Witch, Heinemann (London, England), 1993, translated by Joan Holden, S. French (New York, NY), 1997.

(With Franca Rame) *Plays, Two* (contains *Can't Pay? Won't Pay!,The Open Couple,* and *An Ordinary Day*), Methuen (London, England)), 1994.

Plays, Methuen Drama (London, England), 1997.

Johan Padan and the Discovery of the Americas, Grove Press (New York, NY), 2001.

We Won't Pay! We Won't Pay! and Other Plays: The Collected Plays of Dario Fo, edited by Franca Rame, translated by Ron Jenkins, Theatre Communications Group (New York, NY), 2001.

Also author of *The Devil with Boobs.*

OTHER PLAYS; PRODUCED ONLY

Il Dito nell'occhio (title means "A Finger in the Eye"), first produced in Milan at Piccolo Teatro, June, 1953.

I Sani da legare (title means "A Madhouse for the Sane"), first produced in Milan at Piccolo Teatro, 1954.

Ladri, manachini e donne nude (title means "Thieves, Dummies, and Naked Women"), first produced in Milan at Piccolo Teatro, 1958.

Gli arcangeli non giocano a flipper (title means "Archangels Don't Play Pinball,") first produced in Milan at Teatro Odeon, September, 1959.

Isabella, tre caravelle, e un cacciaballe (title means "Isabella, Three Ships, and a Con Man"), first produced in Milan at Teatro Odeon, 1963.

L'Anomal bicefalo (title means "Two-Headed Anomaly"), frist produced in Milan at Piccolo Teatro, 2003.

Also author of numerous other plays produced in Italy, including *Aveva due pistole con gli occhi bianchi e neri* (title means "He Had Two Pistols with White and Black Eyes"), 1960; *Grande pantomima con bandiere e pupazzi piccoli e medi* (title means "Grand Pantomime with Flags and Small and Medium-Sized Puppets"), October, 1968; *Fedayn,* 1971; *Il Fabulazzo osceno* (title means "The Obscene Fable"), 1982; and *Hellequin, Arlekin, Arlechino,* 1986. Other stage credits include an adaptation of Bertolt Brecht's *Threepenny Opera,* for Teatro Stabile di Torino and Teatro Il Fabbricone of Prato, and *Patapumfete,* for the clown duo I Colombaioni.

OTHER

Manuale minimo dell'attore (title means "Basic Handbook for the Actor"), Einuadi (Turin, Italy), 1987, reprinted, 1997.

The Tricks of the Trade, translation by Joe Farrell, Routledge (New York, NY), 1991.

Marino libero! Marino e innocente!, Einaudi (Turin, Italy), 1998.

Teatro, G. Einaudi (Turin, Italy)), 2000.

L'Ascensione di Alessandro Magno portato in cielo da due grifoni: Dal romanzo greco dello pseudo-Callistene vissuto ad Alessandria d'Egitto nel IV secolo d.c., illustrated by Rachele Lo Piano, Sinnos (Rome, Italy), 2001.

Cinquant'anni di storia italiana attraverso il teatro: Dario Fo e Franca Rame: Tournee 2001-2002, M. Baroni (Lucca, Italy)), 2002.

(With Franca Rame) Il Paese dei Mezaràt: I Miei primi sette anni (e qualcuno in più), Feltrinelli (Milano, Italy), 2002.

The Peasants Bible and The Story of the Tiger, translated by Ron Jenkins, Grove Press (New York, NY), 2004.

SIDELIGHTS: Noted Italian playwright and Nobel laureate Dario Fo began refining his animated method of storytelling as a child, listening to the tales told by the locals in San Giano, the small fishing village in northern Italy where he was born. After leaving Milan's Academy of Fine Arts without earning a degree, Fo wrote and performed with several improvisational theatrical groups. He first earned acclaim as a playwright in 1953 with *Il Dito nell'occhio,* a socially satiric production that presented Marxist ideas against a circus-like background. His 1954 attack on the Italian government in *I Sani da legare,* in which Fo labeled several government officials fascist sympathizers, resulted in the cutting of some material from the original script and the mandated presence of state inspectors at each performance of the play to insure that the country's strict libel laws were not violated.

Following a brief stint as a screenwriter in Rome, Fo, together with his wife, actress Franca Rame, returned to the theater and produced a more generalized, less explicitly political brand of social satire. Widely regarded as his best work during this phase of his career, *Gli arcangeli non giocano a flipper* was the first of Fo's plays to be staged outside of Italy. As quoted by Irving Wardle in the London *Times,* the heroic clown in *Archangels* voices the playwright's basic contention, stating, "My quarrel is with those who organize our dreams."

In 1968 Fo and Rame rejected the legitimate theater as an arm of the bourgeoisie and, backed by the Italian Communist party, they formed Nuova Scena, a noncommercial theater group designed to entertain and inform the working class. The plays produced by this company centered on political issues and grew increasingly radical in tone. The communist government withdrew its support from Nuova Scena after the staging of *Grande pantomima con bandiere e pupazzi piccoli e medi,* a satire of Italy's political history in the wake of World War II. The highly symbolic play depicts the birth of capitalism (portrayed by a beautiful woman) from fascism (a huge monster puppet) and the subsequent seduction of communism by capitalism. Through the play Fo demonstrated his disenchantment with the authoritative, antirevolutionary policies of the Italian Communist party, allowing communism to succumb to capitalism's enticement.

Steeped in an atmosphere of political and social unrest, the 1960s proved to be a decade of increased popularity for Fo, providing him with new material and a receptive audience. *Mistero buffo,* generally considered his greatest and most controversial play was first performed in 1969. An improvised production based on a constantly changing script, the play is a decidedly irreverent retelling of the gospels that indicts landowners, government, and, in particular, the Catholic Church as public oppressors. Fo based the show's format on that of the medieval mystery plays originally parodied by *giullari,* strolling minstrel street performers of the Middle Ages. *Mistero buffo* was written in Italian as a series of sketches for a single actor—Fo—to perform on an empty stage. The playwright introduces each segment of the work with an informal prologue to establish a rapport with his audience. He links together the satiric religious narratives, portraying up to a dozen characters at a time by himself. The sketches include a reenactment of Lazarus's resurrection, complete with opportunists who pick the pockets of the awestruck witnesses; the tale of a contented cripple's efforts to avoid being cured by Jesus; an account of the wedding feast at Cana as told by a drunkard; and an especially dark portrait of the corrupt Pope Boniface VIII.

Writing in *American Theatre,* Ron Jenkins considered Fo's black humor and "sense of moral indignation" most effectively illuminated in a fable from *Mistero buffo* titled "The Birth of the Giullare," which explains how the minstrel received his narrative gift. A former peasant, the *giullare* had been humiliated and victimized by corrupt politicians, priests, and landowners. In his despair, he decides to kill himself but is interrupted by a man asking for water. The man is Jesus Christ, who, in kissing the peasant's lips gives him the facility to mesmerize an audience—and deflate the very authorities that had oppressed him—with his words. Jenkins remarked, "Fo performs the moment of the miracle with an exhilarating sense of musicality. . . . The triumph of freedom over tyranny is palpable in [his] every sound and movement."

According to Charles C. Mann in the *Atlantic Monthly,* Fo took pleasure in the Vatican's description of the play, which was taped and broadcast on television in 1977, as "the most blasphemous" program ever televised. *Mistero buffo* was nevertheless a critical and popular success throughout Europe. The staging of the play in London in 1983 single-handedly saved from bankruptcy the financially ailing theater in which it was performed. Despite the reception of his masterpiece abroad, Fo was unable to perform the play in the United States until 1986 when he and Rame were finally granted permission to enter the country. The couple had been denied visas in 1980 and 1984 because of their alleged involvement in fund-raising activities for an Italian terrorist organization. Fo and his wife dismissed the accusation and maintained their innocence. Through the efforts of civil libertarian and cultural groups in Europe and the United States, Fo and Rame ultimately received visas, and *Mistero buffo* opened in New York in the spring of 1986. Jenkins termed the play "a brilliant one-man version of biblical legends and church history" whose comedy "echo[es] the rhythms of revolt."

Fo's penchant for justice prompted him to compose the absurdist play *Morte accidentale di un anarchico,* produced in English as *Accidental Death of an Anarchist,* in response to the untimely death of anarchist railway man Giuseppi Pinelli in late 1969. Pinelli's death was apparently connected to efforts by right-wing extremists in Italy's military and secret service agencies to discredit the Italian Communist party by staging a series of seemingly leftist-engineered bombings. The railway worker was implicated in the worst of these bombings, the 1969 massacre at Milan's Agricultural Bank. While being held for interrogation, Pinelli fell—it was later shown that he was pushed—from the fourth-floor window of Milan's police headquarters.

In *Accidental Death,* Fo introduces a stock medieval character, the maniac, into the investigation of the bombing to illuminate the truth. Fo commented in *American Theatre,* "When I injected absurdity into the situation, the lies became apparent. The maniac plays the role of the judge, taking the logic of the authorities to their absurd extremes," thus demonstrating that Pinelli's death could not have occurred in the way the police had described. John Lahr reported in the *Los Angeles Times* that because of their part in the exposure of the police cover-up, Fo was assaulted and jailed and Rame kidnapped and beaten in the first few years that the play was staged.

Accidental Death of an Anarchist was a smash hit in Italy, playing to huge crowds for more than four years. When officials pressured a theater in Bologna to halt plans for production, the play was alternatively staged in a sports stadium for an audience of more than six thousand people. After receiving rave reviews throughout Europe—Lahr, writing in *New Society,* called the show "loud, vulgar, kinetic, scurrilous, smart, [and] sensational. . . . Everything theatre should be"—and enjoying a thirty-month run in London, *Accidental Death* opened in the United States in 1984, only to close a short time later.

Because Fo's plays are often either loosely translated or performed in Italian and center on historical, political, and social events that bear more significance for audiences in Italy than in the States, American versions of the playwright's works are frequently considered less dazzling than their Italian counterparts. In an article for the *New York Times,* Mel Gussow pointed out that "dealing with topical Italian materials in colloquial Italian language . . . presents problems for adapters and directors." For instance, a few critics found the presence of a translator on stage during *Mistero buffo* mildly distracting. And many reviewers agreed that the English translation of *Accidental Death* lacked the power of the Italian production. Frank Rich insisted in the *New York Times* that adapter Richard Nelson's introduction of timely American puns into the *Accidental Death* script "wreck[ed] the play's farcical structure and jolt[ed] both audience and cast out of its intended grip."

Fo's 1978 collaboration with Rame, *Tutta casa, letto e chiesa,* produced in the United States as *Orgasmo Adulto Escapes from the Zoo,* also "may have lost some of its punch crossing the Atlantic," asserted David Richards in the *Washington Post.* A cycle of short sketches written for a single female player, *Orgasmo* focuses on women's status in a patriarchal society. Richards felt that, to an American audience in the mid-1980s when the play was produced in the United States, "the women in *Orgasmo* seem to be fighting battles that have long been conceded on these shores." Still, if not timely, the performances were judged favorably for their zest and honesty in portraying Italian sexism.

The Tricks of the Trade, published in 1991, is a collection of notes, talks, and workshop transcripts by Fo that deal with numerous aspects of the theater and their historical origins and modern roles: mimes and clowns, masks, and puppets and marionettes. Fo also discusses his own plays and his distinctive approach to playwriting and performing. "*The Tricks of the Trade* offers inspiration for theatre practitioners of all sorts, while celebrating a revival of the power and predominance of the politically inspired clown," remarked James Fisher in *Drama Review.* Writing in *World Literature Today,* Giovanni d'Angelo commented that the book "is technically robust and exhaustive" and termed Fo's style "fluent and graceful."

In the *New York Times* Gussow noted, "For Mr. Fo, there are no sacred cows, least of all himself or his native country," and concluded that Fo's social commentary is more "relevant" than "subversive." Commenting on the underlying philosophy that shapes and informs his works, Fo asserted in *American Theatre,* "My plays are provocations, like catalysts in a chemical solution. . . . I just put some drops of absurdity in this calm and tranquil liquid, which is society, and the reactions reveal things that were hidden before the absurdity brought them out into the open."

Fo's winning of the Nobel Prize for Literature in 1997 caused quite a stir. Italian literature enjoys a long, distinguished history, going back to the fourteenth century to the work of Petrarch and Boccaccio. When Fo won the coveted prize many people were surprised. They thought him "a mere writer and clownish performer of rather buffoonish comedies," wrote Jack Helbig for *Booklist.* However, audiences who have witnessed his works, continued Helbig, "have seen his anarchistic farces descry serious intent just below their mad comic surfaces." In a statement expressing the reasons for giving the prize to Fo, the academy stated that it was awarded for Fo's commitment to uphold the dignity of the downtrodden in modern society. Upon winning the prize, Fo reportedly telephoned his wife, Rame, referring to her as Mrs. Nobel, acknowledging her lifelong commitment to their shared work.

Fo's *Mistero Buffo* was the first of his plays to be staged in New York in the spring of 1986. The following year, he and his wife won an Obie Award under the category of special citations. More recently, a revival of Fo's *Johan Padan and the Discovery of the Americas,* was presented at the American Repertory Theatre in Cambridge, MA, in 2001. In a review for *American Theatre,* Jenkins noted that despite the fact that Fo adapted his play from sixteenth-century explorers' diaries, "its sly satirical examination of racism, religious warfare, ethnic cleansing and the mass migration of homeless refugees resonates with today's headlines." In this play, Johan Padan is a stowaway on one of Christopher Columbus's ships. However, when Padan arrives in the New World, he sides with the Native Americans in their fight against Columbus and his men. As *Variety*'s Markland Taylor put it, Johan does so, having learned that "the so-called savages of the Americas are a good deal less savage than the Europeans." *Boston Herald* theatre critic Terry Byrne found that this particular play "blends Fo's best skills as a traditional storyteller and political satirist." The play was staged in several U.S. cities, including New York, as a fiftieth anniversary celebration of Fo's career on stage with Rame.

The 2001 publication of *We Won't Pay! We Won't Pay! and Other Plays: The Collected Plays of Dario Fo* once again brought Fo's name to the forefront of discussions about drama in the States. *Library Journal* reviewer Thomas E. Luddy described Fo and Rame as "modern commedia dell'arte entertainers," and claimed that this new study of their collaborative work was "a much-needed critical review." The title of this book comes from one of Fo's most often performed plays. In an article about the titled play, after it was staged back in 1998, *Los Angeles Times'* Laurie Winer, referred to *We Won't Pay! We Won't Pay!* as a classical example of how Fo earned his Nobel Prize, with the play's main theme of upholding the rights of those less fortunate. Winer wrote that the play "blends wacky kitchen-sink comedy with diatribes on how the workers need to grab power from capitalist crooks."

Fo, in his seventies, continues to work. As Maureen Paton wrote in an interview with Fo for the London *Times:* he "still has plenty to rebel against." Despite the fact that he has spent time in jail in Italy for his writing and performance, that his wife has suffered abuse from people who disagreed with the couple's creative material, that his theatre was burnt, and an attempt was made to set his house on fire, Fo has never lacked the courage to express exactly what is on his mind.

Fo was called "a Left-leaning anti-cleric," by Bruce Johnston in London's *Daily Telegraph;* and "a clown with a tongue that slashed the establishment, including the Vatican," by the *Boston Herald*'s Iris Fanger. No matter what he is called, Fo continues to speak in what Winer described as his "anarchic voice," the same one that was heard by the Nobel committee when they awarded him the prize in Stockholm.

If his critics and opponents thought their verbal or physical attacks would intimidate Fo, his scathing 2003 play *Two-Headed Anomaly,* which was performed at Milan's Piccolo Teatro, proved them wrong. This time, Fo turns his attention to Italy's notorious prime minister, Silvio Berlusconi. In the satire, Fo attacks the prime minister for a variety of abuses of power, including passing laws for his own benefit, creating a media monopoly, and censoring journalistic criticism of the government. At one stage in the play, the prime minister, played by Fo, has Russian leader Vladimir Putin's brain transplanted into his head, making him a drunken, confused, Russian speaking, two-and-a-half foot dwarf. Much of the play focuses on the prime minister with his wife, played by Fo's wife, Rame. "These scenes give the play its greatest force. Berlusconi is depicted as a petulant adolescent who is constantly in need of approval while Lario is like a stern mother figure humoring her unruly, mischievous child with patronizing words," wrote Antonion D'Ambroso in the *Progressive*. D'Ambroso went on to note that the play "represents Fo at his best, placing him in the tradition of Moliere and Ruzzante Beolco, the father of the commedia dell'arte." The play has so outraged some of those in power that Italian senator Marcello Dell'Utri, an associate of the prime minister, brought suit against Fo, asking for $1.25 million in damages. Nick Vivarelli, writing in *Variety,* quoted Fo as responding, "It's just caricature. Any elements from reality have been widely reported and even written in books. The truth is, this is an attempt to shut us up. But we aren't going to stop." Fo is also author of *The Peasants Bible and The Story of the Tiger,* in which Fo takes five monologues from various Italian folklore stories and reworks them for his own satirical purposes.

BIOGRAPHICAL AND CRITICAL SOURCES:

BOOKS

Artese, Erminia, *Dario Fo parla di Dario Fo,* Lerici (Cosenza, Italy), 1977.

Behan, Tom, *Dario Fo: Revolutionary Theatre,* Pluto Press (London, England), 2000.

Contemporary Literary Criticism, Gale (Detroit, MI), Volume 32, 1985, Volume 109, 1998.

Farrell, Joseph, and Antonio Scuderi, editors, *Dario Fo: Stage, Text, and Tradition,* Southern Illinois University Press (Carbondale, IL), 2000.

Fellini, Federico, *Federico Fellini & Dario Fo: Disegni Geniali,*Mazzotta (Milan, Italy), 1999.

Hirst, David L., *Dario Fo and Franca Rame,* Macmillan (London, England), 1989.

McAvoy, R. C., editor, *Dario Fo and Franca Rame: The Theatre Workshops at Riverside Studios,* Red Notes (London, England), 1983.

Mitchell, Tony, *Dario Fo: People's Court Jester,* Methuen (London, England), 1984.

Pertile, Lino, "Dario Fo," in *Writers & Society in Contemporary Italy,* St. Martin's Press (New York, NY), 1984, pp. 167-90.

Trussler, Simon, editor, *File on Fo,* Methuen (London, England), 1989.

PERIODICALS

American Theatre, June, 1986; February 1998, Ron Jenkins, "The Nobel Jester," pp. 22-24; October, 2001, Ron Jenkins, review of *Johan Padan and the Discovery of the Americas,* p. 12.

Aperture, summer, 1993; Ron Jenkins, "Drawing from the Imagination: The Comic Art of Dario Fo," pp. 12-19.

Atlantic Monthly, September, 1985.

Booklist, February 1, 2002, Jack Helbig, review of *We Won't Pay! We Won't Pay! and Other Plays: The Collected Plays of Dario Fo,*p. 917.

Boston Herald, April 19, 1999, Iris Fanger, review of *We Won't Pay! We Won't Pay!,* p. O39; September 10, 2001, Terry Byrne, review of *Johan Padan and the Discovery of the Americas,* p. O36.

Choice, March, 1992, p. 1090.

Daily Telegraph (London, England), November 17, 2000, Bruce Johnston, "Dario Fo Is Tipped As Milan Mayor."

Drama, summer, 1979; third quarter, 1985, Phoebe Tait, "Political Clown," pp. 28-29.

Drama Review, September, 1972, A. Richard Sogliuzzo, "Dario Fo: Puppets for Proletarian Revolution," pp. 71-77; June 1975, Suzanne Cowan, "The Throw-Away Theatre of Dario Fo," pp. 102-13; winter, 1992, James Fisher, review of *Tricks of the Trade,* p. 171.

Library Journal, February 15, 2002, Thomas E. Luddy, review of *We Won't Pay! We Won't Pay! and Other Plays: The Collected Plays of Dario Fo,* p. 143.

Los Angeles Times, January 16, 1983; January 21, 1983; September 3, 1998, Laurie Winer, "Nobel Prize Winner's Anarchic, Loony Tone Comes through in *We Won't Pay!,*" pp. 6, 29.

Modern Drama, June, 1985, Martin W. Walsh, "The Proletarian Carnival of *Fo's Non si paga! Non si paga!,*" pp. 211-222; December, 1989, Mimi D'Aponte, "From Italian Roots to American Relevance: The Remarkable Theatre of Dario Fo," pp. 532-544; March, 1990, Joylynn Wing, "The Performances of Power and the Power of Performance: Rewriting the Police State in Dario Fo's *Accidental Death of an Anarchist,*" pp. 139-149; spring, 1998, Joseph Farrell, "Variations on a Theme: Respecting Dario Fo," pp. 19-29.

National Catholic Reporter, November 13, 1992.

New Republic, December 17, 1984.

New Society, March 13, 1980.

New Statesman, August 7, 1981.

New Yorker, February 23, 1981.

New York Times, December 18, 1980; April 17, 1983; August 5, 1983; August 14, 1983; August 27, 1983; February 15, 1984; October 31, 1984; November 16, 1984; May 29, 1986; May 30, 1986; May 9, 1987; November 27, 1987.

New York Times Book Review, February 2, 1998, p. 31.

Opera News, October, 1993.

Partisan Review, 1984, Joel Schechter, "The Un-American Satire of Dario Fo," pp. 112-119.

Progressive, April, 2004, Antonion D'Ambroso, "The Playwright vs. the Prime Minister," review of *Two-Headed Anomaly,* p. 32.

Theatre, spring, 1979, Suzanne Cowan, "Dario Fo, Politics, and Satire: An Introduction to *Accidental Death of an Anarchist,*" pp. 7-11.

Theatre Journal, October 1993, J. L. Wing, "The Iconicity of Absence: Dario Fo and the Radical Invisible," pp. 303-315.

Times (London, England), November 17, 1984; September 22, 1986; September 25, 1986; May 15, 2002, Maureen Paton, "Still a Worthy Fo: Interview," p. 4.

Times Literary Supplement, December 18, 1987.

Variety, August 4, 1982; May 11, 1992; September 17, 2001, Markland Taylor, review of *Johan Padan and the Discovery of the Americas,* p. 28; January 19-January 25, Nick Vivarelli, "Beauty of a 'Beast' Dispute: Berlusconi Play Adds Court Date to Its Run," p. 5.

Washington Post, August 27, 1983; November 17, 1984; January 17, 1985; June 12, 1986.

World Literature Today, autumn, 1992, Giovanni d'Angelo, review of *Tricks of the Trade,* p. 707.

ONLINE

Nobel Prize Internet Archive, http://almaz.com/nobel/ (July 18, 2002).*

* * *

FOERSTEL, Herbert N. 1933-

PERSONAL: Born October 6, 1933, in St. Louis, MO; son of William Herbert (a musician) and Margaret (maiden name, Schneider; present surname, Boe) Foerstel; married Lenora Shargo; children: Jonathan, Helen, Karen. *Ethnicity:* "German/Irish." *Education:* Hamilton College, B.A., 1955; Rutgers University, M.L.S., 1959; Johns Hopkins University, M.S., 1970. *Politics:* Independent. *Hobbies and other interests:* Music.

ADDRESSES: Office—c/o Author Mail, Greenwood Press, 88 Post Road West, Westport, CT 06881-5007.

CAREER: Author and librarian. Towson State University, Towson, MD, fine arts librarian, 1959-66; University of Maryland at College Park, began as science librarian, became head of Engineering and Physical Sciences Library and, later, head of branch libraries, 1967-96. National Security Archive, member of board of directors, 1988—. *Military service:* U.S. Army, 1955-58.

AWARDS, HONORS: Hugh Hefner First Amendment Award, 1988; *Choice: Current Reviews for Academic Libraries* chose *Surveillance in the Stacks* as a "best academic book," 1990.

WRITINGS:

Surveillance in the Stacks: The FBI's Library Awareness Program, Greenwood Press (Westport, CT), 1991.

Secret Science: Federal Control of American Science and Technology, Praeger (Westport, CT), 1993.

Banned in the USA: A Reference Guide to Book Censorship in Schools and Public Libraries, Greenwood Press (Westport, CT), 1994, republished, 2002.

(With daughter, Karen Foerstel) *Climbing the Hill: Gender Conflict in Congress,* Praeger (Westport, CT), 1996.

Free Expression and Censorship in America: An Encyclopedia, Greenwood Press (Westport, CT), 1997.

Banned in the Media: A Reference Guide to Censorship in the Press, Motion Pictures, Broadcasting, and the Internet, Greenwood Press (Westport, CT), 1998.

Freedom of Information and the Right to Know: The Origins and Applications of the Freedom of Information Act, Greenwood Press (Westport, CT), 1999.

From Watergate to Monicagate: Ten Controversies in Modern Journalism and Media, Greenwood Press (Westport, CT), 2001.

Refuge of a Scoundrel: The Patriot Act in Libraries, Libraries Unlimited (Westport, CT), 2004.

Contributor of articles and reviews to periodicals.

SIDELIGHTS: Herbert N. Foerstel once told *CA:* "I had always claimed that the most essential quality of good writing was clarity, the accurate representation of the author's thoughts. Then one day my brother, an English professor, corrected me. Above all, he said, a writer must have something to say. By emphasizing a technical aspect of writing, I had simply assumed motivation, conviction, content itself. After all, why would anyone bother to write without the impulse to speak the truth? Perhaps the two go hand in hand. Have a point of view. Express it clearly."

Foerstel has expressed his point of view in his books about individual freedoms, in particular freedom of speech and expression and censorship. His first book, *Surveillance in the Stacks: The FBI's Library Awareness Program,* is, according to *RQ*'s Mary Nell Bryant, "an authoritative, thoroughly researched, highly readable exposé of the history of the FBI's attempts to infiltrate libraries and engage the cooperation of librarians in the abridgement of the library rights of library users." In the book, Foerstel explains to readers how the FBI has undermined their freedoms. He discusses the FBI's top-secret program to gain reports on library usage by foreigners, as well as FBI requests to see library circulation records to determine who was reading what. In *Secret Science: Federal Control of American Science and Technology,* Foerstel turns the same inquisitive eye on government's role in the censorship of scientific and technological information. A *Publisher's Weekly* reviewer explained that the topic Foerstel discusses in *Secret Science* is extremely complicated and felt that "the short focal length of Foerstel's view severely limit the reader's grasp" of the topic.

Critics responded more favorably to *Banned in the U.S.A.: A Reference Guide to Book Censorship in Schools and Public Libraries.* As its title suggests, the book takes an in-depth look at the censorship of certain books in schools and public libraries. Foerstel tackles the subject by presenting a survey of book-banning incidents from 1976 to 1992, court rulings in book-banning cases, interviews and stories from authors often banned by schools and libraries, and a list of the fifty most frequently banned books. Foerstel later produced a revised and expanded edition of the book that includes changes in book-banning legislation and

updated interviews with authors between 1996 and 2000. *Library Journal* contributor Katherine Merrill deemed *Banned in the U.S.A.* "an enlightening analysis of censorship." *School Library Journal*'s Pat Scales concluded, "Librarians need this book, but patrons who want to better understand the threats to their First Amendment rights should be led to it as well."

Foerstel wrote *Climbing the Hill: Gender Conflict in Congress* with his daughter, Karen Foerstel. Nancy A. Humphreys of the *Affilia Journal of Women and Social Work* called *Climbing the Hill* a "short, informative, highly readable book" that discusses the historical impact of women who have been elected to Congress, such as Jeannette Rankin, Barbara Mikulski, and Debbie Stabenow. Humphreys observed, "If you want to understand how women struggle and successfully cope in an extremely sexist environment, you will find the book inspiring."

Foerstel returns to First Amendment rights in *Free Expression and Censorship in America: An Encyclopedia.* In this book, he provides readers with some of the key issues, subjects, and people involved in censorship debates today. Foerstel briefly covers issues pertinent to books, television, movies, and music. *Libraries and Culture* critic Nathaniel Feis noted that while many of popular music's most outspoken and controversial stars were not mentioned, the book "provides good basic information on the subject of free expression," and is still "a valuable reference tool for anyone researching or just curious about the state of free expression in America today." Foerstel further examined censorship in popular media in his book *Banned in the Media: A Reference Guide to Censorship in the Press, Motion Pictures, Broadcasting, and the Internet,* which *Booklist* reviewer Charles Harmon described as "the perfect book to hand to students writing papers on censorship."

In *Freedom of Information and the Right to Know: The Origins and Applications of the Freedom of Information Act,* Foerstel advocates for freer access to information controlled by the government. The book provides a brief history of the laws regarding government information and a discussion of the Freedom of Information Act and the problems faced by people who have "the right to know." Foerstel's book, *From Watergate to Monicagate: Ten Controversies in Modern Journalism and Media,* examines the controls placed on media by the government and media corporations. Throughout the book the author discusses why the public no longer trusts the media, and attempts to explain how journalistic standards are lowered by corporate controls. Susan Colowick of *Library Journal* dubbed the book "an eye-opener for anyone who may not realize the extent of corporate and government influence on the media."

BIOGRAPHICAL AND CRITICAL SOURCES:

PERIODICALS

Affilia Journal of Women and Social Work, fall, 1997, Nancy A. Humphreys, review of *Climbing the Hill: Gender Conflict in Congress,* p. 371.

American Reference Books Manual, 1999, review of *Banned in the Media: A Reference Guide to Censorship in the Press, Motion Pictures, Broadcasting, and the Internet,* p. 345.

Booklist, January 1, 1994, Charles Harmon, review of *Banned in the U.S.A.: A Reference Guide to Book Censorship in Schools and Public Libraries,* p. 836; July, 1997, review of *Free Expression and Censorship in America: An Encyclopedia,* p. 1834.

Book Report, January, 1999, review of *Banned in the Media,* p. 80; March, 2002, review of *From Watergate to Monicagate: Ten Controversies in Modern Journalism and Media,* p. 77.

Bookwatch, December, 2001, review of *From Watergate to Monicagate,* p.3.

Choice: Current Reviews for Academic Libraries, January, 1999, review of *Banned in the Media,* p. 879; March, 2002, P.E. Kane, review of *From Watergate to Monicagate,* p. 1231; February, 2003, R.M. Roberts, review of *Banned in the U.S.A.,* p. 959.

Journalism and Mass Communication Quarterly, spring, 1999, Randall Sumpter, review of *Banned in the Media,* p. 165.

Libraries and Culture, fall, 1999, Nathaniel Feis, review of *Free Expression and Censorship in America,* p. 427; winter, 1999, Melonie Alspaugh, review of *Banned in the U.S.A.,* p. 88.

Library Journal, August, 2001, Susan M. Colowick, review of *From Watergate to Monicagate,* p. 125; December, 2002, Katherine E. Merrill, review of *Banned in the U.S.A.,* p. 105.

Publishers Weekly, March 8, 1993, review of *Secret Science: Federal Control of American Science and Technology,* p. 60.

Reference and Research Book News, November, 2001, review of *From Watergate to Monicagate,* p. 220.

RQ, summer, 1991, Mary Nell Bryant, review of *Surveillance in the Stacks: The FBI Library Awareness Program,* p. 592.

School Library Journal, March, 2003, Pat Scales, review of *Banned in the U.S.A.,* p. 263.

Teacher Librarian, May, 1999, Jennifer Barth, review of *Banned in the U.S.A.,* p. 64.

Voice of Youth Advocates, April, 2002, review of *From Watergate to Monicagate,* p. 67.

ONLINE

University of Maryland, College of Behavioral Sciences Web site, http://www.bsos.umd.edu/ (March 14, 2003), reviews of *Free Expression and Censorship in America, Banned in the Media,* and *Freedom of Information and the Right to Know: The Origins and Applications of the Freedom of Information Act.**

*   *   *

FOWLER, Sydney
See WRIGHT, S(ydney) Fowler

*   *   *

FRANZKE, Andreas 1938-

PERSONAL: Born September 27, 1938, in Breslau, Germany (now Wroclaw, Poland); son of Walter and Erna (Gloede) Franzke; children: Hendrikje, Titus. *Education:* Attended University of Heidelberg, 1962-63, and University of Würzburg, 1963-64; University of Marburg, Ph.D., 1969. *Religion:* Protestant.

ADDRESSES: Home—A. M. Rüppurrer Schloss 3A, Karlsruhe D-76199, Germany. *Office*—Reinhold-Frank-Straße 81, Karlsruhe D-76133, Germany; fax: 72-184-8150.

CAREER: Staatliche Akademie der Bildenen Künste, Karlsruhe, Germany, professor of art history, 1969—, dean, 1988-2000. University of Michigan, guest professor, 1985.

WRITINGS:

August Lucas (1803-63), Eduard Roether Verlag (Darmstadt, West Germany), 1972.

Jean Dubuffet, Beyeler (Basel, Switzerland), 1975, English translation by Joachim Neugröschel, 1976.

Georg Philipp Schmitt: (1808-1873): e. Heidelberger Maler d. 19. Jh., Müller (Karlsruhe, West Germany), 1977.

(Coauthor) *Kalinowski: Zeichnungen, Dessins, Bilder, Tableaux, Caissons*, Edition Rothe (Heidelberg, West Germany), 1978.

(Editor, with Michael Schwarz) *Christian Boltanski: 17. 1.-5. 3. 1978, Bad. Kunstverein e.V., Karlsruhe*, Bad. Kunstverein (Karlsruhe, West Germany), 1978.

Antoni Tàpies Werk und Zeit (title means "The Work and Life of Antoni Tàpies"), Hatje Cantz (Ostfildern, West Germany), 1979.

Jean Dubuffet Zeichnungen (title means "Drawings by Jean Dubuffet"), Rogner & Bernard (Munich, West Germany), 1980.

Dubuffet, translated by Robert Erich Wolf, Abrams (New York, NY), 1981.

Skulpturen und Objekte von Malern des 20. Jahrhunderts (title means "Sculptures and Objects by Painters of the Twentieth Century"), DuMont Buchverlag (Cologne, West Germany), 1982, reprinted, 2000.

(With Günther Wirth) *Kunst der 50er Jahre in Baden-Württemberg: eine Ausstellung aus Anlass des 30jährigen Bestehens des Landes Baden-Württemberg*, Der Künstlerbund (Stuttgart, West Germany), 1982.

Joan Miró, Skulpturen: 24. September bis 13. November 1983, Städtische Galerie im Prinz-Max-Palais . . ., Die Galerie (Karlsruhe, West Germany), 1983.

Erich Ohser-E. O. Plauen, der Zeichner, 1903-1944: Staatsgalerie Stuttgart, Graphische Sammlung, 4. Juli-23. August 1987, Die Galerie (Karlsruhe, West Germany), 1987.

Max Beckmann Skulpturen, Piper (Munich, West Germany), 1987.

Jean Dubuffet: Petites Statues de la vie precaire (includes English translation; title means "Jean Dubuffet: Small Statues of Precarious Life"), Verlag Gachnang & Springer (Stuttgart, West Germany), 1988.

George Baselitz, Prestel-Verlag (Munich, West Germany), 1988, English translation by David Britt, 1989.

Die Bildhauer der Kunstakademie Karlsruhe von 1864 bis heute: Ausstellung im Neubau für Bildhauer, Bismarckstraße 67, 5. bis 14. Juli 1989, Staatliche Akademie der Bildenden Künste Karlsruhe (Karlsruhe, West Germany), 1989.

Dubuffet, DuMont Buchverlag (Cologne, Germany), 1990.

Tàpies, Prestel-Verlag (Munich, Germany), 1992, English translation by John William Gabriel, 1992.

Alfred Jensen: Bilder und Arbeiten auf Papier von 1952 bis 1978, Daniel Blau Verlag (Munich, Germany), 1992.

Mark Rothko: Multiforms, Daniel Blau Verlag (Munich, Germany), 1993.

(Editor) Stephan Balkenhol, *Plätze, Orte, Situationen*, Cantz Edition (Ostfildern, Germany), 1996.

(Coauthor) *Alberto Giacometti: Zeichnungen, druckgrafische Unikate und Ergänzungen zum Werkverzeichnis der Druckgrafik von Lust: 17. April-21. Juni 1997, Galerie Klewan, München*, Die Galerie (Munich, Germany), 1997.

Lucian Freud, Radierungen (etchings; includes English translation), Kerber Verlag (Bielefeld, Germany), 1997.

(Editor, with Ernst-Gerhard Güse) *Jean Dubuffet, Figuren und Köpfe: auf der Suche nach einer Gegenkultur*, Hatje Cantz (Ostfildern, Germany), 1999.

Stephan Balkenhol: vor Ort, Hatje Cantz (Ostfildern, Germany), 2001.

Antoni Tàpies Lithographien, Museum moderner Kunst-Stiftung (Berlin, Germany), 2001.

(Editor) *Jean Dubuffet: Biographie im Lanfschritt*, Verlag der Buchhandlung Walther Koenig (Cologne, Germany), 2002.

Author of exhibition catalogs and other shorter works, including "Bertholin-Objekte: Badischer Kunstverein e.V., 18. Januar bis 5.Marz 1978," Der Kunstverein (Karlsruhe, West Germany), 1978. Contributor to books, including *Picasso: Druckgraphik, illustrierte Bücher, Zeichnungen, Collagen und Gemälde aus dem Sprengel Museum Hannover,* by Magdalena M. Moeller, Propyläen (Frankfurt am Main, West Germany), 1986; author of introduction, *Chaissac, 1910-1964,* Galerie Nathan (Zurich, Switzerland), 1987; and *Don Quijote,* by Reinhold Metz, Prestel-Verlag (Munich, Germany), 1991.

SIDELIGHTS: Andreas Franzke once told *CA:* "As a student I became familiar with the art and the ideas of Jean Dubuffet. Later on I became a friend of the artist, and I worked with him for many years. He considerably influenced my ideas about art. In my opinion Dubuffet is one of the leading painters of post-World War II Europe, and his impact and influence on American artists is substantial. He was discovered by collectors and museums in America far earlier than in his native France."

BIOGRAPHICAL AND CRITICAL SOURCES:

PERIODICALS

New York Times Book Review, March 28, 1982.

* * *

FRENCH, Marilyn 1929-
(Mara Solwoska)

PERSONAL: Born November 21, 1929, in New York, NY; daughter of E. Charles and Isabel (Hazz) Edwards; married Robert M. French, Jr. (a lawyer), June 4, 1950 (divorced, 1967); children: Jamie, Robert M. III. *Education:* Hofstra College (now University), B.A., 1951, M.A., 1964; Harvard University, Ph.D., 1972. *Hobbies and other interests:* Amateur musician; parties, cooking, travel.

ADDRESSES: Home—New York, NY. *Agent*—Charlotte Sheedy Literary Agency, 145 West 86th St., New York, NY 10024.

CAREER: Writer and lecturer. Hofstra University, Hempstead, NY, instructor in English, 1964-68; College of the Holy Cross, Worcester, MA, assistant professor of English, 1972-76; Harvard University, Cambridge, MA, Mellon Fellow in English, 1976-77. Artist-in-residence at Aspen Institute for Humanistic Study, 1972.

MEMBER: Modern Language Association of America, Society for Values in Higher Education, Virginia Woolf Society, James Joyce Society, Phi Beta Kappa.

WRITINGS:

The Book As World: James Joyce's "Ulysses," Harvard University Press (Cambridge, MA), 1976, reprinted, Paragon House (New York, NY), 1993.

Marilyn French

The Women's Room (novel), Summit Books (New York, NY), 1977, with an afterword by Susan Faludi, Ballantine Books (New York, NY), 1993.

The Bleeding Heart (novel), Summit Books (New York, NY), 1980.

Shakespeare's Division of Experience, Summit Books (New York, NY), 1981.

Beyond Power: On Women, Men, and Morals (essays), Summit Books (New York, NY), 1985.

Her Mother's Daughter (novel), Summit Books (New York, NY), 1987.

(Author of introduction) Edith Wharton, *Summer,* Macmillan (New York, NY), 1987.

(Author of afterword) Jane Wagner, *The Search for Signs of Intelligent Life in the Universe: Now a Major Motion Picture Starring Lily Tomlin,* HarperCollins (New York, NY), 1991.

The War against Women (nonfiction), Summit (New York, NY), 1992.

Our Father (novel), Little, Brown (Boston, MA), 1994.

My Summer with George, Knopf (New York, NY), 1996.

A Season in Hell: A Memoir, Knopf (New York, NY), 1998.

From Eve to Dawn: A History of Women, McArthur (Toronto, Ontario, Canada), 2002.

Also author of two unpublished novels. Contributor of articles and stories, sometimes under pseudonym Mara Solwoska, to journals, including *Soundings* and *Ohio Review.*

ADAPTATIONS: The Women's Room was produced a television movie, 1980.

SIDELIGHTS: Novelist, educator, and literary scholar Marilyn French is perhaps best known for her cogent synthesis of the late-twentieth-century feminist perspective. "My goal in life," she once asserted in an *Inside Books* interview with Ray Bennett, "is to change the entire social and economic structure of western civilization, to make it a feminist world." "Feminism isn't a question of what kind of genitals you possess," she explained, "it's a kind of moral view. It's what you think with your head and feel with your heart." French, whose own feminism was heightened by her life experiences, was married with children before she read Simone de Beauvoir's *The Second Sex,* a book thematically concerned with the importance of women not living through men. Considered by many to be the first text of the twentieth-century feminist movement, the book greatly impressed and influenced French, and soon thereafter she began to write short stories that expressed her own feelings and frustrations. Divorced in 1967, she earned a doctorate from Harvard through fellowships, and then launched an impressive academic career marked by the publication of her thesis, *The Book As World: James Joyce's "Ulysses."* In 1977, the success of French's explosive and provocative first novel *The Women's Room,* allowed her to pursue writing full-time. The work also became a major novel of the women's movement.

"I wanted to tell the story of what it is like to be a woman in our country in the middle of the twentieth century," French explained to a *New York Times* interviewer about *The Women's Room.* Calling it "a collective biography of a large group of American citizens," Anne Tyler described the novel's characters in the *New York Times Book Review:* "Expectant in the 40's, submissive in the 50's, enraged in the 60's, they . . . arrived in the 70's independent but somehow

unstrung, not yet fully composed after all they've been through." The novel is about Mira, a submissive and repressed young woman whose conventional childhood prepares her for a traditional marriage that ends in divorce and leaves her liberated but alone. "The tone of the book is rather turgid, but exalted, almost religious," noted Anne Duchene in the *Times Literary Supplement,* "a huge jeremiad for a new kind of Fall, a whole new experience of pain and loss."

Writing about *The Women's Room* in the *Washington Post Book Review,* Brigitte Weeks contended that "the novel's basic thesis—that there is little or no foreseeable future for coexistence between men and women—is powerfully stated, but still invokes a lonely chaos repellent to most readers." Uncomfortable with what she perceives as the woman-as-victim perspective in *The Women's Room,* Sara Sanborn elaborated in *Ms.:* "My main objection is not that French writes about the sufferings of women; so have the best women writers. But the women of, say, George Eliot or Virginia Woolf, hampered as they are, live in the world of choice and consequence. They are implicated in their own fates, which gives them both interest and stature. The characters in this book glory in the condition which some men have ascribed to women: they are not responsible." In her interview with *People* magazine's Gail Jennes, French stated: "Books, movies, TV teach us false images of ourselves. We learn to expect fairy-tale lives. Ordinary women's daily lives—unlike men's—have not been the stuff of literature. I wanted to legitimate it and I purposely chose the most ordinary lives [for the characters in the novel]—not the worst cases. . . . I wanted to break the mold of conventional women's novels." However, in the *New York Times Book Review,* Rosellen Brown noted that *The Women's Room* "declared the independence of one victimized wife after another."

"French wonders not only if male-female love is *possible,* but whether it's *ethical* in the contemporary context," wrote Lindsey Van Gelder in a *Ms.* review of French's second novel, *The Bleeding Heart.* "How, in other words, does one reconcile one's hard-won feminist insights about the way the System works with one's longing to open one's heart completely to a man who, at the very least, benefits from an oppressive System buttressed, in part, by women's emotional vulnerability?" *The Bleeding Heart* centers on Dolores, a liberated professor of Renaissance literature, who is on leave and researching a new book at Oxford

University when she meets Victor, an unhappily married father of four in England on business. Compromising her feminist principles by engaging in an impassioned but frustratingly combative affair with him, Dolores ultimately realizes that she cannot live with Victor without descending into predictably prescribed roles. Commenting in *Newsweek* that "French makes her point and touches lots of raw contemporary nerves," Jean Strouse queried, "What happens when nobody wants to be the wife?" According to Brown, *The Bleeding Heart* represents "an admirably honest admission of the human complications that arise after a few years of lonely integrity: What now? Must one wait for love until the world of power changes hands? Is there a difference between accommodation and compromise among lovers? Accommodation and surrender? How to spell out the terms of a partial affirmation?"

In the *Village Voice,* Laurie Stone observed the political thesis of *The Bleeding Heart:* "Although a feminist may love a man, she will ultimately have to reject him, since men axiomatically live by values inimical to women." Describing it as "a novel of love and despair in the seeming ruins of post-'60s angst and the ill-defined emotional territory of the '70s," Thomas Sanchez suggested in the *Los Angeles Times Book Review* that the work "is less a novel of people and their fierce concerns for survival than a melodrama of symbols clothed in philosophical and political garb." Furthermore, Sanchez called *The Bleeding Heart* "maddening" in the sense that "French has mistaken politics for prose." But according to R. Z. Sheppard in *Time,* French softened her militancy in the work: "Her soul on ice, Marilyn French sounded like a feminist Eldridge Cleaver [in *The Women's Room*]. *The Bleeding Heart* suggests a slight thaw. Its core is a seemingly endless and inconclusive dialogue—SALT talks in the gender wars." And *Nation* contributor Andrea Freud Loewenstein suggested that although *The Bleeding Heart* is "a depressed and depressing book," it is "not a destructive one." In the words of Alice Hoffman in the *New York Times Book Review,* "French continues to write about the inner lives of women with insight and intimacy. What she's given us this time is a page-turner with a heart."

French's novel *Our Father* depicts the troubled "family reunion" that occurs after a wealthy man, Stephen Upton, suffers a stroke, sparking a visit from his four estranged daughters—all of whom have different

mothers. Each hoping to gain either money or acknowledgment from their father, the women initially compete and bicker. The daughters' discovery that they have all been the victims of incest during their childhood, however, becomes a source of bonding and mutual support. Reviews of the work have been mixed. Citing an element of flatness in French's characters and scenes, Georgia Jones-Davis in the *Los Angeles Times Book Review* commented: "French has written a polemic, not a novel. . . . [The work] is too preachy and badly written to count as literature and too static to be good mind candy." Maude McDaniel, reviewing the book for Chicago's *Tribune Books,* also found the author's prose style "pedestrian," but nevertheless argued that *Our Father* "should strike a chord with every woman who is willing to think honestly about the place of femaleness in the world." While noting that the novel lacks realism in terms of character and environmental detail, Meg Wolitzer of the *New York Times Book Review* also found the book fascinating: "*Our Father* is a big novel that is fueled by anger, revenge, and the possibilities of recovery," Wolitzer noted. "It is overly long and often wildly melodramatic, but somehow these failings also give it an odd power."

A criticism frequently leveled at French's fiction is that "her novels suffer from a knee-jerk feminist stereotype in which all men are at worst, brutal and, at best, insensitive," noted Susan Wood in the *Washington Post Book World.* Astonished at the bitterness and anger French expresses in *The Women's Room* and *The Bleeding Heart,* for instance, critics have cited the author's strident anti-male stance. For example, Libby Purves wrote in the London *Times* that *The Women's Room* is "a prolonged—largely autobiographical—yell of fury at the perversity of the male sex. . . . The men in the novel are drawn as malevolent stick figures, at best appallingly dull and at worst monsters." And referring in the *Chicago Tribune Book World* to a "persistently belligerent anti-male bias" in *The Bleeding Heart,* Alice Adams felt the novel's one-sided characterization only serves to disenfranchise many readers who might otherwise read and learn from French's literature. Richard Phillips commented in the *Chicago Tribune* that "to read one of her novels . . . means wincing through hundreds of pages of professed revulsion over the male species of human kind. Man means power, control, rage. Even the nice guys finish last. Men are bastards. Women suffer. It is a message written with all the subtlety of a sledgehammer, but one that, French argues, is only a mirror reflection of what men themselves are taught from birth: contempt for women." But, as French explained to Phillips, "Contempt for women is not an accident, it is not a by-product of our culture. It is the heart. The culture is founded on it. It is the essential central core; without it, the culture would fall apart."

"Just as feminists have identified and denounced misogyny in books written by men, it behooves us all to arraign those books which exude a destructive hatred of men," opined Suzanne Fields in the *Detroit News*. "Such feelings can infect and calcify in dangerous ways. To intersperse torrid sex scenes with tirades against men for the imagined crime of being men merely allows villains and victims to exchange places. The rules of the game, weighted as they are to create those villains and victims, go unchallenged." However, to those critics who have charged that French portrays male characters as "stick figures," "empty men," and "cardboard villains," French responded in the *New York Times*: "The men are there as the women see them and feel them—impediments in women's lives. That's the focus. . . . Aristotle managed to build a whole society without mentioning women once. Did anyone ever say: 'Are there women in (Joseph Conrad's) *Nigger of the Narcissus*?'"

Praising French's skill in eliciting response from her readers, Weeks declared that "as a polemic [*The Women's Room*] is brilliant, forcing the reader to accept the reactions of the women as the only possible ones." Noting that "the reader, a willing victim, becomes enmeshed in mixed feelings," Weeks observed that the novel "forces confrontations on the reader mercilessly." Although Weeks acknowledged the novel's flaws, she concluded that the novel is "full of life and passions that ring true as crystal. Its fierceness, its relentless refusal to compromise are as stirring as a marching song." Yet, as Van Gelder pointed out in *Ms.*, despite the fact that it "is a book whose message is 'the lesson all women learn: men are the ultimate enemy,'" men do not seem to be "especially threatened by the book"; those who choose to read it probably have some degree of commitment to feminism in the first place. "The best compliment I can pay it is that I kept forgetting that it was fiction," remarked *New York Times* contributor Christopher Lehmann-Haupt. "It seized me by my preconceptions and I kept struggling and arguing with its premises. Men can't be that bad, I kept wanting to shout at the narrator. There must be room for accommodation

between the sexes that you've somehow overlooked. And the damnable thing is, she's right."

In *Her Mother's Daughter*, a forgiving look at motherhood, French writes about the maternal legacy bequeathed to daughters by examining four generations of an immigrant family through the experiences of its women. Anastasia, the narrator, attempts to overcome several generations of wrongs by living like a man, sexually free and artistically and commercially successful. Her success, however, is juxtaposed with the hardships and sufferings endured by the women before her, and her emancipation, according to Anne Summers in the *Times Literary Supplement*, "is shown to be more illusory than real; despite every conceivable change in outward forms, it is the older women's experience which imprints itself on her inner life." Reviewing the novel in Chicago's *Tribune Books*, Beverly Fields indicated that *Her Mother's Daughter* focuses on "the ways in which female submission to male society, with its accompanying suppression of rage, is passed like contagion from mother to daughter." Marie Olesen Urbanski observed in the *Los Angeles Times Book Review* that "the more educated or liberated the mother is, the more pervasive is her sense of a guilt from which there is no absolution. . . . *Her Mother's Daughter* celebrates mothers. It depicts the high price mothers pay for children who say they do not want, but who must have their sacrifices. . . . Has Mother's Day come at last?"

In other nonfiction works French seeks the origins of male dominance in society. In *Shakespeare's Division of Experience*, for example, she posits that the female's capacity to bear children has historically aligned her with nature and, consequently, under man's compulsion to exercise power over it. In the *New York Times Book Review*, Geoffrey H. Hartman described the subject of the book as "the relationship between political power and the 'division' of experience according to gender principles. It is a division that has proved disastrous for both sexes, she writes: To the male is attributed the ability to kill; to the female the ability to give birth; and around these extremes there cluster 'masculine' and 'feminine' qualities, embodied in types or roles that reinforce a schizoid culture and produce all sorts of fatal contradictions." Calling *Shakespeare's Division of Experience* "the finest piece of feminist criticism we have yet had," Laurence Lerner noted in the *Times Literary Supplement* that the author's "concern is not merely with Shakespeare." Recognizing that French "believes the identification of moral qualities with genders impoverishes and endangers our society," Lerner added that she thinks "every human experience should be reintegrated." Lerner continued that "whereas for Shakespeare the greatest threat may have lain in nature, it now lies in control; she therefore confesses an animus against 'the almost total dedication to masculine values that characterizes our culture.'"

Remarking that "French is intelligent, nothing if not ingenious, and obviously sincere," Anne Barton suggested in the *New York Review of Books* regarding *Shakespeare's Division of Experience* that "there is something very limiting . . . about the assumption upon which all her arguments are based." For example, Barton continued, "Although she does grudgingly admit from time to time that rationality, self-control, individualism, and 'permanencies' may have some little value, she is distrustful of 'civilization,' and of the life of the mind. She also leaves a major contradiction in her position unexplored. On the one hand, she indignantly denies that women are any 'closer to nature' than men. . . . On the other hand, it is not clear that the qualities she values, and according to which she would like to see life lived by both sexes, are all—in her terms—feminine." According to S. Schoenbaum in the *Washington Post Book World*, French "accepts what is after all common knowledge: that the gender principles aren't gender-specific—biological males can accommodate feminine values, and females aren't exempt from masculine power struggles. And, along with overlap, there exists the possibility for synthesis."

Beyond Power: On Women, Men, and Morals, wrote Lawrence Stone in the *New York Times Book Review,* "is a passionate polemic about the way men have treated women over the past several millenniums." And according to Paul Robinson in the *Washington Post Book World,* "Nothing in her previous books . . . prepares one for the intellectual range and scholarly energy" of the work, "which is nothing less than a history of the world (from the cavewomen to the Sandinistas) seen through the critical prism of contemporary feminism." Mary Warnock explained in the *Times Literary Supplement* that French's "general thesis is that men, who have hitherto governed the world, have always sought power above all else, and, in the interests of power, have invented the system of patriarchy which dominates all Western art, philosophy,

religion, and education. Above all it now dominates industry and politics."

Agreeing with French's thesis, Stone stated of *Beyond Power:* "The history of the treatment of women by men in the last 2,500 years of Western civilization is truly awful. One therefore has to sympathize with her passionate indignation and admire the single-minded zeal with which she has pursued her theory through the millenniums." Nevertheless, Stone found the book flawed. For instance, pointing to the "relentless cruelty and selfishness" anthropologists have discovered among some of the primitive societies French has perceived as utopian, Stone commented: "French's attempt to resuscitate the noble savage in feminist drag is not convincing. Moreover, worship of a female does not do much to affect the lot of women one way or the other." Observing that "she is a formidable woman to argue with," Purves wondered whether the patriarchal system, whether "strife, competition, rivalry, the concentration of power, and even war itself," is not responsible for even a few benefits to the world. French responded by explaining, "We are always told this. That commercial links and inventions and knowledge of other nations come from war, but who is to say that these things wouldn't have happened anyway? There is no way we can know how the world would have been without men's domination." Calling it "a brilliant study of power and control showing how those two related systems have affected the lives of men and women throughout human history," Richard Rhodes concluded in the *Chicago Tribune Book World* that "*Beyond Power* ranks high among the most important books of the decade."

French's *The War against Women* surveys the oppression of women on a global scale. Considering such activities as ritualized female genital mutilation in Africa and bride burning in India, along with economic disparities between women and men, French argues that women have become "increasingly disempowered, degraded, and subjugated" by patriarchal societies. Comparing the book with Susan Faludi's more popular feminist tract, *Backlash: The Undeclared War against Women,* Julie Wheelwright of the *New Statesman* found *The War against Women* simplistic in light of then-current developments in contemporary feminist thought. In particular, Wheelwright objected to French's insistence on the universal victimization and "moral superiority" of women. In contrast, Isabelle de Courtivron, writing in the *New York Times Book Re-*

view, praised "French's chilling and well-documented research," noting the disturbing validity of many of her observations.

From Eve to Dawn traces the history of women in three volumes. As Marian Botsford Fraser explained in a review for the Toronto *Globe and Mail,* the book revisits *Beyond Power:* "Before there were patriarchal states, there were matrilineal societies; something equivalent to the Big Bang happened to the human race about 10,000 years ago; states and patriarchy resulted and changed profoundly the nature of all societies; understanding this history will enable the world to move beyond patriarchy, but not to matriarchy which would also be a bad thing. Matriarchy, in which women have power over men, has never existed, according to French." Fraser admired the author's "chutzpah" in writing the book, but found *From Eve to Dawn* "impossible to read except in short bursts, or by browsing." What it lacks, Fraser pointed out, is a "narrative, story-telling quality." "It is a fascinating cornucopia of historical tidbits and arcane detail," the critic concluded, citing "a half-page on the Tlingit of Alaska, a page on the !Kung of the Kalahari Desert, an 'overview' of ancient Mesopotamia," and short examinations of the world's three major religions among the book's focus. "If you are satisfied with just a superficial graze . . . or can use the book as introductory . . . it has served [its] purpose," Fraser concluded.

BIOGRAPHICAL AND CRITICAL SOURCES:

BOOKS

Contemporary Literary Criticism, Gale (Detroit, MI), Volume 10, 1979, Volume 18, 1981, Volume 60, 1990.

PERIODICALS

Booklist, March 15, 1992; October 15, 1993.
Chicago Tribune, May 4, 1980; February 7, 1988.
Chicago Tribune Book World, March 9, 1980; June 23, 1985.
Detroit News, April 20, 1980.
Economist, March 21, 1992.
Entertainment Weekly, April 24, 1992.
Globe and Mail (Toronto, Ontario, Canada), July 6, 2002, Marian Botsford Fraser, review of *From Eve to Dawn.*
Ladies' Home Journal, October, 1987.

Library Journal, November 15, 1977; October 15, 1987; May 1, 1992; November 15, 1993.
Los Angeles Times Book Review, May 4, 1980; April 19, 1981; August 25, 1985; October 18, 1987; February 27, 1994, p. 12.
Modern Language Review, January, 1979.
Ms., January, 1978; April, 1979; May, 1980; April, 1987; April, 1989; July-August, 1990; March-April, 1991.
Nation, January 30, 1988.
New Statesman, February 21, 1986; April 3, 1992, p. 44.
Newsweek, March 17, 1980; January 24, 1994, p. 66.
New York, October 12, 1987.
New York Review of Books, June 11, 1981.
New York Times, October 27, 1977; March 10, 1980; March 16, 1981.
New York Times Book Review, October 16, 1977; November 11, 1977; March 16, 1980; March 22, 1981; June 12, 1983; June 23, 1985; October 25, 1987; July 17, 1988; September 24, 1989; July 5, 1992, p. 8; January 16, 1994, p. 12.
Observer (London, England), January 26, 1986.
People, February 20, 1978; January 24, 1994.
Psychology Today, August, 1985.
Publishers Weekly, August 29, 1977; August 21, 1978; March 7, 1980; September 11, 1987; September 2, 1988; March 2, 1992; October 18, 1993.
Spectator, April 4, 1992, p. 39.
Time, March 17, 1980; July 29, 1985.
Times (London, England), March 18, 1982; January 22, 1986; October 15, 1987; October 19, 1987.
Times Literary Supplement, February 18, 1977; April 21, 1978; May 9, 1980; June 4, 1982; January 24, 1986; October 23, 1987; June 19, 1992, p. 3.
Tribune Books (Chicago, IL), October 11, 1987; January 2, 1994.
Village Voice, March 24, 1980.
Virginia Quarterly Review, Volume 54, number 2, 1978.
Washington Post, May 7, 1980.
Washington Post Book World, October 9, 1977; March 9, 1980; March 8, 1981; June 2, 1985; October 18, 1987.
Women's Review of Books, October, 1986; April, 1988.*

*   *   *

FULLER, Kathleen
See GOTTFRIED, Theodore Mark

G

GAINES, Donna 1951-

PERSONAL: Born March 21, 1951, in Brooklyn, NY; daughter of Herbert Denmark and Betty Bradley (a band vocalist); adopted daughter of Arthur Gaines (in business). *Education:* State University of New York at Binghamton, B.A., 1974; Adelphi University, Garden City, NY, M.S.W., 1977; State University of New York at Stony Brook, M.A. in social work, 1984, Ph.D. in sociology, 1990.

ADDRESSES: Home—Carle Place, NY. *Office*—662 Franklin Ave., Suite 388, Garden City, NY 11530. *Agent*—Charlotte Sheedy, Charlotte Sheedy Literary Agency, 41 King St., New York, NY 10014. *E-mail*—donna@donnagaines.com.

CAREER: Writer, journalist, social worker, and sociologist. State University of New York at Binghamton, assistant director of High Hopes Counseling Center, 1973-74; Social worker in private practice, 1976—; *Verstehen,* editorial board, 1983-84; State University of New York at Stony Brook, research associate of Institute for Social Analysis, 1991; Graduate Center of the City University of New York, member of MassCult Research Group. Taught at Barnard College of Columbia University and the graduate faculty of New School University; served as workshop presenter; provided consulting services to youth defense attorneys, clergy, school administrators, community leaders, and international reporters; participated in several published interviews, documentaries, radio programs, as a guest on television programs, including *USA Today.*

MEMBER: American Sociological Association (founder and chair of Culture Section, 1985-86), National Writers Union, Authors Guild, National Rifle Association, People for the Ethical Treatment of Animals, American Civil Liberties Union, Eastern Sociological Society.

AWARDS, HONORS: Levenstein fellowship.

WRITINGS:

Teenage Wasteland: Suburbia's Dead End Kids, Pantheon (New York, NY), 1991, reprinted, with a new afterword, University of Chicago Press (Chicago, IL), 1998.
A Misfit's Manifesto: The Spiritual Journey of a Rock & Roll Heart (memoir), Villard (New York, NY), 2003.

Author of columns "She's Gotta Hack It," *Village Voice,* 1988—, and "Long Island Woman," *Long Island Monthly,* 1989-90. Contributor of articles and reviews to periodicals, including *Newsday, Spin,* and *Rolling Stone.* Also contributor to underground fanzines, trade and scholarly collections, professional journals, and textbooks. Has published poetry, song lyrics, and liner notes for music albums, and has shown photographs.

SIDELIGHTS: Donna Gaines once told *CA:* "It never occurred to me to become a writer. I am a sociologist and advocate. My desire to write is motivated by having something to say that might uplift the human race." With two published books examining the steadfast relationship between teenage rebellion and depression and heavy metal music, as well as many published articles on similar topics, Gaines is considered an expert on the melancholia of troubled youth and their search for outlets, both empowering and destructive.

Gaines's first book, *Teenage Wasteland: Suburbia's Dead End Kids,* considers the strength and validity of the link between disenfranchised, middle-class, suburban youth and the dark, soulless aspects of heavy metal culture. Gaines began composing the book after two related teen suicide incidents rocked suburban residents of northern New Jersey, who were astonished and guilt-ridden. On March 11, 1987, four burnt-out teenagers committed suicide by locking themselves in an abandoned garage, sitting in a running car, and inhaling carbon monoxide. The following week, two teens entered the same garage and reenacted the scene. Perhaps to answer the question "Why?," Gaines began a study of teenagers in economic and social situations similar to those of the departed. In her book, Gaines approaches her subjects as if she, herself, were still an unfulfilled teenager, chronicling their confessions and observations with the air of an insider. While the colored hair, ripped clothing, and dark personae of some of these teens may be an obvious display of the connection between heavy metal music and teenage depression, Gaines patiently draws out of her subjects the influence of this type of music on their lives.

"Music is their religion. Metal and its subgenres are used by these kids to articulate their experiences and to stake out their rebellion. It gives them a look, a solidarity with other burnouts from other communities, and a voice," deduced Allen Shelton in a review of *Teenage Wasteland* for the *Journal of Contemporary Ethnography.* Though Shelton felt that "the relationship between popular culture and dominant culture is underdeveloped," he observed that "Gaines is at her best in explicating how metal infuses the burnouts' biographies," and that "the text is powered by her street persona." In a review for *Publishers Weekly,* Genevieve Stuttaford wrote of the social value of Gaines's work, remarking that "her reflections on the primacy of death in the culture of these nomads in a middle-class society are expressed in an earthy, colloquial style that marks the author's empathy with alienated youth." Stuttaford concluded that the work is "a hard-hitting, disturbing report urging adults to 'renew our social contract with young people.'"

While her first book presents an amalgam of disturbed youths, Gaines's second book, *A Misfit's Manifesto:*

The Spiritual Journey of a Rock & Roll Heart, is a reflection of her own teenage struggles during a time when heavy metal dominated popular culture. Gaines recounts her upbringing in suburban Rockaway, Queens, and Long Island as an overweight, substance-abusing, Jewish teenager. She reveals her innermost thoughts on this person she had once been, as well as the self-destructive outlets she sought to kill the pain of being a teenager: diet pills, cocaine, alcohol, and sex. She then traces her steps toward becoming the respected sociologist, feminist, and renowned writer she is today, with the music remaining as the only contradictory path of her life.

While many reviewers praised the author for her candid and harsh revelations, others considered them of little value. A *Kirkus Reviews* contributor observed that Gaines "convincingly conveys the complications of the 'underworld' culture and its lifeline to troubled nonconformists," but remarked that "Gaines's prime fascination is herself and her presence in locating so many lowlife/bohemian cultural touchstones." Expressing a similar sentiment, one *Publishers Weekly* reviewer stated that "while a compelling memoir delivers a yarn with a deeper level of understanding, Gaines does a whole lot of boasting, but fails to make much sense of it, as if confessing were equal to self-analysis." However, Carol J. Binkowski in *Library Journal* maintained that *A Misfit's Manifesto* is "witty, poignant, and painfully honest," and praised Gaines as "a magnetic writer who provides an absorbing study in contrasts" and "a keen observer of the sociology of time, place, and pop musical trends."

Commenting on the musically driven aspects of Gaines's upbringing, a *New City Chicago* contributor wrote that Gaines "gravitates toward the dark and ugly truths of alienation, which are both expressed and somewhat relieved by the music she loves." This reviewer concluded with a statement of the book's societal value: "Having spent a lifetime understanding her own disenchantment from all angles, Gaines is in an ideal position to clarify the problems of adolescence for others." In a *Spin* review, the author joked about how she might cope with the plethora of criticism her book received: "I worry about how I'll react if reviewers say something mean about me personally," she stated. "But I have all sorts of ways to protect myself. One is, I collect guns."

BIOGRAPHICAL AND CRITICAL SOURCES:

PERIODICALS

Booklist, February 1, 2003, Mike Tribby, review of *A Misfit's Manifesto: The Spiritual Journey of a Rock & Roll Heart,* p. 963.

Bookwatch, August, 1992, review of *Teenage Wasteland: Suburbia's Dead End Kids,* p. 3.

Book World, May 31, 1992, review of *Teenage Wasteland,* p. 12.

Contemporary Sociology, March, 1992, Richard Lachmann, review of *Teenage Wasteland,* pp. 261-262.

Journal of Contemporary Ethnography, October, 1992, Allen Shelton, review of *Teenage Wasteland,* pp. 399-402.

Journal of Reading, April, 1994, review of *Teenage Wasteland,* p. 596.

Journal of Youth Services in Libraries, spring, 1994, review of *Teenage Wasteland,* p. 310.

Kirkus Reviews, December 15, 2002, review of *A Misfit's Manifesto,* p. 1820.

Kliatt Young Adult Paperback Book Guide, September, 1992, review of *Teenage Wasteland,* p. 40.

Library Journal, February 1, 2003, Carol J. Binkowski, review of *A Misfit's Manifesto,* pp. 90-91.

New York Times Book Review, June 16, 1991, p. 20.

Publishers Weekly, November 18, 2002, review of *A Misfit's Manfiesto,* p. 48.

Tribune Books (Chicago, IL), July 12, 1992, review of *Teenage Wasteland,* p. 8.

Voice of Youth Advocates, February, 1992, review of *Teenage Wasteland,* p. 404.

Wilson Library Bulletin, February, 1992, Cathi Dunn Mac Rae, review of *Teenage Wasteland,* pp. 86-87.

ONLINE

Donna Gaines Web site, http://www.donnagaines.com/ (January 22, 2004).

KEXP Radio, http://www.kexp.prg/ (January 22, 2004), "Donna Gaines."

Ramones: Rock and Roll Hall of Fame, http://www. kauhajoki.fi/˜jplaitio/halloffame.html/ (January 22, 2004), "Rock & Roll Hall of Fame 2002 Induction Essay for the Ramones by Dr. Donna Gaines."

Random House Web site, http://www.randomhouse. com/ (January 22, 2004), "About *A Misfit's Manifesto.*"

Village Voice Web site, http://www.villagevoice.com/ (December 10, 2003), column "Not 53rd & 3rd: Joey Ramone Gets His Place (in the 9-to-5 world and beyond)."*

*   *   *

GARNER, Alan 1934-

PERSONAL: Born October 17, 1934, in Cheshire, England; son of Colin and Marjorie Garner; married Ann Cook, 1956 (marriage ended); married Griselda Greaves, 1972; children: (first marriage) Adam, Ellen, Katharine; (second marriage) Joseph, Elizabeth. *Education:* Attended Magdalen College, Oxford.

ADDRESSES: Home—Blackden, Holmes Chapel, Cheshire CW4 8BY, England.

CAREER: Author; writer and director of documentary films. *Military service:* British Army; became second lieutenant.

MEMBER: Portico Library Club (Manchester, England).

AWARDS, HONORS: Carnegie Medal, 1967, and Guardian Award, 1968, both for *The Owl Service;* Lewis Carroll Shelf Award, 1970, for *The Weirdstone of Brisingamen;* first prize, Chicago International Film Festival, for *Images,* 1981; Mother Goose Award for *A Bag of Moonshine,*1987; Phoenix Award, Children's Book Association, 1996, for *The Stone Book.*

WRITINGS:

The Weirdstone of Brisingamen: A Tale of Alderley, Collins (London, England), 1960, published as *The Weirdstone: A Tale of Alderley,* F. Watts (New York, NY), 1961, revised edition, Walck (New York, NY), 1969, reprinted, Magic Carpet Books (San Diego, CA), 1998.

The Moon of Gomrath, Walck (New York, NY), 1963, published as *The Moon of Gomrath: A Tale of Alderley,* Magic Carpet Books, (San Diego, CA), 1998.

Elidor, Walck (New York, NY), 1965, reprinted, Magic Carpet Books (San Diego, CA), 1999.

Holly from the Bongs, Collins (London, England), 1966.

The Owl Service, Walck (New York, NY), 1967, reprinted, Magic Carpet Books (San Diego, CA), 1999.

The Old Man of Mow, illustrated by Roger Hill, Doubleday (New York, NY), 1967.

(Editor) *A Cavalcade of Goblins*, illustrated by Krystyna Turska, Walck (New York, NY), 1969, published as *The Hamish Hamilton Book of Goblins*, Hamish Hamilton (London, England), 1969.

Red Shift (also see below), Macmillan (New York, NY), 1973.

The Breadhorse, Collins (London, England), 1975.

The Guizer, Greenwillow Books (New York, NY), 1976.

The Stone Book, Collins (London, England), 1976.

Tom Fobble's Day, Collins (London, England), 1977.

Granny Reardun, Collins (London, England), 1977.

The Aimer Gate, Collins (London, England), 1978.

The Golden Brothers, Collins (London, England), 1979.

The Girl of the Golden Gate, Collins (London, England), 1979.

The Golden Heads of the Well, Collins (London, England), 1979.

The Princess and the Golden Mane, Collins (London, England), 1979.

Alan Garner's Fairytales of Gold, Philomel Books (New York, NY), 1980.

The Lad of the Gad, Collins (London, England), 1980, Philomel Books (New York, NY), 1981.

Alan Garner's Book of British Fairytales, Collins (London, England), 1984.

A Bag of Moonshine (folk stories), Delacorte (New York, NY), 1986.

The Stone Book Quartet, Dell (New York, NY), 1988.

(Reteller) *Jack and the Beanstalk*, illustrated by Julek Heller, Doubleday (New York, NY), 1992.

Once upon a Time, Though It Wasn't in Your Time, and It Wasn't in My Time, and It Wasn't in Anybody Else's Time. . . ., Dorling Kindersley (New York, NY), 1993.

The Alan Garner Omnibus (contains *Elidor, The Weirdstone of Brisingamen,* and *The Moon of Gomrath*), Lions, 1994.

(Reteller) *Little Red Hen*, illustrated by Norman Messenger, D. K. Publishers (New York, NY), 1996.

Strandloper, Harvill Press (London, England), 1996.

Lord Flame (play), Harvill Press (London, England), 1996.

Pentecost (play), Harvill Press (London, England), 1997.

The Voice That Thunders, Harvill Press (London, England), 1997.

(Reteller) *The Well of the Wind*, D. K. Publishers (New York, NY), 1998.

Thursbitch, Harvill (London, England), 2003.

Also author of play *Holly from the Bongs*, 1965, and of dance drama *The Green Mist*, 1970; author of libretti for *The Bellybag* (music by Richard Morris), 1971, and *Potter Thompson* (music by Gordon Crosse), 1972; author of plays *Lamaload*, 1978, *Lurga Lom*, 1980, *To Kill a King*, 1980, *Sally Water*, 1982, and *The Keeper*, 1983; author of screenplays for documentary films *Places and Things*, 1978, and *Images*, 1981, and for feature film *Strandloper*, 1992; author of film adaptation of *Red Shift*, 1978. Member of International Editorial Board, Detskaya Literatura Publishers (Moscow), 1991—.

SIDELIGHTS: Considered among the most important children's authors of the later twentieth century, British author Alan Garner is noted for his use of folk traditions and the multiple layers of meaning contained in his stories. His early books, including *The Weirdstone of Brisingamen: A Tale of Alderley, The Moon of Gomrath,* and *Elidor,* are reminiscent of the fantasy literature popularized by J. R. R. Tolkien. With more recent works as *The Owl Service* and *The Stone Book Quartet*, however, Garner's interest in fantasy has become more closely enmeshed with the realistic English landscape of his childhood, and his efforts to preserve the folk tales and cultural heritage of his native England have been cited as exemplary by several reviewers.

Born into a family of craftsmen who have lived for several generations near Alderley Edge in Cheshire, England, Garner proved unsuited for pursuing the way of life that had been in his family for many years. Following an education at Manchester Grammar School, Garner attended Magdalen College, Oxford, where he read classics. Returning to Cheshire without completing his degree, he began working on his first work of fiction, *The Weirdstone of Brisingamen*. His development as a writer was closely related to his embrace of his Cheshire homeland and dialect, reflecting what

Roderick McGillis in the *Dictionary of Literary Biography* called his "romantic quest to rediscover the mother tongue."

Though Garner was once considered a "children's" author, the increasing complexity of his stories has led many reviewers to reevaluate their original assessment of his work. For many, the turning point in his status was the publication of *The Owl Service,* an eerie tale of supernatural forces that interweaves ancient symbolism from Welsh folklore with a modern plot and original details. A story "remarkable not only for its sustained and evocative atmosphere, but for its implications," *The Owl Service* is "a drama of young people confronted with the challenge of a moral choice; at the same time it reveals, like diminishing reflections in a mirror, the eternal recurrence of the dilemma with each generation," according to a writer in *Children's Book World.* A critic from the *Christian Science Monitor* described it as "a daring juxtaposition of legend from the *Mabinogion,* and the complex relationship of two lads and a girl [in which] old loves and hates are . . . reenacted. Mr. Garner sets his tale in a Welsh valley and touches with pity and terror the minds of the reader who will let himself feel its atmosphere. This is not a book 'for children'; its subtle truth is for anyone who will reach for it." A writer for the *Times Literary Supplement* echoed this sentiment, noting that with *The Owl Service* "Garner has moved away from the world of children's books and has emerged as a writer unconfined by reference to age-groups; a writer whose imaginative vein is rich enough to reward his readers on several different levels."

In an essay excerpted in the *Times Literary Supplement,* Garner himself alluded to the many levels of meaning in his work. Speaking of his readers, he explained: "The age of the individual does not necessarily relate to the maturity. Therefore, in order to connect, the book must be written for all levels of experience. This means that any given piece of text must work at simple plot level, so that the reader feels compelled to turn the page, if only to find out what happens next; and it must also work for me, and for every stage between. . . . I try to write onions."

One book by Garner that is so complex that some critics have viewed it as almost impenetrable is *Red Shift,* a novel comprised of three different stories with separate sets of characters who are linked only by a Bronze Age axe-head, which functions as a talisman, and a rural setting in Cheshire. Composed almost wholly of dialogue, *Red Shift* jump-cuts from the days of the Roman conquest to the seventeenth century to the present time. Writing in *Horn Book,* Aidan Chambers compared the book to "a decorated prism which turns to show—incident by incident—first one face, then another. In the last section, the prism spins so fast that the three faces merge into one color, one time, one place, one set of people, one meaning." Michael Benton believed that *Red Shift* "expresses the significance of place and the insignificance of time. . . . Certainly in style and structure the book is uncompromising: the familiar literary surface of the conventional novel is stripped away and one is constantly picking up hints, catching at clues, making associations and allowing the chiselled quality of the writing to suggest new mental landscapes."

Despite the fact that Garner's novels are difficult, especially for young American readers unfamiliar with the local British dialects he employs so freely, Garner "takes his craft very seriously, gives far more time to each book than the majority of present-day writers and has probably given more thought to the theory and practice of writing for children than anyone else," wrote Frank Eyre in *British Children's Books in the Twentieth Century.*

Derived from the folklore of the British Isles, Garner's *A Bag of Moonshine* presents twenty-two short stories that some have described as fables of human cunning and folly. Critics have praised Garner's use of the folk tradition, including what E. F. Bleiler in the *Washington Post Book World* termed "fascinating rustic and archaic turns of phrase." Neil Philip concurred in the *Times Educational Supplement,* observing that "Garner has taken a number of lesser-known English and Welsh stories and, as it were, set them to music, establishing in each text a tune or cadence based on local speech patterns." Also a unique retelling of folk tales for children, Garner's *Once upon a Time* presents "The Fox, the Hare, and the Cock," "The Girl and the Geese"—both Russian tales—and "Battibeth," which Joanne Schott of *Quill & Quire* described as "a surrealistic and dreamlike story of a girl's search for her mother's missing knife."

Alan Garner's Fairytales of Gold employs the author's successful technique of drawing upon the plots and themes of traditional stories and then embellishing this material with a highly original use of language and detail. The collection presents four English tales: "The Golden Brothers," "The Girl of the Golden Gate," "The Three Golden Heads of the Well," and "The Princess and the Golden Mane." Reviewers observed that Garner's retellings maintain the general moral perspective, along with many of the thematic tenets of the original stories: the magic power of words, the use of incantations, the motif of fantastic quests, and the morality of kindness rewarded and evil punished. "Garner's interest is in reanimating a tradition of British stories; he laments the passing of traditional fairy tales that were meant for the whole family, not just the children," commented Roderick McGillis in the *Dictionary of Literary Biography*. "The fairy tales he recreates are a link to the British past, and, as he writes, 'a healthy future grows from its past.'"

With *The Stone Book,* Garner presents a "quartet" of interrelated stories depicting four generations of a working-class family in Cheshire, England, spanning the mid-nineteenth-century through the World War II era. Set in Victorian England, the first volume of the series, *The Stone Book,* tells the story of a young girl who begins to learn the significance of history, cultural meaning, and time when her father takes her to a remote cave and tells her to "read" the ancient paintings on the wall. "The ultimate idea [of the book] shines through with an elemental wisdom," asserted Paul Heins in *Horn Book,* noting that the book reflects "the continuity of life, the perception of a collective past." *Granny Reardun,* the second volume of the series, treats the theme of family and history through another angle, depicting a boy who decides to abandon his grandfather's stone masonry trade in favor of apprenticeship to a blacksmith. The saga continues with the final stories of the quartet, *The Aimer Gate,* in which the destructive impact of World War I is addressed, followed by *Tom Fobble's Day,* a coming-of-age story in which a young boy acquires the courage and confidence to sled down one of the highest hills he can find. Although reviewers occasionally question the accessibility of Garner's historical setting and English idiom to contemporary American children, *The Stone Book* has consistently received high praise for the multilayered quality of its treatment of the theme of family history. Offering a laudatory assessment of the series in *Times Literary Supplement,* Margaret Meek commented: "In the Stone Book Quartet we have moved away from a kind of nineteenth-century writing which is still found in books for twentieth-century children. This is a book of our day, for all its Victorian and Edwardian settings."

Reviewing Garner's *The Well of the Wind,* a reviewer for *Publishers Weekly* called the piece "a thought-provoking fantasy full of enchantment," in which a quest taken by abandoned siblings ends in the brother and sister finding their parents. In *Booklist* reviewer Stephanie Zvirin commented that *The Well of the Wind* "is pure fantasy, and the language, lyrical and quiet, is replete with imagery that blossoms outward" from the plot. *Thursbitch* unveils an eighteenth-century mystery surrounding the death of a packman in the snow. The body is found eerily surrounded by a woman's footprints. M. John Harrison, reviewing the novel for the London *Guardian,* commented that, as a demanding novel, *Thursbitch* "isn't a story that takes life lightly, nor does it expect to be taken lightly in turn."

Garner's 1997 essay collection *The Voice That Thunders* is a work that Shelley Cox described in a *Library Journal* review as "an informal autobiography," one that contains both talks and lectures. In *Commonweal* Daria Donnelly praised the collection, noting that while Garner consistently "extends the reach of children's literature," in his essays in particular "he argues that the rise of a separate sphere called children's literature has had spirit-wasting effects. It has put adults beyond the reach of myth and tales that they urgently need." In addition, Donnelly noted, according to Garner "it has left children vulnerable to the didactic and the reductive in both literature and the teaching of literature."

BIOGRAPHICAL AND CRITICAL SOURCES:

BOOKS

British Children's Books in the Twentieth Century, Dutton (New York, NY), 1971.
Contemporary Literary Criticism, Volume 17, Gale (Detroit, MI), 1981.
Dictionary of Literary Biography, Volume 161: *British Children's Writers since 1960, First Series,* Gale (Detroit, MI), 1996.

PERIODICALS

Booklist, March 1, 1981, p. 963; August 1998, p. 2006.
Books for Keeps, May, 1987, p. 15.
Children's Book World, November 3, 1968.

Children's Literature in Education, March, 1974.

Christian Science Monitor, November 2, 1967.

Commonweal, April 7, 2000, Daria Donnelly, review of *The Voice That Thunders,* p. 23; June 16, 2000, p. 26.

Globe and Mail (Toronto, Ontario, Canada), April 4, 1987.

Guardian, October 18, 2003, M. John Harrison, review of *Thursbitch.*

Horn Book, October, 1969, p. 531; February, 1970, p. 45; October, 1973; December, 1976, p. 636; April, 1979, p. 192; October, 1979, p. 533.

Kirkus Reviews, December 1, 1993, p. 1523.

Library Journal, December 15, 1970, p. 4349; October 15, 1998, p. 70.

New York Times Book Review, October 22, 1967, p. 62; October 28, 1973; July 22, 1979.

Observer (London, England), October 7, 1979, p. 39.

Publishers Weekly, September 14, 1998, p. 68.

Quill & Quire, January, 1994, p. 39.

School Library Journal, October, 1976, p. 116; March, 1981, p. 132; March, 1982, p. 157; April, 1987, p. 94; March, 1994, p. 215.

Spectator, April 12, 1975, p. 493.

Times Educational Supplement, December 5, 1986, p. 25.

Times Literary Supplement, May 25, 1967; November 30, 1967; September 28, 1973; March 25, 1977; December 2, 1977; September 29, 1978; November 30, 1984; November 28, 1986, p. 1346; December 5, 1995; May 24, 1996, p. 24.

Tribune Books (Chicago, IL), November 10, 1985.

Village Voice, December 25, 1978.

Washington Post Book World, July 8, 1979; November 10, 1985; November 9, 1986, p. 19; November 8, 1992, p. 11.*

* * *

GODFREY, Ellen (Rachel) 1942-

PERSONAL: Born September 15, 1942, in Chicago, IL; daughter of William and Mary Swartz; married W. David Godfrey (a writer), August 21, 1969; children: Jonathan, Rebecca, Samuel. *Education:* Stanford University, B.A., 1963.

ADDRESSES: Home—Victoria, British Columbia, Canada. *Agent*—Lucinda Vardey Literary Agency, 228 Gerrard St. E, Toronto, Ontario M5A 2E8, Canada. *E-mail*—ellen@ellengodfrey.com.

CAREER: Teacher in Ghana, c. 1963-65; worked as a freelance marketer and promoter, c. late-1960s to early 1970s; Press Porcépic, Ltd. (publishing and software company), Victoria, British Columbia, president, 1976-86; Softwords, Ltd. (software company), Victoria, chief executive officer, 1986-96; full-time writer, 1996—. Former member of board of directors, University of Victoria Coop Council; former president, Vancouver Island Advanced Technology Center; member of advisory council, Working Opportunity Fund; member of board of governors, Royal Roads University; member of Council of Science and Technology, Canada; member of advisory board, British Columbia Information Highway.

MEMBER: International Association of Crime Writers, Crime Writers of Canada, Mystery Writers of America, Sisters in Crime.

AWARDS, HONORS: Special Edgar Allan Poe Award and Edgar Award nomination, Mystery Writers of America, 1982, for *By Reason of Doubt.*

WRITINGS:

The Case of the Cold Murderer (mystery novel), Musson Book (Don Mills, Ontario, Canada), 1976.

Murder among the Well-to-Do (mystery novel), Paperjacks (Don Mills, Ontario, Canada), 1977.

By Reason of Doubt: The Belshaw Case (true crime), Clarke, Irwin (Toronto, Ontario, Canada), 1982.

Murder behind Locked Doors (mystery novel), Penguin (New York, NY), 1989.

Georgia Disappeared (mystery novel), Penguin (New York, NY), 1993.

"WOMEN'S RESCUE COMPANY" SERIES; MYSTERY NOVELS

Murder on the Loose, Contemporary Books (Chicago, IL), 1998.

Murder on the Lover's Bridge, Contemporary Books (Chicago, IL), 1998.

Murder in the Shadows, Contemporary Books (Chicago, IL), 1999.

SIDELIGHTS: Ellen Godfrey is a former software company executive who has turned her love of mystery novels into a writing career. Interestingly, rather than

English literature, Godfrey started off studying history and minoring in anthropology at Stanford University; after she graduated, she and her future husband traveled to Ghana, where they taught English for two years. They returned to settle in Canada, her husband's native country, and started a family while he taught at the University of Toronto and they both raised beef cattle in Ontario. But, as Godfrey related on her Web site, "it was shortly after our return from Africa that my addiction to mystery novels became so severe I began to write them as well as read them. My first two books, *The Case of the Cold Murderer* and *Murder among the Well-to-Do,* were set in Toronto, where we lived for a time, and also in Erin, Ontario, where we later lived and farmed."

About the same time her first novels came out, Godfrey and her husband started a publishing company, Press Porcépic, Ltd., which later evolved into a software company. Despite running the company and raising children, however, she still managed to produce another book, the Special-Edgar-winning *By Reason of Doubt: The Belshaw Case.* An account of a real-life crime, the book involves a renowned anthropologist who is accused of killing his wife after her body is found in Switzerland. He is put on trial, and the case seems to be going against him when his daughter, a television actress, suddenly brings new evidence to light.

After the Godfreys moved to Victoria, British Columbia, in 1986, they started a new software company, Softwords, Ltd. Ellen Godfrey managed to produce two more books during this time: *Murder behind Locked Doors* and *Georgia Disappeared,* both of which feature the character Jane Tregar, a corporate headhunter who finds herself caught up in solving unscrupulous business maneuvers that lead to murder.

In 1996, Godfrey finally decided to devote herself full time to writing, and her first project was to write three short novels in the "Women's Rescue Company" series. Part of the "Thumbprint Mysteries" concept originated by author Joan Lowry Nixon, these short books are designed to attract adults who are struggling with their reading skills. *Murder on the Loose* is written at a fourth-grade reading level; *Murder on the Lover's Bridge* is written at a sixth-grade level; and *Murder in the Shadows* is for those with eighth-grade reading skills. Of these books, the author commented, "I tried to write my books so anyone could read them

and enjoy them, and I suspect if I hadn't told you they were designed for adult literacy courses, you wouldn't have noticed."

BIOGRAPHICAL AND CRITICAL SOURCES:

PERIODICALS

Books in Canada, June, 1988, review of *Murder behind Locked Doors,* p. 27.
Maclean's, November 16, 1981, Eleanor Wachtel, review of *By Reason of Doubt: The Belshaw Case,* p. 67; June 20, 1988, Jack Batten, review of *Murder behind Locked Doors,* p. 54.
Publishers Weekly, July 22, 1988, Sybil Steinberg, review of *Murder behind Locked Doors,* p. 45.
Times Literary Supplement, August 14, 1992, review of *Georgia Disappeared,* p. 19.
Washington Post Book World, September 18, 1988, review of *Murder behind Locked Doors,* p. 6.

ONLINE

Ellen Godfrey Web site, http://www.ellengodfrey.com/ (November 11, 2003.)*

* * *

GOLDBERG, Bruce (Edward) 1948-

PERSONAL: Born November 18, 1948, in New York, NY; son of Samuel and Florence (Nussbaum) Goldberg. *Ethnicity:* "Caucasian." *Education:* Southern Connecticut State College, B.A. (magna cum laude), 1970; University of Maryland, D.D.S., 1974; Loyola College, M.S., 1984. *Hobbies and other interests:* Parasailing, tennis, travel, history, parapsychology, metaphysics, alternative medicine.

ADDRESSES: Home and office—4300 Natoma Ave., Woodland Hills, CA 91364; fax: 818-704-9189. *E-mail*—karma4u@webtv.net.

CAREER: Operator of a dental practice and a hypnotherapy practice, both Baltimore, MD, 1976-89; hypnotherapist in Los Angeles, CA, 1989—. Los Angeles

Bruce Goldberg

Academy of Clinical Hypnosis, president, 1990—; consultant to major American television networks. *Military service:* U.S. Naval Reserve.

MEMBER: American Psychological Society, Academy of Psychomatic Medicine, American Association of Applied and Preventive Psychology, Academy of Stress and Chronic Disease, Association for Past Life Research and Therapy (life member).

AWARDS, HONORS: Fellow, Academy of General Dentistry, 1982; Sealah Award, Association for Parapsychology Healing and Research, 1987; inducted into International Hypnosis Hall of Fame, 1987.

WRITINGS:

Past Lives, Future Lives: Accounts of Regression and Progression through Hypnosis, Newcastle (North Hollywood, CA), 1982, published as *Past Lives, Future Lives,* Ballantine (New York, NY), 1988.
The Search for Grace: A Documented Case of Murder and Reincarnation, privately printed (Sedona, AZ), 1994, Llewelyn (St. Paul, MN), 1997.

Peaceful Transition, Llewelyn (St. Paul, MN), 1997.
Soul Healing, Llewelyn (St. Paul, MN), 1997.
Unleash Your Psychic Powers, Sterling Publishing (New York, NY), 1997.
Astral Voyages, Llewelyn (St. Paul, MN), 1998.
Look Younger, Live Longer, Llewelyn (St. Paul, MN), 1998.
New Age Hypnosis, Llewelyn (St. Paul, MN), 1998.
Protected by the Light: The Complete Book of Psychic Self-Defense, Llewelyn (St. Paul, MN), 1998.
Time Travelers from Our Future: An Explanation of Alien Abduction, Llewelyn (St. Paul, MN), 1998, published as *Time Travelers from Our Future: A Fifth Dimension Odyssey,* Blue Star Productions (Sun Lakes, AZ), 1999.
Lose Weight Permanently and Naturally, Xlibris (Philadelphia, PA), 2000.
Custom Design Your Own Destiny, Millennial Mind Publishing (Salt Lake City, UT), 2000.
Self Hypnosis: Easy Ways to Hypnotize Your Problems Away, New Page Books (Franklin Lakes, NJ), 2001.
Dream Your Problems Away: Heal Yourself While You Sleep, New Page Books (Franklin Lakes, NJ), 2003.

Author of "Hypnotic Highways," a column in *Fate.* Contributor of articles to professional journals.

Goldberg's work has been translated into Hungarian, Italian, German, Spanish, Romanian, Russian, Japanese, Korean, and Portuguese.

ADAPTATIONS: A television drama based on *The Search for Grace: A Documented Case of Murder and Reincarnation* was broadcast by the Columbia Broadcasting System.

SIDELIGHTS: Hypnotherapist Bruce Goldberg received a B.A. in biology and chemistry from Southern Connecticut State College. He attended dental school at the University of Maryland, where he earned a D.D.S. degree. In 1976 he opened a dental practice in Baltimore, MD, where he also practiced as a hypnotherapist during the same period. He received an M.S. in counseling and psychology in 1984. Goldberg closed both Baltimore practices in 1989, and began practicing hypnotherapy in Los Angeles.

BIOGRAPHICAL AND CRITICAL SOURCES:

PERIODICALS

Publishers Weekly, April 24, 1995, p. 19.

GOTTFRIED, Ted
   See GOTTFRIED, Theodore Mark

*   *   *

GOTTFRIED, Theodore Mark 1928-
   (Ted Gottfried; pseudonyms: Lorayne Ashton, Kathleen Fuller, Benjamin Kyle)

PERSONAL: Born October 19, 1928, in Bronx, NY; son of Harry Mark (a toolmaker) and Jennie Gottfried; married Leanore Traugot, June 25, 1950 (divorced, 1970); married Harriet Klein, September 25, 1976; children: (first marriage) Julie Ellen, Daniel Mark, Katherine Anne, Toby Jean, Valerie Dawn; stepchildren: Melanie, Lisa. *Education:* University of Miami, B.A.; attended New York School of Journalism, 1947, and New School for Social Research, 1948-49. *Religion:* Unitarian Universalist.

ADDRESSES: Home—19 Stuyvesant Oval, New York, NY 10009. *Agent*—Richard Curtis Associates, Inc., 164 East 64th St., New York, NY 10021.

CAREER: Warner Brothers, Inc., New York, NY, publicist, 1947-51; worked as assistant manager of a theater, publicist for Skymaster Airline, and reporter and film reviewer for *Boxoffice* (magazine), all New York, NY, 1951; Checker Cab Co., New York, NY, cab driver, 1952-55; Premier Peat Moss, New York, NY, advertising manager, 1955; Penthouse Publications, New York, NY, editor, 1956-57; Stearn Publications, New York, NY, 1957-62, began as editor, became managing editor, then executive editor; Westpart Publications, New York, NY, editor of *Dude* and *Gent* (magazines), 1963; freelance writer, 1963—; editor of *High Society* (magazine), 1976-77; Drake Publications, New York, NY, publisher, 1977-78. Has also taught writing and worked with community action groups, including Coalition for the Homeless.

MEMBER: National Writers Union (founding member).

WRITINGS:

UNDER NAME TED GOTTFRIED

Georges Clemenceau, Chelsea House (New York, NY), 1987.

The House of Diamond, Lynx, 1988.
Enrico Fermi: Pioneer of the Atomic Age, Facts on File (New York, NY), 1992.
Gun Control: Public Safety and the Right to Bear Arms, Millbrook Press (Brookfield, CT), 1993.
The Citadel Treasury of Famous Movie Lines, Carol Publishing Group, 1994.
Libya: Desert Land in Conflict, Millbrook Press (Brookfield, CT), 1994.
Privacy: Individual Right vs. Social Needs, Millbrook Press (Brookfield, CT), 1994.
Alan Turing: The Architect of the Computer Age, Franklin Watts (New York, NY), 1997.
Alexander Fleming: Discoverer of Penicillin, Franklin Watts (New York, NY), 1997.
The American Media, Franklin Watts (New York, NY), 1997.
Capital Punishment: The Death Penalty Debate, Enslow Publishers (Springfield, NJ), 1997.
Eleanor Roosevelt: First Lady of the Twentieth Century, Franklin Watts (New York, NY), 1997.
James Baldwin: Voice from Harlem, Franklin Watts (New York, NY), 1997.
Pornography: Debating the Issues, Enslow Publishers (Springfield, NJ), 1997.
The Holocaust and Nazi Germany, Enslow Publishers (Springfield, NJ), 1998.
The Holocaust Children, Enslow Publishers (Springfield, NJ), 1998.
The Holocaust Victims, Enslow Publishers (Springfield, NJ), 1998.
Homelessness: Whose Problem Is It?, Millbrook Press (Brookfield, CT), 1999.
Police under Fire, Twenty-first Century Books (Brookfield, CT), 1999.
The Israelis and Palestinians: Small Steps to Peace, Millbrook Press (Brookfield, CT), 2000.
Martyrs to Madness: The Victims of the Holocaust, illustrated by Stephen Alcorn, Twenty-first Century Books (Brookfield, CT), 2000.
Nazi Germany: The Face of Tyranny, illustrated by Stephen Alcorn, Twenty-first Century Books (Brookfield, CT), 2000.
Stephen Spielberg: From Reels to Riches, Franklin Watts (New York, NY), 2000.
Should Drugs Be Legalized?, Twenty-first Century Books (Brookfield, CT), 2000.
Children of the Slaughter: Young People of the Holocaust, illustrated by Stephen Alcorn, Twenty-first Century Books (Brookfield, CT), 2001.
Deniers of the Holocaust: Who They Are, What They Do, Why They Do It, illustrated by Stephen Alcorn, Twenty-first Century Books (Brookfield, CT), 2001.

Displaced Persons: The Liberation and Abuse of Holocaust Survivors, illustrated by Stephen Alcorn, Twenty-first Century Books (Brookfield, CT), 2001.

Heroes of the Holocaust, illustrated by Stephen Alcorn, Twenty-first Century Books (Brookfield, CT), 2001.

Teen Fathers Today, Twenty-first Century Books (Brookfield, CT), 2001.

Earvin "Magic" Johnson: Champion and Crusader, Franklin Watts (New York, NY), 2001.

The 2000 Election, Millbrook Press (Brookfield, CT), 2002.

The Death Penalty: Justice or Legalized Murder?, Twenty-first Century Books (Brookfield, CT), 2002.

The Road to Communism, illustrated by Melanie Reim, Twenty-first Century Books (Brookfield, CT), 2002.

The Stalinist Empire, illustrated by Melanie Reim, Twenty-first Century Books (Brookfield, CT), 2002.

Northern Ireland: Peace in Our Time?, Millbrook Press (Brookfield, CT), 2002.

The Great Fatherland War: The Soviet Union in World War II, Twenty-first Century Books (Brookfield, CT), 2003.

The Cold War: The Rise and Fall of the Soviet Union, Twenty-first Century Books (Brookfield, CT), 2003.

Homeland Security versus Constitutional Rights, Twenty-first Century Books (Brookfield, CT), 2003.

The Quest for Peace: A History of Anti-War Movements in America, Twenty-first Century Books (Brookfield, CT), 2004.

OTHER

(Under pseudonym Benjamin Kyle) *Qaddafi* (young adult nonfiction), Chelsea House (New York, NY), 1987.

(Under pseudonym Lorayne Ashton) *Rebels,* Ballantine/Ivy (New York, NY), 1988.

Also author of five books in the "Riverview" series under the pseudonym Kathleen Fuller, for Ballantine/Ivy, 1987-89. Author of adult novels under various pseudonyms. Also author of numerous speeches, articles, reviews, and short stories published in *Redbook, Philadelphia Inquirer,* and *Farmer's Almanac,* among others.

SIDELIGHTS: Under the name Ted Gottfried, Theodore Mark Gottfried has written numerous thought-provoking nonfiction books for middle-grade and high-school readers. Gottfried tackles some of the most controversial issues in modern life, including the death penalty, teen parenthood, the legalization of drugs, pornography, and homelessness. Rather than expressing his own opinion, however, Gottfried presents many positions and allows his readers to draw their own conclusions. Gottfried has also written multiple works on the Nazi Holocaust and its emotional and political fallout, as well as a series on the history of the Soviet Union. His books are characterized by concise chapters and sidebars that use historical figures and situations to illustrate his main points. *Booklist* correspondent Ann O'Malley noted that the value of Gottfried's books lies in "clear, accessible writing style and the presentation of a complex issue . . . in appropriate fashion for beginning research students."

Gottfried has authored several biographies of prominent twentieth-century individuals, including French politician Georges Clemenceau, American author James Baldwin, former First Lady Eleanor Roosevelt, and scientist Alexander Fleming. *Georges Clemenceau* earned praise for the clarity of the writing style, the attractiveness of the book's format, and the quality of the author's research. Herman Sutter in *School Library Journal* faulted *James Baldwin: Voice from Harlem* for its "stale critical analysis" but neverthtless felt that the book offers students "a straightforward introduction" to Baldwin's life and career. Also in *School Library Journal,* Phyllis Graves called *Eleanor Roosevelt: First Lady of the Twentieth Century* "an objective, easy-to-read biography." Allison Trent Bernstein in *School Library Journal* commended *Alexander Fleming: Discoverer of Penicillin* as "a good choice for readers looking for a short biography of an interesting scientist."

Gottfried received similar accolades for his young adult biography *Enrico Fermi: Pioneer of the Atomic Age,* a look at one of the scientists who helped to develop the atomic bomb. Todd Morning remarked in *School Library Journal:* "Gottfried is adept at explaining complex principles of physics," as well as the political situation in Italy at the time Fermi decided to emigrate.

Few authors have been willing to tackle the subject of pornography for a young adult audience. It is particularly difficult to write about a topic with which one presumes children have had scant contact. *Pornography: Debating the Issues* is Gottfried's attempt to introduce serious students to the issues surrounding the uses and abuses of pornography throughout history. The author includes a chapter on the definition of pornography and how it differs from culture to culture and from one time period to the next. Carol Fazioli in *School Library Journal* complimented Gottfried for tackling the "thorny subject" but added that the text "gets tangled up in disorganization." Conversely, Anne O'Malley in *Booklist* felt that the title offers "reasonable, balanced tones" and "clear, accessible writing."

Gottfried's other analyses of controversial topics for young adults, including *Gun Control: Public Safety and the Right to Bear Arms* and *Privacy: Individual Right vs. Social Needs,* have been lauded for their balanced presentation of the issues, and critics also noted the books' ample documentation. Similarly successful efforts at objectivity and usefulness to students were noted in Gottfried's *Libya: Desert Land in Conflict.* While *Bulletin of the Center for Children's Books* reviewer Roger Sutton found the coverage of some areas too summarized, he also claimed that Gottfried accomplished the difficult job of placing Libya "within an understandable historical and religious context."

Capital Punishment: The Death Penalty Debate and *The Death Penalty: Justice or Legalized Murder?* challenge readers to choose a side literally in a life-or-death decision. Again Gottfried does not allow his own opinion to intrude in the two texts, but rather presents data about law and history, pictures of the instruments of execution, and primary documents both for and against capital punishment. Hazel Rochman in *Booklist* observed that in *Capital Punishment* Gottfried "does an excellent job of bringing the discussion right up to the present." *School Library Journal* correspondent Kim Harris declared *The Death Penalty* "a competent overview" and felt its presentation to be "well organized."

Few writers have done more to present the Holocaust to young readers than Gottfried. He has written more than a half dozen books on various aspects of the tragedy, from its child victims and its survivors to profiles of the leaders who put the slaughter into action. *Booklist* contributor Gillian Engberg noted that,

taken together, Gottfried's books on Nazi Germany "offer highly readable, comprehensive accounts of the social and political events." In her *Booklist* review of *Children of the Slaughter: Young People of the Holocaust,* Hazel Rochman praised Gottfried's "clear, direct prose" and his ability to "present the history without rhetoric or exploitation." In his *School Library Journal* review of the same title, Jack Forman called the work a "unique and instructive treatent." Considering *Deniers of the Holocaust: Who They Are, What They Do, Why They Do It* in *Booklist,* Hazel Rochman praised the "spacious design, with lots of subheads, photos, and dramatic woodcuts."

Martyrs to Madness: The Victims of the Holocaust covers not only the Nazis' Jewish victims but also the gypsies, homosexuals, handicapped people, and other civilians who were lost to slaughter. In her *School Library Journal* review of the book, Mary R. Hoffmann noted that Gottfried "has put a fascinating spin on the Holocaust" and added that all of the author's Holocaust titles make "fine additions to Holocaust collections." Gillian Engberg in *Booklist* also praised the "highly readable, comprehensive accounts" offered in *Martyrs to Madness.*

In addition to his books on the Holocaust, Gottfried has written a four-volume history of the Soviet Union. The series begins with *The Road to Communism* and continues in *The Stalinist Empire, The Great Fatherland War: The Soviet Union in World War II,* and *The Cold War: The Rise and Fall of the Soviet Union.* Roger Leslie in *Booklist* noted that Gottfried's "historical accounts are accurate, lively, and compelling." Jack Forman in *School Library Journal* likewise concluded that Gottfried's study "untangles the Byzantine complexities of Russian history while remaining true to the facts." In her *School Library Journal* appreciation of *The Stalinist Empire,* Elizabeth Talbot cited the work as "exceptionally well written."

Gottfried continues to present controversial issues in readable books, exploring international issues in *Northern Ireland: Peace in Our Time?* and *The Israelis and Palestinians: Small Steps to Peace,* and important domestic topics in *The 2000 Election, Teen Fathers Today,* and *Homeland Security versus Constitutional Rights.* In a *School Library Journal* review of *Teen Fathers Today,* Nicole M. Marcuccilli observed that Gottfried "discusses frankly the harsh realities of teen fatherhood and the burdens it presents for the future."

School Library Journal correspondent Linda Greengrass called *Northern Ireland: Peace in Our Time?* "a straightforward history of the long-term, religion-based conflict." Students confused about the strange outcome of the 2000 election can find an explanation of George Bush's victory in *The 2000 Election.* Although *School Library Journal* contributor Mary Mueller found the book "superficial" and noted that it "may actually confuse some readers," Ilene Cooper in *Booklist* maintained that "the design of this book is particularly nice."

On one aspect of Gottfried's work many critics seem to agree. They note with regularity, no matter what subject the author tackles, his works make excellent source material for students seeking to do reports, presentations, or beginning studies of history or sociology.

BIOGRAPHICAL AND CRITICAL SOURCES:

PERIODICALS

Booklist, November 15, 1987, p. 568; September 15, 1994, p. 122; February 1, 1997, Hazel Rochman, review of *Capital Punishment: The Death Penalty Debate,* p. 931; April 15, 1997, Anne O'Malley, review of *Pornography: Debating the Issues,* p. 1415; May 15, 1997, Hazel Rochman, review of *James Baldwin: Voice from Harlem,* p. 1569; November 15, 1997, Hazel Rochman, review of *Eleanor Roosevelt: First Lady of the Twentieth Century,* p. 554; December 1, 1997, Hazel Rochman, review of *Alexander Fleming: Discoverer of Penicillin,* p. 621; April 1, 1999, John Peters, review of *Homelessness: Whose Problem Is It?,* p. 1397; December 15, 1999, Shelle Rosenfeld, review of *Police under Fire,* p. 777; April 1, 2000, Roger Leslie, review of *Should Drugs Be Legalized?,* p. 1447; July, 2000, Gillian Engberg, review of *Martyrs to Madness: The Victims of the Holocaust* and *Nazi German: The Face of Tyranny,* p. 2023; May 15, 2001, Hazel Rochman, review of *Children of the Slaughter: Young People of the Holocaust* and *Heroes of the Holocaust,* p. 1741; September 1, 2001, Hazel Rochman, review of *Deniers of the Holocaust: Who They Are, What They Do, Why They Do It,* and *Displaced Persons: The Liberation and Abuse of Holocaust Surivviors,* p. 94; July, 2002, Ilene Cooper, review of *The*

2000 Election, p. 1840; October 15, 2002, Hazel Rochman, review of *The Road to Communism,* p. 398; May 1, 2003, Roger Leslie, review of *The Cold War,* p. 1587.

Bulletin of the Center for Children's Books, May, 1994, Roger Sutton, review of *Libya: Desert Land in Conflict,* p. 287.

Kirkus Reviews, August 1, 1993, p. 1001.

School Library Journal, March, 1988, p. 20; April, 1993, Todd Morning, review of *Enrico Fermi: Pioneer of the Atomic Age,* p. 146; August, 1993, p. 196; April, 1994, pp. 160-161; July, 1997, Carol Fazioli, review of *Pornography,* p. 104; July, 1997, Herman Sutter, review of *James Baldwin,* p. 104; July, 1997, Jo-Anne Weinberg, review of *Capital Punishment,* p. 104; December, 1997, Phyllis Graves, review of *Eleanor Roosevelt,* p. 137; February, 1998, Allison Trent Bernstein, review of *Alexander Fleming,* p. 116; September, 1999, Libby K. White, review of *Homelessness,* p. 233; January, 2000, Ann G. Brouse, review of *Police under Fire,* p. 145; December, 2000, Mary R. Hoffmann, review of *Martrys to Madness,* p. 161; June, 2001, Jack Forman, review of *Children of the Slaughter,* p. 172; August, 2001, Marcia W. Posner, review of *Heroes of the Holocaust,* p. 196; December, 2001, Nicole M. Marcuccilli, review of *Teen Fathers Today,* p. 160; March, 2002, Linda Greengrass, review of *Northern Ireland: Peace in Our Time?,* p. 250; March, 2002, Kim Harris, review of *The Death Penalty: Justice or Legalized Murder?,* p. 250; April, 2002, Mary Mueller, review of *The 2000 Election,* p. 172; November, 2002, Elizabeth Talbot, review of *The Stalinist Empire,* p. 186; November, 2002, Jack Forman, review of *The Road to Communism,* p. 186; June, 2003, Beth Jones, review of *The Cold War,* p. 161; July, 2003, Joyce Adams Burner, review of *Teen Fathers Today,* p. 79.*

*   *   *

GRAFTON, Sue 1940-

PERSONAL: Born April 24, 1940, in Louisville, KY; daughter of Chip Warren (an attorney and writer) and Vivian Boisseau (a high school chemistry teacher; maiden name, Harnsberger) Grafton; married third husband Steven F. Humphrey (a professor of philosophy), October 1, 1978; children: (first marriage) Leslie

Sue Grafton

Flood; (second marriage) Jay Schmidt, Jamie Schmidt. *Education:* University of Louisville, B.A., 1961. *Hobbies and other interests:* Walking, reading, cooking, bridge.

ADDRESSES: Home—Montecito, CA, and Louisville, KY. *Office*—P.O. Box 41447, Santa Barbara, CA 93140. *Agent*—Molly Friedrich, Aaron Priest Agency, 708 Third Ave., 23rd Floor, New York, NY 10017-4103.

CAREER: Screenwriter and author. Has worked as a hospital admissions clerk, cashier, and clerical/medical secretary. Lecturer, Los Angeles City College, Long Beach, CA, City College, University of Dayton, Dayton, OH, and various writers' conferences, including Los Angeles Valley College, Albuquerque, Smithsonian Campus on the Mall, Antioch Writers Conference, Yellow Springs, OH, and Midwest Writers Conference, Canton, OH.

MEMBER: Writers Guild of America (West), Mystery Writers of America (president, 1994-95), Private Eye Writers of America (president, 1989-90).

AWARDS, HONORS: Christopher Award, 1979, for teleplay *Walking through the Fire;* Mysterious Stranger Award, Cloak and Clue Society, 1982-83, for *A Is for Alibi;* Shamus Award for best hardcover private eye novel, Private Eye Writers of America, and Anthony Award for best hardcover mystery, Mystery Readers of America, both 1985, both for *B Is for Burglar;* Macavity Award for best short story, and Anthony Award, both 1986, both for "The Parker Shotgun"; Edgar Award nomination, Mystery Writers of America, 1986, for teleplay *Love on the Run;* Anthony Award, 1987, for *C Is for Corpse;* Doubleday Mystery Guild Award, 1989, for *E Is for Evidence;* American Mystery Award, best short story, 1990, for "A Poison That Leaves No Trace"; Falcon Award for best mystery novel, Maltese Falcon Society of Japan, and Doubleday Mystery Guild Award, both 1990, both for *F Is for Fugitive;* Doubleday Mystery Guild Award, Shamus Award, and Anthony Award, all 1991, all for *G Is for Gumshoe;* Doubleday Mystery Guild Award, and American Mystery Award, both 1992, both for *H Is for Homicide;* Doubleday Mystery Guild Award, 1993, for *I Is for Innocent,* and 1994, for *J Is for Judgment;* Shamus Award, 1995, and Doubleday Mystery Guild Award, 1995, both for *K Is for Killer.*

WRITINGS:

DETECTIVE NOVELS, EXCEPT AS NOTED

Keziah Dane (novel) Macmillan (New York, NY), 1967.

The Lolly-Madonna War (novel; also see below), P. Owen (New York, NY), 1969.

A Is for Alibi (Mystery Guild main selection; also see below), Holt (New York, NY), 1982.

B Is for Burglar (Mystery Guild main selection; also see below), Holt (New York, NY), 1985.

C Is for Corpse (Mystery Guild main selection; also see below), Holt (New York, NY), 1986.

D Is for Deadbeat, Holt (New York, NY), 1987.

E Is for Evidence, Holt (New York, NY), 1988.

F Is for Fugitive, Holt (New York, NY), 1989.

G Is for Gumshoe, Holt (New York, NY), 1990.

H Is for Homicide, Holt (New York, NY), 1991.

I Is for Innocent, Holt (New York, NY), 1992.

(Editor) *Writing Mysteries: A Handbook,* Writer's Digest (Cincinnati, OH), 1992, 2nd edition, 2002.

Kinsey and Me (short stories), Bench Press (Columbia, SC), 1992.

J Is for Judgment, Holt (New York, NY), 1993.

K Is for Killer, Holt (New York, NY), 1994.

L Is for Lawless (Mystery Guild and Literary Guild main selections), Holt (New York, NY), 1995.

M Is for Malice, Holt (New York, NY), 1996.

N Is for Noose, Holt (New York, NY), 1998.

(Editor, with Otto Penzler) *The Best American Mystery Stories 1998,* Houghton Mifflin (Boston, MA), 1998.

O Is for Outlaw, Holt (New York, NY), 1999.

Three Complete Novels ("A" Is for Alibi, "B" Is for Burglar, and "C" Is for Corpse) Wings Books (New York, NY), 1999.

P Is for Peril, Penguin Putnam (New York, NY), 2001.

Q Is for Quarry, Penguin Putnam (New York, NY), 2002.

R Is for Ricochet, Penguin Putnam (New York, NY), 2004.

Contributor of "Kinsey Millhone" short stories to anthologies, including *Mean Streets: The Second Private Eye Writers of America Anthology,* edited by Robert J. Randisi, 1986; *Sisters in Crime,* edited by Marilyn Wallace, 1989; and *A Woman's Eye,* edited by Sara Paretsky and Martin H. Greenburg, 1991. Contributor to periodicals, including *California Review* and *Redbook.* The "Kinsey Millhone" novels have been translated into numerous languages, including Dutch, Russian, Polish, Spanish, and French, and have also been released as audiobooks.

SCREENPLAYS AND TELEPLAYS

(With Rodney Carr-Smith) *Lolly-Madonna XXX* (adapted from Sue Grafton's novel *The Lolly-Madonna War*), Metro-Goldwyn-Mayer, 1973.

Walking through the Fire (adapted from the novel by Laurel Lee), Columbia Broadcasting Corp. (CBS-TV), 1979.

Sex and the Single Parent (adapted from the book by Jane Adams), CBS-TV, 1979.

Nurse (adapted from the book by Peggy Anderson), CBS-TV, 1980.

Mark, I Love You (adapted from the book by Hal Painter), CBS-TV, 1980.

(With husband, Steven F. Humphrey) *Seven Brides for Seven Brothers* (pilot), CBS-TV, 1982.

(With Steven F. Humphrey) *A Caribbean Mystery* (adapted from the novel by Agatha Christie), CBS-TV, 1983.

(With Steven F. Humphrey and Robert Aller) *A Killer in the Family,* American Broadcasting Co. (ABC-TV), 1983.

(With Steven F. Humphrey and Robert Malcolm Young) *Sparkling Cyanide* (adapted from the novel by Agatha Christie), CBS-TV, 1983.

(With Steven F. Humphrey) *Love on the Run,* National Broadcasting Co. (NBC-TV), 1985.

(With Steven F. Humphrey) *Tonight's the Night,* ABC-TV, 1987.

Contributor of scripts to television series, including *Rhoda,* 1975. Story editor with Humphrey for television series *Seven Brides for Seven Brothers,* 1982-83.

SIDELIGHTS: Sue Grafton, according to Andrea Chambers in *People,* "is perhaps the best of the new breed of female mystery writers, who are considered the hottest segment of the market." In her mystery stories featuring California private investigator Kinsey Millhone, Grafton has chosen to feature a heroine rather than the traditional male hero. Nonetheless, as Deirdre Donahue observed in *USA Today,* "Grafton draws on elements of the classic private-eye genre." In Millhone, David Lehman of *Newsweek* told prospective readers, "you'll find a thoroughly up-to-date, feminine version of Philip Marlowe, Raymond Chandler's hard-boiled hero."

The hard-boiled detective story traditionally features a male protagonist and a lot of action—gunplay, bloodshed, and general mayhem. Heroes such as Dashiell Hammett's Sam Spade, Raymond Chandler's Marlowe, and Ross MacDonald's Lew Archer defined masculinity for a generation of readers with their "loner" mentalities and their sensitivity to the profound difference between the mean streets and the normal world. Yet Grafton's Millhone is as popular as any of her precursors, male or female. *New York Times Book Review* contributor Vincent Patrick suggested that the reason behind her popularity is that Millhone is, in fact, a traditional hero: "Chandler's concept of a detective hero was that 'he must be the best man in his world, and a good enough man for any world.' Gender aside, Kinsey [Millhone] fills that prescription perfectly."

Along with Sara Paretsky, Grafton is credited with establishing female detectives in the hard-boiled genre. The two authors introduced their characters, V. I. Warshawski and Kinsey Millhone, within a few months of each other in 1982. "There had been female sleuths in crime fiction before, of course," wrote Josh Rubins in the *New York Times Book Review,* "like the eponymous heroine of the 1910 book *Lady Molly of Scotland Yard,* Miss Marple, Nancy Drew and Amanda Cross's Kate Fansler. There had even been a thoroughly believable homicide cop named Christie Opara (in Dorothy Uhnak's landmark police novels of the 1960's and 70's). . . . However, Kinsey and V. I. were the first women to . . . [bury] the stereotypes about 'lady detectives' and [clear] a path for the dozens of tough-minded, ready-for-anything heroines who have become a major element in the genre."

Other than establishing a heroine in a traditionally male role, Grafton, according to certain critics, has left intact the framework of the hard-boiled detective story. Ed Weiner wrote in the *New York Times Book Review* that neither Grafton nor her peers "have gone so far as to redefine the genre. They play it fairly safe and conventional. But in their work there is thankfully little of the macho posturing and sluggish rogue beef-cake found so often in the male versions, no Hemingwayesque mine-is-bigger-than-yours competitive literary swaggering." *Women's Review of Books* contributor Maureen T. Reddy declared that Grafton's books "implicitly question, and undermine, received wisdom about gender-specific character traits, but are not otherwise feminist." Instead, Weiner explained, "she has successfully replaced the raw, masculine-fantasy brutality and gore of the [Robert] Parkers and [Jonathan] Valins and [Elmore] Leonards with heart-pounding, totally mesmerizing suspense." "Millhone . . . got our attention by crashing the private eyes' stag party," Rubins declared. She's "kept it by building, in fits and starts, [her] own rather lonely, increasingly distinctive worlds."

Grafton has also kept readers and attracted new ones by allowing Millhone to develop throughout her novels. "Grafton, always competent, comes roaring out of the '80s with an expanded vision of her heroine and a willingness to take risks," declared *Chicago Tribune* contributor Kevin Moore in a review of *G Is for Gumshoe.* "People buy and read Grafton's books because they believe in Kinsey Millhone, and want to know what's happening in her life," wrote Dick Adler in a *Chicago Tribune* review of *J Is for Judgment* several years later. "In her ten books [Grafton] has managed . . . to create a deeper, softer, more approachable central character."

But some of the elements in the series remain the same. "Like those Saturday afternoon serials of yore," declared *Washington Post Book World* reviewer Maureen Corrigan, writing about *K Is for Killer,* "many a mystery novel has tied its readers up in knots over some subplot complication and abandoned them on the railroad tracks of anticipation, only to delay rescue till the next installment." Corrigan traced some new complications introduced in the previous volume, *J Is for Judgment* (Millhone, introduced as an orphan in the beginning of the series, turns out to have some distant relatives), and noted that "curious Kinsey fans will fling open *K Is for Killer* . . . and race through its pages only to discover . . . that Kinsey is still mulling over what to do about her relatives." In an earlier example taken from *G Is for Gumshoe,* Millhone moves back into her apartment which had been partly destroyed by a bomb in the previous book. "You know you are deep in the land of fiction," wrote *New York Times Book Review* contributor Alex Kozinski, "when you find a landlord in Southern California willing to rent a newly renovated apartment for $200 a month, particularly to a tenant known to be a target for bombers."

This question of resolution is something that regularly troubles Grafton. The writer once stated that her late father C. W. Grafton (who published three mysteries during his lifetime) was "very passionate about mystery novels, which he wrote at the office in the evenings. . . . At this point, I would love to sit down and talk to him about plotting, which to me is the great 'bug-a-boo' of mystery." In order to bring the plots under control, Grafton told Enid Nemy of the *New York Times,* she keeps a comprehensive notebook containing all the information she has researched on a topic. "Every three or four weeks, I go through it and highlight what interests me," she said. "Then the story emerges, and from that, the angle of attack, who hires Kinsey, what she's hired to do. Sometimes I walk down roads that don't go anywhere." When plot complications held up the publication of *K Is for Killer,* for instance, reported *Wall Street Journal* contributor Tom Nolan, hundreds of readers called their bookstores to complain. Grafton told Nolan, "A bookstore owner in Pasadena called me and said, 'You have no idea what rumors are circulating!'"

In the fourteenth installment in the series, *N Is for Noose,* Millhone leaves her home base of Santa Teresa, California, to investigate circumstances surrounding the death of Sheriff Tom Newquist in Nota Lake, Nevada. Although Newquist apparently died of natural causes, his wife, Selma, suspects the stress of a recent case involving a double homicide was what brought it on. As Millhone seeks the dead Sheriff's missing notebook, she confronts hostile townsfolk and endures a serious beating. Writing in *Library Journal*, Wilda Williams observed that *N Is for Noose* serves up less violence and plot action than the average Millhone caper, with "more emphasis on character" and "an almost melancholic mood." While praising "Grafton's easy-reading prose and her heroine's sharp humor," a *Publishers Weekly* reviewer lodged a similar reaction, complaining of "a slew of plot weaknesses." However, Emily Melton of *Booklist* found *N Is for Noose* to be "one of the best to date in Grafton's supremely popular series." Melton also commented: "Grafton has such a strong following . . . that virtually anything she writes shoots to the top of the best-seller lists. Fortunately, the fame is, by and large, well deserved."

In *O Is for Outlaw* Grafton further develops Millhone's history and character as the private investigator is drawn into a case involving her own past. Dubbed "one of the very best entries in a long-lived and much-loved series" by a *Publishers Weekly* reviewer, the mystery begins with an undelivered letter discovered in an abandoned storage locker. The fourteen-year-old letter concerns Millhone's first ex-husband, Mickey Magruder, a former vice officer once accused of beating a man to death. It contains evidence that might exonerate Mickey of the crime, which not only caused his expulsion from the police force but prompted Millhone to divorce him only months into their marriage. The plot thickens and accelerates as Mickey is shot with Millhone's gun and hospitalized in a coma. Millhone must delve back into the sixties and the Vietnam War to discover Mickey's assailant and determine his own guilt or innocence. "Kinsey is sassier than ever," noted Karen Anderson of *Library Journal*, "the supporting characters are amusingly eccentric, and the mysteries, both past and present, are intriguing." According to Melton, in *O Is for Outlaw* Grafton delivers "a novel of depth and substance that is, in every way, the class of the series."

Entering the new millennium with *P Is for Peril*, Millhone finds herself embroiled in a missing persons case involving a rich doctor, a disgruntled and suspicious ex-wife, Medicare fraud at a nursing home, a confused teenager, and an ex-stripper. Meanwhile, the sleuth has become romantically involved with the twin brother of her office landlord, a man accused of murdering his parents ten years earlier. "As always," remarked Connie Fletcher in *Booklist*, "Grafton gives us a truly complex heroine, marvelous depictions of Southern California architecture and interiors, and a writing style that can make a weed path interesting." Williams gave Grafton "an A for maintaining her series's high standard of excellence."

On her Web site, Grafton shares with fans the evolution of *R is for Ricochet*. Referring to the extensive notes she keeps when writing, she explains: "I'd written the first 15 pages of the manuscript, double-spaced. At that same point in time, I had 100 pages, single-spaced, written in my journal. . . . On January 26, 2004, twenty-three months from the time I began, I completed the manuscript, which was 500 pages, double-spaced. The 9 journals I'd written simultaneously totaled 516 single-spaced pages. Yes, I'm nuts."

"When I decided to do mysteries," Grafton explained to Bruce Taylor in an interview in *Armchair Detective*, "I chose the classic private eye genre because I like playing hardball with the boys. I despise gender-segregated events of any kind." Part of Millhone's appeal lies in Grafton's concept of her character, whom she sees as "a stripped-down version of me," she told Taylor. "She's the person I would have been had I not married young and had children. She'll always be thinner and younger and braver, the lucky so-and-so. Her biography is different, but our sensibilities are identical. At the core, we're the same. . . . Because of Kinsey, I get to lead two lives—hers and mine. Sometimes I'm not sure which I prefer." In a question and answer session on the McDougal Littell Web site, Grafton stated: "I do enjoy being a writer. The truth is, there's nothing I'd rather do with my life, but writing is 'fun' in the same way lifting weights is fun. It's hard and it hurts."

BIOGRAPHICAL AND CRITICAL SOURCES:

BOOKS

Kaufman, Natalie Hevener, and Carol McGinnis Kay, *"G" Is for Grafton: The World of Kinsey Millhone,* Henry Holt (New York, NY), 1997.

PERIODICALS

Armchair Detective, spring, 1988; winter, 1989; fall, 1989, p. 368; spring, 1991, p. 229.

Belles Lettres, summer, 1990.

Booklist, February 15, 1998, Emily Melton, review of *N Is for Noose,* p. 948; June 1, 1999, Emily Melton, review of *O Is for Outlaw,* p. 1742; March 15, 2001, Connie Fletcher, review of *P Is for Peril,* p. 1332.

Chicago Tribune, May 6, 1990, p. 6; May 4, 1992, p. 3; May 4, 1993, p. 3.

English Journal, February, 1992, p. 95.

Globe and Mail (Toronto, Ontario, Canada), June 20, 1987; May 21, 1988.

Kirkus Reviews, March 1, 2001, review of *P Is for Peril,* p. 296.

Library Journal, March 1, 1998, Wilda Williams, review of *N Is for Noose,* p. 127; August 1999, Karen Anderson, review of *O Is for Outlaw,* p. 146; April 15, 2001, Wilda Williams, review of *P Is for Peril,* p. 131.

Los Angeles Times Book Review, August 4, 1985; May 14, 1989; May 12, 1991; October 8, 1995.

Newsweek, June 7, 1982; June 9, 1986.

New Yorker, June 27, 1994.

New York Times, May 8, 1991, p. C19; August 4, 1994, pp. C1, C10.

New York Times Book Review, May 23, 1982; May 1, 1988, pp. 11-12; May 21, 1989, p. 17; May 27, 1990, p. 13; July 28, 1991, p. 8; May 24, 1992, p. 25; May 2, 1993, p. 22; May 1, 1994, p. 24; October 8, 1995, p. 24.

People, July 10, 1989, Andrea Chambers, "Make No Bones about It, Sue Grafton's Detective Heroine Is a Real Pistol," p. 81; May 9, 1994, Lorenzo Carcaterra, review of *K is for Killer,* p. 29.

Publishers Weekly, February 16, 1998, review of *N Is for Noose,* p. 206; April 5, 1985, p. 66; March 14, 1986, p. 104; August 30, 1999, review of *O Is for Outlaw,* p. 55; May 21, 2001, review of *P Is for Peril,* p. 84.

Reason, December, 1994, p. 52.

Spectator, September 27, 1969.

USA Today, July 27, Deirdre Donahue, 1989.

Wall Street Journal, August 29, 1995, Tom Nolan, p. A12.

Washington Post Book World, May 18, 1986, pp. 8, 13; June 21, 1987; May 19, 1991; May 24, 1992, p. 6; April 17, 1994.

Women's Review of Books, December, 1986, p. 8; July, 1989.

ONLINE

McDougal Littell Web site, http://www.mcdougallittell.com/ (June 6, 2001), "Your Conversation with Sue Grafton."

Sue Grafton Web site, http://www.suegrafton.com/ (August 4, 2004).*

*   *   *

GRAY, Chris Hables 1953-

PERSONAL: Born August 23, 1953, in Bishop, CA; son of George (a transportation engineer and manager) and Benita (a mass transit consultant; maiden name, Hables) Gray; married Jane Lovett Wilson (a sociologist), March 3, 1986; children: Corey Alexander Grayson, Zackary Hables Grayson. *Ethnicity:* "Twenty different ethnicities—Californian, in other words." *Education:* Stanford University, B.A., 1975; University of California—Santa Cruz, Ph.D., 1991. *Politics:* "Anti-Authoritarian." *Religion:* "Biophile." *Hobbies and other interests:* California, soccer, football, frisbee, basketball, gardening, travel and camping, long walks ("with or without our dogs"), personal rituals, nonviolent direct action, reading, owls, "trying to keep up with the marvelous discoveries of science."

ADDRESSES: Home—606 Fifth Ave., Great Falls, MT 59401. *Office*—Department of Computer Science, University of Great Falls, 1301 20th St. S, Great Falls, MT 59405. *E-mail*—cgray@ugf.edu.

CAREER: South Africa Catalyst Project, research director and traveling organizer, 1979-81; University of California—Santa Cruz, lecturer, 1989-91; Oregon State University, Corvallis, adjunct assistant professor of history, 1992-96; University of Great Falls, Great Falls, MT, associate professor of computer science and cultural studies of science and technology, 1996—, Web master, 1996—. Zetetic Software, Inc., consultant, project developer, and technical writer, 1987-90; Square One Software, Inc., lead writer and consultant, 1991-93; Hewlett-Packard, Corvallis, writer and consultant at Inkjet printer cartridge factory, 1994-95; Argentina Autonomista Project, cofounder, 2002. Goddard College, professor of interdisciplinary studies, 1994—; Masaryk University, guest professor and

Eisenhower fellow, 1995; Union Institute and University, faculty member, 2000—; guest speaker at other institutions in the United States and abroad, including Bates College, Brown University, Danish Institute of International Affairs, State University of New York—Buffalo, and Bogazici University. Participant in national and international conferences; guest on numerous media programs; consultant on military technology for the television series *White Heat* and *The Cyborg Commeth,* both British Broadcasting Corp. Member of civic action groups; coach for youth soccer teams; Cascade County Guardian Ad Litem Program, board member, 1997-99. Formerly worked as a security guard, mover, painter, legal clerk, woodworker, secretary, child-care aide, gardener, cook, mechanic, saw-mill hand, insulator, and carpenter.

MEMBER: Association for the Advancement of Computing in Education, American Studies Association, Computer Professionals for Social Responsibility (chair of Weapons and Peace Working Group, 1999—), Society for the History of Technology, Society for the Social Studies of Science, History of Science Society, Cultural Studies of Science and Technology Research Group.

AWARDS, HONORS: Grants from Silicon Valley Research Group, 1986, and Institute on Global Conflict and Cooperation, 1987-88; first prize, Esalen Revisioning Philosophy Essay Contest, 1989; fellow, Department of Space History, Smithsonian Institution, 1990, and National Endowment for the Humanities; humanities fellow, Oregon State University, 1992-94; fellowship in aerospace history, National Aeronautics and Space Administration and American Historical Association, 1993-94; research achievement awards, University of Great Falls, 1997, 2002.

WRITINGS:

Power-Learning: Developing Effective Study Skills, Educational Operating Systems (Merced, CA), 1992.
(Contributing editor) *The New Columbia Encyclopedia,* 5th edition, Columbia University Press (New York, NY), 1993.
(Editor, with Heidi Figueroa-Sarriera and Steven Mentor) *The Cyborg Handbook,* Routledge (New York, NY), 1995.

(Editor) *Technohistory: Using the History of American Technology in Interdisciplinary Research,* Krieger (Malabar, FL), 1996.
Postmodern War: The New Politics of Conflict, Guilford Press (New York, NY), 1997.
Cyborg Citizen: Politics in the Posthuman Age, Routledge (New York, NY), 2001.

Also author or editor of several software manuals, guides for computer training programs, and other technical writing. Contributor to books, including *Cyborg Worlds: Programming the Military Information Society,* Columbia University Press (New York, NY), 1989; *Prosthetic Territories: Politics and Culture,* edited by Mark Driscoll and Gabriel Baum, Westview Press (Boulder, CO), 1995; *Directions and Implications of Advanced Computing 1900,* Volume 3, edited by D. Schuler, Ablex (New York, NY), 1997; *Menfred Clynes: A Festschrift,* edited by Martha Mills, 1999; and *The Viet Nam War and Postmodernity,* edited by Michael Bibby, Burning Cities Press (Tucson, AZ), 2000; author of entries in encyclopedias. General coeditor of "Technologies" book series, Continuum Publishing (New York, NY), 2000—. Author of about a dozen short stories and an unpublished novel. Contributor of articles and reviews to periodicals, including *Black Rose, Science and Technology Studies, AI and Society: Journal of Human and Machine Intelligence, Nomad: Interdisciplinary Journal of the Humanities, Arts, and Sciences, Science-Fiction Studies, Research in Philosophy and Technology, Studies in the History and Philosophy of Science, Cultural Anthropology, Cultural Values,* and *Journal of Men's Studies.* Coeditor of special issue, *Journal of Urban and Cultural Studies,* 1991.

The book *Postmodern War: The New Politics of Conflict* has been translated into Chinese and Turkish. *Cyborg Citizen: Politics in the Posthuman Age* was translated into German.

WORK IN PROGRESS: Terror and Peace: Information, Globalization, and Power, for Routledge (New York, NY); *NASA and the Cyborg: Human-Machine Integration and Space Exploration,* Continuum Publishing (New York, NY).

SIDELIGHTS: Chris Hables Gray's books inhabit the space where scientific and cultural writings overlap. As editor of *The Cyborg Handbook,* he garnered praise for gathering together an unusual and fruitful collection of writings by scientists, cultural critics, and fiction writers on the topic of cyborg technology and its increasing role in both the physical and metaphorical realms of postmodern life. In *Postmodern War* Gray relies upon his knowledge of the ways in which the American military utilizes technology to help change the experience of war by altering what it requires of soldiers. He also points out the greater ease of warring—and thus the greater likelihood of war—in the postmodern era.

The Cyborg Handbook brings together works of both fiction and nonfiction in an amalgam that some critics found both refreshing and unique. From a wide variety of contributors, including classic science-fiction writer Philip K. Dick, postmodernist cultural critic Donna Haraway, and space scientists Manfred Clynes and Nathan Kline, the pieces in Gray's collection share a fascination with the ways in which humanity is changing or is capable of changing through technological augmentation of the human body. Thus, the book contains "the sort of material that one might expect writers on the history, sociology, anthropology, or cultural politics of technology to use as primary research material," observed Matthew Fuller in the *American Book Review*. According to Edward Rothstein, writing in the *New York Times,* many items included focus "on how these beings [cyborgs] break down distinctions between the genders, transform our conception of the body and undo any supposed restrictions on humanity made by nature and culture," and added that "the study of cyborgs ends up saying quite a bit about how culture and society are being interpreted." Though John Alderman, writing for the online publication *Hotwired*, commented "Too many of . . . [the] essays give the popular imagination as much weight as fact, which comes across as refreshing openmindedness or confusing pomposity, depending on the writer," he praised essays and interviews from such contributors as Jacke E. Steele, Motokazu Hori, and Patricia Cowings, and wrote, "This vast collection includes some engaging essays, the best of them from members of the 'hands-on' scientific fields."

Gray brings his knowledge of the ever-expanding role of technology in human, and particularly in military, operations to an investigation of war in *Postmodern War: The New Politics of Conflict.* He traces the changes in United States military strategy since World War II, which, culminating in the Gulf War of the early 1990s, have led to an ever-greater dependence on the technological augmentation of the soldier. This dependence has resulted in a change of the war experience for participants to something altogether different from the face-to-face conflicts of the past. For example, David Keymer, who reviewed *Postmodern War* in *Library Journal,* paraphrased Gray's characterization of the Gulf War as a conflict wherein "advanced technology allowed the Allies to kill their adversaries without personal contact and without empathy." Although a *Publishers Weekly* contributor noted that Gray may have limited his audience to those with "a good command of cyber-age and deconstructionist vocabularies," the reviewer added that even readers skeptical of the author's fundamentally antiwar stance will find in *Postmodern War* "an incentive to expand their definitions of reality."

Gray once told *CA:* "One of the strangest things about being a published author is being reviewed. Some reviews are infuriating, such as one of the *Cyborg Handbook* that claimed that cyborgs were old hat (when the age of cyborgs has just begun!). Book review editors could at least find someone who can understand the book to review it. Would they find someone who can't understand physics to review a physics book?

"A bad review can still be satisfying, such as the attack on *Postmodern War* in the *Proceedings of the Naval Institute* that while complaining about the 'academic gobbleygook' did present the central arguments of the book clearly enough to attract the notice of the many people in the military that I know agree with my opinion.

"Many reviews have been excellent, such as John Alderman in the 'webzine' *Hotwired* and Edward Rothstein in the *New York Times* on the *Cyborg Handbook* and Francis Beer on *Postmodern War* in the *American Political Science Review*. Perhaps my favorite is a review by Shaar Murray in the British paper the *Independent* that reviewed *Postmodern War* along with a novel about future war in a very insightful essay called 'Virtual Wars with Actual Corpses.' I also loved Mark Dery's very favorable comments on *Cyborg Citizen: Politics in the Post-human Age* in *Wired*.

"I guess the reviews that are most aggravating are by people who I sincerely doubt ever read the book at all.

There are many mixed reviews which, on close reading, don't say anything about the book that couldn't be deduced from the cover blurb.

"The very best reviews are usually from actual readers or people who have heard me on the radio or seen me on C-SPAN talking about the book and plan to buy it. I've received dozens of very kind letters from folks like these, and sometimes even gifts, such as a book of paintings by the artist Nabil Kanso who quite correctly felt that we shared the same vision about contemporary war. For dealing with bad reviews I think of these readers, and I've collected the bad reviews on my Web site where I reply to them in detail, often with the response letters that I couldn't get printed where the review was published. At last authors have a public way of responding to unfairness, incompetence, and downright stupidity in reviews."

BIOGRAPHICAL AND CRITICAL SOURCES:

PERIODICALS

American Book Review, June-July, 1996, Matthew Fuller, review of *The Cyborg Handbook,* p. 28.

American Political Science Review, December, 1997, Francis Beer, review of *Postmodern War: The New Politics of Conflict,* pp. 1005-1006.

Choice, April 1, 1997; October, 2001, J. Beidler, review of *Cyborg Citizen: Politics in the Posthuman Age,* p. 343.

Independent, July 19, 1997, Shaar Murray, review of *Postmodern War,* p. 8.

Library Journal, September 1, 1995, p. 204; June 1, 1997, David Keymer, review of *Postmodern War,* pp. 112, 114.

New Scientist, November 11, 1995, p. 43.

New York Review of Books, October 9, 1997, pp. 10-13.

New York Times, January 8, 1996, Edward Rothstein, review of *The Cyborg Handbook,* p. 39.

Proceedings of the U.S. Naval Institute, September, 1997, review of *Postmodern War,* p. 118.

Publishers Weekly, April 28, 1997, review of *Postmodern War,* p. 62.

San Francisco Bay Guardian, January 24, 1996, p. 24.

Sight and Sound, November, 1995, p. 37.

Wired, May, 2001, Mark Dery, review of *Cyborg Citizen.*

ONLINE

Cyborg Citizen by Chris Hables Gray, http://www.routledge-ny.com/cyborgcitizen/ (March 6, 2004).

Hotwired, http://www.hotwired.com/ (February, 1996), John Alderman, review of *The Cyborg Handbook.*

*   *   *

GREENFELD, Karl Taro 1964-

PERSONAL: Born 1964, in Japan.

ADDRESSES: Agent—c/o Author Mail, Random House, 1745 Broadway, New York, NY 10019.

CAREER: Journalist and editor. Deputy editor of *Time Asia* and has worked as a managing editor for the Japanese monthly, *Tokyo Journal,* and as Tokyo correspondent for the *Nation.*

WRITINGS:

Speed Tribes: Days and Nights with Japan's Next Generation, HarperCollins (New York, NY), 1994.

Standard Deviations: Growing Up and Coming Down in the New Asia, Villard (New York, NY), 2002.

SIDELIGHTS: Born to an American father and a Japanese mother in Japan, Karl Taro Greenfeld was raised in the United States. He returned at the age of twenty-three to Japan, where he worked for a journal for expatriate Americans and as Tokyo correspondent for the American weekly the *Nation.* Greenfeld's 1994 nonfiction book, *Speed Tribes: Days and Nights with Japan's Next Generation,* presents a series of profiles of Japanese youth during the country's period of great economic prosperity in the late 1980s. Greenfeld interviewed members of motorcycle gangs, workers in the pornography industry, nightclub frequenters, overworked students, and drug dealers. "These are entertaining characters, familiar to those who have spent time in Japan," commented Alan Poul in a review of *Speed Tribes* for the *New York Times Book Review.*

Critics praised Greenfeld's finely detailed portraits and ability to capture distinct cultural types in *Speed Tribes*. A *Publishers Weekly* reviewer found a discrepancy between the fast-paced and glamorous lifestyles Greenfeld portrays and the seamy reality that comes through. "These 'speed tribes' . . . come across as depressing and sordid, rather than 'dazzling' or rich," said the *Publishers Weekly* reviewer. And critic Poul noted that Greenfeld doesn't highlight the differences between his characters' lives and that of similar American types: "Greenfeld's attempt to forge a cohesive portrait of a hip Japanese Generation X rings hollow because he rarely addresses the cultural currents that not only make these kids what they are, but also set them apart from their Western counterparts." Nonetheless, wrote Poul, "*Speed Tribes* is an entertaining read."

Standard Deviations: Growing Up and Coming Down in the New Asia is Greenfeld's memoir of his wild times running in an elite fast lane around Asia. A *Publishers Weekly* reviewer commented, "He offers unique glimpses into Asia and apparently frank self-revelation," but he "never fleshes out either theme." A *Kirkus Reviews* contributor described the book as "an exhausting journey through one man's ego as all the drugs and girls in Asia gradually wear him out." Elsa Gaztambide commented in her review for *Booklist* that Greenfeld "unabashedly shares the experiences of a youth that reach far beyond the average person's wildest dreams."

BIOGRAPHICAL AND CRITICAL SOURCES:

PERIODICALS

Booklist, September 1, 1994, review of *Speed Tribes: Days and Nights with Japan's Next Generation,* p. 8; June 1, 2002, Elsa Gaztambide, review of *Standard Deviations: Growing Up and Coming Down in the New Asia,* p. 1672.
Book World, November 20, 1994, review of *Speed Tribes,* p. 4.
Entertainment Weekly, October 21, 1994, review of *Speed Tribes,* p. 62.
Kirkus Reviews, July 1, 1994, review of *Speed Tribes,* p. 901; May 1, 2002, review of *Standard Deviations,* p. 636.
Library Journal, September 1, 1994, review of *Speed Tribes,* p. 202.
Los Angeles Times Book Review, January 22, 1995, review of *Speed Tribes,* p. 12.
Nation, December 28, 1992, pp. 807-808, 810-812.
New York Times Book Review, October 16, 1994, review of *Speed Tribes,* p. 36.
Publishers Weekly, July 11, 1994, review of *Speed Tribes,* pp. 69-70; May 13, 2002, review of *Standard Deviations,* p. 59.
Time, November 28, 1994, review of *Speed Tribes,* p. 87.
Times Educational Supplement, April 28, 1995, review of *Speed Tribes,* p. 13.
Village Voice Literary Supplement, September, 1994, review of *Speed Tribes,* p. 33.*

H

HALBERSTAM, David 1934-

PERSONAL: Born April 10, 1934, in New York, NY; son of Charles A. (a surgeon) and Blanche (a teacher; maiden name, Levy) Halberstam; married; wife's name Elzbieta (an actress), June 13, 1965 (divorced, 1977); married Jean Sandness Butler, June 29, 1979; children: Julia. *Education:* Harvard University, B.A., 1955. *Hobbies and other interests:* Reading detective and suspense novels, watching late movies on television, fishing.

ADDRESSES: Home—New York, NY, and Nantucket, MA. *Agent*—Robert Solomon, 488 Madison Ave. New York, NY 10019.

CAREER: Daily Times Leader, West Point, MS, reporter, 1955-56; *Nashville Tennessean,* Nashville, TN, reporter, 1956-60; *New York Times,* New York, NY, staff writer, 1960-67, foreign correspondent in the Congo (now Zaire), 1961-62, Vietnam, 1962-63, Warsaw, Poland, 1965, and Paris, France, 1966; *Harper's,* New York, NY, contributing editor, 1967-71.

MEMBER: Society of American Historians, Adlai Stevenson Institute of International Affairs (fellow).

AWARDS, HONORS: Page One Award, Newspaper Guild of New York, 1962; George Polk Memorial Award, Long Island University, 1963; Louis M. Lyons Award, 1964; Pulitzer Prize, Columbia University, 1964, for international reporting; Overseas Press Club Award, 1973; Political Book Award, 1986, for *The*

David Halbertstam

Reckoning; American Book Award, Before Columbus Foundation, 1988, for *The Reckoning;* Elijah Lovejoy Award, Colby College, 1997; Bob Considine Award from St. Bonaventure College, Robert Kennedy Award, and Robert Melcher Book Award from Unitarian Church, all 1999, all for *The Children;* various honorary degrees.

WRITINGS:

FICTION

The Noblest Roman, Houghton Mifflin (Boston, MA), 1961.
(Editor) *Stephen Crane, Great Stories of Heroism and Adventure,* Platt (New York, NY), 1967.
One Very Hot Day (novel), Houghton Mifflin (Boston, MA), 1968.

NONFICTION

The Making of a Quagmire: America and Vietnam During the Kennedy Era, Random House (New York, NY), 1965.
The Unfinished Odyssey of Robert Kennedy, Random House (New York, NY), 1969.
Ho, Random House (New York, NY), 1971.
The Best and the Brightest, Random House (New York, NY), 1972, reprinted with a new foreword by John McCain, Modern Library (New York, NY), 2001.
The Powers That Be, Knopf (New York, NY), 1979.
The Breaks of the Game, Knopf (New York, NY), 1981.
On a Very Hot Day, Warner Books (New York, NY), 1984.
The Amateurs: The Story of Four Young Men and Their Quest for an Olympic Gold Medal, Morrow (New York, NY), 1985.
The Reckoning, Morrow (New York, NY), 1986.
The Summer of '49, Morrow (New York, NY), 1989.
The Next Century, Morrow (New York, NY), 1991.
(Editor) *The Best American Sports Writing, 1991,* Houghton Mifflin (Boston, MA), 1991.
The Fifties, Villard (New York, NY), 1993.
October 1964, Villard (New York, NY), 1994.
(Editor) *The Kansas Century: One Hundred Years of Championship Jayhawk Basketball,* Andrews & McMeel (Kansas City, MO), 1997.
The Children, Random House (New York, NY), 1998.
(Editor) *The Best American Sports Writing of the Century,* Houghton Mifflin (Boston, MA), 1999.
Playing for Keeps: Michael Jordan and the World He Made, Random House (New York, NY), 1999.
War in a Time of Peace: Bush, Clinton, and the Generals, Scribner (New York, NY), 2001.
(Author of text) *New York September 11: As Seen by Magnum Photographers,* PowerHouse Books (New York, NY), 2001.

Firehouse, Hyperion (New York, NY), 2002.
Teammates, Hyperion (New York, NY), 2003.
(Editor) *Defining a Nation: Our America and the Sources of Its Strength,* National Geographic (Washington, DC), 2003.

Contributor of articles to magazines, including *Atlantic Monthly, Esquire, Harper's Bazaar,* and *McCall's.* Columnist for ESPN.com.

WORK IN PROGRESS: A book on the Korean War and a book about the 1958 baseball championship series between the New York Giants and the Baltimore Colts, both for Hyperion.

SIDELIGHTS: David Halberstam's best-selling books are characterized by voluminous research and an anecdotal, novelistic narrative style. Although the subjects he tackles have ranged from the Japanese auto industry to rowers competing to enter the Olympic Games, Halberstam has consistently been attracted by the question of power and to those individuals who are able to influence events in the United States. Three of his best-known books, *The Best and the Brightest, The Powers That Be,* and *The Reckoning,* have been described collectively as a trilogy on power in America.

Beginning his career as a war correspondent and political reporter, Halberstam was assigned to South Vietnam by the *New York Times* in 1962, and his controversial articles often questioned the official version of events in the Vietnam War. In 1964 he was awarded a Pulitzer Prize for international reporting, and after that, he continued to examine the war in a series of books and in many magazine articles. In *The Best and the Brightest,* Halberstam traces American entanglement in Vietnam and criticizes the leaders of the Kennedy and Johnson administrations for this involvement; he also offers biographical studies of the presidents themselves, and of McGeorge Bundy, then-Secretary of Defense Robert S. McNamara, then-Secretary of State Dean Rusk, economist Walt W. Rostow, General Maxwell Taylor, and General William C. Westmoreland.

In *The Powers That Be,* Halberstam makes the case that the media helped shape recent American politics and society through depictions of the histories of four news reporting giants: *Time,* Columbia Broadcasting System (CBS), the *Washington Post,* and the *Los Angeles Times.* Former CBS correspondent Daniel Schorr, reviewing the book for the *Progressive,* thought Halberstam showed himself to be squarely on the side of the reporters. Schorr observed, "The price of compelling narrative [in this book] is acceptance of the author's perspective. Halberstam's own experience and feeling inevitably color his story." In an article for *Time,* Paul Gray also commented on Halberstam's inclusion of personal feeling, remarking that Halberstam, despite his prodigious research, "listens selectively, and at times relentlessly forces his material in the direction he wants it to go. . . . [His] picture is educational but also highly interpretative."

In the *New Statesman* Godfrey Hodgson expressed disappointment that Halberstam restricted himself to only four opinion-makers. Despite this, Hodgson found Halberstam to be quite readable. "The sheer energy of his infatuation with what he calls power (and I would call influence) carries you along with him," wrote Hodgson. Although questioning the lack of analysis and explanation "of how these empires of the written and the spoken word are held together," the critic admitted, "I lay back, let the tide carry me down the river, took no notice of the mistakes floating past like flotsam, or of the interesting landscapes we were ignoring on the bank, and found myself enjoying it."

In *The Breaks of the Game* and *The Amateurs,* Halberstam turns his investigative reporting and characteristic narrative style to the world of sports. *The Breaks of the Game* examines the gritty world of professional basketball, and *The Amateurs* looks at top-level rowing among the four men's single sculls who competed for the right to represent the United States in the 1984 Olympics. Halberstam told a *New York Times Book Review* interviewer that he was upset by the televised 1984 Winter Olympics because of the "hype" involved. He explained that he selected sculling as a subject precisely because the athletes had no expectations of fame or remuneration.

David Guy, writing in the *Chicago Tribune Book World,* characterized *The Amateurs* this way: "Halberstam has written a penetrating, fascinating and remarkably suspenseful narrative about one of the last truly non-professional sports in the country, amateur rowing, and in particular about rowing's most prestigious event, the single scull." *New York Times* reviewer

Christopher Lehmann-Haupt noted that the subject of *The Amateurs* is "the psychology of competitive rowing. It's about the need to drive oneself through various levels of pain if one wants to win at sculling." As in some of his other work, Halberstam enlivens the story with biographical information, in this case offering the biographies of the four competitors. Critiquing the book for the *Washington Post Book World,* John Jerome noted, "In his usual fashion Halberstam interviews everyone, triangulates every opinion, gets incisive insights and hard judgments even from the oarsmen's mothers. The result is pure reporting on a level undreamt of elsewhere in sports."

With *The Reckoning,* the final volume in what many view as his trilogy on power in America, Halberstam discusses the history of two automobile makers—Ford in the United States and Nissan in Japan—from World War II to the mid-1980s. Halberstam selected the number-two auto company in each country as his subjects because this approach was journalistically more manageable than writing about the largest and most powerful automakers. John F. Baker, who interviewed Halberstam for *Publishers Weekly,* described the book as "a study of American arrogance and blindness and Japanese self-sacrifice and tenacity—and [it] is up-to-date enough to register the recent entry on the auto scene of Korea as an unlikely rival to Japan for the rich American market." Halberstam told Baker: "I like to think the book has value as an alarm clock, telling Americans there's something very out of sync with their society." *Washington Monthly* contributor James Fallows voiced a similar view: "*The Reckoning*'s importance is in helping to shake us out of our complacency."

The Reckoning "does more than scold, however," noted James Flanigan in the *Los Angeles Times Book Review.* He explained, "One of the book's strengths is its reporting on Japanese recent history, on how a devastated nation became an economic power." In the *New York Times,* Peter T. Kilborn related that "Halberstam spent five years at this enterprise, and it shows. For all that has been written of the two countries' industrial competition, much of his work is new and telling." Famed economist John Kenneth Galbraith, writing in the *New York Times Book Review,* called Halberstam's research "formidable," and pointed out that the author persists beyond the exterior of the story: "He seeks out executives, workers and trade unionists and tells of their lives, aspirations, achievements, disappointments, failures and, especially as regards the managers at Ford, of their unending, vanity-inspired and functionally damaging bureaucratic jealousies and infighting."

Some reviewers, though, criticized Halberstam for the unattributed stories that he relates in making his case about the two automakers. Although Fallows praised *The Reckoning* as "a thorough and engrossing case study" and gave the book a largely positive review, he also thought that the revealing anecdotes and mini-biographies at the heart of Halberstam's work are judgments rather than "truth" and should be presented as such. Fallows likewise noted that "it would be fairer to give the reader some idea of the deduction, interpretation, and yes, guesswork that lie behind the stories." In Chicago's *Tribune Books,* Peter Collier registered a similar objection: "A nonfiction novelist at heart, Halberstam is somewhat cavalier about documentation. He includes a list of the people he interviewed for the book, but doesn't use footnotes. This is not a pedantic quibble: In a place like Detroit, where everyone has a private agenda and speaks with a sharpened tongue, it is valuable to know who is saying what about whom." But some commentators emphasized that Halberstam's writing style and the scope of his projects lend themselves to taking a distinct critical stance, whether it be to praise or to blame. Nevertheless, *Washington Post Book World* contributor Robert Kuttner declared, "Like Halberstam's other books, this one is a tour de force of reporting, synthesis and storytelling. Admirers of Halberstam will recognize the familiar formula; his critics will be freshly annoyed by it."

With *The Summer of '49* Halberstam once again took up the subject of professional sports, this time major league baseball. He portrays the 1949 American League pennant race, in which the Boston Red Sox suddenly overtook their arch-rivals, the New York Yankees, only to lose the championship in the final game of the season. The story is told through accounts of two opposing baseball heroes: Joe DiMaggio of the Yankees and Ted Williams of the Red Sox. Justin Kaplan, writing in the *New York Times Book Review,* described the book as "vigorous, altogether engrossing, loaded with dugout insight and wonderful vignettes." In addition to chronicling the pennant race, Halberstam identifies this season as a turning point in baseball—the time in which sport gave way to show business. As Thomas H. Kean noted in the *Wall Street*

Journal, "In the days following World War II, baseball was, as Mr. Halberstam says, 'not so much a sport but a blinding national myth.' It was the way for the children of immigrants to escape and to excel." In summing up Halberstam's achievement, *Time* magazine's Martha Duffy wrote, "This new work may be his most appealing, mainly because it is quirky and informal, and the author leaves his moral fervor in the bat rack."

In *The Next Century,* a slim volume that examines America since Vietnam, Halberstam makes a case he has made before: Americans have ignored growing problems such as weakening educational standards and a decline in economic productivity to the detriment of the nation's future. Some critics have pointed out that the book's title is a misnomer since Halberstam examines the twentieth century in great detail, but never quite predicts what the next century will hold. Dan Tucker, reviewing the book in the *Chicago Tribune,* called *The Next Century* "an attempt to sort out the main forces at work on American society and the world, and to see in what directions they seem to be pushing us."

The *New York Times'* Lehmann-Haupt stated, "As one prominent Japanese he [Halberstam] talked to sees it, what America needs is some sort of shock to jar it 'out of its complacency, an event on the order of *Sputnik.'* The Next Century* is far from shock therapy. But by addressing readers intelligently instead of bludgeoning them with dire statistics, it catches the ear." Several critics praised Halberstam for resisting the temptation to blame Japan for its success. Bill Bradley, then a U.S. senator, commented in the *New York Times Book Review* that *The Next Century* "is one of the few books to recognize that the challenge facing the United States is not finding a scapegoat for our economic blunders but making the most of our physical and mental capabilities, improving our productivity in an open, democratic structure."

Halberstam examines the political, historical, and sociological perspective of the decade from 1950 to 1960 in his book *The Fifties.* He discusses events that run the gamut from the politics of the Eisenhower years to the success of the television series *I Love Lucy.* In a review for the *Washington Post,* Stephen Birmingham called *The Fifties* "absorbing" and credited Halberstam with "customary balance and thoroughness." But John Podhoretz, writing in the

Wall Street Journal, pointed out that Halberstam's anecdotes about the suburbanization of America and the rise of McDonald's are familiar ones, and he faulted Halberstam for cataloguing events rather than analyzing why the memory of this particular decade holds such appeal for Americans. Podhoretz wrote, "Mr. Halberstam is so intent on avoiding controversy that he cannot and will not take sides in the debate on the meaning of the decade he has written 800 pages about." *Chicago Tribune* reviewer Herbert Gold voiced a similar objection, but remarked favorably on those sections of the book that investigate less well-known events. Observed Gold: "Chapter 25, about the overthrow of Mossadegh and the installation of the Shah of Iran, has some bite because the story is less familiar. It's a nice and nasty interlude in which we find the aged Winston Churchill congratulating Kermit Roosevelt of the CIA on a well-managed coup."

Halberstam's *October 1964* finds the author returning to a memorable baseball season, this time the 1964 season in which the St. Louis Cardinals defeated the New York Yankees to win the World Series. Through colorful vignettes of the two teams' unusually articulate and influential players, Halberstam draws parallels between the events of the 1964 season and the groundbreaking social changes that were affecting every aspect of American culture at the time, from race relations to the contentious Vietnam War to the growing power of the media. In particular, Halberstam focuses on the racial issues that came into play during the season. While the Yankees had long been a dominant force, their aging, mostly white roster stood in stark contrast to that of the upstart Cardinals. Under the direction of cantankerous owner August Busch, the beer magnate, the Cardinals roster included many young black stars: Bob Gibson, Lou Brock, and Curt Flood. Halberstam points out that the integrated Cardinals team was free of racial strife; its victory in the World Series symbolized the sport's transformation from one focused on power and high-scoring innings to one featuring speed and aggressive base running.

Writing in the *Los Angeles Times Book Review,* Allen Barra remarked that "the overview afforded by *October 1964* is splendid." *Washington Post Book World* contributor Frank Mankiewicz commented that "Halberstam describes the final game of the 1964 series accurately and so dramatically, I almost thought I had forgotten the ending." James E. B. Breslin, however, critiquing for the *New York Times Book Review,*

compared *October 1964* unfavorably to *The Summer of '49,* noting that Halberstam "does not have the intimate emotional connection to the 1964 season that he did to 1949" and as a result "takes only a half-hearted swing at social history," instead concentrating on "individuals who transcend that history." Nevertheless, Breslin termed the book "engaging."

After writing *The Children,* an award-winning study of young people involved in the civil rights movement in the early 1960s, Halberstam returned to the subject of sports with *Playing for Keeps: Michael Jordan and the World He Made,* a biography of the man whom some observers consider the greatest pro basketball player ever. "Air Jordan" played for the Chicago Bulls from 1984 to 1999—with a brief detour to attempt a baseball career—and led the Bulls to multiple NBA championships. (He came out of retirement in 2001 to play with the Washington Wizards.) Halberstam chronicles the athlete's success on the basketball court, something due, the author says, not only to Jordan's great natural ability but also to his disciplined efforts; he also explores Jordan's rise as a media star with high-profile commercial endorsements, and seeks to explain Jordan's significance for basketball as a whole.

In the words of *New Statesman* contributor John Dugdale, "Jordan was a deus ex machina for a sport in a slump when he entered the professional ranks in 1984—so miraculously answering the dreams of hard-boiled businessmen that they could scarcely believe their luck; but also, David Halberstam suggests, himself benefitting as commodity and salesman by arriving just when the smart new NBA commissioner David Stern was revamping basketball's image." Jordan's brilliant playing, good looks, gentlemanly manner, and hard-to-resist charm—evident in his commercials for Nike shoes, McDonald's restaurants, and other consumer products—gave him a sterling public persona, but Halberstam shows there is more to the story, Dugdale and other critics observed. "Jordan emerges simple in essence and ambiguous in context," remarked L. S. Klepp in *Entertainment Weekly.* "The simple essence is his relentless will to be better than anyone else, to win and win with a vengeance. . . . But for all his devotion to the game, Jordan had a lot to do with the way it veered into tawdry entertainment." Klepp explained that Halberstam's "underlying theme" is that Jordan's role in popularizing pro basketball "didn't corrupt him but did corrupt the sport," and that his successors are unlikely to handle themselves with such grace as he did. Not that Jordan lacks faults: Dugdale reported, "His evident intelligence never extended to political issues"—he was "bewildered" by protests against Nike's use of child labor in developing countries.

Several other reviewers pointed out Halberstam's willingness to deal with all aspects, admirable and less so, of Jordan's character. "Jordan, as drawn by Halberstam, is generous, loyal, thoughtful but flawed," related Ira Berkow in the *New York Times Book Review,* adding that "he is, Halberstam underscores, no Jackie Robinson, Muhammad Ali or Paul Robeson in the civil rights arena." Berkow praised Halberstam by saying, "He skillfully skirts hagiography and writes as credible reporter." *USA Today* writer Erik Brady noted that Halberstam's treatment of Jordan "is mostly admiring, though not entirely," and that "Jordan emerges in all his complexity, as do his lessers." Brady termed *Playing for Keeps* "a meticulously reported book," depicting Jordan and his teammates, coaches, and other associates "in revealing, delicious detail." Dugdale called the book "as ambitious and omnicompetent as its subject" and "much richer than a conventional sports biography." Berkow criticized the book for "an occasional excess of information regarding peripheral aspects of Jordan's life and lapses in which the language is less than carefully or thriftily wrought." He concluded, though, that "Halberstam overall has succeeded in lending perspective to the world Michael Jordan both made and inherited, as well as in portraying Michael Jordan the man and not the icon."

Halberstam left sports for international affairs with *War in a Time of Peace: Bush, Clinton, and the Generals.* This book examines U.S. foreign policy in the 1990s, as pursued by presidents George Bush and Bill Clinton. Following the breakup of the Soviet Union, the United States faced no opposing superpower but dealt with small wars around the world—in Iraq, Bosnia, Somalia, and other places. It was sometimes slow to intervene in these conflicts, though, and unsure of what constituted U.S. interests after the end of the cold war. *War in a Time of Peace* is designed as a companion to *The Best and the Brightest.* Many of the political and military leaders of the 1990s—of whom Halberstam provides detailed portrayals in the newer work—had been young adults during the Vietnam War; some had served in it, and it was a haunting memory.

"Still, Halberstam is smart enough to avoid concluding that the memory of Vietnam drove the major military decisions of the Clinton administration or, as it turned out in some cases, the nondecisions," observed Jane Perlez in the *New York Times Book Review. New York Times* reviewer Richard Bernstein noted that this memory "was a major element in the almost paralyzing caution" of Clinton and his advisers, "but it was far from the only factor. Among the others was the simple fact that George Bush's striking victory against Iraq in the gulf war did not give him much political lift at home, and for the Clinton administration, political lift at home was all important. Meanwhile, the calamity of the Somalia operation, which involved the loss of 18 soldiers in a grisly mob attack in 1993, cast a shadow over all future operations." Halberstam portrays the United States as "groping for a strategy, a vision of what it should do in a turbulent and unsettled post-cold war world to stabilize it at low cost," related *Nation* contributor Dusko Doder, and finally discovering, during the 1999 Kosovo conflict, "that things in the world could be changed by a minimum, casualty-free application of American air power."

Doder was not wholly convinced by Halberstam's endorsement of this means of warfare. "In making the argument for the use of air power, Halberstam presents a fuzzy account of the collapse of the Bosnian Serbs in 1995," Doder wrote, also maintaining that the book lacks "Halberstam's bone-deep knowledge and refined critical powers that gave his Vietnam book a firm spine of political argument. He does not know the Balkans; as a result, he brings little knowledge or insight gained firsthand." Doder added that in light of the terrorist attacks on the United States on September 11, 2001—which occurred after *War in a Time of Peace* went to press—and the subsequent war in Afghanistan, "the book's seductive concept that a war can be won by air power alone is now being put to a real test. . . . Given the short American political attention span, the air bombardments in the Balkans could be presented as victories even though they resolved none of the problems on the ground, where U.S. troops continue doing constabulary duty to keep peace in Bosnia and Kosovo. The war against terrorism is something of an entirely different magnitude, and it will engage our attention for a long time." To some other reviewers, though, Halberstam's book retained great relevance after September 11. "Now that foreign affairs have come home to the United States in the most crushing of ways," commented Perlez, "are [Americans] ready to read an account of foreign policy and its makers by one of the most astute writers in the trade? If they want to learn about the past decade, they should. If they want to think seriously about the future, they must." Bernstein granted that "the situation in Afghanistan is different, but it would be difficult to imagine a better, more detailed and informed account of how the country has handled its recent crises than Mr. Halberstam's new book." After the September 11 attacks, Halberstam came out with two books on the tragedy: *New York September 11: As Seen by Magnum Photographers,* a book of photos from the event accompanied by text by Halberstam, and *Firehouse,* which is the story of the valiant firefighters who died trying to save lives at the World Trade Center.

In *Defining a Nation: Our America and the Sources of Its Strengths,* Halberstam enlists thirty-six leading historians and writers to ask why our country "for all its flaws, for all the things I dissent from, remains so powerful a beacon to so many of the less favored of the world." He introduces essays by contributors like Walter Cronkite, Louis Auchincloss, Joan Didion, Anna Quindlen, and Anthony Lewis that define key issues and events that have shaped the American character, from Paul Revere's ride to Margaret Sanger's campaign for birth control. Halberstam explains that he chose immigration, innovation, and egalitarianism as his themes and focuses on the country's last 100 years because until the eve of World War I, America "was still growing in its body." Each contributor illuminates an aspect of America's uniqueness: for Richard Reeves it's the changes wrought by the GI Bill, for Julia Reed it's regional cooking, for Nick Kotz it's farming, for Bill Geist it's cars or, as he puts it, "freedom machines." Halberstam pens essays on inventor Henry Ford and the Civil Rights Movement, two of his favorite subjects.

Whether Halberstam is writing about basketball's Air Jordan or the U.S. military's air power, his books are often best-sellers, even when they receive mixed reviews from critics. His many readers seem to agree with James Fallows's judgment of *The Reckoning:* "Because the book is so richly detailed, so complete in its coverage, and so readable page-by-page and anecdote-by-anecdote, the complaints about it, which will come, need to take second place to its virtues."

BIOGRAPHICAL AND CRITICAL SOURCES:

BOOKS

Downie, Leonard, Jr., *The New Muckrakers: An Inside Look at America's Investigative Reporters,* New Republic Books (Washington, DC), 1976.

Dygert, James H., *The Investigative Journalist: Folk Heroes of a New Era,* Prentice-Hall (Englewood Cliffs, NJ), 1976.
Prochnau, William W., *Once upon a Distant War,* Times Books (New York, NY), 1995.

PERIODICALS

Business Week, October 8, 2001, "Not Halberstam's Best or Brightest," p. 18.
Chicago Tribune, September 27, 1987; February 25, 1991; June 20, 1993.
Chicago Tribune Book World, May 6, 1979; November 15, 1981; July 14, 1985.
Commentary, June, 1999, Joseph Epstein, "He Flew through the Air," p. 46; January, 2002, Jacob Heilbrunn, review of *War in a Time of Peace: Bush, Clinton, and the Generals,* p. 58.
Entertainment Weekly, February 5, 1999, L. S. Klepp, "The Air up There," p. 62.
Foreign Affairs, November-December, 2001, Michael Hirsh, "America Adrift: Writing the History of the Post Cold Wars," p. 158.
Globe & Mail (Toronto, Ontario, Canada), December 13, 1986; February 16, 1991, p. C7.
Library Journal, October 1, 2001, James R. Holmes, review of *War in a Time of Peace,* p. 124.
Los Angeles Times Book Review, November 23, 1986, pp. 1, 13; March 31, 1991, p. 6; August 21, 1994, p. 4.
Nation, November 26, 2001, Dusko Doder, "Air Power Politics," p. 22.
National Review, November 5, 2001, Andrew J. Bacevich, "Fog of Wars," p. 62.
New Republic, December 3, 2001, Robert Kagan, "How We Unlearned the Art of War: When America Blinked," p. 29.
New Statesman, May 25, 1973; October 5, 1979; April 3, 2000, John Dugdale, "Fateful Tango," p. 58.
Newsweek, November 20, 1972; April 30, 1979; April 17, 1989.
New York Review of Books, January 25, 1973.
New York Times, April 25, 1979; June 17, 1979; July 18, 1985; October 20, 1986; April 18, 1987; February 11, 1991, p. C14; August 11, 1994, p. C18; January 19, 1999, Michiko Kakutani, "When He Shot, He Scored: Jordan the Man and Athlete," p. E1; October 10, 2001, Richard Bernstein, "A New and Cautious Age in American Intervention," p. E8.

New York Times Book Review, November 12, 1972; April 22, 1979; June 17, 1979; January 10, 1982; August 11, 1985; October 26, 1986, pp. 1, 57-58; May 7, 1989; February 17, 1991, p. 9; August 14, 1994, p. 9; January 31, 1999, Ira Berkow, "Looking Over Jordan," p. 11; September 30, 2001, Jane Perlez, "The 90's Wars," p. 8.

Progressive, January, 1973; July, 1979.

Publishers Weekly, December 11, 1978; October 17, 1986, pp. 44-45; February 14, 1994.

Time, April 30, 1979; November 2, 1981; July 29, 1985; May 22, 1989.

Tribune Books (Chicago, IL), October 5, 1986, pp. 1, 3; April 2, 1989.

USA Today, December 2, 1999, Erik Brady, "*Keeps Pumps Fresh Air into Jordan Profile.*"

Wall Street Journal, June 26, 1989; June 23, 1993.

Washington Monthly, April, 1987, pp. 39-45; September, 2001, Nicholas Thompson, review of *War in a Time of Peace,* p. 41.

Washington Post, May 9, 1979; June 7, 1979; October 31, 1986.

Washington Post Book World, November 12, 1972; April 22, 1979; November 15, 1981; June 30, 1985, pp. 1, 8; October 19, 1986, pp. 1, 11; March 3, 1991, p. 11-12; May 23, 1993; August 21, 1994, p. 1.*

*   *   *

HAMMICK, Georgina 1939-

PERSONAL: Born May 24, 1939, in Hampshire, England; daughter of George Douglas (an army officer) and Patricia (a housewife; maiden name, Marsh) Heyman; married Charles C. W. Hammick, October 24, 1961 (divorced, 1983); children: Thomas, Kate, Rose. *Ethnicity:* British. *Education:* Attended Academie Julian, Paris, 1956-57; attended Salisbury School of Art, 1957-58. *Politics:* Social democrat. *Religion:* Anglican. *Hobbies and other interests:* Gardening, wild life (especially birds), walking.

ADDRESSES: Home—Bridgewalk House, Brixton Deverill, Warminster, Wiltshire BA12 7EJ, England. *Agent*—Rachel Calder, Sayle Literary Agency, Bickerton House 25-27 Bickerton Rd., London N19 5JT, England.

CAREER: Teacher of English and art, 1959-61; worked at Hammicks Bookshops Ltd., beginning in 1968, became director, 1970-80; tutor in creative writing and writer-in-school, 1980—. Served on panels of Literature Southern Arts, Greater London Arts, and English PEN.

MEMBER: Writers Guild of Great Britain, Authors Lending and Copyright Society, National Trust, English PEN, Royal Society of Literature.

AWARDS, HONORS: Shortlisted for Whitbread Award for first novel, 1996; Royal Society of Literature fellow, 2001; Society of Authors' Travel Scholarship.

WRITINGS:

(With Angus Nicolson, Valerie Owen, and others) *A Poetry Quintet,* Gollancz (London, England), 1976.

People for Lunch (short stories), Methuen (London, England), 1987.

Spoilt, Chatto & Windus (London, England), 1992.

(Editor) *The Virago Book of Love & Loss: Stories of the Heart,* Virago Press (London, England), 1992.

The Arizona Game, Chatto & Windus (London, England), 1996.

Green Man Running, Chatto & Windus (London, England), 2002.

Contributor of short stories to anthologies, including *Best of Fiction Magazine, Best Short Stories, 1987, Best Short Stories, 1988,* and *Best Short Stories from Stand,* and in magazines, including *Fiction, Stand, Listener, Critical Quarterly,* and *Woman's Journal.*

Author of garden column in *Books.*

SIDELIGHTS: Georgina Hammick's first two books of short stories, *People for Lunch* and *Spoilt,* are what her "considerable reputation rests upon," according to the *Reader's Guide to Twentieth-Century Writers,* which also described Hammmick's stories as "distinguished by unobtrusive craftsmanship, and the quest for the exact work."

Debra West-Maciaszek of *Studies in Short Fiction* praised Hammick for her choice of pieces in the anthology *Love & Loss: Stories of the Heart* that do not reflect "Harlequin romances, but writing by women that is powerful, tight and multidimensional." A reviewer for *Publishers Weekly* described it as a "solid, durable anthology."

Hammick's first novel, *The Arizona Game,* earned praise from *Richmond Review* contributor Sara Rance for fulfilling the "promise of her short stories." *Daily Telegraph* writer Abigail Willis also praised Hammick for having produced in *Green Man Running* "a shrewd, tender look at human contrariness and the cowardly things we sometimes do to feel better about ourselves." Jessica Mann of the *Sunday Telegraph* commented on Hammick's "originality and wit," but also remarked that "her undeniable brilliance seems diluted in a full-length novel."

Hammick once told *CA:* "Authors who have influenced my writing include George Eliot, Virginia Woolf, Katherine Mansfield, Anton Chekhov, Elizabeth Bowen, Elizabeth Bishop, Elizabeth Taylor (the writer, not the actress!), Raymond Carver, Alice Munro, Ellen Gilchrist, and John Cheever. My working habits are slow. I am constantly revising drafts—five or six for each story. My advice to students is to read and to keep reading."

BIOGRAPHICAL AND CRITICAL SOURCES:

BOOKS

Parker, Peter, editor, *A Reader's Guide to Twentieth-Century Writers,* Oxford University Press (New York, NY), 1996, pp. 303-304.

PERIODICALS

Daily Telegraph (London, England), February 16, 2002, Abigail Willis, review of *Green Man Running.*
Publishers Weekly, August 31, 1992, review of *The Virago Book of Love & Loss: Stories of the Heart,* p. 65.
Spectator (London, England), July 11, 1992, Candida Crewe, review of *Spoilt,* p. 32; August 17, 1996, Anita Brookner, review of *The Arizona Game,* p. 25.
Studies in Short Fiction, Debra L. West-Maciaszek, review of *The Virago Book of Love & Loss,* p. 517.

Sunday Observer (London, England), February 10, 2002, Justine Ettler, review of *Green Man Running.*
Sunday Telegraph (London, England), February 17, 2002, Jessica Mann, review of *Green Man Running.*
Sunday Times (London, England), review of *Green Man Running,* p. 296.
Times Literary Supplement, July 24, 1992, Abigail Levene, review of *Spoilt,* p. 21; December 4, 1992, Ana Nicholls, review of *The Virago Book of Love & Loss,* p. 24; March 1, 2002, Sarah Curtis, review of *Green Man Running,* p. 23.

ONLINE

Richmond Review Online, http://www.richmondreview. co.uk/ (February 8, 2003), Sara Rance, review of *The Arizona Game.*

*   *   *

HARRIS, Lynn 1969-

PERSONAL: Born February 3, 1969, in Boston, MA; daughter of James (a professor of linguistics, now retired) and Florence (an educational writer); married Rabbi David Adelson, 2003. *Ethnicity:* "Caucasian." *Education:* Yale University, B.A, 1990. *Hobbies and other interests:* Playing ice hockey.

ADDRESSES: Home—Brooklyn, NY. *Office*—Just Friends Productions, P.O. Box 150214, Brooklyn, NY 11215. *E-mail*—lynn@breakupgirl.net.

CAREER: Journalist, author, comedian, and commentator. Performer in New York, NY, at comedy clubs and literary readings. Columnist for *Glamour,* contributor to *Salon.com, New York Times, GQ, New York Observer,* and other publications. Member of Brooklyn Blades (women's hockey team).

WRITINGS:

(With Larry Berger) *Tray Gourmet: Be Your Own Chef in the College Cafeteria,* illustrations by Chris Kalb, Lake Isle Press, 1992.

(With J. D. Heiman) *MTV's "Singled Out" Guide to Dating*, Pocket Books (New York, NY), 1996.

He Loved Me, He Loves Me Not: A Guide to Fudge, Fury, Free Time, and Life beyond the Breakup, illustrations by Chris Kalb, Avon (New York, NY), 1996.

Breakup Girl to the Rescue!: A Superhero's Guide to Love . . . and Lack Thereof, Little, Brown (Boston, MA), 2000.

Miss Media, IUniverse (Lincoln, NE), 2004.

Contributor of articles to periodicals, including *Glamour*, *Salon.com*, *GQ*, *New York Times*, and the *New York Observer*.

SIDELIGHTS: Lynn Harris is a comic performer and writer who is known for her humorous observations about male-female relationships. Her writings include two volumes published in 1996: *MTV's "Singled Out" Guide to Dating*, on which she collaborated with J. D. Heiman, and *He Loved Me, He Loves Me Not: A Guide to Fudge, Fury, Free Time, and Life beyond the Breakup*, a humorous self-help book for women trying to survive the end of a relationship. The latter title inspired Harris's alter ego, a cartoon character named "Breakup Girl," who "dons a red cape and matching baseball cap to fend off bad relationships, mend broken ones and help get your stuff back," to quote *Milwaukee Journal Sentinel* contributor Christopher Borrelli.

Harris and illustrator Christopher Kalb not only created Breakup Girl, they also gave her maximum exposure through her own Web site and a book titled *Breakup Girl to the Rescue!: A Superhero's Guide to Love . . . or Lack Thereof*. Breakup Girl's advice—part commonsense wisdom from Harris herself, part suggestions from a professional psychotherapist—is dispensed in comic panels and straight question-and-answer format. Harris's aim is to ease the inevitable suffering young men and women endure when they end relationships. In the *Boston Herald*, Robin Vaughan had this to say about Breakup Girl: "If her persona is a bit kooky, her style of advice is sensible, human and often hilarious."

Harris told the *Los Angeles Times* that she gets some of her stand-up comedy ideas from the letters Breakup Girl receives. Harris has also been through breakups of her own and knows they are more than just fodder for laughs. She said: "No matter how strong we are,

no matter what level of power or stature we achieve in society, we are still—for better or worse—ruled by our relationships. Bending steel bars—that's impressive. But mending broken hearts? That's power! The heart rules us . . . but Breakup Girl rules the heart."

BIOGRAPHICAL AND CRITICAL SOURCES:

PERIODICALS

Booklist, August, 2000, Nancy Spillman, review of *Breakup Girl to the Rescue!: A Superhero's Guide to Love . . . or Lack Thereof*, p. 2162.

Boston Herald, August 25, 2000, Robin Vaughan, "Girl's Fans Break Up Laughing," p. S18.

Entertainment Weekly, August 2, 1996, Nikki Amdur, review of *He Loved Me, He Loves Me Not*, p. 54.

Library Journal, March 1, 2000, Pamela A. Matthews, review of *Breakup Girl to the Rescue!*, p. 111.

Los Angeles Times, February 12, 1999, Erika Milvy, "Feeling Broken Up?: Breakup Girl to the Rescue," p. 6.

Milwaukee Journal Sentinel, May 18, 2000, Christopher Borrelli, "Popular Breakup Girl Site on Web Soothes, Advises Solace-Seekers," p. 4.

People, February 14, 2000, Samantha Miller, "Online: Siteseeing on the Net," p. 23.

ONLINE

Breakup Girl.com, http://www.breakupgirl.com/ (November 6, 2003)

Cybergirl, http://wwwcybergirl.com/ (February 6, 2003), "Meet Lynn Harris."

*   *   *

HEGI, Ursula 1946-

PERSONAL: Born May 23, 1946, in Düsseldorf, West Germany; came to the United States in 1965, naturalized citizen, 1970; daughter of Heinrich and Johanna (Maas) Koch; married Ernest Hegi (a management consultant), October 21, 1967 (divorced, 1984); companion to Gordon Gagliano (an architect); children: Eric, Adam. *Education:* University of New Hampshire, B.A., 1978, M.A., 1979.

Ursula Hegi

ADDRESSES: Home—Nine Mile Falls, WA 99026. *Agent*—c/o Author Mail, Simon & Schuster, 1230 Avenue of the Americas, New York, NY 10020.

CAREER: University of New Hampshire, Durham, lecturer in English, beginning 1978; currently professor of fiction writing, Eastern Washington University. Participates in writing conferences; gives poetry and fiction readings. Serves on the board of National Book Critics Circle.

MEMBER: Associated Writing Programs.

AWARDS, HONORS: Nominee, PEN/Faulkner Award, 1994, for *Stones from the River.*

WRITINGS:

Intrusions (novel), Viking (New York, NY), 1981.
Unearned Pleasures and Other Stories, University of Idaho Press (Moscow, ID), 1988.
Floating in My Mother's Palm (novel), Poseidon Press (New York, NY), 1990.
Stones from the River, Poseidon Press (New York, NY), 1994.

Salt Dancers, Simon & Schuster (New York, NY), 1995.
Tearing the Silence: Being German in America, Simon & Schuster (New York, NY), 1997.
The Vision of Emma Blau, Simon & Schuster (New York, NY), 2000.
Hotel of the Saints: Stories, Simon & Schuster (New York, NY), 2001.
Trudi & Pia, Atheneum Books for Young Readers (New York, NY), 2003.
Sacred Time, Simon & Schuster (New York, NY), 2004.

Contributor to magazines, including *McCall's, Feminist Studies, Ms., Blue Buildings, Bradford Review,* and *Kayak.*

ADAPTATIONS: The Vision of Emma Blau was adapted for audio by Simon & Schuster Audio.

SIDELIGHTS: Ursula Hegi was born in Düsseldorf, Germany, in 1946, less than a year after the end of World War II. She immigrated to the United States at the age of eighteen, married, and raised two sons before beginning studies at the University of New Hampshire. In short stories, novels, and nonfiction, Hegi rehearses the pain of internal shame—shame that is the product not of what one has done but of what one is. Hegi's characters are, like herself, German Americans born in the immediate aftermath of World War II and surrounded by people directly or indirectly implicated in wartime atrocities who steadfastly refuse to speak about the war. Her first novel, *Intrusions,* is the author's only attempt to overlay a story with humor and a modernist technique. *Floating in My Mother's Palm,* her second novel, essentially tells the author's own story of growing up in the first generation after World War II, cushioned from knowledge of the part her parents and countrymen played in the atrocities of that war by their perfect silence on the subject but nonetheless attuned to the guilt and self-hatred she sees in the adults around her.

Reading more like a collection of interconnected stories than a traditional novel, *Floating in My Mother's Palm* is set in the fictional German town of Bergdorf, a place Hegi has returned to several times in her fiction. The interwoven lives of the villagers are the stuff of these stories, which "glow with the luminosity of Impressionist paintings," commented Sybil Steinberg in *Publishers Weekly.*

Among the secondary characters in *Floating in My Mother's Palm* is Trudi Montag, the town librarian, a dwarf who seems to know everyone's secrets. Trudi became the central character in Hegi's next novel, *Stones from the River,* a highly celebrated treatment of life in a German town just before and during the rise of Hitler. Because Trudi is a dwarf, the townspeople fail to treat her like a person and end up spilling their secrets in front of her as though she weren't there. During the war, Trudi is able to hide several Jews, in part because of this invisibility. Reviewers were quick to draw comparisons between Hegi's dwarf and another famous fictional dwarf living through the Nazi era in Germany, that created by Günter Grass in *The Tin Drum.* "For both authors [Hegi and Grass]," noted Victoria J. Barnett in the *Christian Century,* "the Third Reich is part of a continuum (for Hegi, of silence; for Grass, of moral chaos) that begins long before 1933 and is not broken after 1945. Further, they contend that the failure to deal honestly with the past ensures the continuance of moral corruption." Thus, the importance of telling stories, of Trudi's stories, whatever their partiality or intent, lies in breaking the silence. "Telling a story and living a life—this compelling novel makes us see how little difference there is between them," observed Bill Ott in *Booklist.* Likewise, *New York Times* contributor Suzanne Ruta remarked: "In [Trudi's] progress from malicious gossip to serene artist, she hints at the ambiguous roots of the writer's vocation."

Stones from the River earned a nomination for the PEN/Faulkner Award and was chosen for *Oprah's* talk show reading club. The novel was quickly followed by *Salt Dancers,* set in the author's adopted home of Washington State, where a forty-one-year-old woman decides to confront her abusive father in the hope of healing old wounds that might cause her to abuse her own unborn child. *Christian Century* contributor Sondra B. Willobee viewed *Salt Dancers* as a recovery novel, one in which the protagonist essentially travels the road from childhood injury through understanding to recovery. "Julia is distinguished from the heroines of other recovery novels by her awareness of her own cruelty and her willingness to understand the roots of her parents' pain," Willobee observed. Like Hegi's other protagonists, Julia learns the importance of moving out of the silence of memories and into the realm of stories. Returning home to confront her father, she realizes that she had forgotten a myriad of good times in her childhood, and along with new insights, she gains renewed relationships with her father, her estranged brother, and with the mother who had abandoned her years before.

For John Skow, who reviewed *Salt Dancers* for *Time,* Hegi's 1995 novel is too programmatic, too closely aligned to the recovery model, to be successful as fiction. The novel's conclusion is especially flawed, according to Skow: "This slack stuff is soap opera, and even a writer as gifted as Hegi can't dress it up as anything else." For other reviewers, Hegi's skills as a writer allowed her to overcome any flaws in her plot. *Booklist* reviewer Margaret Flanagan averred: "In achingly beautiful prose that exacts a huge emotional toll, the author at once shatters and rebuilds the myth of the family unit." Similarly, a contributor to *Publishers Weekly* compared *Salt Dancers* favorably with Hegi's *Stones from the River* and *Floating in My Mother's Palm,* concluding: "There is both poignancy and suspense in Julia's journey through her past, and the surprises she encounters in herself as well as others lead to a healing resolution that has the open-ended feel of real life." And for Abby Frucht, who reviewed *Salt Dancers* for the *New York Times,* Hegi's novel compared favorably with other contemporary accounts of childhood abuse reckoned in adult terms by writers such as Kaye Gibbons, Dorothy Allison, and Mona Simpson: "Perhaps it is the peculiar authority of the narrative voice in Ursula Hegi's latest novel—its refusal either to sentimentalize or sensationalize, its insistence on undulating intuitively through the various part of the story—that makes *Salt Dancers* seem fresh."

Hegi turned to nonfiction with *Tearing the Silence: On Being German in America.* The book is based on the author's interviews with more than two hundred people who, like her, were born in Germany during or just after World War II and later immigrated to the United States. *Tearing the Silence* offers representative discourses on such *verboten* topics as racial prejudice and what these German Americans knew about their parents' involvement with Nazism. "The stories differ strikingly, but for the most part they share a common element: shame for the sins of their fathers," observed Sally Eckhoff for *Salon.com.* Although a *Publishers Weekly* reviewer proclaimed, "These are powerful portraits of survivors of Hitler's legacy," *Nation* contributor Amei Wallach complained that in choosing to write nonfiction, Hegi forfeits her best tools: she is "a novelist who knows perfectly how to tune nuance, charge scenes and beguile language. But at the very moment that she has chosen to write about the subject closest to her, her own story, she abandons what she's best at, on the wrongheaded assumption that fact is more convincing that fiction." Other critics felt differently, however. For example, Kay Meredith Dusheck contended in *Library Journal:* "This singular work is an important addition to a greater understanding of the Holocaust."

In *The Vision of Emma Blau,* Hegi returns to fiction and the fictional world of Burgdorf, Germany, with an epic story of a family of German immigrants whose lives are ruined by the obsession of one of its members. Near the turn of the twentieth century, Stefan Blau leaves his home town of Burgdorf to come to the East Coast of the United States. After arriving, he has a vision of a young girl dancing in a courtyard, and resolves to make that vision a reality by building the Wasserburg, a luxury hotel set on the banks of a lake in New Hampshire. His singular focus on attaining that goal leads him to neglect his family. After the death of his first two wives in childbirth, Stefan returns to Burgdorf to find a third wife. He returns to New Hampshire with Helene Montag, aunt of Trudie Montag, the librarian in *Stones from the River,* who appears briefly in *Floating in My Mother's Palm.* "This book started in my head long before I wrote *Stones,*" Hegi explained to an interviewer for *Publishers Weekly.* "I started it right after *Floating,* and when *Stones* crowded it aside, I had already begun to think about this boy who runs away from Germany to the United States."

Critical response to *The Vision of Emma Blau* was generally positive. In a review in the *Atlantic,* Phoebe-Lou Adams counted among the assets of the novel "a large cast of convincing Blaus, tenants, relatives back in Germany, and Winnipesaukee [New Hampshire] locals." Hegi's account of the family of German Americans in the 1950s was also remarked upon. "In *The Vision of Emma Blau,* [Hegi] tells a story whose scope is an entire century, one filled with insight into a family legacy of secrets, the difficulties of assimilation, intergenerational misunderstanding and half-truths grown unmanageable over time," observed Valerie Ryan in the *Seattle Times.* A contributor to *Publishers Weekly* similarly acknowledged "Hegi's gift for depicting family dynamics and sexual relationships, including the concealed sorrows and tensions that motivate behavior," adding, "but it is her larger perspective of a family's cultural roots that grants her novel distinction."

In *Sacred Time,* Hegi again shows her penchant for and ability to portray the complex dynamics of a large family. In this novel, she leaves Germany for the United States, following—for more than fifty years—the lives of a turbulent and chaotic yet charming Italian-American family living in the Bronx, New York. A reviewer for *Publishers Weekly* described the opening as "boisterously funny," but pointed out that the subsequent family tragedy creates a "moving if occasionally manipulative" novel. Beth E. Anderson, reviewing *Sacred Time* for *Library Journal,* commented that "Hegi puts her readers smack in the center of the psychological morass" while creating quirky characters that provide the reader with comic relief in what would otherwise be an unremittingly grim story. Caledonia Kearns, reviewing the book for the *Boston Globe,* wrote, "It is to Hegi's credit that she has created characters whose intensity and love for one another ring true."

BIOGRAPHICAL AND CRITICAL SOURCES:

BOOKS

Bauermeister, Erica, *Five Hundred Great Books by Women,* Penguin (New York, NY), 1994.

PERIODICALS

Atlantic, March, 2000, Phoebe-Lou Adams, review of *The Vision of Emma Blau,* p. 116.

Booklist, March 15, 1994, Bill Ott, review of *Stones from the River,* p. 1327; August, 1995, Margaret Flanagan, review of *Salt Dancers,* p. 1929; July, 1997, Mary Carroll, review of *Tearing the Silence,* p. 1793; November 15, 1999, Grace Fill, review of *The Vision of Emma Blau,* p. 580.

Boston Globe, May 23, 2004, Caledonia Kearns, review of *Sacred Time,* section L, p. 9.

Christian Century, August 10, 1994, Victoria J. Barnett, review of *Stones from the River,* p. 755; April 24, 1996, Sondra B. Willobee, review of *Salt Dancers,* p. 464.

Chronicle of Higher Education, December 7, 1994, Peter Monaghan, "A Writer Confronts Her German Ghosts," p. A6.

Entertainment Weekly, March 21, 1997, Lisa Schwarzbaum, review of *Stones from the River,* p. 65.

Glamour, March, 1994, Laura Mathews, review of *Stones from the River,* p. 156.

Kirkus Reviews, May 1, 1997, review of *Tearing the Silence.*

Library Journal, March 1, 1990, Mary Soete, review of *Floating in My Mother's Palm,* p. 116; January, 1994, Michael T. O'Pecko, review of *Stones from the River,* p. 160; July, 1995, Patricia Ross, review of *Salt Dancers,* p. 120; June 1, 1997, Kay Meredith Dusheck, review of *Tearing the Silence,* p. 122; December, 1999, Eleanor J. Bader, review of *The Vision of Emma Blau,* p. 186; December 2003, Beth E. Anderson, review of *Sacred Time,* p. 166.

Mother Jones, July-August, 1990, Georgia Brown, review of *Floating in My Mother's Palm,* p. 56.

Nation, July 28, 1997, Amei Wallach, review of *Tearing the Silence,* p. 31.

Newsweek, April 18, 1994, Laura Shapiro, review of *Stones from the River,* p. 63.

New York Times, March 18, 1990, Edward Hoagland, review of *Floating in My Mother's Palm,* section 7, p. 5; March 20, 1994, Suzanne Ruta, "The Secrets of a Small German Town"; August 27, 1995, Abby Frucht, "Like a Motherless Child"; August 17, 1997, Walter Reich, "Guilty Long Ago"; February 13, 2000, Diana Postlethwaite, review of *The Vision of Emma Blau.*

New York Times Book Review, March 20, 1994, Jon Elsen, "What Wasn't Taught in School," p. 2.

Publishers Weekly, January 5, 1990, Sybil Steinberg, review of *Floating in My Mother's Palm,* p. 62; January 17, 1994, review of *Stones from the River,* p. 400; March 14, 1994, Kitty Harmon, interview with Hegi, p. 52; May 22, 1995, review of *Salt Dancers,* p. 46; June 16, 1997, review of *Tearing the Silence,* p. 55; November 29, 1999, review of *The Vision of Emma Blau,* p. 51; October 6, 2003, review of *Sacred Time,* p. 57.

Seattle Times, February 6, 2000, Valerie Ryan, "An Insightful *Vision*: Ursula Hegi Continues to Write about Matters German."

Time, August 21, 1995, John Skow, review of *Salt Dancers,* p. 68.

USA Today, December 2, 1999, Jacqueline Blais, "*Stones* Breaks the Grip of Silence."

Wall Street Journal, April 8, 1997, Amy Gamerman, "Behind the Scenes at Oprah's Book Club," p. A20; February 4, 2000, Gabriella Stern, review of *The Vision of Emma Blau,* p. W8.*

ONLINE

Barnes & Noble.com, http://www.barnesandnoble.com/ "Meet the Writers—Ursula Hegi," (August 20, 2004).

Salon.com, http://www.salon.com/ (June 30, 1997), Sally Eckhoff, review of *Tearing the Silence.**

*   *   *

HERNANDEZ, Gilbert 1957(?)-

PERSONAL: Born c. 1957; married; wife's name Carol.

ADDRESSES: Home—Woodland Hills, CA. *Agent*—c/o Fantagraphics Books, 7563 Lake City Way, Seattle, WA 98115.

CAREER: Graphic novelist, 1982—. Worked as a janitor.

WRITINGS:

Heartbreak Soup, Fantagraphics Books (Westlake Village, CA), 1987.

(With Jaime Hernandez, Mario Hernandez, and Dean Motter) *The Return of Mister X,* Warner (New York, NY), 1987.

The Reticent Heart and Other Stories, Fantagraphics Books (Seattle, WA), 1988.

Birdland, Eros Books (Seattle, WA), 1992.

Poison River, Fantagraphics Books (Seattle, WA), 1994.

Yeah!, Fantagraphics Books (Seattle, WA), 1999.

Fear of Comics, Fantagraphics books (Seattle, WA), 2000.

Luba in America, Fantagraphics Books (Seattle, WA), 2001.

Palomar: The Heartbreak Soup Stories, Fantagraphics Books (Seattle, WA), 2003.

Cocreator of and contributor to the adult comic book "Love and Rockets." Hernandez's work has been translated into six languages.

SIDELIGHTS: The work of graphic novelist Gilbert Hernandez has evoked comparisons to Latin American magical realist writer Gabriel Garcia Marquez and to Midwestern American humorist Garrison Keillor. Critics have praised the serious, provocative textual content and skilled artistry of Hernandez's work. "Gilbert's protagonists always seem to be moving in a sort of exodus through panoramas of history. The stories have exhaustive scale, imagining the history of the Americas in breaks and displacements," said Jeff Chang of *ColorLines* magazine.

With his brother Jaime, Hernandez is the creative force behind the successful adult comic book series "Love and Rockets." The two artists are often credited with helping to usher in a new era of appreciation for the genre. Hernandez, along with brothers Jaime and Mario, grew up in a large Mexican-American family where his creative urges were fueled by an early fascination with vintage films. Both Jaime and Gilbert have drawn on their Hispanic roots for the material in "Love and Rockets." While Jaime's stories focus on barrio life in contemporary America, Hernandez chronicles the characters and events of the mythical Central American village of Palomar. Both Jaime's stories and Gilbert's Palomar tales have been collected into book editions such as *Heartbreak Soup,* published in 1987. It was followed by *The Reticent Heart and Other Stories* in 1988 and *Poison River* in 1994.

Heartbreak Soup is the original story to be set in Palomar. It focuses upon the newcomer, Luba, who poses a threat to Chelo, the resident banmacradera (a woman who gives baths to men), since they share the same profession. Their conflict is resolved ingeniously and peacefully, and Luba becomes a permanent resident of Palomar. Patty Campbell, in a review of *Heartbreak Soup* for the *Wilson Library Bulletin,* wrote that "Hernandez draws us into the daily dramas of his characters' lives with amused compassion and enormous humanity." Mark Sinker, reviewing the book for the *New Statesman,* called it "one of the few extended strips where the comparison with the novel (in particular the magic realist novel) really makes much sense." Sinker praised Hernandez's believable portrayal of female characters and concluded that "it's surely no accident that the most innovative and perceptive of the new American comics comes from the heart of a rising culture" found in an increasingly Hispanic United States.

Luba's life prior to her arrival in Palomar is documented in *Poison River,* a tale filled with politics, love and gangsters. "It is an ambitious work. . . . [and] I found the storytelling technique fascinating," said J. Stephen Bolhafner in his *Love and Rockets* Web site review. A *Publishers Weekly* contributor called *Poison River* "an epic Latin American melodrama of lost identity, political violence and polymorphous sexuality."

Hernandez is also the coauthor of a futuristic tale of an architect gone amiss in *The Return of Mister X,* published in 1987, and an erotic comic, *Birdland,* published in 1992. A *Los Angeles Times* article quoted acclaimed British graphic novelist Alan Moore as stating: "Hernandez uses a genuinely poetic eye to show us all the rich and shadowy passions that surge behind the bland facade of normal life. . . . [He] shows us a little of what humans are actually worth, and while some of it, predictably, is bad news, there are moments of understated optimism that are both touching and illuminating."

In 1999, Hernandez made a foray into the world of children's comic books with the publication of *Yeah!,* a book that revolves around an all-girl rock band. Honey, Krazy and WooWoo, members of the band, are intergalactic superstars recognized on every other planet but their home territory, Earth. "It's sort of a modernized *Josie and the Pussycats* meets the *Spice Girls,*" Hernandez told *Los Angeles Times* contributor Jordan Raphael. *Time* writer Andrew D. Arnold felt that girls, as well as their parents, would appreciate *Yeah!* He praised Hernandez's "clean line and lively colors" that fill the comic's pages. Raphacl asked Hernandez how he manages to appeal to children's inner fantasies when he has no children of his own. Hernandez explained that he watches children's cartoons on television and listens to the conversations of young girls when he and his wife are at the mall. The cartoonist concluded: "Maybe that's why I do this: I have no children, so I create my own."

Fear of Comics was Hernandez's first collection of new adult comics since he and Jaime ended their work on "Love and Rockets" in 1994. This volume contains stories of a supernatural nature that describe the ghost of a mother who searches for her murdered children, a magical tree that gives helpful advice about love, and a gremlin that invades a small village. Hernandez also includes new stories about old characters from "Love and Rockets." *Booklist* reviewer Gordon Flagg noted that Hernandez's comics provide "an effective vehicle for Latin American-style magic realism." Although *Library Journal* contributor Stephen Weiner has appreciated much of the Hernandez's work in the past, he found *Fear of Comics* to be a "disjointed collection."

After a seven-year hiatus, Hernandez continued the saga of the legendary Luba in his work *Luba in America.* In this second volume of the "Love and Rockets" series, she leaves Palomar behind and travels to the United States to stay with her half-sisters, Fritzi (a lisping psychiatrist) and Petra (a lab technician).

"*Love and Rockets, Volume II* is our second wind," said Hernandez in a *Time* interview with Andrew D. Arnold. *Booklist* reviewer Gordon Flagg appreciated Hernandez's "expressive cartooning, masterful design, and . . . compelling characterizations." "The collection . . . [is] accessible even to the Luba neophyte," stated Robert Ito of *Los Angeles Magazine.* A *Publishers Weekly* reviewer praised Hernandez's "precise and anatomically impeccable" black and white drawings. He concluded that the artist's work is "engagingly bizarre, sexy, and unpredictably funny." "[*Luba in America*] is an awesome blend of political intrigue, sexuality and Gilbert's characteristically human portrayal of his characters," remarked a critic for *Fantagraphics Books.* And *ColorLines* magazine writer Jeff Chang wrote, "Here is the fundamental beauty of *Love and Rockets*: the heroism emanates from the quotidian and the grey. This second edition of *Love and Rockets* arrives at a time when art seems both more useless and more necessary than ever. Art cannot speak to the new horrors yet, but it must calm our souls."

BIOGRAPHICAL AND CRITICAL SOURCES:

PERIODICALS

Aztlan: A Journal of Chicano Studies, fall, 1999, Rachel Rubin, review of *Love and Rockets,* pp. 171-189.

Booklist, January 15, 1988, p. 819; March 1, 1988, p. 1088; August, 1994, p. 2012; January 1, 2001, Gordon Flagg, review of *Fear of Comics,* p. 896; April 1, 2002, Gordon Flagg, review of *Luba in America,* p. 1291.

Chicago Tribune, September 24, 1992.

ColorLines, spring, 2002, Jeff Chang, "Locas Rule: Los Bros Hernandez' *Love and Rockets* Is Back, and the Timing Has Never Been Better," pp. 39-42.

Entertainment Weekly, March 29, 2002; December 19, 2003, review of *Palomar: The Heartbreak Soup Stories,* p. L2T22.

Hispanic, May, 2002, p. 14.

Library Journal, March 15, 1990, p. 53; June 15, 2001, Stephen Weiner, review of *Fear of Comics,* p. 66; January, 2004, Khadijah Caturani, review of *Palomar,* p. 80.

Los Angeles, September, 2001, Robert Ito, review of *Luba in America,* p. 139.

Los Angeles Times, July 16, 1991, p. 6F; June 13, 1999, Jordan Raphael, review of *Yeah!,* p. 2

New Statesman and Society, July 29, 1988, pp. 48-49.

Publishers Weekly, August 5, 1988, p. 80; January 6, 1989, p. 51; August 22, 1994, review of *Poison River,* p. 52; March 25, 2002, review of *Luba in America,* p. 48; October 20, 2003, Heidi McDonald, "Gilbert Hernandez's *Palomar,*" author interview, p. S12; November 10, 2003, review of *Palomar,* p. 45.

Science Fiction Chronicle, January, 1988, p. 52.

Time, March 6, 2000, Andrew D. Arnold, review of *Yeah!,* p. 76; February 19, 2001, Andrew D. Arnold, "Graphic Sketches of Latino Life," p. 64.

Village Voice Literary Supplement, December, 1992, p. 28.

Wilson Library Bulletin, February, 1988, p. 81.

ONLINE

Gilbert Hernandez Home Page, http://www.fantagraphics.com/ (May 11, 2003), review of *Luba in America.*

Love and Rockets Web site, http://www.geocities.com/Area51/zone/9923/luvrock.html/ (May 11, 2003), J. Stephen Bolhafner, review of *Poison River.*

Salon.com, http://www.salon.com/ (May 11, 2003), Amy Benfer, "Real Women." review of *Love and Rockets.**

* * *

HIGHAM, John 1920-2003

PERSONAL: Born October 26, 1920, in Jamaica, NY; died July 26, 2003; son of Lloyd Stuart and Margaret (Windred) Higham; married Eileen Moss, August 26, 1948; children: Constance, Margaret, Jay, Daniel. *Edu-*

cation: Johns Hopkins University, B.A., 1941; University of Wisconsin, M.A., 1942, Ph.D., 1949.

CAREER: American Mercury, New York, NY, editorial assistant, 1945-46; University of California, Los Angeles, instructor, 1948-50, assistant professor, 1950-54; Rutgers University, New Brunswick, NJ, associate professor, 1954-58, professor, 1958-60; University of Michigan, Ann Arbor, professor of history, 1960-68, Moses Coit Tyler Professor of History, 1968-71, 1972-73; Johns Hopkins University, Baltimore, MD, John Martin Vincent Professor of History, beginning 1971. Visiting associate professor, Columbia University, 1958-59; Commonwealth Fund Lecturer, University College, University of London, 1968; Phi Beta Kappa visiting scholar, 1972-73; Fulbright lecturer, Kyoto American Studies Seminar, 1974. Ecole des Hautes Etudes en Sciences Sociales, Paris, France, directeur d'etudes, 1981-82. Member of board of directors, American Immigration Conference, 1956-60. Member, Institute for Advanced Study, 1973-74. *Military service:* U.S. Army Air Forces, 1943-45; served in Italy as historian for Twelfth Air Force; became staff sergeant.

MEMBER: American Studies Association (president of Middle Atlantic States chapter, 1956-57), Organization of American Historians (member of executive committee, 1964-67, 1974-77; president, 1973-74), American Historical Association (member of council and executive committee, 1971-74), American Antiquarian Society, Society of American Historians, American Academy of Arts and Sciences, Immigration and Ethnic History Society (vice president, 1976-79; president, 1979-82), New Society Letters Lund (Sweden), Michigan Society of Fellows, Century Club.

AWARDS, HONORS: American Historical Association John H. Dunning Prize, 1956, for *Strangers in the Land: Patterns of American Nativism*; Princeton University Council for the Humanities fellow, 1960-61; Center for Advanced Studies in the Behavioral Sciences fellow, 1965-66; Woodrow Wilson International Center for Scholars fellow, 1976-77; Lifetime Achievement Award, Immigration and Ethnic History Society, 2002.

WRITINGS:

Strangers in the Land: Patterns of American Nativism, 1860-1925, Rutgers University Press (New Bruns-

swick, NJ), 1955, 2nd edition, Atheneum (New York, NY), 1963, reprinted, Rutgers University Press (New Brunswick, NJ), 2002.

(Editor and coauthor) *The Reconstruction of American History,* Harper (New York, NY), 1962, reprinted, Greenwood Press (Westport, CT), 1980.

(With Felix Gilbert and Leonard Krieger) *History,* Prentice-Hall (Englewood Cliffs, NJ), 1965, reprinted, Garland Publishing (New York, NY), 1985.

(Contributor) *The Origins of Modern Consciousness,* edited by John Weiss, Wayne State University Press (Detroit, MI), 1965.

From Boundlessness to Consolidation: The Transformation of American Culture, 1848-1860, Clements Library, University of Michigan (Ann Arbor, MI), 1969.

Writing American History: Essays on Modern Scholarship, Indiana University Press (Bloomington, IN), 1970.

History: Professional Scholarship in America, Harper & Row (New York, NY), 1973.

Send These to Me: Jews and Other Immigrants in Urban America, Atheneum (New York, NY), 1975.

(Editor) *Ethnic Leadership in America,* Johns Hopkins Press (Baltimore, MD), 1978.

(Editor, with Paul Conkin) *New Directions in American Intellectual History*, Johns Hopkins University Press (Baltimore, MD), 1979.

(With Michael Crystal) *Loose on Liquidators: The Role of a Liquidator in a Voluntary Winding-Up,* 2nd edition, Jordan (Bristol, England), 1981.

(Editor) *Civil Rights and Social Wrongs: Black-White Relations since World War II,* Pennsylvania State University Press (University Park, PA), 1997.

Hanging Together: Unity and Diversity in American Culture, edited by Carl J. Guarneri, Yale University Press (New Haven, CT), 2001.

Also editor, "The Meaning of American History" series, Harper. Contributor to professional journals. Member of editorial board, *American Quarterly,* 1964-67; consulting editor, *Comparative Studies in Society and History*, beginning 1972.

SIDELIGHTS: John Higham broke into the historical nonfiction forefront in 1955, when he published *Strangers in the Land: Patterns of American Nativism, 1860-1925.* According to George M. Fredrickson of the *New York Review of Books,* the book was "well received when it came out in 1955, and it has remained to this day the standard account of America's anti-immigrant ideologies, movements, and policies." It was obvious that Higham had a firm grasp on the American condition and the history that created it. His premise was that the natives of our land have the least amount of opportunity, largely due to the immigrants who are much more apt to succeed in our capitalist society. In an interview with *U.S. News & World Report,* Higham conveyed that "opportunity arises out of motion, out of changing places." He continued, "It's the immigrants who can move most dramatically, who can change their lives most spectacularly. They are not bound by their standing in society." Higham surmised that Americans may pursue opportunities in less tangible ways, giving the examples of culture and spirit, "freedom to define one's own goals, freedom to reconsider the character of one's life, freedom to invent, develop and imagine." He believed that is what America will be recognized for throughout time.

Higham's book *Hanging Together,* shows his "greatest impact and influence on the interpretation of America's past . . . through dozens of carefully crafted, thoughtful and perceptive articles," wrote Allen Davis in *American Studies International:* "It can stand as a tribute to a lifetime achievement." Davis believed that Higham really found his niche in the well-thought articles, as apposed to his recurrent "history of history writing in America" themes Higham addressed in other books. *Library Journal*'s Andrew Brodie Smith described the book as addressing "the subject of national character and the mechanisms by which people of divergent ethnic and class backgrounds have come together to identify as Americans throughout the country's history." Smith also wrote that, although some of the essays are decades old, they still are applicable to current conditions. A reviewer for *Publishers Weekly* commented that the book "focuses on the constant reinvention of the 'American'."

"Although Higham's parents came from a Midwestern Protestant background, he grew up in Queens, had Jewish and Catholic friends, and thus became sensitive from an early age to the diverse character of American Society," wrote Fredrickson. It is clear this had an effect on his world view as *Hanging Together* shows "deep understanding of the plight of the oppressed or marginalized groups that have sought higher status both within historical memory and in society at large," explained Fredrickson. This understanding, no doubt, helped Higham in his editorial capacity for the book *Civil Rights and Social Wrongs*

Civil Rights and Social Wrongs addresses the strained relations between blacks and whites since World War II. Higham not only edited the book, but also contributed an article to the collection. Brian Faire of the *Journal of American Ethnic History* explained how "the book situates readers principally in the 1940s postwar period, examining black-white relations and racial attitudes since then." Faire believed the book "reveals significant nuances on controversial topics frequently omitted from policy debates," continuing that "Higham writes as a participant/critic, with an insider's perspective and passion." Faire noted that "Higham's historical review is unsurprisingly first-rate."

Higham's publication, *Send These To Me* is based largely on a paper he read for a meeting of the American Historical Association. Focusing on natives, it explores how immigrants influenced American culture, including the symbols used to represent this country and ideology of what the country stands for. The book was first published in 1975, and was re-issued after a multitude of revisions in 1984. The book also examines anti-Semitism in America, suggesting that the problem is not rooted out of the European uprising spawning World War II, but rather "was primarily a social phenomenon reflecting the insecurities of middle- and upper-class gentiles at a time of great social mobility," according to Fredrickson. Fredrickson explained that Higham once again acted as a mediator between the differing views, bringing cohesion where there was little. It is clear that Higham had a unique perspective, and he employed this perspective to bring more understanding to society for generations of today, and those to come.

BIOGRAPHICAL AND CRITICAL SOURCES:

PERIODICALS

African American Review, March 22, 2000, Allen Matusow, review of *Civil Rights and Social Wrongs: Black-White Relations since World War II,* p. 153.
American Journal of Sociology, July, 1982, review of *New Directions in American Intellectual History,* p. 214.
American Studies International, October, 2001, Allen F. Davis, review of *Hanging Together: Unity and Diversity in American Culture,* pp. 77-79.

Choice, March, 1982, review of *Strangers in the Land: Patterns of American Nativism, 1860-1925,* p. 876; review of May, 1998, J. H. Smith, review of *Civil Rights and Social Wrongs,* p. 1590.

Contemporary Sociology January, 1999, Mihcael E. Hodge, review of *Civil Rights and Social Wrongs,* p. 39.

Ethnic and Racial Studies, January, 1990, Barbara Ballis Lal, review of *Strangers in the Land,* 2nd edition, p. 142; November, 1998, John Edwards, review of *Civil Rights and Social Wrongs,* p. 1183.

History, fall, 1988, review of *Strangers in the Land,* p. 6; fall, 2001, L. Moody Simms, Jr., review of *Hanging Together,* pp. 12-13.

International Migration Review, winter, 1989, Donald L. Zelman, review of *Strangers in the Land,* 2nd edition, p. 952.

Journal of American Ethnic History, fall-winter, 1990, John Bodnar, review of *Strangers in the Land,* 2nd edition, p. 80; summer, 1999, Bryan K. Fair, review of *Civil Rights and Social Wrongs,* pp. 167-175.

Journal of American History, March, 1999, Michael Omi, review of *Civil Rights and Social Wrongs,* p. 1671.

Journal of Southern History, May, 1999, Willard B. Gatewood, review of *Civil Rights and Social Wrongs,* p. 438.

Library Journal, August 1, 2001, Andrew Brodie Smith, review of *Hanging Together,* p. 142.

New York Review of Books, February 28, 2002, George M. Fredrickson, "Wise Man," review of *Hanging Together,* pp. 37-39.

Publishers Weekly, May 7, 2001, review of *Hanging Together,* p. 235.

Reference & Research Book News, May, 1998, review of *Civil Rights and Social Wrongs,* p. 43.

Social Forces, June, 1999, review of *Civil Rights and Social Wrongs,* p. 1638.

U.S. News & World Report, July 4, 1983, "It's the Immigrants Who Can Move Dramatically," interview with John Higham, p. 43.

Virginia Quarterly Review, summer, 1998, review of *Civil Rights and Social Wrongs,* p. 100.*

* * *

HILLERMAN, Tony 1925-

PERSONAL: Born May 27, 1925; son of August Alfred (a farmer) and Lucy (Grove) Hillerman; married Marie Unzner, August 16, 1948; children: Anne, Janet, Anthony, Monica, Stephen, Daniel. *Education:* At-

Tony Hillerman

tended Oklahoma State University, 1943; University of Oklahoma, B.A., 1946; University of New Mexico, M.A., 1966. *Politics:* Democrat. *Religion:* Roman Catholic. *Hobbies and other interests:* Trout fishing.

ADDRESSES: Agent—c/o Author Mail, Houghton Mifflin, 222 Berkeley St., Boston, MA 02116-3764.

CAREER: Borger News Herald, Borger, TX, reporter, 1948; *Morning Press-Constitution,* Lawton, OK, city editor, 1948-50; United Press International, Oklahoma City, OK, political reporter, 1950-52, Santa Fe, NM, bureau manager, 1952-54; *New Mexican,* Santa Fe, political reporter and executive editor, 1954-63; University of New Mexico, Albuquerque, associate professor, 1965-66, professor, 1966-85, chair of department, 1966-73, assistant to the president, 1975-80, professor emeritus of journalism, 1985—; writer. *Military service:* U.S. Army, 1943-45; received Silver Star, Bronze Star, and Purple Heart.

MEMBER: International Crime Writers Association, Mystery Writers of America (president, 1988), Albuquerque Press Club, Sigma Delta Chi, Phi Kappa Phi.

AWARDS, HONORS: Edgar Allan Poe Award, Mystery Writers of America, 1974, for *Dance Hall of the Dead;* Golden Spur award, Western Writers of America, 1987; Special Friend of Dineh award, Navajo Tribal Council, 1987; National Media Award, American Anthropological Association, 1990; Public Services Award, Department of the Interior, 1990; Arrell Gibson Lifetime Award, Oklahoma Center for the Book, 1991; Grandmaster Award, Mystery Writers of America, 1991; Ambassador award, Center for the Indian, 1992; Grand prix de litterature policiere; inducted into Oklahoma Hall of Fame, 1997; Jack D. Rittenhouse Award, Rocky Mountain Book Publishers Association, 1998; Agatha Award, 2002, for *Seldom Disappointed;* D.Litt., University of New Mexico, 1990, and Arizona State University, 1991.

WRITINGS:

MYSTERY NOVELS

The Blessing Way, Harper (New York, NY), 1970.
The Fly on the Wall, Harper (New York, NY), 1971.
Dance Hall of the Dead, Harper (New York, NY), 1973, reprinted, 2003.
Listening Woman, Harper (New York, NY), 1978.
People of Darkness, Harper (New York, NY), 1980.
The Dark Wind, Harper (New York, NY), 1982.
The Ghostway, Harper (New York, NY), 1984.
Skinwalkers, Harper (New York, NY), 1986.
A Thief of Time, Harper (New York, NY), 1988.
Talking God, Harper (New York, NY), 1989.
Coyote Waits, Harper (New York, NY), 1990.
Sacred Clowns, HarperCollins (New York, NY), 1993.
The Fallen Man, HarperCollins (New York, NY), 1996.
The First Eagle, HarperCollins (New York, NY), 1998.
Hunting Badger, HarperCollins (New York, NY), 1999.
The Wailing Wind, HarperCollins (New York, NY), 2002.
The Sinister Pig, HarperCollins (New York, NY), 2003.
Skeleton Man, HarperCollins (New York, NY), 2004.

COLLECTIONS

The Joe Leaphorn Mysteries, Harper (New York, NY), 1989.
The Jim Chee Mysteries, Harper (New York, NY), 1992.

Leaphorn and Chee: Three Classic Mysteries Featuring Lt. Joe Leaphorn and Officer Jim Chee, Harper (New York, NY), 1992.

OTHER

The Boy Who Made Dragonfly: A Zuni Myth (juvenile), Harper (New York, NY), 1972.
The Great Taos Bank Robbery and Other Indian Country Affairs, University of New Mexico Press (Albuquerque, NM), 1973, published as *The Great Taos Bank Robbery: And Other True Stories of the Southwest,* Perennial (New York, NY), 2001.
(Editor) *The Spell of New Mexico,* University of New Mexico Press (Albuquerque, NM), 1984.
Indian Country: America's Sacred Land, illustrated with photographs by Bela Kalman, Northland Press (Flagstaff, AZ), 1987.
(Author of foreword) Erna Fergusson, *Dancing Gods: Indian Ceremonials of New Mexico and Arizona,* University of New Mexico Press (Albuquerque, NM), 1988.
Hillerman Country: A Journey through the Southwest with Tony Hillerman, illustrated with photographs by Barney Hillerman, HarperCollins (New York, NY), 1991.
(With Ernie Bulow) *Talking Mysteries: A Conversation with Tony Hillerman,* University of New Mexico Press (Albuquerque, NM), 1991.
(Editor) *Best of the West: An Anthology of Classic Writing from the American West,* HarperCollins (New York, NY), 1991.
(Author of foreword) Ernie Bulow, *Navajo Taboos,* Buffalo Medicine Books, 1991.
(Author of introduction) Howard Beyan, editor, *Robbers, Rogues, and Ruffians: True Tales of the Wild West,* Clear Light (New York, NY), 1991.
(With others) *The Perfect Murder: Five Great Mystery Writers Create the Perfect Crime,* Harper Prism (New York, NY), 1991.
New Mexico, Rio Grande, and Other Essays, illustrated with photographs by David Muench and Robert Reynolds, Graphic Arts Center, 1992.
(Editor) *The Mysterious West,* HarperCollins (New York, NY), 1994.
(Author of introduction), Robert Allen Rutland, *A Boyhood in the Dustbowl 1926-34,* University Press of Colorado (Boulder, CO), 1995.
Finding Moon (novel), HarperCollins (New York, NY), 1995.

(Editor, with Rosemary Herbert) *The Oxford Book of American Detective Stories,* Oxford University Press (New York, NY), 1996.

(Editor) *The Best American Mystery Stories of the Century,* Houghton Mifflin (Boston, MA), 2000.

Seldom Disappointed: A Memoir, HarperCollins (New York, NY), 2001.

Kilroy Was There: A GI's War in Photographs, photographs by Frank Kessler, Kent State University Press (Kent, OH), 2004.

Contributor to books, including *Crime Lovers Casebook,* edited by Jerome Charyn, Signet (New York, NY), 1996; and also to periodicals, including *New Mexico Quarterly, National Geographic,* and *Reader's Digest.*

ADAPTATIONS: Many of Hillerman's mysteries have been recorded on audiocassette; the novel *Coyote Waits* was adapted for an episode the PBS series *American Mystery!*

SIDELIGHTS: A versatile novelist, Tony Hillerman "created the American Indian policier," according to critic Herbert Mitgang in the *New York Times,* and also "breaks out of the detective genre," as Daniel K. Muhlestein noted in the *Dictionary of Literary Biography.* Hillerman "is a writer of police procedurals who is less concerned with the identity of his villains than with their motivation," Muhlestein further commented. "Most mystery writers begin with plot. Hillerman begins with setting." Setting, for Hillerman, is the sprawling, arid, high plateau of the Southwest: the Four Corners region of Arizona, Utah, Colorado, and New Mexico that comprise Navajo country. Into this vast, empty space he sets his two protagonists, Jim Chee and Joe Leaphorn, detectives with the Navajo Tribal Police, who solve crimes using the most modern police methods as well as the most traditional of Navajo beliefs: a sense of *hozro,* or harmony. Hillerman has written more than a dozen Leaphorn-Chee mysteries, books that have garnered him awards ranging from the Mystery Writers of America to the Navajo Tribal Council's commendation to France's esteemed Grand prix de litterature policiere.

Hillerman's interest in the American Southwest is evident in both his popular mystery series and nonfiction works that explore the natural wonders of the region. A student of southwestern history and culture,

Hillerman often draws his themes from the conflict between modern society and traditional Native American values and customs. The complex nature of this struggle is perhaps most evident in the author's works featuring Leaphorn and Chee, whose contrasting views about heritage and crime-fighting form an interesting backdrop to their criminal investigations. The intricate nature of Hillerman's plots, combined with detailed descriptions of people, places, and exotic rituals, has helped make his novels—from the first in the series, 1970's *The Blessing Way,* to the 1999 *Hunting Badger*—popular with readers and critics alike. Hillerman's novels are, as so many critics have observed, much more than mere police procedurals. His use of character and setting have pushed them beyond the bounds of the detective genre, a fact supported by their large sales in mainstream fiction.

Hillerman is no stranger to the world he portrays in his novels and nonfiction. Born on May 27, 1925, the youngest of three children of August Alfred and Lucy Grove Hillerman, he grew up in rural Oklahoma, where his parents farmed and ran a local store. Hillerman loved reading and books as a youth, and in those days before television and without even enough money for batteries for the radio, he also formed an appreciation for oral storytelling. He would listen to the men who gathered at his parents' store to tell stories and tall tales, and learned pacing, timing, and the importance of detail. Hillerman's youth was thus spent, as Muhlestein noted, "poor in money but rich in the tools of a future writer."

Hillerman also learned, according to Muhlestein, "what it meant to be an outsider," by attending a boarding school for Potawatomie Indian girls. Doubly removed because of both race and gender, Hillerman internalized this feeling of being an outsider, but also formed a deep and abiding respect for Indian ways and culture. As important as that message was, he also learned another: the significance of class in America. As a youngster Hillerman viewed himself as a country boy, one who got his haircuts at home, not at a barber shop. If the world were divided into urban and rural, he would opt for the latter.

After graduating from high school, Hillerman began college at Oklahoma State University, but then joined the army to fight in World War II. He took part in the D-Day landings, was wounded in Alsace, and earned a Silver Star, among other decorations. His letters home, which found their way into the hands of a journalist, were so detailed and spirited that the newspaperman convinced the young returning soldier to take up a career in writing.

Enrolling in journalism courses, Hillerman also worked part-time to support his education. It was in 1945, while driving a truckload of drilling pipe from Oklahoma to New Mexico, that he first encountered the Navajo and their reservation. The Navajos he first saw were engaged in a curing ceremony called the Enemy Way, during which a young Navajo fresh from service in the war, like Hillerman himself, was being cured of the foreign contamination and brought back into harmony with his own people. "When I met the Navajos I now so often write about," Hillerman recalled to Ernie Bulow in *Talking Mysteries,* "I recognized kindred spirits. Country boys. More of us. Folks among whom I felt at ease." In 1948, Hillerman graduated from the journalism program at the University of Oklahoma. He was also married that year to Marie Unzner; the couple would eventually have one child together and adopt five additional children.

Hillerman took several newspaper jobs in and around Oklahoma, Texas, and New Mexico before joining the staff of the Santa Fe *New Mexican* in 1954. He stayed with that paper until 1963, working at the end of his journalism career as executive editor. But he had a longing to become a novelist, and with the encouragement of his wife, left journalism behind to study writing, soon becoming a journalism professor at the University of New Mexico, where he remained until 1985. It was while he was a professor of journalism that he wrote his first novel, *The Blessing Way,* in which he introduces Joe Leaphorn, a fiftyish Navajo with the Tribal Police on the reservation. Leaphorn, however, was almost cut out of this manuscript at the urging of Hillerman's agent. Finally, an editor at Harper & Row wrote an enthusiastic critique of the manuscript, wanting Hillerman to increase Leaphorn's role, and the writer's first major protagonist was born.

In this debut novel, the motive for the murder of a young Navajo is witchcraft in the shape of a Navajo Wolf, akin to a werewolf. According to Geoff Sadler, a contributor for *Contemporary Popular Writers,* this novel "is a tense, exciting adventure that mixes espionage with witchcraft." Hillerman's second novel, *Fly on the Wall,* is a story of political corruption with a journalist serving as the chief investigator. Returning

with his third novel to Navajo country, as he has remained with all but one more of his novels, Hillerman next sent his reserved, logical, and partially assimilated detective, Leaphorn, into Zuni country to investigate tribal rites in *The Dance Hall of the Dead.* This second "Leaphorn" novel, which earned its author the Edgar Allan Poe Award from the Mystery Writers of America, begins with the murder of Ernesto Cata, a Zuni boy who is in training for an important ceremonial role in his tribe. Suspicion falls on a Navajo boy, George Bowlegs, but when Bowlegs is in turn murdered, Leaphorn follows clues and his instinct to a white archaeologist who killed the boys to keep them from disclosing that he had been fudging finds at his excavation site. Hillerman's third "Leaphorn" novel, *Listening Woman,* finds the Navajo detective investigating two homicides and becoming trapped in an underground cavern with terrorists and their hostages. "The novel combines clever plotlines with sharp character insights and a taut, nail-biting payoff," wrote Sadler.

With *People of Darkness* Hillerman introduces a second major protagonist, Jim Chee, who, like Leaphorn, is a Navajo tribal officer, but who, unlike Leaphorn is more traditional, less experienced, younger, and more in flux. One major reason for creating Chee was that Hillerman had sold the television rights for his Leaphorn character; he also knew he needed a different kind of protagonist, someone younger and less sophisticated than Leaphorn. In this story, Chee, a part-time ceremonial singer who is also drawn to the white lifestyle and the possibility of a career in the FBI, investigates a burglary at a wealthy white man's house which leads to a thirty-year-old crime aboard an oil rig. Chee's second adventure, *The Dark Wind,* has the younger Navajo detective chasing criminals involved in a cocaine ring who have killed several Navajos. In *The Ghostway,* Chee is off to Los Angeles in pursuit of two Navajos who are stealing luxury cars. But when the thieves return to the reservation, one of them is killed in his uncle's hogan (dwelling). Chee's heritage comes to the fore when he discovers that whoever laid the young man out for burial neglected one of the ceremonies and was thus not really a Navajo. Such a connection with tradition might come in handy in Chee's work, but not in his love life, for it isolates him from his white schoolteacher lover who ultimately leaves the reservation. Reviewing *The Ghostway* in *Entertainment Weekly,* a contributor noted that you don't have to be "a regular at Tribal Policeman Jim Chee's pow-wows to dig *The Ghostway,* one of the freshest of Hillerman's whodunits."

After finishing *The Ghostway,* Hillerman bought back the rights to Joe Leaphorn, and in his next novel, *Skinwalkers,* he pairs the detective with Chee, as he has continued to do in succeeding titles. The two investigators act as foils to one another: Leaphorn the older, more mature and methodical detective, and Chee the more quixotic, impulsive loner. The Skinwalkers of the title are Navajo ghosts, and the novel, which starts out with a shotgun attack on Chee, has witchcraft at its very heart. Leaphorn helps the younger detective get to the bottom of this attack and others on the reservation. A Golden Spur Award winner, *Skinwalkers* is a "strong, neatly worked novel with a shocking climax," according to Sadler. Writing in *People,* Campbell Geeslin noted that Hillerman "packs his novels with compelling details of Navajo life and beautiful descriptive passages about the land and weather." Geeslin concluded, "Chee . . . is a perfect guide through Hillerman's effective, dreamlike world."

Skinwalkers was, according to Michael Neill in *People,* Hillerman's "commercial breakthrough," selling 40,000 copies in hardcover and 100,000 in paperback. Yet it was his next title, *A Thief of Time,* that secured him a place on the best-seller charts and propelled Hillerman to national attention. Beginning with a murder at an Anasazi historical site, the book features a psychopathic killer and more development of the relationship between Leaphorn and Chee. In this novel, Leaphorn has to cope with his wife's death as well as his own impending retirement. As Hillerman's main recurring characters, Leaphorn and Chee serve a dual function. On one level, the officers act as guides into a world of traditions and customs unfamiliar to most readers; on another level, Hillerman's depiction of Leaphorn and Chee's day-to-day struggles—with bureaucratic red tape, discrimination, and intimate relationships—helps readers understand the difficulty of living in what amounts to two worlds with different, and often contradictory, sets of rules.

This culture clash is not always depicted in a negative light, however. In books such as *Listening Woman* and *The Ghostway,* Leaphorn and Chee use both standard police procedures and their special knowledge of tribal customs to solve a wide variety of baffling crimes. In *Listening Woman,* Leaphorn finds clues to a double murder in a group of ritual sand paintings. An oddly-performed death ceremony puts Chee on the trail of a missing girl and a killer in *The Ghostway.* Stolen pottery from a "lost" tribe becomes the focus of

Leaphorn's investigation into artifact trafficking in *A Thief of Time,* a book that is at once "careful with the facts," and one that "transmutes knowledge into romance," as a contributor to *Time* magazine wrote. Karl G. Fredrikkson and Lilian Fredrikkson called *A Thief of Time* "probably Hillerman's best novel," in the *St. James Guide to Crime and Mystery Writers,* and they further noted, "History and tradition play integral parts in all Hillerman's novels and especially in this one." The Fredrikksons concluded that the main theme of all Hillerman's work "is the clash between the Navajo Way and the so-called American Way of Life, between tradition and the emptiness of modern society."

As with *Dance Hall of the Dead* and *A Thief of Time,* Hillerman's novel *Talking God* deals with anthropology. This time, both Chee and Leaphorn desert the reservation for Washington, D.C., in search of missing Native American artifacts. "The plot," noted Louise Bernikow in a *Cosmopolitan* review, "comes to a crashing finale in the Smithsonian Institute, and the evil that has disturbed the spirits of the Navajo is laid to rest." Bernikow also commented that Hillerman's story "is complicated, emotional, and incredibly suspenseful." In *Coyote Waits,* an officer in the Navajo Tribal Police, Delbert Nez, is gunned down, and Leaphorn and Chee set out to find his killer. It looks as if a Navajo shaman might be responsible for the killing, until other suspects turn up, including a Vietnamese teacher. Behind it all lurks the mythic Navajo character representing chaos, the Coyote of the title. Phoebe-Lou Adams, writing in the *Atlantic,* felt the plot "is a humdinger even by the high Hillerman standard," while a writer for *Entertainment Weekly* dubbed it "sturdy work from an incorruptible craftsman." Reviewing the title in *People,* Neill concluded, "Hillerman's elevation into the best-seller ranks is a great justice of American popular writing. While his novels are mysteries, they are also exquisite explorations of human nature—with a great backdrop." Reviewing *Coyote Waits,* a contributor for *Publishers Weekly* commented, "Hillerman weaves an understated, powerful tale from strands of ancient Navajo mythology, modern greed and ambition, and above all, the sorrows and delights of characters."

In *Sacred Clowns,* the duo investigate the seemingly unrelated murders of a shop teacher at the mission school and a sacred clown dancer, a Hopi koshare. In this novel, Chee is increasingly attracted to the Navajo lawyer, Janet Pete, while Leaphorn considers a relationship with a linguistics professor. "Telling his story the Navajo way," wrote a contributor to *Publishers Weekly,* "Hillerman fully develops the background of the cases . . . so that the resolutions . . . ring true with gratifying inevitability." Gene Lyons, writing in *Entertainment Weekly,* noted that even "devoted readers . . . will find *Sacred Clowns* just a bit different from earlier books in the series." Lyons pointed to the essentially "comic" structure and tone of the novel.

One interesting aspect of Hillerman's novels is that his protagonists have not stayed rooted in time, but rather have developed and aged: Leaphorn has retired, yet keeps a hand in police affairs, while Chee begins to settle down. The pair took a hiatus in the mid-1990s while Hillerman turned his hand to various other projects, including *The Mysterious West* and another novel set in Vietnam, *Finding Moon.* Then in 1997, the duo returned with *The Fallen Man.* In this novel, mountaineers find a skeleton near the summit of Ship Rock in northwestern New Mexico. The skeleton in question turns out to be that of a member of a local white family who disappeared eleven years earlier. Leaphorn, who remembers the earlier disappearance, comes back into action, though Chee, now a lieutenant, at first bristles at his intrusion. Meantime also the romance between Chee and ambitious attorney Janet Pete, whom he is courting, takes twists and turns. "As always," noted a reviewer for *Publishers Weekly,* "Hillerman treats Indian tradition and modern troubles . . . with unsentimental respect, firmly rooting his mystery in the region's distinctive peoples and geography." Sikki Andur, writing in *Entertainment Weekly,* called this thirteenth novel "a scenic ride through a land where police are more worried about cattle rustling than dope dealing," and where "a cop who's been shot doesn't crave revenge—he wants harmony." *Booklist* reviewer Stephanie Zvirin commented, "As usual, Hillerman masterfully sets the scene, conveying contemporary culture and weaving in intriguing side plots to add depth to character and scene." Zvirin concluded that "with all Hillerman's stories, it's the oblique way" of getting to the end "that pulls [the reader] along."

The First Eagle, published in 1998, features another scientist who comes from outside to the "res," a theme found in several of Hillerman's books. This time it is a missing female biologist who has been tracking the Bubonic plague in the prairie dogs of the Southwest. Leaphorn is hired by the scientist's grandmother to find her; meanwhile Chee is investigating the bludgeon death of a Navajo Police officer at the site where the biologist was last seen. "Hillerman's trademark melding of Navajo tradition and modern culture is captured with crystal clarity in this tale of an ancient scourge's resurgence in today's word," noted a reviewer for *Publishers Weekly. Booklist*'s Zvirin felt that "Hillerman's respect and deep affection for his creations and their community" runs through all of the subplots and twists of action. *Hunting Badger,* published in 1999, was inspired by an actual manhunt in the Four Corners region in which the search for the killers was badly bungled by the FBI. In Hillerman's scenario, there is a robbery at an Ute casino, and the security officer there is killed in the process. Chee is drawn into the case along with Leaphorn. Reviews of this fifteenth book in the series were somewhat mixed. Wilda Williams, writing in *Library Journal,* felt that the novel "offers a paint-by-the-numbers plot with cardboard characters," but that "diehard fans will want this." However a reviewer for *Publishers Weekly* wrote that "Hillerman is in top form" with *Hunting Badger,* and *Booklist*'s Bill Ott dubbed *Hunting Badger* "a return to form for Hillerman." Ott concluded, "Nobody uses the power of myth to enrich crime fiction more effectively than Hillerman."

In *The Sinister Pig* readers are provided with "an intricate pattern of ingenious detective work, comic romance, tribal custom, and desert atmosphere" which provide "multifaceted reading pleasure" according to reviewer Connie Fletcher of *Booklist.* The novel once again follows Hillerman's usual cast of characters as they try to solve a mystery involving a body discovered on Navajo land and its connection to billions of dollars owed to the Native Americans as oil royalties. Christine C. Menefee, reviewing the novel for *School Library Journal,* stated that readers "should enjoy the broader geographical and social canvas . . . in this tale of ordinary people unraveling knots of fraud and skullduggery."

Hillerman has also been commended for his nonfiction works and for anthologies that explore the natural beauty and unique history of the Southwest. In *New Mexico, Rio Grande, and Other Essays,* the author discusses a number of topics, including how geographical, political, and historical factors helped the Pueblo Indians thrive when many other tribes fell prey to conquering forces. In *The Mysterious West,* Hillerman as editor pulls together previously unpublished stories from writers such as J. A. Jance and Marcia Muller, while in *The Oxford Book of American Detective Stories* and *The Best American Stories of the Century* he shows his ties to the mystery genre are as strong as those to the Southwest. But in the final analysis, Hillerman is known for his Chee-Leaphorn books and their evocation of Navajo country. In these books, the author explores, as Muhlestein noted in *Dictionary of Literary Biography,* "the themes he cares about most deeply: the question of identity, the tension between the desire to assimilate and the need to retain native traditions, the shortcomings of Anglo justice, and the spiritual illness of white culture." As Fred Erisman commented in *Tony Hillerman,* "Leaphorn and Chee, as Navajos, give readers a sense of the demands of Southwestern life. In a larger sense, though, that they are Navajo is incidental; they are human as well as Navajo, and as they . . . grapple with the realities of their people, their place, and their time, their responsibilities help all readers to decipher the palimpsest of human life in all its complexity and all its majesty."

BIOGRAPHICAL AND CRITICAL SOURCES:

BOOKS

Bulow, Ernie, and Tony Hillerman, *Talking Mysteries: A Conversation with Tony Hillerman,* University of New Mexico Press (Albuqurerque, NM), 1991.

Contemporary Literary Criticism, Volume 62, Gale (Detroit, MI), 1990.

Contemporary Popular Writers, St. James Press (Detroit, MI), 1997.

Dictionary of Literary Biography, Volume 206: *Twentieth-Century American Western Writers, First Series,* Gale (Detroit, MI), 1999.

Erisman, Fred, *Tony Hillerman,* Boise State University, 1989.

Greenberg, Martin, editor, *The Tony Hillerman Companion: A Comprehensive Guide to His Life and Work,* HarperCollins (New York, NY), 1994.

Reilly, John M., *Tony Hillerman: A Critical Companion,* Greenwood Press (Westport, CT), 1996.

St. James Guide to Crime and Mystery Writers, 4th edition, St. James Press (Detroit, MI), 1996.

Sobol, John, *Tony Hillerman: A Public Life,* ECW Press, 1994.

PERIODICALS

Armchair Detective, fall, 1990, p. 426.

Atlantic, September, 1990, Phoebe-Lou Adams, review of *Coyote Waits,* p. 121; January, 1992, p. 115.

Booklist, October 1, 1994, p. 243; September 15, 1995, p. 116; March 1, 1996, p. 1125; November 1, 1996, Stephanie Zvirin, review of *The Fallen Man,* p. 459; October 15, 1997, p. 424; November 15, 1998, p. 604; June 1, 1999, p. 1853; July, 1999, Stephanie Zvirin, review of *The First Eagle,* p. 1829; April 1, 2000, p. 1437; May 1, 2000, Bill Ott, review of *Hunting Badger,* p. 1595; September 1, 2000, p. 144; May 1, 2003, Connie Fletcher, review of *The Sinister Pig,* p. 1547.

Cosmopolitan, June, 1989, Louise Bernikow, review of *Talking God,* p. 48.

Economist, August 14, 1993, pp. 83-84.

Entertainment Weekly, January 31, 1992, review of *Coyote Waits,* p. 54; April 3, 1992, review of *The Ghostway,* p. 47; September 17, 1993, Gene Lyons, review of *Sacred Clowns,* p. 82; November 3, 1995, p. 59; November 15, 1996, Sikki Andur, review of *The Fallen Man.*

Kirkus Reviews, February 1, 1996, p. 179.

Library Journal, November 1, 1994, p. 77; March 1, 1996, p. 109; March 15, 1997, p. 102; July, 1998, p. 136; January, 1999, p. 184; November 15, 1999, Wilda Williams, review of *Hunting Badger,* p. 98; April 1, 2000, p. 150; Janurary 2004, Sandy Glover, review of *The Sinister Pig,* p. 186.

Los Angeles Times Book Review, January 21, 1990, p. 14; May 27, 1990, p. 10; December 16, 1990; November 17, 1991, p. 12; January 5, 1992, p. 9; October 3, 1993, p. 12.

New Yorker, August 23, 1993, p. 165.

New York Times, June 10, 1989, Herbert Mitgang, "Hillerman Adds Tribal Rites of Washington to the Navajos," p. 15; February 16, 2000, p. B2.

New York Times Book Review, December 23, 1990, p. 20; October 20, 1991, p. 36; February 2, 1992, p. 28; August 30, 1992, p. 14; October 17, 1993, p. 36; October 22, 1995, p. 29; November 21, 1999, p. 80.

People, February 9, 1987, Campbell Geeslin, review of *Skinwalkers,* p. 16; July 18, 1988, Michael Neill, "A Keen Observer in a World Not His Own," p. 85; August 27, 1990, Michael Neill, review of *Coyote Waits,* p. 22.

Publishers Weekly, October 24, 1980; May 11, 1990, review of *Coyote Waits,* p. 250; July 26, 1993, review of *Sacred Clowns,* p. 60; September 12, 1994, p. 85; September 4, 1995, p. 48; February 12, 1996, p. 63; October 21, 1996, review of *The Fallen Man,* p. 73; July 13, 1998, review of *The First Eagle,* p. 65; October 18, 1999, p. 74; November 22, 1999, p. 16; January 3, 2000, review of *Hunting Badger,* p. 40; March 6, 2000, p. 85.

Quadrant, July, 2000, p. 118.
School Library Journal, February, 1994, p. 136;
    March, 1995, p. 235; December 2003, Christine
    C. Menefee, review of *The Sinister Pig,* p. 176.
Time, July 4, 1988, review of *A Thief of Time,* p. 71.
Tribune Books (Chicago, IL), September 2, 1990;
    September 26, 1993, p. 6.
Wall Street Journal, August 13, 1998, p. A12.
Washington Post Book World, May 27, 1990, p. 12;
    July 26, 1992, p. 1; September 5, 1993, p. 4.
Writer's Digest, January, 2000, pp. 8-9.*

*   *   *

HORN, Michiel 1939-

PERSONAL: Born September 3, 1939, in the Netherlands; immigrated to Canada, 1952; naturalized
Canadian citizen, 1958; son of Daniel (an architect
and forest service official) and Antje Elisabeth (Re-
itsma) Horn; married Cornelia Schuh, December 29,
1984; children: Daniel Andre, Patrick Benjamin. *Ethnicity:* "Dutch." *Education:* University of British
Columbia, B.A., 1963; University of Toronto, M.A.,
1965, Ph.D., 1969.

ADDRESSES: Home—18 Walder Ave., Toronto, Ontario M4P 2R5, Canada. *Office*—York University, 2275
Bayview Ave., Toronto, Ontario M4N 3M6, Canada;
fax: 416-487-6852. *E-mail*—mhorn@glendon.yorku.
ca.

CAREER: Bank of Montreal, Victoria, British Columbia, Canada, bank officer, 1956-58; York University,
Glendon College, Toronto, Ontario, Canada, lecturer,
1968-69, assistant professor, 1969-73, associate professor, 1973-82, professor of history, 1982—, department
chair, 1982-93, associate principal of the college,
1978-81, director of Canadian Studies, 1986-89.
Member of advisory committees for North York
Historical Board and for a local architectural
conservancy.

MEMBER: Royal Society of Canada (fellow), Canadian Association of University Teachers (member of
executive committee, 1973-75), Ontario Confederation
of University Faculty Associations (chair, 1976-77),
York University Faculty Association (chair, 1972-73),
Massey College Common Room Club, Glendon
Squash Club.

AWARDS, HONORS: Woodrow Wilson fellow, 1963-
64; grants from Canada Council, 1974-75. and Social
Science and Humanities Research Council of Canada,
1986-89, 1990-91; Book Award, Canadian Association
of Foundations in Education, 2000; Milner Memorial
Award, Canadian Association of University Teachers,
2002.

WRITINGS:

*The League for Social Reconstruction: Intellectual
    Origins of the Democratic Left in Canada, 1930-
    1942,* University of Toronto Press (Toronto, On-
    tario, Canada), 1980.
*A Liberation Album: Canadians in the Netherlands,
    1944-45* (based on the film *Liberation!*), edited by
    David Kaufman, McGraw-Hill Ryerson (New
    York, NY), 1980.
(With Edgar McInnis) *Canada: A Political and Social
    History,* Holt, Rinehart & Winston of Canada (Tor-
    onto, Ontario, Canada), 1982.
Years of Despair, Grolier (Toronto, Ontario, Canada),
    1986.
*Becoming Canadian: Memoirs of an Invisible Im-
    migrant,* University of Toronto Press (Toronto,
    Ontario, Canada), 1997.
Academic Freedom in Canada: A History, University
    of Toronto Press (Toronto, Ontario, Canada), 1999.

Author of the booklet "The Great Depression of the
1930s in Canada," Canadian Historical Association
(Ottawa, Ontario, Canada), 1984. Contributor to books,
including *Dutch Immigration to North America,* edited
by Herman Ganzevoort and Mark Boekelman, Multi-
cultural History Society of Ontario (Toronto, Ontario,
Canada), 1983; and *"Building the Co-operative Com-
monwealth": Essays on the Democratic Socialist
Tradition in Canada,* edited by J. William Breenan,
Canadian Plains Research Center, University of Regina
(Regina, Saskatchewan, Canada), 1984. Contributor to
periodicals, including *Canadian Forum, Journal of
Canadian Studies, Dalhousie Review, BC Studies,* and
Canadian Historical Review.

EDITOR

(And contributor) *The Dirty Thirties: Canadians in the
    Great Depression,* Copp Clark (Toronto, Ontario,
    Canada), 1972.

(With Ronald Sabourin) *Studies in Canadian Social History,* McClelland & Stewart (Toronto, Ontario, Canada), 1974.

(And author of introduction) Frank R. Scott, *A New Endeavour: Selected Political Essays, Letters, and Addresses,* University of Toronto Press (Toronto, Ontario, Canada), 1986.

Academic Freedom: The Harry Crowe Memorial Lectures, York University Press (Toronto, Ontario, Canada), 1987.

The Depression in Canada: Responses to Economic Crisis, Copp Clark Pittman (Toronto, Ontario, Canada), 1988.

WORK IN PROGRESS: York University Remembered: A History; literary translations from Dutch into English, focusing on the novels of Maarten 't Hart.

SIDELIGHTS: Born into a middle-class Dutch household that contained six sons, Michiel Horn was uprooted in 1952 when his parents decided to move to British Columbia to start life anew. Their purpose was primarily economic and, looking back at the experience in his 1997 memoir, *Becoming Canadian: Memoirs of an Invisible Immigrant,* Horn was ambivalent about the decision. As quoted in a *Canadian Forum* review by Clyde Sanger, he had "no significant complaints" about having become a Canadian, but wrote, "All the same, had I been given my druthers in 1952, I would probably have chosen to stay in Baarn." Horn expressed skepticism about immigration for the purpose of gaining a better livelihood. In his experience, such experiments were far from guaranteed to work. His own father, an architect in Holland, had to settle for being a minor bureaucrat in a provincial Forest Service in Canada, Sanger explained. Immigration to escape political, ethnic or religious persecution, Horn felt, was much more valid motivation.

Horn's professional reputation has been based on his decades of solid historical work, his specialties being Canadian society and politics of the 1930s and 1940s and, additionally, the role of Canadians in liberating the Netherlands during World War II. One of these works is *The League for Social Reconstruction: Intellectual Origins of the Democratic Left in Canada, 1930-1942.* Despite its forbiddingly scholarly title, it was received as a readable, instructive, and even entertaining book on Canadian social history by that nation's mainstream media. According to Kenneth Mc-

Naught, a reviewer for *Quill & Quire,* the League for Social Reconstruction was a Depression-era progressive movement with borderline socialist leanings, often compared to the Fabian Society in England. The League had its origins in the work of certain professors at the University of Toronto and at McGill University in Montreal, and their work for the cause was professionally perilous in a time and place where academic freedom was hardly a sacred ideal.

"Horn is at his best depicting [the professors'] work," noted McNaught; "and the story of these dedicated crusaders for social justice is an exciting one." Calling the book "carefully written" and "balanced," McNaught stated that Horn had "widely adopted a social as well as intellectual approach and this should make the book of interest to anyone concerned with our social-political history." *Books in Canada* reviewer Albert Moritz commented favorably on Horn's "basically narrative and even anecdotal" approach and his rich use of researched detail, and added, "Horn's strength is the complete and affectionate depiction of this group, mixed with clear accounts of its thought and a sharp but genial eye for shortcomings and flaws." A *Choice* reviewer praised the book, declaring that "the title is about the only dull phrase" in this work. The *Choice* reviewer continued, writing that *The League for Social Reconstruction* "is . . . written with intelligence, vivacity, even charm." Recommending the volume as an introduction to the history of Canada in the 1930s, the reviewer cited Horn's expertise and called the opus one of the finest on its topic. It was an achievement, the reviewer concluded, that should grace the shelves of every library in North America with any claim to an interest in the subject of Canada.

Paul J. Stortz reviewed *Becoming Canadian* in the *Journal of Ethnic and Migration Studies,* noting that a strength of the book is how it "introspectively challenges how effortlessly Horn became a 'productive' citizen of Canada, and how comfortable he was in assuming that role. . . . Throughout the biography, Horn relates impressions and experiences which he and others in his life denote as Canadianisms—conservative instead of risky approaches, accommodation, tolerance, social infrastructures, and federal policies of multiculturalism, being able to paddle a canoe—but the definition of Canada, cogently queried especially in the final chapter, ends up fundamentally elusive, in a sense as quixotic as the country itself."

In writing *Academic Freedom in Canada: A History,* Horn drew on archival research at more than twenty Canadian universities, as well as six public archives. He traces academic freedom from 1860 to present time, including, for example, previously unpublished data about why certain academics were fired or forced to resign, and how others were retained but kept under control. He cites individual cases and issues including resistance to Darwin's theories, capitalism, the roles of women and minorities, and the influence of biblical criticism. A writer for *Creative Resistance* online noted that Horn also looks at modern challenges to academic freedom, including "political correctness." "He shows," wrote the critic, "how the seeds of today's changing demands on universities can be found in the vicissitudes of the past, and contends that Canadian academics owe it to their fellow citizens to use their freedom for the common good."

BIOGRAPHICAL AND CRITICAL SOURCES:

BOOKS

Horn, Michiel, *Becoming Canadian: Memoirs of an Invisible Immigrant,* University of Toronto Press (Toronto, Ontario, Canada), 1997.

PERIODICALS

American Historical Review, October, 1981, p. 958; December, 2000, review of *Academic Freedom in Canada: A History.*
Books in Canada, June-July, 1981, Albert Moritz, review of *The League for Social Reconstruction: Intellectual Origins of the Democratic Left in Canada, 1930-1942,* pp. 20-21.
Canadian Forum, December, 1980, p. 38; June, 1997, Clyde Sanger, review of *Becoming Canadian,* pp. 40-41.
Canadian Historical Review, March, 1989, pp. 117-118; March, 2001, Paul Axelrod, review of *Academic Freedom in Canada,* p. 187.
Canadian Public Administration, summer, 2000, David M. Cameron, review of *Academic Freedom in Canada,* p. 218.
Choice, March, 1981, review of *The League for Social Reconstruction,* p. 1013.
Journal of Ethnic and Migration Studies, July, 1999, Paul J. Stortz, review of *Becoming Canadian,* p. 548.

Quill & Quire, February, 1981, Kenneth McNaught, review of *The League for Social Reconstruction,* p. 46.
University of Toronto Quarterly, winter, 2000, T. H. Adamowski, review of *Academic Freedom in Canada,* p. 294.

ONLINE

Creative Resistance, http://www.creativeresistance.ca/ (March 26, 2004), review of *Academic Freedom in Canada.*

*   *   *

HOWARTH, William Louis 1940-

PERSONAL: Born November 26, 1940, in Minneapolis, MN; son of Nelson Oliver (an attorney) and Mary (Prindiville) Howarth; married Barbara Ann Brown (a teacher), August 16, 1963 (divorced, 1994); children: Jennifer Lynn, Jeffrey Todd. *Education:* University of Illinois, B.A. (with honors), 1962; University of Virginia, M.A., 1963, Ph.D., 1967.

ADDRESSES: Home—95 Herrontown Lane, Princeton, NJ 08540. *Office*—Department of English, McCosh 22, Princeton University, Princeton, NJ 08544. *E-mail*—howarth@princeton.edu.

CAREER: Princeton University, Princeton, NJ, instructor, 1966-68, assistant professor, 1968-73, associate professor, 1973-81, professor of English, 1981—. Princeton Environmental Institute, board member and associate faculty; Center for American Places, past chair.

MEMBER: Modern Language Association of America, American Studies Association, Thoreau Society (president, 1975), Phi Beta Kappa.

AWARDS, HONORS: Huntington Library fellow, 1968; John E. Annan Bicentennial Preceptor, 1970-73; National Endowment for the Humanities fellow, 1976-77; awards from Center for the Study of Religion, 1999-2000, and Center for Theology and Natural Science, 2000.

WRITINGS:

(Editor) Robert F. Stowell, *A Thoreau Gazetteer,* Princeton University Press (Princeton, NJ), 1970.

(Editor) *Twentieth-Century Interpretations of Poe's Tales,* Prentice-Hall (Englewood Cliffs, NJ), 1971.

(Compiler, with others) *Nature in American Life: A Preliminary Bibliographical Guide; with Supplement, 1971 and 1972,* [Princeton, NJ], 1972.

The Literary Manuscripts of Henry David Thoreau, Ohio State University Press (Columbus, OH), 1974.

(Editor) *The John McPhee Reader,* Farrar, Straus & Giroux (New York, NY), 1976.

(Editor, with Carl F. Hovde and Elizabeth Hall Witherell) Henry David Thoreau, *A Week on the Concord and Merrimack Rivers,* Princeton University Press (Princeton, NJ), 1978, published as *The Illustrated "A Week on the Concord and Merrimack Rivers,"* 1983.

(Editor) Henry David Thoreau, *Walden, and Other Writings,* Modern Library (New York, NY), 1981.

(Author of commentary) Henry David Thoreau, *Thoreau in the Mountains,* Farrar, Straus & Giroux (New York, NY), 1982.

The Book of Concord: Thoreau's Life As a Writer, Viking (New York, NY), 1982.

(Editor) Henry David Thoreau, *Journal 1, 1837-44,* Princeton University Press (Princeton, NJ), 1984.

Traveling the Trans-Canada, National Geographic Society (Washington, DC), 1987.

(Editor) Clarence King, *Mountaineering in the Sierra Nevada,* Viking Penguin (New York, NY), 1989.

(Author of commentary) *Walking with Thoreau: A Literary Guide to the New England Mountains,* Beacon Press (Boston, MA), 2001.

Contributor to books, including *Literary Journalism in the Twentieth Century,* Oxford University Press (New York, NY), 1991; *The Changing American Countryside,* University Press of Kansas (Lawrence, KS), 1995; *The Ecocriticism Reader,* University of Georgia Press (Athens, GA), 1996; *Textures of Place,* University of Minnesota Press (Minneapolis, MN), 2001; and *Coming into John McPhee Country,* University of Utah Press (Salt Lake City, UT), 2003. Editor in chief of "The Writings of Henry D. Thoreau," 1972-80. Contributor of articles and reviews to *National Geographic, Smithsonian, Washington Post,* and *Sewanee Review.*

SIDELIGHTS: William Louis Howarth is the author and editor of several books on the life and writings of Henry David Thoreau. He helped to launch the editing of Thoreau's voluminous journal, which spans the years 1837 to 1861. *The Book of Concord: Thoreau's Life As a Writer* is Howarth's critical study of the journal. It details "the themes of Thoreau's life and the evolution of the marvelous journal," according to Clay Jenkinson in the *Los Angeles Times Book Review.*

In what *Sierra* contributor Henry Middleton described as a determination "to feel Thoreau's life as well as understand it," Howarth walked the same trails, climbed the same mountains, and canoed the same streams as Thoreau once did. In a review of *The Book of Concord,* however, *New Republic* contributor Leon Edel suggested that Howarth's attempts to emulate Thoreau's life impair his objectivity. "There is somehow a want of 'distance' from his subject; he is too close, too easily admiring, too defensive." Peter Davison, on the other hand, wrote in the *Washington Post Book World:* "Howarth climbs inside Thoreau's inkwell and tells us how and why he wrote, to what end, out of what fears and aspirations, and with what circuitous progress toward a 'final' text. It would be hard to imagine a critic's account that more faithfully pursues the mystery of the writing process."

Recently Howarth described himself to *CA* as "an author and critic of literary nonfiction, chiefly on places, natural history, and geography; and an early founder of ecocriticism, working at the intersection of literary history and evolutionary theory."

BIOGRAPHICAL AND CRITICAL SOURCES:

PERIODICALS

Los Angeles Times Book Review, December 5, 1982, Clay Jenkinson, review of *The Book of Concord: Thoreau's Life As a Writer.*

New Republic, October 18, 1982, Leon Edel, review of *The Book of Concord.*

New York Times Book Review, September 12, 1982.

Sewanee Review, winter, 1984.

Sierra, January-February, 1983, Henry Middleton, review of *The Book of Concord.*

Southern Humanities Review, winter, 1985.

Washington Post Book World, November 7, 1982, Peter Davison, review of *The Book of Concord.*

ONLINE

William Howarth, Professor of English, Princeton University; Associate Faculty, Princeton Environmental Institute, http://www.princeton.edu/~howarth/ (March 8, 2004).

*   *   *

HUTTON, Paul Andrew 1949-

PERSONAL: Born October 23, 1949, in Frankfurt, West Germany (now Germany); son of Paul Andrew (an American soldier) and Louise (a homemaker; maiden name, Johnson) Hutton; married Vicki Bauer, July 25, 1972 (divorced, August, 1984); children: Laura Bauer. *Education:* Indiana University, Bloomington, B.A., 1972, M.A., 1974, Ph.D., 1981.

ADDRESSES: Office—Department of History, 1104 Mesa Vista Hall, University of New Mexico, Albuquerque, NM 87131. *E-mail*—wha@unm.edu.

CAREER: Educator and writer. Utah State University, Logan, visiting instructor, 1977-80, assistant professor of American history, 1980-84; University of New Mexico, Albuquerque, assistant professor, 1984-86, became associate professor and then professor of history. Executive director, Western History Association; vice president, Western Writers of America.

Has appeared in, written, or narrated more than 100 television documentaries, many available on video cassette, for CBS, NBC, PBS. TBS, TNN, A&E, Discovery, Disney, and the History Channel, including *The Real West,* 67 episodes, 1992-1994; "River Pirates," episode of *In Search of History,* 1999; "America's Changing West," episode of *Colores,* KNME (PBS), 1999; "Betrayal at Little Big Horn," episode of *The New Explorers,* 1998; "Law and Order in the Real West," 1998; "George Armstrong Custer: America's Golden Cavalier," episode of *Biography,* 1997.

MEMBER: Organization of American Historians, Western History Association, Historians Film Committee.

AWARDS, HONORS: Spur Award, Western Writers of America, 1986, Evans Biography Prize, Brigham Young University, 1986, Ray Allen Billington Award, Organization of American Historians, 1987, and Texas Literary Award, Southwestern Booksellers Association, 1987, all for *Phil Sheridan and His Army.*; Vivian A. Paladin Award for best essay to appear in *Montana: The Magazine of Western History,* Montana Historical Society, 1991, for "Correct in Every Detail"; John M. Carroll Literary Award, Little Big Horn Associates, 1992, for *The Custer Reader;* President's Award, Western Writers of America, 1998; Western Heritage Award for outstanding magazine article of 1995, National Cowboy Hall of Fame, 1996, for "Showdown at the Hollywood Coral"; Western Heritage Award for outstanding magazine article of 1998, 1999, for "T. R. Takes Charge"; Stirrup Award, Western Writers of America, 1999, for "Dee Brown: A Life with Books."

WRITINGS:

(Editor) *Custer and His Times,* Little Big Horn Associates (LaGrange Park, IL), 1981.
Phil Sheridan and His Army, University of Nebraska Press (Lincoln, NE), 1985.
(Editor) Henry Eugene Davies, *Ten Days on the Plains,* Southern Methodist University Press (Dallas, TX), 1985.
Soldiers West: Biographies from the Military Frontier, University of Nebraska Press (Lincoln, NE), 1987.
(Editor) *The Custer Reader,* University of Nebraska Press (Lincoln, NE), 1992.
(Editor, with Robert C. Ritchie) *Frontier and Region: Essays in Honor of Martin Ridge,* University of New Mexico Press (Albuquerque, NM), 1997.

Contributor to periodicals, including *TV Guide, American West, Texas Monthly, American History Illustrated, Frontier Times,* and *True West. Western History Quarterly,* assistant editor, 1977-79, associate editor, 1979-84; *New Mexico Historical Review,* editor, 1984—.

SIDELIGHTS: Paul Andrew Hutton is an award-winning writer of books, articles, and documentaries pertaining to the history of the American West. *Frontier and Region: Essays in Honor of Martin Ridge,* of which Hutton is coeditor, is a compilation of twelve essays by twelve western scholars (including Hutton) that won considerable acclaim from reviewers.

Ridge was an important and highly regarded historian and a familiar figure at American and western history conferences around the nation. He was editor of the *Journal of American History* from 1996 to 1997 and director of research at the Huntington Library until his retirement in 1992. "Through the years, he advised, directed, and encouraged hundreds of senior and younger scholars in their manifold projects," wrote Richard W. Etulain for the *Journal of American History.* Most essays in this collection, prepared by Ridge's colleagues and students, were written from research undertaken, at least in part, at the Huntington. All essays were delivered as papers upon Ridge's retirement.

David M. Emmons explained in the *Pacific Historical Review* that a collection of this type is called a "festschrifte," German for "happy writings." He commented: "These are festive and celebratory, usually offered up in honor of the career of someone the essayists know and especially like. . . . Ridge is a wonderful historian and a warm and generous man." Hutton, one of Ridge's students, wrote in what Etulain called a "very helpful" introduction to the book that the essays "have no social, ideological, or historiographical axe to grind, but rather seek to reaffirm the vitality of traditional approaches to the history of the American West" and that they "lack the somewhat contentious tone of much of the recent scholarly debate on the West." This fact, commented Emmons, is attributable to Ridge, the essayists' mentor: "All were done with the same conspicuous lack of rancor or grandstanding that marked Ridge's career."

The collection consists of a wide range of topics divided into four sections. The first comprises essays by well-known regional historians such as James H. Madison, who deals with differences between the Midwest and the West; Walter Nugent, who focuses on "finding" the West; and James P. Ronda, who investigates how rivers provided a means of western exploration. In the second section, Richard Lowitt, Donald J. Pisani, Charles E. Rankin, and Melody Webb look at controversies surrounding water rights and the development of national parks and explore Western journalism and federalism.

Part three, titled "The Popular West," is what Etulain called "lively essays on Old West figures such as Davey Crockett, Annie Oakley, and Buffalo Bill Cody." These essays are written by Hutton, Glenda Riley, and Richard White. Louis Hart pointed out in

Wild West that Hutton's essay reveals that "the greatest impetus to the growth of the Crockett legend came from the Crockett almanacs." Part four contains essays by Albert L. Hurtado and Howard R. Lamar that focus on historian Herbert E. Bolton and four authors who, noted Etulain, "imaginatively used the frontier in their writings."

Of the entire collection, Etulain commented: "Taken together, these essays illustrate the broad range of interests of the diligent historian they honor."

BIOGRAPHICAL AND CRITICAL SOURCES:

PERIODICALS

Journal of American History, September, 1998, Richard W. Etulain, review of *Frontier and Region: Essays in Honor of Martin Ridge,* pp. 717-718.
Pacific Historical Review, February 1999, David M. Emmons, review of *Frontier and Region,* p. 136.
Wild West, October 1998, Louis Hart, review of *Frontier and Region,* p. 73.*

* * *

HYMAN, Paula (E.) 1946-

PERSONAL: Born September 30, 1946, in Boston, MA; daughter of Sydney M. (an accountant) and Ida (a bookkeeper; maiden name, Tatelman) Hyman; married Stanley Rosenbaum (a physician), June 7, 1969; children: Judith, Adina. *Education:* Hebrew College of Boston, B.J.Ed., 1966; Radcliffe College, B.A., 1968; Columbia University, M.A., 1970, Ph.D., 1975. *Religion:* Jewish.

ADDRESSES: Office—Judaic Studies Program, Yale University, 451 College St., New Haven, CT. *E-mail*—paula.hyman@yale.edu.

CAREER: Columbia University, New York, NY, assistant professor of history, beginning 1974; Jewish Theological Seminary of America, former dean of the Seminary College of Jewish Studies; Yale University, New Haven, CT, currently Lucy Moses Professor of Modern Jewish History and chairperson of the Judaic

Studies Program. Member of advisory committee for the Women's Studies in Religion program, Harvard Divinity School. Member of board of directors of Leo Baeck Institute, beginning 1979; member of American Jewish Congress Commission on Youth and Culture.

MEMBER: American Historical Association, American Association for Jewish Research (vice president), National Foundation for Jewish Culture (chairperson of the academic council), Ezrat Nashim (founding member), Association for Jewish Studies (member of board of directors, 1978—), Coordinating Committee on Women in the Historical Profession.

AWARDS, HONORS: National Endowment for the Humanities grant, 1977; American Council of Learned Societies fellowship, 1979; Dartmouth Medal, American Library Association, Association of Jewish Libraries Award, New York Public Library Award, and the National Jewish Book Award in Women's Studies, all 1997, all for *Jewish Women in America: An Historical Encyclopedia;* Akiba Award, American Jewish Committee, 1999; honorary degree, Jewish Theological Seminary, 2000, Hebrew Union College, 2002.

WRITINGS:

(With Charlotte Baum and Sonya Michel) *The Jewish Woman in America,* Dial (New York, NY), 1976.

From Dreyfus to Vichy, Columbia University Press (New York, NY), 1979.

(Editor, with Steven M. Cohen) *The Jewish Family: Myths and Reality,* Holmes & Meier (New York, NY), 1986.

The Emancipation of the Jews of Alsace: Acculturation and Tradition in the Nineteenth Century, Yale University Press (New Haven, CT), 1991.

Gender and Assimilation in Modern Jewish History: The Roles and Representation of Women, University of Washington Press (Seattle, WA), 1995.

(Editor, with Deborah Dash Moore) *Jewish Women in America: An Historical Encyclopedia,* Routledge (New York, NY), 1997.

The Jews of Modern France, University of California Press (Berkeley, CA), 1998.

(Editor and author of introduction) Puah Rakovska, *My Life As a Radical Jewish Woman: Memoirs of a Zionist Feminist in Poland,* Indiana University Press (Bloomington, IN), 2001.

Contributor to Jewish studies and feminist journals, including *Ms.*

SIDELIGHTS: Paula Hyman is "a distinguished historian of the modern Jewish experience," according to Hasia R. Diner in *Lilith: The Independent Jewish Women's Magazine.* Among Hyman's books are *Jewish Women in America: An Historical Encyclopedia* and *The Jews of Modern France.*

Jewish Women in America: An Historical Encyclopedia, edited by Hyman and Deborah Dash Moore, is a 1,700-page "magnificently massive treasure," as Phyllis Chesler wrote in *Tikkun.* The two-volume set contains some 800 biographies of Jewish- American women who lived from 1654, when the first Jewish woman arrived in America, until the present day. Also included are over 100 topical essays on a host of subjects related to Jewish cultural history, including education, politics, and the arts. Mary F. Salony in *Library Journal* called *Jewish Women in America* "an excellent biographical source." Diner found the work's "quantity and quality of information [to be], seemingly, comprehensive" and concluded that the encyclopedia was "a formidable accomplishment."

The Jews of Modern France is a "concise study of French Jews since the Great Revolution of 1789," wrote Irwin Wall in *Judaism: A Quarterly Journal of Jewish Life and Thought.* Hyman especially chronicles the efforts of the French-Jewish community to enjoy the advantages of emancipation and legal tolerance while not losing their traditional culture through assimilation with the larger Christian society. The particulars of French history, including the country's ingrained anti-Semitism and its experience of the Holocaust and Nazi collaboration, makes the story of French Jewry fundamentally different from that of other countries, although it shares some of the same concerns and recurring problems. Elliott Abrams, writing in *First Things: A Monthly Journal of Religion and Public Life,* described *The Jews of Modern France* as "an examination of the struggle to achieve a sustainable Jewish identity in a culture both similar to and different from our own." David A. Bell in the *New Republic* found Hyman's book to be an "excellent general history of modern French Jewry."

BIOGRAPHICAL AND CRITICAL SOURCES:

PERIODICALS

Annals of the American Academy of Political and Social Science, March, 1981, David L. Schalk, review of *From Dreyfus to Vichy,* p. 221.

First Things: A Monthly Journal of Religion and Public Life, April, 1999, Elliott Abrams, review of *The Jews of Modern France,* p. 68.

Historian, autumn, 1992, Albert S. Lindemann, review of *The Emancipation of the Jews of Alsace: Acculturation and Tradition in the Nineteenth Century,* p. 127.

History Today, October, 1980, Robert Anderson, review of *From Dreyfus to Vichy,* p. 61.

Journal of Modern History, June, 1993, p. 393.

Judaism: A Quarterly Journal of Jewish Life and Thought, winter, 2001, Irwin Wall, review of *The Jews of Modern France,* p. 117.

Library Journal, February 1, 1998, Mary F. Salony, review of *Jewish Women in America: An Historical Encyclopedia,* p. 76.

Lilith: The Independent Jewish Women's Magazine, July 1, 1997, Hasia R. Diner, review of *Gender and Assimilation in Modern Jewish History: The Roles and Representation of Women.*

New Leader, June 2, 1980, David Singer, review of *From Dreyfus to Vichy,* p. 18.

New Republic, February 28, 2000, David A. Bell, "The Ordeal of Legitimacy: The Fitful History of French Jewry," p. 37.

Tikkun, May-June, 1998, Phyllis Chesler, review of *Jewish Women in America,* p. 72.

I

INGERSOLL, Earl G(eorge) 1938-

PERSONAL: Born May 6, 1938, in Spencerport, NY; son of Earl D. (a carpenter) and Rose (a homemaker; maiden name, Neth) Ingersoll; married Mary Cosgrove (a teacher), June 17, 1960; children: Jeffrey, Timothy. *Education:* University of Rochester, B.A., 1960; Syracuse University, M.A., 1963; University of Wisconsin—Madison, Ph.D., 1971. *Hobbies and other interests:* Gardening.

ADDRESSES: Home—173 Dewey St., Churchville, NY 14428. *Office*—c/o State University of New York College at Brockport, Brockport, NY 14420; fax: 716-395-2391. *E-mail*—eingerso@brockport.edu.

CAREER: State University of New York College at Brockport, instructor, 1964-71, assistant professor, 1971-87, associate professor, 1987-91, professor, 1991-96, distinguished teaching professor of English, 1996-2002.

MEMBER: International Association for the Fantastic in the Arts, D. H. Lawrence Society of North America (member of executive council, 1994-96; president, 1998-2000), Modern Language Association of America, College English Association, Doris Lessing Society, Margaret Atwood Society, Lawrence Durrell Society, Canadian Association of Irish Studies, New York College English Association (president, 1994-96), Irish-American Cultural Institute.

WRITINGS:

Representations of Science and Technology in British Literature since 1880, Peter Lang Publishing (New York, NY), 1992.

Engendered Trope in Joyce's "Dubliners," Southern Illinois University Press (Carbondale, IL), 1996.

D. H. Lawrence, Desire, and Narrative, University Press of Florida (Gainesville, FL), 2001.

Contributor of more than fifty articles to language and literature journals, including *Conradiana, College Language Association Journal, Journal of Men's Studies, Midwest Quarterly, Studies in the Novel, Journal of the Fantastic in the Arts,* and *Doris Lessing Newsletter.*

EDITOR

(With Judith Kitchen and Stan Sanvel Rubin) *The Post-Confessionals: Conversations with American Poets of the Eighties,* Fairleigh Dickinson University Press (Madison, NJ), 1989.

Margaret Atwood: Conversations, Ontario Review Press (Princeton, NJ), 1990, revised edition, Virago Press (London, England), 1992.

Conversations with May Sarton, University Press of Mississippi (Jackson, MS), 1991.

Doris Lessing: Conversations, Ontario Review Press (Princeton, NJ), 1994, published as *Putting the Question Differently,* HarperCollins (London, England), 1996.

Lawrence Durrell: Conversations, Associated University Presses (Madison, NJ), 1998.

Conversations with Rita Dove, University Press of Mississippi (Oxford, MS), 2003.

(With Keith Cushman) *D. H. Lawrence: New Worlds,* Fairleigh Dickinson University Press (Madison, NJ), 2003.

SIDELIGHTS: Earl G. Ingersoll once told *CA:* "As a reader of literary criticism, I have often been attracted to the connections writers make between contemporary theory and literary works that I may have read many times in preparation for the classroom. Often, if the theorizing is especially provocative, it stimulates me to see ways in which theory can open other texts. When I write, I would like to create a little of that excitement as I work at opening a text, so that readers can participate in the process and go on to do their own. What I write is an effort toward repaying the debt I owe to the dozens of critics and theorists who have opened familiar texts for me.

"I like to think that my book *Engendered Trope in Joyce's 'Dubliners'* is a case in point. I first read Joyce as a college student some forty years ago, and I have discussed at least some of these stories with students almost every year since. The *Dubliners* study grew out of a half-dozen essays that I wrote on individual stories after reading material by several readers of Jacques Lacan. Of these, Barbara Johnson, Jane Gallop, and Jerry Aline Flieger helped me to read Joyce's stories in the context of the gender associations implicit in Lacan's two key tropes of metonymy and metaphor. I hope to be carrying forward what I have called a New Psychoanalytic Criticism. Following in the footsteps of Peter Brooks, I want to redirect attention away from psychoanalyzing authors or fictional characters toward looking at the text as a structure of conflicting desires.

"I would like also to put in a word for the impact of technology. Virtually all of my professional writing and editing dates from my discovery of word processing. There is just no way to exaggerate how much I have benefited from being freed of the drudgery involved in transforming handwritten manuscripts into work that can be sent out for evaluation. Also, I was never one of those who could compose at a typewriter because I was inhibited by the continual appearance of typographical errors. Now I find myself writing very little by hand. I have been fascinated by this 'interface' with the computer monitor with its pulsating prompt signal, encouraging me to make words appear. I am struck by the tropes we use in word processing, such as 'memory.' In my less rational moments I can almost convince myself that, if the machine has memory, perhaps it has stored away somewhere all the brilliant and eloquent writing I *think* I have done—that is, until I go back later to revise it and discover it has vanished."

ISAACS, Susan 1943-

PERSONAL: Born December 7, 1943, in Brooklyn, NY; daughter of Morton (an electrical engineer) and Helen (a homemaker; maiden name, Asher) Isaacs; married Elkan Abramowitz (an attorney), August 11, 1968; children: Andrew, Elizabeth. *Education:* Attended Queens College (now Queens College of the City University of New York). *Politics:* Democratic. *Religion:* Jewish.

ADDRESSES: Agent—c/o Owen Laster, William Morris Agency, 1325 Avenue of the Americas, New York, NY 10019.

CAREER: Novelist, essayist, and screenwriter. *Seventeen* magazine, New York, NY, 1966-70, began as assistant editor, became senior editor; freelance writer, 1970-76; political speech writer for Democratic candidates in Brooklyn and Queens, New York, and for president of the borough of Queens, New York, NY; movie producer.

MEMBER: International Association of Crime Writers, PEN (executive board member, 1993-97), Mystery Writers of America (national board member, chair of committee for freedom of speech, president, 2001), National Book Critics Circle, Creative Coalition, International Association of Crime Writers, Adams Round Table, American Society of Journalists and Authors, Adams Round Table, Poets & Writers (member of board of directors, 1994-99, Chairman, 1999—), Feminists for Free Expression, Queens College Foundation (trustee), Walt Whitman Birthplace Association (trustee), North Shore Child and Family Guidance Association (trustee), Nassau County Coalition against Domestic Violence Advisory Board.

AWARDS, HONORS: D.Litt., Dowling College, 1988; Queens College Barnes & Noble Writers for Writers Award, 1996; John Steinbeck Award, 1999.

WRITINGS:

NOVELS

Compromising Positions (also see below), Times Books (New York, NY), 1978.
Close Relations, Lippincott (Philadelphia, PA), 1980.

Susan Isaacs

Almost Paradise, Harper (New York, NY), 1984.
Shining Through, Harper (New York, NY), 1988.
Magic Hour, HarperCollins (New York, NY), 1991.
After All These Years, HarperCollins (New York, NY), 1993.
Lily White, HarperCollins (New York, NY), 1996.
Red, White, and Blue, HarperCollins (New York, NY), 1998.
Long Time No See, HarperCollins (New York, NY), 2001.
Any Place I Hang My Hat, Scribner (New York, NY), 2004.

OTHER

Compromising Positions (screenplay; based on her novel of the same name), Paramount, 1985.
(And coproducer) *Hello Again* (screenplay), Buena Vista, 1987.
Brave Dames and Wimpettes: What Women Are Really Doing on Page and Screen, Ballantine (New York, NY), 1999.

Also contributor of reviews to newspapers, including *New York Times, Newsday, Washington Post,* and *Los Angeles Times.*

ADAPTATIONS: Shining Through was adapted for film by David Seltzer and released by Twentieth Century-Fox, 1992.

SIDELIGHTS: Susan Isaacs's popular and critically acclaimed novels feature a distinctive type of heroine. In her books, a *Time* reviewer summarized, "secretaries, housewives, the faceless masses of womanhood, all run into phone booths, change clothes, and come out like Cleopatra with the rectitude of Eleanor Roosevelt." This transformation begins when common people come in contact with uncommon events. Isaacs's characters confront murder, political intrigue, even World War II espionage. In spite of such daunting circumstances, the typical Isaacs protagonist displays an engaging sense of humor and a "can-do" attitude which ultimately prevails.

Isaacs achieved critical notice with her first novel, 1978's *Compromising Positions,* a book that Chicago *Tribune* contributor Clarence Petersen described as "the seeming result of an Erica Jong-Joan Rivers collaboration on a Nancy Drew mystery." The protagonist of the book is Judith Singer, a bored homemaker who seeks an outlet for her underemployed intelligence by playing detective after her periodontist is found murdered. Judith's list of suspects grows as she discovers that several of her neighbors—the attractive, upwardly mobile wives of successful men—had not only been seduced by the dentist, but were photographed in pornographic poses. While investigating the murder, Judith is romanced by a police officer, and then confronted by her dull but dutiful husband. In the end, she discovers a vital clue in the photographs that resolves the mystery. *Compromising Positions'* blend of humor, mystery, and a generous dash of sexual situations made it a best-seller. Critical response was also encouraging, though more reserved. *New York Times Book Review* contributor Jack Sullivan praised the novel's direction and humor, but criticized its lack of consistency. "What begins as a brilliant parody of suburban potboilers," Sullivan wrote, "ends by becoming one itself." A *Publishers Weekly* reviewer was more positive, noting that "the dialogue is ribald and wisecracking, the action fast and furious every step of the way."

Isaacs draws on her experience as a political speech writer in her second novel, *Close Relations.* The protagonist, Marcia Green, is a divorced woman working for a New York gubernatorial candidate. Against the backdrop of the campaign, Marcia becomes involved with two men—one Jewish and one Catholic—and her sexual encounters with each are treated in graphic detail. *Washington Post Book World* reviewer Susan Cheever noted Isaacs's refreshing portrayal of a female character who possesses "the kind of sexual appetites that have traditionally been a male prerogative—at least in literature." *Publishers Weekly* contributor Barbara A. Bannon was also impressed with *Close Relations,* emphasizing the book's "snappy dialogue yielding up laughs on every page, the love story tender and satisfying, the plot pulsing with adrenalin."

Isaacs's next effort, *Almost Paradise,* also turns on a love story, this one between Nick Cobleigh, member of a wealthy family and a successful actor, and Jane Heissenhuber, a lower-class woman who was raised by abusive parents. In a contemporary twist on the Cinderella story, poor Jane marries rich Nick, but they do not live happily ever after. Jane suffers from frigidity and agoraphobia; Nick has several extramarital affairs. The couple eventually separate, but are about to be reconciled when a sudden death brings the story to a close.

Almost Paradise received a cooler critical reaction than its Isaacs-penned predecessors. *Los Angeles Times Book Review* contributor Kenneth Atchity was particularly critical of the novel's conclusion, terming it a "shockingly happenstance, tragic ending." *New York Times* reviewer Michiko Kakutani also found fault with the book. "The characters not only speak in clichés," Kakutani wrote, "most of them *are* clichés." Other reviews were more favorable. Anna Shapiro, writing in the *New York Times Book Review,* found flaws in the novel but suggested that "one is reading too absorbedly to notice." Shapiro also praised Isaacs's pacing, emphasizing the author's ability to "keep the plot boiling."

For 1988's *Shining Through,* Isaacs moves away from her contemporary settings. Drawing readers back to World War II, she presents an intrigue that revolves around a secretary who becomes an American spy. This new subject matter challenged Isaacs, causing her to struggle with her portrayal of Linda Voss, the novel's protagonist. "She's not that easy to capture," Isaacs once explained. "There are enormous changes in the character; she goes from being a rather ordinary

legal secretary to be something of a hero, having gotten involved in the war." In the course of her adventure, Linda, a Jew, puts herself at risk by posing as a cook in Nazi Germany; romance also figures in the saga as she tries to win the affections of her married boss. *New York Times Book Review* contributor Anne Tolstoi Wallach compared the book to films from the 1940s, "in which someone pretty much like us takes incredible risks for unimpeachable motives and wins just what *we* wanted." Wallach also applauded Isaacs's successful exploration of new subjects: "Like her girl-next-door heroines, she takes risks and her readers reap the rewards."

Having begun her literary career with the mystery *Compromising Positions,* Isaacs returned to familiar ground with her next effort, *Magic Hour.* Here the sleuth is Steve Brady, a Bridgehampton, Long Island, homicide detective and one of the few male protagonists to be found in Isaacs's work. Brady is a Vietnam veteran with a past record of abusing drugs and alcohol. Though he is engaged to be married, his plans undergo a sudden change when a movie producer is found murdered. In the course of the investigation, Brady falls for Bonnie, the victim's ex-wife and one of several suspects in the case. When the facts point to Bonnie as the murderer, Brady is forced to choose between his heart and his duty as a detective.

New York Times Book Review contributor Helen Dudar found that "it takes a while for the story to develop the kind of narrative drive a light novel of this sort wants." Despite this shortcoming, though, Dudar complimented Isaacs's "wicked eye for small, telling detail," and was impressed by the author's satiric portraits of affluent Long Island residents. Ultimately, Dudar found that reading *Magic Hour* "is like polishing off an entire box of chocolates. You know it can't be nourishing, but it *is* fun." Carolyn Banks, writing in the *Washington Post Book World,* was more enthusiastic, noting that "the plot is streamlined and the time-frame is short and the voice we hear is witty, and coming-right-at-us-real. . . . Isaacs never writes a *mere* mystery . . . but something more."

Isaacs continues her line of successful whodunits with *After All These Years.* The heroine, Rosie, is married to Richie, a recent millionaire due to his software company who has taken to being called Rick, among other affectations of his new wealth. Promptly after a lavish celebration of their silver wedding anniversary,

Rick/Richie announces he is leaving Rosie for his beautiful—and younger—VP, Jessica. Later, however, Rosie finds Rick/Richie dead from a knife wound on her kitchen floor and, knowing herself to be the primary suspect—her fingerprints are on the knife—she sets out to find her husband's true killer. Although, as Barbara Raskin noted in the *New York Times Book Review,* "it's not hard to figure out who will win," the critic declared, "Still, you gotta laugh." Other reviewers also found *After All These Years* to be an enjoyable, if light, tale. "This is a good, fast, illogical read for the beach or plane; just don't ask questions. In a fairy tale, all things are possible," remarked Dorothy Uhnak in the *Washington Post Book World.* Taffy Cannon, contributor to the *Los Angeles Times Book Review,* found deeper meaning in the tale: *After All These Years* "could stand on its own as a credible mystery, but it's more than that. It seriously examines the plight of the discarded wife." Cannon concluded, however, that, "More to the point . . . it's pure fun and perfectly timed for summer reading."

In *Lily White* Isaacs combines elements of a murder mystery with a family history reminiscent of a therapy session. Lily White is a criminal defense lawyer in the suburb of Shorehaven, a far cry from her previous role in the Manhattan district attorney's office. She takes on the case of Norman, a con man accused of the murder of his latest victim. While chronicling Lily's efforts to find Norman innocent, Isaacs relates Lily's dysfunctional family history. Reviewers were mixed in their opinions of Isaacs's experiment. Calling it a "one-volume vacation reader," Elaine Kendall, writing for the *Los Angeles Times Book Review,* found "the route somewhat more circuitous than necessary." Jon Katz, contributing to the *New York Times Book Review,* lauded *Lily White* as "a big, fat, happy feast of a book," but noted, "the effect [of the two tales] is inevitably herky-jerky." *Time* reviewer John Skow was even more critical: "The flashback chapters [into Lily's family history] turn a tidy, well-told book into a fat, soggy one."

Isaacs breaks with her usual suspense novel format in *Red, White, and Blue,* a multigenerational tale of Jewish immigrants who strive for success in America. Though the book begins by chronicling the family's difficult early years in their adoptive country, it eventually develops a more romantic story line involving two characters who are distantly related. Lauren Miller is a reporter for a newspaper and Charlie Blair is an FBI agent. Both are investigating a white supremacy group in Wyoming, which quest leads to their meeting. Mary Frances Wilkens, reviewing the novel for *Booklist,* found that in *Red, White, and Blue* "Isaacs smoothly combines what could have been two different novels into one." Though a writer for *Publishers Weekly* praised Isaacs's research and considered her depictions of the white supremacist movement to be convincing, the critic felt that the book's "sappy" love story "overwhelms" the narrative. Wilkens, however, deemed the story "creative and exciting" and "superbly entertaining." Barbara E. Kemp agreed in her *Library Journal* review, writing that *Red, White, and Blue* "pose[s] . . . deeper questions about what it means to be an American."

In *Brave Dames and Wimpettes: What Women Are Really Doing on Page and Screen,* Isaacs examines how women are typically portrayed in television, film, and fiction. She finds that, as Laura Ellingson explained in a *Women and Language* review, "too many of the heroines offered up as icons for women are really wimpettes, whom we would be wise to reject rather than emulate. In contrast, too few brave dames provide inspiration and sound role models for women." Isaacs describes a wimpette as someone who is seemingly beautiful and strong, but is actually weak and is just trying to be what everyone else wants her to be. In contrast, a brave dame is a woman who is "passionate about something besides passion." Ellingson noted that "this book has several strengths to recommend it as a supplementary text for undergraduate courses," including the fact that "many of the examples are very recent, so students will have seen many of the movies and television programs and may identify with icons they feel are from their own generation." Yet other reviewers expressed less enthusiasm for the book. A critic for *Publishers Weekly* suggested that Isaacs's "foray into cultural criticism quickly turns into an object lesson on oversimplification" and concluded that "though no 'wimpette,' Isaacs fails to deliver deep insights or hardened convictions. She remains a popular entertainer at heart." Ellingson, while observing that Isaacs "recognizes that cultural prescriptions for pleasing plots surround us from the very beginning of our lives," nonetheless finds merit in many depictions of women. "Isaacs's text," the critic concluded, "can be a great help in articulating what is good and bad about female characters in the media."

After twenty years and a multitude of events, Isaacs brings back the character from her debut novel in *Long*

Time No See. The book brings readers up to speed on what has happened with Judith Singer over the past two decades, reintroducing some familiar characters while adding several new ones into the mix. The plot revolves around a "perfect housewife" who is reported missing following a trip to the store on Halloween. Eventually the body is discovered and that is where Judith steps in with enthusiasm. The book goes on to chronicle the list of suspects, which includes the victim's husband, Greg. In the end Judith solves the murder and ends the mystery.

A reviewer for *Publishers Weekly* wrote of *Long Time No See* that "the twenty years between Isaacs's best-selling *Compromising Positions* and this second book to feature amateur sleuth Judith Singer have not affected the author's talent for snappy dialogue and astringent assessments of cant and pretension," but added that "Judith's investigation, despite several clever twists, goes on too long, as does the murderer's bizarre confession." On the whole, though, the book and its protagonist enjoyed positive reviews, with Barbara Kemp writing in *Library Journal* that "the familiar mix of murder, humor, and wry social observation will delight [Isaacs's] many readers." *Booklist* reviewer Carrie Bissey added that "a gripping plot with skillfully rendered secondary characters and plenty of tart humor make this sequel every bit as entertaining as its predecessor."

Isaacs draws on her experience in politics to create Amy Lincoln, the protagonist of her thriller *Any Place I Hang My Hat.* As a reporter covering the campaign of the 2004 Democratic presidential nominee, Senator Thomas Bowles, Lincoln discovers that the senator has an illegitimate son. Rather than racing to the newsdesk with the scoop of the scandal, Amy is forced to confront her own past, "abandonment by her mother when she was only a baby, visitations to her father in prison, and being raised by her shoplifting grandmother," which ultimately creates the crux of the novel, her desire to help Freddy Carasco, the Senator's son, "reunite with his birth family," as Mary Frances Wilkens wrote in *Booklist.* Wilkens added that, "while Isaacs's plots often drift precariously close to cliché, she usually rights the ship with her keen sense of humor and character." A critic for *Publishers Weekly* concurred, noting that "the parade of lavishly and loopishly described secondary characters and gossipy New York scene-setting give the novel its zing."

In addition to her success as a novelist, Isaacs has also done well in transforming her tales for the screen. Her first exposure to the film industry came when she wrote the screenplay for *Compromising Positions.* Since that time she has written and coproduced a second movie, *Hello Again,* and has seen *Shining Through* adapted for the big screen. Whatever genre she is working in, Isaacs finds the writing process to be demanding but rewarding. She once explained: "There are always those days that you think you'd have been better off as a computer programmer, that you say to yourself, why am I doing this? I have no talent for it. Days when the prose is leaden, the work is lonely. . . . But most of the time, I enjoy it. It seems to me it's a legitimized way of telling yourself stories, and I guess very often I get that same thumb-sucking pleasure that a child gets from daydreaming. That part of it I like a lot."

BIOGRAPHICAL AND CRITICAL SOURCES:

BOOKS

Contemporary Literary Criticism, Volume 32, Gale (Detroit, MI), 1985.
Isaacs, Susan, *Brave Dames and Wimpettes: What Women Are Really Doing on Page and Screen,* Ballantine (New York, NY), 1999.

PERIODICALS

Bloomsbury Review, November, 1999, review of *Brave Dames and Wimpettes,* p. 19.
Booklist, May 1, 1996, p. 1469; September 15, 1998, Mary Frances Wilkens, review of *Red, White, and Blue,* p. 173; July, 2001, Carrie Bissey, review of *Long Time No See,* p. 1950; July, 2004, Mary Frances Wilkens, review of *Any Place I Hang My Hat.*
Books, June, 1997, review of *Lily White,* p. 19.
Chicago Tribune Book World, March 25, 1984; September 1, 1985; September 4, 1985.
Detroit News, November 9, 1980; March 18, 1984.
Entertainment Weekly, April 18, 1997, review of *Lily White,* p. 63; November 13, 1998, review of *Red, White, and Blue,* p. 70; February 5, 1999, review of *Brave Dames and Wimpettes,* p. 64.
Kirkus Reviews, September 15, 1998, review of *Red, White, and Blue,* p. 1313; December 15, 1998, review of *Brave Dames and Wimpettes,* p. 1776.

Kliatt, July, 1997, review of *Lily White,* p. 48; May, 1999, review of *Red, White, and Blue,* p. 63; July, 1999, review of *Brave Dames and Wimpettes,* p. 57; September, 1999, review of *Red, White, and Blue,* p. 58.

Ladies' Home Journal, September, 2001, Shana Aborn, "A Woman of Mystery" (interview), p. 38.

Library Journal, February 15, 1997, review of *Lily White,* p. 175; October 15, 1998, Barbara E. Kemp, review of *Red, White, and Blue,* p. 98; January, 1999, Melanie C. Duncan, review of *Red, White, and Blue,* p. 188; February 1, 2000, Laurie Selwyn, review of *Red, White, and Blue,* p. 133; August, 2001, Barbara E. Kemp, review of *Long Time No See,* p. 161.

Los Angeles Times, September 1, 1980; August 30, 1985.

Los Angeles Times Book Review, March 4, 1984, Kenneth Atchity, review of *Almost Paradise;* July 11, 1993, Taffy Cannon, review of *After All These Years,* p. 2; July 28, 1996, Elaine Kendall, review of *Lily White,* p. 4.

Newsweek, May 1, 1978.

New Yorker, May 15, 1978.

New York Times, February 1, 1984; August 30, 1985; September 30, 2001, Karen Karbo, "Nice Lawn!"

New York Times Book Review, April 30, 1978, Jack Sullivan, review of *Compromising Positions;* February 12, 1984, Anna Shapiro, review of *Almost Paradise;* September 11, 1988, Anne Tolstoi Wallach, review of *Shining Through,* p. 13; January 20, 1991, Helen Dudar, review of *Magic Hour,* p. 12; July 11, 1993, Barbara Raskin, review of *After All These Years,* p. 26; June 30, 1996, Jon Katz, review of *Lily White,* p. 19; April 13, 1997, review of *Lily White,* p. 32; December 20, 1998, Nora Krug, review of *Red, White, and Blue,* p. 18.

People, April 24, 1978; April 30, 1984.

Publishers Weekly, January 9, 1978; January 23, 1978; July 25, 1980; September 12, 1980; January 4, 1985; May 13, 1996, p. 54; September 7, 1998, review of *Red, White, and Blue,* p. 82; December 14, 1998, review of *Brave Dames and Wimpettes,* p. 68; February 1, 1999, review of *Brave Dames and Wimpettes,* p. 36; July 23, 2001, review of *Long Time No See,* p. 47; August 2, 2004, review of *Any Place I Hang My Hat.*

St. Louis Post-Dispatch, October 20, 1998, Sue Ann Wood, "Susan Isaacs Remains Serious in Her Latest Installment," p. D3.

Time, October 3, 1988; July 15, 1996, John Skow, review of *Lily White,* p. 68.

Times (London, England), April 3, 1997, Bronwen Maddox, "Carving a Career out of Murder, Betrayal, and Adultery," p. 21.

Times Literary Supplement, November 3, 1978.

Washington Post, September 3, 1985; November 8, 1998, Mike Musgrove, review of *Red, White, and Blue,* p. 4; September 2, 2001, Carolyn Banks, "Horsing Around," p. T10.

Washington Post Book World, August 31, 1980, Susan Cheever, review of *Close Relations;* February 12, 1984; January 27, 1991, Carolyn Banks, review of *Magic Hour,* p. 1; July 4, 1993, Dorothy Uhnak, review of *After All These Years,* p. 3; November 8, 1998, review of *Red, White, and Blue,* p. 4.

Women and Language, fall, 1999, Laura L. Ellingson, review of *Brave Dames and Wimpettes,* p. 37.

Writer, February, 1997, Lewis Burke Frumkes, "A Conversation with . . . Susan Isaacs" (interview), pp. 25-27.

ONLINE

Susan Isaacs Web site, http://www.susanisaacs.com/ (August 25, 2004).*

*   *   *

IVO, Lêdo 1924-

PERSONAL: Born February 18, 1924, in Maceió, Alagoas, Brazil; son of Floriano (a lawyer) and Euridice Placido de Araujo Ivo; married Maria Leda Sarmento de Medeiros, June 25, 1946; children: Patricia, Maria da Graca, Gonçalo. *Education:* University of Brazil, J.D., 1949.

ADDRESSES: Home—Rua Fernando Ferrari, 61 apto. 710, 22231 Botafogo, Rio de Janeiro, Brazil; fax: 2-551-9801. *E-mail*—seecretaria@academia.org.br.

CAREER: Journalist based in Rio de Janeiro, Brazil, 1943-71; writer, 1971—. Gives readings from his works, including the sound recording *Brazilian Poet Lêdo Ivo Reading from His Work,* Archive of Hispanic Literature on Tape (Washington, DC), 1975.

MEMBER: Brazilian Academy of Letters.

AWARDS, HONORS: Graca Aranha Prize, 1947, for *As alianças;* PEN Club of Brazil Prize, Jabuti Prize, Poetry Prize from Cultural Foundation of Brazil, and Casimiro de Abreu Prize, all 1972, all for *Finesterra;* Walmap Prize, 1973, for *Ninho de cobras: Uma História mal contada;* Memory Book Prize from Cultural Foundation of Brasilia, 1979, for *Confissões de um poeta;* Mario de Andrade Prize, 1982, for collected literary work.

WRITINGS:

POETRY

As Imaginações (title means "Imaginations"), Pongetti (Rio de Janeiero, Brazil), 1944.

Ode e elegia (title means "Ode and Elegy"), Pongetti (Rio de Janeiro, Brazil), 1945, 3rd edition, Orfeu (Rio de Janeiro, Brazil), 1967.

Ode ao crepúsculo (title means "Ode to Twilight"), Pongetti (Rio de Janeiro, Brazil), 1948.

Acontecimento do soneto (title means "Birth of the Sonnet"), O Livro Inconsútil (Barcelona, Spain), 1948, Orfeu (Rio de Janeiro, Brazil), 1950.

Cântico (title means "Canticle"), illustrated by Emeric Marcier, José Olympio (Rio de Janeiro, Brazil), 1949, 2nd edition, Orfeu (Rio de Janeiro, Brazil), 1969.

Linguagem (title means "Language"), José Olympio (Rio de Janeiro, Brazil), 1951.

Ode equatorial, illustrated by Anísio Medeiros, Hipocampo (Niteroi, Brazil), 1951.

Um Basileiro em Paris, e O Rei da Europa (title means "A Brazilian in Paris, and The King of Europe"), Orfeu (Rio de Janeiro, Brazil), 1955.

Magias (title means "Witchcrafts"), AGIR (Rio de Janeiro, Brazil), 1960.

Uma Lira dos vinte anos (title means "A Lyre of Twenty Years"), Livraria São José (Rio de Janeiro, Brazil), 1962.

Estação Central (title means "Central Power Station"), Tempo Brasileiro (Rio de Janeiro, Brazil), 1964, 2nd edition, Orfeu (Rio de Janeiro, Brazil), 1968.

Antologia poética (title means "Anthology of Poems"), Editôra Leitura (Rio de Janeiro, Brazil), 1965.

Cinqüenta poemas escolhidos pelo autor (title means "Fifty Poems Selected by the Author"), Ministério da Educação e Cultura, Serviço de Documentação (Rio de Janeiro, Brazil), 1966.

Finisterra (title means "Land's End"), José Olympio (Rio de Janeiro, Brazil), 1972, translation by Kerry Shawn Keys published as *Landsend: Selected Poems,* Pine Press (Harrisburg, PA), 1998.

O Sinal semafórico (title means "The Semaphore Signal"), José Olympio (Rio de Janeiro, Brazil), 1974.

Central poética: Poemas escolhidos (title means "Collected Poems"), Editora Nova Aguilar (Rio de Janeiro, Brazil), 1976.

O Soldado raso (title means "The Common Soldier"), illustrated by Genésio Fernandes, Edições Pirata (Recife, Brazil), 1980, expanded edition with illustrations by Marcelo Bartholomei, Massao Ohno Editor (Sao Paulo, Brazil), 1988.

A Noite misteriosa (title means "The Mysterious Night"), Editora Record (Rio de Janeiro, Brazil), c. 1982.

Os Melhores poemas de Lêdo Ivo (title means "The Best Poems of Lêdo Ivo"), Global Editora (Sao Paulo, Brazil), 1983.

Calabar, Editora Record (Rio de Janeiro, Brazil), 1985.

Cem sonetos de amor (title means "100 Sonnets of Love"), José Olympio (Rio de Janeiro, Brazil), 1987.

Mar oceano (title means "Ocean Sea"), Editora Record (Rio de Janeiro, Brazil), 1987.

Crepúsculo civil, Editora Record (Rio de Janeiro, Brazil), 1990.

Antologia poética, selected by Walmir Ayala, Ediouro (Rio de Janeiro, Brazil), 1991.

Curral de peixe, 1991-1995, Editora Topbooks (Rio de Janeiro, Brazil), 1995.

Noturno romano, Impressoes do Brasil Editora (Teresopolis, Brazil), 1997.

O Rumor da noite, Editora Nova Fronteira (Rio de Janeiro, Brazil), 2000.

Work represented in anthologies, including *Introduction to Modern Brazilian Poetry,* Clube de Poesia do Brasil, 1954.

NOVELS

As Alianças (title means "Alliances"), AGIR (Rio de Janeiro, Brazil), 1947, 33rd edition, Parma (Sao Paulo, Brazil), 1991.

O Caminho sem aventura (title means "The Road without Adventure"), Progresso Editorial, 1947, 3rd edition, illustrated by Newton Cavalcanti, Editora Record (Rio de Janeiro, Brazil), 1983.

O Sobrinho do general (title means "The General's Nephew"), Editôra Civilização Brasileira (Rio de Janeiro, Brazil), 1964, new edition, Editora Record (Rio de Janeiro, Brazil), c. 1981.

Ninho de cobras: Uma História mal contada, José Olympio (Rio de Janeiro, Brazil), 1973, translation by Kern Krapohl published as *Snakes' Nest; or, A Tale Badly Told,* New Directions (New York, NY), 1981.

A Morte do Brasil (title means "The Death of Brazil"), Editora Record (Rio de Janeiro, Brazil), 1984.

OTHER

Lição de Mario de Andrade (title means "The Lesson of Mario de Andrade"), Ministério de Educação e Saúde, Serviço de Documentação (Rio de Janeiro, Brazil), 1952.

O Preto no branco: Exegese de um poema de Manuel Bandeira (criticism), Livraria São José (Rio de Janeiro, Brazil), 1955.

A Cidade e os dias: Crônicas e histórias (history), Edições O Cruzeiro (Rio de Janeiro, Brazil), 1957, 2nd edition published as *Rio, a cidade e os dias: Crônicas e histórias,* Tempo Brasileiro (Rio de Janeiro, Brazil), 1965.

(Editor and author of introduction and notes) Raimundo Corrêa, *Poesia* (essays), AGIR (Rio de Janeiro, Brazil), 1958.

O Girassol às avessas (essays), Assoc. Bras. do Congresso pela Liberdade da Cultura (Rio de Janeiro, Brazil), 1960.

Use a passagem subterrânea (short stories; title means "Please Use the Underground Way"), Difusão Européia do Livro (Sao Paulo, Brazil), 1961, 2nd edition, Editora Record (Rio de Janeiro, Brazil), 1984.

Paraísos de papel (critical essays; title means "Paradises of Paper"), Conselho Estadual de Cultura, Comissão de Literatura (Sao Paulo, Brazil), 1961.

Ladrão de flor (essays; title means "Thief of Flowers"), ELOS (Rio de Janeiro, Brazil), 1962.

O Universo poético de Raul Pompéia; em apéndice: Canções sem metro, e Textos esparsos (criticism; title means "The Poetic Universe of Raul Pompeia"), Livraria São José (Rio de Janeiro, Brazil), 1963, 2nd edition, Academia Brasileira de Letras (Rio de Janeiro, Brazil), 1996.

O Fautim e outras histórias cariocas (short stories), Bloch Educação (Rio de Janeiro, Brazil), 1966.

Poesia observada: Ensaios sôbre a criação poética e matérias afins (critical essays; title means "Poetry Observed: Essays on Poetry Criticism and Related Matters"), Orfeu (Rio de Janeiro, Brazil), 1967.

80 crônicas exemplares, compiled by Herberto Sales, De Ouro (Rio de Janeiro, Brazil), 1968.

Modernismo e modernidade (criticism; title means "Modernism and Modernity"), Livraria São José (Rio de Janeiro, Brazil), 1972.

Estado de Alagoas (juvenile nonfiction; title means "The State of Alagoas"), Bloch Educação (Rio de Janeiro, Brazil), 1976.

Teoria e celebração (critical essays; title means "Theory and Celebration"), Livraria Duas Cidades (Sao Paulo, Brazil), 1976.

Confissões de um poeta (autobiography and critical essays; title means "Confessions of a Poet"), Difusão Editorial (Sao Paulo, Brazil), 1979.

A Ética da aventura (criticism; title means "The Ethics of the Adventure"), F. Alves (Rio de Janeiro, Brazil), 1982.

(Editor) *Os Melhores poemas de Castro Alves,* Global Editora (Sao Paulo, Brazil), 1983.

O Menino de noite (juvenile), Companhia Editora Nacional (Sao Paulo, Brazil), 1984.

10 contos escolhidos, Horizonte (Brasilia, Brazil), 1986.

O Canário azul (juvenile), Scipione (Sao Paulo, Brazil), 1990.

O Aluno relapso (autobiography; title means "The Lapsed Schoolboy"), illustrated by Gonçalo Ivo, Massao Ohno Editor (Sao Paulo, Brazil), 1991.

A República da desilusão (essays), Topbooks (Rio de Janeiro, Brazil), 1995.

Os Melhores contos de Lêdo Ivo, Global Editora (Sao Paulo, Brazil), 1995.

(Presenter) Sebastião Guimarães Passos, *Poesias: Versos de um simples; Horas mortas,* Academia Brasileira de Letras (Rio de Janeiro, Brazil), 1997.

Un Domingo perdido, Global Editora (Sao Paulo, Brazil), 1998.

O Rato na sacristia (juvenile), Global Editora (Sao Paulo, Brazil), 2000.

Also translator of various works by Jane Austen, Guy de Maupassant, Arthur Rimbaud, and Fyodor Dostoyevsky into Portuguese.

Ivo's works have been translated into Spanish, Italian, and Dutch.

SIDELIGHTS: Lêdo Ivo is a prolific and versatile Brazilian literary figure. Best known in his native land for his verse collections, Ivo captured national attention in 1944 with his first volume of poems, *As Imaginações,* and has since written numerous other works of poetry, several of which have won literary prizes in Brazil. The author identified early in his career with the neomodernist Brazilian literary movement known as the "Generation of 1945," rejecting the stylistic innovations of modernism in favor of classical forms and rhythms, especially those present in the sonnet. Yet the body of Ivo's poetic work defies categorization, revealing a broad range of themes in language by turns effusive and spare.

Critics have noted that Ivo's poetic vision is also evident in his novels. Ivo also relies on allusive language and evocative place descriptions to create a mood of exotic mystery in *Ninho de cobras: Uma História mal contada,* his first novel to be translated into English (as *Snakes' Nest; or, A Tale Badly Told*). Set in the northern Brazilian port of Maceió during the Getulio Vargas dictatorship of the 1940s, the narrative functions at once as a mystery novel, political allegory, and philosophical meditation on the nature of good and evil. *Ninho de cobras* features an unreliable narrator whose circumlocutions and outright deceptions—according to some critics—might be attributed to malice, political necessity, or simply the moral uncertainty that defines most human endeavor. Reviewing the translated version, *Snakes' Nest,* in the *Los Angeles Times,* Alan Cheuse praised Kern Krapohl's "fine translation" of this "startlingly compact and beautiful" work. Ivo's "piercing imagery and powerful not so 'badly' told tale turns unscribbled lives into a short novel of astonishing pith and depth," the critic added.

Ivo's other writings include volumes of short stories and critical essays and translations of prominent fiction works into Portuguese. In 1984, he published another novel, *A Morte do Brasil.* Offering a deeply pessimistic vision of Brazil's present and future, the novel takes the form of a detective story in which a cynical protagonist awakens to his country's lost grandeur and moral degradation in the course of a murder investigation.

Ivo once told *CA:* "I live by writing, but I sometimes envy people who live their lives remote from art, distanced from the words and materials which engender the creation of poetry—people who are simply absorbed by the very pattern of life."

BIOGRAPHICAL AND CRITICAL SOURCES:

BOOKS

Ivo, Lêdo, *Confissoes de um poeta,* Difusão Editorial (Sao Paulo, Brazil), 1979.

Ivo, Lêdo, *O Aluno relapso,* Massao Ohno Editor (Sao Paulo, Brazil), 1991.

Meyer, Doris, editor, *Lives on the Line,* University of California Press (Berkeley, CA), 1988.

PERIODICALS

Los Angeles Times, January 7, 1982, Alan Cheuse, review of *Snakes' Nest: A Tale Badly Told.*

New Yorker, December 14, 1987.

New York Times, February 16, 1982, Edwin McDowell, "U.S. Is Discovering Latin America's Literature."

Times (London, England), March 23, 1989, Stuart Evans, "From a View to a Death."

World Literature Today, spring, 1984; spring, 1985.

J

JACOBS, Harvey 1930-

PERSONAL: Born January 7, 1930, in New York, NY; son of Louis (a dentist) and Laura Jacobs; married Estelle Rose (an artist), October 18, 1956; children: Adam. *Education:* Syracuse University, B.A., 1950; Columbia University, graduate study, 1950-51.

ADDRESSES: Home—New York, NY. *Agent*—c/o Author Mail, St. Martin's Press, 175 Fifth Ave., New York, NY) 10010. *E-mail*—celgo@aol.com.

CAREER: Weizman Institute of Science, New York, NY, public relations, 1954-55; worked for *Village Voice*, New York, NY, and published *East* (newspaper), 1956-57; American Broadcasting Co., New York, NY, director of industry affairs, 1958-73. Syracuse University Writers' Workshop, instructor, 1958-59.

MEMBER: Writers Guild of America, PEN, Dramatists Guild.

AWARDS, HONORS: Playboy Fiction Award for story, "The Lion's Share"; Earplay Award for Drama from Writers Guild of America.

WRITINGS:

The Egg of the Glak (short stories), Harper (New York, NY), 1969.
(With David Martin) *Famous Fingerprints* (cartoons), Grosset & Dunlap (New York, NY), 1969.
(With David Martin) *Mrs. Portnoy's Retort: A Mother Strikes Back!* (cartoons), Allograph Publishers (New York, NY), 1969.
Summer on a Mountain of Spices (novel), Harper (New York, NY), 1976.
The Juror: A Novel, F. Watts (New York, NY), 1980.
Beautiful Soup: A Novel for the Twenty-first Century, Celadon Press (New York, NY), 1993.
American Goliath: Inspired by the True, Incredible Events surrounding the Mysterious Marvel Known to the Astonished World As the Cardiff Giant, St. Martin's Press (New York, NY), 1997.

Also author of scripts of specials for ABC-TV, NBC-TV, and Children's Television Workshop. Contributor of short stories to *Transatlantic Review, Esquire, Playboy, Mademoiselle, Cosmopolitan, New Worlds, Realist, Midstream, Paris Review,* and other periodicals.

Syracuse University Library houses a collection of Jacobs's manuscripts.

SIDELIGHTS: Harvey Jacobs writes imaginative, lively novels and stories with unusual characters in unusual situations. An essayist for the *St. James Guide to Science-Fiction Writers* noted that Jacobs's "stories use a satiric, even whimsical tone to examine what it means to be human, how we treat our selves and one another, and the often absurd rules we set up to govern our own behavior. Most of Jacobs's fiction is skillfully written and sufficiently oddball that it appears as frequently in slick mainstream magazines as in purely science fiction publications, and his bizarre vision of the modern world has been compared to Magic Realism, fantasy, and surrealist fiction."

Beautiful Soup: A Novel for the Twenty-first Century is set in a future where people are required to wear bar codes on their foreheads. The bar codes tell each person's identity and social status. The novel focuses on the dilemma of Jim Wander, a man whose privileged status is stripped as the result of a supermarket accident that changes his bar code and leaves him with the identity of a can of pea soup. A series of bizarre characters and adventures ensue. "Despite the relentlessly absurd plot," the *St. James Guide to Science-Fiction Writers* essayist explained, "the novel is a caustic indictment of the pressure for conformity and our willingness to relinquish control of our own lives." In the *Los Angeles Times Book Review*, James Sallis described *Beautiful Soup* as "a wonderful and wonderfully funny book. The fun house is open late tonight."

The main character of *American Goliath: Inspired by the True, Incredible Events surrounding the Mysterious Marvel known to the Astonished World As the Cardiff Giant* is George Hull, who is inspired to mischief by a preacher's claim that there were giants in America at the time described in the biblical Book of Genesis. Hull takes advantage of the fact that there is an archaeological dig nearby, and has sculptors create bogus fossils of giants. The "find" creates waves that are so big, even P. T. Barnum is envious. The story is further animated by the appearance of such figures as Ralph Waldo Emerson, Oliver Wendell Holmes, and John D. Rockefeller. Jacobs's novel is based on the actual events surrounding the Cardiff Giant Hoax of 1869. A *Publishers Weekly* reviewer wrote that "this quaint tapestry is further enlivened with enough lewd misbehavior to put a smile on even the stoniest face." Linda Barrett Osborne called the book "entertaining and clever" in her *Chicago Sun-Times* review. Further, she observed, "In his cynical assessment of human nature, George puts his finger on a certain truth—that a country just emerging from civil war needs to believe in miracles, in healing." William O'Rourke, reviewing the book for the *World and I*, found it to be "an entirely successful satire" and "a riot of dedicated humbug and slapstick denunciation."

In addition to his more fantastical writing, Jacobs has also written the novel *Summer on a Mountain of Spices*, set in the Catskill Mountains of New York and recounting a typical tourist season at one of the many resort hotels in the region. The novel has become, according to Phil Brown, in an interview with Jacobs posted at the Catskills Institute Web site, "an under-

ground favorite . . . with the Catskill reading crowd." Jacobs explained to Brown why he chose to write about the Catskills: "Everything I'd read or seen about the so-called Jewish Alps struck me as hoaky and one-dimensional and I wanted to do something more worthy, meaningful and honest. There was also the fact that my family ran one of those small family hotels and the people involved were not getting any younger. I suppose part of my motivation was to give them some small gift."

"Jacobs is not a prolific writer, but he is a uniformly good one . . . ," explained the essayist for the *St. James Guide to Science-Fiction Writers*. "His voice, though infrequently heard, is one of intelligent wit and an insightful perception of humanity's gift for the absurd, and his reputation in the field, considering the relatively small size of his genre work, is a testimony to the impact those few stories have made on readers."

BIOGRAPHICAL AND CRITICAL SOURCES:

BOOKS

St. James Guide to Science-Fiction Writers, 4th edition, St. James Press (Detroit, MI), 1996.

PERIODICALS

Chicago Sun-Times, November 23, 1997, Linda Barrett Osborne, review of *American Goliath: Inspired by the True, Incredible Events surrounding the Mysterious Marvel Known to the Astonished World As the Cardiff Giant*, p. 25.
Locus, February, 1993, p. 25.
Los Angeles Times Book Review, January 10, 1993, James Sallis, review of *Beautiful Soup: A Novel for the Twenty-first Century*, p. 6.
Magazine of Fantasy and Science Fiction, June, 1998, Robert K. J. Killheffer, review of *American Goliath*, p. 39.
Nation, September 22, 1969, p. 287.
New York Times Book Review, December 14, 1969, p. 44.
Publishers Weekly, August 11, 1997, review of *American Goliath*, p. 382.
Washington Post Book World, December 21, 1980, p. 4.
World and I, February, 1998, William O'Rourke, review of *American Goliath*, p. 279.

ONLINE

Catskills Institute Web site, http://www.brown.edu/ Research/Catskills_Institute/ (May 27, 2003), Phil Brown, "Interview with Harvey Jacobs."*

*　　*　　*

JENKINS, T(erence) A(ndrew) 1958-

PERSONAL: Born May 30, 1958, in England; son of Griffith Hugh (a factory worker) and Ivy (Deering) Jenkins. *Education:* University of East Anglia, B.A. (with first class honors), 1979; Cambridge University, Ph.D., 1984. *Hobbies and other interests:* Numismatics, classical music (piano).

ADDRESSES: Office—History of Parliament, Wedgwood House, 15 Woburn Sq., London WC1H 0NS, England; fax: 0171-255-1442. *E-mail*—tjenkins@ histparl.ac.uk.

CAREER: Cambridge University, Cambridge, England, British Academy postdoctoral fellow, 1987-90; University of East Anglia, Norwich, England, lecturer, 1990-91; University of Exeter, Exeter, England, lecturer, 1991-92; University of East Anglia, lecturer, 1992-94, 1995-96; University of Bristol, Bristol, England, lecturer, 1996-97; History of Parliament, London, England, senior research officer, 1998—.

MEMBER: Royal Historical Society (fellow).

AWARDS, HONORS: Prince Consort Prize for History, Cambridge University, 1988, for *Gladstone, Whiggery, and the Liberal Party, 1874-1886.*

WRITINGS:

Gladstone, Whiggery, and the Liberal Party, 1874-1886, Oxford University Press (Oxford, England), 1988.
(Editor) *The Parliamentary Diaries of Sir John Trelawny, 1858-1865,* Royal Historical Society (London, England), 1990.

The Liberal Ascendancy, 1830-1886, Macmillan (New York, NY), 1994.
(Editor) *The Parliamentary Diaries of Sir John Trelawny, 1868-1873,* Royal Historical Society (London, England), 1994.
Disraeli and Victorian Conservatism, Macmillan (New York, NY), 1996.
Parliament, Party, and Politics in Victorian Britain, Manchester University Press (New York, NY), 1996.
Sir Robert Peel, St. Martin's Press (New York, NY), 1999.
Britain: A Short History, One World Publishers (Oxford, England), 2001.

Contributor to periodicals, including *Historical Journal, English Historical Review, Modern History Review,* and *Parliamentary History.*

SIDELIGHTS: T. A. Jenkins once told *CA:* "I wrote stories from an early age (seven or eight years old) and experimented with poetry in my teens—no talent at all! As the author of works on political history, I suppose I have found a way of combining my scholarly interests with my desire to write. This is probably why my work tends to be rather more in the narrative style than is currently fashionable.

"I have always been fascinated with the Victorian era. It was a time of rapid and profound change, yet there was also an underlying continuity. My interests include the role of the aristocracy within the political system and the process by which Britain's political culture adapted itself in the face of economic and social change. (It was a two-way process, as I see it.) My recent research has emphasized the importance of the parliamentary dimension to politics, which has hitherto been largely neglected by scholars working on the Victorian period."

*　　*　　*

JIANG, Ji-li 1954-

PERSONAL: Name is pronounced "Gee-lee Chiang"; born February 3, 1954, in Shanghai, China; daughter of Xi-reng (an actor) and Ying (in sales; maiden name, Chen) Jiang. *Education:* Attended Shanghai Teachers' College, 1978-80, and Shanghai University, 1980-84; University of Hawaii at Manoa, B.A., 1987.

Ji-li Jiang

ADDRESSES: Home—4 Commodore Dr., No. 444, Emeryville, CA 94608. *E-mail*—jjiang8888@aol.com.

CAREER: Aston Hotels and Resorts, Honolulu, HI, corporate operations analyst, 1987-92; University Health System, Chicago, IL, budgeting director, 1995-96; East West Exchange, Inc., Emeryville, CA, founder and president.

MEMBER: American Chinese Zhi-Qing Association, American Chinese Intellectuals Association, PEN American Center West, Northern California Children's Bookseller's Association, South Bay Area Reading Council.

AWARDS, HONORS: Red Scarf Girl was awarded a Notable Children's Trade Book in the Field of Social Studies citation, National Council for the Social Studies, Books in the Middle: Outstanding Titles of 1997, *Voice of Youth Advocates,* Books for Youth Editors' Choice, American Library Association Booklist, Best Books of 1997 designation, *Publishers Weekly*; Nonfiction Honor List designation, *Voice of Youth Advocates,*

and Book Links Lasting Connections Citation, American Library Association, all 1997; Children's Literature Award, California Bay Area Book Reviewers Association, Book of Distinction, *River Bank Review,* Parents' Choice Gold Award and Story Book Award, Judy Lopez Memorial Award, Notable Children's Book, Best Book for Young Adults, all 1998; and Pennsylvania Young Readers' Choice Award, 1999-2000.

WRITINGS:

Red Scarf Girl: A Memoir of the Cultural Revolution, HarperCollins (New York, NY), 1997.
Magical Monkey King: Mischief in Heaven, Harper-Collins (New York, NY), 2004.

WORK IN PROGRESS: Research on "the differences and conflict between the East and West, in terms of culture, custom, philosophy, value, et cetera."

SIDELIGHTS: Red Scarf Girl is Ji-li Jiang's autobiographical account of her very difficult adolescence during Chairman Mao Tse Tung's 1966 Cultural Revolution in China. A talented girl with a seemingly bright future, Jiang embraced the revolutionary ideals of her day, until the movement degenerated into a witch hunt for anyone "tainted" by capitalism. Because Jiang's paternal grandfather was a wealthy landowner, her entire family faced severe persecution. "Jiang describes in terrifying detail the ordeals of her family and those like them, including unauthorized search and seizure, persecution, arrest and torture, hunger, and public humiliation," noted Janice M. Del Negro in a *Bulletin of the Center for Children's Books* review of Jiang's memoir. Roger Sutton, reviewing the work for *Horn Book,* called *Red Scarf Girl* "a rare personal glimpse of the upheaval China suffered during the 1960s" and added that "the child's point of view is firmly maintained" and the "conflict between political and family expectations is well portrayed." *School Library Journal* contributor John Philbrook praised the book as "a page-turner" and as "excellent discussion material," asserting that Jiang's "the writing style is lively and the events often have a heart-pounding quality about them." Similarly, Kat Kan, writing in *Voice of Youth Advocates,* contended that Jiang's "compelling story makes history come alive for teens, much as Anne Frank's diary has done for decades."

In the *Magical Monkey King: Mischief in Heaven,* Jiang retells a classic Chinese trickster story about a monkey who, part Earth and part Heaven, finds a new home for his threatened family while attempting to trick Jade Emperor and other powerful creatures. "It takes Buddha himself to rein Monkey in and lock him up until he learns from his mistakes," noted Denise Wilms in a *Booklist* review of Jiang's retelling. In *Kirkus Reviews* a contributor noted, "Clever, arrogant, far longer on appetite than attention span, Monkey makes an engaging antihero whose acquaintance young readers . . . will be glad to make."

Raised in a creative and affluent household, Jiang once commented: "When I was a little girl, I dreamed of being an actress. During the Cultural Revolution, although my talent was praised, I was turned down again and again for professional art troupes because of my family's political background. In 1976 the Cultural Revolution ended. New policies were supposed to be implemented. For the first time I might have a chance at achieving my dream, and I was excited. I sent in my application to the Shanghai Drama Institute and waited for the audition. Then I received a letter saying that my district had denied my participation again. I was in despair. I was making plastic flowers in a very small factory and earning seventy cents per day in Chinese currency, equivalent to about twenty-five cents in the United States. This [was] . . . my last chance, since the next year I would be too old to enter the program.

"Time passed, and I moved to America. My first year in Honolulu, I lived with an American family. They were very interested in my life in China. Using my very limited English, I shared some of my stories with them. One day I got a present from them, a copy of *The Diary of Anne Frank*. Inside they wrote: 'In the hope that some day we will read *The Diary of Ji-li Jiang*.'. . . . Not long after I started to work for a hotel chain, one of my co-workers asked me, 'Ji-li, how come you don't have bound feet?' I was shocked: this was like asking 'how come you don't wear a corset?' I realized then how little some Americans knew about China and the Chinese people. I made up my mind to write my story at once. We had experienced a holocaust, too. Few people knew about it. So finally I started writing my story."

Jiang has continued to promote understanding of her native country by founding her own company, East West Exchange, Inc., which promotes and facilitates cultural exchange. "I believe it is very important to increase understanding between the east and the west," the author noted, adding that, on a personal level, it has been "very rewarding to bridge the gap between China and western countries."

BIOGRAPHICAL AND CRITICAL SOURCES:

PERIODICALS

ALAN Review, winter, 1998.
Booklist, October 1, 1997, p. 331; April 15, 2002, p. 1397.
Bulletin of the Center for Children's Books, February, 1998, p. 206.
Horn Book, January-February, 1998, p. 76.
Instructor, October, 1997, p. 48.
Kirkus Reviews, September 1, 1997, p. 1391; April 15, 2002, p. 571
Publishers Weekly, July 28, 1997, p. 75; November 10, 1997, p. 28.
School Library Journal, December, 1997, p. 139.
Voice of Youth Advocates, February, 1998, p. 365; June, 1998, p. 145.

ONLINE

Ji-li Jiang Web site, http://www.jilijiang.com/ (August 24, 2004).

*   *   *

JOHNSON, Angela 1961-

PERSONAL: Born June 18, 1961, in Tuskegee, AL; daughter of Arthur (an autoworker) and Truzetta (an accountant; maiden name, Hall) Johnson. *Education:* Attended Kent State University. *Politics:* Democrat.

ADDRESSES: Home—Kent, OH. *Agent*—c/o Author Mail, Orchard Books, 387 Park Ave. S, New York, NY 10016.

CAREER: Volunteers in Service to America (VISTA), Ravenna, OH, child development worker, 1981-82; freelance writer of children's books, 1989—.

MEMBER: Authors Guild, Authors League of America.

Angela Johnson

AWARDS, HONORS: Best Books, *School Library Journal,* 1989, for *Tell Me a Story, Mama;* Ezra Jack Keats New Writer Award, United States Board on Books for Young People, 1991; Coretta Scott King Honor Book, American Library Association Social Responsibilities Round Table, 1991, for *When I Am Old with You;* Editor's Choice, *Booklist,* Best Books, *School Library Journal,* and Coretta Scott King Author Award, all for *Toning the Sweep;* Coretta Scott King Author Award, 1998, for *Heaven;* Coretta Scott King Honor Book citation, 1998, for *The Other Side: Shorter Poems;* MacArthur Foundation "genius grant," 2003.

WRITINGS:

Tell Me a Story, Mama, illustrated by David Soman, Orchard Books (New York, NY), 1989.

Do Like Kyla, illustrated by James Ransome, Orchard Books (New York, NY), 1990.

When I Am Old with You, illustrated by David Soman, Orchard Books (New York, NY), 1990.

One of Three, illustrated by David Soman, Orchard Books (New York, NY), 1991.

The Leaving Morning, illustrated by David Soman, Orchard Books (New York, NY), 1992.

The Girl Who Wore Snakes, illustrated by James Ransome, Orchard Books (New York, NY), 1993.

Julius, illustrated by Dav Pilkey, Orchard Books (New York, NY), 1993.

Toning the Sweep: A Novel, Orchard Books (New York, NY), 1993, reprinted, 2000.

Joshua by the Sea, illustrated by Rhonda Mitchell, Orchard Books (New York, NY), 1994.

Joshua's Night Whispers, illustrated by Rhonda Mitchell, Orchard Books (New York, NY), 1994.

Mama Bird, Baby Birds, illustrated by Rhonda Mitchell, Orchard Books (New York, NY), 1994.

Rain Feet, illustrated by Rhonda Mitchell, Orchard Books (New York, NY), 1994.

Humming Whispers, Orchard Books (New York, NY), 1995.

Shoes Like Miss Alice's, illustrated by Ken Page, Orchard Books (New York, NY), 1995.

The Aunt in Our House, illustrated by David Soman, Orchard Books (New York, NY), 1996.

The Rolling Store, illustrated by Peter Catalanotto, Orchard Books (New York, NY), 1997.

Daddy Calls Me Man, illustrated by Rhonda Mitchell, Orchard Books (New York, NY), 1997.

Songs of Faith, Orchard Books (New York, NY), 1998.

Heaven, Simon & Schuster (New York, NY), 1998.

The Other Side: Shorter Poems, Orchard Books (New York, NY), 1998.

Maniac Monkeys on Magnolia Street, illustrated by John Ward, Random House (New York, NY), 1999.

The Wedding, illustrated by David Soman, Orchard Books (New York, NY), 1999.

Those Building Men, illustrated by Mike Benny, Scholastic (New York, NY), 1999.

Down the Winding Road, illustrated by Shane W. Evans, DK Ink, 2000.

Gone from Home: Short Takes (stories), Dell (New York, NY), 2001.

When Mules Flew on Magnolia Street, Alfred A. Knopf (New York, NY), 2001.

Rain Feet, illustrated by Rhonda Mitchell, Orchard Books (New York, NY), 2001.

Running Back to Ludie, Orchard Books (New York, NY), 2002.

Looking for Red, Simon & Schuster (New York, NY), 2002.

I Dream of Trains, illustrated by Loren Long, Simon & Schuster (New York, NY), 2003.

The First Part Last, Simon & Schuster (New York, NY), 2003.

A Cool Moonlight, Dial Books (New York, NY), 2003.

Just Like Josh Gibson, illustrated by Beth Peck, Simon & Schuster (New York, NY), 2003.

Violet's Music, illustrated by Laura Huliska-Beith, Dial Books (New York, NY), 2004.

Bird, Dial Books (New York, NY), 2004.

Contributor to several anthologies, including *Gone from Home: Short Takes,* DK Publishing, 1998, and *In Daddy's Arms I Am Tall,* Simon & Schuster (New York, NY), 2003.

ADAPTATIONS: Humming Whispers was recorded on audio cassette and released by Recorded Books, 1997.

SIDELIGHTS: Angela Johnson is the winner of a 2003 MacArthur Foundation "genius grant," a half-million-dollar prize awarded to a select few individuals in the arts and sciences who are thought to be making unique contributions to the betterment of society. In Johnson's case the award recognizes her ability to craft sensitive children's books about African-American family life and the wider issues of growing up in the modern world.

Johnson first drew the attention of critics through her picture books presenting warm portraits of African-American children and their relationship to parents, grandparents, siblings, and friends. Many reviewers have pointed out, however, that Johnson's stories capture emotions and experiences that are familiar to young readers of all cultures. Her books for and about older children tackle difficult issues such as divorce, the death of a sibling, and chronic illness with emphasis on learning to survive and thrive such devastating events. "Johnson is a master at representing human nature in various guises at different levels," asserted *Twentieth-Century Children's Writers* contributor Lucille H. Gregory. Gregory also noted a "high consistency" in Johnson's books, a commendation underscored by Rudine Sims Bishop in *Horn Book,* who maintained that all of Johnson's works "feature charming first-person narrators. . . . The characters are distinct individuals, but their emotions are ones shared across cultures."

Reaching a wide audience is exactly what Johnson strives for in her writing. As she once commented: "In high school I wrote punk poetry that went with my razor blade necklace. At that point in my life my writing was personal and angry. I didn't want anyone to like it. I didn't want to be in the school literary magazine, or to be praised for something that I really didn't want understood. Of course, ten years later, I hope that my writing is universal and speaks to everyone who reads it. I still have the necklace, though."

Many of Johnson's books for children feature young black protagonists narrating events that are common to children their age. In *Tell Me a Story, Mama,* which Rudine Sims Bishop called an "impressive debut" in *Horn Book,* a little girl asks her mother for a familiar bedtime story and ends up doing most of the storytelling herself as she reminds her mother of each favorite part. *Horn Book* reviewer Maria Salvadore, one of a number of commentators offering a favorable assessment of Johnson's first book, observed: "By providing a glimpse of one African-American family, Johnson has validated other families' experiences, regardless of racial or ethnic background."

In subsequent works Johnson has continued to feature characters whose lives are enriched by familial affection and reassurance. In *Do Like Kyla,* a young narrator describes how she imitates her older sister all day long. But when it's time for bed, the young girl revels in the fact that "Kyla does like me." *When I Am Old with You* spotlights a boy who describes to his grandfather the things they will do together when the boy catches up to him in age. The young narrator of *One of Three* relates the fun she has being one of three sisters, as well as the frustration of not being able to join in some of the things her older siblings do. Reviewing *One of Three,* a *Publishers Weekly* critic praised Johnson for her "perceptive and understated text," while Karen James, writing in *School Library Journal,* admired the way Johnson captured "the underlying love and strength of positive family relationships."

Unusual pets join the young protagonists in *The Girl Who Wore Snakes* and *Julius.* In the former, Ali's strong interest in snakes, which she wears as jewelry, surprises everyone in her family except her snake-loving aunt. *Julius,* illustrated by Dav Pilkey, features a young girl named Maya who receives Julius, an Alaskan pig, from her grandfather. Together, Maya and Julius teach each other new tricks and enjoy a variety of adventures. Betsy Hearne, writing in the

Bulletin of the Center for Children's Books, called *Julius* a "gleeful celebration of silliness."

In 1993, Johnson published her first work for older children, *Toning the Sweep.* In this novel, fourteen-year-old Emily participates in the final days of her cancer-stricken grandmother's life by videotaping the ailing woman as she visits with friends, recalling stories of the past. "Full of subtle nuance, the novel is overlaid with meaning about the connections of family and the power of friendship," maintained *School Library Journal* contributor Ellen Fader. *Booklist* reviewer Quraysh Ali lauded the work, asserting: "With ingenuity and grace, Johnson captures the innocence, the vulnerability, and the love of human interaction as well as the melancholy, the self-discovery, and the introspection of adolescence." Mary M. Burns in *Horn Book* cited for special note "the skill with which the author moves between times past and times present without sacrificing her main story line or diluting the emotional impact."

Humming Whispers, another young adult work, tells the story of Sophie, an aspiring dancer who becomes worried that she is developing the schizophrenia that afflicts her older sister. Hazel Rochman characterized the novel in *Booklist* as "a bleak contemporary story of suffering, lit with the hope of people who take care of each other in the storm." *School Library Journal* contributor Carol Schene observed that while "there are no easy answers" for the characters in the book, "the frailty and strength of the human spirit" displayed by each one makes the story memorable. Elizabeth Bush, writing in the *Bulletin of the Center for Children's Books,* stated that the author "ably demonstrates the pervasive effects of mental illness on an entire family," and a *Kirkus Reviews* critic praised the way Johnson "carefully and richly fleshes out the characters."

Johnson returned to picture books with *Shoes Like Miss Alice's* and *The Rolling Store.* In the former work, Sara is hesitant about being with a new babysitter. Her fears are quickly dispelled, however, and a bond is formed when Miss Alice changes into a different pair of shoes for each special activity they do together. "Tucked in the tale is a nice message about being open to new people walking into your life," noted *Booklist* reviewer Ilene Cooper. In *The Rolling Store,* a young black girl tells her white friend a family story about a general store on wheels that used to serve her

grandfather's rural community when he was a boy. With help from the visiting grandfather, the girls create their own mobile store out of a small red wagon. "Johnson's family story has a certain nostalgic appeal," noted *Bulletin of the Center for Children's Books* editor Janice M. Del Negro. *Booklist* reviewer Stephanie Zvirin deemed *The Rolling Store* "a sweet, upbeat story."

The author drew particularly favorable reviews for her novel *Heaven.* Fourteen-year-old Marley is the beloved only child in a happy family—until, by accident, she discovers that her parents are actually her uncle and aunt, and her real father is an itinerant "uncle" she hardly knows. This revelation leads Marley to investigate exactly what constitutes a family unit and how her identity is shaped by those who love her. Praising the book for its "plain, lyrical writing," *Booklist* contributor Hazel Rochman concluded that the author "makes us see the power of loving kindness."

Johnson has also written collections of poems and has contributed to poetry anthologies. One of her best known poetry books is *The Other Side: Shorter Poems.* This work was inspired by the fact that her grandmother's hometown of Shorter, Alabama, was razed for redevelopment. During a nostalgic trip to the small town, Johnson wrote about her memories of growing up there. Nancy Vasilakis in *Horn Book* called *The Other Side* an "intriguing collection" and a "captivating narrative," while a *Publishers Weekly* critic noted that the book offers "an unforgettable view of an insightful young woman growing up in the South."

Not all of Johnson's novels are so serious in tone. *Maniac Monkeys on Magnolia Street* and its sequel *When Mules Flew on Magnolia Street* introduce Charlie, a youngster who must adjust to new friends and new surroundings after moving to Magnolia Street. Told from Charlie's point of view, the two stories reveal how the youngster adapts to new situations by being "open to the small wonders around her," to quote Helen Rosenberg in *Booklist.* In her *Booklist* review of *When Mules Flew on Magnolia Street,* Denise Wilms likewise praised the "small slices of life" that Johnson serves to early readers.

Difficult family situations inform the novels *Running Back to Ludie* and *Looking for Red.* In *Running Back to Ludie,* a teenaged narrator explores her mixed emotions as she prepares to meet the mother who abandoned her to live in the woods. Joanna Rudge Long in *Horn Book* felt that the free verse style of the work helps to highlight the young person's feelings of rejection and reconciliation. "Johnson's exploration of the process is subtle and beautifully wrought," the critic concluded. *Looking for Red* offers a more straightforward narrative with a dark secret at its core. Red's sister Mike is still reeling from grief in the wake of his disappearance, and she receives small solace from Red's equally traumatized friends. Only as the story proceeds does the reader realize that Mike and Red's friends share some of the responsibility for his accidental death. "The strength of this story is the accurate portrayal of the surreal nature of grief laden with guilt," observed Jean Gaffney in *School Library Journal*. In *Horn Book,* Joanna Rudge Long praised the "luminous ease" with which Johnson depicts the characters, "both their estrangement from reality and their eventual return toward it."

A Cool Moonlight tells the story of Lila, a child stricken with xeroderma pigmentosum, a rare oversensitivity to sunlight. Forced to live a nocturnal lifestyle, Lila takes solace in imaginary friends until her ninth birthday, when she comes to terms with her individuality. Once again in *Horn Book* Joanna Rudge Long commended the novel, particularly for Johnson's "deft touches that make this spare portrait so effective."

Readers first met Bobby, the hero of *The First Part Last,* in *Heaven.* In *The First Part Last,* Johnson spins the story of Bobby's unexpected teenage parenthood, how it compromises his ambitions to be an artist but in return offers him the opportunity to love his infant daughter and connect with his parents. The responsibility for a helpless infant is scary—and at times frustrating—but Bobby is sustained by his fond memories of the past and moments of enjoyment in the present. A *Publishers Weekly* critic of *The First Part Last* liked the way Johnson "skillfully relates the hope in the midst of pain."

Johnson is still creating at least one new picture book per year. One successful title is *I Dream of Trains,* a poignant look at engineer Casey Jones through the eyes of a fictional black field worker. A young boy toiling in the heat lives for the moment when the mighty engine roars by and dreams of the day when he will board a train and leave the hard work behind.

He is bolstered in his fantasy by the knowledge that some of those who work with the mighty Casey Jones are black men. In *Black Issues Book Review* Suzanne Rust wrote: "Bold and provocative in prose, picture and content," *I Dream of Trains* is "a work worthy of any contemporary collection."

Since 1989, Johnson has published one or more books per year and continues to write at a steady pace. The author once remarked: "I don't believe the magic of listening to Wilma Mitchell read us stories after lunch will ever be repeated for me. Book people came to life. They sat beside me in Maple Grove School. That is when I knew. I asked for a diary that year and have not stopped writing. My family, especially my grandfather and father, are storytellers and those spoken words sit beside me too." As a "genius grant" recipient, Johnson will be awarded one-hundred-thousand dollars each year through 2008.

BIOGRAPHICAL AND CRITICAL SOURCES:

BOOKS

Children's Literature Review, Volume 33, Gale (Detroit, MI), 1994, pp. 93-96.
Twentieth-Century Children's Writers, 4th edition, St. James (Detroit, MI), 1995, pp. 493-494.

PERIODICALS

Black Issues Book Review, July-August, 2003, Suzanne Rust, review of *I Dream of Trains,* p. 65.
Booklist, April 1, 1993, Quraysh Ali, review of *Toning the Sweep,* p. 1432; February 15, 1995, Hazel Rochman, review of *Humming Whispers,* p. 1072; March 15, 1995, Ilene Cooper, review of *Shoes Like Miss Alice's,* p. 1334; February 15, 1997, Stephanie Zvirin, review of *The Rolling Store,* p. 1026; September 15, 1998, Hazel Rochman, review of *Heaven,* p. 219; November 15, 1998, Helen Rosenberg, review of *The Other Side: Shorter Poems,* p. 579; January 1, 1999, Helen Rosenberg, review of *Maniac Monkeys on Magnolia Street,* p. 878; February 15, 2000, Michael Cart, review of *Down the Winding Road,* p. 1118; November 15, 2000, Anna Rich, review of *Heaven,* p. 657; January 1, 2001, Denise Wilms, review of

When Mules Flew on Magnolia Street, p. 960; February 15, 2001, Henrietta M. Smith, review of *Rain Feet,* p. 1161; January 1, 2002, review of *Running Back to Ludie,* p. 858; September 1, 2003, Hazel Rochman, review of *The First Part Last,* p. 122; October 1, 2003, Carolyn Phelan, review of *A Cool Moonlight,* p. 324; October 1, 2003, Gillian Engberg, review of *I Dream of Trains,* p. 328.

Bulletin of the Center for Children's Books, May, 1993, Betsy Hearne, review of *Julius,* p. 284; April, 1995, Elizabeth Bush, review of *Humming Whispers,* p. 278; May, 1997, Janice M. Del Negro, review of *The Rolling Store,* pp. 325-326.

Horn Book, September-October, 1992, Rudine Sims Bishop, "Books from Parallel Cultures: New African-American Voices," p. 620; March-April, 1993, Ellen Fader, review of *Julius,* pp. 196-197; September-October, 1993, Mary M. Burns, review of *Toning the Sweep,* p. 603; March-April, 1995, Maria Salvadore, "Making Sense of Our World," p. 229; November, 1998, Nancy Vasilakis, review of *The Other Side,* p. 750; November-December, 2001, Joanna Rudge Long, review of *Running Back to Ludie,* p. 766; July-August, 2002, Joanna Rudge Long, review of *Looking for Red,* p. 463; September-October, 2003, Joanna Rudge Long, review of *A Cool Moonlight,* p. 611.

Kirkus Reviews, April 1, 1995, review of *Humming Whispers,* p. 470.

New York Times Book Review, November 16, 2003, Marsha Wilson Chall, "One-Track Minds," p. 24.

Publishers Weekly, August 9, 1991, review of *One of Three,* p. 56; August 3, 1998, review of *Heaven,* p. 86; November 16, 1998, review of *The Other Side,* p. 76; November 23, 1998, review of *Maniac Monkeys on Magnolia Street,* p. 67; March 22, 1999, review of *The Wedding,* p. 91; March 6, 2000, review of *Down the Winding Road,* p. 109; May 27, 2002, review of *Looking for Red,* p. 60; June 16, 2003, review of *The First Part Last,* p. 73; October 20, 2003, review of *I Dream of Trains,* p. 53, and *A Cool Moonlight,* p. 55.

School Library Journal, October, 1991, Karen James, review of *One of Three,* p. 98; April, 1993, Ellen Fader, review of *Toning the Sweep,* p. 140; April, 1995, Carol Schene, review of *Humming Whispers,* p. 154; January, 2001, Maria B. Salvadore, review of *When Mules Flew on Magnolia Street,* p. 101; March, 2001, Susan Helper, review of *Those Building Men,* p. 236; October 22, 2001, review of *Running Back to Ludie,* p. 77; December, 2001,

Nina Lindsay, review of *Running Back to Ludie,* p. 164; July, 2002, Jean Gaffney, review of *Looking for Red,* p. 120; September, 2003, Maria B. Salvadore, review of *A Cool Moonlight,* p. 215; October, 2003, Catherine Threadgill, review of *I Dream of Trains,* p. 126.*

*   *   *

JONES, Adam Mars
See MARS-JONES, Adam

*   *   *

JONES, Edward P. 1950-

PERSONAL: Born October 5, 1950. *Education:* Attended College of the Holy Cross, Worcester, MA, and University of Virginia.

ADDRESSES: Home—4300 Old Dominion Drive, No. 914, Arlington, VA 22207.

CAREER: Fiction writer. Columnist for *Tax Notes.*

AWARDS, HONORS: National Book Award finalist, and Ernest Hemingway Foundation/PEN Award, both 1992, both for *Lost in the City;* Lannan Foundation Literary Award and fellowship, 2003; National Book Award nomination for fiction, 2003, and National Book Critics Circle award, and Pulitzer Prize for fiction, both 2004, all for *The Known World.*

WRITINGS:

Lost in the City (short stories), photographs by Amos Chan, Morrow (New York, NY), 1992.
The Known World, Amistad (New York, NY), 2003.

SIDELIGHTS: Called "a poignant and promising first effort" by *Publishers Weekly,* Edward P. Jones's first book, *Lost in the City,* was greeted with critical and popular acclaim. The work was nominated for the 1992 National Book Award, an honor last granted to a short-story collection six years earlier. The appeal of the

Edward P. Jones

fourteen-story collection lies in the realness of the people and the experiences that Jones presents. Each of the stories profiles African-American life in Washington, D.C. The characters are all lost in the nation's capital, some literally, others figuratively. They are black working-class men and women who struggle to preserve their families, communities, neighborhoods, and themselves amid drugs, violence, divorce, and other crises. Jones's assortment of characters include a mother whose son buys her a new home with drug money, a husband who repeatedly stabs his wife as their children sleep, and a girl who watches her pigeons fly from her home after their cages are destroyed by rats. They are all stories that "affirm humanity as only good literature can," remarked Michael Harris in the *Los Angeles Times Book Review.* "There's no secret to it, or only the final, most elusive secret: Jones has near-perfect pitch for people. . . . Whoever they are, he reveals them to us from the inside out."

Washington Post writer Mary Ann French noted that in *Lost in the City* Jones "creates sympathy through understanding—a sadly needed service that is too

seldom performed." *Washington Post Book World* reviewer Jonathan Yardley commented that the assembled stories are set in the 1950s, 1960s, and 1970s, "so there is little sense of the drug-and-crime haunted place that the inner city has become." Nevertheless, Yardley added, "danger and death are never far in the background." While the stories usually convey a sense of hope despite some bleak settings and horrible events, "Jones is no sentimentalist," according to the critic. Rather, he is "a lucid, appealing writer. He puts on no airs, tells his stories matter-of-factly and forthrightly, yet his prose is distinctive and carries more weight than first impressions might suggest."

The Known World, Jones's first novel and second published book, generated even more critical acclaim than his short-story collection. In 2004 the work won the Pulitzer Prize and the National Book Critics Circle award for fiction, both on the heels of a National Book Award for fiction nomination in 2003. *The Known World* begins with the antebellum story of African-American Henry Townsend, a farmer, bootmaker, and former slave. Townsend, an intelligent man with a fondness for John Milton's *Paradise Lost,* has taken an unusual adviser: William Robbins, a powerful man residing in Manchester County, Virginia. Under Robbins's guidance, Townsend rises economically to become a landowner and, ironically, a slave owner. When he dies, his widow, Caldonia, cannot carry on alone and things at the Townsend plantation begin to deteriorate: slaves run off in the night, and families with once-strong bonds start to turn on one another. Outside the farm, everything else, in other words, "the known world," is falling apart, too: free black people are sold into slavery and rumors of slave rebellions circulate widely, setting white families on edge and destroying their trust in the blacks who have worked for them for years.

According to Champ Clark, writing in *People,* readers of *The Known World* "will be rewarded many times over by Jones's masterful ability to convey even the most despicable aspects of the nation's history with humanity and poetic language." In *Booklist,* Vanessa Bush described the novel as "a profoundly beautiful and insightful look at American slavery and human nature." "Jones moves back and forth in time," she explained, "making the reader omniscient, knowing what will eventually befall the characters despite their best and worst efforts, their aspirations and their moral failings." *Newsweek* reviewer Susannah Meadows was less enthusiastic about the novel, writing that while "The human mystery that drives the narrative is the question of how a freed man could own another, . . . Jones never quite solves the puzzle of Henry's odd spiritual kinship with his former master." Mark Harris, reviewing the book for *Entertainment Weekly,* cited the "difficulty and occasional randomness of Jones's storytelling." This "doesn't seem accidental," Harris maintained. Jones "is writing about a landscape in which families, identities, and the very notion of self can be destroyed in the course of a casual business transaction—and he doesn't want you to get too comfortable tracing a single life across a tidy narrative line."

In an interview with Robert Fleming of *Publishers Weekly,* Jones explained his use of a dispassionate voice when describing the brutal episodes that take place in *The Known World* by noting that he wanted "to highlight the inhumanity of the whole situation of slavery." "I didn't want to preach," he added. "It was my goal to be objective, to not put a lot of emotion into this, to show it all in a matter-of-fact manner. But still I knew I was singing to the choir. In a case like this, you don't raise your voice, you just state the case and that is more than enough."

Sarah Anne Johnson, in an interview with Jones for the *Writer,* asked the author where he found his inspiration for *The Known World.* "You just wake up one morning with some image or some words in your head, and you go from there," Jones replied. "The first thing that set me off with *The Known World* was the image of Henry Townsend on his deathbed in the first few pages. You have to figure out how he got to be in the bed and who's in the room with him. Then you branch out further and further until finally you have all the pages that are in the book right now."

Despite praising Jones's award-winning novel, several critics have noted that *The Known World* is not an easy read. A contributor to *Kirkus Reviews* described the first hundred pages as "daunting," saying, "The reader struggles to sort out initially quickly glimpsed characters and absorb Jones's handling of historical background information." But then the novel gains "overpowering momentum," the critic added, and becomes "a harrowing tale that scarcely ever raises its voice." "By focusing on an African-American slave-holder," Edward B. St. John noted in *Library Journal,* "Jones forcefully demonstrates how institutionalized

slavery jeopardized all levels of civilized society so that no one was really free." The novel, St. John continued, is "a fascinating look at a painful theme." "Everyone in *The Known World* exhibits good, bad, and every other shade of humanity inside their actions," added Carroll Parrott Blue in *Black Issues Book Review.* "Jones uses his hard-won mastery of craft to gently entice us to stare directly into the face of our universally human quest for freedom."

BIOGRAPHICAL AND CRITICAL SOURCES:

BOOKS ·

Contemporary Literary Criticism, Yearbook 1992, Volume 76, Gale (Detroit, MI), 1992.

PERIODICALS

Black Issues Book Review, November-December, 2003, Carroll Parrott Blue, review of *The Known World,* p. 50.
Booklist, September 15, 2003, Vanessa Bush, review of *The Known World,* p. 211.
Entertainment Weekly, August 22, 2003, Mark Harris, review of *The Known World,* p. 134.
Kirkus Reviews, July 15, 2003, review of *The Known World,* p. 928.
Library Journal, August, 2003, Edward B. St. John, review of *The Known World,* p. 131.
Los Angeles Times Book Review, July 12, 1992, p. 6.
Newsweek, September 8, 2003, Susannah Meadows, review of *The Known World,* p. 57.
New York Times, June 11, 1992, p. C18; August 23, 1992, section 7, p. 16.
People, September 29, 2003, Champ Clark, review of *The Known World,* p. 45.
Publishers Weekly, March 23, 1992, p. 59; August 11, 2003, Robert Fleming, interview with Jones, p. 254.
Washington Post, July 22, 1992, pp. G1, G4; October 6, 1992, p. B4.
Washington Post Book World, June 21, 1992, p. 3.
Writer, August, 2004, Sarah Anne Johnson, interview with Jones, p. 20.*

*   *   *

JONES, John Bush 1940-

PERSONAL: Born August 3, 1940, in Chicago, IL; son of Aaron J., Jr. (a theater owner) and Dorothy (Bush) Jones; married Sandra Carson (a law student), May 18, 1968; children: Aaron Carson. *Education:* Attended Harvard University, 1958-59; Northwestern University, B.S. (with distinction), 1962, M.A., 1963, Ph.D., 1970.

ADDRESSES: Home—Lawrence, KS. *Office*—c/o Department of English, University of Kansas, Lawrence, KS 66045.

CAREER: Happy Medium Theater, Chicago, IL, assistant stage manager, 1960-61; Wagon Wheel Playhouse, Warsaw, IN, lighting designer and stage manager, 1962; Northwestern University, Evanston, IL, instructor in English 1965-68; University of Kansas, Lawrence, assistant professor, 1968-72, associate professor, 1972-77, professor of English, beginning 1977; retired. Founder and stage director of Northwestern University Gilbert and Sullivan Guild and (with wife) University of Kansas Mount Oread Gilbert and Sullivan Company; International Conference on Gilbert and Sullivan, chair, 1970.

MEMBER: Modern Language Association of America, American Educational Theater Association, Savage Club (London, England).

AWARDS, HONORS: Grants from Newberry Library grant, 1971, and American Philosophical Society, 1972.

WRITINGS:

W. S. Gilbert: A Century of Scholarship and Commentary, New York University Press (New York, NY), 1970.

(Editor) *Readings in Descriptive Bibliography,* Kent State University Press (Kent, OH), 1974.

(Editor and author of introduction, with George L. Vogt) *Literary and Historical Editing,* University of Kansas Libraries (Lawrence, KS), 1981.

Our Musicals, Ourselves: A Social History of the American Musical Theater, University Press of New England (Hanover, NH), 2003.

Contributor to *Encyclopedia Americana.* Special drama correspondent, *Kansas City Star.* Contributor to literary and library journals.

BIOGRAPHICAL AND CRITICAL SOURCES:

PERIODICALS

Library Journal, May 1, 2003, Laura Anne Ewald, review of *Our Musicals, Ourselves: A Social History of the American Musical Theater,* p. 116.*

K

KALFUS, Ken 1954-

PERSONAL: Born April 9, 1954, in Bronx, NY; son of Martin (a businessman) and Ida Kalfus; married Inga Saffron (a journalist), May 2, 1991; children: Sky. *Education:* Attended Sarah Lawrence College, 1972-74; attended New York University, 1974-76.

ADDRESSES: Agent—Caroline Dawnay, PFD, Drury House, 34-43 Russell St., London WC2B 5HA, England. *E-mail*—72754.2514@compuserve.com.

CAREER: Journalist and author, 1990—.

AWARDS, HONORS: Short-story collection *Pu-239 and Other Russian Fantasies* was nominated for the PEN/Faulkner Award for Fiction, 1999.

WRITINGS:

(Editor and author of introduction) Christopher Morley, *Christopher Morley's Philadelphia,* illustrated by Walter Jack Duncan and Frank H. Taylor, Fordham University Press (Fordham, NY), 1990.
Thirst (short stories), Milkweed Editions (Minneapolis, MN), 1998.
Pu-239 and Other Russian Fantasies (short stories), Milkweed Editions (Minneapolis, MN), 1999.
The Commissariat of Enlightenment: A Novel, Ecco (New York, NY), 2003.

SIDELIGHTS: Journalist Ken Kalfus grew up in Long Island, New York, but has lived around the world in locations as diverse as Belgrade, Dublin, and Moscow.

Accordingly, his debut collection of short stories, titled *Thirst,* offers an eclectic and varied treat for the reader, according to several reviewers. Kalfus was contacted by Milkweed Editions when an editor there read Kalfus's writing in *Harper's.* In response to the editor's request, Kalfus submitted several stories, and the editor's choices were published in book form. According to critic Mary Ann Grossmann of the *Saint Paul Pioneer Press,* the author's stories reflect his international experiences. *Voice Literary Supplement* critic Dwight Garner commented on the author's outlook, concluding that Kalfus is the "rare writer whose travels haven't colored his prose with cosmopolitan cynicism." Garner compared Kalfus to Hemingway in his ability to "let moments speak for themselves."

Thirst, according to Grossmann, contains the common themes of human dislocation and situational uncertainty. Kalfus admits that uncertainty is central to both his writing style and personal outlook. Grossmann joined other critics in finding the theme of uncertainty particularly effective in the short story "A Line Is a Series of Points." The story allows readers a glimpse into the psyche of refugees who have been homeless for so long that wandering has become a way of life; it is based on Kalfus's observations of Muslim refugees who had been forced out of a Bosnian village by Serbs. Kalfus was struck by the sense of denationalization that he observed, and the sense that such people could have "come from anywhere." A *Publishers Weekly* reviewer further praised *Thirst* as "skilled and versatile" and alternating between "postmodern playfulness and darker realism." This reviewer liked the daring aspect of some of the stories, as well as the element of surprise in the collection. Among the stories are "Cats in Space," which features suburban teenagers who set a cat adrift in a hot air balloon and later rescue the animal; "Night and Day You Are the One," which features a sleep-deprived character who walks back and forth between two different worlds in the same city; the title story, which finds an Irish au pair and a Moroccan student becoming romantically involved in Paris; and "The Joy and Melancholy Baseball Trivia Quiz," which suggests deeper meaning behind sports statistics.

Applauding Kalfus for subtly showing the reader that "sometimes the really significant truths are those found closest to home," Garner recalled in the *Voice Literary Supplement* that *Thirst* was the most effective debut book he had seen in a year. James Held of the *Philadelphia Inquirer* advised the reader to "unexpect the expected," and gave the author credit for capturing the humor inherent in our pursuits of deeper questions such as "knowing and being." Ron Carlson of the *New York Times Book Review* described Kalfus's style as one where the reader is never completely comfortable and the stories are laced with "fundamental strangeness."

After living in Russia for four years, Kalfus published a second collection of five short stories and one novella titled *Pu-239 and Other Russian Fantasies.* The stories in this collection take place in Russia at various times between Joseph Stalin's regime and the present. "What is most wonderful about the variety of these stories is Kalfus's restraint," commented *Review of Contemporary Fiction* contributor Paul Maliszewski. "While Kalfus is an American author, this is not Russia as seen through American eyes," Maliszewski continued. Similarly, Paul Richardson wrote in *Russian Life,* "It is exceptionally difficult for a foreigner to write fiction about Russia and get it right. Ken Kalfus gets it right. Again and again." In the book's title story, "Pu-239 and other Russian Fantasies," readers meet Timofey, a nuclear engineer who learns that he has absorbed fatal amounts of radiation. In an effort to leave his family with some means of support after he dies, Timofey attempts to sell weapons-grade plutonium on the black market. His clientele, however, ignorantly assume that the powder is an illicit drug. In "Anzhelika 13," a young girl begins menstruating on the day of Joseph Stalin's death and associates the biological event with Russia's mourning.

"Kalfus shows a striking talent for transcultural understanding, and for depicting the very strange," noted one *Publisher's Weekly* contributor in a review

of *Pu-239 and other Russian Fantasies.* Many reviewers were taken aback by the author's technique, which seemed to gain power with this second publication. "Kalfus is a rare writer of fiction whose passages of description feel like action," wrote Laura Miller for *Salon.com.* "It's as if he were injecting his readers with a serum that renders them, in a rush, intimately familiar with the texture of the Russian experience," Miller acknowledged. In a review of *Pu-239 and other Russian Fantasies* published on the *Stranger* book review Web site, Evan Sult expressed a dissenting opinion of Kalfus's fiction. "It's not the Russian characters or perspective that fail. . . . It's the writing itself. . . . Kalfus has a problem linking his narrative voice to the characters he writes." This, however, was not the popular view of the book, which left most reviewers wanting more. "Hopefully, it won't be long before readers see a novel from this master storyteller," remarked Veronica Scrol in *Booklist,* and upon hearing of the pending publication of Kalfus's first novel, Miller wrote, "Ah, something at last to look forward to in the next millennium."

The Commissariat of Enlightenment begins in pre-revolutionary Russia in the year 1910. Eminent author Leo Tolstoy is dying in a railway station in the small Russian town of Astapavo. Nikolai Grisbin, a young and ambitious cinematographer for a French newsreel company, joins the throng of media that congregate in the tiny town in hopes of capturing on film Tolstoy's last moments on Earth. On the way to Astapavo, Grisbin meets Professor Vorobev, a scientist and embalmer who wishes to embalm Tolstoy's body with his self-proclaimed revolutionary preservation skills, to which he attests by presenting a preserved rat. While in Astapavo, Grisbin meets revolutionary Russian figures Joseph Stalin and Vladimir Lenin. Stalin, who is quietly collecting political allies, convinces Grisbin to use his cinematic skills for propaganda purposes. After the revolution and Lenin's rise to power, in the year 1919, Grisbin changes his name to Astapov and goes to work for the Commissariat of Enlightenment, a Russian agency dealing in political propaganda. Here Grisbin truly realizes the dark power of film as he takes part in manipulating and controlling images and stories, ultimately determining what will become Russia's political history. When Lenin is close to death, Professor Vorobev is called on to preserve him. The novel ends at the crumbling of the Soviet Union.

Kalfus's first novel was widely reviewed. "Told in supple, witty prose, the story exhibits all the vigorous intelligence and vision readers have come to expect form Kalfus," stated a *Publishers Weekly* reviewer of *The Commissariat of Enlightenment.* "It's not moral complexity or clashes of opinion that interest Ken Kalfus, but the driving force of single ideas, the questioning, gives a relentless impetus to the narrative that makes this novel compelling to read," remarked Barry Unsworth in a *New York Times Books* Web site review. Unsworth continued with a popular observation on the author's powers to overtake the reader with an almost chemical force: "Some scenes of action and description are realized so vividly that they almost have the force of hallucination." Similarly, John Freeman wrote in the *Star Tribune,* "Kalfus mixes a stiff cocktail out of history's sad ingredients. In fact, it goes down so smoothly you almost don't feel the burn." Not all reviewers praised the book, however. In the *Houston Chronicle,* Evan Miles Williamson revealed one of the novel's problems: "Rather than let the reader draw conclusions from the events being dramatized, Kalfus repeatedly clubs readers over the head with his thesis: History is manipulable, and our culture is controlled by the propaganda machines of the media." Summing up popular opinion of the book, and making the prevalent comparison of Kalfus to revered Russian writer Nikolai Gogol, a *Kirkus Reviews* contributor called the book "a brilliant fusion of satire, science fiction, and political commentary," adding, "Gogol is probably tearing his hair out, wishing he'd dreamed this up." Remarking on his development as a writer since the publication of *Thirst,* Kalfus revealed to Garner in a *Salon.com* interview, "I certainly felt that when I was writing those stories that aiming for spareness in my work was a way of avoiding screwing it up with things that weren't relevant. I think my style has become a bit more lush. I think I'm more confident."

BIOGRAPHICAL AND CRITICAL SOURCES:

PERIODICALS

Bloomsbury Review, September, 1999, review of *Pu-239 and Other Russian Fantasies,* p. 13.

Book, March-April, 2003, Beth Kephart, review of *The Commissariat of Enlightenment,* pp. 78-79.

Book: The Magazine for the Reading Life, review of *Pu-239 and Other Russian Fantasies,* p. 70.

Booklist, August, 1999, Veronica Scrol, review of *Pu-239 and Other Russian Fantasies,* p. 2027; January 1, 2003, review of *The Commissariat of Enlightenment,* pp. 847-848.

Choice, March, 1999, review of *Thirst,* p. 1266.

Entertainment Weekly, February 14, 2003, review of *The Commissariat of Enlightenment,* p. 76.

Esquire, November, 1999, *Pu-239 and Other Russian Fantasies,* p. 82.

Harper's, February, 2003, John Leonard, review of *The Commissariat of Enlightenment,* pp. 67-68.

Hungry Mind Review, fall, 1999, review of *Pu-239 and Other Russian Fantasies,* p. 32.

Kirkus Reviews, July 15, 1999, review of *Pu-239 and Other Russian Fantasies,* p. 1074; December 1, 2002, review of *The Commissariat of Enlightenment,* p. 1720.

Library Journal, August, 1999, Jim Dwyer, review of *Pu-239 and Other Russian Fantasies,* p. 144.

Newsday, August 20, 1998.

New Yorker, November 22, 1999, review of *Pu-239 and Other Russian Fantasies,* p. 202.

New York Times Book Review, July 26, 1998, p. 9; September 26, 1999, review of *Pu-239 and Other Russian Fantasies,* p. 10; October 3, 1999, review of *Thirst,* p. 104; December 5, 1999, review of *Pu-239 and Other Russian Fantasies,* p. 77, and review of *Thirst,* p. 105.

Philadelphia Inquirer, June 28, 1998.

Publishers Weekly, April 27, 1998, p. 45; July 12, 1999, review of *Pu-239 and Other Russian Fantasies,* p. 72; March 20, 2000, review of *The Commissariat of Enlightenment,* p. 20; January 6, 2003, review of *The Commissariat of Enlightenment,* p. 37.

Review of Contemporary Fiction, spring, 2000, Paul Maliszewski, review of *Pu-239 and Other Russian Fantasies,* p. 183; summer, 2003, Tim Feeney, review of *The Commissariat of Enlightenment,* p. 138.

Russian Life, January, 2000, Paul Richardson, review of *Pu-239 and Other Russian Fantasies,* p. 58.

Saint Paul Pioneer Press, August 30, 1998.

Times Literary Supplement, July 9, 1999, review of *Thirst,* p. 23.

Voice Literary Supplement, June, 1998, pp. 73-74.

Yale Review, October, 2001, review of *Pu-239 and Other Russian Fantasies,* p. 129.

ONLINE

Curled Up with a Good Book Web site, http://www.curledup.com/ (April 16, 2003), review of *The Commissariat of Enlightenment.*

Esquire Web site, http://esquire.com/ (April 16, 2003), Adrienne Miller, review of *The Commissariat of Enlightenment.*

HarperCollins Web site, http://www.harpercollins.com/ (April 16, 2003), description of *The Commissariat of Enlightenment.*

Houston Chronicle Web site, http://www.chron.com/ (February 25, 2004), Eric Miles Williamson, "Soviet-Set Page-Turner Offers Warning," review of *The Commissariat of Enlightenment.*

Mostly Fiction Web site, http://mostlyfiction.com/ (February 25, 2004), Mary Whipple, review of *The Commissariat of Enlightenment.*

New York Times Books Web site, http://www.nytimes.com/ (April 11, 2003), Barry Unsworth, "Ambiguous Light," review of *The Commissariat of Enlightenment.*

PFD Literary Agency Web site, http://www.pfd.co.uk/ (February 25, 2004), "Author Ken Kalfus."

PIF Magazine Web site, http://www.pifmagazine.com/ (February 25, 2004), Ryan Boudinot, "Interview with Ken Kalfus."

Reading Group Guides Web site, http://www.readinggroupguides.com/ (February 25, 2004), description of *The Commissariat of Enlightenment.*

Salon.com, http://www.salon.com/ (April 16, 2003), Laura Miller, review of *Pu-239 and Other Russian Fantasies,* and Dwight Garner, "The Salon Interview: Ken Kalfus."

Star Tribune Web site, http://www.startribune.com/ (April 16, 2003), John Freeman, review of *The Commissariat of Enlightenment.*

Stranger, http://www.thestranger.com/ (April 16, 2003), Evan Sult, review of *Pu-239 and Other Russian Fantasies.**

*   *   *

KAYMOR, Patrice Maguilene
See SENGHOR, Léopold Sédar

*   *   *

KELLOGG, Frederick 1929-

PERSONAL: Born December 9, 1929, in Boston, MA; son of Frederick Floyd (a cardiologist) and Stella Harriet (a homemaker; maiden name, Plummer) Kellogg; married Patricia Hanbery, August 21, 1954 (died, April 24, 1975); children: Kristine Marie Calvert. *Ethnicity:* "European." *Education:* Stanford University, A.B., 1952; University of Southern California, M.A., 1958; Indiana University—Bloomington, Ph.D., 1969. *Politics:* Liberal. *Hobbies and other interests:* Opera, drama, ballet, art, literature, classical music.

ADDRESSES: Home—1018 East Greenlee Pl., Tucson, AZ 85719. *Office*—Department of History, 215 Social Sciences Bldg., University of Arizona, Tucson, AZ 85721; fax: 520-621-2422. *E-mail*—kellogg@u.arizona.edu.

CAREER: Boise State University, Boise, ID, instructor, 1962-64, assistant professor, 1964-65, associate professor of history, 1966-67; University of Arizona, Tucson, instructor, 1967-68, assistant professor, 1969-71, associate professor of history, 1971—. University of Idaho, visiting assistant professor, 1965. International Commission for the History and Theory of Historiography, member, 1980—; Idaho Historical Conference, founder, 1964; member of Idaho State Coordinating Committee for the Promotion of History and National Coordinating Committee for the Promotion of History. *Southeastern Europe,* managing editor, 1974—.

MEMBER: American Historical Association, American Association for the Advancement of Slavic Studies, Society for Romanian Studies, Southeast European Studies Association, Institutul de istorie Alexandru D. Xenopol (honorary member).

AWARDS, HONORS: Scholar of U.S.-Romania Cultural Exchange, 1960-61; senior Fulbright scholar in Romania, 1969-70; grants from American Council of Learned Societies (for the U.S.S.R.), 1970-71, International Research and Exchanges Board (for Romania), 1972-73, 1973-74, 1977, 1982, Republic of Romania, 1977, Polska Rzeczypospolita Ludowa, 1979, and Republic of Bulgaria, 1981; Certificate of Recognition, Society for Romanian Studies, 1993; Nicolae Iorga Prize, Romanian Academy, 1997, for *The Road to Romanian Independence;* named honorary editor, *Romanian Cultural Studies,* 1999—.

WRITINGS:

(Editor) Cornelia Bodea, *The Romanians' Struggle for Unification, 1834-1849,* Publishing House of the Academy of the Socialist Republic of Romania (Bucharest, Romania), 1970.

A History of Romanian Historical Writing (mono-graph), Charles Schlacks, Jr. (Bakersfield, CA), 1990.
The Road to Romanian Independence, Purdue University Press (West Lafayette, IN), 1995.

Editor in chief of the series "The Laws of Romania," Charles Schlacks, Jr. (Bakersfield, CA). Contributor to books, including *The 1848 Revolutions in the Romanian Principalities,* edited by Cornelia C. Bodea, Romanian Library (New York, NY), 1975; and *Labyrinth of Nationalism/Complexities of Diplomacy: Essays in Honor of Charles and Barbara Jelavich,* edited by Richard Frucht, Slavica (Columbus, OH), 1992. Contributor to history journals, including *East European Quarterly, Journal of Central European Affairs, Canadian Review of Studies in Nationalism, Romanian Bulletin,* and foreign-language periodicals.

The monograph *A History of Romanian Historical Writing* was also published in Romanian.

WORK IN PROGRESS: A monograph, *Romania and the Romanians,* for Hoover Institution Press (Stanford, CA).

SIDELIGHTS: Frederick Kellogg once told *CA:* "Along with many contemporaries I seek to understand our global milieu. My thoughts about it all have been chaotic, but penning on paper and a word processor enables me to espy some harmony.

"History attracted me because of the romance, mystery, and adventure of bygone days. Romania seemed especially mysterious. Indeed, my urge to scribble about Romanian yesterdays stemmed largely from a lack of reliable information in English about Carpatho-Danubia, the Romanian-inhabited region of Eastern Europe comprising the eastern Carpathian Mountains, the lower Danube River, and the northwestern shore of the Black Sea.

"After picking several intriguing subjects, I teed off by exploring archives and libraries in America, England, Austria, Germany, France, Russia, and Romania. I soon realized that studying Romanian alone would not suffice. I must also handle Slavic, Uralic, Altaic, and additional Indo-European tongues. Yet posing ques-

tions, collecting data, and learning languages were only the start. I needed to make sense of my findings. A glimmer came once I began to write.

"My endeavors have had two major thrusts. One is historiography. For instance, *A History of Romanian Historical Writing* looks at Romanian and foreign notions about Carpatho-Danubia from the fifteenth century onward. I chose this topic to assist English readers in recognizing the richness of the Romanians' heritage, and to provide a launching pad for fresh research into the Romanian past. My second thrust is diplomacy. *The Road to Romanian Independence* probes Romania's passage from political dependency to national sovereignty, from the 1860s to 1880. I selected this theme, again, owing to a paucity of relevant scholarly works, to sift the Danubian Romanians' challenges from the neighboring empires of Russia, Austria-Hungary, and Turkey, as well as to shed light on Romania's quest for material progress, its civil rights, and its relations with other peoples and regimes in southeastern and western Europe.

"These two thrusts readied me to contemplate the Romanians' goals and efforts, along with their accomplishments and persisting problems, on a broad canvas depicting their economy, society, politics, and culture. I discovered thereby some tentative approaches to my current project embracing Romania and the Romanians from prehistory to the present."

*   *   *

KENNEDY, William 1928-

PERSONAL: Born January 16, 1928, in Albany, NY; son of William J. (a deputy sheriff) and Mary Elizabeth (a secretary; maiden name, MacDonald) Kennedy; married Ana Daisy (Dana) Sosa (a former actress and dancer), January 31, 1957; children: Dana Elizabeth, Katherine Anne, Brendan Christopher. *Education:* Siena College, B.A., 1949.

ADDRESSES: Home—R.D. 3, Box 508, Averill Park, NY 12018. *Office*—Department of English, State University of New York at Albany, 1400 Washington Ave., Albany, NY 12222; NYS Writers Institute, Washington Avenue, Albany, NY 12222-0001. *Agent*—Liz Darhansoff, 1220 Park Ave., New York, NY 10028.

CAREER: Post Star, Glen Falls, NY, assistant sports editor and columnist, 1949-50; *Times-Union,* Albany, NY, reporter, 1952-56, special writer, 1963-70, and film critic, 1968-70; *Puerto Rico World Journal,* San Juan, assistant managing editor and columnist, 1956; Miami *Herald,* Miami, FL, reporter, 1957; correspondent for Time-Life publications in Puerto Rico, and reporter for Dorvillier (business) newsletter and Knight Newspapers, 1957-59; *Star,* San Juan, Puerto Rico, founding managing editor, 1959-61; full-time fiction writer, 1961-63; book editor of *Look* magazine, 1971; State University of New York at Albany, lecturer, 1974-82, New York State Writers Institute, founder and professor of English, 1983—. Writers Institute at Albany, founder, 1983, director, 1984—. Visiting professor of English, Cornell University, 1982-83. Cofounder, Cinema 750 film society, Rennselaer, NY, 1968-70; organizing moderator for series of forums on the humanities, sponsored by the National Endowment for the Humanities, New York State Library, and Albany Public Library. Panelist, New York State Council on the Arts, 1980-83. American Academy of Arts and Letters, member, beginning in 1993. *Military service:* U.S. Army, 1950-52; served as sports editor and columnist for Army newspapers; became sergeant.

MEMBER: Writers Guild of America, PEN, American Academy of Arts and Letters.

AWARDS, HONORS: Award for reporting, Puerto Rican Civic Association (Miami, FL), 1957; Page One Award, Newspaper Guild, 1965, for reporting; *Times-Union* won the New York State Publishers Award for Community Service, 1965, on the basis of several of Kennedy's articles on Albany's slums; National Association for the Advancement of Colored People award, 1965, for reporting; Writer of the Year Award, Friends of the Albany Public Library, 1975; National Endowment for the Arts fellowship, 1981; MacArthur Foundation fellowship, 1983; National Book Critics Circle Award, 1983, and Pulitzer Prize for fiction, 1984, both for *Ironweed;* New York State Governor's Arts Award, 1984; honored by citizens of Albany and the State University of New York at Albany with "William Kennedy's Albany" celebration, September 6-9, 1984; Before Columbus Foundation American Book Award, 1985, for *O Albany!;* Brandeis University Creative Arts Award, 1986; L.H.D., Russell Sage College, 1980, Rensselaer Polytechnic Institute, 1987, Fordham University, 1992, and Trinity College, 1992;

Litt.D., Siena College, 1984, and College of St. Rose, 1985; Commander, Order of Arts and Letters (France), 1993; PEN/Faulkner Award nomination, 2003, for *Roscoe.*

WRITINGS:

The Ink Truck (novel), Dial (New York, NY), 1969.

Legs (novel), Coward (New York, NY), 1975.

Billy Phelan's Greatest Game (novel), Viking (New York, NY), 1978.

Getting It All, Saving It All: Some Notes by an Extremist, New York State Governor's Conference on Libraries, 1978.

Ironweed (novel), Viking (New York, NY), 1983.

O Albany!: An Urban Tapestry (nonfiction), Viking (New York, NY), 1983, published as *O Albany! Improbable City of Political Wizards, Fearless Ethnics, Spectacular Aristocrats, Splendid Nobodies, and Underrated Scoundrels,* Penguin, 1985.

(With son, Brendan Kennedy) *Charley Malarkey and the Belly Button Machine* (juvenile), Atlantic Monthly Press (New York, NY), 1986.

(With Francis Coppola and Mario Puzo) *The Cotton Club,* St. Martin's Press (New York, NY), 1986.

(Author of introduction) *The Making of Ironweed,* Penguin Books, 1988.

Quinn's Book, Viking (New York, NY), 1988.

Very Old Bones, Viking (New York, NY), 1992.

Riding the Yellow Trolley Car: Selected Nonfiction, Viking (New York, NY), 1994.

(With Brendan Kennedy) *Charlie Malarkey and the Singing Moose* (juvenile), Viking (New York, NY), 1994.

The Flaming Corsage (novel), Viking (New York, NY), 1996.

The Albany Trilogy (contains *Legs, Billy Phelan's Greatest Game,* and *Ironweed*), Penguin (New York, NY), 1996.

(With Mary Lynch Kennedy and Hadley M. Smith) *Writing in the Disciplines: A Reader for Writers,* Prentice Hall (Englewood Cliffs, NJ), 1996.

Conversations with William Kennedy, edited by Neila C. Seshachari, University Press of Mississippi (Jackson, MS), 1997.

Roscoe (novel), Viking (New York, NY), 2002.

Contributor to books, including *Gabriel García Màrquez* (criticism), Taurus Ediciones, 1982; and *The Capitol in Albany,* Aperture, 1985. Contributor of articles, interviews, and reviews to periodicals, including *New York Times Magazine*, *National Observer*, *New York Times Book Review*, *Washington Post Book World*, *New Republic*, and *Look*.

SCREENPLAYS

(With Francis Ford Coppola) *The Cotton Club*, Orion Pictures, 1984.

Ironweed (based on Kennedy's novel), Tri-Star Pictures, 1987.

Also author of screenplay *Legs* for Gene Kirkwood and *Billy Phelan's Greatest Game* for Pepper-Prince Company.

SIDELIGHTS: Novels by Irish-American writer William Kennedy did not receive much critical attention when they first appeared. He was known primarily as a respected and versatile journalist who had worked for Albany, New York's *Times-Union*, the Miami *Herald*, and San Juan, Puerto Rico's *Star*. *Columbia Journalism Review* writer Michael Robertson cited former editor William J. Dorvillier's comment that Kennedy was "one of the best complete journalists—as reporter, editor, whatever—that I've known in sixty years in the business." But when Kennedy's 1983 novel *Ironweed* won the Pulitzer Prize, his fiction was given new life and three early novels were reissued and became best-sellers. Hollywood also took note; director Francis Ford Coppola enlisted Kennedy to write the screenplay for *The Cotton Club*, and he also wrote screen versions of his three other books.

O Albany!, written before *Ironweed*'s spectacular reception secured long-overdue literary recognition for Kennedy, is based in part upon a series of articles Kennedy wrote about city neighborhoods for the *Times-Union* in the mid-1960s. *Publishers Weekly* reviewer Joseph Barbato maintained that the essays in *O Albany!* provide readers with a "nonfiction delineation of Kennedy's imaginative source—an upstate city of politicians and hoodlums, of gambling dens and ethnic neighborhoods, which for all its isolation remains, he insists 'as various as the American psyche' and rich in stories and characters." Christopher Lehmann-Haupt agreed in the *New York Times* that "even more absorbing than the detail and the enthusiasm is the raw material of Mr. Kennedy's fiction,

present on every page [of the essays]. Even if one doesn't give a damn for Albany, it is always interesting to watch the author's imagination at play in the city and its history, for one is witnessing the first steps in a novelist's creative process." As Kennedy explains in his introduction to the work, "I write this book not as a booster of Albany, which I am, nor as an apologist for the city, which I sometimes am, but rather as a person whose imagination has become fused with a single place, and in that place finds all the elements that a man ever needs for the life of the soul."

Legs, Billy Phelan's Greatest Game, and *Ironweed* are all set in the Albany of the 1930s. Margaret Croyden stated in the *New York Times Magazine* that the books "are inexorably linked to [Kennedy's] native city . . . during the Depression years, when Albany was a wideopen city, run by Irish bosses and their corrupt political machine. This sense of place gives Kennedy's work a rich texture, a deep sense of authenticity." Susan Chira of the *New York Times* added that Albany, "often dismissed by outsiders as provincial and drab, lives in Mr. Kennedy's acclaimed fiction as a raucous town that symbolizes all that was glorious and corrupt, generous and sordid in the America of the 20s and 30s."

The Ink Truck is a novel about an Albany newspaper strike featuring a main character described by *Time* reviewer R. Z. Sheppard as "a columnist named Bailey, a highly sexed free spirit with a loud checkered sports jacket, a long green scarf and a chip on his shoulder as big as the state capitol." "It is my hope," Kennedy told *Library Journal* in 1969, that *The Ink Truck* "will stand as an analgesic inspiration to all weird men of good will and rotten luck everywhere." The novel, Sheppard related, culminates in "a poignant conclusion, yet it does not show Kennedy at his full spellbinding power. Much of the book is inspired blarney, fun to read and probably fun to write."

This political landscape dominates Kennedy's novels. Kennedy wrote in *O Albany!* that "it was a common Albany syndrome for children to grow up obsessed with being a Democrat. Your identity was fixed by both religion and politics, but from the political hierarchy came the way of life: the job, the perpetuation of the job, the dole when there was no job, the loan when there was no dole, the security of the neighborhood, the new street-light, the new sidewalk, the right to run your bar after hours or to open a card-game on the sneak. These things came to you not by right of citizenship. Republicans had no such rights. They came to you because you gave allegiance to Dan O'Connell and his party."

Kennedy's knowledge of Albany's political machinery is firsthand. A Toronto *Globe and Mail* reporter indicated that Kennedy's "father sold pies, cut hair, worked in a foundry, wrote illegal numbers, ran political errands for the Democratic ward heelers, and was rewarded by the Machine by being made a deputy sheriff." And, as Croyden explained, William Sr. "often took his son with him to political clubs and gambling joints where young Bill Kennedy, with his eye and ear for detail and for the tone and temper of Irish-Americans, listened and watched and remembered." Kennedy, wrote Doris Grumbach in the *Saturday Review*, "knows every bar, hotel, store, bowling alley, pool hall, and whorehouse that ever opened in North Albany. He knows where the Irish had their picnics and parties—and what went on at them; where their churches were; where they bet on horses, played the numbers, and bet on poker. He can re-create with absolute accuracy the city conversations."

One of the few Kennedy novels that does not rely heavily on firsthand experience is *Legs*, for which he did extensive research on the gangster era. *Legs*, according to *Washington Post* reviewer Curt Suplee, is a "fictional biography" of Jack "Legs" Diamond, the "vicious" Irish-American gangster-bootlegger "who in 1931 was finally shot to death" at an Albany rooming house. Kennedy's novel chronicles "'Legs' attempts to smuggle heroin, his buying of politicians, judges and cops," and his womanizing, related W. T. Lhamon in the *New Republic*. A bully and a torturer who frequently betrayed associates, Diamond made many enemies. Several attempts were made on his life, and to many people, he seemed unkillable. Though vicious, Diamond was also a glamorous figure. *Listener* critic Tony Aspler indicated that writer F. Scott Fitzgerald met the gangster on a transatlantic crossing in 1926, and in the words of *Times Literary Supplement* writer Philip French, Diamond "may have been the model" for Fitzgerald's character Jay Gatsby. Legs Diamond, pointed out Suplee, "evolved into a national obsession, a godsend for copy-short newsmen, a mesmerizing topic in tavern or tearoom. Yet profoundly evil."

Kennedy's second novel in the "Albany" cycle, *Billy Phelan's Greatest Game*, explores the same territory.

As *Newsweek* reviewer Peter S. Prescott related, "The year is 1938, the time is almost always after dark, and the characters . . . are constantly reminded of times further past, of the floods and strikes, the scandals and murders of a quarter century before." The plot of the novel is related by reporter Martin Daugherty. Through his eyes, wrote Suplee, "we watch Billy—a pool shark, bowling ace and saloon-wise hustler with a pitilessly rigid code of ethics—prowl among Albany's nighttown denizens. But when kidnappers abduct the sole child of an omnipotent clan (patterned on the family of the late Dan O'Connell, of Albany's Democratic machine), Billy is pushed to turn informer, and faces competing claims of conscience."

Billy Phelan's Greatest Game received a smattering of mildly favorable critical attention, as did *Legs*, but did not sell particularly well; all three of the author's earlier novels sold only a few thousand copies. The first one hundred pages of *Ironweed*—detailing the story of Billy's father who left the family when Billy was nine—were originally accepted by Viking, but the book later lost the marketing backing it needed. In 1979 Kennedy agreed it would be best to submit the novel elsewhere. It was rejected twelve more times, and the author was disillusioned—past fifty and in debt—when Saul Bellow wrote Viking, admonishing them for slighting Kennedy's talent and asking them to reconsider their decision not to publish *Ironweed*. Viking heeded Bellow's letter, in which the Nobel Prize-winner referred to Kennedy's "Albany" novels, calling them "a distinguished group of books."

By itself, *Ironweed* did not appear to be a good publishing risk. The subject matter is relentlessly downbeat. *Ironweed* portrays "the world of the down-and-outer, the man who drifts by the windows of boarding houses and diners with a slouch hat and a brain whose most vivid images are twenty years old," noted *Detroit News* critic James F. Veseley. Prior to publication, editors took issue with the book's unconventional use of language. *New York Review of Books* critic Robert Towers wrote that, in *Ironweed*, Kennedy "largely abandons the rather breezy, quasi-journalistic narrative voice of his previous fiction and resorts to a more poetically charged, often surrealistic use of language as he re-creates the experiences and mental states of an alcoholic bum." As Kennedy told a Toronto *Globe and Mail* reporter, "They . . . objected that the book was overwritten, they didn't understand what I was doing in terms of language, they felt that no bum would ever talk like Francis does, or think like he does, that they thought of him only as a bum. They didn't understand that what I was striving for was to talk about the central eloquence of every human being. We all have this unutterable eloquence, and the closest you can get to it is to make it utterable at some point, in some way that separates it from the conscious level of life."

The figures in *Ironweed* are drawn from portraits Kennedy gathered for a nonfiction study of the street people of Albany, called *Lemon Weed*. Rejected by publishers, *Lemon Weed*, a collection of interviews with the homeless, was set aside while Kennedy worked on *Billy Phelan's Greatest Game*. After concentrating on its main character, Francis Phelan, the author decided to reshape the *Lemon Weed* material using the fictional Francis's point of view. Thus, "the specifics in *Ironweed*—the traction strike, professional baseball, Irish immigrant experiences, a vast Irish cemetery, an Irish neighborhood, the Erie Canal and so forth—are the elements of life in Albany," Kennedy told Croyden. "Some people say that *Ironweed* might have had any setting, and perhaps this is true. But the values that emerged are peculiar to my own town and to my own time and would not be the same in a smaller city, or a metropolis, or a city that was not Irish, or wasn't large enough to support a skid row."

Ironweed, "which refers to a tough-stemmed member of the sunflower family," according to Lehmann-Haupt, "recounts a few days in the life of an Albany skid-row bum, a former major-league third-baseman with a talent for running, particularly running away, although his ambition now, at the height of the Depression, has been scaled down to the task of getting through the next twenty minutes or so." Once Phelan ran from Albany after he threw a rock at a scab and killed him during a trolley strike, setting off a riot, but he was later in the habit of leaving the town and his family to play in the leagues every baseball season. When he accidentally dropped his newborn son— breaking his neck and killing him—while attempting to change the child's diapers, Francis ran from town and abandoned his family for good.

Now Phelan is back in Albany after twenty-two years, as Towers noted, "lurching around the missions and flophouses of the city's South End." On a cold Halloween night and the following All Saints' Day in

1938, the weekend of Orson Welles's *War of the Worlds* broadcast, Phelan "encounters the ghosts of his friends, relatives, and murder victims, who shout at him on buses, appear in saloons wearing corsages, talk with him from their graves in St. Agnes's cemetery," related Mark Caldwell in the *Voice Literary Supplement*.

Kennedy's next novel, *Quinn's Book,* set in pre-Civil War Albany, begins another cycle centered on residents of New York's capitol city. In the beginning, pre-teen narrator Daniel Quinn witnesses a spectacular drowning accident on the banks of the Hudson River followed by a deviant sexual act in which a whore, presumed drowned, miraculously revives. It is also his first meeting with "Maud the wondrous," a girl he saves from drowning, who becomes the love of his life. "The end is a whirl of events that include sketches of high life in Saratoga and accounts of horse races, boxing matches and a draft riot," Richard Eder related in the *Los Angeles Times Book Review*. He continued, "Daniel shocks a fashionable audience with a bitterly realistic account of his Civil War experiences. Hillegond is savagely murdered; her murderer is killed by two owls jointly and mysteriously controlled by Maud and a magical platter owned by Daniel. The two lovers are lushly and definitively reunited." With these events, said Eder, *Quinn's Book* "elevates portions or approximations of New York history—Dutch, English, Irish—into legend."

Most reviews of *Quinn's Book* were favorable. Although George Garrett, writing in Chicago's *Tribune Books,* called *Quinn's Book* "one of the most bloody and violent novels" he has read, the gore is necessary to tell the whole truth about life in Albany, the critic added. In this regard, Garrett elaborated, the author's "integrity is unflinching. Yet this is, too, a profoundly funny and joyous story, as abundant with living energy as any novel you are likely to read this year or for a long time to come." Some readers feel that the idiomatic language Kennedy uses to evoke a past era sometimes misses the mark; however, countered T. Coraghessan Boyle in the *New York Times Book Review,* "The language of *Quinn's Book* rises above occasional lapses, and Quinn, as the book progresses, becomes increasingly eloquent, dropping the convoluted syntax in favor of a cleaner, more contemporary line. And if the history sometimes overwhelms the story, it is always fascinating. . . . Kennedy does indeed have the power to peer into the past, to breathe life into it and make it indispensable, and Quinn's battle to control his destiny and win Maud is by turns grim, amusing and deeply moving. In an era when so much of our fiction is content to accomplish so little, *Quinn's Book* is a revelation. Large-minded, ardent, alive on every page with its author's passion for his place and the events that made it, it is a novel to savor." Concluded Toronto *Globe and Mail* reviewer H. J. Kirchhoff, "This is historical fiction suffused with mysticism and myth. . . . *Quinn's Book* is superlative fiction."

In *The Flaming Corsage,* another contribution to the "Albany saga," Kennedy covers the twenty-eight years between 1884 and 1912, concentrating on the marriage between Edward Daugherty, an Irish-American playwright, and Katrina, the daughter of a patrician family that traces its roots back to English Puritan revolutionary Oliver Cromwell. In *The Flaming Corsage,* Kennedy dramatizes the conflict between Irish immigrants and the culture they struggled to adopt. Michael Gorra, writing for the *New York Times,* noted that "[never] before have we seen so clearly the degree to which Mr. Kennedy is not only a regional writer but an ethnic one. In the past, almost all his characters have been Irish Catholics, but here that's underlined by Edward's pursuit of the Episcopalian Katrina, a pursuit that offers a fuller sense of the society against which Irish America is defined." James B. Denigan, writing in *America,* called *The Flaming Corsage* "a complex, subtly sequenced novel that, in a florid tapestry of linguistic virtuosity, buttonholes readers with a compelling tale of guile, shame and conflict. In his novels, with their physical strength and vitality, obsession with capricious success and faith in a willful democracy hell-bent on denying class identity, Kennedy reconfirms that Albany is indeed a microcosm of America." Some critics, like Gorra, found *The Flaming Corsage* to be "less than the sum of its parts." The critic concluded, however, that narrative requirements of novel cycles are complex, and qualifies his criticism of Kennedy's latest effort: "It adds little to the Albany cycle as a whole; but neither, and despite my reservations, does it seriously detract from Mr. Kennedy's achievement."

Kennedy's fascination with Albany continues in his seventh novel, *Roscoe.* Although a fictional story about Roscoe Conway, a Democratic party boss immediately after World War II, *Roscoe,* like many of Kennedy's "Albany" novels, has a factual basis. "Most of the characters are based on real historical figures, the lead-

ers of Albany's infamous O'Connell political machine," Sandy English explained in an online review of the novel for the World Socialist Web site. English lamented that it is difficult to "distinguish Kennedy's voice from Roscoe's, . . . at times it is not clear whether the sentiments are the protagonist's or the author's." Noting Kennedy's talent for portraying Irish Americans who, while "self-destructive and melancholic, . . . are also wildly comic and vibrantly alive," David W. Madden added in his *Review of Contemporary Fiction* appraisal that in *Roscoe* the author "has created a rich tapestry of mid-twentieth-century America . . . home to schemers and swindlers, crooked politicians and charming rogues, the America often unacknowledged in the euphoria of the war years." Calling *Roscoe* the "most overtly political novel in Kennedy's Albany cycle," *Book* reviewer Don McCleese added that the novel eschews formal conventions for vitality. "As the author approaches his mid-seventies," the critic explained, "he plainly has plenty on his mind and little patience with formalistic conventions. . . . Kennedy is less concerned with dotting 'i's and crossing 't's than with letting the reader know how things really work—in Albany, on earth, in heaven."

BIOGRAPHICAL AND CRITICAL SOURCES:

BOOKS

Contemporary Literary Criticism, Gale (Detroit, MI), Volume 6, 1976, Volume 28, 1984, Volume 34, 1985, Volume 53, 1989.

McCaffery, Larry, and Sinda Gregory, *Alive and Writing: Interviews with American Authors of the 1980s,* University of Illinois Press (Champaign, IL), 1987.

Reilly, Edward C., *William Kennedy,* Twayne (New York, NY), 1991.

Van Dover, J. K., *Understanding William Kennedy,* University of South Carolina Press (Columbia, SC), 1991.

PERIODICALS

America, May 19, 1984; November 21, 1992, p. 410; January 29, 1994, James E. Rocks, review of *Riding the Yellow Trolley Car,* p. 29; September 14, 1996, p. 28.

Book, January-February, 2002, Don McCleese, review of *Roscoe,* p. 64.

Booklist, January 1, 2003, review of *Roscoe,* p. 792.

Chicago Tribune, January 23, 1983.

Christianity Today, May 13, 1988, p. 63.

Classical and Modern Literature, summer, 1988, pp. 247-63.

Commonweal, October 13, 1978; September 9, 1983; May 20, 1988, p. 308; May 19, 1989, p. 298; May 22, 1992, p. 28; September 13, 1996, Daniel M. Murtaugh, review of *The Flaming Corsage,* p. 36.

Critique, spring, 1986, pp. 167-184.

Detroit News, January 30, 1983; February 26, 1984.

Economist, March 2, 2002, review of *Roscoe.*

Entertainment Weekly, April 24, 1992, p. 60; July 9, 1993, p. 45; June 17, 1994, p. 66.

Esquire, March, 1985.

Gentlemen's Quarterly, June, 1993, p. 47.

Globe and Mail (Toronto, Ontario, Canada), September 1, 1984; December 15, 1984; May 21, 1988.

Hudson Review, summer, 1983.

Library Journal, October 1, 1969; April 15, 1996, p. 122; September 1, 1996, p. 228.

Listener, May 6, 1976.

Los Angeles Times, December 14, 1984.

Los Angeles Times Book Review, December 26, 1982; September 23, 1984; May 22, 1988.

New Republic, May 24, 1975; February 14, 1983; June 27, 1988, p. 41.

New Statesman & Society, June 17, 1988, p. 44.

Newsweek, June 23, 1975; May 8, 1978; January 31, 1983; February 6, 1984; May 9, 1988, p. 72.

New York, May 23, 1988, p. 93.

New Yorker, February 7, 1983; January 11, 1988, p. 78; April 27, 1992, p. 106; January 21, 2002, review of *Roscoe,* p. 83.

New York Review of Books, March 31, 1983; August 13, 1992, p. 54.

New York Times, January 10, 1983; September 17, 1983; December 23, 1983; September 22, 1984; March 12, 1987; July 19, 1987; September 18, 1987; December 13, 1987; May 16, 1988; May 2, 1996, pp. B5, C19.

New York Times Book Review, January 23, 1983; November 13, 1983; January 1, 1984; September 30, 1984; October 2, 1986; January 25, 1987, p. 3; May 22, 1988, p. 1; May 20, 1990, p. 1; May 10, 1992, p. 1; May 16, 1993, p. 11; May 19, 1996, p. 7; May 4, 1997, p. 32; June 1, 1997, p. 52.

New York Times Magazine, August 26, 1984.

Observer (London, England), October 20, 1969.

Paris Review, fall, 1989, pp. 35-59.

People, December 24, 1984; January 18, 1988; May 25, 1992, p. 31; June 24, 1996, p. 29.

Playboy, June, 1988, p. 22.

Poets & Writers, March-April, 1994, pp. 42-49.

Publishers Weekly, December 9, 1983; May 18, 1988, p. 71; February 3, 1992, p. 62; March 15, 1993, p. 76; June 6, 1994, p. 64; March 4, 1996, p. 52; March 17, 1997, p. 81.

Review of Contemporary Fiction, summer, 2002, David W. Madden, review of *Roscoe,* p. 227.

Rolling Stone, September 30, 1993, p. 18.

Saturday Review, April 29, 1978.

Time, January 24, 1983; October 1, 1984; December 17, 1984; May 16, 1988, p. 92; April 27, 1992, p. 68; May 13, 1996, p. 92.

Times Literary Supplement, October 5, 1984.

Tribune Books (Chicago, IL), May 8, 1988.

Twentieth Century Literature, spring, 1999, Brock Clarke, "'A Hostile Decade': The Sixties and Self-Criticism in William Kennedy's Early Prose," p. 1.

Voice Literary Supplement, February, 1983; October, 1984.

Washington Post, October 5, 1969; May 18, 1975; December 28, 1983.

Washington Post Book World, January 16, 1983; January 29, 1984; October 14, 1984; May 8, 1988.

World Literature Today, summer, 1994, Marvin J. LaHood, review of *Riding the Yellow Trolley Car,* p. 580; spring, 1997, Marvin J. LaHood, review of *The Flaming Corsage,* p. 386.

ONLINE

World Socialist Web site, http://www.wsws.org/ (January, 2004), Sandy English, review of *Roscoe.**

*   *   *

KEYES, Ralph 1945-

PERSONAL: Surname rhymes with "eyes"; born January 12, 1945, in Cincinnati, OH; son of Scott (a regional planner) and Charlotte Esther (a writer; maiden name, Shachmann) Keyes; married Muriel Gordon (a college administrator), February 13, 1965; children: David Gordon, Scott Michael. *Education:* Antioch College, B.A., 1967; London School of Economics and Political Science, graduate study, 1967-68.

ADDRESSES: Home—690 Omar Circle, Yellow Springs, OH 45387. *Agent*—Colleen Mohyde, Doe Coover Agency, 58 Sagamore Ave., Medford, MA 02155. *E-mail*—ralph@ralphkeyes.com.

CAREER: Newsday, Long Island, NY, assistant to publisher and feature writer, 1968-70; Prescott College, visiting assistant professor, 1971 and 1974; Temple University, Philadelphia, PA, lecturer, 1979; Widener University, Chester, PA, lecturer, 1983. Center for Studies of the Person, La Jolla, CA, fellow, 1970-79. Has also taught at Antioch College. Frequent speaker and leader of workshops and seminars on behavioral topics.

MEMBER: Authors Guild, Authors League of America, Antioch Writers' Workshop (member, board of directors).

AWARDS, HONORS: Woodrow Wilson Foundation fellow; San Diego Press Club Headliner of the Year for literature, 1976; fiction citation, *Athenaeum* (Philadelphia, PA).

WRITINGS:

We, the Lonely People: Searching for Community, Harper (New York, NY), 1973.
Is There Life after High School?, Little, Brown (Boston, MA), 1976.
The Height of Your Life, Little, Brown (Boston, MA), 1980.
Chancing It: Why We Take Risks, Little, Brown (Boston, MA), 1985.
Timelock: How Life Got So Hectic and What You Can Do about It, HarperCollins (New York, NY), 1991.
"Nice Guys Finish Seventh": False Phrases, Spurious Sayings, and Familiar Misquotations, HarperCollins (New York, NY), 1992.
(Editor) *Sons on Fathers: A Book of Men's Writing* (anthology), HarperCollins (New York, NY), 1992.
The Courage to Write: How Writers Transcend Fear, Holt (New York, NY), 1995.
(Editor) *The Wit and Wisdom of Harry Truman: A Treasury of Quotations, Anecdotes, and Observations,* Gramercy (New Brunswick, NJ), 1999.
(Editor) *The Wit and Wisdom of Oscar Wilde: A Treasury of Quotations, Anecdotes, and Observations,* Gramercy (New Brunswick, NJ), 1999.

Whoever Makes the Most Mistakes Wins: The Paradox of Innovation, Simon & Schuster (New York, NY), 2002.
The Post-Truth Era, St. Martin's Press (New York, NY), 2004.

Contributor of articles to magazines, including *Newsweek, Nation, Playboy, Mademoiselle, Human Behavior, Popular Psychology, Car and Driver, Change, West, Parade, Esquire, New York, Reader's Digest, Publishers Weekly, Cosmopolitan, Antioch Review, Family Weekly, Gentlemen's Quarterly,* and *Village Voice.* Also contributor to newspapers, including *New York Times, Los Angeles Times,* and *Philadelphia Inquirer.*

ADAPTATIONS: Is There Life after High School? was adapted for the stage as a musical comedy and produced on Broadway, 1982.

SIDELIGHTS: In his books Ralph Keyes explores obstacles ranging from learning how to deal with loneliness in an increasingly dehumanized and mobile society to the obvious—and not so obvious—difficulties associated with being unusually tall or short. Relying on statistical information, results from questionnaires, and comments obtained during personal interviews, Keyes blends a touch of humor and occasional sadness with his factual findings to come up with highly readable and entertaining "studies" of the insecurities troubling countless American adults. But why, he is often asked, does he choose to dwell almost exclusively on the negative aspects of human existence? The answer, notes Keyes, is simple: "Failure is more universal than success and I'm looking for universal subjects. I'm much more interested in exploring areas where I feel room for growth."

One of Keyes's most popular endeavors in this field focuses on what he believes to be the ultimate American experience: high school. *Is There Life after High School?* features Keyes's customary blend of facts and humor, and a certain nostalgia as well, as he recounts the trials and tribulations of adolescence as seen through the eyes of various celebrities and non-celebrities. According to some reviewers, this method is especially appealing when it is applied to a subject such as high school, for it always comes as a relief to readers to know that Henry Kissinger was the fat kid nobody would eat lunch with and that the bully who used to push Mike Nichols's head under water and stand on it is now a used-car salesman.

Taking into account these stories and other types of information, Keyes concludes that being included in or rejected from the popular group in high school is integral to shaping a person's future. He distinguishes between high school "innies" and "outies," with the "in" group consisting of male jocks and their female equivalents—cheerleaders—and the "out" group consisting of everyone who is *not* a jock or a cheerleader. In short, he offers some comfort to the "outies" of the world: he claims that they are better off in the long run. Writing about the book in the *Chicago Tribune Book World,* Susan Brownmiller pointed out, "The winners of the high school celebrity sweepstakes are not necessarily the ones who sail from success to success in the afterlife. . . . The standards of conformity by which they judge themselves and the rest of us do not prepare them completely for the varied games of individual achievement that adult persons play."

Lois Gould, commenting in the *New York Times Book Review,* called *Is There Life after High School?* a "painstaking—and pain-inducing—autopsy on high school." "High school, like youth itself," Gould added, "is best appreciated from a safe distance—say, twenty years. Even then, it hurts when you laugh. And if you stop laughing, it hurts worse. Ralph Keyes knows all this only too well. He is, like most of us, a lifelong sufferer from high school dis-ease. . . . Painful as it is to revive these horrors by publishing them, it is, for some, the only thing that helps."

For Francis H. Curtis, writing in *Best Sellers, Is There Life after High School?* falls somewhat short of expectations, for "while [it] does make a valid point or two, Keyes has tried to capitalize on research to give it authenticity and on sex and foul language to make it a seller. This turns an interesting topic and a valuable contribution to the literature into a treatise that fails to be much of either." In the *Christian Science Monitor,* R. J. Cattani criticized Keyes for being "a high school fan, a reunion buff" who "writes more with nostalgia than irony," but the reviewer concluded that *Is There Life after High School?* "roars with adolescent enthusiasm and apprehension. . . . [The author] should find many readers among those who now and then take out their senior yearbooks." Writing in the *Washington Post Book World,* L. J. Davis observed, "Reading this thoroughly engaging little study is like finding our adoption papers; we always knew it was true. High school in America is a universal

but singularly worthless social experience that spectacularly rewards the meaningless skills of a few, traumatizes the majority, and marks us for life. . . . Keyes doesn't tell us what to do about it, but it is nice to know that we aren't alone."

Keyes dealts with the social ramifications of height in his 1980 book, *The Height of Your Life,* which, as John Leonard explained in the *New York Times,* "has to do with the war between the talls and the smalls; how our own height relative to someone else's affects our perceptions of ourselves, our self-esteem; what it feels like to be abnormal on either end of the scale . . . how always having to look up at other people is, literally, a pain in the neck." In addition to trivia such as heights of well-known people—chef Julia Child is six feet two inches, for example—and general facts—we all shrink an inch or two after age thirty—Keyes ruminates on how height breeds stereotype and even discrimination. Leonard found *The Height of Your Life* to be "an odd, breezy book, quick to record a joke, occasionally rueful, that gathers a kind of sadness as it moves along. . . . I am made to realize how crucial size is in social dynamics, and how cruel those dynamics are."

Keyes's next book, *Chancing It: Why We Take Risks,* was prompted, Lee Powell reported in *People,* by "a feeling of restlessness—one he believed others of his generation were sharing." Keyes explains: "People were talking the way I felt . . . wanting to take more risks." The questions, Powell stated, were why "and what constituted a risk in the first place?" More than five hundred interviews later, with an assortment of subjects as diverse as nuns and go-go dancers, policemen and drug dealers, Keyes wrote *Chancing It,* in which he sets forth his finding that there are two kinds, or levels, of risk: one that poses physical excitement and danger and another that involves personal chance-taking, such as revealing private emotions or making long-term commitments. The two levels of risk are usually mixed within any individual, though most people tend to prefer one kind to the other. Humiliation, Keyes elaborated to Powell, is "the universal risk," the one we are willing to avoid by taking other serious—even potentially fatal—risks. For example, Keyes told Powell, "high-wire walker Philippe Petit, who denies taking risks, told me he once worked on a cable that was dangerously loose just to avoid the embarrassment of walking away." Keyes suggests that we analyze our own risk-taking styles with the goals of finding productive outlets for our preferred risk-taking method—such as finding a job driving an ambulance or washing windows on a high-rise building for physical risk-takers—and taking some carefully chosen risks from the level we are less comfortable with to provide a "balanced diet of risks," Zick Rubin quoted Keyes as saying in the *New York Times Book Review.*

John Urquhart, writing for the *Philadelphia Inquirer,* labeled *Chancing It* "an entertaining, insightful tour through the psychology of risk-taking, with all its paradoxes and contradictions." Urquhart added that the book "helps readers recognize the contradictions in their own risk-taking behavior, and it makes the case that accepting risk is an essential part of a full and healthy life." While Rubin called Keyes "an entertaining writer with a light touch," he took exception to Keyes's analysis of the psychology of risk taking, which the critic considered "too loose and facile to be truly enlightening." Rubin believed that the author "overemphasizes the role of personality and underemphasizes the role of situational factors in determining the risks we take." Despite Urquhart's objection that the book lacks "practical pieces of information about risks in today's life," such as health risks associated with smoking and drunken driving, the reviewer concluded that "what you get from *Chancing It . . .* is a richly exampled, well-written account of the diversity of human judgment and behavior in the face of choices involving the fear of possible loss."

In 1992 Keyes saw the publication of two books, *"Nice Guys Finish Seventh": False Phrases, Spurious Sayings, and Familiar Misquotations* and *Sons on Fathers: A Book of Men's Writing,* the latter an anthology which he edited. *Sons on Fathers* includes almost eighty essays and poems Keyes collected for about twenty years. The selections are by men who have written strongly emotional pieces about their fathers and include such luminaries as Ernest Hemingway's son Patrick and writer Robert Bly, as well as other authors, poets, novelists, and journalists. Mary Carroll, writing for *Booklist,* noted that "*Sons on Fathers* is a celebration, a meditation, a plaint, and a eulogy"; the work was deemed an "important collection" by a reviewer for *Library Journal.*

"Nice Guys Finish Seventh" is a volume of research dedicated to clarifying the origin and wording of such common expressions as "Winning isn't everything, it's the only thing," "There ain't no such thing as a free lunch," "Play it again, Sam," and hundreds of others. The book's title has its roots in the saying "Nice guys finish last," which has been attributed to Brooklyn Dodger manager Leo Durocher speaking of rival team the New York Giants. Keyes explained that Durocher actually said, as he waved to the Giants' dugout, "The nice guys are all over there. In seventh place." In addition, Keyes pointed out, seventh place wasn't even last. A reviewer for the *Wilson Library Bulletin* stated that the work is "basic to reference collections," and Mary Carroll in *Booklist* noted Keyes's "interesting, often surprising facts about who said what when . . . deserves a place in most quotation collections."

Keyes explores how authors confront their fears of writing in his book *The Courage to Write: How Writers Transcend Fear.* Explaining that writers undergo something similar to the stage fright experienced by actors, Keyes "confronts anxieties like finding a worthy project, exposing self on paper, writing about loved ones and personal taboos, submitting work and facing editors," according to Ed Peaco in the *Antioch Review.* One suggestion Keyes makes is for writers to harness their fears to help them through their anxiety. As a critic for *Publishers Weekly* quoted Keyes, "many writing problems 'are really courage problems.'"

In *Whoever Makes the Most Mistakes Wins: The Paradox of Innovation,* Keyes and coauthor Richard Farson argue that taking risks and failing are absolutely necessary to success. The question they ask, Paul B. Brown explained in *CioInsight,* is "How can you make companies, and the people who work inside them, more adventurous?" They find that people who experience failure are often more open to risk-taking and innovation, while successful people are prone to be cautious and do what they have always done. To spark more innovation in employees, Keyes and Farson propose, companies should be more tolerant of employees who take a risk and fail. As Jane Applegate put it in the *Long Island Business News,* "The book aims to destigmatize failure and question our obsession with success."

Keyes once told *CA:* "For most of my adult life I have been a freelance writer. Like so many who do it for a living, I don't enjoy writing as such. (Peter De Vries once said, 'I love being a writer. What I can't stand is the paperwork.') Yet I do like much that surrounds the writing process: developing story ideas, interviewing subjects, doing research. Creating a whole from these parts can be quite satisfying. There are few types of work with more tangible evidence of how you've spent your time than writing. Nor is there a better shot at immortality.

"Because so much of my writing gets onto 'touchy' ground, I nearly always try to soften it with humor. Just as the smoothest Scotch can pack the hardest punch, heavy messages are best conveyed with light prose. Although I don't see my work as a tool for righting social wrongs, I do hope it gives aid and comfort to readers by suggesting that they're not alone in having reactions to life which may feel embarrassing. Confronting 'negative' thoughts and feelings directly can have positive outcomes. (Unburdening myself with *Is There Life after High School?* made it possible for me to attend my twentieth class reunion, and enjoy it immensely)."

"The longer I write, the simpler I'd like my writing to be; a well-cleaned piece of glass through which the reader can see clearly to the content inside. The ideal would be prose so transparent that readers wouldn't even be aware of my fingers at the keyboard. . . . The hardest work of writing, I find, is concealing how much effort it takes, and beating down the urge to show off."

BIOGRAPHICAL AND CRITICAL SOURCES:

PERIODICALS

Antioch Review, winter, 1996, Ed Peaco, review of *The Courage to Write: How Writers Transcend Fear,* p. 111.

Best Sellers, September, 1976, Francis H. Curtis, review of *Is There Life after High School?*

Booklist, January 1, 1985, p. 604; May 15, 1992, p. 1646; October 1, 1992.

Chicago Tribune Book World, June 13, 1976, Susan Brownmiller, review of *Is There Life after High School?*

Christian Science Monitor, July 21, 1976, R. J. Cattani, review of *Is There Life after High School?*

CioInsight, June 1, 2002, Paul B. Brown, review of *Whoever Makes the Most Mistakes Wins: The Paradox of Innovation.*

ETC, winter, 1993, William E. Coleman, Jr., review of *Nice Guys Finish Seventh : False Phrases, Spurious Sayings, and Familiar Misquotations,* p. 512.

Lambda Book Report, December, 1996, D. Killian, review of *The Wit and Wisdom of Oscar Wilde: A Treasury of Quotations, Anecdotes, and Observations,* p. 25.

Library Journal, May 15, 1976; June 15, 1992, review of *Sons on Fathers: A Book of Men's Writing;* April 15, 1995, Charles C. Nash, review of *The Courage to Write,* p. 87.

Long Island Business News, June 14, 2002, Jane Applegate, review of *Whoever Makes the Most Mistakes Wins,* p. 23A.

Los Angeles Times, May 8, 1980.

Men's Health, May, 1994, Mark Kram, review of *The Height of Your Life,* p. 24.

Newsweek, May 19, 1980.

New York Daily News, September 8, 1985.

New York Times, April 14, 1980, John Leonard, review of *The Height of Your Life,* p. C17.

New York Times Book Review, June 13, 1976, Lois Gould, review of *Is There Life after High School?,* p. 8; February 3, 1985, Zick Rubin, review of *Chancing It: Why We Take Risks,* p. 7.

People, May 13, 1985, Lee Powell, review of *Chancing It.*

Philadelphia Inquirer, February 17, 1985, John Urquhart, review of *Chancing It.*

Publishers Weekly, March 27, 1995, review of *The Courage to Write,* p. 68; April 8, 2002, review of *Whoever Makes the Most Mistakes Wins,* p. 223.

Washington Post Book World, May 30, 1976, L. J. Davis, review of *Is There Life after High School?*

Wilson Library Bulletin, January, 1993, review of *"Nice Guys Finish Seventh."*

Wisconsin State Journal (Madison, WI), June 16, 2002, William Wineke, review of *Whoever Makes the Most Mistakes Wins,* p. F3.

ONLINE

Ralph Keyes Web site, http://www.ralphkeyes.com/ (November 13, 2003).

*   *   *

KING, Stephen (Edwin) 1947-
(Richard Bachman, Eleanor Druse, Steve King, John Swithen)

PERSONAL: Born September 21, 1947, in Portland, ME; son of Donald (a merchant sailor) and Nellie

Stephen King

Ruth (Pillsbury) King; married Tabitha Jane Spruce (a novelist), January 2, 1971; children: Naomi Rachel, Joseph Hill, Owen Phillip. *Education:* University of Maine at Orono, B.Sc., 1970. *Politics:* Democrat. *Hobbies and other interests:* Reading (mostly fiction), jigsaw puzzles, playing the guitar ("I'm terrible and so try to bore no one but myself"), movies, bowling.

ADDRESSES: Agent—Arthur Greene, 101 Park Ave., New York, NY 10178.

CAREER: Writer. Has worked as a janitor, a laborer in an industrial laundry, and in a knitting mill. Hampden Academy (high school), Hampden, ME, English teacher, 1971-73; University of Maine, Orono, writer-in-residence, 1978-79. Owner, Philtrum Press (publishing house), and WZON-AM (rock 'n' roll radio station), Bangor, ME. Has made cameo appearances in films, including *Knightriders,* 1981, *Creepshow,* 1982, *Maximum Overdrive,* 1986, *Pet Sematary,* 1989, and *The Stand,* 1994; has also appeared in American Express credit card television commercial. Served as judge for 1977 World Fantasy Awards, 1978. Participated in radio honor panel with George A. Romero,

Peter Straub, and Ira Levin, moderated by Dick Cavett, WNET, 1980.

MEMBER: Authors Guild, Authors League of America, Screen Artists Guild, Screen Writers of America, Writers Guild.

AWARDS, HONORS: Carrie named to *School Library Journal*'s Book List, 1975; World Fantasy Award nominations, 1976, for *Salem's Lot,* 1979, for *The Stand* and *Night Shift,* 1980, for *The Dead Zone,* 1981, for "The Mist," and 1983, for "The Breathing Method: A Winter's Tale," in *Different Seasons;* Hugo Award nomination, World Science Fiction Society, and Nebula Award nomination, Science Fiction Writers of America, both 1978, both for *The Shining;* Balrog Awards, second place in best novel category, for *The Stand,* and second place in best collection category for *Night Shift,* both 1979; named to the American Library Association's list of best books for young adults, 1979, for *The Long Walk,* and 1981, for *Firestarter;* World Fantasy Award, 1980, for contributions to the field, and 1982, for story "Do the Dead Sing?"; Career Alumni Award, University of Maine at Orono, 1981; Nebula Award nomination, Science Fiction Writers of America, 1981, for story "The Way Station"; special British Fantasy Award for outstanding contribution to the genre, British Fantasy Society, 1982, for *Cujo;* Hugo Award, World Science Fiction Convention, 1982, for *Stephen King's Danse Macabre;* named Best Fiction Writer of the Year, *Us Magazine,* 1982; Locus Award for best collection, Locus Publications, 1986, for *Stephen King's Skeleton Crew;* Bram Stoker Award for Best Novel, Horror Writers Association, 1988, for *Misery;* Bram Stoker Award for Best Collection, 1991, for *Four Past Midnight;* World Fantasy award for short story, 1995, for *The Man in the Black Suit;* Bram Stoker Award for Best Novelette, Horror Writers Association, 1996, for *Lunch at the Gotham Cafe;* O. Henry Award, 1996, for "The Man in the Black Suit"; Bram Stoker Award for Best Novel, 1997, for *The Green Mile;* Bram Stoker Award for Best Novel, 1999, for *Bag of Bones;* Bram Stoker Award nominee in novel category (with Peter Straub), 2001, for *Black House;* Medal for Distinguished Contribution to American Letters, National Book Award, 2003; *The Stand* was voted one of the nation's 100 best-loved novels by the British public as part of the BBC's The Big Read, 2003.

WRITINGS:

NOVELS

Carrie: A Novel of a Girl with a Frightening Power (also see below), Doubleday (New York, NY), 1974, movie edition published as *Carrie,* New American Library/Times Mirror (New York, NY), 1975, published in a limited edition with introduction by Tabitha King, Plume (New York, NY), 1991.

Salem's Lot (also see below), Doubleday (New York, NY), 1975, television edition, New American Library (New York, NY), 1979, published in a limited edition with introduction by Clive Barker, Plume (New York, NY), 1991.

The Shining (also see below), Doubleday (New York, NY), 1977, movie edition, New American Library (New York, NY), 1980, published in a limited edition with introduction by Ken Follett, Plume (New York, NY), 1991.

The Stand (also see below), Doubleday (New York, NY), 1978, enlarged and expanded edition published as *The Stand: The Complete and Uncut Edition,* Doubleday (New York, NY), 1990.

The Dead Zone (also see below), Viking (New York, NY), 1979, movie edition published as *The Dead Zone: Movie Tie-In,* New American Library (New York, NY), 1980.

Firestarter (also see below), Viking (New York, NY), 1980, with afterword by King, 1981, published in a limited, aluminum-coated, asbestos-cloth edition, Phantasia Press (Huntington Woods, MI), 1980.

Cujo (also see below), Viking (New York, NY), 1981, published in limited edition, Mysterious Press (New York, NY), 1981.

Pet Sematary (also see below), Doubleday (New York, NY), 1983.

Christine (also see below), Viking (New York, NY), 1983, published in a limited edition, illustrated by Stephen Gervais, Donald M. Grant (Hampton Falls, NH), 1983.

(With Peter Straub) *The Talisman,* Viking Press/ Putnam (New York, NY), 1984, published in a limited two-volume edition, Donald M. Grant (Hampton Falls, NH), 1984.

The Eyes of the Dragon (young adult), limited edition, illustrated by Kenneth R. Linkhauser, Philtrum Press, 1984, new edition, illustrated by David Palladini, Viking (New York, NY), 1987.

It (also see below), limited German edition published as *Es,* Heyne (Munich), 1986, Viking (New York, NY), 1986.

Misery (also see below), Viking (New York, NY), 1987.

The Tommyknockers (also see below), Putnam (New York, NY), 1987.

The Dark Half (also see below), Viking (New York, NY), 1989.

Needful Things (also see below), Viking (New York, NY), 1991.

Gerald's Game, Viking (New York, NY), 1992.

Dolores Claiborne (also see below), Viking (New York, NY), 1993.

Insomnia, Viking (New York, NY), 1994.

Rose Madder, Viking (New York, NY), 1995.

The Green Mile (serialized novel), Signet (New York, NY), Chapter 1, "The Two Dead Girls" (also see below), Chapter 2, "The Mouse on the Mile," Chapter 3, "Coffey's Hands," Chapter 4, "The Bad Death of Eduard Delacroix," Chapter 5, "Night Journey," Chapter 6, "Coffey on the Mile," March-August, 1996, published as *The Green Mile: A Novel in Six Parts,* Plume (New York, NY), 1997.

Desperation, Viking (New York, NY), 1996.

(And author of foreword) *The Two Dead Girls,* Signet (New York, NY), 1996.

Bag of Bones, Viking (New York, NY), 1998.

Hearts in Atlantis, G. K. Hall (Thorndike, ME), 1999.

The Girl Who Loved Tom Gordon, Scribner (New York, NY), 1999.

Dreamcatcher, Simon & Schuster (New York, NY), 2001.

(With Peter Straub) *Black House* (sequel to *The Talisman*), Random House (New York, NY), 2001.

(Editor) Ridley Pearson, *The Diary of Ellen Rimbauer: My Life As Rose Red,* Hyperion (New York, NY), 2001.

From a Buick 8, Scribner (New York, NY), 2002.

(Under name Eleanor Druse) *The Journals of Eleanor Druse: My Investigation of the Kingdom Hospital Incident,* Hyperion (New York, NY), 2004.

Also author of early unpublished novels "Sword in the Darkness" (also referred to as "Babylon Here"), "The Cannibals," and "Blaze," a reworking of John Steinbeck's *Of Mice and Men.*

"THE DARK TOWER" SERIES

The Dark Tower: The Gunslinger (also see below), Amereon (New York, NY), 1976, published as

The Gunslinger, New American Library (New York, NY), 1988, published in limited edition, illustrated by Michael Whelan, Donald M. Grant (Hampton Falls, NH), 1982, 2nd limited edition, 1984, revised and expanded edition, Viking (New York, NY), 2003.

The Dark Tower II: The Drawing of the Three (also see below), illustrated by Phil Hale, New American Library (New York, NY), 1989.

The Dark Tower III: The Waste Lands (also see below), illustrated by Ned Dameron, Donald M. Grant (Hampton Falls, NH), 1991.

The Dark Tower Trilogy: The Gunslinger; The Drawing of the Three; The Waste Lands (box set), New American Library (New York, NY), 1993.

The Dark Tower IV: Wizard and Glass, Plume (New York, NY), 1997.

The Dark Tower V: Wolves of the Calla, Plume (New York, NY), 2003.

The Dark Tower VI: The Songs of Susannah, Donald M. Grant (Hampton Falls, NH), 2004.

The Dark Tower VII, Scribner (New York, NY), 2004.

NOVELS; UNDER PSEUDONYM RICHARD BACHMAN

Rage (also see below), New American Library/Signet (New York, NY), 1977.

The Long Walk (also see below), New American Library/Signet (New York, NY), 1979.

Roadwork: A Novel of the First Energy Crisis (also see below) New American Library/Signet (New York, NY), 1981.

The Running Man (also see below), New American Library/Signet (New York, NY), 1982.

Thinner, New American Library (New York, NY), 1984.

The Regulators, Dutton (New York, NY), 1996.

SHORT FICTION

(Under name Steve King) *The Star Invaders* (privately printed stories), Triad/Gaslight Books (Durham, ME), 1964.

Night Shift (story collection; also see below), introduction by John D. MacDonald, Doubleday (New York, NY), 1978, published as *Night Shift: Excursions into Horror,* New American Library/Signet (New York, NY), 1979.

Different Seasons (novellas; contains *Rita Hayworth and the Shawshank Redemption: Hope Springs Eternal* [also see below]; *Apt Pupil: Summer of Corruption*; *The Body: Fall from Innocence*; and *The Breathing Method: A Winter's Tale*), Viking (New York, NY), 1982.

Cycle of the Werewolf (novella; also see below), illustrated by Berni Wrightson, limited portfolio edition published with "Berni Wrightson: An Appreciation," Land of Enchantment (Westland, MI), 1983, enlarged edition including King's screenplay adaptation published as *Stephen King's Silver Bullet,* New American Library/Signet (New York, NY), 1985.

Stephen King's Skeleton Crew (story collection), illustrated by J. K. Potter, Viking (New York, NY), 1985, limited edition, Scream Press, 1985.

My Pretty Pony, illustrated by Barbara Kruger, Knopf (New York, NY), 1989, limited edition, Library Fellows of New York's Whitney Museum of American Art, 1989.

Four Past Midnight (contains "The Langoliers," "Secret Window, Secret Garden," "The Library Policeman," and "The Sun Dog"; also see below), Viking (New York, NY), 1990.

Nightmares and Dreamscapes, Viking (New York, NY), 1993.

Lunch at the Gotham Cafe, published in *Dark Love: Twenty-two All Original Tales of Lust and Obsession,* edited by Nancy Collins, Edward E. Kramer, and Martin Harry Greenberg, ROC (New York, NY), 1995.

Everything's Eventual: 14 Dark Tales, Scribner (New York, NY), 2002.

Also author of short stories "Slade" (a western), "The Man in the Black Suit," 1996, and, under pseudonym John Swithen, "The Fifth Quarter." Contributor of short story "Squad D" to Harlan Ellison's *The Last Dangerous Visions;* contributor of short story "Autopsy Room Four" to *Robert Bloch's Psychos,* edited by Robert Bloch. Also contributor to anthologies and collections, including *The Year's Finest Fantasy,* edited by Terry Carr, Putnam (New York, NY), 1978; *Shadows,* edited by Charles L. Grant, Doubleday (New York, NY), Volume 1, 1978, Volume 4, 1981; *New Terrors,* edited by Ramsey Campbell, Pocket Books (New York, NY), 1982; *World Fantasy Convention 1983,* edited by Robert Weinberg, Weird Tales, 1983; *The Writer's Handbook,* edited by Sylvia K. Burack, Writer (Boston, MA), 1984; *The Dark Descent,* edited by David G. Hartwell, Doherty Associates, 1987; *Prime Evil: New Stories by the Masters of Modern Horror,* by Douglas E. Winter, New American Library (New York, NY), 1988; and *Dark Visions,* Gollancz (London, England), 1989.

SCREENPLAYS

Stephen King's Creep Show: A George A. Romero Film (based on King's stories "Father's Day," "The Lonesome Death of Jordy Verrill" [previously published as "Weeds"], "The Crate," and "They're Creeping Up on You"; released by Warner Bros. as *Creepshow,* 1982), illustrated by Berni Wrightson and Michele Wrightson, New American Library (New York, NY), 1982.
Cat's Eye (based on King's stories "Quitters, Inc.," "The Ledge," and "The General"), Metro Goldwyn-Mayer/United Artists, 1984.
Stephen King's Silver Bullet (based on and published with King's novella *Cycle of the Werewolf*; released by Paramount Pictures/Dino de Laurentiis's North Carolina Film Corp., 1985), illustrated by Berni Wrightson, New American Library/Signet (New York, NY), 1985.
(And director) *Maximum Overdrive* (based on King's stories "The Mangler," "Trucks," and "The Lawnmower Man"; released by Dino de Laurentiis's North Carolina Film Corp., 1986), New American Library (New York, NY), 1986.
Pet Sematary (based on King's novel of the same title), Laurel Production, 1989.
Stephen King's Sleepwalkers, Columbia, 1992.
(Author of introduction) Frank Darabont, *The Shawshank Redemption: The Shooting Script,* Newmarket Press (New York, NY), 1996.
Storm of the Century (also see below), Pocket Books (New York, NY), 1999.
(Author of introductions with William Goldman and Lawrence Kasdan) William Goldman and Lawrence Kasdan, *Dreamcatcher: The Shooting Script,* Newmarket Press (New York, NY), 2003.

TELEPLAYS

Stephen King's Golden Years, CBS-TV, 1991.
(And executive producer) *Stephen King's The Stand* (based on King's novel *The Stand*), ABC-TV, 1994.
(With Chris Carter) *Chinga,* (episode of *The X-Files,*) Fox-TV, 1998.

Storm of the Century, ABC-TV, 1999.
Rose Red (also see below), ABC-TV, 2001.
Stephen King's Kingdom Hospital, ABC-TV, 2004.
Desperation, USA, c. 2004.

Also author of *Battleground* (based on short story of same title; optioned by Martin Poll Productions for NBC-TV), and "Sorry, Right Number," for television series *Tales from the Dark Side,* 1987.

RECORDINGS

The Dark Tower: The Gunslinger, New American Library (New York, NY), 1988.
The Dark Tower II: The Drawing of the Three, New American Library (New York, NY), 1989.
The Dark Tower III: The Waste Lands, Penguin-HighBridge Audio (St. Paul, MN), 1991.
Needful Things, Penguin-HighBridge Audio (St. Paul, MN), 1991.

OMNIBUS EDITIONS

Stephen King (contains *The Shining, Salem's Lot, Night Shift,* and *Carrie*), W. S. Heinemann/Octopus Books (London, England), 1981.
(And author of introduction) *The Bachman Books: Four Early Novels* (contains *Rage, The Long Walk, Roadwork,* and *The Running Man*), New American Library (New York, NY), 1985.
Another Quarter Mile: Poetry, Dorrance (Philadelphia, PA), 1979.
Stephen King's Danse Macabre (nonfiction), Everest House (New York, NY), 1981.
The Plant (privately published episodes of a comic horror novel in progress), Philtrum Press (Bangor, ME), Part 1, 1982, Part 2, 1983, Part 3, 1985.
Black Magic and Music: A Novelist's Perspective on Bangor (pamphlet), Bangor Historical Society (Bangor, ME), 1983.
Dolan's Cadillac, Lord John Press (Northridge, CA), 1989.
Stephen King (contains *Desperation* and *The Regulators*) Signet (New York, NY), 1997.
Stephen King's Latest (contains *Dolores Claiborne, Insomnia* and *Rose Madder*) Signet (New York, NY), 1997.

OTHER

Nightmares in the Sky: Gargoyles and Grotesques (nonfiction), photographs by F. Stop FitzGerald, Viking (New York, NY), 1988.

On Writing: A Memoir of the Craft, Scribner (New York, NY), 2000.

Author of e-book *The Plant,* self-published first two chapters on his Web site (www.stephenking.com), August, 2000; also published a short story, "Riding the Bullet," as an e-book, March, 2000. Author of weekly column "King's Garbage Truck" for *Maine Campus,* 1969-70, and of monthly book review column for *Adelina,* 1980. Contributor of short fiction and poetry to numerous magazines, including *Art, Castle Rock: The Stephen King Newsletter, Cavalier, Comics Review, Cosmopolitan, Ellery Queen's Mystery Magazine, Fantasy and Science Fiction, Gallery, Great Stories from Twilight Zone Magazine, Heavy Metal, Ladies' Home Journal, Magazine of Fantasy and Science Fiction, Maine, Maine Review, Marshroots,* Marvel comics, *Moth, Omni, Onan, Playboy, Redbook, Reflections, Rolling Stone, Science-Fiction Digest, Startling Mystery Stories, Terrors, Twilight Zone Magazine, Ubris, Whisper,* and *Yankee.* Contributor of book reviews to the *New York Times Book Review.*

Most of King's papers are housed in the special collection of the Folger Library at the University of Maine at Orono.

ADAPTATIONS: Many of King's novels have been adapted for the screen. *Carrie* was produced as a motion picture in 1976 by Paul Monash for United Artists, screenplay by Lawrence D. Cohen, directed by Brian De Palma, featuring Sissy Spacek and Piper Laurie, and was also produced as a Broadway musical in 1988 by Cohen and Michael Gore, developed in England by the Royal Shakespeare Company, featuring Betty Buckley; *Salem's Lot* was produced as a television miniseries in 1979 by Warner Brothers, teleplay by Paul Monash, featuring David Soul and James Mason, and was adapted for the cable channel TNT in 2004, with a teleplay by Peter Filardi and direction by Mikael Salomon; *The Shining* was filmed in 1980 by Warner Brothers/Hawks Films, screenplay by director Stanley Kubrick and Diane Johnson, starring Jack Nicholson and Shelley Duvall, and it was filmed for television in 1997 by Warner Brothers,

directed by Mick Garris, starring Rebecca De Mornay, Steven Weber, Courtland Mead, and Melvin Van Peebles; *Cujo* was filmed in 1983 by Warner Communications/Taft Entertainment, screenplay by Don Carlos Dunaway and Lauren Currier, featuring Dee Wallace and Danny Pintauro; *The Dead Zone* was filmed in 1983 by Paramount Pictures, screenplay by Jeffrey Boam, starring Christopher Walken; was adapted as a cable television series starring Anthony Michael Hall by USA Network, beginning 2002; *Christine* was filmed in 1983 by Columbia Pictures, screenplay by Bill Phillips; *Firestarter* was produced in 1984 by Frank Capra, Jr., for Universal Pictures in association with Dino de Laurentiis, screenplay by Stanley Mann, featuring David Keith and Drew Barrymore; *Stand by Me* (based on King's novella *The Body*) was filmed in 1986 by Columbia Pictures, screenplay by Raynold Gideon and Bruce A. Evans, directed by Rob Reiner; *The Running Man* was filmed in 1987 by Taft Entertainment/Barish Productions, screenplay by Steven E. de Souza, starring Arnold Schwarzenegger; *Misery* was produced in 1990 by Columbia, directed by Reiner, screenplay by William Goldman, starring James Caan and Kathy Bates; *Graveyard Shift* was filmed in 1990 by Paramount, directed by Ralph S. Singleton, adapted by John Esposito; *Stephen King's It* (based on King's novel *It*) was filmed as a television miniseries by ABC-TV in 1990; *The Dark Half* was filmed in 1993 by Orion, written and directed by George A. Romero, featuring Timothy Hutton and Amy Madigan; *Needful Things* was filmed in 1993 by Columbia/Castle Rock, adapted by W. D. Richter and Lawrence Cohen, directed by Fraser C. Heston, starring Max Von Sydow, Ed Harris, Bonnie Bedelia, and Amanda Plummer; *The Tommyknockers* was filmed as a television miniseries by ABC-TV in 1993; *The Shawshank Redemption,* based on King's novella *Rita Hayworth and Shawshank Redemption: Hope Springs Eternal,* was filmed in 1994 by Columbia, written and directed by Frank Darabont, featuring Tim Robbins and Morgan Freeman; *Dolores Claiborne* was filmed in 1995 by Columbia; *Thinner* was filmed by Paramount in 1996, directed by Dom Holland, starring Robert John Burke, Joe Mantegna, Lucinda Jenney, and Michael Constantine; *Night Flier* was filmed by New Amsterdam Entertainment/Stardust International/Medusa Film in 1997, directed by Mark Pavia, starring Miguel Ferrer, Julie Entwisle, Dan Monahan, and Michael H. Moss; *Apt Pupil* was filmed in 1998 by TriStar Pictures, directed by Bryan Singer, starring David Schwimmer, Ian McKellen, and Brad Renfro; *The Green Mile* was filmed in 1999 by Castle Rock, directed by Frank

Darabont, who also wrote the screenplay, starring Tom Hanks; *Hearts in Atlantis* was filmed in 2001 by Castle Rock, directed by Scott Hicks, screenplay written by William Goldman, starring Anthony Hopkins; *Dreamcatcher* was released in 2003 by Warner Brothers and Castle Rock Entertainment and was directed by Lawrence Kasdan, written by William Goldman, starring Morgan Freeman. Several of King's short stories have also been adapted for the screen, including *The Boogeyman,* filmed by Tantalus in 1982 and 1984 in association with the New York University School of Undergraduate Film, screenplay by producer-director Jeffrey C. Schiro; *The Woman in the Room,* filmed in 1983 by Darkwoods, screenplay by director Frank Darabont, broadcast on public television in Los Angeles, 1985 (released with *The Boogeyman* on videocassette as *Two Mini-Features from Stephen King's Nightshift Collection* by Granite Entertainment Group, 1985); *Children of the Corn,* produced in 1984 by Donald P. Borchers and Terrence Kirby for New World Pictures, screenplay by George Goldsmith; *The Word Processor* (based on King's "The Word Processor of the Gods"), produced by Romero and Richard Rubenstein for Laurel Productions, 1984, teleplay by Michael Dowell, broadcast November 19, 1985, on *Tales from the Darkside* series and released on videocassette by Laurel Entertainment, 1985; *Gramma,* filmed by CBS-TV in 1985, teleplay by Harlan Ellison, broadcast February 14, 1986, on *The Twilight Zone* series; *Creepshow 2* (based on "The Raft" and two unpublished stories by King, "Old Chief Wood'nhead" and "The Hitchhiker"), was filmed in 1987 by New World Pictures, screenplay by Romero; *Sometimes They Come Back,* filmed by CBS-TV in 1987; "The Cat from Hell" is included in a three-segment anthology film titled *Tales from the Darkside—The Movie,* produced by Laurel Productions, 1990; *The Lawnmower Man,* written by director Brett Leonard and Gimel Everett for New Line Cinema, 1992; *The Mangler,* filmed by New Line Cinema, 1995; and *The Langoliers,* filmed as a television miniseries by ABC-TV in 1995; the short fiction "Secret Window, Secret Garden" was adapted into the film *Secret Window,* distributed by Columbia Pictures, written and directed by David Koepp; 2004; the short story "All That You Love Will Be Carried Away" from the collection *Everything's Eventual* has been adapted and made into a short film by James Renner; film rights to the short story "1408" from the collection *Everything's Eventual* has been optioned by Dimension Films.

WORK IN PROGRESS: In collaboration with Stewart O'Nan, a nonfiction work chronicling the 2004 season of the Boston Red Sox.

SIDELIGHTS: "With Stephen King," mused Chelsea Quinn Yarbro in *Fear Itself: The Horror Fiction of Stephen King,*"you never have to ask 'Who's afraid of the big bad wolf?'—You are. And he knows it." Throughout a prolific array of novels, short stories, and screen work in which elements of horror, fantasy, science fiction, and humor meld, King deftly arouses fear from dormancy. The breadth and durability of his popularity alone evince his mastery as a compelling storyteller. "Nothing is as unstoppable as one of King's furies, except perhaps King's word processor," remarked Gil Schwartz in *People,* which selected King as one of twenty individuals who had defined the decade of the Eighties. And although the critical reception of his work has not necessarily matched its sweeping success with readers, colleagues and several critics alike discern within it a substantial and enduring literary legitimacy. In *American Film,* for instance, Darrell Ewing and Dennis Meyers called him "the chronicler of contemporary America's dreams, desires, and fears."

While striking a deep and responsive chord within its readers, the genre of horror is frequently trivialized by critics who tend to regard it, when at all, less seriously than mainstream fiction. In an interview with Charles Platt in *Dream Makers: The Uncommon Men and Women Who Write Science Fiction,* King suspected that "most of the critics who review popular fiction have no understanding of it as a whole." Regarding the "propensity of a small but influential element of the literary establishment to ghettoize horror and fantasy and instantly relegate them beyond the pale of so-called serious literature," King told Eric Norden in a *Playboy* interview, "I'm sure those critics' nineteenth-century precursors would have contemptuously dismissed [Edgar Allan] Poe as the great American hack." But as King contends in "The Horror Writer and the Ten Bears," his foreword to *Kingdom of Fear:* "Horror isn't a hack market now, and never was. The genre is one of the most delicate known to man, and it must be handled with great care and more than a little love." Furthermore, in a panel discussion at the 1984 World Fantasy Convention in Ottawa, reprinted in *Bare Bones: Conversations on Terror with Stephen King,* he predicted that horror writers "might actually have a serious place in American literature in a hundred years or so."

King's ability to comprehend "the attraction of fantastic horror to the denizen of the late twentieth century," according to Deborah L. Notkin in *Fear*

Itself, partially accounts for his unrivaled popularity in the genre. But what distinguishes him is the way in which he transforms the ordinary into the horrific. Pointing out in the *Atlantic Monthly* that horror frequently represents "the symbolic depiction of our common experience," Lloyd Rose observed that "King takes ordinary emotional situations—marital stress, infidelity, peer-group-acceptance worries—and translates them into violent tales of vampires and ghosts. He writes supernatural soap operas." But to Gary Williams Crawford in *Discovering Stephen King,* King is "a uniquely sensitive author" within the Gothic literary tradition, which he described as "essentially a literature of nightmare, a conflict between waking life and the darkness within the human mind." Perpetuating the legacy of Edgar Allan Poe, Nathaniel Hawthorne, Herman Melville, Henry James, and H. P. Lovecraft, "King is heir to the American Gothic tradition in that he has placed his horrors in contemporary settings and has depicted the struggle of an American culture to face the horrors within it," explained Crawford, and because "he has shown the nightmare of our idealistic civilization." Observing that children suspend their disbelief easily, King argued in his *Danse Macabre* that, ironically, they are actually "better able to deal with fantasy and terror *on its own terms* than their elders are." In an interview for *High Times,* for instance, he marveled at the resilience of a child's mind and the inexplicable, yet seemingly harmless, attraction of children to nightmare-inducing stories: "We start kids off on things like 'Hansel and Gretel,' which features child abandonment, kidnapping, attempted murder, forcible detention, cannibalism, and finally murder by cremation. And the kids love it." Adults are capable of distinguishing between fantasy and reality, but in the process of growing up, laments King in *Danse Macabre,* they develop "a good case of mental tunnel vision and a gradual ossification of the imaginative faculty"; thus, he perceives the task of the fantasy or horror writer as enabling one to become "for a little while, a child again." In *Time* King discussed the prolonged obsession with childhood that his generation has had. "We went on playing for a long time, almost feverishly," he recalled. "I write for that buried child in us, but I'm writing for the grown-up too. I want grown-ups to look at the child long enough to be able to give him up."

The empowerment of estranged young people is a theme that recurs throughout King's fiction. "If Stephen King's kids have one thing in common," declared young-adult novelist Robert Cormier in the *Washington Post Book World,* "it's the fact that they all are losers. In a way, all children are losers, of course—how can they be winners with that terrifying adult world stacked against them?" His first novel, *Carrie,* is about a persecuted teenaged girl. "The novel examines female power," stated *Dictionary of Literary Biography* contributor Carol Senf, "for Carrie gains her telekinetic abilities with her first menstruation." "It is," Senf concluded, "a compelling character study of a persecuted teenager who finally uses her powers to turn the table on her persecutors. The result is a violent explosion that destroys the mother who had taught her self-hatred and the high-school peers who had made her a scapegoat." An alienated teenaged boy is the main character in King's *Christine,* and *Rage* features Charlie Decker, a young man who tells the story of his descent into madness and murder. In *The Shining* and *Firestarter,* Danny Torrance and Charlie McGee are alienated not from their families—they have loving, if sometimes weak, parents—but through the powers they possess and by those who want to manipulate them: evil supernatural forces in *The Shining,* the U.S. Government in *Firestarter.* Children also figure prominently, although not always as victims, in *Salem's Lot, The Tommyknockers, Pet Sematary, The Eyes of the Dragon,* and *The Talisman.*

King's most explicit examination of alienation in childhood, however, comes in the novel *It.* The eponymous IT is a creature that feeds on children—on their bodies and on their emotions, especially fear. IT lives in the sewers of Derry, Maine, having arrived there ages ago from outer space, and emerges about every twenty-seven years in search of victims. "*It* begins, demonically enough, in 1957," explained *New York Review of Books* contributor Thomas R. Edwards, "when a six-year-old boy has his arm torn off by what appears to be a circus clown lurking down a storm drain. . . . King organizes the tale as two parallel stories, one tracing the activities of seven unprepossessing fifth-graders—'The Losers' Club'—who discovered and fought the horror in 1958, the other describing their return to Derry in 1985 when the cycle resumes." The surviving members of the Losers' Club return to Derry to confront IT and defeat IT once and for all. The only things that appears to hurt IT are faith, humor, and childlike courage. "Only brave and imaginative children, or adults who learn to remember and honor their childish selves," Edwards concluded, "can hope to foil It, as the Losers finally do in 1985."

"*It* involves the guilts and innocences of childhood and the difficulty for adults of recapturing them,"

Christopher Lehmann-Haupt stated in the *New York Times*. "*It* questions the difference between necessity and free will. *It* also concerns the evil that has haunted America from time to time in the forms of crime, racial and religious bigotry, economic hardship, labor strife and industrial pollution." The evil takes shape among Derry's adults and older children, especially the bullies who terrorize the members of the Losers' Club.

Not surprisingly, throughout most of King's adolescence, the written word afforded a powerful diversion. "Writing has always been it for me," King indicated in a panel discussion at the 1984 World Fantasy Convention in Ottawa, reprinted in *Bare Bones*. Science fiction and adventure stories comprised his first literary efforts. Having written his first story at the age of seven, King began submitting short fiction to magazines at twelve, and published his first story at eighteen. In high school, he authored a small, satiric newspaper titled "The Village Vomit"; and in college he penned a popular and eclectic series of columns called "King's Garbage Truck." He also started writing the novels he eventually published under the pseudonymous ruse of Richard Bachman—novels that focus more on elements of human alienation and brutality than supernatural horror. After graduation, King supplemented his teaching salary through various odd jobs and by submitting stories to men's magazines. Searching for a form of his own, and responding to a friend's challenge to break out of the machismo mold of his short fiction, King wrote what he described to Abe Peck in *Rolling Stone College Papers* as "a parable of women's consciousness." Retrieving the discarded manuscript from the trash, though, King's wife, Tabitha, who is a writer herself, suggested that he ought to expand it. And because King completed the first draft of *Carrie* at the time William Peter Blatty's *The Exorcist* and Thomas Tryon's *The Other* were being published, the novel was marketed as horror fiction, and the genre had found its juggernaut. Or, as Don Herron put it in *Fear Itself,* "Like a mountain, King is there."

"Stephen King has made a dent in the national consciousness in a way no other horror writer has, at least during his own lifetime," stated Alan Warren in *Discovering Stephen King*. "He is a genuine phenomenon." A newsletter—"Castle Rock"—has been published since 1985 to keep his ever-increasing number of fans well informed; and Book-of-the-Month Club has been reissuing all of his best-sellers as the

Stephen King Library collection. In his preface to *Fear Itself,* "On Becoming a Brand Name," King described the process as a fissional one in that a "writer produces a series of books which ricochet back and forth between hardcover and softcover at an ever increasing speed." Resorting to a pseudonym to get even more work into print accelerated the process for King; but according to Stephen P. Brown in *Kingdom of Fear,* although the ploy was not entirely "a vehicle for King to move his earliest work out of the trunk," it certainly triggered myriad speculations about, as well as hunts for, other possible pseudonyms he may also have used. In his essay "Why I Was Bachman" in *The Bachman Books: Four Early Novels by Stephen King,* King recalled that he simply considered it a good idea at the time, especially since he wanted to try to publish something without the attendant commotion that a Stephen King title would have unavoidably generated. Also, his publisher believed that he had already saturated the market. King's prodigious literary output and multimillion-dollar contracts, though, have generated critical challenges to the inherent worth of his fiction. Deducing that he has been somehow compromised by commercial success, some critics imply that he writes simply to fulfill contractual obligations. But as King told Norden, "Money really has nothing to do with it one way or the other. I love writing the things I write, and I wouldn't and 'couldn't' do anything else."

King writes daily, exempting only Christmas, the Fourth of July, and his birthday. He likes to work on two things simultaneously, beginning his day early with a two- or three-mile walk: "What I'm working on in the morning is what I'm *working* on," he said in a panel discussion at the 1980 World Fantasy Convention in Baltimore, reprinted in *Bare Bones*. He devotes his afternoon hours to rewriting. And according to his *Playboy* interview, while he is not particular about working conditions, he is about his output. Despite chronic headaches, occasional insomnia, and even a fear of writer's block, he produces six pages daily; "And that's like engraved in stone," he told Joyce Lynch Dewes Moore in *Mystery*.

Aware that "people want to be scared," as he related to Abe Peck in a *Rolling Stone College Papers* interview, and truly delighted to be able to accommodate them, King rejects the criticism that he preys on the fears of others. As he explained to Jack Matthews in a *Detroit Free Press* interview, some people simply avoid his books just as those who are afraid of speed and heights, especially in tandem, shun roller coasters. And that, he declared to Paul Janeczko in *English Journal,* is precisely what he believes he owes his readers—"a good ride on the roller coaster." Regarding what he finds to be an essential reassurance that underlies and impels the genre itself, King remarked in *Danse Macabre* that "beneath its fangs and fright wig" horror fiction is really quite conservative. Comparing horror fiction with the morality plays of the late middle ages, for instance, he believes that its primary function is "to reaffirm the virtues of the norm by showing us what awful things happen to people who venture into taboo lands." Also, there is the solace in knowing "when the lights go down in the theatre or when we open the book that the evildoers will almost certainly be punished, and measure will be returned for measure." But King admitted to Norden that despite all the discussion by writers generally about "horror's providing a socially and psychologically useful catharsis for people's fears and aggressions, the brutal fact of the matter is that we're still in the business of public executions."

"Death is a significant element in nearly all horror fiction," wrote Michael A. Morrison in *Fantasy Review,* "and it permeates King's novels and short stories." Noting in *Danse Macabre* that a universal fear with which each of us must personally struggle is "the fear of dying," King explained to Bob Spitz in a *Penthouse* magazine interview that "everybody goes out to horror movies, reads horror novels—and it's almost as though we're trying to preview the end." But he submitted that "if the horror story is our rehearsal for death, then its strict moralities make it also a reaffirmation of life and good will and simple imagination—just one more pipeline to the infinite." While he believes that horror is "one of the ways we walk our imagination," as he told Matthews, he does worry about the prospect of a mentally unstable reader patterning behavior after some fictional brutality. Remarking that "evil is basically stupid and unimaginative and doesn't need creative inspiration from me or anybody else," King told Norden, for instance, that "despite knowing all that rationally, I have to admit that it is unsettling to feel that I could be linked in any way, however tenuous, to somebody else's murder."

An example of King's ability to "pour new wine from old bottles" is his experimentation with narrative structure. In *It, Carrie,* and *The Stand,* declared Tony Magistrale in the study *Landscape of Fear: Stephen*

King's American Gothic, King explores story forms—"stream of consciousness, interior monologues, multiple narrators, and a juggling of time sequences—in order to draw the reader into a direct and thorough involvement with the characters and events of the tale." Both *The Dark Half* and *Misery,* according to George Stade in the *New York Times Book Review,* are "parable[s] in chiller form of the popular writer's relation to his audience." In *Gerald's Game's* Jessie Burlingame has lost her husband to heart failure. He "has died after handcuffing her to the bed at their summer home," Senf explained in the *Dictionary of Literary Biography,* "and Jessie must face her life, including the memory that her father had sexually abused her, and her fears alone." *Dolores Claiborne* is the story of a woman suspected of murdering her employer, a crusty old miser named Vera Donovan. Dolores maintains her innocence, but she freely confesses that she murdered her husband thirty years previously when she caught him molesting their daughter.

"There are a series of dovetailing, but unobtrusive, connections," stated *Locus* contributor Edward Bryant, "linking the two novels and both Jessie and Dolores." Like *It,* both *Gerald's Game* and *Dolores Claiborne* are set in the town of Derry, Maine. They are also both psychological portraits of older women who have been subjected to sexual abuse. *Dolores Claiborne* differs from *Gerald's Game,* however, because it uses fewer of the traditional trappings of horror fiction, and it is related entirely from the viewpoint of the title character. *Dolores Claiborne* "is, essentially, a dramatic monologue," stated Kit Reed in the *Washington Post Book World,* "in which the speaker addresses other people in the room, answers questions and completes a narrative in actual time." "All but the last page is one long quote from Dolores Claiborne," asserted a *Rapport* reviewer. "King has taken horror literature out of the closet and has injected new life into familiar genres," Senf concluded. "He is not afraid to mix those genres in fresh ways to produce novels that examine contemporary American culture."

Insomnia, King's 1994 novel, continues the example set by *Gerald's Game* and *Dolores Claiborne.* It is also set in Derry, and its protagonist is an elderly man named Ralph Roberts, a retired salesman, newly widowed and suffering severely from insomnia. Ralph begins to see people in a new way: their auras become visible to him. "Ralph finds himself a man in a classic situation, a mortal in conflict with the fates—literally," declared *Locus* reviewer Bryant. "How much self-determination does he really possess? And how much is he acted upon?" Ralph also finds himself in conflict with his neighbor Ed Deepeneau, a conservative Christian and antiabortion activist who beats his wife and has taken up a crusade against a visiting feminist speaker. "There are some truly haunting scenes in the book about wife abuse and fanaticism, as well as touching observations about growing old, but they're quickly consumed by more predictable sensationalism," remarked Chris Bohjalian in the *New York Times Book Review.* "In a world teeming with timeless, omnipotent entities," declared novelist Kinky Friedman in the *Washington Post Book World,* "King has provided Ralph Roberts, that ancient vulnerable, white-haired widower, with the ultimate weapon, the power of the human spirit."

King delighted his readers and astounded his critics by issuing three new major novels in 1996: *Desperation, The Regulators*—under the pseudonym Richard Bachman—and *The Green Mile,* the last a Depression-era prison novel serialized in six installments. A *Publishers Weekly* reviewer said that "if the publishing industry named a Person of the Year, this year's winner would be Stephen King." The critic noted that, with *Desperation,* "King again proves himself the premier literary barometer of our cultural clime." Released on the same day from two different publishers, *Desperation* and *The Regulators* have interlocking characters and plots; each works as a kind of distorted mirror image of the other. In *Desperation,* which many critics agree is the better book, a group of strangers drive into Desperation, Nevada, where they encounter a malign spirit (Tak) in the body of police officer Collie Entragian. The survivors of this apocalyptic novel are few, but include David Carver, an eleven-year-old boy who talks to God, and John Edward Marinville, an alcoholic novelist. Robert Polito, writing for the *New York Times,* noted that "King's peculiar knack as a novelist is to strip away much of the complexity and nearly all of the art from a terrifying vision of an unknowable universe ruled by a limited, perhaps evil God and insinuate that Gnosticism into the rituals and commodities of everyday America." Polito admired King's capacity to tap into the collective unconscious of America at the end of the millennium but regretted that "the recurrent silliness shrugs off the horror and the social anger." Mark Harris, writing for *Entertainment Weekly,* however, remarked that King "hasn't been this intent on scaring readers—or been this suc-

cessful at it—since *The Stand,*" noting that "King has always been pop fiction's most compassionate sadist." In *Desperation,* King grapples with the nature of God, but Polito claimed that the "bromide" that "God is Love" can't dispel the novel's dark and cruel vision of the universe. King recorded the audio version of *Desperation* himself.

While *The Regulators* received little critical praise, King's experiment in serialization with *The Green Mile* captured the imagination of both readers and critics. An *Entertainment Weekly* reviewer called it a novel "that's as hauntingly touching as it is just plain haunted," and a *New York Times* contributor claimed that in spite of "the striking circumstances of its serial publication," the novel "manages to sustain the notes of visceral wonder and indelible horror that keep eluding the Tak books." Set in the Deep South in 1932, *The Green Mile*—a prison expression for death row—begins with the death of twin girls and the conviction of John Coffey for their murder. Block superintendent Paul Edgecombe, who narrates the story years later from his nursing home in Georgia, slowly unfolds the story of the mysterious Coffey, a man with no past and with a gift for healing.

King's next major novel, *Bag of Bones,* appeared in 1998. This tale of a writer struggling with both grief for his dead wife and writer's block while living in a haunted cabin met with a great deal of acclaim from critics. Also acclaimed was the following year's *Hearts in Atlantis,* which Tom De Haven described in *Entertainment Weekly* as "a novel in five stories, with players sometimes migrating from one story to the next." De Haven went on to note that "there's more heartbreak than horror in these pages, and a doomy aura that's more generational than occult." He also reported that the "last two stories are drenched in sadness, mortality, regret, and finally absolution," concluding that *Hearts in Atlantis* "is wonderful fiction." Similarly, Ray Olson praised the volume in *Booklist* as "a rich, engaging, deeply moving generational epic." *The Girl Who Loved Tom Gordon* also saw print in 1999. This novel, short by King's standards, centers on a nine-year-old girl from a broken home who gets lost in a forest for two weeks. She has her radio with her, and survives her ordeal by listening to Boston Red Sox games and imagining conversations with her hero, Red Sox relief pitcher Tom Gordon.

While these books were making their way to readers, however, King suffered a serious health challenge. On

June 19, 1999, he was struck by a van while walking alongside a road near his home, sustaining injuries to his spine, hip, ribs, and right leg. One of his broken ribs punctured a lung, and he nearly died. He began a slow progress towards recovery, cheered by countless cards and letters from his fans. During his recovery, he began experimenting with publishing his fiction electronically. In August, 2000, King self-published the first two installments of his e-book *The Plant* on his Web site. Pricing the installments at one dollar each, King promised to publish additional chapters if at least 75 percent of those who download the first two installments paid for them. King also published a short story, "Riding the Bullet," in March, only distributed as an e-book publication in a number of formats. This tale was eventually reprinted in the 2002 collection *Everything's Eventual: 14 Dark Tales.*

King had also begun work on a writer's manual before his accident, and the result, 2000's *On Writing: A Memoir of the Craft,* sold more copies in its first printing than any previous book about writing. In addition to King's advice on crafting fiction, however, the book includes a great deal of autobiographical material. The author chronicles his childhood, his rise to fame, his struggles with addiction, and the horrific accident that almost ended his life. "King's writing about his own alcoholism and cocaine abuse," noted John Mark Eberhart in the Kansas City *Star,* "is among the best and most honest prose of his career." Similarly, Jack Harville reported in the Charlotte *Observer* that "the closing piece describes King's accident and rehabilitation. The description is harrowing, and the rehab involves both physical and emotional recovery. It is beautifully told in a narrative style that would have gained Strunk and White's approval." Some of the novels King has published since the beginning of the twenty-first century, including *Dreamcatcher* and *From a Buick 8,* have brought strong comparisons from critics with his earlier novels; in these specific cases, *It* and *Christine,* respectively. These books, however, were followed by an announcement King made in 2002 that he is planning to retire from publishing. In an interview with Chris Nashawaty in *Entertainment Weekly,* King clarified, "First of all, I'd never stop writing because I don't know what I'd do between nine and one every day. But I'd stop publishing. I don't need the money." Yet *Dreamcatcher* and *From a Buick 8* have garnered praise from reviewers as well. Rene Rodriguez in the *Miami Herald* maintained that "*Dreamcatcher* marks [King's] bracing return to all-out horror, complete with trademark grisly gross-outs, a panoramic cast of

deftly drawn characters and a climactic race against time, with the fate of the planet hanging in the balance." Salem Macknee in the Charlotte *Observer,* noting surface similarities between *From a Buick 8* and *Christine,* assured readers that "this strange counterfeit of a Buick Roadmaster is no rerun. Stephen King has once again created an original, a monster never seen before, with its own frightful fingerprint."

King also received a great deal of praise for *Everything's Eventual.* Among other stories, the collection includes a few that he previously published in the *New Yorker.* Notable among these is "The Man in the Black Suit," which won the 1996 O. Henry Award for best short story and brought King comparisons with great nineteenth-century American fiction writer Nathaniel Hawthorne. "As a whole," concluded Rodriguez in another *Miami Herald* review, "*Everything's Eventual* makes a perfect showcase for all of King's strengths: His uncanny talent for creating vivid, fully realized characters in a few strokes, his ability to mine horror out of the mundane, . . . and his knack for leavening even the most preposterous contraptions with genuine, universal emotions."

Although he does not necessarily feel that he has been treated unfairly by the critics, King has described what it is like to witness the written word turned into filmed images that are less than generously received by reviewers. "Whenever I publish a book, I feel like a trapper caught by the Iroquois," he told Peck in *Rolling Stone College Papers.* "They're all lined up with tomahawks, and the idea is to run through with your head down, and everybody gets to take a swing. . . . Finally, you get out the other side and you're bleeding and bruised, and *then* it gets turned into a movie, and you're there in front of the same line and everybody's got their tomahawks out again." Nevertheless, in his essay "Why I Was Bachman," he readily admitted that he really has little to complain about: "I'm still married to the same woman, my kids are healthy and bright, and I'm being well paid for doing something I love." And despite the financial security and recognition, or perhaps because of its intrinsic responsibility, King strives to improve at his craft. "It's getting later and I want to get better, because you only get so many chances to do good work," he stated in a panel discussion at the 1984 World Fantasy Convention in Ottawa. "There's no justification not to at least try to do good work when you make the money."

According to Warren in *Discovering Stephen King,* there is absolutely nothing to suggest that success has been detrimental to King: "As a novelist, King has been remarkably consistent." Noting, for instance, that "for generations it was given that brevity was the soul of horror, that the ideal format for the tale of terror was the short story," Warren pointed out that "King was among the first to challenge that concept, writing not just successful novels of horror, but long novels." Moreover, said Warren, "his novels have gotten longer." King once quipped in the *Chicago Tribune Magazine* that his "philosophy has always been take a good thing and beat it 'til it don't move no more." Although some critics fault him for overwriting, Warren suggested that "the sheer scope and ambitious nature of his storytelling demands a broad canvas." Referring to this as "the very pushiness of his technique," the *New York Times*' Lehmann-Haupt similarly contended that "the more he exasperates us by overpreparing, the more effectively his preparations eventually pay off."

Influenced by the naturalistic novels of writers such as Theodore Dreiser and Frank Norris, King confessed to Janeczko that his personal outlook for the world's future is somewhat bleak. On the other hand, one of the things he finds most comforting in his own work is an element of optimism. "In almost all cases, I've begun with a premise that was really black," he said in a panel discussion at the 1980 World Fantasy Convention in Baltimore, reprinted in *Bare Bones*. "And a more pleasant resolution has forced itself upon that structure." But as Andrew M. Greeley maintained in *Kingdom of Fear*: "Unlike some other horror writers who lack his talents and sensitivity, Stephen King never ends his stories with any cheap or easy hope. People are badly hurt, they suffer and some of them die, but others survive the struggle and manage to grow. The powers of evil have not yet done them in." According to Notkin, though, the reassurance King brings to his own readers derives from a basic esteem for humanity itself: "For whether he is writing about vampires, about the death of 99 percent of the population, or about innocent little girls with the power to break the earth in half, King never stops emphasizing his essential liking for people."

"There's unmistakable genius in Stephen King," admitted Walter Kendrick in the *Village Voice,* adding that he writes "with such fierce conviction, such blind and brutal power, that no matter how hard you fight—and needless to say, I fought—he's irresistible." The less reserved critical affirmations of King's work extend from expressions of pragmatism to those of metaphor. Lehmann-Haupt, for example, a self-professed King addict, offered his evaluation of King's potential versus his accomplishments as a writer of horror fiction: "Once again, as I edged myself nervously toward the climax of one of his thrillers, I found myself considering what Stephen King could accomplish if he would only put his storytelling talents to serious use. And then I had to ask myself: if Mr. King's aim in writing . . . was not entirely serious by some standard that I was vaguely invoking, then why, somebody please tell me, was I holding on to his book so hard that my knuckles had begun to turn white?" Douglas E. Winter assessed King's contribution to the genre in his study *Stephen King: The Art of Darkness* this way: "Death, destruction, and destiny await us all at the end of the journey—in life as in horror fiction. And the writer of horror stories serves as the boatman who ferries people across that Reach known as the River Styx. . . . In the horror fiction of Stephen King, we can embark upon the night journey, make the descent down the dark hole, cross that narrowing Reach, and return again in safety to the surface—to the near shore of the river of death. For our boatman has a master's hand."

While King has played with the idea of giving up publishing his writings, his legion of fans continues to be delighted that the idea has not yet become a reality. In 2004, under the pseudonym of Eleanor Druse, King published *The Journals of Eleanor Druse: My Investigation of the Kingdom Hospital Incident*. He has also continued with his "Dark Tower" series (the illustrated novels featuring Roland the gunslinger) with the publication of *The Dark Tower V: Wolves of the Calla* in 2003. The book was published more than five years after the publication of the previous installment in the series, *The Dark Tower IV: Wizard and Glass*. King also completed the final two installments of the series in 2004, including *The Dark Tower VI: The Songs of Susannah* and *The Dark Tower VII: The Dark Tower.* In a surprise for fans, King introduced himself as a character in the sixth installment, which a *Publishers Weekly* reviewer called a "gutsy move" and commented, that "way there's no denying the ingenuity with which King paints a candid picture of himself." As noted by Gregory Kirschling in *Entertainment Weekly,* King announced in 2004 that he was also working on a new novel. Kirschling quoted the author as saying, "I don't know how well it's going, but the nice thing about it is, having announced my retirement, I don't feel like I'm under any pressure."

BIOGRAPHICAL AND CRITICAL SOURCES:

BOOKS

Badley, Linda, *Writing Horror and the Body: The Fiction of Stephen King, Clive Barker and Anne Rice,* Greenwood Press (Westport, CT), 1996.

Beahm, George W., *The Stephen King Story,* revised and updated edition, Andrews & McMeel (Kansas City, MO), 1992.

Beahm, George W., editor, *The Stephen King Companion,* Andrews & McMeel (Kansas City, MO), 1989.

Blue, Tyson, *Observations from the Terminator: Thoughts on Stephen King and Other Modern Masters of Horror Fiction,* Borgo Press (San Bernardino, CA), 1995.

Collings, Michael R., *Stephen King As Richard Bachman,* Starmont House (Mercer Island, WA), 1985.

Collings, Michael R., *The Works of Stephen King: An Annotated Bibliography and Guide,* edited by Boden Clarke, Borgo Press (San Bernardino, CA), 1993.

Collings, Michael R., *Scaring Us to Death: The Impact of Stephen King on Popular Culture,* 2nd edition, Borgo Press (San Bernardino, CA), 1995.

Contemporary Literary Criticism, Gale (Detroit, MI), Volume 12, 1980, Volume 26, 1983, Volume 37, 1985, Volume 61, 1990.

Davis, Jonathan P., *Stephen King's America,* Bowling Green State University Popular Press (Bowling Green, OH), 1994.

Dictionary of Literary Biography, Volume 143: *American Novelists since World War II, Third Series,* Gale (Detroit, MI), 1994.

Dictionary of Literary Biography Yearbook: 1980, Gale (Detroit, MI), 1981.

Docherty, Brian, editor, *American Horror Fiction: From Brockden Brown to Stephen King,* St. Martin's Press (New York, NY), 1990.

Hoppenstand, Gary, and Ray B. Browne, editors, *The Gothic World of Stephen King: Landscape of Nightmares,* Bowling Green State University Popular Press (Bowling Green, OH), 1987.

Keyishian, Amy, and Marjorie Keyishian, *Stephen King,* Chelsea House (Philadelphia, PA), 1995.

King, Stephen, *Stephen King's Danse Macabre* (nonfiction), Everest House (New York, NY), 1981.

King, Stephen, *The Bachman Books: Four Early Novels,* New American Library (New York, NY), 1985.

Magistrale, Tony, editor, *Landscape of Fear: Stephen King's American Gothic,* Bowling Green State University Popular Press (Bowling Green, OH), 1988.

Magistrale, Tony, editor, *A Casebook on "The Stand,"* Starmont House (Mercer Island, WA), 1992.

Magistrale, Tony, editor, *The Dark Descent: Essays Defining Stephen King's Horrorscape,* Greenwood Press (Westport, CT), 1992.

Magistrale, Tony, *Stephen King: The Second Decade—"Danse Macabre" to "The Dark Half,"* Twayne (New York, NY), 1992.

Platt, Charles, *Dream Makers: The Uncommon Men and Women Who Write Science Fiction,* Berkley (New York, NY), 1983.

Russell, Sharon A., *Stephen King: A Critical Companion,* Greenwood Press (Westport, CT), 1996.

Saidman, Anne, *Stephen King, Master of Horror,* Lerner Publications (Minneapolis, MN), 1992.

Schweitzer, Darrell, editor, *Discovering Stephen King,* Starmont House (Mercer Island, WA), 1985.

Short Story Criticism, Volume 17, Gale (Detroit, MI), 1995.

Underwood, Tim, and Chuck Miller, editors, *Fear Itself: The Horror Fiction of Stephen King,* Underwood-Miller, 1982.

Underwood, Tim, and Chuck Miller, editors, *Kingdom of Fear: The World of Stephen King,* Underwood-Miller, 1986.

Underwood, Tim, and Chuck Miller, editors, *Bare Bones: Conversations on Terror with Stephen King,* McGraw-Hill (New York, NY), 1988.

Underwood, Tim, and Chuck Miller, editors, *Feast of Fear: Conversations with Stephen King,* Carroll & Graf (New York, NY), 1992.

Underwood, Tim, and Chuck Miller, editors, *Fear Itself: The Early Works of Stephen King,* foreword by King, introduction by Peter Straub, afterword by George A. Romero, Underwood-Miller, 1993.

Winter, Douglas E., *Stephen King: The Art of Darkness,* New American Library (New York, NY), 1984.

PERIODICALS

American Film, June, 1986, article by Darrell Ewing and Dennis Meyers.

Atlantic Monthly, September, 1986.

Book, November-December, Chris Barsanti, review of *The Dark Tower V: Wolves of the Calla,* p. 75.

Booklist, July, 1999, Ray Olson, review of *Hearts in Atlantis,* p. 1893; May 1, 2004, Ray Olson, review of *The Dark Tower V: Song of Susannah,* p. 1483.

Boston Globe, October 10, 1980; April 15, 1990, p. A1; May 16, 1990, p. 73; July 15, 1990, p. 71; September 11, 1990, p. 61; October 31, 1990, p. 25; November 17, 1990, p. 12; December 5, 1990, p. 73; July 16, 1991, p. 56; September 28, 1991, p. 9; November 22, 1991, p. 1; August 21, 1992, p. 21; August 30, 1992, p. 14; May 8, 1993, p. 21; May 24, 1993, p. 43; October 16, 1994, p. 14; May 13, 1995, p. 21.

Chicago Tribune, August 26, 1990, p. 3; October 29, 1990, p. 5; November 16, 1990, p. 1; November 30, 1990, p. C29; June 29, 1992, p. 3; November 18, 1992, p. 3; November 7, 1993, p. 9; October 26, 1994, p. 1; May 14, 1995, p. 5.

Chicago Tribune Magazine, October 27, 1985.

Christian Science Monitor, January 22, 1990, p. 13.

Detroit Free Press, November 12, 1982, Jack Matthes, interview with author.

Detroit News, September 26, 1979.

English Journal, January, 1979; February, 1980; January, 1983; December, 1983; December, 1984.

Entertainment Weekly, October 14, 1994, pp. 52-53; June 16, 1995, p. 54; March 22, 1996, p. 63; April 26, 1996, p. 49; May 31, 1996, p. 53; June 28, 1996, p. 98; August 2, 1996, p. 53; September 6, 1996, p. 67; October 4, 1996, p. 54; October 18, 1996, p. 75; December 27, 1996, p. 28; February 7, 1997, p. 111; April 11, 1997, p. 17; April 25, 1997, p. 52; November 28, 1997, p. 41; September 17, 1999, Tom De Haven, "King of *Hearts:* He May Be the Master of Horror, but Stephen King Is Also Adept at Capturing Everyday America. In *Hearts in Atlantis,* His Take on the 60s, including the Effects of Vietnam, Is Scarily Accurate," p.72; September 27, 2002, Chris Nashawaty, "Stephen King Quits," p. 20; June 25, 2004, Gregory Kirschling, review of *The Dark Tower V: Song of Susannah,* p. 172.

Esquire, November, 1984.

Fantasy Review, January, 1984, Michael A. Morrison.

Film Journal, April 12, 1982.

High Times, January, 1981; June, 1981.

Library Journal, March 1, 2004, Kristen L. Smith, review of *The Dark Tower V: Wolves of the Calla,* p. 126; May 15, 2004, Nancy McNicol review of *The Dark Tower V: Song of Susannah,* p. 115.

Locus, September, 1992, pp. 21-22, 67; November, 1992, pp. 19, 21; February, 1994, p. 39; October, 1994, pp. 27, 29.

Los Angeles Times, April 23, 1978; December 10, 1978; August 26, 1979; September 28, 1980; May 10, 1981; September 6, 1981; May 8, 1983; November 20, 1983; November 18, 1984; August 25, 1985; March 9, 1990, p. F16; October 29, 1990, p. F9; November 18, 1990, p. F6; November 30, 1990, p. F1; July 16, 1991, p. F1; May 28, 1992, p. E7; April 16, 1995, p. 28; November 7, 1997, p. D4.

Los Angeles Times Book Review, August 29, 1982; July 15, 1990, p. 12; June 9, 1991, p. 6; April 23, 1995, p. 14.

Maclean's, August 11, 1986.

Miami Herald, March 21, 2001, Rene Rodriguez, review of *Dreamcatcher;* March 27, 2002, Rene Rodriguez, review of *Everything's Eventual.*

Midwest Quarterly, spring, 2004, Tom Hansen, "Diabolical Dreaming in Stephen King's 'The Man in the Black Suit,'" p. 290.

Mystery, March, 1981.

New Republic, February 21, 1981.

New Statesman, September 15, 1995, p. 33.

Newsweek, August 31, 1981; May 2, 1983.

New Yorker, January 15, 1979; September 30, 1996, p. 78.

New York Review of Books, October 19, 1995, p. 54.

New York Times, March 1, 1977; August 14, 1981; August 11, 1982; April 12, 1983; October 21, 1983; November 8, 1984; June 11, 1985; April 4, 1987; January 25, 1988; June 17, 1990, p. 13; October 27, 1990, p. A12; November 16, 1990, p. C38; December 2, 1990, p. 19; June 3, 1991, p. C14; July 14, 1991, p. 25; October 2, 1991, p. C23; June 29, 1992, p. C13; November 16, 1992, p. C15; March 15, 1993, p. D6; June 27, 1993, p. 23; September 17, 1993, p. B8; April 24, 1995, p. C12; May 12, 1995, p. D18; June 26, 1995, p. C16; November 11, 1995, p. 39; April 7, 1996, p. E2; August 5, 1996, p. D7; October 26, 1996, 15; April 25, 1997, p. D22; October 27, 1997, p. C1; November 5, 1997, p. E3; November 7, 1997, pp. A30, D10; February 6, 1998, p. B10.

New York Times Book Review, May 26, 1974; October 24, 1976; February 20, 1977; March 26, 1978; February 4, 1979; September 23, 1979; May 11, 1980; May 10, 1981; September 27, 1981; August 29, 1982; April 3, 1983; November 6, 1983; November 4, 1984; June 9, 1985; February 22, 1987; December 6, 1987; May 13, 1990, p. 3; September 2, 1990, p. 21; September 29, 1991, pp. 13-14; August 16, 1992, p. 3; December 27, 1992, p. 15; October 24, 1993, p. 22; October 30,

1994, p. 24; March 24, 1995, p. C14; July 2, 1995, p. 11; October 20, 1996, p. 16.

New York Times Magazine, May 11, 1980.

Observer (Charlotte, NC), October 4, 2000, Jack Harville, review of *On Writing: A Memoir of the Craft;* Salem Macknee, review of *From a Buick 8.*

Observer (London, England), October 1, 1995, p. 15.

Penthouse, April, 1982, Bob Spitz, interview with author.

People, March 7, 1977; December 29, 1980; January 5, 1981; May 18, 1981; January 28, 1985; fall, 1989; April 1, 1996, p. 38; October 7, 1996, p. 32; October 21, 1996, p. 16; April 28, 1997, p. 15; January 19, 1998, p. 45.

Playboy, June, 1983, interview with author.

Publishers Weekly, January 17, 1977; May 11, 1984; March 13, 1996, p. 26; April 1, 1996, p. 22; May 13, 1996, p. 26; June 24, 1996, p. 43; August 5, 1996, p. 292; August 26, 1996, p. 34; September 9, 1996, p. 27; October 7, 1996, p. 20; April 7, 1997, p. 52; July 14, 1997, p. 65; October 27, 1997, p. 21; November 10, 1997, p. 10; April 19, 2004, review of *The Dark Tower VI: Song of Susannah,* p. 37.

Rapport, Volume 17, number 3, p. 20.

Rolling Stone College Papers, winter, 1980; winter, 1983.

Saturday Review, September, 1981; November, 1984.

Science Fiction Chronicle, December, 1995; June, 1997, p. 43.

Star (Kansas City, MO), October 4, 2000, John Mark Eberhart, review of *On Writing.*

Time, August 30, 1982; July 1, 1985; October 6, 1986; December 7, 1992, p. 81; September 2, 1996, p. 60.

Tribune Books (Chicago, IL) June 8, 1980.

Village Voice, April 29, 1981; October 23, 1984; March 3, 1987.

Voice Literary Supplement, September, 1982; November, 1985.

Wall Street Journal, July 7, 1992, p. B2; October 5, 1992, p. B3; November 7, 1997, p. B8.

Washington Post, August 26, 1979; April 9, 1985; May 8, 1987; October 29, 1990, p. B8; July 16, 1991, p. B1; April 13, 1992, p. C7; May 21, 1993, p. 16; May 27, 1993, p. D9; May 14, 1995, p. G1.

Washington Post Book World, May 26, 1974; October 1, 1978; August 26, 1980; April 12, 1981; August 22, 1982; March 23, 1983; October 2, 1983; November 13, 1983; June 16, 1985; August 26, 1990, p. 9; September 29, 1991, p. 9; October 31, 1991, p. C7; July 19, 1992, p. 7; December 13, 1992, p. 5; October 10, 1993, p. 4; October 9, 1994, p. 4; March 6, 1995, p. D6.

ONLINE

Stephen King Web site, http://www.stephenking.com/ (June 28, 2002).*

* * *

KING, Steve
See KING, Stephen (Edwin)

* * *

KITZINGER, Sheila 1929-

PERSONAL: Born March 29, 1929, in Taunton, England; daughter of Alexander and Clare (Bond) Webster; married Uwe W. Kitzinger (dean of a French business school); children: Celia, Nell, Tess, Polly, Jenny. *Education:* Ruskin College, Oxford, Diploma (social anthropology; with distinction), 1951; St. Hugh's College, Oxford, B.Litt. (anthropology), 1956. *Politics:* Labour. *Religion:* Society of Friends (Quaker). *Hobbies and other interests:* Painting.

ADDRESSES: Home—The Manor, Standlake, near Witney, Oxfordshire OX29 7RH, England. *Office*—National Childbirth Trust, 9 Queensborough Ter., London W2, England. *Agent*—Hilary Rubinstein, A. P. Watt and Son, 26/28 Bedford Row, London WC1R 4HL, England.

CAREER: University of Edinburgh, Edinburgh, Scotland, researcher on race relations in Britain, 1951-53; National Childbirth Trust, London, England, prenatal teacher and counselor, 1958—; teacher of midwifery, Wolfson School of Health Sciences. Lecturer in England for Department of Education and Science, at universities and teacher training colleges, and to nurses and social workers; lecturer in United States for International Childbirth Education Association and American Society for Psychoprophylaxis in Obstetrics, 1972; has also lectured and conducted workshops in Canada, Sweden, and South Africa.

MEMBER: Institute of Health Educators.

AWARDS, HONORS: Joost de Blank Award for research, 1972; honorary professor, Thames Valley University.

WRITINGS:

The Experience of Childbirth, Gollancz (London, England), 1962, 4th edition, Taplinger (New York, NY), 1972.

An Approach to Antenatal Teaching (booklet), National Childbirth Trust (London, England), 1968.

Giving Birth: The Parent's Emotions in Childbirth, Gollancz (London, England), 1971, Taplinger (New York, NY), 1972.

(Editor) *Episiotomy: Physical and Emotional Aspects,* National Childbirth Trust (London, England), 1972, revised edition published as *Episiotomy and the Second Stage of Labor,* Pennypress (Seattle, WA), 1984.

Counselling for Childbirth, Bailliere Tindall, 1977.

Journey through Birth (cassette tapes), International Childbirth Education Association, 1977.

Women As Mothers, Fontana Books (London, England), 1978.

(Editor, with John A. Davis) *The Place of Birth: A Study of the Environment in Which Birth Takes Place with Special Reference to Home Confinements,* Oxford University Press (New York, NY), 1978.

Birth at Home, Oxford University Press (New York, NY), 1979.

Education and Counseling for Childbirth, Schocken Books (New York, NY), 1979.

The Complete Book of Pregnancy and Childbirth, Knopf (New York, NY), 1984, revised edition, 1996, published as *The New Pregnancy and Childbirth: Choices and Challenges,* Dorling Kindersley (London, England), 2003, 4th edition, Knopf (New York, NY), 2004.

Well-Being: An Introduction to Health, Scott, Foresman (Glenview, IL), 1980.

Women's Experience of Sex, Putnam (New York, NY), 1983.

Birth over Thirty, Penguin Books (New York, NY), 1985.

Being Born, Grosset & Dunlap (New York, NY), 1986.

The Experience of Breastfeeding, Penguin Books (New York, NY), 1987.

Your Baby, Your Way: Making Pregnancy Decisions and Birth Plans, Pantheon Books (New York, NY), 1987.

Breastfeeding Your Baby, Knopf (New York, NY), 1989, revised edition, 1998.

Giving Birth: How It Really Feels, Noonday Press (New York, NY), 1989.

The Crying Baby, Penguin Books (New York, NY), 1990.

Homebirth: The Essential Guide to Giving Birth outside of the Hospital, Dorling Kindersley (New York, NY), 1991, 2nd edition published as *Birth Your Way,* Dorling Kindersley (London, England), 2002.

(Editor) *The Midwife Challenge,* Pandora (London, England), 1991.

(With daughter, Celia Kitzinger) *Tough Questions: Talking Straight with Your Kids about the Real World,* Harvard Common Press (Boston, MA), 1991.

Birth over Thirty-five, Sheldon Press (London, England), 1994.

The Year after Childbirth: Surviving and Enjoying the First Year of Motherhood, Scribner (New York, NY), 1994, published as *The Year after Childbirth: Enjoy Your Body, Your Relationships, and Yourself in Your Baby's First Year,* Fireside Press (New York, NY), 1996.

Ourselves As Mothers: The Universal Experience of Motherhood, Addison-Wesley (Reading, MA), 1995.

Becoming a Grandmother: A Life Transition, Scribner (New York, NY), 1996.

A Celebration of Birth, 1997.

(With Celia Kitzinger) *Talking with Children about Things That Matter,* Pandora (London, England), 2000.

Rediscovering Birth, Pocket Books (New York, NY), 2000.

Contributor to books, including: Alioune Diop, editor, *Les Etudiants noirs parlent,* Presence Africaine, 1952; M. L. Kellmer Pringle, editor, *Caring for Children,* Longmans, Green, 1969, Humanities, 1970; Michael Horowitz, editor, *Peoples and Cultures of the Caribbean,* Natural History Press, 1971; and Margaret Laing, editor, *Women on Women,* Sidgwick & Jackson, 1972. Narrator for video *Developing Midwifery Skills: Looking Forward to a Home Birth,* Mark-It Television, 2000. Contributor of articles and reviews to *New Society, Vogue, Nursing Mirror, Journal for the Scientific Study of Religion,* and other periodicals.

Kitzinger's books have been translated into nineteen languages.

SIDELIGHTS: Sheila Kitzinger has written extensively on childbirth, particularly on home birth. Her *Complete Book of Pregnancy and Childbirth,* which has sold some 500,000 copies worldwide, is a standard in its field, while *The Experience of Childbirth,* published in 1962, presents "a radical woman-centered view of birth," as a writer for *Mothering* explained. Noemie Maxwell in *Library Journal* described Kitzinger as "a well-known birth educator and activist."

Kitzinger's *Experience of Childbirth* broke new ground, not with its subject matter but with its approach. Julie Akhurst, writing online for *Junior* magazine, recounted that, "as an anthropologist, Kitzinger wrote about birth as a highly personal, sexual and social event. No one had ever done so before, but it rang a bell with millions of women." In addition, Kitzinger was among the first to popularize relaxation and breathing techniques now commonly used throughout the world. She also argued on behalf of home birth, a topic she has continued to champion over the years.

In *The Complete Book of Pregnancy and Childbirth,* Kitzinger covers such issues as how to choose a doctor, whether to give birth at home or in a hospital, prenatal concerns, labor, and delivery. Mary Frances Wilkens in *Booklist* noted that "no other source offers such a complete and educated look at childbirth choices for mothers-to-be." But Kitzinger goes beyond such questions to argue that, as she states, "the woman is active birthgiver rather than a passive patient." This approach, according to Naomi Yavneh in *Whole Earth,* "really sets this book apart" and makes *The Complete Book of Pregnancy and Childbirth* "a best bet for the woman who wants a healthy and informed pregnancy."

Kitzinger once wrote: "Birth, like death, is an experience in which we all share. It can either be a disruption in the flow of human existence, a fragment which has little or nothing to do with loving and being loved or with the passionate longing which created the baby, or it can be lived with beauty and dignity, and labour itself be a celebration of joy. Birth is a part of a woman's very wide psychosexual experiences and is intimately concerned with her feelings about and sense of her own body, her relations with others, her role as a woman, and the meaning of her personal identity. I feel that in choosing to write about childbirth I am at the hub of life."

BIOGRAPHICAL AND CRITICAL SOURCES:

PERIODICALS

Booklist, November 1, 1994, Denise Perry Donavin, review of *Ourselves As Mothers: The Universal Experience of Motherhood,* p. 463; September 15, 1996, Mary Frances Wilkens, review of *The Complete Book of Pregnancy and Childbirth,* p. 179.
Family Matters, winter, 2000, review of *Talking with Children about Things That Matter,* p. 71.
Lancet, April 3, 1999, "Sheila Kitzinger," p. 1198.
Library Journal, November 15, 1991, KellyJo Houtz Parish, review of *Homebirth: The Essential Guide to Giving Birth Outside of the Hospital,* p. 102; November 1, 1996, Rebecca Cress-Ingebo, review of *The Complete Book of Pregnancy and Childbirth,* p. 100; September 15, 2000, Noemie Maxwell, review of *Rediscovering Birth,* p. 106.
Midwifery Today, autumn, 2002, Cher Mikkola, review of *Birth Your Way,* p. 63.
Mothering, September, 1999, "Living Treasures: Sheila Kitzinger," p. 96.
Ms., January-February, 1995, Barbara Findlen, "Bold Type: Childbirth Is Powerful," p. 69.
Natural Health, May-June, 1995, Ellen Grimm, review of *Ourselves As Mothers,* p. 166.
Nursing Times, January 4, 1995, Joanna Trevelyan, review of *The Year after Childbirth: Surviving the First Year of Motherhood,* p. 51; September 6, 1995, Joanna Trevelyan, "Home Birth and Other Alternatives to Hospital," p. 62; November 16, 2000, Anne Gulland, "Back to the Basics," p. 10.
Publishers Weekly, July 12, 1991, review of *Tough Questions: Talking Straight with Your Kids about the Real World,* p. 62; July 22, 1996, review of *Becoming a Grandmother,* p. 221.
Special Delivery, winter, 1991, Rahima Baldwin, review of *Homebirth,* p. 15; spring, 2000, Annmarie G. Klyzub Kalmar, review of *Developing Midwifery Skills: Looking Forward to a Home Birth,* p. 26.
Whole Earth, summer, 1998, Naomi Yavneh, review of *The Complete Book of Pregnancy and Childbirth,* p. 79.

Junior Online, http://www.juniormagazine.co.uk/ (March 20, 2003), Julie Akhurst, "Sheila Kitzinger: The Woman Who Changed Childbirth."

Sheila Kitzinger Web site, http://www.sheilakitzinger. com/ (November 12, 2003).*

*   *   *

KIZER, Carolyn (Ashley) 1925-

PERSONAL: Born December 10, 1925, in Spokane, WA; daughter of Benjamin Hamilton (a lawyer and planner) and Mabel (a biologist and professor; maiden name, Ashley) Kizer; married Charles Stimson Bullitt, January 16, 1948 (divorced, 1954); married John Marshall Woodbridge (an architect and planner), April 11, 1975; children: (first marriage) Ashley Ann, Scott, Jill Hamilton. *Education:* Sarah Lawrence College, B.A., 1945; graduate study at Columbia University, 1945-46, and University of Washington, 1946-47; studied poetry with Theodore Roethke, University of Washington, Seattle, 1953-54. *Politics:* Independent. *Religion:* Episcopalian.

ADDRESSES: Home—19772 Eighth St. E, Sonoma, CA 95476; Paris, France.

CAREER: Poet, educator, and critic. *Poetry Northwest,* Seattle, WA, founder and editor, 1959-65; National Endowment for the Arts, Washington, DC, first director of literary programs, 1966-70; University of North Carolina at Chapel Hill, poet-in-residence, 1970-74; Ohio University, Athens, McGuffey Lecturer and poet-in-residence, 1975; Iowa Writer's Workshop, University of Iowa, Iowa City, professor of poetry, 1976; University of Maryland, College Park, professor, 1976-77; Stanford University, Stanford, CA, professor of poetry, spring, 1986; Princeton University, Princeton, NJ, senior fellow in the humanities, fall, 1986; Fannie Hurst Professor of Literature at Washington University, St. Louis, MO, 1971; lecturer at Barnard College, spring, 1972; acting director of graduate writing program at Columbia University, 1972; visiting professor of writing, University of Arizona, Tucson, 1989, 1990, and University of California—Davis, 1991; Coal Royalty Chair, University of Alabama, 1995. Partici-

Carolyn Kizer

pant in International Poetry Festivals, London, England, 1960, 1970, Yugoslavia, 1969, 1970, Pakistan, 1969, Rotterdam, Netherlands, 1970, Knokke-le-Zut, Belgium, 1970, Bordeaux, 1992, Dublin, 1993, and Glasgow, 1994. Volunteer worker for American Friends Service Committee, 1960; specialist in literature for U.S. State Department in Pakistan, 1964-65; director of literary programs for the National Endowment for the Arts; poet-in-residence at the University of North Carolina and Ohio University. Member of founding board of directors of Seattle Community Psychiatric Clinic.

MEMBER: International PEN, Amnesty International, Association of Literary Magazines of America (founding member), Poetry Society of America, Poets and Writers, Academy of American Poets (chancellor), American Civil Liberties Union.

AWARDS, HONORS: Masefield Prize, Poetry Society of America, 1983; Washington State Governors Award, and San Francisco Arts Commission award, both 1984, both for *Mermaids in the Basement: Poems for Women;*

award in literature, American Academy and Institute of Arts and Letters, 1985; Pulitzer Prize in poetry, 1985, for *Yin: New Poems*; Frost Medal, Poetry Society of America, Theodore Roethke Memorial Foundation Poetry Award, and President's Medal, Eastern Washington University, all 1988; D.Litt., Whitman College, 1986, St. Andrew's College, 1989, Mills College, 1990, and Washington State University, 1991.

WRITINGS:

POETRY

Poems, Portland Art Museum (Portland, OR), 1959.

The Ungrateful Garden, Indiana University Press (Bloomington, IN)), 1961.

Knock upon Silence, Doubleday (New York, NY), 1965.

Midnight Was My Cry: New and Selected Poems, Doubleday (New York, NY), 1971.

Mermaids in the Basement: Poems for Women, Copper Canyon Press (Port Townsend, WA), 1984.

Yin: New Poems (contains selections from *Mermaids in the Basement*), BOA Editions (Brockport, NY), 1984.

The Nearness of You: Poems for Men, Copper Canyon Press (Port Townsend, WA), 1986.

Harping On: Poems 1985-1995, Copper Canyon Press (Port Townsend, WA), 1996.

Cool, Calm, & Collected: Poems 1960-2000, Copper Canyon Press (Port Townsend, WA), 2000.

Pro Femina: A Poem, University of Missouri Press (Kansas City, MO), 2000.

(Coeditor) *American Poetry: The Twentieth Century,* Library of America (New York, NY), 2000.

OTHER

(Editor, with Elaine Dallman and Barbara Gelpi) *Woman Poet—The West,* Women-in-Literature (Reno, NV), 1980.

(Editor) Robertson Peterson, *Leaving Taos,* Harper (New York, NY), 1981.

(Editor) Muriel Weston, *Primitive Places,* Owl Creek Press (Seattle, WA), 1987.

(Translator) *Carrying Over* (poetry), Copper Canyon Press (Port Townsend, WA), 1988.

(Editor) *The Essential John Clare,* Ecco Press (Hopewell, NJ), 1992.

Proses: Essays on Poems & Poets, Copper Canyon Press (Port Townsend, WA), 1993.

(Editor) *One Hundred Great Poems by Women,* Ecco Press (Hopewell, NJ), 1995.

Picking and Choosing: Essays on Prose, Eastern Washington University Press (Cheney, WA), 1995.

(Compiler and author of introduction) Jeffrey Greene, *American Spiritualists,* Northeastern University Press (Boston, MA), 1998.

Contributor to numerous anthologies, including *New Poems by American Poets,* Ballantine (New York, NY), 1957; *New Poets of England and America,* Meridian Publishing (Salinas, CA), 1962; *Anthology of Modern Poetry,* Hutchinson (London, England), 1963; *Erotic Poetry,* Random House (New York, NY), 1963; and *New Modern Poetry,* Macmillan (New York, NY), 1967.

Translator of *Sept versants, sept syllables* (title means "Seven Sides, Seven Syllables"). Also contributor to various periodicals, including *Poetry, New Yorker, Kenyon Review, Spectator, Paris Review, Shenandoah, Antaeus, Grand Street,* and *Poetry East.*

SIDELIGHTS: Although Carolyn Kizer's poetry collections are not vast in number, they bear witness to her much-praised meticulousness and versatility. Critics noted although that Kizer's subject matter has changed over the years, the caliber of her art has remained high. In 1985 her collection *Yin: New Poems*—twelve years in the making—won the Pulitzer Prize in poetry. Kizer is "a writer to treasure," maintained Elizabeth B. House in a *Dictionary of Literary Biography* essay. "She has created poetry that will endure. . . . Faced with the human inevitability of loss and destruction, Kizer, in both poetry and life, celebrates the joys of art, friendship, family, and good works. Undoubtedly, she has earned a secure niche in American letters."

"Like some people, Carolyn Kizer is many people," noted *Washington Post* reviewer Meryle Secrest. Kizer received her B.A. degree from Sarah Lawrence College in 1945 and then went on to do graduate work at both Columbia University and the University of Washington. During the mid-1950s, she studied poetry at the University of Washington under the tutelage of Theodore Roethke. According to *American Women Writers,* Kizer believes that it was "her study of the craft with Theodore Roethke at the University of Washington in the early 1950s that finally turned her into a self-assured poet." Later, Kizer cofounded the prestigious Seattle-based *Poetry Northwest,* a journal she edited from its inception in 1959 until 1965. In 1964 Kizer went to Pakistan as a U.S. State Department specialist and taught at various institutions, including the distinguished Kinnaird College for Women. Among her other activities, Kizer was the first director of literary programs for the newly created National Endowment for the Arts in 1966, a position she held until 1970. As literary director, she promoted programs to aid struggling writers and literary journals, and she worked to have poetry read aloud in inner city schools. In addition to teaching and lecturing nationwide, Kizer has translated Urdu, Chinese, and Japanese poetry. According to Kizer, "What is so marvelous about living today is that it is possible to extend, like a flower, spreading petals in all directions," recorded Secrest.

House claimed that, as a poet, Kizer deals equally well with subjects that have often been treated by women and those that have not. "Tensions between humans and nature, civilization and chaos," are topics no more and no less congenial to her than are love affairs, children, and women's rights. According to House, in Kizer's first two poetry collections, *The Ungrateful Garden* and *Knock upon Silence,* the poet employs grotesque imagery—"lice cozily snuggling in a captured bat's wing, carrion birds devouring the last pulp of hell-bound bodies," and other unsettling topics—but the poet is not fearful of femininity and sentimentality. Sometime in the past, Roethke composed a list of common complaints made against women poets that included such things as lack of sense of humor, narrow range of subject matter, lamenting the lot of women, and refusing to face up to existence. In *Alone with America: Essays on the Art of Poetry in the United States since 1950,* Richard Howard maintained that Kizer has first incurred and then overcome these complaints. "She does not fear—indeed she *wants*—to do all the things Roethke says women are blamed for, and indeed I think she does do them. . . . But doing them or not, being *determined* to do them makes her a different kind of poet from the one who manages to avoid the traps of his condition, and gives her a different kind of success," noted Howard.

The Ungrateful Garden, Kizer's first major collection, appeared in 1961. Devoted in large part to the

examination of people's relationships to nature, it is a candid work, according to *Saturday Review* critic Robert D. Spector. Because "candor is hardly ever gentle, her shocking images are brutal," the critic continued. Kizer "abuses adult vanity by setting it alongside a child's ability to endure the removal of an eye. Pretensions to immortality are reduced to rubbish by 'Beer cans on headstones, eggshells in the [cemetery] grass.'" In the title poem and in one of her better-known pieces, "The Great Blue Heron," Kizer presents her belief that nature has no malevolence toward man, that the two simply exist side by side. In "The Great Blue Heron," according to House, "the heron is a harbinger of death, but [Kizer] never suggests that the bird is evil. As part of nature, he merely reflects the cycle of life and death that time imposes on all living creatures."

In *The Ungrateful Garden,* House also observed Kizer emphasizing the distance between humans and nature, and also the perils of modern governments quashing individual identity. Kizer demonstrates that a reprieve from the terrors of nature and government can be found in human relationships, and especially in poetry. In the poem "From an Artist's House," for example, the poet celebrates the unchanging nature of verse. On the whole, D. J. Enright of the *New Statesman* feels there are "some remarkably good things in this strong-tasting collection, thick with catastrophes and fortitude."

Whereas *Poetry* critic William Dickey considered *The Ungrateful Garden* to showcase a poet "more concerned with the manner of [her poems'] expression than with the material to be expressed," *Saturday Review* contributor Richard Moore commented that Kizer's third poetry collection, *Knock upon Silence,* contains relaxed meters and simple diction: "There are no verbal fireworks, no fancy displays." As with much of Kizer's poetry, an Eastern influence is present in *Knock upon Silence,* with its calm, cool, sensitive verse. The collection consists of two long poems—"A Month in Summer" and "Pro Femina"—a section called "Chinese Imitations," and several translations of the eighth-century Chinese poet Tu Fu. "She's at the top of her form, which is to say, devastating in her observations of the human animal," wrote Gene Baro in the *New York Times Book Review.* "How true, one thinks, when this poet writes about feminine sensibility or about love."

Of the two longer poems included in *Knock upon Silence,* "A Month in Summer" received mixed reviews. This diary of love gone sour, which contains both prose segments and occasional haiku, is viewed by Moore as the "weakest part of [Kizer's] book. . . . It is moving in places, witty in others; but there is also a tendency to be straggling and repetitive." In contrast, Bewley cited this piece as "the heart and triumph" of *Knock upon Silence:* "It manages to compress within a very few pages alive with self-irony and submerged humor, more than most good novelists can encompass in a volume."

The other long selection in *Knock upon Silence,* "Pro Femina," is comprised of three conversational poems that discuss the role of the liberated woman in the modern world, particularly the woman writer. "Pro Femina" is a satiric piece keenly aware of the fact that women still confront obstacles related to their gender: "Keeping our heads and our pride while remaining unmarried; / And if wedded, kill guilt in its tracks when we stack up the dishes / And defect to the typewriter."

Kizer turns, in part, to different matters in her collection *Midnight Was My Cry: New and Selected Poems,* which contains several previously published poems and sixteen new ones. Though she remains dedicated to meter and Eastern restraint—"the poet's mind continually judges, restrains, makes passion control itself," wrote Eric Mottram in *Parnassus*—her newer poems express an interest in the social and political problems of the contemporary world, especially those of the 1960s. These poems center on antisegregation sit-ins, the Vietnam conflict, and the assassination of Senator Robert Kennedy. For *Poetry* contributor Richard Howard, Kizer has "reinforced her canon by some dozen first-rate poems, observant, solicitous, lithe."

Catching the literary world a little by surprise, Kizer published two poetry volumes in 1984, *Mermaids in the Basement: Poems for Women* and *Yin: New Poems. Mermaids in the Basement* received minor critical attention, perhaps because it contains several poems from her previous collections, including "A Month in Summer" and "Pro Femina," the latter one of her best-known poems satirizing as it does liberated women writers by mimicking the hexameter used by the ancient misogynist poet Juvenal. According to Patricia Hampl in the *New York Times Book Review,* "the craft for which . . . Kizer is known serves her well in [the poem] 'Thrall'; a remarkable compression allows her

to review the entire disappointing history of her relationship with her father. . . . There is a great effort toward humor in these poems. But the tone is uneven; the humor, as well as the outrage, seems arch at times." *Yin,* in contrast, received a favorable critical reception from the outset, winning the Pulitzer Prize for poetry in 1985. "One could never say with certainty what 'a Carolyn Kizer poem' was—until now. . . . Now we know a Kizer poem is brave, witty, passionate, and not easily forgotten," contended *Poetry* critic Robert Phillips.

The word "yin" is Chinese for the feminine principle, and many of the poems in this award-winning collection focus on feminine perceptions and creativity. In her joint review of *Mermaids in the Basement* and *Yin,* Hampl considered the prose memoir in *Yin* titled "A Muse" to be "a real find. . . . This piece, about . . . Kizer's extraordinary mother, is not only a fascinating portrait, but a model of detachment and self-revelation." "A Muse" examined Kizer's childhood feelings about the ambitions her mother had for her: "The poet describes a . . . mama smothering her precocious offspring with encouragement. . . . Only with the woman's death does the speaker's serious life as an artist begin," assessed Joel Conarroe in the *Washington Post Book World.* In addition, "Semele Recycled" is considered an imaginative treat with its description of a modern-day Semele symbolically torn apart at the sight of her lover and then made whole again.

Probably the most admired piece in the *Yin* collection is the poem "Fanny." Written in Roman hexameter, this 224-line poem is the proposed diary of Robert Louis Stevenson's wife, Frances (Fanny), as she nurses her husband during the last years of his life. Remarked Kizer in Penelope Moffet's *Los Angeles Times* review: "'Fanny' is about what happens to women who are the surrogate of gifted men. Women who look after the great writers, whether mothers, sisters, wives, or daughters. What they do with their creativity, because they can't engage in open or active competition. I think 'Fanny' [is] a political poem, if you consider feminism a political issue, as I do." In addition, Conarroe claimed "Fanny" is "Keatsian in the sensuousness of its imagery, the laughing of its odors and textures. Kizer gives a shattering sense of a woman's sacrifice and isolation while communicating vividly the terrible beauty of the woman's obsession with her husband's health." Whereas Suzanne Juhasz in *Library Journal* considered *Yin* a "mixed bag, or blessing," most reviewers agree with Phillips that *Yin* "is a marvelous book."

Kizer's *The Nearness of You* serves as a "companion piece" to *Mermaids in the Basement,* as it is a collection of poetry on men. According to Charles Libby in the *New York Times Book Review,* the collection "shows evidence that writing about the other sex involves different struggles than writing about one's own. Despite many local triumphs, the new collection is in many ways less striking, technically and psychologically more self-conscious [than *Mermaids in the Basement*]." In *Contemporary Women Poets,* essayist John Montague noted, with relief, "In an era when a shrill feminism threatens to tilt the scales of past injustice, Kizer's view of the sexual universe contains polarity without hostility." Meanwhile Diane Wakoski, appraising *The Nearness of You* for the *Women's Review of Books,* found the work somewhat uneven, but concluded, "What this book convinces me of, finally, is that Carolyn Kizer is a poet of occasion, of person and personality. When she becomes historical or formal, when she attempts either love-lyrics or story poems, she is mediocre at best. . . . But as the ambassador of goodwill in the poetry world . . . as the woman longing for a family of artists and intellectuals who will replace the one she lost in growing up and leaving her father—yes, yes, yes. Believable, strong, someone who deserves to be remembered."

Kizer's subsequent collection, *Harping On: Poems 1985-1995,* was not published until 1996. Christine Stenstrom, writing for *Library Journal,* noted that Kizer's "political poems satisfy less than those vividly recalling parents and friends in small masterpieces of verse narrative." In *Publishers Weekly,* a critic described Kizer's voice in the book as "distinctly irreverent," her politics "left-leaning," and noted of her poetry that "Kizer employs everything from slanted rhymes to venerable forms like the villanelle and pantoum with a chatty grace that makes the intricacy of her structures all but invisible." Commenting on the satire that wires its way throughout the poems in *Harping On, New Leader* reviewer Phoebe Pettingell maintained that while the poet comes across as a "clever, tough-minded, and erudite" harpy "exercising her slashing wit on her self as often as others," the poetry scene of the 1990s "needs her voice, whether hectoring, prophesying, seducing, or informing, to raise our consciousness with the eloquence of her subtle lyrics."

Kizer's essays and criticism have been gathered in several volumes, including 1994's *Proses: Essays on Poems and Poets.* Kate Fitzsimmons, reviewing the book for the *San Francisco Review of Books,* found Kizer's writing to be engaging. "The joy Kizer experiences in reading other poets is infectious," Fitzsimmons concluded. "Whether she is writing about the lives of poets or their poetry, her enthusiasm for their work is evident, nearly tactile." While Doris Lynch in *Library Journal* praised the effort, a *Publishers Weekly* reviewer was less impressed, commenting that if the book had been written by a more-obscure writer, "it would fade quickly into blessed obscurity."

Antioch Review critic Carol Moldaw called Kizer's *Cool, Calm & Collected: Poems 1960-2000,* "consistently and fearlessly irreverent," and noted that Kizer uses "wit and irony to drive her points home." She added that "almost all of her poems have points, the way roses have thorns." Moldaw continued, "Kizer's poetic voice is one of the most engagingly warm human voices we have, and it would be a mistake to take this enormous, if hard to define, feat for granted. While in her poems from the 50s, Kizer has already begun to stake out the territory she will later make her own . . . and by the 60s she is already writing 'Chinese Imitations,'" but "it is in the 70s and 80s that you feel her hit her stride." Robert Phillips of the *Houston Chronicle* noted that *Cool, Calm & Collected* appears in Kizer's seventy-fifth year and that it "ranks among her best." He observed that one of Kizer's greatest strengths is her use of mythology. "Rather than dragging out the usual versions of the familiar tales, she goes the sources of the myths with surprising results," he explained.

Writing in *Booklist* Ray Olson observed that "Kizer's four decades of work demonstrate a highly skilled and witty formal poet who yet has been an avant-gardist thematically. Well before many others, she adopted the personae of goddesses in poems that remain more feminine and more feminist than many poems published yesterday." In the same publication, Patricia Monaghan reflected that Kizer "has produced dozens of tender, passionate poems of age and loss. . . . The stately power of her verse has never failed her."

Although the more pointed aspects of her verse are often couched in sarcasm and stylistic intricacy, Kizer considers herself a political poet. As she remarked to Moffet: "Because I do not feel that [it] is a steady undercurrent, just as feminism is, there are these parallel streams that I hope infuse everything that I do. And I find that stream getting more and more strong in my work. But I don't ever want to be hortatory or propagandistic." With regard to the quantity of poetic output—Kizer is not known for being especially prolific herself—she had this to say to inexperienced poets: "I think a lot of younger poets get terrible anxiety that they'll be forgotten if they don't have a book all the time. Well, maybe they will be forgotten, but if they're any good they'll come back."

In an interview with Allan Jalon for the *Los Angeles Times,* Kizer explained her writing style: "I'm not a formalist, not a confessional poet, not strictly a free-verse poet." Jalon described Kizer as, "Tough without being cold, sometimes satirical (she's a great admirer of Alexander Pope)," and noted that "her work expresses a wordly largeness that repeatedly focuses on the points at which lives meet. 'That's my subject,'" concluded Kizer. "No matter how brief an encounter you have with anybody, you both change."

BIOGRAPHICAL AND CRITICAL SOURCES:

BOOKS

Contemporary Authors Autobiography Series, Volume 5, Gale (Detroit, MI)), 1987.
Contemporary Literary Criticism, Gale (Detroit, MI), Volume 15, 1980, Volume 39, 1986.
Contemporary Women Poets, St. James Press (Detroit, MI), 1997.
Dictionary of Literary Biography, Volume 169: *American Poets since World War II, Fifth Series,* Gale (Detroit, MI), 1996.
Encyclopedia of American Literature, Continuum (New York, NY), 1999.
Howard, Richard, *Alone with America: Essays on the Art of Poetry in the United States since 1950,* Atheneum (New York, NY), 1969.
Kizer, Carolyn, *The Ungrateful Garden,* Indiana University Press (Bloomington, IN), 1961.
Kizer, Carolyn, *Knock upon Silence,* Doubleday (New York, NY), 1965.
Malkoff, Karl, *Crowell's Handbook of Contemporary American Poetry,* Crowell (New York, NY), 1973.
Rigsbee, David, editor, *An Answering Music: On the Poetry of Carolyn Kizer,* Ford-Brown (Boston, MA), 1990.

PERIODICALS

Antioch Review, winter, 2002, Carol Moldaw, review of *Cool, Calm & Collected: Poems, 1960-2000,* p. 166.
Approach, spring, 1966.
Booklist, November 1, 2000, Patricia Monoghan, review of *Cool, Calm & Collected,* p. 513; March 15, 2001, Ray Olson, review of *Cool, Calm & Collected,* p. 1349.
Hollins Critic, June, 1997.
Houston Chronicle, December 24, 2000, Robert Phillips, "Two Modern Masters: Collected Poems of Kizer, Kunitz, Prove Luminary Works," p. 13.
Hudson Review, spring, 1972; summer, 1985, pp. 327-340; summer, 2001, R. S. Gwynn, *Cool, Calm & Collected,* p. 341.
Library Journal, July, 1984; November 1, 1993, p. 93; July, 1996, p. 120; April 1, 2000, Daniel L. Guillory, review of *American Poetry: The Twentieth Century,* p. 105.
Los Angeles Times, January 13, 1985; March 5, 2001, Allan M. Jalon, "Everything, Forever, Everything Is Changed; A Glimpse of Einstein, the Bombing of Hiroshima, the Plight of Women; Moments Are Blazing Images in Carolyn Kizer's Poetry."
Michigan Quarterly Review, John Taylor, "Cool? Calm? Collected? A Meditation of Carolyn Kizer's Poetry," p. 162-173.
New Leader, February 254, 1997, p. 14.
New Statesman, August 31, 1962.
New York Review of Books, March 31, 1966; September 21, 2000, Brad Leithauser, review of *American Poetry,* pp. 70-74.
New York Times Book Review, March 26, 1967; November 25, 1984; March 22, 1987, p. 23; December 17, 2000, Melanie Rehak, "Freedom and Poetry," p. 23; April 2, 2000, William H. Pritchard, "Eliot, Frost, Ma Rainey, and the Rest," p. 10.
Paris Review, spring, 2000, Barbara Thompson, "Carolyn Kizer: The Art of Poetry," pp. 344-346.
Parnassus, fall-winter, 1972.
Poetry, November, 1961; July, 1966; August, 1972; March, 1985; November, 1985.
Prairie Schooner, fall, 1964.
Publishers Weekly, October 18, 1993, p. 70; August 26, 1996, p. 94; September 18, 2000, review of *Cool, Calm, & Collected,* p. 105.
San Francisco Chronicle, March 30, 2002, "Milosz, Straight Win California Book Awards," p. D5.

San Francisco Review of Books, October-November, 1994, p. 20.
Saturday Review, July 22, 1961; December 25, 1965.
Shenandoah, winter, 1966.
Tri-Quarterly, fall, 1966.
Village Voice, November 5, 1996.
Washington Post, February 6, 1968.
Washington Post Book World, August 5, 1984; February 1, 1987, p. 6.
Women's Review of Books, September, 1987, p. 6.
World Literature Today, summer, 1997.

ONLINE

Academy of American Poets Web site, http://www. poets.org/poets/ (May 13, 2003), "Carolyn Kizer."
St. Martin's Press Web site, http://www.bedford stmartins.com/ (May 13, 2003), "Carolyn Kizer."*

* * *

KONING, (Angela) Christina 1954-

PERSONAL: Born April 8, 1954, in Kuala Belait, Borneo; daughter of Geert Julius (an engineer) and Angela Vivienne (a teacher; maiden name, Thompson) Koning; married Eamonn Stephen Vincent, May 16, 1981 (divorced, 1994); children: Anna Cordelia, James Connor. *Ethnicity:* "White (English/Dutch)." *Education:* Girton College, Cambridge, M.A. (with honors), 1975; attended Newcastle College of Art, 1975-76; doctoral study at University of Edinburgh, 1976-78. *Politics:* "Left of center." *Religion:* "Agnostic." *Hobbies and other interests:* Art, music, travel, gardening.

ADDRESSES: Home and office—London, England. *Agent*—Derek Johns, A. P. Watt Ltd., 20 John St., London WC1N 2DR, England. *E-mail*—ckoning@ interbase.co.uk.

CAREER: Tate Gallery, worked as publications assistant, 1978; Transworld Publishers Ltd., export sales assistant, 1978-81; freelance writer and reviewer. Interbase UK (Internet recruitment agency for journalists), part-time employee. Lecturer at educational institutions, including University of Greenwich, 1993-94, Universidad Católica Andres Bello and Universidad Simon Bolívar, both in Venezuela, 1994, Birkbeck

College, London, 1999, 2002-03, Oxford University, University of Greenwich, and American Institute for Foreign Study; judge of writing competitions. Appeared on British television programs, including *Espresso,* Channel 5, and *Woman's Hour,* British Broadcasting Corp.

AWARDS, HONORS: Encore Prize, 1999, for *Undiscovered Country;* travel scholarship, Society of Authors, 2001.

WRITINGS:

A Mild Suicide (novel), Lime Tree, 1992.
(Assistant editor and contributor) *The Oxford Guide to Twentieth Century Literature,* Oxford University Press (Oxford, England), 1996.
The Good Reading Guide to Children's Books, Bloomsbury (London, England), 1997.
Undiscovered Country (novel), Penguin (London, England), 1998.
Fabulous Time (novel), Penguin (London, England), 2000.

Assistant editor of the anthology *New Writing,* British Council (London, England). Work represented in anthologies, including *A Treasury for Mothers,* Michael O'Mara, 1998. Columnist for *Guardian,* 1987-89. Contributor of articles, stories, and reviews to magazines and newspapers, including *Time Out, New Statesman, Women's Review, New Socialist, She, Times* (London, England), *Observer, Roman Holiday, London for Kids,* and *You.* Books editor, *Cosmopolitan* and *M.*

WORK IN PROGRESS: A Slight Return, a novel set in Jamaica; *A China Passage,* a novella; *The Company You Keep,* a short story collection.

SIDELIGHTS: Christina Koning told *CA:* "What motivates me as a writer and interests me as a reader is primarily to do with style. All the writers I admire— James Joyce, F. Scott Fitzgerald, E. M. Forster, Elizabeth Bowen—are stylists first and foremost. I enjoy the insights into the human heart afforded by Iris Murdoch's novels, the highly charged emotions and exotic landscapes of Jean Rhys, and the anarchic humor of Martin Amis. These are writers I go back to time and again; if I have a favorite writer, it's probably Jane Austen. When I was younger, I identified with Lizzie Bennet and Emma Woodhouse; now it's Anne Elliott in *Persuasion* whose dilemmas interest me more.

"Because my time is so taken up with teaching and journalism, I have to be quite disciplined about my writing. Like most writers, I carry a notebook around with me to jot down ideas and bits of dialogue as they occur. I find I write best in libraries, away from domestic distractions. My second novel, *Undiscovered Country,* contains a brief description of the famous blue-and-gold domed reading room at the British Museum, where much of the book was written. I used to love the feeling of being surrounded by all that literary history: all those novels and poems and political treatises that had come into being in that hallowed space.

"When I'm starting something new, there's usually the germ of an idea—usually no more than a single image—around which my thoughts focus. With my first novel, *A Mild Suicide* (set in Edinburgh in 1977), I was haunted by the image of a woman looking out of a window at a man who has just left her; in *Undiscovered Country* it was a memory of childhood: myself aged about four, sitting on the veranda at my parents' house in Maracaibo, and looking at the light falling through the mosquito screens on the floor. *Fabulous Time,* my third novel, opens with a woman painting a rose. The artist in question was based on an elderly and very eccentric relative of mine. When we were taken to see her, her house was always a terrible mess, because she was more interested in painting than cleaning. I always knew I would write about her some day.

"The novel *A Slight Return* came about after I attended a murder trial as an observer. The book is set in Jamaica, where I lived as a child, and combines memories of that time with more contemporary reflections on what it means to be an expatriate. I'm very interested in ideas of exile and 'strangeness.' Perhaps because of my peripatetic childhood (my parents worked for the Shell oil company, and we moved around a lot when I was small) or because I'm half Dutch and half English, I've never felt I really 'belong' to any one country. The part of London where I now live is very ethnically mixed, with people from a number of former British colonies, including Jamaica.

In writing *A Slight Return,* I wanted to explore what it means to belong to two cultures.

"Themes of exile and estrangement are also central to *Undiscovered Country.* The novel, which is seen through the eyes of Tony, an eleven-year-old girl, focuses on a group of English, Dutch, and American expatriates living and working in the Venezuelan oil fields during the early 1950s. I was struck by the way that people of that era, who had experienced the trauma of World War II, tried to make a new life for themselves and their families in the aftermath of catastrophe. Of course, this didn't always work out; and one of the things that interested me most in writing the novel was the extent to which one can—or cannot—escape the past.

"*Fabulous Time,* a black comedy set partly in Sussex in 1967 and partly in Shanghai in 1910, also considers the interconnectedness of past and present. I suppose, at its simplest, the novel is about the fact that actions have consequences. It's also about the tricks the heart can play. Everyone in the book is in love with someone who doesn't—or can't—reciprocate these feelings. Even though there are darker things in the book (the plot centers around a plan by two of the characters, Sandy and Ray, to murder Sandy's Aunt Connie for her money) it is also about the triumph of goodness. It was only when I had finished the novel that I realized this, of course. However much I plan the structure, or try and preordain how my characters will behave, they always surprise me in the end. And after all, what would be the point of writing if you knew what you were going to say before you started?"

BIOGRAPHICAL AND CRITICAL SOURCES:

PERIODICALS

Guardian, February 26, 1998.
Independent, February 23, 1998.
Observer, January 18, 1998.
Scotsman, January 24, 1998.
Spectator, February 7, 1998.
Sunday Telegraph, February 15, 1998.
Times (London, England), January 24, 1998.
Times Literary Supplement, February 13, 1998; February 16, 2001, Robert Irwin, review of *Fabulous Time,* p. 22.

KUENG, Hans
    See KÜNG, Hans

*   *   *

KÜNG, Hans 1928-

PERSONAL: Born March 19, 1928, in Sursee, Lucerne, Switzerland; son of Hans (a merchant) and Emma (Gut) Küng. *Education:* Pontifical Gregorian University, Rome, Italy, licentiate in philosophy, 1951, licentiate in theology, 1955; Institut Catholique, Sorbonne, University of Paris, Dr.Theol., 1957; also studied in Berlin, Germany, London, England, Amsterdam, Netherlands, and Madrid, Spain. *Hobbies and other interests:* Classical music, water sports, skiing.

ADDRESSES: Home and office—Foundation for a Global Ethic, Waldhäuserstraße 23, D-72076 Tübingen, Germany. *E-mail*—hans.kung@uni-tuebingen.de.

CAREER: Ordained Roman Catholic priest, 1954; performed pastoral work at St. Leodegar, Lucerne, Switzerland, 1957-59; University of Münster, Münster, Germany, assistant in dogmatic theology, 1959-60; University of Tübingen, Tübingen, Germany, ordinary (full) professor of fundamental theology, 1960-63, ordinary professor of dogmatic and ecumenical theology, 1963-80 (removed and censored by the Vatican), ordinary professor of ecumenical theology, 1980-96, director of Institute for Ecumenical Research, 1963-96, professor emeritus, 1996—; Foundation for a Global Ethic, Tübingen, president, 1995—. Appointed *peritus* (official theological consultant) at Second Vatican Council, 1962. Yale University, Terry Lecturer, 1978; visiting professor at Union Theological Seminary, New York, NY, 1968, University of Basel, 1969, University of Chicago Divinity School, 1981, University of Michigan, 1983, University of Toronto, 1985, and Rice University, 1987; guest lecturer at numerous universities in Europe, Asia, Australia, and the United States.

MEMBER: PEN Center of West Germany, Arbeitsgemeinschaft Deutschspachige Dogmatiker, PEN American Center.

AWARDS, HONORS: LL.D., University of St. Louis, 1963, University of Toronto, 1984; D.D., Pacific School of Religion, 1966, University of Glasgow, 1971, Cambridge University, 1985, University of Dublin, 1995, and University of Wales—Swansea, 1999; HH.D., Loyola University of Chicago, 1970; Ludwig Thoma Medal, 1975; L.H.D., University of Michigan, 1985, Ramapo College of New Jersey, 1999, and Hebrew Union College-Jewish Institute of Religion, Cincinnati, OH, 2000; Oskar Pfister Award, American Psychiatric Association, 1986; Silver Medal, University of Tübingen, 1996; Interfaith Gold Medallion, International Council of Christians and Jews, 1998; Theodor-Heuss-Prize, Theodor-Heuss-Foundation, 1998; named honorary citizen of Sursee, Switzerland, 1998, Syracuse, Italy, 2002, and Tübingen, Germany, 2002; Ernst-Robert-Durtius Literary Award, 2001; Göttingen Peace Award, 2002.

WRITINGS:

Die Anwendung der grundlegenden betriebswirtshaftlichen Erkenntnisse im Rechnungswesen der chemischen Industrie, Buchdruckerei Muri, Schertenlieb & Malzacher (Muri-Bern, Switzerland), 1951.
Rechtfertigung: die Lehre Karl Barths und eine katholische Besinnung, Johannes Verlag (Einsiedeln, Switzerland), 1957, 4th enlarged edition, 1964, translation by Thomas Collins, Edmund E. Tolk, and David Granskou published as *Justification: The Doctrine of Karl Barth and a Catholic Reflection,* Thomas Nelson (New York, NY), 1964, published with a letter from Karl Barth, Burns & Oates (London, England), 1966, 40th anniversary edition with new foreword by Hermann Häring, Westminster John Knox Press (Louisville, KY), 2003.
Konzil und Wiedervereinigung: Erneuerung als Ruf in die Einheit, Herder (Freiberg im Breisgau, Germany), 1960, translation by Cecily Hastings published as *The Council and Reunion,* Sheed & Ward (New York, NY), 1961, published as *The Council: Reform, and Reunion,* 1962, new edition, Image Books (Garden City, NY), 1965.
Damit die Welt glaube: Briefe an junge Menschen, Pfeiffer (Munich, Germany), 1962, 5th edition, 1968, translation by Cecily Hastings published as *That the World May Believe,* Sheed & Ward (New York, NY), 1963, published as *That the World May Believe: Letters to Young People,* Sheed & Ward (London, England), 1963.
Strukturen der Kirche, Herder (Freiburg im Breisgau, Germany), 1962, translation by Salvator Attanasio published as *Structures of the Church,* preface by

Cardinal Richard Cushing, Thomas Nelson (New York, NY), 1964, published with a new preface, Crossroad (New York, NY), 1982.

Kirche im Konzil, Herder (Freiberg im Breisgau, Germany), 1963, 2nd edition, 1964, translation by Cecily Hastings published as *The Council in Action: Theological Reflections on the Second Vatican Council,* Sheed & Ward (New York, NY), 1963, translation by Cecily Hastings and N. D. Smith published as *The Living Church: Reflections on the Second Vatican Council,* Sheed & Ward (London, England), 1963, translation by Cecily Hastings, William Glen-Doepel, and H. R. Bronk published as *The Changing Church,* 1965.

Freiheit in der Welt: Sir Thomas More, Benziger (Einsiedeln, Switzerland), 1964, translation by Cecily Hastings published as *Freedom in the World: Sir Thomas More* (also see below), Sheed & Ward (New York, NY), 1965.

Theologe und Kirche, Benziger (Einsiedeln, Switzerland), 1964, translation by Cecily Hastings published as *The Theologian and the Church* (also see below), Sheed & Ward (New York, NY), 1965.

Kirche in Freiheit, Benziger (Einsiedeln, Switzerland), 1964, translation by Cecily Hastings published as *The Church and Freedom* (also see below), Sheed & Ward (New York, NY), 1965.

Christenheit als Minderheit: Die Kirche unter den Weltreligionen (also see below), Benziger (Einsiedeln, Switzerland), 1965.

Freiheit des Christen, Sheed & Ward (New York, NY), 1966, translation by Cecily Hastings published as *Freedom Today* (includes *Freedom in the World: Sir Thomas More, The Theologian and the Church, The Church and Freedom,* and a translation of *Christenheit als Minderheit: Die Kirche unter den Weltreligionen*), Sheed & Ward (New York, NY), 1966.

Gott und das Leid, Benziger (Einsiedeln, Switzerland), 1967.

The Church, translated from German by Ray Ockenden and Rosaleen Ockenden, Sheed & Ward (New York, NY), 1967, abridged German edition published as *Was ist Kirche?,* Herder (Freiberg im Breisgau, Germany), 1970.

Wahrhaftigkeit: Zur Zukunft der Kirche, Herder (Freiberg im Breisgau, Germany), 1968, translation by Edward Quinn published as *Truthfulness: The Future of the Church,* Sheed & Ward (New York, NY), 1968.

Menschwerdung Gottes: eine Einführung in Hegels theologisches Denken als Prolegomena zu einer künftigen Christologie, Herder (Freiberg im Breisgau, Germany), 1970, translation by J. R. Stephenson published as *The Incarnation of God: An Introduction to Hegel's Theological Thought As a Prolegomena to a Future Christology,* Crossword (New York, NY), 1987.

Unfehlbar? Eine anfrage, Benziger (Einsiedeln, Switzerland), 1970, translation by Edward Quinn published as *Infallible? An Inquiry,* Doubleday (Garden City, NY), 1971, translation by Eric Mosbacher published as *Infallible? An Enquiry,* Collins (London, England), 1971, expanded edition with preface by Herbert Haag published as *Infallible?: An Unresolved Inquiry,* Continuum (New York, NY), 1994.

Wozu Priester? Ein Hilfe, Benziger (Einsiedeln, Switzerland), 1971, translation by Robert C. Collins published as *Why Priests? A Proposal for a New Church Ministry,* Doubleday (Garden City, NY), 1972, translation by John Gumming published as *Why Priests?,* Collins (London, England), 1972, new edition, SCM Press (London, England), 1991.

Hans Küng, edited by Martin Redfern, Sheed & Ward (New York, NY), 1972.

Was in der Kirche bleiben muss., Benziger (Einsiedeln, Switzerland), 1973, translation published as *What Must Remain in the Church,* Collins (London, England), 1977.

Christ sein, R. Piper (Munich, Germany), 1974, published as *Die christliche Herausforderung,* 1980, translation by Edward Quinn published as *On Being a Christian,* Doubleday (Garden City, NY), 1976, abridged translation published as *The Christian Challenge,* 1979, new edition, SCM Press (London, England), 1991.

Zwanzig Thesen zum Christsein, R. Piper (Munich, Germany), 1975.

(With Pinchas Lapide) *Jesus im Widerstreit: Ein jüdisch-christlicher Dialog,* Kösel (Munich, Germany), 1976, translation by Edward Quinn published as *Brother or Lord? A Jew and a Christian Talk Together about Jesus,* Fount Paperbacks (London, England), 1977.

Was ist Firmung?, Benziger (Einsiedeln, Switzerland), 1976.

Heute noch an Gott glauben?, R. Piper (Munich, Germany), 1977.

Existiert Gott? Antwort auf die Gottesfrage der Neuzeit, R. Piper (Munich, Germany), 1978, translation by Edward Quinn published as *Does God Exist? An Answer for Today,* Doubleday (Garden

City, NJ), 1980, new edition, SCM Press (London, England), 1991.

Signposts for the Future (essays; includes "On Being a Christian"), Doubleday (Garden City, NY), 1978.

Freud and the Problem of God (Terry lectures), translated by Edward Quinn, Yale University Press (New Haven, CT), 1979, enlarged edition, 1990.

Kirche, gehalten in der Wahrheit?, Benziger (Zurich, Switzerland), 1979, translation by Edward Quinn published as *The Church—Maintained in Truth? A Theological Meditation*, Seabury Press (New York, NY), 1980.

24 Thesen zur Gottesfrage, R. Piper (Munich, Germany), 1979.

(With Edward Schillebeeckx, David Tracey, and others) *Consensus in Theology? A Dialogue with Hans Küng, Edward Schillebeeckx*, edited by Leonard Swidler, Westminster Press (Philadelphia, PA), 1980.

Kunst und Sinnfrage, Benziger (Zurich, Switzerland), 1980, translation by Edward Quinn published as *Art and the Question of Meaning*, Crossroad (New York, NY), 1981.

Wegzeichen in die Zukunft: Programmatisches fuer eine christlichere Kirche, Rowohlt (Reinbek, Germany), 1980.

Glauben an Jesus Christus, Benziger (Zurich, Switzerland), 1982.

Ewiges Leben?, R. Piper (Munich, Germany), 1982, translation by Edward Quinn published as *Eternal Life? Life after Death As a Medical, Philosophical, and Theological Problem*, Doubleday (Garden City, NJ), 1984, new edition, SCM Press (London, England), 1991.

(With others) *Christentum und Weltreligionen: Hinführung zum Dialog mit Islam, Hinduismus und Buddhismus*, R. Piper (Munich, Germany), 1984, translation by Peter Heinegg published as *Christianity and the World Religions: Paths of Dialogue with Islam, Hinduism, and Buddhism*, Doubleday (Garden City, NY), 1986, new edition, SCM Press (London, England).

(With David Tracy) *Theologie, wohin? Auf dem Weg zu einem neuen Paradigma*, Benziger (Zurich, Switzerland), 1984.

(With Walter Jens) *Dichtung und Religion: Pascal, Gryphius, Lessing, Hölderlin, Novalis, Kierkegaard, Dostojewski, Kafka*, Kindler (Munich, Germany), 1985, translation by Peter Heinegg published as *Literature and Religion: Pascal, Gryphius, Lessing, Hölderlin, Novalis, Kierkegaard, Dostoyevsky, Kafka*, Paragon House (New York, NY), 1991.

(With Norbert Greinacher) *Katholische kirche, wohin? Wider den Verrat am Konzil*, R. Piper (Munich, Germany), 1986.

(With Walter Jens, Karl-Josef Kuschel, and others) *Theologie und Literatur: Zum Strand des Dialogs*, Kindler (Munich, Germany), 1986.

Church and Change: The Irish Experience, Gill & Macmillan (Dublin, Ireland), 1986.

Theologie im Aufbruch: Eine ökumenische Grundlegung, R. Piper (Munich, Germany), 1987, translation by Peter Heinegg published as *Theology for the Third Millennium: An Ecumenical View*, Doubleday (New York, NY), 1988.

Woran man sich halten kann, translation by David Smith and others published as *Why I Am Still a Christian*, edited by E. C. Hughes, Abingdon Press (Nashville, TN), 1987.

(With Walter Jens) *Anwälte der Humanität: Thomas Mann, Hermann Hesse, Heinrich Böll*, Kindler (Munich, Germany), 1989.

(With Julia Ching) *Christianity and Chinese Religions* (originally published as *Christentum und Chinesische Religion*), Doubleday (New York, NY), 1989.

Reforming the Church Today: Keeping Hope Alive, (originally published as *Die Hoffnung bewahren: Schriften zur Reform der Kirche*), translated by Peter Heinegg and Francis McDonagh, Crossroad (New York, NY), 1990.

Projekt Weltethos, R. Piper (Munich, Germany), 1990, translation by John Bowden published as *Global Responsibility: In Search of a New World Ethic*, Crossroad (New York, NY), 1991, published with new preface, SCM Press (London, England), 1991.

Das Judentum, R. Piper (Munich, Germany), 1991, translation by John Bowden published as *Judaism: Between Yesterday and Tomorrow*, Crossroad (New York, NY), 1992, published as *Judaism: The Religious Situation of Our Time*, SCM Press (London, England), 1992.

Credo: das Apostolische Glaubensbekenntnis Zeietgenossen erklärt, R. Piper (Munich, Germany), 1992, translation by John Bowden published as *Credo: The Apostle's Creed Explained for Today*, Doubleday (New York, NY), 1993.

Mozart, Spuren der Transzendenz, R. Piper (Munich, Germany), 1992, translation by John Bowden published as *Mozart: Traces of Transcendence*, William B. Eerdmans Publishing (Grand Rapids, MI), 1993.

Die Schweiz ohne Orientierung? Europäische Perspektiven, Benziger (Zurich, Switzerland), 1992.

Great Christian Thinkers, Continuum (New York, NY), 1994.

Das Christentum: Wesen und Geschichte, R. Piper (Munich, Germany), 1994, translation published as *Christianity: Essence, History and Future,* Continuum (New York, NY), 1995.

(With Walter Jens and others) *Dying with Dignity: A Plea for Personal Responsibility,* translated by John Bowden, Continuum (New York, NY), 1995, published as *A Dignified Dying: A Plea for Personal Responsibility,* SCM Press (London, England), 1995.

Weltethos f'r Weltpolitik und Weltwirtschaft, R. Piper (Munich, Germany), 1997, translation by John Bowden published as *A Global Ethic for Global Politics and Economics,* Oxford University Press (New York, NY), 1998.

The Catholic Church: A Short History, translated by John Bowden, Modern Library (New York, NY), 2001.

Die Frau im Christentum, R. Piper (Munich, Germany), 2001.

Erkämpfte Freiheit: Erinnerungen, R. Piper (Munich, Germany), 2002.

Tracing the Way: Spiritual Dimensions of the World Religions, translated by John Bowden, Continuum (New York, NY), 2002.

Wozu Weltethos? Religion und Ethik in Zeiten der Globalisierung, Herder (Freiburg, Germany), 2002.

My Struggle for Freedom: Memoirs, translated by John Bowden, William B. Eerdmans Publishing (Grand Rapids, MI), 2003.

Shorter works include "Gottesdienst, warum?," Benziger (Einsiedeln, Switzerland), 1976. Contributor to books, including *Begegnung der Christen: Festschrift O. Karrer,* edited by Maxmilian Rösle and Oscar Cullman, Evangelisches Verlagswerk (Stuttgart, Germany), 1959, translation edited by D. J. Callahan, Heiko A. Oberman, and Daniel O'Hanlon published as *Christianity Divided: Protestant and Catholic Theological Issues,* Sheed & Ward (New York, NY), 1961; *Einsicht und Glaube: Festschrift G. Söhngen,* edited by Joseph Ratzinger and Heinrich Fries, Herder (Freiberg im Breisgau, Germany), 1962; *Looking toward the Council: An Inquiry among Christians,* Herder (Freiberg im Breisgau, Germany), 1962; and *Freedom and Man,* edited by John Courtney Murray, P. J. Kenedy (New York, NY), 1965. Contributor of more than 500 articles to periodicals in Germany, Switzerland, the Netherlands, England, and the United States, including *Cross Currents, Sign, Catholic Digest, Sunday Visitor, New York Times, Commonweal, Christian Century, Irish Times, Journal for the Study of Christian Culture,* and *Critic.*

Some of Küng's writings have been translated into French and Chinese.

EDITOR

(With Yves Congar and Daniel O'Hanlon) *Konzilsreden,* Benziger (Einsiedeln, Switzerland), 1964, translation published as *Council Speeches of Vatican II,* Paulist Press (Glen Rock, NJ), 1964.

(And contributor) *The Church and Ecumenism,* Paulist Press (New York, NY), 1965.

Do We Know the Others?, Paulist Press (New York, NY), 1966.

(And author of preface) *The Sacraments: An Ecumenical Dilemma,* Paulist Press (New York, NY), 1967.

(And author of preface) *The Unknown God?* (translation of *Are We Searching for God?* by Joseph Möller, *The God of the Beginnings and of Today* by Herbert Haag, and *Encounter with God* by Gotthold Hasenhüttl; originally published separately in German), Sheed & Ward (New York, NY), 1967.

(And contributor) *Apostolic Succession: Rethinking a Barrier to Unity,* Paulist Press (New York, NY), 1968.

(And author of preface) *Life in the Spirit* (translation of volumes by Karl H. Schelkle, Thomas A. Sartory, and Michael Pfliegler originally published separately in German), Sheed & Ward (New York, NY), 1968.

The Future of Ecumenism, Paulist Press (New York, NY), 1969.

Post-Ecumenical Christianity, Herder (New York, NY), 1970.

Papal Ministry in the Church, Herder (New York, NY), 1971, published as *The Petrine Ministry in the Church,* Burns & Oates (London, England), 1971.

(With Walter Kasper) *The Plurality of Ministries,* Herder (New York, NY), 1972.

(With Walter Kasper) *Polarization in the Church,* Herder (New York, NY), 1973.

Fehlbar? Eine Bilanz, Benziger (Zurich, Switzerland), 1973.

(With Walter Kasper) *Christians and Jews,* Seabury Press (New York, NY), 1974.

(With David Tracy and Johann B. Metz) *Toward Vatican III: The Work That Needs to Be Done,* Seabury Press (New York, NY), 1978.

(With Jürgen Moltmann) *Why Did God Make Me?,* Seabury Press (New York, NY), 1978.

(With Jürgen Moltmann) *An Ecumenical Confession of Faith?,* Seabury Press (New York, NY), 1979.

(With Jürgen Moltmann) *Conflicts about the Holy Spirit,* Seabury Press (New York, NY), 1979.

(With Jürgen Moltmann) *Conflicting Ways of Interpreting the Bible,* Seabury Press (New York, NY), 1980.

(With Jürgen Moltmann) *Who Has the Say in the Church?,* Seabury Press (New York, NY), 1981.

(With Jürgen Moltmann) *The Right to Dissent,* Seabury Press (New York, NY), 1982.

(With Jürgen Moltmann) *Mary in the Churches,* Seabury Press (New York, NY), 1983.

(With Jürgen Moltmann) *Christianity among World Religions,* T. & T. Clark (Edinburgh, Scotland), 1986.

(With Leonard Swidler) *The Church in Anguish: Has the Vatican Betrayed Vatican II?,* Harper (New York, NY), 1987.

(With Jürgen Moltmann) *A Council for Peace,* T. & T. Clark (Edinburgh, Scotland), 1988.

(With David Tracy) *Paradigm Change in Theology,* two volumes (originally published as *Theologie—Wohin?* and *Das Neue Paradigma von Theologie*), translated by Margaret Kohl, Crossroad (New York, NY), 1989.

(With Jürgen Moltmann) *The Ethics of World Religions and Human Rights,* Trinity Press International (Philadelphia, PA), 1990.

(With Jürgen Moltmann) *Fundamentalism As an Ecumenical Challenge,* SCM Press (London, England), 1992.

(With Karl-Josef Kuschel) *Weltfrieden durch Religionsfrieden: Antworten aus den Weltreligionen,* R. Piper (Munich, Germany), 1993.

(With Karl-Josef Kuschel) *A Global Ethic: The Declaration of the Parliament of the World's Religions,* special edition, Continuum (New York, NY), 1993.

(With Jürgen Moltmann) *Islam: A Challenge for Christianity,* Orbis Books (Maryknoll, NY), 1994.

(And author of preface) *Ja zum Weltethos: Perspektiven für die Suche nach Orientierung,* R. Piper (Munich, Germany), 1995, translation published as *Yes to a Global Ethic: Voices from Religion and Politics,* Continuum (New York, NY), 1996.

(With Karl-Josef Kuschel) *Wissenschaft und Weltethos,* R. Piper (Munich, Germany), 1998.

(With H. Schmidt) *A Global Ethic and Global Responsibilities: Two Declarations,* SCM Press (London, England), 1998.

(With Berthold Leibinger and Werner Spies) *Auf sicherem Fundament: Festschrift für Erwin Teufel,* Deutsche Verlags-Anstalt (Stuttgart, Germany), 1999.

(With Dieter Senghaas) *Friedenspolitik: ethische Grundlagen internationaler Beziehungen,* R. Piper (Munich, Germany), 2003.

Editor of the series "Theologische Meditationen," Benziger (Einsiedeln, Switzerland), beginning 1964, and "Concilium"; coeditor of the series "Ökumenische Forschungen," Herder (Einsiedeln, Switzerland), and "Ökumenische Theologie." Associate editor, *Tübinger Theologische Quartalschrift,* 1960-80, *Journal of Ecumenical Studies,* beginning 1964, and *Revue Internationale de Theologie Concilium,* beginning 1965; member of editorial board, *Buddhist-Christian Studies,* 1987—, *Currents of Encounter: Studies on the Contact between Christianity and Other Religions, Beliefs, and Cultures,* 1988—, *Journal of Religious Pluralism,* 1989—, *Christian Culture Review,* 1990—, and *International Journal for Philosophy of Religion,* 1991—; member of executive editorial committee, *Concilium.*

SIDELIGHTS: Swiss-born theologian Hans Küng is credited with modernizing the outlook of the Roman Catholic Church from a rigidly anti-Protestantism viewpoint that grew out of the historic Council of Trent (1545) to the far more liberal one reflected by the standards established in Vatican Council II, called by Pope John XXIII in 1962. Over a span of more than four decades, Küng has advanced from his initial study of Roman Catholic institutions, through an examination of the basic tenets of Catholicism, to directly addressing the question of whether or not God exists. His work became well known on an international level during the 1960s, due to his extensive lecturing and wide-ranging travel. Among Küng's numerous works, many of which have been translated into English, are *Unfehlbar? Eine anfrage, Ewiges Leben?,* and *Ja zum Weltethos: Perspektiven für die Suche nach Orientierung,* a collection of essays that he edited in 1996.

Küng's quest for greater freedom within the strictures of the Catholic Church underlies much of his work, including his *magnum opus, Christ sein.* In the theologian's first book, *Rechtfertigung: die Lehre Karl Barths und eine katholische Besinnung,* Küng attempts to reconcile the beliefs of noted Protestant theologian Karl Barth with Roman Catholicism with regards to grace, or "justification"—the means by which an individual is ultimately reconciled with God—one of the most-divisive issues of the Reformation. Showing that modern Protestantism as outlined by Barth is an outgrowth of centuries of modifications, the author concludes that "there is a fundamental agreement between Karl Barth's position and that of the Catholic Church seen in its totality."

In *Unfehlbar? Eine anfrage,* Küng delves deeper into the workings of the modern Church and traces the roots of a belief held by many Catholics for centuries: that in regard to major pronouncements, the pope cannot err. Citing numerous instances of papal error, Küng contends that the Church and, by extension, the pope, are human and capable of making mistakes; only God is infallible. While papal infallibility was dogmatized by the First Vatican Council's designation of the pope as "Vice-God of Man" in 1870, it began quietly to be questioned in the years following. Küng's purpose in publishing his work was to openly articulate that questioning and argue for the repudiation of the century-old dogma. While *Commonweal* reviewer Gregory Baum took issue with the author over what he termed Küng's "vehement, though brilliant polemical style" and the theologian's unwillingness to concede that though mistakes were made throughout history, many were later corrected, Martin E. Martin praised the work as "a reverent book by a disappointed man who urges that Catholicism live not by the propositions of the church but by Christ's gospel," in his review of *Infallible* for the *New York Times Book Review.*

In *Ewiges Leben?,* Küng focuses on man's quest for eternal life through faith. Divided into three sections, the volume presents the problem, outlines the history of philosophical thought on the subject of eternal life, and then examines the manner in which several different religious traditions attempt to come to terms with it.

Once again taking the role of religious arbitrator, Küng attempts to bridge theological gaps between Christians and Jews in *Das Judentum.* Ranging from a study of the Jewish Jesus to the Catholic Church's relentless persecution of the Jews throughout history, Küng confronts the issues dividing two of the world's major religions. Again the scholar divides his work into three sections: the history of Judaism, from its tribal beginnings through its modern incarnation—what Küng sees as assimilation into Christian-dominated cultures; contemporary issues such as Christians' post-Holocaust guilt, and the problems surrounding the establishment of the modern state of Israel; and a conclusion that predicts the future course of Judaism. While the 753-page volume was praised by several critics for what a *Choice* reviewer deemed "a major work," *Commonweal* critics Eugene Fisher and Jack Bemporad took issue with Küng, citing the theologian's "needlessly harsh rhetoric" with regard to the Jewish people and his lack of scholarship in presenting such a broad topic. "Küng's aim may simply have exceeded his reach," the reviewers maintained, adding that although the project may have been "well intentioned," "Jewish readers—with good cause—are likely to find this volume, which purports after all to present *their* faith and *their* traditions, to be insensitive and inaccurate."

Despite his early fame and mainstream acceptance as a theological scholar—Küng served as an advisor to the Second Vatican Council—his increasingly unconventional views resulted in restrictions being placed on his teaching position at the University of Tübingen after he was censored by the Vatican in 1980. However, he remains an influential voice in Roman Catholic circles, and his works continue to be widely read. Because of demand for his work, many of Küng's essays for German publications have been collected and translated into English, including *Theology for the Third Millennium: An Ecumenical View,* containing works dating from the 1960s through the 1980s. Readers of this collection can clearly discern the evolution of Küng's thought during his controversial career, as he seeks to create a new paradigm with regard to the way Roman Catholics will view the Church in the coming thousand years. While his theology continues to be considered radical—even heretical—in some circles, Küng maintains a deep loyalty to the Christian foundations of his faith, a loyalty shared by many progressive and liberal-minded Roman Catholics.

BIOGRAPHICAL AND CRITICAL SOURCES:

BOOKS

Anatharackal, T., *Towards a Theocentric Normative Christology: A Critical Analysis of the Christologi-*

cal Project of Hans Küng within the Framework of the Theology of Religions, Catholic University of Louvain (Louvain, Belgium), 2002.

Becker, Rolf, *Hans Küng und die Ökumene: evanglische Katholizität als Modell,* Matthias-Grünewald-Verlag (Mainz, Germany), 1996.

Duggan, G. H., *Hans Küng and Reunion,* Newman Press (Mahwah, NJ), 1964.

Eingel, U. and Walter Jens, *Um nichts als die Wahrheit,* R. Piper (Munich, Germany), 1978.

Greinacher, Norbert and Herbert Haag, editors, *Der Fall Küng: e. Dokumentation,* R. Piper (Munich, Germany), 1980.

Häring, Hermann and J. Nolte, *Diskussion um Hans Küng "Die Kirche,"* [Vienna, Austria], 1971.

Häring, Hermann and Karl-Joseph Kuschel, editors, *Hans Küng: Weg und Werk,* R. Piper (Munich, Germany), 1978, translation by Robert Nowell published as *Hans Küng: His Work and His Way,* Fount Paperbacks (London, England), 1979.

Häring, Hermann and Karl-Joseph Kuschel, editors, *Hans Küng: New Horizons for Faith and Thought,* Continuum (New York, NY), 1993.

Häring, Hermann, *Hans Küng: Breaking Through,* SCM Press (London, England), 1998.

Hinsdale, Mary Ann, *Hans Küng's Use of Scripture: Theological, Hermeneutical, and Socio-Critical Perspectives,* Peter Lang (New York, NY), 1996.

Jens, Walter, *Literature & Religion,* translated from the German by Peter Heinegg, Paragon House (New York, NY), 1991.

Jens, Walter and Karl-Josef Kuschel, *Dialog mit Hans Küng,* R. Piper (Munich, Germany), 1996, translation published as *Dialogue with Hans Küng,* SCM Press (London, England), 1997.

Kiwiet, John, *Hans Küng,* Word Books (Waco, TX), 1985.

Küng, Hans, *Rechtfertigung: die Lehre Karl Barths und eine katholische Besinnung,* Johannes Verlag (Einsiedeln, Switzerland), 1957, 4th enlarged edition, 1964, translation by Thomas Collins, Edmund E. Tolk, and David Granskou published as *Justification: The Doctrine of Karl Barth and a Catholic Reflection,* Thomas Nelson (New York, NY), 1964, published with a letter from Karl Barth, Burns & Oates (London, England), 1966, 40th anniversary edition with new foreword by Hermann Häring, Westminster John Knox Press (Louisville, KY), 2003.

Küng, Hans, *My Struggle for Freedom: Memoirs,* translated by John Bowden, William B. Eerdmans Publishing (Grand Rapids, MI), 2003.

Nowell, Robert, *A Passion for Truth: Hans Küng and His Theology,* Crossroad (New York, NY), 1981.

Rebeiro, Manual, *The Church As the Community of the Believers: Hans Küng's Concept of the Church As a Proposal for an Ecumenical Ecclesiology,* Volumes 1-2, Intercultural Publications (New Delhi, India), 2001.

Robinson, Donald, *The 100 Most Important People in the World Today,* Putnam (New York, NY), 1970.

Swidler, Leonard, *Küng in Conflict,* Doubleday (Garden City, NY), 1981.

PERIODICALS

America, October 19, 1963; May 22, 1965; April 20, 1968; November 20, 1976; September 22, 1979; July 19-26, 1980; March 25, 1989, p. 274; April 22, 1989, p. 374; April 14, 1990, p. 384; October 31, 1992, p. 332; October 21, 1995, p. 23.

Best Sellers, April 15, 1971; July 1, 1972; April, 1977; July, 1978; September, 1979.

Choice, October, 1992, review of *Das Judentum,* p. 318.

Christian Century, September 1, 1965; June 1, 1966; September 11, 1968; May 19, 1971; March 2, 1977; November 24, 1978; September 24, 1980; September 12, 1984, pp. 842-843; January 4, 1989, p. 21; March 15, 1989, p. 290; March 7, 1990, p. 254; May 29, 1991, p. 599; October 16, 1991, p. 945; March 17, 1993, p. 299; March 2, 1994, p. 231; May 18, 1994, p. 530; December 20, 1995, p. 1250.

Commonweal, July 5, 1963; August 7, 1964; February 5, 1965; May 6, 1966; February 28, 1969; April 9, 1971, Gregory Baum, review of *Unfehlbar? Eine anfrage,* pp. 103-105; August 25, 1972; May 23, 1975; December 3, 1976; March 4, 1977; June 24, 1977; March 3, 1978; February 29, 1980; May 9, 1980; November 7, 1980; January 29, Eugene Fisher and Jack Bemporad, review of *Das Judentum,* 1993, pp. 29-30; April 7, 1995, p. 29; December 15, 1995, p. 22.

Critic, October, 1963; December, 1964-January, 1965; April, 1965; June, 1966; June, 1968; December, 1968; July, 1971; spring, 1977; October, 1979; October, 1980; November, 1980.

Detroit Free Press, September 25, 1983.

Economist, January 22, 1977; April 20, 1991, p. 89.

Los Angeles Times, November 14, 1980.

Los Angeles Times Book Review, January 4, 1987; July 29, 1987.

National Catholic Reporter, September 24, 1993, p. 11.

National Review, May 3, 1966; July 23, 1990, p. 45.

New Perspectives Quarterly, spring, 1991, p. 44.

New Republic, May 15, 1971; July 21, 1979; July 28, 1979; November 8, 1980.

New Statesman, January 16, 1981.

Newsweek, January 25, 1971; July 16, 1973; December 6, 1976; July 8, 1991, B. Ivry, "The Christian Thing to Do"; August 12, 1996, "New Rules to Live By," p. 54.

New Yorker, February 7, 1977.

New York Review of Books, May 15, 1968, p. 16; August 22, 1968; February 7, 1980.

New York Times, June 11, 1967; February 8, 1980.

New York Times Book Review, October 27, 1963; March 7, 1965; May 5, 1968; April 4, 1971, Martin E. Martin, review of *Unfehlbar?,* p. 6; September 17, 1972; December 19, 1976; July 22, 1979; January 11, 1981; April 19, 1981; May 6, 1984.

New York Times Magazine, October 12, 1975.

Observer, January 16, 1977.

Publishers Weekly, September 26, 1980; October 5, 1990, p. 85; October 26, 1990, p. 60; March 9, 1992, p. 44; April 11, 1994, p. 30; June 12, 1995, p. 28; April, 22, 1996, p. 65.

Saturday Review, June 9, 1962; December 21, 1963; March 29, 1969; April 10, 1971.

Spectator, January 22, 1977.

Third Way: The Modern World through Christian Eyes, Volume 24, number 1, 2001, R. McCloughry, "Thinking Big," pp. 18-21.

Time, July 8, 1962; September 20, 1963; February 23, 1968; July 16, 1973; March 3, 1975; January 3, 1977.

Times (London, England), January 8, 1987.

Times Literary Supplement, October 21, 1965; August 25, 1966; August 1, 1968; November 21, 1980; September 25, 1987.

Washington Post Book World, November 28, 1976.

ONLINE

Stiftung Weltethos für interkulturelle und interreligiöse Forschung, Bildung und Begegnung, http://www.uni-tuebingen.de/stiftung-weltethos/ (March 17, 2004).

KUTTNER, Robert (Louis) 1943-

PERSONAL: Born April 17, 1943, in New York, NY; son of Arthur Paul Kuttner and Pauline M. Levy; married Sharland Grace Trotter (a psychologist and author), December 19, 1971 (deceased, 1997); married Joan Fitzgerald, May 7, 2000; children: (first marriage) Gabriel A., Jessica A. *Education:* Oberlin College, A.B., 1965; University of California, Berkeley, M.A., 1966; London School of Economics, certification, 1963-64. *Hobbies and other interests:* Tennis, photography, writing poetry.

ADDRESSES: Office—American Prospect, 5 Broad St., Boston, MA 02109-2901. *E-mail*—kuttner@prospect.org.

CAREER: Pacifica Radio, correspondent and program director, New York, NY, 1968-71; Village Voice, Washington, DC, editor, 1971-1973; *Washington Post,* Washington, DC, national staff writer, 1974-75; U.S. Senate Committee on Banking, Housing, and Urban Affairs, Washington, DC, chief investigator, 1975-1978; *Working Papers,* MA, editor, 1980-83; *New Republic,* economics writer and editor, 1983-1991; *Business Week,* columnist, 1984; *Boston Globe,* Boston, MA, and *Washington Post Syndicate,* Washington, DC, columnist, 1985—; *American Prospect: A Journal for the Liberal Imagination,* founder and coeditor, c. 1989—; *Village Voice,* New York, NY, editor, Washington, DC; *Working Papers for a New Society,* editor-in-chief; *New Republic,* economics editor; *Business Week,* contributing columnist; also worked as a syndicated columnist. Has worked in noncommercial radio and television in California, including KQED-TV, San Francisco, CA; visiting professor at Boston University, 1980-82, and Brandeis University, 1991-1992, 2003, both Boston, MA, University of Massachusetts, 1987-88, and Harvard University's John F. Kennedy Institute of Politics, Cambridge, MA. Served as assistant to I. F. Stone, Washington, DC, 1966; legal assistant to Congressman W. F. Ryan, Washington, DC, 1967-68; the executive director of U.S. president Jimmy Carter's National Commission on Neighborhoods, 1978, founder and board member of the Economic Policy Institute, 1986, member of the board of directors of Families USA, Boston, MA, 1989-96, and Florence Fund, 1999. Has made appearances on National Public Radio (NPR), and on television programs, including *Firing Line,* syndicated and Public Broadcasting Systems (PBS), *Crossfire,* Cable Network News (CNN), *American Broadcasting Co. (ABC) News Nightline,* ABC, and *The NewsHour with Jim Lehrer,* PBS.

MEMBER: National Academy of Social Institutions.

AWARDS, HONORS: Woodrow Wilson fellow, University of California, 1965-66; Paul Hoffman award, UN Development Program, 1966; Kennedy fellow, Harvard University, 1979; Jack London award for labor journalism, United Steelworkers of America, 1982; John Hancock Award for excellence in business and financial journalism, 1988; Sidney Hillman award, Sidney Hillman Foundation, 1998; fellow, McCormack Institute, 1978-1988, John Guggenheim Memorial Foundation, 1988, Radcliffe Public Policy Center, 1988-2000; L.L. D., Swarthmore College, 1999

WRITINGS:

Revolt of the Haves: Tax Rebellions and Hard Times, Simon & Schuster (New York, NY), 1980.

The Economic Illusion: False Choices between Prosperity and Social Justice, Houghton Mifflin (Boston, MA), 1984.

The Life of the Party: Democratic Prospects in 1988 and Beyond, Viking (New York, NY), 1987.

Managed Trade and Economic Sovereignty, Economic Policy Institute (Washington, DC), 1989.

Export Controls: Industrial Policy in Reverse, Economic Policy Institute (Washington, DC), 1991.

The End of Laissez Faire: National Purpose and the Global Economy after the Cold War, Knopf (New York, NY), 1991.

(Editor) *Ticking Time Bombs: The New Conservative Assaults on Democracy,* New Press (New York, NY), 1996.

Everything for Sale: The Virtues and Limits of Markets, Knopf (New York, NY), 1997.

(Editor) *Making Work Pay: America after Welfare,* Free Press (New York, NY), 2002.

(With wife, Sharland Trotter) *Family Re-Union: Reconnecting Parents and Children in Adulthood,* Free Press (New York, NY), 2002.

Contributing editor, *More,* Washington, DC, 1973-78. Also contributor of articles to periodicals, including the *American Prospect: A Journal for the Liberal*

Imagination, Atlantic Monthly, Boston Globe, Business Week, Dissent, Harvard Business Review, New Republic, New Yorker, New York Times Magazine, Village Voice, Washington Post, and *Working Papers for a New Society.*

SIDELIGHTS: Columnist, editor and commentator Robert Kuttner is one of the most prominent advocates of a liberal vision for American politics. According to *Washington Post Book World* critic James K. Glassman, "In the first one hundred pages of *Revolt of the Haves,* Robert Kuttner tells the entertaining tale of the passage of Proposition 13, the California initiative that cut the state's property taxes by six billion dollars." Kuttner then goes on to discuss subsequent tax initiatives in states such as Michigan and Idaho, but, unlike many contemporary pundits, argues that tax revolts like these initiatives are not part of a conservative, antigovernment trend but rather a protest that the wrong people—i.e., the working and middle classes—are bearing a tax burden which should be reserved for the wealthy and large corporations. Glassman described *Revolt of the Haves* as "a call to arms for liberals to lead the tax revolt." Though the critic did not agree completely with the author's analysis of the situation, he felt Kuttner "presents his case lucidly." Though Jack Clark in *Commonweal* noted that "something remains unsatisfying in Kuttner's conclusion" in *Revolt of the Haves,* he nevertheless remarked that the author "meticulously analyzes the welfare state, American-style, and concludes, correctly in my view, that its purposes are structurally undermined by subservience to the corporate rich."

In *The Economic Illusion: False Choices between Prosperity and Social Justice,* Kuttner argues that economic prosperity is best achieved through government guidance of business rather than through a free market policy with as few legal strictures upon it as possible. In Kuttner's words, "Societies with strong unions and highly refined social bargaining machinery do a much better job of maintaining full employment, promoting distributive justice, reconciling technological progress with social needs, and moderating inflation." A *Booklist* contributor labeled *The Economic Illusion* "an effectively stimulating volume in the equity-efficiency debate." Putting these things into more partisan terms, J. Holton Wilson in the *Library Journal* concluded that "liberals will find much to their liking in this work; conservatives will find little."

The Life of the Party: Democratic Prospects in 1988 and Beyond is Kuttner's attempt to steer the Democratic party back to its traditional roots. In the book, he expresses the opinion that rather than becoming more conservative to compete with the popular Reagan-era Republicans, Democrats should adopt what A. D. McNitt in *Choice* described as "a program that would emphasize economic reforms and social programs designed to benefit the broadest possible segment of society." To make such a program work, Kuttner claims the government "would have to combine our several disparate programs, each with its own bureaucracy, into a functioning, coherent system, with a clear set of goals." Though Eric B. Schnurer in the *Los Angeles Times Book Review* noted that Kuttner "spends the entire book attacking reliance on market solutions, failing to differentiate between the laissez faire of Reagannomics and progressive market regulating," he described *The Life of the Party* as "by far the best discussion that I have read in years of both the substance and politics of the Democratic Party's future."

The End of Laissez Faire presents Kuttner's theory that during the Cold War, the United States preached the doctrine of free market capitalism but involved a great deal of its national economy in military-related production in order to win the arms race against the then-Soviet Union. Kuttner asserts that since the Cold War has ended, the United States would do well to abandon even the pretense of belief in free markets in favor of adopting a national economic policy guided by the government. He also recommends developing a global defense alliance rather than having the United States shoulder most of the burden of policing international affairs. A *Publishers Weekly* reviewer wrote that "this closely argued book administers a potent dose of economic reality." *Washington Post Book World* critic Robert Skidelsky, however, was not so sure that Kuttner's proposed solutions would work. "The thesis is compelling," he stated, "but the question remains: Can a national ideology and government institutions fashioned for hegemony adapt to a non-hegemonic world?"

Kuttner edited *Ticking Time Bombs: The New Conservative Assaults on Democracy* in 1996. The pieces within the volume are reprinted from the *American Prospect,* the publication Kuttner helped to found. Contributing essayists include Robert Putnam, Theda Skocpol, Lester Thurow, Louis Lowenstein, Stanley Greenberg, and Marshall Ganz; these writers and others discuss topics such as the impact of money on

politics and voter apathy. *Booklist* reviewer Mary Carroll described *Ticking Time Bombs* as a "lively collection of articles."

Kuttner returns to the task of arguing against a free-market economy in his 1997 volume, *Everything for Sale.* According to a *Publishers Weekly* contributor, the author maintains that "market norms drive out nonmarket norms such as civility, commitment to the public good, personal economic security, and liberty." According to other reviewers, Kuttner takes a more moderate view than he has in the past. As *Washington Post Book World* contributor Suzanne Garment observed, Kuttner writes that "America's choice has been not between capitalism and socialism but between a mixed economy and unfettered laissez faire." *Library Journal* contributor Steven J. Mayover praised *Everything for Sale* as a "thorough, scholarly approach to current economics relative to the political scene."

In 2002 Kuttner published two books. He edited *Making Work Pay: America after Welfare.* As the subtitle suggests, the volume contains essays by several authors on how various aspects of the welfare system in the United States have evolved since the large scale policy changes that took place during the administration of U.S. President William Jefferson Clinton. Kuttner also collaborated on a more personal project, however, with his late wife, Sharland Trotter. Before her death late in 1997, the couple penned most of *Family Re-Union: Reconnecting Parents and Children in Adulthood.* The book draws on both authors' personal experiences as parents and as adult children of their own parents, as well as Trotter's expertise as a psychologist. *Family Re-Union* also includes a discussion of how Trotter's diagnosis with and subsequent death from cancer affected the lives of her adult children.

BIOGRAPHICAL AND CRITICAL SOURCES:

BOOKS

Kuttner, Robert, *The Economic Illusion: False Choices between Prosperity and Social Justice,* Houghton Mifflin (Boston, MA), 1984.
Kuttner, Robert, *The Life of the Party: Democratic Prospects in 1988 and Beyond,* Viking (New York, NY), 1987.

PERIODICALS

American Political Science Review, summer, 1998, review of *The Life of the Party,* p. 991.

Annals of the American Academy of Political and Social Science, November, 1998, review of *The Life of the Party,* p. 151.

Booklist, November 15, 1984, review of *The Economic Illusion,* pp. 404, 406; January 4, 1987, review of *The Economic Illusion,* p. 12; January 15, 1991, review of *The End of Laissez Faire: National Purpose and the Global Economy after the Cold War,* p. 986; September 1, 1996, p. 43; May 1, 2002, Vanessa Bush, review of *Family Re-Union: Reconnecting Parents and Children in Adulthood,* p. 1486.

Book World, November 9, 1980, review of *Revolt of the Haves: Tax Rebellions and Hard Times,* p. 7; July 10, 1988, review of *The Life of the Party,* p. 12; March 3, 1991, review of *The End of Laissez-Faire,* p. 1; February 2, 1997, review of *Everything for Sale: The Virtues and Limits of Markets,* p. 8.

Business Week, October 21, 1996, p. 19.

Choice, April, 1981, review of *Revolt of the Haves,* p. 1161; March, 1988, review of *The Life of the Party,* p. 1176.

Commonweal, March 27, 1981, review of *Revolt of the Haves,* p. 180; February 12, 1998, review of *The Life of the Party,* p. 89; February 28, 1997, review of *Everything for Sale,* p. 21.

Dissent, spring, 1985, review of *The Economic Illusion,* p. 240; spring, 1988, review of *The Life of the Party,* p. 237; summer, 1991, review of *The End of Laisez-Faire,* p. 432; spring, 1998, review of *Everything for Sale,* p. 97.

Economist, April 13, 1991, review of *The End of Laissez-Faire,* p. 831; February 15, 1997, review of *Everything for Sale,* p. 3.

Journal of Politics, February 1982, review of *Revolt of the Haves,* p. 277.

Kirkus Reviews, September 1, 1980, review of *Revolt of the Haves,* p. 1210; August 1, 1984, review of *The Economic Illusion,* p. 734; October 1, 1987, review of *The Life of the Party,* p. 1438.

Kliatt Young Adult Paperback Book Guide, summer, 1988, review of *The Life of the Party,* p. 40.

Library Journal, October 1, 1980, review of *Revolt of the Haves,* p. 2066; January, 1985, review of *The Economic Illusion,* p. 83; December, 1987, review of *The Life of the Party,* p. 100; October 1, 1990,

p. 124; February 15, 1991, review of *The End of Laissez-Faire,* p. 205; January, 1997, pp. 115-116; March 15, 2002, Pam Matthews, review of *Family Re-Union,* p. 97.

Los Angeles Times Book Review, December 6, 1987, review of *The Life of the Party,* p. 2; March 10, 1991, review of *The End of Laissez-Faire,* p. 8; January 26, 1997, review of *Everything for Sale,* p. 9; December 6, 1987, p. 2.

National Review, May 5, 1997, review of *Everything for Sale,* p. 52.

New Leader, September 17, 1984, review of *The Economic Illusion,* p. 18; December 16, 1996, review of *Everything for Sale,* p. 34.

Newsweek, February 10, 1997, review of *Everything for Sale,* p. 67.

New Yorker, November 19, 1984, review of *The Economic Illusion,* p. 190; May 20, 1991, review of *The End of Laissez-Faire,* p. 108.

New York Review of Books, February 28, 1985, review of *The Economic Illusion,* p. 37; November 7, 1991, review of *The End of Laissez-Faire,* p. 46.

New York Times Book Review, October 19, 1980, review of *Revolt of the Haves,* p. 7; October 21, 1984, review of *The Economic Illusion,* p. 44; November 15, 1987, review of *The Life of the Party,* p. 9; July 10, 1988, review of *The Life of the Party,* p. 32; March 10, 1991, review of *The End of Laissez-Faire,* p. 3; June 9, 1991, review of *The End of Laissez-Faire,* p. 22; January 26, 1997, review of *Everything for Sale,* p. 11.

Progressive, September, 1991, review of *The End of Laissez-Faire,* p. 41; March, 1997, review of *Everything for Sale,* p. 39.

Public Administration Review, May, 1993, review of *The End of Laissez-Faire,* p. 268.

Publishers Weekly, September 19, 1980, review of *Revolt of the Haves,* p. 152; August 17, 1984, review of *The Economic Illusion,* p. 50; October 16, 1987, review of *The Life of the Party,* p. 75; December 21, 1990, review of *The End of Laissez-Faire,* p. 40; November 25, 1996, p. 65; April 15, 2002, review of *Family Re-Union,* p. 57.

Rapport, February, 1997, review of *Everything for Sale,* p. 36.

Reason, June, 1997, review of *Everything for Sale,* p. 56.

Times Literary Supplement, May 31, 1991, review of *The End of Laissez-Faire,* p. 10; November 21, 1997, review of *Everything for Sale,* p. 21.

Wall Street Journal, November 6, 1980, review of *Revolt of the Haves,* p. 32; November 12, 1987, review of *The Life of the Party,* p. 36; April 9, 1991, review of *The End of Laissez-Faire,* p. A20; January 22, 1997, review of *Everything for Sale,* p. A12.

Washington Monthly, October, 1984, review of *The Economic Illusion,* p. 52; March, 1988, review of *The Life of the Party,* p. 48; March, 1991, review of *The End of Laissez-Faire,* p. 59.

Washington Post Book World, November 9, 1980, p. 7; March 3, 1991, pp. 1, 10; February 2, 1997, p. 8.

Wilson Library Journal, October, 1990, pp. 114.

Wilson Quarterly, January, 1985, review of *The Economic Illusion,* p. 150; Volume 2, 1988, review of *The Life of the Party,* p. 145.*

*   *   *

KYLE, Benjamin
  See GOTTFRIED, Theodore Mark

L

LAHIRI, Jhumpa 1967-

PERSONAL: Born 1967, in London, England; daughter of a librarian and a teacher; married Alberto Vourvoulias (a journalist), January 15, 2001; children: Octavio. *Education:* Barnard College, B.A.; Boston University, M.A. (English), M.A. (creative writing), M.A. (comparative literature and the arts), Ph.D. (Renaissance studies).

ADDRESSES: Home—New York, NY. *Agent*—c/o Author Mail, Houghton Mifflin, 222 Berkeley St., Boston, MA 02116-3764.

CAREER: Writer.

AWARDS, HONORS: O. Henry Award, 1999, for "Interpreter of Maladies"; Pulitzer Prize for Fiction, 2000, for *Interpreter of Maladies;* shortlisted for M. F. K. Fisher Distinguished Writing Award, James Beard Foundation, 2001; Transatlantic Review Award, Henfield Foundation; fiction prize, *Louisville Review;* fellow, Fine Arts Work Centre, Provincetown; named one of the twenty best young writers in America by the *New Yorker.*

WRITINGS:

Interpreter of Maladies, Houghton Mifflin (Boston, MA), 1999.
(Author of introduction) Xavier Zimbardo, *India Holy Song* (photography collection), Rizzoli (New York, NY), 2000.
The Namesake, Houghton Mifflin (Boston, MA), 2003.

Jhumpa Lahiri

ADAPTATIONS: "A Temporary Matter," one of the stories from *Interpreter of Maladies,* was adapted for a film directed by Mira Nair.

SIDELIGHTS: London-born writer Jhumpa Lahiri, the daughter of Bengali parents, has spent considerable time with her extended family in Calcutta, India. This locale serves as the setting for three of the nine stories in her debut collection, *Interpreter of Maladies,* which won the Pulitzer Prize for fiction in 2000. The stories in the collection, three of which had already appeared in the *New Yorker,* deal with such themes as marital problems, experiences of Indian immigrants to the United States, and translations of not only language, but experience. *Newsweek* reviewer Laura Shapiro wrote that Lahiri "writes such direct, translucent prose you almost forget you're reading." Caleb Crain wrote in the *New York Times Book Review* that Lahiri's collection "features marriages that have been arranged, rushed into, betrayed, invaded, and exhausted. Her subject is not love's failure, however, but the opportunity that an artful spouse (like an artful writer) can make of failure—the rebirth possible in a relationship when you discover how little of the other person you know. In Lahiri's sympathetic tales, the pang of disappointment turns into a sudden hunger to know more."

The stories in *Interpreter of Maladies* include the title story, which earned an O. Henry Award in 1999, as well as "A Temporary Matter," which was adapted as a film by Indian filmmaker Mira Nair, and "This Blessed House," among others. "This Blessed House" is the story of Indian newlyweds Twinkle and Sanjeev, who are at odds over Twinkle's laid-back habits and her fascination with the Christian knickknacks left by the previous homeowners. They include a Nativity snow globe, a paint-by-number picture of the wise men, and a Virgin Mary lawn ornament. Crain wrote that Lahiri "is not out to convert Hindus here, nor is she indulging in sarcasm at the expense of sincere belief. But not even religion is sacred to her writerly interest in the power of a childlike sympathy, going where it ought not go."

Other stories featured in the collection include "When Mr. Pirzada Came to Dine," the story of ten-year-old Lilia who learns about the politics and hardships of India from a family friend; "Third and Final Continent," which tells of a librarian putting together the basics in his rented room in anticipation of the arrival of his wife; and "Mrs. Sen," the story of a lonely Indian wife trying to make do in the United States. She wears her beautiful saris as she prepares fresh fish which reminds her of her native Calcutta. She is sustained by aerograms from her family, who envy her, and the little boy she cares for, who learns what it's like to be isolated and lonely. In an interview in *Newsweek,* Lahiri told Vibhuti Patel that Mrs. Sen is based on her mother, who babysat in their home. "I saw her one way," she explained, "but imagined that an American child may see her differently, reacting with curiosity, fascination, or fear to the things I took for granted."

Because Lahiri was not born in India, her stories set in India have been criticized by some reviewers as inauthentic and stereotypical. *Time International* reviewer Nisid Hajari wrote that two of the stories set in Calcutta "survive on little more than smoothness. . . . The reader is lulled by Lahiri's rhythmic sentences and, for her Western audiences, no doubt by the Indian setting. Lahiri hits her stride closer to home—on the uncertain ground of the immigrant." Other reviewers, however, have offered Lahiri nothing but praise. A *Publishers Weekly* reviewer wrote, "Lahiri's touch in these nine tales is delicate, but her observations remain damningly accurate, and her bittersweet stories are unhampered by nostalgia." Hajari, too, offered praise, saying, "The whole is assured and powerful, and it is perhaps not too harsh a criticism to say that readers should look forward to Lahiri's second book." Prema Srinivasan, writing for *Hindu,* called *Interpreter of Maladies* "eminently readable," and noted that its author "talks about universal maladies in detail, with a touch of humour and sometimes with irony which is never misplaced." In a *New York Times Book Review* article, Michiko Kakutani called *Interpreter of Maladies* an "accomplished collection. . . . Ms. Lahiri chronicles her characters' lives with both objectivity and compassion while charting the emotional temperature of their lives with tactile precision. She is a writer of uncommon elegance and poise, and with *Interpreter of Maladies* she has made a precocious debut."

Lahiri's much-praised debut into the world of fiction led to a lot of speculation surrounding the appearance of her second effort, a novel titled *The Namesake. The Namesake* deals with identity, the importance of names, and the effect the immigrant experience has on family ties. Gogol Ganguli finds himself saddled with a pet name, rather than a proper Bengali first name. Since he does not find out the significance of his name and its connection to a major incident in his father's life until he is older, the name seems empty to him. Gogol too feels somehow incomplete, and this feeling adds to his confusion and insecurity as an outsider trapped between two cultures: that of India, his parents' homeland, and that of the United States, his country of birth. While Gogol's parents followed the conventions of an arranged marriage, their son does not hold his family's cultural heritage in that high a regard, and wants more than his parents seem to have. Gogol's inner turmoil is also reflected in his unsuccessful romantic relationships. It is not until Lahiri's dissatisfied young protagonist comes to understand who his parents are that things begin to come together for him.

A contributor to *Time* magazine praised Lahiri's *The Namesake* as "delicate, moving," as did *Women's Review of Books* critic Mendira Sen, who wrote that this "beautifully crafted and elegantly written novel will speak to many." In the *Antioch Review,* Ed Peaco noted that, despite the lack of action on the part of the novel's fictional protagonist, "Lahiri's delicate details and soft rhetorical touch create an absorbing reading experience in which characters become friends in the sense that we can rely on them for wit, insight, and affirmation." Praising the author for her "spare, lyrical prose," *Herizons* contributor Irene D'Souza added that *The Namesake* is a "wondrous, gentle book" whose major strength is that it "demystifies a culture that often finds itself at odds with the majority."

BIOGRAPHICAL AND CRITICAL SOURCES:

PERIODICALS

Antioch Review, summer, 2004, Ed Peaco, review of *The Namesake,* p. 581.
Book, September-October, 2003, pp. 52, 77.
Booklist, June 1, 2003, Donna Seaman, review of *The Namesake,* p. 123; November 15, 2003, Donna Seaman, "Voices of India," p. 574.
Entertainment Weekly, April 28, 2000, p. 100; September 19, 2003, Gregory Kirschling, review of *The Namesake,* p. 40; September 19, 2003, Jennifer Reese, "A Name to Remember," p. 88.
Esquire, October, 2000, Sean Flynn, "Jhumpa Lahiri," p. 172.
Explicator, summer, 2001, Simon Lewis, review of *Interpreter of Maladies,* p. 219; winter, 2004, Jennifer Bess, review of *Interpreter of Maladies,* p. 125.
Herizons, summer, 2001, Irene D'Souza, review of *Interpreter of Maladies,* p. 32; summer, 2004, Irene D'Souza, review of *The Namesake,* p. 36.

Hindu, April 12, 2000, "Pulitzer for Jhumpa Lahiri"; February 5, 2001, "Beyond Bengal and Boston."
Kenyon Review, summer, 2004, David H. Lynn, "Virtue of Ambition," p. 160.
Kirkus Reviews, June 1, 2003, review of *The Namesake,* p. 773.
Library Journal, July, 2003, Starr E. Smith, review of *The Namesake,* p. 123.
Nation, October 23, 2004, David Bromwich, "The Man without Qualities," p. 36.
New Leader, September-October, 2003, Benjamin Austen, "In the Shadow of Gogol," p. 86.
Newsweek, July 19, 1999, Laura Shapiro, "India Calling: The Diaspora's New Star," p. 67; August 25, 2003, Barbara Kantrowitz, review of *The Namesake,* p. 61.
Newsweek International, September 20, 1999, Vibhuti Patel, "Maladies of Belonging."
New York Times, April 11, 2000, Felicity Barringer, "Author's First Book Wins Pulitzer for Fiction"; September 28, 2003, Stephen Metcalf, "Out of the Overcoat," p. 11.
New York Times Book Review, July 11, 1999, p. 11; August 6, 1999.
Publishers Weekly, April 19, 1999, review of *Interpreter of Maladies,* p. 59; July 26, 1999, p. 20; July 7, 2003, Edward Nawotka, interview with Lahiri, p. 49; September 15, 2003, Daisy Maryles, "See Jhumpa Jump," p. 17.
Spectator, January 17, 2004, Lee Langley, "Cola versus Curry," p. 39.
Time International, September 13, 1999, Nisid Hajari, "The Promising Land," p. 49.
Times of India, April 16, 2000, Ratnottama Sengupta, "Mira Nair to Film Jhumpa Lahiri Story."
Town and Country, January, 2004, p. 55.
Washington Post Book World, September 14, 2003, Christopher Tilghman, review of *The Namesake,* p. 10.
Women's Review of Books, March, 2004, Mendira Sen, "Names and Nicknames," p. 9.
World and I, January, 2004, Linda Simon, review of *The Namesake,* p. 230.

ONLINE

Bookbrowse.com, http://www.bookbrowse.com/ (August 3, 2004), "A Conversation with Jhumpa Lahiri."

Houghton Mifflin Web site, http://www.houghton mifflinbooks.com/ (August 3, 2004).

PBS Web site, http://www.pbs.org/ (August 3, 2004), Elizabeth Farnsworth, interview with Lahiri.

PIF Magazine Online, http;//www.pif.com/ (August 3, 2004), Arun Aguiar, interview with Lahiri.*

*   *   *

LAVERY, David 1949-

PERSONAL: Born August 27, 1949, in Oil City, PA; son of Donald J. (a time clerk) and Martha S. (a homemaker) Lavery; married Joyce Kling (director of the Nashville chapter of the National Conference for Community and Justice), July, 1979; children: Rachel Alden, Sarah Caitlin. *Ethnicity:* "Caucasian." *Education:* Clarion University, B.S., 1971; St. Cloud State University, M.A., 1973; University of Florida, Ph.D., 1978. *Politics:* Liberal Democrat. *Religion:* "Nonpracticing Catholic." *Hobbies and other interests:* Classical music, HTML design.

ADDRESSES: Home—2246 Wiltshire Dr., Murfreesboro, TN 37129. *Office*—Department of English, Middle Tennessee State University, Murfreesboro, TN 37132; fax 615-898-5098. *E-mail*—dlavery@mtsu.edu

CAREER: Educator and author. College of St. Benedict, St. Joseph, MN, instructor in English, 1975-76; University of North Florida, Jacksonville, adjunct assistant professor of English, 1979-80; Seattle University, Seattle, WA, visiting assistant professor of English, 1980-81; East China Normal University, Shanghai, foreign expert in English, 1981; University of Alabama, Huntsville, interim assistant professor of English, 1981-83; Northern Kentucky University, Highland Heights, assistant professor, 1983-88, director of freshman English, 1986-88; University of Memphis, Memphis, TN, associate professor of communication and film studies, 1988-93; Middle Tennessee State University, Murfreesboro, professor of English, 1993—, department head, 1993-97; *Literature/Film Quarterly,* editor, 1993—.

MEMBER: South Atlantic Modern Language Association (secretary, 1986-87), Owen Barfield Society (an affiliate of the Rocky Mountain Modern Language Association; founder, 2003), Rocky Mountain Modern Language Association, Wallace Stevens Society, Popular Culture Association in the South, Tennessee Philological Association, Phi Beta Kappa, Media Ecology Association.

AWARDS, HONORS: Teaching Assistant of the Year, University of Florida, 1978; Teacher of the Year, University of Alabama, Huntsville, 1983; Bronze Award for Independent Video, Worldfest, Houston, 1996, and honorable mention, Columbus International Film and Video Festival, 1996, both for *Owen Barfield: Man and Meaning;* four-time Pushcart Prize nominee; Kraszna-Krausz Book Award nominee for *Full of Secrets: Critical Approaches to Twin Peaks.*

WRITINGS:

Late for the Sky: The Mentality of the Space Age, Southern Illinois University Press (Carbondale, IL), 1992.

(Editor and contributor) *Full of Secrets: Critical Approaches to "Twin Peaks,"* Wayne State University Press (Detroit, MI), 1994.

(Editor, with Angela Hague and Marla Cartwright, and contributor) *Deny All Knowledge: Reading "The X-Files,"* Syracuse University Press (Syracuse, NY), 1996.

(Editor, with Rhonda V. Wilcox, and contributor) *Fighting the Forces: What's at Stake in Buffy the Vampire Slayer,* Rowman & Littlefield (Lanham, MD), 2002.

(Editor and contributor) *This Thing of Ours: Investigating the Sopranos,* Columbia University Press (New York, NY), 2002.

(Editor, with Angela Hague) *Teleparody: Predicting/ Preventing the TV Discourse of Tomorrow,* Wallflower Press (London, England), 2002.

Re-Weaving the Rainbow: The Thought of Owen Barfield, Galda & Wilch Verlag (Cambridge, MA), 2003.

How to Gut a Book: Essay on Imagination and the Evolution of Consciousness (e-book), iUniverse. com, 2004.

The Encyclopedia of Native American Literature, edited by R. Velie and Jennifer McClinton-Temple, Facts on File (New York, NY), 2005.

Investigating Angel, edited by Stacey Abbott, I. B. Tauris (London, England), 2005.

Nineteenth-Century American Fiction on Screen: An Anthology of Critical Essays, edited by R. Barton Palmer, Cambridge University Press (New York, NY), 2005.

Also editor of *Post Script: Essays in Film and the Humanities* series (1987) and coeditor of *Slayage: The Online International Journal of Buffy Studies.* Also coauthor and coproducer of the film *Owen Barfield: Man and Meaning,* 1994. Contributor to books, including *The Cult Film Experience: Beyond All Reason,* edited by J. P. Telotte, University of Texas Press (Austin, TX), 1991; *The Remote Control Device in the New Age of Television,* edited by James R. Walker and Rob Bellamy, Praeger (New York, NY), 1993; *Seeing Beyond: Movies, Visions, and Values,* edited by Richard P. Sugg, Golden String Press (New York, NY), 2001; *Conspiracy Theories in American History: An Encyclopedia,* edited by Peter Knight, ABC-Clio (Santa Barbara, CA), 2003; *Professional Wrestling: The Myth, the Mat, and American Popular Culture,* by Marc Leverette, Edwin Mellen (Lewiston, NY), 2003; *50 Key Television Programs,* edited by Glen Creeber, Arnold (London, England), 2004.

Contributor of articles, poetry, short fiction, and reviews to periodicals, including *Journal of Humanistic Psychology, Journal of Evolutionary Psychology, Wallace Stevens Journal, Film Criticism, Journal of Popular Film and Television, Television Quarterly, Seven,* and *Georgia Review.* Member of editorial board of *Studies in Popular Culture,* 1997— , and *Intensities: The Online Journal of Cult Media,* 2000—. Organizer, Slayage Conference on *Buffy the Vampire Slayer,* 2004.

WORK IN PROGRESS: Contributions to the following forthcoming books: *Art, Science, and Morality: Creative Journeys,* edited by Doris B. Wallace; *The Coen Brothers: On Screen, in Print, and Beyond,* edited by Keith Perry and Joseph Walker; *Beyond Fandom: Media Aficionados, Academics, and Allergics,* edited by Matt Hills and Jonathan Gray; *Grave Concerns: Critical Approaches to Six Feet Under,* edited by Kim Akass and Janet McCabe.

SIDELIGHTS: David Lavery once told *CA:* "My interests are truly eclectic: television studies, film and film theory, autobiography, the creative process, the evolution of consciousness. Underlying and uniting them all, however, is a preoccupation with the nature of imagination in all its forms. My primary motivations for writing are to discover what I think about a given subject and to advance our understanding of the imagination. A variety of inspirations have brought me to my subjects, though I always seem to end up working on projects that seem to need to be done.

"I am an early riser and write almost exclusively in the very early morning. I write all drafts on the computer. Writers who have influenced me include Rainer Maria Rilke, Wallace Stevens, Owen Barfield, Jorge Luis Borges, James Hillman, Loren Eiseley, and William Irwin Thompson."

As a professor at Middle Tennessee State University, Lavery demonstrates his "truly eclectic" nature by teaching courses in subjects he loves: American literature, television studies, and film and film theory. He has produced several analyses of popular television series, but a favorite topic is the television series *Buffy the Vampire Slayer.* Lavery has taught a course, coedited an online journal, coedited a book, and organized a conference all based on the *Buffy* television series and movie. Aside from *Buffy,* Lavery has also analyzed television shows such as *Seinfeld, The Sopranos, Six Feet Under, The X-Files, Angel,* and *Twin Peaks.*

Lavery coedited *Fighting the Forces: What's at Stake in Buffy the Vampire Slayer,* a compilation of essays about the popular television show, with Rhonda Wilcox. The television show is about the adventures of Buffy, a strong (both physically and mentally) teenage girl, struggling not only with normal, everyday teen angst, but also with vampires, demons, and the forces of darkness that roam the streets of Sunnydale and the halls of Sunnydale High School. The book examines obvious topics, such as feminism and role reversal, in addition to the underlying themes that have made the show a cult hit. According to Dorothy Kuykendal in *Extrapolation,* "Wilcox and Lavery have opened an intriguing doorway to fans of the show, giving us opportunities to reflect on aspects of the show we have never examined before." Kuykendal continued, noting that the essays in the collection offer "some interesting parallels between Buffy and the traditional lonely, misunderstood Romantic hero. . . . an intriguing exploration of the interdependence between the show's creators and its main supporters," as well the issues of "postmodern politics, the psychological impact of death and suffering as presented by the show, and the rhetoric of music. . . ." Kuykendal concluded, "The style of these essays is overall quite accessible, and the reader's interest is sure to be caught by the piquant feel of the collection itself. Have a look. And don't walk the streets alone after dark in Sunnydale." Deborah Netburn of the *New York Observer* compared *Fighting the Forces* to other

Buffy-related collections, noting, "The essays come at the show from a better variety of perspectives (race, religion, psychoanalysis, gender, cultural history); and the book has a broader—if more academic—appeal."

Lavery compiled another group of essays in *This Thing of Ours: Investigating the Sopranos,* this time focusing on the hit HBO television series. As Peter Mattessi noted in *Metro Magazine,* "Lavery has brought together a diverse collection that encompasses foreign perspectives, close textual readings, cultural analysis, and contemporary gender theory, as well as the local viewpoint of a native New Jerseyan." The essays are divided into several parts, including discussions of media context, men and women, genre and narrative techniques, and cultural contexts. "There is no question that *This Thing of Ours* is a thoroughly considered collection," Mattessi commented, continuing, "Similarly, the contributors' unconcealed enthusiasm for *The Sopranos* makes for exciting reading, and a wonderful tendency to adopt the language of the show in their writing."

Lavery coedited *Teleparody: Predicting/Preventing the TV Discourse of Tomorrow* with Angela Hague. The book, which Matt Duvall of the *PopMatters* Web site called, "humorous and yet frightening at the same time," is a collection of fake essays and book reviews on books that have not been published. Duvall noted, "The humor of *Teleparody: Predicting/Preventing the TV Discourse of Tomorrow* is also the source of its impact: these things sound like real scholarly papers." The book parodies traditional reviews and analyses of television shows, proving that scholars can find a hidden subtext in almost any show they watch. Duvall concluded, "This book should frighten us in the same way the original *War of the Worlds* broadcast frightened so many people—not because it's real, but because it *could* be."

BIOGRAPHICAL AND CRITICAL SOURCES:

PERIODICALS

Extrapolation, fall, 2002, Dorothy Kuykendal, review of *Fighting the Forces: What's at Stake in Buffy the Vampire Slayer,* p. 352.

Film Quarterly, fall, 1997, John P. McCarthy, review of *Full of Secrets: Critical Approaches to "Twin Peaks,"* p. 49.

Metro Magazine, spring, 2003, Peter Matessi, review of *This Thing of Ours: Investigating the Sopranos,* p. 186.

News-Press (Fort Myers, FL), February 20, 2002, Miriam Pereira, "Webwatch: www.slayage.tv," p. 10E.

New York Observer, March 25, 2002, Deborah Netburn, "Media Studies Does Buffy—And Buffy, As Always, Prevails," p. 26.

New York Times Book Review, September 15, 2002, David Kelly, "Deconstruct This!," review of *This Thing of Ours,* p. 8.

Reference and Research Book News, May, 1995, review of *Full of Secrets,* p. 41; May, 1997, review of *Deny All Knowledge: Reading "The X-Files,"* p. 123.

Science Fiction Chronicle, March, 1992, review of *Late for the Sky: The Mentality of the Space Age,* p. 16.

Science-Fiction Studies, November, 1997, Nicola Nixon, review of *Deny All Knowledge,* p. 513.

Times Higher Education Supplement, March 28, 1997, Graham McCann, review of *Deny All Knowledge,* p. 23.

University Press Book News, June, 1992, review of *Late for the Sky,* p. 6.

Wilson Library Bulletin, September, 1992, Tom Carpenter, review of *Late for the Sky,* p. 107.

ONLINE

Columbia University Press Web site, http://www.columia.edu/cu/cup/ (January 15, 2003), description of *This Thing of Ours.*

David Lavery's Home Page, http://www.mtsu.edu/~dlavery/ (March 18, 2004).

Film-Philosophy Web site, http://www.film-philosophy.com/ (July, 2003), Jonathan Gray, review of *Teleparody: Predicting/Preventing the TV Discourse of Tomorrow.*

PopMatters, http://www.popmatters.com/ (December 11, 2002), Matt Duvall, review of *Teleparody.*

Slayage: The Online International Journal of Buffy Studies Web site, http://www.slayage.tv/ (March 18, 2004), "About David Lavery."

Vampyres Only Web site, http://www.vampyres.com/ (October 6, 2002), Deborah Netburn, review of *Fighting the Forces.**

*   *   *

LAWSON, Philip
See Di FILIPPO, Paul

LEAVITT, David 1961-

PERSONAL: Born June 23, 1961, in Pittsburgh, PA; son of Harold Jack (a professor) and Gloria (a homemaker; maiden name, Rosenthal) Leavitt. *Education:* Yale University, B.A., 1983.

ADDRESSES: Office—Department of English, University of Florida, 4008 Turlington Hall, P.O. Box 117310, Gainesville, FL 32611-7310. *E-mail*—dleavitt@ufl.edu.

CAREER: Writer. Viking-Penguin, New York, NY, reader and editorial assistant, 1983-84; taught at Princeton University; University of Florida, Gainesville, professor of creative writing, 2000—.

MEMBER: PEN, Authors Guild, Authors League of America, Phi Beta Kappa.

AWARDS, HONORS: Willets Prize for fiction, Yale University, 1982, for "Territory"; O. Henry Award, 1984, for "Counting Months"; nomination for best fiction, National Book Critics Circle, 1984, and PEN/Faulkner Award for best fiction, PEN, 1985, both for *Family Dancing;* National Endowment for the Arts grant, 1985; Visiting Foreign Writer, Institute of Catalan Letters, Barcelona, Spain, 1989; Guggenheim fellow, 1990; Literary Lion, New York Public Library.

WRITINGS:

Family Dancing (short stories), Knopf (New York, NY), 1984.

The Lost Language of Cranes (novel), Knopf (New York, NY), 1986.

Equal Affections (novel), Weidenfeld & Nicolson (London, England), 1989.

A Place I've Never Been (short stories), Viking (New York, NY), 1990.

While England Sleeps (novel), Viking (New York, NY), 1993, reprinted with a new preface by the author, Houghton Mifflin (Boston, MA), 1995.

(Editor, with Mark Mitchell) *Penguin Book of Gay Short Stories,* Viking (New York, NY), 1994.

(With Mark Mitchell) *Italian Pleasures,* Chronicle Books (San Francisco, CA), 1996.

David Leavitt

Arkansas: Three Novellas (includes "The Term Paper Artist," "The Wooden Anniversary," and "Saturn Street"), Houghton Mifflin (Boston, MA), 1997.

(Editor and author of introduction, with Mark Mitchell) *Pages Passed from Hand to Hand: The Hidden Tradition of Homosexual Literature in English from 1748 to 1914,* Houghton Mifflin (Boston, MA), 1997.

The Page Turner (novel), Houghton Mifflin (Boston, MA), 1998.

Martin Bauman; or, A Sure Thing (novel), Houghton Mifflin (Boston, MA), 2000.

(Editor and author of introduction, with Mark Mitchell) E. M. Forster, *Selected Stories,* Penguin (New York, NY), 2001.

(With Mark Mitchell) *In Maremma: Life and a House in Southern Tuscany,* Counterpoint (Washington, DC), 2001.

The Marble Quilt (stories), Houghton Mifflin (Boston, MA), 2001.

Florence, a Delicate Case, Bloomsbury (New York, NY), 2002.

Collected Stories, Bloomsbury (New York, NY), 2003.

The Body of Jonah Boyd (novel), Bloomsbury (New York, NY), 2004.

Contributor to periodicals, including *Esquire, Harper's, New Yorker, New York Times Book Review, New York Times Magazine,* and *Village Voice.*

ADAPTATIONS: The Lost Language of Cranes was adapted for film by the British Broadcasting Corp. (BBC), 1991. *The Page Turner* was adapted for film by Spanish director Ventura Pons, as *Food of Love,* 2002.

SIDELIGHTS: Lauded for his insightful and empathetic characterizations, author David Leavitt has gained recognition as as one of the leaders of the gay literature movement in the United States. According to Daniel J. Murtaugh in the *Dictionary of Literary Biography,* "While Leavitt has converted the experiences of gay men and women into a matter of interest for the mainstream reader, he remains one of the most poignant and subjective tellers of what it means to be gay and how a gay person survives in a world of family, education, or business not necessarily receptive to sexual difference." Leavitt published his first story, "Territory," in the *New Yorker* at the age of twenty-one. The story of a mother and her homosexual son, it was the first of its kind to be published in that magazine, and it created "a small stir in the city's more conservative circles," according to an *Interview* writer. Leavitt also published pieces in other periodicals, including *Esquire* and *Harper's,* and in 1984 published his first book, a collection of short stories titled *Family Dancing.*

Family Dancing showcases Leavitt's insights into some of the more offbeat, troubling aspects of domestic life. Among the stories noted by critics are "Radiation," about a slowly dying cancer victim, "Out Here," which concerns sibling guilt, and "Aliens," in which a young girl believes herself to be an extraterrestrial creature. "Territory" is included in this collection, and several other works in the volume also address homosexual concerns, including "Dedicated," and "Out Here," in which one of the characters is a lesbian.

Family Dancing earned acclaim as an impressive debut volume. *Newsweek's* David Lehman, hailing the 1980s boom in short-story writing, called Leavitt's book "a first collection of unusual finesse," and Michiko Kakutani wrote in the *New York Times* that *Family Dancing* is "an astonishing collection" with "the power to move

us with the blush of truth." In a review for the *Washington Post,* Dennis Drabelle praised Leavitt as "remarkably gifted," and reserved particular commendation for his tales of homosexuality. Leavitt, Drabelle contended, "captures the deep-rooted tensions between adult gays and their families and the efforts of childless gays to carve out families among their peers." Drabelle concluded that Leavitt's insights had "only just been tapped."

Leavitt devotes his first novel, *The Lost Language of Cranes,* to an in-depth depiction of homosexual life. While the main character's romantic experiences are rather typical—he falls in love, loses his lover, and finds a more suitable mate—a subplot involving the protagonist's father delves into traumas specific to homosexuality. The father is a married man who spends Sunday afternoons indulging in his passion for patronizing pornography theaters. After learning that his son is a homosexual, he too makes his own difficult confession.

The Lost Language of Cranes chronicles more than just the elements of a homosexual life, however. It also addresses more universal issues regarding love and traces the hope, pain, ecstasy, and suffering that are all a part of romantic involvement. Other issues explored in the novel include the notion of family life, as Leavitt delineates the tensions and disappointments of the family as it is altered by the son's and the father's revelations. In addition, the anguish of the wife and mother is also evoked through her increased withdrawal from familial crises. Her disappointment, together with the father's anguish and the son's alternately exhilarating and crushing experiences with love, adds another dimension to Leavitt's work.

The Lost Language of Cranes garnered much critical acclaim. Susan Wood wrote in the *Washington Post* that Leavitt's novel "has much to recommend it," and Philip Lopate noted in the *New York Times Book Review* that the book is "readable and literate." An enthusiastic reviewer for Chicago's *Tribune Books* described the novel as "well-written and frankly interesting," and added that "Leavitt's style is compelling, and the subject matter . . . is equally elucidative." Similarly, Dorothy Allison wrote in the *Village Voice* that "Leavitt catches beautifully the terror and passion of new love" and shows a profound understanding of love's "tentativeness." She further declared that *The Lost Language of Cranes* "places David Leavitt firmly among the best young authors of his generation," and concluded that his novel gave her "new hope for modern fiction."

Critics of *The Lost Language of Cranes* were especially impressed with Leavitt's skill in portraying compelling characters and his ability to evoke the tension and turmoil, as well as the fulfillment and ecstasy, of love. The reviewer for *Tribune Books* declared that Leavitt "opens up the gay world to readers" and added that the narrative is "mature, quick-paced and fascinating." Likewise, Allison wrote that the novel's various characters are "so fully realized" that she found herself "tense with fear for each of them." Allison commended Leavitt for his artistry in evincing such a response from readers. "It is David Leavitt's strength that he could inspire that kind of fear in me and win me back when his characters did not find true love or happiness," Allison noted. "At every moment I believed in them, and these days that is so rare as to suggest genius."

Leavitt's second novel, *Equal Affections*, which *Listener* reviewer John Lahr called a "tale of the extraordinariness of ordinary family suffering," centers around Louise Cooper, who is dying of cancer, and the members of her family who must deal with this reality. Louise's husband, Nat, is a computer visionary whose visions have never amounted to much. Her son Danny is a gay lawyer living in bland, immaculate monogamy in the suburbs with Walter, who has not fully committed to the relationship. Daughter April is a famous folk singer who "discovers" her true lesbian nature and turns her singing to feminist issues. Louise's bitterness over lost opportunities, her crisis of faith, and her impending death color her interactions with her husband and family. As Louise's twenty-year bout with cancer draws to a close, the family deals with this strain as well as their individual problems: Nat is having an affair with another woman, Danny endures Walter's Internet philandering, and April is artificially inseminated with donor sperm from a culturally aware San Francisco homosexual.

Equal Affections received mixed reviews. Acknowledging her disappointment in Leavitt's first novel, *The Lost Language of Cranes*, Beverly Lowry wrote in the *New York Times Book Review* that, in contrast, *Equal Affections* "does not compromise itself with easy answers. It is a gritty, passionate novel that should settle the question of David Leavitt's abilities. . . .

He has the talent for a lifelong career." Lahr called the novel "adroit," while a *New York* writer found it to be "limp, dreary business." *Washington Post Book World* contributor Alan Hollinghurst praised Leavitt's characterizations, but observed that the "emotional drama . . . is distinctly soggy. Leavitt's characters are notoriously lachrymose, but here there's really too much tearful sentiment, spunky goodness and curtain-line corniness: this is a sleepie that turns into a weepie." London *Observer* correspondent Candia McWilliam was more enthusiastic, terming *Equal Affections* an "attentive, unsparing book."

In Leavitt's second collection of short stories, *A Place I've Never Been*, most of his tales focus on gay characters dealing with relationships. "When You Grow to Adultery" finds the protagonist leaving an old lover for a new one, and in "My Marriage to Vengeance," a lesbian character's former lover marries a man. In the title story, a woman finally realizes that her gay friend Nathan is too wrapped up in his own self-pity to contribute to their friendship. A mother tests the limits of her AIDS-stricken son's waning strength in "Gravity," and a heterosexual couple who have lost their respective spouses to cancer begin an affair in "Spouse Night."

Many critics praised *A Place I've Never Been*. Charles Solomon in the *Los Angeles Times Book Review* called Leavitt's writing "fine, polished prose that is refreshingly free of the drip-dry nihilism of his Brat Pack contemporaries." James N. Baker declared in *Newsweek* that Leavitt "is not an oracle nor is he a groundbreaker. . . . He remains what he has always been: a writer of conventional stories who casts an incisive, ironic eye on families and lovers, loyalty and betrayal." Reviewer Harriet Waugh wrote in the *Spectator*: "Short stories, unlike novels, have to be perfect. *A Place I've Never Been* . . . very nearly is." In her *New York Times Book Review* piece on the work, Wendy Martin called *A Place I've Never Been* a "fine new collection of short fiction," and Clifford Chase described Leavitt's short fiction as "at once wrenching and satisfying" in his review for the *Village Voice Literary Supplement.*

Leavitt's third novel, *While England Sleeps*, is set in the 1930s against the backdrop of the Spanish Civil War, and follows the love story between Brian Botsford, a literary aristocrat, and Edward Phelan, a lower-class ticket-taker on the London Underground. Brian ends the affair, and in an attempt to deny his homo-sexuality marries a woman whom his wealthy aunt thinks is suitable. Distraught, Edward joins the fight in Spain, but he soon deserts the military and lands in prison. Brian follows his lover to Spain and secures Edward's release, but Edward dies of typhoid on the voyage home.

While England Sleeps borrowed a segment of its plot from British poet Stephen Spender's 1948 autobiography, *World within World,* a fact first revealed by Bernard Knox in his review for the *Washington Post.* Leavitt admitted using an episode from Spender's life as a springboard for his novel and wrote in the *New York Times Magazine* that he had initially included an acknowledgment to Spender, "but had been advised by an in-house lawyer at Viking to omit the reference." He also defended his book on the basis that it is an historical novel and maintained that it "diverged from Spender's account in many more ways than it converged with it." Spender brought suit in London against Leavitt for copyright infringement. Viking agreed to withdraw the book until Leavitt revised the manuscript according to some seventeen points cited in the Spender suit; once this had been done, however, Viking declined to publish the revised version. However, in the fall of 1995, Houghton Mifflin released the new version with an added preface by Leavitt that addresses the book's legal controversy.

Despite the controversy, the *Los Angeles Times* short-listed *While England Sleeps* for its fiction prize after it had been withdrawn from its initial publication, and *While England Sleeps* continued to receive much publicity from reviewers. In a *New York Times* review, Christopher Lehmann-Haupt lauded Leavitt's authentic portrayal of the prewar European era and his depiction of the region's divergent social classes. In the scenes that take place in Spain, Lehmann-Haupt added, "the theme of sexual deception is chillingly replicated in the way the Communist leaders treat their followers." Lehmann-Haupt concluded that *While England Sleeps* should be credited for climbing "out of its preoccupation with sex and [making] a significant comment on the political issues of its time." Conversely, Jeremy Treglown noted in the *Times Literary Supplement* that "style is one thing about which Spender hasn't complained, yet the book's main offence lies in its novelettishness." D. T. Max observed in the *Los Angeles Times Book Review:* "A careful reading of *World within World* shows Spender's charge of

plagiarism to be over the top—all the novel's words seem Leavitt's own—but a charge of laziness would be far harder to disprove, and the knowledge of it mars an otherwise graceful, romantic novel."

In his next foray into short fiction, *Arkansas: Three Novellas,* Leavitt once again explores issues of gay love and life, this time mixing directly autobiographical elements into the work. In "The Term Paper Artist," a young writer—named David Leavitt—tries to break through a case of writer's block caused by an accusation of plagiarism by an English poet. In an interview with Celestine Bohlen in the *New York Times,* Leavitt described his intent with this novella: "It is so common to write autobiographical fiction in which your own experience is thinly disguised. I thought it could be very interesting to do the opposite with a story where even a tiny amount of research into my life would prove it did not happen . . . and thereby turn the convention inside out." The volume's other two novellas, "The Wooden Anniversary" and "Saturn Street," both deal with characters whose lovers have died and who are struggling with moving on with their lives. "The Wooden Anniversary" is set in Italy, where Leavitt himself now lives.

Although *Arkansas* received some favorable critical reception, *New York Times* reviewer Michiko Kakutani termed the work "disappointing," criticizing the author's handling of sexual events as "repetitious, tiresome and sophomoric" and noting that "this sort of adolescent writing is unworthy of the richly talented Mr. Leavitt."

The Marble Quilt, published in 2001, reestablished Leavitt's critical standing as an author of short fiction, even as he experimented with "different formats and styles," according to *Booklist* reviewer Michael Spinella. "The Infection Scene" balances a story about the petulant Lord Alfred "Bosie" Douglas, young lover to nineteenth-century writer Oscar Wilde and later that same man's downfall, with a modern-day tragedy about AIDS; "The Black Box" finds two men drawn together as one mourns the recent loss of a lover in a tragic plane crash; and "The List" follows the gossip-ridden e-mail dialogue among a group of gay academics. The title story, about a murdered man whose life, as narrated by his former boyfriend during a police inquiry, is shown to be rife with contradictions, "is infused with an anger that exists . . . just below its dense writerliness," noted a *Publishers*

Weekly contributor, adding that in *The Marble Quilt* Leavitt "achieves an electric narrative energy."

Leavitt's 1998 novel, *The Page Turner,* deals with the dual themes of love and ambition. Aspiring concert pianist Paul Porterfield, the book's narrator, is given the chance to turn pages for renowned artist Richard Kennington during a concert in California. The two men meet a few months later in Italy and begin a brief affair that is halted by Kennington's loyalty to a longtime partner and by Paul's realization that his talent does not equal Kennington's. The book also explores Paul's milieu in New York City and his mother's struggle to come to terms with the dissolution of her marriage. In her *New York Times* review of the book, Kakutani maintained that the novel "represents something of a rediscovery of the methods and ambitions of *Family Dancing.* It is by no means a perfect novel . . . but . . . it intermittently shimmers with the magical talent that first announced itself a decade and a half ago." Elizabeth Gleick also praised *The Page Turner* in the *New York Times Book Review* as "a perfectly enjoyable read" and "a portrait of the aspiring artist as a young man." Gleick continued: "Love and striving for selfhood may be inseparable, but in this novel the author achieves clarity, even flashes of poetry, only when grappling with the turning points in an artistic life."

The "artistic life" also informs *Martin Bauman; or, A Sure Thing,* Leavitt's *roman à clef* about the New York publishing world. The central character of this novel, Martin Bauman, is a youthful prodigy who publishes a groundbreaking short story with gay themes in an important literary magazine—and who thereafter has to struggle with his disillusion at the venality of the publishing business and with the dire predictions of his demanding college instructor, Stanley Flint. *Martin Bauman* "gives every appearance of being an extended, merciless excoriation of Leavitt's younger self—depicted here as a boy with a propensity for cheating on exams, a coddled yet chronically needy child-man not above betraying the people he loves when they prove insufficiently forthcoming with their reassurance," wrote Laura Miller in the *New York Times Book Review.* Miller added: "The pettiness of writers is so disheartening because, at its best, the experience of reading is so sublime; naturally, we expect better of the people who can engineer such a miracle. That Leavitt depicts his own generation of 'hot' young writers as not just preoccupied with reputation but also ap-

parently indifferent to the alchemy of reading itself may be the most damning thing of all." A *Publishers Weekly* reviewer felt that the New York literary scene "is given a sound drubbing in this comedy of egos and coming-of-age tale. . . . Readers hip to the New York book biz will be tickled throughout by Leavitt's thinly veiled satiric references to various literary institutions." Kakutani, writing in the *New York Times,* found the book to be "as poignant and funny an account of literary apprenticeship as that found in the opening pages of William Styron's *Sophie's Choice.*"

In *The Body of Jonah Boyd* Judith "Denny" Denham reflects on a significant Thanksgiving dinner, thirty years before, at the house of her then employer/lover and his family. Sometime throughout the evening one of the members of the party, novelist Jonah Boyd, irretrievably misplaces his most recent manuscript, setting him off on a path of despair. "Leavitt drops you into this family, allows you to muck around in its glorious dysfunction, and then extracts you in an ingenious way," explained Henry Goldblatt in a review for *Entertainment Weekly.* Marc Kloszewski in *Library Journal* commented that *The Body of Jonah Boyd* is a "generally breezy and humorous book whose charms outweigh any flaws; many readers will enjoy it," while Ray Olson of *Booklist* acknowledged, "Followers of Leavitt's career may note that his nemesis, plagiarism, figures in here, while homosexuality, formerly prevalent in his fiction, does not, and conclude that this is his best novel."

In addition to his own writing, Leavitt has edited several well-received works with his companion, Mark Mitchell. The *Penguin Book of Gay Short Stories,* for instance, consists of pieces that focus on gay men and includes a wide variety of writers, both contemporary and historical, among them Larry Kramer, D. H. Lawrence, Graham Greene, Christopher Isherwood, Edna O'Brien, and James Purdy. Writing in the *New Statesman & Society,* Richard Canning bemoaned the omission of non-American and non-English writers as well as pre-1900 writers, questioning the inclusion of pieces that seem at odds with the authors' stated criteria. "Leavitt's preference for 'self-contained, autonomous works' rather than novel extracts is shelved for particular favourites." Nonetheless, Canning recommended the anthology as "no less comprehensive than any work subject to such criteria could be." Peter Parker in the *Observer* similarly questioned the scope of the pieces included, noting that the volume reflects Leavitt's own writing terrain—conservative, mainstream, "suburban-sensitive"—at the expense of angrier or more explicitly sexual literature. But Peter Parker, while admitting some reservations about inclusion criteria in his *Times Literary Supplement* review, commended Leavitt and Mitchell for choosing "so many stories of such high literary quality."

Leavitt and Mitchell also edited *Pages Passed from Hand to Hand: The Hidden Tradition of Homosexual Literature in English from 1748 to 1914.* The anthology includes excerpts from novels, stories, and obscure manuscripts that depict gay passion, sometimes in veiled form due to cultural taboos and censorship. According to Robert Dawidoff in the *Advocate,* the pieces, though of other eras and in some cases previously unknown to readers, "are often hauntingly familiar, partly because they have been incorporated into the gay literature we know but also because they concern the same uncomfortable and confused feelings gays experience even now." Dawidoff concluded that the book "belongs in every gay library. . . . It is like a time capsule, carefully secreted in the cornerstone of our gay foundation and now restored to us as a reminder and a treasure."

Leavitt's success has made him one of the few mainstream writers whose work deals primarily with homosexual themes. As Martin explained in the *New York Times Book Review:* "Leavitt has the wonderful ability to lead the reader to examine heterosexist assumptions without becoming polemical. In prose that is often spare and carefully honed, he sensitizes us to the daily difficulties of homosexual life—of negotiating public spaces, for example, where holding hands or a simple embrace becomes problematic." She added: "Leavitt's insight and empathy serve . . . to enlighten, to make us realize that human sexuality is a continuum of possibilities that encompasses the subtle as well as the sensational."

BIOGRAPHICAL AND CRITICAL SOURCES:

BOOKS

Contemporary Literary Criticism, Volume 34, Gale (Detroit, MI), 1985.
Dictionary of Literary Biography, Volume 130: *American Short Story Writers since World War II,* Gale (Detroit, MI), 1993.

PERIODICALS

Advocate, October 19, 1993, pp. 51-55; December 28, 1993, p. 76; February 17, 1998, Robert Dawidoff, review of *Pages Passed from Hand to Hand: The Hidden Tradition of Homosexual Literature in English from 1748 to 1914,* p. 53; March 31, 1998, Robert L. Pela, review of *The Page Turner,* p. 74.
Booklist, February 15, 1998, Ray Olson, review of *The Page Turner,* p. 982; August, 2000, Donna Seaman, review of *Martin Bauman; or, A Sure Thing,* p. 2074; September 2, 2001, Michael Spinella, review of *The Marble Quilt,* p. 51; April 1, 2004, Ray Olson, review of *The Body of Jonah Boyd,* p. 1348.
Entertainment Weekly, April 30, 2004, Henry Goldblatt, review of *The Body of Jonah Boyd,* p. 171.
Esquire, May, 1985.
Harper's, April, 1986.
Interview, March, 1985.
Kirkus Reviews, February 15, 1998, review of *The Page Turner.*
Library Journal, June 1, 1995; February 1, 1998, David Azzolina, review of *Pages Passed from Hand to Hand,* p. 86; February 15, 1998, Roger W. Durbin, review of *The Page Turner,* p. 170; September 1, 2000, Brian Kenney, review of *Martin Bauman; or, A Sure Thing,* p. 250; July, 2001, review of *The Marble Quilt,* p. 128; May 1, 2004, Marc Kloszewski, review of *The Body of Jonah Boyd,* p. 140.
Listener, June 15, 1989, John Lahr, review of *Equal Affections,* p. 25.
London Review of Books, May 23, 1991, pp. 22-23.
Los Angeles Times Book Review, March 5, 1989, p. 6; August 4, 1991, p. 1991; October 3, 1993, pp. 3, 12.
National Review, December 27, 1993, p. 72.
New Republic, April 6, 1998, Denis Donoghue, review of *Pages Passed from Hand to Hand,* p. 36.
New Statesman & Society, November 12, 1993, p. 38; March 11, 1994, p. 41.
Newsweek, January 14, 1985; February 13, 1989, p. 78; September 3, 1990, p. 66; November 8, 1993, p. 81.
New York, January 30, 1989; October 18, 1993, pp. 139-140.
New York Times, October 30, 1984; October 14, 1993, p. C20; February 20, 1994, p. D14; February 25, 1997, p. B1; March 11, 1997, p. B2; March 27, 1998, Michiko Kakutani, "Ambition, Manipula-

tion and a Misguided Mother"; September 29, 2000, Michiko Kakutani, "The Writing Life: Never Unexamined, Often Nasty."

New York Times Book Review, September 2, 1984; October 5, 1986; February 12, 1989, p. 7; August 26, 1990, p. 11; October 3, 1993, p. 14; September 4, 1994, p. 10; April 26, 1998, Elizabeth Gleick, "On the Other Side of Arrival"; October 8, 2000, Laura Miller, "Who's Who?"

New York Times Magazine, July 9, 1989, pp. 28-32; April 3, 1994, p. 36.

Observer (London, England), May 28, 1989, p. 46; February 6, 1994, p. 21.

Partisan Review, winter, 1994, pp. 80-95.

Publishers Weekly, August 24, 1990, pp. 47-48; February 21, 1994; February 2, 1998, review of *The Page Turner,* p. 79; August 7, 2000, review of *Martin Bauman; or, A Sure Thing,* p. 74; July 30, 2001, review of *The Marble Quilt,* p. 56.

Spectator, March 9, 1991, Harriet Waugh, review of *A Place I've Never Been,* p. 28.

Time, November 8, 1993, p. 27.

Times Literary Supplement, June 9-15, 1989, p. 634; October 29, 1993, p. 20; February 4, 1994, p. 20.

Tribune Books (Chicago, IL), September 21, 1986.

Village Voice, October 14, 1986, Dorothy Allison, review of *The Lost Language of Cranes.*

Village Voice Literary Supplement, December, 1990, Clifford Chase, review of *A Place I've Never Been,* pp. 10-11.

Washington Post, November 19, 1984; March 2, 1985; October 7, 1986; February 17, 1994, p. A1.

Washington Post Book World, January 22, 1989, p. 4; October 7, 1990, p. 7; September 12, 1993, p. 5.

ONLINE

PureFiction.com, http://www.purefiction.com/ (December 12, 2000), interview with Leavitt.*

*   *   *

LEHMAN, Peter 1944-

PERSONAL: Born December 25, 1944, in Janesville, WI; son of Ernest and Anne (Heinemann) Lehman; married second wife, Melanie Magisos, June 16, 1983; children: (first marriage) Eleanor. *Education:* University of Wisconsin—Madison, B.S. (with honors), 1967,

graduate study, 1967-68, M.A., 1973, Ph.D., 1978; graduate study at Queens College of the City University of New York, 1968-69.

ADDRESSES: Home—1525 South Moonlight Dr., Tucson, AZ 85748. *Office*—Department of Drama, University of Arizona, Tucson, AZ 85721.

CAREER: English teacher at public junior high schools in New York, NY, 1968-71; Ohio University, Athens, visiting professor, 1975-77, assistant professor of film and director of annual Film Conference, 1977-83, co-director of conference, 1984; University of Arizona, Tucson, associate professor of film, 1983—, and member of faculty of interdisciplinary humanities. University of California—Santa Barbara, visiting lecturer, summer, 1982.

MEMBER: Society for Cinema Studies.

WRITINGS:

(Coauthor) *Authorship and Narrative in the Cinema: Issues in Contemporary Aesthetics and Criticism,* Putnam (New York, NY), 1977.

(With William Luhr) *Blake Edwards,* Ohio University Press (Athens, OH), 1981.

(Editor) *Close Viewings: An Anthology of New Film Criticism,* Florida State University Press (Tallahassee, FL), 1990.

Running Scared: Masculinity and the Representation of the Male Body, Temple University Press (Philadelphia, PA), 1993.

(Editor and author of introduction) *Defining Cinema,* Rutgers University Press (New Brunswick, NJ), 1997.

(With William Luhr) *Thinking about Movies: Watching, Questioning, Enjoying,* Harcourt Brace (Fort Worth, TX), 1998.

(Editor) *Masculinity: Bodies, Movies, and Culture,* Routledge (New York, NY), 2000.

Roy Orbison: The Invention of an Alternative Rock Masculinity, Temple University Press (Philadelphia, PA), 2003.

Contributor to books, including *Cinema Histories, Cinema Practices,* edited by Patricia Mellencamp and Philip Rosen, American Film Institute, 1984; and

American Film Directors since World War II, edited by Randall Clark, Gale (Detroit, MI), 1985. Contributor of articles and reviews to magazines, including *Velvet Light Trap, Film Reader,* and *Cineaste.* Editor, *Wide Angle: Film Quarterly of Theory, Criticism, and Practice;* member of editorial advisory board, *Ca Cinema.*

SIDELIGHTS: Peter Lehman once told *CA:* "When I was a freshman in college, I saw the film *The Pink Panther* and enjoyed it so much that I went back to see it over and over. I memorized the scenes which I thought were funny and in the process I discovered how much of the humor had to do with composition, use of space, and cutting patterns. I'd had no film education of any kind, and this was my real discovery of some of the significant elements of the medium. Years later, when I became a film graduate student, I wanted to write my master's thesis or doctoral dissertation on Blake Edwards. I could not find an advisor who would agree that it was a worthwhile project (one professor sarcastically referred to Edwards as 'that party-going director'), so I chose John Ford instead. I resolved, however, that, at the first opportunity, I would do on my own what I could not do in academia at that time."

BIOGRAPHICAL AND CRITICAL SOURCES:

PERIODICALS

Library Journal, June 1, 2003, Bill Piekarski, review of *Roy Orbison: The Invention of an Alternative Rock Masculinity.**

*   *   *

LEROY, Gilles 1958-

PERSONAL: Born December 28, 1958, in Paris, France; son of Andre and Eliane (Mesny) Leroy. *Education:* Attended Hypokhagne, Khagne.

ADDRESSES: Office—c/o Mercure de France SA, Editions Gallimard, 26, rue de Conde, F-75006 Paris, France. *E-mail*—gill.leroy@wanadoo.fr.

CAREER: Writer.

AWARDS, HONORS: Prix de la Nouvelle, Nanterre, 1992, for *Les Derniers seront les premiers;* Prix Valery-Larbaud, 1999, for *Machines à sous.*

WRITINGS:

Habibi (novel), Editions Michel de Maule (Paris, France), 1987.
Maman est morte (nonfiction; title means "Mother Is Dead"), Editions Michel de Maule (Paris, France), 1990.
Les Derniers seront les premiers (short stories; title means "The Last Shall Be the First"), Mercure de France (Paris, France), 1991.
Madame X (novel), Mercure de France (Paris, France), 1992.
Les Jardins publics (novel), Mercure de France (Paris, France), 1994.
Les Maîtres du monde (novel), Mercure de France (Paris, France), 1996.
Machines à sous (novel), Mercure de France (Paris, France), 1998.
Soleil noir (novel), Mercure de France (Paris, France), 2000.
L'Amant russe (novel), Mercure de France (Paris, France), 2002.
Fragiles (novel), Mercure de France (Paris, France), 2003.
Grandir (novel), Mercure de France (Paris, France), 2004.

SIDELIGHTS: Gilles Leroy has drawn from his childhood growing up in a working-class and middle-class family in the suburbs of Paris to create novels and short stories. His first novel, *Habibi,* revolves around the tragic passions of two adolescent boys. It was followed three years later by the nonfiction work *Maman est morte,* an account of the author's grief over the death of his mother. Gerard-Julien Salvy reported in *Le Figaro Magazine:* "*Maman est morte* is an unusual book, for it says something truly new: allegory has given way to the feelings that exist beyond the facts. Without sadness somehow, Gilles Leroy has written an astonishing book."

In *Les Derniers seront les premiers,* a collection of nine short stories, Leroy portrays the marginalized in society: children and adolescents, the lonely elderly, little-known writers, the poor, and singers of forgotten songs. Leroy explained to a contributor to *Figaroscope,* "In less than ten years, I lost my entire family. I wanted to pay my respects to all of the people I loved. They became the characters in my book. I wanted to reconstruct a sort of legacy." In the title story, the narrator is a reporter assigned to interview stars whose careers are on the wane; in "Les Coups et blessures," Leroy describes the relationship of two teenagers; and in "Hors la loi," he recounts what happens when a father discovers his son shoplifting. In "La Compagnie des femmes," he depicts two young women sharing their secrets with each other while riding a train home from a blackmarket venue, then describes them many years later when they accidentally encounter each other and find that their roles of "needy" and "satisfied" have been reversed. *Les Derniers seront les premiers* garnered good reviews. "This is a sensitive collection—grim, tense, and compassionate. With a knowing eye and sparkling style, Leroy has created a spellbinding work," declared Laurence Vidal in *Le Figaro.* J. M. Mi also praised the work in his review for *Lire,* stating, "the stories of these characters whose fate is sealed are very moving. Gilles Leroy proves here that he is a talented writer."

The short novel *Madame X* revolves around an aging "sexaholic" who holds court in a dilapidated movie theater in Paris and the narrator who becomes her friend, known only as the Sentimental One. At one point, the two meet for drinks at a bar and the narrator invites Madame X to a bowling alley, where she tells the story of her lost true love, an American businessman. James Kirkup, writing in the *Times Literary Supplement,* called *Madame X* both "extraordinary" and "strange and unclassifiable, with a subject at once pathetic and shocking." He concluded, "This is a sharply observed little tale about the death of our simple human joys; its language, like its heroine, is discreet, classic and poignant."

Leroy once told *CA:* "I spent my childhood reading all the books I could get my hands on. When I was ten years old, I discovered literature with *The Red and the Black* by Stendhal, which I read in a single night. I believe that night I began to write, without setting a pencil to paper, without even being aware of my desire to write. Ten years later, I made another important discovery: William Faulkner and his novel *Sanctuary.* Several days later, I wrote my first novel. Was there a link between these two aesthetic 'shocks' and the

books I write? I don't know. I believe they have in common the search for truths that neither the sciences nor ethics can teach us. These truths take the form of violence and metaphor: Julien Sorel's crushed head in *The Red and the Black* and the cornstalk sword in *Sanctuary* are what might be called unforgettable images, and perhaps for me the foundations of writing.

"A book is always wrested from chaos. To write is to engage in a battle to create a part of the world, to take from it some flashes of insight. The chaos in my life was to have lost my entire family in several years. I found myself still a young man and all alone, deprived of my origins, which are also social references, landmarks from which to move forward. I felt as if I were not the heir but the depository of a history that while inevitably personal was also the history of the century. It is a concrete history, lived by people 'without history' as anonymous lives are called.

"Both sides of my family lived in Paris, in the outlying, rural suburbs that are part of the suburbs today. Among them were small business people—furriers, butchers—and workers in metal, clothes manufacturing, and printing. Inspired by their circumstances and destinies, I felt the need to create in my recent books a certain world: my own topography (imaginary settings, a little like Yoknapatawpha county in Faulkner's works) and my own 'society' of people who go from one work to another. This is still the kind of novel that I write today and should be with *Les Derniers seront les premiers* and *Madame X,* the final part of a trilogy.

"Finally, I want to say that I do not believe in the idea of a 'writing career.' Today that is the greatest danger for anyone who writes books. Writing is a vocation, not a job. To want to make a career, which many authors do, is to take part in spite of oneself in the system that wants to make the book a product of consumption like any other. In my [unpublished] novel *L'Aviateur* I evoked the life of one of my great-aunts, who worked in a printing factory. Sometimes she brought home from work books that were damaged or soiled and thus couldn't be sold, so they were left for the workers. She solemnly put them in her library to give to me later. She was very proud of her library and realized, I think, that she belonged to a sort of worker's aristocracy that took part in the development of knowledge. It was as if the product of her labor transcended her modest condition. And for me, who received these works, the feeling of respect was too strong for me to be able today to call the books products, that is, to imagine readers as clients. The only true danger for a writer is to want to please."

BIOGRAPHICAL AND CRITICAL SOURCES:

PERIODICALS

Figaroscope, November 13, 1991.
Le Figaro, June 1, 1990, Laurence Vidal, review of *Les Derniers seront les premiers,*
Le Figaro Magazine, June 1, 1990, Gerard-Julien Salvy, review of *Maman est morte.*
Le Monde, October 18, 1991, p. 21; November 9, 1991.
Lire, December, 1991, J. M. Mi, review of *Les Derniers seront les premiers,* p. 122.
Times Literary Supplement, February 5, 1993, James Kirkup, review of *Madame X,* p. 12.

*   *   *

LESCHAK, Peter M. 1951-

PERSONAL: Born May 11, 1951, in Chisholm, MN; son of Peter (a miner) and Agnes (in retail sales; maiden name, Pavelich) Leschak; married Pamela Cope (a writer), May 4, 1974. *Ethnicity:* "Russian/ Croatian." *Education:* Attended College of St. Thomas, St. Paul, MN, 1969-70; Ambassador College, B.A., 1974.

ADDRESSES: Home—Box 51, Side Lake, MN 55781. *E-mail*—pleschak@cpinternet.com.

CAREER: Lumberjack in Roseburg, OR, 1973; printer in Baton Rouge, LA, 1974; water plant operator in Chisholm, MN, 1975-79; City of Hibbing, Hibbing, MN, operator of waste water plant, 1979-84; writer, 1984—. Fire chief of French, MN, volunteer fire department and wildland firefighter for the Minnesota Department of Natural Resources.

MEMBER: Authors Guild, Minnesota Fire Chiefs Association, Minnesota Wildland Firefighters Association, Northeastern Minnesotans for Wilderness.

WRITINGS:

Letters from Side Lake: A Chronicle of Life in the North Woods, Harper (New York, NY), 1987.
The Bear Guardian: Northwoods Tales and Meditations, North Star Press (St. Cloud, MN), 1990.
Bumming with the Furies: Out on the Trail of Experience, North Star Press (St. Cloud, MN), 1993.
Seeing the Raven: A Narrative of Renewal, University of Minnesota Press (Minneapolis, MN), 1994.
Hellroaring, North Star Press (St. Cloud, MN), 1994.
The Snow Lotus: Exploring the Eternal Moment, University of Minnesota Press (Minneapolis, MN), 1996.
Rogues and Toads: A Poetry Collection, North Star Press (St. Cloud, MN), 1999.
Trials by Wildfire: In Search of the New Warrior Spirit, Pfeifer-Hamilton (Duluth, MN), 2000.
Ghosts of the Fireground: Echoes of the Great Peshtigo Fire and the Calling of a Wildland, HarperSanFrancisco (San Francisco, CA), 2002.

Author of regular column in *TWA Ambassador,* 1985-86. Contributor to magazines. Contributing editor of *Twin Cities,* 1984-86, and *Minnesota Monthly,* 1984-89.

WORK IN PROGRESS: Deep Sky.

SIDELIGHTS: Peter M. Leschak grew up in a small mining town in northern Minnesota. In 1969 he left the Mesabi Iron Range to attend college in the city of St. Paul. The author never felt comfortable with city life, however; so, after earning his college degree, Leschak returned to rural Minnesota. He and his wife settled near Side Lake, where they built a log home and began to explore the wilderness around them. Their experiences form the core of *Letters from Side Lake: A Chronicle of Life in the North Woods.* "Mr. Leschak is an acute observer with genuine affection for his material," wrote John Tallmadge in the *New York Times Book Review.* His book is a collection of "dozens of stories told in a breezy, journalistic style." *Washington Post Book World* critic Vic Sussman likewise found Leschak "a fine writer with an eye both for natural wonder and for irony . . . [and with a] great sense of humor that carries this lively book along." He added: "Leschak's engaging essays are happily free of bile, evangelism, and Thoreauvian moralizing on the evils of modern life." Sussman saw *Letters from Side Lake* as a celebration of "the beauty and adventure of the north woods . . . and the simplicity of small-town life."

In addition to his writing, Leschak has another vocation—or a "calling," as a *Publishers Weekly* writer put it. He is a wildlands firefighter, battling blazes that threaten hundreds of thousands of woodland acres. "These firefighters aren't pulling kitties out of trees," noted a *Baltimore City Paper* article by Scott Carlson. "They're saving ancient sequoias and million-dollar retirement homes." Leschak chronicled a firefighter's lot in the 2002 book *Ghosts of the Fireground: Echoes of the Great Peshtigo Fire and the Calling of a Wildland.* This part-history, part-memoir recounts the Peshtigo, Wisconsin, wildfire of 1871, which killed 1,200 people and charred 1,800 square miles of land. The Peshtigo disaster is told through the eyewitness account of a priest who survived the blaze; Leschak, himself trained for the ministry, uses spiritual references throughout the book, "citing sources as diverse as Carl Jung, Friedrich Nietzsche, William James and Walker Percy," according to a *Publishers Weekly* contributor. As Leschak wrote in *Ghosts of the Fireground:* "Wildlife firefighting is a path to pain and not to a fat stock portfolio. There is mystery here—the romantic attraction of hardship and hazard amid a corpulent society obsessed with mammon."

Carlson remarked that Leschak "found what amounts to a new religion fighting fire, one influenced by Christian notions of suffering." Indeed, "there's plenty of zeal-touched imagery here," stated a *Kirkus Reviews* critic, who added that the "urgency and drama . . . never feel overstated but aptly fit the circumstances." In his assessment of *Ghosts of the Fireground,* Carlson felt the author "brings to life the horror of being trapped in . . . Peshtigo as it burned," while a *Publishers Weekly* reviewer likewise found such scenes "crackle with energy." In describing the duties of a present-day firefighter, the author "explains the theory and practice," commented Dean Neprud of the *Star Tribune,* "in crisp, factual prose. The emphasis is on logistics and backbreaking labor, but he adds a sense of urgency that helps one understand firefighting's 'gritty verity of action and life.'"

In a 2002 interview with Fred Turner for *National Geographic Adventure,* Leschak compared his job at the dawn of the twenty-first century with the tech-

niques used just a few decades earlier. Both yesterday and today, managing wild areas with controlled fire is part of the job. "Fifteen years ago I worked fires—and notice I don't say 'fought' fires, I say 'worked fires'—[in] some of the most forbidding, rattlesnake-infested land on the continent," Leschak said. "There were no structures at the time, but now there are people there with houses and it's become very complicated and very expensive to fight fires in these former 'wilderness' areas. Yet if we wish to maintain forests, as opposed to tree plantations, then fire is an integral part of the natural life cycle."

Leschak told *CA:* "I agree with novelist Philip Roth that 'We writers are lucky: nothing truly bad can happen to us. It's all material.' One of the goals of a writer is to weave his own life into the tapestry of the culture. We're entertainers as well as reporters and teachers, and if we wish to reach others, we must be willing to offer a piece of ourselves. If you can tell a story (and all writing boils down to that) in such a way that the reader feels he knows you, then you are successful. In the terms of our ancient forebears, we are closer to the shaman than the scribe. It's just too bad it doesn't pay better."

BIOGRAPHICAL AND CRITICAL SOURCES:

PERIODICALS

Kirkus Reviews, May 15, 2002, review of *Ghosts of the Fireground: Echoes of the Great Peshtigo Fire and the Calling of a Wildland,* p. 718.
New York Times Book Review, June 28, 1987, John Tallmadge, review of *Letters from Side Lake: A Chronicle of Life in the North Woods;* February 12, 1995; September 15, 2002, Stewart O'Nan, "New Age Firefighting: To the Author, Fighting Fire Is God's Work, Both Now and Long Ago," p. 22.
Publishers Weekly, July 15, 2002, review of *Ghosts of the Fireground,* p. 66.
St. Paul Pioneer Press-Dispatch, July 7, 1993.
Star Tribune (Minneapolis, MN), July 21, 2002, Dean Neprud, "Trial by Fire," p. 14F.
Wall Street Journal, July 9, 2002, p. D6.
Washington Post Book World, July 12, 1987, Vic Sussman, review of *Letters from Side Lake.*

ONLINE

Baltimore City Paper, http://www.citypaper.com/ (August 19, 2002), Scott Carlson, "Hot Stuff."

National Geographic Adventure, http://www.news. nationalgeographic.com/ (August 19, 2002), Fred Turner, "Firefighter-Author on Battling Colorado Blazes, Scandal."

*   *   *

LESSEM, Don 1951-

PERSONAL: Born December 2, 1951, in New York, NY; son of Lawrence (a dentist) and Gertrude (a psychologist; maiden name, Goldman) Lessem; divorced; children: Rebecca, Erica. *Ethnicity:* "Caucasian." *Education:* Brandeis University, B.A. (cum laude), 1973; also attended University of Massachusetts—Boston, 1976, and Massachusetts Institute of Technology, 1988. *Politics:* "Anarchist." *Religion:* Jewish. *Hobbies and other interests:* Travel, sports.

ADDRESSES: Home and office—Fax: 617-527-7752. *Agent*—Al Zuckerman, Writers House, 21 West 26th St., New York, NY 10010. *E-mail*—dinodonl@aol. com.

CAREER: Dinosaur Productions, president, 1995—; Dinosaur Exhibitions, president, 1996—. Jurassic Foundation, founder. Writer and consultant; technical advisor for films and theme parks, including the film *Jurassic Park.*

MEMBER: Society of Vertebrate Paleontology.

AWARDS, HONORS: Winner of several awards from National Science Teachers Association for his children's books.

WRITINGS:

Life Is No Yuk for the Yak: A Book of Endangered Animals, illustrated by Linda Bourke, Crane Russak (New York, NY), 1977.
How to Flatten Your Nose, Klutz Press, 1980.
Aerphobics: The Scientific Way to Stop Exercising (humor), William Morrow (New York, NY), 1980.
The Worst of Everything: The Experts' Listing of the Most Loathsome and Deficient in Every Realm of Our Lives, McGraw-Hill (New York, NY), 1988.

Don Lessem

(With John R. Horner) *Digging Up Tyrannosaurus Rex,* Crown (New York, NY), 1992.
Kings of Creation: How a New Breed of Scientists Is Revolutionizing Our Understanding of Dinosaurs, illustrated by John Sibbick, Simon & Schuster (New York, NY), 1992, published as *Dinosaurs Rediscovered: New Findings Which Are Revolutionizing Dinosaur Science,* Touchstone (New York, NY), 1993.
(With John R. Horner) *The Complete T. Rex: How Stunning New Discoveries Are Changing Our Understanding of the World's Most Famous Dinosaur,* Simon & Schuster (New York, NY), 1993.
(With Donald F. Glut) *The Dinosaur Society's Dinosaur Encyclopedia,* Random House (New York, NY), 1993.
The Iceman, Crown (New York, NY), 1994.
Jack Horner: Living with Dinosaurs, illustrated by Janet Hamlin, Scientific American Books for Young Readers (New York, NY), 1994.
Inside the Amazing Amazon: Incredible Fold-out Cross Sections of the World's Greatest Rainforest, illustrated by Michael Rothman, Crown (New York, NY), 1995.

Ornithomimids: The Fastest Dinosaur, illustrated by Donna Braginetz, Carolrhoda Books (Minneapolis, MN), 1996.

Raptors! The Nastiest Dinosaurs, illustrated by David Peters, Little, Brown (Boston, MA), 1996.

Seismosaurus: The Longest Dinosaur, illustrated by Donna Braginetz, Carolrhoda Books (Minneapolis, MN), 1996.

Troodon: The Smartest Dinosaur, illustrated by Donna Braginetz, Carolrhoda Books (Minneapolis, MN), 1996.

Utahraptor: The Deadliest Dinosaur, illustrated by Donna Braginetz, Carolrhoda Books (Minneapolis, MN), 1996.

Dinosaur Worlds: New Dinosaurs, New Discoveries, Boyds Mills Press (Honesdale, PA), 1996.

Supergiants! The Biggest Dinosaurs, illustrated by David Peters, Little, Brown (Boston, MA), 1997.

Bigger Than T. Rex: The Discovery of Gigantosorus, the Biggest Meat-Eating Dinosaur Ever Found, illustrated by Robert F. Walters, Crown (New York, NY), 1997.

All the Dirt on Dinosaurs, illustrated by Kevin Wasden, Tor Kids (New York, NY), 1998.

Dinosaurs to Dodos: An Encyclopedia of Extinct Animals, illustrated by Jan Sovak, Scholastic (New York, NY), 1999.

Scholastic Dinosaur Dictionary, Scholastic (New York, NY), 2001.

Biggest Dinosaurs, illustrated by John Bindon, Grosset & Dunlap (New York, NY), 2001.

Baby Dinosaurs, illustrated by John Bindon, Grosset & Dunlap (New York, NY), 2001.

Giants of the Sky, illustrated by John Bindon, Grosset & Dunlap (New York, NY), 2002.

(With Hall Train) *Triceratops,* Candlewick Press (Cambridge, MA), 2002.

Monsters of the Sea, illustrated by John Bindon, Grosset & Dunlap (New York, NY), 2002.

(With Hall Train) *T. Rex,* Candlewick Press (Cambridge, MA), 2002.

The Dinosaur Atlas: A Complete Look at the World of Dinosaurs, illustrated by John Bindon, Firefly Books (Buffalo, NY), 2003.

Scholastic Dinosaurs A to Z: The Ultimate Dinosaur Encyclopedia, illustrated by Jan Sovak, Scholastic (New York, NY), 2003.

Dino Don's Dinosaur Atlas, Key Porter Books (Toronto, Ontario, Canada), 2003.

Television writer and program host for the series *Discovery* and *Nova,* both for Public Broadcasting Service. Columnist, *Highlights for Children.*

WORK IN PROGRESS: The Smallest Dinosaurs, Giant Meat-Eating Dinosaurs, Duck-Billed Dinosaurs, Armored Dinosaurs, Giant Plant-Eating Dinosaurs, and *Horned Dinosaurs,* all in "Meet the Dinosaurs" series, illustrated by John Bindon, publication by Lerner Publications (Minneapolis, MN) expected in 2005.

SIDELIGHTS: Don Lessem once commented to *CA:* "Dinosaurs are my writing life, at least much of it. My job as I see it is to communicate the latest discoveries of dinosaurs to anyone who gives a hoot, especially kids. I do so via exhibits I build, such as 'Lost World' or 'Chinese Dinosaurs'; writing a column for *Highlights* magazine; creating the largest dinosaur charity; recreating the largest dinosaurs; advising on theme parks and movies; writing and hosting *Nova* and *Discovery* documentaries; AND writing books.

"While I've also written books on Amazon animals and mummies, I got onto dinosaurs visiting a Montana dig for a newspaper while a science journalism fellow at Massachusetts Institute of Technology in 1988. I love the new discoveries, the remote locales, the characters who study dinosaurs, and the scavenger hunting that is much of the science. Many people, at least those under the age of ten, share that interest, fortunately, or I'd be working nights at McDonald's."

Lessem, whose engaging style and evident excitement about his topics, coupled with his dedication to providing accurate, accessible information on his subjects, has authored books popular with readers and critics alike. Nicknamed "Dino Don," Lessem is best known for his volumes on dinosaurs and the scientists who have dedicated their lives to uncovering the mysteries of these long-extinct animals. His first books, including *Life Is No Yuk for the Yak,* in which profiles of endangered species are accompanied by lighthearted limericks and Linda Bourke's cartoon illustrations, often combine science with a humorous approach. The majority of his books outline the history of and current findings about a wide variety of dinosaurs—their discovery, habits, environments, and time periods.

In addition to writing about dinosaurs, Lessem is the author of a book on the Amazon rainforest, *Inside the Amazing Amazon: Incredible Fold-out Cross Sections of the World's Greatest Rainforest,* in which the text augments oversize fold-out illustrations by Michael

Rothman that detail plant and animal life in the world's largest rainforest. He is also the creator of *The Iceman,* a book describing the discovery of a 5,000-year-old mummy in the mountains of Europe and what scientists gleaned from it about the life of prehistoric Europeans, and *Jack Horner: Living with Dinosaurs,* a biography about John R. Horner, the chief curator of paleontology at the University of Montana and the scientific advisor on the film *Jurassic Park;* he is also a friend of the author. A writer who studied biobehavioralism and science journalism, Lessem is the founder of several dinosaur-related organizations, including the Dinosaur Foundation, Dinosaur Productions, and Dinosaur Exhibitions.

Notable among Lessem's many books on dinosaurs is *Dinosaur Worlds: New Dinosaurs, New Discoveries,* a work in which several of the most important sites where dinosaur remains have been found are introduced to the reader; Lessem also provides information on the environments, prey, and life cycles of a large number of the creatures. This "is a book that report writers and dinophiles won't want to miss," commented Stephanie Zvirin in *Booklist.* Lessem's books on individual dinosaurs include *Raptors! The Nastiest Dinosaurs, Ornithomimids: The Fastest Dinosaur, Troodon: The Smartest Dinosaur, Seismosaurus: The Longest Dinosaur,* and *Utahraptor: The Deadliest Dinosaur,* all part of a series on special dinosaurs published by Carolrhoda in 1996. In these books, Lessem gathers information on the discovery of the fossil remains of each dinosaur type and the paleontologists who found them as well as on how information about their abilities and habits has been deduced from the fossil evidence; in addition, the author speculates about possible evolutionary descendants of his subjects. "Lessem treats a popular topic adeptly, humorously, and with a balance of information that is both relevant and stimulating to read," remarked Olga Kuharets in a review of *Seismosaurus* and *Utahraptor* in *School Library Journal.* In her *Booklist* review of *Ornithomimids* and *Troodon,* Frances Bradburn commented that these "finely crafted" books offer "a fascinating look at how paleontologists discover the fossilized remains of these huge beasts." In addition, Lessem's texts are praised by critics for their clarity and organization of a wealth of fascinating material.

The Dinosaur Atlas: A Complete Look at the World of Dinosaurs is divided into the three eras in which dinosaurs lived, the Triassic, Jurassic, and Cretaceous periods. Each section includes its own map showing where the various dinosaurs of the period were found on the continents as they then existed. The text studies each dinosaur and the environment in which it lived and is accompanied by facts in a sidebar titled "Dino Don Says." The book offers information on digs that students can visit, as well as Web sites that provide related information. In a review for *Resource Links,* Judy Cottrell wrote that *The Dinosaur Atlas* "is a wonderful book which takes a geographical approach to the study of dinosaurs."

Scholastic Dinosaurs A to Z: The Ultimate Dinosaur Encyclopedia, written at the elementary school level, presents dinosaurs alphabetically along with complete details about each. Common names point to the original scientific names, and many of the dinosaurs are shown in full-page color illustrations. Lessem tells readers how to participate in a dig and offers a bibliography of books, Web sites, videos, expeditions, and museums. *School Library Journal*'s Steven Engelfried called the volume "an attractive and useful resource."

Lessem's dedication to introducing children and adults to the lives of the scientists behind the scientific discoveries has yielded such works as *Kings of Creation: How a New Breed of Scientists Is Revolutionizing Our Understanding of Dinosaurs* and *Jack Horner: Living with Dinosaurs.* In *Kings of Creation,* the author presents an overview of the explosion of new information that has become available over the last three decades, in which the popular image of dinosaurs has been completely revised by a group of scientists who have uncovered signs of intelligence, speed, and nurturing in species previously thought to be stupid, slow, and hostile even to their own offspring. Leading scientists, significant digs, and the new theories are all presented in a work in which Lessem, according to a reviewer for *Publishers Weekly,* "presents a lively sampling of current and significant work on dinosaurs worldwide. . . . This is the best book on the subject since Robert Bakker's *Dinosaur Heresies* and a treat for buffs."

In Lessem's book about Horner, the paleontologist with whom Lessem has written two books and with whom he worked as a consultant on the immensely popular film *Jurassic Park,* the author presents both personal background about Horner and his most famous scientific discoveries.

Lessem's books on dinosaurs and paleontologists have garnered widespread praise for their accumulation of a wealth of information on a topic of interest to many children. This information is consistently presented in an attractive, uncluttered format, in prose that critics consider both clear and inspirational, displaying the author's own enthusiasm for his subject. Lessem's books on the scientists whose lives have been dedicated to revising and augmenting what is known about dinosaurs display similar qualities, according to the author's reviewers.

"My aspiration," Lessem once commented, "is to continue providing children with what for so long they have lacked—current and accurate information on new scientific discoveries and the methods behind them in hopes of feeding their mania for dinosaurs and spreading it to all of science as a lifetime interest.

"I'm doing so most recently by not only writing but 'packaging' books, providing illustrators and graphics for publishers. I hope to continue as long as dinosaurs are still alive, at least in the imaginations of many of us."

BIOGRAPHICAL AND CRITICAL SOURCES:

PERIODICALS

American Scientist, May-June, 1993, Thomas J. Rossbach, review of *Kings of Creation: How a New Breed of Scientists Is Revolutionizing Our Understanding of Dinosaurs,* p. 1480.

Appraisal, winter, 1995, pp. 112-114; winter-spring, 1996, pp. 35-36.

BioScience, March, 1995, Philip W. Signor, review of *The Complete T. Rex: How Stunning New Discoveries Are Changing Our Understanding of the World's Most Famous Dinosaur,* p. 221.

Booklist, April 1, 1992, Jon Kartman, review of *Kings of Creation,* p. 1419; January 15, 1993, Hazel Rochman, review of *Digging Up Tyrannosaurus Rex,* p. 896; April 15, 1993, John Kartman, review of *The Complete T. Rex,* p. 1480; April 15, 1994, review of *The Dinosaur Society's Dinosaur Encyclopedia,* p. 1551; November 1, 1994, Ilene Cooper, review of *The Iceman,* p. 496; November 15, 1994, Denia Hester, review of *Jack Horner: Living with Dinosaurs,* p. 596; October 1, 1995,

Carolyn Phelan, review of *Inside the Amazing Amazon: Incredible Fold-out Cross Sections of the World's Greatest Rainforest,* p. 310; February 15, 1996, Frances Bradburn, review of *Ornithomimids: The Fastest Dinosaur* and *Troodon: The Smartest Dinosaur,* p. 1014; September 1, 1996, Stephanie Zvirin, review of *Raptors! The Nastiest Dinosaurs,* p. 121; p. 997; November 15, 1996, Stephanie Zvirin, review of *Dinosaur Worlds: New Dinosaurs, New Discoveries,* pp. 583-584; December 15, 2003, review of *Scholastic Dinosaurs A to Z: The Ultimate Dinosaur Encyclopedia,* p. 766; March 1, 2004, review of *The Dinosaur Atlas: A Complete Look at the World of Dinosaurs,* p. 1228.

Book Report, May-June, 1997, Joyce B. Fisher, review of *Dinosaur Worlds,* p. 42.

Bulletin of the Center for Children's Books, September, 1994, p. 17; December, 1994, p. 135.

Kirkus Reviews, May 15, 1994, p. 702; November 15, 1994, p. 1534; December 1, 1995, p. 1703.

Library Journal, April 15, 1992, Amy Brunvand, review of *Kings of Creation,* p. 118.

People, June 21, 1993, Jill Rachlin, review of *The Complete T. Rex,* p. 27; July 5, 1993, William Plummer, "Mr. Dinosaur," p. 69.

Publishers Weekly, March 2, 1992, review of *Kings of Creation,* p. 58; November 4, 1996, p. 78; January 20, 2003, "Dino-mite!," p. 85.

Quarterly Review of Biology, June, 1993, Edwin H. Colbert, review of *Kings of Creation,* p. 255.

Resource Links, October, 2003, Judy Cottrell, review of *The Dinosaur Atlas,* p. 25.

School Library Journal, March, 1978, p. 138; July, 1994, Jeanette Larson, review of *The Iceman,* p. 111; January, 1996, Susan Oliver, review of *Inside the Amazing Amazon,* p. 120; April, 1996, Cathryn A. Camper, review of *Ornithomimids* and *Troodon,* p. 147; September, 1996, Olga Kuharets, review of *Seismosaurus: The Longest Dinosaur* and *Utahraptor: The Deadliest Dinosaur,* p. 218; October, 1996, Cathryn A. Camper, review of *Raptors!,* pp. 135-136; December, 1996, Cathryn A. Camper, review of *Dinosaur Worlds,* p. 131; September, 1997, Cathryn A. Camper, review of *Supergiants! The Biggest Dinosaurs,* p. 232; December, 1997, Cathryn A. Camper, review of *Bigger Than T. Rex: The Discovery of Gigantosorus, the Biggest Meat-Eating Dinosaur Ever Found,* p. 140; December, 2003, Steven Engelfried, review of *The Dinosaur Atlas* and *Scholastic Dinosaurs A to Z,* p. 170.

Science Teacher, October, 1993, Richard Thomas, review of *Dinosaurs Rediscovered: New Findings Which Are Revolutionizing Dinosaur Science,* p. 80.

Scientific American, December, 1993, Philip Morrison and Phylis Morrison, review of *Digging Up Tyrannosaurus Rex,* p. 132; December, 1994, Philip Morrison and Phylis Morrison, review of *The Iceman,* p. 121.

Wilson Library Bulletin, April, 1994, James Rettig, review of *The Dinosaur Society's Dinosaur Encyclopedia,* p. 88.

* * *

LIPEZ, Richard 1938-
(Richard Stevenson)

PERSONAL: Born November 30, 1938, in Lock Haven, PA; son of Harris (a radio station manager) and Helen (Seltzer) Lipez; married Hedy Harris, 1968 (marriage ended c. 1989); companion of Joe Wheaton (a sculptor), since 1990; children: Sydney, Zachary. *Education:* Lock Haven State College, B.A., 1961; graduate study at Pennsylvania State University. *Politics:* Democrat.

ADDRESSES: Home—161 Otis Rd., Otis, MA 01253.

CAREER: Journalist. Peace Corps, volunteer in Addis Ababa, Ethiopia, 1962-64, program evaluator in Washington, DC, 1964-67; Action for Opportunity, Pittsfield, MA, executive director, 1968-70; freelance writer, 1970—. *Berkshire Eagle,* editorial writer.

WRITINGS:

(With Peter Stein) *Grand Scam,* Dial Press (New York, NY), 1979.

Contributor of articles and stories to periodicals, including *Harper's, Newsday, Washington Post, Progressive, Atlantic, New Times, Redbook,* and *Newsweek;* contributor of reviews to *Washington Post.*

"STRACHEY" MYSTERY SERIES; UNDER PSEUDONYM RICHARD STEVENSON

Death Trick, St. Martin's Press (New York, NY), 1981.
On the Other Hand, Death, St. Martin's Press (New York, NY), 1984.

Ice Blues, St. Martin's Press (New York, NY), 1986.
Third Man Out, St. Martin's Press (New York, NY), 1993.
Shock to the System, St. Martin's Press (New York, NY), 1995.
Chain of Fools, St. Martin's Press (New York, NY), 1996.
Strachey's Folly, St. Martin's Press (New York, NY), 1998.
Tongue Tied, St. Martin's Press (New York, NY), 2003.

SIDELIGHTS: Richard Lipez has written a series of mystery novels under the pseudonym Richard Stevenson. These novels, featuring gay private investigator Donald Strachey and his lover, Timothy Callahan, are "some of the funniest, smartest PI novels around," according to D. L. Browne in an online review for *Thrilling Detective.* "The guy is just a terrific writer! Maybe even brilliant."

As might be expected, gay characters and issues appear throughout each one of the "Donald Strachey" books. In *Third Man Out,* for example, John Rutka, a gay activist, is on a crusade to "out" gays in his community who refuse to come out publicly. When Rutka turns up dead, Strachey must sort through the many suspects to find the killer. *A Shock to the System* concerns Dr. Crockwell, a psychiatrist who cures gays who want to change their lives. But when former patient Paul Haig, the son of a wealthy and politically prominent family, is found murdered, the police name Crockwell as a prime suspect, while Haig's mother insists that her son's lover is to blame. *Strachey's Folly* finds the detective, Timothy, and Peace Corps friend Maynard Sudbury visiting the AIDS quilt in Washington, D.C. The quilt includes a panel for each of those who have died of AIDS. The trio are startled to find a political writer back home memorialized on the quilt, although they know for certain the man is alive and healthy. Soon after, the quilt is vandalized, Maynard is shot, and Strachey must fight local police bias and political corruption to unravel the mystery. Whitney Scott of *Booklist* called *Strachey's Folly* "a gripping, fast-paced mystery."

Two constants in the "Strachey" books, a critic for *Publishers Weekly* explained, are "Strachey's customary wry humor and engaging at-home scenes with lover Timmy." Charles Harmon in *Booklist* acknowledged that "the detective's tranquilly domestic rela-tion-ship with his longtime lover stands in refreshing contrast to affairs in most other gay novels, with their less contented leading characters."

Speaking of the series as a whole, Browne summed up: "Stevenson is one of the best PI writers out there. I suspect his Don Strachey series isn't taken as seriously as it should be . . . because they're so funny. Funny, yes, but smart. And you don't have to be gay to enjoy Stevenson's clever, crafty mysteries. True, the books are often political in theme, but the tone is non-strident and convincing."

BIOGRAPHICAL AND CRITICAL SOURCES:

PERIODICALS

Booklist, February 15, 1992, Ray Olson, review of *Third Man Out,* p. 1092; January 1, 1996, Charles Harmon, review of *A Shock to the System,* p. 798; November 1, 1996, Charles Harmon, review of *Chain of Fools,* p. 483; June 1, 1998, Whitney Scott, review of *Strachey's Folly,* p. 1735.

Lambda Book Report, May-June, 1992, Austin Wallace, review of *Third Man Out,* p. 46.

Library Journal, March 1, 1986, Jo Ann Vicarel, review of *Ice Blues,* p. 111; July, 1998, Rex E. Klett, review of *Strachey's Folly,* p.141.

New York Times Book Review, October 14, 1984, Newgate Callendar, review of *On the Other Hand, Death,* p. 46; May 18, 1986, review of *Ice Blues,* p. 38.

Publishers Weekly, June 15, 1984, review of *On the Other Hand, Death,* p. 75; January 17, 1986, review of *Ice Blues,* p. 63; December 20, 1991, review of *Third Man Out,* p. 67; November 20, 1995, review of *A Shock to the System,* p. 69.

Wilson Library Bulletin, June, 1986, Kathleen Maio, review of *Ice Blues,* p. 68.

ONLINE

Richard Stevenson Mysteries Web site, http://members.aol.com/FansPage/ (April 18, 2003).

Thrilling Detective, http://www.thrillingdetective.com/ (December, 2002), D. L. Browne, review of "Strachey" series.

LISLE, Janet Taylor 1947-

PERSONAL: Born February 13, 1947, in Englewood, NJ; daughter of Alden (in insurance) and Janet (an architect) Taylor; married c. 1970 (divorced); married Richard Lisle (in international banking), 1976; children: Elizabeth. *Education:* Smith College, B.A., 1969; studied journalism at Georgia State University.

ADDRESSES: Home—Little Compton, RI. *Agent*—Gina Maccoby, P.O. Box 60, Chappaqua, NY 10514.

CAREER: Writer. Has worked as a journalist in Georgia and New York; VISTA (Volunteers in Service to America), volunteer, Atlanta, GA, c. 1970.

AWARDS, HONORS: Best Books for Young Adults, American Library Association (ALA), Best Books, *School Library Journal,* Editors' Choice, *Booklist,* all 1985, Parents' Choice Award, Parents' Choice Foundation, 1986, and Best of the '80s, *Booklist,* all for *Sirens and Spies;* Golden Kite Honor Book for Fiction, Society of Children's Book Writers, Best Children's Books, *Parents' Magazine,* and Editors' Choice, *Booklist,* all 1987, all for *The Great Dimpole Oak;* Best Books, *School Library Journal,* Editors' Choice, *Booklist,* and Parents' Choice, all 1989, and Newbery Honor Book, ALA, 1990, all for *Afternoon of the Elves;* Best Books, *School Library Journal, New York Times Book Review, Boston Globe,* and *Parents' Magazine,* all 1991, all for *The Lampfish of Twill;* Best Books, *School Library Journal,* "Pick of the Lists," American Booksellers Association (ABA), and Best Books, Bank Street Child Study Children's Books Committee, for *Forest;* Notable Books selection, Bank Street Child Study Children's Books Committee, 1994, for *The Gold Dust Letters,* and 1995, for *Looking for Juliette;* Best Books, *School Library Journal,* 1995, for *A Message from the Match Girl;* Scott O'Dell Award for Historical Fiction, *Riverbank Review* "book of distinction" citation, ALA Notable Children's Book, and "Fanfare" citation, *Horn Book,* all 2001, all for *The Art of Keeping Cool;* ALA Notable Children's Book citation and "best book" citation, *School Library Journal,* both 2001, both for *The Lost Flower Children.*

WRITINGS:

The Dancing Cats of Applesap, illustrated by Joelle Shefts, Bradbury Press (Scarsdale, NY), 1984, Aladdin Books (New York, NY), 1993.

Janet Taylor Lisle

Sirens and Spies, Bradbury Press (Scarsdale, NY), 1985, Collier Books (New York, NY), 1990.

The Great Dimpole Oak, illustrated by Stephen Gammell, Orchard Books (New York, NY), 1987, reprinted, Puffin Books (New York, NY), 1999.

Afternoon of the Elves, Orchard Books (New York, NY), 1989.

The Lampfish of Twill, illustrated by Wendy Anderson Halperin, Orchard Books (New York, NY), 1991.

Forest, Orchard Books (New York, NY), 1993.

The Gold Dust Letters, Orchard Books (New York, NY), 1994.

Looking for Juliette, Orchard Books (New York, NY), 1994.

A Message from the Match Girl, Orchard Books (New York, NY), 1995.

Angela's Aliens, Orchard Books (New York, NY), 1996.

The Lost Flower Children, Philomel Books (New York, NY), 1999.

The Art of Keeping Cool, Atheneum (New York, NY), 2000.

How I Became a Writer and Oggie Learned to Drive, Philomel Books (New York, NY), 2002.

The Crying Rocks, Atheneum (New York, NY), 2003.

ADAPTATIONS: Afternoon of the Elves was adapted as a stage play, 1993, and is collected in *Theatre for Young Audiences: Around the World in 21 Plays.*

SIDELIGHTS: Janet Taylor Lisle is the author of young adult and juvenile novels that explore the relationships and boundaries between the miraculous and the everyday. Blending humor and realistic character development, Lisle creates worlds full of both fantasy and fact. She revels in dancing cats, backyard elves, and forests shared by squirrels and humans leading parallel lives. Set primarily in the northeastern United States where Lisle was raised and continues to live, early Lisle titles such as *Sirens and Spies, The Great Dimpole Oak,* and *Afternoon of the Elves* were all award-winners and garnered the author a wide readership. Later titles include the four companion volumes of the "Investigators of the Unknown" series. Whatever the topic or setting, "Lisle's books are uniformly delightful," according to Andrea Cleghorn in an essay in *Children's Books and Their Creators.* And if she employs elements of fantasy in her books, it is in order to delve more deeply into the hidden recesses of human life. As Lisle noted in an essay for *Something about the Author Autobiography Series (SAAS),* "The investigation of reality, both the inward and outward sort, is at the core of the stories I like to write."

Lisle has been writing since she was a child. The only daughter—and oldest child—in a family of five siblings, she grew up in rural Rhode Island and Connecticut. She enjoyed her special position as the sole girl in the family, and she and her brothers were avid readers from an early age, consuming J. R. R. Tolkien and Robert Louis Stevenson until they felt "in a trance" from the stories, as she recalled in *SAAS.* Her tranquil childhood in Farmington, Connecticut, changed radically when she went to a private school in the sixth grade. "I was a new girl," Lisle wrote in *SAAS,* "an outsider, and even though I recognized some of the students in my class from home, I felt shy and out of place." Worse, she began to have academic troubles, something that had never occurred before. Math, particularly, was a weak spot, but she soon compensated with a talent for soccer that won her friends and recognition. Yet always throughout school, English classes were her safe haven. From the age of ten, Lisle was composing stories both at school and increasingly on her own at home. When her teachers became more concerned with such things as spelling and sentence structure over content, Lisle turned to "secret writing," as she called it in *SAAS*.

Attending Smith College, Lisle majored in English, but her study of the great writers daunted her with the high benchmark they set. "I did not take a single writing class at Smith College," Lisle noted in *SAAS*. "In a completely unforeseen way, my education had silenced me." Out of college, she married and worked as a volunteer for VISTA (Volunteers in Service to America) for a time. Then she returned to school and earned a degree in journalism. Thereafter she worked for a decade as a journalist, writing both hard news and features. The daily grind of deadline writing was another kind of school for Lisle, and helped give her a facility for speedy organization.

A new marriage and the birth of her child put Lisle on a different path, however. In 1981 she gave up journalism and started writing for children. A writer's workshop helped with this decision, and the inspiration of some childhood memories resulted in her first book, *The Dancing Cats of Applesap,* the story of a shy ten-year-old girl who manages to save her town's drugstore and soda fountain by bringing some amazing cats together. As Ilene Cooper noted in a *Horn Book* article about Lisle, the story was "an utterly original fantasy," about cats that dance in a drugstore after hours to the guitar strums of the owner. Melba Morris, the protagonist of the book, brings Applesap, New York, notoriety when she helps spread the news about the cats in Mr. Jiggs's old-fashioned drugstore. This notoriety, in turn, saves the drugstore. "This story has elements found in the most enduring works of children's fiction: humor, inventiveness, and a message gently relayed," Cooper noted, writing in *Booklist*. Anne Osborn, in *School Library Journal,* called the book a "gentle but rewarding story" and "not so much a cat fantasy as a novel of character development and growth."

Lisle followed this initial publication with a more realistic young adult novel, *Sirens and Spies,* the story of two sisters and their secret-bearing violin teacher. As Lisle explained in *SAAS,* "I contrived to place a pair of sisters at the center of the story so that I could experience a little of the doubleness of sisterhood," the doubleness she was missing in her own youth surrounded by four younger brothers. Mary and Elsie take violin lessons from Miss Fitch, with Elsie being the favorite. It is therefore surprising to Mary when

her sister turns against the aged teacher, accusing her of being a collaborator with the Germans during the Second World War in her native France. But when Miss Fitch is injured in her home by an intruder, Mary helps to unravel the secret in the teacher's past. Nancy Choice, writing in the *Voice of Youth Advocates,* called the book a "moving story about friendship, forgiveness, and the awful power of secrets." Zena Sutherland in the *Bulletin of the Center for Children's Books* noted that *Sirens and Spies* is a "truly sophisticated book," while David A. Lindsey in *School Library Journal* dubbed it "a piece of quality fiction."

Lisle wrote a quartet of imaginative novels for children and young adults from 1987 to 1993, including *The Great Dimpole Oak, Afternoon of the Elves, The Lampfish of Twill,* and *Forest.* Something of a technical tour de force, *The Great Dimpole Oak* cuts back and forth from Paris to Bombay to small town America where a majestic oak tree is weaving its subtle magic over all concerned. Everyone who comes into contact with the tree is affected in this "feat of originality and plotting," according to a critic in *Publishers Weekly,* who concluded: "A beautifully orchestrated novel, this is short yet deeply satisfying." Anita Silvey, writing in *Horn Book,* found everything about the book, from writing to cover art, "marked by exquisite taste," and concluded that Lisle's third novel "contains no echoes of other creators' voices."

"A fascinating portrayal of a manipulative yet touching friendship" is how Annette Curtis Klause summed up Lisle's next book, *Afternoon of the Elves,* in *School Library Journal.* The outcast, Sara-Kate, befriends the younger, more popular Hillary by showing her an elf village in her back yard, but Hillary also discovers the truth about Sara-Kate: that she is alone caring for her sick mother and desperately trying to cope with domestic duties and unpaid bills. Neither Hillary nor the reader are ever quite sure of the reality of the elves, but once social services intervenes and takes Sara-Kate from her mother, Hillary sets the tiny village up in her own yard. In the *Bulletin of the Center for Children's Books,* Betsy Hearne described *Afternoon of the Elves* as "a carefully developed story focused on two children who influence each other in realistic, subtle stages."

In *The Lampfish of Twill,* the magic is underwater. An old fisherman leads Eric down a whirlpool into an ancient and glorious world at the center of the Earth.

A *Publishers Weekly* contributor compared *The Lampfish of Twill* favorably to other classics of the imagination such as *Wrinkle in Time* and *The Lion, the Witch, and the Wardrobe,* and noted that it "tickles the imagination and challenges preconceived notions about reality and illusion." A *Kirkus Reviews* commentator called it "a splendid, unique fantasy" in which "fantastical creatures help convey truths that transcend the harsh realities of a world whose rituals and prejudices are all too familiar."

With *Forest,* the magic is more traditional, involving the exploits of twelve-year-old Amber and a sentient squirrel named Woodbine. Amber unwittingly sets off a war between humans and the other forest animals when she builds a tree house too deep in the forest. Carol Fox, reviewing the book in the *Bulletin of the Center for Children's Books,* concluded that Lisle "has created a world of innocence marked with heartache, truth infused with absurdity, and wisdom relinquished to recklessness—all in the guise of animal fantasy." In *Publishers Weekly* a reviewer noted that this "expertly crafted promotion of open-mindedness and tolerance is sure to hold its audience's attention."

Lisle has also written a series of four middle-grade novels titled collectively "Investigators of the Unknown." The stories, which include *The Gold Dust Letters, Looking for Juliette, A Message from the Match Girl,* and *Angela's Aliens,* recount a year in the lives of four nine-year-olds who, while investigating magic, begin to discover truths about themselves and their families. In the initial volume, Angela receives letters, covered in gold dust, from a lonely, old-fashioned fairy. Investigating these letters with her friends, Georgina and Poco, leads Angela to a new understanding of her father. "Lisle celebrates the imagination's power to help ease wounds," maintained a *Publishers Weekly* critic in a starred review of *The Gold Dust Letters.* Starr LaTronica noted in *School Library Journal* that the author had created a "multifaceted novel to be appreciated on many levels."

The magic and reality-checks continue with the second novel in the series, *Looking for Juliette,* in which Angela moves to Mexico for the year, leaving her cat, Juliette, with Poco. But when Juliette turns up missing, Poco and Georgina blame the elderly Miss Bone, who is caretaking Angela's house. Walter, another classmate, introduces a Ouija board to the hunt. Ellen Fader noted in *School Library Journal* that the book

"is well plotted, and replete with humor, interesting characters, and enough shivers and surprises to satisfy readers." Ilene Cooper called the work "a magical mix" in her *Booklist* review.

With the third title in the series, *A Message from the Match Girl,* Georgina and Poco try to help Walter, an orphan who believes he is being haunted by, and receiving messages from, his dead mother. A contributor to *Kirkus Reviews* called the book "a tantalizing mystery of mother love," and a *Publishers Weekly* critic called it a "poignant story." The series was rounded off with the return of Angela from Mexico in *Angela's Aliens.* Because she seems to have become a different person—taller and more adult and somber—after being away, Poco, Georgina, and Walter suspect that Angela has been abducted by aliens and then returned in an altered state. In *Publishers Weekly* a reviewer noted that Lisle's magic would work on even the "most down-to-earth readers," and that as with all the books in the series—indeed, with all of Lisle's books—*Angela's Aliens* is more concerned with "opening the door to possibilities in human relationships than on solving supernatural mysteries."

A *Publishers Weekly* reviewer described *The Lost Flower Children* as a "blend of gentle fantasy and tough reality." Bereft after the death of their mother, nine-year-old Olivia and her peculiar five-year-old sister, Nellie, are sent to spend the summer with Great-Aunt Minty. Olivia's isolation is complete, as she must care for Nellie and deal with her own grief with little help from her doddering aunt. Then Olivia finds an old book in which she reads a story about children placed under a spell by garden fairies. Only when a buried tea set is dug up will the children be free of the spell and able to continue their lives. Taken by the story, Nellie begins to dig in Aunt Minty's overgrown garden—and she begins to uncover a child's tea set, cup by cup. Lisle's suggestive ending allows readers to come to their own conclusions about the restoration of the magical children. In her *Booklist* review of the work, Shelle Rosenfeld called *The Lost Flower Children* "an irresistible mystery resulting in personal transformation." A *Horn Book* critic praised the story as "a tantalizing, delicately told book" that will ". . . take readers into completely unexplored territory, setting them free to imagine what they will."

Lisle won the prestigious Scott O'Dell Award for *The Art of Keeping Cool,* a historical novel set in Rhode Island during World War II. Robert's father goes off to fight in the war, and Robert, his sister, and his mother must move in with his paternal grandparents. There Robert and his cousin Elliot are at the mercy of their grandfather's temper, but they take strength in each other. Elliot, a talented artist, has also befriended an expatriate German painter named Abel Hoffman, but in the wartime climate of fear, the townspeople conclude that Hoffman is a spy. "This is a powerful story of World War II at home," wrote Hazel Rochman in *Booklist*. "Lisle weaves together the thrilling war action and the spy mystery." A *Publishers Weekly* reviewer called the novel "an intriguing web of family secrets and wartime fears" that ". . . brings universal themes of prejudice and loss to a personal level." *School Library Journal* correspondent Cyrisse Jaffee likewise characterized *The Art of Keeping Cool* as "a heartfelt story about family dynamics and the harmful power of prejudice and hatred."

Switching gears, Lisle next wrote *How I Became a Writer and Oggie Learned to Drive*, a humorous, fast-paced novel about the dual thrills of living dangerously and writing, told in the voice of a twelve-year-old boy who is determined to become a writer. Archie Jones's story "The Mysterious Mole People" starts as bedtime entertainment for his younger brother, Oggie, six, who is trying to cope with newly separated parents and split living arrangements. But the story soon develops into an all-consuming passion. Writing secretly in the closet at night, Archie begins to see how his real-life troubles with a tough neighborhood gang are spilling over into his fiction, and vice-versa, how his writing gives him a way to speak about his deepest feelings. Lisle's story is "a book about writing that is both serious and unpretentious," wrote Susan Marie Swanson in *Riverbank Review*. Carol A. Edwards in *School Library Journal* concluded that the book's real essence lies in "how fiction and life are different and equally useful to one another."

Lisle returned to a Rhode Island setting for *The Crying Rocks*, a story about thirteen-year-old Joelle's search for her origins. Found by the railroad tracks when she was five, and adopted by an older couple, Joelle recalls nothing of her early years, until Carlos, a classmate, tells her she resembles seventeenth-century Narragansett Indians in an old painting in the public library. The teens begin to research these early natives, hiking trails in nearby woods and exploring the Crying Rocks, where the weeping of children can sometimes be heard. In a starred review for *Voice of Youth*

Advocates, Diane Emge wrote: "Again Lisle demonstrates her skill at creating characters rich with personality." *Horn Book* correspondent Peter D. Sieruta called the work "a multilayered novel that explores the strong but subtle connections between the past and present." *Booklist* contributor Ilene Cooper concluded: "Lisle's fluidly written story fascinates."

"I believe in the unknown," Lisle once commented. "There is a great deal we don't know about our world, like how big the universe is or what makes our brains work." And as she concluded in *SAAS*, "What we know and believe must always be qualified by what we don't know yet. New facts are arriving daily, however, new ways of thinking and seeing. . . . The stories are there to be told, and unless there's some unseen system at work that's set on preventing me, I expect to keep on writing them."

BIOGRAPHICAL AND CRITICAL SOURCES:

BOOKS

Kovac, Deborah, *Meet the Authors: 25 Writers Talk about Their Writing,* Scholastic (New York, NY), 1995.

Silvey, Anita, editor, *Children's Books and Their Creators,* Houghton Mifflin (Boston, MA), 1995, p. 410.

Something about the Author Autobiography Series, Volume 14, Gale (Detroit, MI), 1992, pp. 157-166.

Twentieth-Century Children's Writers, 4th edition, St. James Press (Detroit, MI), 1995.

PERIODICALS

Booklist, July, 1984, Ilene Cooper, review of *The Dancing Cats of Applesap,* p. 1550; September 15, 1994, Ilene Cooper, review of *Looking for Juliette,* p. 136; May 15, 1999, Shelle Rosenfeld, review of *The Lost Flower Children,* p. 1690; September 15, 2000, Hazel Rochman, review of *The Art of Keeping Cool,* p. 237; February 1, 2002, Ilene Cooper, review of *How I Became a Writer and Oggie Learned to Drive,* p. 939; October 15, 2003, Ilene Cooper, review of *The Crying Rocks,* p. 405.

Bulletin of the Center for Children's Books, June, 1985, Zena Sutherland, review of *Sirens and Spies,* pp. 188-189; October, 1988, Betsy Hearne, review of *Afternoon of the Elves,* p. 37; January, 1994, Carol Fox, review of *Forest,* p. 160.

Horn Book, January-February, 1988, Anita Silvey, review of *The Great Dimpole Oak,* p. 64; November-December, 1988, Ilene Cooper, "New Voices, New Visions: Janet Taylor Lisle," pp. 755-758; May, 1999, review of *The Lost Flower Children,* p. 333; March-April, 2002, Peter D. Sieruta, review of *How I Became a Writer and Oggie Learned to Drive,* p. 214; November-December, 2003, Peter D. Sieruta, review of *The Crying Rocks.*

Kirkus Reviews, October 1, 1991, review of *The Lampfish of Twill,* p. 1288; October 1, 1995, review of *A Message from the Match Girl,* p. 1432.

New York Times Book Review, February 11, 2001, Marigny Dupuy, review of *The Art of Keeping Cool,* p. 27.

Providence Journal Bulletin (Providence, RI), April 10, 1996, Jerry O'Brien, "Janet Taylor Lisle Creates Truly Human Characters That Are Real to Young Readers."

Publishers Weekly, October 9, 1987, review of *The Great Dimpole Oak,* p. 88; September 13, 1991, review of *The Lampfish of Twill,* p. 80; August 30, 1993, review of *Forest,* p. 97; January 10, 1994, review of *The Gold Dust Letters,* p. 62; September 25, 1995, review of *A Message from the Match Girl,* p. 57; September 16, 1996, review of *Angela's Aliens,* p. 84; April 12, 1999, review of *The Lost Flower Children,* p. 75; September 4, 2000, review of *The Art of Keeping Cool,* p. 108; March 11, 2002, review of *How I Became a Writer and Oggie Learned to Drive,* p. 73; November 17, 2003, review of *The Crying Rocks,* p. 65.

School Library Journal, October, 1984, Anne Osborn, review of *The Dancing Cats of Applesap,* p. 159; August, 1985, David A. Lindsey, review of *Sirens and Spies,* p. 78; September, 1989, Annette Curtis Klause, review of *Afternoon of the Elves,* p. 254; April, 1994, Starr LaTronica, review of *The Gold Dust Letters,* pp. 128-129; August, 1994, Ellen Fader, review of *Looking for Juliette,* p. 158; October, 2000, Cyrisse Jaffee, review of *The Art of Keeping Cool,* p. 164; March, 2002, Carol A. Edwards, review of *How I Became a Writer and Oggie Learned to Drive,* p. 234.

Voice of Youth Advocates, December, 1985, Nancy Choice, review of *Sirens and Spies,* p. 320; February, 2004, Diane Emge, review of *The Crying Rocks,* p. 494.

ONLINE

Janet Taylor Lisle, http://www.janettaylorlisle.com/ (December 15, 2003), author's home page, with interview.

Penguin Putnam, http://www.penguinputnam.com/ (December 15, 2003), "Janet Taylor Lisle."

Riverbank Review, http://www.riverbankreview.com/ (March 27, 2004), author profile and review of *How I Became a Writer and Oggie Learned to Drive.*

*   *   *

LoCICERO, Donald 1937-

PERSONAL: Born November 14, 1937, in Brooklyn, NY; son of Peter and Nancy (Passanate) LoCicero; married Cecelia Molfetto, August 16, 1958; children: Darius Jason. *Education:* Brooklyn College of the City University of New York, B.A., 1960; Rutgers University, M.A., 1964, Ph.D., 1965; University of Tübingen, post-doctoral study.

ADDRESSES: Home—2815 West Greenleaf St., Allentown, PA 18104. *E-mail*—donlo14@enter.net.

CAREER: State University of New York College at Oneonta, associate professor of German, 1965-66; Cedar Crest College, Allentown, PA, began as assistant professor, became professor of international languages, creative writing, and comparative literature and served as coordinator of comparative literature and director of Honors Program, 1966-2001; full-time writer, 2001—.

WRITINGS:

NOVELS

The Twisted Star, E. M. Press (Haymarket, VA), 1992.

Fate's Marionettes, Qunzhong Publishing House (Beijing, China), 1998, AmErica House (Frederick, MD), 2001.

The American War, Qunzhong Publishing House (Beijing, China), 2001, iUniverse (Lincoln, NE), 2002.

A Guy from Brooklyn, iUniverse (Lincoln, NE), 2002.

The Other Sex, iUniverse (Lincoln, NE), 2002.
You Never Know, iUniverse (Lincoln, NE), 2003.
Apparatus, iUniverse (Lincoln, NE), 2003.

OTHER

(Editor, with Vincent LoCicero) *Humor and Witz,* Harper (New York, NY), 1968.
Novellentheorie: The Practicality of the Theoretical, Mouton (Hawthorne, NY), 1970.

Contributor of articles and reviews to journals. Editor and chief contributor, *Mafkikker,* a literary magazine.

SIDELIGHTS: Donald LoCicero told *CA:* "The Twisted Star* is the first novel in a historical trilogy. It presents a detailed account of the disintegration of the German nation during the years of World War I and through the dark Nazi period. It portrays the fates of two families, one Jewish and one Aryan. Heinrich Hartstein and others experience the horrors of the concentration camp. The family of Karl Linsdorff, Heinrich's Aryan best friend, is also central in the work: I describe the suffering they endure as a result of their refusal to accept Nazi doctrines. While the novel's primary focus is on the pernicious effects of racism and bigotry, it also demonstrates the power of love and friendship. In the end, there are many questions: How was a civilized country like Germany able to spawn the Holocaust? Why did so many Jews remain in the Third Reich until it was too late to flee? Where were the democracies when it would have been possible to halt the atrocities? Why did God permit such an unthinkable horror?

"The second volume in the trilogy, *Fate's Marionettes,* continues the story of Heinrich Hartstein, a survivor of the Nazi death camp Treblinka, and his best friend and brother-in-law, Karl Linsdorff, who suffers through the battle of Stalingrad and the siege of Leningrad, serving as a noncombatant field surgeon. Captured by the Red Army as he attempts to defect from the Wehrmacht, Karl languishes for years in the gulags of Siberia.

"Meanwhile, Heinrich struggles to regain the will to live and to adjust to a new life in America, eventually finding a cause which gives his life purpose. Supplied with false papers by the Jewish underground move-ment, he travels to Palestine to join in the war for an independent Jewish state. After the foundation of Israel, he becomes disillusioned with the pervasive hate and violence between Arabs and Jews and returns to the United States.

"Finally free after many years of captivity, Karl also makes his way to the United States. Heinrich and Karl are also reunited. All is not happy, however, since a war in Southeast Asia looms ahead.

"The final work in the trilogy, *The American War,* takes place in the United States, Israel, and Vietnam. The central character of the work is Franz Linsdorff, son of the former Wehrmacht field physician Karl Linsdorff and nephew of the concentration camp survivor, Heinrich Hartstein. A pacifist, Franz follows his father's lead and dedicates himself to the study of medicine. Out of a sense of duty and loyalty to his adopted country, he enlists in the American army when hostilities break out between America and North Vietnam. Sent to Vietnam as a medic, Franz serves valiantly until he is severely wounded during the Tet offensive.

"This work presents a comprehensive picture of American society during the war that is known in Vietnam as the American War. Along with descriptions of battle, the novel details the peace movement in the States, which Franz joins upon his return home. Another major theme is the plight of returning soldiers, many of whom are unable to adjust to 'normal' life after Vietnam.

"Another novel, *A Guy from Brooklyn,* presents an insight into the complexity of human nature. Unlike the mafia don in the television series *The Sopranos,* however, Guy Lorenzo is engaged in a life-defining journey from the tough Brooklyn streets to the halls of higher learning. The novel presents an account of how it was to grow up during the 1950s in Brooklyn, New York. The reader can follow Guy and his family as they escape the rat- and roach-infested slums of Williamsburg to settle in East New York. The first awaken-ings of interest in the opposite sex, membership in a tough street gang, academic failure and success, and ultimately true love—these are some of the signposts along Guy's journey to adulthood.

"*The Other Sex* is intended as an erotic, absurd, and profound romp through the labyrinth of human sexual identity. The adventures of Helen and Harold Kern, a devoted couple who wake up one morning transfigured into each other, will make you shake your head in disbelief. Will Harold's mother-in-law change her negative attitude toward him now that he carries her future grandchild? Can the burned-out pastor of their church offer spiritual aid to them in their bizarre circumstances? Will the young social worker, Ms. Turnball, be able to give them a pragmatic course of action to follow? Are they given legal counsel by the famous transvestite lawyer, or medical relief from their trusted family doctor? People are not always, if ever, what and who they seem to be."

*　　*　　*

LUPER, Steven 1956-

PERSONAL: Born June 15, 1956, in Washington; son of Donald (in the military) and Barbara (Biggs) Luper; married; wife's name Ann Marie. *Education:* Baylor University, B.A., 1977; Harvard University, Ph.D., 1982.

ADDRESSES: Home—San Antonio, TX. *Office*— Department of Philosophy, Trinity University, 715 Stadium Dr., San Antonio, TX 78212; fax: 210-999-8353. *E-mail*—sluper@trinity.edu.

CAREER: Trinity University, San Antonio, TX, professor of philosophy, 1982—. Methodist Hospital, past member of Bioethics Committee.

MEMBER: American Philosophical Association, Greenpeace.

WRITINGS:

Invulnerability: On Securing Happiness, Open Court (La Salle, IL), 1996.

Social Ideals and Policies: Readings in Social and Political Philosophy, Mayfield (Mountain View, CA), 1999.

Living Well: Introductory Readings in Ethics, Harcourt Brace College Publishers (Fort Worth, TX), 2000.

A Guide to Ethics, McGraw-Hill (New York, NY), 2002.

EDITOR

The Possibility of Knowledge: Nozick and His Critics, Rowman & Littlefield (Totowa, NJ), 1987.

Problems of International Justice, Westview Press (Boulder, CO), 1988.

(With Curtis Brown) *The Moral Life,* Holt (Fort Worth, TX), 1991, 2nd edition, 1997.

(With Curtis Brown) *Drugs, Morality, and the Law,* Garland Publishing (New York, NY), 1994.

Existing: An Introduction to Existential Thought, Mayfield (Mountain View, CA), 2000.

The Skeptics, Ashgate Publishing (Aldershot, England), 2002.

Essential Knowledge, Longman (New York, NY), 2003.

Editor, *Synthese,* 1988 and 1991, and *Monist,* 1991.

M

MADIGAN, Mary Jean Smith 1941-

PERSONAL: Born February 26, 1941, in Nanticoke, PA; daughter of Melvin (a construction supervisor) and Irene (Bellegia) Smith; married Richard Allen Madigan, June 11, 1960 (divorced, 1975); children: Richard Allen, Dana Smith, Reese Jennings. *Education:* Attended Drew University, 1958-60; Cornell University, A.B., 1962; American University, M.A., 1968.

ADDRESSES: Home—565 North Broadway, Hastings-on-Hudson, NY 10706.

CAREER: Hudson River Museum, Yonkers, NY, curator of American history and decorative art, 1970-75, curator of exhibitions, 1975-77, assistant director of museum, 1977-78. *Art and Antiques,* editor in chief, 1978-83, editor and publisher, 1983. Opportunity Resources for the Arts, director of museum program, 1978.

MEMBER: National Trust for Historic Preservation, Victorian Society in America, American Association of Museums, American Society of Magazine Editors, Authors Guild, Authors League of America, Phi Beta Kappa.

AWARDS, HONORS: Harry N. Grier fellow, 1975.

WRITINGS:

The Photography of Rudolf Eickemeyer, Hudson River Museum (Yonkers, NY), 1971.
Eastlake Influenced American Furniture, Hudson River Museum (Yonkers, NY), 1973.

The Sculpture of Isidore Konti, Hudson River Museum (Yonkers, NY), 1975.
(With others) *Steuben Glass: An American Tradition in Crystal,* Abrams (New York, NY), 1982, revised and enlarged edition, 2003.
(Editor, with Susan Colgan) *Early American Furniture,* Billboard Publications (New York, NY), 1983.
(Editor, with Susan Colgan) *Prints and Photographs,* Billboard Publications (New York, NY), 1983.

Contributor of articles and reviews to art periodicals and museum journals.

BIOGRAPHICAL AND CRITICAL SOURCES:

PERIODICALS

Chicago Tribune Book World, December 5, 1982.
Library Journal, July, 2003, Therese Duzinkiewicz Baker, review of *Steuben Glass: An American Tradition in Crystal.*
Los Angeles Times Book Review, December 12, 1982.
Washington Post Book World, November 28, 1982.*

* * *

MAILLET, Antonine 1929-

PERSONAL: Born May 10, 1929, Bouctouche, New Brunswick, Canada; daughter of Leonide (a teacher) and Virginie (a teacher; maiden name, Cormier) Maillet. *Education:* College Notre-Dame d'Acadie, Moncton, B.A., 1950; University of Moncton, M.A., 1959; University of Montréal, LL.D., 1962; Laval University, Ph.D., 1970.

Antonine Maillet

ADDRESSES: Agent—c/o Author Mail, Northwest Passages, 628 Penzer St., Kamloops, British Columbia V2C 3G5, Canada.

CAREER: Writer. Taught at College Notre-Dame d'Acadie, Moncton, New Brunswick, Canada, 1954-60, University of Moncton, New Brunswick, 1965-67, College des Jesuites, Québec City, Québec, Canada, 1968-69, Laval University, Québec City, 1971-74, University of Montréal, Montréal, Québec, 1974-75, National Drama School, Montréal, Québec, 1989-91; visiting professor, University of Berkeley, 1983; State University of New York at Albany, 1985. University of Moncton, associate professor of French studies, chancellor, 1989-2001. Member of board of directors of Baxter and Alma Ricard Foundation; member of Ordre des francophones d'Amerique, 1984, High Council of the Francophonie, 1987, Academy of Large Montréalais, 1991, and Literary Council of the Foundation Prince Pierre of Monaco.

MEMBER: PEN, Association des Ecrivains de Langue Française, Royal Society of Canada, Academie Canadienne-Française, Societe des Auteurs et Compos-

iteurs Dramatiques de France, Society of Arts and Letters of France. Academy of Science of the Institute of Bologna, Italy.

AWARDS, HONORS: Prize for best Canadian play, Dominion Drama Festival, 1958, for *Poire-Acre;* Prix Littéraire Champlain from Conseil de la Vie Française, 1960, for *Pointe-aux-Coques;* Canada Council Prize, 1960, for *Les Jeux d'enfants sont faits;* grants from Canada Council, 1962-63, 1963-64, 1969-70, 1974-75, and 1977, and Québec Department of Cultural Affairs, 1972-73; Governor-General's Literary Award, 1972, for *Don l'Orignal;* grand prize for literature of the Ville de Montréal, 1973, Prix des Volcans from L'Auvergne, 1975, and France-Canada Prize, Association France-Québec, 1975, all for *Mariaagélas;* named Officer of the Order of Canada, 1976; Prix Littéraire de la Presse, 1976, for *La Sagouine;* Prix Goncourt finalist, 1977, and Four Juries Prize, 1978, both for *Les Cordes-de-Bois;* Prix Goncourt, 1979, for *Pélagie-la-Charrette;* Chalmers Canadian Play Award, Ontario Arts Council, 1980, for *La Sagouine;* named Officer, French Academic Palms, 1980; member of Knights of the Order of Pleiad, Frédéricton, New Brunswick, 1981; companion, Order of Canada, 1982; officer, National Order of Québec, 1990; appointed to Queen's Privy Council for Canada, 1992; translation prize from Association Québecoise des Critiques de Théâtre, 1992-93, for *La Nuit des Rois;* named commander, Ordre du mérite Culturel de Monaco, 1993; Great Prize Paul Féval de Littérature Popular, Company of the Men of Letters of France, 1997, for *Le Chemin Saint-Jacques;* Prize Samuel de Champlain, 2002; Prize of Excellence, Pascal Pear Tree, Council of Arts of New Brunswick, 2002; Prize Montfort for Literature, 2003; named officer, Legion of Honor (France), 2004. Honorary degrees from universities, including University of Moncton, 1972; Carleton University (Ottawa, Ontario), 1978; University of Alberta (Edmonton, Alberta), 1979; Mount Allison University (Sackville, New Brunswick), 1979; St. Mary's University (Halifax, Nova Scotia), 1980; University of Windsor, 1980; Acadia University, 1980; Laurentian University of Sudbury, 1981; Dalhousie University, 1981; McGill University, 1982; University of Toronto, 1982; Queen's University (Kingston, Ontario), 1982; Francis Xavier University, 1984; St. Thomas University (Fredericton, New Brunswick), 1986; Mount St. Vincent University, 1987; Université Ste. Anne, 1987; Bowling Green State University, 1988; Université Laval, 1988; Université de Lyon, 1989, Simon Fraser University, 1989; Concordia University, 1990; University of Maine, 1990;

British Columbia University, 1991; Royal Military College of Canada, 1992; University of New England, 1994; University of New Brunswick, 1997: Memorial University of Newfoundland, 2000; University of Victoria, 2001; and University of the Island of Prince Édouard, 2004.

WRITINGS:

NOVELS

Pointe-aux-Coques, Fides, 1958, reprinted, Leméac (Montréal, Québec, Canada), 1972.

On a mangé la dune, Beauchemin, 1962, reprinted, Leméac (Montréal, Québec, Canada), 1977.

Don l'Orignal, Leméac (Montréal, Québec, Canada), 1972, translation by Barbara Godard published as *The Tale of Don l'Orignal,* Clark & Irwin (Toronto, Ontario, Canada), 1978, reprinted, Goose Lane Editions (Frédéricton, New Brunswick, Canada), 2004.

Mariaagélas, Leméac (Montréal, Québec, Canada), 1973, translation by Ben Z. Shek, published as *Mariaagélas: Maria, Daughter of Gélas,* Simon & Pierre (Toronto, Ontario, Canada), 1986.

Emmanuel a Joseph a Dâvit (title means "Emmanual with Joseph and David"), Leméac (Montréal, Québec, Canada), 1975.

Les Cordes-de-Bois (title means "Cords of Wood"), Grasset (Paris, France), 1977.

Pélagie-la-Charrette, Leméac (Montréal, Québec, Canada), 1979, translation by Philip Stratford, published as *Pélagie: The Return to a Homeland,* Doubleday (New York, NY), 1982, translation published as *Pélagie: The Return to Acadie,* Goose Lane Editions (Frédéricton, New Brunswick, Canada), 2004.

Cent ans dans les bois (title means "Hundred Years in the Woods"), Leméac (Montréal, Québec, Canada), 1981.

La Gribouille, Grasset (Paris, France), 1982.

Crache-a-Pic, Leméac (Montréal, Québec, Canada), 1984, translation by Philip Stratford published as *The Devil Is Loose,* Lester & Orpan Dennys (Toronto, Ontario, Canada), 1986.

Le Huitième jour (title means "The Eighth Day") Leméac (Montréal, Québec, Canada), 1986, translation by Wayne Grady, Lester & Orpan Dennys (Toronto, Ontario, Canada), 1989.

L'Oursiade, Leméac (Montréal, Québec, Canada), 1990.

Comme un cri du coeur, Essential Editions (Montréal, Québec, Canada), 1992.

Les Confessions de Jeanne de Valois, Leméac (Montréal, Québec, Canada), 1992.

Le Chemin Saint-Jacques (title means "The St-Jacques Road") Grasset (Paris, France) , 1997.

L'Ile-aux-Puces, Leméac (Montréal, Québec, Canada), 1996.

Chronique d'une sorcière de vent (title means "Chronicle of a Witch of the Wind"), Grasset (Paris, France), 2000.

Madame Perfecta, Leméac (Montréal, Québec, Canada), 2001.

Le Temps me dure, Leméac (Montréal, Québec, Canada), 2003.

PUBLISHED PLAYS

Les Crasseux (one act), Holt (New York, NY), 1968, revised edition, 1974.

La Sagouine (monologues; first broadcast by Radio Canada, 1970, adapted for television and broadcast by Canadian Broadcasting Corporation (CBC), 1975), Leméac (Montréal, Québec, Canada), 1971-74, English translation by Luis de Cespedes, Simon & Pierre (Toronto, Ontario, Canada), 1979.

Gapi et Sullivan, Leméac (Montréal, Québec, Canada), 1973, English translation by Luis de Cespedes, Simon & Pierre, (Toronto, Ontario, Canada), 1987.

Évangéline Deusse (title means "Evangeline the Second"), Leméac (Montréal, Québec, Canada), 1975, translated by Luis de Cespedes, Simon & Pierre (Toronto, Ontario, Canada), 1987.

Gapi, Leméac (Montréal, Québec, Canada), 1975.

La Veuve enragée, Leméac (Montréal, Québec, Canada), 1977.

Le Bourgeois Gentleman (title means "The Middle-Class Gentleman"), Leméac (Montréal, Québec, Canada), 1978.

La Contrebandière, Leméac (Montréal, Québec, Canada), 1981.

Les Drôlatiques, horrifiques, et épouvantables aventures de Panurge, ami de Pantagruel, d'après Rabelais, Leméac (Montréal, Québec, Canada), 1983.

Garrochés en paradis (title means "Garrochés in Paradise"; produced in Montréal, Québec, 1986), Leméac (Montréal, Québec, Canada), 1986.

Margot la folle (first produced in Ottawa, Ontario, Canada, 1987), Leméac (Montréal, Québec, Canada), 1987.

William S. (first produced in Ottawa, Ontario, 1991), Leméac (Montréal, Québec, Canada), 1991.

Fountain; or, The Comedy of the Animals (first produced at Théâtre of the Green Curtain, 1995), Leméac (Montréal, Québec, Canada), 1995.

UNPUBLISHED PLAYS

Entr'acte (two-act), first produced in Bathurst, New Brunswick, Canada, at Dominion Drama Festival, 1957.

Poire-Acre (two-act), first produced in Sackville, New Brunswick, Canada, at Dominion Drama Festival, 1958.

Bulles de Savon (one-act), first produced with College Notre Dame d'Acadie in Moncton, New Brunswick, Canada, 1959.

Les Jeux d'enfants sont faits (two-act), first produced in Halifax, Nova Scotia, Canada, at Dominion Drama Festival, 1960.

Mariaagélas, first produced in Montréal, Québec, Canada, at Theatre du Rideau Vert, 1973.

Emmanuel a Joseph a Davit (based on the novel of the same name), first produced in Montréal, Québec, Canada, 1978.

La Joyeuse criee (two-act; title means "The Merry One Shouted"), first produced in Montréal, Québec, Canada, at Theatre du Rideau Vert, 1982.

NONFICTION

Rabelais et les traditions populaires en Acadie (doctoral thesis), Préface de Luc Lacourcière, Lavel University Press (Québec, Canada), 1971.

L'Acadie pour quasiment rien (title means "Acadia for Almost Nothing"), Leméac (Montréal, Québec, Canada), 1973.

(With others) *Les Acadiens, Piétons de l'Atlantique,* ACE (Paris, France), 1984.

TRANSLATOR

Tom Jones, *The Fantasticks,* produced by National Center of Arts, Ottawa, Canada, 1988.

(Into French) William Shakespeare, *Richard III,* Leméac (Montréal, Québec, Canada), 1989.

Willy Russell, *Valentine,* produced at Théâtre of the Green Curtain, Ottawa, Canada, 1990.

(Into French) William Shakespeare, *La Nuit des Rois,* (first produced in Ottawa, Ontario, Canada, 1993), Leméac (Montréal, Québec, Canada), 1993.

(Into French) Ben Jonson, *La Foire de Saint-Barthélemy* (title means "Bartholomew Fair"), Leméac (Montréal, Québec, Canada), 1994.

(Into French; and adapter) William Shakespeare, *The Tempest,* Leméac (Montréal, Québec, Canada), 1997.

Din, produced at Théâtre of the Green Curtain, Ottawa, Canada, 1999.

(Into French) William Shakespeare, *Hamlet,* produced at Théâtre of the Green Curtain, Ottawa, Canada, 1999.

(Into French) George Bernard Shaw, *Pygmalion,* produced at Théâtre of the Green Curtain, Ottawa, Canada, 1999.

OTHER

Par derrière chez mon perè (short stories), Leméac (Montréal, Québec, Canada), 1972.

Christophe Cartier de la noisette dit nounours (children's story), Hachette / Leméac (Montréal, Québec, Canada), 1981, translation by Wayne Grady published as *Christopher Cartier of Hazelnut, also Known as Bear,* Methuen (Toronto, Ontario, Canada), 1984.

Also author of television script *Echec au destin,* 1983. Contributor to periodicals, including *En Route, Modes et travaux, Le Monde,* and *Les Nouvelles littéraires.*

Author's works have been translated into several languages, including German and Rumanian.

ADAPTATIONS: Les Confessions de Jeanne de Valois was adapted as a musical drama by Vincent de Tourdonnet and produced in Montréal, Québec, Canada, 1997. *Pélagie-la-Charrette* was adapted into a musical, *Pélagie,* by Vincent de Tourdonnet and produced at National Arts Center Theatre/CanStage, Toronto, Ontario, Canada, 2004. *Gapi* was adapted into a film released by the CBC in 1982. *La Sagouine* was made into a television series.

SIDELIGHTS: The first author to write in her local French-Canadian vernacular about the French-descended Canadians known as Acadians, Antonine

Maillet has earned recognition as a spokesperson for Acadia and a preserver of its cultural and linguistic traditions and identity. Throughout her novels, plays, and nonfiction pieces written over several decades, Maillet relates the story of the Acadian people. From her first novel, *Pointe-aux-Coques,* published in 1958, to her doctoral dissertation completed in 1970 that catalogued more than 500 archaic French phrases still used in Acadia, to more recent works that tell tales as seen through the eyes of mature heroines, Maillet's focus has been to bring the culture of Acadia to life. Her work has been adapted into musicals and television series and has led to increased tourism in her region. She has also been widely acknowledged for her writing, and has earned numerous prestigious literary awards and honorary degrees from more than thirty institutions.

In the pages of her books and on the stage, Maillet's main characters are often simple, common women from the "wrong side of the tracks." Poor and illiterate, and speaking in their own tongue, they find the courage and will to overcome shortcomings and improve their station in life. Writing of the protagonist of Maillet's novel *Les Confessions de Jeanne de Valois,* an online contributor to *Northwest Passages* wrote that the narrator "recounts her life story and shares her thoughts on everything from religion to the role of women in Acadian culture," and "it becomes clear to the reader that the voice of the author freely mingles with that of the character, continually blurring the line between biography and autobiography."

Acadia, the setting for much of Maillet's work, was colonized by the French in the early seventeenth century, and in the mid-eighteenth century it was viewed as a threat by the British government, which controlled Canada at the time. In 1755, in what is known as *La Dispersion,* the British burned down Acadia's capital city, Grand Pre, killed the Acadians' livestock, and forced as many Acadians as they could find into ships which deposited them at various spots along the Atlantic coast from Maine to Georgia. Many eventually settled in Louisiana. The region is now inhabited by descendants of Acadians who either avoided La Dispersion or returned afterward, and the region has a shared heritage, passed on largely through storytellers, and a language derived from seventeenth- and eighteenth-century French that is different in many ways from both the French spoken in Québec and that spoken in modern France.

In 1971, Maillet captured public attention with the theatrical premiere of *La Sagouine.* Considered by some critics to be Maillet's masterpiece, *La Sagouine* is a monologue of an old Acadian cleaning woman as she washes the floor, considers the history of her "beaten and forgotten people," and puzzles over what remains of her Acadian heritage. As Maillet noted, of the evolution of the *La Sagouine* character: "I didn't invent the word *sagouine,* but I practically put it into common language. Before, you had the masculine *le sagouin,* but *la sagouine* didn't exist that much in French. It's hardly in the dictionary. In spoken Acadian we would use it, though not very often. We would use the diminutive more, *la sargailloune,* which was a little pejorative, and for that reason I didn't want to give that name to my heroine. So I called her La Sagouine, which was a little better. Now everybody who works as a cleaning woman is a *sagouine,* since I wrote the book."

The influence of the novel and play has been felt beyond the world of literature. "The village of Bouctouche," Maillet explained, "is officially called the town of La Sagouine. We have the *Jeux d'Acadie,* which means more or less the Olympics of Acadia, which we have every year; they're called the Jeux d'Acadie au Pays de La Sagouine, the Acadian Games at La Sagouine's Country. So the people identify themselves now as coming from the country of Sagouine, which means to be Acadian."

Another Maillet novel that has earned critical acclaim was her 1973 work, *Mariaagélas,* which concerns a young Acadian woman who smuggles alcohol during the period of Prohibition in the United States. This book became, in 1975, the first of Maillet's novels to be published in France and one of twenty-five books considered for France's most prestigious literary award, the Prix Goncourt.

Maillet came even closer to winning the Prix Goncourt in 1977 with her novel *Les Cordes-de-Bois,* losing by only one vote. The novel concerns a hilltop settlement on the New Brunswick coast that is populated by a group of disreputable people known as the Mercenaires. Led by courageous, determined women, the Mercenaires are comprised of social outcasts, including orphans, criminals, vagabonds, idiots, and the infirm, and they are beleaguered by the "respectable" population at the foot of the hill. "The feud between the two groups," remarked Emile J. Talbot in

World Literature Today, "takes on the dimensions of a moral struggle which . . . justifies the humanity of the poor and lowly." In relating this struggle, the narrator, ostensibly drawing from several Acadian storytellers' accounts of the past while incorporating their techniques and styles of delivery, presents a few different versions of the "facts," thus allowing the renegade community to gain what Talbot described as "a legendary dimension." Moreover, Talbot concluded, "The use of Acadian French, earthy and colorful, the humor of many of the situations, the fascinating array of unusual characters, all contribute to a delightful evocation of a culture little known outside its region."

Pélagie-la-Charrette won the 1979 Prix Goncourt, its author becoming the first non-European to earn this coveted award. In the novel, Maillet relates the story of a group of displaced Acadians who, fifteen years after La Dispersion scattered them throughout the American colonies, begin a return trek by oxcart to their homeland. The main character of the story is the group's leader, Pélagie, a widow whose strength, patience, and determination to take her family and other fellow exiles back to Acadia results in her being called, in English translation, Pélagie-the-Cart. The novel's other characters include Pélagie's lover, an exiled Acadian named Beausoleil who lives aboard his hijacked British schooner, the *Grand'Goule,* and periodically assists Pélagie and her company in times of trouble; Pélagie's four children; the crippled medicine woman Celina; and the ninety-year-old storyteller, Belonie.

During the grueling ten-year journey through the American colonies to Acadia, Pélagie and her original companions are joined by other displaced Acadians, some of whom complete the trip, others of whom turn back or head for the French subculture of colonial Louisiana. The oxcart caravan endures the American Revolution, Indian warfare, "famine, drought, rains, epidemics, quarrels, defections" before arriving in the much-dreamed-about homeland. Pélagie, however, does not finish the journey. Just before reaching Acadia, she dies, but not before hearing that her homeland is still inaccessible; the British still rule Acadia, and Acadians must live undercover if they live in Acadia at all.

The survivors of Pélagie's trek and their descendents do settle in Acadia, albeit secretly, and one hundred years later narrate *Pélagie-la-Charrette,* passing on Pélagie's story in the oral tradition by which they learned it themselves. The narrators at times disagree with each other and offer varying accounts of their ancestors' ten-year journey. But together, as an *Atlantic* reviewer explained, they "gradually weave a tale with the quality of legend—everything is larger than life but blurred around the edges." This legendary or mythic quality of Maillet's work was also noted by David Plante in his *New York Times Book Review* critique of *Pélagie-la-Charrette.* Remarked Plante, "The novel is narrated . . . by 'descendents of the carts,' . . . and in the recounting Pélagie and Beausoleil take on the aura of mythological figures . . . in the end they become people of legend."

The character of Pélagie has also become what Henry Giniger of the *New York Times* described as "a symbol and champion of the [Canadian] French-speaking minority's determination to survive on an English-speaking continent." In her stoic strength and patient persistence she represents the stubborn will of the Acadians to retain their heritage despite the discriminatory treatment by English-speaking Canadians that exists to this day. Moreover, in winning the Prix Goncourt for *Pélagie-la-Charrette,* Maillet gained for the Acadian language recognized legitimacy in the literary world and renewed hope among Acadians that their linguistic and cultural traditions will be preserved and respected. The story of Pélagie, as Mark Abley explained in his *Times Literary Supplement* review of *Pélagie-la-Charrette,* "is written from a proud sense of community and Maillet's individual voice seems all the stronger for it."

Maillet once commented of the logistics involved in committing to paper a language formulated in the seventeenth century that existed solely through oral tradition. "When I wrote *Pélagie* and *La Sagouine,* I had to create a written language that had never been written in my country. That language that was Rabelais's or Molière's was written by those authors, but it's not quite the same language that we have, because it had evolved in a different country. We have an American French language. I had to figure out how I could handle that as a written language. I had to invent some kind of a syntax, a style. That was my originality, in a sense. . . . I had to invent a grammar, almost, and to find a way of spelling words that had never been spelled before. I wanted to capture the flavor of the spoken language, and I had to get the pronunciation right, which meant inventing an accent."

Furthermore, although the character of Pélagie is fictional, "she's a symbol really of the kind of women who figured in the stories that were told to me. I created the character, but what happened to her is history." In 2004, Canada and France observed the 400th anniversary of the founding of Acadia, and *Pélagie-la-Charrette* was performed as the musical, *Pelagie: An Acadian Odyssey.*

In *Chronique d'une sorciere de vent,* Maillet lets an elderly nun tell the old tale of a beautiful Acadian woman, Carlagne, who, although married, "appeals equally to other men and to women," according to Steven Daniell in a review for *World Literature Today.* In the story, Carlagne becomes romantically involved with both Marijoli, the wife of a blacksmith, and Yophie, who many think is the devil himself. According to Daniell, "The nun fills her tale with a wide variety of explicit and implicit omens that lend an air of suspense and doom." One such omen, on the night of the Titanic disaster, is the birth of Carlagne and Yophie's illegitimate daughter, whom Marijoli and her husband adopt. Added Daniell, "Minute details about local custom, myth, or even construction add further texture to the story." Summarized Daniell, "Since this novel belongs to a large collection of stories about the same community . . . , familiarity with a broad range of Maillet's works is a distinct advantage. However, as with any well-written novel, *Chronique d'une sorciere de vent* stands alone quite well, and it can even serve nicely as an introduction to the works of one of today's preeminent French-language writers."

In one of her later novels, *Madame Perfecta,* Maillet retains her theme of using common woman heroines, this one, a Spanish immigrant housemaid, inspired by her own Spanish housekeeper she had employed years earlier. In the novel, the maid reflects on her life in her strange new homeland, Canada, the hardships of the homeland she left behind, including those created by Franco and the Spanish Civil War, and the trials and tribulations of creating a new life in her adopted home.

In *Le Temps me dure* Maillet brings back the character, Radi, a young girl who had appeared in two other works, *On a mangé la dune* and *Le Chemin Saint-Jacques,* a series that has been considered to consist of autobiographical novels. *Le Temps me dure* tracks a dialogue between two incarnations of Radi, who keep traveling back and forth in time. The mature woman,

now called Radegonde, tries to come to grips with some of the intense moments of her childhood, while the little girl looks to the future and the reaching of her dreams.

In additon to her original writings, Maillet has brought the works of English playwrights to the French-speaking public through her many translations, including French-language versions of William Shakespeare's *Richard III, The Tempest,* and *Hamlet;* Ben Jonson's *Bartholomew Fair;* Tom Jones's *The Fantasticks;* and George Bernard Shaw's *Pygmalion.*

In her speech accepting an honorary degree from the Memorial University of Newfoundland, as archived on the Library and Archives Canada Web site, Maillet told the tale of the two frogs that have somehow landed in a bowl of cream. One frog panicks and drowns. The other, though accepting his fate, does not give up and thus tries for hours to scramble out, eventually finding himself on top of a pile of butter. Relating this tale to the story of her people, she commented, "Now we all descend from that little frog, otherwise we wouldn't be here . . . ; that's part of evolution. We are here because we descend from one that survived. We are survivors of a survivor who fought. I think this is a story of your country and mine, or your people and mine, maybe of the whole of the country. . . . We are the lucky ones. We won the lottery." Further encouraging the graduating students at that commencement address, Maillet added, "Every time I wake up, I look: the sun is there for me, the sea is there for me, the world is there for me. . . . Go and give back to the world something to remember you, do something in science, in medicine, in arts, in social work, in everything. Do something so that the world will remember and be grateful that you are alive."

BIOGRAPHICAL AND CRITICAL SOURCES:

BOOKS

Contemporary Literary Criticism, Volume 54, Gale (Detroit, MI), 1989.
Dictionary of Literary Biography, Volume 60, *Canadian Writers since 1960,* Gale (Detroit, MI), 1987.
Godin, Jean-Cleo, and Laurent Mailhot, editors, *Theatre Québecois,* HMH, 1980, pp. 147-164.

Le Blanc, Rene, editor, *Derriere la charrette de Pélagie: Lecture analytique du roman d'Antonine Maillet, "Pélagie-la-Charrette,"* Presses de l'Université Sainte-Anne, 1984.

Smith, Donald, *Voices of Deliverance: Interviews with Québec & Acadian Writers,* Anansi (Toronto, Ontario, Canada), 1986, pp. 243-268.

PERIODICALS

Acadiensis, spring, 1983, pp. 171-180.
American Review of Canadian Studies, summer, 1988, pp. 239-248.
Atlantic, April, 1982.
Atlantic Provinces Book Review, May, 1982.
Books in Canada, May, 1982.
Canadian Children's Literature, number 41, 1986, p. 63.
Canadian Forum, October, 1986, pp. 36-38.
Canadian Literature, spring, 1981, pp. 157-161; spring, 1988, pp. 43-56; winter, 1988, pp. 143-149; spring, 1989, pp. 193-196; winter, 1992, pp. 192-194.
Canadian Theatre Review, number 46, 1986, pp. 58-64, 65-71.
Chicago Tribune, January 2, 1983.
Figaro, September 14, 1979; September 23, 1979; November 20, 1979.
French Review, May, 1985, p. 919.
Le Monde, September 14, 1979; November 20, 1979.
L'Express, September 8, 1979; December 8, 1979.
Maclean's, May 5, 1980.
New Brunswick Telegraph Journal, Rosella Melanson, "What Is Lost in a Good Translation Is Precisely the Best," August, 2001.
New Statesman, July 2, 1982.
New York Times, November 20, 1979; December 5, 1979.
New York Times Book Review, March 7, 1982.
Philadelphia Inquirer, October 16, 1983.
Québec Studies, number 4, 1986, pp. 220-336.
Queen's Quarterly, fall, 1992, pp. 642-652.
Quill & Quire, February, 1985, p. 14; June, 1986, p. 37; August, 1986, p. 43.
Studies in Canadian Literature, number 2, 1981, pp. 211-220.
Times Literary Supplement, December 3, 1982.
Toronto Star, February 13, 1982.
Washington Post Book World, March 28, 1982.

World Literature Today, summer, 1978, pp. 429-430; autumn, 1982, p. 646; autumn, 2000, Steven Daniell review of *Chronique d'une sorciere de vent,* p. 74.

ONLINE

Globe and Mail Online, http://www.theglobeandmail.com/ (April 7, 2004), Kamal Al-Solaylee, "Acadia on Our Minds."
Government of Canada, Collections Web site, http://collections.ic.gc.ca/ (August 4, 2004), "Antonine Maillet, Visionary Epic Storyteller."
Library and Archives Canada Web site, http://www.collectionscanada.ca/ (October 7, 1994), "Lectures, Antonine Maillet."
McGill Tribune of McGill University Web site, http://www.mcgilltribune.com/ (March 25, 2002), Ric Lambo, "Reading across the Divide: Music and Prose."
Northwest Passages Web site, http://www.nwpassages.com/ (August 4, 2004), "*Pélagie—The Return to Acadie.*"
Pays de la Sagouine Web site, http://www.sagouine.com/ (August 4, 2004), "The Author and Her Characters."*

*   *   *

MARS-JONES, Adam 1954-

PERSONAL: Born October 26, 1954, in London, England; son of William Lloyd (a judge) and Sheila (an attorney; maiden name, Cobon) Mars-Jones. *Education:* Cambridge University, B.A., 1976, M.A., 1978.

ADDRESSES: Agent—Peters, Fraser, and Dunlop, 503-504 The Chambers, Chelsea Harbour, Lots Rd., London SW10 0XF, England.

CAREER: Writer; *Independent,* London, England, film critic, 1986-97; *Times,* London, England, film critic, 1998-2000.

AWARDS, HONORS: Benjamin C. Moomaw Prize for Oratory, University of Virginia; Hoyns fellow for creative writing; Somerset Maugham Award, 1982, for *Lantern Lecture.*

WRITINGS:

Fabrications (stories), Knopf (New York, NY), 1981, published with an additional title story as *Lantern Lecture,* Faber (London, England), 1981.

(Editor) *Mae West Is Dead: Recent Lesbian and Gay Fiction,* Faber (London, England), 1983.

(With Edmund White) *The Darker Proof: Stories from a Crisis,* Faber (London, England), 1987, New American Library (New York, NY), 1988.

Venus Envy, Chatto & Windus (London, England), 1990.

Monopolies of Loss, Knopf (New York, NY), 1993.

The Waters of Thirst, Faber (London, England), 1993, Knopf (New York, NY), 1994.

Blind Bitter Happiness, Chatto & Windus (London, England), 1997.

Contributor to books, including *The Penguin Book of Modern British Short Stories,* edited by Malcolm Bradbury, Penguin, 1987; *Best Short Stories, 1988,* edited by Giles Gordon and David Hughes, Heinemann, 1988; *Best Short Stories, 1989,* edited by Giles Gordon and David Hughes, Heinemann, 1989; *The Faber Book of Gay Short Stories,* edited by Edmund Wilson, Faber, 1991; and *The Oxford Book of English Love Stories,* edited by John Sutherland, Oxford University Press, 1996. Contributor to periodicals, including *Guardian, Times Literary Supplement, Observer, Granta, Quarto,* and *Index on Censorship.*

SIDELIGHTS: British-born fiction writer Adam Mars-Jones first caught critical attention with his 1981 story collection *Lantern Lecture*—published in a slightly abridged version as *Fabrications* in the United States—which was hailed as a triumphant debut by Galen Strawson in the *Times Literary Supplement.* Assessing the book, Strawson found that "there is something punk, in the modern sense of the word, about this extremely clever and original collection of stories. It's to do with the emotionally deadpanned style of delivery, the technical impassivity of the allusive, *cloisonne* construction."

In 1987, in response to the social emergency surrounding AIDS, Mars-Jones collaborated with Edmund White to produce *The Darker Proof: Stories from the Crisis.* This collection deals "less with the disease and its case-histories than with the effect it has had on the consciousness of people who are living in close proximity to it," according to Anne Billson in a London *Times* interview with Mars-Jones. As the interview related, Mars-Jones has maintained a personal interest in the subject matter by acting as a "buddy"—someone readily available to provide physical and moral support—to a pair of AIDS victims. While he told Billson that he never before considered writing about the disease from the standpoint of a buddy, he saw that "the book wouldn't have been written if I hadn't buddied, because I wouldn't have had a sense of knowing the reality [of AIDS] rather than just the culture of it."

Calling Mars-Jones's work in *The Darker Proof* "an important discovery," *Washington Post* critic Richard McCann added that the writer "devotes his considerable intelligence and compassion to the exploration of smaller moments in which characters renegotiate their daily lives." While the Mars-Jones style is "highly discursive," wrote McCann, it still "allows him to build toward powerfully dramatic realizations, particularly when he writes, as he often does, of the guilty and grief-stricken transactions between the sick and the (still) well." An essayist for *Contemporary Novelists* compared *The Darker Proof* with the earlier *Lantern Lecture:* "Albeit devoid of the exciting experimental structures of *Lantern Lecture,* the same basic strengths of Mars-Jones's writing come through in *The Darker Proof.* The humor . . . springs from an awareness of the maximum possible motivations and interpretations of any action, and his subject matter of whatever kind, is imbued with absolute precision."

Mars-Jones continues writing fictionally about AIDS in his *Monopolies of Loss,* a collection of nine stories. "Through snapshots of the epidemic," wrote Pamela Wine in the *Journal of the American Medical Association,* "Mars-Jones's stories fashion a collage of lives staggered from fear and death." Kasia Boddy, writing in the *Dictionary of Literary Biography,* quoted Mars-Jones's introduction to the collection: "His goal was to explore the illness from as many perspectives as possible: how it felt 'to be well in a sick world, to be sick in a well world, to be part of a relationship in which sickness was an atmospheric feature, to write about close relationships, personal relationships, and impersonal relationships, the new style of relationship that the epidemic sort of forged.'" A *Publishers Weekly* critic found "a Chekhovian resonance" in the story "A Small Spade," in which a man accompanies his AIDS-infected lover to a hospital emergency room for minor surgery and comes to realize that their future together will be filled with similar visits.

In the novel *The Waters of Thirst,* Mars-Jones tells of William, a gay man who is dying of AIDS in a London hospital, as he looks back over his life. William has worked as a voice-over actor in television and has had a longtime relationship with his companion, Terry. In his present condition, brought on by kidney failure, he spends his hours fantasizing about a gay porn star whose career he has followed. "The novel climaxes with William waking to discover—fantastically—the porn star Hunter lying in the hospital bed with him," Richard Canning revealed in the *New Statesman.* "With this book-length monologue," Ray Olson wrote in *Booklist,* "Mars-Jones consolidates his status as the premier writer of fiction about dying gay men—an odd niche for anyone to fill."

Boddy concluded of Mars-Jones that the writer continues to experiment with new styles of short fiction. "The stories in *Monopolies of Loss* are radically different in theme and style from those in *Lantern Lecture,*" the critic noted, while "In *The Waters of Thirst* he takes on the challenge of the novel with verve and originality. . . . What unites all Mars-Jones's writings is a sharp intelligence, a distrust of easy emotion . . . , and a precise and expert handling of language."

BIOGRAPHICAL AND CRITICAL SOURCES:

BOOKS

Contemporary Novelists, 7th edition, St. James Press (Detroit, MI), 2001.

Dictionary of Literary Biography, Volume 207: *British Novelists since 1960, Third Series,* Gale (Detroit, MI), 1999.

Woods, Gregory, *A History of Gay Literature: The Male Tradition,* Yale University Press (New Haven, CT), 1998.

PERIODICALS

Advocate, April 5, 1994, Brian Hickman, review of *The Waters of Thirst,* p. 74.

Booklist, April 1, 1993, Ray Olson, review of *Monopolies of Loss,* p. 1410; March 1, 1994, Ray Olson, review of *The Waters of Thirst,* p. 1181.

Gay Times, November, 1992, Sebastian Beaumont, review of *Monopolies of Loss.*

Harper's, November, 1981, Jeffrey Burke, review of *Fabrications,* p. 82.

Journal of the American Medical Association, March 2, 1994, Pamela Wine, review of *Monopolies of Loss,* p. 717.

Lambda Book Report, July-August, 1992, Richard McCann, "Writing AIDS," p. 10; May-June, 1993, John Weir, review of *Monopolies of Loss,* p. 26.

Library Journal, September 15, 1981, Janet Wiehe, review of *Fabrications* p. 1753; November 1, 1983, review of *Mae West Is Dead: Recent Lesbian and Gay Fiction,* p. 2100; April 1, 1993, Brian Kenney, review of *Monopolies of Loss,* p. 134; April 15, 1994, Kevin M. Roddy, review of *The Waters of Thirst,* p. 113.

Los Angeles Times Book Review, November 1, 1981.

New Statesman, October 2, 1981, Martin Amis, review of *Lantern Lecture,* p. 21; November 11, 1983, Harriett Gilbert, review of *Mae West Is Dead,* p. 30; September 25, 1992, Richard Canning, review of *Monopolies of Loss,* p. 57; June 25, 1993, Richard Canning, review of *The Waters of Thirst,* p. 38.

New Yorker, May 30, 1994, review of *The Waters of Thirst,* p. 111.

New York Times Book Review, June 13, 1993, Meg Wolitzer, review of *Monopolies of Loss,* p. 18; March 20, 1994, Jonathan Dee, review of *The Waters of Thirst,* p. 25.

Observer (London, England), July 1, 1990; May 31, 1994, review of *The Waters of Thirst.*

Publishers Weekly, September 11, 1981, review of *Fabrications* p. 59; September 23, 1983, Sally A. Lodge, review of *Mae West Is Dead,* p. 69; February 5, 1988, Penny Kaganoff, review of *The Darker Proof: Stories from a Crisis,* p. 89; February 15, 1993, review of *Monopolies of Loss,* p. 188; February 28, 1994, review of *The Waters of Thirst,* p. 73.

Scotsman, July 3, 1993, Ali Smith, review of *The Waters of Thirst.*

Times (London, England), February 23, 1983; June 29, 1987; August 9, 1987.

Times Literary Supplement, October 9, 1981, Galen Strawson, review of *Lantern Lecture.*

Washington Monthly, July-August, 1988, Joe Arena, review of *The Darker Proof,* p. 58.

Washington Post, May 30, 1988, Richard McCann, review of *The Darker Proof.*

Washington Post Book World, November 1, 1981.

ONLINE

Contemporary Writers, http://www.contemporary writers.com/ (November 13, 2003).

*   *   *

MARTÍNEZ-FERNÁNDEZ, Luis 1960-

PERSONAL: Born January 14, 1960, in Havana, Cuba; son of Celestino Martínez (a photographer and retired executive) and Luisa Fernández; married, 1984; wife's name Margaret A. (a professor); children: Luis, Alberto, Andres. *Ethnicity:* "Hispanic." *Education:* University of Puerto Rico, B.A. (with high honors), 1982, M.A., 1985; Duke University, Ph.D., 1990. *Politics:* Independent. *Religion:* Protestant. *Hobbies and other interests:* Travel, reading.

ADDRESSES: Office—Department of Hispanic, Caribbean, and Latin American History, Rutgers University, 235 Tillett Hall, 53 Avenue E, Piscataway, NJ 08854-8040. *E-mail*—lumartin@rci.rutgers.edu.

CAREER: Augusta State University, Augusta, GA, assistant professor of Latin American, Caribbean, and U.S. history, 1990-92; Colgate University, Hamilton, NY, assistant professor of Latin American and Caribbean history, 1992-94; Rutgers University, Piscataway, NJ, associate professor of history and Caribbean studies, beginning 1997, chair of Department of Hispanic, Caribbean, and Latin American History, beginning 1998.

MEMBER: American Historical Association, Association of Caribbean Historians, Conference on Latin American History, Caribbean Studies Association, Historical Society, Latin American Studies Association.

AWARDS, HONORS: J. B. Duke fellowship, 1986-1988; international travel grant, Tinker Foundation, 1987; Beveridge travel grant, American Historical Association, 1988; National Hispanic Scholar, 1987, 1988; grant from National Endowment for the Humanities, 1993; fellow of Pew Evangelical Scholars Program, 1994-95; fellowship for scholarly excellence, Rutgers University Board of Trustees, 1997-98; has also received other awards, grants, and fellowships.

WRITINGS:

Torn between Empires: Economy, Society, and Patterns of Political Thought in the Hispanic Caribbean, 1840-1878, University of Georgia Press (Athens, GA), 1994.

Fighting Slavery in the Caribbean: The Life and Times of a British Family in Nineteenth-Century Havana, M. E. Sharpe (Armonk, NY), 1998.

(Coeditor) *Encyclopedia of Cuba: People, History, Culture,* two volumes, Greenwood Press (Westport, CT), 2003.

Work represented in anthologies. Contributor of articles to periodicals, including *Magazine of History, Latin American Research Review, Caribbean Studies, Diplomatic History, New West Indian Guide, Americas, Revista/Review Interamericana, Cuban Studies,* and *Slavery and Abolition.*

SIDELIGHTS: Luis Martínez-Fernández has had a lifelong interest in the Hispanic countries of the Caribbean. He has researched and written extensively on the histories of Cuba, Puerto Rico, and the Dominican Republic, with emphasis on the nineteenth and twentieth centuries. He has also lived throughout Latin America; when he was two years old, he and his family left Havana, Cuba, as refugees fleeing from the communist regime of Fidel Castro, and came to the United States. They did not stay long; when Martínez-Fernández's father accepted a management job with International Harvester in Peru, the family moved to Lima. In 1968 a military coup led them to move again, this time to San Juan, Puerto Rico. After completing his undergraduate education and receiving a master's degree in history at the University of Puerto Rico, he moved to the United States to pursue a doctorate in history at Duke University.

Torn between Empires: Economy, Society, and Patterns of Political Thought in the Hispanic Caribbean, 1840-1878 is a comparative study of the economy, society, and political culture of Cuba, Puerto Rico, and the Dominican Republic in the mid-nineteenth century. Martínez-Fernández discusses changes in each country's balance of power and its relationship to changes in the countries' heritage of insularity, colonialism, and slavery. The book covers the years between 1840, when British consul and abolitionist

David Turnbull arrived in Havana, to 1878, when the first Cuban war of independence from Spain ended. Avi Chomsky, reviewing *Torn between Empires* for *Americas,* remarked: "What is new in Martínez-Fernández's account is the way he focuses his lens, moving easily from internal events in the United States to events in the three country/colonies of the Hispanic Caribbean . . . , to Spain, to Great Britain, and back again, showing the intricate links between local and international events and ideas." *Journal of Latin American Studies* contributor Jean Stubbs responded favorably to *Torn between Empires,* declaring: "For guiding us through the terrain of imperial rivalries still with us today, as well as on its own intrinsic merit, this is a book that should be on every Caribbean history reading list."

Fighting Slavery in the Caribbean: The Life and Times of a British Family in Nineteenth-Century Havana draws on diaries, letters, and other papers to tell the story of George and Grace Backhouse, a British couple who went to Cuba in the mid-1800s to serve on the Anglo-Spanish Havana Mixed Commission for the Suppression of the Slave Trade. Fighting slavery was an uphill battle at the time: most influential people in Cuba were strongly pro-slavery because the island's economy relied on slave labor. In addition to the difficulties of their anti-slavery struggle, the Backhouses were immersed in an unfamiliar culture and were often isolated and lonely. Through their story, the book shows the Cuban slave trade, its role in the sugar industry, and relations between races and genders on the island. Martínez-Fernández told Michelle Adam in *Hispanic Outlook,* "I began to read [George and Grace Backhouse's] diaries, and I fell in love with this family. They had children like me. They faced a lot of the same issues." Later, he said, "His diary came to an end, and I opened an envelope. There were newspaper notices of his death. He had been killed in Cuba. From that day on, I knew I had to tell his story." Martínez-Fernández also wrote the book because he is fascinated with Cuba's history. "I am convinced," he told Adam, "that in order to understand the current political situation of Cuba, you need to understand the nineteenth century when the political climate crystallized." And, he told Alberto Alvarez in the *Daily Targum,* "The lives of the Backhouses are like a window to the way life was lived in Cuba." Thomas Davis, in his review of *Fighting Slavery in the Caribbean* for *Library Journal,* called the volume an "elegant narrative" and a "fascinating peek into mid-nineteenth-century Cuba."

Martínez-Fernández's research for the book helped him not only to understand the history of Cuba, but also to understand his own roots and personal history. When he was thirty-four, he returned to Cuba for the first time to do research for the book. He told Adam, "I felt uncannily at home. The smells, people's accents, the skies, the architecture. It was almost as if I had never left." He visited his grandfather and heard his entire family history for the first time. It was not until he went to Cuba, he told Adam, that he realized he was truly Cuban. Before then, the experience of emigration had marked him and his family with a sense of exile and rootlessness. "The experience of emigration becomes internalized within families," he told Adam. "It becomes a family pattern, which is painful in many ways."

Martínez-Fernández once commented: "As is the case with most authors, I find pleasure in learning that readers enjoy my work and find it useful. Although I write about serious subjects, some of the most rewarding praise that my work has received is that it reflects a sense of humor. That is my advice to my students: 'Keep a sense of humor and enjoy what you do.'"

BIOGRAPHICAL AND CRITICAL SOURCES:

PERIODICALS

Americas, July, 1996, Avi Chomsky, review of *Torn between Empires: Economy, Society, and Patterns of Political Thought in the Hispanic Caribbean, 1840-1878,* pp. 174-175.

Daily Targum, April 24, 1998, article by Alberto Alvarez.

Hispanic Outlook, October 9, 1998, article by Michelle Adam, p. 14.

Journal of Latin American Studies, February, 1996, Jean Stubbs, review of *Torn between Empires,* pp. 266-270.

Library Journal, March 15, 1998, Thomas Davis, review of *Fighting Slavery in the Caribbean: The Life and Times of a British Family in Nineteenth-Century Havana,* p. 82; May 15, 2003, Lee Arnold, review of *Encyclopedia of Cuba: People, History, Culture,* p. 78.

Rutgers Focus, February 13, 1998, p. 4.*

*   *   *

MATTHEW, Christopher C(harles) F(orrest) 1939-

PERSONAL: Born May 8, 1939, in London, England; son of Leonard Douglas and Doris Janet Matthew; married, October, 1979; children: three. *Education:* Oxford University, B.A., 1963, M.A., 1989.

ADDRESSES: Office—35 Drayton Gardens, London SW10 9RY, England; fax: 0207-244-7004.

CAREER: La Colline School of Languages, La Tour de Peilz, Switzerland, lecturer in English, 1963-64; London Press Exchange Ltd., London, England, advertising copywriter, 1964-66; J. Walter Thompson Co. Ltd., London, copywriter, 1966-68; Masius, Wynne-Williams, London, copywriter, 1968-70; Thomson Group Marketing, London, copywriter, 1970; freelance writer and broadcaster, 1970—.

AWARDS, HONORS: Arts Council award, 1977.

WRITINGS:

Diary of a Somebody (fiction), illustrated by Peter Brookes, Hutchinson (London, England), 1978.
A Different World: Stories of Great Hotels, photographs by Ben Martin, Paddington Press (New York, NY), 1978.
The Long-Haired Boy (fiction), Hamish Hamilton (London, England), 1979, Atheneum (New York, NY), 1980.
Loosely Engaged, Hutchinson (London, England), 1980.
The Crisp Report, Hutchinson (London, England), 1981.
(Editor, with Benny Green, and coauthor of annotations and introduction) Jerome K. Jerome, *Three Men in a Boat,* Pavilion Books (London, England), 1982.
The Junket Man, Severn House (Sutton, Surrey, England), 1983.
How to Survive Middle Age, Pavilion Books (London, England), 1983.
Family Matters, Hodder & Stoughton (London, England), 1986.
The Amber Room, Sinclair-Stevenson (London, England), 1995.
A Nightingale Sang in Fernhurst Road: A Schoolboy's Journal of 1945, John Murray (London, England), 1998.
Now We Are Sixty (poetry), illustrated by David Eccles, John Murray (London, England), 1999, Viking (New York, NY), 2001.
Knocking On, John Murray (London, England), 2001.
Now We Are Sixty (and a Bit), John Murray (London, England), 2003.
Madonna's Plumber (radio play), British Broadcasting Corp., 2003.

Writer for *The Good Guys,* a series broadcast by London Weekend Television, 1992-93. Contributor to British magazines and newspapers, including *Daily Mail.* Editor, *Times Travel Guide,* 1973-75.

ADAPTATIONS: The Long-Haired Boy was adapted for television and broadcast as *A Perfect Hero* by London Weekend Television in 1991.

WORK IN PROGRESS: Summoned by Betjeman, a solo stage show celebrating the life and work of Sir John Betjeman.

BIOGRAPHICAL AND CRITICAL SOURCES:

PERIODICALS

Times Literary Supplement, November 24, 1978; March 7, 1980; November 21, 1980.

*   *   *

McCARTHY, Kevin M. 1940-

PERSONAL: Born October 15, 1940, in Dumont, NJ; son of Dennis L. and Dorothy (King) McCarthy; married second wife, Karelisa Hartigan, December 22, 1992; children: Catherine, Brendan, Erin, Matthew. *Education:* LaSalle College, B.A. (cum laude), 1963; University of North Carolina—Chapel Hill, M.A., 1966, Ph.D., 1970.

ADDRESSES: Home—3815 Southwest Fifth Pl., Gainesville, FL 32607. *Office*—Department of English, 4008 Turlington Hall, University of Florida, Gainesville, FL 32611; fax: 352-392-0860.

CAREER: U.S. Peace Corps, Washington, DC, volunteer English teacher in Turkey, 1963-65; University of Florida, Gainesville, assistant professor, 1969-74, associate professor, 1974-91, professor of English and linguistics, 1991—. Lebanese National University, Fulbright lecturer and chair of department of English, 1971-72; University of South Florida, associate professor, 1975; King Saud University, Fulbright lecturer,

1982-84; Aegean Institute, Poros, Greece, lecturer, 1992. Southeastern Conference on Linguistics, member of executive committee, 1971-74.

MEMBER: Marjorie Kinnan Rawlings Society (executive director, 2000—), Florida College English Association (president, 1975-76), Linguistic Circle of Florida (president, 1970-71), University of Florida Language and Literature Club (president, 1975-76).

AWARDS, HONORS: Scholarship for Egypt from Portland State University, 1968; travel grant, American Philosophical Society, 1970; Charlton Tebeau Award, Florida Historical Society, 1994, for *African Americans in Florida: An Illustrated History;* Patrick Smith Literary Prize, Library of the Florida Historical Society, 1999, for *"A River in Flood" and Other Florida Stories by Marjory Stoneman Douglas.*

WRITINGS:

(With Joel H. Siegel) *Grammar and the Teaching of English,* MSS Publishing, 1970.
Grammar and Usage, Harcourt, Brace, Jovanovich (New York, NY), 1980.
Saudi Arabia: A Desert Kingdom (juvenile), Dillon Press (Minneapolis, MN), 1986.
Grammar and Paragraphs, Harcourt, Brace, Jovanovich (New York, NY), 1986.
The History of Gilchrist County, Trenton Women's Club (Trenton, FL), 1986.
The AVT Learning System in Writing: Grammar and Paragraphs, HBJ Media Systems Corp. (Orlando, FL), 1986.
(Editor) *Florida Stories,* University Presses of Florida (Gainesville, FL), 1989.
(Editor) *Nine Florida Stories by Marjory Stoneman Douglas,* University of North Florida Press (Jacksonville, FL), 1990.
Florida Lighthouses, University Presses of Florida (Gainesville, FL), 1990.
Thirty Florida Lighthouses, Pineapple Press (Sarasota, FL), 1992.
(Editor) *The Book Lover's Guide to Florida,* Pineapple Press (Sarasota, FL), 1992.
Thirty Florida Shipwrecks, Pineapple Press (Sarasota, FL), 1992.
(With Maxine D. Jones) *African Americans in Florida: An Illustrated History,* Pineapple Press (Sarasota, FL), 1993.

(With James P. Jones) *The Gators and the Seminoles: Honor, Guts, and Glory,* Maupin Press (Gainesville, FL), 1993.
Twenty Florida Pirates, Pineapple Press (Sarasota, FL), 1994.
The Hippocrene U.S.A. Guide to Black Florida, Hippocrene Press (New York, NY), 1994.
Baseball in Florida, Pineapple Press (Sarasota, FL), 1996.
Twentieth-Century Florida Authors, Mellon Press (New York, NY), 1996.
(Editor) *More Florida Stories,* University Presses of Florida (Gainesville, FL), 1996.
Lighthouses of Ireland, Pineapple Press (Sarasota, FL), 1997.
Guide to the University of Florida and Gainesville, Pineapple Press (Sarasota, FL), 1997.
Georgia's Lighthouses and Historic Coastal Sites, Pineapple Press (Sarasota, FL), 1998.
(Editor) *Alligator Tales,* Pineapple Press (Sarasota, FL), 1998.
(Editor) *"A River in Flood" and Other Florida Stories by Marjory Stoneman Douglas,* University Presses of Florida (Gainesville, FL), 1998.
Native Americans, in Florida, Pineapple Press (Sarasota, FL), 1999.
Fightin' Gators: A History of University of Florida Football, Arcadia Publishing (Charleston, SC), 2000.
Christmas in Florida, Pineapple Press (Sarasota, FL), 2000.
(With Ernest Jernigan) *Ocala,* Arcadia Publishing (Charleston, SC), 2001.
Florida Outhouses, Infinity Publishing (Haverford, PA), 2002.
Babe Ruth in Florida, Infinity Publishing (Haverford, PA), 2002.
(With Betty Stewart-Dowdell) *African Americans at the University of Florida,* University of Florida Sesquicentennial Committee (Naples, FL), 2003.

Author of workbooks and other curriculum materials. Contributor of about forty articles and reviews to language, literature, and linguistic journals, popular magazines including *Florida* and *North Florida Living,* and newspapers. Editor, *Newsletter of the Marjorie Kinnan Rawlings Society,* 1990—; associate editor, *Marjorie Kinnan Rawlings Journal of Florida Literature,* 1989-97.

SIDELIGHTS: Kevin M. McCarthy once told *CA:* "Having lived in the Middle East for five years, I came to appreciate its history, customs, and languages. I went on to do a master's thesis on the influence of the Middle East on American literature and a Ph.D. dissertation on Arabic and Turkish. I wrote the book on Saudi Arabia in order to clear up many of the misconceptions outsiders have of that country and to share some of the wonderful experiences I had there. I have since discovered Florida and its wealth of subjects to write about: lighthouses, shipwrecks, pirates, football, literature, etc."

*   *   *

MOMADAY, N(avarre) Scott 1934-

PERSONAL: Surname is pronounced "*Ma*-ma-day"; born Navarre Scott Mammedaty, February 27, 1934, in Lawton, OK; son of Alfred Morris (a painter and teacher of art) and Mayme Natachee (a teacher and writer; maiden name, Scott) Mommedaty; married Gaye Mangold, September 5, 1959 (divorced); married Regina Heitzer, July 21, 1978 (divorced); children: (first marriage) Cael, Jill, Brit (all daughters); (second marriage) Lore (daughter). *Education:* Attended Augusta Military Academy; University of New Mexico, A.B., 1958; Stanford University, M.A., 1960, Ph.D., 1963.

ADDRESSES: Office—University of Arizona, 445 Modern Languages Building, P.O. Box 210067, Tucson, AZ 85721. *E-mail*—natachee@aol.com.

CAREER: Artist, author, and educator. University of California, Santa Barbara, assistant professor, 1963-65, associate professor of English, 1968-69; University of California, Berkeley, associate professor of English and comparative literature, 1969-73; Stanford University, Stanford, CA, professor of English, 1973-82; University of Arizona, Tucson, professor of English and comparative literature, 1982—, regents professor of English; former teacher at New Mexico State University. Has exhibited drawings and paintings in galleries. Museum of American Indian, Heye Foundation, New York, NY, trustee, 1978—. National Endowment for the Humanities, National Endowment for the Arts, consultant, 1970—.

MEMBER: PEN, Modern Language Association of America, American Studies Association, Gourd Dance Society of the Kiowa Tribe.

N. Scott Momaday

AWARDS, HONORS: Academy of American Poets prize, 1962, for poem "The Bear"; Guggenheim fellowship, 1966-67; Pulitzer Prize for fiction, 1969, for *House Made of Dawn*; inducted into Kiowa Gourd Clan, 1969; National Institute of Arts and Letters grant, 1970; shared Western Heritage Award with David Muench, 1974, for nonfiction book *Colorado: Summer/ Fall/Winter/Spring*; Premio Letterario Internazionale Mondelo (Italy), 1979; inducted into Academy of Achievement, 1993.

WRITINGS:

(Editor) *The Complete Poems of Frederick Goddard Tuckerman,* Oxford University Press (New York, NY), 1965.

(Reteller) *The Journey of Tai-me* (Kiowa Indian folktales), with original etchings by Bruce S. McCurdy, University of California Press, (Santa Barbara, CA) 1967, enlarged edition published as *The Way to Rainy Mountain,* illustrated by father,

Alfred Momaday, University of New Mexico Press (Albuquerque, NM), 1969.

House Made of Dawn (novel), Harper (New York, NY), 1968, reprinted, 1989.

Colorado: Summer/Fall/Winter/Spring, illustrated with photographs by David Muench, Rand McNally (Chicago, IL), 1973.

Angle of Geese and Other Poems, David Godine (Boston, MA), 1974.

(And illustrator) *The Gourd Dancer* (poems), Harper (New York, NY), 1976.

The Names: A Memoir, Harper (New York, NY), 1976, reprinted, University of Arizona Press (Tucson, AZ), 1996.

(Author of foreword) An Painter, *A Coyote in the Garden,* Confluence (Lewiston, ID), 1988.

The Ancient Child (novel), Doubleday (New York, NY), 1989.

(Contributor) Charles L. Woodward, *Ancestral Voice: Conversations with N. Scott Momaday,* University of Nebraska Press (Lincoln, NE), 1989.

(Author of introduction) Marcia Keegan, *Enduring Culture: A Century of Photography of the Southwest Indians,* Clear Light (Santa Fe, NM), 1991.

In the Presence of the Sun: A Gathering of Shields, Rydal (Santa Fe, NM), 1992.

In the Presence of the Sun: Stories and Poems, 1961-1991 (poems, stories, art), St. Martin's Press (New York, NY), 1992.

(Author of introduction) Gerald Hausman, *Turtle Island Alphabet: A Lexicon of Native American Symbols and Culture,* St. Martin's Press (New York, NY), 1992.

Circle of Wonder: A Native American Christmas Story, Clear Light (Santa Fe, NM), 1994.

Conversations with N. Scott Momaday, University Press of Mississippi (Jackson, MS), 1997.

The Man Made of Words: Essays, Stories, Passages, St. Martin's Press (New York, NY), 1997.

In the Bear's House, St. Martin's Press (New York, NY), 1999.

Also author of film script of Frank Water's novel, *The Man Who Killed the Deer.* Contributor of articles and poems to periodicals; a frequent reviewer on Indian subjects for the *New York Times Book Review.*

WORK IN PROGRESS: A study of American poetry in the middle period, *The Furrow and the Plow: Science and Literature in America, 1836-1866* (tentative title), for Oxford University Press; a book on storytelling, for Oxford University Press.

SIDELIGHTS: N. Scott Momaday's poetry and prose reflect his Kiowa Indian heritage in structure and theme, as well as in subject matter. "When I was growing up on the reservations of the Southwest," he told Joseph Bruchac in the *American Poetry Review,* "I saw people who were deeply involved in their traditional life, in the memories of their blood. They had, as far as I could see, a certain strength and beauty that I find missing in the modern world at large. I like to celebrate that involvement in my writing." Roger Dickinson-Brown indicated in the *Southern Review* that Momaday has long "maintained a quiet reputation in American Indian affairs and among distinguished *literati*" for his brilliance and range, "his fusion of alien cultures, and his extraordinary experiments in different literary forms."

Momaday is half Kiowa. His mother, Mayme Natachee Scott, is descended from early American pioneers, although her middle name is taken from a Cherokee great-grandmother. Momaday's memoir also includes anecdotes of such Anglo-American ancestors as his grandfather, Theodore Scott, a Kentucky sheriff. His mother, however, preferred to identify with her imagined Indian heritage, adopting the name Little Moon when she was younger and dressing Indian style. She attended Haskell Institute, an Indian school in Kansas, where she met several members of the Kiowa tribe. Eventually she married Momaday's father, also a Kiowa. The author grew up in New Mexico, where his mother, a teacher and writer, and his father, an artist and art teacher, found work among the Jemez Indians in the state's high canyon and mountain country, but he was originally raised among the Kiowas on a family farm in Oklahoma. Although Momaday covers his Anglo-American heritage in the memoir, he prefers, like his mother, "to imagine himself *all* Indian, and to 'imagine himself' back into the life, the emotions, the spirit of his Kiowa forebears," commented Edward Abbey in *Harper's.* He uses English, his mother's language, according to Abbey, to tell "his story in the manner of his father's people; moving freely back and forth in time and space, interweaving legend, myth, and history." In *Modern American Poetry,* Kenneth M. Roemer remarked that Momaday's culturally rich childhood led him to "fall in love with Kiowa, Navajo, Jemez Pueblo, Spanish, and English words."

Momaday's *The Names: A Memoir* explores the author's heritage in autobiographical form. It is composed of tribal tales, boyhood memories, and genealogy, reported *New York Times Book Review* critic Wallace Stegner. Momaday's quest for his roots, wrote Abbey, "takes him back to the hills of Kentucky and north to the high plains of Wyoming, and from there, in memory and imagination, back to the Bering Straits." Stegner described it as "an Indian book, but not a book about wrongs done to Indians. It is a search and a celebration, a book of identities and sources. Momaday is the son of parents who successfully bridged the gulf between Indian and white ways, but remain Indian," he explained. "In boyhood Momaday made the same choice, and in making it gave himself the task of discovering and in some degree inventing the tradition and history in which he finds his most profound sense of himself." *New York Review of Books* critic Diane Johnson agreed that "Momaday does not appear to feel, or does not discuss, any conflict of the Kiowa and white traditions; he is their product, an artist, heir of the experiences of his ancestors and conscious of the benignity of their influence."

Momaday does not actually speak Kiowa, but, in his work, he reveals the language as not only a reflection of the physical environment, but also a means of shaping it. The title of *The Names,* reported Richard Nicholls in *Best Sellers,* refers to all "the names given by Scott Momaday's people, the Kiowa Indians, to the objects, forms, and features of their land, the southwestern plains, and to its animals and birds." When he was less than a year old, Momaday was given the name Tsoaitalee or "Rock-Tree-Boy" by a paternal relative, after the 200-foot volcanic butte in Wyoming, which is sacred to the Kiowas and is known to Anglo-Americans as Devil's Tower. "For the Kiowas it was a place of high significance," Abbey pointed out. "To be named after that mysterious and mythic rock was, for the boy, a high honor and a compelling one. For among the Indians a name was never merely an identifying tag but something much more important, a kind of emblem and ideal, the determining source of a man or woman's character and course of life."

Momaday's first novel, *House Made of Dawn,* tells "the old story of the problem of mixing Indians and Anglos," reported *New York Times Book Review* critic Marshall Sprague. "But there is a quality of revelation here as the author presents the heart-breaking effort of his hero to live in two worlds." In the novel's fractured narrative, the main character, Abel, returns to the prehistoric landscape and culture surrounding his reservation pueblo after his tour of duty in the Army during World War II. Back home, he kills an albino. He serves a prison term and is paroled, unrepentant, to a Los Angeles relocation center. Once in the city, he attempts to adjust to his factory job, like his even-tempered roommate, Ben, a modern Indian, who narrates parts of the novel. During his free time, Abel drinks and attends adulterated religious and peyote-eating ceremonies. He can't cope with his job; and, "because of his contempt," Sprague indicated, he's brutally beaten by a Los Angeles policeman, but returns again to the reservation "in time to carry on tradition for his dying grandfather," Francisco. The novel culminates in Abel's running in the ancient ritual dawn race against evil and death.

According to Kerr, the book is "a creation myth—rife with fabulous imagery, ending with Abel's rebirth in the old ways at the old man's death—but an ironic one, suffused with violence and telling a story of culture loss." The grandfather, he maintained, "heroic, crippled, resonant with the old ways, impotent in the new—acts as a lodestone to the novel's conflicting energies. His incantatory dying delirium in Spanish flexes Momaday's symbolic compass . . . , and around his dying the book shapes its proportions." Francisco is "the alembic that transmutes the novel's confusions," he commented. "His retrospection marks off the book's boundaries, points of reference, and focal themes: the great organic calendar of the black mesa—the house of the sun (which locates the title)—as a central Rosetta stone integrating the ceremonies rendered in Part One, and the source place by which Abel and [his brother] could 'reckon where they were, where all things were, in time.'"

Momaday meets with difficulties in his attempt to convey Indian sensibility in novelistic form, Kerr related. The fractured narrative is open to criticism, in Kerr's opinion, and the "plot of *House Made of Dawn* actually seems propelled by withheld information, that besetting literary error." Of the novel's structure, Dickinson-Brown wrote that the sequence of events "is without fixed order. The parts can be rearranged, no doubt with change of effect, but not always with recognizable difference. The fragments thus presented are the subject. The result is a successful depiction but not an understanding of what is depicted: a reflection, not a novel in the comprehensive sense of the word." Kerr also objected to the author's overuse of "quiet, weak constructions" in the opening paragraph and indicated that "repetition, polysyndeton, and *there* as subject continue to deaden the narrative's force well into the book." *Commonweal* reviewer William James Smith agreed that "Momaday observes and renders accurately, but the material seems to have sunken slightly beneath the surface of the beautiful prose." The critic maintained, however, that the novel should also be regarded as "a return to the sacred art of storytelling and myth-making that is part of Indian oral tradition," as well as an attempt "to push the secular mode of modern fiction into the sacred mode, a faith and recognition in the power of the word." And a *Times Literary Supplement* critic pointed out Momaday's "considerable descriptive power," citing "a section in which Tosamah [a Los Angeles medicine man/priest] rehearses the ancient trampled history of the Kiowas in trance—like visionary prose that has moments of splendour."

In a review of *The Way to Rainy Mountain, Southern Review* critic Kenneth Fields observed that Momaday's writing exemplifies a "paradox about language which is often expressed in American Indian literature." Momaday himself has written that "by means of words can a man deal with the world on equal terms. And the word is sacred," commented Fields. "On the other hand . . . the Indians took for their subject matter those elusive perceptions that resist formulation, never entirely apprehensible, but just beyond the ends of the nerves." In a similar vein, Dickinson-Brown maintained that Momaday's poem "Angle of Geese" "presents, better than any other work I know . . . perhaps the most important subject of our age: the tragic conflict between what we have felt in wilderness and what our language means." What Momaday must articulate in *The Way to Rainy Mountain,* Fields argued, is "racial memory," or "the ghostly heritage of [his] Kiowa ancestors," and "what it means to feel himself a Kiowa in the modern American culture that displaced his ancestors."

Described by Fields as "far and away [Momaday's] best book," *The Way to Rainy Mountain* relates the story of the Kiowas journey 300 years ago from Yellowstone down onto the plains, where they acquired horses, and, in the words of John R. Milton in the *Saturday Review,* "they became a lordly society of sun priests, fighters, hunters, and thieves, maintaining this position for 100 years, to the mid-nineteenth century," when they were all but destroyed by the U.S. Cavalry in Oklahoma. And when the sacred buffalo began to disappear, Fields wrote, "the Kiowas lost the sustain-ing illumination of the sun god," since, as Momaday explains, the buffalo was viewed as "the animal representation of the sun, the essential and sacrificial victim of the Sun Dance." "Momaday's own grandmother, who had actually been present at the last and abortive Kiowa Sun Dance in 1887, is for him the last of the Kiowas," related Fields.

In *The Way to Rainy Mountain,* Momaday uses form to help him convey a reality that has largely been lost. His text is made up of twenty-four numbered sections grouped into three parts, "The Setting Out," "The Going On," and "The Closing In." These parts are in turn divided into three different passages, each of which is set in a different style typeface. The first passage in each part is composed of Kiowa myths and legends, the second is made up of historical accounts of the tribe, and the third passage is a personal autobiographical rendering of Momaday's rediscovery of his Kiowa homeland and roots. Fields explained that in form, the book "resembles those ancient texts with subsequent commentaries which, taken altogether, present strange complexes of intelligence; not only the author's, but with it that of the man in whose mind the author was able to live again."

By the end of the last part, however, wrote Nicholas, the three passages begin to blend with one another, and "the mythic passages are no longer mythic in the traditional sense, that is Momaday is creating myth out of his memories of his ancestors rather than passing on already established and socially sanctioned tales. Nor are the historical passages strictly historical, presumably objective, accounts of the Kiowas and their culture. Instead they are carefully selected and imaginatively rendered memories of his family. And, finally, the personal passages have become prose poems containing symbols which link them thematically to the other two, suggesting that all three journeys are products of the imagination, that all have become interfused in a single memory and reflect a single idea." Dickinson-Brown considered the book's shape a well-controlled "associational structure," distinctively adapted to the author's purpose. The form, according to Fields, forced Momaday "to relate the subjective to the more objective historical sensibility. The writing of the book itself, one feels, enables him to gain both freedom and possession. It is therefore a work of discovery as well as renunciation, of finding but also of letting go."

After *The House Made of Dawn,* Momaday wrote mainly nonfiction and poetry. He did not write another novel for twenty years. "I don't think of myself as a novelist. I'm a poet," he told *Los Angeles Times* interviewer Edward Iwata. Yet, in 1989, the poet completed his second novel, *The Ancient Child*. Building this book around the legend behind his Indian name, Tsoaitalee, Momaday uses the myth to develop the story of a modern Indian artist searching for his identity. A number of reviewers lauded the new novel. Craig Lesley, for one, wrote in the *Washington Post* that *The Ancient Child* "is an intriguing combination of myth, fiction and storytelling that demonstrates the continuing power and range of Momaday's creative vision." A "largely autobiographical novel," according to Iwata, *The Ancient Child* expresses the author's belief that "dreams and visions are pathways to one's blood ancestry and racial memory."

In addition to his poetry and fiction, Momaday is also an accomplished painter. His diverse skill is evident in *In the Presence of the Sun: Stories and Poems, 1961-1991*. The collection includes numerous poems from Momaday's early poetic career; twenty new poems; a sequence of poems about the legendary outlaw Billy the Kid; stories about the Kiowas' tribal shields; and sixty drawings by the author. "A slim volume, [*In the Presence of the Sun*] contains the essence of the ancestral voices that speak through him. It is a refined brew of origins, journeys, dreams and the landscape of the deep continental interior," remarked Barbara Bode in the *New York Times Book Review*.

In the Bear's House is a mixture of paintings, poems, dialogues, and prose relating to the bear, an animal of spiritual significance to the Kiowas. "Momaday's blend of biblical and Native American spirituality and language seems almost old-fashioned in light of more separatist studies that have dominated since he first arrived on the scene back in the 60s," remarked a *Kirkus Reviews* contributor. However, the same contributor noted that "Momaday's clean, sharp measures enhance a number of well-made poems that date mostly from recent times." The critic further observed, "The bold brushstrokes of Momaday's paintings echo the power and precision of his poetry and prose."

Momaday views his heritage objectively and in a positive light. He explains much of his perspective as a writer and as a Native American in *Ancestral Voice: Conversations with N. Scott Momaday*, the result of a series of interviews with Charles L. Woodward. *World Literature Today* contributor Robert L. Berner called

the volume "an essential tool of scholarship" in analyzing and understanding Momaday and his work. Discussing his heritage with Bruchac, Momaday commented: "The Indian has the advantage of a very rich spiritual experience. As much can be said, certainly, of some non-Indian writers. But the non-Indian writers of today are culturally deprived, I think, in the sense that they don't have the same sense of heritage that the Indian has. I'm told this time and time again by my students, who say, 'Oh, I wish I knew more about my grandparents; I wish I knew more about my ancestors and where they came from and what they did.' I've come to believe them. It seems to me that the Indian writer ought to make use of that advantage. One of his subjects ought certainly to be his cultural investment in the world. It is a unique and complete experience, and it is a great subject in itself."

BIOGRAPHICAL AND CRITICAL SOURCES:

BOOKS

Allen, Paula Gunn, *Recovering the Word: Essays on Native American Literature*, edited by Brian Swann and Arnold Krupat, University of California Press (Berkeley, CA), 1987, pp. 563-579.

Blaeser, Kimberly, *Narrative Chance: Postmodern Discourse on Native American Indian Literatures*, edited by Gerald Vizenor, University of New Mexico Press (Albuquerque, NM), 1989, pp. 39-54.

Brumble, H. David, III, *American Indian Autobiography*, University of California Press (Berkeley, CA), 1988, pp. 165-80.

Contemporary Literary Criticism, Gale (Detroit, MI), Volume 2, 1974, Volume 19, 1981, Volume 85, 1995, Volume 95, 1997.

Dictionary of Literary Biography, Volume 143: *American Novelists since World War II, Third Series*, Gale (Detroit, MI), 1994, Volume 175: *Native American Writers of the United States*, Gale (Detroit, MI), 1997, Volume 256: *Twentieth-Century American Western Writers, Third Series*, 2002, pp. 203-218.

Encyclopedia of World Biography, 2nd edition, Gale (Detroit, MI), 1998.

Gridley, Marion E., editor, *Indians of Today*, I.C.F.P., 1971.

Gridley, Marion E., *Contemporary American Indian Leaders*, Dodd (New York, NY), 1972.

Hogan, Linda, *Studies in American Indian Literature: Critical Essays and Course Designs,* edited by Paula Gunn Allen, Modern Language Association of America (New York, NY), 1983, pp. 169-177.

Krupat, Arnold, *The Voice in the Margin: Native American Literature and the Canon,* University of California Press (Berkeley, CA), 1989.

Lincoln, Kenneth, *Native American Renaissance,* University of California Press (Berkeley, CA), 1983, pp. 82-121.

Momaday, N. Scott, *The Way to Rainy Mountain,* University of New Mexico Press (Albuquerque, NM), 1969.

Momaday, N. Scott, *The Names: A Memoir,* Harper (New York, NY), 1976.

Native North American Literature, Gale (Detroit, MI), 1994.

Owens, Louis, *Other Destinies: Understanding the American Indian Novel,* University of Oklahoma Press (Norman, OK), 1992.

Roemer, Kenneth, editor, *Approaches to Teaching Momaday's "The Way to Rainy Mountain,"* Modern Language Association of America (New York, NY), 1988.

St. James Guide to Young Adult Writers, 2nd edition, St. James Press (Detroit, MI), 1999.

Schubnell, Matthias, *N. Scott Momaday: The Cultural and Literary Background,* University of Oklahoma Press (Norman, OK), 1985.

Trimble, Martha Scott, *Fifty Western Writers: A Bio-Bibliographical Sourcebook,* edited by Fred Erisman and Richard W. Etulain, Greenwood Press (Westport, CT), 1982, pp. 313-324.

Velie, Alan R, *Four American Indian Literary Masters: N. Scott Momaday, James Welch, Leslie Marmon Silko, and Gerald Vizenor,* University of Oklahoma Press (Norman, OK), 1982.

PERIODICALS

American Indian Quarterly, May, 1978; winter, 1986, pp. 101-117; summer, 1988, pp. 213-220.

American Literature, January, 1979; October, 1989, p. 520.

American Poetry Review, July-August, 1984.

American West, February, 1988, pp. 12-13.

Atlantic, January, 1977.

Best Sellers, June 15, 1968; April, 1977.

Bloomsbury Review, July-August, 1989, p. 13; July-August, 1993, p. 14; November- December, 1994, p. 25.

Booklist, February 1, 1999, Ray Olson, review of *In the Bear's House,* p. 957.

Canadian Literature, spring, 1990, p. 299.

Commonweal, September 20, 1968.

Denver Quarterly, winter, 1978, pp. 19-31.

Harper's, February, 1977.

Indiana Social Studies Quarterly, Autumn, 1975, Joseph F. Trimmer, "Native Americans and the American Mix: N. Scott Momaday's *House Made of Dawn,*" pp. 75-91.

Journal of Popular Culture, fall 1999, review of *The Ancient Child,* p. 23.

Kirkus Reviews, March 15, 1999, review of *In the Bear's House,* p. 411.

Listener, May 15, 1969.

Los Angeles Times, November 20, 1989.

Los Angeles Times Book Review, December 27, 1992, p. 6.

Nation, August 5, 1968.

New Yorker, May 17, 1969.

New York Review of Books, February 3, 1977, pp. 19-20, 29.

New York Times, May 16, 1969; June 3, 1970.

New York Times Book Review, June 9, 1968, Marshall Sprague, review of *House Made of Dawn,* p. 5; June 16, 1974; March 6, 1977; December 31, 1989; March 14, 1993, p. 15.

Observer, May 25, 1969.

Publishers Weekly, September 19, 1994, p. 28; February 22, 1999, review of *In the Bear's House,* p. 91.

Saturday Review, June 21, 1969.

Sewanee Review, summer, 1977.

Social Studies, July, 1998, review of *The Man Made of Words,* p. 189.

South Dakota Review, winter, 1975-76, Charles A. Nicholas, review of *The Way to Rainy Mountain,* pp. 149-158.

Southern Review, winter, 1970; January, 1978, Roger Dickinson Brown, review of *House Made of Dawn,* pp. 30-32; April, 1978.

Southwest Review, summer, 1969; spring, 1978, Baine Kerr, review of *House Made of Dawn,* pp. 172-173.

Spectator, May 23, 1969.

Studies in American Fiction, Spring, 1983, Michael W. Raymond, review of *House Made of Dawn,* pp. 61-71.

Times Literary Supplement, May 22, 1969.

Tribune Books (Chicago, IL), October 1, 1989; December 4, 1994, p. 9.

Voice of Youth Advocates, October, 1998, review of *The Man Made of Words,* p. 255.

Washington Post, November 21, 1969; November 28, 1989.

Western American Literature, May, 1977, pp. 86-87; November, 1993, Eric Todd Smith, review of *In the Presence of the Sun,* pp. 274-275; spring 1999, review of *The Names* and *House Made of Dawn,* p. 7.

World Literature Today, summer, 1977; winter, 1990, p. 175; summer, 1993, p. 650.

ONLINE

Modern American Poetry, http://www.English.uiuc.edu/maps/poets/ (May 30, 2003), Kenneth Roemer, "N. Scott Momaday: Biographical, Literary, and Multicultural Contexts."*

*   *   *

MOORE, Gwyneth
See BANNISTER, Patricia Valeria

*   *   *

MOORE, Louis 1946-

PERSONAL: Born May 11, 1946, in Houston, TX; son of Louis A., Sr. (in sales) and Grace (Mauldin) Moore; married Kay Wheeler (a journalist), August 30, 1969; children: Matthew Justin, Catharine Louisa. *Education:* Baylor University, B.A., 1968, graduate study, 1968-69; Southern Baptist Theological Seminary, M.Div., 1972. *Religion:* Baptist.

ADDRESSES: Home and office—217 Asheboro Place, Franklin, TN 37064.

CAREER: Houston Chronicle, Houston, TX, religion editor, 1972-86; *Plano Star Courier,* Plano, TX, editor, 1986-88; Collin County Community College, Plano, professor of journalism, 1988-89; Southern Baptist Christian Life Commission, Nashville, TN, associate director for publications, beginning 1989; Belmont College, Nashville, part-time journalism teacher, beginning 1989. Editorial coordinator of Harte-Hanks Community Newspapers, 1986-88; member of Harte-Hanks Editorial Council; cochair of Harte-Hanks Contest Committee, 1987. Member of advisory board of Collin County Mental Health-Mental Retardation Authority; past member of board of directors of *Houston Chronicle* Credit Union.

MEMBER: American Society of Newspaper Editors, Religion Newswriters Association (president, 1984-86), Associated Press Managing Editors, Plano Chamber Orchestra Association.

AWARDS, HONORS: Schachern Award from Religion Newswriters Association, 1977, for the best religion section produced by a secular daily newspaper; first place award from Texas United Press International column writing contest, 1986, for a column on the Soviet Jews; first prize from Suburban Newspapers of America writing contest, 1987, for best feature story; eleven awards from Harte-Hanks writing and photography contests, 1987.

WRITINGS:

(With wife, Kay Moore) *When You Both Go to Work: How Two-Paycheck Families Can Stay Active in the Church,* Word Books (Waco, TX), 1982.

(With Kay Moore and Del Harris) *Playing the Game,* Word Books (Waco, TX), 1983.

(With Kay Moore and Grant Teaff) *Winning: It's How You Play the Game,* Word Books (Waco, TX), 1985.

(Editor, with Kay Moore, and contributor) *The Guideposts Biblical Commentary on the General Epistles,* Guideposts, 1986.

(Editor) Tim Hansel, *Eating Problems for Breakfast,* Word Books (Waco, TX), 1988.

(Editor, with Richard D. Land) *The Earth Is the Lord's: Christians and the Environment,* Broadman Press (Nashville, TN), 1992.

(Editor, with Richard D. Land) *Citizen Christians: The Rights and Responsibilities of Dual Citizenship,* Broadman Press (Nashville, TN), 1994.

(Editor, with Richard D. Land) *Life at Risk: The Crises in Medical Ethics,* Broadman & Holman (Nashville, TN), 1995.

Contributor to periodicals.

SIDELIGHTS: Louis Moore told *CA* that his major writing interests are "religious topics, sports figures, and family issues."

BIOGRAPHICAL AND CRITICAL SOURCES:

PERIODICALS

Christian Herald, September, 1982, review of *When You Both Go to Work: How Two-Paycheck Families Can Stay Active in the Church,* p. 64.

Florida Times Union, October 25, 1999, Bruce Bryant-Friedland, "Baptist Tract Warns Hindus of 'Hopeless Darkness,'" p. A1.*

* * *

MORGAN, Edmund S(ears) 1916-

PERSONAL: Born January 17, 1916, in Minneapolis, MN; son of Edmund Morris (a professor of law) and Elsie (Smith) Morgan; married Helen Mayer (an historian), June 7, 1939; married Marie Caskey (an historian), June 22, 1983; children: (first marriage) Penelope, Pamela. *Education:* Harvard University, A.B., 1937, Ph.D., 1942; London School of Economics, University of London, graduate study, 1937-38. *Hobbies and other interests:* Woodturning.

ADDRESSES: Home—244 Livingston St., New Haven, CT 06511. *Office*—Department of History, Yale University, New Haven, CT 06520.

CAREER: Massachusetts Institute of Technology, Cambridge, instrument maker in Radiation Laboratory, 1942-45; University of Chicago, Chicago, IL, instructor in social sciences, 1945-46; Brown University, Providence, RI, assistant professor, 1946-49, associate professor, 1949-51, professor of history, 1951-55; Yale University, New Haven, CT, professor of history, 1955-65, Sterling Professor of History, 1965-86, professor emeritus, 1986—. Johnson Research Professor, University of Wisconsin, 1968-69. Member of council, Institute of Early American History and Culture, 1953-56, 1958-60, and 1970-72; trustee of Smith College, 1984-89.

MEMBER: Society of American Historians, American Antiquarian Society, Organization of American Historians (president, 1971-72), American Philosophical Society, American Academy of Arts and Sciences,

Connecticut Academy of Arts and Sciences, Massachusetts Historical Society, Colonial Society of Massachusetts, British Academy, Royal Historical Society.

AWARDS, HONORS: Research fellow, Huntington Library, 1952-53; William Clyde DeWane Medal, 1971; Douglass Adair Memorial Award, 1972; Bruce Catton Award, 1992; Organization of American Historians Distinguished Services Award, 1998; National Humanities Medal, 2000; National Book Critics Circle Award nomination, 2003, for *Benjamin Franklin;* honorary degrees from Rutgers University, Brown University, Colgate University, Washington College, William and Mary, University of New Haven, Williams College, Lawrence University, and Smith College.

WRITINGS:

The Puritan Family: Religion and Domestic Relations in Seventeenth-Century New England, Boston Public Library (Boston, MA), 1944, new edition, Harper (New York, NY), 1966.

Virginians at Home: Family Life in the Eighteenth Century, Colonial Williamsburg (Williamsburg, VA), 1952.

(With Helen M. Morgan) *The Stamp Act Crisis: Prologue to Revolution,* University of North Carolina Press (Chapel Hill, NC), 1953, 3rd edition, 1994.

The Birth of the Republic, 1763-1789, University of Chicago Press (Chicago, IL), 1956, 3rd edition, 1992.

The Puritan Dilemma: The Story of John Winthrop, Little, Brown (Boston, MA), 1958.

The American Revolution: A Review of Changing Interpretations, Service Center for Teachers of History (Washington, DC), 1958.

The Gentle Puritan: A Life of Ezra Stiles, 1727-1795, Yale University Press (New Haven, CT), 1962, reprinted, Norton (New York, NY), 1984.

(With others) *The National Experience: A History of the United States,* Harcourt (New York, NY), 1963.

Visible Saints: The History of a Puritan Idea, New York University Press (New York, NY), 1963.

(With others) *The Emergence of the American,* Educational Services, 1965.

Roger Williams: The Church and the State, Harcourt (New York, NY), 1967.

So What about History?, Atheneum (New York, NY), 1969.

American Slavery, American Freedom: The Ordeal of Colonial Virginia, Norton (New York, NY), 1975.

The Challenge of the American Revolution, Norton (New York, NY), 1976.

The Meaning of Independence: John Adams, George Washington, and Thomas Jefferson, University Press of Virginia (Charlottesville, VA), 1976, 2nd edition, 2004.

The Genius of George Washington, Norton (New York, NY), 1980.

Inventing the People: The Rise of Popular Sovereignty in England and America, Norton (New York, NY), 1988.

Benjamin Franklin, Yale University Press (New Haven, CT), 2002.

The Genuine Article, Norton (New York, NY), 2004.

EDITOR

Prologue to the Revolution: Sources and Documents on the Stamp Act Crisis, 1764-1766, University of North Carolina Press (Chapel Hill, NC), 1959.

The Founding of Massachusetts: Historians and the Sources, Bobbs-Merrill (Indianapolis, IN), 1964.

The American Revolution: Two Centuries of Interpretation, Prentice-Hall (Englewood Cliffs, NJ), 1965.

Puritan Political Ideas, 1558-1794, Bobbs-Merrill (Indianapolis, IN), 1965, 2nd edition, Hackett Publishing, 2003.

The Diary of Michael Wigglesworth, 1653-1657: The Conscience of a Puritan, Harper (New York, NY), 1965.

Contributor to *The Mirror of the Indian*, Associates of the John Carter Brown Library, 1958. Author of introduction to *Paul Revere's Three Accounts of His Famous Ride*, Massachusetts Historical Society, 1961, 2nd edition, 1968. Also contributor of articles and reviews to historical journals. Member of editorial board, *New England Quarterly*.

SIDELIGHTS: Described by Michael Kammen in the *Washington Post Book World* as "one of the most distinguished historians of the United States," Edmund S. Morgan is the author of over fifteen books that have challenged traditional assumptions about the forces that shaped early American history, including the lives and beliefs of the Puritans and the impetus

for the Revolutionary War. With works such as *The Stamp Act Crisis: Prologue to Revolution, The Puritan Dilemma: The Story of John Winthrop*, and *Inventing the People: The Rise of Popular Sovereignty in England and America*, Morgan has earned a reputation as an historian of people as well as of ideas, and as a writer of wide appeal. Bruce Kuklick, writing in *Books and Culture*, maintained that "Edmund Morgan is arguably the finest living American historian."

Much of Morgan's acclaim has resulted from not only his ideas, but also his attention to the lives of human beings. In an essay for the *Dictionary of Literary Biography*, William D. Liddle explained that "Morgan's writings generally exhibit an affinity for people, a preoccupation with the details of their daily lives, and a concern for even the most mundane events and experiences when they touch upon things human. Attracted to the concrete and averse to abstractions, Morgan traces the history of ideas in their specific settings." In the opinion of Pauline Maier in the *New York Times Book Review*, he is "a man with a rare gift for telling the story of the past simply and elegantly without sacrificing its abundant complexity." Morgan has been able to reach wide audiences "by writing in language distinguished by simplicity, precision, grace, and wry humor. To achieve clarity and resonance he assumes that his audience is brighter than he is but completely ignorant of his subject and therefore dependent on the information he makes available. With Morgan, this is a formula for writing remarkable history," Liddle asserted. Because of this, Morgan's work appeals to audiences as diverse as Harvard scholars and the junior high school students who have read his *So What about History?*

Morgan's ideas have sparked lively debates for more than forty years. "The intellectual history of the American Revolutionary era was rewritten by scholars who followed the path marked out by Edmund S. Morgan," Liddle noted. For Liddle, Morgan's achievement is singular because the historian has never made such an influence his goal. "There is no 'Morgan thesis' on the American Revolution or on any other subject, and there is no 'Morgan school' either," Liddle added. "As he never became a disciple, so he never sought disciples."

Morgan's influence has been particularly strong in the study of the early Puritans, the subject of the historian's first book, *The Puritan Family: Essays on Religion and Domestic Relations in Seventeenth-Century New England,* published in 1944, and of many that followed. "Rarely have the Puritans emerged from modern scholarship as more human figures than in these writings," Liddle claimed. Liddle called *The Puritan Dilemma: The Story of John Winthrop,* first published in 1958, "a beautifully written volume," later adding: "Perhaps the book's most conspicuous and characteristic feature is the human touch with which its author treats complex beliefs and ideas."

Morgan returned to America's earlier history in his 1962 biography *The Gentle Puritan: A Life of Ezra Stiles, 1727-1795,* a work that illuminates the man whose writings Morgan had often used as source material for his own. For historians, Maier wrote, the book is "the inside favorite" among Morgan's works. In 1963, he published *Visible Saints: The History of a Puritan Idea,* which explained Puritan thought in the light of their policies toward church membership.

Morgan's writings on the Revolutionary War are considered integral to an understanding of the early United States. Among those books considered most important is *The Stamp Act Crisis: Prologue to Revolution,* written with Morgan's first wife, Helen M. Morgan, and published in 1953. Using a method that Liddle noted "has been described as seeking 'historical objectivity through cumulative partiality,'" Morgan looks at what had not previously been considered a significant British/colonist conflict in the instigation of the American Revolution, the Stamp Act, and reveals its importance through the eyes of six of its major figures. In this respect, Morgan's methods are considered revolutionary as well.

American Slavery, American Freedom: The Ordeal of Colonial Virginia is, in Liddle's opinion, "arguably Morgan's most important book; it is unquestionably his most controversial work." The book argues that it was the practice of owning slaves that spurred Virginians to want to be free of the British, in turn paving the way for revolution. "When Virginians became remarkably eloquent about the threat of 'slavery' and the danger to their 'liberties' in new British measures of the 1760s and 1770s, Morgan saw in their rhetoric a vital link between the very real freedom they enjoyed, the bondage they imposed on others, and 'a conglomeration of republican ideas' from which the ideology of Revolution was drawn," Liddle explained. Maier admired the "hilarious comparison of Indians with the barbarous Englishmen of seventeenth-century Virginia," and wrote that the book "will delight anyone with a taste for the human comedy and good writing."

In *The Genius of George Washington,* published in 1980, Morgan's analysis of the first president is backed up by excerpts from his subject's own letters. According to the *Atlantic Monthly,* Morgan's thesis is that Washington's true acumen lay in his "superb understanding of power," a side of the first president that had not previously been widely explored, and one that is reinforced by Washington's personal correspondence.

Morgan's *Inventing the People: The Rise of Popular Sovereignty in England and America* received a great deal of attention from critics and colleagues alike. Morgan's study of what he describes as the "political fictions" behind the notion of government by representation, *Inventing the People* argues that it was James Madison's fear of diversity leading to division that led him to "invent" the "fiction" of the "one people" upon which the U.S. Constitution is based. Samuel H. Beer commented in the *New Republic* that the problem was one of size: "On the one hand, as Morgan observes, the country was already so far united that its government had to be conducted [in Morgan's words,] 'in terms of a whole continent.' On the other hand, because of the weakness of the federal authority under the Articles of Confederation, the forces of localism dominated at the center as well as the periphery. How to overcome localism, [Morgan] says, was 'the central problem' confronting the aspiration for self-government." According to Kammen, the power of the book is that it explores the roots of "American notions concerning governmental power: where it actually lies, where we prefer to *believe* it ultimately resides and how the relationship between those two—fact and fiction—shapes our perception of political representation." As such, *Inventing the People* provoked a wide range of responses.

In the *New York Review of Books,* Keith Thomas contended that in *Inventing the People,* Morgan neglects to consider several other historical examples (including the French Revolution) of the developments of the same "fictions" that Morgan considers peculiar to the birth of the United States. However, Thomas wrote that when Morgan leaves off what the critic sees as the author's dependence on the work of other historians, he "puts forward original arguments of his own. In a series of brilliant chapters he probes the myths that sustained eighteenth-century American notions of liberty, and he reveals in each case the huge gulf between the high-sounding platitudes and the brutal realities of political life." Kammen called *Inventing the People* "a creative synthesis of considerable significance." Despite concerns that the historian may have overstated the extent to which colonists were devoted to the idea of equality at the time of the Revolution, Kammen assessed that Morgan has "made a penetrating contribution to our understanding of the origins of American political culture."

In 2002, Morgan published *Benjamin Franklin,* "the best short biography of Franklin ever written," according to T. J. Schaeper in *Library Journal.* Morgan's version of Franklin's life focuses on the Founding Father's desire to lead a "useful life," beyond his financial and scientific achievements. This desire led Franklin into public service, which he saw as a way to give his life a meaning beyond the strictly personal. Relying on Franklin's writings, and on his own extensive knowledge of the scholarship already published on Franklin, Morgan tries to capture the essence of Franklin's way of thought. Walter Russell Mead in *Foreign Affairs* called Morgan's book "a concise, excellent, and eminently readable biography." The critic for *Publishers Weekly* believed that "this wonderful biography of an extraordinary man results from a perfect marriage of subject and scholar."

BIOGRAPHICAL AND CRITICAL SOURCES:

BOOKS

Dictionary of Literary Biography, Volume 17: *Twentieth-Century American Historians,* Gale (Detroit, MI), 1983.

PERIODICALS

Atlantic Monthly, May, 1981, review of *The Genius of George Washington,* p. 81.
Booklist, August, 2002, Gilbert Taylor, review of *Benjamin Franklin,* p. 1916.
Books and Culture, January-February, 2003, Bruce Kuklick, review of *Benjamin Franklin,* p. 12.

Foreign Affairs, January-February, 2003, Walter Russell Mead, review of *Benjamin Franklin.*
Houston Chronicle, November 15, 2002, Lee Cearnal, review of *Benjamin Franklin.*
Kirkus Reviews, June 15, 2002, review of *Benjamin Franklin,* p. 861.
Library Journal, September 15, 2002, T. J. Schaeper, review of *Benjamin Franklin,* p. 70.
Los Angeles Times Book Review, March 13, 1988, review of *Inventing the People,* p. 4.
New England Quarterly, June, 1994, p. 202.
New Republic, August 1, 1988, Samuel H. Beer, review of *Inventing the People: The Rise of Popular Sovereignty in England and America,* p. 49.
New York Review of Books, November 24, 1988, Keith Thomas, review of *Inventing the People,* p. 43.
New York Times, June 28, 1965.
New York Times Book Review, July 3, 1988, Pauline Maier, review of *Inventing the People,* p. 10.
Publishers Weekly, July 1, 2002, review of *Benjamin Franklin,* p. 64.
Spectator, December 24, 1988, review of *Inventing the People,* p. 70.
Washington Post Book World, April 24, 1988, Michael Kammen, review of *Inventing the People,* p. 7.
Yale Review, winter, 1969.

*   *   *

MORRIS, Gerald (Paul) 1963-

PERSONAL: Born October 29, 1963, in Riverside, WI; son of Russell A. (a missionary) and Lena May (a missionary) Morris; married Rebecca Hughes (a registered nurse), August 2, 1986; children: William, Ethan, Grace. *Education:* Oklahoma Baptist University, B.A., 1985; Southern Baptist Theological Seminary, M.Div., 1989, Ph.D., 1994. *Politics:* Democrat. *Religion:* Baptist.

ADDRESSES: Home—624 North 16th Ave., Wausau, WI 54401. *Office*—P.O. Box 2014, Wausau, WI 54401-2014. *E-mail*—fbcw@pcpros.net.

CAREER: Southern Baptist Theological Seminary, Louisville, KY, adjunct professor of Hebrew and biblical interpretation, 1994-95; Ouachita Baptist University, Arkadelphia, AR, assistant professor of biblical

Gerald Morris

studies, 1995-96; teacher at Christian school in Arkadelphia, 1997; HortCo Landscaping, Norman, OK, contract laborer, 1997-98; First Baptist Church, Wausau, WI, pastor, 1998—.

MEMBER: Society of Biblical Literature, American Academy of Religion, Society of Children's Book Writers and Illustrators, Minnesota-Wisconsin Baptist Convention.

WRITINGS:

(As Gerald Paul Morris) *Prophecy, Poetry, and Hosea,* Sheffield Academic Press, 1996.

(Old Testament editor) *Life and Times Historical Reference Bible,* Thomas Nelson (Nashville, TN), 1998.

The Squire's Tale (novel), Houghton Mifflin (Boston, MA), 1998.

The Squire, His Knight, and His Lady (novel), Houghton Mifflin (Boston, MA), 1999.

The Savage Damsel and the Dwarf, Houghton Mifflin (Boston, MA), 2000.

Parsifal's Page, Houghton Mifflin (Boston, MA), 2001.

The Ballad of Sir Dinadan, Houghton Mifflin (Boston, MA), 2003.

The Princess, the Crone, and the Dung-Cart Knight, Houghton Mifflin (Boston, MA), 2004.

WORK IN PROGRESS: Dear DJ, a "contemporary semi-epistolary novel"; research on narrative techniques in the biblical books of I and II Kings.

SIDELIGHTS: Gerald Morris once commented: "I began my first novel when I was in the eighth grade. It was a perfectly dreadful western in which sharp-eyed gunslingers squinted into the sun and tough-as-boot-leather old-timers called people 'young 'un' and spat into the dust. The early chapters were, providentially, lost.

"I returned to writing novels when I went to graduate school. Writing fiction was an antidote to the gaseous prose I was churning out for my professors. Maybe because I wrote as a sort of simplifying exercise, I chose to write for children and adolescents. A child's world is no simpler than an adult's, but children often see their world with clearer eyes. These first attempts at children's novels received some very fine, preprinted rejection cards in a variety of pretty colors. Pastels were big in the late 1980s. Then my first child, William, was born, to be followed two years later by Ethan, then Grace. Life was busier then, so I put the novels aside.

"Then, for a while, I was an academic. I finished my doctorate and became a professor of Hebrew and biblical interpretation for a couple of years. When my last academic contract ended, I was rather at loose ends, and so I decided to rework some of those old novels. This time, one was accepted—*The Squire's Tale.* Encouraged, I kept writing. Meanwhile, I tutored Greek, taught middle schoolers, taught English as a second language, did some substitute teaching, and worked for a landscaper. At the end of that time, I became the pastor of the First Baptist Church of Wausau, Wisconsin. So now, I suppose, I write children's novels as an antidote to my own sermons."

Morris has now written a series of rollicking novels based on the old Arthurian legends of Thomas Mallory and other writers. Where these older sources seek seriousness of purpose and embroil their tales in allegory, Morris's more modern versions concentrate on the humanity of secondary characters and the way in which great quests sometimes boil down to small moments of self-discovery. *Booklist* reviewer Sally Estes noted that in his works, Morris puts "a humorous spin on Camelot and its denizens while still providing plenty of adventure, dimensional characters, and fresh, modern dialogue."

In his first book for children, *The Squire's Tale,* Morris uses the Arthurian legend as inspiration for his story about a young lad who serves as squire for Sir Gawain. Uncertain of his parentage, fourteen-year-old Terence decides to leave the wizard who raised him and join Sir Gawain on his quest to become The Maiden's Knight. As he follows the adventures of the future Knight of the Round Table, Terence not only discovers who his real parents are, but also what his destiny will be. The novel offers a different view of Sir Gawain as he is seen through the eyes of Terence, a perspective that *School Library Journal* reviewer Helen Gregory claimed was "both original and true to the legend of Gawain." She went on to suggest that "readers who savor swashbuckling tales of knighthood will enjoy this adventure." *Horn Book* critic Ann A. Flowers praised Morris's characters, saying: "Both Sir Gawain and Terence are remarkably engaging figures, holding our attention and affection." Shelle Rosenfeld noted in a *Booklist* review that in addition to being a "well-written, fast read," *The Squire's Tale* also offers readers "well-drawn characters, excellent, snappy dialogue, detailed descriptions of medieval life, and a dry wit."

Terence and Gawain continue their adventures in *The Squire, His Knight, and His Lady,* a sequel to *The Squire's Tale.* A *Kirkus Reviews* critic dubbed the work "an ideal follow-up to the first book and just as full of characters who are brave, loyal, and admirably human." In this story, Sir Gawain accepts a challenge in King Arthur's stead to meet the Knight of the Green Chapel, and sets out to find him with the assistance of his young squire, Terence. The two are joined in their quest by Lady Eileen, after rescuing her from her evil uncle. Together, the trio encounters a cannibal hag, a sea monster, the treacherous Marquis of Alva, and the Green Knight in disguise at an enchanted castle. "Laced with magic, humor, and chivalry," noted *Horn Book* reviewer Anne St. John, "this reworking of 'Sir Gawain and the Green Knight' . . . provides an engaging introduction to the original tale." A *Publishers*

Weekly commentator asserted: "Morris retells various medieval legends with plenty of action, tongue-in-cheek humor and moments of keen perception."

Another episode from Mallory's *Le Morte d'Arthur* forms the basis for *The Savage Damsel and the Dwarf.* Sixteen-year-old Lady Lynet travels to Camelot in the company of a wise dwarf, in the hopes that some knight will come to the aid of her besieged home. Lynet finds little sympathy at Arthur's court beyond a ragged kitchen servant named Beaumains. Beaumains is actually a brash knight in disguise, however, and if Lynet can keep him from picking quarrels with every other knight he meets on the way, he might actually be the hero she needs to defeat the villain. In *Horn Book,* Morris is quoted as having said: "It is a pure pleasure and an honor to retell this story . . . to fill in some of the gaps, and maybe turn a few things upside down." Beth Wright in *School Library Journal* found *The Savage Damsel and the Dwarf* "great fun and will be enjoyed by fans of the genre."

Parsifal's Page offers a new spin on another Arthurian hero, again from the point of view of his servant. The son of a blacksmith, Piers longs for a more noble life and thinks he has found his chance when he becomes page to the ignorant and backward Parsifal. When Piers's attempts to educate Parsifal backfire and cause Piers to be fired, he joins forces with Gawain and Terence. Together they try to locate Parsifal, who is missing and presumed to be in danger. In her *Horn Book* review of the work, Anne St. John noted that readers already familiar with Morris's series would enjoy re-encountering familiar characters, but "this newest adventure also stands on its own." St. John added that the legendary but believable figures in the tale "provide a perfect backdrop for Piers's growing understanding of his role in the world."

Sir Dinadan, hero of *The Ballad of Sir Dinadan,* has been described by several reviewers as one of Morris's most engaging characters. With a quick wit and the ability to see humor in every situation, Dinadan is an artist at heart—specifically a musician. His martial-minded father has other ideas, however, and Dinadan is knighted against his will and sent off to make his way as a soldier. Among his varied tasks, Dinadan helps his cloddish brother Tristram deal with a decidedly unlikable Iseult, as well as helping a deposed king win back his throne. Throughout, young Dinadan continues to mature while still maintaining his individuality as an artist and a thinker. *Booklist* correspondent Carolyn Phelan described *The Ballad of Sir Dinadan* as "a witty tale of adventure and reflection," and Steven Engelfried praised the book in *School Library Journal* for Morris's "skilled storytelling" that provides ". . . a lighthearted introduction to the period."

Morris once discussed his inspirations: "My faith is important to me. (This is good. We pastors are *encouraged* to believe something, after all.) All the same, I don't see myself as a 'Christian novelist.' I am, rather, a novelist who is a Christian, and a pastor, and a teacher, and a landscaper." And, clearly, a devotee of the tales of King Arthur.

BIOGRAPHICAL AND CRITICAL SOURCES:

PERIODICALS

Booklist, April 15, 1998, Shelle Rosenfeld, review of *The Squire's Tale,* pp. 1436-1437; May 1, 1999, Shelle Rosenfeld, review of *The Squire, His Knight, and His Lady,* p. 1587; March 1, 2000, GraceAnne A. DeCandido, review of *The Savage Damsel and the Dwarf,* p. 1244; April 15, 2000, Sally Estes, "The Denizens of Camelot Series," p. 1544; April 15, 2001, Carolyn Phelan, review of *Parsifal's Page,* p. 1558; May 1, 2003, Carolyn Phelan, review of *The Ballad of Sir Dinadan,* p. 1589.

Horn Book, July-August, 1998, Ann A. Flowers, review of *The Squire's Tale,* p. 492; March-April, 1999, Anne St. John, review of *The Squire, His Knight, and His Lady,* p. 210; May, 2000, review of *The Savage Damsel and the Dwarf,* p. 317; May, 2001, Anne St. John, review of *Parsifal's Page,* p. 333; May-June, 2003, Peter D. Sieruta, review of *The Ballad of Sir Dinadan,* p. 353.

Kirkus Reviews, April 1, 1999, review of *The Squire, His Knight, and His Lady,* p. 536.

Publishers Weekly, March 15, 1999, review of *The Squire, His Knight, and His Lady,* p. 60.

School Library Journal, July, 1998, Helen Gregory, review of *The Squire's Tale,* p. 97; May, 2000, Beth Wright, review of *The Savage Damsel and the Dwarf,* p. 174; April, 2001, Cheri Estes, review of *Parsifal's Page,* p. 146; April, 2003, Steven Engelfried, review of *The Ballad of Sir Dinadan,* p. 166.*

N

NELSON, Richard 1950-

PERSONAL: Born October 17, 1950, in Chicago, IL; son of Richard Finis (a sales representative) and Viola (a dancer; maiden name, Gabriel) Nelson; married Cynthia B. Bacon, May 21, 1972; children: Zoe Elizabeth, Jocelyn Anne. *Education:* Hamilton College (Clinton, NY), B.A., 1972.

ADDRESSES: Home—32 South St., Rhinebeck, NY 12572. *Agent*—Peter Franklin, William Morris Agency, 1350 Sixth Ave., New York, NY 10019; Patricia Mac-Naughton, MLR, 200 Fulham Rd., London SW10 9PN, England.

CAREER: Playwright and director. Playwright, 1972—; Brooklyn Academy of Music Theater Company (BAM), New York, NY, literary manager, 1979-81; Goodman Theater of the Art Institute of Chicago, Chicago, IL, associate director, 1980-83; Tyrone Guthrie Theater, Minneapolis, MN, dramaturge, 1981-82.

Also directed the stage productions for his plays *Between East and West* (with Ted D'Arms), *Goodnight Children Everywhere, Madame Melville, The General from America,* and the unpublished plays *James Joyce's The Dead, Franny's Way,* and *My Life with Albertine.* Also worked on lighting design for several Broadway and Off-Broadway productions, and appeared on an episode of *Working in the Theatre* for the City University of New York, 2000.

MEMBER: PEN.

AWARDS, HONORS: Thomas J. Watson travel fellowship, 1972; Office for Advanced Drama Research grant, 1976, for *Conjuring an Event;* National Endowment for the Arts creative writing fellowship, 1979, 1985; Obie Award for distinguished play writing, *Village Voice,* 1979, for *The Vienna Notes;* Rockefeller Foundation grants, 1979, 1988; Obie Award for innovative programming, *Village Voice,* 1980; Guggenheim fellowship, 1983; ABC Playwriting Award, American Broadcasting Companies (ABC) Television, 1985, for *Principia Scriptoriae;* National Endowment for the Arts playwriting fellowships, 1986, 1987; Playwrights USA Award, Home Box Office (HBO), 1986, for *Between East and West; Time Out* London Theatre Award, 1987, for *Principia Scriptoriae;* Giles Cooper Award for best radio play, 1988, for *Languages Spoken Here;* Lila Wallace Writers Award, Reader's Digest Fund, 1991-93; Antoinette Perry ("Tony") Award nomination for best play, 1992, for *Two Shakespearean Actors;* Lannan Literary Award, 1995; and Antoinette Perry ("Tony") Award for best book of a musical, 2000, for *James Joyce's The Dead.*

WRITINGS:

PUBLISHED STAGE PLAYS

The Killing of Yablonski: Scenes of Involvement in a Current Event (produced in Los Angeles, CA, at the Mark Taper Forum/Lab, 1975), published in *Plays by Richard Nelson: Early Plays, Volume 1,* Broadway Play Publishing (New York, NY), 1998.
Conjuring an Event (produced in Los Angeles, CA, at the Mark Taper Forum/Lab, 1976; produced in New York, NY, at the American Place Theater,

March 19, 1978), published in *An American Comedy and Other Plays,* PAJ Publications (New York, NY), 1986, published in *Plays by Richard Nelson: Early Plays, Volume 1,* Broadway Play Publishing (New York, NY), 1998.

Scooping (one-act monologue; produced in Washington, DC, at the Arena Stage, 1977), published in *Plays by Richard Nelson: Early Plays, Volume 1,* Broadway Play Publishing (New York, NY), 1998.

Jungle Coup (produced in New York, NY, at Playwrights Horizons Theatre, June 22, 1978), published in *Plays from Playwrights Horizons,* Broadway Play Publishing (New York, NY), 1987, published in *Plays by Richard Nelson: Early Plays, Volume 1,* Broadway Play Publishing (New York, NY), 1998.

The Vienna Notes (produced in Minneapolis, MN, at the Tyrone Guthrie Theater, October 6, 1978; produced in New York, NY, at Playwrights Horizons Theatre, January 18, 1979), published in *Wordplays,* PAJ Publications (New York, NY), 1980, published in *Plays by Richard Nelson: Early Plays, Volume 2,* Broadway Play Publishing (New York, NY), 1998.

Bal (produced by Chicago Theatre Group, in Chicago, IL, at the Goodman Theater, February 29, 1980), published in *An American Comedy and Other Plays,* PAJ Publications (New York, NY), 1986, published in *Plays by Richard Nelson: Early Plays, Volume 2,* Broadway Play Publishing (New York, NY), 1998.

Rip Van Winkle or "The Works" (produced in New Haven, CT, at the Yale Repertory Theater, December 4, 1981), Broadway Play Publishing (New York, NY), 1986.

The Return of Pinocchio (produced in Seattle, WA, at Empty Space, March, 1983; produced in New York, NY, by Double Image Theater, September, 1986), published in *An American Comedy and Other Plays,* PAJ Publications (New York, NY), 1986, published in *Plays by Richard Nelson: Early Plays, Volume 2,* Broadway Play Publishing (New York, NY), 1998.

(And codirector, with Ted D'Arms) *Between East and West* (two-act; produced in Seattle, WA, at the Seattle Repertory Theater, March 23, 1984; produced in London, England, at the Hampstead Theatre Club, December, 1987), published in *New Plays USA 3,* edited by James Leverett and M. Elizabeth Osborne, Theatre Communications Group (New York, NY), 1986, published by Faber & Faber (Boston, MA), 1989, published in *Prin-*

cipia Scriptoriae [and] *Between East and West,* Faber & Faber (Boston, MA), 1991.

An American Comedy (produced in Los Angeles, CA, at the Mark Taper Forum, October 13, 1986), published in *An American Comedy and Other Plays,* PAJ Publications (New York, NY), 1986.

An American Comedy and Other Plays (includes *An American Comedy, Bal, The Return of Pinocchio,* and *Conjuring an Event*), PAJ Publications (New York, NY), 1986.

Principia Scriptoriae (two-act; produced in New York, NY, at Manhattan Theatre Club, March 25, 1986; produced by the Royal Shakespeare Company, in London, England, 1986), Theatre Communications Group (New York, NY), 1986, published in *Principia Scriptoriae* [and] *Between East and West,* Faber & Faber (Boston, MA), 1991.

Chess (book for the two-act musical; produced on Broadway at the Imperial Theater, 1988; music by Benny Andersson and Bjön Ulvaeus, lyrics by Tim Rice, based on an idea by Tim Rice), Samuel French (New York, NY), 1989.

Some Americans Abroad (two-act; produced in Stratford-upon-Avon, England, by the Royal Shakespeare Company, July, 1989; produced in New York, NY, at the Mitzi E. Newhouse Theatre, 1990), Faber & Faber (Boston, MA), 1989.

Sensibility and Sense (produced in New York, NY, at the Mitzi E. Newhouse Theatre, 1989), Faber & Faber (Boston, MA), 1989.

Two Shakespearean Actors (produced in Stratford-upon-Avon, England, 1990; produced by the Royal Shakespeare Company, in New York, NY, at Lincoln Center Theatre, 1991), Faber & Faber (Boston, MA), 1990.

Columbus and the Discovery of Japan (produced by the Royal Shakespeare Company, in London, England, at the Barbican Theatre, 1992), Faber & Faber (Boston, MA), 1992.

(With Alexander Gelman) *Misha's Party* (produced in London, England, at the Pit, 1993; produced in Williamstown, MA, at the Williamstown Theatre Festival, MainStage Theatre, 1997), Faber & Faber (Boston, MA), 1993.

(And director) *The General from America* (produced by the Royal Shakespeare Company in London, England, at Barbican Theatre, 1996; produced by the Milwaukee Repertory Company), published in *Madame Melville* [and] *The General from America,* Grove Press (New York, NY), 2000, published separately, Samuel French (New York, NY), 2003.

(And director) *Goodnight Children Everywhere* (produced in Stratford-upon-Avon, England, by the Royal Shakespeare Company, 1997; produced in New York, NY, at Playwrights Horizons Theatre, 1999), Faber & Faber (Boston, MA), 1997.

Plays by Richard Nelson: Early Plays, Volume 1 (contains *The Killing of Yablonski, Scooping, Jungle Coup,* and *Conjuring an Event*), Broadway Play Publishing (New York, NY), 1998.

Plays by Richard Nelson: Early Plays, Volume 2, (contains *The Vienna Notes, Bal,* and *The Return of Pinocchio,*), Broadway Play Publishing (New York, NY), 1998.

Plays by Richard Nelson: Early Plays, Volume 3, Broadway Play Publishing (New York, NY), 1999.

Richard Nelson: Plays 1 (contains *Some Americans Abroad, Two Shakespearean Actors, New England, Principia Scriptoriae,* and *Left*), Faber & Faber (Boston, MA), 1999.

UNPUBLISHED STAGE PLAYS

Roots in Water (a collection of twelve vignettes), produced in Woodstock, NY, at River Arts Repertory, summer, 1988.

Life Sentences (expanded version of Nelson's television special "The End of a Sentence"), produced in New York, NY, at Second Stage, 1993.

New England, produced in London, England, at the Barbican Theatre, 1994; produced in New York, NY, at the Manhattan Theatre Club, 1995.

(And director) *Franny's Way* (one act), produced in New York, NY, at Playwrights Horizons Theatre, 2001.

Also author, with Colin Chambers, of the unpublished children's play *Kenneth's First Play.*

RADIO PLAYS

Languages Spoken Here (produced on BBC Radio-3, 1987), published in *Best Radio Plays of 1987,* Methuen (London, England), 1988.

Roots in Water (radio version of the stage play), produced as a radio play on BBC-Radio 3, 1989.

Eating Words (produced on BBC-Radio 3, 1989), published in *Best Radio Plays of 1989,* Methuen (London, England), 1989.

Also author of radio plays for WUHY-FM titled "The Unrequited Lovers' Manual," "Hank Aaron's 715th," "The Fall of Agnew," and "Watergate: An Audio Memory." Also author of radio plays for other stations, including "Advice to Eastern Europe" (1990) and "The American Wife" (1994).

TELEVISION PRODUCTIONS

(With Elinor Karpf and Stephen Karpf) *Terror in the Sky* (television movie), CBS, 1971.

Houston, We've Got a Problem (television movie), ABC, 1974.

Sensibility and Sense (two-act television version of the stage play for *American Playhouse* series), PBS, 1990.

The End of a Sentence (television play for series *American Playhouse*), directed by David Jones and produced by Nondas Voll for WETA-TV, 1991.

Also author of unproduced television script "A Shock of Recognition." Also author of a television episode for the series *Kojak,* CBS, 1973.

TRANSLATIONS AND ADAPTATIONS

Don Juan (adaptation of a work by Moliere; produced in Washington, DC, at the Arena Stage, April 3, 1979), Broadway Play Publishing (New York, NY), 1989.

(With Helga Ciulei) *The Wedding* (translation of a work by Bertolt Brecht; first of two-part production titled "The Marriage Dance: An Evening of Farce"), produced in New York, NY, at Brooklyn Academy of Music, May 22, 1980.

The Suicide (adaptation of a work by Nikolai Erdman; produced in Chicago, IL, at the Goodman Theatre, 1980), Broadway Play Publishing (New York, NY), 2000.

Il Campiello (adaptation of a work by Carlo Goldoni; produced in New York, NY, at the Acting Company, 1980), Theatre Communications Group (New York, NY), 1981.

Jungle of Cities (adaptation of a work by Bertolt Brecht), produced in New York, NY, at the Playhouse Theatre, Brooklyn Academy of Music, 1981.

The Marriage of Figaro (adaptation of a work by Pierre-Augustin Caron de Beaumarchais; produced in Minneapolis, MN, at the Tyrone Guthrie

Theater, July 15, 1982; produced on Broadway at the Circle in the Square Theater, October, 1985), Broadway Play Publishing (New York, NY), 1991.

Three Sisters (adaptation of a work by Anton Chekhov), produced in Minneapolis, MN, at the Tyrone Guthrie Theater, 1984.

Accidental Death of an Anarchist (adaptation of a work by Dario Fo; based on a literal translation by Susan Cowan), produced in Washington, DC, at the Arena Stage, February 3, 1984; produced on Broadway at the Belasco Theater, November 15, 1985), Samuel French (New York, NY), 1987.

Ethan Frome (screenplay; based on the novel by Edith Wharton), directed by John Madden, Miramax Films, 1993.

The School for Husbands (adaptation of *The Moliere Comedies* by Moliere), produced in New York, NY, at Roundabout Theatre, 1995.

The Imaginary Cuckold (adaptation of a work by Moliere), produced in New York, NY, at Roundabout Theatre, 1995.

(And director; and lyricist with Shaun Davey) *James Joyce's The Dead* (musical based on the story by James Joyce; produced in New York, NY, at Playwrights Horizons Theatre, 1999), music by Shaun Davey, Stage & Screen (Garden City, NY), 1995.

(And director) *Madame Melville* (one act; produced in London, England, at Vaudeville Theatre, 2000-2001; produced in New York, NY, at the Promenade Theatre, 2001; adapted from a work by Charles Isherwood), published in *Madame Melville* [and] *The General from America,* Grove Press (New York, NY), 2000.

Enrico IV (adaptation of a work by Luigi Pirandello), produced in San Francisco, CA, at Geary Theatre, American Conservatory Theatre, 2001.

(And lyricist and director) *My Life with Albertine* (based on the "Albertine" section of Marcel Proust's *Remembrance of Things Past*), music by Ricky Ian Gordon, produced in New York, NY, at Playwrights Horizons Theatre, 2003.

Also author of *Jitterbugging* (adaptation), produced in 1989, and *The Father* (adaptation of a work by August Strindberg), produced in New York, NY, at Criterion Center Stage.

OTHER

(Author of introduction and editor) *Strictly Dishonorable and Other Lost American Plays,* Theatre Communications Group (New York, NY), 1986.

(With David Jones) *Making Plays: The Writer-Director Relationship in the Theatre Today,* edited by Colin Chambers, Faber & Faber (Boston, MA), 1995.

Contributor to periodicals, including seven-part series on the trial of labor leader Tony Boyle for *Philadelphia Drummer,* 1974, and essays for *Performing Arts Journal.*

SIDELIGHTS: Playwright Richard Nelson is known for his portrayals of individuals, often writers, whose personal beliefs and professional obligations come into conflict with their political convictions. Nelson's dramatic works *The Killing of Yablonski, Conjuring an Event, Jungle Coup,* and *Scooping,* for example, which were collected and published in 1998 as *Plays by Richard Nelson, Volume 1,* form a series that examines the extent to which the media coverage of a news event is influenced by individual biases and journalistic choices. His Obie Award-winning *Vienna Notes* focuses on an American senator preparing to present a chapter of unpublished memoirs at an international conference. Nelson is also recognized for his numerous adaptations—including *The Marriage of Figaro* and *The Accidental Death of an Anarchist*—that incorporate topical references to American culture and politics, as well as the famous *My Life with Albertine,* a reflection of lost love. Nelson often relies on history and ponderings of the past to provide rich backgrounds for his works.

Many of Nelson's works have appeared on Broadway, including *Chess,* which is set during the last rounds of the 1972 world chess championship match. The musical focuses on the match's two final players: Bobby Fischer, an American, and Boris Spassky, a Russian. The air of the play is permeated with Cold War attitudes that have not yet warmed, putting a greater importance on the chess match, its players almost ambassadors. Bobby's assistant and former lover, Florence, falls in love with the gentle, unhappily married Russian, ultimately battling his wife for his affections. *Variety* reviewer Rita Katz Farrell wrote that the play "might have worked better with more emphasis on the flawed human beings at its core rather than the flawed politics of the Cold War." Beverly Creasey from *Theater Mirror,* however, stated that the best part of the play was "the corruption of a pure love of the game of chess by Commissars and Cold Warriors playing a ruthless international game in which human lives and emotions are irrelevant pawns." This reviewer felt that while Nelson wrote an "excellent book," the play's music detracted from its value.

Nelson again strives to represent historical happenings with *Two Shakespearean Actors,* a Broadway play about the Astor Place riots in New York City. In 1849, American actor Edwin "Ned" Forrest starred in a production of *Macbeth* at the Broadway Theater, while the British actor William Macready starred in a production of the same work, staged at the Astor Place Opera House. Tensions grew in the city as the two productions continued to run simultaneously, until they exploded one night in Greenwich Village. Fans of Forrest and Macready maimed and killed one another in support of the actors, ultimately setting the Village aflame.

As New Yorkers die and the Village burns, Forrest and Macready take cover in Forrest's theater, discussing acting and performing for one another in an empty theater. Their arrogance is apparent throughout the play, but especially when the actors become irritated by the gunshots outside. At one point, Forrest yells, "I told you before, to just leave us alone!" David Richards of the *New York Times* wrote that this "outburst, I think, goes to heart of Mr. Nelson's drama. For his two celebrated actors, the imagined world is more important than the real world."

Back Stage reviewer David Sheward criticized Nelson's play, stating, "Instead of thoroughly examining the reasons why the performance of a play would cause such a bloody rampage, Nelson settles for easy targets like the exaggerated styles of nineteenth-century thespians and such in-jokes as forgotten lines and funny stage stories." It is Sheward himself, however, who points out the "study in contrasts between Anglo and American viewpoints and values" offered in *Two Shakespearean Actors.* These contrasts create a tension present from the play's opening and become the cultural culprit of the riots upon its close. *Two Shakespearean Actors* was nominated for a 1992 Tony award for best play.

One of Nelson's most famous works, *Principia Scriptoriae,* was published in 1991 in *Principia Scriptoriae* [and] *Between East and West. Principia Scriptoriae* concerns two young intellectuals who meet when imprisoned in an unidentified Latin American country

for distributing subversive political leaflets. Ernesto Pico is the Cambridge-educated native who wrote the pamphlet, and Bill Howell, his cell mate, is a naive and arrogant American activist beginning a career in journalism. Act I focuses on the relationship that develops between the aspiring writers as they converse about their disparate cultures, politics, and literary tastes, with machine gun fire and the screams of tortured prisoners in the background indicating what awaits them. Act II takes place fifteen years later at an international diplomatic meeting in the country, which has since become a left-wing dictatorship. Howell and Ernesto meet again, this time to observe and write about the negotiations in progress over the fate of a poet imprisoned for supporting the previous regime. The writers are torn between their sympathy for a fellow writer and their hatred for his affiliation with the government that tortured them. They struggle, according to the *New York Times'* Frank Rich, with the question of whether to "condemn totalitarianism regardless of the political fashions it wears."

Principia Scriptoriae received mixed reviews upon its 1986 Manhattan premiere. Some critics felt the play poorly represented the responsibilities of writers in repressive societies. The *New York Post's* Clive Barnes, for example, deemed the play "interesting," but felt that its "political implications—right is right, left is left, and dictatorship, left or right, is wrong—lies [sic] listlessly on the table." Other critics, however, admired the play's powerful emotional tension and engagement with complex issues. "The prison scenes created a sense of human courage holding out against panic that will not easily be forgotten," observed Jeremy Kingston in the London *Times,* and Rich noted that the play "makes for an unusually weighty slice of new American theater." The play was similarly praised by New York *Daily News* drama critic Douglas Watt, who appreciated its "stimulating dialogue" and concluded that "*Principia Scriptoriae* [was] excellently acted, finely directed, and engrossing." The other play in this publication, *Between East and West,* was first produced in 1984 and features a Czech immigrant couple (a director, Gregor, and his actress wife, Erma) that has trouble fitting into American society. Erma reads Chekhov's *Three Sisters* for an audition piece but cannot quell her accent. "Language defines behavior in the play, and Nelson develops a more finely modulated, minimalist, understated, and oblique dialogue that persists in later plays," wrote Richard H. Palmer in *Reference Guide to American Literature.* Nelson received a *Time Out* London Theatre Award for *Principia Scriptoriae,* as well as an ABC Playwriting Award following the play's television production.

The characters in the historically based *Goodnight Children Everywhere* are London-born siblings, who were separated and sent to Canada and Wales during the London air raids of World War II, and are finally able to reunite at the play's beginning. In this play, which was first produced in 1997 and published in 2000, Betty, Ann, and Vi wait for their younger brother, Peter, to arrive. The four reunite after six years' separation to find one another startlingly different. As they catch up on lost years, it is revealed that Betty, the oldest, had stayed with their parents until their death, while Peter was sent to live with a cruel uncle, and Ann and Vi stayed with a Welsh family who attempted to teach them the value of hard work. The psychological turmoil of war and familial separation has left these young people with abnormal behavioral problems, which at first surface in odd behaviors, but become darker and more dangerous as the play continues. Ann, who has married a man twice her age and is pregnant with his child, is now drawn to Peter, who is only seventeen-years-old and is still struggling to find himself. The sexual tension between the two persists as the others try not to notice. Vi, an actress, is busy using her sexuality to woo work out of directors, while Betty, a nurse, has relegated herself to spinsterhood at the young age of twenty-one.

In *Back Stage,* Elias Stimac called *Goodnight Children Everywhere* "a gripping drama," stating, "Nelson has masterfully mapped out the intertwining family dynamics, and evokes sympathy and shock from viewers in equal measure." Charles McNulty wrote in *Variety* that "while there's no denying the subtle intelligence of the work, the dramatic core seems somewhat underdeveloped." McNulty continued, however, stating that "what's most compelling about the playwright's handling of his particular family's traumatic legacy is the way sexuality encodes so much of the psychological damage."

Nelson next published *Madame Melville* [and] *The General from America.* In *The General from America,* which premiered in 1996, Nelson turns to history once again to examine the events surrounding Benedict Arnold's famous betrayal of his country. Nelson shows playgoers how General Arnold was charged with profiteering by George Washington, who stripped him of his rank and sent him to work at West Point. This

and other events led to the infamous act in which Arnold sold military secrets to the British and America, synonymizing the name "Benedict Arnold" with "traitor." Critic Charles Isherwood wrote in *Daily Variety* that "Nelson takes such a dim view of everyone's behavior that one may surmise the production's gloomy look was intended to be metaphorical." Commenting on the play's historical value, *Curtain Up* reviewer Elyse Sommer pointed out that Nelson "does not try to whitewash Arnold's treason. What the play does instead is to put it into the context of history, to show us why and how a man could be both patriot and turncoat." Sommer also observed, "Despite an at time grating use of colloquial language, Nelson and his actors do a good job in establishing the mood of the times and depicting the other players in the drama of Arnold's downfall."

Madame Melville, the accompanying play in the publication, first premiered in London in 2000. It tells the story of a fifteen-year-old boy seduced into an affair with his Parisian literature teacher, Claudie Melville. Played on the stage by a twenty-year-old Macaulay Culkin, Carl ruminates on the lessons he learned from Madame Melville, who not only taught him about literature, but also about art, philosophy, and love. "Nelson's writing is more delicate than the foregoing précis would suggest, even if his subject is on the precocious side," commented Isherwood in *Variety.* "His direction is subtly cued to the currents of hesitancy and affection between this odd couple," continued Isherwood.

Set in 1957 and filled with sexual and emotional turmoil, *Franny's Way,* like *Madame Melville,* is also a reflective play. When it begins, an older Franny recollects her teenage sexual awakening, which took place on a trip to New York City. Seventeen-year-old Franny and her fifteen-year-old sister, Dolly, travel to Greenwich Village, accompanied by their grandmother, to visit their cousin. Sally and her husband Phil have lost a baby, which has put a great deal of tension on both their marriage and their sexual relationship. Sally enjoys having the sisters in her home because it distracts her from her uncomfortable life, but at the play's end, she is not the only one distracted by Franny. When Dolly and her grandmother go to a play, Franny sneaks off to meet a boyfriend. The rendezvous does not go well, and Franny returns to find Sally and Phil clumsily attempting to rekindle dead desire. Meanwhile, Dolly has arranged a secret meeting with the sisters' estranged mother, enraging Franny upon her return. The tension mounts as Franny and Phil become uncomfortably close, leading to the sexual encounter that closes the play. "The play is effective at establishing an atmosphere of thwarted desire," wrote Isherwood in a review for *Variety,* but he pointed out that "the production works hard for low-key poignance, which can prove elusive when it is so diligently bidden." Isherwood did, however, deem the play a "delicately observed, gently nostalgic epiphan[y]."

Reflection on life's former circumstances again surfaces in Nelson's *My Life with Albertine,* the 2003 adaptation of a section of Marcel Proust's epic novel *Remembrance of Things Past.* In the play, the older Marcel torturously reminisces the greatest love of his life and the reasons it went wrong. The story begins in 1919, when seventeen-year-old Marcel travels to Paris to visit his grandmother and meets Albertine, a young, free-spirited, and beautiful woman who steals his heart. Albertine, the audience learns, cannot commit to the confines of love, and as she pulls away from Marcel, his passion for her becomes greater, leading to the saddened state of his present character.

In a review of *My Life with Albertine,* Isherwood observed in *Daily Variety* that Nelson's adaptation is "a delicate, stylishly presented production that attempts to honor both the spirit and the letter of the original," but complained that it is also "both static and choppy, and ultimately pedantic in its attempts to impart the reflections on love's illusions and life's mysteries that are developed with such tender rapture throughout Proust's novel." Critic John Rowell raised an interesting question in a review of the play for *Show Business Weekly:* "Was the 'Albertine' section of *Remembrance* begging to be musicalized?" Rowell, however, explained that he admires Nelson's adaptation, calling it a "meticulously crafted, beautifully mounted chamber piece that had been written, directed, and designed by theater craftspeople of impeccable taste and skill."

BIOGRAPHICAL AND CRITICAL SOURCES:

BOOKS

Berney, K. A., editor, *Contemporary American Dramatists,* St. James Press (London, England), 1994.
Contemporary Dramatists, 6th edition, St. James Press (Detroit, MI), 1999.

Comtemporary Theatre, Film, and Television, Volume 39, Gale (Detroit, MI), 2002.
Nelson, Richard, *Two Shakespearean Actors,* Faber & Faber (Boston, MA), 1990.
Riggs, Thomas, editor, *Reference Guide to American Literature,* 4th edition, St. James Press (Detroit, MI), 2000.

PERIODICALS

American Historical Review, October, 1998, review of *A Culture of Confidence,* p. 1349.
American Theatre, December, 1995, review of *Making Plays: The Writer-Director Relationship in the Theatre Today,* p. 30; December, 1996, review of *The General from America,* p. 20.
Back Stage, February 7, 1992, David Sheward, review of *Two Shakespearean Actors,* pp. 23-24; June 18, 1999, Elias Stimac, review of *Goodnight Children Everywhere,* p. 56.
Chicago Tribune, May 5, 1988.
Christian Science Monitor, November 20, 1984; April 16, 1986.
Daily News (New York, NY), November 16, 1984; October 11, 1985; April 10, 1986.
Daily Variety, March 28, 2002, Charles Isherwood, review of *Franny's Way,* p. 20; November 22, 2002, Charles Isherwood, review of *The General from America,* p. 4; March 14, 2003, Charles Isherwood, review of *My Life with Albertine,* pp. 10-11.
Economist (U.S.), August 8, 1992, review of *Columbus and the Discovery of Japan,* p. 78.
Los Angeles Times, October 7, 1983.
New Leader, February 10, 1992, Stefan Kanfer, review of *Two Shakespearean Actors,* p. 22.
New Republic, April 14, 2003, Robert Brustein, "On Theater—Why Plays Fail," review of *My Life with Albertine,* p. 25.
New York, April 15, 1985.
New York Post, November 19, 1984; October 11, 1985; April 12, 1986.
New York Times, February 21, 1978; March 21, 1978; November 16, 1984; October 11, 1985; April 3, 1986; April 10, 1986; April 30, 1986; September 24, 1986; January 17, 1988; April 24, 1988; April 29, 1988; May 8, 1988; January 26, 1992, David Richards, review of *Two Shakespearean Actors.*
Theatre Journal, March, 1997, review of *Making Plays,* p. 95.

Time, April 28, 1986.

Times (London, England), December 18, 1987.

Times Literary Supplement, April 28, 1995, review of *Making Plays,* p. 9.

Variety, May 31, 1999, Charles McNulty, review of *Goodnight Children Everywhere,* p. 42; February 14, 2000, Rita Katz Farrell, review of *Chess,* p. 50; May 14, 2001, Charles Isherwood, review of *Madame Melville,* p. 31; April 1, 2002, Charles Isherwood, review of *Franny's Way,* p. 41.

Wall Street Journal, November 20, 1984.

ONLINE

Curtain Up Web site, http://www.curtainup.com/ (May 30, 2003), Elyse Sommer, review of *Goodnight Children Everywhere;* (March 5, 2004), Elyse Sommer, review of *The General from America.*

New York Metro Web site, http://www.newyorkmetro.com/ (May 30, 2003), John Simon, review of *Goodnight Children Everywhere;* (March 5, 2004), John Simon, review of *The General from America.*

Peter Gill Web site, http://dspace.dial.pipex.com/town/parade/abj76/PG/pieces/richard_nelson.shtml (May 30, 2003), "Richard Nelson."

Show Business Weekly Web site, http://www.showbusinessweekly.com/ (March 5, 2004), John Rowell, review of *My Life with Albertine.*

Theatre Database Web site, http://www.theatredb.com/ (March 4, 2004), "Richard Nelson."

Theatre Mirror Web site, http://www.theatermirror.com/ (1997), Beverly Creasey, review of *Chess.**

*   *   *

NELSON, Ted (W.) 1931-

PERSONAL: Born June 22, 1931, in McCloud, CA; son of DeWitt (a forester) and Sadiebelle (a lecturer; maiden name, Friedley) Nelson; married Sharlene Patten (a writer), July 17, 1955; children: Gregg, Janise Nelson Gates. *Ethnicity:* "Caucasian." *Education:* Attended Pomona College, 1949-51; University of California—Berkeley, B.S., 1954; University of Michigan, M.F., 1957. *Politics:* Republican. *Religion:* Methodist. *Hobbies and other interests:* Sailing, backpacking, skiing, oil painting, playing the banjo.

ADDRESSES: Home and office—824 South Marine Hills Way, Federal Way, WA 98003.

CAREER: Diamond Match Co., Lyman Springs, CA, resident forester, 1957-64; Weyerhaeuser Co., Tacoma, WA, 1964-91, retiring as vice president of Timberlands, Washington division; writer, 1991—. Member of board of directors, China Relations Council and World Affairs Council. *Military service:* U.S. Army, Infantry, 1954-56; became first lieutenant.

MEMBER: Forest History Society (member of board of directors, 1992—), Society of American Foresters, National Maritime Historical Society, Society of Children's Book Writers and Illustrators, U.S. Lighthouse Society, Washington Forest Protection Association (honorary trustee, 1991), Oregon Historical Society, Washington State Historical Society, Japan-America Society (member of board of directors), Tacoma Yacht Club.

WRITINGS:

WITH WIFE, SHARLENE NELSON

(And with Joan LeMieux) *Cruising the Columbia and Snake Rivers: Eleven Cruises in the Inland Waterway,* Pacific Search Press (Seattle, WA), 1981, revised edition, 1986.

The Umbrella Guide to Washington Lighthouses, Umbrella Books (Friday Harbor, WA), 1990, revised edition, 1998.

The Umbrella Guide to California Lighthouses, Epicenter Press (Seattle, WA), 1993, revised edition, 1999.

The Umbrella Guide to Oregon Lighthouses, Epicenter Press (Seattle, WA), 1994.

Bull Whackers to Whistle Punks: Logging in the Old West, Franklin Watts (Danbury, CT), 1996.

The Umbrella Guide to Exploring the Columbia-Snake River Inland Waterway, Epicenter Press (Seattle, WA), 1997.

Mount St. Helens National Volcanic Monument, Children's Press (Danbury, CT), 1997.

Olympic National Park, Children's Press (Danbury, CT), 1997.

Hawaii Volcanoes National Park, Children's Press (New York, NY), 1998.

Mount Rainier National Park, Children's Press (New York, NY), 1998.

William Boeing: Builder of Planes, Children's Press (New York, NY), 1999.

The Golden Gate Bridge, Children's Press (New York, NY), 2001.
Brett Favre, Capstone Books (Mankato, MN), 2001.
The Makah, Franklin Watts (Danbury, CT), 2003.
The Nez Percé, Franklin Watts (Danbury, CT), 2003.
Jedediah S. Smith, Franklin Watts (Danbury, CT), 2004.

Author of booklets about forestry.

WORK IN PROGRESS: Nonfiction articles for children.

BIOGRAPHICAL AND CRITICAL SOURCES:

PERIODICALS

Booklist, August, 1996, p. 1899.
Library Journal, June 1, 1990, p. 158.
School Library Journal, July, 1996, p. 94.

*   *   *

NOVAK, Matt 1962-

PERSONAL: Born October 23, 1962, in Trenton, NJ; son of Theresa (a factory worker; maiden name, Belfiore) Novak. *Education:* Attended Kutztown State University, 1980-81; School of Visual Arts, New York, NY, B.F.A., 1985. *Hobbies and other interests:* Reading, biking, hiking, gardening, and cooking.

ADDRESSES: Home—Pennsylvania. *Agent*—c/o Author Mail, Simon & Schuster, 1230 Avenue of the Americas, New York, NY 10020. *E-mail*—mattnovak@ truevine.net.

CAREER: Pegasus Players, Sheppton, PA, puppeteer, 1979-83; Walt Disney World, Orlando, FL, animation artist, 1983; St. Benedict's Preparatory School, Newark, NJ, art teacher, beginning 1986; Parsons School of Design, instructor, beginning 1986; Walt Disney Studios, Orlando, FL, animation artist, 1989-92; Pennsylvania College of Art and Design, instructor, 2001—; University of the Arts, Philadelphia, PA, instructor, 2003—.

MEMBER: Society of Children's Book Writers and Illustrators, Authors Guild.

AWARDS, HONORS: Mouse TV was a *School Library Journal* Best Book of the Year and a Parents' Choice Honor recipient; *Newt* received the International Reading Association Children's Choice Award.

WRITINGS:

SELF-ILLUSTRATED JUVENILES

Rolling, Bradbury Press (New York, NY), 1986.
Claude and Sun, Bradbury Press (New York, NY), 1987.
Mr. Floop's Lunch, Orchard Books (New York, NY), 1990.
Elmer Blunt's Open House, Orchard Books (New York, NY), 1992.
The Last Christmas Present, Orchard Books (New York, NY), 1993.
Mouse TV, Orchard Books (New York, NY), 1994.
Gertie and Gumbo, Orchard Books (New York, NY), 1995.
Newt, HarperCollins (New York, NY), 1996.
The Pillow War, Orchard Books (New York, NY), 1998.
The Robobots, DK Books (New York, NY), 1999.
Jazzbo Goes to School, Hyperion (New York, NY), 1999.
Jazzbo and Googy, Hyperion (New York, NY), 2000.
Little Wolf, Big Wolf, HarperCollins (New York, NY), 2000.
No Zombies Allowed, Atheneum (New York, NY), 2001.
Too Many Bunnies, Roaring Brook Press (Brookfield, CT), 2004.

Also author of *On Halloween Street,* Simon & Schuster.

ILLUSTRATOR

Pat Upton, *Who Does This Job?,* Bell Books (Honesdale, PA), 1991.
Lee Bennett Hopkins, *It's about Time* (poems), Simon & Schuster (New York, NY), 1993.

Dayle Ann Dodds, *Ghost and Pete,* Random House (New York, NY), 1995.

Heather Feldman, *Little Slugger,* Random House (New York, NY), 1997.

Susan Hightower, *Twelve Snails to One Lizard: A Tale of Mischief and Measurement,* Simon & Schuster (New York, NY), 1997.

SIDELIGHTS: Matt Novak has written and illustrated a number of picture books for children. Among his most popular titles are *The Pillow War, Jazzbo Goes to School, Jazzbo and Googy,* and *No Zombies Allowed.*

In *The Pillow War* young siblings Millie and Fred get into an argument over who will sleep with their dog Sam. Taking up pillows, the pair begin a pillow fight that leads them out of their bedroom, down the stairs, and into the street. Soon their neighbors join in the battle with their own pillows until the whole neighborhood is in an uproar. By the time Millie comes up with the idea of taking turns sleeping with Sam, the dog has come up with his own surprising solution to the problem. A critic for *Publishers Weekly* noted Novak's "refreshingly quirky wit." Stephanie Zvirin in *Booklist* called *The Pillow War* "a funny-bone tickler that little ones will like."

Jazzbo Goes to School finds a young bear going with his mother to find a new school. The first one they visit is far too strict; even the birds outside are not allowed to sing during lessons. The second school, called the Willy Nilly School, is far too permissive; the children just play all day. But the third school, called the Super School, seems just right, and the teacher explains that they really need to have Jazzbo join them. A critic for *Publishers Weekly* believed that Novak's story could help "turn a frightening subject into utter merriment."

Jazzbo returns in *Jazzbo and Googy,* in which the little bear meets an eager but clumsy pig named Googy. Googy means well, but he ends up spilling things, knocking other children down, and ruining school projects. Only when he saves Jazzbo's teddy bear from landing in a mud puddle is Googy able to show that he is not so bumbling as he seems to be. "Children will see parts of themselves in the overly enthusiastic porcine," according to Sheilah Kosco in *School Library Journal,* "and find this tale to be reassuring."

No Zombies Allowed finds two witches, Wizzle and Woddle, planning their annual monsters ball. But when they look at the photographs from last year's ball, they remember some of the guests' bad behavior. The zombies kept dropping their eyes into the punch bowl; the skeletons called everyone else "fatso"; and the werewolves coughed up furballs. Soon Wizzle and Woddle are removing certain monsters from the guest list. This year's party will be perfect. Eventually they realize that, if they are going to be so picky about who they invite, there will be no party at all. Martha V. Parravano in *Horn Book* found *No Zombies Allowed* to be "a nice little send-up of messagey picture books, presented with the lightest possible touch." Carol L. MacKay, reviewing the book for *School Library Journal,* noted that "the text is engaging, the dialogue is ironic, and the characters are true to form." Ultimately, Novak "creates a bewitchingly funny world," according to a critic for *Kirkus Reviews.*

Novak once told *CA:* "My work deals primarily with nature. I want to impart my amazement at nature's beauty to children so that they may gain a sense of the importance of all of it. I grew up in a small town, surrounded by fields and woodland, so these things are important to me. A lot of children don't have the opportunity to experience living in such an environment. I write and illustrate books I would want to buy myself. That's how I judge my own work."

BIOGRAPHICAL AND CRITICAL SOURCES:

PERIODICALS

Booklist, September 1, 1995, Stephanie Zvirin, review of *Gertie and Gumbo,* p. 89; February 15, 1998, Stephanie Zvirin, review of *The Pillow War,* p. 1020; June 1, 1999, Susan Dove Lempke, review of *The Robobots,* p. 1844.

Horn Book, September-October, 2002, Martha V. Parravano, review of *No Zombies Allowed,* p. 556.

Kirkus Reviews, July 15, 2002, review of *No Zombies Allowed,* p. 1040.

Publishers Weekly, August 7, 1995, review of *Gertie and Gumbo,* p. 460; March 24, 1997, review of *Twelve Snails to One Lizard: A Tale of Mischief and Measurement,* p. 82; February 9, 1998, review of *The Pillow War,* p. 94; June 14, 1999, review of *Jazzbo Goes to School,* p. 68; September 23, 2002, review of *No Zombies Allowed,* p. 71.

School Library Journal, October, 1995, Marilyn Taniguchi, review of *Gertie and Gumbo,* p. 110; March, 1996, Sharron McElmeel, review of *Ghost and Pete,* p. 173; July, 1996, Gale W. Sherman, review of *Newt,* p. 70; May, 1997, John Sigwald, review of *Twelve Snails to One Lizard,* p. 100; March, 1998, Julie Cummins, review of *The Pillow War,* p. 185; June, 1999, Anne Connor, review of *The Robobots,* p. 104; August, 1999, Mary Ann Carcich, review of *Jazzbo Goes to School,* p. 140; January, 2000, Pat Leach, review of *Little Wolf, Big Wolf,* p. 108; June, 2000, Sheilah Kosco, review of *Jazzbo and Googy,* p. 123; August, 2002, Carol L. MacKay, review of *No Zombies Allowed,* p. 162.

ONLINE

Matt Novak's Web site, http://www.mattnovak.com/ (April 17, 2003).

*   *   *

NYLANDER, Jane C. 1938-

PERSONAL: Born January 27, 1938, in Cleveland, OH; daughter of James Merritt (a paperboard manufacturer) and Jeannette (a homemaker) Cayford; married Daniel Harris Giffen, November 30, 1964 (divorced, June, 1970); married Richard Conrad Nylander (a museum curator), July 8, 1972; children: (first marriage) Sarah Louise, Thomas Harris; (second marriage) Timothy Frost. *Education:* Brown University, A.B. (with distinction), 1959; University of Delaware, M.A., 1961.

ADDRESSES: Home—17 Franklin St., Portsmouth, NH 03801.

CAREER: Historical Society of York County, York, PA, curator, 1961-62; New Hampshire Historical Society, Concord, curator, 1962-69; Old Sturbridge Village, Sturbridge, MA, curator of ceramics and textiles, 1969-84, senior curator, 1985-86; Strawbery Banke, Inc., Portsmouth, NH, director, 1986-92; Society for the Preservation of New England Antiquities, Boston, MA, director, 1992-93, president, 1993-2002. New England College, instructor, 1963-64; Monadnock Community College, instructor, 1964-68; Boston University, adjunct associate professor, 1978-85, adjunct professor, 1993—; University of New Hampshire, adjunct assistant professor, 1987-92. Worcester Historical Museum, trustee, 1978-84; Historic Deerfield, Inc., trustee, 1981—, head of Museum Committee, 1992-94, head of strategic planning committee, 2003—; Jones Museum, trustee, 1986-88; Portsmouth Athenaeum, trustee, 1987-90; Decorative Arts Trust, member of board of governors, 1991—; Wentworth-Coolidge advisory committee, member, 1991—; Historic Massachusetts, Inc., member of board of directors, 1992-93; Bentley College, member of board of advisers of New England Heritage Center, 1993-2001. Committee to Preserve Historic Flags Belonging to the State of New Hampshire, member, 1991-92; lecturer on New England social history and domestic life; consultant to local and national museums.

MEMBER: American Antiquarian Society, American Association of Museums, American Association for State and Local History, National Trust for Historic Preservation, Costume Society of America (member of board of directors, 1977-83; member of regional board of directors, 1984-85), National Society of the Colonial Dames of America, Warner House Association, Costume Society (England), New England Historic Genealogical Society, Colonial Society of Massachusetts (member of council, 1993-95), New Hampshire Historical Society, Japan-America Society of New Hampshire (member of board of directors, 1988-92), Friends of Historic Deerfield, Boston Museum of Fine Arts, Society of Winterthur Graduates.

AWARDS, HONORS: Charles F. Montgomery Award, Decorative Arts Society, 1985, for contribution to the book *The Great River;* Distinguished Sophomore Book Prize from Boston University, 1993, for *Our Own Snug Fireside: Images of the New England Home, 1760-1860;* Doctor of Fine Arts, New England College, 1994; Roger and Ann Webb Award, Historic Massachusetts, 1995 (with Richard C. Nylander); John F. Ayer Award, Bay State Historical League, 2002; Boston History Award, Bostonian Society, 2002.

WRITINGS:

Fabrics for Historic Buildings: A Guide to Selecting Reproduction Fabrics, Preservation Press (Washington, DC), 1977, 5th edition, John Wiley (New York, NY), 1995.

Our Own Snug Fireside: Image and Reality in the New England Home, 1750-1860, Knopf (New York, NY), 1993.

(With Diane Viera) *Windows on the Past: Four Centuries of New England Homes,* Bullfinch Press (Boston, MA), 2000.

Contributor to *The Great River,* Wadsworth Atheneum, 1985; *Upholstery in America and Europe,* Norton (New York, NY), 1987; *An American Sampler: Folk Art from the Shelburne Museum,* National Gallery of Art (Washington, DC), 1987; and *The Art of Family* (Boston, MA), 2002. Contributor of articles and reviews to history, museum, and antique journals, including *Connoisseur, Early American Life, Historic Preservation, Historical New Hampshire, Antiques,* and *Old Time New England.*

WORK IN PROGRESS: A study of collecting and exhibiting decorative arts in nineteenth-century New England.

SIDELIGHTS: Jane C. Nylander is a specialist on domestic life in New England from the mid-eighteenth century to the mid-nineteenth century. As president of the Society for the Preservation of New England Antiquities, she was charged with acquiring and maintaining a museum and library of artifacts and written materials that cover every aspect of life in pre-Civil War era communities. Nylander presents the results of her research into colonial life in her book *Our Own Snug Fireside: Image and Reality in the New England Home.* This volume draws upon old diaries and letters, advertising billets, artifacts, and other sources to reconstruct daily routines in middle-class and upper-middle-class households prior to the

Civil War. Although the book was primarily meant as a scholarly resource, the widespread interest in re-creating history accurately brought more readers to the work. According to Denise Perry Donavin in *Booklist,* Nylander's "approach is absorbing," while the photographs and period art work "add pizzazz and authenticity." A *Publishers Weekly* reviewer called *Our Own Snug Fireside* a "delightfully intimate portrayal of New England home life."

BIOGRAPHICAL AND CRITICAL SOURCES:

PERIODICALS

American Historical Review, December, 1994, Jan Lewis, review of *Our Own Snug Fireside: Images of the New England Home, 1760-1860,* p. 1751.

Booklist, March 15, 1993, Denise Perry Donavin, review of *Our Own Snug Fireside,* p. 1294.

Journal of American History, June, 1994, Karin Calvert, review of *Our Own Snug Fireside,* p. 246.

New York Times Book Review, August 29, 1993, Martha Saxton, review of *Our Own Snug Fireside,* p. 16.

Publishers Weekly, February 22, 1993, review of *Our Own Snug Fireside,* p. 73.

ONLINE

Yale University Press, http://www.yale.edu/ (April 9, 2003), synopsis and reviews of *Our Own Snug Fireside.*

O-P

OWENS, John E. 1948-

PERSONAL: Born June 13, 1948, in Widnes, England; son of William Thomas (a grocer) and Catherine (a shopkeeper; maiden name, Jones) Owens; married October 1, 1971; wife's name Margaret Patricia; children: Daniel Scott, Rachel Hannah. *Ethnicity:* "European." *Education:* University of Reading, B.A. (with honors), 1973; attended University of Warwick, 1973-75; University of Essex, Ph.D., 1982.

ADDRESSES: Home—Colchester, England. *Office*—Centre for the Study of Democracy, University of Westminster, 100 Park Village E, London W1N 3SR, England; fax: 0207-911-5164. *E-mail*—owensj@westminster.ac.uk.

CAREER: Polytechnic of Central London, London, England, lecturer, 1978-85; University of Essex, Colchester, England, lecturer in government, 1985-86; University of Westminster, London, senior lecturer, 1986-98, reader, 1998-2002, professor of U.S. government and politics, 2002—. University of Essex, visiting fellow at Economic and Social Research Council Data Archive, 1984-85, 1986-87, 1993-95; Brookings Institution, guest scholar, 1990, 1991, 1993, 1995, 1997, 1999, 2000-02; Texas A & M University, visiting fellow at Center for Presidential Studies, 1999; consultant to Library of Congress and British Broadcasting Corp.

MEMBER: International Political Science Association, Political Studies Association of the United Kingdom (chair of American Politics Group, 1992-94), American Political Science Association (Legislative Studies Section), Western Political Science Association, Southern Political Science Association.

AWARDS, HONORS: Grants from American Politics Group, Political Studies Association of the United Kingdom, 1978-98; Moody grant, Lyndon Baines Johnson Foundation, 1982-83; grants from U.S. Information Service, 1985, 1991, Nuffield Foundation, 1987-89, 1993-95, and Everett McKinley Dirksen Congressional Leadership Center, Pekin, IL, 1988-89.

WRITINGS:

(With John Keane) *After Full Employment,* Hutchinson University Press (Dover, NH), 1986.
(With Michael Foley) *Congress and the Presidency: Institutional Politics in a Separated System,* St. Martin's Press (New York, NY), 1996.
(Editor, with Dean McSweeney, and contributor) *The Republican Takeover of Congress,* St. Martin's Press (New York, NY), 1998.
(Editor, with Erwin C. Hargrove, and contributor) *Political Leadership Skills in Context,* Rowman & Littlefield (Lanham, MD), 2003.

Contributor to books, including *The State, Finance, and Industry: A Comparative Analysis of Post-war Trends in Six Advanced Industrial Economies,* edited by Andrew Cox, Wheatsheaf (Brighton, England), 1986; *Superpower Politics: Change in the United States and the Soviet Union,* edited by Michael Pugh and Philip Williams, Manchester University Press

(New York, NY), 1990; *New Developments in American Politics 3,* edited by Gillian Peele, Christopher J. Bailey, and others, Chatham House Publishers (Chatham, NJ), 1998; *American Politics: 2000 and Beyond,* edited by Alan R. Grant, Ashgate Publishing (Burlington, VT), 2000; and *Governing America: The Politics of Divided Democracy,* edited by Robert Singh, Oxford University Press (New York, NY), 2003. Contributor of articles and reviews to periodicals, including *Roll Call, Critical Social Policy, Social Studies Review, British Journal of Political Science,* and *Political Studies.* Book review editor, *American Politics Review,* 1992-2002; member of editorial board, *Presidential Studies Quarterly,* 1998—, and *Journal of Legislative Studies,* 2000—.

BIOGRAPHICAL AND CRITICAL SOURCES:

ONLINE

John Owens: Professor of U.S. Government and Politics, http://www.wmin.ac.uk/sshl/new/politics/owens.htm/ (May 1, 2001).

*   *   *

PARTRIDGE, Frances (Catherine) 1900-2004

PERSONAL: Born March 15, 1900, in London, England; died February 5, 2004; daughter of William Cecil (an architect) and Margaret (Lloyd) Marshall; married Ralph Partridge, March 2, 1933 (died, 1960); children: Lytton Burgo (deceased). *Education:* Newnham College, Cambridge, graduated (with honors), 1921. *Politics:* "Liberal and pacifist." *Hobbies and other interests:* Music, collecting and identifying wild flowers, reading (particularly history, memoirs, philosophy, and biographies).

CAREER: Translator and author. Worked at a bookstore, 1921-28.

MEMBER: International PEN, Royal Literary Society (fellow).

AWARDS, HONORS: D.Litt., University of London, 2000; Commander of the Order of the British Empire, 2000.

WRITINGS:

(Editor, with husband, Ralph Partridge) *The Greville Memoirs, 1814-1860,* eight volumes, Macmillan (London, England), 1938.
A Pacifist's War, Hogarth Press (London, England), 1978.
Love in Bloomsbury: Memories, Little, Brown (Boston, MA), 1981, published as *Memories,* Gollancz (London, England), 1983.
(With Julia Strachey) *Julia: A Portrait of Julia Strachey,* Little, Brown (Boston, MA), 1983.
Everything to Lose: Diaries, 1945-1960, Little, Brown (Boston, MA), 1985.
Friends in Focus: A Life in Photographs, Chatto & Windus (London, England), 1987.
A Bloomsbury Album, Little, Brown (Boston, MA), 1987.
Good Company: Diaries: January 1967-December 1970, HarperCollins (London, England), 1994.
Hanging On: Diaries, December 1960-1963, Flamingo (London, England), 1994.
Other People: Diaries, September 1963-December 1966, Flamingo (London, England), 1994.
Life Regained: Diaries, January 1970-December 1971, Weidenfeld & Nicolson (London, England), 1998.
(Editor) *Diaries: 1939-1972,* Phoenix Press (London, England), 2001.
Ups and Downs: Diaries, 1972-1975, Weidenfeld & Nicolson (London, England), 2001.

TRANSLATOR; FROM THE SPANISH

Mercedes Ballesteros de Gailbrois, *Nothing Is Impossible,* Harvill (London, England), 1956.
Vincent Blasco-Ibañez, *Blood and Sand,* Elek, 1958.
Vincent Blasco-Ibañez, *The Naked Lady,* Elek, 1959.
Miguel A. Asturias, *The President,* Atheneum (New York, NY), 1963.
Jose L. Aranguren, *Human Communication,* McGraw-Hill (New York, NY), 1967.
Pedro L. Entralgo, *Doctor and Patient,* McGraw-Hill (New York, NY), 1969.
Alejo Carpentier, *War of Time,* Knopf (New York, NY), 1970.
Rita Guibert, *Seven Voices,* Knopf (New York, NY), 1973.
Alejo Carpentier, *Reasons of State,* Knopf (New York, NY), 1976.

TRANSLATOR; FROM THE FRENCH

Iovleff Bornet, *Something to Declare,* Harvill (London, England), 1957.

Joseph Dessel, *The Enemy in the Mouth,* Hart-Davis, 1961.

Gabriel Estivals, *A Gap in the Wall,* Collins (London, England), 1963.

Raymond Cogniat, *Seventeenth-Century Painting,* Viking (New York, NY), 1964.

Vassily Photiades, *Eighteenth-Century Painting,* Viking (New York, NY), 1964.

Olivier Beigbeider, *Ivory,* Putnam (New York, NY), 1965.

Pierre Nordon, *Conan Doyle: A Biography,* J. Murray, 1966, Holt (New York, NY), 1967.

Jacques Bonssard, *The Civilization of Charlemagne,* McGraw-Hill (New York, NY), 1967.

Gilbert Martineau, *Napoleon's St. Helena,* J. Murray, 1968, Rand McNally (Chicago, IL), 1969.

Gilbert Martineau, *Napoleon Surrenders,* J. Murray, 1974.

Gilbert Martineau, *Napoleon's Last Journey,* J. Murray, 1976.

Gilbert Martineau, *Madame Mere,* J. Murray, 1978.

Translator of magazine articles from French and Spanish. Contributor to *New Statesman, Spectator,* and *Times Literary Supplement.*

SIDELIGHTS: A translator of books in Spanish and French for many years, Frances Partridge gave up this work at the age of seventy to write original works based on the diaries she kept while living in the company of members of the famous Bloomsbury group. Members of this group of early-twentieth-century British intellectuals included Virginia Woolf and her husband, Leonard, Lytton Strachey, E. M. Forster, John Meynard Keynes, Vanessa and Clive Bell, Duncan Grant, and others who followed an idealistic philosophy influenced by G. E. Moore's *Principia Ethica.* Partridge (then Frances Marshall) became involved with the Bloomsburyites when she fell in love with Ralph Partridge, who was at the time married to Dora Carrington. Dora and Ralph Partridge lived, in turn, with Lytton Strachey in a well-known *ménage à trois* at Ham Spray in Hampshire. This arrangement ended when Strachey died of cancer and Dora subsequently committed suicide. Soon afterwards, Ralph Partridge married Frances and the two lived happily until his death in 1960.

While the story behind this and other affairs among the Bloomsburyites has become the subject of many, often gossipy, books, critics note that Partridge provides a new perspective on the lives of these people in her personal accounts. Caroline Moorehead, for example, described *Love in Bloomsbury* in the London *Times* as "a book about friendship, among people who really cared about friends, about its rules and limits and the determining power of its influence." *New York Times* critic Anatole Broyard added that Partridge "is natural, unassuming and observing, neither a spy, a gossip nor one of the charmed circle herself, but someone who was always there and deeply interested in the others."

Each of Partridge's books about the Bloomsbury group covers a different period and subject of its history. *A Pacifist's War* covers the years during World War II, *Love in Bloomsbury: Memories* involves the times between world wars, and *Julia: A Portrait of Julia Strachey* focuses on one of the group's enigmatic if personally troubled members as well as a longtime friend of Partridge. *Everything to Lose: Diaries, 1945-1960* is somewhat less concerned with Bloomsbury and instead centers on the life the author enjoyed with her husband after World War II. In a *Spectator* article concerning all these books, Moorehead wrote that "if John Updike is the poet of unhappy marriage, Frances Partridge is that of friendship, an attachment whose rules and demands she understands and conveys extraordinarily well. Furthermore, she lacks the malice of some of the Bloomsbury writers; she can be mocking and exigent but she is not merciless. It is her own particular and very agreeable voice that leaves its mark on every page."

Because Partridge often goes into great detail in her descriptions of the daily lives of the Bloomsbury group, some reviewers have found parts of her books to be slow reading. *Times Literary Supplement* contributor Margaret Forster remarked that the descriptions of Robert Kee's love affairs are uninteresting to read, "as are the commonplace comings and goings of most of [Partridge's] friends." But, Forster added, "there is also . . . the inspiring theme of Partridge's love for her husband." Other critics, such as *Washington Post Book World* reviewer Stanley Weintraub, praised the author for the writing skills she demonstrates in her diaries. "Nothing of Frances Partridge's other writing evidences the verve for vivid description of her diaries," stated Weintraub. "From the opening pages her knack for capsulizing sensory impressions is remarkable."

Partridge's books about Bloomsbury are significant, according to *New York Times Books Review* critic Samuel Hynes in his review of *Love in Bloomsbury,* in that the author has written more than an account of life among British intellectuals in the early twentieth century; "she has [also] written a social history of what happened to young persons of her sex and class in England in a time of great social change." Partridge's portrayal of these people succeeds, opined Jean Strouse in *Newsweek,* because "there is no reverential talk of genius, no poppycock about intellect's finest hour. Instead, she draws deft sketches from her personal impressions of the 'Bloomsburies.'" Concluded *New York Times Book Review* contributor Caryn James, Partridge "has outlived the ghostly presences of Bloomsbury and refused to become a living relic of her era. Still assessing, still irreverent, she is Bloomsbury's living legacy."

Ups and Downs: Diaries, 1972-1975 was written a decade after the death of Partridge's husband. In it she still struggles with that loss, trying to make meaning in her life. She continued to live, surrounded by friends, and record her own candid observations and thoughts about their lives. Lindsay Duguid commented in the *Times Literary Supplement* that such observations, while "entertainingly abrasive," are "balanced by her sympathetic concern and appreciation of kindness as well as her gusto for life's pleasures."

BIOGRAPHICAL AND CRITICAL SOURCES:

PERIODICALS

Los Angeles Times Book Review, September 13, 1981; September 4, 1983.
Newsweek, October 5, 1981.
New York Times, September 30, 1981; August 26, 1983.
New York Times Review of Books, September 27, 1981; October 16, 1983; May 4, 1986.
Spectator, February 21, 1981; December 7, 1985; November 17, 2001, Richard Shone, review of *Ups and Downs: Diaries, 1972-1975,* p. 52.
Times (London, England), January 29, 1981; March 17, 2001, Tim Teeman, "The Last Voice of Bloomsbury," p. W6.
Times Literary Supplement, August 4, 1978; February 13, 1981; May 13, 1983; October 25, 1985; September 4, 1998, Anne Chisholm, review of

Life Regained: Diaries, January 1970-December 1971, p. 5; November 30, 2001, Lindsay Duguid, "The Longest Lap," p. 14.
Washington Post Book Review, April 13, 1986.*

*   *   *

PERINBANAYAGAM, Robert S(idharthan) 1934-

PERSONAL: Born February 14, 1934, in Rangoon, Burma; came to the United States, 1962; son of Saravanamuttu H. (a professor) and Amirtha (Singham) Perinbanayagam. *Education:* University of Ceylon, B.A., 1959; University of Minnesota, M.A., 1964, Ph. D., 1967. *Politics:* "Humanist." *Religion:* "Humanist."

ADDRESSES: Home—321 East 66th St., New York, NY 10021. *Office*—Department of Sociology, Hunter College of the City University of New York, 695 Park Ave., New York, NY 10021.

CAREER: University of Missouri—Columbia, instructor, 1966-67, assistant professor of sociological theory and collective behavior, 1967-70; New School for Social Research, New York, NY, assistant professor of sociology, 1970-72; Hunter College of the City University of New York, New York, NY, assistant professor, 1972-76, associate professor, 1977-85, professor of social theory and social psychology, 1985—.

MEMBER: American Sociological Association, American Association for Asian Studies, Society for the Study of Symbolic Interaction.

WRITINGS:

The Karmic Theater: Self, Society, and Astrology in Jaffna, University of Massachusetts Press (Cambridge, MA), 1982.
Signifying Acts, Southern Illinois University Press (Carbondale, IL), 1985.
Discursive Acts, Aldine Publishing (Hawthorne, NY), 1991.
The Presence of Self, Rowman & Littlefield (Lanham, MD), 2000.

Contributor to books, including *Social Psychology through Symbolic Interaction,* edited by G. P. Stone and Harvey A. Farberman, Wiley (New York, NY), 1981; and *The Psychology of the Social Situation,* edited by Adrian Furnham and Michael Argyle, Pergamon (New York, NY), 1981.

SIDELIGHTS: Perinbanayagam once reported to *CA* that his goal is to "discover and report the sources of meaning and significance in everyday life."

BIOGRAPHICAL AND CRITICAL SOURCES:

PERIODICALS

Contemporary Sociology, September, 2002, Gordon Shepherd, review of *The Presence of Self,* p. 560.
Journal of Phenomenological Psychology, spring, 2001, Gerald L. Peterson, review of *The Presence of Self,* p. 89.

*   *   *

PERL, Lila
   (Lila Perl Yerkow)

PERSONAL: Born in New York, NY; daughter of Oscar and Fay (Rosenthal) Perl; married Charles Yerkow (a writer). *Education:* Brooklyn College (now Brooklyn College of the City University of New York), B.A.; additional study at Columbia University and New York University.

ADDRESSES: Home—160-20 Cryders Lane, Beechhurst, NY 11357. *Office*—c/o Author Mail, Benchmark Books, Marshall Cavendish Corp., 99 White Plains Rd., P.O. Box 2001, Tarrytown, NY 10591.

CAREER: Writer, educator, and lecturer. Judge of Golden Kite Award for Society of Children's Book Writers; fellow of MacDowell Colony; teacher of writing to children.

AWARDS, HONORS: American Library Association Notable Book Award, 1965, for *Red-Flannel Hash and Shoo-Fly Pie;* American Institute of Graphic Arts award, 1967, for *Rice, Spice, and Bitter Oranges;* National Science Teachers Association award, 1973, for *The Hamburger Book,* and 1987, for *Mummies, Tombs, and Treasure;* Notable Children's Trade Book in the Field of Social Studies, National Council for the Social Studies/Children's Book Council, 1975, for *Slumps, Grunts, and Snickerdoodles,* 1977, for *Hunter's Stew and Hangtown Fry,* 1980, for *Junk Food, Fast Food, Health Food,* 1986, for *Blue Monday and Friday the Thirteenth,* 1987, for *Mummies, Tombs, and Treasure,* 1988, for *Don't Sing before Breakfast, Don't Sleep in the Moonlight,* and 1989, for *The Great Ancestor Hunt; Boston Globe/Horn Book* Nonfiction Honor Book citation, 1981, for *Junk Food, Fast Food, Health Food;* Best Books for the Teen Age citation, New York Public Library, 1988, for *The Secret Diary of Katie Dinkerhoff;* Parents' Choice Story Book Award, 1991, for *Fat Glenda Turns Fourteen.*

WRITINGS:

FOR ADULTS

What Cooks in Suburbia, Dutton (New York, NY), 1961.
The Delights of Apple Cookery, Coward (New York, NY), 1963.
The House You Want: How to Find It, How to Buy It, McKay (New York, NY), 1965.
The Finishing Touch: A Book of Desserts, New American Library (New York, NY), 1970.

JUVENILE NONFICTION

Red-Flannel Hash and Shoo-Fly Pie: American Regional Foods and Festivals, World Publishing (New York, NY), 1965.
Rice, Spice, and Bitter Oranges: Mediterranean Foods and Festivals, World Publishing (New York, NY), 1967.
Foods and Festivals of the Danube Lands: Germany, Austria, Czechoslovakia, Hungary, Yugoslavia, Bulgaria, Romania, Russia, World Publishing (New York, NY), 1969.
Yugoslavia, Romania, Bulgaria: New Era in the Balkans, Thomas Nelson (New York, NY), 1970.
Living in Naples, Thomas Nelson (New York, NY), 1970.

Living in Lisbon, Thomas Nelson (New York, NY), 1971.

Ethiopia: Land of the Lion, Morrow (New York, NY), 1972.

East Africa, Kenya, Tanzania, Uganda, Morrow (New York, NY), 1973.

The Hamburger Book: All about Hamburgers and Hamburger Cookery, illustrated by Ragna Tischler Godard, Seabury Press (New York, NY), 1973.

America Goes to the Fair: All about State and County Fairs in the U.S.A., Morrow (New York, NY), 1974.

Ghana and Ivory Coast: Spotlight on West Africa, Morrow (New York, NY), 1975.

Slumps, Grunts, and Snickerdoodles: What Colonial America Ate and Why, Seabury Press (New York, NY), 1975.

The Global Food Shortage, Morrow (New York, NY), 1976.

Egypt: Rebirth on the Nile, Morrow (New York, NY), 1977.

Hunter's Stew and Hangtown Fry: What Pioneer America Ate and Why, Seabury Press (New York, NY), 1977.

Mexico: Crucible of the Americas, Morrow (New York, NY), 1978.

Eating the Vegetarian Way: Good Food from the Earth, Morrow (New York, NY), 1980.

Junk Food, Fast Food, Health Food: What America Eats and Why, Houghton Mifflin (Boston, MA), 1980.

Guatemala, Central America's Living Past, Morrow (New York, NY), 1982.

Red Star and Green Dragon: Looking at New China, Morrow (New York, NY), 1983.

Piñatas and Paper Flowers: Holidays of the Americas in English and Spanish, Clarion Books (New York, NY), 1983.

Candles, Cakes, and Donkey Tails: Birthday Symbols and Celebrations, Clarion Books (New York, NY), 1984.

Blue Monday and Friday the Thirteenth, Clarion Books (New York, NY), 1986.

Mummies, Tombs, and Treasure: Secrets of Ancient Egypt, Clarion Books (New York, NY), 1987.

Don't Sing before Breakfast, Don't Sleep in the Moonlight: Everyday Superstitions and How They Began, Clarion Books (New York, NY), 1988.

The Great Ancestor Hunt: The Fun of Finding Out Who You Are, Clarion Books (New York, NY), 1989.

From Top Hats to Baseball Caps, from Bustles to Blue Jeans: Why We Dress the Way We Do, Clarion Books (New York, NY), 1990.

Molly Picon: A Gift of Laughter, Jewish Publication Society (Philadelphia, PA), 1990.

It Happened in America: True Stories from the Fifty States, Holt (New York, NY), 1992.

Isaac Bashevis Singer: The Life of a Storyteller, Jewish Publication Society (Philadelphia, PA), 1994.

(With Marion Blumenthal Lazan) *Four Perfect Pebbles: A Holocaust Story,* Greenwillow Books (New York, NY), 1996.

Dying to Know—About Death, Funeral Customs, and Final Resting Places, Twenty-first Century Books (Brookfield, CT), 2001.

Behind Barbed Wire: The Story of Japanese-Americans Internment during World War II, Benchmark Books (Tarrytown, NY), 2002.

North across the Border: The Story of the Mexican Americans, Benchmark Books (Tarrytown, NY), 2002.

To the Golden Mountain: The Story of the Chinese Who Built the Transcontinental Railroad, Benchmark Books (Tarrytown, NY), 2003.

Terrorism, Benchmark Books (Tarrytown, NY), 2003.

Cloning, Benchmark Books (Tarrytown, NY), 2004.

The Ancient Egyptians, Franklin Watts (New York, NY), 2004.

The Ancient Maya, Franklin Watts (New York, NY), 2005.

Some books published under the name Lila Perl Yerkow.

JUVENILE FICTION

No Tears for Rainey, Lippincott (Philadelphia, PA), 1969.

Me and Fat Glenda, Seabury Press (New York, NY), 1972.

That Crazy April, Seabury Press (New York, NY), 1974.

The Telltale Summer of Tina C., Seabury Press (New York, NY), 1975.

Dumb Like Me, Olivia Potts, Seabury Press (New York, NY)1976.

Don't Ask Miranda, Seabury Press (New York, NY), 1979.

Pieface and Daphne, Clarion Books (New York, NY), 1980.

Hey, Remember Fat Glenda?, Ticknor & Fields (New York, NY), 1981.

Annabelle Starr, E. S. P., Clarion Books (New York, NY), 1983.

Tybee Trimble's Hard Times, Clarion Books (New York, NY), 1984.

Marleen, the Horror Queen, Clarion Books (New York, NY), 1985.

Fat Glenda's Summer Romance, Clarion Books (New York, NY), 1986.

The Secret Diary of Katie Dinkerhoff, Scholastic (New York, NY), 1987.

Fat Glenda Turns Fourteen, Clarion Books (New York, NY), 1991.

SIDELIGHTS: Lila Perl's nonfiction work for young readers is invigorated by her own sense of adventure. She enjoys traveling to far-flung locations and tackling difficult historical issues such as the Holocaust and the internment of Japanese Americans during World War II. She has also written numerous books about aspects of life often taken for granted: holiday customs, superstitions, the foods we eat, and the clothing we wear. Perl once noted, "Doing research, as one must for nonfiction, is fascinating to me, keeping in mind (as I must) that young readers should find the finished material appealing, accessible, and as exciting as a good work of fiction." One of Perl's best-known nonfiction titles is *Four Perfect Pebbles: A Holocaust Story*, in which Marion Blumenthal Lazan remembers a Jewish childhood during the years of World War II. In a *Booklist* review of the work, Hazel Rochman wrote: "Perl weaves the history of the Holocaust with a survivor's personal memories of what happened to her family. The writing is direct and devastating, with no rhetoric or sensationalizing. The truth is in what's said and in what's left out."

Most of Perl's fiction is aimed at young teens who are struggling to find personal and social identity. One of her favorite recurring characters is Fat Glenda, a youngster with weight control issues who gradually comes to accept herself. A *Publishers Weekly* reviewer noted that the issue addressed in the Fat Glenda books "is overwhelmingly interesting to many young people." Perl once explained: "*Fat Glenda . . .* seems to have touched a nerve in all of us. Although I was never fat, I was able to empathize with her insecurity and vulnerability. (Perhaps all of us are 'fat' on the inside?) Leavened with good humor *and* humor, the stories about Glenda appear to have made her a favorite heroine with readers, who feel they can relate to her."

Perl once told *CA:* "Writing is a learning experience for me—a never-ending source of intellectual and emotional stimulation. I love it with a passion and hope that the thrust of my own joy in the undertaking is conveyed in some measure to my readers. The feedback letters from readers of my young people's novels are an immense source of gratification. Every single letter is answered.

"With all due respect to fictional works based on history or personal reminiscence, and to fantasy," Perl added, "I feel that the times in which we are living are too complex, too challenging to be ignored, particularly by the writer of young people's literature. Contemporary settings and characters, situations and problems, in both fiction and nonfiction, lay claim to me. My concern is to sort out some of the turmoil, evoke, elucidate, and enrich the life of the imagination within that frame of reference."

BIOGRAPHICAL AND CRITICAL SOURCES:

PERIODICALS

Booklist, May 1, 1994, Hazel Rochman, review of *Isaac Bashevis Singer: The Life of a Storyteller*, p. 1600; April 1, 1996, Hazel Rochman, review of *Four Perfect Pebbles: A Holocaust Story*, p. 1361; December 1, 2001, Roger Leslie, review of *Dying to Know—About Death, Funeral Customs, and Final Resting Places*, p. 638; January 1, 2002, Ilene Cooper, review of *North across the Border: The Story of Mexican Americans*, p. 834.

Publishers Weekly, April 12, 1991, review of *Fat Glenda Turns Fourteen*, p. 59; March 25, 1996, review of *Four Perfect Pebbles*, p. 86.

School Library Journal, December, 2001, Jennifer Ralston, review of *Dying to Know*, p. 170; February, 2003, Ginny Gustin, review of *To the Golden Mountain: The Story of the Chinese Who Built the Transcontinental Railroad*, p. 168.

ONLINE

Four Perfect Pebbles Web site, http://www.fourperfect pebbles.com/ (April 17, 2003).*

*   *   *

POMERANCE, Bernard 1940-

PERSONAL: Born 1940, in Brooklyn, NY. *Education:* Attended University of Chicago.

ADDRESSES: Agent—Alan Brodie Representation Ltd., 211 Piccadilly, London W1J 9HF, England.

CAREER: Playwright. Cofounder of Foco Novo Theatre Group, London, England.

AWARDS, HONORS: Antoinette Perry ("Tony") Award for best play and best director, New York Drama Critics Circle Award, Drama Desk Award, and Obie Award, all 1979, all for *The Elephant Man.*

WRITINGS:

PLAYS

High in Vietnam Hot Damn (first produced by Foco Novo Theatre Group, London, England, 1971), published in *Gambit 6,* 1972.

Hospital (first produced by Foco Novo Theatre Group, London, England, 1971), published in *Gambit 6,* 1972.

Thanksgiving before Detroit (first produced by Foco Novo Theatre Group, London, England, 1971), published in *Gambit 6,* 1972.

Foco Novo, produced by Foco Novo Theatre Group, London, England, 1972.

Someone Else Is Still Someone, produced by Foco Novo Theatre Group, London, England, 1974.

A Man's a Man (adaptation of a play by Bertolt Brecht), produced in London, England, 1975.

The Elephant Man (first produced at Hampstead Theatre, London, England; produced Off-Broadway at Theater of St. Peter's Church, January 14, 1979; produced on Broadway at Booth Theater, April 19, 1979; produced on Broadway at Royale Theatre, 2002), Grove (New York, NY), 1979.

Quantrill in Lawrence (also see below; first produced in London, England, 1980), Faber (London, England), 1981.

Melons (also see below), first produced at Pit Theatre, London, England, 1985, produced in New Haven, CT, 1987.

The Collected Plays of Bernard Pomerance (includes *Superhighway, Quantrill in Lawrence, Melons,* and *Hands of Light*), Grove Press (New York, NY), 2001.

POETRY

We Need to Dream All This Again: An Account of Crazy Horse, Custer, and the Battle for the Black Hills, Penguin (New York, NY), 1987.

SIDELIGHTS: When Bernard Pomerance left his native New York City to settle in London in the early 1970s, his ambition was to be a novelist. Before long, however, he realized that drama was his strength. Pomerance became involved with the left-wing fringe theatre groups that were flourishing in London at the time. Teaming up with director Roland Rees, he founded the Foco Novo Theatre Group, which has subsequently produced many of his plays, including *High in Vietnam Hot Damn* and *Someone Else Is Still Someone.* The play that first brought Pomerance to the attention of the general public was *The Elephant Man,* which had a long and successful run at the Hampstead Theatre before being brought to New York City in January of 1979, where it met with widespread critical acclaim.

Pomerance's award-winning play is based on the true story of Englishman John Merrick (1836-1890). Merrick was afflicted with a disease (scientists now believe it was neurofibromatosis, a genetic disorder) that grotesquely deformed him. His head was thirty-six inches in circumference, large growths covered his body, and his hips were so deformed that he could barely walk. He earned a living as a sideshow freak before he was befriended by Frederick Treves, a prominent surgeon. In addition to providing Merrick with a home at London Hospital, Treves sought to introduce the young man to Victorian society. Under Treves' guidance, Merrick became a figure in London society, visited by members of the Royal Family and aristocrats. Pomerance first learned of Merrick from his brother. A book written by Treves, *The Elephant Man and Other Reminiscences,* and a study of Merrick by Ashley Montagu, which included Treves' memoirs, was also useful.

One of the problems in staging *The Elephant Man* is how to convey the sense of Merrick's hideously misshapen body. In a prefatory note to *The Elephant Man,* Pomerance wrote, "Any attempt to reproduce his [Merrick's] appearance and his voice naturalistically—if it were possible—would seem to me not only counterproductive, but the more remarkably successful it was, the more distracting it would be." Instead of relying on make-up and padding to suggest Merrick's deformity, Pomerance uses a clever theatrical device. Early in the play, Treves brings Merrick to London Hospital to lecture about him. In the course of the lecture the audience views enlarged photographs of the real Merrick. "The pictures are so horrifying, so explicit in their detail, that we transfer the image to the actor beside the screen, even though he is simply contorting his body," Martin Gottfried observed in the *Saturday Review.* Other critics also found that they had no difficulty in believing that the actor on the stage was horribly deformed. Many paid tribute to the talent of Philip Anglim, who played the part of Merrick in the New York production. Through his twisted motions and muffled speech, Anglim convinced the audience that the man he was playing was so repulsive that people would shriek and run away from him in terror.

However deformed his body, Merrick is portrayed in the play as an intelligent and sensitive man. His innocence often causes him to challenge the ideas and assumptions presented to him by his more worldly benefactors. According to Richard Eder in the *New York Times,* Pomerance "has made Merrick not an abstraction, but a most individual exemplar of Natural Man. His deformities are external; they stand for the deformities, social and moral, that twist the lives of those who crowd about him; but his spirit is clear, vulnerable and acute." As the play progresses, Merrick's pure and questioning spirit is subdued. The drama, Eder explained, is a "haunting parable about natural man trading his frail beauty and innocence for the protection and prison of society."

The two other principal characters in the play are Treves and Madge Kendal. Treves, *New Yorker* contributor Edith Oliver pointed out, is portrayed as "a complex man, responsible, encouraging, and sympathetic, but a Victorian whose spontaneous kindness seems to conflict with his squeamishness about sex and his utter trust in rules and standards." The kindly physician teaches Merrick how to conform to society, but he tragically comes to realize that this educational process has had many detrimental effects on both the physical and mental health of his patient.

Initially, Treves has difficulty finding anyone who would care for the horribly deformed Merrick. He resorts to hiring an actress, Madge Kendal, to visit Merrick in the hopes that she can use her acting skills to hide her repulsion. Merrick and Kendal become close friends. He is able to express his deepest feelings to her, and in a moving scene she reaches out to this sexually repressed man by undressing to the waist for him. Both characters benefit from their relationship.

Several critics observed that the driving tension of *The Elephant Man* fell off in the second act. John Simon,

writing in *New York* magazine, described the first act as "terse, thoughtful, theatrical in the best sense, and devoid of spurious rhetoric—a lesson from Brecht well learned, with an added touch of humanity often lacking in the master." However, he felt that the second act suffers from "some insufficiently developed marginalia . . . , some less than revelatory speechifying . . . , some top-heavy irony with a few minor characters reduced to over-convenient contrivances. Above all, too many, and conflicting, layers of symbolism." Eder offered an explanation as to why the second act is the weaker half of the play: "In part it is inevitable: the opening up of the Elephant Man is more exciting than his decline. And furthermore many of the themes that are dramatized at the beginning remain to be expounded at the end. They are expounded very well indeed, but some of the play's immediacy flags a bit."

In viewing *The Elephant Man* as a whole, however, reviewers were generous with their praise. Gottfried commented that its flaws "do not fatally mar the play, for what counts most is its overwhelming humanity; its tragedy and compassion; its soaring poetry; the theatrical beauty it makes of the contrast between innocence, deformity, and the stark Victorian staging." *"The Elephant Man,"* Stanley Kauffmann maintained in the *New Republic,* "is the best new American play since 1972," while T. E. Kalem, writing in *Time,* felt that the drama is "lofted on poetic wings and nests in the human heart."

A 2002 Broadway revival of *The Elephant Man* received mixed reviews. Lasting only one-hundred minutes, the revival is a condensed version of the original, casting Billy Crudup as Merrick. Like his predecessor, Crudup portrays Merrick without makeup or padding. Noted Roy Sorrels in a review of the play published on the *Culture Vulture* Web site, "Without mask or padding, the actor's face, body, and voice are left unimpeded to reveal the character. The absence of mask allows Merrick to be a mirror for each of the main characters of the play, each of whom sees some feature of his or her own personality reflected." On *Talkin' Broadway's Broadway Reviews* Web site, Matthew Murray observed, "When Crudup walks, it's with an anguished shoulder roll and stiff legs, the effect being one of clockwork precision, as effortless to him, apparently, as anyone not possessing such an affliction may walk."

The revival features Kate Burton as Mrs. Kendal, the actress asked to befriend Merrick. Sorrels felt that

Burton "gives the character a fascinating sense of depth." He went on to explain, "First seen as a strutting, overdressed, self-consciously witty but apparently shallow woman, she slowly morphs, through her growing relationship with Merrick, into a fully dimensional, flawed, yet beautiful woman."

Despite the stunning success of *The Elephant Man*, Pomerance remains a mysterious figure. He fled back to England shortly after *The Elephant Man* opened in New York City in the 1970s. In a rare interview, he talked with Michael Owen of the *New York Times* about his conception of drama. "The most important element in theater is the audience's imagination," he remarked. "What is in them, is in me. It goes back to the function of memory. My function is—I don't know the proper word—is to remind them that this too is true, though our consciousness may deny it. I don't mean to tell them something they do not already know. I'm not bringing hot news. My interest in the audience is to remind them of a common thing and, if only temporarily, they do then become a unity, a community."

Pomerance's play *Melons* was produced in London, England, in the 1985-1986 season. Writing a report on the London theater scene for the *New York Times*, Benedict Nightingale said that this play was "recognizably the fruit of the same moral imagination, it too is about a noble savage oppressed and exploited by a civilization with less claim to true virtue than himself." *Melons* is set on a New Mexico Pueblo Indian reservation in 1906, where an old Apache warrior leader named Caracol (called John Lame Eagle by the white men) is living in seclusion. Caracol is confronted by a former enemy, ex-cavalry officer Stolsky, who is now working for an oil company that wishes to survey the Indian's land, an assignment that needs Caracol's cooperation.

Irving Wardle, reviewing *Melons* for the London *Times*, felt that the play's confusing structure diminished its appeal. "Instead of proceeding in a straight line toward an inescapable tragic outcome," he wrote, "the action undergoes labyrinthian contortions, as Caracol embarks on prolonged speeches evoking the massacre of his family and his reunion with them, events loop into flashbacks and double-flashbacks." Nightingale suggested that the play might have worked better as a "ruminative monologue" for the central character alone. Both reviewers, however, had high praise for actor Ben Kingsley in the role of Caracol/John Lame Eagle. In 1987, *Melons* was given its American premiere by the Yale Repertory Theater. Despite strong performances in all the major roles, *New York Times* reviewer Mel Gussow reported that the play was "thoughtful drama, but its portent has to be mined from beneath the verbiage." As had reviewers of the London performance, Gussow was jarred by the bloody conclusion of the play, in which Caracol ritualistically beheads two geologists.

In 1987, Pomerance also published *We Need to Dream All This Again: An Account of Crazy Horse, Custer, and the Battle for the Black Hills.* This book-length narrative poem recreates the events surrounding the 1876 Battle of the Little Big Horn. Martin Kirby in the *New York Times Book Review* called Pomerance's verse "prosy" and described the narrative as "mixing pathos and satire." Kirby felt that Pomerance was unsuccessful in the devices he used in an attempt to revitalize what has become a cliche Indian/white confrontation. He objected particularly to the use of "arch, smirking metaphors derived from current popular culture—'Crazy Horse goes not left or right, but—imagine Dr. J. driving on Bill Russell—takes it straight to Red Cloud.'"

BIOGRAPHICAL AND CRITICAL SOURCES:

BOOKS

Contemporary Dramatists, 6th edition, St. James Press (Detroit, MI), 1999.

Contemporary Literary Criticism, Volume 13, Gale (Detroit, MI), 1980.

Graham, Peter W., and Fritz H. Oehlschlaeger, *Articulating the Elephant Man: Joseph Merrick and His Interpreters*, Johns Hopkins University Press (Baltimore, MD), 1992.

Pomerance, Bernard, *The Elephant Man*, Grove (New York, NY), 1979.

PERIODICALS

Chicago Tribune, June 6, 1979.

Drama, winter, 1972; autumn, 1974; winter, 1977-1978.

Harper's, April, 1987, p. 31.

Library Journal, May 15, 1987, p. 98.

New Republic, February 17, 1979; May 12, 1979.

Newsweek, February 5, 1979, p. 67.

New York, May 7, 1979.

New Yorker, January 29, 1979; April 30, 1979, pp. 45-46.

New York Times, January 15, 1979; February 4, 1979; April 15, 1979; April 20, 1979, p. 7; April 21, 1979; May 1, 1979; June 3, 1979; August 14, 1979; January 26, 1986; November 14, 1987.

New York Times Book Review, August 23, 1987, Martin Kirby, review of *We Need to Dream All This Again: An Account of Crazy Horse, Custer, and the Battle for the Black Hills,* p. 17.

Publishers Weekly, April 3, 1987, p. 66.

Saturday Review, March 17, 1979, Martin Gottfried, review of *The Elephant Man,* p. 60.

Time, January 29, 1979, p. 64.

Times (London, England), December 20, 1985.

Variety, November 11, 1987, p. 97.

Washington Post, May 20, 1979.

Western American Literature, winter, 1988, p. 358.

ONLINE

Talkin' Broadway's Broadway Reviews Web site, http://www.talkinbroadway.com/world/ElephantMan.html/ (April 14, 2002), Matthew Murray, review of *The Elephant Man.*

Culture Vulture Web site, http://www.culturevulture.net/Theater3/ElephantMan.htm/ (April 18, 2002), Roy Sorrels, review of *The Elephant Man.*

*   *   *

POTOK, Andrew 1931-

PERSONAL: Born July 12, 1931, in Warsaw, Poland; immigrated to the United States, 1940; naturalized citizen, 1943; son of Leon (an engineer) and Anna (a designer; maiden name, Maximilian) Potok; married Joan Henley, January 30, 1954 (divorced, 1963); married Charlotte Clifford (a designer and ceramist), October 10, 1967; children: (first marriage) Mark, Sarah; (second marriage) Jed Clifford, Maya Clifford. *Education:* Yale University, B.A., 1953; Union Graduate School, Ph.D., 1976. *Politics:* "Liberal." *Religion:* Jewish.

ADDRESSES: Home and office—East Hill, Plainfield, VT 05667. *Agent*—Phyllis Wender, Rosenstone/Wender, 3 East 48th St., Fourth Floor, New York, NY 10017.

CAREER: Painter, 1955-72; writer. Counselor to the blind.

MEMBER: PEN, Authors Guild, Vermont Association for the Blind (member, board of directors), Vermont Council on the Arts (member, board of trustees).

AWARDS, HONORS: National Endowment for the Arts fellow in creative writing, 1983.

WRITINGS:

Ordinary Daylight: Portrait of an Artist Going Blind (memoir), Holt (New York, NY), 1980, reprinted, Bantam (New York, NY), 2003.

My Life with Goya (novel), Arbor House (New York, NY), 1986.

A Matter of Dignity: Changing the Lives of the Disabled, Bantam (New York, NY), 2002.

Contributor of articles to periodicals, including *Quest, Moment,* and *Life.*

SIDELIGHTS: Andrew Potok, a former painter, is the author of several books, among them his memoir, *Ordinary Daylight: Portrait of an Artist Going Blind. Ordinary Daylight* is an account of Potok's loss of eyesight and that event's meaning in terms of his work, his identity, and his personal relationships. The author inherited a condition known as retinitis pigmentosa from his father. This disease causes the retina to become more opaque, so that it has difficulty distinguishing form, light, and color. Beginning in his early forties, Potok gradually became completely blind. Having been an artist all his life, the author at first could not accept his inability to paint. But despite his diminishing sense of self-worth, he grew determined to continue living a full life. At a rehabilitation center in Massachusetts, Potok learned to walk with a cane and to read and write using the Braille system of raised dots. He was also taught by a sculptor to imagine colors and forms so that he would not lose his visual memory. After he left the center, the author decided to work toward a doctorate in psychology and begin a new career as a counselor, helping other victims of his disease learn to accept and cope with blindness.

Several years after embarking on his new career, Potok read of a woman in England who claimed to have a miracle cure for retinitis pigmentosa. He left his clients behind and traveled to England, in desperate hope that his sight might be restored. The woman subjected Potok to repeated stings from bees she claimed were specially treated in order to cleanse him of his affliction. Having learned that he had passed the disease on to his daughter Sarah—for which he felt tremendous guilt—the author subjected her to the treatment as well. But it soon became clear that the cure was ineffective, and the author returned to his family in Vermont. After spending some time feeling sorry for himself, Potok realized "something that should have been clear to me from the beginning: the only thing that could replace the creative activity in the center of my life would be another creative activity." He substituted writing for painting and used words to describe the painful loss he had experienced. In order to review and edit what he had written, Potok had someone else read each draft into a tape recorder. The author was now able to see beyond his pain and appreciate his wife's success as a potter. David Mamet, writing in the *Chicago Tribune,* referred to Potok as "anecdotal, funny, charming, and very direct." *New York Times Book Review* contributor Anne Roiphe stressed the universal element of Potok's experience. "*Ordinary Daylight,*" Roiphe stated, "concerns not just a blind artist but the human ordeal."

Following *Ordinary Daylight,* Potok's next book was a work of fiction. *My Life with Goya,* which he published in 1986, deals with a young Polish Jew's new life in America following World War II. Ten-year-old Adam Krinsky, an artist who emulates the eighteenth-century Spanish painter Francisco José de Goya, escapes from Warsaw in 1940 with his uncle, Bolek Casimir. Four years later, they are living in New York City with old friends, including Maggie, who is Adam's age. Each of the main characters pursues a dream: Bolek re-creates the fur business he left behind, Maggie becomes an actress in Hollywood films, and Adam finds success as a painter. Potok—who has crafted his main character using details from his own life—explores Adam's relationships with his uncle, with Maggie, and with his art.

Taking an advocate's stance, Potok produced *A Matter of Dignity: Changing the World of the Disabled* in 2001. Using interviews, the author presents portraits of therapists, researchers, and activists—some disabled, some not—who have worked to more fully integrate disabled persons into mainstream American life. It is not a simple task; as recently as the 1960s, Potok notes in his book, many U.S. communities enforced what he calls "ugly laws," prohibiting people with disabilities "or in any other way deformed" from being seen in public places. More recently, as the book reports, some seventy percent of the disabled were reported as unemployed; those who do work have often been underutilized because of perceived deficiencies of skill. The author categorizes disability "politically, as another form of ethnicity." *A Matter of Dignity* chronicles the work of such people as Ted Hunter, a blind computer expert who created JAWS, a screen-talking software; Mary Lou Breslin, founder of the Disability Rights and Defense Fund; and Chai Feldblum, who helped craft the Americans with Disabilities Act of 1990. Potok also narrates the story of how he was paired with his first guide dog, "a giant move, not only in shrugging off my natural fears about putting my life in the hands of a dog, but in being unequivocally identified from then on as a blind man."

At the same time, in *A Matter of Dignity* Potok takes a stand against individuals, organizations, and issues he considers counter to the cause of the disabled. Actor Christopher Reeve, a quadriplegic, is criticized for lobbying for spinal-cord injury cures while "losing sight of the pressing need for civil rights and ongoing care," as Potok writes. He also addresses the research into genetic selection, prenatal diagnosis, and the human genome project, which theoretically could alter the genetics of generations to come. To these issues the author comments: "It is interesting to consider this rage for cleanliness and 'purity' in light of the human genome project, which dreams of perfectibility, a disease-free, disability-free humanity, a more efficient and happy workforce, the conquest of death."

"While careful not to present a completely cheery portrait of the world of the disabled," noted a *Publishers Weekly* reviewer, Potok "discusses such positive developments as the new academic Society for Disability Studies." The author's message of empowerment in *A Matter of Dignity* lifts the book beyond a work that "evokes pity," in the words of *St. Louis Post-Dispatch* critic Stephen Lyons. "Instead, Potok reminds us that the attributes of ingenuity, compassion and justice come from the heart and mind, and are always present in every human being: 'disabled' or not."

BIOGRAPHICAL AND CRITICAL SOURCES:

BOOKS

Potok, Andrew, *Ordinary Daylight: Portrait of an Artist Going Blind,* Holt (New York, NY), 1980.

Potok, Andrew, *A Matter of Dignity: Changing the Lives of the Disabled,* Bantam (New York, NY), 2002.

PERIODICALS

Chicago Tribune, May 4, 1980, David Mamet, review of *Ordinary Daylight,* p. 3.

Kirkus Reviews, December 1, 2001, review of *A Matter of Dignity,* p. 1669.

Library Journal, April 1, 1980, Joan Kapstein, review of *Ordinary Daylight,* p. 851; June 15, 1986, Marcia G. Fuch, review of *My Life with Goya,* p. 79.

New Yorker, October 27, 1986, review of *My Life with Goya,* p. 144.

New York Times, March 3, 1980, "For Blinded Painter, a New Meaning to Words," p. D7; April 18, 1980, Anatole Broyard, review of *Ordinary Daylight,* p. C26.

New York Times Book Review, May 11, 1980, Anne Roiphe, review of *Ordinary Daylight,* p. 12; September 7, 1986, Jay Neugeboren, review of *My Life with Goya,* p. 22.

Publishers Weekly, February 22, 1980, review of *Ordinary Daylight,* p. 97; Mary 2, 1986, review of *My Life with Goya,* p. 64; November 12, 2001, review of *A Matter of Dignity,* p. 45.

St. Louis Post-Dispatch, February 10, 2002, Stephen Lyons, "Author Focuses on Accomplishments, Not Circumstances of Disabled People," p. F8.

Washington Post, July 7, 1980, review of *Ordinary Daylight,* p. D2.*

*   *   *

PULLMAN, Philip 1946-

PERSONAL: Born October 19, 1946, in Norwich, England; son of Alfred Outram (an airman) and Audrey (homemaker; maiden name, Merrifield) Pullman; married Judith Speller (a teacher), August 15, 1970; children: James, Thomas. *Education:* Oxford Univer-

Philip Pullman

sity, B.A., 1968; Weymouth College of Education, earned teaching degree. *Politics:* Liberal. *Hobbies and other interests:* Drawing, music.

ADDRESSES: Agent—A. P. Watt, 20 John St., London WC1N 2DR, England; Ellen Levine, 432 Park Ave. S, Suite 1205, New York, NY 10016.

CAREER: Author, playwright, scriptwriter, and educator. Teacher at Ivanhoe, Bishop Kirk, and Marston middle schools, Oxford, England, 1970-86; writer, 1986—. Lecturer at Westminster College, North Hinksey, Oxford, 1988-95.

MEMBER: Society of Authors (chairman, 2001-03).

AWARDS, HONORS: Lancashire County Libraries/ National and Provincial Children's Book Award and Best Books for Young Adults listing, *School Library Journal,* both 1987, Children's Book Award, International Reading Association, Preis der Leseratten, ZDF

Television (Germany), and Best Books for Young Adults listing, American Library Association (ALA), all 1988, all for *The Ruby in the Smoke;* Best Books for Young Adults listing, ALA, 1988, and Edgar Allan Poe Award nomination, Mystery Writers of America, 1989, both for *Shadow in the North;* Carnegie Medal, British Library Association, 1996, *Guardian* Children's Fiction Award, *The Guardian,* 1996, both for *Northern Lights,* Top of the List in youth fiction, *Booklist,* 1996, for *The Golden Compass* (U.S. edition of *Northern Lights*); Smarties Award, Rowntree Mackintosh Co., 1996, for *The Firework-Maker's Daughter;* Whitbread Book of the Year Award and Whitbread Children's Book Award, both 2001, both for *The Amber Spyglass;* Securicor Omega Express Author of the Year and Whitaker/BA Author of the Year, both 2002.

WRITINGS:

"SALLY LOCKHART" SERIES; YOUNG ADULT HISTORICAL FICTION

The Ruby in the Smoke, Alfred A. Knopf (New York, NY), 1985.

The Shadow in the Plate, Oxford University Press (Oxford, England), 1987, published as *Shadow in the North,* Alfred A. Knopf (New York, NY), 1988.

The Tiger in the Well, Alfred A. Knopf (New York, NY), 1990.

The Tin Princess, Alfred A. Knopf (New York, NY), 1994.

"HIS DARK MATERIALS" YOUNG ADULT FANTASY NOVELS

Northern Lights, Scholastic (England), 1995, published as *The Golden Compass,* Alfred A. Knopf (New York, NY), 1996.

The Subtle Knife, Alfred A. Knopf (New York, NY), 1997.

The Amber Spyglass, Alfred A. Knopf (New York, NY), 2000.

Lyra's Oxford, illustrated by John Lawrence, Alfred A. Knopf (New York, NY), 2003.

OTHER YOUNG ADULT FICTION

How to Be Cool (humorous fiction), Heinemann (London, England), 1987.

The Broken Bridge, Macmillan (London, England), 1990, Alfred A. Knopf (New York, NY), 1992.

The White Mercedes (realistic fiction), Macmillan (London, England), 1992, Alfred A. Knopf, 1993.

(Editor) *Detective Stories: Chosen by Philip Pullman,* illustrated by Nick Hardcastle, Kingfisher (New York, NY), 1998.

FOR CHILDREN; FICTION

Count Karlstein, or The Ride of the Demon Huntsman (picture book), Chatto & Windus (London, England), 1982, new edition, illustrated by Patrice Aggs, Doubleday (London, England), 1991, new edition, illustrated by Diana Bryan, Alfred A. Knopf (New York, NY), 1998.

Spring-Heeled Jack: A Story of Bravery and Evil (graphic novel), illustrated by David Mostyn, Doubleday (London, England), 1989, Alfred A. Knopf (New York, NY), 1991.

The Wonderful Story of Aladdin and the Enchanted Lamp (retelling), illustrated by David Wyatt, Picture Hippo, 1995.

The Firework-Maker's Daughter (fantasy), Corgi, 1996, illustrated by S. Saelig Gallagher, Arthur A. Levine Books (New York, NY), 1999.

Clockwork, or All Wound Up, illustrated by Peter Bailey, Doubleday (London, England), 1996, new edition, illustrated by Leonid Gore, Scholastic/Arthur A. Levine Books (New York, NY), 1998.

I Was a Rat!, illustrated by Kevin Hawkes, Alfred A. Knopf (New York, NY), 2000.

Puss in Boots: The Adventures of That Most Enterprising Feline, illustrated by Ian Beck, Alfred A. Knopf (New York, NY), 2000.

"THE NEW CUT GANG" SERIES

Thunderbolt's Waxworks, illustrated by Mark Thomas, Viking (New York, NY), 1994.

The Gas-Fitter's Ball, illustrated by Mark Thomas, Viking (New York, NY), 1995.

OTHER

Ancient Civilizations (nonfiction), illustrated by G. Long, Wheaton (Exeter, England), 1978.

PLAYS

Sherlock Holmes and the Adventure of the Sumatran Devil (produced at Polka Children's Theatre, Wimbledon, 1984), published as *Sherlock Holmes and the Adventure of the Limehouse Horror,* Thomas Nelson (London, England), 1993.

The Three Musketeers (adapted from Alexandre Dumas's novel), produced at Polka Children's Theatre, Wimbledon, England, 1985.

Frankenstein (adapted from Mary Shelley's novel), produced at Polka Children's Theatre, Wimbledon, England, 1987), Oxford University Press (Oxford, England), 1990.

Puss in Boots, produced at Polka Children's Theater, Wimbledon, England, 1997.

ADULT NOVELS

Galatea (fantasy), Gollancz (London, England), 1978, Dutton (New York, NY), 1979.

Pullman is also the author of scripts for television. Author of introduction, John and Mary Gribbin, *The Science of "His Dark Materials,"* Hodder & Stoughton (London, England), in press.

ADAPTATIONS: How to Be Cool was televised by Granada-TV in the United Kingdom, 1988. *The Golden Compass* and *The Amber Spyglass* were made into sound recordings. The first three books in the "His Dark Materials" series have been optioned by New Line Cinema for production as motion pictures. Two plays based on "His Dark Materials," adapted by Nicholas Wright, were produced at the National Theatre, London, 2003-04.

WORK IN PROGRESS: A novel, *The Book of Dust,* in the "His Dark Materials" series.

SIDELIGHTS: The English bestow two prestigious literary prizes every year: the Whitbread Award and the Booker Prize. In 2001, Philip Pullman won the Whitbread Book of the Year Award for *The Amber Spyglass,* an unprecedented accolade for someone who is seen primarily as a writer for younger readers. Never before had the Whitbread Book of the Year been awarded to a young adult novel, or any children's book for that matter—in fact, the Whitbread has a category for children's literature, and *The Amber Spyglass* won *that* award too. Most critics agree that the award comes as recognition for Pullman's unique and imaginative "His Dark Materials" trilogy, comprising *The Golden Compass, The Subtle Knife,* and *The Amber Spyglass.* Drawing its energy from myth, science fiction, classical literature, the Bible, and specula-

tive philosophy, Pullman's trilogy succeeds for children as a ripping good-versus-evil adventure, and for teens and adults as a thoughtful venture into alternative realities.

Considered a writer of great range, depth, and imagination, Pullman is recognized as one of the most talented creators of children's literature to have entered the field in the last quarter century. The author of fiction, nonfiction, and picture books as well as a playwright and reteller, he is best known for writing fantasy and historical fiction for young adults, and historical fiction and fantasy for primary and middle graders. Pullman is lauded as a gifted storyteller who adds a distinctive, original touch to such literary forms as the mystery, the thriller, the horror story, and the problem novel. As a writer of historical fiction, he usually sets his books in Victorian England, a period that he is credited for recreating with accuracy. His works are often praised for their meticulous research, and he uses prior eras or fantasy worlds to treat themes with strong parallels to contemporary society such as feminism, prejudice, and adjustment to new technology. Pullman is known as the creator of four books about Sally Lockhart, a brave and independent young woman who solves mysteries in nineteenth-century London. Filled with underworld atmosphere, larger-than-life characters, and cliff-hanging suspense as well as thoughtful, provocative themes, these works have inspired Pullman's comparison to classic novelists such as Charles Dickens and Wilkie Collins.

The author is far more famous, however, as the creator of the "His Dark Materials" series, the best-selling epic tales set in an Arctic-like region that revolve around the concept of daemons, animal familiars that contain the souls of their human counterparts, and the quest of Lyra Belacqua, a feisty, shrewd teenager, to find the origin of Dust, a mysterious substance integral to the composition of the universe. Called "science fantasies" by their author in an interview in *Publishers Weekly,* these novels are regarded as extraordinary works that combine exciting adventures with thought-provoking philosophical content. Although many of Pullman's books are considered sophisticated and demanding, most reviewers note their accessibility while acknowledging the author's ability to explore moral and ethical issues in riveting stories. Chris Routh of *School Librarian* commented that Pullman "has already confirmed his status as one of today's top storytellers," while Anne E. Deifendeifer, writing in

Children's Books and Their Creators, noted, "At their best, Pullman's novels, daring and inventive, are page turners that immediately hook readers into the story and often introduce them to the Victorian age." In his entry in *Twentieth-Century Young Adult Writers,* Keith Barker claimed, "Pullman plays with the rules of fiction as few young-adult writers attempt to do." The critic concluded that the author's "unpredictability of plot and character coupled with the sheer readability of his novels earn them the right to be widely read."

Born in Norwich, England, to Alfred Pullman, an airman for the Royal Air Force, and his wife, Audrey, a homemaker and amateur dramatist who also worked for the British Broadcasting Corporation (BBC), Pullman spent much of his early life traveling. At the age of six, he went to live in Southern Rhodesia, now Zimbabwe, where his father was sent on assignment. "Africa," Pullman wrote in his essay in *Something about the Author Autobiography Series (SAAS),* "was full of strange things," including some wonderful smells such as roasting mealies (corn on the cob). He remembered, "I loved that smell so much that when years and years later I happened to smell it unexpectedly in a street market in London, where someone was roasting mealies to sell, I found tears springing to my eyes." When his father's tour of duty ended, Pullman returned to England, where he spent happy times with his grandfather and grandmother in Drayton, a small village in Norfolk. His grandfather, a clergyman in the Church of England, was rector of the church there. His grandfather, Pullman noted in *SAAS,* was "the centre of the world. There was no one stronger than he was, or wiser, or kinder. . . . When I was young he was the sun at the centre of my life." In addition to his other attributes, Pullman's grandfather was an accomplished storyteller; his grandson remembered, "He took the simplest little event and made a story out of it."

After his father was killed on a mission in Africa, Pullman and his younger brother went to live in Norfolk while their mother went to London to look for work. Shortly thereafter, Pullman's mother received a letter saying that her husband was to receive the Distinguished Flying Cross, an award that was presented to the family by Queen Elizabeth at Buckingham Palace. Later, Pullman discovered that his father, who had incurred gambling debts and was involved in extramarital affairs, was suspected of committing suicide by crashing his plane. Pullman wrote,

"Sometimes I think he's really alive somewhere, in hiding, with a different name. I'd love to meet him."

When Pullman was nine, his mother married an airman friend of her late husband's. When his stepfather was sent to Australia on assignment, the family went with him. Pullman made a spectacular discovery in Australia—comic books. He wrote in *SAAS,* "When one day my stepfather brought me a Superman comic, it changed my life. I'd been a reader for a long time, but a reader of books; I'd never known comics. When I got this one, I devoured it and demanded more. I adored them." Most of all, the author remembered, "I adored Batman. Those poorly printed stories on their cheap yellowing newsprint intoxicated me, enthralled me, made me dizzy with passion." In evaluating what he loved about the Batman comics, Pullman noted, "What I wanted was to *brood* over the world of Batman and dream actively. It was the first stirring of the storytelling impulse. I couldn't have put it like this, but what I wanted was to take characters, a setting, words, and pictures and weave a pattern out of them; not *be* Batman, but write about him." He added, "I knew instinctively at once, that the telling of stories was delicious, and it all belonged to me."

In Australia, Pullman began telling ghost stories to his school friends and to his brother in their bedroom at night. The author recalled, "I don't know whether he enjoyed it, or whether he even listened, but it wasn't for his benefit; it was for mine. I remember vividly the sense of diving into the dark as I began the story, with no idea at all what was going to happen or whether the story would 'come out' as I called it, by which I meant make sense or come to a neat end. I remember the exhilaration of the risk: Would I find something to say? Would I dry up? And I remember the thrill, the bliss, when, a minute ahead of getting there, I saw a twist I could give to the end, a clever way of bringing back that character who'd come into it earlier and vanished inconclusively, a neat phrase to tie it all up with. Many other things happened in Australia, but my discovery of storytelling was by far the most important."

After moving back to the United Kingdom, Pullman settled in Llanbedr, a village on the north coast of Wales where he would spend the next decade. "[Of] all the things I remember from those years," he wrote in *SAAS,* "the most exciting came when I discovered art." When Pullman was fifteen, he became interested in the history of painting. A book called *A History of Art* was "more precious to me than any Bible," Pullman wrote. He also began drawing. Pullman learned the Welsh landscape by sketching it, and, he noted, "came to care for it with a lover's devotion." In his young adult novel *The Broken Bridge,* a work that the author called "a love letter to a landscape" in *SAAS,* he describes a young woman who makes the same discoveries. As a teenager, Pullman also became enthralled by poetry. One of his English teachers, Enid Jones, was instrumental in developing his interest; he wrote in *SAAS,* "I owe her a great debt." Jones introduced Pullman to Milton, Wordsworth, and the English metaphysical poets and, he remembered, "took me to places I never dreamed of. . . ." In addition to learning reams of poetry by heart, Pullman began writing poems in literary forms such as the sonnet, the rondeau, and the ballad; in the process, he recalled, "I developed a great respect for craftsmanship."

After winning a scholarship to Oxford to study English, Pullman became the first person in his family to attend university. However, he wrote in *SAAS,* "it wasn't long before I found out that I didn't enjoy English as much as I thought I would, anyway. I was doing it because I wanted to learn how to write, but that wasn't what they were interested in teaching." While at Oxford, Pullman realized that he was destined to be a storyteller, not a poet. After graduation, he began to write a novel. Shortly thereafter, he moved to London and worked at a men's clothing store and in a library while writing three pages a day—a regime to which he still adheres—in his spare time. In 1970, Pullman married Judith Speller, a teacher; the couple has two sons. His wife influenced Pullman's next career move; he wrote in *SAAS,* "I liked what she told me about [teaching]." After attending Weymouth College of Education, Pullman got his degree and began teaching middle school in Oxford.

For twelve years, Pullman taught Greek mythology to his students by telling them stories of the gods and heroes, including oral versions of *The Iliad* and *The Odyssey.* Writing in *SAAS,* the author confirmed that the "real beneficiary of all that storytelling wasn't so much the audience as the storyteller. I'd chosen—for what I thought, and think still, were good educational reasons—to do something that, by a lucky chance, was the best possible training for me as a writer. To tell great stories over and over again, testing and refining the language and observing the reaction of the

listeners and gradually improving the timing and the rhythm and the pace, was to undergo an apprenticeship that probably wasn't very different, essentially, from the one that Homer himself underwent three thousand years ago."

In 1978, Pullman published his first novel, *Galatea,* a book for adults that outlines how flautist Martin Browning, searching for his missing wife, embarks on a series of surreal adventures. Now considered a cult classic among aficionados of science fiction and fantasy literature, the novel is described by its author in *SAAS* as "a book I can't categorize." He added, "I'm still proud of it." After completing *Galatea,* Pullman began writing and producing plays for his students; he wrote in *SAAS,* "I enjoyed doing school plays so much that I've written for children ever since." Pullman's first book for young people is *Ancient Civilizations,* a nonfiction title about the cultures of several Mediterranean, Eastern, Middle Eastern, and South American countries that R. Baines of *Junior Bookshelf* called "a lively and informative work."

Pullman's next book, *Count Karlstein,* is an adaptation of a story that the author had originally written as a play. The book was also published as a graphic novel. Taking his inspiration from Victorian pulp fiction and from such tales of derring-do as Anthony Hope's *The Prisoner of Zenda,* Pullman created a gothic farce set in a Swiss castle that describes how a fourteen-year-old servant girl and her English tutor foil a plot by the evil Count Karlstein to sacrifice his two young nieces to Zamiel, the Demon Huntsman, in exchange for riches. Writing in the *New Statesman,* Charles Fox noted, "To compare this book with T. H. White's *Mistress Masham's Repose* is to risk hyperbole, yet it shares a similar concern with making the improbable seem remarkably precise." Pullman has also adapted *The Three Musketeers, Frankenstein,* and a story featuring Sherlock Holmes into plays, and has turned the latter two into books of his own. In his review of *Frankenstein* in *School Librarian,* Derek Paget claimed, "Pullman's is a good adaptation, keeping a firm grip on the perennial fascination of the story. . . ." Noting the adapter's inclusion of a section on genetic engineering as well as his suggestions for lesson plans in English and drama, Paget concluded that *Frankenstein* is "certainly a book for the library, and would be worth a production by youth or school drama groups."

In 1986, Pullman published *The Ruby in the Smoke,* a historical novel for young adults that became the first of his series of books about Sally Lockhart. A thriller set in Victorian London that was inspired by the English melodramas of the period, *Ruby* concerns the whereabouts of a priceless stone that mysteriously disappeared during the Indian mutiny. Sixteen-year-old Sally, a recently orphaned girl who is savvy about such subjects as business management, military strategy, and firearms, becomes involved in the opium trade when she receives a cryptic note written in a strange hand soon after hearing word of her father's drowning off Singapore. Like its successors, *The Ruby in the Smoke* includes abundant—often violent—action, murky atmosphere, and an examination of Victorian values from a modern perspective. Writing in *British Book News Children's Books,* Peter Hollindale claimed, "This is a splendid book. . . . It is a first-rate adventure story." David Churchill commented in the *School Librarian:* "There are not many books that offer such promise of satisfaction to so many children, of both sexes, of secondary age." Brooke L. Dillon in *Voice of Youth Advocates (VOYA)* noted the "beautifully crafted writing" and "the fact that Pullman respects his teenaged audience enough to treat them to a complex, interwoven plot." Writing in *SAAS,* Pullman claimed, "With *The Ruby in the Smoke* I think I first found my voice as a children's author."

The next volume in the series, *The Shadow in the Plate,* was published in the United Kingdom in 1987, and as *Shadow in the North* in the United States the next year. In this novel, Sally, now a financial consultant, and Frederick Garland, a photographer turned detective who was introduced in the previous story, solve a mystery with connections to the aristocracy, the Spiritualism movement, and a conspiracy that involves the production of an ultimate weapon. Pullman introduces readers to such issues as the moral implications of the Industrial Revolution while profiling Sally's growing love for Frederick. At the end of the novel, Frederick is killed, and Sally announces that she is pregnant with his child. Writing in *School Librarian,* Dennis Hamley called *The Shadow in the Plate* a "super read and a story to mull over afterwards for a significance which belies its outward form," while Michael Cart in *School Library Journal* noted that Pullman "once again demonstrates his mastery of atmosphere and style." Peter Hollindale claimed in *British Book News Children's Books* that the work "could mystify and disturb young children who may have liked the earlier one" and noted that it "is part of a children's trilogy, not *Bleak House.*" However, *Junior Bookshelf* contributor Marcus Crouch concluded that

Shadow "is the kind of tale in which the reader willingly suspends critical judgement in favour of a wholehearted 'good read.'"

In the third volume of the "Sally Lockhart" series, *The Tiger in the Well,* Sally is a successful tycoon as well as a single mother with a two-year-old daughter, Harriet. When Sally receives a court summons informing her that she is being sued for divorce by a man she does not know, the heroine is faced with the prospect of losing her daughter and her property. After her court date, Sally—who has lost custody of Harriet as well as her home and her job—disappears into the Jewish ghetto of London's East End in order to find out who is behind the ruse. Pullman outlines Sally's developing social conscience through her experiences, which expose her to an anti-Semitic campaign, while drawing parallels between her treatment and that of the ghetto residents. Writing in *Voice of Youth Advocates,* Joanne Johnson noted that, as in his previous books in the series, Pullman "has recreated nineteenth-century London in good detail. His portrayal of the chauvinism rampant in British law during that time is a lesson to all." Marcus Crouch commented in *Junior Bookshelf:* "Not for the first time in the sequence, but with greater relevance, the name of Dickens comes to mind." The critic concluded that, like its predecessors, *The Tiger in the Well* "is compulsively readable. Unlike them the strong action runs parallel with sound social observations." Writing in *Books for Keeps,* Geoff Fox commented that the book "tastes delicious like the Penny Dreadfuls beloved of one of the novel's characters. . . . At another level, the book is a social document with the detail of Mayhew and the compassion of Dickens."

The final volume of the "Sally Lockhart" series, *The Tin Princess,* takes place in Central Europe rather than in Victorian London. A swashbuckling adventure set in the tiny kingdom of Razkavia, which lies between Germany and Austria, the novel introduces two new protagonists, Cockney Adelaide, a former prostitute featured in *The Ruby in the Smoke* who is now queen of Razkavia, and her friend and translator, Becky Winter. During the course of the story, Adelaide and Becky become caught up in political intrigue and romance, and Sally Lockhart makes a cameo appearance. Writing in *Booklist,* Ilene Cooper noted that the author's passion for details "gets in the way" and that "too many names and places and plot twists" confuse the readers; however, the critic concluded, fans of Pullman's writing "should find much to enjoy here." Roger Sutton in the *Bulletin of the Center for Children's Books* commented in a similar vein, noting that the plot "is far too complicated for its own good" but concluded that while Pullman "appreciates the excesses of Victorian melodrama he is never seduced by them."

With the popular and critical reaction to "His Dark Materials," a series named for a phrase from John Milton's *Paradise Lost,* Pullman became an international phenomenon. Originally envisioned as a trilogy, the "His Dark Materials" series has expanded to more volumes and has been optioned for film. It is one of those rare publishing successes that finds as many readers among adults as it does among children and is particularly popular with college students—and their professors, who sometimes use it in classes on how to write children's literature. "The books can obviously be read at more than one level," observed John Rowe Townsend in *Horn Book.* "To younger readers they offer narratives of nonstop excitement with attractive young central characters. Adolescents and adults, putting more experience into their reading, should be able to draw more out. There are features of 'His Dark Materials' that will give older readers a great deal to think about." The chief elements that Pullman asks his older readers to ponder are no less than the nature of God, Satan, and the power that organized religion exerts on the independent mind. Townsend concluded: "This [work] has weight and richness, much that is absorbing and perceptive, and ample food for serious thought. It has flaws; but a large, ambitious work with flaws can be more rewarding than a cabined and confined perfection and 'saying something truthful and realistic about human nature' is surely what all fiction, including fantasy, should be trying to do."

In the first volume, which was published in the United Kingdom in 1995 as *Northern Lights* and in the United States in 1996 as *The Golden Compass,* Pullman describes an alternate world—parallel to our own but featuring technology from a hundred years ago as well as inventions from the future and the recent past—in which humans and daemons in animal form are tied with emotional bonds that if broken cause considerable damage, even death. Lyra, a young orphan girl with the skills of a natural leader, lives with her daemon Pantalaimon at Oxford. After children around the country begin disappearing and her uncle Lord Asriel is imprisoned during an expedition to the Arctic,

Lyra embarks on a journey North with an alethiometer, a soothsaying instrument that looks like a golden compass. There she discovers that the youngsters are being held in a scientific experimental station where they are subjected to operations to separate them from their daemons. As the story progresses, Pullman discloses that Lyra, the key figure in an ancient prophecy, is destined to save her world and to move into another universe. Writing in the *Times Educational Supplement* about *Northern Lights,* Jan Mark noted: "Never did anything so boldly flout the usual protective mimicry of the teen read. This novel really does discuss the uniqueness of humanity—the fact of the soul." Julia Eccleshare commented in *Books for Keeps:* "The weaving together of story and morality is what makes *Northern Lights* such an exceptional book. Never for a moment does the story lose ground in the message it carries." Writing in *Horn Book* about the U.S. edition, Ann A. Flowers called *The Golden Compass* an "extraordinary, compelling fantasy. . . . Touching, exciting, and mysterious by turns, this is a splendid work." Although Jane Langton claimed in the *New York Times Book Review* that the novel does not achieve the stature of *The Lord of the Rings, A Wizard of Earthsea,* or *The Mouse and His Child,* the critic concluded that "it is still very grand indeed. There is scene after scene of power and beauty."

While writing *Northern Lights/The Golden Compass,* Pullman knew that he was creating a significant work. He told Julie C. Boehning of *Library Journal,* "I felt as if everything I'd read, written, and done in my whole life had been in preparation for this book." In 1996, *Northern Lights* was awarded the Carnegie Medal, Great Britain's highest literary award specifically for children's literature.

In the next novel in the series, *The Subtle Knife,* Lyra meets Will Parry, a boy from Oxford who escapes into an alternative city after killing a man. Like Lyra, Will is destined to help save the universe from destruction; in addition, he possesses a counterpart to her golden compass, a knife that can cut through anything—even the borders between worlds. While Lyra and Will search for Dust and for Will's explorer father, it becomes evident that Lord Asriel, Lyra's guardian from the first book, is preparing to re-stage the revolt of the angels against God and that Lyra has been chosen to be the new Eve. *Horn Book* critic Ann A. Flowers commented that Pullman "offered an exceptional romantic fantasy in *The Golden Compass,* but

The Subtle Knife adds a mythic dimension that inevitably demands even greater things from the finale." Sally Estes in *Booklist* noted, "Often the middle book in a trilogy is the weakest; such is not the case here." Estes called *The Subtle Knife* a "resoundingly successful sequel." Writing in *Voice of Youth Advocates* about both *The Subtle Knife* and its predecessor, Jennifer Fakolt commented that these volumes "are, simply, magnificent. Pullman has the power of a master fantasist. He imbues an age-old classical struggle with a new mythic vision, the depth and realization of which are staggering." Fakolt concluded that the "two titles stand in equal company with the works of J. R. R. Tolkien and C. S. Lewis."

In an interview with Julia Eccleshare in *Books for Keeps,* Pullman discussed the background of "His Dark Materials": "What I really wanted to do was *Paradise Lost* in 1,200 pages. From the beginning I knew the shape of the story. It's the story of The Fall which is the story of how what some would call sin, but I would call consciousness, comes to us. The more I thought about it the clearer it became. It fell naturally into three parts. Though it's long, I've never been in danger of getting lost because the central strand is so simple." Pullman's central thrust is to reveal the Biblical God as an elderly, powerless figurehead, manipulated by a head angel named Metatron, who is power-hungry and autocratic in the extreme. Lord Asriel and his wife, Mrs. Coulter—both ambiguous figures capable of both good and evil—oppose Metatron and the powers of Heaven. It is Lyra and Will, and their various fantastic helpers, who finally bring about, in Volume Three, *The Amber Spyglass,* literally the death of God.

Published to much anticipation in 2000, *The Amber Spyglass* is perhaps the most successful of the first three "His Dark Materials" novels. It won the Whitbread Award over the shortlisted adult novels, biographies, and nonfiction published in Great Britain in 2000 and prompted an author tour of the United States as well. The novel culminates with Will and Lyra descending into the realm of death and returning to life again, reversing the loss of Dust from the universe, and—by expressing their love for one another—putting an end to the iron autocracy led by Metatron and the demented deity. "The witches and wizards in the 'Harry Potter' books will seem like cartoon characters compared with those in Pullman's religious pantheon," declared Ilene Cooper in *Booklist.* "The first two books

in the series exposed the Church as corrupt, bigoted, and evil. Now Pullman takes on Heaven itself. . . . 'His Dark Materials' has taken readers on a wild, magnificent ride that, in its totality, represents an astounding achievement." Eva Mitnick in *School Library Journal* found the message in *The Amber Spyglass* "clear and exhilarating," adding that the book offers "a subtle and complex treatment of the eternal battle between good and evil."

In interviews, Pullman has maintained that he used the vehicle of fantasy in "His Dark Materials" to make starkly realistic points about human nature. He told *School Library Journal:* "When I found myself writing this book, what I wanted to do was to use the apparatus of fantasy in order to do what writers of realism are more typically interested in doing, namely, to explore this business about being a human being—what it feels like and what it's like, what it means for us to grow up, to pass away from our childhood, to suffer, to learn, to grow, to develop, to die, and so on. And that's what I mean by saying that it's not really a work of fantasy. It's as realistic as I could make it."

Pullman has also had success with his stand-alone titles for readers of various ages. For example, *How to Be Cool,* a humorous satire published in 1987 in which a group of teens expose a government agency that decides which fashions will be hip, was called "a perfect gift for iconoclastic teenagers" by Peter Hollindale of *British Book News Children's Supplement; How to Be Cool* was made into a television program by Granada-TV in 1988. *The Broken Bridge,* a young adult novel published in 1990, is considered a major departure for its author. The story features Ginny Howard, a sixteen-year-old Haitian/English girl living with her single father in a small Welsh town. Anxious to begin her career as a painter, Ginny learns that she is illegitimate, that she has a half-brother, and that her mother, whom she assumed was dead, is actually alive. Ginny meets this parent—who tells her that she is a painter, not a mother—and learns about her father's abused childhood, while evaluating her own heritage, character, and direction. Writing in the *New York Times Book Review,* Michael Dorris said, "It's a credit to the storytelling skill of Philip Pullman that this contemporary novel succeeds as well as it does. As the plot tumbles forward, . . . the writing remains fresh, the settings original and the central characters compelling." Nancy Vasilakis in *Horn Book* praised Pullman for "skillfully manipulating the conventions of the mystery and the problem novel," while a critic in *Publishers Weekly* saw "the emotional truths that Pullman reveals" as being "so heartfelt and raw that they hardly read like fiction."

Pullman returned to nineteenth-century London for the setting of his "New Cut Gang" series, comic mysteries for middle graders that feature a gang of urchins in the 1890s. In a review of the first book in the series, *Thunderbolt's Waxworks,* D. A Young in *Junior Bookshelf* commented that Pullman "creates a convincing picture of his chosen time and place with the lightest of touches," while Jan Mark, reviewing the same title in *Carousel,* noted that the narrative introduces "an extraordinary vocabulary of scientific terms and nineteenth-century slang. You get very educated without noticing it." Pullman has also written works that reflect his fascination with folktale and myth. In *The Firework-Maker's Daughter,* a book that won the Smarties Award in 1996, the author describes how Lila, the daughter of a fireworks maker who is in the final stages of apprenticeship, goes on a quest with Hamlet, a talking white elephant that belongs to the king of her country, and Chulak, the elephant's keeper. Their journey takes them to the lair of the Fire-fiend, a figure who holds the key to firework making. In the process, Lila discovers herself. A critic in *Reading Time* said, "This is the stuff of myths. . . . It is an exciting story, not only for its own sake but for the other layer of meaning which lurks beneath the surface." Writing in *Magpies,* Rayma Turton commented, "Lila is all a feminist could ask for," and concluded that *The Firework-Maker's Daughter* is "the work of a master storyteller."

Clockwork, or All Wound Up, a short novel with echoes of *Faust* and the ballet *Coppelia,* is noted for weaving an examination of the process of storytelling with a spine-tingling tale. The book describes how Fritz, a talented tale-spinner, and Karl, a clockmaker's apprentice who has failed to complete his latest assignment, a clockwork child, are joined with the subject of one of Fritz's stories, Dr. Kalmerius, a clockmaker thought to have connections with the Devil. Writing in *School Librarian,* Chris Routh called *Clockwork* "a fantastic and spine-chilling tale," adding that it "begs to be read in one sitting (who could bear to put it down?)." The critic concluded by asking, "Who said the art of storytelling is dead?" George Hunt of *Books for Keeps* described the book as a "fascinating meditation on the intricate machinations of narrative," and simultaneously "a funny, frighten-

ing, and moving story." Writing in *Carousel,* Adèle Geras concluded, "This story could not be more modern, yet it has the weight and poetry of the best folktales. Not to be missed on any account."

In *I Was a Rat!,* a scruffy little boy tries to convince people that he actually is a rat. By some trick of magic he was turned into a boy in order to accompany a woman to a ball—and then, at the stroke of midnight, he was playing when he should have been transformed back into a rat. Now he seeks help wherever he can find it—from the tabloid press, from his adoptive parents, and from the new princess herself, who he remembers as his old friend Mary Jane. The story turns the *Cinderella* fairy tale on its head in a humorous way but also manages to make points about modern society and the way people respond to unconventional requests. A *Horn Book* reviewer described *I Was a Rat!* as a "playful spoofing of sensational news stories, mob mentality, and the royal family." In a starred review of the work, *School Library Journal* correspondent Connie Tyrrell Burns noted that, while Pullman is having fun here, he still "leaves readers with some thought-provoking ideas."

Pullman once explained in *SAAS:* "I am first and foremost a storyteller. In whatever form I write—whether it's the novel, or the screenplay, or the stage play, or even if I tell stories (as I sometimes do)—I am always the servant of the story that has chosen me to tell it and I have to discover the best way of doing that. I believe there's a pure line that goes through every story and the more closely the telling approaches that pure line, the better the story will be. . . . The story must tell me." When asked by Kit Alderdice in *Publishers Weekly* what he finds most satisfying about his career, Pullman responded, "The fundamental thing that I do find important and gratifying is that I simply have the time—never as much time as I would like—but I simply have the time to sit here and enjoy the company of my stories and my characters. That's an enormous pleasure, and a great privilege." He added in *SAAS,* "Sometimes I can hardly believe my luck."

BIOGRAPHICAL AND CRITICAL SOURCES:

BOOKS

Children's Literature Review, Volume 20, Gale, 1990, pp. 185-188.
Gallo, Donald, editor, *Speaking for Ourselves, Too,* National Council of Teachers of English, 1993.

Silvey, Anita, editor, *Children's Books and Their Creators,* Houghton Mifflin (Boston, MA), 1995, p. 544.

Something about the Author Autobiography Series, Volume 17, Gale (Detroit, MI), pp. 297-312.

Squires, Claire, *Philip Pullman's "His Dark Materials" Trilogy: A Reader's Guide,* Continuum (New York, NY), 2003.

Twentieth-Century Young Adult Writers, St. James Press (Detroit, MI), 1994, pp. 543-544.

PERIODICALS

Book, September, 2000, Jennifer D'Anastasio and Kathleen Odean, "Built to Last," p. 88; November-December, 2002, Anna Weinberg, "Are You There, God? It's Me, Philip Pullman," p. 11.

Booklist, February 15, 1994, Ilene Cooper, review of *The Tin Princess,* p. 1075; July, 1997, Sally Estes, review of *The Subtle Knife,* p. 1818; October 1, 2000, Ilene Cooper, "Darkness Visible—Philip Pullman's Amber Spyglass," p. 354.

Bookseller, June 29, 2001, Caroline Sylge, "Performing Books," p. 8.

Books for Keeps, May, 1992, Geoff Fox, "Philip Pullman," p. 25; September, 1996, Julia Eccleshare, "Northern Lights and Christmas Miracles," p. 15; March, 1997, George Hunt, review of *Clockwork, or All Wound Up,* p. 25.

British Book News Children's Books, March, 1986, Peter Hollindale, review of *The Ruby in the Smoke,* pp. 33-34; December, 1986, Peter Hollindale, review of *The Shadow in the Plate,* pp. 30-31; March, 1988, Peter Hollindale, review of *How to Be Cool,* p. 30.

Bulletin of the Center for Children's Books, February, 1994, Roger Sutton, review of *The Tin Princess,* pp. 199-200.

Carousel, spring, 1997, Adèle Geras, review of *Clockwork, or All Wound Up,* p. 19; spring, 1997, Jan Mark, review of *Thunderbolt's Waxworks,* p. 19.

Commonweal, November 17, 2000, Daria Donnelly, "Big Questions for Small Readers," p. 23.

Horn Book, March-April, 1992, Nancy Vasilakis, review of *The Broken Bridge,* p. 211; July-August, 1996, Ann A. Flowers, review of *The Golden Compass,* pp. 464-465; September-October, 1997, Ann A. Flowers, review of *The Subtle Knife,* pp. 578-579; January, 2000, review of *I Was a Rat!,* p. 82; July-August, 2002, John Rowe Townsend, "Paradise Reshaped," p. 415.

Junior Bookshelf, April, 1982, R. Baines, review of *Ancient Civilizations,* p. 75; December, 1986, Marcus Crouch, review of *The Shadow in the Plate,* pp. 229-230; June, 1991, Marcus Crouch, review of *The Tiger in the Well,* p. 127; December, 1994, D. A. Young, review of *Thunderbolt's Waxworks,* pp. 231-232; November, 2000, Gregory Maguire, review of *The Amber Spyglass,* p. 735.

Library Journal, February 15, 1996, Julie C. Boehning, "Philip Pullman's Paradise," p. 175.

Magpies, May, 1997, Rayma Turton, review of *The Firework-Maker's Daughter,* p. 35.

National Review, March 25, 2002, Andrew Stuttaford, "Sunday School for Atheists," p. 56.

New Statesman, December 3, 1982, Charles Fox, "Once and Future Image," pp. 21-22; October 30, 2000, Amanda Craig, "Burning Dazzle," p. 53.

Newsweek, October 30, 2000, "Pullman's Progress," p. 80.

New York Times Book Review, May 17, 1992, Michael Dorris, "Galloping Adolescence," p. 24; May 19, 1996, Jane Langton, "What Is Dust?," p. 34.

Publishers Weekly, January 1, 1992, review of *The Broken Bridge,* p. 56; May 30, 1994, Kit Alderdice, "In the Studio with Philip Pullman," pp. 24-25; September 25, 2000, review of *The Amber Spyglass,* p. 119; September 25, 2000, Kit Alderdice, "PW Talks with Philip Pullman," p. 119; December 18, 2000, Shannon Maughan, "Whose Dark Materials?," p. 25.

Reading Time, May, 1997, review of *The Firework-Maker's Daughter,* p. 30.

School Librarian, June, 1986, David Churchill, review of *The Ruby in the Smoke,* p. 174; December, 1986, Dennis Hamley, review of *The Shadow in the Plate,* p. 368; November, 1990, Derek Paget, review of *Frankenstein,* p. 157; May, 1997, Chris Routh, review of *Clockwork, or All Wound Up,* p. 90.

School Library Journal, May, 1988, Michael Cart, review of *Shadow in the North,* p. 112; March, 2000, Connie Tyrrell Burns, review of *I Was a Rat!,* p. 241; October, 2000, Eva Mitnick, review of *The Amber Spyglass,* p. 170.

Times Educational Supplement, July 21, 1995, Jan Mark, review of *Northern Lights,* p. 23.

Voice of Youth Advocates, October, 1987, Brooke L. Dillon, review of *The Ruby in the Smoke,* p. 206; December, 1990, Joanne Johnson, review of *The Tiger in the Well,* p. 288; June, 1998, Jennifer Fakolt, review of *The Golden Compass* and *The Subtle Knife,* p. 133.

R

RANDALL, Monica 1944-

PERSONAL: Born March 14, 1944, in Oyster Bay, NY. *Education:* Attended Fashion Institute of Technology, 1964, New York University, 1965, and C.W. Post College of Long Island University, 1966. *Religion:* Unitarian-Universalist.

ADDRESSES: Home and office—P.O. Box 75, Oyster Bay, NY 11771. *Agent*—Connie Clausen, Connie Clausen Associates, 250 East 87th St., New York, NY 10028.

CAREER: Author, photographer, lecturer, historic preservationist, and location scout. President of Locations, Inc., 1968-80; director of North Shore Preservation Society, beginning 1980. *Exhibitions:* Randall's photographs have been displayed at the Cooper-Hewitt Museum, New York, NY, and are in the permanent collection of the Metropolitan Museum of Art, New York, NY.

MEMBER: International Platform Association, Society for the Preservation of Long Island Antiquities.

WRITINGS:

Mansions of Long Island's Gold Coast, Hastings House (New York, NY), 1979, revised edition, Rizzoli International Publications (New York, NY), 2003.
Phantoms of the Hudson Valley: The Glorious Estates of a Lost Era, Overlook Press (Woodstock, NY), 1995.

Winfield: Living in the Shadow of the Woolworths, St. Martin's Press/Thomas Dunne (New York, NY), 2003.

Contributor to magazines and newspapers, including *Newsday.*

SIDELIGHTS: Monica Randall is best known for her books that document the architectural heritage of Long Island's Gold Coast era. She has also extensively researched the family histories of those who built some of the grandest homes on Long Island. Her *Mansions of Long Island's Gold Coast* and *Winfield: Living in the Shadow of the Woolworths* are testimonials to those grand houses built mostly in the early twentieth century. Additionally, Randall has turned her focus to some of the grand old homes of New York's Hudson River Valley in another photo-journalistic essay, *Phantoms of the Hudson Valley: The Glorious Estates of a Lost Era.* Randall's interest in the great houses "isn't just a passion," according to *Booklist*'s Michelle Kaske; "it has been a life's work."

Randall, who grew up on Long Island's North Shore, formed an early love for the mansions that even in the 1950s were becoming derelict and waiting for demolition. As teenagers, she and her two sisters managed to get into some of these old houses before they were destroyed and were able to save some of the artifacts of a disappearing time. Soon she began photographing these same estates and then started a business as a location finder for movies and advertising using these same locales as backdrop. Her first book, *Mansions of Long Island's Gold Coast,* appeared in 1979; a revised edition came out in 2003. The book is both a photographic record of the mansions as well as a history of the families that built them.

Randall's *Phantoms of the Hudson Valley* documents some of the great mansions built between New York City and Albany, mostly in the nineteenth century. Many of these near-castles, such as Wyndcliff, built by Elizabeth Schermerhorn Jones, lie in ruins awaiting destruction; others are in private hands; and still others have been renovated and are open to the public. Wyndcliff, built in 1852, is indicative of what has befallen many of these enormous structures, built by the wealthy of New York as country seats. Its property has been sold off to developers over the years while it has remained empty for decades. Put on the real estate market for a few hundred thousand dollars, it is expected to be razed by new owners and redeveloped. When built, it was so opulent as to give rise to the saying, "Keeping up with the Joneses." Reviewing Randall's book in the *New York Times Book Review,* Robert R. Harris felt that Randall manages to "capture the haunting atmosphere of great wealth's trappings gone to seed." Harris also commented that while the author/photographer includes "entertaining lore along with her pictures," she is also a "little too receptive to tales of ghosts walking the riverbanks."

A predilection for ghosts and paranormal events is even more evident in Randall's 2003 book *Winfield,* a personal history of the mansion built by five-and-dime owner F. W. Woolworth. Built for nine million dollars in the early twentieth century, Winfield is among the most fantastic of the mansions built along the North Shore of Long Island, the so-called Gold Coast. Woolworth, a staunch believer in the occult and time travel, lived in his mansion only two years before his death in 1919. The home stayed in the Woolworth family for another decade and then was sold to a nephew of R. J. Reynolds, the tobacco baron. It subsequently went through several other ownerships; in the late 1970s Randall, taken with the mansion from the time she was a child, lived there herself and experienced the charm and mystery of the house firsthand. In her book, Randall investigates many of the tales that have developed around the house, specifically those dealing with séances, strange sounds heard in the distant rooms, and other haunting tales. "'This book is a much bigger story than chasing ghosts,'" Randall told N. C. Maisak in the *New York Times.*

A contributor for *Publishers Weekly* agreed with Randall, noting that the author "achieves an ideal balance between the bizarre and the compelling." Not all reviewers appreciated the blend of memoir and architectural history, however. Elaine Machleder, writing in *Library Journal,* for example, found it to be a "confused paranormal fantasy based on limited history," and a contributor for *Kirkus Reviews* called the book an "odd memoir" whose "plausibility isn't helped by purple prose." *Booklist'*s Kaske, on the other hand, felt that the fans of writer Jane Eyre "will love this memoir laced with romance and gothic atmosphere."

BIOGRAPHICAL AND CRITICAL SOURCES:

PERIODICALS

Booklist, April 15, 2003, Michelle Kaske, review of *Winfield: Living in the Shadow of the Woolworths,* p. 1440.
Kirkus Reviews, February 1, 2003, review of *Winfield,* p. 216.
Library Journal, February 15, 2003, Elaine Machleder, review of *Winfield,* p. 152.
New York Times, September 14, 2003, N. C. Maisak, "Nickels and Dimes Built This Mansion," p. LI16.
New York Times Book Review, May 25, 1997, Robert R. Harris, review of *Phantoms of the Hudson Valley: The Glorious Estates of a Lost Era,* p. 17.
Publishers Weekly, March 17, 2003, review of *Winfield,* p. 62.*

*   *   *

REGALIA, Nanzi
See COLLINS, Nancy A(verill)

*   *   *

ROESKE, Paulette 1945-

PERSONAL: Surname is pronounced "*Res*-key"; born September 30, 1945, in Bloomington, IL; daughter of Paul Henry Rudolph (a pharmacist and store manager) and Helen Virginia (Reise) Roeske; married John Terrence Becker, June 17, 1967 (divorced, 1978); married Robert L. Reid, June 14, 1999; children: Adrienne Lee. *Education:* University of Iowa, B.A., 1967;

Paulette Roeske

Northwestern University, M.A., 1968; Warren Wilson College, M.F.A., 1982. *Hobbies and other interests:* Tae kwondo (first-degree black belt), dressage.

ADDRESSES: Home—7525 Syls Dr., Evansville, IN 47712. *Office*—University of Southern Indiana, School of Liberal Arts, Department of English, 8600 University Blvd., Evansville, IN 47712-3596. *E-mail*—proeske@usi.edu; pauletteroeske@aol.com.

CAREER: Educator, author, and editor. Harper High School, Chicago, IL, English teacher, 1968-69; College of Lake County, Grayslake, IL, professor of English, 1969-2001, Reading Series founder and director, 1983-2001; *Willow Review,* founder and editor, 1983—; Christ Church College, Canterbury, England, teacher, 1995; University of Southern Indiana, Evansville, professor of creative writing, 2002-2003. School of the Art Institute of Chicago, member of board of directors of Poetry Center of Chicago (vice president, 1987-92; program committee chair, 1992-98; Ragdale Foundation, member of selection committee, 1989-2002; Chicago Chapter of the American Composers Forum, member of advisory committee,

1999—; Harlaxton College, Grantham, England, poet-in-residence, 2003; judge of poetry competitions; workshop leader; gives readings from her works.

MEMBER: Academy of American Poets, Associated Writing Programs, Modern Language Association, Modern Poetry Association, Poetry Society of America, Poets and Writers, PEN Midwest Associates, PEN International, Society of Midland Authors, Illinois Writers, Inc.

AWARDS, HONORS: Poets and Patrons Award for Free Verse, 1978; Jo-Anne Hirschfield Memorial Poetry Award, Evanston Library, 1979, for "Dream of Trains"; Illinois Arts Council, Literary Awards, 1981, 1989, 1990, fellowship, 1989; winner of Chicago Cultural Center Poetry Competitions, 1983, for "Shortcut through the Park" and "Waiting for This," and 1989, for "Sestina: Her Life with Chopin"; New Poetry Broadsides Award, 1983, for "Waiting for This"; Pushcart Prize nominations, 1986, for poems in *Indiana Review,* and 1988; award from *South Coast Poetry Journal,* 1988; Goodman Award, Thorntree Press, 1989; resident, Ragdale Foundation, 1990, 1991, 1992, 1995; first place award, Chester H. Jones Foundation National Poetry Competition, 1990; Teaching Excellence Award, National Institute for Staff and Organizational Development, 1991; first place award, poetry chapbook competition, Illinois Writers, Inc., 1992, for *The Body Can Ascend No Higher;* fellow of National Endowment for the Humanities at the Chinese Culture and Civilization Institute, 1993; Fulbright fellow, 1994; Japan Foundation fellow, 1995; Carl Sandburg Award, 1996, for *Divine Attention;* Three Oaks Prize in Fiction, Story Line Press, 2002, for *Bridge of Sighs: A Novella and Stories.*

WRITINGS:

Breathing under Water (poems), Stormline Press (Urbana, IL), 1988.
The Body Can Ascend No Higher (poetry chapbook), Illinois Writers (Normal, IL), 1992.
Divine Attention (poems), Louisiana State University Press (Baton Rouge, LA), 1995.
Anvil, Clock & Last (poems), Louisiana State University Press (Baton Rouge, LA), 2001.
Bridge of Sighs: A Novella and Stories (fiction), Story Line Press (Ashland, OR), 2002.

Work represented in anthologies, including *The Anthology of Magazine Verse and Yearbook of Contemporary American Poetry,* edited by Alan F. Pater, Monitor (Beverly Hills, CA), 1983; *Woman Poet: The Midwest,* edited by Elaine Dallman, Women-in-Literature, Inc. (Reno, NV), 1985; *Benchmark: Anthology of Contemporary Poetry in Illinois,* edited by James McGowan and Lynn DeVore, University of Illinois Press (Urbana, IL), 1988; *The Yellow Shoe Poets: Selected Poems 1964-1999,* edited by George Garrett, Louisiana State University Press (Baton Rouge, LA), 1999; *Essential Love: Poems about Mothers and Fathers, Daughters and Sons,* edited by Ginny Lowe Connors, Poetworks/Grayson Books (West Hartford, CT), 2000; *Illinois Voices: An Anthology of Twentieth-Century Poetry,* edited by Kevin Stein and G. E. Murray, University of Illinois Press (Urbana, IL), 2001; *Vespers: Contemporary Poems of Religion and Spirituality,* edited by Virgil Suárez and Ryan G. Van Cleave, University of Iowa Press (Iowa City, IA), 2003; and *Proposing on the Brooklyn Bridge: Poems about Marriage,* edited by Ginny Lowe Connors, Poetworks/Grayson Books (West Hartford, CT), 2003. Contributor of dozens of poems to periodicals, including *Poetry, Poetry Northwest, Ascent, Georgia Review, Virginia Quarterly, Chariton Review, Threepenny Review, Indiana Review, Chicago Review, Hawaii Review, JAMA: The Journal of the American Medical Association, Short Fiction Review,* and *Other Voices.* Contributor of stories to periodicals, such as *Glimmer Train, Louisiana Literature, Short Fiction Review, Short Story Review, Other Voices,* and others. Work represented in numerous anthologies, including *Sarajevo Anthology,* edited by John Babbitt, Carolyn Feucht, and Andie Stabler, Elgin College (Elgin, IL), 1993; *Crossing Boundaries,* edited by Susan J. Bandy and Anne S. Darden, Human Kinetics (Champaign, IL), 1999; *The Yellow Shoe Poets: Selected Poems 1964-1999,* edited by George Garrett, Louisiana State University Press (Baton Rouge), 1999; *Knowing Stones: Poems of Exotic Places* edited by Maureen Tolman Flannery, JOhn Gordon Blake Publisher, Inc., 2000; *Essential Love,* edited by Ginny Connors, Poetworks (West Hartford, CT), 2000; *Illinois Voices: An Anthology of Contemporary Poetry from Illinois,* edited by G. E. Murray and Kevin Stein, University of Illinois Press (Urbana, IL), 2001; *Vespers: Religion & Spirituality in Twenty-first Century America,* edited by Virgil Suarez and Ryan G. Van Cleave, University of Iowa Press (Iowa City, Iowa), 2003; *Proposing on the Brooklyn Bridge: Poems about Marriage,* edited by Ginny Lowe Connors, Poetworks (West Hartford, CT), 2003; *Where We Live: Illinois Poets* (e-book) edited by Kathleen Kirk,

greatunpublished.com, 2003; *Crude: Poems at the End of the Age of Oil,* edited by Jennifer Bosveld, Pudding House Press (Johnstown, OH) in press.

SIDELIGHTS: Paulette Roeske once told *CA:* "I settled on the notion of writing poems in 1978, at age thirty-three, when it occurred to me, as the divorced mother of a five-year-old daughter, that I could improve my lot by completing graduate work that would permit advancement on the salary scale at the College of Lake County, where I had been teaching freshman composition to dazed Vietnam veterans. My less than 'anything-for-art's-sake' motive catapulted me from column A to column E, disproving Robert Frost's maxim, 'Never write a poem to pay a bill, because you won't.'

"The following year, "Dream of Trains," one of my first poems, was selected by Lisel Mueller to tie for first place in the Evanston Library's first annual Jo-Anne Hirschfield Memorial Poetry Competition. Lisel would later become my first teacher and a lifelong friend, who would continue to offer her sure hand, her cool wisdom and clarity in all matters, both on and off the page. These many years later, she is the one I imagine looking over my shoulder as I write.

"Frost, of course, was right, but by the time I learned that, I was already being paid in spiritual currency, and it was too late to turn back.

"I came to writing through reading, a habit cultivated in childhood as an escape from the noise of the family. The only closed door ever respected was the bathroom door, so it was there my life as a reader began. After childhood's typical fare, I turned to autobiography—these even before Nancy Drew and Cherry Ames, those stalwart young women who never learned the extent of their limitations, and long before *Gone with the Wind,* which I read at an age young enough to believe it was pornographic, although that was not a word I knew.

"On the bottom shelf in the grade school library, the autobiographies, arranged alphabetically, occupied several running feet. The books were all the same length, about a hundred pages, I should imagine, with large, uniform print that gave the impression of reading one multivolume story with a large cast of characters. I began with Clara Barton and, even before I reached Benjamin Franklin, the end of the shelf reared up like a spooked horse, and beyond it, what? The end.

"Always an unhappy child, I had finally found something I liked. The tight fist of panic clenched in my stomach at the thought of reading the last word in the last book at the end of that shelf. Looking back, I think my fear that the story would end was my childhood apprehension of mortality.

"My fascination with stories directed me through undergraduate and graduate school as an English major whose blissful task it was to read a book a week for each of five literature courses that comprised my schedule by the time I was a junior. I loved everything I read, but preferred the Russian novels—for their length, still hoping, I suppose, to stave off the end.

"When I began to write, my poems, in contrast, were short lyrics with no story at all. Only at Goddard College in my work with Stephen Dobyns did I come to study his poems and realize the narrative potential in my own subjects. This was the first development in my writing. The result was the long narratives in *Divine Attention,* which Li-Young Lee referred to as 'an autobiographical novel.'"

Divine Attention won the Carl Sandburg Award and much praise from critics. Each poem relates very human characters with real experiences. Roeske writes about ordinary struggles and problems, but transcends the ordinary to a world of imagination and art. *Anvil, Clock, & Last* features poems that focus on the ways pieces of life fit together. Much like the precise fittings of a clock, Roeske's poetry shows how all things in life are somehow connected. Whether she is writing about pain, loss, or love, Roeske is said to capture human emotions clearly and gracefully.

In Roeske's next work, *Bridge of Sighs: A Novella and Stories,* the author moves from poetry to prose. The central story in the collection is the novella titled *The Ecstasy of Magda Brummel.* Looking to escape from a past filled with sadness and loss, Magda embarks on a trip through Italy with her friend Harry. As the story progresses, Magda tries to revive herself and begin anew. Each of the short stories supports a running theme of "relationships and the way conflagrations in the past can scorch the present," wrote a *Kirkus Reviews* contributor. Though the *Kirkus Reviews* critic initially found *Bridge of Sighs* "filled with emotional cripples," upon further reflection the critic claimed, "but when all is done, her people don't seem a whole lot different from the rest of us." Most critics thought that Roeske deftly captures the thoughts, emotions, and struggles in her characters' relationships while maintaining the precision of her writing. *Booklist*'s Whitney Scott praised, "Roeske's writing is strong throughout, easily keeping one's interest."

BIOGRAPHICAL AND CRITICAL SOURCES:

PERIODICALS

Booklist, October 15, 2002, Whitney Scott, review of *Bridge of Sighs: A Novella and Stories,* p. 389.
Chicago Tribune, May 15, 1995.
Kirkus Reviews, September 15, 2002, review of *Bridge of Sighs,* p. 1349.

ONLINE

Paulette Roeske Web site, http://web.usi.edu/proeske/ (April 14, 2004).
Society of Midland Authors Web site, http://www.midlandauthors.com/roeske.html/ (April 14, 2004), "Paulette Roeske," biography and comments.

*   *   *

RUURS, Margriet 1952-

PERSONAL: Born December 2, 1952, in the Netherlands; daughter of H. Bodbyl and W. Bodbyl-Schut; married Kees Ruurs (a parks and recreation manager), 1972; children: Alexander, Arnout. *Education:* Simon Fraser University, graduate study. *Hobbies and other interests:* Gardening, travel, hiking, camping, family activities.

ADDRESSES: Home—4282 Poplar Dr., Armstrong, British Columbia V0E 1B6, Canada; fax: 780-790-0011. *E-mail*—ruurs@shaw.ca.

Margriet Ruurs

CAREER: Teacher of creative writing enrichment and presenter of writing workshops for children in various schools and by e-mail; workshop presenter at Okanagan University College in British Columbia, Canada. Speaker at children's literature and technology conferences.

AWARDS, HONORS: Honor title selection in "Tellable" stories for ages 4-7 category, *Storytelling World Awards*, International Reading Association, 1997, and "Our Choice Catalogue" selection, Canadian Children's Book Centre, both for *Emma's Eggs;* "Our Choice Catalogue" selections for *A Mountain Alphabet* and *Emma's Eggs;* White Raven selection for *A Pacific Alphabet.*

WRITINGS:

Apenkinderen, Leopold (Netherlands), 1982.

(Translator into Dutch) Judith Viorst, *Alexander and the Terrible, Horrible, No Good, Very Bad Day,* Leopold (Netherlands), 1985.

Fireweed (picture book), illustrated by Roberta Mebs, Burns & Morton (Whitehorse, Yukon, Canada), 1986.

Big Little Dog, illustrated by Marc Houde, Penumbra (Waterloo, Ontario, Canada), 1992.

The R.C.M.P (nonfiction), KGR Learning Aides (Netherlands), 1992.

On the Write Track! A Guide to Writing, Illustrating, and Publishing Stories (adult), Pacific Educational Press (Vancouver, British Columbia, Canada), 1993.

A Mountain Alphabet (picture book), illustrated by Andrew Kiss, Tundra Books (New York, NY), 1996.

Emma's Eggs (picture book), illustrated by Barbara Spurll, Stoddart Kids (Toronto, Ontario, Canada), 1996.

Emma and the Coyote (picture book), illustrated by Barbara Spurll, Stoddart Kids (Toronto, Ontario, Canada), 1999.

The Power of Poems: Teaching the Joy of Writing Poetry, Maupin House (Gainesville, FL), 2001.

Virtual Maniac: Silly and Serious Poems for Kids, illustrated by Eve Tanselle, Maupin House (Gainesville, FL), 2001.

When We Go Camping, illustrated by Andrew Kiss, Tundra Books (New York, NY), 2001.

A Pacific Alphabet, illustrated by Dianna Bonder, Whitecap Books (Vancouver, British Columbia, Canada), 2001.

Logan's Lake, Hodgepog Books (Edmonton, Alberta, Canada), 2001.

Emma's Cold Day, illustrated by Barbara Spurll, Stoddart Kids (Toronto, Ontario, Canada), 2001.

Wild Babies, illustrated by Andrew Kiss, Tundra Books (New York, NY), 2003.

My Librarian Is a Camel, Boyds Mills Press (Honesdale, PA), 2004.

Also author of *Spectacular Spiders,* Integrated Activities for Primary Classrooms, Pacific Edge Publishing. Contributor of articles and poetry to numerous magazines. Editor of an online magazine for children's writing.

ADAPTATIONS: Big Little Dog was published in Braille by the Canadian National Institute for the Blind in 1994.

WORK IN PROGRESS: Animal Alpha Bed, a rhyming picture book, for Boyds Mills Press (Honesdale, PA).

SIDELIGHTS: Born in the Netherlands, Margriet Ruurs has lived in many places, including California, Oregon, Northern Alberta, and the Yukon; currently, she resides in British Columbia. A teacher of creative writing, she is best known as the creator of picture books that characteristically combine a lighthearted approach with a reverence for nature; she is also the author of fiction for middle graders and nonfiction for children and adults.

Ruurs is perhaps most widely recognized as the creator of *A Mountain Alphabet,* an alphabet book in alliterative text that is set in the Canadian Rockies and is structured as a hike through the mountain ranges. The book is illustrated by Andrew Kiss, a well-known oil painter of wildlife, who provides twenty-six pictures that each emphasize a letter of the alphabet. Both the text and the art represent the variety of plant and animal life to be found in the Rockies; Ruurs includes both an introduction and an appended alphabet to provide further information about the scenes depicted. Critics note that not all the items beginning with a particular letter were mentioned in the text, though all are listed in the back of the book; this, along with the hidden letter itself, is considered an invitation to young readers to closely examine each illustration. The "book will help young readers to explore this ecosystem," maintained Barbara Chatton in *School Library Journal.* Chatton added, "While this title provides a valuable resource, it will need adult intervention to help youngsters 'read' the pictures so that they can get the most out of it." *Quill & Quire* reviewer Janet Mc-Naughton commented, "Some picture books find their real audience with adults who have a special affinity with the subject matter. *A Mountain Alphabet* may well be one of those."

In *Emma's Eggs,* Ruurs tells a humorous story while displaying her knowledge and love of animal life. In this picture book, the author features a mixed-up hen who notices what the humans on her farm are doing with her eggs (for example, scrambling them for eating, or decorating and hiding them for an Easter egg hunt), and tries to accommodate them by herself scrambling her eggs or hiding them. Eventually, however, Emma realizes exactly what her eggs are for. "The story is well written," noted Bridget Donald in *Quill & Quire.* "The narrative descriptions and dialogue convey the energy of Emma's human-like ambitions while preserving a strong sense of her chicken nature." There have been several sequels to *Emma's Eggs.*

In addition to her picture books, Ruurs is the author of *Big Little Dog,* the story of a boy and his sled dog that is, according to *Quill & Quire* reviewer Fred Boer, "told simply and effectively, with both drama and suspense." Ruurs is also the author of an informational book on the Royal Canadian Mountain Police and an instructional book on how to get published; she is a poet as well, and has translated a popular children's book by Judith Viorst into Dutch.

Ruurs once commented to *CA:* "Nothing is more fun than playing with words! I started writing stories and poems when I was in grade one. I wrote lots of stories and, thank goodness, my mom kept the scribblers with the poems I wrote when I was little.

"Reading, too, was a favorite pastime. I still read several books a week. I have books in my living room, books in my family room, books in my bedroom, and even books in my bathroom!

"Writing *A Mountain Alphabet* seems easy when you flip through the book now, but it took me almost two years to get the words just right, to say exactly what I wanted to say about life in the mountains. And I hope you have as much fun as I did trying to find all the hidden objects and letters in the book's illustrations!

"I like picture books. I read lots of them and do story-time in the public library every week. I was, therefore, thrilled when *Emma's Eggs* was awarded the 1997 honor title by the *Storytelling World* Awards.

"I love writing poetry. English is my second language and so it was hard for me to write poetry for a while but now I write poetry in both Dutch and English and do some translating as well.

"I teach lots of creative writing workshops in elementary schools and enjoy encouraging kids to write and read as much as they can. When I was little I thought that all authors were either very old or dead. . . . Now I like telling kids that they, too, can be authors. Being an author means you get to create lots of stories and use your imagination all the time. You have to keep your eyes and ears open for all the stories around. But it also means doing lots of rewriting and editing. That can be hard work but also does improve the final story, so it's worth it!

"I love being home and creating stories—first in my head and eventually on the computer. But I also enjoy traveling to schools and libraries to meet the kids who read my books. A book sitting on the shelf is just cardboard and paper, but a book in the hands of a reader comes to life! I write the stories but you make the book a book by reading it!"

Recently Ruurs added: "Writing for children is the genre that I like best. I read almost only books for children: picture books, novels, and poetry. Working in schools across North America allows me to test unpublished stories as well as to share my published books with children. Speaking at literacy conferences, I travel to many different places. Meeting teachers and librarians gives me materials for new books to write. I like showing kids the process of getting an idea, weaving it into a story or poem, and the rewriting process. I also show them how illustrators work and how books are designed and printed. Children, animals, and my love of the outdoors continue to inspire me with new ideas."

BIOGRAPHICAL AND CRITICAL SOURCES:

PERIODICALS

Booklist, December 15, 2001, Ilene Cooper, review of *When We Go Camping,* p. 741.
Books for Young People, June, 1987, p. 6.
Books in Canada, May, 1993, p. 31.
Canadian Children's Literature, fall, 2002, Ulrich Teucher, review of *Emma's Eggs,* p. 77.
Canadian Materials, October, 1993, p. 184; January, 1994, p. 11.
Instructor, January-February, 2002, review of *The Power of Poems: Teaching the Joy of Writing Poetry,* p. 13.
Publishers Weekly, July 17, 2000, review of *When We Go Camping,* p. 166; November 12, 2001, review of *A Pacific Alphabet,* p. 62.
Quill & Quire, May, 1993, Fred Boer, review of *Big Little Dog,* p. 34; August, 1996, Bridget Donald, review of *Emma's Eggs,* p. 42; December, 1996, Janet McNaughton, review of *A Mountain Alphabet,* pp. 36-37; May, 2001, review of *When We Go Camping,* p. 33.
Resource Links, February, 2002, Heather Hamilton, review of *Emma's Cold Day,* p. 8; April, 2002, Michael Jung, review of *A Pacific Alphabet,* p. 9.
School Library Journal, February, 1997, Barbara Chatton, review of *A Mountain Alphabet,* pp. 97-98; July, 2001, Susan Marie Pitard, review of *When We Go Camping,* p. 88; February, 2002, Alison Kastner, review of *A Pacific Alphabet,* p. 112; February, 2003, Patricia Manning, review of *Wild Babies,* p. 137.

ONLINE

Margriet Ruurs, Children's Author, http://www.margrietruurs.com/ (April 5, 2004).

S

SADDLEMYER, (Eleanor) Ann 1932-

PERSONAL: Born November 28, 1932, in Prince Albert, Saskatchewan, Canada; daughter of Orrin Angus (a lawyer) and Elsie Sarah (Ellis) Saddlemyer. *Education:* University of Saskatchewan, B.A., 1953; graduate study (honors in English), 1953-55; Queen's University at Kingston, M.A., 1956; University of London, Ph.D., 1961. *Politics:* NDP (New Democratic Party of Canada). *Religion:* Protestant. *Hobbies and other interests:* Contemporary theatre, music, and art; collecting books and prints of 1880-1915; the histories of the Irish and Canadian theatres, women's biography.

ADDRESSES: Office—10876 Madrona Dr., Sidney, British Columbia, V8L 5N9 Canada. *E-mail*—saddlemy@uvic.ca.

CAREER: University of Victoria, Victoria, British Columbia, Canada, instructor, 1956-57, 1960-62, assistant professor, 1962-64, associate professor, 1964-68, professor of English, 1968-71, adjunct professor, 1995—; University of Toronto, professor of English, Victoria College, 1971-95, professor emerita, 1995—, Massey College, master, 1988-95, master emerita, 1995—, Graduate Drama Centre, director, 1972-77, acting director, 1985-86. Berg Professor, New York University, 1975.

MEMBER: Modern Language Association of America, Association of Canadian University Teachers of English, Canadian Association of University Teachers, Canadian Association of Irish Studies, International Association for the Study of Anglo-Irish Literature (founding member; past chair), Society for Theatre Research, Association of Canadian Theatre Research (founding president).

AWARDS, HONORS: Canada Council short-term grant, 1962, 1963; Guggenheim fellowship, 1965-66; Canada Council research fellow, 1968; Royal Society of Canada fellow, 1976; Ontario distinguished service award, 1985; Connaught senior research fellow, 1986-87; Rose Mary Crawshay Award, British Academy, 1986; Royal Society of Arts fellow, 1987; the Association for Canadian Theatre Research created the Ann Saddlemyer Award, 1989; Alumni Award, University of Toronto, 1991; Woman Distinguished Award, Young Women's Christian Association (YWCA); Officer of the Order of Canada, 1995; Rosenthal Award, Yeats Society of New York, 2001; D.Litt., University of Victoria, 1989, McGill University, 1989, University of Windsor, 1990, University of Saskatchewan, 1991, and University of Toronto, 1999; L.L.D., Queen's University, 1977, and Concordia University, 2000; shortlisted for James Tait Black Memorial Book Prize, 2003, for *Becoming George: The Life of Mrs. W. B. Yeats.*

WRITINGS:

(Editor, with Robin Skelton) *The World of W. B. Yeats,* University of Washington Press (Seattle, WA), 1965, 2nd edition, 1967.
In Defense of Lady Gregory, Playwright, Dolmen Press (Dublin, Ireland), 1966.
(Editor) J. M. Synge, *Collected Works,* Volumes 3 and Volume 4; *Plays,* two volumes, Oxford University Press (New York, NY), 1968, published as *J. M. Synge: Plays,* 1969.

(Editor) *The Plays of Lady Gregory,* four volumes, Colin Smythe (Gerrards Cross, Buckinghamshire, England), 1970.

(Editor) *Letters to Molly: J. M. Synge to Maire O'Neill,* Harvard University Press (Cambridge, MA), 1971.

(Compiler) *A Selection of Letters from John M. Synge to Lady Gregory and W. B. Yeats,* Cuala Press (Dublin, Ireland), 1971.

(With others) *Accessibility Study of the University of Victoria and Camosun College,* British Columbia Ministry of Human Resources (Victoria, British Columbia, Canada), 1978.

(Editor) *Theatre Business: The Letters of the First Abbey Theatre Directors,* Penn State University Press (University Park, PA), 1982.

(Editor) *The Collected Letters of John Millington Synge,* two volumes, Clarendon Press (Oxford, England), 1983-84.

(Editor, with Colin Smythe) *Lady Gregory Fifty Years After,* Colin Smythe (Gerrards Cross, Buckinghamshire, England), 1987.

Wisdom, Magic, Sensation: W. B. Yeats in the 1930s, Memorial University (St. Johns, Newfoundland, Canada), 1988.

(Editor) *Early Stages: Theatre in Ontario, 1800-1914,* University of Toronto Press (Toronto, Ontario, Canada), 1990.

(Editor) J. M. Synge, *The Playboy of the Western World and Other Plays,* Oxford University Press (New York, NY), 1995.

(Editor, with Richard Plant) *Later Stages: Essays on Ontario Theatre from the First World War to the 1970s,* University of Toronto Press (Toronto, Ontario, Canada), 1997.

Becoming George: The Life of Mrs. W. B. Yeats, Oxford University Press (New York, NY), 2002.

Writer of lecture series for Canadian Broadcasting Corp. Contributor to *Irish Book, Anglo-Soviet Journal, Canadian Literature, Dalhousie Review, Queen's Quarterly, Theatre Research, Modern Drama, Theatre Survey, Massachusetts Review, Quill & Quire,* and other journals. Member of editorial board, *Yeats Studies, Irish University Review, Journal of Irish Literature, Modern Drama, English Studies in Canada,* and *Canadian Theatre Review.* Founding coeditor, *Theatre History in Canada,* 1978-86.

SIDELIGHTS: Ann Saddlemyer has written extensively on Canadian and Irish theatre. Adrian Frazier, writing in the *Irish Times,* stated: "The books of Ann Saddlemyer are landmarks: editions of Synge's letters and plays, groundbreaking histories of the Abbey Theatre in *The World of W. B. Yeats,* and a massive recuperation of the Abbey's most popular early playwright in *Lady Gregory: Fifty Years After.* She made Seamus Heaney's *Field Work* possible by lending him her Wicklow house in which to write it. If Ireland gave a prix, as France does, to foreign friends, it would have awarded the title ollamh strainsear to Ann Saddlemyer."

Saddlemyer's books on Canadian theatre include *Early Stages: Theatre in Ontario, 1800-1914* and *Later Stages: Essays on Ontario Theatre from the First World War to the 1970s,* which together provide an overview of theatrical activity in Ontario for nearly two hundred years. Among the subjects covered in the first volume are garrison theatre, touring entertainers, circuses, dime museums, and vaudeville. The second volume traces the development of professional theatre in Ontario, chronicling the rise of stock companies, theatre festivals, and university theatres. Denis Johnston, in a review for *Theatre Research in Canada,* found that "perhaps the greatest achievement in *Early Stages* is the sense of it being a unified and comprehensive whole—rare in collections of essays. Each essay is complete and thorough in itself, and each refers pertinently to its companion pieces." Writing of *Later Stages* in *Canadian Literature: A Quarterly of Criticism and Review,* Kym Bird found the volume to be a "monumental contribution. . . . Like its predecessor, it is the first detailed overview of theatre in its period." "Together with its earlier sister volume," Ronald Vince wrote in *Theatre Research International,* "*Later Stages* will be required reading for anyone interested in the theatre in Ontario or indeed in Canada."

Becoming George: The Life of Mrs. W. B. Yeats is Saddlemyer's biography of Georgie Hyde Lees, the wife of Irish poet William Butler Yeats. Saddlemyer's biography, some 800 pages in length, covers Georgie's life from childhood through her married life until her death thirty years after her husband's passing. Hilary Spurling in the *New York Times* found Saddlemyer's book to be "patiently researched [and with] previously unpublished and scrupulously documented detail." Brenda Maddox in the *Guardian* found that Saddlemyer had "delivered the life of this remarkable woman in encyclopaedic detail." John Banville of the *New York Review of Books* reported, "Ann Saddlemyer has written a profound, exhaustive, and richly evocative life of this truly remarkable woman." Kildare Dobbs wrote in the *Toronto Globe & Mail,* "In her wise, majestic biography, Ann Saddlemyer seems to see all and understand all; her book is a masterpiece, an extraordinary achievement."

BIOGRAPHICAL AND CRITICAL SOURCES:

PERIODICALS

Canadian Historical Review, September, 1984, review of *The History of Theatre in Ontario,* p. S15.
Canadian Literature: A Quarterly of Criticism and Review, winter, 1992, Richard Paul Knowles, review of *Early Stages: Theatre in Ontario, 1800-1914,* p. 132; spring, 2000, Kym Bird, review of *Later Stages: Essays on Ontario Theatre from the First World War to the 1970s,* p. 170.
Canadian Theatre Review, summer, 1998, Patrick B. O'Neill, review of *Later Stages,* p. 89.
Choice: Current Reviews for Academic Libraries, March, 2003, G. Grieve-Carlson, review of *Becoming George: The Life of Mrs. W. B. Yeats,* p. 1186.
Economist, August 27, 1983, review of *The Collected Letters of John Millington Synge: Volume One, 1871-1907,* p. 65; November 10, 1984, review of *The Collected Letters of John Millington Synge, Volume Two, 1907-1909,* p. AB9.
Guardian (London, England), October 26, 2002, Brenda Maddox, review of *Becoming George,* p. 12.
International Association for the Study of Irish Literatures Newsletter, July 20, 2000.
Irish Times (Dublin, Ireland), October 12, 2002, Olivia Kelly, "Literati Light Up Kildare Street," p. 57; November 2, 2002, Adrian Frazier, "Seized by a Superior Power?," p. 59.
Journal of Canadian Studies, spring, 1994, Craig Stewart Walker, review of *Early Stages,* p. 156.
New York Review of Books, April 10, 2003, John Banville, review of *Becoming George,* p. 46.
New York Times, October 20, 2002, Hilary Spurling, review of *Becoming George,* p. 27.
Spectator, October 5, 2002, P. J. Kavanagh, review of *Becoming George,* p. 42.
Theatre Research in Canada, Volume 19, number 1, 1998, Denis Johnston, reviews of *Early Stages* and *Later Stages,* pp. 86-91.
Theatre Research International, autumn, 1992, Mary Elizabeth Smith, review of *Early Stages,* p. 246; autumn, 1998, Ronald Vince, review of *Later Stages,* p. 289.

Toronto Globe & Mail, 2003, Kildare Dobbs, review of *Becoming George.*
University of Toronto Quarterly, winter, 1998, Denyse Lynde, review of *Later Stages,* p. 534.
Victorian Studies, winter, 1989, Linda Ray Pratt, review of *Lady Gregory: Fifty Years After,* p. 265.

ONLINE

Ann Saddlemyer's Home Page, http://www.pgil-eirdata.org/html/pgil_gazette/scholars/ (April 17, 2003).*

*   *   *

SANDFORD, John
    See CAMP, John (Roswell)

*   *   *

SARRAUTE, Nathalie 1900-1999

PERSONAL: Born July 18, 1900, in Ivanovo-Voznessensk, Russia; died October 19, 1999, in Paris, France; daughter of Ilya (a chemist) and Pauline (a writer; maiden name, Chatounovsky) Tcherniak; married Raymond Sarraute (a barrister), July 28, 1925 (divorced, 1940; remarried, 1956); children: Claude, Anne, Dominique. *Education:* Sorbonne, University of Paris, licence d'anglais, 1920, licence en droit; 1925; attended Oxford University, 1921; additional study in Berlin, 1921-22; University of Paris, studied law, 1922.

CAREER: Attorney, 1925-39; fictionwriter, beginning 1939.

AWARDS, HONORS: Formentor Prize and Prix Internationale de Litterature, both 1964, both for *The Golden Fruits;* doctor honoris causa, Trinity College, Dublin, 1976, University of Kent at Canterbury, 1980, and Oxford University, 1991; Grand Prix National, 1982; Prix Cavour, 1984.

WRITINGS:

FICTION: IN ENGLISH TRANSLATION

Tropismes (sketches), Denoel (Paris, France), 1939, revised edition, Editions de Minuit (Paris, France), 1957, translation by Maria Jolas published as *Tro-*

Nathalie Sarraute

"Disent les imbeciles" (novel), Gallimard (Paris, France), 1976, translation by Maria Jolas published as *"Fools Say,"* Braziller (New York, NY), 1977.

L'Usage de la parole (sketches), Gallimard (Paris, France), 1980, translation by Barbara Wright published as *The Use of Speech,* Braziller (New York, NY), 1983.

Tu ne t'aimes pas, Gallimard (Paris, France), 1989, translation by Barbara Wright published as *You Don't Love Yourself* (novel), Braziller (New York, NY), 1990.

Ici, Gallimard (Paris, France), 1995, translation by Barbara Wright published as *Here: A Novel,* George Braziller (New York, NY), 1997.

CRITICISM

L'Ere du soupcon: Essais sur le roman, Gallimard (Paris, France), 1956, translation by Maria Jolas published as *The Age of Suspicion: Essays on the Novel* (also see below), Braziller (New York, NY), 1963.

Paul Valery et l'enfant d'elephant (first published in *Les Temps modernes,* January, 1947) [and] *Flaubert le precurseur* (first published in *Preuves,* February, 1965), Gallimard (Paris, France), c. 1986.

PLAYS

Le Silence [and] *Le Mensonge* (both plays first broadcast on German radio, both produced in Petit Odeon at Theatre de France, January 14, 1967), Gallimard (Paris, France), 1967, translation by Maria Jolas published in England as *Silence* [and] *The Lie,* Calder & Boyars (London, England), 1969.

Isma; ou, Ce qui s'appelle rien (produced at Espace Pierre-Cardin, February 5, 1973) [and] *Le Silence* [and] *Le Mensonge,* Gallimard (Paris, France), 1970.

Theatre (contains *C'est beau,* first performed at Theatre d'Orsay, October 24, 1975, *Elle est la,* first performed at Theatre d'Orsay, January 15, 1980, *Isma, Le Mensonge,* and *Le Silence*), Gallimard (Paris, France), 1978, translation by Maria Jolas and Barbara Wright published as *Collected Plays of Nathalie Sarraute* (contains *It Is There, It's Beautiful, Izzum, The Lie,* and *Silence*), J. Calder (London, England), 1980, Braziller (New York, NY), 1981.

pisms (also see below), Braziller (New York, NY), 1967, reprinted, Riverrun Press (New York, NY), 1986.

Portrait d'un inconnu (novel), with preface by Jean-Paul Sartre, Robert Marin (Paris, France), 1948, reprinted, Gallimard (Paris, France), 1977, translation by Maria Jolas published as *Portrait of a Man Unknown,* Braziller (New York, NY), 1958.

Martereau (novel), Gallimard (Paris, France), 1953, translation by Maria Jolas published as *Martereau,* Braziller (New York, NY), 1959.

Le Planetarium (novel), Gallimard (Paris, France), 1959, 2nd edition, 1967, translation by Maria Jolas published as *The Planetarium,* Braziller (New York, NY), 1960.

Les Fruits d'or (novel), Gallimard (Paris, France), 1963, translation by Maria Jolas published as *The Golden Fruits,* Braziller (New York, NY), 1964.

Entre la vie et la mort (novel), Gallimard (Paris, France), 1968, translation by Maria Jolas published as *Between Life and Death,* Braziller (New York, NY), 1969.

Vous les entendez? (novel), Gallimard (Paris, France), 1972, translation by Maria Jolas published as *Do You Hear Them?,* Braziller (New York, NY), 1973.

Also author of *For No Good Reason,* first produced in New York City in 1985.

OTHER

Tropisms [and] *The Age of Suspicion,* Calder & Boyars (London, England), 1964.
Enfance (autobiography), Gallimard (Paris, France), 1983, translation by Barbara Wright published as *Childhood,* Braziller (New York, NY) 1984.
(With Simone Benmussa) *Nathalie Sarraute: Qui êtes-vous,* edited by Simone Benmussa, La Manufacture (Lyon, France), 1987.
Ouvrez, Gallimard (Paris, France), 1997.

Contributed to many publications such as *Visages d'aujourd'hui,* Plon, 1960; *The Writer's Dilemma,* Oxford University Press, 1961; *The Novel Today: Edinburgh International Festival 1962—International Writers' Conference; Programme and Notes,* edited by Andrew Hook, R. R. Clark, 1962; *Les Critiques de notre temps et Camus,* edited by Jacqueline Levi-Valensi, Garnier, 1970; *Violoncelle qui resiste,* Eric Losfeld, 1971; *Gespraeche mit,* Europaverlag, 1972; *Nouveau roman: Hier, aujourd'hui* (text not reviewed by Sarraute), edited by Jean Ricardou and Francoise von Rossum-Guyon, Union Generale d'Editions, 1972; *Words and Their Masters,* Doubleday, 1974; *Comment travaillent les ecrivains,* Flammarion, 1978; and *Du monologue interieur a la sousconversation,* edited by Frida S. Weissman, Nizet, 1978. Sarraute's works have been translated into other languages, including German, Hebrew, Italian, Russian, and Spanish. Contributor to numerous journals and periodicals, including the *New York Times Book Review, Washington Post Book World, Times Literary Supplement, Cahiers Renaud Barrault, Le Monde, Les Temps modernes, Nouvelle Revue Française,* and *Preuves.*

ADAPTATIONS: Childhood was adapted as a play by Simone Benmussa and premiered in Paris in 1984. The American premiere, both adapted and directed by Benmussa, was produced in 1985 at the Samuel Beckett Theater, New York City, featuring Glenn Close in the starring role.

SIDELIGHTS: As one of the outstanding writers and theoreticians of the "New Novel" in France, Nathalie Sarraute consistently sought to create innovative forms of narrative that apprehend the psychological reality beneath the surface of daily events and conversations. Her work received little critical attention until the publication of her theoretical work, *L'Ere du soupcon: Essais sur le roman (The Age of Suspicion: Essays on the Novel),* and her novel *Les Fruits d'or (The Golden Fruits).* Sarraute's novels are complex studies of human interaction that reject traditional elements of character and plot, while challenging the reader to reassess common assumptions about literature and its relationship to life.

One of the hallmarks of Sarraute's literary work is the "tropism." Borrowing the term from the biological sciences—where it characterizes an involuntary reaction to external stimuli, as when a plant turns toward light or heat—Sarraute uses it to describe the subtle psychological responses of people to objects, words, and other human beings. In the *Listener,* Sarraute explained tropisms as movements that "glide quickly round the border of our consciousness" and "compose the small, rapid, and sometimes very complex dramas concealed beneath our actions, our gestures, the words we speak, our avowed and clear feelings." *Tropisms,* Sarraute's earliest work, is composed of short texts that investigate what Valerie Minogue, in *Nathalie Sarraute and the War of the Words,* called "the teeming sub-surface of life, anonymously yet intimately observed." The reader is thrust into the midst of a world of unidentified characters (nameless women gossiping in a tea salon, passersby in front of a shop window) who experience sensations that are dramatically and poetically rendered through imagery, rhythm, and repetition. Character development and plot are minimal, Sarraute explained, because such novelistic traits tend to particularize experience and to distract the reader from Sarraute's portrayal of an underlying psychological reality common to everyone.

In *The Age of Suspicion,* the author develops many of her critical and theoretical stances regarding the novel and clarifies her own creative goals. In an interview for the 1984 issue of *Digraphe* devoted to her work, Sarraute defined the "real" as "what hasn't yet taken on the conventional forms" and held that the writer's task is not to copy or imitate accepted reality, but to invent new forms that will help the reader perceive new realities. In her investigation of the human psyche, Sarraute makes a case for formal innovations that shape the experience of the reader. Instead of calling for controlled analyses of carefully defined feelings, she develops the notion of the "subconversation," which renders verbally "what is dissimulated behind the interior monologue: a countless profusion of sensations, of images, of feelings, of memories . . . which no interior language expresses." She thus portrays instinctive, instantaneous reactions before they become fully understood and named, insisting that the passage from subconversation to dialogue must be continuous: no standard formulas like "she said" or "George murmured" are to interrupt the flow of "these interior dramas made up of attacks, triumphs, defeats, caresses." Sarraute uses imagery to present the unnameable sensations that make up the tropism. As Gretchen Rous Besser pointed out in *Nathalie Sarraute,* the novelist often utilizes the imagery of animals and insects "whose instinctive reactions are consonant with the prerational nature of tropistic reactions."

In his preface to Sarraute's first novel, *Portrait d'un inconnu (Portrait of a Man Unknown),* Jean-Paul Sartre characterized the work as an antinovel because it contests traditional novelistic conventions. A first-person narrator, who remains a nameless voice, "is speaking or writing or dreaming or reflecting" about a father and daughter whose relationship fascinates and perhaps obsesses him. The boundaries between the narrator's imagination and his actual knowledge about the couple tend to blur because there are no linguistic markers to distinguish between fact and fiction, between objective reality and creative interpretation.

The characters of Sarraute's second novel, *Martereau,* include an entire family, creating more complex interpersonal interactions. Except for Martereau, characters are identified only by personal pronouns or family relationships. The readers must make their way through this labyrinth of shifting connections by remaining attentive to certain repeated words and rhythms, which Minogue called Sarraute's "signposts." This technique stresses the characters' common ground, instead of individualizing them according to an established set of categories. Sarraute's works define labels, proper names, and abstractions as tools to conceal the multifaceted aspects of life. Martereau is, at first, one of these stock individuals, a "traditional novel character," said Sarraute in *Digraphe,* "in the way that we see the people around us"—that is, from the outside. But as the novel progresses, the external appearance disintegrates.

Regarding her novel *Le Planetarium ("The Planetarium"),* Sarraute remarked in the *Listener:* "Here I

met with greater difficulties than in my previous books." Sarraute's third novel is populated by a large cast of characters with proper names, but, again, elaborate descriptions of place and time are absent. Sarraute may have named the characters to supply the reader with more recognizable markers because of the complex interaction between characters, but the names do not serve as a claim to uniqueness, for the novel concludes with the comment: "I think that we are all a little like that," and the characters' similarities ultimately loom larger than their differences. In a 1965 *Tel Quel* article, Lucette Finas commented on the novel's quick psychological maneuvers and reversals: "All the dialogues have their victim and their tormenter who exchange roles from one page to the next, sometimes from one retort to the next."

With the publication of her next three novels, *Les Fruits d'or (The Golden Fruits), Entre la vie et la mort (Between Life and Death),* and *Vous les entendez? (Do You Hear Them?),* Sarraute adroitly focuses her attention on artistic creation and critical reception. *The Golden Fruits* follows the path of an imaginary novel as it is created, critically received, heralded, and then forgotten. Like the various objects in *The Planetarium,* it serves as a pretext around which a group of anonymous voices battle for superiority of literary judgment, juxtaposing everyday colloquial language and poetic metaphors that capture the underlying emotions of the moment. Sarraute uses many elliptical sentences that trail off without finishing. These fragmentary remarks underscore the commonplace quality of the discussions and, as Sarraute explained in a letter to *CA,* imply that the reader is "supposed to know how they would finish." But they also suggest that thoughts and impressions are formed and "cross our minds very quickly. There is no time to waste for building correct, well-rounded sentences."

The Golden Fruits highlights the process of reading, experiencing, and evaluating literature, and Sarraute calls her reader to participate actively in the interrogation. The tropism is not just a phenomenon to be perceived and understood by readers, but reenacted as they move toward and away from the speakers' comments about the imaginary novel. Although critical positions abound in the novel, no single stance (or voice) can triumph over the others. One voice comments near the end of the book: "Art as you say, a work of art is never a sure value. . . . One is often wrong, that's natural. How can one know? Who can say that he knows?" The open-ended questions of Sarraute's novel suggest that any work of art undergoes a continual re-evaluation according to the needs of a particular society at a given moment in history.

In *Between Life and Death,* Sarraute turns her attention to the writer's activity, pondering the act of creation from the inside, as well as the writer's interactions with his public. In this work, which she has stated is not autobiographical, Sarraute is more concerned with problems in the perception of writers than with the portrait of a specific individual. She refers to the writer as a "he" rather than a "she," which distances Sarraute from her work and avoids an identification between them. The reader shares in the writer's solitary moments of joy and anguish as he labors over his manuscript, wondering whether his writing is original, facile, or interesting, whether it is alive or dead. Once he has written something, the writer splits himself in two to evaluate his effort.

Sarraute completed the trilogy of *The Golden Fruits* and *Between Life and Death* with *Do You Hear Them?,* focusing, as she said in her interview with Bree, on "the relationship between the work of art, the environment into which it falls, and its fate in general." In his home, a man and his friend contemplate a small stone figurine of primitive art while the man's children are heard laughing upstairs. The domestic drama lies in the tension between the father's love of the statue and his love for his children, who rebel against what they see as his quasi-religious devotion to art, favoring free artistic creation untrammeled by rules and a weighty sense of tradition. The father interprets the children's effervescent laughter as, in turns, carefree and innocent or mocking and deceitful. Besser noted how the metaphorical descriptions of the children's gleeful voices pass from poetic cliche ("Tiny bells. Tiny drops. Fountains. Gentle water-falls. Twittering of birds.") to ominous images of persecution: "Soon the 'titters' grow 'sharp as needles,' and the water drips on its victim like a Chinese torture." When Besser asked Sarraute which of the two opposing conceptions of art she would herself choose, the novelist responded that she could identify with both. Sarraute told Besser about the novel, "I wanted to show a kind of interaction between consciousnesses which are extremely close to one another to the extent that they almost fuse and communicate by a kind of osmosis. . . . What each one feels and attributes to another becomes any one of the others at any given moment."

In her next two works, *"Disent les imbeciles"* (*"Fools Say"*) and *L'Usage de la parole* (*The Use of Speech*), Sarraute pushes the novelistic genre to the limit. In fact, *The Use of Speech* is often not considered a novel at all. Neither work presents one story line or character to unite the fragmented episodes. Instead, the author creates a series of interpersonal exchanges in which anonymous voices react to the effects of linguistic labeling, to the power of cliches to imprison the individual in stock phrases and concrete descriptions. The episodes are unified by the relentless study of the way language intervenes in the development of ideas and of human identity. Of *"Fools Say,"* Ellen E. Munley commented in *Contemporary Literature,* "Sarraute scrutinizes the tropistic proximity and distance, the fusion and separation created by language. Words speak actions. . . . Words create a cast of characters erected at a distance." Minogue described the setting of *"Fools Say"* as "a terrorist world, against which Nathalie Sarraute raises a voice that insists that any idea, however comforting, or however disconcerting it may be, must be treated as an idea, not as an appurtenance of a personality, group, class, nation, or race."

The Use of Speech is a collection of ten essays or sketches more reminiscent of *Tropisms* than of a conventional novel. Again, Sarraute focuses her attention on the resonances of certain verbal expressions. Munley commented that *The Use of Speech* differs from Sarraute's previous works in that "it contains a self-styled narrator—doctor of words who joins all of its loosely connected vignettes by virtue of her presence." This narrator does not directly participate as one of the characters in the vignettes, which perhaps anticipates Sarraute's subsequent interest in writing an account of her early years in her autobiographical *Enfance* (*Childhood*).

You Don't Love Yourself continues to explore self and identity in a novel devoid of conventional plot or characterization. Consisting of interior dialogues between various parts of a single personality, the novel is a study of the themes of self-love and self-hate. "This is Mrs. Sarraute's rendering of the language of the self," noted *New York Times Book Review* reviewer Ginger Danto, "notably the self that does not love itself, whose fractured ego ebbs now into self-loathing and illusion, now into envy and regret-subjective musings possibly, but not necessarily, provoked by circumstance."

It might seem surprising that Sarraute, who has steadfastly questioned the status of personal identity and unequivocal factual truth, wrote *Childhood*, a series of autobiographical texts about her early relationships with her families and her first experiences in language. But for Sarraute, autobiography is still literature, another terrain for prospecting the subterranean tropisms of her own experiences. Instead of the singular "I" usually found in autobiography, this work contains *two* narrators in dialogue: while one voice narrates episodes from the past, the other admonishes, encourages, censures, and interprets what the first has presented. Sarraute makes no attempt to connect the various episodes she relates, for identity is conceived as split or fragmented, and interpretation is acknowledged in the text as a necessary component of memory. The author's personae and her past are recognized as fictive re-creations like those in her other literary works.

Sarraute's last two books follow the same conventions as her previous works. *Ici (Here)* is a compilation of sketches in which the author meditates on words and how their interpretations can impact different interactions. Nancy Pearl noted in *Booklist* that Sarraute's books "frustrate readers who expect the conventional in contemporary fiction, and *Here* is no exception." While a *Publishers Weekly* reviewer expressed a similar sentiment, the reviewer also lauded *Ici,* calling it "brilliant and innovative," and concluding that "Sarraute's eye for the perfect metaphor, and ear for the rhythms of thought, are reason enough to read this stunning work." Sarraute's last work, *Ouvrez,* contains eighteen short, untitled vignettes on language's ambiguities. The author's sentiments are revealed through random conversations. Reviewer John L. Brown contended in *World Literature Today* that Sarraute "still maintains . . . a reputation as one of the most innovative writers of her time and also one of the most difficult to categorize, not only as a novelist, but also, and especially, as a theoretician who has explored in numerous essays such as *Ouvrez* what she considers new ways of perceiving reality, of understanding human behavior."

BIOGRAPHICAL AND CRITICAL SOURCES:

BOOKS

Alberes, R.-M., *Metamorphoses du roman,* Albin Michel (Paris, France), 1966.

Allemand, Andre, *L'Oeuvre romanesque de Nathalie Sarraute,* Editions de la Baconniere (Neuchatel, Switzerland), 1980.

Alter, Robert, *Partial Magic: The Novel As a Self-Conscious Genre,* University of California Press, 1975.

Barbour, Sarah, *Nathalie Sarraute and the Feminist Reader: Identities in Process,* Associated University Presses, 1993.

Barrere, J.-B., *La Cure d'amaigrissement du roman,* Albin Michel (Paris, France), 1964.

Beetz, Kirk H., *Beacham's Encyclopedia of Popular Fiction,* Beacham's Publishing (Osprey, FL), 1996.

Beja, Morris, *Epiphany in the Modern Novel,* University of Washington Press, 1971.

Bell, Sheila Margaret, compiler, *Nathalie Sarraute: A Bibliography,* Grant & Cutler, 1982.

Benmussa, Simone, *Entretiens avec Nathalie Sarraute,* Le Renaissance du Livre (Tournai, Belgium), 1999.

Besser, Gretchen Rous, *Nathalie Sarraute,* Twayne, 1979.

Bloch-Michel, J., *Le Present de l'indicatif: Essai sur le nouveau roman,* Gallimard, 1963.

Boisdeffre, Pierre de, *Le Roman depuis 1900,* Presses Universitaires de France (Paris, France), 1979.

Butor, Michel, *Repertoire II,* Editions de Minuit, 1964.

Calin, Francoise, *La Vie retrouvee: Etude de l'oeuvre romanesque de Nathalie Sarraute,* Minard (Paris), 1976.

Chapsal, Medeleine, *Les Ecrivains en personne,* Juilliard (Paris, France), 1960.

Contemporary Literary Criticism, Gale (Detroit, MI), Volume 1, 1973, Volume 2, 1974, Volume 4, 1975, Volume 8, 1978, Volume 10, 1979, Volume 31, 1985, Volume 80, 1994.

Contemporary World Writers, 2nd edition, St. James Press (Detroit, MI), 1993.

Cranaki, Mimica, and Yvon Belaval, editors, *Nathalie Sarraute,* Gallimard, 1965.

Daellenbach, Lucien, *Le Recit speculaire,* Le Seuil (Paris, France), 1977.

Dictionary of Literary Biography, Volume 83: *French Novelists since 1960,* Gale (Detroit, MI), 1989.

Dictionary of Twentieth Century Culture, Volume 2: *French Culture 1900-1975,* edited by Catherine Savage Brosman, Gale (Detroit, MI), 1995.

Edel, Leon, *The Modern Psychological Novel,* revised edition, Grosset & Dunlap-Universal Library, 1964.

Eliez-Ruegg, Elizabeth, *La Conscience d'autrui et la conscience des objets dans l'oeuvre de Nathalie Sarraute,* Lang (Berne, Switzerland), 1972.

Encyclopedia of World Literature in the Twentieth Century, 3rd edition, edited by Leonard S. Klein, St. James Press (Detroit, MI), 1999.

Frohock, W. M., editor, *Image and Theme: Studies in Modern French Fiction:* Harvard University Press, 1969.

Goldmann, Lucien, *Pour une sociologie du roman,* Gallimard, 1964.

Hassan, Ihab, *The Dismemberment of Orpheus,* Oxford University Press, 1971.

Heath, Stephen, *The Nouveau Roman: A Study in the Practice of Writing,* Temple University Press, 1972.

International Dictionary of Theatre, Volume 2: *Playwrights,* edited by Mark Hawkins-Dady, St. James Press (Detroit, MI), 1994.

Jaccard, Jean-Luc, *Nathalie Sarraute,* Juris (Zurich, Switzerland), 1967.

Jansen, Steen, *Analyse de la forme dramatique du Mensonge de Nathalie Sarraute precedee de Nathalie Sarraute, Le Mensonge,* Akademisk Forlag, 1976.

Janvier, Ludovic, *Une Parole exigeante: Le Nouveau Roman,* Editions de Minuit, 1964.

Jefferson, Ann, *Nathalie Sarraute: Fiction and Theory,* Cambridge University Press (New York, NY), 2000.

Knapp, Bettina, *Off-Stage Voices: Interviews with Modern French Dramatists,* Whitston, 1975.

Knapp, Bettina, *Nathalie Sarraute,* Rodopi (Amsterdam, Netherlands), 1994.

Kostelanetz, Richard, *On Contemporary Literature,* Avon, 1964.

Le Sage, Laurent, *The French New Novel,* Pennsylvania State University Press, 1962.

Levi, Anthony, *Guide to French Literature,* 1789 to the Present, St. James Press (Chicago, IL), 1992.

Magill, *Great Women Writers,* Henry Holt (New York, NY), 1994.

Matthews, J. H., editor, *Un Nouveau Roman?,* La Revue des Lettres Modernes, 1964.

Mauriac, Claude, *L'Alitterature contemporaine,* revised edition, Albin Michel, 1969.

McCarthy, Mary, *The Writing on the Wall and Other Literary Essays,* Harcourt, 1970.

Mercier, Vivian, *The New Novel: From Queneau to Pinget,* revised edition, Farrar, Straus, 1966.

Micha, Rene, *Nathalie Sarraute,* Editions Universitaires (Paris, France), 1966.

Minogue, Valerie, *Nathalie Sarraute and the War of the Words: A Study of Five Novels,* Edinburgh University Press, 1981.

Moore, Harry T., *Twentieth-Century French Literature since World War II,* Southern Illinois University Press, 1966.

Nadeau, Maurice, *The French Novel since the War,* translated by A. M. Sheridan-Smith, Methuen, 1967.

Newman, A. S., *Une Poesie des discours: Essai sur les romans de Nathalie Sarraute,* Droz (Geneva), 1976.

Newsmakers 2000, Issue 2, Gale (Detroit, MI), 2000.

O'Beirne, Emer, *Reading Nathalie Sarraute: Dialogue and Distance,* Clarendon Press (New York, NY), 1999.

Peyre, Henri, *The Contemporary French Novel,* Oxford University Press, 1955.

Peyre, Henri, *French Novelists of Today,* Oxford University Press, 1967.

Phillips, John, *Nathalie Sarraute: Metaphor, Fairy-Tale and the Feminine of the Text,* P. Lang, 1994.

Pierrot, Jean, *Nathalie Sarraute,* J. Corti, 1990.

Podhoretz, Norman, *Doings and Undoings,* Farrar, Straus, 1953, revised edition, 1964.

Rahv, Betty T., *From Sartre to the New Novel,* Kennikat Press, 1974.

Raimond, Michel, *Le Roman depuis la revolution,* Armand Colin (Paris, France), 1967.

Ramsay, Raylene L., *The French New Autobiographies: Sarraute, Duras, and Robbe Grillet,* University Press of Florida, 1996.

Reference Guide to World Literature, 2nd edition, edited by Lesley Henderson, St. James Press (Detroit, MI), 1995.

Ricardou, Jean, *Problemes du nouveau roman,* Le Seuil, 1967.

Ricardou, Jean, *Pour une theorie du nouveau roman,* Le Seuil, 1971.

Ricardou, Jean, and Françoise von Rossum-Guyon, editors, *Nouveau Roman: Hier, aujourd'hui,* Union Generale d'Editions (Paris), 1972.

Ricardou, Jean, *Le Nouveau Roman,* Le Seuil, 1973.

Robbe-Grillet, Alain, *Pour un nouveau roman,* Gallimard, 1964.

Rykner, Arnaud, *Nathalie Sarraute,* Le Seuil, 1991.

Sarraute, Nathalie, *Portrait d'un inconnu,* with preface by Jean-Paul Sartre, Robert Marin, 1948, translation by Maria Jolas published as *Portrait of a Man Unknown,* Braziller, 1958, reprinted, 1990.

Sarraute, Nathalie, *L'Ere du soupcon: Essais sur le roman,* Gallimard, 1956, translation by Maria Jolas published as *The Age of Suspicion: Essays on the Novel,* Braziller, 1963, reprinted, 1990.

Sontag, Susan, *Against Interpretation and Other Essays*, revised edition, Farrar, Straus, 1966.

Stade, George, editor, *European Writers*, Volume 12: *The Twentieth Century*, Scribner (New York, NY), 1990.

Temple, Ruth Z., *Nathalie Sarraute*, Columbia University Press, 1968.

Tison-Braun, Micheline, *Nathalie Sarraute ou la recherche de l'authenticite*, Gallimard, 1971.

Vinson, James, and Daniel Kirkpatrick, editors, *Contemporary Foreign Language Writers*, St. Martin's Press (New York, NY), 1984.

Weightman, John, *The Concept of the Avant-Garde: Explorations in Modernism*, Alcove, 1973.

Wunderli-Mueller, Christine, *Le Theme du masque et les banalites dans l'oeuvre de Nathalie Sarraute*, Juris Druck Verlag (Zurich, Switzerland), 1970.

PERIODICALS

American Scholar, summer, 1963.

Arts, June 3-9, 1959.

Atlantic, June, 1960; March, 1973; May, 1977; April, 1984.

Booklist, July, 1997, Nancy Pearl, review of *Here*, pp. 1800-1801.

Books Abroad, autumn, 1972.

Book Week, February 9, 1964.

Bucknell Review, April, 1976.

Bulletin des jeunes romanistes, Volume 20, 1974.

Cahiers Renaud Barrault, Volume 89, 1975.

Chicago Tribune, October 24, 1999, p. 10.

Christian Science Monitor, February 13, 1964; July 15, 1969; August 22, 1977; August 2, 1984.

Commonweal, December 18, 1959; August 22, 1969.

Contemporary Literature, spring, 1973; summer, 1983.

Critique (Paris, France), Volumes 86-87, 1954; Volumes 100-101, 1955; Volumes 111-112, 1956.

Critique, winter, 1963-64, Volume 14, number 1, 1972.

Digraphe (interview), March, 1984.

Drama, autumn, 1981.

Economist, February 17, 1996, review of *Ici*, pp. S14-S15.

Esprit, Volume 376, 1968.

Essays in French Literature, Volume 3, 1966.

Etudes litteraires, Volume 17, number 2, 1984.

Express (Paris), April 29-May 5, 1968.

French Forum, Volume 5, 1980; spring, 2002, Ann Cothran, review of *Reading Nathalie Sarraute: Dialogue and Distance*, pp. 153-155.

French Review, December, 1959, spring special issue, 1972; October, 1977; February, 1980; March, 1981; April, 1983; April, 1999, review of *Ouvrez*, p. 945.

French Studies, April, 1973, Volume 30, number 1, 1976.

Hudson Review, autumn, 1967; autumn, 1973.

International Fiction Review, January, 1974; January, 1977.

Journal of European Studies, September, 2000, Sheila M. Bell, review of *Reading Nathalie Sarraute: Dialogue and Distance*, p. 338; June, 2001, Martin Crowley, review of *Nathalie Sarraute: Fiction and Theory*, pp. 229-230.

Kentucky Romance Quarterly, Volume 14, number 3, 1969.

Kenyon Review, summer, 1963.

Lettres Françaises, February 4, 1960.

Lettres Nouvelles, April 29, 1959.

Listener, March 9, 1961.

Los Angeles Times, April 17, 1984.

Mercure de France, Volume 336, 1959; Volume 345, 1962; Volume 348, 1963.

Modern Fiction Studies, winter, 1960-61.

Modern Language Notes, Volume 88, number 4, 1973.

Modern Language Review, July, 1978; July, 1982; January, 1986; January, 1987.

Modern Language Studies, Volume 13, number 3, 1983.

Ms., July, 1984.

Nation, March 23, 1962; March 2, 1964.

New Republic, March 21, 1964.

New Statesman, April 15, 1983.

Newsweek, February 10, 1964.

New Yorker, March 26, 1960; May 21, 1960; May 2, 1964; November 22, 1969; May 9, 1977; April 11, 1983.

New York Herald Tribune Book Review, August 3, 1958.

New York Review of Books, March 5, 1964; July 31, 1969; April 19, 1973; October 25, 1984.

New York Times, August 10, 1958; May 30, 1969; July 24, 1970; March 30, 1984.

New York Times Book Review, November 1, 1959; May 15, 1960; February 9, 1964; May 21, 1967; May 18, 1969; February 4, 1973; April 3, 1977; April 1, 1984; November 18, 1990, p. 7.

Nouvelle Revue Française, Volume 54, 1957; Volume 62, 1958; Volume 127, 1963.

Nouvelles litteraires, June 9, 1966.

Performing Arts Journal, winter, 1977.

Preuves, Volume 154, 1963.

PTL: A Journal for Descriptive Poetics and Theory of Literature, April, 1977.

Publishers Weekly, June 9, 1997, review of *Here,* p. 38.

Renascence, summer, 1964.

Review of Contemporary Fiction, spring, 1998, Renee Kingcaid, review of *Here,* p. 233.

Revue de Paris, June, 1958.

Romantic Review, May, 2001, Jennifer Willging, "Partners in Slime: The Liquid and the Viscous Sarraute and Sartre," pp. 277-296.

Salmagundi, spring, 1970.

San Francisco Chronicle, July 10, 1960.

Saturday Review, August 2, 1958; January 2, 1960; June 11, 1960; March 16, 1963; February 15, 1964; May 6, 1967; May 24, 1969; April 2, 1977.

Symposium, winter, 1974.

Tel Quel, Volume 20, 1965.

Time, August 4, 1958; May 23, 1960; February 7, 1964.

Times (London, England), October 21, 1999.

Times Literary Supplement, January 1, 1960; January 30, 1964; July 29, 1965; July 11, 1968; January 1, 1970; February 25, 1972; July 11, 1975; April 4, 1980; July 30, 1982; June 10, 1983; April 11, 1986.

Village Voice, July 31, 1984.

Washington Post Book World, February 18, 1973; May 20, 1984.

World, July 4, 1972.

World Literature Today, summer, 1977; summer, 1979; spring, 1981; autumn, 1983; winter, 1983; summer, 1996, E. Nicole Meyer, review of *Ici,* pp. 654-655; spring, 1998, John L. Brown, review of *Ouvrez,* p. 339.

Yale French Studies, winter, 1955-56; summer, 1959; spring-summer, 1961; June, 1971.

Yale Review, winter, 1959; summer, 1960; autumn, 1973.

ONLINE

France Diplomatie, http://www.france.diplomatie.fr/ (November 19, 2003), "Nathalie Sarraute, or How to Paint the Invisible."

Para Ethos Library, http://www.paraethos.com/ (November 19, 2003), "*The Planetarium,* by Nathalie Sarraute."

Virginia Polytechnic Institute and State University, Center for Digital Discourse and Culture Web site, http://www.cddc.vt.edu/feminism/sarraute/html/ (November 19, 2003), "Nathalie Sarraute."

OBITUARIES:

PERIODICALS

Economist, October 30, 1999, p. 96.

Los Angeles Times, October 20, 1999, p. A24.

New York Times, October 20, 1999, p. C25.*

* * *

SEIDLER, Tor 1952-

PERSONAL: Born June 26, 1952, in Littleton, NH; son of John M. (an investor) and Jean (an actress; maiden name, Burch) Falls. *Education:* Stanford University, B.A., 1972.

ADDRESSES: Home—121 West 78th St., New York, NY 10024.

CAREER: Harcourt Brace Jovanovich, New York, NY, freelance contributor to language arts program, 1976-78; freelance writer, 1978—.

AWARDS, HONORS: Fiction Award, Washington State Writer's Day, 1980, for *The Dulcimer Boy;* Outstanding Children's Book citation, *New York Times,* 1982, for *Terpin;* Children's Book of the Year citation, *Publishers Weekly,* 1986, and Silver Pencil Award (Dutch translation), both for *A Rat's Tale;* Notable Book citation, American Library Association, and Parents' Choice Storybook Award, both 1993, both for *The Wainscott Weasel;* Best Books citations, *Publishers Weekly* and *School Library Journal,* and National Book Award finalist, 1997, all for *Mean Margaret.*

WRITINGS:

FOR CHILDREN

The Dulcimer Boy, illustrated by David Hockney, Viking (New York, NY), 1979, illustrated by Brian Selznick, Laura Geringer Books (New York, NY), 2003.

Terpin, Farrar, Straus & Giroux (New York, NY), 1982, Laura Geringer Books (New York, NY), 2002.

A Rat's Tale, illustrated by Fred Marcellino, Farrar, Straus & Giroux (New York, NY), 1985.

The Tar Pit, Farrar, Straus & Giroux (New York, NY), 1987.

(Reteller) Hans Christian Andersen, *The Steadfast Tin Soldier,* illustrated by Fred Marcellino, HarperCollins (New York, NY), 1992.

The Wainscott Weasel, illustrated by Fred Marcellino, HarperCollins (New York, NY), 1993.

Mean Margaret, illustrated by Jon Agee, HarperCollins (New York, NY), 1997.

The Silent Spillbills, HarperCollins (New York, NY), 1998.

The Revenge of Randal Reese-Rat, illustrated by Brett Helquist, Farrar, Straus & Giroux (New York, NY), 2001.

Brothers below Zero, Laura Geringer Books (New York, NY), 2002.

Brainboy and the Deathmaster, Laura Geringer Books (New York, NY), 2003.

Toes, illustrated by Eric Beddows, Laura Geringer Books (New York, NY), 2004.

OTHER

Take a Good Look (adult novel), Farrar, Straus & Giroux (New York, NY), 1990.

Contributor of articles and reviews to art magazines.

ADAPTATIONS: A sound recording of *A Rat's Tale* was produced by Listening Library (New York, NY), 1998, and a videotape version of *A Rat's Tale* made by a German marionette troupe was later released by Warner Bros. (Burbank, CA) in the United States. Sound recordings have also been produced of *Mean Margaret* and *The Silent Spillbills,* Recorded Books (Prince Frederick, MD), 2000.

SIDELIGHTS: Tor Seidler mixes elements of fairy tale and realism in his highly imaginative novels for young readers. Fate and chance, and the personal risks that people sometimes take when their way of life is threatened, all figure prominently in his books, which include *The Dulcimer Boy, A Rat's Tale,* and the whimsical *The Wainscott Weasel.*

Seidler lived in Burlington, Vermont, before moving with his mother and stepfather to Seattle, Washington. Because his parents were divorced when he was very young, he recalls growing up in two different families, with two different sets of rules. Seidler's mother was an actress; his stepfather was very interested in the stage and established theatre groups in both Vermont and Seattle. Tor's childhood memories with them include watching rehearsals of such productions as Shakespeare's *Richard III,* rich with language, duplicity, and mystery.

Although an early introduction to Thorton Wilder's *The Bridge of San Luis Rey* convinced Seidler that he wanted to be an author, he never actively pursued writing during his school years. Instead, he studied math and science at Stanford University while competing in sports. After graduating from Stanford in 1972, Seidler moved to New York City and accepted a position with a publishing company that would finally inspire him to begin writing with an eye to publication. "I started trying to write children's books after working on elementary school readers for a language arts program at Harcourt, Brace," he once explained. "I always liked children's literature. My stepfather used to tell terrific bedtime stories to my older brother and me. He made up 'episodes' which featured animal characters whose foibles were, in fact, ours."

Seidler's first book, *The Dulcimer Boy,* is a fantasy set in New England. The story follows the adventures of William, whose life has an unusual beginning: he is placed, with his twin brother, Jules, in a basket outside the door of some distant relatives—Mr. and Mrs. Carbuncle—before his widowed father goes off to sea. The only other object the father leaves in the basket is a dulcimer, which William eventually learns to play quite well, using its tones to entertain Jules, who cannot speak. Unfortunately for the boys, the Carbuncles are very selfish people. They mistreat the twins for many years and finally attempt to take the dulcimer and sell it. William, with the dulcimer, runs away in search of his father and of answers to who he really is and how he can rescue his brother from the clutches of the Carbuncles. A *Junior Bookshelf* reviewer hailed *The Dulcimer Boy* as "exquisitely formed, with a fine irony of style, trenchant and economic yet also poetic," noting that Seidler's work incorporates more than a little social satire. Zena Sutherland of the *Bulletin of the Center for Children's Books* noticed the same theme, commenting that in his debut novel, Seidler makes the "Alger-like adventures of the dulcimer boy almost believable and certainly touching."

Seidler's next work of fiction, *Terpin,* tells the story of a U.S. Supreme Court justice who returns to the town where he was raised, after a thirty-year absence, to attend a celebration in his honor. The trip back home brings to mind an event from the distant past that had formed the crux of Terpin's personal philosophy: he recalls an incident from his youth where he told a lie that he believes led to a tragic suicide. A dream occurring shortly after the incident reinforced the young Terpin's decision: always to live and speak the truth. This way of life, of course, made the young man unpopular with both family and friends, in whose opinion his penchant for truthfulness became annoying. *Terpin* was not viewed by critics as a simple story, but rather, in the words of *Bulletin of the Center for Children's Books* reviewer Sutherland, a multilayered tale containing "a wry commentary" on failing to reach one's potential and the superficiality of interpersonal relationships, as well as a "rejection" of several commonplace ethical and moral standards in place in modern society. "The trouble with *Terpin,*" thought a *Junior Bookshelf* critic, "is that at the end one wishes there were much more of it."

In *A Rat's Tale,* Seidler tells the story of Montague Mad-Rat the Younger, a sleek, frisky fellow whose habits are not those of his friends. Instead of the usual rat pursuits through the sewers in his Central Park home, Montague enjoys helping his mother make feathered hats, watching his father build mud castles, and painting. Realizing that he scuttles to a different drummer, Montague ventures outside the park and meets up with the Wharf Rats, who are trying to scout up enough lost loose change to pay off the wharf owner before he hires an exterminator to rid the area of their kind. Here Montague's talents can ultimately be of some use, as his paintings—detailed miniature drawings done on sea shells—prove popular with buyers and bring in the much-needed cash. Noting the satire that runs through *A Rat's Tale, Horn Book* critic Ann A. Flowers commented that the story is "clever in its use of language" and called it "a study of the problems and rewards of nonconformity." Lyle Blake Smythers also noted in his *School Library Journal* review that "although seemingly light entertainment, the novel tackles such topics as death, strength of character, and self-acceptance, and handles them well."

Seidler waited over fifteen years before publishing *The Revenge of Randal Reese-Rat,* a sequel to *A Rat's Tale.*

This time around, the author focuses less on Montague Mad-Rat and more on his rival for Isabel's hand, Randal Reese-Rat. Accused of setting fire to Montague and Isabel's home on their wedding night, the innocent Randal vows revenge on the rat community, which has turned against him. "As in the first title," wrote *Booklist*'s Gillian Engberg, "Seidler creates an elaborate world with a skillful mix of fantasy and realism." According to *School Library Journal* critic Eva Mitnick, "the simple, yet evocative language and warmly depicted characters make this fantasy a delight."

Anthropomorphized rodents also serve as the protagonists of Seidler's *Wainscott Weasel* and *Mean Margaret.* In the first title, which takes place in the wooded areas of eastern Long Island, readers find Bagley Brown, Jr., whose amorous interests are seemingly misplaced when he falls for a green-striped fish named Bridget instead of the smooth-coated weasel Wendy Blackish, who is also an excellent dancer. Although Bridget rejects Bagley's advances, she finally agrees to friendship, although her destiny will be to go out to sea with the rest of her kind. Comparing the author's warm-hearted approach to that of E. B. White in the classic *Charlotte's Web, New York Times Book Review* contributor Karen Brailsford noted that Seidler "is prodding young readers [toward] tolerance and cooperation with the environment—and with themselves." Praising the author's imaginatively plotted story, Stephen Fraser added in *Five Owls* that Seidler's "language is elegant without sounding high-minded, creating a sophisticated yet wholly engaging read."

Horn Book commentator Martha V. Parravano also praised Seidler's prose in a review of his well-received *Mean Margaret,* a comical tale of woodchuck newlyweds whose lives are completely disrupted by the arrival of a human toddler named Margaret who has been abandoned near their burrow. Margaret quickly turns the woodchucks' quiet home into an uninhabitable mess in what Parravano described as a "very funny commentary on the demands and rewards of parenthood." "This witty novel about a cranky toddler and her adoptive parents slyly reverses the people-pets dynamic as it comments on modern relationships," wrote a critic for *Publishers Weekly.*

A bird-loving heroine is presented in Seidler's 1998 book, *The Silent Spillbills,* a "highly imaginative novel [that] offers suspense and offbeat humor," according to a reviewer for *Publishers Weekly*. Thirteen-year-old Katerina Farnsworth is on a crusade to save an endangered bird, the spillbill, whose habitat is threatened by the corporate maneuverings of her grandfather. Katerina, who suffers from stuttering, must learn through the course of the book to speak up for herself. *Booklist* reviewer Ilene Cooper praised the "deceptive effortlessness" of Seidler's writing, which she found "easy to respond to." "Young nature enthusiasts will likely want to see more of Katerina and her eccentric family," concluded the critic for *Publishers Weekly*.

Sibling rivalry is at the center of *Brothers below Zero*, but "Seidler takes on an age-old story line . . . and spins it into a survival story with a soft mystical edge," explained a *Kirkus Reviews* contributor. Tim is constantly outshone by his younger brother, John Henry, until his beloved Great-Aunt Winnifred brings out Tim's hidden talent for painting. Jealous, John Henry defaces one of Tim's paintings, sending Tim on a blind rush into the frigid winter night. The suddenly remorseful John Henry goes after him, leading to an "exciting, satisfying climax" which "blends family dynamics and intense action," Janet Hilbun wrote in *School Library Journal*.

Focusing his attention on computers, Seider published *Brainboy and the Deathmaster* in 2003, a novel featuring Darryl, a twelve-year-old suddenly orphaned after his parents perish in a fire. Placed in a shelter, the young boy takes advantage of the computer equipment and online games placed there by Keith Masterly, a giant in the world of computer gaming. Sensing the boy's talents, Masterly adopts Darryl and places him with the other computer prodigies he has "rescued." In Masterly's sprawling compound, the drugged children work on a sinister plot and are kept out of contact with the rest of the world. His suspicions raised, Darryl attempts to find a way out of his adopted father's complex and save his fellow imprisoned child researchers. Though finding some of the plot elements a bit far-fetched, a *Publishers Weekly* critic nonetheless thought that "the language, invariably crisp and bright, makes for a quick read." Writing in *Horn Book*, Susan P. Bloom predicted that the novel would appeal to a wide audience, claiming "everyone . . . will want to play this thrilling, high-tech game of cat and mouse."

Despite the praise that his fiction has received, Seidler remains modest about his accomplishments as a writer.

"I've been writing pretty much regularly for [several] years," he once commented, "and every once in the while I think I'm beginning to get the hang of it, but most of the time I really wonder."

BIOGRAPHICAL AND CRITICAL SOURCES:

PERIODICALS

Booklist, December 1, 1992, Carolyn Phelan, review of *The Steadfast Tin Soldier,* p. 665; November, 1993, Janice Del Negro, review of *The Wainscott Weasel,* p. 519; December 1, 1997, Michael Cart, review of *Mean Margaret,* p. 619; December 15, 1998, Ilene Cooper, review of *The Silent Spillbills,* p. 750; September 1, 2000, Barbara Baskin, review of *The Silent Spillbills,* p. 142; October 1, 2000, Rod Reid, review of *Mean Margaret,* p. 367; November 1, 2001, Gillian Engberg, review of *The Revenge of Randal Reese-Rat,* p. 479; January 1, 2002, Todd Morning, review of *Brothers Below Zero,* p. 845.

Bulletin of the Center for Children's Books, February, 1980, Zena Sutherland, review of *The Dulcimer Boy,* p. 118; December, 1982, Zena Sutherland, review of *Terpin,* p. 77; February, 1998, Deborah Stevenson, review of *Mean Margaret,* p. 218.

Childhood Education, winter, 2002, Timothy W. Easter, review of *Brothers Below Zero,* p. 111.

Five Owls, February, 1994, Stephen Fraser, review of *The Wainscott Weasel,* p. 62.

Horn Book, March-April, 1987, Ann A. Flowers, review of *A Rat's Tale,* p. 212; March-April, 1993, Ellen Fader, review of *The Steadfast Tin Soldier,* p. 192; January-February, 1998, Martha V. Parravano, review of *Mean Margaret,* p. 80; January-February, 2004, Susan P. Bloom, review of *Brainboy and the Deathmaster,* p. 92.

Junior Bookshelf, October, 1981, review of *The Dulcimer Boy,* p. 217; June, 1984, review of *Terpin,* p. 144.

Kirkus Reviews, December 1, 1998, review of *The Silent Spillbills,* p. 1740; August 15, 2001, review of *The Revenge of Randal Reese-Rat,* p. 1221; January 15, 2002, review of *Brothers Below Zero,* p. 108; September 15, 2003, review of *Brainboy and the Deathmaster,* p. 1182.

New Statesman, November 27, 1987, Marsha Rowe, review of *A Rat's Tale,* p. 35.

New York Times, November 30, 1982, George A. Woods, review of *Terpin,* pp. 23, C16; December 3, 1992, Christopher Lehmann-Haupt, review of *The Steadfast Tin Soldier,* pp. B2, C19.

New York Times Book Review, December 5, 1982, review of *Terpin,* p. 22; January 25, 1987, Kenneth C. Davis, review of *A Rat's Tale,* p. 23; October 18, 1987, Francine Prose, review of *The Tar Pit,* p. 38; December 20, 1992, J. D. Landis, review of *The Steadfast Tin Soldier,* p. 19; November 14, 1993, Karen Brailsford, review of *The Wainscott Weasel,* p. 52; November 16, 1997, M. P. Dunleavey, review of *Mean Margaret,* p. 34; November 18, 2001, Nora Krug, review of *The Revenge of Randal Reese-Rat,* p. 52.

Publishers Weekly, November 19, 1982, review of *Terpin,* p. 77; October 31, 1986, review of *A Rat's Tale,* p. 68; June 22, 1990, review of *Take a Good Look,* p. 46; November 2, 1992, review of *The Steadfast Tin Soldier,* p. 81; September 20, 1993, review of *The Wainscott Weasel,* p. 73; August 18, 1997, review of *Mean Margaret,* p. 93; November 16, 1998, review of *The Silent Spillbills,* p. 75; July 30, 2001, review of *The Revenge of Randal Reese-Rat,* p. 85; January 14, 2002, review of *Brothers Below Zero,* p. 61; March 4, 2002, review of *Terpin,* p. 82; May 19, 2003, review of *The Dulcimer Boy,* p. 76; October 13, 2003, review of *Brainboy and the Deathmaster,* p. 80.

School Library Journal, March, 1983, Trev Jones, review of *Terpin,* p. 197; February, 1983, Linda Boyles, review of *The Steadfast Tin Soldier,* p. 68; January, 1987, Lyle Blake Smythers, review of *A Rat's Tale,* p. 79; December, 1993, Cheri Estes, review of *The Wainscott Weasel,* p. 116; November, 1997, Carrie Schadle, review of *Mean Margaret,* p. 99; July, 1998, Stephanie G. Miller, review of *A Rat's Tale,* p. 57; April, 1999, Susan Oliver, review of *The Silent Spillbills,* p. 142; December, 2000, Carol Robison, review of *Mean Margaret,* p. 79; October, 2001, Eva Mitnick, review of *The Revenge of Randal Reese-Rat,* p. 170; April, 2002, Janet Hilbun, review of *Brothers Below Zero,* p. 157.

ONLINE

East Hampton Star Web Site, http://archive.east hamptonstar.com/ehquery/ (September 17, 1998), Joanne Pilgrim, "Tor Seidler: A World That Mirrors Our Own."*

SENGHOR, Léopold Sédar 1906-2001
(Silmang Diamano, Patrice Maguilene Kaymor, pseudonyms)

PERSONAL: Born October 9, 1906, in Joal, Senegal (part of French West Africa; now Republic of Senegal); died December 20, 2001, in Normandy, France; son of Basile Digoye (a cattle breeder and groundnut planter and exporter) and Nyilane (Bakoume) Senghor; married Ginette Eboue, September, 1946 (divorced, 1956); married Collette Hubert, October 18, 1957; children: (first marriage) Francis-Aphang, Guy-Waly (deceased); (second marriage) Philippe-Maguilen (deceased). *Education:* Baccalaureate degree from Lycée of Dakar, 1928; University of Paris, Sorbonne, agregation de grammaire, 1933, studied African languages at Ecole des Hautes Etudes, Paris, 1929-32.

CAREER: Lycée Descartes, Tours, France, instructor in Greek and Latin classics, 1935-38; Lycée Marcelin Berthelot, St. Maur-des-Fosses, France, instructor in literature and African culture, 1938-40 and 1943-44; Ecole Nationale de la France d'Outre Mer, professor, 1945; French National Assembly, Paris, France, and General Council of Senegal, Dakar, Senegal, elected representative, beginning in 1946; Bloc Democratique Sénégalais, Dakar, founder, 1948; French Government, Paris, delegate to United Nations General Assembly in New York City, 1950-51, Secretary of State for scientific research, and representative to UNESCO conferences, 1955-56, member of consultative assembly, 1958, minister-counselor to Ministry of Cultural Affairs, Education, and Justice, 1959-60, advisory minister, beginning in 1960; City of Thies, Senegal, mayor, beginning in 1956; Senegalese Territorial Assembly, elected representative, beginning in 1957; founder and head of Union Progressiste Sénégalaise, beginning in 1958; Mali Federation of Senegal and Sudan, president of Federal Assembly, 1959-60; Republic of Senegal, President of the Republic, 1960-80, Minister of Defense, 1968-69; Socialist Inter-African, chair of executive bureau, beginning 1981; Haut Conseil de la Francophonie, vice president, beginning 1985. Cofounder, with Lamine Gueye, of Bloc Africain, 1945; representative for Senegal to French Constituent Assemblies, 1945 and 1946; official grammarian for writing of French Fourth Republic's new constitution, 1946; sponsor of First World Festival of Négro Arts, Dakar, 1966; chair of Organisation Commune Africaine et Malgache, 1972-74; established West African Economic Community,

Léopold Sédar Senghor

1974; chair of ECONAS, 1978-79. *Military service:* French Army, infantry, 1934-35; served in infantry battalion of colonial troops, 1939; prisoner of war, 1940-42; participated in French Resistance, 1942-45; received serviceman's cross, 1939-45.

MEMBER: International Confederation of Societies of Authors and Composers (past president), Academie des Sciences morales et politiques, Comite National des Ecrivains, Societe des Gens de Lettres, Societe Linguistique de France, Academy of Overseas Sciences, Black Academy of Arts and Sciences, Academy Française, American Academy of Arts and Letters.

AWARDS, HONORS: Corresponding membership in Bavarian Academy, 1961; International French Friendship Prize, 1961; French Language Prize (gold medal), 1963; International Grand Prize for Poetry, 1963; Dag Hammarskjöld International Prize Gold Medal for Poetic Merit, 1963; Marie Noel Poetry Prize, 1965; Red and Green International Literature Grand Prix, 1966; German Book Trade's Peace Prize, 1968; associate membership in French Academy of Moral and Political Sciences, 1969; Knokke Biennial International Poetry Grand Prix, 1970; membership in Academy of Overseas Sciences, 1971; membership in Black Academy of Arts and Sciences, 1971; Grenoble Gold Medal, 1972; Haile Selassie African Research Prize, 1973; Cravat of Commander of Order of French Arts and Letters, 1973; Apollinaire Prize for Poetry, 1974; Prince Pierre of Monaco's Literature Prize, 1977; Prix Eurafrique, 1978; Alfred de Vigny Prize, 1981; Aasan World Prize, 1981; election to Academie Française, 1983; Jawaharlal Nehru Award, 1984; Athinai Prize, 1985. Also recipient of Grand Cross of French Legion of Honor, Commander of Academic Palms, Franco-Allied Medal of Recognition, membership in Agegres de Grammaire and American Academy of Arts and Letters. Numerous honorary doctorates, including those from Fordham University, 1961, University of Paris, 1962, Catholic University of Louvain (Belgium), 1965, Lebanese University of Beirut, 1966, Howard University, 1966, Laval University (Quebec), 1966, Harvard University, 1971, Oxford University, 1973, and from the universities of Ibadan (Nigeria), 1964, Bahia (Brazil), 1965, Strasbourg (France), 1965, Al-Azan (Cairo, Egypt), 1967, Algiers (Algeria), 1967, Bordeaux-Talence (France), 1967, Vermont, 1971, California at Los Angeles, 1971, Ethiopia Haile Selassie I, 1971, Abidjan (Ivory Coast), 1971, and Lagos (Nigeria), 1972.

WRITINGS:

POETRY

Chants d'ombre (title means "Songs of Shadow"; includes "Femme noire" and "Joal"; also see below), Seuil (Paris, France), 1945.

Hosties noires (title means "Black Sacrifices"; includes "Au Gouverneur Eboue," "Mediterranee," "Aux Soldats Négro-Americains," "Tyaroye," and "Priere de paix"), Seuil (Paris, France), 1948.

Chants pour Naëtt (title means "Songs for Naëtt"), Seghers (Paris, France), 1949.

Chants d'ombre [and] *Hosties noires* (title means "Songs of Shadow" [and] "Black Sacrifices"), Seuil (Paris, France), 1956.

Ethiopiques (includes "Chaka," poetic adaptation of Thomas Mofolo's historical novel *Chaka;* "A New York"; and "Congo"), Seuil (Paris, France), 1956, critical edition with commentary by Papa Gueye N'Diaye published as *Ethiopiques: Poèmes,* Nouvelles éditions africaines (Dakar, Senegal), 1974.

Nocturnes (includes *Chants pour Naëtt,* "Elégie de minuit," and "Elégie a Aynina Fall: Peème dramatique a plusieurs voix" [title means "Elegy for Aynina Fall: Dramatic Poem for Many Voices"]), Seuil (Paris, France), 1961, translation by John Reed and Clive Wake published as *Nocturnes,* Heinemann Educational (London, England), 1969, with introduction by Paulette J. Trout, Third Press (New York, NY), 1971.

Elégie des Alizés, original lithographs by Marc Chagall, Seuil (Paris, France), 1969.

Lettres d'hivernage, illustrations by Marc Chagall, Seuil (Paris, France), 1973.

Paroles, Nouvelles éditions africaines (Dakar, Senegal), 1975.

Oeuvre Poétique, Seuil (Paris, France), 1990, translation and introduction by Melvin Dixon published as *Léopold Sédar Senghor: The Collected Poetry,* University Press of Virginia (Charlottesville, VA), 1991.

La Dialogue de cultures, Seuil (Paris, France), 1993.

Contributor of poems to periodicals, including *Chantiers, Les Cahiers du Sud, Les Lettres Françaises, Les Temps Modernes, Le Temp de la Poésie, La Revue Socialiste, Présence africaine,* and *Prevue.*

CRITICAL AND POLITICAL PROSE

(With Robert Lemaignen and Prince Sisowath Youteyong) *La Communaute imperiale française* (includes "Views on Africa; or, Assimilate, Don't Be Assimilated"), Editions Alsatia (Paris, France), 1945.

(With Gaston Monnerville and Aime Cesaire) *Commemoration du centenaire de l'abolition de l'esclavage,* introduction by Edouard Depreux, Presses Universitaires de France (Paris, France), 1948.

Rapport sur la doctrine et le programme du parti, Présence africaine (Paris, France), 1959, translation published as *Report on the Principles and Programme of the Party,* Présence africaine (Paris, France), 1959, abridged edition edited and translated by Mercer Cook published as *African Socialism: A Report to the Constitutive Congress of the Party of African Federation,* American Society of African Culture (New York, NY), 1959.

Rapport sur la politique générale, [Senegal], 1960.

Nation et voie africaine du socialisme, Présence africaine (Paris, France), 1961, new edition published as *Liberté II: Nation et voie africaine du social-*

isme, Seuil (Paris, France), 1971, translation by Mercer Cook published as *Nationhood and the African Road to Socialism,* Présence africaine (Paris, France), 1962, abridged edition published as *On African Socialism,* translation and introduction by Cook, Praeger (New York, NY), 1964.

Rapport sur la doctrine et la politique générale; ou, Socialisme, unite africaine, construction nationale, (Dakar, Senegal) 1962.

(With Pierre Teilhard de Chardin) *Pierre Teilhard de Chardin et la politique africaine* [and] *Sauvons l'humanite* [and] *L'Art dans la ligne de l'energie humaine* (the first by Senghor, the latter two by Teilhard de Chardin), Seuil (Paris, France), 1962.

(With others) *Le Racisme dans le monde,* Juilliard (Paris, France), 1964.

Theorie et pratique du socialisme sénégalais, (Dakar, Senegal), 1964.

Liberté I: Négritude et humanisme, Seuil (Paris, France), 1964, selections translated and introduced by Wendell A. Jeanpierre published as *Freedom 1: Negritude and Humanism,* [Providence, RI], 1974.

(In Portuguese, French, and Spanish) *Latinite et négritude,* Centre de Hautes Etudes Afro-Ibero-Americaines de l'Université de Dakar (Dakar, Senegal), 1966.

Négritude, arabisme, et francité: Réflexions sur le problème de la culture (title means "Negritude, Arabism, and Frenchness: Reflections on the Problem of Culture"), preface by Jean Rous, Editions Dar al-Kitab Allubmani (Beirut), 1967, republished as *Les Fondements de l'Africanite; ou, Négritude et arabite,* Présence africaine, 1967, translation by M. Cook published as *The Foundations of "Africanite"; or, "Negritude" and "Arbiter,"* Présence africaine (Paris, France), 1971.

Politique, nation, et développement moderne: Rapport de politique générale, Imprimerie Nationale (Rufisque, Senegal), 1968.

Le Plan du décollage économique; ou, La Participation responsable comme moteur de développement, Grande Imprimerie Africaine (Dakar, Senegal), 1970.

Pourquoi une ideologie négro-africaine? (lecture), Universite d'Abidjan (Abidjan, Ivory Coast), 1971.

La Parole chez Paul Claudel et chez les Négro-Africains, Nouvelles éditions africaines (Dakar, Senegal), 1973.

(With others) *Litteratures ultramarines de langue française, genese et jeunesse: Actes du colloque de l'Universite du Vermont,* compiled by Thomas H. Geno and Roy Julow, Naaman (Quebec, Canada), 1974.

Paroles (addresses), Nouvelles éditions africaines (Dakar, Senegal), 1975.

Pour une relecture africaine de Marx et d'Engels (includes "Le socialisme africain et la voie séné-galaise"), Nouvelles éditions africaines (Dakar, Senegal), 1976.

Pour une societe sénégalaise socialiste et democratique: Rapport sur la politique générale, Nouvelles éditions africaines (Dakar, Senegal, 1976.

Liberté III: Négritude et civilisation de l'universel (title means "Freedom 3: Negritude and the Civilization of the Universal"), Seuil (Paris, France), 1977.

(With Mohamed Aziza) *La Poésie de l'action: Conversations avec Mohamed Aziza* (interviews), Stock (Paris, France)), 1980.

Ce que je crois: Négritude, francité, et la civilisation de l'universel, Bernard Grasset (Paris, France), 1988.

Also author of *L'Apport de la poésie nègre,* 1953; *Langage et poésie négro-africaine,* 1954; *Esthetique négro-africain,* 1956; and *Liberté IV: Socialisme et planification,* 1983. Author of four technical works on Wolof grammar. Contributor to books, including *Cultures de l'Afrique noire et de l'Occident,* Societe Europeenne de Culture, 1961; and *La Senegal au Colloque sur le liberalisme planifie et les voies africaines vers le socialisme, Tunis, 1-6 juillet 1975,* Grand Imprimerie Africaine (Dakar), 1975. Author of lectures and addresses published in pamphlet or booklet form, including *The Mission of the Poet,* 1966; *Négritude et germanisme,* 1968; *Problèmes de développement dans les pays sous-développés,* 1975; *Négritude et civilisations mediterraneennes,* 1976; and *Pour une lecture négro-africaine de Mallarme,* 1981. Contributor, sometimes under the pseudonyms Silmang Diamano or Patrice Maguilene Kaymor, of critical, linguistic, sociological, and political writings to periodicals and journals, including *Journal de la Societe des Africanists, Présence africaine,* and *L'Esprit.*

OTHER

(Editor) *Anthologie de la nouvelle poésie nègre et malgache de langue française* [precede de] *Orphee noir, par Jean Paul Sartre* (poetry anthology; title means "Anthology of the New Négro and Malagasy Poetry in French [preceded by] Black Orpheus, by Jean-Paul Sartre"), introduction by Sartre, Presses Universitaires de France (Paris, France), 1948, 4th edition, 1977.

(With Abdoulaye Sadji) *La Belle Histoire de Leuk-le-Lievre* (elementary school text; title means "The Clever Story of Leuk-the-Hare"), Hachette (Paris, France), 1953, reprinted as *La Belle Histoire de Leuk-le-Lievre: Cours elementaire des ecoles d'Afrique noir,* illustrations by Marcel Jeanjean, Hachette (Paris, France), 1961, British edition (in French) edited by J. M. Winch, illustrations by Jeanjean, Harrap (London, England), 1965, adaptation published as *Les Aventures de Leuk-le-Lievre,* illustrations by G. Lorofi, Nouvelles éditions africaines (Dakar, Senegal), 1975.

(Author of introductory essay) *Anthologie des poètes du seizieme siecle* (anthology), Editions de la Bibliotheque Mondiale (Paris, France), 1956.

Melange offerts a Léopold Sédar Senghor: Langues—litterature—histoire anciennes, Nouvelles éditions africaines (Paris, France), 1977.

Espaces: A la recherche d'une ecology de l'esprit, Euroeditor (Luxembourg), 1989.

Le Dialogue des cultures, Seuil (Paris, France)), 1993.

Also author of foreword to *The Astrolabe of the Sea,* by Shams Nadir, 1996. Also author of prose tale *Mandabi* (title means "The Money Order"). Translator of poetry by Mariane N'Diaye. Contributor of selected texts to books, including *Afrique Africaine* (photography), photographs by Michel Huet, Clairfontaine, 1963; *Terre promise d'Afrique: Symphonie en noir et or* (poetry anthology), lithographs by Hans Erni, Andre et Pierre Gonin (Lausanne, Switzerland), 1966; and *African Sojourn* (photography), photographs by Uwe Ommer, Arpel Graphics, 1987. Founder of journals, including *Condition Humaine,* with Aime Cesaire and Leon Gontran Damas, *L'Etudiant Noir,* and, with Alioune Diop, *Présence africaine.*

OMNIBUS VOLUMES

Léopold Sédar Senghor (collection of prose and poems; with biographical-critical introduction and bibliography), edited by Armand Guibert, Seghers, 1961, reprinted as *Léopold Sédar Senghor: Une Etude d'Armand Guibert, avec un choix de poèmes* [et] *une chronologie bibliographique, "Léopold Sédar Senghor et son temps,"* Seghers (Paris, France), 1969.

Selected Poems, edited and translated by John Reed and Clive Wake, introduction by Reed and Wake, Atheneum (New York, NY), 1964.

Poèmes (includes *Chants d'ombre, Hosties noires, Ethiopiques, Nocturnes,* and "Poèmes divers"), Seuil (Paris, France), 1964, 4th edition, 1969, new edition, 1984.

L. S. Senghor: Poète sénégalais, commentary by Roger Mercier, Monique Battestini, and Simon Battestini, F. Nathan (Paris, France), 1965.

(In English translation) *Prose and Poetry,* selected and translated by John Reed and Clive Wake, Oxford University Press (Oxford, England), 1965, Heinemann Educational (London, England), 1976.

(In French with English translations) *Selected Poems/Poésies choisies,* English-language introduction by Craig Williamson, Collings (London, England), 1976.

(In French) *Selected Poems of Léopold Sédar Senghor,* edited, with English-language preface and notes, by Abiola Irele, Cambridge University Press (Cambridge, England), 1977.

Elégies majeures [suivi de] *Dialogue sur la poésie francophone,* Seuil (Paris, France), 1979.

(In English translation) *Poems of a Black Orpheus,* translated by William Oxley, Menard (London, England), 1981.

ADAPTATIONS: Senghor's *Mandabi* was adapted for film by Ousmane Sembene.

SIDELIGHTS: President of the Republic of Senegal from the proclamation of that country's independence in 1960 until he stepped down in 1980, Léopold Sédar Senghor is considered, according to *Time,* "one of Africa's most respected elder statesmen." Yet until 1960, Senghor's political career was conducted primarily in France rather than in Africa. He was a product of the nineteenth-century French educational system, a scholar of Greek and Latin, and a member of the elite Academie Française, but he is best known for developing "negritude," a wide-ranging movement that influenced black culture worldwide. As the chief proponent of negritude, Senghor is credited with contributing to Africa's progress toward independence from colonial rule and, according to Jacques Louis Hymans in his *Léopold Sédar Senghor: An Intellectual Biography,* with "setting in motion a whole series of African ideological movements." Senghor first gained widespread recognition, however, when his first collection of poetry was published in 1945; he followed that volume with a highly esteemed body of verse that has accumulated numerous prestigious honors, most notably consideration for the Nobel Prize in literature.

Senghor, thus, was, as Hymans suggested, "the living symbol of the possible synthesis of what appears irreconcilable: he is as African as he is European, as much a poet as a politician, . . . as much a revolutionary as a traditionalist."

As a child, Senghor demonstrated a lively intelligence and an early ambition to become a priest or a teacher, and was accordingly enrolled in a Catholic elementary school in 1913. The following year he began living in a boarding house four miles from Joal at N'Gasobil, where he attended the Catholic mission school operated by the Fathers of the Holy Spirit. There, Senghor was encouraged to forsake his ancestral culture while he learned Latin and studied European civilization as part of a typical nineteenth-century French teaching program. In 1922 he entered Libermann Junior Seminary in Dakar. In his four years there Senghor acquired a sound knowledge of Greek and Latin classics. Obliged to leave the seminary when he was deemed ill-suited to the priesthood, Senghor, disappointed, entered public secondary school at a French-style lycée in Dakar. There he earned numerous scholastic prizes and distinction for having bested white pupils in academic performance. Senghor obtained his secondary school degree with honors in 1928 and was awarded a half scholarship for continued study in France.

In Paris, Senghor boarded at the Lycée Louis-le-Grand, where top-ranking French students study for entrance exams to France's elite higher education programs. One of Senghor's classmates was Georges Pompidou, later prime minister and, eventually, president of France. Pompidou exposed Senghor to the works of French literary masters Marcel Proust, Andre Gide, and Charles Baudelaire. During this time Senghor was also influenced by the writings of Paul Claudel, Arthur Rimbaud, and Maurice Barres. Senghor's lycée education in Paris emphasized a methodology for rigorous thought and instilled habits of intellectual discipline, skills that Senghor embraced. He meanwhile continued to observe Roman Catholicism and expressed support for a restoration of the French government to monarchical rule. According to Hymans, Senghor in his student days was considered fully assimilated into Paris's intellectual milieu, which began including political and social liberation movements such as socialism, rationalism, humanism, and Marxism.

In *The New Negro,* an anthology published in 1925, Senghor encountered the works of prominent writers such as Paul Laurence Dunbar, W. E. B. Du Bois, Countee Cullen, Langston Hughes, Claude McKay, Zora Neale Hurston, James Weldon Johnson, and Jean Toomer. The anthology's editor, Alain Locke, was a professor of philosophy at Harvard University and a contributor to *La Revue du Monde Noir;* Senghor met him through Nardal as well. When Senghor, Cesaire, and Leon-Gontran Damas, a student from French Guiana, sought a name for the growing francophone interest in African culture, they borrowed from the title of Locke's anthology and dubbed the movement "neonègre" or "nègre-nouveau." These labels were later replaced by "négritude," a term coined by Cesaire. Senghor credits Jamaican poet and novelist Claude McKay with having supplied the values espoused by the new movement: to seek out the roots of black culture and build on its foundations, to draw upon the wealth of African history and anthropology, and to rehabilitate black culture in the eyes of the world. With Cesaire and Damas, Senghor launched *L'Etudiant Noir,* a cultural journal.

In exalting black culture and values, Senghor emphasized what he perceived as differences between the races. He portrayed blacks as possessing intuitive and artistic natures, seeing in them an essential and exuberant emotionalism that whites tend to suppress with reason and intellect. Europe he saw as alien, dehumanized, and dying; in stark contrast, he considered Africa vital, nourishing, and thriving. As racism and fascism swept through Europe in the 1930s, Senghor's attitudes hardened. For a brief period he became disillusioned with Europe and abandoned his religious faith. However, as Hymans has suggested, Senghor began to see that "the same Romantic antirationalism that fathered racism among the Fascists of the 1930s underlay his early reaction against the West." Thus, as Senghor observed the increasing turmoil in Europe caused by Fascist regimes in Italy and Germany and witnessed the dangers of racism, he began to modify his position.

The poems Senghor wrote in the late 1930s were later published in the collection *Chants d'ombre.* For the most part, these poems express Senghor's nostalgia for Africa, his sense of exile, estrangement, and cultural alienation, and his attempt to recover an idealized past. In a style based on musical rhythms, the poet evokes the beauty of the African landscape and peoples, the richness of Africa's past and the protecting presence of the dead, and the innocence and

dignity inherent in his native culture. These poems, critics noted, celebrate an Africa Senghor knew as a child, one transformed by nostalgia into a paradise-like simplicity. In some of the volume's other poems Senghor laments the destruction of the continent's culture and the suffering of its people under colonial rule. One of the collection's frequently cited pieces, "Femme noir," employs sensual yet worshipful language intended to glorify all black women. In "Joal" Senghor returns to his native village, revisiting places and inhabitants he had once known very well; it is, according to Sebastian Okechukwu Mezu in *The Poetry of Léopold Sédar Senghor,* "easily one of the most beautiful poems created by Senghor." When *Chants d'ombre* was published in 1945, it was well received in Paris and brought Senghor to public attention as a voice of black Africa. "In recreating the distant continent by verse," Hymans observed, "Senghor helped blaze the trail that led to the phenomenon of negritude."

World War II intervened between the writing of the poems collected in *Chants d'ombre* and their eventual publication. Germany invaded Poland in September, 1939, and Senghor was immediately called to active duty to protect France at the German border. While the holder of a high academic degree is usually made a commissioned officer, Senghor, as a black man was made a second-class soldier in the Colonial Infantry. France fell to the German assault in June, 1940, the same month Senghor was captured and interned in a German prison camp. At the time of his capture he was almost shot along with some other Senegalese prisoners, but a French officer interceded on his behalf. While in prison Senghor met African peasants who had been recruited into the French Army, and began to identify with their plight. He wrote a number of poems that he sent by letter to his old classmate and friend Georges Pompidou; they were hand-delivered by a German guard who had been a professor of Chinese at the University of Vienna before the war. These poems later formed the core of Senghor's second published collection, *Hosties noires,* which appeared in 1948.

Hosties noires documents Senghor's realization that he was not alone in his exile from Africa, explores his increasing sense of unity with blacks as an exploited race, and elucidates the positive meaning Senghor finds in the sacrifices blacks have made. In poems such as "Au Gouveneur Eboue," which treats a black man's willingness to die for the salvation of the white world, Senghor memorializes blacks fighting for Europe. Elsewhere in *Hosties noires,* Senghor protests the exploitation of black soldiers and attacks western sources of power and violence. In other poems, such as "Mediterranee" and "Aux Soldats Négro-Americains," he rejoices in the common bonds formed with fellow soldiers and with American blacks. And with "Priere de paix" and "Tyaroye," Senghor hopes for unity and peace; while denouncing colonialism, he calls for an end to hatred and welcomes the new life that succeeds death. The collection, according to Mezu, is "the most homogeneous volume of Senghor's poetry, from the point of view not only of theme but also of language and sentiment."

Through the influence of West Indian colleagues, Senghor was released from prison in June, 1942, and resumed teaching at the lycée in suburban Paris where he had earlier served as instructor of literature and African culture. He joined a Resistance group and also participated in activities involving colonial students. During the war, negritude had gained momentum, and when *Chants d'ombre* appeared in 1945, a new group of black intellectuals eagerly embraced Senghor's poetry and cultural theories. That year he published the influential essay "Views on Africa; or, Assimilate, Don't Be Assimilated." In the 1930s, Senghor had concentrated on cultural rather than political issues; after the war, encouraged by colonial reforms extended to French West Africans, he decided to run for election as one of Senegal's representatives in the French National Assembly. With Lamine Gueye, Senghor formed the Bloc Africain to involve the Senegalese people in their political fate. France was forming a new constitution, and in recognition of his linguistic expertise, France's provisional government appointed Senghor the document's official grammarian. Senghor founded the Bloc Democratique Sénégalais (BDS) in 1948; throughout the 1950s the BDS dominated Senegalese politics.

Senghor's literary activities also continued. In 1947, he founded, with Alioune Diop, the cultural journal *Présence africaine.* Along with a publishing house of the same name, *Présence africaine* became, under Diop's direction, a powerful vehicle for black writing worldwide. As editor of *Anthologie de la nouvelle poésie noire et malgache de langue française,* published in 1948, Senghor brought together contemporary poetry written by francophone blacks. An essay titled "Orphee noir" ("Black Orpheus"), by French philoso-

pher and writer Jean-Paul Sartre, introduced the anthology. Sartre's essay outlined the cultural aims of black peoples striving to recapture their heritage. In the process, Sartre defined and gained notoriety for the philosophy of negritude, portraying negritude as a step toward a united society without racial distinction. Many consider "Black Orpheus" to be the most important document of the negritude movement.

A collection of poems Senghor had been working on since 1948 was published as *Ethiopiques* in 1956. These poems reflect Senghor's growing political involvement and his struggle to reconcile European and African allegiances through crossbreeding, both figurative and literal. The year *Ethiopiques* was published, Senghor divorced his African wife to marry one of her friends, a white Frenchwoman; critics have suggested that Senghor's views on crossbreeding represent an attempt to resolve his personal conflict by eliminating the divisive social elements that divided his loyalties. One of *Ethiopiques*' poems, "Chaka," is a dramatic adaptation of Thomas Mofolo's novel about a Zulu hero who forged and ruled a vast domain in the early nineteenth century. Mezu called "Chaka" Senghor's "most ambitious piece." Others have drawn parallels between Senghor's life and the poem's attempt to combine in the character of Chaka, both the poet and politician. In "Chaka," Senghor applied his theories about the combination of music, dance, and poetry found in native African art forms. As Mezu noted, "Senghor aimed to illustrate what he considered an indigenous form of art where music, painting, theatre, poetry, religion, faith, love, and politics are all intertwined." In addition to musical and rhythmic elements, native plants and animals also figure prominently in *Ethiopiques,* whose other poems include "A New York," and "Congo."

Poems Senghor wrote during the tumultuous years leading up to his election as president of Senegal were published in the 1961 collection *Nocturnes,* which featured a group of love poems previously published as *Chants pour Naëtt* in 1949. In *Nocturnes,* Senghor ponders the nature of poetry and examines the poetic process. Critics have noted that in this volume, particularly in poems such as "Elégie de minuit," Senghor reveals his regret for time spent in the empty pomp of political power, his nostalgia for his youth, and his reconciliation with death. Mezu called "Elégie de minuit" the poet's "'last'poem."

After 1960, Senghor wrote mainly political and critical prose, tied closely to the goals, activities, and demands of his political life. During this time he survived an attempted coup d'etat staged in 1962 by Senegal's prime minister, Mamadou Dia. The following year, Senghor authorized the Senegalese National Assembly to draw up a new constitution that gave more power to the president, elected to five-year terms. Known for his ability to hold factions together, he remained in power, reelected in 1968 and 1973, despite more coup attempts, an assassination plot in 1967, and civil unrest in the late 1960s. Much of Senghor's writing from this era outlines the course to which he feels Africa must hold. Commenting on the instability suffered after African nations achieved independence, Senghor told *Time:* "The frequency of coups in Africa is the result of the backwardness in civilization that colonization represented. . . . What we should all be fighting for is democratic socialism. And the first task of socialism is not to create social justice. It is to establish working democracies."

According to Hymans, Senghor's brand of socialism, often called the African Road to Socialism, maps out a middle position between individualism and collectivism, between capitalism and communism. Senghor saw socialism as a way of eliminating the exploitation of individuals that prevents universal humanism. Some of Senghor's writings on this topic were translated by Mercer Cook and published in 1964 as *On African Socialism*. Appraising *On African Socialism* for *Saturday Review*, Charles Miller called its selections "exquisitely intellectual tours de force."

When a new collected edition of Senghor's poetry appeared in 1984, Robert P. Smith, Jr., writing in *World Literature Today* identified Senghor as a "great poet of Africa and the universe." Praising the masterly imagery, symbolism, and versification of the poetry, Smith expressed particular admiration for Senghor's "constant creation of a poetry which builds up, makes inquiries, and expands into universal dimensions," and cited an elegy Senghor wrote for his deceased son as "one of the most beautiful in modern poetry." Critics characterize Senghor's poetic style as serenely and resonantly rhetorical. While some readers detect a lack of tension in his poetry, most admire its lush sensuality and uplifting attitude. Offered as a means of uniting African peoples in an appreciation of their cultural worth, Senghor's poetry, most agree, extends across the chasm that negritude, at least in its early form, seemed to have created in emphasizing the differences between races. "It is difficult to predict whether

Senghor's poetry will excite the same approbation when the prestige of the President and that of the idealist no longer colour people's view of the man," Mezu acknowledged. "The Senegalese poet will certainly survive in the history of the Black Renaissance as the ideologist and theoretician of negritude." Writing in the *Washington Post Book World*, K. Anthony Appiah saw Senghor's poetry as "an integral part of his political and intellectual career rather than as a free-standing accomplishment demanding separate literary treatment."

BIOGRAPHICAL AND CRITICAL SOURCES:

BOOKS

Black Literature Criticism, Gale (Detroit, MI), 1992.

Blair, Dorothy S., *African Literature in French,* Cambridge University Press (Cambridge, England), 1976.

Collins, Grace, *Man of Destiny: Léopold Sédar Senghor of Senegal,* Sights Publications (Mt. Airy, MD), 1997.

Contemporary Literary Criticism, Volume 54, Gale (Detroit, MI), 1989.

Crowder, Michael, *Senegal: A Study in French Assimilation Policy,* Oxford University Press (Oxford, England), 1962.

Hymans, Jacques Louis, *Léopold Sédar Senghor: An Intellectual Biography,* University Press (Edinburgh, Scotland), 1971.

Kluback, William, *Léopold Sédar Senghor: From Politics to Poetry,* P. Lang (New York, NY), 1997.

Markovitz, Irving Leonard, *Léopold Sédar Senghor and the Politics of Negritude,* Atheneum (New York, NY), 1969.

Mezu, Sebastian Okechuwu, *The Poetry of Léopold Sédar Senghor,* Fairleigh Dickinson University Press (Rutherford, NJ), 1973.

Neikirk, Barend van Dyk Van, *The African Image (Negritude) in the Work of Léopold Sédar Senghor,* A. A. Balkema, 1970.

Spleth, Janice, editor, *Critical Perspectives on Léopold Sédar Senghor,* Three Continents Press (Washington, DC), 1991.

Vaillant, Janet G., *Black, French and African: A Life of Léopold Sédar Senghor,* Harvard University Press (Cambridge, MA), 1990.

Vaillant, Janet G., and Brenda Randolph, *A Trumpet for His People: Léopold Sédar Senghor of Senegal,* Sights Publications (Mt. Airy, MD), 1996.

PERIODICALS

Black World, August 14, 1978.
Callaloo, winter, 1990.
Ebony, August, 1972.
Essence, September, 1987.
French Review, May, 1982.
Maclean's, February 24, 1986, p. 22.
New York Review of Books, December 20, 1990, p. 11.
Saturday Review, January 2, 1965.
Time, June 9, 1978; January 16, 1984.
Times Literary Supplement, June 11, 1964.
Washington Post Book World, July 5, 1992, p. 2.
World Literature Today, spring, 1965; autumn, 1978; summer, 1981; winter, 1985; summer, 1990, p. 540.

ONLINE

New York Times Online, http://www.nytimes.com/ (December 21, 2001).

OBITUARIES:

BOOKS

Contemporary Literary Criticism, Volume 54, Gale (Detroit, MI), 1989.
Historic World Leaders, Gale (Detroit, MI), 1998.
Major Twentieth-Century Writers, Gale (Detroit, MI), 1999.
Modern Black Writers, 2nd edition, St. James Press (Detroit, MI), 2000.

PERIODICALS

Chicago Tribune, December 21, 2001, section 2, p. 10.
Los Angeles Times, December 21, 2001, p. B12.
New York Times, December 21, 2001, p. A25.
Times (London, England), December 21, 2001, p. 19.
Washington Post, December 21, 2001, p. B6.*

*   *   *

SEYMOUR, Alan
    See WRIGHT, S(ydney) Fowler

SHIGEKUNI, Julie

PERSONAL: Female. *Ethnicity:* "Japanese American." *Education:* Attended City University of New York, Hunter College, and Sarah Lawrence College.

ADDRESSES: Office—Department of Creative Writing, University of New Mexico, Albuquerque, NM 87131.

CAREER: Writer and editor. University of New Mexico, Albuquerque, assistant professor of creative writing, 1998—. Has also been a writer in residence at Mills College and has taught at Hunter College, Sarah Lawrence College, and the Institute of American Indian Arts.

AWARDS, HONORS: Henfield Award; American Japanese National Literary Award; Josephine Miles Award, PEN Oakland, 1997, for *A Bridge between Us.*

WRITINGS:

A Bridge between Us, Anchor Books (New York, NY), 1995.
Invisible Gardens, Thomas Dunne Books (New York, NY), 2003.

Also author of *Lovely in Her Bones.* Author of short stories contributed to periodicals and anthologies, including "Krista Rising," *On a Bed of Rice: An Asian American Erotic Feast,* edited by Geraldine Kudaka and Russell C. Leong, Anchor Books, 1995. Editor, *Blue Mesa Review.*

SIDELIGHTS: Julie Shigekuni, a fifth-generation Japanese American, explores the relationships between four generations of women in a Japanese-American family in her debut novel, *A Bridge between Us.* Much of the book focuses on Nomi, a member of the youngest generation of the family. Nomi is at odds with her family, which includes her great-grandmother, Reiko, her grandmother, Rio, and Tomoe, her mother. In alternating chapters each of the four women tells her own story of betrayed love, cruelty, obligation, and the intense intimacy of family life. Reiko has grown up under a lie about her mother's reasons for abandoning her, believing that she was a Japanese princess who could not cope with life in the United States without the comforts of servants and other royal luxuries. Despite this maternal loss in her life, Reiko for the most part neglects her own daughter, Rio.

After a failed marriage, Rio returns home to find that her mother has remarried. As the story develops, the plot circles back to Rio's suicide attempt, which lends insight to the character's relationships. Rio's daughter, Tomoe, is a travel agent with traditional values who, along with Reiko, finds seven-year-old Nomi and Rio's personality to be selfish. As Nomi matures she attempts to shrug off the family influences that tie her and develop her own person. Sexually promiscuous to a degree, Nomi becomes pregnant and travels to Japan to give birth and understand her family's past. A reviewer for *Booklist* commented that in doing so, "she is . . . reenacting the journeys of all of her female relatives."

According to critic Lisa Shea, in a review for the *New York Times Book Review,* the manner in which the four women's narratives circle back on themselves allows each of their tales to enlarge the story and "give the novel unexpected heft." Shea remarked that "while Nomi's story could not exist without the specific tensions of her heritage . . . , the lesson one takes . . . is time-honored in every culture. No one makes you pay more dearly for becoming who you are than your own family; all you can do is ask them to forgive you, as you must forgive them, for the person you have become." A *Publishers Weekly* reviewer praised the novel, calling it "visceral, rich in metaphor and intricately crafted," and added that "Shigekuni's impressive debut hums along with subdued grace."

In *Invisible Gardens,* Shigekuni's second novel, the seemingly perfect life of history professor Lily Soto is tainted by dissatisfaction, role confusion, repressed sexual passion, and obsession with death. Lily's husband, Joseph, is a successful pathologist, and her son and daughter are healthy and attractive—her young son, in fact, is still nursing. Despite the semblance of domestic and professional bliss, Lily experiences deep emotional turmoil. She has long had conflicting emotions about her mother, who died suddenly during Lily's final year of college. When her father, in deteriorating physical and mental health, comes to New Mexico to live with them, his arrival brings back an intense flood of memories of her childhood and her mother. To add to her emotional turmoil and midlife

crisis, Lily begins a clandestine affair with colleague Perish Ishida, a physically imperfect, cranky, solitary academic who nevertheless manages to bring emotions and sensations to Lily that she can't get elsewhere—particularly at home. Throughout the novel, symbols and images of death waft around Lily's thoughts and actions. But even while her carefully constructed life seems to be crumbling at all points, Lily retains her intellect, and realizes that she must make important decisions about her family, marriage, and career.

"Shigekuni does an outstanding job creating an alliance between the reader and Lily by subtly delineating the motives behind Lily's actions," observed Irene J. Kim on the *Jade Magazine* Web site. "We are aware of Lily's thought processes, although we may not necessarily agree with them," Kim wrote. Reviewer Jeff Zaleski, writing in *Publishers Weekly,* called the book "mostly a taut, well-modulated tale," but also pointed out that readers of the book "may be a bit baffled by the resolution" that is unexpected and inconclusive. Despite his misgivings about the end of the novel, Zeleski remarked that "Shigekuni beautifully describes Lily's subtle sense of isolation in her marriage." Ellen R. Cohen, reviewing the book in *Library Journal,* declared, "This poignant story will be particularly appreciated by women." A *Kirkus Reviews* critic concluded that *Invisible Gardens* is "as sexy and brief as the love it describes."

BIOGRAPHICAL AND CRITICAL SOURCES:

PERIODICALS

Booklist, January 1, 1995, review of *A Bridge between Us,* pp. 801-802.
Kirkus Reviews, March 1, 2003, review of *Invisible Gardens,* p. 342.
Library Journal, March 15, 2003, Ellen R. Cohen, review of *Invisible Gardens,* p. 117.
Los Angeles Times, June 29, 2003, Susan Salter Reynolds, "That Was *Joy Luck,* This Is Now; Anger, Realism, and Irreverence Distinguish the 'Second Generation' of Asian American Novelists," p. E1.
New York Times Book Review, March 19, 1995, Lisa Shea, review of *A Bridge between Us,* p. 7.
Publishers Weekly, January 2, 1995, review of *A Bridge between Us,* p. 57; June 23, 2003, Jeff Zaleski, review of *Invisible Gardens,* p. 49.

ONLINE

Jade Magazine Web site, http://www.jademagazine. com/ (November 14, 2003), review of *Invisible Gardens.*

Newsday Web site, http://www.newsday.com/ (August 5, 2003), Susan Salter Reynolds, "A New Telling—A Cadre of Young Authors Reflects the Widening Mainstream of the Asian-American Experience."

Recursos Web site, http://www.recursos.org/ (November 14, 2003), profile of Julie Shigekuni.

University of New Mexico Web site, http://www.unm. edu/~english/writing/creative/profiles.html/ (March 5, 1999), biography of Julie Shigekuni.*

*   *   *

SMIRAGLIA, Richard P(aul) 1952-

PERSONAL: Born March 18, 1952, in New York, NY; son of Sylvio Carl (a musician) and Marcia Jane Hinds Jacob Smiraglia. *Ethnicity:* "Caucasian Italian-American." *Education:* Lewis and Clark College, B.A., 1973; Indiana University—Bloomington, M.L.S., 1974; University of Chicago, Ph.D., 1992; General Theological Seminary of the Episcopal Church, M.Div., 1997. *Politics:* Democrat. *Hobbies and other interests:* Trains, cooking.

ADDRESSES: Home—340 Fitzwater St., Philadelphia, PA 19147. *Office*—Palmer School of Library and Information Science, Long Island University, Brookville, NY 11548. *E-mail*—richard.smiraglia@liu. edu.

CAREER: University of Illinois—Urbana-Champaign, Urbana, assistant music catalog librarian, 1974-78, music catalog librarian and associate professor of library administration, 1978-86, visiting instructor, 1985-86; Columbia University, New York, NY, assistant professor of library service, 1987-93; Long Island University, Brookville, NY, professor of library and information science, 1993—. Ordained Episcopal priest, 1998; National Episcopal AIDS Coalition, member, 1992—; pastor of Episcopal churches in New York, NY, 1995-97; pastor for outreach ministry to the "unchurched gay and lesbian community," 1996; as-

sisting priest at Episcopal church in Philadelphia, PA, 1997-98, and at St. Mary's Hamilton Village, 1999-2000; priest in charge at St. Mark's Church, Frankford District, Philadelphia, 2000-01, and St. Philip's Memorial Church, 2002—. Consultant to Union Catalog of Motion Picture Music, Kurt Weill Foundation, and National Museum of American History.

MEMBER: International Society for Knowledge Organization, American Society for Information Science.

AWARDS, HONORS: Shared awards from Music Library Association, 1981, for article "Music in the OCLC Online Union Catalog," and 1999, for "Beyond the Score."

WRITINGS:

Shelflisting Music: Guidelines for Use with the Library of Congress Classification M, Music Library Association (Philadelphia, PA), 1981.

(Music arranger and transcriber) Rochelle A. Wright and Robert L. Wright, *Danish Emigrant Ballads and Songs,* Southern Illinois University Press (Carbondale, IL), 1983.

Cataloging Music: A Manual for Use with AACR2, Soldier Creek (Lake Crystal, MN), 1983, 2nd edition, 1986.

(Editor, with Sheila S. Intner) *Policy and Practice in the Bibliographic Control of Nonbook Materials,* American Library Association (Chicago, IL), 1987.

Music Cataloging: The Bibliographic Control of Printed and Recorded Music in Libraries, Libraries Unlimited (Englewood, CO), 1989.

(Editor) *Describing Archival Materials: The Use of the MARC AMC Format,* Haworth Press (New York, NY), 1990.

(Editor and contributor) *Origins, Content, and Future of AACR2,* revised edition, Association for Library Collections and Technical Services (Chicago, IL), 1992.

Describing Music Materials: A Manual for Use with AACR2 and APPM, 3rd edition, Soldier Creek (Lake Crystal, MN), 1996.

The Nature of a Work: Implications for the Organization of Knowledge, Scarecrow Press (Lanham, MD), 2001.

(Editor and contributor) *Works As Entities for Information Retrieval,* Haworth Press (New York, NY), 2001.

Series editor, "Soldier Creek Music Series," Soldier Creek (Lake Crystal, MN), 1987—, and "Technical Reports Series," Music Library Association (Canton, MA), 1988-94. Contributor to periodicals, including *Journal of the American Society for Information Science and Technology, Knowledge Organization,* and *Notes: Quarterly Journal of the Music Library Association.* Editor, *Library Resources and Technical Services,* 1990-96; member of editorial board, *Cataloging and Classification Quarterly,* 1984-90, 2001—.

BIOGRAPHICAL AND CRITICAL SOURCES:

PERIODICALS

Library Resources and Technical Services, January, 2004, Patrick Le Boeuf, review of *Works As Entities for Information Retrieval,* p. 79.

ONLINE

Richard P. Smiraglia Home Page, http://smiraglia.org/ (April 8, 2004).

*   *   *

SMITH, Ray Campbell 1916-

PERSONAL: Born January 25, 1916, in London, England; son of Harold Frederick (a naval commander) and Daisy Gladys (a homemaker) Smith; married Eileen Joyce Devereux, April 25, 1945; children: Wendy Maralyn Smith Baker, Paul Devereux. *Ethnicity:* "British; English." *Education:* Croydon School of Art, London, degree (with honors), 1952. *Politics:* "Middle of the road." *Religion:* Church of England. *Hobbies and other interests:* Preservation of the countryside and architecture, studying historic buildings.

ADDRESSES: Home—Finchcocks, 5 Wildernesse Mount, Sevenoaks, Kent TN13 3QS, England.

CAREER: Art teacher at grammar schools and secondary schools in and around London, England, 1947-88; writer and artist, 1988—. Creator of instructional videotapes for film companies and television networks.

Paintings included in collections, including those of the National Trust, Lord and Lady Sackville, and the Duke and Duchess of Devonshire. *Military service:* British Army, Royal Artillery, 1939-46; became captain; received Bronze Oak Leaf.

MEMBER: Royal Society of Arts (fellow), British Society of Painters (fellow), British Watercolour Society (associate).

AWARDS, HONORS: SAA (Society for All Artists) Award, best book and video category, 1997.

WRITINGS:

Fresh Watercolour: Bring Light and Life to Your Painting, David & Charles (Newton Abbot, Devon, England), 1991.
Developing Style in Watercolour, David & Charles (Newton Abbot, Devon, England), 1993.
Watercolour for All: A Practical Guide for Beginners and Improvers, David & Charles (Newton Abbot, Devon, England), 1994.
The Art of Watercolour: A Guide to the Skills and Techniques, Reader's Digest Association (Pleasantville, NY), 1995.
Watercolour Work-out: Fifty Landscape Projects from Choosing a Scene to Painting the Picture, David & Charles (Newton Abbot, Devon, England), 1996.
Ray Campbell Smith's Way with Watercolour: Exploring Landscape Painting, David & Charles (Newton Abbot, Devon, England), 1997.
Classic Techniques for Watercolour Landscapes, David & Charles (Newton Abbot, Devon, England), 2002.

Other books include three titles in the "Learn to Paint" series and three titles in the "Step by Step Leisure Arts" series, both Search Press, 1987-2003. Contributor of more than 200 articles and reviews to art magazines.

WORK IN PROGRESS: Another book on watercolor painting.

SIDELIGHTS: Ray Campbell Smith once told *CA:* "Art has always been my consuming passion, and I expressed this in painting and in teaching others to paint. I have contributed to leading art magazines and, when approached by publishers, I agreed to write a book on painting. This quickly became a best-seller and encouraged me to write several more.

"I am interested in a variety of media, but have concentrated on watercolor in recent years. I am inspired by nature and am interested in the imaginative treatment of landscapes and seascapes, with lively color, bold brushwork, and powerful tonal contrasts."

BIOGRAPHICAL AND CRITICAL SOURCES:

PERIODICALS

Booklist, May 1, 2002, Alice Joyce, review of *Classic Techniques for Watercolour Landscapes,* p. 1497.

*   *   *

SMITH, Wilbur (Addison) 1933-

PERSONAL: Born January 9, 1933, in Broken Hill, Northern Rhodesia (now Zambia); son of Herbert James and Elfreda (Lawrence) Smith; married Jewell Slabbert, August 28, 1964 (divorced); married Danielle Thomas, February 1971; children: two sons and one daughter. *Education:* Rhodes University, Bachelor of Commerce, 1954. *Hobbies and other interests:* Fishing and wildlife conservation.

ADDRESSES: Home—Sunbird Hill, 34 Klaassens Road, Constantia 7800, South Africa. *Agent*—Charles Pick Consultancy, Flat 3, 3 Bryanston Place, London W1H 7FN, England. *E-mail*—wilbur.smith@stmartins.com.

CAREER: Affiliated with Goodyear Tire & Rubber Co., Port Elizabeth, South Africa, 1954-58, and H. J. Smith & Son, Ltd., Salisbury, Rhodesia (now Zimbabwe), 1958-63; full-time writer, 1964—.

MEMBER: Chartered Institute of Secretaries, South African Wildlife Society (trustee), Friends of Conservation (trustee), Rhodesian Wildlife Conservation Association, British Sub Aqua Club.

Wilbur Smith

WRITINGS:

When the Lion Feeds, Viking (New York, NY), 1964.
The Train from Katanga, Viking (New York, NY), 1965, published as *The Dark of the Sun,* Heinemann (London, England), 1965.
Shout at the Devil, Coward (New York, NY), 1968.
Gold Mine, Doubleday (New York, NY), 1970.
The Diamond Hunters, Heinemann (London, England), 1971, Doubleday (New York, NY), 1972.
The Sunbird, Heinemann (London, England), 1972, Doubleday (New York, NY), 1973.
Eagle in the Sky, Doubleday (New York, NY), 1974.
Eye of the Tiger, Doubleday (New York, NY), 1974.
Cry Wolf, Doubleday (New York, NY), 1975.
A Sparrow Falls, Doubleday (New York, NY), 1976.
Hungry As the Sea, Doubleday (New York, NY), 1977.
Wild Justice, Doubleday (New York, NY), 1978.
A Falcon Flies, Doubleday, 1979 (New York, NY), published as *Flight of the Falcon,* Doubleday (New York, NY), 1982.
Men of Men, Doubleday (New York, NY), 1980.
The Delta Decision, Doubleday (New York, NY), 1981.

The Angels Weep, Doubleday (New York, NY), 1983.

The Leopard Hunts in Darkness, Doubleday (New York, NY), 1984.

The Burning Shore, Doubleday (New York, NY), 1985.

Power of the Sword, Little, Brown (Boston, MA), 1986.

Rage, Little, Brown (Boston, MA), 1987.

The Courtneys, Little, Brown (Boston, MA), 1988.

A Time to Die, Random House (New York, NY), 1989.

Golden Fox, Random House (New York, NY), 1990.

Elephant Song, Random House (New York, NY), 1991.

The Sound of Thunder, Fawcett (New York, NY), 1991.

River God, St. Martin's Press (New York, NY), 1994.

The Seventh Scroll, St. Martin's Press (New York, NY), 1995.

Birds of Prey, St. Martin's Press (New York, NY), 1997.

Monsoon, St. Martin's Press (New York, NY), 1999.

Warlock, Macmillan (New York, NY), 2001.

The Blue Horizon, St. Martin's Press (New York, NY), 2003.

Writer for British Broadcasting Corp. (BBC) programs.

ADAPTATIONS: The Dark of the Sun was filmed by Metro-Goldwyn-Mayer and released in 1968; *Gold Mine* was filmed by Hemdale and released in 1974; the film rights to *The Leopard Hunts in Darkness* have been purchased by Sylvester Stallone, as have the film rights of two of Smith's other novels. Most of Smith's novels have been adapted for audiocassette.

SIDELIGHTS: A writer of historical adventure sagas, Wilbur Smith is known for his "swashbuckling adventure novels set against the historical backdrop of Africa," as an essayist for *Contemporary Popular Writers* explained. His novels have sold some 100 million copies throughout the world. Smith once told *CA:* "I am essentially a writer of entertainment fiction. So far most of my work is against the background of southern Africa. My interests are the history of this land, its wildlife, and its people. . . . I speak Afrikaans and some African dialects, including Zulu."

Born in Northern Rhodesia, now Zambia, Smith was first discouraged from writing by his father, who thought the profession would not pay well. Speaking to Jonah Hull of the *Out There* Web site about his father, Smith explained: "He was a hard man, but a fair one, who wanted me to do something sensible with my life, like be an accountant. I actually was an accountant for a while in my twenties. That made him happy. When I got seriously into writing, though, he couldn't understand it. I think it puzzled him to his death. He wasn't a man who read many books. In fact, I seriously doubt if he actually read any of my books. Even the first one which I dedicated to him." Following a divorce, which brought on depression, Smith began to write fiction to take himself away from the realities of his daily life. While working a day job with the Rhodesian tax department, he spent his nights working on a novel, *When the Lion Feeds.* The story of an early European pioneer in Southern Africa who fights off the native Zulus and rival Europeans as he searches for gold, the novel proved an enormous success. Smith first gained international success in 1964 with the novel *When the Lion Feeds,* according to a writer for *Geographical.* "His name has since become synonymous with adventure blockbuster writing."

Smith's three related novels—*A Falcon Flies, Men of Men,* and *The Angels Weep*—are concerned with the European conquest of what is now Zimbabwe. In this trilogy, the Ballantynes, a fictional family, challenge the historical figure Cecil Rhodes, who amassed a fortune in South Africa and after whom both the nation of Rhodesia and the Rhodes scholarships were named. The essayist for *Contemporary Popular Writers* explained that "in this series, the novels' plots are intertwined with the tumultuous history of Rhodesia, including the slave trade, diamond mining, and tribal warfare." The *Washington Post*'s Richard Harwood, reviewing *Men of Men,* compared Smith favorably to other historical thriller writers: "Wilbur Smith is more artful than John Jakes and less pedantic than James Michener." Roger Manvell, who reviewed *A Falcon Flies* for *British Book News,* praised Smith for the detail of this work; he observed: "The author, who seems to possess an unrivalled knowledge of his subject, writes with an impressive authenticity, as if he had himself taken part in these varied actions a century and more ago." Cliff Glaviano of *Library Journal* found *A Falcon Flies* to be "full of adventure, romance, sex, blood, and gore and set in central and southern Africa and on the surrounding high seas about 1860."

In *Monsoon* Hal Courtney leaves his African estate to hunt down pirates preying on British shipping off the East African coast in the late 1700s. Taking his three sons into the battle with him, Courtney soon finds that the pirate hunt is only part of his mission; keeping his scheming and ambitious sons alive is also a challenge. Writing in *Booklist,* Vanessa Bush found that "readers who love swashbucklers will enjoy"*Monsoon,* while Kathy Piehl in the *Library Journal* noted: "Smith offers plenty of battles and harrowing escapes for adventure fans." A critic for *Publishers Weekly* concluded: "Once again the veteran author creates a masterful tale of action and suspense set on the high seas, arid deserts and steaming jungles."

Smith explored new historical territory in his three books set in ancient Egypt, *River God, The Seventh Scroll,* and *Warlock.* In these books, set some 4,000 years ago, he weaves a complex tale of royal intrigue, betrayal, and assassination. A tale of fictional pharaohs and eunuchs, *River God* concerns the warrior Tanus and a young woman who loves him, Lostris, whose father conspires to have her married off to the pharaoh instead. Complete with battles involving thousands of soldiers, descriptions of resplendent palaces, and crowds of hundreds of thousands of people on the banks of the Nile greeting their pharaoh, the book was hailed as "compulsively readable" by a *Publishers Weekly* reviewer. Similarly, Brian Jacomb of the *Washington Post Book World* declared it a "majestic novel, one filled to overflowing with passion, rage, treachery, barbarism, prolonged excitement and endless passages of sheer, exquisite color."

Smith followed *River God* with a sequel, *The Seventh Scroll.* Set in the present, the novel is the story of an adventurous search for the tomb of the Pharaoh Mamose, husband of Lostris. At the story's opening, Egyptologist Royan Al Simma and her husband, Duraid, have discovered a scroll from the tomb of Lostris that purports to tell the location of Mamose's tomb. However, Duraid is murdered by a rival. Royan then teams up with Sir Nicholas Quenton-Harper, a wealthy collector mourning the deaths of his wife and child. The two battle villainous rivals, booby traps, and other dangerous events in a race to find the tomb. A *Publishers Weekly* reviewer called the novel "intoxicating."

In *Warlock,* Smith's third novel about ancient Egypt, Taita, lover of the deceased queen Lostris, goes into the desert to live as a hermit. Studying magic, he becomes a mighty warlock with remarkable powers. Because of his power, Taita becomes tutor to young Prince Nefer, heir to the Egyptian throne. He finds that

his magical skills are tested when rivals plot to kill the young prince. According to Kathleen Hughes in *Booklist,* in her review of *Warlock,* "Smith is an excellent storyteller, and the fast-moving action and the exciting plot will hook even those who normally don't appreciate historical fiction." Speaking of the same novel, the critic for *Publishers Weekly* noted that "though timorous readers may wish to steer clear, those willing to brave the blood and gore will be carried away by the sweep and pace of Smith's tale." "This most recent novel by a master storyteller," Jane Baird wrote of *Warlock* in *Library Journal,* "is resplendent with all the power and pageantry of Egypt, the center of civilization of the ancient world."

Some critics have faulted Smith's novels for their politics. Rob Nixon, writing in the *Village Voice Literary Supplement,* for example, criticized Smith for championing colonialism: "At a time when anti-apartheid literature crowds the shelves, *A Time To Die* serves as a reminder that a considerable audience remains for writing that glamorizes South African racism." But many other critics praise Smith for his masterful storytelling. Writing in the *Washington Post Book World,* Bruce VanWyngarden, in his review of *Power of the Sword,* noted that "the book's principal strengths lie in the author's considerable storytelling talents and his compelling way with action sequences. Smith writes with real panache about fighting and riding and shooting and bleeding." Simon Ritchie of the *This Is York* Web site claimed: "Smith must surely be the world's greatest living storyteller."

BIOGRAPHICAL AND CRITICAL SOURCES:

BOOKS

Contemporary Literary Criticism, Volume 33, Gale (Detroit, MI), 1985.
Contemporary Popular Writers, St. James Press (Detroit, MI), 1997.

PERIODICALS

Booklist, March 1, 2001, Kathleen Hughes, review of *Warlock,* p. 1189; March 15, 2003, Margaret Flanagan, review of *The Blue Horizon,* p. 1254.
British Book News, August, 1980.

Geographical, April, 2001, "The Write Stuff," p. 114.

Guardian Weekly, August 19, 1990.

Kirkus Reviews, March 15, 2003, review of *The Blue Horizon,* p. 426.

Library Journal, May 15, 1999, Kathy Piehl, review of *Monsoon,* p. 128; April 15, 2001, Jane Baird, review of *Warlock,* p. 134; December, 2001, Cliff Glaviano, review of audiocassette edition of *Warlock,* p. 199; July, 2002, Cliff Glaviano, reviews of audiocassette editions of *The Angels Weep, The Leopard Hunts in Darkness,* and *Wild Justice,* p. 141; May 15, 2003, Robert Conroy, review of *The Blue Horizon,* p. 127; October 1, 2003, Cliff Glaviano, audiobook review of the audiobook version of *The Blue Horizon,* p. 132.

Listener, April 4, 1974.

Los Angeles Times Book Review, November 22, 1987; April 8, 1990.

M2 Best Books, February 19, 2002, "Best-Selling Author in Trust Fund Legal Battle."

New Statesman, October 20, 1972.

New York Times Book Review, October 25, 1970; April 23, 1972; July 29, 1973; May 30, 1976; September 4, 1977; February 24, 1980; April 26, 1981.

Publishers Weekly, December 6, 1993; March 20, 1995, p. 42; May 1, 1995, p. 38; April 26, 1999, review of *Monsoon,* p. 55; April 9, 2001, review of *Warlock,* p. 49; June 3, 2002, review of audiocassette edition of *Cry Wolf,* p. 32; April 28, 2003, review of *The Blue Horizon,* p. 426.

Spectator, July 6, 1991.

Times (London, England), April 30, 1981; June 16, 1990.

Tribune Books (Chicago, IL), April 21, 1991; February 16, 1992.

Village Voice Literary Supplement, July-August, 1990.

Virginia Quarterly Review, winter, 1978; summer, 1992.

Washington Post, August 3, 1983; August 4, 1984; October 7, 1985; September 20, 1986; October 9, 1987.

Washington Post Book World, September 20, 1986; February 24, 1994.

ONLINE

Liquid Review Web site, http://users.chariot.net.au/~rastous/wilbur.htm/ (April 10, 2003), Stuart Beaton, interview with Wilbur Smith and Danielle Thomas.

Out There Web site, http://www.outthere.co.za/ (October, 1997), Jonah Hull, interview with Wilbur Smith.

This Is York Web site, http://www.thisisyork.co.uk/ (March 19, 2003), Simon Ritchie, "Licence to Thrill."

Wilbur Smith Books Web site, http://www.wilbursmithbooks.com/ (April 10, 2003).*

* * *

SOLWOSKA, Mara
See FRENCH, Marilyn

* * *

STEVENSON, Richard
See LIPEZ, Richard

* * *

STIRLING, Jessica
See COGHLAN, Margaret M.

* * *

STUTSON, Caroline 1940-

PERSONAL: Born September 14, 1940; daughter of Malcolm (a purchasing agent) and Randolph (a librarian; maiden name, Hardy) MacLachlan; married Al Stutson (a wood carver), September 5, 1964; children: A. C., Christine. *Education:* Metro State College, certificate in early education, 1978; attended College of William and Mary, 1958-60, and University of Denver, 1960-62. *Hobbies and other interests:* Hiking, puppetry, gardening, reading, and stitchery.

ADDRESSES: Home—5521 South Cedar St., Littleton, CO 80120. *Agent*—Nancy Gallt, 273 Charlton Ave., South Orange, NJ 07079. *E-mail*—astutson@aol.com.

CAREER: Bemis Public Library, Littleton, CO, children's librarian, 1961-65; writer. Also worked as a kindergarten teacher and special reading teacher in Littleton. Highlands Ranch Library, part-time storyteller and puppeteer.

MEMBER: Society of Children's Book Writers and Illustrators, Colorado Author's League.

AWARDS, HONORS: Named Teacher of Excellence, Colorado Association for Childhood Education, 1991; Top Hand Award, Colorado Author's League, for *Cowpokes.*

WRITINGS:

FOR CHILDREN

By the Light of the Halloween Moon, illustrated by Kevin Hawkes, Lothrop, Lee & Shepard (Boston, MA), 1993.

On the River ABC, illustrated by Anna-Maria Crum, Roberts Rinehart (Boulder, CO), 1993.

Mountain Meadow 1, 2, 3, illustrated by Anna-Maria Crum, Roberts Rinehart (Boulder, CO), 1995.

Prairie Primer A to Z, illustrated by Susan Condie Lamb, Dutton (New York, NY), 1996.

Cowpokes, illustrated by Daniel San Souci, Lothrop, Lee & Shepard (Boston, MA), 1999.

Star Comes Home, illustrated by Rick Reason, Benefactory (Wheeling, IL), 1999.

Night Train, illustrated by Catherine Tillotson, DK Publishing (New York, NY), 2002.

Contributor of poetry to magazines, including *Children's Playmate, Highlights for Children, On the Line,* and *Spider.*

ADAPTATIONS: By the Light of the Halloween Moon was adapted for video by Weston Woods in 1997.

WORK IN PROGRESS: Mama Loves You, illustrated by John Segal, publication by Scholastic (New York, NY) expected in 2005.

SIDELIGHTS: Caroline Stutson once told *CA:* "Looking back at one's life is an interesting process. If enough time has passed, you can see the pieces fitting neatly together. Yet, on a day to day basis, so much seems haphazard and iffy.

"One of the few things I know for sure about my life is that I've always loved books. Shortly before I was born, longer ago than I'll publicly admit, my mother worked as a librarian at the Brooklyn Public Library in New York. I was lucky to have lots of early links with literature, from my mother's reading out loud to me, to a friend of hers who sent me copies of book reviews she wrote for a parenting magazine.

"In addition to listening to and reading books, I always enjoyed playing pretend. My best friend and I were careful to note where our adventure left off when it was time to go home. That way we knew where our chosen characters would begin the next day. Writing for children still lets me play pretend. All those 'what ifs' are great fun, and you get to create your own universe with a happy ending to boot.

"My writing began in kindergarten. I didn't know how to write words then, but every day after school I drew pictures and made up stories to go with the drawings. Later when we had writing assignments, I struggled with the spelling. I still struggle with spelling, but it doesn't stop me from writing any more. I just circle the troublesome words and look up how to spell them later.

"Today, things are so much better for the students I meet when I visit schools promoting my books. Some of their writing involves choice. They get to write about things that really matter to them, and they get to share their work with each other. They also get to respond to the literature they are reading. I can't help feeling a little envious.

"After I graduated from Massapequa High School on Long Island, New York, I went to William and Mary College in Virginia and two years later I transferred to the University of Denver. During those years I changed my mind a million times about what I wanted to do, finally majoring in theater arts—not a very practical decision for making a living.

"I've changed jobs quite a few times too. I've been a reading teacher, a kindergarten teacher, and a children's librarian, all of which connected me to books. Currently, I work part time doing puppet shows and story times at the Highlands Ranch Library in Douglas County, Colorado. In my office at home I have a huge trunk of puppets ready to pop out and be part of a new puppet show each week.

"A big part of my life has been spent being a mom. Our two children are grown now. Our daughter is a lawyer, our son, a police detective, and I am now a grandmother for the first time, having fun reading to my grandson from my ever-growing collection of books."

Stutson's fast-paced debut picture book, *By the Light of the Halloween Moon,* holds a "toe" up for grabs. The toe belongs to a little girl who dangles her legs over a footbridge while playing a fiddle on Halloween night. A cat, a witch, a bat, a graveyard ghoul, a ghost, and a sprite all stream through this boisterous tale, and each character, more pleasurably gruesome than the one before, aims to grab the toe. A *Kirkus Reviews* critic called the poem a "catchy, lilting cumulative tale." Ilene Cooper declared in her review for *Booklist* that this "rousing" tale with "bouncy text" makes a "terrific choice for holiday story hours." Ann A. Flowers of *Horn Book* also praised *By the Light of the Halloween Moon,* describing the book as "rhythmically bouncy and appealing."

In *On the River ABC,* an ant floats down the river on a leaf. As he drifts, wildlife from A to Z pass before his makeshift vessel. Stutson ends her book with factual information about each of these animals that live in the western regions of the United States. *School Library Journal* contributor Kathy Piehl commented favorably on the lyrical quality of Stutson's writing, noting that the author "does not fall into the trap of singsong regularity." Piehl encouraged teachers to use this picture book as a springboard for "children to create similar alphabet books based on trips in their own environment."

With *Prairie Primer A to Z,* Stutson once again presents a rhyming alphabet book, evoking the daily life of a Midwestern farm family in the early 1900s. Letters introduced help to explore life on a farm long ago: B is for "butter in the churn" and P is for "porridge in the pot." Unusual words such as "whirligig" and "velocipede" place the primer back in the era of homesteading. A critic for *Kirkus Reviews* suggested that the book may be too "old-fashioned" for today's "rough-and-ready preschool set," but Paula A. Kiely, writing in *School Library Journal,* called Stutson's book a "pleasant step back in time," pointing out that "young children will enjoy trying to pronounce" these forgotten words. Carolyn Phelan of *Booklist* suggested that the primer be used to introduce "today's young children to another time, another place."

Recently Stutson added: "One of my favorite things to do, when I'm not writing, is visiting schools and talking about the writing process. (I also love finding out what books students are reading.) The questions I'm asked help me focus on unconscious aspects of writing: how do I choose what to write about? How do I get started? How do I decide what to include or exclude?

"Through answering these questions, I've discovered that my best writing topics are those I can't forget—those that put butterflies in my stomach and stir up strong feelings whenever I think about them. I've also learned that I need to write quickly at first. (I often begin with lists I've brainstormed.) Writing fast shuts out the critic inside me who tries to whisper discouraging comments in my ear. Lastly, I've come to realize I need to read my work out loud to myself and, later on, to my treasured critique group to truly know what to include or subtract from my writing."

BIOGRAPHICAL AND CRITICAL SOURCES:

PERIODICALS

Booklist, July, 1993, Ilene Cooper, review of *By the Light of the Halloween Moon,* p. 1977; October 15, 1996, Carolyn Phelan, review of *Prairie Primer A to Z,* p. 437; May 1, 2002, Gillian Engberg, review of *Night Train.*
Children's Book Review Service, December, 1996, p. 41.
Horn Book, November-December, 1993, Ann A. Flowers, review of *By the Light of the Halloween Moon,* p. 728.
Kirkus Reviews, July 15, 1993, review of *By the Light of the Halloween Moon,* pp. 942-943; September 15, 1996, review of *Prairie Primer A to Z,* p. 1408; March 1, 2002, review of *Night Train,* p. 346.
Library Talk, November, 1994, p. 37.
New York Times Book Review, May 11, 1997, p. 24.
Publishers Weekly, March 18, 2002, review of *Night Train,* p. 102.
School Library Journal, September, 1993, Kathy Piehl, review of *On the River ABC;* p. 220; October, 1996, Paula A. Kiely, review of *Prairie Primer A to Z,* p. 107; May, 2002, Wanda Meyers-Hines, review of *Night Train,* p. 128.

ONLINE

Providence Journal Online, http://www.projo.com/ (July 7, 2002), Peter Mandel, review of *Night Train.*

*   *   *

SWITHEN, John
See KING, Stephen (Edwin)

T

TOKER, Franklin K(arl) B(enedict) S(erchuk) 1944-

PERSONAL: Born April 29, 1944, in Montreal, Quebec, Canada; immigrated to the United States, 1964, naturalized U.S. citizen, 1983; son of Maxwell Harris (a dental surgeon) and Ethel (Serchuk-Herzberg) Toker; married Ellen Judith Burack (a fine arts administrator), September 3, 1972; children: Sarah Augusta, Maxwell Abraham, Jeffrey Burack. *Education:* McGill University, B.A., 1964; Oberlin College, A.M., 1966; Harvard University, Ph.D., 1972. *Politics:* "Jeffersonian." *Hobbies and other interests:* Sailing, travel, painting, writing fiction.

ADDRESSES: Home—1521 Denniston Ave., Squirrel Hill, Pittsburgh, PA 15217. *Office*—Department of the History of Art and Architecture, Frick Fine Arts Building, University of Pittsburgh, Pittsburgh, PA 15260; fax: 412-648-2792. *Agent*—William Clark, William Clark Associates, 355 West 22nd St., New York, NY 10011-2650. *E-mail*—ftoker@pitt.edu.

CAREER: Soprintendenza ai Monumenti (historic buildings commission), Florence, Italy, archaeological director of excavation of Florence Cathedral, 1969-74; Carnegie-Mellon University, Pittsburgh, PA, visiting professor, 1974-76, associate professor of history of architecture, 1976-80; University of Pittsburgh, Pittsburgh, professor of history of art and architecture, 1980—. University of Florence, visiting professor, 1989; University of Rome, visiting professor, 1991. Reggio Calabria, president, 1993-94, visiting professor, 1996. Institute for Advanced Study, Princeton, NJ, member, 1985-86.

Franklin K. B. S. Toker

MEMBER: International Center for Medieval Art, Medieval Academy of America (life member), Archeological Institute of America, College Art Association of America (life member), Society of Architectural Historians (life member; president, 1993-94), National Trust for Historic Preservation.

AWARDS, HONORS: Alice Davis Hitchcock Book Award, Society of Architectural Historians, 1971, for

The Church of Notre-Dame in Montreal; Guggenheim fellowship, 1979; grants, National Endowment for the Humanities, 1979, 1992; Arthur Kingsley Porter Prize, College Art Association of America, 1980, for most distinguished article in *Art Bulletin,* 1978; resident, Rockefeller Foundation, Bellagio Center, 1994.

WRITINGS:

The Church of Notre-Dame in Montreal, McGill-Queens University Press (Montreal, Quebec, Canada), 1970, revised translation published as *L'Eglise Notre-Dame de Montreal, son architecture, son passe,* Hurtubise-HMH (Montreal, Quebec, Canada), 1981.
(With Guido Morozzi and J. A. Herrmann) *S. Reparata: L'Antica cattedrale fiorentina* (title means "St. Reparata: The Ancient Cathedral of Florence"), Bonechi (Florence, Italy), 1974.
Pittsburgh: An Urban Portrait, Pennsylvania State University Press (Pittsburgh, PA), 1985, 2nd edition, 1991.
Fallingwater Rising: Frank Lloyd Wright, E. J. Kaufmann, and America's Most Extraordinary House, Alfred A. Knopf (New York, NY), 2003.
(With Lu Donnelly and David Brumble) *Buildings of Pennsylvania: Pittsburgh and Western Pennsylvania,* Oxford University Press (New York, NY), 2004.

Contributor to books, including *Giuseppe Zocchi's Views of Florence,* edited by James Ackerman, Walker (New York, NY), 1967. Contributor to art and architecture journals.

WORK IN PROGRESS: Excavations at the Cathedral of Florence, four volumes, for Pontifical Institute of Mediaeval Studies (Toronto, Ontario, Canada).

SIDELIGHTS: Franklin K. B. S. Toker once told *CA:* "I write about scholarly material and use scholarly method, but I write as an *author,* with the aim of provoking and enlivening rather than deadening a scholarly audience. I am contemptuous of technical jargon in other fields and try to keep it out of my works."

Toker later added: "With *Fallingwater Rising: Frank Lloyd Wright, E. J. Kaufmann, and America's Most*

Extraordinary House, I have finally achieved my objective of writing simultaneously as a scholar and as someone addressing a wide audience of nonspecialists."

BIOGRAPHICAL AND CRITICAL SOURCES:

PERIODICALS

Booklist, November 1, 2003, Keir Graff, review of *Fallingwater Rising: Frank Lloyd Wright, E. J. Kaufmann, and America's Most Extraordinary House,* p. 472.
Kirkus Reviews, August 15, 2003, review of *Fallingwater Rising,* p. 1066.
Library Journal, October 1, 2003, Valerie Nye, review of *Fallingwater Rising,* p. 74.
New York Times, September 29, 2003, Janet Maslin, review of *Fallingwater Rising,* p. E8.

ONLINE

Franklin Toker Home Page, http://www.franklintoker.com/ (April 10, 2004).

*　　*　　*

TOLKIEN, J(ohn) R(onald) R(euel) 1892-1973

PERSONAL: Surname is pronounced "*tohl*-keen"; born January 3, 1892, in Bloemfontein, South Africa; died of complications resulting from a bleeding gastric ulcer and a chest infection, September 2, 1973, in Bournemouth, England; buried in Wolvercote Cemetery, Oxford; son of Arthur Reuel (a bank manager) and Mabel (Suffield) Tolkien; married Edith Mary Bratt (a pianist), March 22, 1916 (died, November 29, 1971); children: John, Michael, Christopher, Priscilla. *Education:* Exeter College, Oxford, B.A., 1915, M.A., 1919. *Religion:* Roman Catholic.

CAREER: Author and scholar. Assistant on *Oxford English Dictionary,* 1918-20; University of Leeds, Leeds, England, reader in English, 1920-24, professor of English language, 1924-25: Oxford University, Oxford, England, Rawlinson and Bosworth Professor

J. R. R. Tolkien

of Anglo-Saxon, 1925-45, Merton Professor of English Language and Literature, 1945-59, fellow of Pembroke College, 1926-45, honorary resident fellow of Merton College, 1972-73. Freelance tutor, 1919; Leverhulme research fellow, 1934-36; Sir Israel Gollancz Memorial Lecturer, British Academy, 1936; Andrew Lang Lecturer, St. Andrews University, 1939; W. P. Ker Lecturer, University of Glasgow, 1953; O'Donnell Lecturer, Oxford University, 1955. *Military service:* Lancashire Fusiliers, 1915-18.

MEMBER: Royal Society of Literature (fellow), Philological Society (vice-president), Science Fiction Writers of America (honorary), Hid Islenzka Bokmenntafelag (honorary).

AWARDS, HONORS: New York Herald Tribune Children's Spring Book Festival award, 1938, for *The Hobbit;* D.Phil., Liege, 1954; D.Litt., University College, Dublin, 1954, and Oxford University, 1972; International Fantasy Award, 1957, for *The Lord of the Rings;* Benson Medal, 1966; Commander, Order of the British Empire, 1972; *Locus* Award for best fantasy novel, 1978, for *The Silmarillion;* Mythopoeic Fantasy

Award, 1981, for *Unfinished Tales; The Lord of the Rings* was voted Britain's number-one best-loved novel (and *The Hobbit* was voted into the top 100) by the British public as part of the British Broadcasting Corporation's "The Big Read," 2003.

WRITINGS:

(Editor, with C. L. Wiseman, and author of introductory note) Geoffrey Bache Smith, *A Spring Harvest* (poems), Erskine Macdonald (London, England), 1918.

A Middle English Vocabulary, Clarendon Press (Oxford, England), 1922.

(Editor, with Eric V. Gordon) *Sir Gawain and the Green Knight,* Clarendon Press (Oxford, England), 1925, 2nd edition, revised by Norman Davis, 1967.

(With Eric V. Gordon and others) *Songs for the Philologists* (verse), Department of English, University College, Oxford (Oxford, England), 1936.

Beowulf: The Monsters and the Critics (originally published in *Proceedings of the British Academy,* 1936; also see below), Oxford University Press (Oxford, England), 1937, new edition published as *Beowulf and the Critics,* Arizona Center for Medieval and Renaissance Studies (Tempe, AZ), 2002.

(Self-illustrated) *The Hobbit; or, There and Back Again* (also see below), Allen & Unwin (London, England), 1937, Houghton Mifflin (Boston, MA), 1938, 5th edition, 2001.

Chaucer As a Philologist, Oxford University Press (Oxford, England), 1943.

Farmer Giles of Ham (also see below), Allen & Unwin (London, England), 1949, Houghton Mifflin (Boston, MA), 1950, 2nd edition, Allen & Unwin (London, England), 1975, Houghton Mifflin (Boston, MA), 1978.

The Lord of the Rings, Houghton Mifflin (Boston, MA), Volume 1: *The Fellowship of the Ring,* 1954, Volume 2: *The Two Towers,* 1954, Volume 3: *The Return of the King,* 1955, with new foreword by the author, Ballantine (New York, NY), 1966, 2nd edition, Allen & Unwin (London, England), 1966, Houghton Mifflin (Boston, MA), 1967, one volume edition, Houghton Mifflin (Boston, MA), 1994.

The Adventures of Tom Bombadil and Other Verses from the Red Book (also see below), Allen & Unwin (London, England), 1962, Houghton Mifflin (Boston, MA), 1963, 2nd edition, Houghton Mifflin (Boston, MA), 1978.

(Editor) *Ancrene Wisse: The English Text of the Ancrene Riwle,* Oxford University Press (Oxford, England), 1962.

Tree and Leaf (includes "On Fairy-Stories" and "Leaf by Niggle" [originally published in *Dublin Review,* 1945]; also see below), Allen & Unwin (London, England), 1964, Houghton Mifflin (Boston, MA), 1965, 2nd edition, Allen & Unwin (London, England), 1975.

The Tolkien Reader (includes "The Homecoming of Beorhtnoth" [originally published in *Essays and Studies,* English Association, 1953; also see below], *Tree and Leaf, Farmer Giles of Ham,* and *The Adventures of Tom Bombadil*), introduction by Peter S. Beagle, Ballantine (New York, NY), 1966.

The Road Goes Ever On: A Song Cycle, music by Donald Swann, Houghton Mifflin (Boston, MA), 1967.

Smith of Wootton Major (also see below), Houghton Mifflin (Boston, MA), 1967, 2nd edition, Allen & Unwin (London, England), 1975, Houghton Mifflin (London, England), 1978.

Smith of Wootton Major [and] *Farmer Giles of Ham,* Ballantine (New York, NY), 1969.

(Translator) *Sir Gawain and the Green Knight, Pearl,* [and] *Sir Orfeo,* edited by son, Christopher Tolkien, Houghton Mifflin (Boston, MA), 1975.

Tree and Leaf, Smith of Wootton Major, The Homecoming of Beorhtnoth, Unwin Books (London, England), 1975.

Farmer Giles of Ham [and] *The Adventures of Tom Bombadil,* Unwin Books (London, England), 1975.

The Father Christmas Letters, edited by Baillie Tolkien, Houghton Mifflin (Boston, MA), 1976.

The Silmarillion, edited by Christopher Tolkien, Houghton Mifflin (Boston, MA), 1977.

Pictures by J. R. R. Tolkien, foreword and notes by Christopher Tolkien, Houghton Mifflin (Boston, MA), 1979.

Unfinished Tales of Numenor and Middle-Earth, edited by Christopher Tolkien, Houghton Mifflin (Boston, MA), 1980.

Poems and Stories, Allen & Unwin (London, England), 1980.

The Letters of J. R. R. Tolkien, selected and edited by Humphrey Carpenter and Christopher Tolkien, Houghton Mifflin (Boston, MA), 1981.

(Author of text and commentary, and translator) *The Old English Exodus,* edited by Joan Turville-Petre, Oxford University Press (Oxford, England), 1981.

Mr. Bliss (reproduced from Tolkien's illustrated manuscript), Allen & Unwin (London, England), 1982, Houghton Mifflin (Boston, MA), 1983.

Finn and Hengest: The Fragment and the Episode, edited by Alan Bliss, Allen & Unwin (London, England), 1982, Houghton Mifflin (Boston, MA), 1983.

The Monsters and the Critics and Other Essays, edited by Christopher Tolkien, Allen & Unwin (London, England), 1983, Houghton Mifflin (Boston, MA), 1984.

The Annotated Hobbit: The Hobbit, or There and Back Again, introduction and notes by Douglas A. Anderson, Houghton Mifflin (Boston, MA), 1988, expanded edition, with illustrations by Tolkien, 2002.

Bilbo's Last Song (verse), illustrated by Pauline Baynes, Riverwood Publishers (Newmarket, Ontario, Canada), 1990.

Tales from the Perilous Realm (includes *Farmer Giles of Ham, The Adventures of Tom Bombadil,* "Leaf by Niggle," and *Smith of Wootton Major*), HarperCollins (London, England), 1997.

Roverandom, Houghton Mifflin (Boston, MA), 1998.

The Hobbit: A 3-D Pop-Up Adventure, HarperFestival (New York, NY), 1999.

Poems from "The Hobbit," Houghton Mifflin (Boston, MA), 1999.

"HISTORY OF MIDDLE EARTH" SERIES; EDITED BY CHRISTOPHER TOLKIEN

The Book of Lost Tales, Part 1, Allen & Unwin (London, England), 1983, Houghton Mifflin (Boston, MA), 1984.

The Book of Lost Tales, Part 2, Houghton Mifflin (Boston, MA), 1984.

The Lays of Beleriland, Houghton Mifflin (Boston, MA), 1985.

The Shaping of Middle-Earth: The Quenta, the Ambarkanta, and the Annals, Houghton Mifflin (Boston, MA), 1986.

The Lost Road and Other Writings: Language and Legend before "The Lord of the Rings," Houghton Mifflin (Boston, MA), 1987.

The Return of the Shadow: The History of "The Lord of the Rings," Part 1, Houghton Mifflin (London, England), 1988.

The Treason of Isengard: The History of "The Lord of the Rings," Part 2, Houghton Mifflin (London, England), 1989.

The War of the Ring: The History of "The Lord of the Rings," Part 3, Houghton Mifflin (London, England), 1990.

Sauron Defeated: The History of "The Lord of the Rings," Part 4, Houghton Mifflin (London, England), 1992.

Morgoth's Ring: The Later Silmarillion, Part One: The Legends of Aman, Houghton Mifflin (Boston, MA), 1992.

The War of the Jewels: The Later Silmarillion, Part Two: The Legends of Beleriland, Houghton Mifflin (Boston, MA), 1994.

The Peoples of Middle-Earth, Houghton Mifflin (Boston, MA), 1996.

OTHER

(Author of foreword) Walter E. Haigh, *A New Glossary of the Dialect of the Huddersfield District,* Oxford University Press (Oxford, England), 1928.

(Author of preface) John R. Clark Hall, *Beowulf and the Finnesburg Fragment: A Translation into Modern English Prose,* edited by C. L. Wrenn, Allen & Unwin (London, England), 1940.

(Author of preface) *The Ancrene Riwle,* translated by M. Salu, Burns & Oates (London, England), 1955.

Contributorto books, including *Oxford Poetry, 1915,* edited by G. D. H. Cole and T. W. Earp, Basil H. Blackwell (London, England), 1915; *A Northern Venture: Verses by Members of the Leeds University English School Association,* Swan Press (London, England), 1923; *Realities: An Anthology of Verse,* edited by G. S. Tancred, Gay & Hancock (London, England), 1927; *Report on the Excavation of the Prehistoric, Roman, and Post-Roman Sites in Lydney Park,* Gloucestershire, Reports of the Research Committee of the Society of Antiquaries of London, Oxford University Press (Oxford, England), 1932; *Essays Presented to Charles Williams,* Oxford University Press (Oxford, England), 1947; *Angles and Britons: O'Donnell Lectures,* University of Wales Press (Cardiff, Wales), 1963; *Winter's Tales for Children: 1,* edited by Caroline Hillier, St. Martin's Press (New York, NY), 1965; William Luther White, *The Image of Man in C. S. Lewis,* Abingdon Press (New York, NY), 1969; Roger Lancelyn Green, *The Hamish Hamilton Book of Dragons,* Hamish Hamilton (London, England), 1970; *A Tolkien Compass,* edited by Jared Lobdell, Open Court, 1975; Mary Salu and Robert T. Farrell, *J. R. R. Tolkien: Scholar and Storyteller,* Cornell University Press (Ithaca, NY), 1979. Contributor of translations to *The Jerusalem Bible,* Doubleday (New York, NY), 1966.

Contributor to *The Year's Work in English Studies,* 1924 and 1925, *Transactions of the Philological Society,* 1934, *English Studies,* 1947, *Studia Neophilologica,* 1948, and *Essais de philologie moderne,* 1951. Contributor to periodicals, including *The King Edward's School Chronicle, Oxford Magazine, Medium Aevum, Dublin Review, Welsh Review,* and *Shenandoah: The Washington and Lee University Review.*

The greater part of the manuscripts of *The Hobbit, The Lord of the Rings, Farmer Giles of Ham,* and *Mr. Bliss* are collected at Marquette University, Milwaukee, WI. Some of Tolkien's letters are collected in the British Broadcasting Corporation Written Archives, the Bodleian Library of Oxford University, the Oxford University Press and its Dictionary Department, the Humanities Research Center of the University of Texas at Austin, and the Wade Collection of Wheaton College, Wheaton, IL.

ADAPTATIONS: Recordings of J. R. R. Tolkien reading from his own works include *Poems and Songs of Middle-Earth, The Hobbit* and *The Fellowship of the Ring* and *The Lord of the Ring,* released by Caedmon Records. Christopher Tolkien reads *The Silmarillion: Of Beren and Luthien,* also for Caedmon Records. Tolkien's illustrations from *Pictures by J. R. R. Tolkien* have been published in various editions of his books, and have appeared on calendars, posters, and postcards. Rankin-Bass animated a version of *The Hobbit* for television in 1977. Ralph Bakshi directed a theater film based on *The Fellowship of the Ring* and bits and pieces of *The Two Towers,* which was released as "The Lord of the Rings" in 1978. A Bunraku-style puppet version of *The Hobbit* was produced in Los Angeles in 1984 by Theatre Sans Fil of Montreal. The three volumes of *The Lord of the Rings* have been adapted to feature films of the same titles: *The Fellowship of the Ring, The Two Towers,* and *The Return of the King.* The first of the three movies was released in 2001, the second in 2002, and the third in 2003. All three movies were directed by Peter Jackson and produced by New Line Cinema; the third film received an Academy Award as best picture, 2004.

SIDELIGHTS: J. R. R. Tolkien is best known to most readers as the author of *The Hobbit* and *The Lord of the Rings,* regarded by Charles Moorman in *Tolkien and the Critics* as "unique in modern fiction," and by Augustus M. Kolich in the *Dictionary of Literary*

Biography as "the most important fantasy stories of the modern period." From 1914 until his death in 1973, Tolkien drew on his familiarity with Northern and other ancient literatures and his own invented languages to create not just his own story, but his own world: Middle Earth, complete with its own history, myths, legends, epics, and heroes. Tolkien's life's work, Kolich continued, "encompasses a reality that rivals Western man's own attempt at recording the composite, knowable history of his species. Not since Milton has any Englishman worked so successfully at creating a secondary world, derived from our own, yet complete in its own terms with encyclopedic mythology; an imagined world that includes a vast gallery of strange beings: hobbits, elves, dwarfs, orcs, and, finally, the men of Westernesse." Tolkien's *Lord of the Rings* trilogy has drawn a readership from multiple generations and has been adapted to award-winning feature films. It is unquestionably one of the most popular and influential fantasy works ever written.

Tolkien began to create his secondary world while still in school, shortly before enlisting to fight in World War I. In 1914, according to Humphrey Carpenter in *J. R. R. Tolkien: A Biography,* Tolkien wrote a poem based on a line from the works of an Old English religious poet. Entitled "The Voyage of Earendel, the Evening Star," the poem marked the first appearance in his work of the mariner who sails across the heavens through the night, and was "the beginning of Tolkien's own mythology"—the stories that, edited by Christopher Tolkien, appeared after the author's death in "The History of Middle Earth" series and *The Silmarillion.* Nearly all of Tolkien's fiction drew on these stories for their background. *The Hobbit* had at first no connection with Tolkien's legendary histories; he wrote it to please his own children and later remarked that "Mr. Baggins got dragged against my original will" into his imagined mythos. *The Lord of the Rings* also moved into the realm of legend until it became the chronicle of the last days of the Third Age of Middle Earth. After *The Lord of the Rings,* Tolkien published a sequence of related poems, *The Adventures of Tom Bombadil,* but the other fiction he published during his lifetime, including the satirical *Farmer Giles of Ham,* the allegorical "Leaf by Niggle," and *Smith of Wootton Major,* one of his last works, drew on other sources.

However, Tolkien held another reputation not as well known to readers of his fantasies: he was "in fact one of the leading philologists of his day," Kolich reported.

His essay "Beowulf: The Monsters and the Critics"—a plea to study the Old English poem "Beowulf" as a poem, and not just as a historical curiosity—is regarded as a classic critical statement on the subject, and his renditions of the Middle English poems "Sir Orfeo," "Sir Gawain and the Green Knight," and "Pearl" into Modern English are used as texts in literature classes. His academic work, teaching English language and literature at Leeds and later at Oxford, heavily influenced his fiction. Tolkien himself wrote that "a primary 'fact' about my work [is] that it is all of a piece, and *fundamentally linguistic* in inspiration."

"'Philology,'" wrote T. A. Shippey in *The Road to Middle Earth,* quoting Tolkien, "is indeed the only proper guide to a view of Middle Earth 'of the sort which its author may be supposed to have desired.'" Carpenter declared, "There were not two Tolkiens, one an academic and the other a writer. They were the same man, and the two sides of him overlapped so that they were indistinguishable—or rather they were not two sides at all, but different expressions of the same mind, the same imagination."

What is philology? The concise edition of the *Oxford English Dictionary*—a book that focuses on the meaning of words through time, rather than just their present definition, and on which Tolkien himself worked—derives the word "philology" from two Greek stems: *philo,* meaning "love of," and *logos,* meaning "words" or "language," and defines it as "the study of literature in a wide sense, including grammar, literary criticism and interpretation, the relation of literature and written records to history, etc." Tolkien was a philologist in the literal sense of the word: a lover of language. It was a passion he developed early and kept throughout his life, exploring tongues that were no longer spoken and creating languages of his own. Carpenter explained: "It was a deep *love* for the look and sound of words [that motivated him], springing from the days when his mother had given him his first Latin lesson." After learning Latin and Greek, Tolkien taught himself some Welsh, Old and Middle English, Old Norse, and Gothic, a language with no modern descendant—he wrote the only poem known to exist in that tongue. Later he added Finnish to his list of beloved languages; the Finnish epic *The Kalevala* had a great impact on his *Silmarillion,* and the language itself, said Carpenter, formed the basis for "Quenya," the High-elven tongue of his stories.

But philology also refers to a discipline: linguistics, the science of language, the application of observed, consistent change of tongues through time to reconstruct languages no longer spoken. After recognizing the common ancestry of certain tongues, philologists devised laws—such as Grimm's Law of Consonants, devised by the great philologist Jacob Grimm, of *Grimm's Fairy Tales* fame—to describe the changes these languages underwent in their development to modern form. Because the changes were regular, these laws make it possible to reconstruct words that do not exist in written records. Reconstructed words are marked with an asterisk (*) to show that the word in question is inferred and does not appear in any known document. Modern philologists have used the principles of linguistics to recover and interpret ancient languages and their literatures ranging from Mycenaean Linear B script—the language contemporary with *The Iliad's* heroes—to the Hittite language of Old Testament times.

Throughout his fiction, from the early tales of *The Silmarillion* to *The Hobbit* and *The Lord of the Rings,* Tolkien exercised his philological talents and training to create an "asterisk-epic"—an inferred history—that revealed elements of the Northern (and especially the English) literature he loved, and of which so little remains. "The dwarf-names of 'Thorin and Company,' as well as Gandalf's," declared Shippey, "come from a section of the Eddic poem *Voluspa,* often known as the *Dvergatal* or 'Dwarves' Roster.'" "In the case of the 'ents,'" stated A. N. Wilson in the *Spectator,* quoting Tolkien, "'as usual with me they grew rather out of their name than the other way about. I always felt that something ought to be done about the peculiar Anglo-Saxon word *ent* for a "giant" or a mighty person of long ago—to whom all old works are ascribed.'" Wilson added that Tolkien "was not content to leave the ents as they appear on the page of *Beowulf,* shadowy, unknown figures of an almost forgotten past." In the opinion of Ursula Le Guin in *The Language of the Night: Essays on Fantasy and Science Fiction:* "That is lovely. That is the Creator Spirit working absolutely unhindered—making the word flesh."

The value of linguistics, or comparative philology, lies in its applicability. Knowing the history of the words forgotten people used can reveal something about the way those people thought and about the modern languages descended from their tongues. Once philolo-

gists recognized the relationship between English and Gothic (the oldest recorded Germanic language), for instance, they were able to explain why certain English words are pronounced and spelled the way they are: "a whole series of things which people said, and still *say,* without in the least knowing why, turn out to have one very old but clear, 100 percent predictable reason. It's almost like genetics," declared Shippey. Historians frequently use linguistic principles to trace patterns of settlement through place names. In England, for example, towns whose names end in the element *-caster* or *-chester* (from the Latin *castrum,* a fort) mark sites where Roman legions built fortifications, according to the *Oxford English Dictionary.* Towns whose names end in *-ham* or *-wich* were once inhabited by speakers of Old English; in that language, *wic* is an encampment or village, while *hamme* can mean a meadow or a manor-house. Towns whose names end in *-by,* however, were settled by invading Vikings; *byr* is an Old Norse term for a dwelling-place. Tolkien, Shippey pointed out, uses place names in a "Celtic 'style,'" to make subliminally the point that hobbits were immigrants too, that their land had a history before them." The Carrock, the rocky island in the middle of the river of Wilderland in *The Hobbit,* is derived from the Welsh *carrecc,* a rock, while the town of Bree in *The Lord of the Rings* comes from a Welsh word for a hill.

One of the reasons that philologists have to rely on terms like place names is that so few manuscript sources have survived from ancient times. "The philologist," wrote E. Christian Kopff in *Chronicles of Culture,* "lives in the tragic world of the partially lost or broken. He knows the eighteenth-century fire that ate away just that page of *Beowulf* that explains why the dragon attacks after so many years." Of the sixteen epic poems that originally told the entire history of the Trojan War and its aftermath, only Homer's *Iliad* and *Odyssey* remain intact; the others survive only in fragments or summaries. But careful examination of the fragments of ancient literature that do survive can often reveal facets of the writer's culture, and can contain echoes of still older tales. In *Finn and Hengest: The Fragment and the Episode,* wrote Kopff, "Tolkien takes a brief and fragmentary tale sung by a bard in *Beowulf* and a fragment of a separate version of the same story that survives on a single manuscript page and tries to reconstruct the history that lies behind the two sources."

This sense of loss helps explain why Tolkien came to write the history of Middle Earth. "Like Walter Scott or William Morris before him," Shippey observed, "he felt the perilous charm of the archaic world of the North, recovered from bits and scraps by generations of inquiry. He wanted to tell a story about it simply, one feels, because there were hardly any complete ones left." In *British Book News,* Jessica Yates suggested that Tolkien "began to write *The Book of Lost Tales* in 1916-17, as his first attempt on 'a mythology for England.' He felt that the English people, as opposed to the Greeks or the Celts for example, had no 'body of . . . connected legend' of their own. All we had was *Beowulf* (imported from Denmark) and our native fairy stories. So partly with the sense of mission and partly as an escape from the horrors of the First World War, he wrote a series of tales about the creation of the world and the coming of the Elves, of evil Melko and the wars of Elves and Men against him."

Tolkien used the evocative power of language to create his English legend. Names in Tolkien's fiction are not merely identifying sounds, Shippey pointed out; they are also descriptions of the people, places and creatures that bear them. The name Gandalf, for instance, is made up of two Norse words: *gandr,* a magical implement (probably a staff), and *alfr,* an elf. Tolkien's Gandalf, therefore, is an elf with a staff, or a wizard. Shippey explains, "Accordingly when Gandalf first appears [in *The Hobbit*], 'All that the unsuspecting Bilbo saw that morning *was an old man with a staff.*' . . . He turns out not to be an elf, but by the end of *The Lord of the Rings* it is clear he comes from Elvenhome." The character Gollum continually refers to himself and to the Ring throughout *The Hobbit* and *The Lord of the Ring* as "my precious"; Douglas A. Anderson, in his notes to *The Annotated Hobbit,* cited Constance B. Hieatt, who declared that "Old Norse gull/goll, of which one inflected form would be *gollum,* means 'gold, treasure, something precious' and can also mean 'ring,' a point which may have occurred to Tolkien." In the last appendix to *The Lord of the Rings,* Shippey pointed out, Tolkien derives the word *hobbit* itself from an Old English asterisk-word—**holbytla,* meaning "hole-dweller" or "-builder"—although he worked out the meaning long after he first used the word. Tolkien also drew on ancient words for inspiration. Shippey traces the origins of the Balrog—the evil creature Gandalf faces on the bridge in Moria—to an article Tolkien published in two parts in the journal *Medium Aevum* on the Anglo-Saxon word *Sigelhearwan,* used to translate Latin biblical references to natives of Ethiopia. Tolkien suggested that

the element *sigel* meant both 'sun' and 'jewel,' and that the element *hearwa* was related to the Latin *carbo,* meaning soot. He further conjectured that when an Anglo-Saxon used the word, he did not picture a dark-skinned man but a creature like the fire-giants of Northern myth. "What was the point of the speculation," asked Shippey, "admittedly 'guess-work,' admittedly 'inconclusive?' It offers some glimpses of a lost mythology, suggested Tolkien with academic caution, something 'which has coloured the verse-treatment of Scripture and determined the diction of poems.' A good deal less boringly, one might say, it had helped to naturalise the 'Balrog' in the traditions of the North, and it had helped to create (or corroborate) the image of the *silmaril,* that fusion of 'sun' and 'jewel' in physical form." In the *New York Review of Books,* Janet Adam Smith suggested that Tolkien's attitude to language "is part of his attitude to history . . . to recapture and reanimate the words of the past is to recapture something of ourselves; for we carry the past in us, and our existence, like Frodo's quest, is only an episode in an age-long and continuing drama."

Tolkien's ability to use ancient tongues—"tending," according to Shippey, "to focus on names and words and the things and realities which lie behind them"—helps create a sense of history within Middle Earth, a feeling many reviewers have noticed. Joseph McLellan wrote in the *Washington Post Book World:* "Tolkien's stories take place against a background of measureless depth. . . . That background is ever-present in the creator's mind and it gives Frodo and company a three-dimensional reality that is seldom found in this kind of writing." Shippey explained that Tolkien's use of language "gave *The Lord of the Rings* a dinosaur-like vitality which cannot be conveyed in any synopsis, but reveals itself in so many thousands of details that only the most biased critical mind could miss them all." *Time and Tide* correspondent C. S. Lewis stated: "In the Tolkinian world, you can hardly put your foot down anywhere from Esgaroth to Forlindon or between Ered Mithrin and Khand without stirring the dust of history."

Although many readers have viewed *The Lord of the Rings* as an allegory of modern history (especially of the Second World War), Tolkien explicitly rejected such an interpretation. In the foreword to the Ballantine edition of *The Lord of the Rings,* he stated, "As for any inner meaning or 'message,' it has in the intention of the author none. It is neither allegorical nor topical." He continued: "I cordially dislike allegory in all its manifestations, and have always done so since I grew old and wary enough to detect its presence. I much prefer history, true or feigned, with its varied applicability to the thought and experience of readers. I think that many confuse 'applicability' with 'allegory'; but the one resides in the freedom of the reader, and the other in the purposed dominations of the author." He expanded on these comments in a letter to his publisher Stanley Unwin in *The Letters of J. R. R. Tolkien:* "There is a 'moral,' I suppose, in any tale worth telling. But that is not the same thing. Even the struggle between light and darkness (as [Rayner Unwin] calls it, not me) is for me just a particular phase of history, one example of its pattern, perhaps, but not The Pattern; and the actors are individuals— they each, of course, contain universals or they would not live at all, but they never represent them as such." Tolkien concluded: "You can make the Ring into an allegory of our own time, if you like, an allegory of the inevitable fate that waits for all attempts to defeat evil power by power. But that is only because all power magical or mechanical does always so work. You cannot write a story about an apparently simple magic ring without that bursting in, if you really take the ring seriously, and make things happen that would happen, if such a thing existed."

Tolkien did, however, suggest that his work had an underlying theme. "*The Lord of the Rings,*" he wrote in a letter to the Jesuit Father Robert Murray published in *The Letters of J. R. R. Tolkien,* "is of course a fundamentally religious and Catholic work; unconsciously so at first, but consciously in the revision." Shippey pointed out that the rejoicing of the forces of the West after the downfall of Sauron in *The Return of the King* is an example of what Tolkien called a "eucatastrophe." Tolkien wrote to his son Christopher that in his essay "On Fairy Stories," he "coined the word 'eucatastrophe': the sudden happy turn in a story which pierces you with a joy that brings tears (which I argued it is the highest function of fairy-stories to produce). And I was there led to the view that it produces its peculiar effects because it is a sudden glimpse of Truth." He went on to explain, "It perceives . . . that this is indeed how things really do work in the Great World for which our nature is made. And I concluded by saying that the Resurrection was the greatest 'eucatastrophe' possible in the greatest Fairy Story—and produces that essential emotion: Christian joy which produces tears because it is qualitatively so like sorrow, because it comes from

those places where Joy and Sorrow are at one." He added: "Of course, I do not mean that the Gospels tell what is *only* a fairy-story; but I do mean very strongly that they do tell a fairy-story: the greatest. Man the story-teller would have to be redeemed in a manner consonant with his nature: by a moving story."

"A good way to understand *The Lord of the Rings* in its full complexity," noted Shippey, "is to see it as an attempt to reconcile two views of evil, both old, both authoritative, each seemingly contradicted by the other." To the orthodox Christian, evil does not exist by itself, but springs from an attempt to separate one's self from God—an opinion expressed most clearly in *The Consolation of Philosophy,* a work by the early medieval thinker Boethius, a Roman senator imprisoned and later executed for his views. Tolkien was probably most familiar with it through King Alfred's Old English translation, made in the ninth century A.D. An alternate view—labelled Manichaean, and considered heretical by the church—is that good and evil are separate forces, equal and opposite, and the world is their battleground. King Alfred's own career, campaigning against marauding Norsemen, wrote Shippey, emphasized the "strong point of a 'heroic' view of evil, the weak point of a Boethian one: if you regard evil as something internal, to be pitied, more harmful to the malefactor than the victim, you may be philosophically consistent but you may also be exposing others to sacrifices to which they have not consented (like being murdered by Viking ravagers or, as *The Lord of the Rings* was being written, being herded into gas-chambers)." In *The Lord of the Rings,* Shippey stated, Tolkien strikes a balance between these two views of evil, using the symbol of the shadow: "Shadows are the absence of light and so don't exist in themselves, but they are still visible and palpable just as if they did." Tolkien's attitude "implies the dual nature of wickedness," which can also be found in the Lord's Prayer: "'And lead us not into temptation; but deliver us from evil.' Succumbing to temptation is our business, one might paraphrase, but delivering us from evil is God's." Shippey concluded: "At any rate, on the level of narrative one can say that *The Lord of the Rings* is neither a saint's life, all about temptation, nor a complicated wargame, all about tactics. It would be a much lesser work if it had swerved towards either extreme."

Nonetheless, Tolkien implies consistently that to take *The Lord of the Rings* too seriously might be a mistake. "I think that a fairy story has its own mode of reflecting 'truth,' different from allegory or (sustained) satire, or 'realism,' and in some ways more powerful," he stated. "But first of all it must succeed just as a tale, excite, please, and even on occasion move, and within its own imagined world be accorded literary belief. To succeed in that was my primary object." Tolkien also wrote: "The tale is after all in the ultimate analysis a tale, a piece of literature, intended to have literary effect, and not real history. That the device adopted, that of giving its setting an historical air or feeling, and (an illusion of ?) three dimensions, is successful, seems shown by the fact that several correspondents have treated it in the same way . . . as if it were a report of 'real' times and places, which my ignorance or carelessness had misrepresented in places or failed to describe properly in others." He concluded: "Having set myself a task, the arrogance of which I fully recognized and trembled at: being precisely to restore to the English an epic tradition and present them with a mythology of their own: it is a wonderful thing to be told that I have succeeded, at least with those who have still the undarkened heart and mind."

BIOGRAPHICAL AND CRITICAL SOURCES:

BOOKS

Authors in the News, Volume 1, Gale (Detroit, MI), 1976.

Blackwelder, Richard E., *A Tolkien Thesaurus,* Garland Press (New York, NY), 1990.

Bloom, Harold, editor, *J. R. R. Tolkien,* Chelsea House (Philadelphia, PA), 2000.

Carpenter, Humphrey, *J. R. R. Tolkien: A Biography,* Allen & Unwin (London, England), 1977, published as *Tolkien: A Biography,* Houghton Mifflin (Boston, MA), 1978.

Carpenter, Humphrey, *The Inklings: C. S. Lewis, J. R. R. Tolkien, Charles Williams and Their Friends,* Allen & Unwin (London, England), 1978, Houghton Mifflin (Boston, MA), 1979.

Carter, Lin, *Tolkien: A Look behind "The Lord of the Rings,"* Houghton Mifflin (Boston, MA), 1969.

Compact Edition of the Oxford English Dictionary, Oxford University Press (Oxford, England), 1971.

Contemporary Literary Criticism, Gale (Detroit, MI), Volume 1, 1973, Volume 2, 1974, Volume 3, 1975, Volume 8, 1978, Volume 12, 1980, Volume 38, 1986.

Curry, Patrick, *Defending Middle-Earth: Tolkien, Myth and Modernity,* St. Martin's Press (New York, NY), 1997.

Day, David, *A Tolkien Bestiary,* Ballantine (New York, NY), 1979.

Day, David, *Tolkien: The Illustrated Encyclopedia,* Collier (New York, NY), 1992.

Day, David, *Tolkien's Ring,* HarperCollins (London, England), 1994.

Dictionary of Literary Biography, Gale (Detroit, MI), Volume 15: *British Novelists, 1930-1959,* 1983, Volume 160: *British Children's Writers, 1914-1960,* pp. 254-271, Volume 255: *British Fantasy and Science-Fiction Writers, 1918-1960,* 2002, pp. 237-250.

Duriez, Colin, *The J. R. R. Tolkien Handbook: A Comprehensive Guide to His Life, Writings, and World of Middle-Earth,* Baker Book House (Grand Rapids, MI), 1992.

Ellwood, Gracia F., *Good News from Tolkien's Middle Earth: Two Essays on the Applicability of "The Lord of the Rings,"* Eerdmans (New York, NY), 1970.

Evans, Robley, *J.R.R. Tolkien,* Warner Paperback Library (New York, NY), 1972.

Flieger, Verlyn, *Splintered Light: Logos and Language in Tolkien's World,* Eerdmans (New York, NY), 1983.

Fonstad, Karen Wynn, *The Atlas of Middle-Earth,* Houghton Mifflin (Boston, MA), 1981.

Foster, Robert, *A Guide to Middle-Earth,* Mirage Press (New York, NY), 1971, revised edition published as *The Complete Guide to Middle-Earth,* Del Rey (New York, NY), 1981.

Fuller, Edmund, and others, *Myth, Allegory and Gospel: An Interpretation; J. R. R. Tolkien, C. S. Lewis, G. K. Chesterton, Charles Williams,* Bethany Fellowship, 1974.

Green, William, *The Hobbit: A Journey into Maturity,* Twayne (New York, NY), 1995.

Hammond, Wayne G., and Christina Scull, *J. R. R. Tolkien: Artist & Illustrator,* Houghton Mifflin (Boston, MA), 1995.

Harvey, David, *Song of Middle Earth,* Allen & Unwin (London, England), 1985.

Helms, Paul, and Paul S. Ritz, *Tolkien's Peaceful War: A History and Explanation of Tolkien Fandom and War,* American Tolkien Society (Highland, MI), 1994.

Isaacs, Neil D., and Rose A. Zimbardo, editors, *Tolkien and the Critics,* University of Notre Dame Press (South Bend, IN), 1968.

Johnson, Judith A., *J. R. R. Tolkien: Six Decades of Criticism,* Greenwood Press (Westport, CT), 1986.

Kocher, Paul H., *Master of Middle-Earth: The Fiction of J. R. R. Tolkien,* Houghton Mifflin (Boston, MA), 1972.

Le Guin, Ursula K., *The Language of the Night: Essays on Fantasy and Science Fiction,* edited and with an introduction by Susan Wood, Putnam (New York, NY), 1979.

Lobdell, Jared, editor, *A Tolkien Compass,* Open Court, 1975.

Neimark, Anne E., *Myth Maker: J. R. R. Tolkien,* illustrated by Brad Weinman, Harcourt Brace (San Diego, CA), 1996.

Noel, Ruth S., *The Languages of Tolkien's Middle-Earth,* Houghton Mifflin (Boston, MA), 1980.

Purtill, Richard L., *Lord of the Elves and Eldils: Fantasy and Philosophy in C. S. Lewis and J. R. R. Tolkien,* Zondervan (Grand Rapids, MI), 1974.

Ready, William B., *The Tolkien Relation: A Personal Inquiry,* Regnery (New York, NY), 1968.

Shippey, T. A., *J. R. R. Tolkien: Author of the Century,* Houghton Mifflin (Boston, MA), 2001.

Shippey, T. A., *The Road to Middle-Earth,* Allen & Unwin (London, England), 1982, Houghton Mifflin (Boston, MA), 1983.

Stevens, David, and Carol D. Stevens, *J. R. R. Tolkien: The Art of the Myth-Maker,* revised edition, R. Reginald (San Bernardino, CA), 1993.

Stimpson, Catherine R., *J. R. R. Tolkien,* Columbia University Press (New York, NY), 1969.

Strachey, Barbara, *Journeys of Frodo: An Atlas of J. R. R. Tolkien's "The Lord of the Rings,"* Ballantine (New York, NY), 1981.

Tolkien, John, and Priscilla Tolkien, *The Tolkien Family Album,* HarperCollins (New York, NY), 1992.

Tolkien, J. R. R., *The Annotated Hobbit,* Houghton Mifflin (Boston, MA), 1988.

Tolkien, J. R. R., *The Lord of the Rings,* Ballantine (New York, NY), 1966.

Tolkien, J. R. R., *The Letters of J. R. R. Tolkien,* selected and edited by Humphrey Carpenter and Christopher Tolkien, Houghton Mifflin (Boston, MA), 1981.

Tyler, J. E. A., *The Tolkien Companion,* Houghton Mifflin (Boston, MA), 1982.

West, Richard C., compiler, *Tolkien Criticism: An Annotated Checklist,* Kent State University Press (Kent, OH), 1970, revised edition, 1981.

Wilson, Colin, *Tree by Tolkien,* Capra, 1974.

PERIODICALS

Atlantic, March, 1965.
Book Week, February 26, 1967.
British Book News, December, 1984.
Chicago Tribune Book World, March 22, 1981.
Christian Century, February 24, 1993, p. 208.
Chronicles of Culture, April, 1985.
Commentary, February, 1967.
Commonweal, December 3, 1965.
Criticism, winter, 1971.
Critique, spring-fall, 1959.
Encounter, November, 1954.
Esquire, September, 1966.
Hudson Review, number 9, 1956-57.
Kenyon Review, summer, 1965.
Los Angeles Times Book Review, January 4, 1981; February 10, 1985.
Nation, April 14, 1956.
New Republic, January 16, 1956.
New Statesman and Society, December 20, 1991, p. 47.
New York Review of Books, December 14, 1972.
New York Times Book Review, March 14, 1965; October 31, 1965; November 16, 1980; May 27, 1984; June 17, 1984.
New York Times Magazine, January 15, 1967.
Saturday Evening Post, July 2, 1966.
Sewanee Review, fall, 1961.
South Atlantic Quarterly, summer, 1959; spring, 1970.
Spectator, November, 1954.
Sunday Times (London, England), September 19, 1982.
Thought, spring, 1963.
Time and Tide, August 14, 1954; October 22, 1955.
Times Literary Supplement, July 8, 1983; July 19, 1985; December 23, 1988.
Washington Post Book World, September 4, 1977; December 9, 1980; February 13, 1983.

OBITUARIES:

PERIODICALS

Newsweek, September 17, 1973.
New York Times, September 3, 1973.
Publishers Weekly, September 17, 1973.
Time, September 17, 1973.
Washington Post, September 3, 1973.*

V-Y

VALLE, Victor Manuel 1950-

PERSONAL: Born November 10, 1950, in Whittier, CA; son of a dairy worker; married Maria Lau; children: Lucina, Alejandra. *Education:* California State University, Long Beach, B.A. (cum laude), 1974, M.A., 1978; Northwestern University, Medill School of Journalism, M.S.J., 1981.

ADDRESSES: Agent—c/o Author Mail, University of Minnesota Press, Mill Place, 111 Third Ave. S, Suite 290, Minneapolis, MN 55401.

CAREER: Poet, journalist, and translator. *Los Angeles Times,* Los Angeles, CA, staff writer; California Polytechnic State University, San Luis Obispo, CA, associate professor of ethnic studies. Artist-in-residence, California Arts Council; participant in the National Endowment for the Humanities Poetry in the Schools Program.

AWARDS, HONORS: Third Irvine Chicago Prize for poetry, 1977, for *Illegal;* Translation Award, from Translation Center of Columbia University, 1979; Pulitzer Prize for food journalism; James Beard Cookbook Award nomination for *Recipe of Memory: Five Generations of Mexican Cuisine.*

WRITINGS:

Illegal, [Los Angeles, CA], 1977.
(With John Valadez) *A Choice of Colors* (video documentary), 1978.

Nicaragua: Lucha de las Américas (radio special), 1979.
La Educación universitaria en El Salvador: Un Espejo roto en los 1980's, CINAS (San Salvador, El Salvador), 1991.
Siembra de vientos: El Salvador, 1960-69, CINAS (San Salvador, El Salvador), 1993.
(With wife, Mary Lau Valle) *Recipe of Memory: Five Generations of Mexican Cuisine,* New Press (New York, NY), 1995.
(With Rodolfo D. Torres) *Latino Metropolis,* University of Minnesota Press (Minneapolis, MN), 2000.

Contributor to anthologies, including *Third Chicano Literary Prize Anthology, 1976-77,* University of California (Irvine, CA), 1977; *Calafia: The California Poetry,* edited by Ishmael Reed, Y'Bird (Berkeley, CA), 1979; *Fiesta in Aztlán,* edited by Toni Empringham, Capra (Santa Barbara, CA), 1981; *201: Homenaje a la ciudad de Los Angeles,* edited by Jesús Mena, [Los Angeles, CA], 1982; *Southern California's Latino Community,* Los Angeles Times (Los Angeles, CA), 1983; and *Autonomía universitaria: Tensiones y esperanzas,* Organization of American States, Department of Educational Affairs (Washington, DC), 1986. Contributor to *Tin Tan, Rara Avis, Rip Rap, Electrum,* and other periodicals. Former associate editor, *Somos* magazine; former literary editor, *Chismearte* magazine.

SIDELIGHTS: Victor Manuel Valle is a poet, journalist, and a teacher in ethnic studies whose writings explore Latino culture and history. According to Enrique R. Lamadrid in the *Dictionary of Literary Biography,* "Valle's poems explore the links and contradictions between the deeply personal and the historical, opposite poles of experience that are usually alienated or dichotomized in most American poetry. In Valle's poetry they reach a powerful synthesis, as he is able to perceive the workings of history in the most insignificant everyday aspects of his life and in those of the people around him." Valle has also published a Mexican cookbook, *Recipe of Memory: Five Generations of Mexican Cuisine,* with his wife, and a sociological study, *Latino Metropolis,* with Rodolfo D. Torres.

Valle was born and raised in Whittier, California, in a family of dairy workers of Mexican descent; many of them were political exiles from Mexico and had been followers of Pancho Villa. Valle once explained, according to Lamadrid, that he had "a rather mundane public life and education. However, privately, I learned to raise mockingbirds, gorreones [sparrows], pigeons, crows, lizards, deer, and about thirteen dogs. . . . The oral tradition of my grandparents and aunts provided me with insight and knowledge on Mexican history. Before my grandfather Alfredo died, my grandma Matilde wrote all his memoirs of *la Revolucion* down. I'll be rewriting them sometime in the future."

Much of Valle's work is inspired by his family background and childhood experiences. Although he began as a poet, more recently his journalistic pieces have taken much of his time. Because he has translated the work of many other writers, he is deeply familiar with contemporary Latin American literature, which gives him a wider perspective than many other writers. In addition to writing poetry and nonfiction and translating, Valle has produced a video program, *A Choice of Colors,* about gangs and graffiti, as well as a radio program, *Nicaragua: Lucha de las Americas* ("Nicaragua: Struggle of the Americas"). He has worked as associate editor of *Somos* magazine and as literary editor of *Chismearte* magazine. He has also run a creative writing workshop for Latino writers in Los Angeles.

Although Valle's poems have appeared in several literary magazines, such as *New, Tin Tan,* and *Rara Avis,* Lamadrid noted that "he is comparatively underpublished as a poet, considering the special qualities of his work." His first book, *Illegal,* which was originally published in a limited underground edition, established his reputation as a poet; it later won the third Irvine Chicago Prize for poetry.

In *Recipe of Memory,* Valle collaborated with his wife on a book which combines old family recipes, some

of them dating back to the 1880s, with a family history filled with anecdotes and photographs and tracing the family's journey from Guadalajara, Mexico, in the nineteenth century to present-day Los Angeles. The result, wrote a critic for *Publishers Weekly,* "blends its ingredients much as Mole Caragueno combines lamb, chiles, peanuts, clove and cinnamon." *Recipe of Memory* was nominated for a James Beard Cookbook Award.

Valle collaborated with Rodolfo D. Torres to write *Latino Metropolis,* an examination of contemporary racial politics in the American urban setting. Looking specifically at the role played by Latinos in Los Angeles, the two authors "challenge existing methodologies of defining urban society in terms of race, calling for the construction of a new urban politics based on the commonalities of culture and class," according to Deborah Bigelow in *Library Journal.*

BIOGRAPHICAL AND CRITICAL SOURCES:

BOOKS

Dictionary of Literary Biography, Volume 122: *Chicano Writers,* Gale (Detroit, MI), 1992.

PERIODICALS

Library Journal, August, 2000, Deborah Bigelow, review of *Latino Metropolis,* p. 136.
Publishers Weekly, October 16, 1995, review of *Recipe of Memory: Five Generations of Mexican Cuisine,* p. 58.*

*   *   *

VERYAN, Patricia
   See BANNISTER, Patricia Valeria

*   *   *

WALTON, Rick 1957-

PERSONAL: Born February 12, 1957, in Provo, UT; son of Bill (a professor of educational psychology) and Wilma (an elementary school teacher) Walton; married Ann Ivie (a computer programmer), April 27, 1983; children: Alan, Patrick, Nicholas, Sarah, David.

Ethnicity: "Caucasian." *Education:* Brigham Young University, B.A., 1980, elementary education certification, 1987, M.A., 2000. *Politics:* Independent. *Religion:* Church of Jesus Christ of Latter-day Saints (Mormons). *Hobbies and other interests:* Playing guitar, reading, travel, playing with his children.

ADDRESSES: Home and office—2880 North 840 E, Provo, UT 84604. *Agent*—Kendra Marcus, BookStop Literary Agency, 67 Meadow View Rd., Orinda, CA 94563. *E-mail*—rick@rickwalton.com.

CAREER: Freelance writer, 1982—. Provo Parks and Recreation Department, projects coordinator, 1983-84; WICAT Systems, editor in education division, 1984-85; elementary schoolteacher, 1987-88; Waterford School, Class V teacher, 1988-89; International Business Machines Co., software designer and creative writer, 1989-90; freelance software designer and writer, 1994—. Church of Jesus Christ of Latter-day Saints, missionary in Brazil, 1976-78; Provo Cultural Affairs Board, resource assistant, 1981-86; Academy Square Foundation, board member, 1984-88; Provo Media Review Commission, member, 1992-94, 1996-98, vice chair, 1993, 1997, chair, 1994, 1998.

MEMBER: Society of Children's Book Writers and Illustrators.

AWARDS, HONORS: Children's Choice selection, International Reading Association, 1990, for *Kiss a Frog! Jokes about Fairy Tales, Knights, and Dragons, Can You Match This? Jokes about Unlikely Pairs, What a Ham! Jokes about Pigs, Fossil Follies! Jokes about Dinosaurs,* and *Clowning Around! Jokes about the Circus,* and 1999, for *So Many Bunnies;* Award in Children's Literature, Association of Mormon Letters, 1996, for *You Don't Always Get What You Hope For;* Gold Award, Oppenheim Toy Portfolio, 2000, for *One More Bunny: Adding from One to Ten,* and 2003, for *Bertie Was a Watchdog;* selection as "best book of the year," *Child* magazine, 2001, for *My Two Hands/My Two Feet.*

WRITINGS:

WITH WIFE, ANN WALTON; "MAKE ME LAUGH" RIDDLE BOOK SERIES

Dumb Clucks! Jokes about Chickens, illustrated by Joan Hanson, Lerner Publications (Minneapolis, MN), 1987.

Something's Fishy! Jokes about Sea Creatures, illustrated by Joan Hanson, Lerner Publications (Minneapolis, MN), 1987.
What's Your Name, Again? More Jokes about Names, illustrated by Joan Hanson, Lerner Publications (Minneapolis, MN), 1988.
Kiss a Frog! Jokes about Fairy Tales, Knights, and Dragons, illustrated by Joan Hanson, Lerner Publications (Minneapolis, MN), 1989.
Can You Match This? Jokes about Unlikely Pairs, illustrated by Joan Hanson, Lerner Publications (Minneapolis, MN), 1989.
What a Ham! Jokes about Pigs, illustrated by Joan Hanson, Lerner Publications (Minneapolis, MN), 1989.
Fossil Follies! Jokes about Dinosaurs, illustrated by Joan Hanson, Lerner Publications (Minneapolis, MN), 1989.
Clowning Around! Jokes about the Circus, illustrated by Joan Hanson, Lerner Publications (Minneapolis, MN), 1989.

WITH ANN WALTON; "YOU MUST BE JOKING" RIDDLE BOOK SERIES

Weather or Not: Riddles for Rain or Shine, illustrated by Susan Slattery Burke, Lerner Publications (Minneapolis, MN), 1990.
On with the Show: Show Me Riddles, illustrated by Susan Slattery Burke, Lerner Publications (Minneapolis, MN), 1990.
I Toad You So: Riddles about Frogs and Toads, illustrated by Susan Slattery Burke, Lerner Publications (Minneapolis, MN), 1991.
Ho-Ho-Ho! Riddles about Santa Claus, illustrated by Susan Slattery Burke, Lerner Publications (Minneapolis, MN), 1991.
Alphabatty: Riddles about the Alphabet, illustrated by Susan Slattery Burke, Lerner Publications (Minneapolis, MN), 1991.
Off Base: Riddles about Baseball, illustrated by Susan Slattery Burke, Lerner Publications (Minneapolis, MN), 1993.
Hoop-La: Riddles about Basketball, illustrated by Susan Slattery Burke, Lerner Publications (Minneapolis, MN), 1993.
Take a Hike: Riddles about Football, illustrated by Susan Slattery Burke, Lerner Publications (Minneapolis, MN), 1993.

OTHER RIDDLE BOOKS

Riddle-Day Saints, illustrated by Howard Fullmer, Deseret Book (Salt Lake City, UT), 1994.

Wholly Cowboy: Cowboy, Cow, and Horse Riddles, illustrated by Pat Bagley, Buckaroo Books (Carson City, NV), 1995.

Dino-Might: Pre-hysterical Dinosaur Riddles, illustrated by Pat Bagley, Buckaroo Books (Carson City, NV), 1995.

The Ghost Is Clear: Riddles about Ghosts, Goblins, Vampires, Witches, and Other Creatures That Cause Shivers in the Night, illustrated by Pat Bagley, Buckaroo Books (Carson City, NV), 1995.

Astro-Nuts! Riddles about Astronauts and the Planets They Love, illustrated by Pat Bagley, Buckaroo Books (Carson City, NV), 1995.

Really Really Bad School Jokes!, illustrated by Renee Williams-Andriani, Candlewick Press (Cambridge, MA), 1998.

Really, Really Bad Summer Jokes, illustrated by Jack Desrocher, Candlewick Press (Cambridge, MA), 1999.

PICTURE BOOKS

Will You Still Love Me? illustrated by Brad Teare, Deseret Book (Salt Lake City, UT), 1992.

How Many How Many How Many, illustrated by Cynthia Jabar, Candlewick Press (Cambridge, MA), 1993.

Noah's Square Dance, illustrated by Thor Wickstrom, Lothrop, Lee & Shepard (New York, NY), 1995.

Once There Was a Bull . . . (frog), illustrated by Greg Hally, Gibbs Smith (Salt Lake City, UT), 1995.

You Don't Always Get What You Hope For, illustrated by Heidi Stetson Mario, Gibbs Smith (Salt Lake City, UT), 1996.

Pig Pigger Piggest, illustrated by Jimmy Holder, Gibbs Smith (Salt Lake City, UT), 1997.

Dance, Pioneer, Dance!, illustrated by Brad Teare, Deseret Book (Salt Lake City, UT), 1997.

So Many Bunnies: A Bedtime ABC and Counting Book, illustrated by Paige Miglio, Lothrop, Lee & Shepard (New York, NY), 1998.

Why the Banana Split, illustrated by Jimmy Holder, Gibbs Smith (Salt Lake City, UT), 1998.

Bullfrog Pops!, illustrated by Chris McAllister, Gibbs Smith (Salt Lake City, UT), 1999.

Little Dogs Say "Rough!," illustrated by Henry Cole, Putnam (New York, NY), 2000.

Herd of Cows, Flock of Sheep, Quiet, I'm Tired, I Need My Sleep!, Gibbs Smith (Layton, UT), 2002.

Cars at Play, Putnam (New York, NY), 2002.

Bunny Day: Telling Time from Breakfast to Bedtime, HarperCollins (New York, NY), 2002.

Bertie Was a Watchdog, Candlewick Press (Cambridge, MA), 2002.

Bunnies on the Go: Getting from Place to Place, HarperCollins (New York, NY), 2003.

Suddenly, Alligator, Gibbs Smith (Layton, UT), 2004.

A Very Hairy Scary Story, Putnam (New York, NY), 2004.

OTHER

(Editor, with Fern Oviatt) *Stories for Mormons,* Bookcraft (Salt Lake City, UT), 1983.

What to Do When a Bug Climbs in Your Mouth and Other Poems to Drive You Buggy, illustrated by Nancy Carlson, Lothrop, Lee & Shepard (New York, NY), 1995.

The Big Book of Scripture Activities, illustrated by Shauna Kawasaki, Deseret Book (Salt Lake City, UT), 1996.

My Two Hands/My Two Feet, illustrated by Julia Gorton, Putnam (New York, NY), 2000.

One More Bunny: Adding from One to Ten, illustrated by Paige Miglio, Lothrop Lee & Shepard (New York, NY), 2000.

That's What You Get!, illustrations by Jimmy Holder, Gibbs Smith (Salt Lake City, UT), 2000.

The Treasure Hunt Book (activity book), Klutz (Palo Alto, CA), 2000.

How Can You Dance?, illustrated by Ana Lopez-Escriva, Putnam (New York, NY), 2001.

That's My Dog!, illustrations by Julia Gorton, Putnam (New York, NY), 2001.

The Bear Came Over to My House, illustrated by James Warhola, Putnam (New York, NY), 2001.

Brain Waves (activity book), Pleasant Co. (Middleton, WI), 2002.

Mini-Mysteries, Pleasant Co. (Middleton, WI), 2004.

Also creator of computer software products, including "Bone," in *PerfectOffice for Kids,* WordPerfect (Orem, UT), 1995; *Richer Than the Pharaoh,* Infovision (Orem, UT), 1996; *Operation Groupwise,* Novell (Orem, UT), 1996; and *Ten Pin Alley,* Saffire (American Fort, UT), 1999.

WORK IN PROGRESS: Mrs. McMurphy's Pumpkin and *Bunny Christmas,* picture books, publication by HarperCollins (New York, NY) expected in 2005; *Boo*

Bunnies, a picture book, HarperCollins (New York, NY), 2006; and *The Remarkable Friendship of Mr. Cat and Mr. Rat,* a picture book, for Putnam (New York, NY).

SIDELIGHTS: Rick Walton once told *CA:* "I talk to lots of groups of kids, and whenever I talk the kids have many questions they want to ask me. This leads to serious problems. When hundreds of kids put their hands in the air, I can't get to them all. After some time the blood leaves the children's hands, and then fingers fall off. And then the principal, teachers, and I have to go around and pick up all those fingers and figure out who they belong to and glue them back on. It takes a long time and the kids miss their lunch, which makes them grumpy. And then they can't do their homework for at least three or four days, and that makes their teachers mad. So for the health of children and sanity of teachers, I've put together this list of frequently asked questions. These questions are in no particular order because kids don't ask their questions in any particular order.

"*When did you start writing?* When I was a kid, I did some writing just for fun. Mostly really silly stuff. But I decided I wanted to be a professional writer when I was in my early twenties. I still write mostly really silly stuff."

Walton commented that he writes, "Because I love the creative process . . . I like playing with words . . . Writing lets me pretend to be someone else . . . I want to leave as much of value as I can when I'm gone . . . I like reading my stories to my kids . . . I like to belong to writers groups . . . I like something I've done to add to the lives of others . . . I like to communicate what I believe about life . . . I like to see my name and ideas in print . . . I've tried every other career, and this is the only one left . . . Money.

"*All that?* And more. I write for the same reason I eat. Because I'd die if I didn't. It's an obsession."

Discussing why he writes for children, Walton commented, "Children's literature is incredibly varied. I like to write for kids because I can write about anything in almost any fashion. I can be more inventive in writing for children than I can in writing for any other audience."

Walton related, "Absolutely everything is a source of ideas. For example, your shoes are giving me an idea for a book right now.

"Some books take me an hour to write. Some take me several days. Some several weeks. It depends on how long the book is, how well the book is developed in my mind, and how much research I have to do."

Walton commented that he enjoys writing. "For others, plumbing might be fun. I hope it is. I have some pipes that need fixing and I hope my plumber enjoys himself, because the job isn't going to be easy." Remarking on what he hates about writing, Walton added, "Deadlines. And not knowing how much money I'm going to get, or when it's coming."

The author speculated that if he was not a writer, he might have become "a tour guide, or a songwriter, or a presidential advisor, or if Harold II hadn't lost the Battle of Hastings in 1066 and the right 100,000 people had died in the right order—King of England."

Walton declared that of all the books he has written, his favorite is "All of them! (It's like asking, 'Who's your favorite kid?') Okay, I admit, I do have some books I like better than others, but I'm not telling you which. I'm more interested in what's YOUR favorite book I've written."

Regarding his favorite books to read, Walton related, "I don't have one favorite book. When I was a kid I read every funny book and every mystery series I could find. Now I read all kinds of books, but my favorite are funny books, the funnier and weirder the better. I like Roald Dahl, Daniel Pinkwater, Babette Cole, Jon Scieszka, Dave Barry, Patrick McManus, David Wiesner, E. Nesbit, and anything you've written."

"I'm working on an early chapter book series and a couple of middle-grade novels. I also want to do some screenwriting and some songwriting. I want to write more poetry. And some fun things for grownups. And I want to write about a million more funny picture books."

It is not likely that anyone could accuse Walton of lacking a sense of humor. He has written dozens of laughter-inducing books for young readers, and is known for his many collections of riddles, as well as his humorous picture books. Perhaps the best-known of Walton's writing is his collection of riddle and joke books. Starting in 1987 with *Dumb Clucks! Jokes about Chickens* and *Something's Fishy! Jokes about Sea Creatures,* he has published numerous volumes of humor relating to sports, animals, names—even Santa Claus and the alphabet.

Born and raised in Utah, Walton is a member of the Church of Jesus Christ of Latter-day Saints, the Mormon Church. He served as a missionary to Brazil from 1976 to 1978, soon after he graduated from high school. Later, at Brigham Young University, he became president of the Brazil Club. In 1980 he graduated from Brigham Young with a bachelor's degree in Spanish and a minor in Portuguese, the language spoken in Brazil.

Walton's education continued after he obtained his degree. In 1980 he went back to Brigham Young for one semester of graduate work in business, but chose not to follow that career path. Deciding to become a teacher, he earned certification in elementary education from Brigham Young in 1987, as well as certification to teach gifted and talented students. Up to that point, he had held a number of jobs, including a year with the parks and recreation department of Provo, Utah. In 1987 he began teaching sixth grade at a local public school, then switched to a private school.

Walton was also interested in computers, and would later publish several items of software. He left teaching to accept a position as software designer for International Business Machines (IBM) Company in 1989. In 1994, he turned to freelance software design and writing. He also returned to Brigham Young University once again, this time to earn his master's degree in English, with an emphasis on creative writing.

Walton's wife, Ann, with whom he has written many of his books, is a computer programmer. They were married in 1983, and have five children. With *Dumb Clucks!* and *Something's Fishy!* in 1987, the Waltons began writing books, illustrated by Joan Hanson, for the Lerner Publications "Make Me Laugh" series. An example of a riddle in *Dumb Clucks!* is "What happened when the chicken ate cement? She laid a sidewalk." As for *Something's Fishy!*, an exemplary riddle would be, "Why did the shark wear a tuxedo? He was dressed to kill."

The Waltons soon took on more subjects with their riddle books in the "Make Me Laugh" series. *School Library Journal* contributor Eva Elisabeth Von Ancken cited *Can You Match This? Jokes about Unlikely Pairs* as the "most fun" of the five "Make Me Laugh" books published by the Waltons in 1989. Examples of its humor include "What do you get when you cross an owl with a duck? A wisequack" and "What do you get when you cross Lassie with a rose? A Collieflower."

Clowning Around! Jokes about the Circus consists of some sixty jokes, such as "Which circus performers can see in the dark? The acro-bats." *School Library Journal* contributor Von Ancken observed that "some of the jokes are rather far-fetched, while others show originality." Other Walton books in the series include *Fossil Follies! Jokes about Dinosaurs* ("What do you get if you feed your nodosaurus gunpowder? Dino-mite"); *What a Ham! Jokes about Pigs* ("What constellation looks like a pig? The Pig Dipper"); *What's Your Name, Again? More Jokes about Names* ("What do you call a girl who babbles? Brooke"); and *Kiss a Frog! Jokes about Fairy Tales, Knights, and Dragons.*

The Waltons also penned a similar collection of books for Lerner's "You Must Be Joking" series, all illustrated by Susan Slattery Burke. These include *Weather or Not: Riddles for Rain or Shine* and *On with the Show: Show Me Riddles* ("Show me a pencil that itches . . . And I'll show you scratch paper.") In 1991, they published *I Toad You So: Riddles about Frogs and Toads* ("What does a frog do if he gets sick? He gets a hoperation"), *Alphabatty: Riddles from A to Z* ("What letter will give you a lift? The L-eva-tor"), and *Ho-Ho-Ho! Riddles about Santa Claus.*

The Waltons have also written a series of sports-related riddle books as part of the larger "You Must Be Joking" series. These include *Off Base: Riddles about Baseball, Hoop-La: Riddles about Basketball,* and *Take a Hike: Riddles about Football.* Ilene Cooper of *Booklist* offered a favorable assessment of these works, noting that there is always a demand for humor with a sporting theme, and Walton's three books "go a long way toward satisfying it."

Walton published several other riddle and joke titles with Buckaroo Books, among them *The Ghost Is Clear,* a collection of riddles about ghosts, goblins, and ghouls. At the same time, however, Walton has enjoyed success in other genres. Among his well-received picture books is *Will You Still Love Me?*, in which a young boy describes a number of situations to his father, asking each time if the father would still love him in that situation. In *You Don't Always Get What You Hope For*, a boy begins his day just hoping that it will be an ordinary one; it turns out to be anything but ordinary.

With *How Many How Many How Many*, written for preschoolers and early primary graders, Walton made a foray into concept books. Described by *Publishers Weekly* as a "nifty counting book," it offers riddles of a more serious kind than those presented in Walton's joke books. Here the riddles are more like mind-teasers, rhyming couplets designed to be answered with a number. To the question, "Spiders like to steal her seat. How many things does Muffet eat?" the answer, of course, is two—curds and whey. The book, which takes readers through the numbers from one to twelve, offers knowledge of many kinds, with questions as to how many legs an ant has or how many positions are on a soccer team. Some of the questions, such as those about the number of planets in the solar system, may be a bit challenging for young readers, as reviewer I. Anne Rowe observed in *School Librarian*. But *School Library Journal* contributor Cynthia K. Richey called the book "a springboard to further learning experiences." Richey also commented favorably on the "multicultural cast" of children depicted in the book, as well as illustrator Cynthia Jabar's "well-designed and uncluttered double-page spreads."

Noah's Square Dance depicts a square dance aboard Noah's Ark, with Noah calling the turns of the dance while his family takes part in the music and the dancing. A critic for *Kirkus Reviews* reported: "The final verse celebrates the end of the storm, but readers will believe that everyone had a good time waiting it out." Brigham Young is cast as square-dance caller in *Dance, Pioneer, Dance!*, a cheerful picture book in which the featured festivities provide a bit of respite for Mormon pioneers traveling to the Great Salt Lake in 1847. Calling the work "exuberant and whimsical," *School Library Journal* contributor John Sigwald maintained: "Teachers can use the handful of Mormon-migration references as an introduction to this American-born Christian sect."

Walton has continued to produce works such as *What to Do When a Bug Climbs in Your Mouth and Other Poems to Drive You Buggy*, a book of "silly poems,"

according to Sally R. Dow in *School Library Journal*. *What to Do* consists of twenty poems about different kinds of bugs, from ants to cockroaches, gnats to centipedes. *Bloomsbury Review* listed it among several recommended books of poetry for children, all of which were distinguished by the fact that the poetry was simple enough for young children to read aloud. *Once There Was a Bull . . . (frog)*, which *Booklist*'s Lauren Peterson called an "amusing tale" that is "noteworthy for its clever design," features a frog who is searching for his hop, which he has lost. In the course of searching, he keeps running into unexpected things. On any given spread from the book, the illustrations and wording lead the reader to think that one thing is coming, when something quite different awaits on the next page. Hence the line, "He landed hard in a patch of grass" is paired with a picture of a field covered in grass; but on the next page, one discovers that the word is actually *grasshoppers*, and the illustration shows a number of them leaping about. The book is built entirely around such compound nouns, and Walton constantly encourages readers to guess what's coming next. Given its intended audience of early primary graders, *Once There Was a Bull . . . (frog)* offers educational opportunities, and a *Publishers Weekly* commentator suggested that it "could easily lend itself to a high-energy read-aloud."

Pig Pigger Piggest retells the familiar story of "The Three Little Pigs," who go by the names of Pig, Pigger, and Piggest. Each of them builds a castle for himself, and each pig's castle is larger than the one that precedes it. Unfortunately for them, however, they are confronted by witches named Witch, Witcher, and Witchest, who demand that the pigs give their castles to them. The witches end up destroying the castles with the help of Huff and Puff, who blow the castles down and turn them into piles of mud. But everything turns out right in the end, when the three pigs propose marriage to the three witches and they live "sloppily ever after." Throughout the book, Walton uses wordplay involving rhymes and comparative terms: hence "cheap sheep," "cheaper sheeper," and "cheapest sheepest." *Publishers Weekly* called this "enjoyably goofy," and dubbed *Pig Pigger Piggest* "definitely a funny book."

In addition to his many traditional books, Walton has authored several electronic books for children, including *Bone*, published in PerfectOffice for Kids, and activities and games such as *Richer Than the Pharaoh*, a game that teaches financial planning skills. He continues to produce entertaining and educational works prolifically, and promises to offer his readers many more laughs in years to come.

BIOGRAPHICAL AND CRITICAL SOURCES:

PERIODICALS

Bloomsbury Review, September-October, 1995.

Booklist, March 15, 1987, p. 1123; May 1, 1989, p. 1544; November 15, 1993, Ilene Cooper, review of *Take a Hike: Riddles about Football, Off Base: Riddles about Baseball,* and *Hoop-La: Riddles about Basketball,* p. 629; September 1, 1995, Carolyn Phelan, review of *Noah's Square Dance,* p. 59; December 15, 1995, Lauren Peterson, review of *Once There Was a Bull . . . (frog),* p. 710; March 15, 1998, April Judge, review of *So Many Bunnies: A Bedtime ABC and Counting Book,* p. 1252; September 15, 1998, Kay Weisman, review of *Dance, Pioneer, Dance!,* p. 233; April 15, 2000, Connie Fletcher, review of *One More Bunny: Adding from One to Ten,* p. 1554; October 1, 2000, Shelle Rosenfeld, review of *My Two Hands/My Two Feet,* p. 350; March 15, 2001, Lauren Peterson, review of *The Bear Came Over to My House,* p. 1406; June 1, 2001, Ilene Cooper, review of *How Can You Dance?,* p. 1897; May 15, 2002, Ilene Cooper, review of *Bunny Day: Telling Time from Breakfast to Bedtime,* p. 1603; January 1, 2003, Julie Cummins, review of *Bunnies on the Go: Getting from Place to Place,* p. 911.

Kirkus Reviews, August 15, 1995, review of *Noah's Square Dance,* p. 1196; December 15, 2001, review of *Bunny Day,* p. 1764; February 1, 2002, review of *Cars at Play,* p. 191; May 1, 2002, review of *Bertie Was a Watchdog,* p. 669; December 1, 2002, review of *Bunnies on the Go,* p. 1775.

Publishers Weekly, October 18, 1993, review of *How Many How Many How Many,* p. 71; November 6, 1995, review of *Once There Was a Bull . . . (frog),* p. 94; July 14, 1997, review of *Pig Pigger Piggest,* p. 83; January 26, 1998, review of *So Many Bunnies,* p. 90; October 26, 1998, review of *Why the Banana Split,* p. 65; June 12, 2000, review of *Little Dogs Say "Rough!,"* p. 73; January 15, 2001, review of *The Bear Came Over to My House,* p. 75; June 11, 2001, review of *That's My Dog!,* p. 84; June 11, 2001, review of *How Can You Dance?,* p. 85; May 6, 2002, review of *Bertie Was a Watchdog,* p. 56.

School Librarian, February, 1994, p. 18.

School Library Journal, August, 1987, pp. 64-65; June, 1989, Eva Elisabeth Von Ancken, review of *What a Ham! Jokes about Pigs, Kiss a Frog! Jokes about Fairy Tales, Knights, and Dragons,* and *Can You Match This? Jokes about Unlikely Pairs,* p. 116; August, 1989, p. 138; June, 1990, Susan H. Williamson, review of *Weather or Not: Riddles for Rain or Shine* and *On with the Show: Show Me Riddles,* p. 133; October, 1991, Dorothy Houlihan and Jane Marino, review of *Ho-Ho-Ho! Riddles about Santa Claus,* pp. 34-35; February, 1994, Cynthia K. Richey, review of *How Many How Many How Many,* p. 99; April, 1995, Sally R. Dow, review of *What to Do When a Bug Climbs in Your Mouth and Other Poems to Drive You Buggy,* p. 129; October, 1995, p. 123; November, 1996, Anne Parker, review of *You Don't Always Get What You Hope For,* pp. 94-95; November, 1997, Carrie A. Guarria, review of *Pig Pigger Piggest,* p. 102; March, 1998, Dawn Amsberry, review of *So Many Bunnies,* p. 189; August, 1998, John Sigwald, review of *Dance, Pioneer, Dance!,* p. 157; January, 1999, John Sigwald, review of *Why the Banana Split,* p. 106; January, 2000, Blair Christolon, review of *Bullfrog Pops!,* p. 112; July, 2000, Lucinda Snyder, review of *One More Bunny,* p. 90; August, 2000, Lisa Dennis, review of *Little Dogs Say "Rough!,"* p. 167; November, 2000, Marian Drabkin, review of *My Two Hands/My Two Feet,* p. 137; April, 2001, Maryann H. Owen, review of *The Bear Came Over to My House,* p. 124; July, 2001, Genevieve Ceraldi, review of *How Can You Dance?,* p. 90; December, 2001, Susan Marie Pitard, review of *That's My Dog!,* p. 114; April, 2002, Susan Marie Pitard, review of *Bunny Day,* p. 126; August, 2002, Judith Constantinides, review of *Bertie Was a Watchdog,* p. 172; September, 2002, Carolyn Janssen, review of *Herd of Cows! Flock of Sheep! Quiet, I'm Tired! I Need My Sleep!,* p. 208; March, 2003, Bina Williams, review of *Bunnies on the Go,* p. 210.

Teaching Children Mathematics, May, 1995, review of *How Many How Many How Many,* p. 586.

Writers Digest, June, 1998.

ONLINE

Rick Walton, Children's Author, http://www.rickwalton.com/ (April 11, 2004).

WARREN, Andrea 1946-

PERSONAL: Born October 30, 1946, in Norfolk, NE; daughter of James V. (a public school administrator) and Ruth (an executive director of a charitable organization; maiden name, Wilson) Warren; married Jay Wiedenkeller, November 22, 1981; children: Alison, Brendon (deceased), Kymberly, Derek. *Ethnicity:* "Caucasian." *Education:* University of Nebraska, B.S., 1968, M.A., 1971; University of Kansas, M.S., 1983. *Hobbies and other interests:* Reading, travel, theater.

ADDRESSES: Home and office—4908 West 71st St., Shawnee Mission, KS 66208-2309. *Agent*—Regina Ryan, 251 Central Park W, New York, NY 10024. *E-mail*—AWKansas@aol.com.

CAREER: High school English teacher in Hastings, NE, 1969-79; University of Kansas, Lawrence, writer and editor, 1979-81; Golf Course Superintendents Association of America, Lawrence, editor of national magazine, 1981; freelance writer, 1982—.

MEMBER: American Society of Journalists and Authors, Orphan Train Heritage Society of America, Writers Place of Kansas City.

AWARDS, HONORS: Boston Globe-Horn Book Award, nonfiction category, 1996, for *Orphan Train Rider: One Boy's True Story;* Society of Midland Authors, citation for "best children's nonfiction," 1997, for *Orphan Train Rider: One Boy's True Story,* award for best children's book, c. 1998, for *Pioneer Girl: Growing Up on the Prairie,* and nonfiction book award, c. 2001, for *Surviving Hitler: A Boy in the Nazi Death Camps;* citations for "notable children's trade book in the field of social studies," National Council for Social Studies and Children's Book Council, 1997, for *Orphan Train Rider: One Boy's True Story,* c. 1998, for *Pioneer Girl: Growing Up on the Prairie,* and c. 2001, for both *Surviving Hitler: A Boy in the Nazi Death Camps* and *We Rode the Orphan Trains;* American Library Association, "notable book" citation, 1997, for *Orphan Train Rider: One Boy's True Story,* and Robert F. Sibert Honor Book Award, most distinguished informational book for children, c. 2001, for *Surviving Hitler: A Boy in the Nazi Death Camps;* citation for "book of distinction," *Hungry Mind Review,* and citation for "best book in social studies for grades

kindergarten through six," Society of School Librarians International, both 1997, Dorothy Canfield Fisher Children's Book Award, Pennsylvania Young Readers' Award, Lamplight Award from National Christian Schools, Young Hoosier Book Award, and Jane Addams Children's Honor Book Award, all for *Orphan Train Rider: One Boy's True Story;* Nonfiction Honor Book Award, Voice of Youth Advocates, 2001, for both *Surviving Hitler: A Boy in the Nazi Death Camps* and *We Rode the Orphan Trains;* included among "top ten biographies for 2001," *Booklist,* for *We Rode the Orphan Trains;* inclusion in master list for William Allen White Book Award, 2003-04, for *Surviving Hitler: A Boy in the Nazi Death Camps;* Children's Book Award, South Carolina Association of School Librarians, and Orbis Pictus Award, outstanding nonfiction for children, National Council of Teachers of English, both for *Pioneer Girl: Growing Up on the Prairie;* Gold Medal, children's nonfiction category, National Association of Parenting Publications, Sydney Taylor Book Award and citation among "notable children's books of Jewish Content," both Association of Jewish Libraries, selection as "outstanding children's book," American Society of Journalists and Authors, and Learned Research Journal Award, national women's committee of Brandeis University, all for *Surviving Hitler: A Boy in the Nazi Death Camps.*

WRITINGS:

JUVENILE

Coming on Strong (novel), Scholastic (New York, NY), 1986.

Searching for Love (novel), Bantam (New York, NY), 1987.

Orphan Train Rider: One Boy's True Story, Houghton Mifflin (Boston, MA), 1996.

Pioneer Girl: Growing Up on the Prairie, Morrow (New York, NY), 1998.

Surviving Hitler: A Boy in the Nazi Death Camps, HarperCollins (New York, NY), 2001.

We Rode the Orphan Trains, Houghton Mifflin (Boston, MA), 2001.

Escape from Saigon: How a Vietnam War Orphan Boy Became an American Boy, Farrar, Straus & Giroux (New York, NY), 2004.

FOR ADULTS

Recovering from Breast Cancer, HarperCollins (New York, NY), 1991.

(With husband, Jay Wiedenkeller) *Everybody's Doing It: How to Survive Your Teenagers' Sex Life (and Help Them Survive It, Too),* Penguin (New York, NY), 1993.

A Mission of Healing: The History of Saint Joseph Health Center, St. Mary's Hospital of Blue Springs, and the Creation of Carondelet Health of Kansas City, Carondelet Health Press (Kansas City, MO), 1999.

Contributor of more than a hundred articles to magazines and newspapers, including *Ladies' Home Journal, American Health, Reader's Digest, American Education, Good Housekeeping,* and *World and I.*

SIDELIGHTS: Andrea Warren once told *CA:* "I have had a varied career, though all of it has in some way connected me to words and the joy of writing, or teaching writing. Under different circumstances, I would have first become a working journalist. Instead, it was a foregone conclusion that I would become a teacher, and no surprise that I selected English as my field, since reading and writing were always my great passions.

"My other teaching assignments included world history, debate, and creative writing. I moved to Lawrence, Kansas, in the summer of 1979, and for the next two years worked as an editor on a women's equity grant studying women in school administration. Shortly before I completed my master's degree in magazine journalism, I was hired to edit a golf magazine. I then worked briefly as a newspaper reporter while starting my freelance writing career, which took off in 1983. I also taught writing and communication workshops and a magazine writing seminar.

"My first two books were young adult novels. The next two were adult trade books. I then moved to history for young readers when I wrote *Orphan Train Rider: One Boy's True Story* and *Pioneer Girl: Growing Up on the Prairie.* At least for the foreseeable future, I will continue to write for young readers, loosely defined as grades five through ten. Those were the years in my life when I was an insatiable reader.

"I grew up in a tiny Nebraska town, and our public library was my refuge. I still remember books I read and re-read there. At the time it never occurred to me that someday I could write books. In fact, it took me several decades to confront my desire to write full-

time. I kept waiting for someone to tell me to do it—to give me permission. I finally had to give myself permission, and it was the hardest and the easiest thing I've ever done.

"*Orphan Train Rider* came readily as a subject. Ever since I first learned of them when I was a child, I had been interested in the orphan trains and the 150,000 American children who rode the rails to new homes. *Pioneer Girl* grew out of my interest in sharing with my readers what it was really like to grow up on the prairie. The book tells the true story of a Nebraska pioneer who lived in a sod house and spent her childhood working hard to help her parents.

"My interests typically lie in the stories of ordinary people and how they work through the challenges of their own lives. I have a special interest in children caught up in circumstances beyond their control, but I have also written many magazine stories about adults who find themselves in extraordinary difficulties, which they meet with grace, perseverance, and courage. When I come across this type of story, I find it irresistible.

"While I love fiction, I am happy at present writing nonfiction history. I might have majored in history and devoted my teaching career to it except for one major problem: I so often found it boring. Wars and treaties and successions of kings and presidents didn't interest me nearly so much as the people behind the facts. I loved historic literature, like *War and Peace,* which taught me the facts, but did so almost surreptitiously because I was so engrossed in the lives of the characters. I have tried to pattern my writing for children in the same way.

"I write every weekday. I keep regular office hours and, when I'm not on the phone or handling billings or some such thing, I am writing. I meet weekly with two other writers here in Kansas City who also make their living by freelancing magazine articles and books, and we critique each others' work and offer support for the vagaries and difficulties of the writer's life. Although my children are grown and away from home, I love working at home, and I have a sunny office that I always enjoy. I share my life with my husband, Jay, and feel fortunate to do so."

BIOGRAPHICAL AND CRITICAL SOURCES:

PERIODICALS

Booklist, July, 1996, p. 1826; January 1, 2001, Hazel Rochman, review of *Surviving Hitler: A Boy in* the Nazi Death Camps, p. 930; November 1, 2001, Hazel Rochman, review of *We Rode the Orphan Trains*, p. 477.

Capper's, March 4, 2003, review of *We Rode the Orphan Trains*, p. 6.

Horn Book, January-February, 1997, pp. 35-39; March, 2001, review of *Surviving Hitler*, p. 235; November-December, 2001, Peter D. Sieruta, review of *We Rode the Orphan Trains*, p. 775.

Ladies' Home Journal, December, 1997, p. 80.

Library Journal, April 1, 1993, p. 118.

Publishers Weekly, October 1, 2001, review of *We Rode the Orphan Trains*, p. 63.

School Library Journal, August, 1996, p. 162; March, 2001, Steven Engelfried, review of *Surviving Hitler,* p. 280; November, 2001, William McLoughlin, review of *We Rode the Orphan Trains*, p. 189.

Times Educational Supplement, January 18, 2002, Tom Deveson, review of *Surviving Hitler,* p. 22.

Writer's Digest, July, 1988, p. 72.

*　　*　　*

WILLIAM, Kate
See ARMSTRONG, Jennifer

*　　*　　*

WINFIELD, Julia
See ARMSTRONG, Jennifer

*　　*　　*

WINGRAVE, Anthony
See WRIGHT, S(ydney) Fowler

*　　*　　*

WITTREICH, Joseph Anthony, Jr. 1939-

PERSONAL: Surname is pronounced "*Wit*-trick"; born July 23, 1939, in Cleveland, OH; son of Joseph Anthony (a supervisor) and Mamie (Pucel) Wittreich. *Ethnicity:* "German/Austrian." *Education:* University of Louisville, B.A., 1961, M.A., 1962; Western Reserve University (now Case Western Reserve University), Ph.D., 1966. *Politics:* Democrat.

ADDRESSES: Home—311 West 83rd St., Apt. 5C, New York, NY 10024. *Office*—English Program, Graduate Center of the City University of New York, 365 Fifth Ave., New York, NY 10016. *E-mail*—jwittreich@gc.cuny.edu.

CAREER: University of Wisconsin—Madison, assistant professor, 1966-70, associate professor, 1970-74, professor of English, 1974-76; University of Maryland—College Park, professor of English, 1977-87; Graduate Center of the City University of New York, New York, NY, distinguished professor of English, 1988—. California State University—Los Angeles, guest lecturer, 1970, 1972.

MEMBER: Modern Language Association of America, Milton Society of America (member of executive committee), Renaissance Society of America.

AWARDS, HONORS: American Philosophical Society fellow, 1967; Henry E. Huntington fellow, 1968, 1976; Folger fellow, 1971, 1974; fellow of National Endowment for the Humanities, 1974, 1976, 1986, Newberry Library, 1974, and Wisconsin Institute for Research in the Humanities, 1975; Guggenheim fellow, 1979.

WRITINGS:

Angel of Apocalypse: Blake's Idea of Milton, University of Wisconsin Press (Madison, WI), 1975.

Visionary Poetics: Milton's Tradition and His Legacy, Huntington Library (San Marino, CA), 1979.

"Image of That Horror": History, Prophecy, and Apocalypse in "King Lear," Huntington Library (San Marino, CA), 1984.

Interpreting "Samson Agonistes," Princeton University Press (Princeton, NJ), 1986.

Feminist Milton, Cornell University Press (Ithaca, NY), 1987.

Shifting Contexts, Duquesne University Press (Pittsburgh, PA), 2002.

Contributor to books, including *Achievements of the Left Hand: Essays on John Milton's Prose Work,* edited by John T. Shawcross and Michael Lieb, University of Massachusetts Press (Amherst, MA), 1974; *Milton Encyclopedia,* edited by John T. Shawcross and others, Bucknell University Press (Lewisburg, PA), 1976; and *Homage to Milton,* edited by Balachandra Raja,

University of Georgia Press (Athens, GA), 1976; author of introduction, *Life of Milton* by William Hayley, facsimile edition, Scholars' Facsimiles and Reprints (Delmar, NY), 1970. Contributor of articles, essays, and reviews to periodicals, including *PMLA, Blake Studies, Studies in Philology, English Language Notes, Milton Quarterly, Milton Studies, Bucknell Review, Keats-Shelley Journal, Huntington Library Quarterly,* and *Journal of English and Germanic Philology.*

EDITOR

(And author of introduction and notes) *The Romantics on Milton: Formal Essays and Critical Asides,* Press of Case Western Reserve University (Cleveland, OH), 1970.

(And author of introduction) *Early Lives of William Blake,* Scholars' Facsimiles and Reprints (Delmar, NY), 1970.

(And author of introduction and notes) *Nineteenth-Century Accounts of William Blake,* Scholars' Facsimiles and Reprints (Delmar, NY), 1970.

Richard Meadowcourt, *Milton's "Paradise Regained": Two Eighteenth-Century Critiques,* facsimile edition, Scholars' Facsimiles and Reprints (Delmar, NY), 1971.

Calm of Mind: Tercentenary Essays on "Paradise Regained" and "Samson Agonistes," Press of Case Western Reserve University (Cleveland, OH), 1971.

(With Stuart Curran, and contributor) *Blake's Sublime Allegory: Essays on "The Four Zoas," "Milton," and "Jerusalem,"* University of Wisconsin Press (Madison, WI), 1973.

(With Eric Rothstein) *Literary Monographs,* University of Wisconsin Press (Madison, WI), Volume 6: *Medieval and Renaissance Literature,* 1975, Volume 7: *Thackery, Hawthorne, Melville, and Dreiser,* 1975, Volume 8: *Mid-Nineteenth-Century Writers: Eliot, De Quincy, Emerson,* 1976.

(And contributor) *Milton and the Line of Vision,* University of Wisconsin Press (Madison, WI), 1975.

(With Richard Ide, and contributor) *Composite Orders: The Genres of Milton's Last Poems,* University of Pittsburgh Press (Pittsburgh, PA), 1983.

(With C. A. Patrides, and contributor) *The Apocalypse in English Renaissance Thought and Literature,* Cornell University Press (Ithaca, NY), 1984.

(With Peter E. Medine) *Soundings of Things Done: Essays in Early Modern Literature in Honor of S. K. Heninger, Jr.,* University of Delaware Press (Newark, DE) 1997.

Blake Studies, member of editorial advisory board, 1968-78, guest editor, 1972; member of editorial advisory board, *Literary Monographs,* 1971-75, *Genre,* 1973—, and *Milton and the Romantics.*

WORK IN PROGRESS: Why Milton Matters.

BIOGRAPHICAL AND CRITICAL SOURCES:

PERIODICALS

Times Literary Supplement, August 16, 1985; February 5, 1988.

*   *   *

WOLF, Marvin J(ules) 1941-

PERSONAL: Born July 23, 1941, in Chicago, IL; son of Frank (a salvage dealer) and Cecille (a homemaker) Wolf; divorced; children: Laura. *Ethnicity:* Jewish. *Education:* Attended American University, 1967, and Newark State College (now Kean College of New Jersey), 1969; University of Maryland, A.A., 1974; California State University, Fullerton, B.A., 1977. *Religion:* Jewish. *Hobbies and other interests:* Photography.

ADDRESSES: Home—13237 Warren Ave., Los Angeles, CA 90066. *Agent*—Judy Coppage, 5411 Camillia Ave., North Hollywood, CA 91601. *E-mail*—marvin. wolf@comcast.net.

CAREER: U.S. Army, career officer in Signal Corps and public affairs, 1959-74, leaving service as captain; Avco Financial Services Corp., Newport Beach, CA, editor, 1974-76; Transamerica Financial Corp., Los Angeles, CA, editor, 1977-78; California State University, Fullerton, instructor in photojournalism, 1977-78; copywriter for Wells, Rich, Greene, 1977-81, and for Deutsch, Shea and Evans, 1985; freelance writer and photographer, 1978—.

MEMBER: Authors Guild, American Society of Journalists and Authors, U.S. Marine Corps Combat Correspondents (honorary life member), National

Order of Battlefield Commissions, Association of the First Cavalry Division, Independent Writers of Southern California (past president).

AWARDS, HONORS: Military: Bronze Star; Purple Heart; Air Medal; Expert Infantryman's Badge. Other: Greater Los Angeles Press Club, 1977, "Best Story in Business Publication"; Gold Quill Awards from International Association of Business Communicators, 1977, for photography; Robert L. Denig Distinguished Service Award, USMC Combat Correspondents Association, 1982; Greater Los Angeles Press Club award of excellence for nonfiction, 1993; Robert G. Anderson Memorial Award, American Society of Journalists and Authors, 1994; Author of the Year (runner up), American Society of Authors and Journalists, 1995; Founder's Award, Independent Writers of Southern California, 1995 and 2001.

WRITINGS:

The Japanese Conspiracy: The Plot to Dominate Industry Worldwide and How to Deal with It, Empire Books, 1983.
(With Katherine Mader) *The Official Guide to Los Angeles Crime Sites,* Facts on File (New York, NY), 1985.
(With Katherine Mader) *Fallen Angels: Chronicles of L. A. Crime and Mystery,* Facts on File (New York, NY), 1986.
(With Armand Grant) *Platinum Crime,* Pocket Books (New York, NY), 1988.
(With Leonard H. Goldenson) *Beating the Odds: The Untold Story behind the Rise of ABC: The Stars, Struggles, and Egos That Transformed Network Television by the Man Who Made It Happen,* Scribner (New York, NY), 1991.
(With Katherine Mader) *Rotten Apples: Chronicles of New York Crime and Mystery, 1689 to the Present,* Ballantine (New York, NY), 1991.
(With Larry Attebery) *Family Blood: The True Story of the Yom Kippur Murders: One Family's Greed, Love, and Rage,* HarperCollins (New York, NY), 1993.
(With Russell Means) *Where White Men Fear to Tread: The Autobiography of Russell Means,* St. Martin's Press (New York, NY), 1995.
(With Katherine Mader) *Perfect Crimes,* Ballantine (New York, NY), 1995.

Space Pioneers: Illustrated History of the Jet Propulsion Laboratory and the Race to Space, General Publishing Group (Los Angeles, CA), 1999.
(With Nguyen Cao Ky) *Buddha's Child: My Life and War in Vietnam,* St. Martin's Press (New York, NY), 2002.

Also photographer for *Streets of Seoul.* Contributor of articles and photographs to magazines and newspapers, including *Geo, Reader's Digest, Chicago Tribune, Los Angeles, Los Angeles Daily News, Los Angeles Magazine, San Francisco Examiner, Variety, Asia, Westways, Science 83,* and *New West.*

ADAPTATIONS: The Bicycle, a screenplay based on a short story of the same name originally published in *Chicago Tribune Magazine.*

WORK IN PROGRESS: Family Jewels, a screenplay.

SIDELIGHTS: Marvin J. Wolf has cowritten a number of books with famous celebrities and political figures, including *Beating the Odds: The Untold Story behind the Rise of ABC: The Stars, Struggles, and Egos That Transformed Network Television by the Man Who Made It Happen, Where White Men Fear to Tread: The Autobiography of Russell Means,* and *Buddha's Child: My Life and War in Vietnam.*

In *Beating the Odds,* Wolf teamed with Leonard H. Goldenson, the longtime head of the American Broadcasting Company (ABC), to tell the story of that television network's rise to prominence. When Goldenson took over the network in 1951, ABC was considered the weakest of four national television networks. But Goldenson showed a remarkable ability to pick outstanding key executives and a willingness to take programming risks. His memoir includes recollections from some of the network's top stars, including Bob Hope and Barbara Walters. "Goldenson spans a significant era, and his contribution to it on so many levels, without sacrificing any of his human values, makes this book so fascinating, valuable and, in many ways, so reflective of this extraordinary executive," according to Fred Hift in *Video Age International.* Genevieve Stuttaford in *Publishers Weekly* concluded: "The book is important reading for students of media history."

Where White Men Fear to Tread is the story of Native American activist Russell Means, the leader of the American Indian Movement (AIM) who led the

Wounded Knee takeover of 1973. The armed confrontation with agents of the Federal Bureau of Investigation (FBI) was provoked by opposition to a corrupt tribal government. A critic for *Publishers Weekly* found that, "assisted by historian Wolf, Means tells his story with vernacular frankness." "Means's book reveals quite a bit about the complexity of being Indian in the late twentieth century," according to Richard White in the *New Republic*, "and even more about the tortuous relations of Indians and whites."

Wolf collaborated with the former South Vietnamese vice president and air force general Nguyen Cao Ky to write *Buddha's Child,* in which Ky provides a behind-the-scenes look at the South Vietnamese government during the 1960s. Among the subjects Ky deals with are the efforts of the government to promote democracy, the reasons behind its crackdown on Buddhist priests, and his own never-implemented military plan to defeat the communist insurgents. The book "provides an insider's look at the political machinations within South Vietnam during the American war," according to a *Publishers Weekly* critic. Gilbert Taylor in *Booklist* believed that "Ky's recollections will certainly contribute to assessments of South Vietnam's viability and fate."

BIOGRAPHICAL AND CRITICAL SOURCES:

PERIODICALS

American Banker, August 30, 1988, Pamela S. Leven, review of *Platinum Crime,* p. 36.
American Film, April, 1991, Shawn Levy, review of *Beating the Odds: The Untold Story behind the Rise of ABC: The Stars, Struggles, and Egos That Transformed Network Television by the Man Who Made It Happen,* p. 10.
Booklist, May 1, 2002, Gilbert Taylor, review of *Buddha's Child: My Life and War in Vietnam,* p. 1501.
Business Week, April 9, 1984, review of *The Japanese Conspiracy: The Plot to Dominate Industry Worldwide and How to Deal with It,* p. 11.
Journal of American History, September, 1996, L. G. Moses, review of *Where White Men Fear to Tread: The Autobiography of Russell Means,* p. 712.
Library Journal, January, 1991, Chet Hagan, review of *Beating the Odds,* p. 112; July, 1991, Lois Walker, review of *Rotten Apples: Chronicles of*

New York Crime and Mystery, 1689 to the Present, p. 114; October 1, 1993, Lois Walker, review of *Family Blood,* p. 110.
New Republic, July 8, 1996, Richard White, review of *Where White Men Fear to Tread,* p. 37.
New York Review of Books, March 28, 1985, Murray Sayle, review of *The Japanese Conspiracy,* p. 33.
New York Times Book Review, April 14, 1991, Michael E. Ross, review of *Beating the Odds,* p. 20; October 15, 1995, Brent Staples, review of *Where White Men Fear to Tread,* p. 9.
Publishers Weekly, March 4, 1988, Penny Kaganoff, review of *Platinum Crime,* p. 104; December 14, 1990, Genevieve Stuttaford, review of *Beating the Odds,* p. 58; September 25, 1995, review of *Where White Men Fear to Tread,* p. 41; March 25, 2002, review of *Buddha's Child,* p. 51.
Video Age International, March, 1991, Fred Hift, review of *Beating the Odds,* p. 7.

ONLINE

Marvin J. Wolf Web site, http://www.marvwolf.com/ (October 1, 2003).

*   *   *

WOODS, Stuart 1938-

PERSONAL: Original surname Lee, legally changed to stepfather's first name in 1955; born January 9, 1938, in Manchester, GA; son of Stuart Franklin (in business) and Dorothy (in business; maiden name, Callaway) Lee. *Education:* University of Georgia, B.A., 1959. *Politics:* Democrat.

ADDRESSES: Agent—Anne Sibbald, Janklow & Nesbit, 445 Park Ave., New York, NY 10022. *E-mail*—stuart@stuartwoods.com.

CAREER: Advertising writer and creative director with firms in New York City, 1960-69, including Batten, Barton, Durstine & Osborne; Papert, Koenig & Lois; Young & Rubicam; and J. Walter Thompson; creative director and consultant with firms in London, England, 1970-73, including Grey Advertising and Dorland; consultant to Irish International Advertising and Hunter Advertising, both in Dublin, both 1973-74; freelance writer, 1973—. Past member of board of directors of Denham's, Inc. *Military service:* Air National Guard, 1960-68, active duty, 1961; served in Germany.

MEMBER: Authors Guild, New York Yacht Club, Royal Yacht Sqadron, The Century Association.

AWARDS, HONORS: Advertising awards from numerous organizations in New York, including Clio award for television writing and Gold Key award for print writing; Edgar Award, Mystery Writers of America, 1980, for *Chiefs;* Prix de Literature Policiere (France), for *Imperfect Strangers.*

WRITINGS:

NOVELS

Chiefs, Norton (New York, NY), 1980.
Run before the Wind, Norton (New York, NY), 1983.
Deep Lie, Norton (New York, NY), 1986.
Under the Lake, Simon & Schuster (New York, NY), 1987.
White Cargo, Simon & Schuster (New York, NY), 1988.
Grass Roots, Simon & Schuster (New York, NY), 1989.
Palindrome, HarperCollins (New York, NY), 1991.
New York Dead, HarperCollins (New York, NY), 1991.
Santa Fe Rules, HarperCollins (New York, NY), 1992.
L.A. Times, HarperCollins (New York, NY), 1993.
Dead Eyes, HarperCollins (New York, NY), 1994.
Heat, HarperCollins (New York, NY), 1994.
Imperfect Strangers, HarperCollins (New York, NY), 1995.
Choke, HarperCollins (New York, NY), 1995.
Dirt, HarperCollins (New York, NY), 1996.
Dead in the Water, HarperCollins (New York, NY), 1997.
Swimming to Catalina, HarperCollins (New York, NY), 1998.
Orchid Beach, HarperCollins (New York, NY), 1998.
Worst Fears Realized, HarperCollins (New York, NY), 1999.
L.A. Dead, Putnam (New York, NY), 2000.
The Run, HarperCollins (New York, NY), 2000.
Cold Paradise, Putnam (New York, NY), 2001.
Orchid Blues, Putnam (New York, NY), 2001.
The Short Forever, Putnam (New York, NY), 2002.

Blood Orchid, Putnam (New York, NY), 2002.
Dirty Work, Putnam (New York, NY), 2003.
Capital Crimes, Putnam (New York, NY), 2003.
Reckless Abandon, Putnam (New York, NY), 2004.
The Prince of Beverly Hills, Putnam (New York, NY), 2004.
Two-dollar Bill, Putnam (New York, NY), 2005.

NONFICTION

Blue Water, Green Skipper (Dolphin Book Club selection), Norton (New York, NY), 1977.
A Romantic's Guide to the Country Inns of Britain and Ireland, Norton (New York, NY), 1979.

Contributor to magazines, including *Yachting.* Contributing editor and restaurant critic for *Atlanta.*

ADAPTATIONS: Chiefs was filmed as a television miniseries, 1983; *Grass Roots* was filmed as a television miniseries, 1993.

SIDELIGHTS: Stuart Woods is a writer of suspenseful thrillers that regularly make their way onto the best-seller lists. Woods has enjoyed equal success with three series—the Will Lee books about modern politics, the Stone Barrington mysteries, and the Holly Barker books featuring a female protagonist and her feisty Doberman sidekick, Daisy. A *Publishers Weekly* reviewer characterized the author's work as a "breezy and irreverent brand of detective fiction, full of mischievous asides." And David Pitt, in a *Booklist* review of *The Run,* commended Woods as a "careful, talented writer" whose stories "should please . . . anyone who loves good political fiction."

Woods began his writing career as an advertising executive but was smitten with the sailing life while living in Europe. Upon receiving an inheritance, he commissioned the construction of his own boat and took to the seas as a sail racer. His first publication, *Blue Water, Green Skipper,* is the story of his own experiences as a novice at transatlantic voyages. He once explained to *CA:* "*Blue Water, Green Skipper* is a memoir deriving from my decision to sail in the 1976 *Observer* Single-Handed Transatlantic Race (OSTAR), though I had only eighteen months to build a boat and learn to sail it. I also sailed in the 1979 Fastnet race, in which many lives were lost." He added: "I expect to continue ocean racing and cruising, including a transatlantic crossing from England to Antigua." This trip was indeed accomplished in 1979.

In reviewing *Blue Water, Green Skipper,* Holger Lundbergh of *Yachting* declared, "The step-by-step account of how this green skipper in a remarkably short time became a seasoned blue-water sailor is beautifully told by a young American from Georgia, a brilliant stylist, a man of humor, courage, and patience." Lundbergh added that the book is "dramatic and inspiring reading of rare quality."

Woods's novels are fast-paced adventures that are frequently set in high society, power politics, or the entertainment world. His first novel, *Chiefs,* introduced Senator Will Lee and his CIA deputy director wife, Kate, who find themselves enmeshed in a series of intrigues on Capitol Hill. The Lees are also featured in *Grass Roots* and *The Run.* A *Publishers Weekly* critic stated that Senator Lee "is for the most part about as likable as a politician can be, and boasts impeccable Democratic stripes."

Woods's most popular works are those featuring the character of Stone Barrington, an ex-cop turned New York City lawyer and detective. Over a series of novels Barrington has evolved from a cash-strapped street-level hero to a wealthy, jet-setting gumshoe with an international clientele. What has remained consistent is Barrington's fondness for romantic encounters with women and his reliance upon his longtime fellow detective Dino Bacchetti to help him solve his cases. A *Publishers Weekly* contributor noted that, when writing Barrington series novels, "Woods is eternally in best-seller mode."

In *Dirt,* for instance, Barrington is hired by a sexually voracious gossip columnist to find out who is faxing damaging information about her to influential people around the city. June Vigor, a reviewer for *Booklist,* found *Dirt* to have "brisk sex, designer name-dropping, and the voyeuristic tingle of dishing dirt on the rich and famous." A *Publishers Weekly* correspondent also praised *Dirt,* noting: "This slickly entertaining suspenser displays Woods at the top of his game with no signs of flagging. . . . [This] superbly paced tale [is] subtly reminiscent of the waggish P. G. Wodehouse, [and] Woods delivers a marvelously sophisticated, thoroughly modern old-fashioned read." Emily Melton

approved of *Swimming to Catalina,* another Barrington adventure, stating in *Booklist* that the novel is "a highly entertaining read that's chock-full of slam-bang action, fast cars, beautiful women, fine wine, and tart, tongue-in-cheek humor. Another outstanding effort."

More recently Woods has introduced another series sleuth, Holly Barker. Holly is a former Army Military Police Battalion commander who was run out of the service after filing a sexual harassment charge against her superior. *Orchid Beach* introduces her story and finds her working as a deputy in the small Florida town that gives the novel its name. Holly solves crimes with the assistance of her father, Ham, and her dog, Daisy. The Florida milieu allows Woods—a part-time Florida resident—to explore the special criminal dynamic of that region. Kristine Huntley in *Booklist* found the Holly Barker series to be "suspenseful" and "exciting . . . sure to please Woods's many fans."

Woods once told *CA:* "Writing fiction is terribly hard work, and I intend to alleviate this oppression by continuing to write about yachting, travel, food and wine, and whatever else takes my fancy. I have found the secret to happiness: finding a way to make a living doing all the things you like best, or, to put it another way, finding a way to make all the things you like to do best tax-deductible."

BIOGRAPHICAL AND CRITICAL SOURCES:

BOOKS

St. James Guide to Horror, Ghost & Gothic Writers, St. James Press (Detroit, MI), 1998.

PERIODICALS

Atlanta Journal-Constitution Magazine, February 8, 1977.
Booklist, December 1, 1994, p. 635; August, 1996, p. 1857; July, 1997, p. 1777; March 15, 1998, p. 1180; September 14, 1998, review of *Orchid Beach,* p. 44; June 1, 1999, Emily Melton, review of *Worst Fears Realized,* p. 1744; April 1, 2000, David Pitt, review of *The Run,* p. 1413; March 1, 2001, Kristine Huntley, review of *Cold Paradise,* p. 1189; February 1, 2002, Kristine Huntley,

review of *The Short Forever,* p. 908; August, 2002, Kristine Huntley, review of *Blood Orchid,* p. 1888; February 15, 2003, Kristine Huntley, review of *Dirty Work,* p. 1019.

Cosmopolitan, January, 1994, p. 18.

Entertainment Weekly, May 7, 1993, p. 53; January 20, 1995, p. 47.

Kirkus Reviews, February 1, 2003, review of *Dirty Work,* p. 181; August 1, 2003, review of *Capital Crimes,* p. 992.

Library Journal, March 1, 1997, p. 141; August, 1997, p. 136; September 15, 1997, p. 118; May 15, 2002, Steven J. Mayover, review of *Orchid Blues,* p. 144.

New York Times, November 24, 1991; October 8, 1995.

People, September 16, 1996, p. 48; May 11, 1998, p. 48.

Publishers Weekly, April 12, 1993, p. 48; June 7, 1993, p. 26; November 1, 1993, p. 65; May 30, 1994, p. 36; December 5, 1994, p. 66; August 12, 1996, p. 65; July 14, 1997, p. 63; September 1, 1997, p. 40; April 6, 1998, p. 58; July 5, 1999, review of *Worst Fears Realized,* p. 57; August 23, 1999, Daisy Maryles, "Not Out of Woods Yet," p. 18; April 24, 2000, review of *The Run,* p. 58; June 5, 2000, Daisy Maryles, "A *Run* on the Charts," p. 17; September 11, 2000, review of *L.A. Dead,* p. 67; April 16, 2001, review of *Cold Paradise,* p. 46; May 7, 2001, Daisy Maryles, "Woods Catches *Cold,*" p. 32; October 1, 2001, review of *Orchid Blues,* p. 34; November 12, 2001, Daisy Maryles, "Woods Goes Skyward," p. 16; January 7, 2002, review of *Orchid Blues,* p. 21; March 25, 2002, review of *The Short Forever,* p. 42; August 26, 2002, review of *Blood Orchid,* p. 39; March 17, 2003, review of *Dirty Work,* p. 52; August 18, 2003, review of *Capital Crimes,* p. 55.

Yachting, September, 1977; September, 1978.

ONLINE

Stuart Woods Home Page, http://www.stuartwoods. com/ (December 26, 2002).

*   *   *

WRIGHT, S(ydney) Fowler 1874-1965

(Sydney Fowler; Alan Seymour; Anthony Wingrave)

PERSONAL: Born January 6, 1874, in Birmingham, England; died February 25, 1965; married Nellie Ash-

barry, 1895 (died, 1918); married Truda Hancock, 1920; children: (first marriage) three sons, three daughters; (second marriage) one son, three daughters. *Education:* King Edward's School, Birmingham, England.

CAREER: Writer and translator. Accountant in Birmingham, England, 1895-1933; Fowler Wright Books Ltd., founder. Empire Poetry League, Birmingham, founder, 1917; *Poetry* (later *Poetry and the Play;* journal of Empire Poetry League), editor, 1920-32; editor for Merton Press (organ of Empire Poetry League).

WRITINGS:

NOVELS

The Amphibians: A Romance of 500,000 Years Hence, Merton Press (London, England), 1925, World (New York, NY), 1949.

Deluge (also see below), Fowler Wright (London, England), 1927, Cosmopolitan (New York, NY), 1928.

The Island of Captain Sparrow, Cosmopolitan (New York, NY), 1928.

The World Below (includes *The Amphibians*), Collins (London, England), 1929, Longman (New York, NY), 1930, published as *The Dwellers,* Panther (London, England), 1954.

Dawn (also see below), Cosmopolitan (New York, NY), 1929.

Elfwin, Longman (New York, NY), 1930.

Dream; or, The Simian Maid, Harrap (London, England), 1931, Greenwood Press (Westport, CT), 1985.

Seven Thousand in Israel, Jarrolds (London, England), 1931.

(With J. M. Denwood) *Red Ike,* Hutchinson (London, England), 1931, published as *Under the Brutchstone,* Coward McCann (New York, NY), 1931.

Beyond the Rim, Jarrolds (London, England), 1932.

Lord's Right in Languedoc, Jarrolds (London, England), 1933.

Power, Jarrolds (London, England), 1933.

David, Butterworth (London, England), 1934.

Prelude in Prague: A Story of the War of 1938, Newnes (London, England), 1935, published as *The War of 1938,* Putnam (New York, NY), 1936.

Four Days War, Hale (London, England), 1936.

Megiddo's Ridge, Hale (London, England), 1937.

The Hidden Tribe, Hale (London, England), 1938.

The Adventure of Wyndham Smith, Jenkins (London, England), 1938.

The Screaming Lake, Hale (London, England), 1939.

Ordeal of Barata, Jenkins (London, England), 1939.

The Siege of Malta: Founded on an Unfinished Romance by Sir Walter Scott, Muller (London, England), 1942.

Spider's War, Abelard Press (New York, NY), 1954.

Deluge: A Romance; and Dawn, Arno (New York, NY), 1975.

Inquisitive Angel, FWB (Ludlow, England), 1996.

Cortéz: For God and Spain, FWB (Ludlow, England), 1996.

Song of Arthur, FWB (Ludlow, England), 1996.

NOVELS; AS SYDNEY FOWLER, UNLESS OTHERWISE INDICATED

The King against Anne Bickerton, Harrap (London, England), 1930, published as *The Case of Anne Bickerton,* Boni (New York, NY), 1930, published as *Rex v. Anne Bickerton,* Penguin (Harmondsworth, England), 1947.

The Bell Street Murders, Macaulay (New York, NY), 1931.

By Saturday, Lane (London, England), 1931.

The Hanging of Constance Hiller, Jarrolds (London, England), 1931, Macaulay (New York, NY), 1932.

Crime & Co., Macaulay (New York, NY), 1931, published as *The Hand-Print Mystery,* Jarrolds (London, England), 1932.

Arresting Delia, Macaulay (New York, NY), 1932.

The Secret of the Screen, Jarrolds (London, England), 1933.

Who Else But She?, Jarrolds (London, England), 1934.

(As Anthony Wingrave) *The Vengeance of Gwa,* Butterworth (London, England), 1935.

Three Witnesses, Butterworth (London, England), 1935.

The Attic Murder, Butterworth (London, England), 1936.

Was Murder Done?, Butterworth (London, England), 1936.

Post-Mortem Evidence, Butterworth (London, England), 1936.

Four Callers in Razor Street, Jenkins (London, England), 1937.

The Jordans Murder, Jenkins (London, England), 1938, Curl (New York, NY), 1939.

The Murder in Bethnal Square, Jenkins (London, England), 1938.

The Wills of Jane Kanwhistle, Jenkins (London, England), 1939.

The Rissole Mystery, Rich & Cowan (London, England), 1941.

A Bout with the Mildew Gang, Eyre & Spottiswoode (London, England), 1941.

Second Bout with the Mildew Gang, Eyre & Spottiswoode (London, England), 1942.

Dinner in New York, Eyre & Spottiswoode (London, England), 1943.

The End of the Mildew Gang, Eyre & Spottiswoode (London, England), 1944.

Too Much for Mr. Jellipot, Eyre & Spottiswoode (London, England), 1945.

Who Murdered Reynard?, Rich & Cowan (London, England), 1947.

With Cause Enough?, Harvill Press (London, England), 1954.

SHORT STORY COLLECTIONS

(As Sydney Fowler) *The New Gods Lead,* Jarrolds (London, England), 1932.

The Witchfinder, Books of Today (London, England), 1945.

Justice, and The Rat (Two Famous Stories), Books of Today (London, England), 1945.

The Throne of Saturn, Arkham House (Sauk City, WI), 1949.

S. Fowler Wright's Short Stories, FWB (Ludlow, England), 1996.

POETRY

(As Alan Seymour) *Scenes from the Morte d'Arthur,* Erskine MacDonald (London, England), 1919.

Some Songs of Bilitis, Poetry (Birmingham, England), 1921.

The Song of Songs and Other Poems, Merton Press (London, England), 1925, Cosmopolitan (New York, NY), 1929.

The Ballad of Elaine, Merton Press (London, England), 1926.

The Riding of Lancelot: A Narrative Poem, Fowler Wright Books (London, England), 1929.

NONFICTION

Police and the Public: A Political Pamphlet, Fowler Wright Books (London, England), 1929.

The Life of Sir Walter Scott: A Biography, Poetry League (London, England), 1932, Haskell House (New York), 1971.

Should We Surrender Colonies?, Readers' Library (London, England), 1939.

EDITOR

Voices on the Wind: An Anthology of Contemporary Verse, three volumes, Merton Press (London, England), 1922-24.

Poets of Merseyside: An Anthology of Present-Day Liverpool Poetry, Merton Press (London, England), 1923.

(With R. Crompton Rhodes) *Poems: Chosen by Boys and Girls,* four volumes, Blackwell (Oxford, England), 1923-24.

Birmingham Poetry 1923-24, Merton Press (London, England), 1924.

From Overseas: An Anthology of Contemporary Dominion and Colonial Verse, Merton Press (London, England), 1924.

Some Yorkshire Poets, Merton Press (London, England), 1924.

A Somerset Anthology of Modern Verse 1924, Merton Press (London, England), 1924.

The County Series of Contemporary Poetry (verse anthologies), thirteen volumes, Merton Press (London, England), 1927-30.

Edward Bulwer-Lytton, *The Last Days of Pompeii: A Redaction,* Vision Press (London, England), 1948.

TRANSLATOR

Dante Alighieri, *The Inferno,* Fowler Wright Books (London, England), 1928.

Alexandre Dumas, *Marguerite de Valois,* Temple (London, England), 1947.

Dante Alighieri, *The Purgatorio,* Oliver & Boyd (Edinburgh, Scotland), 1954.

Dante Alighieri, *The Paradisio,* FWB (Ludlow, England), 1996.

Contributor to anthologies, including *Beyond the End of Time,* edited by Frederik Pohl, Permabooks (Garden City, NY), 1952; *Science-Fiction Adventures in Mutation,* edited by Groff Conklin, Vanguard (New York, NY), 1955.

ADAPTATIONS: Deluge was adapted as a motion picture released by RKO in 1933, starring Sidney Blackmer.

SIDELIGHTS: During a lifetime that spanned over ninety years, S. Fowler Wright worked dutifully as an accountant, married, was widowed, remarried, and fathered and supported ten children. He began writing fantasy novels and stories during middle age and enjoyed subsequent fame and success as a writer of futuristic tales. Like many other science fiction and fantasy writers, Wright sought to convey his ideas on the direction of society through the medium of fiction—and he entertained grave anxieties about the "progress" of science and technology. As Darren Harris-Fain put it in the *Dictionary of Literary Biography,* Wright's voice "was one of caution, if not alarm, about what human beings would do with technological changes and better-organized social structures. . . . Wright was distrustful, if not disdainful, of many modern social and technological developments. The scientific worldview so central to modern science fiction comes under attack in much of Wright's fiction." His pessimistic view notwithstanding, Wright enjoyed success in England and America for his fantasy works and was highly regarded in England as well for his detective and historical novels.

Born and reared in Birmingham, England, Wright spent his early literary career as a poet, a translator of poetry, and an editor of poetry magazines and anthologies. His accomplishments in these fields were particularly noteworthy in light of the fact that he also worked full time as an accountant and cared for ten children during the early decades of the twentieth century. Wright turned to fantasy fiction in the 1920s. *Deluge,* perhaps his greatest popular success, was published in 1927. It was 1924, however, when Wright's own publishing house, Merton Press, issued his first novel, *The Amphibians: A Romance of 500,000 Years Hence.* This novel's structure "recapitulates Homer's *Odyssey,*" according to a writer in the *Encyclopedia of Science Fiction.*

The genesis of *The Amphibians* and its 1929 sequel, *The World Below*—they were originally planned as part of a trilogy—was also influenced by Wright's work on a translation of Dante's *Divine Comedy.* These novels describe a far-future Earth on which three new intelligent species struggle to take the place of extinct humanity. Amphibians are willowy and intellectual, Dwellers are giant-sized scientists, and Killers are reptilian hunters. The novels contain a good deal of social commentary aimed at Wright's own species and epoch. Harris-Fain observed: "Wright was clearly operating within the conventions of [the fantasy] mode in *The Amphibians,* writing about an Earth 500,000 years in the future contested by three intelligent species, none of them human. . . . Wright extrapolates about the far future from an evolutionary viewpoint; he speculates about the possibility of human extinction and the idea of more than one powerful species in conflict; and he does so for more than mere entertainment."

With his 1927 publication of *Deluge,* Wright achieved critical and commercial success for the first time. The book, which echoes the biblical story of Noah, is a disaster novel in which much of England is overwhelmed by waters. A man and two women are among the survivors, and the three of them establish a new society together. Calling *Deluge* "engrossing," Mary S. Weinkauf in *Twentieth-Century Science-Fiction Writers* expressed admiration for Wright's handling of the survivors' emotions: some criminals become more humane, while some formerly ordinary citizens become sociopathic. Criticism at the time of publication was also quite favorable. William Rose Benet summed up the press reaction in the *Saturday Review of Literature:* "A London reviewer . . . after quite inevitably referring to the earlier H. G. Wells in this connection, added these remarks: 'Others have written fantasies of unknown worlds. Mr. Fowler Wright creates one.' The latter sentence is no less than the truth. *Deluge* lives and breathes with actuality in its every detail. It is energized by a profound scorn for the artificial environment our modern industrialism has made for us."

The *Times Literary Supplement* contributor who reviewed *Deluge* differentiated Wright from H. G. Wells, and from Jules Verne, on the grounds that the latter two might have treated the material more sociologically or politically. Wright, creating "an exceedingly good story," concentrated on "the adventures and loves of individual men and women." A critic in the *New York Times* recommended the book as "vastly amusing." Some reviewers, such as those for *Bookman* and *Outlook,* found the author's moralizing on social issues distracting, but even they were enthusiastic about its entertainment qualities. The novel was made into a motion picture in 1933, and Wright retired from accountancy.

In 1928, Wright released *The Island of Captain Sparrow,* whose evident affinities are to Wells's *The Island of Dr. Moreau.* The novel presents a ship's captain who lands on an uncharted island where the bloodthirsty inhabitants are half-human, half-satyr, and where ten-foot-tall birds do the gardening. The captain saves a French-English girl who has successfully hidden on the island for two years, and together they find happiness. Again, reviewers generally concurred in characterizing the novel as well-written; while some found its fantasy element uncongenial, a *Bookman* reviewer termed it "a swift, exciting yarn, with a touch of improbable fantasy which gives it spice." A *Nation and Athenaeum* reviewer called it "a brilliant book," asserting that the author "keeps his imagination in control and writes in a good matter-of-fact way about these creatures of fancy." A contributor to the *New York Herald Tribune Books* recommended it to "all those who like a roaring adventure tale—and who are willing to be kept up at night until the tale is done."

Wright returned to his drowned England of the future with *Dawn,* the 1929 sequel to *Deluge.* Harris-Fain characterized the work as "less a sequel than a companion, as much of the action parallels the story in *Deluge.*" The essayist noted that the novel "was less critically successful than its predecessor, in large part because there is less action and more philosophical discussion on the part of the characters." A reviewer for the *New York Herald Tribune Books,* for instance, asserted that *Dawn* was weighed down by philosophizing on the part of figurehead characters. However, in a review for the *Boston Transcript,* a critic declared that the author "has a truth to impart, and surely there could be no more subtle or dramatic way in which his object could be accomplished." Similarly, the *New York Times* reviewer claimed that Wright had found "a theme of unbounded potentialities, one to intrigue the imagination and to compel a rapt attention."

Although continuing to write fantasy novels, Wright turned to the mystery genre for the first time with *The Case of Anne Bickerton,* which was eventually published in England under two other titles at two different times. A *Saturday Review of Literature* commentator assessed the book's ending as too predictable to make a successful mystery, but the *Bookman* reviewer praised the "brilliant characterizations." The year 1930 also saw the publication of Wright's historical novel *Elfwin,* a tale of the daughter and granddaughter of Alfred the Great and their political and social relations with Danish invaders. Some reviewers found the novel's style to be an unfortunate attempt at Anglo-Saxon simplicity—but Donald Douglas, in *Books,* raved: "Not even the Scandinavian authors have done those early years with such somber richness and poetry drawn from the very blood of life." A *Saturday Review of Literature* piece called *Elfwin* "a historical novel very much above the average, full of meat and shrewdness."

In 1931, Wright published the first volume of a projected trilogy, *Dream; or, The Simian Maid,* which dealt with the adventures of Margaret Cranleigh, who, with the aid of a psychologist-magician, travels into prehistory where ape-humans battle monstrous rats for dominance. A second volume in the trilogy, *The Vengeance of Gwa,* was published in 1935 under the name Anthony Wingrave, and the third volume, *Spiders' War,* which deals with a conflict between future humans and giant spiders, was not published until 1954. It was in 1935 that Wright issued the first volume of a different kind of fantasy, a rather prophetic vision of a near-future world war begun by an authoritarian Germany. Wright had visited Nazi Germany in 1934 with the task of writing newspaper articles, and the additional result was the novels *Prelude in Prague: A Story of the War of 1938,* published in 1935, *Four Days War,* published in 1936, and *Megiddo's Ridge,* published in 1937. Some reviewers of *Prelude in Prague* responded negatively, assessing it as unpersuasive. The critic for the *Saturday Review of Literature* remarked: "As prophecy it does not altogether impress. As a good 'yarn' it frequently holds one's close attention." In contrast, *New York Times* correspondent E. C. Beckwith wrote that *Prelude in Prague* "deals in a most compelling fashion with uncertain world realities, which may be now just over the way, presenting them without exaggerating the likelihood that they must plunge this afflicted earth again into the horrors of Armageddon."

When World War II did arrive, it found Wright turning out mystery novels at a steady rate, an activity that, in England, supported the war effort by furnishing reading matter to soldiers and sailors. Although in the view of the writer in the *Encyclopedia of Science Fiction,* Wright's abilities as an author were diminishing during this period, he published a well-received collection of science fiction stories, *The Throne of Saturn,* in 1949. Two eminent science fiction writers offered praise for the collection: Anthony Boucher, in the *Chicago Sun,* welcomed it as a "deft and delightful assortment of previews, often chilling in their implications, of the aseptic and rational world of tomorrow," and Fritz Leiber, assessing the book for the *Chicago Sunday Tribune,* wrote, "Here is a collection of science-fiction stories characterized by dramatic power, horror and shocking social predictions. . . . The narratives grip the reader's mind with a peculiar fascination."

According to Weinkauf, Wright's best short stories include "Justice," which was published in book form in 1945, and "Original Sin," which was the source for Wright's 1938 novel *The Adventure of Wyndham Smith.* Curiously, it is Wright's short stories that have received greater attention since his death, with collections published in America and abroad as recently as 1996.

Appraising Wright's career as a whole, the *Encyclopedia of Science Fiction* writer rated Wright below Wells as a social commentator, but called him "a strikingly original writer and one of the key figures in the tradition of UK scientific romance." Harris-Fain concluded: "Although Wright's literary career did not really begin until his forties and he did not begin publishing fiction until his fifties, he produced dozens of noteworthy stories and novels in the half of his life remaining." Wright died in 1965, leaving several unpublished manuscripts that have since found their way into print.

BIOGRAPHICAL AND CRITICAL SOURCES:

BOOKS

Dictionary of Literary Biography, Volume 255: *British Fantasy and Science-Fiction Writers, 1918-1960,* Gale (Detroit, MI), 2002, pp. 289-296.

Moskowitz, Sam, *Strange Horizons: The Spectrum of Science Fiction,* Scribner (New York, NY), 1976, pp. 92-106.

Nicholls, Peter, editor, *Encyclopedia of Science Fiction: An Illustrated A to Z,* Granada Publishing (London, England), 1979, pp. 1350-1351.

Stableford, Brian, *Scientific Romance in Britain, 1890-1950,* St. Martin's Press (New York, NY), 1985.

Twentieth-Century Science-Fiction Writers, 3rd edition, edited by Noelle Watson and Paul E. Schellinger, St. James Press (Detroit, MI), 1991, pp. 889-890.

Weinkauf, Mary S., *Sermons in Science Fiction: The Novels of S. Fowler Wright,* Borgo (San Bernardino, CA), 1994.

PERIODICALS

Bookman, May, 1928; September, 1928; September, 1930.
Books, September 28, 1930, p. 35.
Boston Transcript, November 23, 1929, p. 10.
Chicago Sun, February 3, 1950, p. S6.
Chicago Sunday Tribune, January 22, 1950, p. 6.
Foundation, November, 1983, pp. 10-52.
Nation and Athenaeum, June 23, 1928.
New York Herald Tribune Books, July 22, 1928, p. 3; December 15, 1929, p. 10.
New York Times, March 4, 1928, p. 5; November 17, 1929, p. 10; March 1, 1936, p. 23.
Outlook, March 28, 1928; November 6, 1929.
Saturday Review of Literature, March 3, 1928; September 29, 1930; September 13, 1930, March 28, 1936.
Times Literary Supplement, December 15, 1927, p. 963.

ONLINE

Works of Sydney Fowler Wright, http://www.sfw.org.uk/ (December 31, 2002), bibliography of author's works.*

*   *   *

YERKOW, Lila Perl
See PERL, Lila

*   *   *

YOUST, Lionel 1934-

PERSONAL: Born January 19, 1934, in Woodland, WA; son of George (a logger and sawmill owner) and Doris (maiden name, Eagles; later surname, McGuire) Youst; married Hilda Gaitan, July 7, 1961; children: Alice, Julia, Oliver. *Education:* University of Nebraska—Omaha, B.G.S., 1971; graduate study at Creighton University and Humboldt State University. *Politics:* Democrat.

ADDRESSES: Home—12445 Highway 241, Coos Bay, OR 97420. *E-mail*—lyoust@gte.net.

CAREER: Logger in Oregon, California, Washington, and British Columbia, 1949-53; U.S. Air Force, career officer in aircraft maintenance, 1953-75, retiring as major; owner and operator of a charter transportation service in Oregon, 1978-92; writer, 1992—. Also worked as theater director, actor, and playwright.

AWARDS, HONORS: Recipient of military honors, including Bronze Star with oak leaf cluster, Meritorious Service Medal, and Joint Services Commendation Medal.

WRITINGS:

Above the Falls: An Oral and Folk History of Upper Glenn Creek, Coos County, Oregon, privately printed, 1991, revised edition, 2003.
(And producer) *When Everybody Was Working: A Vintage Film of Logging and Lumbering* (documentary videotape), Siskyou National Forest, 1994.
She's Tricky Like Coyote: Annie Miner Peterson, an Oregon Coast Indian Woman, University of Oklahoma Press (Norman, OK), 1997.
(With others, and producer) *Steam Logging in History and in Models* (documentary videotape), PCI Imageworks, 1998.
(With William R. Seaburg) *Coquelle Thompson, Athabaskan Witness: A Cultural Biography,* University of Oklahoma Press (Norman, OK), 2002.

WORK IN PROGRESS: In All the Wars: The Life and Times of Sergeant Joseph Clesson, 1683-1758.

SIDELIGHTS: Lionel Youst once told *CA:* "My motivation for writing is the same as it was for Herodotus. His was 'to preserve from decay the remembrance of what men have done.' I work from interviews, oral histories, local histories, anthropological field notes, newspapers, census records, and other documents both published and unpublished. My goal is to depict the speech, the thought, and the values of ordinary people who otherwise would have no 'history' in the traditional sense.

"In my youth I devoured the 'biographical novels' of Irving Stone; *Clarence Darrow for the Defense* probably influenced me more than any other. Being from the northwest and from a lumbering family, I also devoured the books of Stewart H. Holbrook. *Holy Old Mackinaw* and *The Age of the Moguls* were probably my favorites. In later years I have admired the work of Studs Terkel, and it is because of his example that I have tape-recorded scores of hours of interviews with old-time loggers. I have wanted to preserve the story of their lives and the manner of their speech. I love the sound of colloquial speech and of dramatic action, and so it seems natural that I have had a long avocational interest in the theater. Shakespeare, Ibsen, and Strindberg are my favorites among the world classics. I have acted in the plays of all three and have directed plays of Ibsen and Strindberg. Among contemporary playwrights I am most fond of Sam Shepard and David Mamet because the rhythm and sound of their speech rings true.

"My writing proceeds slowly, usually after years of reading, interviewing, and thinking on a particular theme. I write and rewrite, and I read every draft aloud. If it doesn't flow nicely when read aloud, if there is an awkwardness there, I redo it until it sounds right.

"I have been inspired to write on the subjects I have chosen—the local history of a wilderness homestead in Oregon, the biography of an Oregon Coast Indian woman, and the biography of an Oregon Indian chief—because of disappointment with the manner in which such subjects have been treated in the past. It has been my objective to present my subjects in their own voices, their own manners of speaking, their own modes of thought. My current work, a biography set during the colonial wars, stems from the same objective."

BIOGRAPHICAL AND CRITICAL SOURCES:

PERIODICALS

Journal of the Royal Anthropological Institute, June, 2002, Anthony P. Grant, review of *She's Tricky Like Coyote: Annie Miner Peterson, an Oregon Coast Indian Woman,* p. 405.